Y0-DLC-992

THE LEGAL ENVIRONMENT OF BUSINESS

FOURTH EDITION

THE DRYDEN PRESS SERIES IN BUSINESS LAW

ALLISON AND PRENTICE
The Legal Environment of Business
Fourth Edition

ALLISON, PRENTICE, AND HOWELL
Business Law: Text and Cases
Fifth Edition

ALLISON, PRENTICE, AND HOWELL
Business Law: Text and Cases
Alternate Fifth Edition

ESTEY
The Unions

LIEBERMAN AND SIEDEL
Business Law and the Legal Environment
Third Edition

LIEBERMAN AND SIEDEL
The Legal Environment of Business

MAURER
Business Law: Text and Cases
Second Edition

SPIRO AND HOUGHTELLING
The Dynamics of Law
Third Edition

WARNER
The Legal Environment of Business

JOHN R. ALLISON   ROBERT A. PRENTICE

UNIVERSITY OF TEXAS, AUSTIN   UNIVERSITY OF TEXAS, AUSTIN

THE LEGAL ENVIRONMENT OF BUSINESS

FOURTH EDITION

THE DRYDEN PRESS

HARCOURT BRACE JOVANOVICH COLLEGE PUBLISHERS
FORT WORTH   PHILADELPHIA   SAN DIEGO   NEW YORK
ORLANDO   AUSTIN   SAN ANTONIO
TORONTO   MONTREAL   LONDON   SYDNEY   TOKYO

Editor in Chief	Robert A. Pawlik
Acquisitions Editor	Scott Isenberg
Development Editor	Glenn Martin
Project Editor	Jim Patterson
Production Manager	Marilyn Williams
Designer	Linda Miller
Cover Photo	Copyright © 1992 Abrams/Lacagnina Photography

Copyright © 1993, 1990, 1987, 1984 by The Dryden Press.

All rights reserved. No part of this publication may be reproduced or transmitted in any form or by any means, electronic or mechanical, including photocopy, recording, or any information storage and retrieval system, without permission in writing from the publisher.

Requests for permission to make copies of any part of the work should be mailed to: Permissions Department, Harcourt Brace Jovanovich College Publishers, 8th Floor, Orlando, FL 32887.

Address for Editorial Correspondence
The Dryden Press, 301 Commerce Street, Suite 3700, Fort Worth, TX 76102

Address for Orders
The Dryden Press, 6277 Sea Harbor Drive, Orlando, FL 32887
1-800-782-4479, or 1-800-433-0001 (in Florida)

ISBN: 0-03-093477-X

Library of Congress Catalogue Number: 92-70971

Printed in the United States of America

3 4 5 6 7 8 9 0 1 2   039   9 8 7 6 5 4 3 2 1

The Dryden Press
Harcourt Brace Jovanovich

PREFACE

The first three editions of *The Legal Environment of Business* were published in response to the increased offerings of legal environment courses in business schools as alternatives to traditional business law courses. (These offerings appear under a number of titles at the undergraduate and graduate levels: The Legal Environment of Business, Business and Government, Business and the Legal System, and Business and Society, to name but a few.) Because the text found widespread acceptance in that market, this fourth edition retains the basic format and approach of its predecessors.

Several significant changes and additions, nonetheless, have been made to keep the text abreast of current developments in the dynamic areas of law that collectively fall within the legal environment spectrum. Not only do these improvements properly convey an air of currency and relevance of the subject to our students but, additionally, they ensure that the text continues to meet the standards for Legal Environment of Business courses as set forth by the American Assembly of Collegiate Schools of Business (AACSB).

Changes in the Fourth Edition

The most significant changes and additions are the following:

- A new chapter—Chapter 8, Criminal Law and Business—has been added.
- Chapter 2, Court Systems and Jurisdiction, and Chapter 3, Litigation and Alternative Dispute Resolution, have been completely rewritten.
- Chapter 5, Constitutional Law, has been completely rewritten.
- Chapter 7, Business Ethics, Corporate Responsibility and the Law, has been completely rewritten.
- The three chapters on Antitrust Law from the previous edition have been combined into a single Chapter 14 and completely rewritten.
- Chapter 17, Employment Law/Protection Against Discrimination, has been

almost completely rewritten, with extensive coverage of sexual harassment, the Americans With Disabilities Act of 1990, and the Civil Rights Act of 1991.

- Chapter 19, Environmental Protection Law, has been completely rewritten.

- There has been significant updating and rewriting, as well as the inclusion of many new cases, in most other chapters. The chapters in which substantial changes of this nature have been made include Chapter 9, Contract and Sales Law; Chapter 10, General Tort Law; Chapter 11, Products Liability; Chapter 12, Business Torts; Chapter 13, Agency and Business Organizations; Chapter 15, Securities Regulation; Chapter 16, Protection of Employee Safety and Welfare; and Chapter 20, Consumer Transactions and the Law.

- There is greater emphasis on the international legal environment than in the previous edition. Chapter 21, The Legal Environment of International Business, has been updated and expanded. Moreover, international applications have been integrated into many chapters. For example, there is increased emphasis on international dispute resolution, the role of the Constitution in state and federal regulation of international commerce, international sales law, international protection of intellectual property rights, international implications of securities marketing and trading, and the international application of employment discrimination laws.

Format and Approach

As noted earlier, the strengths of the first two editions—the basic format and conceptual approach—have been retained. The following is a brief description of that format and approach.

Structure: The text is again divided into three parts, but with a somewhat different orientation in the second part. Part I, *Business and the Legal System,* explores the fundamental nature, structure, and processes of our legal system. It also examines in some depth the various sources of our rules of law. Part II, titled *Business and the Law of Commerce,* presents some of the more traditional business-related legal subjects, including contracts and sales, torts and products liability, and agency and business organizations. Part III, *Business and the Regulatory Environment,* discusses several common rationales for government regulation and then examines various federal and state laws that impose constraints on business activities.

Writing Style: We have continued to be mindful of the fact that we are writing this text *for students*. Thus we have not attempted to create a legal reference work, or to expound on topics of our own particular interest, at the expense of a coherent and balanced textbook. Similarly, we have continued to use a lucid, readable writing style. Legal jargon is used only when absolutely necessary, and in those instances it is fully explained. We have also avoided the vice of "rule-stating." Rather than merely setting forth rule after rule, we have provided explanation, background, illustration, and analysis of relevant legal principles.

Coverage: Our topical treatment continues to be evenly balanced. This means that we have tried to align the depth and breadth of our treatment of a given topic with the professional consensus regarding that topic's relative importance. Similarly, a proper balance has been struck between the theoretical and the practical. Ample theoretical foundation is provided, and then is supported by practical illustrations. We have continued to be careful not to go too far in either direction: that is, the theory does not delve into the arcane, and the practical does not overemphasize the "how to."

Case Presentation: Cases are included at pertinent points in each chapter, rather than being lumped together at chapter ends. We continue to present the facts of each case in our own words for the purpose of clarity. Following the summary of facts is the court's opinion, which has—in every case—been edited judiciously to maintain a reasonable length and to focus the student's attention on those points being illustrated. At the same time, we have tried not to over-edit; enough of the opinion is presented to enable the student to participate in the court's analysis, to obtain a sense of the judicial process, and to consider relevant policy implications.

Teaching Aids

This edition is again accompanied by complete instructional support materials. The *Instructor's Manual and Test Bank* includes answers to the end-of-chapter problems and questions, case briefs, and a test bank that includes both objective test items and brief essay questions. The *Study Guide* has been written by Dan Bertozzi, Jr., of California Polytechnic State University.

Acknowledgments

Once again we are grateful to the many people whose assistance was invaluable in the preparation of this edition. In particular, thanks goes to several colleagues at other institutions who reviewed the fourth edition manuscript: Philip Dimarzio, Gene Chambers, Dennis Kuhn, Burke T. Ward, Villanova University; Sheelwant Pawar, Idaho State University; Nancy Hauserman, Nim Razook, University of Oklahoma; Lynn Ward, Bowling Green State University; Dr. Randy Abbott, Southwest State University; Ronald Bird, Rene Cone, Richard Finkley, Governors State University; Susan Grady, University of Massachusetts; Gainesville College; Louis E. Katz, Youngstown State University; John Michael, Margaret Noteman, Marvin Segal, College of DuPage; John H. Shannon, Seton Hall University; Katie Simmons, David Hoch, Louise Holcomb, Gainesville College; Daniel Warner, Western Washington University; Clint Wood, Delta State University; Thomas Brierton, University of the Pacific; W. Arthur Graham, University of Montana; E. C. Hipp, Clemson University; Neal A. Phillips, University of Delaware; Robert T. Rhodes, Texas Christian University; Kent Royalty, St. Mary's University; Deborah A. Ballam, Ohio State University; Thomas Brucker, Sandra Burns, Arkansas State University; Richard L. Coffinberger, George Mason University; Roger Crowe, Pellissippi State Technical Community College; Sylvia Denys, Glen Droguemueller, Charles Foster, University of North Texas; Paul D. Frederickson, University of Wisconsin-Oshkosh; Susan Gardner, California State University-Chico; Andrea Giampetro-Meyer, Loyola College; Carolyn Hotchkiss, Babson College; Janell Kurtz, St. Cloud State University; Melinda Kwart, Robert Lamb, Incarnate Word College; Greg Anderson, Logan Langwith, Richard Larson, Mary May, Brad McDonald, Northern Illinois University; Christine O'Brien, Mike Pustay, Texas A & M University; John Quinn, University of Dayton; Durwood Ruegger, University of Southern Mississippi; Albert

Spaulding, Wayne State University; Larry Strate, University of Las Vegas; and Curtis Terflinger, Wichita State University.

Finally, we wish to thank Scott Isenberg, acquisitions editor; Glenn Martin, developmental editor; Jim Patterson, project editor; Marilyn Williams, production manager; and Linda Miller, designer for their critical roles in developing and producing this fourth edition.

John R. Allison
Robert A. Prentice
August 1992

CONTENTS IN BRIEF

PART I BUSINESS AND THE LEGAL SYSTEM 1

Chapter 1 *Nature and Sources of Law* 2

Chapter 2 *Court Systems, Jurisdiction, and Functions* 22

Chapter 3 *Litigation and Alternative Methods of Dispute Resolution* 48

Chapter 4 *Common and Statutory Law* 88

Chapter 5 *Constitutional Law* 116

Chapter 6 *Lawmaking by Administrative Agencies* 166

Chapter 7 *Business Ethics, Corporate Social Responsiveness, and the Law* 190

Chapter 8 *Criminal Law and Business* 222

PART II BUSINESS AND THE LAW OF COMMERCE 253

Chapter 9 *Contract and Sales Law* 254

Chapter 10 *General Tort Law* 290

Chapter 11 *Products Liability* 324

Chapter 12　*Business Torts*　360

Chapter 13　*Agency and Business Organizations*　392

PART III　BUSINESS AND THE REGULATORY ENVIRONMENT　423

Chapter 14　*Antitrust Law*　428

Chapter 15　*Securities Regulation*　468

Chapter 16　*Employment Law: Protection of Employee Security and Welfare*　504

Chapter 17　*Employment Law: Protection Against Discrimination*　542

Chapter 18　*Employment Law: Labor-Management Relations*　588

Chapter 19　*Environmental Protection Law*　626

Chapter 20　*Consumer Transactions and the Law*　654

Chapter 21　*The Legal Environment of International Business*　692

CONTENTS

PART I — BUSINESS AND THE LEGAL SYSTEM 1

Chapter 1 Nature and Sources of Law 2

Law as a Subject of Study 3
What is Law? 4
Rules and Processes 5
Requisites of a Legal System 6
Some Classifications of Law 9
Legal Misconceptions 12
Law, Justice, and Morals 13
Selecting and Using Attorneys 18

Chapter 2 Court Systems, Jurisdiction, and Functions 22

Court Systems 25
Problems of Jurisdiction 29
Law, Equity, and Remedies 43

Chapter 3 Litigation and Alternative Methods of Dispute Resolution 48

The Adversarial System 50
Litigation: Pretrial Proceedings 52

Litigation: Trial Proceedings 60
Litigation: The Appellate Courts 71
Note on Performance of Judges 77
Alternative Dispute Resolution 80

Chapter 4 COMMON AND STATUTORY LAW 88

Origin of Common Law 90
Common Law—The Doctrine of Stare Decisis 92
Profile of Our Federal and State Statutory Law 97
Statutory Law—The Rationale 98
Limitations on Legislative Bodies 99
Statutory Law and Common Law—A Contrast 104
Statutory Interpretation 106
Selected State Statutes 112

Chapter 5 CONSTITUTIONAL LAW 116

Organization of the Federal Government 118
Authority of Federal and State Governments 121
Protecting Basic Rights 137

Chapter 6 LAWMAKING BY ADMINISTRATIVE AGENCIES 166

Rise of the Administrative Agency 168
The Agency—An Overview 169
Legislative Delegation of Lawmaking Power 170
Functions and Powers 171
Estoppel 184
Recent Developments 185

Chapter 7 BUSINESS ETHICS, CORPORATE SOCIAL RESPONSIVENESS, AND THE LAW 190

What Is Ethics? 193
The Relationship Between Law and Ethics 194
Are There Any Moral Standards? 197
The "Moral Minimum" 198
Is There a Duty to "Do Good"? 202

Excusing Conditions 204
Moral Dilemmas 205
Moral Reasoning and Decision Making 206
Are Corporations Moral Agents? 212
Does Ethics Pay? 215
Corporate Social Responsiveness 217

Chapter 8 CRIMINAL LAW AND BUSINESS 222

Nature of Criminal Law 224
Constitutional Protections 228
General Elements of Criminal Responsibility 231
General Criminal Defenses 234
State Crimes Affecting Business 236
Federal Crimes Affecting Business 241
Computer Crime 246
White Collar Crime 248
International Criminal Enforcement 250

PART II BUSINESS AND THE LAW OF COMMERCE 253

Chapter 9 CONTRACT AND SALES LAW 254

Introduction 256
Elements of a Contract 260
Rescission of Contracts 274
Contracts in Writing 275
Third Parties 276
Contract Interpretation 282
Remedies 283
Title and Risk of Loss 285
Internationalization of Contract Law 287

Chapter 10 GENERAL TORT LAW 290

Scope and Complexity of Tort Law 292
Negligence 293

Major Intentional Torts 305
Other Intentional Torts 316
Special Problems 320

Chapter 11 PRODUCTS LIABILITY 324

Warranty 326
Negligence 344
Strict Liability 345
Federal Consumer Legislation 354
Legislative Limitations on Products Liability Revolution 356

Chapter 12 BUSINESS TORTS 360

Interference with Business Relationships 362
Trademark Infringement 366
Misuse of Trade Secrets 371
Patent Infringement 375
Copyright Infringement 380
International Protection of Intellectual Property 385
Unfair Competition 386

Chapter 13 AGENCY AND BUSINESS ORGANIZATIONS 392

Partnerships 402
Corporations 409
Special Duties in Closely Held Corporations 420

PART III BUSINESS AND THE REGULATORY ENVIRONMENT 423

Transitional Note—Introduction to Government Regulations of Business 424

Chapter 14 ANTITRUST LAW 428

Monopolization 434
Mergers 440

Horizontal Restraints of Trade 447
Vertical Restraints of Trade 455

Chapter 15 SECURITIES REGULATION 468

Introduction to Securities Regulation 470
1933 Act: Regulating the Issuance of Securities 474
1934 Act: Regulating the Trading of Securities 484
State Regulation 499
International Implications 500

Chapter 16 EMPLOYMENT LAW: PROTECTION OF EMPLOYEE SECURITY AND WELFARE 504

The Employee—Independent Contractor Distinction 506
The Employment Relationship and Job Security 507
Protection of Employee Privacy 514
Workers' Compensation Legislation 520
The Occupational Safety and Health Act 528
The Fair Labor Standards Act 533
Unemployment Compensation 538

Chapter 17 EMPLOYMENT LAW: PROTECTION AGAINST DISCRIMINATION 542

Race, Color, National Origin, Sex, and Religion 544
Age Discrimination 579
Discrimination Against People with Disabilities 580

Chapter 18 EMPLOYMENT LAW: LABOR-MANAGEMENT RELATIONS 588

Federal Legislation 591
The Limited Role of State Law 594
The National Labor Relations Board 594
Scope of the NLRA 595
Selecting the Bargaining Representative 598
The Collective Bargaining Process 606
Unfair Labor Practices 614

Chapter 19   Environmental Protection Law   626

Common Law and Pollution   629
National Environmental Policy Act   633
Water Pollution Control   635
Air Pollution Control   638
Solid Waste and Its Disposal   642
Regulation of Toxic Substances   647
Noise Pollution   648
Indoor Pollution   649
International Legal Aspects of Pollution   649
The Environment, Industry, and Society   651

Chapter 20   Consumer Transactions and the Law   654

Deceptive Trade Practices   656
Consumer Credit Protection Act   661
Uniform Consumer Credit Code   675
Real Estate Settlement Procedures Act   679
Additional Consumer Protection Measures   680
Bankruptcy—Relief for the Overextended Consumer   681

Chapter 21   The Legal Environment of International Business   692

International Sales Contract   696
Resolving International Trade Disputes   701
National Regulations of the Export/Import Process   711
Organizing for International Trade   717
Other Ways of Doing Business   721
Regulating the Transnational Corporation   723

Appendix A

The Constitution of the United States of America   727

Appendix B

Sherman Act (As Amended) (Excerpts)   738

Appendix C

Clayton Act (As Amended) (Excerpts) 739

Appendix D

Robinson-Patman Act (Excerpts) 741

Appendix E

Federal Trade Commission Act (As Amended) (Excerpts) 743

Appendix F

Title VII of the 1964 Civil Rights Act (As Amended) (Excerpts) 744

Appendix G

National Labor Relations Act (As Amended) (Excerpts) 747

Glossary 753

Case Index 774

Subject Index 780

PART I

BUSINESS AND THE LEGAL SYSTEM

1
CHAPTER

LAW AS A SUBJECT OF STUDY

A. P. Herbert once wrote: "The general mass, if they consider the law at all, regard it as they regard some monster in the zoo. It is odd, it is extraordinary; but there it is, they have known it all their lives, they suppose that there must be some good reason for it, and accept it as inevitable and natural."[1]

Although the law is not nearly as odd or extraordinary as many persons believe, it is undeniably "there"—an integral part of the environment that has been a source of great interest, even fascination, for centuries.

---

[1] *Uncommon Law*, 1936.

NATURE AND SOURCES OF LAW

Considering the pervasiveness of the law, this is hardly surprising. Almost all human activity is affected by it in one manner or another, and this alone is adequate explanation for such widespread interest. Certainly, anyone contemplating a business transaction of any magnitude today realizes that he or she must consider not only the physical and financial effort it will entail but—to some extent, at least—the legal ramifications as well. And beyond the practical effect law has on individual conduct in specific situations, it possesses additional characteristics that make its study uniquely rewarding.

First, although the law is by no means an occult language understood only by lawyers, it clearly is a subject that is *academically stimulating*. For students to get any real benefit from a course in law, they must at the very least learn to recognize precise legal issues, understand the reasoning of the courts as set forth in their decisions, and subject this reasoning to critical analysis. These activities involve varying degrees of mental exercise; and although this is not always pleasurable, it fosters a degree of mental discipline that is not easily acquired elsewhere.

Second, students should have the opportunity to consider the law as a *societal institution*—to see how it has affected conduct and thought and how it has been influenced by them in return. Whatever the law is, it certainly is not static, and it certainly does not exist in a vacuum.

This approach, which emphasizes the impact of social and economic changes on the law, gives the subject a liberal arts flavor. When viewed in this light, the law and its processes become rewarding to anyone having even a passing interest in economics, sociology, and political science.

WHAT IS LAW?

Ever since the law began to take form, scholars have spent impressive amounts of time and thought analyzing its purposes and defining what it is and what it ought to be—in short, fitting it into a philosophic scheme of one form or another. Although space does not permit inclusion of even the major essays in which these philosophers defend their respective views, their conclusions provide us with useful observations about the nature of law. Consider, for example, the following:

> *We have been told by Plato that law is a form of social control, an instrument of the good life, the way to the discovery of reality, the true reality of the social structure; by Aristotle that it is a rule of conduct, a contract, an ideal of reason, a rule of decision, a form of order; by Cicero that it is the agreement of reason and nature, the distinction between the just and the unjust, a command or prohibition; by Aquinas that it is an ordinance of reason for the common good, made by him who has care of the community, and promulgated [thereby]; by Bacon that certainty is the prime necessity of law; by Hobbes that law is the command of the sovereign; by Spinoza that it is a plan of life; by Leibniz that its character is determined by the structure of society; by Locke that it is a norm*

established by the commonwealth; by Hume that it is a body of precepts; by Kant that it is a harmonizing of wills by means of universal rules in the interests of freedom; by Fichte that it is a relation between human beings; by Hegel that it is an unfolding or realizing of the idea of right.[2]

Although these early writers substantially agree as to the general *purpose* of law—the ensuring of orderliness to all human activity—their *definitions* of the term vary considerably. Today there is still no definition of *law* that has universal approval, even in legal circles—a fact that is no doubt attributable to its inherent breadth. One can understand how very broad the law is by considering just these few widely varying matters with which the law must deal: (1) the standards of care required of a surgeon in the operating room (2) the determination of whether an "exclusive-dealing" provision in a motion picture distributor's contracts constitutes an unfair method of competition under federal law, and (3) the propriety of a witness's testimony when it is challenged as constituting "hearsay" under the rules of evidence.

A brief comment about *sources* of law is in order at this early point. In our legal system (and in most others throughout the world), there are *primary* and *secondary* sources. Primary sources, which contain legally binding rules and procedures, include federal and state constitutions, statutes (legislative enactments), administrative agency regulations, and court decisions; also included are federal treaties and city ordinances. Secondary sources summarize and explain the law, and sometimes criticize and suggest changes in it. Such sources are not legally binding, but are frequently referred to and used by courts, administrative agencies, legislative staff members, and practicing attorneys as aids in determining what the law is or should be. Secondary sources include research articles in academic legal periodicals, restatements (which consist of summaries of and commentary upon specific subject areas of law by experts in those areas), legal texts and encyclopedias, and others.

RULES AND PROCESSES

At the risk of oversimplification, it can be said that two major approaches to the teaching and study of law exist today. The *rule-oriented approach* views the law as consisting of the rules that are in effect within a state or nation at a given time. This is very likely what practicing attorneys have in mind when they speak about the law, and it is a perfectly respectable view. Witness the following definition adopted by the American Law Institute: "[Law] is the

---

[2] Huntington Cairns, *Legal Philosophy from Plato to Hegel* (Baltimore: Johns Hopkins University Press, 1949).

body of principles, standards and rules which the courts . . . apply in the decision of controversies brought before them."[3]

The *process-oriented approach* sees the law in a broader light: The *processes by which the rules and principles are formulated* (rather than the rules and principles themselves) constitute the major element of law. Because law is necessitated solely by human activity, those who emphasize process contend that the ever-changing problems resulting from this activity and *the ways in which the law attempts to solve them* must receive primary emphasis if one is to gain a proper insight into the subject. The following definition expresses this view: "Law is a dynamic process, a system of regularized, institutionalized procedures for the orderly decision of social questions, including the settlement of disputes."[4]

Obviously, the law is both rule and process. Each approach to the teaching and study of law is legitimate; indeed, each is essential and inevitable. The only difference is in emphasis. In this text, process is emphasized in the first few chapters, and rules in many of the later chapters. Our discussion of rules and principles, however, always includes related legal processes.

REQUISITES OF A LEGAL SYSTEM

For a legal system to function properly, particularly within a democratic government such as ours, it must command the respect of the great majority of people governed by it. To do so, the legal rules that compose it must, as a practical matter, possess certain characteristics. They must be (1) relatively certain, (2) relatively flexible, (3) known or knowable, and (4) apparently reasonable.

In the following chapters we consider these requirements more fully and determine the extent to which our legal system satisfies them. For the moment, we give brief descriptions of each of the four.

CERTAINTY

One essential element of a stable society is reasonable certainty about its laws, not only at a given moment but over long periods of time. Many of our activities, particularly business activities, are based on the assumption that legal principles will remain stable into the foreseeable future. If this were not so, chaos would result. For example, no television network would enter into a contract with a professional football league, under which it is to pay millions of dollars for the right to televise league games, if it were not reasonably sure that the law would compel the league to live up to its contractual obligations or to pay damages if it did not. And no lawyer would advise a client on a contemplated course of action without similar assurances.

---

[3] *Restatement, Conflict of Laws 2d*, §4. The American Law Institute, 1971.
[4] James I. Houghteling, Jr., *The Dynamics of Law* (New York: Harcourt Brace Jovanovich, 1963).

Because of these considerations, the courts (and to a lesser extent the legislatures) are generally reluctant to overturn principles that have been part of the law for any appreciable length of time. This is not to say, of course, that the law is static. Many areas of American law are dramatically different than they were 50, or even 25 years ago. However, most of these changes resulted from a series of modifications of existing principles rather than from an abrupt reversal of them. The *Soldano v. O'Daniels* case later in this chapter illustrates one such modification.

FLEXIBILITY

In any nation, particularly a highly industrialized one such as the United States, societal changes occur with accelerating (almost dismaying) rapidity. Each change present new legal problems that must be resolved without undue delay. This necessity was recognized by Justice Cardozo when he wrote that "the law, like the traveler, must be ready for the morrow."[5]

Some problems are simply the result of scientific and technological advances. Before Orville and Wilbur Wright's day, for example, it was a well-established principle that landowners had unlimited rights to the airspace above their property, any invasion of which constituted a *trespass*—a wrongful entry. But when the courts became convinced that the flying machine was here to stay, the utter impracticality of this view became apparent and owners' rights were subsequently limited to a "reasonable use" of their airspace.

Other novel problems result from changing methods of doing business or from shifting attitudes and moral views. Recent examples of the former are the proliferating use of the business franchise and of the general credit card. Attitudinal changes involve such questions as the proper ends of government, the propriety of Sunday sales, and the circumstances in which abortions should be permitted.

Some of these problems, of course, require solutions that are more political than legal in nature. This is particularly true where large numbers of the citizenry are faced with a common problem, such as the many difficulties faced by disabled persons in overcoming stereotypical attitudes and physical barriers, and where the alleviation of the problem may well be thought to constitute a legitimate function of either the state or federal government. The passage by Congress of the Americans with Disabilities Act of 1990 is an example of an attempted solution at the federal level of this particular problem.

Regardless of political considerations, however, many problems (particularly those involving disputes between individuals) can be settled only through the judicial process—that is, by one of the parties instituting legal action against the other. The duty to arrive at a final solution in all such cases falls squarely on the courts, no matter how novel or varied the issues. It is to their credit, but it is also their curse, that Americans increasingly turn to

---

[5] Benjamin N. Cardozo, *The Growth of the Law* (New Haven: Yale University Press, 1924), pp. 19–20.

them for dispute resolution, and not to the churches, schools, or other institutions that are available.

KNOWABILITY

One of the basic assumptions underlying a democracy—and, in fact, almost every form of government—is that the great majority of its citizens are going to obey its laws voluntarily. It hardly need be said that obedience requires a certain knowledge of the rules, or at least a reasonable means of acquiring this knowledge, on the part of the governed. No one, not even a lawyer, "knows" all the law or all the rules that make up a single branch of law; that could never be required. But it is necessary for persons who need legal advice to have access to experts on the rules—lawyers. It is equally necessary that the law be in such form that lawyers can determine their clients' positions with reasonable certainty to recommend the most advantageous courses of action.

REASONABLE-NESS

Most citizens abide by the law. Many do so even when they are not in sympathy with a particular rule, out of a sense of responsibility, a feeling that it is their civic duty, like it or not; others, no doubt, do so simply through fear of getting caught if they do not. But by and large the rules have to appear reasonable to the great majority of the people if they are going to be obeyed for long. The so-called Prohibition Amendment, which met with such wholesale violation that it was repealed in 1933, is the classic example of a rule lacking widespread acceptance. Closely allied with the idea of reasonableness is the requirement that the rules reflect, and adapt to, changing views of morality and justice. Figure 1.1 summarizes the qualities a legal system must possess to function properly.

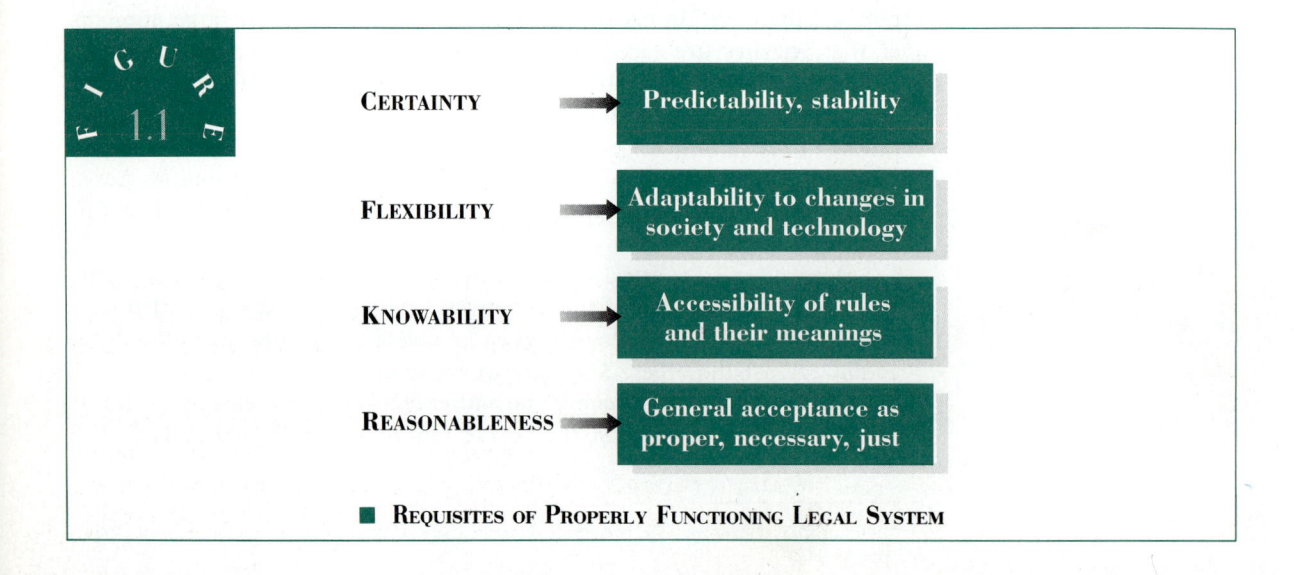

FIGURE 1.1

CERTAINTY →	Predictability, stability
FLEXIBILITY →	Adaptability to changes in society and technology
KNOWABILITY →	Accessibility of rules and their meanings
REASONABLENESS →	General acceptance as proper, necessary, just

■ **REQUISITES OF PROPERLY FUNCTIONING LEGAL SYSTEM**

SOME CLASSIFICATIONS OF LAW

Although the lawmaking and adjudicatory processes are the major concern in Part I, the products that result from the lawmaking process—the rules themselves and the bodies of law that they make up—must not be overlooked. At the outset, particularly, it is useful to recognize some of the more important *classifications of law*.

SUBJECT MATTER

One way of classifying all the law in the United States is on the basis of the *subject matter* to which it relates. Fifteen or 20 branches or subjects are of particular importance, among them

- Administrative law
- Agency
- Commercial paper
- Constitutional law
- Contracts
- Corporation law
- Criminal law
- Domestic relations
- Evidence
- Partnerships
- Personal property
- Real property
- Sales
- Taxation
- Torts
- Wills and estates

Two observations can be made about this classification:

1. The subjects of agency, contracts, and torts are essentially *common law* in nature, whereas the subjects of corporation law, criminal law, sales, and taxation are governed by *statute*. Most of the remaining subjects, particularly evidence and property, are mixed in nature.

2. Several of these subjects obviously have a much closer relationship to the world of business than the others; these are the topics that fall within the usual business law or legal environment courses of a business school curriculum. Agency, contracts, corporation law, and sales are typical examples.

FEDERAL AND STATE LAW

Another way of categorizing all law in this country is on the basis of the governmental unit from which it arises. On this basis, all law may be said to be either *federal law* or *state law*. Although there are some very important areas of fedeal law, as we shall see later, the great bulk of our law is state (or "local") law. Virtually all the subjects in the preceding list, for example, are within the jurisdiction of the individual states. Thus it is correct to say that there are 50 bodies of contract law in the United States, 50 bodies of corporation law, and so on. But this is not as bewildering as it appears, because the rules that constitute a given branch of law in each state substantially parallel those that exist in the other states—particularly in regard to common-law subjects.

COMMON LAW (CASE LAW) AND STATUTORY LAW

The term **common law** has several different meanings. It sometimes is used to refer only to the judge-made rules in effect in England at an early time—the "ancient unwritten law of England." It sometimes is also used to refer only to those judge-made rules of England that were subsequently adopted by the states in this country. In this text, however, we define the term more broadly to mean *all the rules and principles currently existing in any state, regardless of their historical origin, that result from judicial decisions in those areas of law where legislatures hve not enacted comprehensive statutes*. This type of law, examined further in Chapter 4, is frequently referred to as case law, judge-made law, or unwritten law.

The term **statutory law,** by contrast, is generally used to refer to the state and federal *statutes* in effect at a given time—that is, rules that have been formally adopted by legislative bodies rather than by the courts. When *statutory law* is used in contrast to *common law*, it also comprises state and federal constitutions, municipal ordinances, and even treaties. Statutory law is frequently referred to as written law in the sense that once a statute or constitutional provision is adopted, its exact wording is set forth in the final text as passed—although the precise meaning, we should recall, is still subject to interpretation by the courts. The subjects of statutory law and judicial interpretation are also covered in Chapter 4.

CIVIL AND CRIMINAL LAW

Civil Law

The most common types of controversies are civil actions—that is, actions in which the parties bringing the suits (the **plaintiffs**) are seeking to enforce private obligations or duties against the other parties (the **defendants**). **Civil laws,** then, are all those laws that spell out the rights and duties existing among individuals, business firms, and sometimes even government agencies. Contract law, tort law, and sales law all fall within the civil category.

The usual remedy that the plaintiff is seeking in a civil suit is *damages*—a sum of money roughly equivalent to the loss that he or she has suffered as a result of the defendant's wrong. Another civil remedy is the *injunction*—a court decree ordering the defendant to do or not to do some particular thing.

Criminal Law

Criminal law, in contrast to civil law, comprises those statutes by which a state or the federal government prohibits specified kinds of conduct and which additionally provide for the imposition of *fines or imprisonment* on persons convicted of violating them. Criminal suits are always brought by the government whose law has allegedly been violated. In enacting criminal statutes, a legislature is saying that certain activities are so inherently inimical to the public good that they constitute wrongs against organized society as a whole.

In addition to the nature of the liability that is imposed, criminal suits also differ from civil suits in another significant respect. In a criminal action it is necessary that the government's case be proved "beyond a reasonable doubt," whereas in civil actions the plaintiff—the person bringing the suit—need prove his or her allegations only by "a preponderance of the evidence."

Crimes are either *felonies or misdemeanors,* depending on the severity of the penalty that the statute prescribes. A **felony** is the most serious of the two and is usually defined as crime for which the legislature has provided a maximum penalty of either imprisonment for more than one year or death, as in the cases of murder, arson, or rape. **Misdemeanors** are all crimes carrying lesser penalties, most traffic offenses, for example.

Finally, it should be noted that some wrongful acts are of a dual nature, subjecting the wrong doer to both criminal and civil penalties. For example, if X steals Y's car, the state could bring a criminal action against X, and Y could also bring a civil action to recover damages arising from the theft.

PUBLIC AND PRIVATE LAW

Some branches of law deal more directly with the relationship that exists between the government and the individual than do others. On the basis of the degree to which this relationship is involved, law is occasionally classified as public law or private law.

When an area of law is directly concerned with the government–individual (or government–business) relationship, it falls within the *public law* designation. Subjects that are most clearly of this nature are criminal law, constitutional law, and administrative law. Because *criminal laws* deal with acts that are prohibited by a government itself, the violation of which is a "wrong against the state," such laws more directly affect the government–individual relationship than do any of the other laws. To the extent that our federal Constitution contains provisions substantially guaranteeing that certain rights of the individual or business cannot be invaded by federal and state government activities, the subject of *constitutional law* falls within the same category. *Administrative law*—comprising the principles that govern the procedures and activities of government boards and commissions—is of similar nature, in that such agencies are also concerned with the enforcement of certain state and federal statutes (and regulations promulgated thereunder) against individual citizens and businesses.

Many other areas of law, which are primarily concerned with the creation and enforcement of the rights of one individual against another, fall within the *private law* category. Although a state is indeed concerned that all its laws be properly enforced, even when individuals' or business firms' rights alone are being adjudicated, the concern in these areas is distinctly secondary to the interests of the parties themselves. There also are many areas of law that are of a mixed public-private nature; examples include state or federal statutes that regulate business activities and also create rights and obligations that individuals and businesses themselves may enforce.

LEGAL MISCONCEPTIONS

Before proceeding to the more substantive areas of law, we will reflect briefly on two widely held misconceptions about our legal system.

MYTH OF THE ONE RIGHT ANSWER

It is widely believed that there is one "correct" legal answer to any legal controversy. This is true in a good many situations but certainly not as often as many persons believe. The chief reasons for divergent legal opinions are quite explainable:

1. Many rules are expressed in rather general terms to fit varying situations. Consequently, they afford the courts considerable latitude in deciding how they should be applied to specific situations.

2. The ultimate legal processes are in the hands of people, the judges, whose application of rules is always subject, to some extent, to their individual economic and political philosophies and personal moral beliefs. The law, therefore, is not an exact science and never will be.

3. The nature of most legal problems is such that something can be said in behalf of both litigants. The ordinary controversy does not present a clear-cut case of a "good" person suing a "bad" one. In some cases, each party has acted in good faith; in others, each is guilty of some degree of wrong. Additionally, there are some "legal collision" situations, in which one general principle of law may lead to one result while a second will lead to a different result. In such instances each principle will probably have to undergo some modification when applied to particular cases, with results that are not always harmonious.

MYTH OF JUDICIAL ECCENTRICITY

The feeling is sometimes expressed that the law is not based on common sense—that its rules are so esoteric and arbitrary, and the judges and lawyers so preoccupied with them, that the results are not in keeping with reality or with what a reasonable person would expect. This indictment, in very large measure, is false. Cases invariably present practical problems for the courts, and the courts keep the practical considerations in mind in choosing the rules that apply.

Take, for example, this situation. C, a contractor, agrees to build a house according to certain specifications for O, the owner, for $60,000. When the house is completed, by which time O has paid $36,000, O discovers that the family room is 10 inches shorter than the plans specified. O refuses to make further payments for this reason, whereupon C brings suit to recover the balance of $24,000.

Now, as far as contract law is concerned, the principle is well established that a person who breaches a contract is not permitted to recover anything from the other party. The question here is, should that rule be applicable to this specific situation, where that would mean that C would not recover any of the balance? The practical person might well say, "I wouldn't think so—where the defect is so slight, it would seem unfair for C to suffer a loss of $24,000." The law reaches the same conclusion: under a view known as the *doctrine of substantial performance*, a person in C's position is usually permitted to recover most of the unpaid balance (even though he did, technically, breach the contract).

The foregoing does not mean, of course, that the law is perfect or that startling or unfair decisions never occur. They do. But by and large the unreasonable result occurs with much less frequency than reports in the news media would indicate; and even in such cases, the possibility usually exists that an appellate court will subsequently repair much of the damage.

LAW, JUSTICE, AND MORALS

LAW AND JUSTICE

There is a close relationship between law and justice, but the terms are not equivalent. Most results of the application of legal rules are "just"—fair and reasonable. Where this is not so to any degree, the rules are usually changed. Yet it must be recognized that results occasionally "are not fair." Without attempting to defend the law in all such instances, some cautions should nevertheless be voiced.

First, there is never complete agreement as to what is just; there are always some decisions that are just to some people but not to others. And even if there were unanimity of opinion—a perfect justice, so to speak—the facts in many cases are such that it is simply impossible to attain this end.

In some situations, for example, a legal controversy may arise between two honest persons who dealt with each other in good faith, as sometimes occurs in the area of "mutual mistake." Take this case: P contracts to sell land to G for $40,000, both parties mistakenly believing that a General Motors plant will be built on adjoining land. When G learns that the plant will not be built, he refuses to go through with the deal. If a court rules that the mistake frees G of his contractual obligations, the result might be quite unjust as far as P is concerned. And if it rules otherwise, the decision might seem quite unfair to G. Yet a decision must be made, one way or the other.

Second, in some instances it is fairly clear who is right and who is wrong, but the situation has progressed to the point where it is impossible, either physically or legally, to put the "good" person back into the original position. These "bad check" cases will illustrate: A buys a TV set from Z, giving Z her personal check in payment. If the check bounces, it is clear that Z should be allowed to recover the set. But what if the TV has been destroyed by fire while in A's hands? Here the most the law can do is give Z a *judgment* against A—an order requiring A to pay a sum of money to Z equal to the amount of the check, which A may or may not be financially able to do. Or suppose that A had resold the TV to X before Z learned that the check had bounced. Would it not be unfair to permit Z to retake the set from X, an innocent third party?

Because of these considerations, and others to be discussed later, the most the law can seek to accomplish is *substantial* justice in the greatest possible number of cases that come before it.

LAW AND MORALS

Although the terms *law* and *morals* are not synonymous, legal standards and moral standards parallel one another more closely than many people believe. For example, criminal statutes prohibit certain kinds of conduct that are clearly "morally wrong"—murder, theft, arson, and the like. And other rules of law impose civil liability for similar kinds of conduct that although not crimes, are also generally felt to be wrongful in nature—such as negligence, breach of contract, and fraud. To illustrate: S, in negotiating the sale of a race horse to B, tells B that the horse has run an eighth of a mile in 15 seconds on several occasions within the past month. In fact, the animal has never been clocked under 18 seconds, and S knows this. B, believing the statement to be true, purchases the horse. In such a case S's intentional misstatement constitutes the tort of *fraud*, and B—assuming he can prove these facts in a legal action brought against S—has the right to set aside the transaction, returning the horse and recovering the price he has paid.

Why, then, are the terms *law* and *morals* not precisely synonymous? First, there are some situations in which moral standards are higher than those imposed by law. For example, a person who has promised to keep an offer open for a stated period of time generally has the legal right to withdraw the offer before the given time has elapsed (for reasons appearing in a later chapter). Yet many persons who make such offers feel morally compelled to keep their offers open as promised, even though the law does not require this. Second, sometimes the law imposes higher standards than do our morals. For example, no religions or philosophies feature the 65-mile-per-hour speed limit as a major tenet, yet it is illegal to drive faster. Third, many rules of law and court decisions are based on statutory or practical requirements that have little or no relationship to moral considerations. For example, in the area of minors' contracts, we see later that most courts feel, on balance, that it is sound public policy to permit minors to disaffirm (cancel) their contracts until they reach the age of majority, even though the contracts were otherwise perfectly valid and even though the persons with whom they dealt did not overreach or take advantage of them in any way. These observations notwithstanding, a society's moral standards will always heavily influence its legal standards. The relationship between legal standards and moral standards, as well as many related questions, is explored thoroughly in Chapter 7.

The interplay between law and morality is illustrated in the following case. Because the study of law involves to a very great extent the ability to reason from cases, students must have some familiarity with court procedures and jurisdiction. For this reason, major emphasis on cases will begin in the following chapter. The case below is our first, and therefore requires a few prefatory comments:

1. This is a *wrongful death* action authorized by statute to allow close relatives of deceased persons to sue those whose wrongful acts have caused a death. Without such statutes, we could be held liable for carelessly or intentionally injuring someone but could escape civil liability if we killed them. Under a state wrongful death statute, the *wrongful* act must be a *tort* such as negligence or assault and battery, for which the deceased could have filed suit if only injury and not death had occurred. In this case, the basis for the wrongful death action is a claim by the *plaintiff* that the *defendant* committed the tort of negligence. The subject of torts is discussed in Chapters 10, 11, and 12. In addition, the plaintiff is seeking to hold both the bartender and his employer legally responsible for damages. Although it is only the bartender's conduct that is in question, under the law of *agency* the bartender's employer also can be held liable if the bartender was acting within the *scope of his employment* at the time of the incident. The bartender clearly was acting within the scope of his employment in this case. If the court finds the bartender liable and the employer pays the judgment to the plaintiff, the employer will have a legal right to reimbursement from the bartender. As a practical matter, however, employers seldom exercise this right. The law of agency is discussed in Chapter 13.

2. In a civil case, the jury is normally the "judge of the *facts*." The trial judge decides the *law*. However, a judge, for reasons of judicial efficiency, can grant a summary judgment, terminating the case before it is ever tried. Summary judgment is appropriately granted if the evidence in the case so clearly indicates that factually one side or the other is entitled to prevail that a trial would be a waste of time. Only if the judge can conclude that there is "no genuine issue of material fact" should a summary judgment be granted on this ground. The following case involves a situation in which the trial judge had granted a summary judgment for the defendant.

3. If a trial court does grant a summary judgment motion, the losing party can always seek review in an appellate court. If the appellate court finds that the ruling was in error, the case will be returned to the trial court with instructions for a trial on the issue.

SOLDANO v. O'DANIELS

CALIFORNIA COURT OF APPEAL, 190 CAL. RPTR. 310 (1983)

On August 9, 1977, Villanueva pulled a gun and threatened the life of Soldano at Happy Jack's Saloon. A patron of Happy Jack's ran across the street to the Circle Inn and informed the bartender of the threat, asking the bartender either to call the police or allow him to use the phone to call the police. The bartender refused both requests. Soon thereafter, Villanueva shot Soldano to death. The plaintiff in this wrongful death action is Soldano's child. The defendants are the bartender and his employer. The trial judge dismissed the claim in response to the defendants' motion for summary judgment. Plaintiff appeals.

ANDREEN, ASSOCIATE JUSTICE:

Does a business establishment incur liability for wrongful death if it denies use of its telephone to a good samaritan who explains an emergency situation occurring without and wishes to call the police?

... There is a distinction, well rooted in the common law, between action and inaction. It has found its way into the prestigious Restatement Second of Torts, which provides in section 314:

> The fact that the actor realizes or should realize that action on his part is necessary for another's aid or protection does not of itself impose upon him a duty to take such action.

The distinction between malfeasance and nonfeasance, between active misconduct working positive injury and failure to act to prevent mischief not brought on by the defendant, is founded on "that attitude of extreme individualism so typical of anglo-saxon legal thought." (Bohlen, *The Moral Duty to Aid Others as a Basis of Tort Liability*, part I (1908) 56 U.Pa.L.Rev. 217, 219–220.)

Defendant argues that the request that its employee call the police [or permit the requestor to make the call] is a request that it do something. He points to the established rule that one who has not created a peril ordinarily does not have a duty to take affirmative action to assist an imperiled person. ...

The refusal of the law to recognize the moral obligation of one to aid another when he is in peril and when such aid may be given without danger and at little cost in effort has been roundly criticized. Prosser describes the case law sanctioning such inaction as a "refus[al] to recognize the moral obligation of common decency and common humanity" and characterizes some of these decisions as "revolting to any moral sense." (Prosser, *Law of Torts* (4th ed. 1971) §56.)

As noted in *Tarasoff v. Regents of University of California*, 131 Cal. Rptr. 14 (1976), the courts have increased the instances in which affirmative duties are imposed not by direct rejection of the common law rule, but by expanding the list of special relationships which will justify departure from that rule. ... In *Tarasoff*, a therapist was told by his patient that he intended to kill Tatiana Tarasoff. The therapist and his supervisors predicted the patient presented a serious danger of violence. In fact he did, for he carried out his threat. The court held the patient–therapist relationship was enough to create a duty to exercise reasonable care to protect others from the foreseeable result of the patient's illness.

... Here there was no special relationship between the defendant and the deceased. But this does not end the matter.

It is time to re-examine the common law rule of nonliability for nonfeasance in the special circumstances of the instant case.

Besides well-publicized actions taken to increase the severity of punishments for criminal offenses, the Legislature has expressed a social imperative to diminish criminal action. [The court then referred to laws passed to compensate citizens for injuries sustained in crime suppression efforts, to make it a misdemeanor to refuse to relinquish a party line when informed that it is needed to call the police, and to establish an emergency '911' telephone system.]

The above statutes ... demonstrate that "that attitude of extreme individualism so typical of anglo-saxon legal thought" may need limited re-examination in light of current societal conditions and the facts of this case to determine whether the defendant owed a duty to the deceased to permit the use of the telephone. ...

As the [California] Supreme Court has noted, the reluctance of the law to impose liability for nonfeasance, as distinguished from misfeasance, is in part due to the difficulties in setting standards and of making rules workable [citing *Tarasoff*].

CONTINUED

Many citizens simply "don't want to get involved." No rule should be adopted which would require a citizen to open up his or her house to a stranger so that the latter may use the telephone to call for emergency assistance. As Mrs. Alexander in Anthony Burgess' *A Clockwork Orange* learned to her horror, such an action may be fraught with danger. It does not follow, however, that use of a telephone in a public portion of a business should be refused for a legitimate emergency call. Imposing liability for such a refusal would not subject innocent citizens to possible attack by the "good samaritan," for it would be limited to an establishment open to the public during times when it is open to business, and to places within the establishment ordinarily accessible to the public.

... We conclude that the bartender owed a duty to the plaintiff's decedent to permit the patron from Happy Jack's to place a call to the police or to place the call himself.

It bears emphasizing that the duty in this case does not require that one must go to the aid of another. That is not the issue here. The employee was not the good samaritan intent on aiding another. The patron was.

It would not be appropriate to await legislative action in this area. The rule was fashioned in the common law tradition, as were the exceptions to the rule.... The courts have a special responsibility to reshape, refine and guide legal doctrine they have created.

The words of the Supreme Court [in *Rodriguez v. Bethlehem Steel Corp.*, 115 Cal. Rptr. 765 (1974)] on the role of the courts in a common law system are well suited to our obligation here:

> The inherent capacity of the common law for growth and change is its most significant feature. Its development has been determined by the social needs of the community which it serves. It is constantly expanding and developing in keeping with advancing civilization and the new conditions and progress of society, and adapting itself to the gradual change of trade, commerce, arts, inventions, and the needs of the country....

In short, as the United States Supreme Court has aptly said, "This flexibility and capacity for growth and adaptation is the peculiar boast and excellence of the common law." [Citation omitted].

The possible imposition of liability on the defendant in this case is not a global change in the law. It is but a slight departure from the "morally questionable" rule of nonliability for inaction absent a special relationship. It is a logical extension of Restatement section 327 which imposes liability for negligent interference with a third person who the defendant knows is attempting to render necessary aid. However small it may be, it is a step which should be taken.

We conclude there are sufficient justiciable issues to permit the case to go to trial and therefore reverse.

COMMENT

1. As this is our first case, a few comments about the mechanics of case reporting are in order:

   a. The opinion, written by Justice Andreen, is that of an intermediate appellate court in a state system. It hears appeals from California state trial courts, and its decisions can be appealed to the California State Supreme Court.

   b. The ellipsis points (...) appearing in the opinion indicate portions that have been deleted by the authors of this text. Deletions are made to eliminate redundancy or exclude issues irrelevant to points that the case has been selected to illustrate.

   c. When a general principle of law is stated in a decision, the court will frequently *cite* (refer to) earlier cases in which that principle has been established. Here, for example, the court has referred to *Tarasoff v. Regents of University of California* for such a purpose. To facilitate the reading of opinions, the authors have generally omitted such references except where the cited case is heavily relied on to support the decision.

2. A word of caution: It is imperative for readers to acquire the ability *to determine the precise issue of a case*, so they will not leap to unwarranted general conclusions. Could we say, for example, that the instant case establishes the principle that on seeing one person attack another with a knife a bystander has the legal duty to personally intervene to save the victim? Not at all. This court was very careful in stating the issue narrowly and emphasizing that it was only creating a small exception to the traditional rule.

SELECTING AND USING ATTORNEYS

Choosing an attorney can be as important as choosing one's clergyman, banker, or doctor ... and more difficult.

INDIVIDUALS

Individuals frequently require an attorney's services for their business matters as well as for their personal affairs. As sole proprietors of or partners in a business enterprise, individuals facing (or seeking to avoid) legal problems must select an attorney. This is no easy task.

Now that the Supreme Court has made advertising by lawyers permissible,[6] at least a little more information about attorneys is publicly available than was formerly the case. Still, much investigation and consultation may be required before a selection is made, in part because most attorneys (especially successful ones) choose not to advertise. In addition, much attorney advertising is not very informational.

If friends or business associates have had similar problems in the past, their advice may be particularly helpful. If their experience with a specific attorney was quite favorable, that attorney can be contacted. Professionals in the area of concern are also valuable resources. For example, if the legal problem is financial in nature, an individual's banker might provide valuable insight regarding lawyers with experience in that type of case. A call to a nearby law school permits consultation with a professor who specializes in the problem area and will probably know local attorneys who practice that type of law. A trip to a library to consult the *Martindale-Hubbell Law Directory,* which gives significant background information on attorneys and their specialties (and even rates them), can be beneficial. Finally, the Yellow Pages will list the local attorneys and contain the number of a lawyers' referral service sponsored by the local bar association.

---

[6] *Bates v. State Bar of Ariz,* 433 U.S. 350 (1977).

HUMOR AND THE LAW

We believe that when you have finished your study of the law in this course, you will conclude that the law, on balance (though certainly not always), comports with common sense and produces just results in the vast majority of cases. This is not to say that the system is flawless. One of our nation's most colorful federal judges, the Honorable Bruce Selya of the First Circuit Court of Appeals, was once moved to state: "Perhaps the law need not always align itself with common sense, but when that happy coincidence occurs, lawyers and judges should not reflexively recoil from it." *Communications Workers of America v. Western Electric*, 860 F.2d 1137 (1st Cir. 1988).

An individual consulting an attorney must not be hesitant to ask questions, including: How much will I be charged for an initial consultation? Do you frequently handle this type of case? Will my case receive the attention of an experienced lawyer in the firm? How will the fee be structured? How much is your representation likely to cost for the total case?

The matter of fees is a delicate subject, but the client should demand that all specifics be spelled out before hiring an attorney. For many types of cases, lawyers work for an *hourly fee*. The rate charged varies with the geographic area, type of firm, and type of case. Unless the client investigates thoroughly, "comparison shopping" will be impossible. Some types of cases, particularly plaintiffs' personal injury cases, are handled on a *contingency fee* basis. That is, the lawyer's compensation is a percentage of the plaintiff's recovery, *if any*. No recovery usually means no fee for the attorney. Sometimes contingency fees are set on a sliding scale where the attorney receives an agreed percentage if the case is settled out of court, a larger percentage if the case is settled after suit is filed, and a still larger percentage (usually around 33 percent, but sometimes as high as 50 percent) if the case must be tried.

Once a relationship is established, clients must be completely open with their attorneys. Only if attorneys are given all relevant information by their clients can they provide effective counsel. Clients should trust their lawyers unless there is specific evidence of unethical practices, overbilling, or the like. The attorneys are being paid to provide advice, and that advice should normally be trusted just as a patient trusts a surgeon's advice. However, clients should always remember that it is *their case* that is the basis of the relationship. The attorney works for and is paid by the client, not vice versa. Matters of strategy are in the attorney's discretion, but the client has the ultimate choice of whether to file suit, whether to accept a settlement offer, and whether to take an appeal. An attorney who refuses to follow a client's instructions should be discharged.

CORPORATIONS

Corporations are even more dependent on attorneys than individuals. As fictional entities, corporations must appear in court through a licensed attorney. That is, while individuals have the right (although it is not usually the sensible thing to do) to represent themselves in court, corporations do not. Not even the president of the corporation can represent it in court if the president is not an attorney. Much of what was said about selection and use of attorneys by individuals is also applicable to corporations.

Many corporations have "in-house" counsel—lawyers who work for the corporation full time. Other corporations farm out all their legal work to law firms that represent a number of other clients as well. Many larger corporations combine these approaches, with routine matters handled by in-house counsel and litigation and specialty matters handled by outside counsel.

The high cost of litigation, particularly attorneys' fees, is a major concern for corporations. The average manufacturing company spends about 1 percent of its revenues on legal services. Some corporations have reacted to this problem by increasing their reliance on in-house counsel. Others have put their legal business up for competitive bid by law firms. Still others have instituted "legal audits" in which experienced attorneys evaluate a company's practices to detect potential legal troublespots. These troublespots might not be illegal practices, only activities that might invite litigation or inhibit success should litigation ensue. Such "preventive law" is being hailed, much as is preventive medicine. An attorney who can keep the client out of court altogether is probably more valuable as one who can win a case in court.

Corporations, like individuals, must cooperate with their attorneys. Obviously corporations can act only through their employees. Those employees must also be open and cooperative. The Supreme Court has recognized this, holding that the attorney–client privilege applies to communications made by corporate employees to the corporation's attorneys.[7]

Questions and Problems

1. In two cases reaching the U.S. Supreme Court in 1985, the executive branch of the United States government—through action by the Solicitor General—asked the court to overrule its controversial 1973 decision in *Roe v. Wade*, 410 U.S. 113. (In that case the court held that a Texas statute making it a crime for anyone to have an abortion within the state except to save the mother's life violated the implicit right to privacy in the U.S. Constitution.) In effect, this controversial ruling "legalized" abortion to the extent that it gave pregnant women

---

[7] *Upjohn Co. v. United States*, 449 U.S. 383 (1981).

the absolute right to an abortion during the first trimester of their pregnancies, if they so desired.

Leaving aside the precise constitutional question that is raised, do you generally agree or disagree with the 1985 position of the executive branch? In other words, do you feel—because of religious beliefs or moral principles—that state law (as the Reagan administration argued in 1985) or each individual woman (as the Supreme Court held in 1973) should determine the question of abortion? Discuss.

2. While there is no universal agreement as to what law is when viewed in the abstract, there seems to be substantial agreement among philosophers as to what the *primary purpose* of law is.
    a. How would you describe this purpose?
    b. Identify the specific passage or clause in each of the philosophers' quoted observations that substantiates your conclusion.

3. Briefly summarize the main factors that require a nation's legal rules to be flexible and somewhat changing.

4. If X and Y make a contract and X later refuses to go through with the deal, without any legal excuse, we say that X's conduct is a *wrong* but it is not a *crime.* Why is it not a crime? *It is civil*

5. For some years the Washington Interscholastic Activities Association had a rule that prohibited girls from participating on high school football teams in the state. When this rule was challenged by parents of two girls who wanted to go out for football, the Supreme Court of Washington had to decide whether the rule violated the state constitution (*Darrin v. Gould,* 540 P.2d 882, 1975). Leaving aside the precise legal question that was posed, do you think that such a rule is a good one? Discuss.

6. In 1884 a ship sank 1,600 miles from shore. Dudley, Stephens, Brooks, and a 17-year-old boy, Richard Parker, scrambled into a life boat with only two pounds of turnips to eat and no fresh water. They caught a turtle, but by their 12th day in the raft the provisions were completely consumed. Soon thereafter Dudley and Stephens proposed killing the boy for food, but Brooks resisted the idea. Finally, on the 20th day after the shipwreck as the boy lay almost dead, Dudley and Stephens slit his throat and Brooks then joined them in eating him. Four days later a passing ship picked up the three survivors. They were returned to England where Dudley and Stephens were charged with murder. Assume that you are the judge in this case. Assume further that the evidence shows (a) all four men would have been dead by the 24th day had Parker not been eaten and (b) the mandatory penalty for murder is death. What will you do? (*Regina v. Dudley & Stephens,* [1884] L.R., Q.B. 61.)

7. A minor child and its mother brought a paternity action against defendant. Defendant admitted that he was the father of the child and agreed to pay child support but filed a counterclaim against the mother claiming (a) she had falsely represented that she was taking birth control pills, (b) defendant had engaged in sexual intercourse with her in reliance on the misrepresentation, and (c) as a direct result of the birth he had been injured in the form of mental agony and distress and creation of an obligation to support the child financially. The mother moved to dismiss the counterclaim, arguing that even if the facts alleged by defendant were true, he should not be allowed to recover money damages. Discuss: (*Lasher v Kleinberg,* 164 Cal. Rptr. 618, Cal. App. 1980.)

8. A wooden bridge crossing a canal was destroyed by a fire of unknown origin one afternoon. McCarthy soon learned of the fire; he attempted to contact the county commissioners but failed. Simpson also learned of the fire and told another traveler, Ramos, that he would notify somebody about the fire, but he did not do so. At 6:30 the next morning Roberson drove off the bridge in the dark and was killed. No barricades or any type of warning devices were at the site of the burned-out bridge. Roberson's wife brought a wrongful death action against McCarthy and Simpson. Should she prevail? Discuss. (*Roberson v. McCarthy,* 620 S.W.2d 912, Tex. Civ. App. 1981.)

2
CHAPTER

Legal rules and principles take on vitality and meaning only when they are applied to real-life controversies between real persons, when the rules are applied to facts—when, for example, a particular plaintiff is successful or unsuccessful in his or her attempt to recover a specific piece of

land from a particular defendant, or where one company is successful or unsuccessful in recovering damages from another company as a result of an alleged breach of contract on the latter company's part. But the fitting of rules

COURT SYSTEMS, JURISDICTION, AND FUNCTIONS

to facts—the settlings of legal controversies—does not occur automatically. This process, which we call **adjudication,** has to be in somebody's hands. Traditionally, that "somebody" has been the state and federal courts that hear thousands of cases each year.[1] As Figure 2.1 indicates, rules and facts come together in the adjudication process, leading to a decision.

The primary reason, then, for looking at the courts and the work that they do is to gain an overall awareness of this important legal process. There is, however, another reason for doing so. In the following chapters many actual cases are presented. The reader is given the basic facts of a particular controversy, the judgment entered by the trial court on the basis of those facts, and excerpts of the appellate court's decision in affirming or reversing the trial court's judgment. Obviously, some familiarity with court systems and the judicial process will facilitate one's understanding of the legal significance of each step in these proceedings.

In this chapter, then, we take a brief look at the state and federal court systems and at some problems of jurisdiction arising in those systems. We also examine some additional matters, such as venue, conflict of laws, and the law–equity distinction. In Chapter 3, we will study the litigation process, focusing on the functions of the trial and appellate courts, and then we will discuss some alternative methods of dispute resolution.

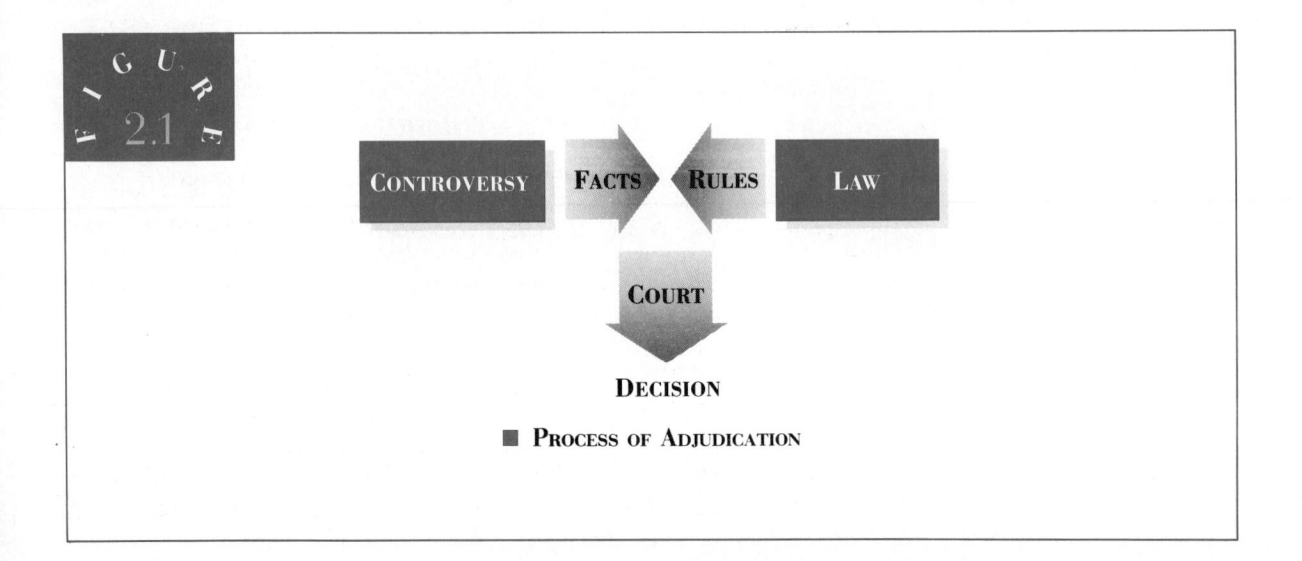

FIGURE 2.1

CONTROVERSY → FACTS ← RULES ← LAW

↓ COURT

DECISION

■ PROCESS OF ADJUDICATION

---

[1] In addition to the state and federal trial courts, many administrative agencies (such as the Federal Trade Commission) also hear certain kinds of controversies—usually those in which the agency is contending that a company has violated the agency's own rules or regulations. (The general subject of administrative agencies, including the role that they play in the adjudicatory process, is covered in Chapter 6.)

COURT SYSTEMS

As a result of our federal system of government, we live under two distinct, and essentially separate, sovereign types of government—the state governments and the federal government. Each has its own laws and its own court system. For this reason, it is necessary to study both systems to acquire an adequate knowledge of the court structures within which controversies are settled.

THE TYPICAL STATE SYSTEM

Although court systems vary somewhat from state to state, most state courts fall into three general categories. In ascending order, they are (1) courts of limited jurisdiction, (2) general trial courts, and (3) appellate courts (which frequently exist at two levels).

Courts of Limited Jurisdiction

Every state has trial courts that are limited as to the kinds of cases they can hear and are thus called **courts of limited jurisdiction.** Examples include justice of the peace courts, municipal courts, traffic courts, probate courts (hearing matters of wills and decedents' estates), and domestic relations courts (handling divorce, custody, and child support cases). Numerically speaking, these courts hear most cases that come to trial. However, they need not be discussed in detail here because many of the matters they hear are relatively minor in nature (such as traffic violations) and others involve very specialized subject matter (such as a dispute over a deceased person's estate).

General Trial Courts

The most important cases involving state law, and the ones we will be most concerned with hereafter, commence in the **general trial courts**. These are courts of "general jurisdiction"; they are empowered to hear all cases except those expressly assigned by statute to the courts of limited jurisdiction discussed above. Virtually all important cases involving contract law, criminal law, and corporation law, for example, originate in the general trial courts. In some states these courts are called "district courts," in others "common pleas courts," and in still others "superior courts." Whatever the specific name, one or more such courts normally exists in every county of every state. Throughout the remainder of the text, we will sometimes refer to these general trial courts simply as *state trial courts* to distinguish them from federal trial courts. When this is done, we are referring to the state trial courts of general jurisdiction rather than to those of limited jurisdiction.

Appellate Courts

All states have one or more **appellate courts,** which hear appeals from judgments entered by the courts below. In some states there is only one such court, usually called the "supreme court," but in the more populous states there is a layer of appellate courts interposed between the trial courts and the supreme court. Such courts decide legal questions; they do not hear testimony of witnesses or otherwise entertain new evidence.

THE FEDERAL COURT SYSTEM

Article III, Section 1 of the U.S. Constitution provides that "the judicial power of the United States shall be vested in one Supreme Court, and in such inferior courts as the Congress may from time to time ordain and establish." The numerous federal courts that exist today by virtue of this section can, at the risk of oversimplification, be placed into three main categories similar to those of the state courts: (1) specialized trial courts, (2) U.S. district courts, and (3) appellate courts—the courts of appeal and the Supreme Court.

Specialized U.S. Courts

Some federal courts have very specialized subject matter jurisdiction. Examples include the U.S. Tax Court, which hears only federal tax cases, and the U.S. Claims Court, which hears only claims against the U.S. government. These and other specialized federal courts are somewhat analogous to the courts of limited jurisdiction in state court systems.

U.S. District Courts

The basic trial courts within the federal system are the *U.S. district courts*, sometimes called federal district courts. Most federal cases originate in these courts.

Congress has created 94 judicial districts, each of which covers all or part of a state or a U.S. territory. The federal districts, with the exceptions noted above, essentially are based on state lines. The less populated states have only one federal district court within their boundaries, whereas most of the remaining states have two, and a few states have three or four. U.S. territories such as Puerto Rico, Guam, and the Virgin Islands each have one federal district court. Every square foot of land in this country and its territories is, geographically speaking, within the jurisdiction of one U.S. district court.

Although the federal district courts are the most important courts in the federal system, they are not really courts of general jurisdiction in the same sense as are the general state courts. State courts of general jurisdiction are essentially a repository of general judicial power; if no other court has jurisdiction over a particular type of case, then a state court of general jurisdiction has power to hear the case. Federal courts, however, are part of the federal government, and the federal government is a government of limited powers under our Constitution. Thus, as we will see shortly, even our most important federal trial courts—the U.S. district courts—have power to hear only those cases that have been specifically placed within their jurisdiction by the Constitution and federal statutory enactments.

Appellate Courts

Above the district courts are two levels of *federal appellate courts*—the U.S. courts of appeal and, above them, the U.S. Supreme Court. There are 13 U.S. courts of appeal. Eleven of these, located in "circuits" across the country, have jurisdiction to hear appeals from the district courts located in the states within their respective boundaries. For example, the U.S. Court of Appeals for the Ninth Circuit in San Francisco hears appeals from decisions of district courts within the states of Alaska, Arizona, California, Hawaii,

Idaho, Montana, Nevada, Oregon, and Washington. Each of these 11 appellate courts also hears appeals from the rulings of federal administrative agencies.

The jurisdiction of the remaining two appellate courts is somewhat different from that of the others. The U.S. Court of Appeals for the District of Columbia hears appeals from the federal district court located in the District, as well as appeals from rulings of federal agencies that are issued there. The other appellate court is the U.S. Court of Appeals for the Federal Circuit, which hears all patent appeals from Patent and Trademark Office boards throughout the country and appeals from decisions of the U.S. Claims Court.

Appeals from judgments of the U.S. courts of appeal, like appeals from judgments of the state supreme courts that present federal questions, can be taken to the U.S. Supreme Court. In most cases, however, these appeals are not a matter of right. Rather, the parties who seek review must petition the Supreme Court for a *writ of certiorari*, and the Court has absolute discretion in deciding which of these cases are sufficiently important to warrant the granting of certiorari.[2] In a typical year the Court can hear only about 150 of the approximately 4,500 appeals that are made.

SOME OBSERVATIONS

The typical state court system and the federal system can be diagrammed as in Figure 2.2. Several general comments can be made about this diagram.

1. The basic trial courts are the U.S. district courts and the state general trial courts; all courts above this level are appellate courts.

2. Trial courts must settle questions of both *fact* and *law,* whereas appellate courts rule on questions of law only. Questions of fact are "what happened" questions: for instance, did the defendant corporations expressly or implicitly agree not to sell goods to the plaintiff? Questions of law, by contrast, are "what is the rule applicable to the facts?" (Much more is said about the fact/law distinction in the next chapter.)

3. Although most decisions of the trial courts are not appealed, a substantial number are. Hereafter we are concerned primarily with the *decisions of the appellate courts*. There are several basic reasons for this. First, state trial courts usually enter a judgment without writing a formal opinion as to their reasoning; and, even if there is such an opinion, it is normally not reported (published). Appellate courts, however, normally do write opinions that are reported, and access to them is available to anyone wishing to look up the rulings of law involved. Second, appellate courts have more opportunity to delineate the legal issues in their opinions for the benefit of lawyers and others who may read them. Third, if the appellate court disagrees with the result reached by the trial court, the appellate court's decision is, of course, controlling.

---

[2] A *writ of certiorari* is an order of a higher court requiring a lower court to forward to it the records and proceedings of a particular case.

FIGURE 2.2

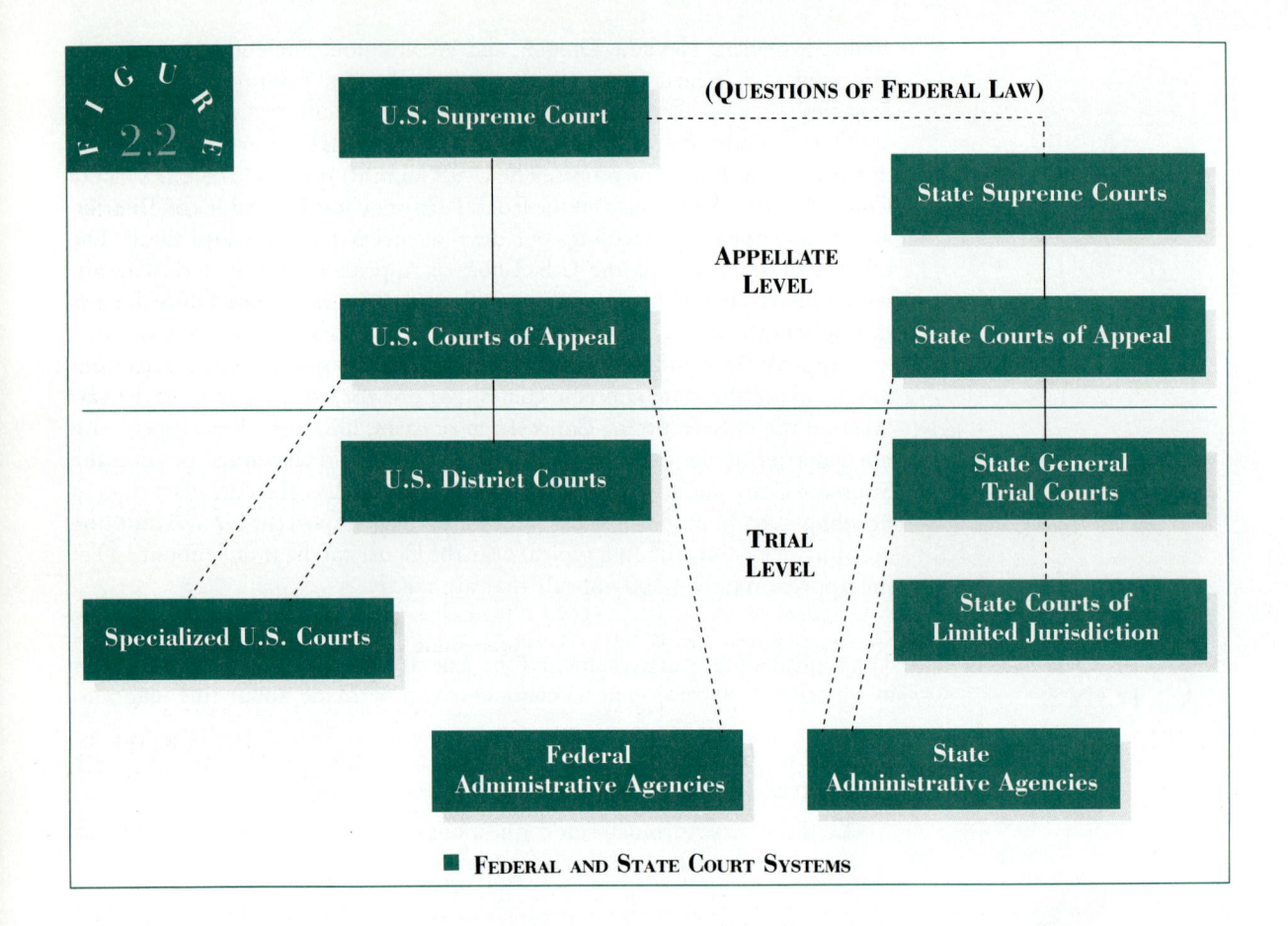

Federal and State Court Systems

```
                            (QUESTIONS OF FEDERAL LAW)
   U.S. Supreme Court  --------------------------------
         |                                            |
         |                                   State Supreme Courts
         |                     APPELLATE              |
         |                      LEVEL                 |
   U.S. Courts of Appeal                      State Courts of Appeal
         |                                            |
   ─────────────────────────────────────────────────────────
         |                                            |
   U.S. District Courts                       State General
                                              Trial Courts
                          TRIAL                       |
                          LEVEL                       |
                                              State Courts of
                                              Limited Jurisdiction
   Specialized U.S. Courts

         Federal                               State
   Administrative Agencies              Administrative Agencies
```

---

4. Once a case is initiated within a given court system, it will normally stay within that system until a final judgment is reached. Thus, if a case is properly commenced in a state court of general jurisdiction, any appeal from the trial court's judgment must be made to the next higher state court rather than to a federal appellate court. And if a case reaches the highest court in the state, its judgment is usually final. In other words, on matters of state law, state supreme courts are indeed supreme.[3] However, should a state supreme court rule on a case that turns on interpretation of a federal statute or a provision of the U.S. Constitution, an appeal could be taken to the U.S. Supreme Court, which has the final word on matters of *federal law*.

5. With regard to the "title" of an appealed case, the state and federal courts follow somewhat different rules. In most state courts, the original

---

[3] The normal terminology is being used here. In a few states, however, the "supreme court" label is given to an intermediate appellate court, with the highest court in the state bearing some other name. The court of last resort in the state of New York, for example, is the Court of Appeals of New York.

plaintiff's name appears first—just as it did in the trial court. Suppose, for example, that Pink (plaintiff) sues Doe (defendant) in a state trial court, where the case is obviously *Pink v. Doe*. If the judgment of the trial court is appealed, the rule followed by most state courts is that the title of the case remains *Pink v. Doe* in the appellate courts, no matter which party is the *appellant* (the one bringing the appeal). In the federal courts and in a few states, however, the appellant's name appears first. Under this rule, if Doe (defendant) loses in a U.S. district court and appeals to a U.S. court of appeals, the title of the case will be *Doe v. Pink* in the higher court. For this reason, when one sees a case in a federal appellate court so entitled, one cannot assume that Doe was the party who originated the action in the trial court. That determination must be made by referring to the facts of the case as set forth in the decision of the appellate court.

PROBLEMS OF JURISDICTION

In a general sense, the term **jurisdiction** refers to the legal power of a governmental body or official to take some type of action. With respect to courts, jurisdiction means the power to adjudicate, that is, to hear and decide a case and render a judgment that is legally binding on the parties. A court normally has such power only if it has both **subject matter jurisdiction** and **personal jurisdiction.** Any action taken by a court without complete jurisdiction has no legal effect.

SUBJECT MATTER JURISDICTION

Subject matter jurisdiction consists of the power to hear a particular kind of case. In each of our states, provisions in the state constitution specify which types of cases are within the subject matter jurisdiction of which types of courts. Typically, state legislative enactments then provide more detail on the subject matter jurisdiction of particular state courts. As we have already seen, some state courts have very limited jurisdiction, and one set of state courts will have more general jurisdiction. In the federal system, the U.S. Constitution specifies in general terms the kinds of cases that are within the subject matter jurisdiction of the federal courts, and federal statutes provide more detail. The federal courts themselves have also added more detail to the jurisdictional rules through their interpretations of the relevant constitutional and statutory provisions.

SUBJECT MATTER JURISDICTION OF THE FEDERAL COURTS

As we have already seen, the federal courts have subject matter jurisdiction over only those kinds of cases that are designated by the U.S. Constitution and federal statutes.

Criminal Cases

Federal courts have jurisdiction over criminal cases in which a violation of a federal criminal statute is alleged. There is a large body of federal criminal law, including statutes making it a crime to smuggle drugs into the U.S., hijack an airplane, commit securities fraud, threaten the president, cross state lines after having committed a state law crime, and so on. Some federal statutes, such as the securities and antitrust laws, include both civil liability and criminal penalty provisions. Congress has power to pass criminal laws, like noncriminal ones, only if there is some basis in the Constitution authorizing it to do so. Many federal criminal laws are based on the constitutional provision that empowers Congress to pass laws regulating interstate commerce, but others are enacted under the power granted by different constitutional provisions.

Civil Cases

We are primarily concerned about the jurisdiction and functions of courts in civil cases. Most of the time it will be obvious whether a particular civil case can be heard by a federal court, but sometimes there are difficult questions. These questions may arise when a plaintiff's attorney thinks it would be in the client's best interest to have the case decided by a federal rather than a state court, but where some of the facts relating to the jurisdictional question are not clear. There can be many reasons why a plaintiff's attorney might prefer to file a case in federal court. For example, if the case has to be filed in a state where the attorney normally does not practice, he may be unfamiliar with the procedures of that state's courts and thus may be more comfortable in a federal court in that state, where the procedures are basically the same as in federal courts in other states. Likewise, if a plaintiff has filed in a state court where the defendant's attorney usually does not practice, the latter might attempt to have the case moved to a federal court for the same reason. Sometimes a question about federal versus state court jurisdiction can arise because the plaintiff has filed a case in federal court but the defendant's attorney sees some strategic advantage in having the case decided by a state court. There are two general categories of civil cases that the Constitution and federal statutes have placed within the subject matter jurisdiction of the federal courts.

Federal Question Cases: Federal courts have subject matter jurisdiction over any civil case in which the plaintiff's claim arises from either the U.S. Constitution, a federal statute, or a federal treaty. For example, if a group of environmentally concerned citizens sues a corporation alleging that it was polluting a stream in violation of the federal Clean Water Act, there would be a **federal question.** The plaintiff's claim must directly raise a question of federal law; if the plaintiff's claim does not raise a federal question, the defendant cannot create federal subject matter jurisdiction by raising a federal question in a defense or counterclaim.

It is common for a plaintiff to assert two or more legal claims based on the same set of factual circumstances. If one of these claims raises a federal question and thereby creates federal subject matter jurisdiction, the federal court also has subject matter jurisdiction over any other claim arising out of the same facts, even if the other claim is based on state law rather than federal law. This type of federal subject matter jurisdiction is called "pendent" or "ancillary" jurisdiction and represents a pragmatic attempt to avoid multiple lawsuits.

Federal jurisdiction based on a federal question may be either *exclusive* or *concurrent*. A claim arising under the U.S. Constitution creates concurrent federal–state jurisdiction, which means that it can be heard by either a federal or state court. A claim arising under a federal statute usually creates concurrent federal–state jurisdiction unless the statute itself says otherwise. A number of federal statutes, such as the patent, copyright, antitrust, and securities laws, specifically provide for exclusive federal court jurisdiction; claims thereunder can be filed only in a federal court.

If a federal question case is taken to a federal court, it is normally done at the outset, in one of the federal district courts. However, if (1) a particular federal question case is one that is characterized by concurrent federal–state jurisdiction, (2) the plaintiff chooses to file the case in a *state* court, and (3) the case proceeds through the state court system until all avenues of appeal in that system are exhausted, either party may ask the U.S. Supreme Court to review the case because of the presence of the federal question. In this situation, as in most others, the U.S. Supreme Court has discretion to hear or not hear the case.

Diversity of Citizenship Cases: Diversity of citizenship creates federal subject matter jurisdiction only if there is an amount in controversy greater than $50,000. When federal jurisdiction exists because of **diversity of citizenship,** it is always concurrent federal–state jurisdiction, and the plaintiff has a choice of filing in a federal court. If the plaintiff chooses state court and the case is heard in the state court system, there can be no appeal to the U.S. Supreme Court or any other federal court. (Thus, the situation is different with a diversity case filed in state court than with a federal question case filed in state court.)

In the case of an individual, citizenship in a state for federal jurisdiction purposes means U.S. citizenship plus residency in that state. The phrase *diversity of citizenship* encompasses several different situations. By far the most important situation included within the phrase is one in which the plaintiff and defendant are citizens of different states. Diversity of citizenship also exists when one party is a citizen of a state in the United States and the other is a citizen of another nation.

In several ways, federal courts have interpreted the diversity of citizenship concept rather narrowly to exclude some kinds of cases that logically might have been included. For example, if a case involves multiple plaintiffs and/or multiple defendants, diversity of citizenship exists only if there is *no common state citizenship on opposite sides of the case.* Thus if P1, a citizen of Nebraska, and P2, a citizen of Kansas, join in a suit against D1, a citizen of New York, and D2, a citizen of Kansas, there is no diversity of citizenship.

If a corporation is a plaintiff or defendant, it is considered to be a citizen of the state where it was *incorporated;* in addition, if it has its *principal place of business* in another state, it is viewed as a citizen of that state as well. Thus, for the purpose of determining whether a federal court has jurisdiction on the basis of diversity of citizenship, it is possible for a corporation to be a citizen of two states. Neither Congress nor the U.S. Supreme Court has defined the term *principal place of business.* Most lower federal courts have held that the state where a company has its headquarters is its principal place of business. Suppose that P, a citizen of New York, sues D Corporation, which was incorporated in Delaware and has its principal place of business in New York. Because there is common state citizenship on opposite sides of the case (New York), a federal court would not have subject matter jurisdiction on the basis of diversity of citizenship.

The original reason for permitting diversity of citizenship cases to be heard by federal courts was to guard against "hometown verdicts"—decisions by juries or judges that are biased against an out-of-state party. If this ever was a problem, there is little if any evidence that it is still a problem. In any event, if there is such a problem, it is unclear how placing these cases in a federal trial court can solve it. Juries in federal courts are taken from the local population just as they are in state courts, and federal judges are almost always from the state where they serve. For these reasons, and also because diversity of citizenship cases involve questions of state law, bills have been introduced in Congress a number of times over the years to eliminate diversity of citizenship as a basis for federal subject matter jurisdiction. No such bill has passed, however.

Removal from State to Federal Court

When concurrent federal–state jurisdiction exists, the plaintiff has the initial choice of filing in state or federal court. If the plaintiff chooses state court, however, the defendant may have a **right of removal.** This means that, within a short time after the plaintiff files the case in state court, the defendant may have the case moved to a federal district court in the same geographic area.

The defendant has a right of removal in any federal question case, so that if the defendant chooses he or she can always have a federal court rule on claims against him or her that are based on federal law. The right also exists in diversity of citizenship cases, except in the situation where the plaintiff filed the suit in the state where the defendant is a citizen.

PERSONAL JURISDICTION

In the great majority of cases, a court must have **personal jurisdiction** in addition to subject matter jurisdiction. Personal jurisdiction is the court's jurisdiction over the parties to the case. In a civil lawsuit, the plaintiff submits to the court's personal jurisdiction by filing the case; thus, any question about personal jurisdiction relates to the defendant.[4] Personal

---

[4] It should be mentioned in the interest of accuracy that a court does have to obtain personal jurisdiction over a plaintiff with respect to a defendant's counterclaim, but this would rarely present any problem.

jurisdiction over the defendant is a requirement in so-called **in personam** cases, in which the plaintiff seeks a judgment that will be legally binding against the defendant (whether an individual, corporation, government agency, or other entity). The judgment might be an award of money damages that the defendant has to pay or some other remedy such as an injunction requiring the defendant to take or refrain from taking some particular action. Most cases are of the *in personam* variety. The other type of case is an **in rem** action, which will be discussed after this section on personal jurisdiction.

In our legal system, personal jurisdiction is a concept that arises only in civil cases, not in criminal ones; the reason is that in a criminal case the defendant must be arrested and bodily brought before the court before he can be tried.

Although the rules for a court's acquisition of personal jurisdiction over a defendant vary somewhat from state to state in this country, these rules all have the same objective. That objective is compliance with the constitutional requirement of *procedural due process*. We will study due process in some detail in Chapter 5, Constitutional Law. What is basically required by procedural due process, however, is (1) adequate notice, (2) a meaningful opportunity to be heard (i.e., a hearing), (3) an impartial decision maker, and (4) in court actions, some significant contact between the defendant and the *forum state*. The forum state is the state where the lawsuit has been filed.

Appearance

As we will see, some of the methods for obtaining personal jurisdiction are different depending on whether the defendant is a *resident* of the forum state or a *nonresident*. However, regardless of the residency of the defendant, the defendant automatically submits to the court's personal jurisdiction if he makes an **appearance.** In this context, the word *appearance* is a term of art. It does not refer to an actual physical presence in court; instead the term refers to the taking of any formal steps to defend the case. Thus if the defendant, normally acting through his attorney, files a motion to dismiss, an answer to the plaintiff's complaint, or almost any other court papers aimed at defending against the claim, the defendant has made an appearance. Once this has happened, the trial court has personal jurisdiction and the defendant cannot thereafter challenge the existence of such jurisdiction. Therefore, if the defendant wishes to contest the court's personal jurisdiction, it must be completed before taking any other action that would constitute an appearance.

The major exception to this rule is the *special appearance*. This is a motion or other formal action taken by the defendant solely for the purpose of challenging the court's personal jurisdiction. If the only action the defendant takes is to challenge the court's personal jurisdiction, this action does not give the court jurisdiction. If the defendant properly makes the special appearance before taking any other formal action in the case but the trial court denies the challenge to its personal jurisdiction, the defendant can then go ahead and defend the case on its merits without losing the right to later have an appellate court rule on the personal jurisdiction question.

Service of Summons

If the defendant has not made an appearance, the plaintiff must see to it that the court acquires personal jurisdiction. Whether the defendant is a resident or nonresident, the preferred method is *personal service of summons*. The **summons** is the formal notice of the lawsuit.[5] A copy of the plaintiff's complaint is usually attached to the summons. Personal service means delivery to the defendant in person while the defendant is physically within the forum state. Traditionally, an officer such as a sheriff, marshal, a deputy sheriff or marshal, or a constable was always used to deliver the summons. In recent years, however, the rules in many places have been changed to permit other persons, such as the plaintiff's attorney, to deliver a summons. In the federal district courts, for example, the rules were changed in the past few years to place responsibility on the plaintiff's attorney for seeing that the summons is served; the actual delivery of the summons to the defendant can be performed by any person at least 18 years old and who is not a party to the lawsuit (such as a clerk in the office of the plaintiff's attorney). Whoever attempts to deliver a summons must make a sworn statement to the court as to whether they were successful or unsuccessful.

In the case of a resident defendant, there are several alternatives to personal service of summons, including (1) permitting the authorized summons-server to leave the summons at the defendant's residence with someone older than a specified age (such as 16 or 18 years), (2) permitting the server to leave it at the defendant's regular place of business, or (3) permitting the server or the court clerk to mail the summons to the defendant's residence or business. In the latter case, registered or certified mail is required in some places, but only first class mail is required in others. In some states, it is required that personal service first be attempted before one of these alternatives can be used; in other places this is not required.

Corporate Defendants

Although many of the rules for acquiring personal jurisdiction over a corporation are the same as for an individual, some are a bit different because of the nature of a corporate entity. The rules regarding the making of an appearance are the same for a corporation as for an individual.

If there is no appearance, there are several possible means for serving summons on a corporation. First, if the corporation has a *registered agent* in the forum state, service on that agent is sufficient. This service may be by personal delivery or by some alternative method permitted in that particular court system. A corporation is supposed to have a registered agent for receiving summonses and other legal notices in the state where it is incorporated and in any other state where it does business. In this regard, "doing

---

[5] In some places, other terms, such as *process* or *citation*, are used instead of the term *summons*. Sometimes the term *service of process* is used in a general sense to describe delivery of any legal papers in a lawsuit, including a summons, a subpoena to testify, and other papers.

business" usually means having some physical presence in the state, not just advertising or receiving mail or telephone orders. In most places, service of summons also may be accomplished by delivering it to an *officer* of the corporation if one is located within the forum state.

Long-Arm Statutes and Due Process

As a general rule, a summons is effective to give a court personal jurisdiction only if it is served on the defendant within the forum state. Thus if P files a suit for breach of contract against D in a state or federal court in Michigan, a summons issued normally must be served on D within Michigan to give the court personal jurisdiction. This requirement presents little problem if D is a resident of Michigan. Not only will it usually be possible to personally deliver the summons to a resident defendant but, as we have already seen, various alternatives are available for accomplishing service of summons to someone who is a resident of the forum state. Also, if a corporate defendant has either its headquarters or a registered agent in the forum state, the requirement is not difficult to meet.

However, if an individual defendant is a resident of some other state or nation or if the corporation has no registered agent in the forum state, serving a summons becomes more difficult. The defendant in such a case is not likely to "hang around" in the forum state so that a summons can be served. If personal jurisdiction cannot be obtained, the plaintiff is faced with the prospect of filing suit in a state (or nation) where personal jurisdiction can be obtained; unless the claim is quite large, the substantial extra expense could mean that pursuing the claim is not economically feasible.

There are certain circumstances in which it is possible for a court to gain personal jurisdiction over a defendant even though that defendant has not made an appearance and has not been served with summons within the forum state. The procedural due process guarantee in the Constitution is essentially aimed at ensuring basic fairness. A number of years ago, the U.S. Supreme Court decided that the due process requirement of basic fairness is satisfied if a nonresident defendant has had significant prior contact with the forum state. (The Court used the term *minimal* contact, but *significant* better describes the concept as it has been applied over the years.) In addition to the contact requirement, the Supreme Court said that a particular state had to have a statutory procedure for making sure that a summons was actually forwarded to the nonresident defendant at its out-of-state address.

In response to this Supreme Court decision, every state has adopted a so-called *long-arm statute* specifying such a procedure. In many states, the long-arm statute specifies that personal jurisdiction can be acquired over a nonresident defendant who has "done business" or committed a "tort" (i.e., wrongful conduct for which civil liability can be imposed) within the forum state. In other states, the statute simply provides that jurisdiction can be acquired in any circumstances in which the defendant's prior contact with the state is sufficient to comply with the fairness requirement of due process. Even if the state statute specifies certain kinds of contact, such as doing business, the application of the statute in a particular case is still subject to court review for compliance with procedural due process.

Long-arm statutes provide that, when the evidence shows that defendant has had sufficient contact with the forum state, the summons is to be sent to a central office in the forum state. In most states, this is the secretary of state's office. The official in charge of that office then has the responsibility to send the summons to the defendant at its out-of-state address.

The courts have divided the due process requirement of significant contacts into two categories. First, suppose that the lawsuit arises from a specific contact that the nonresident defendant had with the forum state. For instance, the defendant may have driven his or her car into the forum state, where he or she had an accident that is now the basis for the lawsuit. Or the plaintiff's complaint may be based on some specific business he or she and the defendant conducted within the forum state. In such a situation, the defendant's contact is sufficient for that particular lawsuit even if it was the defendant's only contact with that state. Second, suppose that the lawsuit arises from actions of the defendant that occurred in some place other than the forum state. In such a case, the long-arm statute can be used to acquire personal jurisdiction against the nonresident defendant only if the defendant's prior contacts with the forum state were of a substantial and continuous nature. The reason for this distinction is, again, basic fairness. When a nonresident defendant has had substantial and continuous contacts with a particular state, the courts believe that it is fair to require the defendant to defend against lawsuits in that state even if the facts leading to the lawsuit arose somewhere else. However, the courts have concluded that it is not fair to haul a nonresident defendant into court if his or her only contact with the state has been of an isolated or insubstantial nature, except in the situation where the lawsuit actually involves the specific actions of the defendant within that state.

Before leaving the discussion of personal jurisdiction, we must make an observation about enforcing court judgments. Suppose that D, a resident of Wisconsin, drove his car to Tennessee for a vacation. While there, he had a collision with a car driven by P, a resident of Tennessee. If P files a lawsuit against D in a Tennessee court, the Tennessee long-arm statute is used to acquire personal jurisdiction over D, and if P wins a judgment for damages, D cannot just go home to Wisconsin and ignore the judgment. If D has "nonexempt" assets back home, P will be able to get the Wisconsin authorities to enforce the Tennessee judgment by seizing D's assets in Wisconsin. More will be said about enforcing court judgments in the next chapter.

The following case illustrates some of the principles we discussed concerning the requirement that a nonresident defendant have had significant contacts with the forum state.

CASE

HELICOPTEROS NACIONALES DE COLOMBIA v. HALL

United States Supreme Court, 466 U.S. 408 (1984)

Petitioner "Helicol," a Colombian corporation, entered into a contract to provide helicopter transportation for Consorcio/WSH, a Peruvian company closely connected to a joint venture headquartered in Houston, Texas, during the company's construction of a pipeline in Peru. One of the helicopters crashed in Peru, killing four U.S. citizens. Respondents, survivors and representatives of the four decedents, filed this suit in Texas state court in Houston.

At the request of Consorcio/WSH, Helicol's chief executive officer had flown to Houston to negotiate the contract; the agreement was signed in Peru. During the years 1970–77, Helicol also purchased helicopters, spare parts, and accessories for more than $4,000,000 from a Fort Worth, Texas, company. Helicol had sent prospective pilots to Fort Worth for training and to ferry the helicopters back to South America and also sent some management and maintenance personnel there for technical consultation. Helicol received into its New York and Florida bank accounts more than $5,000,000 in payments from Consorcio/WSH drawn on a Houston bank.

However, Helicol has never been authorized to do business in Texas and never had an agent for service of summons there. Nor has it ever performed helicopter operations, sold products, solicited business, signed contracts, based employees, recruited employees, owned property, maintained an office or records, or had shareholders in Texas.

Helicol filed a special appearance in the trial court and moved to dismiss for lack of personal jurisdiction. The trial court denied the motion and, after a jury trial, entered a $1,141,200 judgment against Helicol. The Texas Court of Civil Appeals reversed for lack of personal jurisdiction, but the Texas Supreme Court later reinstated the verdict. Helicol then appealed to the U.S. Supreme Court.

BLACKMUN, JUSTICE:

[T]he Texas Supreme Court first held that the State's long-arm statute reaches as far as the Due Process Clause of the Fourteenth Amendment permits. Thus, the only question remaining for the court to decide was whether it was consistent with the Due Process Clause for Texas courts to assert *in personam* jurisdiction over Helicol.

The Due Process Clause of the Fourteenth Amendment operates to limit the power of a State to assert *in personam* jurisdiction over a nonresident defendant. Due process requirements are satisfied when *in personam* jurisdiction is asserted over a nonresident corporate defendant that has "certain minimum contacts with [the forum] such that the maintenance of the suit does not offend 'traditional notions of fair play and substantial justice.'" *International Shoe Co. v. Washington*, 326 U.S. 310 (1945). When a controversy is related to or "arises out of" a defendant's contacts with the forum, the Court has said that a "relationship among the defendant, the forum, and the litigation" is the essential foundation of *in personam* jurisdiction. *Shaffer v. Heitner*, 433 U.S. 186 (1977).

Even when the cause of action does not arise out of or relate to the foreign corporation's activities in the forum State, due process is not offended by a State's subjecting the corporation to its *in personam* jurisdiction when there are sufficient contacts between the State and the foreign [out-of-state] corporation. *Perkins v. Benguet Consolidated Mining Co.*, 342 U.S. 437 (1952). In *Perkins*, the Court addressed a situation in which state courts had asserted general jurisdiction over a defendant foreign corporation. During the Japanese occupation of the Philippine Islands, the president and general manager of a Philippine mining corporation maintained an office in Ohio from which he conducted activities on behalf of the company. He kept company files and held directors' meetings in the office, carried on correspondence relating to the business, distributed salary checks drawn on two active Ohio bank accounts, engaged an Ohio bank to act as transfer agent, and supervised policies dealing with the rehabilitation of the corporation's properties in the

CONTINUED

Philippines. In short, the foreign corporation, through its president, "ha[d] been carrying on in Ohio a continuous and systematic, but limited, part of its general business," and the exercise of general jurisdiction over the Philippine corporation by an Ohio court was "reasonable and just."

All parties to the present case concede that respondents' claims against Helicol did not "arise out of," and are not related to, Helicol's activities within Texas. We thus must explore the nature of Helicol's contacts with the State of Texas to determine whether they constitute the kind of continuous and systematic general business contacts the Court found to exist in *Perkins*. We hold that they do not.

It is undisputed that Helicol does not have a place of business in Texas and never has been licensed to do business in the State. Basically, Helicol's contacts with Texas consisted of sending its chief executive officer to Houston for a contract-negotiation session; accepting into its New York bank account checks payable on a Houston bank; purchasing helicopters, equipment, and training services from Bell Helicopter for substantial sums; and sending personnel to Bell's facilities in Fort Worth for training.

The one trip to Houston by Helicol's chief executive officer for the purpose of negotiating the transportation-services contract with Consorcio/WSH cannot be described or regarded as a contact of a "continuous and systematic" nature, and thus cannot support an assertion of *in personam* jurisdiction over Helicol by a Texas court. Similarly, Helicol's acceptance from Consorcio/WSH of checks drawn on a Texas bank is of negligible significance. Common sense and everyday experience suggest that, absent unusual circumstances, the bank on which a check is drawn is generally of little consequence to the payee and is a matter left to the discretion of the drawer. Such unilateral activity of another party or a third person is not an appropriate consideration when determining whether a defendant has sufficient contacts with a forum State to justify an assertion of jurisdiction.

The Texas Supreme Court focused on the purchases and related training trips in finding contacts sufficient to support an assertion of jurisdiction. We do not agree with that assessment, for the Court's opinion in *Rosenberg Bros. & Co. v. Curtis Brown Co.*, 260 U.S. 516 (1923) makes clear that purchases and related trips, standing alone, are not a sufficient basis for a State's assertion of jurisdiction.

Nor can we conclude that the fact that Helicol sent personnel into Texas for training in connection with the purchase of helicopters and equipment in that State in any way enhanced the nature of Helicol's contacts with Texas. The brief presence of Helicol employees in Texas for the purpose of attending the training sessions is no more a significant contact than were the trips to New York made by the buyer for the [defendant] retail store in *Rosenberg*.

[*Reversed.*]

COMMENT

The result in this case would have been the same if Helicol, the defendant, had been headquartered in Oklahoma rather than the nation of Colombia. In addition, we will see very shortly that the analysis of the personal jurisdiction issue, and the ultimate result, would have been the same if the plaintiff had filed the suit in a *federal* court in Houston rather than a state court there. (A federal court probably would have had subject matter jurisdiction on the basis of diversity of citizenship.)

Foul-Ups in Service of Summons

We should note that although it is rather unusual, occasionally something can go wrong in the summons-serving process. This can happen in the case of either a resident or a nonresident defendant. Suppose that the rules for serving a summons have been complied with, but for some reason the defendant did not actually receive it. For instance, the summons may have been properly left at the defendant's residence with a friend or family member who lost it and forgot to tell the defendant. Suppose also that the defendant did not know about the lawsuit and thus did not answer the plaintiff's complaint and that the plaintiff then received a default judgment against the defendant because of the latter's failure to respond.

Within a certain period of time thereafter (such as a year or two, depending on the state), the defendant may ask the court to set aside the default judgment and give the defendant a chance to defend against the complaint The trial judge will do so if convinced that the defendant really did not receive the summons, had no actual knowledge that the lawsuit had been filed, and has some plausible rebuttal or defense to the complaint.

Note—Personal Jurisdiction in Federal Courts

As a general rule, a federal court in a particular state faces the same constraints on its ability to acquire personal jurisdiction as would a state court in that state. Most of the time, a summons issue by a federal district court is effective only if served within the state where the court is located. The federal court can, however, make use of the state's long-arm statute to obtain personal jurisdiction over a nonresident defendant in the same circumstances in which a state court could do so. There are certain exceptional situations in which a federal court summons has a wider reach than one issued by a state court; in a few types of federal question cases, the federal statute that forms the basis of the plaintiff's claim includes a specific provision permitting nationwide service of summons. One example of this is found in the federal laws regulating the issuance and trading of securities in interstate commerce.

In Rem Cases

As mentioned earlier, a court usually must have personal jurisdiction over a defendant because most lawsuits are of the *in personam* variety. However, if the plaintiff's case is characterized as **in rem,** rather than *in personam,* the court is not required to have personal jurisdiction over a particular party. (It still must have subject matter jurisdiction, however.) A case is an *in rem* one if the plaintiff's objective is to obtain a judgment of the court against some item of *property,* rather than against a particular defendant.

Suppose, for example, that D borrowed money from Bank B and executed a document giving B a mortgage on a home or other piece of real estate. The mortgage makes the real estate collateral for the loan and gives B a right to take ownership and possession of the property if D fails to repay the loan on its agreed terms. If D defaults, B will exercise its right by filing a *mortgage foreclosure* action in court. The object of the action is not D, but instead is the acquisition of title to the property. This is an *in rem* case, and it is not required that the court have personal jurisdiction over D. B can simply have a notice published in a local newspaper, which is not sufficient notice for personal jurisdiction but is sufficient for an *in rem* case to proceed. As a practical matter, if it is possible to get personal jurisdiction over D, B will usually see to it that the court obtains it, so that B can also get an *in personam* "deficiency judgment" against D; this is a judgment for any amount of the loan that may remain unpaid if the proceeds from the sale of the property are inadequate.

Other examples of *in rem* cases include court actions to establish ownership to lost or abandoned property or to give the government title over property that has been forfeited because it was used in connection with certain crimes such as drug dealing.

RELATED MATTERS

If we assume that the court has both subject matter and personal jurisdiction, there still may be other preliminary matters to consider. These other matters might include questions regarding venue, *forum non conveniens,* and conflict of laws.

Venue

If a state district court in Texas has subject matter and personal jurisdiction in a case filed by P, *every* district court in Texas has such jurisdiction. The question of where within the state the lawsuit should be heard is a question of **venue.** Every state has statutes that specify which counties are the appropriate venue. Typically, venue is appropriate in either the county where the defendant resides or where the accident or transaction took place. Sometimes venue may lie in other places; if the case involves real estate, the appropriate venue may be the county where the land is located. If there are two or more permissible venues, the plaintiff normally may choose among them when filing the lawsuit. In the federal court system, federal statutes specify which federal districts are the appropriate venues.

Although venue is not the same as jurisdiction, the rules governing venue questions have some of the same ultimate objectives as the rules pertaining to personal jurisdiction. The main objective is fairness, and a secondary one is efficiency.

Forum Non Conveniens

A court with both subject matter and personal jurisdiction may decline to exercise them if another court, more conveniently connected to the suit, also has both types of jurisdiction. Under the doctrine of ***forum non conveniens,*** the court may choose to transfer the suit or even dismiss it, forcing the plaintiff to file in the more convenient court.

For example, in one case arising out of a defendant's agent carelessly causing a fire in the plaintiff's warehouse in Virginia, the plaintiff sued 400 miles away in New York City where the state court had subject matter jurisdiction over the simple tort case and personal jurisdiction because of defendant corporation's many business contacts in New York. However, the New York court declined to exercise its jurisdiction on grounds that the suit was more conveniently brought in Virginia where the plaintiff and all witnesses were located and where the accident had occurred. The only justification the plaintiff gave for filing in New York—that a New York jury was likely to give a bigger verdict—was inadequate.[6]

---

[6] *Gulf Oil Corp. v. Gilbert,* 330 U.S. 401 (1947).

In determining the most convenient forum, courts will consider private interest factors such as ease of access to sources of proof, costs of obtaining witnesses' attendance, the possibility of a view of the site of the accident, and the convenience of the parties. Public factors to be considered include the imposition of jury service on residents of the community, the congestion of court dockets, and the interest in having local controversies decided at home.

The *forum non conveniens* doctrine can also be applied internationally. For example, a U.S. court of appeals affirmed a decision of the U.S. district court in New York City that used the doctrine as a basis for transferring a case from that federal court in New York to a court in India. The case involved claims against Union Carbide Corp. arising from the tragic leak of toxic gases from a chemical factory that killed more than 2,000 people in Bhopal, India. The federal trial judge took this action only after being convinced that Indian law and procedure were designed to handle such claims and provide substantial justice and that an Indian court would take jurisdiction over the claims. The court also conditioned its dismissal in favor of the Indian courts on Union Carbide's consent to the jurisdiction of the Indian courts and its waiver of any statute of limitations defense.[7] (A statute of limitations specifies a time limit for filing a lawsuit.)

It should be noted that although the term *venue* is not used, the doctrine of *forum non conveniens* actually involves a very specialized and somewhat *ad hoc* type of venue question.

Conflict of Laws

Assume D Corporation, formed in Delaware with its principal place of business in Colorado, hires P from California to do subcontracting work on D's condominiums in New Mexico. The contract is negotiated in California, Colorado, and New Mexico before being signed in Colorado. When New Mexico officials ordered P to stop work because he did not have a license to do such work in New Mexico, D fired him. P sued in Colorado to recover for the work he had performed before being stopped. Several states' laws are potentially applicable to this case. If they all lead to the same result, it does not matter which state's rules are applied. However, in this case, New Mexico law bars P from recovery because he had no license. Colorado and California law would allow him to recover despite the lack of a license. There is a "conflict of laws." To determine which state's laws to apply, we must resort to "choice of law" rules, which are designed to prevent a plaintiff with multiple jurisdictions from which to choose (because all have subject matter and personal jurisdiction) from "forum shopping" for the jurisdiction with the laws most favorable to him or her.

Conflict of laws questions also can arise in international disputes. Recall for a moment the example of the case against Union Carbide Corp. that was transferred from a federal court in New York to a court in India under the

---

[7] *In re Union Carbide Corp. Gas Plant Disaster at Bhopal, India in Dec. 1984,* 809 F.2d 195 (2d. Cir. 1987).

doctrine of *forum non conveniens*. The federal court could have retained jurisdiction and decided the case. If so, it probably would have applied the law of India to decide the case; to do so, the court obviously would have to call on experts in Indian law.

Contract Cases: If the parties stipulate in the contract that, for example, "California law will govern any disputes arising out of this contract," the courts will normally respect that choice if it was fairly bargained and California has at least a passing connection to the parties or the transaction. It is especially desirable for the parties to an international transaction to negotiate and include a clause in their contract specifying which nation's law should be applied to any dispute arising from the deal.

Absent a choice by the parties, the traditional view was to apply the law of the state in which the contract was made to any litigation about the validity of the contract and to apply the law of the state in which the contract was to be performed to any litigation about the performance of the contract. The strong modern trend, however, is to use an "interest" analysis.

Using an interest analysis to determine which state's law to apply, courts would consider such factors as the relevant policies of the forum (Colorado) and of other interested states, the protection of justified expectations (i.e., which state's laws did the parties assume would apply), certainty, predictability, ease of determination of the law to be applied, and uniformity of result.

In contract cases specifically, most modern courts attempt to determine the state with the "most significant relationship" to the parties and the transaction, considering such factors as (1) the place of contracting, (2) the place of negotiation, (3) the place of performance, (4) the location of the subject matter of the contract, and (5) the domicile, residence, nationality, place of incorporation, and place of business of the parties.

In the factual situation outlined above, the Colorado Supreme Court applied New Mexico's law, reasoning that New Mexico's interest in protecting its citizens from substandard construction by unlicensed subcontractors outweighed Colorado's interest in validating agreements and protecting parties' expectations.[8]

Tort Cases: Assume that a husband and wife from New Mexico are killed when a plane the husband is piloting crashes in Texas. The parties intended to return to New Mexico and had no other contacts with Texas. The estate of the wife filed suit against the husband's estate in state court in Texas. Texas' doctrine of interspousal immunity would not allow the suit. New Mexico has no such doctrine; its law would allow the suit. Which state's law should apply? The traditional view is to apply the law of the place of the tort—Texas. But why would Texas courts care whether a New Mexico wife's estate can recover from a New Mexico husband's estate? Again, the strong

---

[8] *Wood Bros. Homes, Inc. v. Walker Adjustment Bureau,* 601 P.2d 1369 (Colo. 1979).

HUMOR AND THE LAW

Note how the judge used principles studied in this chapter, along with a passing reference to "The Devil and Daniel Webster" to dismiss the following suit filed against Satan, wherein plaintiff alleged that "Satan has on numerous occasions caused plaintiff misery and unwarranted threats, against the will of plaintiff, that Satan has placed deliberate obstacles in his path and has caused plaintiff's downfall." The judge wrote:

> We question whether plaintiff may obtain personal jurisdiction over the defendant in this judicial district. The complaint contains no allegation of residence in this district. While the official reports disclose no case where this defendant has appeared as a defendant there is an unofficial account of a trial in New Hampshire where this defendant filed an action of mortgage foreclosure as plaintiff. The defendant in that action was represented by the preeminent advocate of that day, and raised the defense that the plaintiff was a foreign prince with no standing to sue in an American Court. This defense was overcome by overwhelming evidence to the contrary. Whether or not this would raise an estoppel in the present case we are unable to determine at this time.
>
> We note that the plaintiff has failed to include with his complaint the required form of instructions for the United States Marshal for directions as to service of process. [Dismissed.]

Mayo v. Satan and His Staff, 54 F.R.D. 282 (W.D.Pa. 1971).

---

modern trend is to move away from an automatic choice of the law of the place of the tort to an interest analysis. Modern courts often use the following factors in deciding which state has the "most significant relationship" to the occurrence and the parties (1) the place where the injury occurred; (2) the place where the conduct causing the injury occurred; (3) the domicile, residence, nationality, place of incorporation, and place of business of the parties; and (4) the place where the relationship, if any, between the parties is centered. In this case, New Mexico law was applied.[9]

LAW, EQUITY, AND REMEDIES

In the next chapter we will examine the major steps in the process of adjudication, paying particular attention to the roles played by the trial and

---

[9] *Robertson v. McKnight,* 609 S.W.2d 534 (Tex. 1980).

appellate courts in that process. We will see that in all legal controversies the plaintiff is asking for a **remedy**—an order addressed to the defendant, requiring that person either to pay money or to do (or not to do) a particular act. A remedy, then, is "the means by which a plaintiff's right is enforced, or the violation of a right is prevented, redressed, or compensated."[10] All remedies are either "legal" or "equitable" in nature, a fact that can be explained only by a brief glimpse at the development of the early court systems in England.

COURTS OF LAW

Some 900 years ago the first Norman kings of England established a system of courts by designating individuals throughout the country to be their personal representatives in the settling of certain kinds of legal disputes. These representatives could grant only very limited types of relief: (1) money damages, (2) possession of real estate, or (3) possession of personal property.

In setting disputes, the courts made up their own rules as they went along, based largely on the customs and moral standards then prevailing, plus their own ideas of "justice" in particular situations. The formulation of rules in this manner, a process that continues today in some branches of law, gave birth to the *common law* (which we will study in more detail in Chapter 4). The royal courts ultimately became known as **courts of law,** and the remedies that they granted were *remedies at law.*

COURTS OF EQUITY

When plaintiffs needed relief other than what the courts of law could grant, they often petitioned the king. Such petitions were frequently decided by the king's chancellor, who granted relief when he thought the claim was a fair one. Out of the rulings of successive chancellors arose a new body of "chancery" rules and remedies for cases outside the jurisdiction of the courts of law. This developed eventually into a system of **courts of equity,** as distinct from the courts of law.

A plaintiff who wanted a legal remedy, such as money damages, would bring an **action at law** in a court of law. A plaintiff wanting some other relief, such as an **injunction** (e.g., an order forcing D to stop grazing cattle on land belonging to P) or a **decree of specific performance** (e.g., an order commanding D to live up to a contract to sell land to P) brought an **action in equity** in an equity court. Other common equitable actions, in addition to those asking for injunctions and decrees of specific performance, include (1) divorce actions, (2) mortgage foreclosure suits, and (3) actions for an accounting, brought by one member of a partnership against another.

THE PRESENT SCENE

Although the distinction between legal and equitable remedies as diagrammed in Figure 2.3 persists today, there has been a fusion of law and equity courts in virtually all states. This means that separate courts of law and equity, as such, have been eliminated. Instead, the basic trial courts in

---

[10] *Black's Law Dictionary*, Fifth Edition, Copyright 1979 by West Publishing Co.

FIGURE 2.3

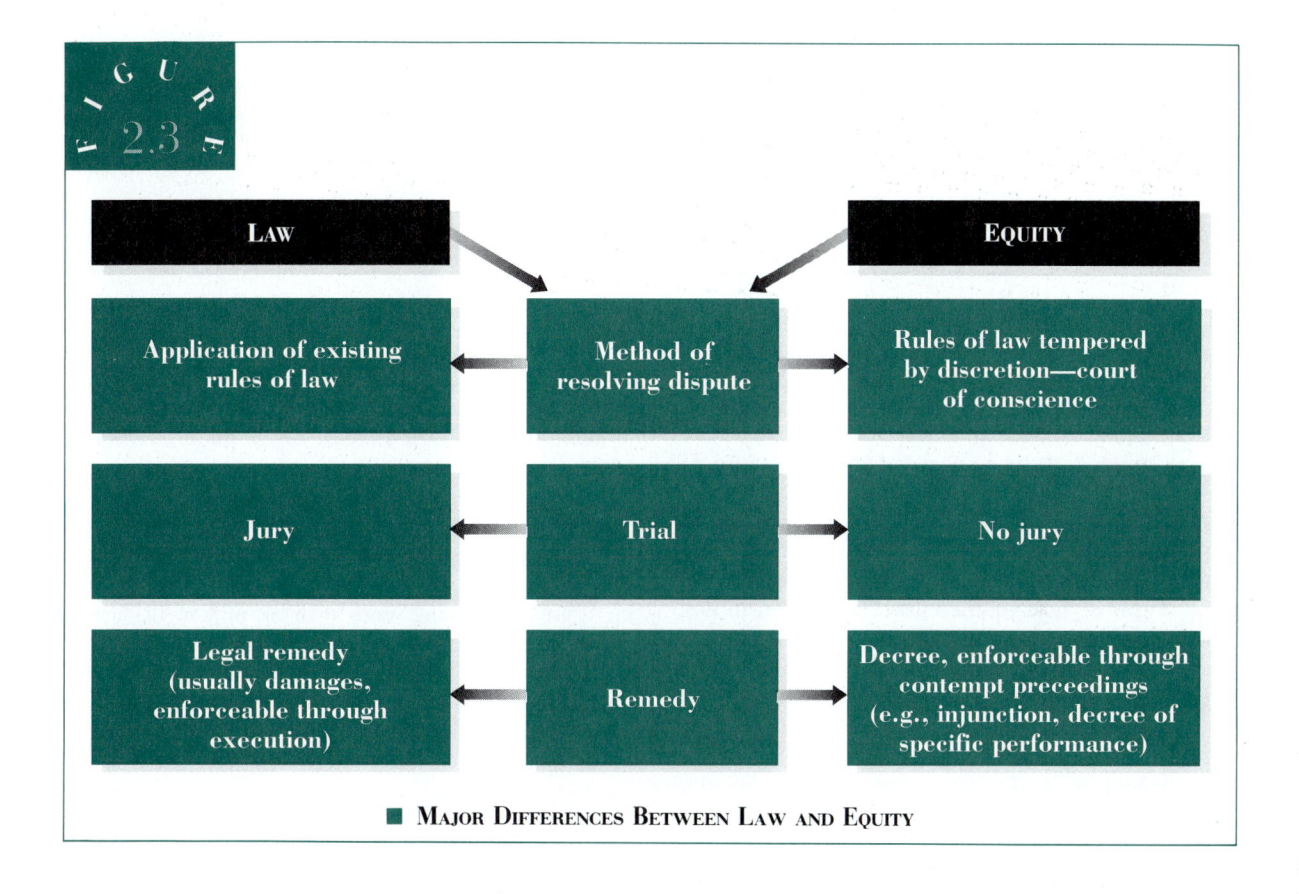

LAW		EQUITY
Application of existing rules of law	Method of resolving dispute	Rules of law tempered by discretion—court of conscience
Jury	Trial	No jury
Legal remedy (usually damages, enforceable through execution)	Remedy	Decree, enforceable through contempt proceedings (e.g., injunction, decree of specific performance)

■ **Major Differences Between Law and Equity**

the state and federal systems are empowered to hear both legal and equitable actions.

Today, the basic distinctions between the two kinds of actions are these:

1. Whether an action is one at law or in equity depends solely on the *nature of the remedy* that the plaintiff is seeking.

2. There is *no jury* in an equitable action. Questions of both fact and law are decided by the court, that is, the trial judge.

3. Proceedings in equitable actions are *less formal* than those at law, particularly in regard to the order in which witnesses' testimony can be presented and the determination of admissibility of their evidence.

4. Equitable remedies are considered to be exceptional. Therefore, when determining whether to grant an equitable remedy, a court considers certain factors that it would not consider in a typical money damage suit. For example, even if the plaintiff has proved that the defendant has violated the plaintiff's legal rights, a court may refuse to grant an injunction or other equitable remedy in any of the following situations: (1) The plaintiff does not have "clean hands"—that is, has been guilty of unfair conduct in his or her dealings with the defendant; (2) an award of money damages—a "remedy at law"—would adequately redress the harm done to plaintiff, so that an equitable remedy is not necessary; or (3) the granting of an equitable remedy might interfere substantially with the rights of some third party who is not involved in the case.

Questions and Problems

1. A Michigan Department of Transportation rule required that all railroads have "adequate toilet facilities" for the health of their employees. About one-third of plaintiff CSXT's locomotives do not have toilets. CSXT protested, and a state administrative law judge upheld the rule. CSXT then filed suit in federal court, claiming that the state rule was inconsistent with federal regulations, which do not require toilets. The Michigan Department of Transportation argued that the federal court should refuse to hear the case (abstain) because of the ongoing proceedings at the state level. The question arose as to whether a state court would have jurisdiction to decide a lawsuit involving federal statutes and regulations. Would it? (*CSXT, Inc. v. Pitz*, 883 F.2d 468, 6th Cir. 1989.)

2. Rate, a Georgia lawyer, is owed $55,000 in legal fees by Jackson, a Florida resident. Although Rate could have brought suit to recover the debt in a federal court in Florida on grounds of diversity of citizenship, he chose, instead, to file his suit in a Florida court in the county in which Jackson lives. If Jackson now asks that the suit be transferred to a federal court, will his request have to be granted? Explain.

3. While walking across Gomez's property one evening, North is injured when he falls into an unguarded excavation. When North brings a negligence action against Gomez in the proper state court to recover damages, that court applies the rule that a trespasser cannot hold a landowner liable even if he is guilty of negligence, and the court dimisses the action. North appeals the decision to the state supreme court, which affirms the rule of nonliability. In this case, is the ruling of the state supreme court final: (If North were to appeal to the U.S. Supreme Court, would it refuse to consider the case?) Why or why not?

4. On December 21, 1985, an Arrow Air Corp. charter plane carrying 248 soldiers from active duty in the Middle East back to Fort Campbell, Kentucky, crashed in Newfoundland, killing all aboard. Relatives of the victims sued Arrow in Kentucky. Arrow moved to dismiss for lack of personal jurisdiction. Evidence showed that Arrow was incorporated in Delaware with its main office in Florida. Arrow hangared an aircraft in Kentucky in 1983, flying five cargo flights per week. It also made flights into Kentucky for the Military Airlift Command in 1984–85, earning more than $2 million in charter revenue. The crash in question was Arrow's second flight into Fort Campbell. Arrow had no bank accounts or phone number in Kentucky. Does a Kentucky court have personal jurisdiction? (*In re Air Crash Disaster at Gander Newfoundland*, 660 F.Supp. 1202, W.D.Ky. 1987.)

5. Plaintiffs bought an Audi automobile in New York. Later, while moving to Arizona they were involved in a serious collision in Oklahoma when the Audi caught fire after being struck from behind. Filing in Oklahoma, plaintiffs sued the New York retailer from whom they had purchased the car and the wholesaler who had provided the car to the retailer. These defendants claimed that because they only sold cars in New York, an Oklahoma court had no personal jurisdiction over them. Does the Oklahoma long-arm statute reach this far? Discuss. (*World-Wide Volkswagen Corp. v. Woodson*, 444 U.S. 286, 1981.)

6. Dennis married Francie in West Virginia in 1976. They spent their married life in New Jersey, where their children were born. In July 1987, they decided to separate. Francie moved herself and the children to San Francisco. Dennis visited Los Angeles on a business trip and then went to San Francisco to see the kids. When he arrived, Francie had him served with a summons and a divorce petition. Dennis went back to New Jersey and had his lawyer file a special appearance in California—a motion to dismiss the California suit for lack of personal jurisdiction. Should the motion be granted, given Dennis's lack of contacts with California? Discuss. (*Burnham v. Superior Court of California*, 110 S.Ct. 2105, 1990.)

7. The plaintiff corporation, incorporated in Michigan, hired the defendant from Florida to operate a helicopter to spray agricultural chemicals on fields in Ohio. In a contract written and signed by the plaintiff in Michigan and later signed by the defendant in Florida, the defendant agreed that if he left the plaintiff's employ he would not enter into a competing business. After 2 years, the defendant left plaintiff's employ and did begin a competing business in Ohio. The plaintiff sued in Ohio to enforce the convenant not to compete. Such a covenant is void under Michigan law but enforceable if reasonable under the laws of Florida and Ohio. Which state's law should be applied by the Ohio court? Discuss. (*S&S Chopper Service, Inc. v Scripter*, 394 N.E.2d 1011, Ohio App. 1977.)

8. The defendant airline, a Delaware corporation headquartered in New York, invited several Illinois travel agents to take an expense-paid vacation to Mexico. While in Mexico, one of the travel agents was killed by unknown assailants. His wife, the plaintiff, sued the airline in Illinois, claiming that its Illinois employees knew at the time of the invitation that portions of Mexico near the trip site were overrun with bands of armed guerrillas, yet they negligently failed to take precautions for the safety of her husband. Mexico's law would allow recovery on the plaintiff's theory; Illinois law would not. Which law should apply? Discuss. (*Semmelroth v. American Airlines*, 448 F.Supp. 730, E.D.Ill. 1978.)

9. Durant was left paralyzed from the waist down when his tractor struck the defendant's guide wire. Durant sued the defendant on a theory of negligent maintenance, filing the suit in Lee County, South Carolina. The defendant filed a motion to change the suit's venue to Sumter County on grounds of convenience to witnesses. Nine of defendant's employees, who would also be witnesses, filed affidavits stating that they would have to travel 23 miles to the Lee County Courthouse. The plaintiff responded with an affidavit indicating that because of his paralysis he was difficult to move and that the Lee County rescue squad had agreed to transport him to and from the Lee County Courthouse but no further. Should the court grant the motion to change venue on *forum non conveniens* grounds? Discuss. See *Durant v. Black River Electric Cooperative, Inc.*, 248 S.E.2d 264 (S.C. 1978.)

CHAPTER 3

Many American novels, movies, and television programs feature courtroom scenes to produce dramatic tension for the readers and viewers. This is appropriate, because courtroom battles can produce high drama. Nothing quite matches the tension that litigants and attorneys feel when a jury verdict is about to be announced in open court.

This chapter will look at the litigation process, from the initiation of a civil suit through the trial process all the way to final appeal. After this examination, you will be better able to appreciate the context in which these

LITIGATION AND ALTERNATIVE METHODS OF DISPUTE RESOLUTION

few dramatic moments occur. You will also understand that litigation can be extremely complicated, expensive, and time-consuming. Indeed, litigation is usually something to be avoided. But when you cannot avoid litigation, it pays to understand the process.

Our discussion focuses on procedures in civil lawsuits rather than in criminal prosecutions. Although many of the procedures in the two types of proceedings are the same, there also are a number of important differences. Some of these differences are noted in Chapter 8, Criminal Law and Business. In addition, a few differences between civil and criminal procedures will be mentioned in this chapter.

After we have studied the civil litigation process, we will explore some other ways of resolving disputes, especially those that arise in business. These other methods, which are sometimes grouped together under the name *alternative dispute resolution,* include arbitration, mediation, and other techniques. Such methods are being used with greater frequency today in an effort to resolve some disputes more quickly, less expensively, and without destroying valuable relationships.

THE ADVERSARIAL SYSTEM

Before studying the process of civil litigation, it is important to note that both civil and criminal proceedings in the United States are based on the so-called **adversarial system.** This approach to litigation is one of the key features of American law inherited from England.[1] The term *adversarial* has a very specialized meaning in this context. Even in a nation that does not use the adversarial system, the parties to a lawsuit or a criminal prosecution obviously are adversaries. However, when we use the term *adversarial* to describe the English/American approach to litigation, we are referring primarily to the amount of control that the parties and their attorneys have over the procedure.

Under the adversarial system, the parties themselves (acting through their attorneys) research the law and develop the facts. They decide which issues are going to be presented, which legal arguments are going to be made, what evidence should be gathered and presented, and how the evidence is to be introduced in court. The trial judge does not make these decisions; indeed, the judge normally takes no action unless a party specifically requests it. For example, if one party's attorney attempts to introduce some testimony or physical evidence that is not legally admissible, the judge usually will not keep the evidence out unless the other party's attorney makes an objection. If

---

[1] Although America derives its adversarial system from England, today the American courts typically use a more extreme version of the adversarial system than do the English courts; in other words, the degree of party control (rather than judge control) over the litigation process is usually even greater in the United States than in England.

an attorney overlooks a relevant legal argument and fails to make it, the judge normally will not take the initiative to include that argument in the legal analysis of the case.

Although the parties and their attorneys have the primary control over the issues and evidence, the trial judge obviously has the duty to exercise ultimate supervisory authority over the entire process. In addition, within the adversarial framework the rules relating to control over issues and evidence can vary somewhat from one court system to another. For example, in some states in the United States, as well as in the federal district courts, trial judges may sometimes ask questions of witnesses if they believe that an attorney's questioning is not eliciting certain important testimony. Similarly, in some states and in the federal courts, trial judges can "comment on the weight of the evidence"—make comments to the jury about the strength of particular testimony or other evidence. In other states, judges cannot do these things. Finally, as caseloads and delays increase, more trial judges in the adversarial system probably will take a greater degree of control over the process in the future than they usually have in the past. However, the general idea that the parties and their attorneys should have primary control is so firmly embedded that it will undoubtedly continue as a fundamental element in our system of litigation.

The adversarial system can be contrasted with the so-called **inquisitorial system** of litigation used in European nations and, indeed, in most other parts of the world that did not inherit the English legal system. In general, the trial judge (or panel of judges)[2] in the inquisitorial system has much more control over the process, and the parties have much less than in the adversarial system. The judge often will have the authority to decide which issues will be addressed, although the parties certainly will provide important input. The judges are usually in charge of the investigation and gathering of evidence; they do not do this personally but have investigators who answer directly to them. Judges make rulings and take various other actions on their own initiative rather than merely responding to the parties' requests for action.[3] It should be noted, finally, that there is significant variation in procedural details among the many countries that use the inquisitorial system, just as there is variation within the adversarial system.

There are good and bad points about both of these systems. The adversarial system requires fewer judges and more lawyers than the inquisitorial system. The inquisitorial system requires that more of the time

---

[2] In many other countries, it is more common to have a panel of three or more trial judges in significant cases, rather than the single trial judge that typically presides over a trial in the United States.

[3] There are other differences in the two systems that cannot be discussed here in detail. For example, in many countries that use the inquisitorial system, the trial in a civil lawsuit is not a single, highly intensive event. Instead, it may consist of a series of several conferences among the judges, parties, and attorneys. The process of investigation and evidence-gathering takes place not only before the first conference but also between later conferences. Each meeting brings the case closer to a conclusion. This kind of process can work in these countries because juries of citizens are not used.

HUMOR AND THE LAW

One of our greatest freedoms is the right to go to the judicial system to vindicate our rights. In a nation of 250 million people, there will be an unfortunately large number of crackpots and malcontents who will file suits better left unfiled. We are reminded of the woman who sued actor Leonard Nimoy, who played Spock on the 1960s television show "Star Trek" for violating her intergalactic patent rights to the knife, fork, spoon, and Phillips screwdriver. *Steele v. Nimoy*, No. 77-0507-CV-W-4 (W.D.Mo. 1978).

When insistent litigants are incarcerated with time on their hands, they may sue repeatedly. When one state prison inmate filed his 140th (or so) lawsuit, the poor federal judge who had handled many of them was prompted to begin his opinion:

"This is another chapter in the H_____ F_____ saga. No longer am I tempted to call it the final chapter, as desirable as that would be to me. I mention mournfully that only the finality of death—his or mine—would enable the other of us to sue the term "final" in that way. And, of course, if mine comes first, I have no doubt that another judge will someday express lamentations such as these. They will be packaged and labelled, by reason of tradition, as opinions."

Franklin v. State of Oregon, 563 F.Supp. 1310 (D.Or. 1983).

---

and energy devoted to a case be expended by public officials (judges and investigators) than by the parties and attorneys. Thus, the adversarial system shifts more of the cost to the private sector, whereas the inquisitorial system places more of the cost in the public sector. The adversarial system also puts primary responsibility for developing the facts in the hands of those (parties and their attorneys) who have a natural incentive to do a more thorough job. However, putting this responsibility in the hands of the parties and their attorneys also means that the fact-gathering process may be aimed more at seeking strategic advantage than finding the truth.

LITIGATION: PRETRIAL PROCEEDINGS

Pretrial proceedings consist of two stages, the **pleading stage** and the **discovery stage.** We will look at each of these steps briefly.

THE PLEADING STAGE

The typical suit is commenced by the plaintiff, through an attorney, filing a **complaint** (or petition) with the court having jurisdiction of the case. At the same time, the plaintiff asks the court to issue a summons to the defendant.

After receiving the summons, the defendant has a prescribed period of time in which to file a response of some sort, normally an **answer,** to the complaint. After that has been completed, the plaintiff can file a **reply** to the answer. The complaint, answer, and reply make up the *pleadings* of a case, the main purpose of which is to permit the court and the parties to ascertain the actual points in issue.

The Complaint

The *complaint* sets forth the plaintiff's version of the facts and ends with a "prayer" (request) for a certain remedy based on these facts. The plaintiff alleges those facts which, if ultimately proved by the evidence, will establish a legally recognized claim against the defendant. Suppose, for example, that the plaintiff bought a boat from the defendant, a dealer. The plaintiff claims that the boat leaks badly. After the two parties are unable to resolve their differences, the plaintiff institutes a lawsuit by filing a complaint. The complaint may allege that the parties made an agreement for the sale of the boat on a particular date for a particular price, the price was paid and the boat delivered, the plaintiff used the boat and found that it leaked, the defective condition of the boat is in violation of a warranty made by the dealer, and the plaintiff has suffered economic harm because the boat is worth far less in its defective condition than it would have been worth if not defective. If these facts are ultimately proved, the plaintiff has a good claim against the defendant for breach of warranty. However, the plaintiff might also allege that the defendant intentionally lied about the condition of the boat, thus committing the tort of fraud or perhaps violating a state deceptive trade practice statute.

In most complaints, the remedy requested by the plaintiff is an award of money damages to be paid by the defendant to compensate the plaintiff for his or her loss. If the plaintiff seeks some other remedy, such as an injunction, it will be requested in the complaint. Sometimes the plaintiff's complaint may request multiple remedies, such as damages for past harm and an injunction to prevent future harm. In the boat example, the plaintiff might request money damages for breach of warranty or perhaps fraud. This is not the type of case in which the plaintiff would seek an injunction. He might, however, request the equitable remedy of *rescission,* an order of the court cancelling the contract, along with *restitution,* a return of the purchase price.

The Answer

The defendant usually responds to the complaint by filing an *answer*. The answer may include several components. One thing it always contains is a *denial* of the plaintiff's allegations. In some places, the defendant is permitted to make a *general denial,* which simply denies all the plaintiff's allegations together. In other court systems, the rules require a defendant to deny each allegation individually; any allegation not denied is deemed to be admitted. The rules in some systems permit a general denial in most cases, but require specific denials of certain types of allegations. Regardless of the form, a denial is essentially a formality that places the plaintiff's allegations in issue and places the burden on the plaintiff to prove the assertions he or she has made.

It must be remembered that the plaintiff in a civil lawsuit (and the prosecution in a criminal case) bears the overall burden of proof. In other words, if the plaintiff does not ultimately produce evidence that convinces the jury (or judge if there is no jury) of the correctness of the allegations in the complaint, the plaintiff loses. Although the defendant must respond with an answer, he or she is not obligated to *prove* anything. Nevertheless, if a defendant believes that the facts create a legally recognized *defense* (sometimes called an *affirmative defense*) against the plaintiff's claim, he or she will assert the defense in the answer after the denial. A defense defeats the plaintiff's claim *even if the plaintiff is able to prove those facts that establish all the elements of his or her claim.* Asserting a defense consists of alleging those facts that, if ultimately proved by the defendant, will establish a legally recognized defense against the plaintiff's claim. For virtually every type of civil claim, the law recognizes one or more defenses. In the boat example, the defendant might allege as a defense to the breach of warranty claim that there was a *disclaimer* in the sale contract stating clearly and conspicuously that the boat was a reconditioned one and was being sold on an "as is" basis. If proved, this allegation would defeat the plaintiff's breach of warranty claim. Such a defense would not defeat a fraud claim, however. (In criminal cases, there are also legally recognized defenses against virtually all types of criminal charges.)

When asserting a defense, the defendant does not make a claim or request a remedy but simply tries to defeat the plaintiff's claim. Sometimes, however, the defendant may wish to assert a claim against the defendant in the form of a **counterclaim.** The defendant will allege facts that, if proved by the defendant, will establish a legally recognized claim against the plaintiff, and the defendant will ask for money damages or some other remedy. Either party alone might prevail on its claim, or both may prevail; in the latter event, the amount of the smaller judgment will be subtracted from the amount of the larger judgment.

Most counterclaims arise from the same set of circumstances that led to the plaintiff's claim (a so-called *compulsory* counterclaim). In such a case, the rules in most court systems require that the defendant assert the claim in this case as a counterclaim if it is to be asserted at all; he or she cannot keep quiet about it now and later sue the plaintiff (with their roles and names obviously reversed) on the claim. However, if the defendant's claim against the plaintiff arises from an unrelated set of circumstances, it is a so-called *permissive* counterclaim, and the defendant has a choice of asserting a counterclaim in the present case or suing separately.

In the boat example, the defendant might assert a counterclaim alleging that the plaintiff had not paid all the boat's purchase price, in violation of the sale contract, and request damages in the amount of the unpaid portion. It is not a rare occurrence for a plaintiff to have the tables turned on him or her by a counterclaim and make the plaintiff regret that he or she ever filed a lawsuit. The existence of a potential counterclaim sometimes may persuade a plaintiff not to file a complaint in the first place; at the very least, a realistic possibility that the other party may be able to prove a counterclaim can dramatically affect the bargaining positions of the parties as they attempt to negotiate a settlement.

The Reply

If the defendant raises new matter—additional facts—in his or her answer, the plaintiff must file a reply. In this pleading, the plaintiff will either deny or admit the new facts alleged in the answer.

Motion to Dismiss

Although technically it is not part of the pleadings, the **motion to dismiss**[4] must be mentioned at this point. The defendant will file such a motion instead of an answer if he or she believes that the plaintiff has no claim even if all the allegations in the complaint are true. In this motion, the defendant asserts that the plaintiff has not even stated a "cause of action"—that is, that even if plaintiff's allegations are true (which the defendant is not admitting), the law does not recognize such a claim. The motion does not refer to any evidence but merely takes aim at the allegations made in the plaintiff's complaint. Suppose, for example, that Ralph, the owner of a retail store in Milwaukee, is upset about some of the business practices of a competing retailer in town. In a private conversation between Ralph and George, the president of the other retailer, Ralph says, "You and your people are liars and cutthroats; you screw your customers whenever you think you can get away with it; you have the morals of a gutter rat." The conversation is not overheard by anyone else, and Ralph does not repeat any of it to anyone. If George sues Ralph for the tort of defamation, alleging these facts, Ralph will probably file a motion to dismiss and the court will grant it. Even if what Ralph said about George and his company was false, the tort of defamation (slander or libel) can occur only if false defamatory statements about someone are *communicated* to a third party. Thus, George and his company have no claim against Ralph even if events were exactly as George described in his complaint.

If the court grants the motion to dismiss, the plaintiff will be given an opportunity to amend the complaint. If the problem cannot be corrected by an amendment to the complaint, the court will dismiss the plaintiff's case. However, if the court denies the defendant's motion to dismiss, the defendant will then file an answer.

Like other actions of a trial judge, its ruling on a motion to dismiss can be appealed to a higher court. The plaintiff can begin such an appeal

---

[4] The terminology used in referring to this particular type of "motion to dismiss" follows the rules of civil procedure that have, in recent years, been adopted by many states. The earlier name for this same pleading device—the "demurrer"—continues to be used in a few states, however. In such states, what has been said here in regard to the motion to dismiss applies with equal force to the demurrer.

immediately if the trial court grants the motion to dismiss, because this results in a final determination of the case at that level. However, if the trial judge denies the motion to dismiss, the defendant must wait until the case ends at the trial level before appealing; in this situation, the trial judge's ruling on the motion to dismiss probably will be only one of several grounds for the appeal.

The motion to dismiss is the first of several types of motions that give the trial judge an opportunity to end the litigation early when he or she is convinced that there is no doubt about the outcome and thus no reason to continue.

Defendant's Failure to Respond

Assuming that the court has jurisdiction, the defendant must respond within a specified time period by filing either a motion to dismiss or an answer. This time period is 20 days in the federal district courts and about the same amount of time in most state courts. The "clock starts ticking" when the defendant receives the summons and complaint. If the defendant does not respond during this period, the court may grant a **default judgment** against the defendant. By failing to respond, the defendant has given up his or her right to contest liability. The only issue to be determined is the amount of money damages to which the plaintiff is entitled, or the appropriateness of some other remedy the plaintiff may be seeking. The court will conduct a hearing at which the plaintiff presents evidence on the question of damages or other requested remedy.

THE DISCOVERY STAGE

In early years, cases moved directly from the pleading stage to the trial stage. This meant that each party, going into the trial, had little information as to the specific evidence that the other party would rely on in presenting his or her case. Trial proceedings, as a result, often became what was commonly described as a "cat and mouse" game, with the parties often bringing in evidence that suprised their opponents. This situation was a natural outgrowth of the control parties have over evidence gathering and presentation in the adversarial system.

The undesirability of these proceedings was finally perceived by lawyers and judges, with the result that the Federal Rules of Civil Procedure, adopted in 1938, provided means (called "discovery proceedings") by which much of the evidence that each party was going to rely on in proving his or her version of the facts would be fully disclosed to the other party before the case came on for trial. The most common discovery tools recognized by these federal rules, which have now been essentially adopted by the states, are *depositions, interrogatories,* and *requests for production of documents.*

A deposition is testimony of a witness that is taken outside of court. Such testimony is given under oath, and both parties to the case must be notified so that they can be present when the testimony is given and thus have the opportunity to cross-examine the witness. Depositions are taken for these reasons: (1) to learn what the key witnesses know about the case; (2) to gain leads that will help obtain additional information; (3) to preserve the testimony of witnesses who might die or disappear; and (4) to establish a foundation for cross-examination of witnesses who might later change their stories.

Interrogatories are written questions submitted by one party to the other, which must be answered under oath. Use of this device is a primary way by which the questioning party may gain access to evidence that otherwise would be solely in the possession of his or her adversary.

A demand for documents permits a party to gain access to those kinds of evidence—such as business records, letters, and hospital bills—that are in the possession of the other party. Under modern rules of civil procedure the party seeking the documents has the right to obtain them for purposes of inspection and copying.

A party must make a good faith effort to comply with the other party's legitimate discovery request. The court can impose various sanctions on parties and attorneys who do not make such an effort. These penalties may include the assessment of discovery costs, attorney's fees, or monetary penalties. In cases of flagrant disregard of legitimate discovery requests, the court can even dismiss a claim or defense or grant a default judgment against the offending party. The following case provides an example of such a situation.

PROFILE GEAR CORP. v. FOUNDRY ALLIED INDUSTRIES, INC.

U.S. SEVENTH CIRCUIT COURT OF APPEALS 937 F.2D 351 (1991)

Profile Gear Corp. manufactures and sells gears, gear assemblies, and various machine tool products. Under a contract with the U.S. government, Profile supplied replacement final drive assemblies for the Bradley fighting vehicle. Profile entered a contract with Foundry Allied Industries, under which Foundry was to supply Profile with aluminum castings that were a major component part of Profile's final drive assemblies. A dispute arose between Profile and Foundry over the contract terms. Profile claimed that all the contract terms were in a purchase order and other forms it sent to Foundry, and these terms obligated Foundry to supply 2,434 sets of castings at a fixed price of $455 per set. Foundry claimed, however, that the contract included the terms and conditions contained in a quotation that Foundry sent to Profile. One of these terms permitted Foundry to raise the price as the cost of aluminum increased. Profile refused to pay for castings it received after Foundry raised the price. Profile filed suit for breach of contract in federal district court (there was diversity of citizenship), claiming damages of $120,000.

Foundry asserted a counterclaim for breach of contract, claiming damages of $320,000.

During pretrial, Profile and its attorney repeatedly refused to make various documents available in response to legitimate discovery requests by Foundry. In addition, Profile and its attorney lied to Foundry's attorney and to the district judge on several occasions about the nonexistence of documents or about its inability to find or obtain them. On four different occasions, the district judge levied monetary penalties against Profile and its attorney for this behavior. The conduct continued, however; ultimately, the

CONTINUED

district judge gave Profile notice that default judgment would be entered against Profile on Foundry's counterclaim if Profile did not immediately comply with various discovery requests. Profile did not do so, and the court granted default judgment for Foundry on its counterclaim in an amount of $360,000 (damages plus interest).

Eschbach, Circuit Judge:

"For a long time courts were reluctant to enter default judgments, and appellate courts were reluctant to sustain those that were entered.... Those times are gone." *Metropolitan Life Insurance Co. v. Estate of Cammon*, 929 F.2d 1120 (7th Cir. 1991).... The story begins with Profile Gear's response to interrogatories that the defendant Foundry served on July 28, 1989. Instead of answering the interrogatories, Profile responded "See Complaint" and "See Documents Produced," which the District Court properly characterized as evasive conduct. [On September 14,] the District Court imposed a sanction of $250, and ordered Profile to "respond to all outstanding discovery requests by September 25, 1989."...

Meanwhile, Profile [moved for sanctions against Foundry.] Its motion stated that Foundry had offered to produce certain documents for Profile's Chicago counsel only in Racine, Wisconsin. In fact, this problem had been resolved and the documents offered in Chicago. At a September 19 hearing, the District Court asked, "You told me in your motion that you have to go to Racine to see the documents. That is not the fact, is it?" To which Profile's counsel answered, "No, no, your Honor." The District Court issued a second sanction of $250 against Profile's counsel "for pursuing this motion when he knew the representations were not true."

The District Court issued more substantial sanctions three months later, on January 17, 1990. At this point, Profile had been caught in a clear lie. Profile had responded "none" in answer to requests for documents concerning other disputes involving the contract language at issue in this case. Yet, in depositions, a Profile employee admitted the existence of such a dispute. And when documents were finally produced, they showed that Profile's counsel sent and received letters regarding this dispute just one month before stating that no documents existed....

Two other incidents were similar. As of January 17, 1990, Profile admitted receiving at least three quotations for aluminum castings. Profile claimed that these quotations were missing from its files, but offered essentially no explanation for their absence. So too, Profile failed to produce a two page statement that it had asked a former employee to prepare. The statement was mailed to Profile, but Profile's counsel denied receiving it. The District Court concluded that, "in a strict credibility contest, [Profile's counsel] would not prevail over the reliability of the United States mail."

In addition, Profile refused to disclose the minutes of meetings of its own board of directors because "they are not within the immediate control of Profile's officers or counsel," and it refused to disclose monthly and quarterly financial reports because they concerned a "unique defense" that was otherwise unspecified.... This conduct led to a third set of sanctions. [On January 17, 1990,] the District Court ordered Profile to pay various of Foundry's attorneys' fees and "to immediately engage in a thorough search for all documents described in Foundry's document request that remain undisclosed.... These documents shall be produced by February 1, 1990." The District Court also warned, "Should Profile fail to fully comply with this order, the court will determine whether to enter [default] judgment in favor of Foundry."...

Instead of complying, Profile for the first time claimed that it had 100,000 documents to produce, and this volume of material would take 30 days to assemble. This failure by Profile to meet another firm deadline led to a fourth sanction.... [T]he District Court ordered Profile to post a bond by March 1, 1990 in the amount of Foundry's counterclaim, and warned that a default judgment would be entered if the bond was not posted. [Profile did not post the bond.]

The District Court's findings of intentional delay and repeated dishonesty are adequately supported [by evidence in the record].... [T]he District Court did not abuse its discretion in entering a default judgment. For comparison, we note that this Court [i.e., the Court of Appeals] has stated that a district court need not impose any lesser sanctions prior to entering the sanction of default judgment.... A district court is not required to fire a warning shot prior to issuing a default judgment as a sanction. And even absent a finding of dishonesty, we have affirmed numerous default judgments due to dilatory tactics....
AFFIRMED.

COMMENT

1. It should be emphasized that, as punishment for Profile, the trial court granted a default judgment to Foundry on its counterclaim without regard to whether Foundry had proved this claim. Thus the court's action was very different from the action of a court in granting a summary judgment, which will be discussed shortly.

2. Although Profile's attorney was guilty of substantial misconduct in the case, Profile probably would not have a good malpractice claim against its attorney, because the evidence strongly suggested that Profile's management either directed or at least knew about and agreed to most of this conduct. Profile had a different attorney on appeal.

Abuse of the Discovery Process

Almost everyone who is knowledgeable about the American litigation process agrees that it is better to permit pretrial discovery than to have "trial by ambush." Most of them also admit, however, that the discovery process is plagued by frequent abuses. Discovery can be misused for the purpose of causing delay or confusion or imposing extra costs on the other party. One party may flood the other with voluminous and unnecessary interrogatories, take far more depositions than necessary, conduct depositions in an inefficient and wasteful manner, ask for a much larger volume of documents than necessary, respond to the other party's request for documents with truckloads of material when a few boxes would do, and engage in other tactics intended to wear the other party down. Just as the original need for pretrial discovery was an outgrowth of the adversarial system, so too are these abuses of discovery.

Trial judges generally possess the same power to punish parties and their attorneys for abusing the discovery process as they have to punish them for failing to comply with legitimate discovery requests. Traditionally, however, too few trial judges have exercised adequate supervisory control over pretrial discovery. Often times, this failure probably has been attributable to the fact they simply have had too many cases on their dockets. Although an increasingly heavy case load may cause a judge to have less time to supervise the pretrial proceedings in each case, it also makes it even more important that the judge exercise tighter control over all aspects of every case. Many judges are finding that they have to be good managers as well as good judges. In recent years, necessity has been leading more and more trial judges to exercise tighter control over the pretrial discovery process and other aspects of litigation. This is especially evident in the federal district courts, where it is becoming commonplace for judges to hold pretrial conferences with the attorneys, at which schedules and deadlines are established for conducting discovery and dealing with other pretrial matters. It also is becoming more common for trial judges, particularly federal district judges, to impose various penalties on parties and their attorneys for abuse of discovery. In the federal system, as well as in some state court systems, *magistrates* are increasingly used as judicial assistants to perform various tasks including supervision of pretrial discovery. As has happened in other matters over the

SUMMARY JUDGMENT

years, it is likely that many state courts will follow the lead of the federal courts in supervising discovery more closely and punishing abuses of discovery more severely. Indeed, courts in some states have already begun to do so. There still is much room for improvement, however.

At or near the end of discovery, one party or the other (and occasionally both) may file a motion for **summary judgment** as to one or more of the issues in the lawsuit. In filing such a motion a party is arguing to the judge, in essence, that the evidence produced by discovery makes it so clear that the moving party is legally entitled to prevail that a trial would be a waste of time. A judge should grant such a motion only if a thorough review of the evidence obtained through discovery indicates that there is "no genuine issue as to any material fact"—that is, that there is no real question as to any important factual matter. Although summary judgment can be granted against either party, the fact that the plaintiff has the burden of proof means that summary judgments for the defendant are more common than for the plaintiff. Thus, if a defendant files a motion for summary judgment, it will be granted unless the plaintiff has presented at least enough evidence during discovery to create a genuine issue on all the required elements of its claim. However, if a plaintiff files the motion, the court will grant it only if (1) the plaintiff has produced enough evidence to prove the elements of its claim, (2) the defendant has failed to present evidence that creates doubt about any of these elements, and (3) the defendant also has failed to present evidence sufficient to create a genuine issue regarding an affirmative defense.

Judges traditionally have been reluctant to grant summary judgment motions, especially when a jury trial has been requested. In recent years, however, the U.S. Supreme Court has urged the federal district courts to make more use of summary judgment when there really does not seem to be much doubt about the ultimate outcome. In *Celotex Corp. v. Catrett*, 477 U.S. 317 (1986), the Court stated that "summary judgment procedure is properly regarded not as a disfavored procedural shortcut, but rather as an integral part of the Federal Rules [of Civil Procedure], which are designed to 'secure the just, speedy and inexpensive determination of every action.'" Not only are federal courts making increasing use of summary judgment, but it is very likely that more state courts also will do so as heavier case loads put greater pressure on judicial resources.

LITIGATION: TRIAL PROCEEDINGS

THE TRIAL STAGE

Unless a lawsuit is settled out of court or disposed of by the granting of a motion to dismiss or motion for summary judgment, it will eventually come up for trial. In the **trial stage** a jury may be impaneled, evidence presented, a verdict returned, and a judgment entered in favor of one of the parties.

Trial by Jury

In most civil lawsuits in which the plaintiff is seeking a so-called remedy at law, there is a constitutional right to jury trial. Because most lawsuits involve claims for money damages, such a right usually exists. In the federal courts, the right to trial by jury in civil cases is guaranteed by the Seventh Amendment of the U.S. Constitution. (For federal criminal cases, the right to jury trial is found in the Sixth Amendment.) Almost all state constitutions provide similar guarantees for cases tried in state courts.

When there is a right to jury trial, a jury will be impaneled if either party formally requests one. Failure to demand a jury trial constitutes a waiver of the right to one. The jury is a fact-finding body; its function is to consider all of the evidence and determine to the best of its ability what really happened. The jury determines whether particular testimony or other evidence is believable ("credible") and how much strength it seems to have as proof of the alleged facts. The jury is required to follow the judge's instructions as to the applicable legal principles. If neither party requests a jury, the trial judge performs the fact-finding role in addition to the judicial function. When there is no jury, the trial judge usually is required to prepare formal written "Findings of Fact" and "Conclusions of Law" after hearing the case. Although it is increasingly common today for both parties to waive a jury trial, especially in business disputes, there are still a great many jury trials. Most of the discussion in the remainder of this chapter assumes that there is a jury.

The use of juries drawn randomly from the local population is another unique feature of litigation inherited from the English system.[5] The jury system is sometimes criticized as being inefficient and unpredictable. Critics offer several arguments to support the claim that the jury system is an inferior method for resolving disputes, including the following:

1. Jurors do not have to meet any particular educational requirements.

2. Jurors do not have the experience or training to sift through substantial amounts of evidence, weigh it, and make carefully reasoned decisions.

3. Untrained and inexperienced decision makers are likely to be influenced too easily by irrelevant sympathies or by the rhetoric of a highly skillful attorney.

4. Many of the rules of procedure and evidence that lengthen and complicate lawsuits exist only to accommodate an untrained and inexperienced fact-finding body.

Supporters of the jury system counter with a number of their own arguments, such as the following:

1. General experience in "living" is more important for deciding the average case than is any kind of specialized training or experience.

---

[5] Although juries are no longer used extensively in civil lawsuits in England, they continue to be used there in criminal cases.

2. Juries serve as a limited but valuable check on the power of the judicial branch of government.

3. Juries provide a means for direct, continuous input of community values into the legal system.

Impaneling a Jury

However one may feel about the jury as an institution, it will no doubt continue to be an integral part of our legal system for a long time to come. When a jury is to be impaneled, names of prospective jurors are drawn from a list of those who have been randomly selected from public records (voter registration, driver license, etc.) for possible duty during the term. Each prospective juror is questioned in an effort to make sure that the jury will be as impartial as possible. This questioning is conducted by the plaintiff's and defendant's attorneys, a judge, or by all three, depending on the practice in the particular court system. This preliminary questioning of prospective jurors is called the *voir dire* examination. (*Voir dire,* from the French, means "to speak the truth.")

If questioning indicates that a particular person probably would not be capable of making an impartial decision, the judge will excuse the person by granting a **challenge for cause** made by one of the attorneys. A challenge for cause may be granted, for example, if it is shown that a prospective juror has a close friendship, family relationship, or business association with one of the parties or attorneys, a financial interest in the case, or a clear bias resulting from any other aspect of the action.

The attorney for each party also has a limited number of **peremptory challenges** (or "strikes"). Such challenges permit the attorney to have a prospective juror removed without giving any reason for doing so. The U.S. Supreme Court has ruled, however, that attorneys in civil or criminal cases, or government prosecutors in criminal cases, violate the *equal protection clause* of the U.S. Constitution if they exclude jurors because of their race. Proving this, of course, may be very difficult.

Once the number of prospective jurors who have survived both kinds of challenges reaches the number required by law to hear the case, they are sworn in and the case proceeds. Traditionally the number of jurors has been 12, but in recent years courts in quite a few states and in the federal system have reduced the number of jurors in civil cases, with eight being a common number.

Presentation of Evidence

After the attorneys for both sides have made opening statements outlining their cases, the plaintiff begins to present its case. As we have seen, the plaintiff has the *burden of proof*—the duty to prove the facts alleged in the complaint. In a normal civil case, the plaintiff must convince the fact-finder of the truth of the allegations by a preponderance of the evidence—in other words, the plaintiff has to tilt the scales somewhat in its favor on each of the alleged facts. The plaintiff attempts to meet this burden by presenting evidence to support his or her version of the facts. This evidence may consist of the sworn testimony of witnesses, as well as physical evidence such as documents, photographs, and so on. When an item of physical evidence is introduced in court, it is usually required that a witness with personal knowledge about the item give sworn testimony about its authenticity. A witness who gives false testimony while under oath may be convicted of the crime of *perjury*.

The testimony of a witness is normally elicited by questions from an attorney. When a witness is called to testify in court by the plaintiff's attorney, that attorney questions the witness first. This is called the *direct examination*. As a general rule, an attorney cannot ask *leading questions* during the direct examination. The attorney for the other side must object, however, before the judge will order the attorney to stop asking leading questions. A leading question is one that suggests its own answer, that is, it "puts words into the witness's mouth." "You saw the defendant's car smash into the plaintiff's car while the defendant was going at a high rate of speed, didn't you?" is a leading question. If the attorney calls an *adverse witness*, however, the rule against leading questions does not apply. An adverse witness is either the opposing party to the case or some other witness for the other side. After each of the plaintiff's witnesses testifies, the defendant's attorney has an opportunity to conduct a *cross-examination* of that witness. The attorney is permitted to ask leading questions in cross-examination. The purpose of cross-examination is to discredit or cast doubt on the witness's testimony. For example, a cross-examination might divulge that (1) pertinent facts in the direct examination were omitted, (2) a witness's powers of observation were poor, (3) the witness made a statement in the past (such as in a deposition) that is inconsistent with his or her present testimony, thus creating doubt about his or her credibility, or (4) the witness is not completely disinterested because he or she stands to gain or lose something from the outcome of the case. At the judge's discretion, the plaintiff's attorney may then have a chance to conduct a *redirect examination* to deal with any new matters that might have developed during cross-examination. The judge similarly has discretion to permit another cross-examination after the redirect, but this is unusual.

After the plaintiff has completed its presentation of evidence, the defendant then has the same opportunity. The defendant's purpose will be to offer evidence tending to show that the plaintiff's allegations are not correct. If the defendant had asserted a defense or counterclaim, he or she also will offer evidence to meet the burden of proof on those allegations. The procedures and rules are the same when the defendant presents evidence as when the plaintiff was doing so, except that the roles obviously are reversed on direct, cross-, and redirect examination.

Rules of Evidence

Before going on, a brief mention of the **rules of evidence** is necessary. These rules attempt to ensure that the evidence presented in a court of law is relevant to the issues and is as accurate and reliable as possible. The rules of evidence apply whether there is a jury performing the fact-finding role or whether the trial judge is doing so. The rules are more important, however, and are often applied more strictly in a trial before a jury than in one before a judge. As mentioned earlier, even if evidence is inadmissible under the rules of evidence, it will be excluded only if the attorney for the other side objects. Such an objection is made during the trial when an attempt is made to introduce the evidence. Before trial, however, if an attorney can identify inadmissible evidence that the other side probably will try to present in court and can convince the judge that the other side may be able to "sneak in" some of this evidence before the attorney has a chance to object, the judge may grant a motion ordering the other side not to make the attempt.

Although the rules of evidence are so numerous and complex that a complete treatment is impossible here, we can provide a flavor of them by discussing three kinds of evidence that are commonly excluded by the rules.[6]

Irrelevant Evidence: If a witness is asked a question that can have no possible bearing on any of the disputed facts, the opposing attorney may object on the basis that the answer would constitute **irrelevant evidence.** In a personal injury suit arising from an accident, for example, such matters as the defendant's religious beliefs or the fact that he or she was convicted of a charge of reckless driving several years earlier would have no bearing on the present case. Objections to such evidence would be "sustained" by the court. Documents or other physical evidence can also be excluded on grounds of irrelevancy.

Hearsay: In our common experience, we all know that second-hand information is usually not as reliable as first-hand information. The law takes this fact into account by holding that, in general, **hearsay evidence** is not admissible in court. Hearsay evidence may take the form of oral testimony by a witness, or it may consist of a statement in a written document that is offered as evidence. Oral or written evidence is hearsay if (1) it consists of a statement made by some person who is not testifying personally in court and (2) the evidence is offered in court for the purpose of proving the truth of that statement. Thus if an issue in a particular case is whether a trucker delivered a shipment of goods to the X Company on a certain day, witness W (a jogger in the vicinity at the time) could testify that she saw packages being unloaded from a truck on the day in question. But neither W nor any other witness would normally be allowed to testify that she was *told by a third party*, Z, that Z saw goods being unloaded on the day in question. In the latter situation, W's testimony would be inadmissible hearsay because it related a statement of Z,

---

[6] Cases brought in the federal courts are governed by the Federal Rules of Evidence, which Congress adopted in 1975. The rules of evidence applied in state courts are adopted by the various state legislatures or by state supreme courts (under authority delegated by the state legislature). The state rules vary somewhat but are generally uniform on the major points. The federal rules of evidence are widely acknowledged as representing the most modern view of evidentiary rules, and are increasingly being adopted at the state level.

who is not testifying in person, and the evidence is being offered for the purpose of proving the content of Z's statement.

There are many situations in which second-hand statements can be placed into evidence because they are not offered for the purpose of proving the truth of the statements. In a breach of contract case, for example, the plaintiff or some other witness may testify in court that the defendant (D) said "I will sell you my car for $10,000." This would not be hearsay, because the witness's testimony is not being offered for the purpose of proving that the internal content of D's statement is true. Indeed, D's statement cannot be characterized as true or false; there may be a question about whether D actually said it, but there can be no issue about the truth or falsity of the statement's content. Sometimes such a statement is called a "verbal act." Another example would be, in a defamation case brought by P against D, the statement allegedly made by D that "P is a thief, a liar, and a cheat." A witness's testimony in court that D said this would be offered for the purpose of proving that D actually said such a thing and not for the purpose of proving the content of D's statement as a factual matter.

Even if evidence constitutes hearsay, sometimes it is nevertheless admissible under an exception to the hearsay rule. Exceptions exist for situations in which, despite being within the definition of hearsay, particular kinds of evidence are likely to possess a relatively high degree of reliability. For example, a ledger or other business record includes "statements" of the person who made the entry in the record; these statements relate to the factual details of particular actions or business transactions. If the person who made the entry is not testifying personally about his or her recollection of a certain transaction, but instead the business record is offered to prove particular facts about the transaction, the business record is hearsay. There is, however, a well-established exception for business records. Such records are usually made with care because the business firm relies on them for many important purposes. The exception usually applies if a witness in custody of the records can testify under oath that the record was made "in the usual course of business" and was made at or near the time of the act or transaction being recorded.

Opinion: Sometimes a witness is asked for or volunteers information that he or she believes to be true but that is not based on the witness's personal knowledge. As a general rule, such **opinion evidence,** whether in oral or written form, is not legally admissible. For example, in an auto accident case, a witness properly could testify that he or she had observed the defendant's car weaving back and forth on a highway shortly before the accident. On the basis of this observation, however, the witness could not testify that the defendant was "obviously drunk." Evidence normally is supposed to take the form of information based on direct observation; the drawing of inferences, the forming of opinions, and the reaching of conclusions are tasks for the jury (or the judge if there is no jury).

Opinion evidence is not always excluded. On technical matters that lie outside the knowledge of ordinary jurors, it is frequently necessary that qualified experts be permitted to state their opinions as an aid to the jury's or judge's determination of what facts probably occurred. Thus a physician may give an opinion as to cause of death or as to whether a particular course of medical treatment is generally accepted within the medical community. Similarly, a civil engineer may give an opinion as to the likely cause of a bridge collapsing. Unless the attorney for one party agrees ("stipulates") that a particular witness called by the other party is qualified to testify as an expert, the judge must make a ruling on whether the witness is so qualified. In the average situation, a person called as an expert witness is stipulated as such by the other side.

Motion for Directed Verdict

After all the plaintiff's evidence has been presented, the defendant's attorney often makes a **motion for directed verdict.** This motion makes the same assertion as the earlier motion for summary judgment, except that the motion for directed verdict is based on more evidence, including the personal testimony of witnesses in court. The motion asserts that the plaintiff's evidence on one or more of the required elements of its case is either nonexistent or so weak that there is no genuine issue of disputed fact. Thus, "reasonable minds could not differ" on the factual question, and the judge should decide the case "as a matter of law" instead of sending it to the jury. Sometimes it is said that the motion raises the issue of whether there is a "jury question."

If the defendant's motion for directed verdict is denied, the defendant then presents its case as discussed earlier. At the close of the defendant's case, the plaintiff can make a motion for directed verdict. The motion contends that the plaintiff's evidence on the required elements of its claim is so overwhelming and the defendant's rebuttal evidence is so weak that reasonable minds could not differ in the conclusion that the plaintiff has met its burden of proof. Again, the motion asks the judge to decide the case as a matter of law and not send it to the jury. The defendant can also make a motion for directed verdict at this time, regardless of whether he or she had earlier made one after presentation of the plaintiff's case. Motions for directed verdict are denied in most cases, because once a case has progressed this far there usually are genuine issues of fact that must be resolved.

Instructions to the Jury

When a case is submitted to the jury, the judge provides instructions to guide the jury in its deliberations. These instructions are often read aloud to the jury in open court; in some states, a written copy of these instructions is then given to the jury before they begin their deliberations. The instructions typically contain several parts, including (1) general rules of conduct, such as requirements that the jurors (a) refrain from discussing the case with anyone except other jurors in formal deliberations until the case is over and they are discharged and (b) not speculate about the effect that insurance coverage or attorney fees might have on the ultimate judgment; (2) definitions of certain relevant legal terms; and (3) the court's *charge* to the jury.

CHAPTER 3   LITIGATION AND ALTERNATIVE METHODS OF DISPUTE RESOLUTION   67

The charge is the core of the instructions that gives the jury a legal framework for performing its job. A charge may be *general* or *special* or a combination of the two types, depending on the court system. In the same system, diffferent types of charge may be used in different types of cases; in a particular state, for instance, a special charge might be used in civil cases and a general charge in criminal ones. Although the general charge is most common, mixed special–general charges are increasing in usage. A general charge outlines and explains the relevant legal principles for the jury; it then asks them to decide the relevant facts and reach a verdict either for the plaintiff or for the defendant. (In a criminal case, the charge would ask for a verdict of guilty or acquittal.) A special charge is a series of questions to the jury; each question relates to a disputed fact and asks for a yes or no answer. If a special charge is used in a typical money damage case, there will be a final question about damages that asks for an answer in the form of a dollar amount, assuming that previous questions have been answered favorably to the plaintiff.

The following case illustrates the critical importance of the judge's instructions to the jury.

Not everything is 100% Black/White

RILEY v. WILLIS

COURT OF APPEAL OF FLORIDA 585 So. 2d 1024 (1991)

Juanita Willis, a minor, and her sister were walking along the side of Highway 50 in Brooksville with their dog between them. The dog was not on a leash. Juanita walked closest to the road. Joseph Riley was driving on Highway 50, which he used every day to travel to and from work. Just as Riley's truck pulled even with the girls, the dog darted toward the road. Juanita leaned into the road and was struck by the front of Riley's truck. Juanita, plaintiff, filed suit against Riley, defendant, alleging that Riley's negligence was the cause of her injuries. (See Chapter 10 for a discussion of the tort of negligence.) Riley raised the defense of contributory negligence. Under Florida law, as in most states today, if the jury finds that both the plaintiff and the defendant are negligent, the plaintiff's damages are reduced by the percentage that his or her negligence contributed to the occurrence. However, if the plaintiff's negligence contributed more to the occurrence than did the defendant's, the plaintiff cannot receive any money damages.

In the trial, Riley testified that he saw the two girls and slowed from 45 mph to about 35 mph as he approached but did not sound his horn or move to the left of his lane. He also stated that after his truck pulled alongside the girls, he lost sight of them and did not see the dog bolt or Juanita bend into the road.

At the close of the evidence, the trial judge gave the jury instructions about what a plaintiff has to prove to establish a claim of negligence against the defendant and what a defendant has to prove to establish a defense of contributory negligence. In addition, the court included an instruction setting forth a Florida statute detailing the special duty of a motorist to avoid "obstructions" in the roadway by moving to the left of the center of the highway. This instruction had been requested by Juanita's attorney. However, the judge refused to include an instruction, requested by Riley's attorney, concerning a county ordinance that required people to keep their dogs on a leash. The jury found that the plaintiff's negligence contributed 40 percent to the incident and the

CONTINUED

defendant's 60 percent. The trial judge entered judgment requiring defendant to pay 60 percent of the amount of damages found by the jury to have been suffered by the plaintiff.

Riley appealed on the following grounds: (1) The trial judge should not have included the jury instruction about a motorist's special duty to avoid obstructions. (2) The trial judge should have included the jury instruction about the county ordinance requiring an owner to keep his or her dog on a leash, because Juanita's dog was not on a leash and this contributed substantially to the accident.

GOSHORN, JUDGE:

Riley asserts that an instruction governing a motorist's duty to avoid an obstacle was improperly given. The instruction contained section 316.081(1)(b), Florida Statutes (1987), which provides in relevant part: "(1) Upon all roadways of sufficient width, a vehicle shall be driven upon the right half of the roadway, except as follows: (b) When an obstruction exists making it necessary to drive to the left of the center of the highway; provided any person so doing shall yield the right-of-way to vehicles traveling in the proper direction upon the unobstructed portion of the highway within such distance as to constitute an immediate hazard...."

The controversy surrounding the instruction concerns the word "obstruction" and whether evidence of an obstruction hindering Riley was presented at trial. The term "obstruction" is not defined by Chapter 316. Black's Law Dictionary 972 (rev. 5th ed. 1979) defines "obstruction" as "a hindrance, obstacle or barrier." The evidence presented at trial is unrefuted that at the time of the accident Riley's view was unobstructed and the road was clear. It is also unrefuted that Juanita did not bend into the path of Riley's oncoming truck until the truck was practically upon her. Prior to that moment, Juanita and Ebony [her sister] were walking along the side of the road. The obvious inference from the instruction is that Juanita herself was an obstacle that Riley was statutorily obligated to avoid. Yet no testimony or other evidence was presented that Juanita posed an obstacle to the oncoming truck, making it necessary for Riley to drive to the left of the center of the highway.

Jury instructions must be supported by facts in evidence and an instruction not founded upon evidence adduced at trial constitutes error. Whether that error requires reversal depends on whether the improper instruction in some manner affected the jury's deliberations by misleading or confusing it.... The instruction at issue in [this case] quite likely confused and misled the jury by creating the erroneous impression that Riley was obligated to somehow avoid Juanita when she reached out into the road and became an "obstacle" simultaneously with Riley's passing. The giving of the improper instruction requires reversal.

Riley also appeals the trial court's refusal to instruct the jury on Hernando County Ordinance 86-2, section 6-5, the local leash law: "The owner, harborer, keeper or person having custody or care of an animal shall ensure that: (1) All dogs, except police dogs on active duty, shall be kept under physical restraint by a responsible person at all times while off the premises of the owner, harborer or keeper." The trial court refused to grant the instruction because no evidence was presented that Juanita owned the dog. However, the ordinance is also applicable to a person who is a "harborer, keeper or person having custody or care of an animal." The record is undisputed that the dog was walking unleashed between Juanita and Ebony until it darted toward the road and Juanita tried to grab it....

A party is entitled to have the jury instructed upon its theory of the case when there is evidence to support the theory. In *Orange County v. Piper*, 523 So. 2d 196 (Fla. 5th DCA) this court set forth three elements that must be met in order to establish that failure to give a requested jury instruction constitutes reversible error: (1) The requested instruction accurately states the applicable law, (2) The facts in the case support giving the instruction, and (3) The instruction was necessary to allow the jury to properly resolve all issues in the case. [The requested instruction met these requirements.] Riley's theory of the case attempted to show that, but for the girls' failure to walk the dog on a leash, the dog would not have darted toward the road and Juanita would not have lunged into Riley's oncoming truck. Riley's requested instruction sought to bolster his claim that Juanita's own negligence resulted in the accident; her failure to comply with the local leash law was a direct and proximate cause of her accident. Indeed, violation of a municipal ordinance is prima facie evidence of negligence. The failure to give the requested instruction was reversible error. [Reversed and remanded for a new trial.]

After the Verdict

After the jury has reached its verdict, the court usually enters a judgment in conformity with it. Occasionally this does not happen, however, because the losing party still has an opportunity to make two additional types of motions. One is the **motion for judgment notwithstanding the verdict** (or motion for judgment N.O.V., an abbreviation for the Latin equivalent, *non obstante veredicto*). This motion makes the same contention earlier made in the motion for directed verdict; it essentially asserts that the judge earlier should have granted a directed verdict in favor of the movant and should not have let the case go to the jury because the evidence was so one-sided in the movant's favor. Although a judge rarely grants this motion, it does provide the judge with something of a "safety valve" if a jury goes completely against the evidence.

The other post-verdict motion that may be filed by the party who suffered an adverse jury verdict is the **motion for new trial.** This motion alleges that the trial judge committed one or more errors in the trial that probably affected the outcome. The errors alleged in such a motion may include erroneous rulings on objections to evidence, erroneous wording of the instructions that misstated the applicable law, and so on. A motion for new trial is usually a prerequisite for appeal; a party normally must give a trial judge the opportunity to correct his or her own mistakes by granting a new trial before the party can complain about these mistakes to an appellate court.

The following case illustrates the reasoning employed by a court in ruling on a motion for judgment notwithstanding the verdict.

BEEBE-OWEN v. WESTERN OHIO PIZZA, INC.

Court of Appeals of Ohio 1991 Ohio App. LEXIS 3034 (1991)

Mrs. Sharon Beebe-Owen, the plaintiff, had worked for Western Ohio Pizza for seven years as the director of management information services, managing various computer systems.

(Hereafter, the last name Owen will be used, because the appeals court used the shortened version in its decision.) As a result of an incident between Sharon Owen and Eric Marcus, another employee of Western Ohio Pizza, she filed a lawsuit against Marcus and Western.

On April 4, 1988, Sharon Owen, Eric Marcus, and six other employees traveled in a van from their place of work in Dayton, Ohio, to Cincinnati to watch a Cincinnati Reds baseball game. In the lawsuit, the evidence established that Eric and Sharon drank beer at the ball game although she denied becoming intoxicated. The evidence also established that Eric at various times during the day kissed and hugged Sharon. Sharon testified that Eric kissed her after the game — "he just reached out and pulled me by the shoulders and embraced me." In cross-examination, she testified: "He hugged me at the ballpark, he kissed me at the ballpark, he hugged me a couple of times in the van, he kissed me a couple of times in the van. He tried to unsnap my bra in the van when I asked him not to, Sure, he had his hands on me more than that."

CONTINUED

After the game the group returned to Dayton and went to the Olive Garden Restaurant. Sharon testified that while she was walking toward the restaurant she heard footsteps and Eric threw his arms around her shoulders "and hit me really hard and just pushed me to the ground and ended up falling on my leg." However, Eric testified to a different version of the incident, saying that he "put his arms around her to give her a hug and she stumbled and we fell in a heap."

Phyllis Phillips, a secretary at Western Ohio and one of the eight who attended the baseball game, gave the following testimony: She had nothing to drink that day. She sat with three other employees in a different part of the ballpark than Sharon and Eric; when the game ended she went over to where Sharon and Eric were seated and saw Sharon with her arm around Eric and she was kissing his ear. Sharon was staggering when she got up to leave her seat, and she was loud and her speech was slurred. While they were standing by a souvenir stand she observed Sharon go up to Eric and put her arm around him and hug and kiss him. Sharon had her arm around Eric in the van on the return trip and was kissing him. She did not see Sharon and Eric fall in the restaurant parking lot but heard something and saw them lying on the ground laughing.

Janet Heitman, research coordinator for Western Ohio, was the "designated driver" for the trip to the ball game and also did not drink alcohol that day. Her testimony about the conduct of Eric and Sharon during the trip was practically identical to that of Phyllis Phillips. She also stated that both Sharon and Eric appeared to be under the influence of alcohol and that on the way back five people were "smashed into the back seat" and were engaged in horseplay. She stated she did not see Eric and Sharon fall in the parking lot but saw Eric kneeling over her and Sharon was laughing. She said Sharon could not get up. Sharon was taken by ambulance to a hospital, where she underwent surgery for a severe knee injury and remained hospitalized for ten days.

The defendant also introduced into evidence the written notes made by a nurse when Sharon was admitted to the hospital; the notes were made as a regular part of the admission process. One of the nurse's statements in the notes was that Sharon had told her that she had been hurt while "playing with a friend, who had tackled her." The plaintiff's attorney did not challenge the notes as hearsay evidence, so the court made no ruling on this point; however, it is likely that the notes were within an exception to the hearsay rule.

Sharon worked three days in June, from mid-July until November 7, 1988, and two weeks in December 1988. She applied for workers' compensation medical benefits and Western Ohio certified her claim on June 16, 1988; she received these benefits. Her full salary was continued by Western until March 12, 1989. Western asked her to obtain information from her physician as to when she could return to full employment. When she failed to provide the requested medical information to her supervisor, her salary was discontinued.

On March 30, 1989, Sharon Owen and her husband filed this lawsuit, asserting various claims against Eric Marcus and Western Ohio Pizza. Shortly thereafter, both she and her husband, who also worked for Western, were terminated. The trial judge granted summary judgment in favor of Western on all claims, and in favor of Eric on most of the claims. The claims of Sharon's husband also did not survive summary judgment. However, Sharon's claim against Eric for the tort of assault and battery remained alive and went to trial. A mixed general–special charge was used in the jury instructions. In response to specific questions, the jury found that Eric had been negligent but that he had not committed the intentional tort of assault and battery, because the jury concluded that Eric was not guilty of an "intentional offensive physical contact without consent" as required by the law for an assault and battery claim.

The jury rendered a general verdict against Eric for $41,000 in damages.

Both sides filed motions for judgment notwithstanding the verdict. Eric's motion asserted that he could not be held liable at all for simple negligence, because he was a co-employee, this was a work outing, and workers' compensation benefits were Sharon's only legal remedy. Sharon's motion argued that the jury's finding that Eric was guilty of only negligence, and not assault and battery, was so contrary to the overwhelming evidence that Eric should have been found guilty of

CONTINUED

assault and battery by the judge as a matter of law. The trial judge granted Eric's motion and denied Sharon's and entered judgment in favor of Eric. Sharon appealed.

BROGAN, JUDGE:

[First, the appellate court agreed with the trial court's decision to grant Eric's motion for judgment notwithstanding the verdict. This was a work outing, and Sharon and Eric were within the scope of their employment at the time. In such a situation, an employee has no legal claim against the employer or a fellow employee for mere negligence; the benefits provided under state workers' compensation law are the only remedy. The employee can maintain a claim for an intentional wrong such as assault and battery, if it can be proved. The jury was properly instructed on these matters but apparently did not adequately understand the instructions and found Eric liable for damages after finding that he was only negligent. Thus, the trial court was correct to grant Eric's motion for judgment N.O.V.]

[Turning to Sharon's claim that the trial court should have granted her motion for judgment N.O.V. because the evidence overwhelmingly proved assault and battery on Eric's part, the court of appeals stated:] The test to be applied by a trial court in ruling on a motion for judgment notwithstanding a verdict is the same as that for a motion for a directed verdict. The evidence must be construed most strongly in favor of the party against whom the motion is made, and where there is substantial evidence to support his side of the case, upon which reasonable minds may reach different conclusions, the motion must be denied. The jury could have reasonably believed Marcus' version of the incident where he fell on Mrs. Owen. The trial court appropriately denied the motion [and submitted this question to the jury].... The judgment will be affirmed.

LITIGATION: THE APPELLATE COURTS

NATURE AND ROLE OF APPELLATE COURTS

If a party is dissatisfied with the outcome in the trial court, and his or her attorney believes that legally material errors may have been committed in the trial, the party may wish to appeal the trial court's decision to a higher court.

The function of an *appellate court* is very different from that of a trial court. An appellate court does not hear evidence or make any factual determinations; instead the court seeks to determine whether material errors were committed by the trial court. A material error is one that probably affected the outcome. If a case is appealed to the highest court in a particular system after having been heard by an intermediate level appellate court, the high court essentially "reviews the review" of the intermediate appellate court.

In most appellate courts, the party who is appealing is usually referred to as the *appellant;* the other party is the *appellee*. Sometimes different terms are used, such as *petitioner* and *respondent*. When an appellate court writes its opinion in a case, it normally uses either of these sets of terms to refer to the parties. Occasionally, however, the court's opinion will refer to the parties by their original trial court designations—plaintiff and defendant.

An appellate court always includes at least three judges, and often more. When the court has more than three members, it sometimes expands its capacity for work by dividing into panels of three judges for each case. When this is done, the entire membership of the court has the authority to review the decision of the three-judge panel, although it usually does not do so. For example, the various U.S. courts of appeal, which have from 6 to 28 judges, usually divide into three-member panels to hear cases, and only rarely does the entire membership of one of these courts review a panel decision. The U.S. Supreme Court, however, does not divide into panels; all nine of its justices participate in deciding each case.

THE PROCESS OF APPEAL

The Record

The appellant's attorney begins the appeal by filing a notice of appeal and by requesting that the clerk of the trial court prepare the *record* of the case and send it to the appellate court. There is a fee for preparation of the record. The most important part of the record is the *transcript* of the trial. During the trial, an official court reporter was recording every word of the proceedings, including all the attorney's questions, witnesses' answers, attorney's objections, and the judge's rulings. The transcript is a typewritten copy of this verbatim account. Copies of the pleadings, motions, jury instructions, and other official papers in the case also are included in the record if they are relevant to some point being raised on appeal. In addition, the record may include items of physical evidence that were introduced and considered in the trial court; such items might include a written contract, business records, a map or photograph, and so on.

Written Briefs

The appellant's attorney prepares an *appellant's brief* and files it with the appellate court. The brief sets forth errors that the appallate claims were made by the trial judge. These alleged errors usually relate to the trial judge's actions in (1) ruling on motions, (2) ruling on objections to evidence, or (3) stating the relevant law in the jury instructions. The remainder of the brief then presents arguments, based on applicable legal principles, that the cited actions of the trial judge amounted to material errors. The appellee's attorney then responds with the *appellee's brief* (or *reply brief*), in which it is argued that under applicable law the trial judge's actions were correct (or even if erroneous, the errors did not affect the outcome and were "harmless").

Oral Arguments

Appellate courts usually schedule several periods of time during the year in which the parties to appeals are permitted to make *oral arguments*. During one two-week period, for example, an appellate court might hear oral arguments in 50 or so cases. In each case, the attorney's for each side will have a brief period (typically from 30 to 60 minutes) to clarify and emphasize the most important points in their written briefs and to give the appellate court judges an opportunity to ask questions.

APPELLATE COURT'S DECISION

As we mentioned earlier, an appellate court serves a very different role than that of a trial court. The court studies the record, considers the legal points made in the briefs and oral arguments, does legal research, and decides whether one or more material errors occurred in the trial.

Review of Trial Court's Factual Determinations

Some of the points raised by the appellant may require the appellate court to study the evidence that appears in the record, such as the transcript of witnesses' testimony and physical evidence that has been included in the record. For example, if the appellant claims that the trial judge erred in ruling on a motion for summary judgment, directed verdict, or judgment N.O.V., the appellate court must determine whether the evidence in the record created a genuine fact issue or whether it was overwhelming in the other direction. The court does not, however decide what the facts are; fact-finding is a trial court function. Indeed, even if the judges on the appellate court believe that they might have reached a different conclusion had they been performing the fact-finding task in the trial court, they normally will not overturn the trial court's (jury's or trial judge's) factual determinations as long as there is any substantial evidence in the record to support those conclusions. Appellate court judges recognize that the jury or judge that performed the fact-finding role was in a better position to assess the evidence, especially when key evidence took the form of testimony from witnesses who testified and were cross-examined in person. Moreover, in any multilevel decision-making system, it makes very little sense to redo everything at successive levels.

Review of Trial Court's Legal Determinations

Much of the appellate court's attention is focused on pure legal questions, that is, reviewing the trial judge's rulings on legal questions. For example, when the trial judge rules on a motion to dismiss or when it frames the instructions to the jury, it makes decisions as to what the applicable legal principles are. In some cases, especially when there is no jury, the trial judge makes formal written "conclusions of law." These legal principles may derive from precedents (prior decisions in other cases—see Chapter 4), federal or state statutes, administrative agency regulations, or constitutional provisions. In response to the appellant's contentions on appeal, the appellate court decides whether the trial court's interpretations and applications of these legal principles were correct. An appellate court is not so reluctant to overturn the trial court's legal determinations as it is to reverse factual determinations.

Decision Making

The appellate court judges deliberate individually on a case and consult with each other. They decide the case by majority vote. If the majority concludes that no material errors occurred, it *affirms* the lower court's decision, usually sending the case back to the trial court for appropriate action to enforce the judgment. If the court decides that some material error was committed, it *reverses* the lower court's decision. (Sometimes the terms *vacate* or *set aside* are used instead of *reverse*.) Occasionally an appellate court may reverse the decision outright and order a contrary judgment. In most cases of reversal, however, the appellate court *remands* the case to the lower court, where some type of further proceeding will be conducted in accordance with the appellate court's opinion. The further proceeding in the lower court may be of a very limited nature, such as merely requiring the trial judge to reconsider some portion of the decision by applying a slightly different legal standard to the already-established facts. Sometimes, however, the additional proceeding necessary to correct the error after remand may be a completely new trial.

Appellate Court's Opinion

One of the judges is assigned the primary responsibility for writing the court's formal opinion; however, the key language of the opinion is the product of agreement among the judges in the majority. If a judge does not agree with some of the reasoning or language of the opinion but still agrees with the overall result, he or she may wish to write a separate concurring opinion setting forth areas of disagreement. If the decision is not unanimous, a judge who disagrees with the majority decision has the opportunity to write a dissenting opinion setting forth his or her views. Although a dissenting opinion has no effect on the outcome of that case, a persuasive dissent on a close and controversial issue may provide "ammunition" for continuing debate on the question in future cases (or in future legislative debates).

As we have already mentioned, an appellate court usually upholds a jury's or a trial judge's factual findings but is not so reluctant to reverse on the basis of errors of law committed by the trial judge. The following case presents an interesting example of this proposition. Technically, the error asserted by the appellant is that one of the important factual findings of the jury was not supported by any substantial evidence in the record. In reversing the decision, however, the appeals court actually does so on the basis of the trial judge's erroneous interpretation of the law in submitting a particular issue to the jury. Things are not always (or even usually) neat and tidy.

Lehr v. Vance

Court of Appeals of Ohio 1991 Ohio App. LEXIS 3922 (1991)

At the time of the incident that led to this lawsuit, Delores Lehr and John Vance were married but separated. They owned two vehicles, a 1986 Ford van and a 1986 Honda Prelude. The evidence in the case did not indicate whose name or names were on the titles of the vehicles, and because there had not yet been a divorce there was no court judgement splitting up their property. After their separation, Delores, the plaintiff, took possession of the 1986 Honda Prelude, and John, the defendant, kept the van. Each of them apparently had keys to both vehicles. In the trial John testified that shortly after they separated, he received an anonymous telephone call informing him that the Honda Prelude would be returned to him if he put the keys to the vehicle and $100 in his mailbox. The caller said that the car could then be recovered at

CONTINUED

a bowling alley parking lot at the intersection of Route 161 and Cleveland Avenue. John did as the caller suggested and acquired possession of the Honda. After the Honda was taken from her possession, Delores took the Ford van from John's residence, apparently stating to either the defendant or the police that she needed some form of transportation. John testified in court that later the same day, he received a second telephone call, again from an unidentified caller, informing him that if he wanted to have the van returned to him, he should place $100 and the keys to the van in his mailbox.

John testified that he believed that the anonymous calls were from an agent of his wife for the purpose of extorting money from him in exchange for the return of the automobiles. He said that he based his belief on a prior incident in which Delores had taken his clothing and required him to "buy" the clothes back from her. He had no other evidence to support this belief, however. John testified that he asked the caller if Delores was responsible for the proposed exchange, which the caller denied.

A short while later, Delores was at her parents' home when her mother noticed someone entering the Ford van, which was parked in the driveway next to the home. Delores testified in court that she approached the vehicle and stepped onto the running board inquiring as to who the person was and what he was doing. This individual's identity was never established in court. Delores said that as she attempted to question this person, he suddenly drove the van from the driveway and proceeded onto the street with her still standing on the running board holding on to the side of the van. She stated that the driver ignored her pleas to stop and drove at a high rate of speed, keeping her from safely stepping from the van. Then the driver of the van suddenly applied the brake, throwing Delores from the van onto the roadway.

As a result of being thrown from the van, Delores received serious injuries. She sued John, claiming that the driver was acting as John's agent in trying to seize the van, and that John was thus liable for the driver's recklessness. John responded by claiming that Delores caused her own injury by jumping on the running board of the van as the driver was trying to leave; he also asserted that the driver was not his agent but was someone Delores was using to help with a scheme to extort money from John. The jury rendered a verdict in favor of John on the basis that Delores's own negligence contributed more than 50% to her injuries; under the law of Ohio (and most other states), this meant that she lost the case. The jury thus made no finding on the question of who the driver was working for. Delores appealed, claiming that the verdict was contrary to the overwhelming evidence and that the trial judge should have granted either a judgment N.O.V. or a new trial.

STRAUSBAUGH, JUDGE:

[The appeals court drew an analogy from statutes and case law in Ohio that concern the right of a "secured creditor" to act on its own, without court action, to seize the collateral held by a debtor who has defaulted on the debt. A secured creditor is one owning a security interest in a specific item of personal property that serves as collateral for a debt. Under the law of Ohio and most other states, the secured creditor has the right to use "self-help"—to seize the property on its own, without court action—only if the creditor can do so without a "breach of the peace." The court recognized that the present case did not involve a seizure of collateral by a secured creditor, but it did involve a seizure of property by one claiming a legal interest in it. The court stated that the situation was analogous, and the same basic rules should apply; the one claiming a right to the property could not seize it if doing so involved a breach of the peace. A breach of the peace is an intentional or reckless act and is not simple negligence. Thus, if a breach of the peace occurred, any contributory negligence on Delores's part was not a defense against her claim; contributory negligence is a defense only against a claim of simple negligence. Elaborating, and quoting from a prior decision of the Ohio Supreme Court, the appeals court stated:]

Fundamental public policy requires the discouragement of extrajudicial conduct which is fraught with the likelihood of resulting violence.... Breach of the peace... includes an act which is likely to produce violence, which reasonably tends to provoke or excite others to break the peace and which is not performed under judicial process.... Where a creditor legally enters upon the private premises of his debtor for the purpose of repossessing collateral security kept thereon and is (1) physically confronted by one in charge of such premises, (2) told to desist his efforts at

CONTINUED

repossession, and (3) instructed to depart from the premises, the refusal by the creditor to heed such commands constitutes a breach of the peace . . . and such creditor thereafter stands as would any other person who unlawfully refuses to depart from the land of another.

We find the policy emanating from the foregoing decision [of the Ohio Supreme Court] to be sound and equally applicable herein. Given the clearly wanton and reckless conduct of the unidentified driver of the van, we find that contributory negligence is not a defense in the present case. [Thus, the trial court should not have submitted a contributory negligence issue to the jury.] When first confronted by plaintiff, the driver should have ended his efforts to take possession of the van. When he instead sped away with plaintiff holding on to the side of the van and then suddenly stopped, the driver should have known that his conduct would likely injure plaintiff. Defendant would therefore be . . . responsible for all of the acts of the driver during his efforts to take the van if it is determined that the driver was acting as defendant's agent. However, [the defendant will not be liable if it is found that the driver was not acting as his agent. When the case is reheard, the only issue will be whether the driver was the defendant's agent. If he was, the trial court should then] allow the jury to determine the amount of damages to which plaintiff is entitled. The judgment of the trial court is hereby reversed and the cause is remanded for further proceedings consistent with the law and this opinion.

ENFORCEMENT OF JUDGMENTS

If a judgment for the plaintiff survives the appellate process (or if no appeal was ever taken), the plaintiff may still have to worry about enforcing the judgment. In the relatively unusual case in which the court's judgment grants an injunction or other equitable remedy, the court will enforce the judgment by fining or jailing the defendant for *contempt of court* if the defendant fails to comply. In the typical case, however, the judgment awards an amount of money damages to the plaintiff. If the defendant is financially well-off, well-insured for this type of claim, or is a corporation with adequate assets, enforcement of a money judgment will probably present no major obstacles. It can be very difficult, however, to collect a judgment from some people. Indeed, the probable collectability of any judgment is one of the things a party often must take into account in deciding whether to file a lawsuit in the first place.

If the defendant refuses to pay a valid judgment, the plaintiff will ask the court to issue a **writ of execution.** This writ empowers a law enforcement official to seize defendant's nonexempt property and sell it at auction until enough money is raised to satisfy the judgment.

Another procedure is a **writ of garnishment,** which orders a third party holding property belonging to the defendant to deliver the property to the custody of the court. In most cases, the third party is a bank, stock broker, or other entity holding funds or securities belonging to the defendant. A writ of garnishment may also be issued against a third party who owes a debt to the defendant, ordering the third party to pay the debt to the plaintiff instead of the defendant. If the writ of garnishment targets some type of property other than money, a law enforcement officer will sell the property at auction and the proceeds will be applied to pay the judgment. Many (but not all) states even allow garnishment of wages—a court order to the defendant's employer to pay a specified percentage of the defendant's wages or salary to the plaintiff every week or month until the judgmet is fully paid. As we will see in Chapter 20, federal law places a limit on the portion of a person's wages that can be taken by garnishment.

In speaking of "nonexempt" assets, we are referring to the fact that all states have *exemption laws* specifying that certain types of property cannot be seized for the purpose of satisfying a court judgment. The laws vary quite a bit among the states, some states having very liberal statutes exampting much valuable property and others having extremely limited statutes exempting very little. The most common type of property protected by exemption laws is an individual's *homestead,* or residence; however, many states provide for such an exemption only up to a limited dollar amount.

In the discussion of personal jurisdiction, we mentioned that nonresident defendant cannot just go back to his or her home state and ignore a judgment. If a defendant has no nonexempt assets in the forum state, the plaintiff can have the judgment enforced by execution or garnishment in any other state where the defendant has such assets. As long as the court that issued the judgment had subject matter and personal jurisidiction, the authorities in other states are required by the U.S. Constitution's *full faith and credit clause* to enforce the judgment. Although it is more difficult to enforce a judgment by trying to seize assets located in another nation, it often can be performed if such assets can be identified. The United States is a party to bilateral and multilateral treaties with many countries that obligate each nation to honor the valid court judgments of the other country or countries that have signed the treaty.

Regardless of whether a plaintiff can collect his judgment—in fact, regardless of whether he wins or loses the lawsuit—once a case is finally concluded, the plaintiff is finished. The doctrine of *res judicata* ("the thing has been adjudicated") specifies that a plaintiff cannot start over by filing another claim against the defendant based on the same general facts. The plaintiff is barred from reasserting not only the same claim, but also any other claim the he or she reasonably could have asserted the first time around. If the later claim arises from the same general events as the earlier claim, the doctrine of *res judicata* applies even if the plaintiff has come up with some new evidence. Figure 3.1 pictures the entire process of civil litigation by means of a flow chart.

NOTE ON PERFORMANCE OF JUDGES

The overall performance of a legal system obviously depends to a great extent on the character and competence of its judges. For this reason, particularly, it is distressing to note that the judges of this country have, as a

FIGURE 3.1

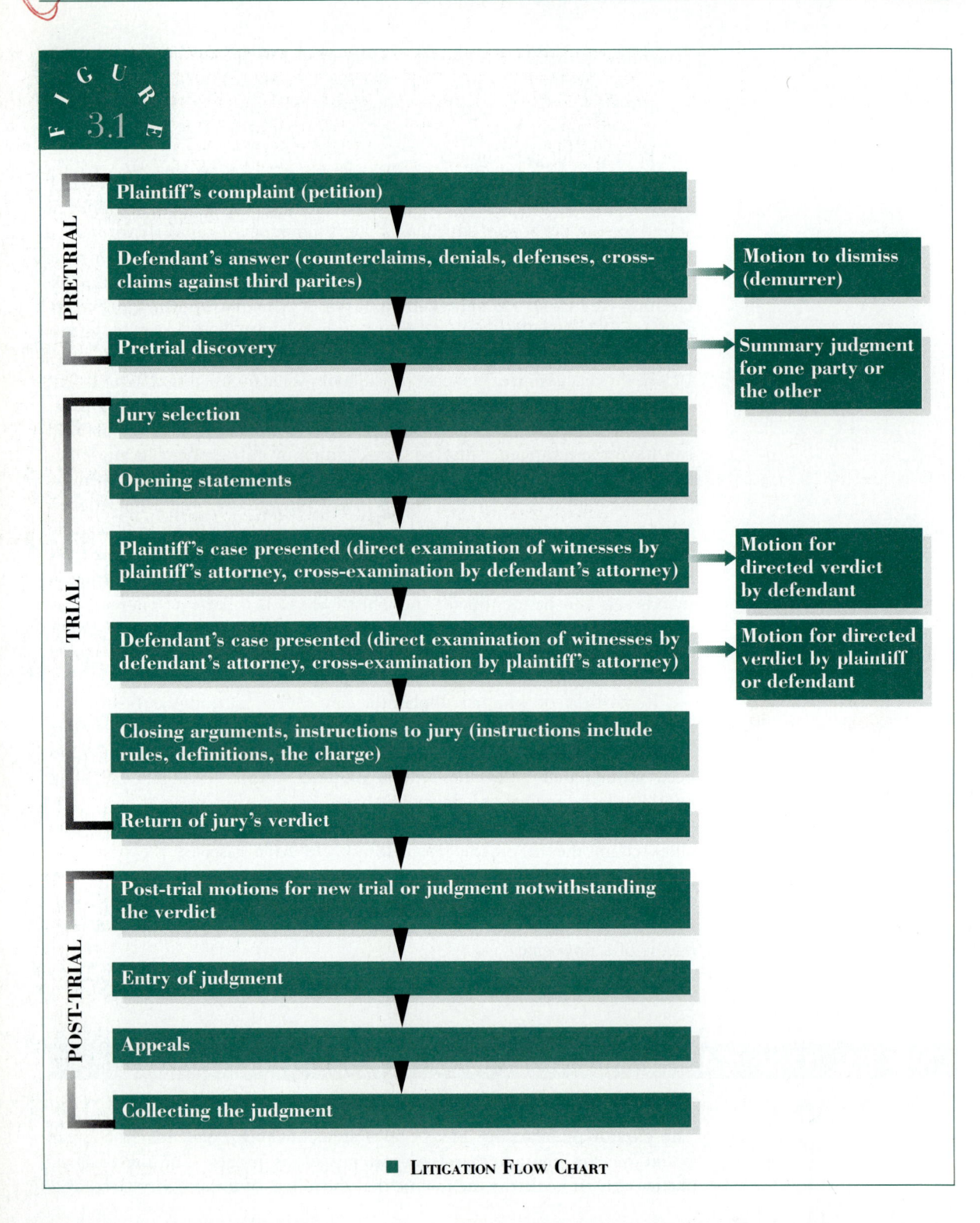

PRETRIAL
- Plaintiff's complaint (petition)
- Defendant's answer (counterclaims, denials, defenses, cross-claims against third parites) → Motion to dismiss (demurrer)
- Pretrial discovery → Summary judgment for one party or the other

TRIAL
- Jury selection
- Opening statements
- Plaintiff's case presented (direct examination of witnesses by plaintiff's attorney, cross-examination by defendant's attorney) → Motion for directed verdict by defendant
- Defendant's case presented (direct examination of witnesses by defendant's attorney, cross-examination by plaintiff's attorney) → Motion for directed verdict by plaintiff or defendant
- Closing arguments, instructions to jury (instructions include rules, definitions, the charge)
- Return of jury's verdict

POST-TRIAL
- Post-trial motions for new trial or judgment notwithstanding the verdict
- Entry of judgment
- Appeals
- Collecting the judgment

■ **LITIGATION FLOW CHART**

class, come in for rather heavy criticism over the years. Although much of this criticism may be unjustified, there is cause for concern.

Three factors are chiefly responsible. First, judges' salaries are often lower than the income that can be earned in private practice by good attorneys. Second, in the United States, persons who aspire to a career in the judiciary are not required to take special training or to go through an apprenticeship of a year or two, as is the case in many countries. Third, the judges of our state courts have traditionally been elected. This has frequently resulted in the nomination of candidates by the political parties on the basis of their party service and loyalty, rather than on ability and experience. And, once elected, incumbent judges have not easily been dislodged even when their performance has been mediocre or worse.

In recent years, in an effort to alleviate the short-comings resulting from the election of judges, more than 30 states and the District of Columbia have adopted some form of "merit plan" selection of judges. Although these plans vary to some extent, they all are based on the idea that when a judicial vacancy occurs, a judicial nominating commission develops a list of three to five persons whom they feel to be the best qualified for the job. (These commissions are nonpartisan in nature and are usually composed equally of lawyers and nonlawyers.) The list of names is submitted to the governor, who selects one person to fill the vacancy. Thereafter, appointees must indicate before their terms of office expire whether they wish to stand for another term. If so, the appointee runs unopposed in the next general election, with the voters simply indicating whether they are satisfied with the performance rendered during the first term of office. If the appointee loses on this vote, the appointive process then begins anew.

Generally speaking, there has been less criticism of federal judges than state judges. Most criticism of federal judges tends to be based on their ideological slant rather than on their competence. Although there are a great many very fine state court judges and some federal court judges who are not as capable as we might wish, on a nationwide basis the average federal court judge is probably somewhat more able than the average state judge. This is true at both the trial and appellate court levels.

Federal judges are nominated for appointment by the president. The Federal Bureau of Investigation (under the Attorney General) conducts a thorough background check on nominees, and the American Bar Association reviews their records and issues an opinion to the Attorney General on their qualifications to serve. This information is available to the U.S. Senate, which must confirm the president's nominations. If confirmed, federal judges have lifetime tenure unless they are found guilty of impeachable conduct by Congress. The nature of the selection process, plus the fact that a federal judgeship carries more prestige than a position on a state court, usually seems to result in relatively high quality on the federal bench.

Whether in the state or federal courts, being a judge is becoming an increasingly stressful occupation in modern times, especially at the trial court level. In many parts of the country, state and federal trial judges face such heavy caseloads that they simply cannot do as good a job as they are capable of doing. In particular, the number of criminal cases has increased so dramatically that judges are able to devote less and less time to the civil cases on their dockets. The constitutional requirement of a speedy criminal trial means that the criminal cases get priority. Many federal judges, for example, have discovered that they have to spend most of their time hearing federal drug cases, instead of the far more interesting civil cases they envisioned hearing when they were appointed. To maintain, much less improve, the quality of the judiciary, relief must be provided in a number of forms. More judges, more magistrates to supervise discovery and other pretrial processes, and greater use of alternative dispute resolution mechanisms are but a few of the possible reforms that may help.

ALTERNATIVE DISPUTE RESOLUTION

We have already noted some of the criticisms directed at the American legal system, as well as some of the responses from the supporters of the system. There can be no question that in the United States, there is an enormous amount of litigation that consumes tremendous resources. Many people, particularly in the business community, argue that Americans are too eager to sue, there are too many lawsuits of questionable merit, and these lawsuits take too much time and cost far too much money. They also commonly assert that there are too many lawyers with too much influence.

Others contend that there is much value in the way we traditionally have resolved many controversies in the United States. One can argue, for instance, that we tend to use formal litigation more than people in most other countries for several legitimate reasons. (1) We are the most heterogeneous, diffuse, and open society the world has ever known. These characteristics tend to produce more use of formal adjudication than in more homogeneous, static societies. (2) We place great value on the "rule of law," rather than the "rule of men," another factor that tends to cause people to look to courts for the interpretation and enforcement of rules. (3) We are not, nor would we want to be, a passive people who accept wrongs with fatalistic resignation as is the custom in some societies. (4) One of the strong legal traditions we inherited from England is the attitude that the courts have authority to formulate legal principles when there is no legislation applicable to a case. Because courts in our system have this limited type of lawmaking power, we naturally use them to set norms of behavior for society to a greater extent than people do in nations with a different system. (5) Our legal profession is much better educated than in most nations, with attorneys being more independent and more readily available to people who feel that their rights have been violated. In some parts of the world, the scarcity of lawyers leads people to obtain help from organized crime syndicates (such as the Yakuza in Japan) in making and collecting claims.

It also bears mentioning that a lot of the increase in litigation rates in recent years is not the result of greedy individuals trying to "make a killing" by filing claims against businesses, but instead is attributable to greatly increased filings of cases (1) by corporations against other corporations as a strategic business maneuver and (2) by and against government agencies.

Although there is much disagreement about whether there really are *too many* lawsuits in the United States, most knowledgeable observers agree that the litigation process is not nearly as efficient as it should be—lawsuits commonly take far too much time and money. In addition, in the case of disputes between business firms, lawsuits tend to decrease the chances that they will be able to maintain a valuable commercial relationship with each other. Although litigation is sometimes necessary and courts will always play a central role in dispute resolution in this country, recent times have witnessed widespread efforts to use other methods.

These other methods are frequently referred to as **alternative dispute resolution** (ADR) techniques. Although these methods do not always work and certainly are not a cure-all for society's problems, they often enable the parties to a dispute to lessen the "sharpness" of the adversarial system, replacing it with an increased emphasis on trust, respect, and win–win solutions.

NEGOTIATED SETTLEMENT

Before we address specific methods of ADR, it is important first to point out that most disputes never get to the courtroom. Sometimes a person or business will just "lump it," that is, take a loss rather than pursue a claim. A corporation may do this to keep a valued customer or supplier, perhaps thinking that this particular problem is a one-time occurrence. Also, people sometimes do not pursue claims because they decide that it not worth it; the perceived likelihood of winning or the size of the claim may lead to a conclusion that pressing a claim will be more trouble and expense than it is worth. Sometimes, instead of lumping it, a party may be able to reach a compromise with the other without ever going to court.

Even when lawsuits are filed, at least 90 percent of them are resolved without a trial. Some of these are disposed of by some pretrial action of the judge, such as the granting of summary judgment. A large percentage of claims filed in court are resolved by a negotiated out-of-court settlement, with part of the agreement being the dropping of all claims and counterclaims.

The problem with the traditional practice of filing suit and then ultimately settling it out of court is that it usually has been performed very inefficiently. Parties and their attorneys generally have not started thinking seriously about settlement talks until the trial date is very near, thousands of dollars and many months (or years) having already been spent on pretrial discovery and strategic maneuvering. It seems that parties and their attorneys often have felt that they just were not "ready" to talk settlement until just before trial. Thus, enormous time and money traditionally have been spent preparing for an event (the trial) that usually does not happen. In addition, spending so much time, money, and energy battling each other during a lengthy pretrial process tends to make the parties harden their positions, escalating the intensity of the conflict.

ARBITRATION

Arbitration is a very old method for resolving disputes but in recent years has beome increasingly popular. In arbitration, the parties select an arbitrator (or a panel of three arbitrators), submit very brief pleadings, and present evidence and arguments to the arbitrator. The arbitrator makes a decision, usually called an "award," which is legally enforceable like a court judgment if the parties had agreed beforehand that it would be binding. Thus, arbitration resembles litigation in that there is actually an adjudication by a third party whose decision is binding.

Despite this superficial resemblance to litigation, arbitration is quite different in many ways. Most of these differences translate into cheaper, faster, and less painful dispute resolution. These differences also increase the chances that the parties can walk away from the process with a commercial relationship still intact. The parties have the ability to control the entire process. They select the decision maker, who may be an expert in the subject matter of the dispute. They also can decide what rules and procedures to use. Unlike litigation, the proceeding can be kept entirely private, which often may be very important to the disputants. There is no required pretrial discovery, although the parties do frequently agree to exchange documents before the arbitration hearing. The parties can decide whether the arbitrator is required to strictly follow particular rules of law and evidence; they usually do not, in which case the arbitrator's duty is just to do justice between the parties. There is essentially no appeal from an arbitrator's award, and a court will not review the arbitrator's factual or legal determinations. A court normally will set aside an arbitration award and require a new arbitration hearing only if the evidence shows that the award was affected by fraud or collusion or if there was some serious procedural error such as lack of notice to one of the parties. Although arbitration has a number of advantages over litigation, one can readily see that there are also some important trade-offs that the parties should know about before agreeing to arbitrate.

Arbitration is generally categorized as either *labor arbitration* or *commercial arbitration*. Labor arbitration involves the resolving of disputes within the labor–management context, usually when the particular group of employees is represented by a union. The relationship between the company and unionized employees is based primarily on a collective bargaining agreement. Almost all collective bargaining agreements include a multistage process for resolving workplace disputes, with legally binding arbitration as the last step. Most of these disputes involve claims by employees that they have been fired or otherwise disciplined without the adequate justification that the contract requires. The federal Taft-Hartley Act makes collective bargaining agreements, including arbitration provisions, legally binding.

The term *commercial arbitration* is usually used to describe almost all other forms of arbitration.[7] It includes the use of arbitration to resolve disputes arising from almost any kind of business transaction, including construction contracts, agreements for the sale of goods (supplies, equipment, etc.), insurance arrangements, joint ventures, and many others. In the United States, the Federal Arbitration Act (FAA) makes commercial arbitration agreements and arbitrator awards legally enforceable if the underlying business transaction affected interstate commerce. If there is no significant effect on interstate commerce, state arbitration statutes in every state usually make the arbitration agreement and award enforceable, although some of these state laws are less "friendly" to arbitration than the FAA.

In addition, most of the world's significant trading nations are parties to one or more multilateral treaties under which they agree to enforce arbitration agreements and awards in international commercial transactions involving citizens of other nations that signed the particular treaty. The most important of these treaties is the 1958 United Nations Convention on the Enforcement of Arbitral Awards.

Most commercial arbitration agreements (domestic or international) are of the *predispute* variety (or "future disputes"); this is a clause in some type of commercial contract by which the parties agree that if there is any future dispute arising from the transaction, they will submit that dispute to legally binding arbitration. It is also possible for parties to make an agreement to arbitrate after a dispute has already occurred, but this is not usually what happens.

Although the parties to an arbitration agreement can agree as they wish, they usually specify that the arbitration will be coordinated and supervised by an established arbitration organization. In domestic commercial arbitration, the oldest and most frequently used organization is the American Arbitration Association (AAA), which handles about 55,000 commercial arbitration cases per year. In international commercial arbitration, there are several important sponsoring organizations, including the AAA, the International Chamber of Commerce in Paris, and the London Court of Arbitration (which is not a court despite its name).

Although most arbitration is still voluntary, the trial courts in more than 20 states and 20 federal districts have adopted *court-annexed arbitration*. These programs generally apply to cases involving money damage claims below certain amounts, which range from a few thousand dollars to $150,000 (and a few state programs have no limits). In this form of arbitration, shortly after the lawsuit is filed, the trial judge refers the case to arbitration, with a panel of local attorneys serving as arbitrators. The parties must participate in the arbitration, but the award is not legally binding if either party formally demands a regular trial within a short time after the award (usually 30 days).

---

[7] Even when the dispute is between employer and employee, if no union or collective bargaining agreement is involved the arbitration is commonly classified as commercial.

MEDIATION

Other forms of ADR are quite different than arbitration. The various other types do not produce a decision that is legally binding on the parties. Instead, these methods are aimed at facilitating agreed settlements by (1) creating a structure that encourages the parties to get together and seriously negotiate much earlier, before they have hardened their positions and spent so much time and money, (2) trying to build trust and respect between the parties, (3) making the parties more realistic about the weaknesses of their positions and the strengths of the other side's positions before the dispute has escalated very far, and (4) creating an environment in which the parties are more likely to think of creative solutions to their problems that can benefit both sides rather than thinking about the dispute only in legalistic and dollar terms.

The most important version of this type of ADR is **mediation,** another old method being used much more in recent years. Like ADR generally, most mediation is entirely voluntary; it is created and controlled by the parties. The third party chosen by the disputants to help them find a solution to their differences is called a *mediator.* A mediator does not impose a solution but tries to help the parties themselves achieve one. Various approaches are used in mediation, depending on the wishes of the parties, the nature of the dispute, and the skill and personality of the mediator. The mediator may do as little as persuade the parties to talk to each other. Going further, he or she might help the parties agree on an agenda for a meeting and provide a suitable environment for negotiation. The mediator might point out that particular proposals are unrealistic, help the parties formulate their own proposals, and even make proposals for them to consider. In some situations, he or she may try very hard to persuade them to accept a settlement he or she believes is reasonable.

Mediation has facilitated resolution of a wide range of disputes, such as many kinds of business disputes, international political conflicts, labor disputes, landlord–tenant disagreements, disputes between divorcing spouses, and multi-party controversies over environmental protections. It also can be very useful in combination with some other form of ADR, such as arbitration. For example, when IBM claimed that Fujitsu had illegally copied the former's mainframe operating system software, they spent several years and a great deal of time, money, and energy unsuccessfully trying to negotiate a settlement. They reached certain settlement agreements, but disagreements continued to break out, largely because of the technical complexity of the problem. The parties agreed to arbitration by a law professor experienced in dispute resolution and a retired computer industry executive. (The use of a two-member panel was unusual.) The arbitrators recognized that the controversy presented factual disputes about past copying that would be almost impossible to resolve. They focused primarily on the future, ordering Fujitsu to provie a complete accounting of its use of programs under the earlier settlement agreement and requiring the parties to participate in mediation regarding programs falling outside the earlier agreement. The arbitrators became mediators; through mediation, new agreements were reached, after which the professor and executive resumed their role as arbitrators and incorporated the new agreements into a binding arbitration order.

Although most mediation is voluntary, a number of states and a few federal districts are using court-annexed mediation, in whch a trial judge refers the parties to mediation shortly after the case is filed. Although participation in this type of mediation is required, the mediator still does not impose an outcome on the parties.

SUMMARY JURY TRIAL

Unlike most ADR techniques, the **summary jury trial** (SJT) can be used only after a lawsuit has been filed. The trial judge usually selects cases for SJT that he or she thinks (1) are unlikely to be settled by the parties through normal negotiation and (2) will probably require substantial trial time. The parties have either performed some amount of pretrial discovery already, or if not, they are given an opportunity to conduct limited discovery before the SJT. A small (such as six members) jury is selected in the same way that regular juries are chosen. To ensure that the jurors take their responsibility seriously, they are not informed that their decision is nonbinding.

The parties are then given a few hours to summarize their positions and their evidence (sometimes including key portions of videotaped deposition testimony) and to give closing arguments. After the jury renders a verdict, the parties are urged to negotiate a settlement based on the additional guidance that the jury's reaction to the case provides. Despite the fact that "hard" cases are usually chosen for SJT, it has generally enjoyed a very high success rate, with most of the cases settling shortly after the SJT. The procedure tends to puncture inflated expectations and make parties choose more realistic settlement positions.

MINITRIAL

The **minitrial,** which has been used almost exclusively in disputes between corporations, involves summary presentations of evidence and arguments (similar to the presentations in an SJT) by opposing attorneys to a panel consisting of a neutral advisor and high-ranking executives from each company. The company representatives, who should have settlement authority, retire for direct settlement negotiations shortly after the presentations. They may seek the opinion of the neutral advisor before beginning settlement talks or only after negotiations have stalled. The exact design of the procedure, like the decision to use it in the first place, depends on the agreement of the parties. The minitrial has had a number of notable successes in complex, difficult disputes involving some of America's largest and best known companies. For example, almost immediately after a minitrial, Allied Corporation and Shell Oil settled a contract dispute that had been dragging on for almost ten years, including four years of expensive litigation.

REGULATORY NEGOTIATION

Regulatory negotiation, sometimes called "reg-neg" or negotiated rule making, has been a reasonably successful alternative to traditional administrative agency rule making. Agency regulations are often challenged in court, commonly taking years to finally receive court approval or disapproval. A number of federal and state agencies have avoided such litigation through a process in which the agency meets with representatives from interested groups to negotiate the content of regulations before they are formally proposed. The negotiations frequently involve a neutral third party acting as a mediator. The scope and validity of a rule produced through this process is much less likely to be challenged; in fact, the procedure sometimes produces both an agreed-on regulation *and* an agreement not to file a lawsuit challenging the regulation. The Environmental Protection Agency has been one of the leaders among federal agencies in using regulatory negotiation for new water and air quality regulations.

FUTURE OF ADR

Other forms of ADR have been used, often consisting of variations or hybrids of the methods we have discussed. Given the time and expense associated with traditional litigation and non-ADR negotiation, the use of ADR is likely to increase. In Texas, for example, the legislature stated in a recent law that "it is the policy of the State to encourage the peaceable resolution of disputes ... and the early settlement of pending litigation through voluntary settlement procedures." The law charges the courts of the state with the responsibility to carry out that policy by encouraging use of arbitration, meditation, SJTs, minitrials, and the like.

QUESTIONS and PROBLEMS

1. After ten years of litigation, a federal antitrust case was submitted to a formally summoned jury. However, the attorneys were given only a half-day in which to present their case and the decision of the jury was not binding. Why would such a procedure be undertaken?

2. Wydel Associates, a partnership, sued Thermasol, Ltd., on a breach of contract claim. Thermasol moved to dismiss the lawsuit because the contract contained a clause stating that any dispute should be arbitrated in New York rather than litigated. Wydel argued that the arbitration clause was not binding because the law of the state in which its partnership was formed provided that any partnership agreement to submit a claim to arbitration must be signed by *all* the partners. This contract had been signed by only one Wydel partner. Should the court dismiss the suit? *Wydel Associates v. Thermasol Ltd.*, 452 F.Supp. 739 (W.D.Tex 1978).

3. The Brockton Bank sued First United, a broker-dealer, after the defendant induced the bank to purchase a 90-day $1,000,000 CD from a bank (Penn Square) that failed. In discovery, Brockton sought to determine how much research First United had performed before making the recommendation to purchase. Four times during discovery, the defendant made untimely and only partial responses to court orders to produce documents. After arguing unsuccessfully for months that certain documents should be protected from discovery, the defendant claimed that the documents had been discarded long before. Suspecting the documents had been destroyed, the trial judge ordered the defendant's president to appear in court. The president did not appear, his attorney stating, "My client chooses not to obey." What should the court do? *Brockton Sav. Bank v. Peat, Marwick & Mitchell*, 771 F.2d (1st Cir. 1985).

4. In a report on the plaintiff's business, the defendant television station reported "[W]e spoke to Judge Rissman ... he says they've [customers of the plaintiff] got a good case." The plaintiff sued for defamation, claiming that this conversation never took place. The defendant moved to dismiss the suit on grounds that the conversation did take place and that it was just one man's opinion, anyway. Should the court dismiss? *Action Repair, Inc. v. American Broadcasting Co.*, 776 F.2d 143 (7th Cir. 1985).

5. The defendant company built a swimming pool for Denault. On January 9, 1978, the defendant's president was served with a summons in a lawsuit filed by Denault. Denault claimed the defendant's sloppy building of the pool forced her to make $2000 in repairs. Under the court rules, an answer was due from the defendant on January 29. The defendant tried to answer on January 31, but the court refused to accept the filing because it was untimely. The court entered a default judgment against defendant and set a hearing to establish damages. The defendant moved to set aside the default judgment on grounds of "excusable neglect," pointing out that its president had received two summons in the same week and thought Denault's had been served at the same time as the other summons, on January 13. Should the judge set aside the default judgment? *Denault v. Holloway Builders, Inc.*, 248 S.E.2d 265 (S.C. 1978).

6. Under a kickback scheme devised by Moore, a purchasing agent, one of the bidders on a construction project, submitted several price sheets; the purchasing agent read that bidder's price list last, choosing the highest one that was still low enough to get the bid. On discovering the extra sheets, Moore's secretary, Marren, exclaimed: "I've found the evidence I've been waiting for for a long time!" Marszalek overheard this statement. At Moore's criminal trial, Marszalek was asked about this statement because Marren died before trial. Should Marszalek be allowed to testify about the statement: *United States v. Moore*, 791 F.2d 566 (7th Cir. 1986).

7. On behalf of her children who had heart value problems, Fontent sued Upjohn Company, claiming that a drug Upjohn manufactured caused the defects. During discovery, the plaintiff was asked which experts she would call to testify that the drug had actually caused the defects. She responded, "Unknown at the present time." After more time for discovery, Upjohn moved for summary judgment on grounds that the plaintiff had produced no evidence to indicate that the drug had caused the heart defects. The plaintiff responded by pointing out that Upjohn had produced no evidence showing that the drug did *not* cause the defects and by arguing that the question of causation is inherently a jury question and inappropriate for resolution on a summary judgment motion. Should Upjohn's motion be granted? *Fontenot v. Upjohn Co.*, 780 F.2d 1190, 5th Cir. 1986.

8. A plane owned by Douglas landed at the Los Angeles airport and received permission from the tower to enter runway 22. Because of the shape of his plane, the Douglas pilot was not in a position to see clearly ahead, so he zigzagged the plane at 15° angles as he taxied to improve his forward vision. However, the plane collided with a P-51 owned by the government, which was parked along the side of runway 22. The pilot of the government plane, which was painted a brown camouflaged Army color, said after the accident: "I am sorry. I had no business being there. I have been here for about ten minutes. I called for a truck and they haven't come after me yet." The government sued Douglas for negligence; Douglas raised a contributory negligence defense. At the close of the evidence, the government moved for a directed verdict in its favor on the questions of respective negligence. The judge denied the motion and the jury found for Douglas. On appeal, the government argued that the judge erred in failing to grant its directed verdict motion. Discuss. *United States v. Douglas Aircraft Co.*, 169 F.2d 755 (9th Cir. 1948).

9. According to one court: "Lawsuits have become particularly inappropriate devices for resolving minor disputes. They are clumsy, noisy, unwieldy and notoriously inefficient. Fueled by bad feelings, they generate much heat and friction, yet produce little that is of any use. Worst of all, once set in motion, they are well-nigh impossible to bring to a halt." Is this a fair assessment? Does it help explain the trend toward use of alternative methods of dispute resolution? *Blackburn v. Goettel-Blanton*, 898 F.2d 95, 9th Cir. 1990.

CHAPTER 4

There are several basic processes by which law is made: (1) the formulation of rules by the courts—the judges—in deciding cases coming before them in those areas of law in which no statutes apply; (2) the enactment and interpretation of statutes; (3) the interpretation and application of constitutional provisions; and (4) the promulgation of rules and regulations by administrative agencies. In this chapter we look at the first and second of these lawmaking processes. First we show how **common law** *(or case law)*

COMMON AND STATUTORY LAW

is formed by the courts. Then we turn our attention to the enactment and interpretation of statutory law.

ORIGIN OF COMMON LAW

As we described in Chapter 2, the early king's courts in England largely made up the law on a case-by-case basis. If, for example, a plaintiff asked for damages for breach of contract in a situation in which the defendant denied that a contract ever existed, the court had to spell out the nature of a contract—that is, specify the minimum elements that the court felt must exist for it to impose contractual liability on the defendant. Similarly, if a defendant admitted making the contract in question but sought to escape liability for reasons of illness or military service, the court had to decide what kinds of defenses ought to be legally recognizable—defenses that should free the defendant from his or her contractual obligations.

Over a period of time, then, as more and more cases were settled, a rudimentary body of contract law came into being. Thereafter, when other cases arose involving contractual matters, the courts quite naturally looked to the earlier cases to see what principles of law had been established. The same procedure was followed in many other branches of law, and the legal rules that arose in this manner constituted the common law, or **case law,** of England.

The common-law rules that had developed in England became the law of our early colonies. And, when those colonies achieved statehood, they adopted those rules as a major part of their respective bodies of law. As the territories became states, they followed suit so that at one time the major portion of the law of all states (with the exception of Louisiana) was common law in nature.[1]

THE CURRENT SCENE

Gradually, the state legislatures began to pass increasing numbers of statutes, with the result that today most branches of the law are statutory in nature. For example, all states now have comprehensive statutes governing the areas of corporation law, criminal law, tax law, municipal corporations, and commercial law. Some of these statutes have been based largely on the common-law principles that were in effect earlier. Others, however, have been passed to create bodies of rules that did not exist previously or that expressly overrule common-law principles.

Despite the ever increasing amount of statutory law in this country (which we examine in some detail later in this chapter), several branches of law today are still essentially common law in nature in 49 of our states—particularly the subjects of *contracts, torts,* and *agency.* In these areas, in which

---

[1] Louisiana continues to be governed by the *civil-law* (as distinguished from common law) system of law. Under such a system, adopted by most European countries, virtually all law is "codified"—that is statutory.

FIGURE 4.1

COMMON LAW

- Origin — Created by the judicial branch through decisions in cases decided by the courts
- Form — Diffuse—rules found in fact-patterns and decisions of prior cases
- Scope — Narrow—limited to actual cases
- Effect of social and political forces — Indirect—judges somewhat insulated from political pressures

■ Common Law

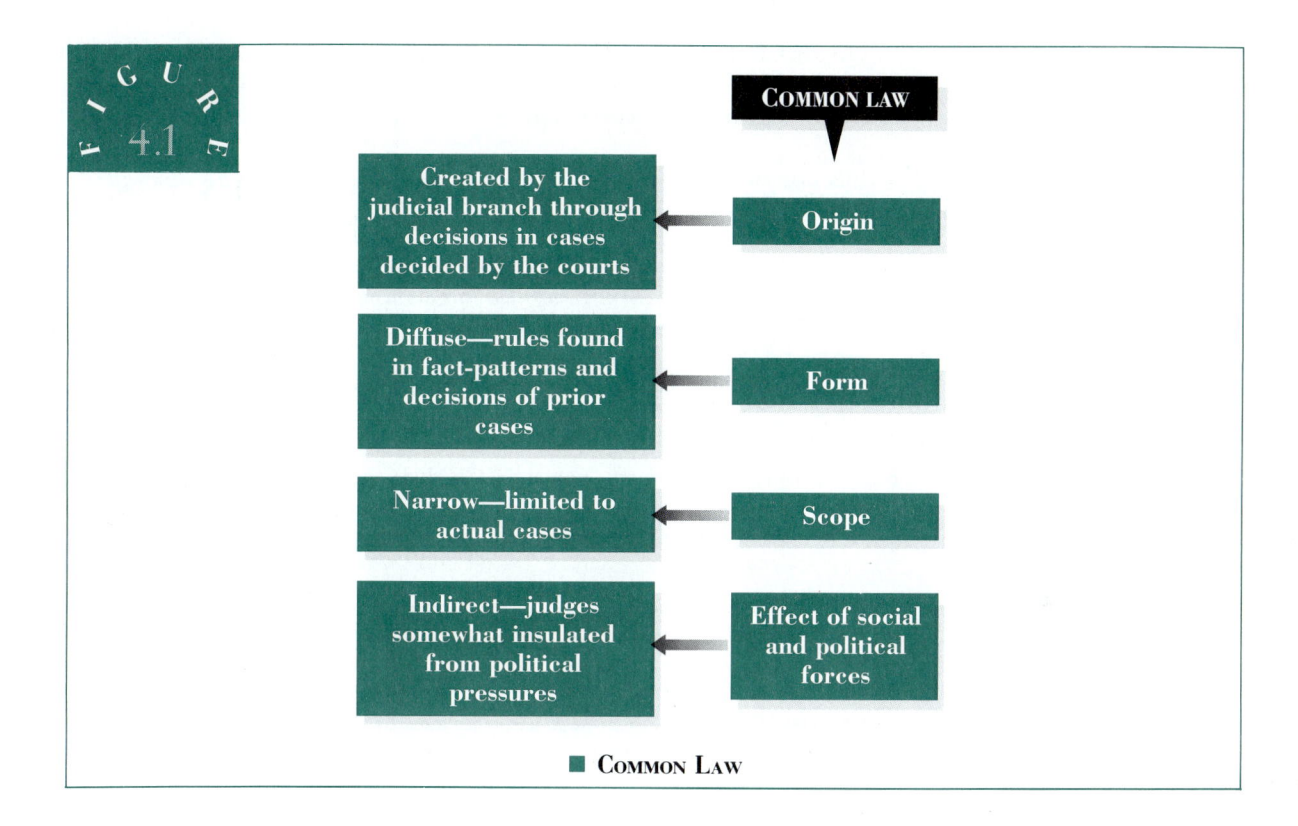

the legislatures have not seen fit to enact comprehensive statutes, the courts still settle controversies on the basis of judge-made or **case law**—the rules formulated by the courts in deciding earlier cases over the years, as illustrated in Figure 4.1. (Although many of these rules had their origin in England, as has been indicated, our definition of common law also includes those addtional rules that have originated in the state courts in this country.)

In deciding each case, judges bear the twin burden of attempting to provide "justice" for the case at hand while at the same time setting a precedent that will serve the greater interests of society when applied in future cases. The common-law rules, like legislative statutes, must serve public policy interests—the "community common sense and common conscience." Therefore, courts have laid great stress on the customs, morals, and forms of conduct that are generally prevailing in the community at the time of decision. There is no doubt that occasionally the judge's personal feelings as to what kinds of conduct are just and fair, what rule would best serve societal interests, and simply what is "right or wrong" enter the picture.

ROLE OF THE JUDGE

Benjamin N. Cardozo, an associate justice of the U.S. Supreme Court, contended that four "directive forces" shaped the law, and especially the common law, as follows: (1) philosophy (logic); (2) history; (3) custom; and (4) social welfare (or sociology).

In this lecture on the role of philosophy in the law, Cardozo briefly commented on the special tasks of the judge in interpreting statutes and constitutions, and then continued:

> *We reach the land of mystery when constitution and statute are silent, and the judge must look to the common law for the rule that fits the case. . . . The first thing he does is to compare the case before him with the precedents, whether stored in his mind or hidden in the books. . . . Back of precedents are the basic juridical conceptions which are the postulates of judicial reasoning, and farther back are the habits of life, the institutions of society, in which those conceptions had their origin, and which, by a process of interaction, they have modified in turn. . . . If [precedents] are plain and to the point, there may be need of nothing more.* Stare decisis *is at least the everyday working rule of the law. . . .*[2]

Early in that same lecture, however, Cardozo cautioned that the finding of **precedent** was only part of the judge's job and indicated how the law must grow beyond the early precedents, in these words:

> *The rules and principles of case law have never been treated as final truths, but as working hypotheses, continually retested in those great laboratories of the law, the courts of justice. . . . In [the] perpetual flux [of the law,] the problem which confronts the judge is in reality a twofold one: he first must extract from the precedents the underlying principle, the ratio decidendi [the ground of decision]; he must then determine the path or direction along which the principle is to move and develop, if it is not to wither and die. . . .*
>
> *The directive force of a principle may be exerted along the line of logial progression; this I will call the rule of analogy or the method of philosophy; along the line of historical development; this I will call the method of evolution; along the line of the customs of the community; this I will call the method of tradition; along the lines of justice, morals and social welfare, the mores of the day; and this I will call the method of sociology. . . .*[3]

COMMON LAW—THE DOCTRINE OF *STARE DECISIS*

The heart of the common-law process lies in the inclination of the courts generally to follow precedent—to stand by existing decisions. This policy, as we were told by Cardozo, is referred to as the doctrine of ***stare decisis.*** Under this approach, when the fact-pattern of a particular controversy is established, the attorneys for both parties search for earlier cases involving similar fact-patterns in an effort to determine whether applicable principles of law have been established. If this research produces a number of similar cases (or

---

[2] *Stare decisis* means literally, "to stand by decisions."
[3] Benjamin N. Cardozo, *The Nature of the Judicial Process* (1921). Excerpts are used by permission of the Yale University Press.

even one) within the state where a rule has been applied by the appellate courts, the trial court will ordinarily feel constrained to follow the same rule in settling the current controversy. (But, as we will see later, this does not mean that the courts are reluctant to abandon a precedent if it produces clear injustice under "contemporary conditions.")

TYPES OF PRECEDENT

Authority originating in courts above the trial court in the appellate chain is called **mandatory authority.** The judge must follow it. Thus, a state trial judge in Ohio will follow the rulings of the Ohio Supreme Court if there are any precedents from this court; if not, the judge will follow the prior decisions of Ohio's intermediate appellate courts. The intermediate appellate courts will do the same thing, and the Ohio Supreme Court will follow its own precedents. In matters of federal law, the Ohio Supreme Court will follow the holdings of the U.S. Supreme Court. A judge who does not follow mandatory authority is not impeached or shot at dawn but certainly runs a strong risk of reversal.

So strong is the hold of mandatory authority that judges will usually follow it even though they violently disagree with its reasoning and result. The following case illustrates this fact. The case involves a claim of *negligence*, which we shall study in detail in Chapter 10. It means simply that the defendant was more careless than a reasonable person would have been under the circumstances and should be liable for injuries that result. The case also involves a defense of governmental immunity, which stems from the ancient English doctrine that the King (or in this case the government) "can do no wrong" and therefore cannot be sued absent his consent. The decision is by a Michigan intermediate appellate court, sitting between the trial court and the Michigan Supreme Court in the appellate chain.

EDWARDS V. CLINTON VALLEY CENTER

COURT OF APPEALS OF MICHIGAN, 360 N.W.2d 606 (1984)

The plaintiff is the estate of Jean Edwards, who was fatally stabbed by a former mental patient. The defendant is a government mental hospital that refused to admit the killer after she was brought to the facility by police when she threatened to "kill someone." The plaintiff alleges that the defendant's refusal to admit the killer was negligent. The trial judge dismissed the suit on a purely legal ground—governmental immunity. The plaintiff appealed.

BRONSON, PRESIDING JUDGE:

Under the rule of *stare decisis*, this Court is bound to follow decisions of the Michigan Supreme Court, even if we disagree with them. The rule of *stare decisis*, founded on considerations of expediency and sound principles of public policy, operates to preserve harmony, certainty, and stability in the law. However, the rule "was never intended to perpetuate error or to prevent the consideration of rules of law to be applied to the everchanging business, economic, and political life of a

CONTINUED

community." *Parker v. Port Huron Hospital*, 105 N.W.2d 1 (1960).

In *Perry v. Kalamazoo State Hospital*, 273 N.W.2d 421 (1978), the majority of the Supreme Court held that governmental immunity for tort liability extends to the day-to-day care public mental hospitals provide. An attempt to distinguish the instant case from *Perry* could not possibly withstand logical or honest analysis. As a member of the Court of Appeals, I am obligated to follow the decisions of our higher court. For that reason, and that reason alone, the order of summary judgment is affirmed.

I feel compelled, however, to register my fundamental disagreement with the result adopted by the *Perry* majority. I am much more inclined to follow the narrow interpretation of governmental immunity advanced by the dissenters, because the operation of a mental hospital is not an activity which can be done only by the government, it is not a governmental function within the meaning of [the Michigan statutes establishing governmental immunity], and, therefore, a mental hospital should not be immune from liability for its torts.

If ever a factual situation invited reconsideration of the wisdom of a broad interpretation of what is, in the first place, an archaic doctrine, it is presented in the instant case. The Pontiac police bring Wilma Gilmore to the state-operated Clinton Valley Center. Gilmore threatens to kill someone. Gilmore had been previously institutionalized at the center. The center refuses to admit Gilmore. Four days later, Gilmore once again goes to the police and repeats her homicidal threats. She is told to leave.

Two days later, Gilmore enters the apartment of Jean Edwards and fatally stabs her in the arms, throat, and abdomen. Of note is that nowhere in the record does the center offer a reason for its refusal to admit Gilmore.

I fail to see how summarily relieving the hospital of responsibility for such obvious gross negligence, without requiring of it even the slightest explanation, serves any viable public interest or protects the people of our state. Instead, it harshly imposes the entire risk of the center's negligence on Jean Edwards and her family. The time has come for either the Legislature or our Supreme Court to preserve and promote justice by modifying the doctrine of governmental immunity.

Affirmed.

What if a trial judge searches the law books and discovers that there is no precedent in the state on the legal question presented? In such a case, the judge may examine the decisions of courts of other state. For example, assume a state trial judge in Oregon is faced with the question of whether a landlord who did not attempt to lease an apartment after a tenant moved out in the middle of a lease should be barred from suing the tenant for damages. No Oregon cases address the issue, and the only case "on point" was rendered by the Alabama Supreme Court. Must the Oregon judge follow the Alabama precedent? No. Because the Oregon judge's decision cannot be appealed to the Alabama Supreme Court, the latter's rulings are not mandatory authority.

The Alabama decision would constitute **persuasive authority.** That is, the Oregon judge can study the Alabama decision and, on finding it persuasive, may choose to follow it. However, if the judge finds the decision not to be persuasive, the judge need not apply its rationale in Oregon.

What if there are two existing precedents, that of the Alabama Supreme Court and one from the North Dakota Supreme Court, that reach diametrically opposed results on the same issue? Again, they are both only presuasive authority for the Oregon judge who can study them and follow the one that seems more reasonable. Of course, the judge can also reject both persuasive precedents and create yet a third approach to the issue. Despite the importance of stability to the law, the majesty of the common law lies in its flexibility and adaptability. Although judges revere stability, they will change a rule when they become convinced that it was wrongly established and never served society's interests or that while it was a good rule when established, changing social, moral, economic, or technological factors have rendered it outmoded. If no valid reason supports a common-law rule, no matter how long it has been established, the judges should and usually will change it.

Sometimes common-law rules change slowly. Exceptions or qualifications to the rule will slowly appear in the case law. Most of the history of the common law is of a slow evolution as the law keeps pace with a changing society. Refer back to *Soldano v. O'Dariels* in Chapter 1. That case not only illustrates a minor change in the slow evolution of the law regarding our duties to our fellow man, it contains some eloquent language extolling the virtues of our flexible common law.

Sometimes the law will change dramatically, as when modern judges decide an established rule no longer serves society and must be scrapped, as the following case illustrates.

FLAGIELLO v. PENNSYLVANIA HOSPITAL

SUPREME COURT OF PENNSYLVANIA 208 A.2d 193 (1965)

Mrs. Flagiello, a patient in the Pennsylvania Hospital in Philadelphia, fell and broke an ankle while being moved by two of its employees. She brought this action against the hospital to recover damages, alleging that the employees were guilty of negligence. The defendant hospital moved for a judgment on the pleadings, contending that under the case law of Pennsylvania, it was well established that a charitable institution was not responsible for the wrongs of its employees. The trial court sustained this motion and entered judgment for the defendant. The plaintiff appealed to the Supreme Court of Pennsylvania.

MUSMANNO, JUSTICE:

... The hospital has not denied that its negligence caused Mrs. Flagiello's injuries. It merely announces that it is an eleemosynary institution, and, therefore, owed no duty of care to its patient. It declares in effect that it can do wrong and still not be liable in damages to the person it has wronged. It thus urges a momentous exception to the generic proposition that in law there is no wrong without a remedy. From the earliest days of organized society it became apparent to man that society could never become a success unless the collectivity of mankind guaranteed to every member of society a remedy for a palpable wrong inflicted on him by another member of that society. In 1844 Justice Storrs of the Supreme Court of Connecticut crystallized into epigrammatic lanaguage that wise concept, as follows: "An injury is a wrong; and for the redress of every wrong there is a remedy; a wrong is a violation of one's right; and for the vindication of every right there is a remedy." *Parker v. Griswold,* 17 Conn. 288.

[The court addressed itself to several specific arguments advanced by the defendant to support it contention that

CONTINUED

charitable institutions were not, and should not be, subject to the general rule stated above. One of these arguments was that, on economic grounds alone, the imposition of liability on charitable institutions would be financially ruinous to them. The court rejected this argument, noting first that, as a general rule, a defendant is never permitted to escape liability as to valid claims solely on the ground that an entry of a judgment against him would be financially burdensome to him, or might even force him into bankruptcy. The court also noted that the rule of immunity as to charitable institutions originated in this country at a time when most of their patients paid nothing for the services they received and that the rule was an effort by the courts to preserve the meager assets of such institutions. Judge Musmanno further observed that conditions have now changed; that so-called charitable hospitals operate on the same basis as ordinary business establishments; that in 1963 "the fees received from patients in the still designated charitable hospitals in Pennsylvania constituted 90.92 percent of the total income of such hospitals," and the plaintiff did, in fact, pay defendant $24.50 a day for services rendered her. On these facts, the court rejected defendant's claim of immunity based on financial considerations. The court then turned to the remaining major contention of the defendant, specifically, that the rule of immunity as to charitable hospitals was so firmly established in the case law of Pennsylvania, including cases decided by the Pennsylvania Supreme Court, that, under the doctrine of *stare decisis*, the rule could not now be abandoned by the courts. In that regard Judge Musmanno, in a lengthy examination of cases, concluded that the immunity doctrine originated in an early English case that was soon overruled there, that the American courts seemed to adopt the rule of that case blindly, without examining the validity of the reasons ostensibly underlying it, and further noted that approximately half the states in this country have now rejected the doctrine of immunity. The court then continued:]

Failing to hold back both the overwhelming reasons of rudimentary justice for abolishing the doctrine, and the rising tide of out-of-state repudiation of the doctrine, the defendant hospital and the Hospital Association of Pennsylvania fall back for defense to the bastion of *stare decisis*. It is inevitable and proper that they should do so. Without *stare decisis*, there would be not stability in our system of jurisprudence.

Stare decisis channels the law. It erects lighthouses and flys the signals of safety. The ships of jurisprudence must follow that well-defined channel which, over the years, has been proved to be secure and trustworthy. But it would not comport with wisdom to insist that, should shoals rise in a heretofore safe course and rocks emerge to encumber the passage, the ship should nonetheless pursue the original course, merely because it presented no hazard in the past. The principle of *stare decisis* does not demand that we follow precedents which shipwreck justice. . . .

There is nothing in the records of the courts, the biographies of great jurists, or the writings of eminent legal authorities which offers the slightest encouragement to the notion that time petrifies into unchanging jurisprudence a palpable fallacy. [Emphasis added.] As years can give no sturdiness to a decayed tree, so the passing decades can add no convincing flavor to the withered apple of sophistry clinging to the limb of demonstrated wrong. There are, of course, principles and precepts sanctified by age, and no one would think of changing them, but their inviolability derives not from longevity but from their universal appeal to the reason, the conscience and the experience of mankind. No one, for instance, would think of challenging what was written in Magna Charta, the Habeas Corpus Act or the Bill of Rights of the Constitution of the United States. . . .

While age adds venerableness to moral principles and some physical objects, it occasionally becomes necessary, and it is not sacrilegious to do so, to scrape away the moss of the years to study closely the thing which is being accepted as authoritative, inviolable, and untouchable. The Supreme Court of Michigan said sagaciously in the case of *Williams v. City of Detroit*, 364 Mich. 231, that "it is the peculiar genius of the common law that no legal rule is mandated by the doctrine of *stare decisis* when that rule was conceived in error or when the times and circumstances have so changed as to render it an instrument of injustice."

The charitable immunity rule proves itself an instrument of injustice and nothing presented by the defendant shows it to be otherwise. In fact, the longer the argument for its preservation the more convincing is the proof that it long ago outlived its purpose if, indeed, it ever had a purpose consonant with sound law. "Ordinarily, when a court decides to modify or abandon a court-made rule of long standing, it starts out by saying

CONTINUED

that 'the reason for the rule no longer exists.' In this case, it is correct to say that the 'reason' originally given for the rule of immunity never did exist." *Pierce v. Yakima Valley Hospital Ass'n*, 260 P.2d 765.

A rule that has become insolvent has no place in the active market of current enterprise. *When a rule offends against reason, when it is at odds with every precept of natural justice, and when it cannot be defended on its own merits, but has to depend alone on a discredited genealogy, courts not only possess the inherent power to repudiate, but, indeed, it is required, by the very nature of judicial function, to abolish such a rule.* [Emphasis added.]

We, therefore, overrule *Michael v. Habnemann*, 404 Pa. 424, and all other decisions of identical effect, and hold that the hospital's liability must be governed by the same principles of law as apply to other employers. . . .

Reversed and remanded.

PROFILE OF OUR FEDERAL AND STATE STATUTORY LAW

While a significant portion of our law is still common law in nature, most of our federal and state law today results from the enactment of **statutes** by legislative bodies. These are the formally adopted rules that constitute our *statutory law*, the second of the major sources of law.[4] All states, for example, have comprehensive statutes governing such subjects as banking law, criminal law, education, consumer sales, and motor vehicle law.

Similarly, at the federal level, sweeping statutes in the areas of antitrust law, labor law, food and drug regulation, and securities law have long been in effect. Newer (and usually narrower) statutes are added every year, including, for example, the Consumer Product Safety Act of 1972, the Bankruptcy Reform Act of 1978, and the Trademark Counterfeiting Act of 1984. Figure 4.2 summarizes the origin, form, scope, and effect of statutory law.

In this section our first objectives are to look at the reasons for the existence of statutory law, to become acquainted with the basic rules that delineate the jurisdictions of the federal and state governments, and to note the contrasts between statutory and common law. We then turn our attention to the closely related area of statutory interpretation—the process by which the courts spell out the precise meaning of statutes that are applicable to the particular cases coming before them—and conclude with a summary

---

[4] The term *statutory law*, when broadly used in contrast to *common law*, includes not only laws passed by legislative bodies but, additionally, U.S. treaties, the federal and state constitutions, and municipal ordinances. In this chapter, however, the term is used in its more customary sense, referring only to acts of the state legislatures and of Congress.

FIGURE 4.2

STATUTORY LAW

- **Origin** → Created by the legislative branch through a formal lawmaking process
- **Form** → Official codified text
- **Scope** → Broad—subject only to constitutional limitations
- **Effect of social and political forces** → Direct—through the political process

■ Statutory Law

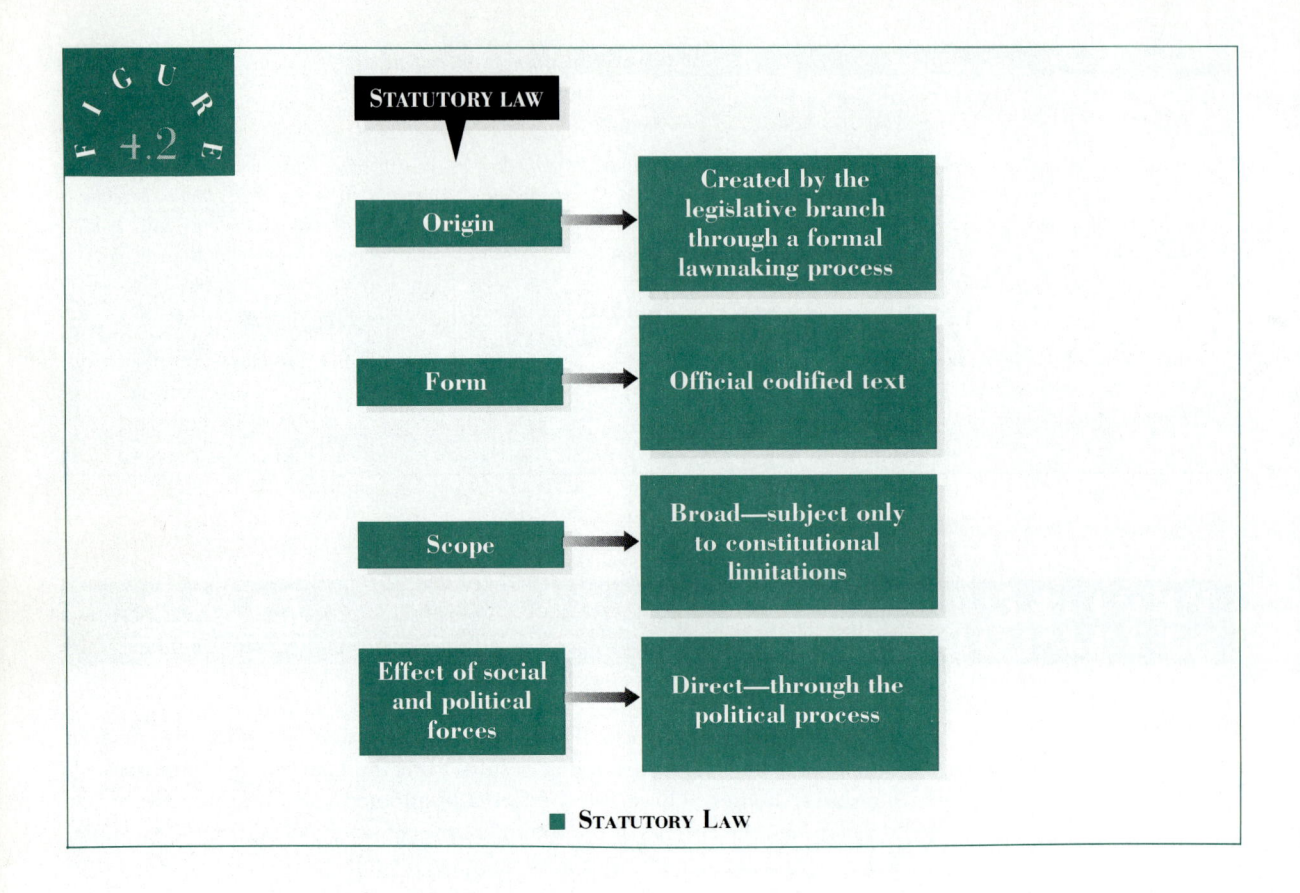

of selected state statutes that are of special significance to the business community.[5] As a back-drop for a better understanding of the issues that are addressed in this chapter, however, a brief description of the vast scope of our statutory law is first in order.

STATUTORY LAW—THE RATIONALE

There are many reasons for the existence of statutory law, three of which deserve special mention.

1. One of the primary functions of any legislative body is to adopt measures having to do with the *structure and day-to-day operation* of the govern-

---

[5] Many federal statutes, as well as some state enactments, are discussed in later chapters on topics such as employment law, securities regulation, and environmental protection.

ment of which it is a part. Thus many federal statutes are of the "nuts and bolts" variety, relating to such matters as the operation of the federal court system, the Internal Revenue Service, and the administration and employment rules of the U.S. Civil Service Commission. In a similar vein, many state statutes relate to such matters as the property tax laws, the operation of school systems, and the setting forth of powers of municipalities within their borders.

2. Many activities are of such a nature that *they can hardly be regulated by common-law principles* and the judicial processes. In the area of criminal law, for example, it is absolutely essential for the general populace to know what acts are punishable by fine and imprisonment; the only sure way to set forth the elements of specific crimes is through the enactment of federal and state criminal statutes. Similarly, the activities of corporations are so complex and so varied that they do not lend themselves to judicial regulation. Few judges, for example, have either the expertise to deal with such questions as the conditions under which the payment of corporate dividends should be permitted or the time to deal with the spelling out of such conditions on a case-by-case basis. Thus the only practical way to deal with these and other problems is by the drafting of detailed statutes, which, in total, make up the comprehensive corporation laws of the states.

3. A third function of a legislature is to change expressly (or even overrule) common-law rules when it believes such modifications are necessary, and—even more commonly—to enact statutes to *remedy new problems* to which common-law rules do not apply. Thus a state legislature might pass a statute making nonprofit corporations (such as hospitals) liable for the wrongs of their employees to the same extent as are profit-making corporations, thereby reversing the early common-law rule of nonliability for such employers. Or a legislature, aware of increasing purchases of its farmlands by foreign citizens—a situation not covered by common-law rules—might react to this perceived evil by passing a statute placing limits on the number of acres aliens may own or inherit. (More than 20 states today have such statutes, and approximately ten have passed laws that prohibit aliens who live outside the United States from owning *any* farmlands within these states' borders.)

LIMITATIONS ON LEGISLATIVE BODIES

PROCEDURAL REQUIREMENTS

All state constitutions (and, to a lesser extent, the federal Constitution) contain provisions about the manner in which statutes shall be enacted. As a general rule, acts that do not conform to these requirements are void. For example, virtually all state constitutions provide that revenue bills "shall originate in the House of Representatives," a requirement that also appears in the federal Constitution. Typical state constitutions also contain provisions (1) restricting the enactment of "special" or "local" laws that affect

HUMOR AND THE LAW

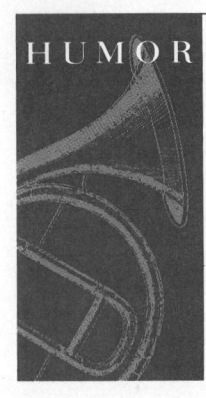

Lawyers and judges are often accused of using technical legal reasoning to evade common sense solutions. Such beliefs led to publication of the following apocryphal Canadian opinion.

Regina v. Ojibway
(August 1965)

Blue, Judge: This is an appeal by the Crown by way of a stated case from a decision of the magistrate acquitting the accused of a charge under the Small Birds Act, R.S.O., 1960, c. 724, s.2. The facts are not in dispute. Fred Ojibway, an Indian, was riding his pony through Queen's Park on January 2, 1965. Being impoverished, and having been forced to pledge his saddle, he substituted a downy pillow in lieu of the said saddle. On this particular day the accused's misfortune was further heightened by the circumstance of his pony breaking its right foreleg. In accord with Indian custom, the accused then shot the pony to relieve it of its awkwardness.

The accused was then charged with having breached the Small Birds Act, s.2, of which states: "2. Anyone maiming, injuring or killing small birds is guilty of an offence and subject to a fine not in excess of two hundred dollars." The learned magistrate acquitted the accused, holding, in fact, that he had killed his horse and not a small bird. With respect, I cannot agree.

In light of the definition section my course is quite clear. Section 1 defines "bird" as "a two legged animal covered with feathers." There can be no doubt that this case is covered by this section.

Counsel for the accused made several ingenious arguments to which, in fairness, I must address myself. He submitted that the evidence of the expert clearly concluded that the animal in question was a pony and not a bird, but this is not the issue. We are not interested in whether the animal in question is a bird or not in fact, but whether it is one in law. Statutory interpretation has forced many a horse to eat birdseed for the rest of his life.

Counsel also contended that the neighing noise emitted by the animal could not possibly be produced by a bird. With respect, the sounds emitted by an animal are irrelevant to its nature, for a bird is no less a bird because it is silent.

Counsel for the accused also argued that since there was evidence to show that the accused had ridden the animal, this pointed to the fact that it could not be a bird but was actually a pony. Obviously, this avoids the issue. The issue is not whether the animal was ridden or not, but whether it was shot or not, for to ride a pony or a bird is of no offence at all. I believe counsel now sees his mistake.

Counsel contends that the iron shoes found on the animal decisively disqualify it from being a bird. I must inform counsel, however, that how an animal dresses is of no concern to this court.

Counsel relied on the decision in *Re Chicadee*, where he contends that in similar circumstances the accused was acquitted. However, this is a horse of a different colour. A close reading of that case indicates that the animal in question there was not a small bird, but, in fact, a midget of a much larger species. Therefore, that case is inapplicable to our facts.

Counsel finally submits that the word "small" in the title Small Birds Act refers not to "Birds" but to "Act," making it The Small Act relating to Birds. With respect, counsel did not do his homework very well, for the Large Birds Act, R.S.O. 1960 c.725, is just as small. If pressed, I need only refer to the Small Loans Act R.S.O. 1960, c.727 which is twice as large as the Large Birds Act.

It remains then to state my reason for judgment which, simply, is as follows: Different things may take on the same meaning for different purposes. For the purpose of the Small Birds Act, all two-legged, feather-covered animals are birds. This, of course, does not imply that only two-legged animals qualify, for the legislative intent is to make two legs merely the minimum requirement. The statute therefore contemplated multi-legged animals with feathers as well. Counsel submits that having regard to the purpose of the statute only small animals "naturally covered" with feathers could have been contemplated. However, had this been the intention of the legislature, I am certain that the phrase "naturally covered" would have been expressly inserted just as 'Long' was inserted in the Longshoreman's Act.

Therefore, a horse with feathers on its back must be deemed for the purposes of this Act to be a bird, and *a fortiori*, a pony with feathers on its back is a small bird.

Counsel posed the following rhetorical question: If the pillow had been removed prior to the shooting, would the animal still be a bird? To this let me answer rhetorically: Is a bird any less of a bird without its feathers?

Appeal allowed.
H. Pomerantz & S. Breslin, 8 CRIMINAL LAW QUARTERLY 137 (1965)

---

only a portion of the citizenry, (2) requiring that the subject of every act be set forth in its title, and (3) prohibiting a statute from embracing more than one subject. Additionally, all constitutions prescribe certain formalities in regard to the enactment processes themselves, such as specific limitations on the time and place of the introduction of bills, limitations on the amendment of bills, and the requirement that bills have three separate readings before final passage.

These kinds of provisions, although appearing to be unduly technical, actually serve meritorious purposes. For example, although legislatures normally strive to pass statutes of general application, it is necessary that some laws operate only on certain classes of persons or in certain localities of a state. Such special or local laws are valid only if the basis of their classification is reasonable; two of the purposes of the constitutional provisions mentioned above are to ensure such reasonableness and to guarantee that the classes of persons covered be given notice of the consideration of the bill before its passage. Similarly, the purpose of requiring that the subject of an act be expressed in its title is to ensure that legislators voting on a bill are fully apprised as to its subject, thereby guarding against the enactment of "surprise" legislation. And the purpose of the requirement that a bill contain one subject is to prevent the passage of omnibus bills (those that bring together entirely unrelated, or incongruous, matters).

REQUIREMENT OF CERTAINTY

All statutes are subject to the general principle of constitutional law that they be "reasonably definite and certain." Although the Constitution itself does not expressly contain such a provision, the courts have long taken the view that if the wording of a statute is such that persons of ordinary intelligence cannot understand its meaning, the statute violates the due process clause of the Constitution and is thus invalid.[6] In such instances, it is said that the statute is "unconstitutionally vague."

As a practical matter, most statutes that are challenged on the ground of vagueness or uncertainty are upheld by the courts. This is because most statutes are, in fact, drafted carefully and because the courts are extremely reluctant to declare a statute unconstitutional if they can avoid doing so. Thus, if the wording of a statute is subject to two possible but conflicting interpretations, one of which satisfies constitutional requirements and the other of which does not, the former interpretation will be accepted by the courts if they can reasonably do so.

An application of the vagueness analysis in a criminal case occurred in *Kolender v. Lawson,* 461 U.S. 352 (1983), in which the U.S. Supreme Court struck down, on the ground of vagueness, a California statute that required persons who loitered or wandered on the streets to provide "credible and reliable" identification and to account for their presence when requested to do so by a peace officer. The court, speaking through Justice Sandra Day O'Connor, said, "It is clear that the full discretion accorded to the police whether the suspect has provided a 'credible and reliable' identification necessarily entrusts lawmaking to the moment-to-moment judgment of the policeman on his beat," and "furnishes a convenient tool for harsh and discriminatory enforcement by local prosecuting officials against particular groups deemed to merit their displeasure."

In a case involving regulation of business, rather than criminal charges, the courts will not be as demanding in applying the vagueness test, as the next case illustrates.

---

[6] *State v. Jay J. Garfield Bldg. Co.,* 3 P.2d 983 (Ariz. 1931).

U.S. v. Sun and Sand

U.S. Second Circuit Court of Appeals, 725 F.2d 184 (1984)

The Consumer Products Safety Commission (CPSC) issued an administrative complaint charging that Sun and Sand Imports had imported and transported in interstate commerce flammable children's sleepwear in violation of the Flammable Fabrics Act (FFA). The garments in question are sold in sizes that fit infants and toddlers, are made of soft stretchable fabric with no trim, have attached feet and a front zipper running from neck to crotch, and are, admittedly, made of flammable fabric. The trial judge enjoined importation of the garments pending conclusion of CPSC administrative proceedings.

Sun and Sand appealed, arguing that the regulatory definition of sleepwear is void for vagueness under the due process clause of the Fifth Amendment.

TIMBERS, CIRCUIT JUDGE:

Children's sleepwear is defined in a regulation promulgated under the FFA as

> any product of wearing apparel up to and including size 6X, such as nightgowns, pajamas, or similar or related items, such as robes, intended to be worn primarily for sleeping or activities relating to sleeping. Diapers and underwear are excluded from this definition.

In addition, the CPSC uses the following factors to determine whether an item of chidren's clothing is sleepwear within the meaning of the regulation: the nature of the product and its suitability for use by children for sleeping or activities related to sleeping; the manner in which the product is distributed and promoted; and the likelihood that the product will be used by children primarily for sleeping or activities related to sleeping in a substantial number of cases.

Before turning to the merits of Sun and Sand's vagueness challenge, we must determine what standard to apply. A provision is void for vagueness if it is so vague that it gives no warning to the challenger that his conduct is prohibited. In *Village of Hoffman Estates v. The Flipside, Hoffman Estates, Inc.*, 455 U.S. 489 (1982), the Supreme Court held that a more relaxed standard is to be applied to economic regulations which do not implicate fundamental rights and provide only for civil penalties. The instant case involves an economic regulation. Sun and Sand argues that the more restrictive standard should apply because the FFA provides criminal penalties for willful violations. The critical distinction is that criminal penalties are imposed only for *willful* violations of the FFA. A scienter requirement may mitigate the vagueness of a law.*

Moreover, the CPSC here sought only a cease and desist order. Sun and Sand remains free to assert a vagueness defense in any criminal action which may ensue.

---

*"Scienter" indicates an intent to violate the law.

We hold that the definition of children's sleepwear set forth in the regulation promulgated under the FA is sufficiently specific. Moreover, the CPSC's criteria for determining whether an article of clothing is primarily sleepwear provide guidance to the manufacturer, as do the examples provided by the cease and desist orders published in the *Federal Register*. In addition, the agency is willing to give pre-enforcement advice to manufacturers concerned with the applicability of the FFA to their products. We find these factors persuasive. We decline Sun and Sand's invitation to require an unworkable level of specificity. In *Boyce Motor Lines, Inc. v. United States*, 342 U.S. 337, 340 (1952), the Supreme Court recognized that because "few words possess the precision of mathematical symbols, most statutes must deal with untold and unforeseen variations in factual situations, and the practical necessities of discharging the business of government inevitably limit the specificity with which legislators can spell out prohibitions."

Sun and Sand focuses upon a 1978 memorandum by a compliance officer to the CPSC stating that "[d]ifferences between CPSC and firms regarding particular garments may then be litigated, as necessary, to resolve differences of opinion as to the intended use of the garments and to establish case precedents." Statutes and regulations, however, are not impermissibly vague simply because it may be difficult to determine whether marginal cases fall within

CONTINUED

their scope. *United States v. National Dairy Products Corp.,* 372 U.S. 29, 32 (1963). The burden upon a manufacturer of defending a cease and desist proceeding in a marginal case does not render the standard vague. It is not unfair to require that "one who deliberately goes perilously close to an area of proscribed conduct shall take the risk that he may cross the line." *Boyce Motor Lines, supra.* Only a reasonable degree of certainty is necessary. We hold that that requirement has been complied with here.

[The court then concluded that the trial court had properly held Sun and Sand's products to be within the statute because, *inter alia:* (1) they had the same characteristics as infant sleepwear, especially the attached feet; (2) Sun and Sand does not promote them as playwear; (3) customers in several stores were shown Sun and Sand's garments when they asked for sleepwear; (4) Sun and Sand's garments were intermingled with sleepwear in many stores; and (5) the garments bore a "striking similarity" to classic sleepwear garments.]

Affirmed.

STATUTORY LAW AND COMMON LAW — A CONTRAST

Statutory law and common law differ in several significant respects. The most obvious of these are the *processes* by which each comes into being and the *form* of each after it becomes operative.

PROCESSES AND FORM

Legislative acts become law only after passing through certain formal steps in both houses of the state legislatures (or of Congress) and, normally, by subsequent approval of the governor (or the president). The usual steps are (1) introduction of a bill in the house or senate by one or more members of that body; (2) referral of the bill to the appropriate legislative committee, where hearings are held; (3) approval of the bill by that committee and perhaps others; (4) approval of the bill by the house and senate after full debate; and (5) signing of the bill by the executive (or legislative vote overriding an executive veto). At each of these stages the opponents of the bill are given considerable opportunity to raise objections, with the result that the bill may be voted down or may pass only after being substantially amended. *Common-law rules,* by contrast, are creatures of the judicial branch of government; they are adopted by the courts for settling controversies involving points of law on which the legislature has not spoken.

In addition to these obvious contrasts between the two types of law, other are equally significant. We note these briefly.

SOCIAL AND POLITICAL FORCES

The social and political forces within a state have a greater and more evident impact on statutory law than on common law. Judges are somewhat more insulated from such pressures than are legislatures. Additionally, the steps required in the enactment of statutes enable representatives of vocal special-interest groups (who are frequently at odds with one another) to attract considerable publicity to their causes. And, of course, the raw political power that each is able to exert on the legislators plays a significant, although not always controlling, part in the final disposition of a bill.

In addition to the political and financial pressures that have always been wielded by lobbyists, the past 20 years have seen an enormous increase in the activities of political action committees (PACs). Whereas lobbyists' activities are intended to sway the votes of lawmakers, PACs direct their efforts to raising funds for the election of candidates who will support their particular causes. A hint of the power of PACs can be gained from just three statistics: (1) more than 4,000 PACs are registered with the Federal Elections Commission, representing virtually every business, union, and special interest group imaginable; (2) spending by PACs for the 1990 elections was estimated to be more than $150 million, even though there was no presidential race that year; and (3) about 95 percent of the incumbents in the U.S. House of Representatives win reelection every term, a statistic that many attribute in large part to the fact that PACs tend to support incumbents.

LEGISLATIVE OPTIONS

Although judges are required to settle controversies that come before them, legislatures generally have no duty to enact legislation. Thus legislatures have the option of refraining from the passage of laws when there is little public sentiment for them or when competing groups are so powerful that inaction is, politically, the better part of valor.

LEGISLATIVE SCOPE

Subject only to the relatively few constitutional limitations placed on it, the legislative power to act is very broad. Thus legislatures are not only free to enact statutes when case law is nonexistent, but they also can pass statutes that expressly overrule common-law principles. Examples of the latter are those statutes involving the legality of married women's contracts. Under English and early American common law, it was firmly established that married women lacked the capacity—the legal ability—to contract, and thus any agreements they entered into while married had no effect. Today, all states have enacted statutes that give married women the same rights to contract as those enjoyed by other citizens.

As for jurisdictional scope, legislatures have the power to pass broad statutes encompassing all aspects of a given subject, whereas the courts can "make law" only in deciding the cases that come before them. Every state, for example, has comprehensive corporation acts, in which virtually all aspects of corporate activities, from incorporation procedures to dissolution procedures, are specified in detail. Similarly, every state has an all-encompassing criminal code, within which the criminal offenses in the state are defined.

STATUTORY INTERPRETATION

We have seen that legislative bodies make law whenever they enact statutes. By doing so, they formally state what kinds of conduct they are requiring or prohibiting in specified situations and what results they expect from the passage of these laws on the rights and duties of affected parties.

But the true scope and meaning of a particular statute is never known with precision until it is formally construed by the courts in settling actual disputes arising under it. This search for legislative intent, which usually necessitates a *statutory interpretation*, is thus another major source of our law. **Interpretation** is the process by which a court determines the precise legal meaning of a statute as it applies to a particular controversy.

INTERPRETATION: A NECESSARY EVIL?

Whenever a dispute arises in which either of the parties is basing his or her case on the wording of a particular statute, one might think that the court's job would be mechanical in nature; that is, once the facts were established, a careful reading of the statute would make it clear what result the legislature intended in such a situation. Although this is often true, there are many instances in which it is not.

To bring the nature of the problem into sharper focus, consider the following situation. X flies a stolen airplane from one state to another and is convicted under a U.S. statute that makes the interstate movement of stolen motor vehicles a federal crime. In this statute, a motor vehicle is defined as "an automobile, automobile truck, automobile wagon, motorcycle, or any other self-propelled vehicle not designed for running on rails." Is an airplane a "motor vehicle" under this law? The problem is that the words of the statute are broad enough to embrace aircraft if they are given a literal interpretation; yet it is at least arguable that Congress did not really intend such a result. (The U.S. Supreme Court answered no to the question, with Justice Holmes saying that the term *vehicle* is "commonly understood as something that moves or runs on land, not something which flies in the air"—although he did admit that "etymologically the term might be considered broad enough to cover a conveyance propelled in the air".[7]

PLAIN-MEANING RULE

The primary source of legislative intent is, of course, the language that makes up the statute itself. In the relatively rare case when a court feels that the wording of an act is so clear as to dictate but one result and that the result is not "patently absurd," the consideration of other factors is unnecessary. If, for example, a state statute provides that "every applicant for examination

---

[7] *McBoyle v. United States*, 283 U.S. 25 (1931).

and registration as a pharmacist shall be a citizen of the United States," a state pharmacy board would have to refuse to process the application of an alien even though he or she may have *applied for* U.S. citizenship as of the date of the pharmaceutical examination.[8] In cases of this sort (and occasionally in others in which the language is somewhat less precise), the courts say that the statute possesses a **plain meaning** and that interpretation is thus unnecessary.

AIDS TO INTERPRETATION

Many statutes, however, do not easily lend them themselves to the plain-meaning rule. There are several reasons why courts frequently must interpret statutes before applying them, including the following: (1) Legislatures sometimes draft statutes with an element of "deliberate imprecision," intentionally giving the courts a degree of latitude in applying the statute. They may do this because they legitimately recognize the difficulty of defining certain concepts in the abstract or because they want to avoid making a specific decision on a controversial political issue. (2) Even if a legislature tries to define all the key elements of a statute with great precision, the effort sometimes fails because some concepts are extremely difficult to define without reference to a specific set of facts. (3) The complex process of amendment and deletion as a bill goes through the legislature sometimes leads to a product that is less clear than the originally introduced bill. (4) The choice of particular language may have been the result of compromise among factions in the legislature, which sometimes leads to a lack of clarity. (5) At its best, language is imperfect, and few words are susceptible to but one meaning.

Therefore, in many cases a court must interpret a statute before using it as a basis for deciding a case. Even when a court asserts that a statute has a plain meaning, it often bolsters its conclusion by resorting to various interpretive aids. The aids or devices used by a court to ascertain the legislative intent may be grouped into several categories.

First, a court sometimes refers to a dictionary or other standard reference source. It is presumed that legislative bodies use words in their common, ordinary sense, and a standard dictionary may be the best starting point to determine common English usage. If anyone claims that the legislature used a word in an unusual or technical sense, that party has the burden of proving it. General rules of grammar and punctuation are also usually followed unless there is a clear indication that the legislature intended otherwise.

Second, the court will examine the law's **textual context,** which involves reading the statute as a whole rather than concentrating solely on the language in question. Sometimes other language in that section of the statute, or perhaps similar language in another section of the same statute, may provide

---

[8] *State v. Dame,* 249 P.2d 156 (Wyo. 1952).

a clue as to what the legislature intended. This is simply an application of one of the cardinal principles of communication—do not take words out of their context.

Third, a court might examine the statute's **legislative history.** Comprehensive legislative histories are available for federal statutes, and less comprehensive histories are available for the statutory enactments of several states. A statute's legislative history may consist of several components. All bills are considered by one or more committees of the legislature, which holds hearings on the bill at which testimony and other evidence is presented by proponents and opponents of particular positions. Sometimes a verbatim *transcript* of all the oral testimony, written statements, and other evidence is published. After the committee has held hearings and deliberated, it will vote on whether to send the bill to the full body (house or senate) with a favorable or unfavorable recommendation. The committee often prepares a written report to accompanying its recommendation. Dissenting committee members may also write a minority report. These *committee reports* are also part of the legislative history. Finally, the transcript of the *floor debates* when the entire body considers the bill forms part of the legislative history, as well. In the case of federal legislation, these transcripts are published in the *Congressional Record.* The legislative history, especially the hearing transcripts and committee reports, can provide a wealth of information about the background and purpose of the law, the reasons for using particular language, how and why amendments and deletions were made, and other relevant matters.

Fourth, the statute's **circumstantial context** may be taken into account by a court seeking to discern the meaning of legislative language. This term simply describes the conditions or social problem that led the legislature to act. If, for example, the law was passed to fight organized crime, the courts will construe ambiguous language to help achieve that purpose. Evidence of the circumstantial context may be derived from several sources, including the legislative history.

Fifth, a court will consider *precedent* when interpreting a statute. Thus, prior judicial interpretations of the same statute, or of similar language in another statute, may be taken into account.

Regardless of the reason why a particular statute needs to be interpreted, and regardless of the particular interpretive aids employed, the court's sole task is to do the best it can to determine the legislative intent. The court's job is not to improve on what the legislature said or to make the statute mean what the court thinks it *should* mean. Even though determining what the legislature meant can be an elusive goal, the courts must do the best they can.

A final comment on statutory interpretation relates to the concept of *implied repeal.* Sometimes a party to a case will contend that some provision of a statute was implicitly repealed by later action of the same legislative body. The courts operate from a strong presumption against implied repeal; a court will find that a legislature intended to amend, repeal, or make an exception to an earlier statute only if the evidence of such intent is very clear. For example, in *Tennessee Valley Authority v. Hill,* 437 U.S. 153 (1978), the TVA, a federal government–owned corporation, was 80 percent finished with the construction of a major dam project on the Little Tennessee River when an ichthyologist from the University of Tennessee discovered a previously unknown species of "snail darter" in the river. At the time, this was the only known habitat of the fish, and there was no way of knowing whether efforts to transplant the species to another habitat would be successful. In accord with the federal Endangered Species Act, the Secretary of the Interior placed the snail darter on the endangered species list. This statute required all federal agencies and departments to take all "action necessary to insure" that their programs and activities would not jeopardize endangered species or damage their critical habitats. A lawsuit was brought in federal district court seeking an injunction that would prohibit the TVA from completing the project because it would destroy the snail darter's habitat. The TVA claimed that Congress, by appropriating funds to the project for several years, had implicitly created an exception to the Endangered Species Act for "substantially completed federal projects." The Supreme Court invoked the presumption against implied repeal and held that if Congress wanted to create an exception to the Endangered Species Act it had to express its intent clearly. Applying the statute exactly as it was written, the Court affirmed the lower court's decision granting an injunction against the TVA. Not long afterward, Congress passed legislation specifically giving TVA permission to complete the project.

The next case, which involves the federal Racketeering Influenced and Corrupt Organizations Act (RICO), provides an example of a statute that has proved to be very difficult to interpret. Part of the reason for this difficulty is that the target of the statute, organized crime, cannot be defined easily. There is no doubt that the statute was aimed primarily at the infiltration of legitimate business by the Mafia and other organized criminal operations. However, in more than 90 percent of the cases in which RICO's civil liability provisions have been used, the defendants were legitimate businesses, including stock brokerage firms such as Merrill Lynch and Dean Witter, CPA firms such as Arthur Andersen and Price Waterhouse, banks such as Citibank and Continental Illinois, and manufacturers such as Boeing and Miller Brewing. The problem is that the severe civil penalties in RICO, including the automatic tripling of damage awards, were probably intended by Congress to be used only against "mobsters." To slow down the spate of RICO lawsuits, some federal courts interpreted RICO's provisions to require that plaintiffs show that defendants had been previously *convicted* of certain specified "racketeering acts." The U.S. Supreme Court was called on to resolve the meaning of the statute. As you read the opinion, identify which interpretative aids the Court uses. Also, take note of the Court's effort to not stray very far from the specific language that Congress used. In this case, as in a number of others, the Court is essentially saying, "This is what the actual language of the statute seems to say; if this isn't what the legislature really intended, we wish they would change the law and tell us exactly what they do mean."

Sedima v. Imrex Co., Inc.

U.S. Supreme Court, 105 S.Ct 3275 (1985)

Plaintiff Sedima entered into a joint venture with the defendant Imrex Co. to provide electronic components to a Belgian firm. The buyer was to order parts through Sedima; Imrex was to obtain the parts in America and ship them to Europe. Sedima and Imrex were to split the net proceeds. After Imrex filled $8,000,000 in orders, Sedima became convinced that Imrex was inflating bills, cheating Sedima out of a portion of its proceeds by collecting for nonexistent expenses.

Sedima sued Imrex and two of its officers under the Racketeering Influenced and Corrupt Organizations Act (RICO). It contains both criminal provisions and the civil provisions that Sedima invoked. Sedima claimed that Imrex had by its presentation of inflated, fraudulent bills committed mail and wire fraud, which are "racketeering" acts within the meaning of RICO.

The trial court dismissed the RICO claims, and the Court of Appeals affirmed for the reason, among others, that the complaint was defective for failing to allege that the defendants had been convicted of mail and wire fraud. Sedima appealed.

White, Justice:

RICO takes aim at "racketeering activity," which it defines as any act "chargeable" under several generically described state criminal laws, any act "indictable" under numerous specific federal criminal provisions, including mail and wire fraud, and any "offense" involving bankruptcy or securities fraud or drug-related activity that is "punishable" under federal law. Section 1962, entitled "Prohibited Activities," outlaws the use of income derived from a "pattern of racketeering activity" to acquire an interest in or establish an enterprise engaged in or affecting interstate commerce; the acquisition or maintenance of any interest in an enterprise "through a pattern of racketeering activity"; conducting or participating in the conduct of an enterprise through a pattern of racketeering activity; and conspiring to violate any of these provisions.

Congress provided criminal penalties. In addition, it set out a far-reaching civil enforcement scheme, §1964, including the following provision for private suits:

> Any person injured in his business or property, by reason of a violation of section 1962 of this chapter may sue therefor in any appropriate United States district court and shall recover threefold the damages he sustains and the cost of the suit, including a reasonable attorney's fee. §1964(c).

The Court of Appeals found the complaint defective for not alleging that the defendants had already been criminally convicted of the predicate acts of mail and wire fraud, or of a RICO violation. This element of the civil cause of action was inferred from §1964(c)'s reference to a "violation" of §1962, the court also observing that its prior conviction requirement would avoid serious constitutional difficulties, the danger of unfair stigmatization, and problems regarding the standard by which the predicate acts were to be proved....

As a preliminary matter, it is worth briefly reviewing the legislative history of the private treble damages action. The civil remedies in the bill passed by the Senate, S. 30, were limited to injunctive actions by the United States....

During hearings on S. 30 before the House Judiciary Committee, Representative Steiger proposed the addition of a private treble damages action "similar to the private damage remedy found in the antitrust laws.... [T]hose who have been wronged by organized crime should at least be given access to a legal remedy. In addition, the availability of such a remedy would enhance the effectiveness of [RICO's] prohibitions." The American Bar Association also proposed an amendment "based upon the concept of Section 4 of the Clayton Act [i.e., the treble (triple) damage provision in the federal antitrust laws]."

Over the dissent of three members, who feared the treble damages provision would be used for malicious harassment of business competitors, the Committee approved the amendment....

The Senate did not seek a conference and adopted the bill as amended in the House. The treble damages provision had been drawn to its attention while the legislation was still in the House, and had received the endorsement of Senator

CONTINUED

McClellan, the sponsor of S. 30, who was of the view that the provision would be "a major new tool in extirpating the baneful influence of organized crime in our economic life."

The language of RICO gives no obvious indication that a civil action can proceed only after a criminal conviction. The word "conviction" does not appear in any relevant portion of the statute. To the contrary, the predicate acts involve conduct that is "chargeable" or "indictable," and "offense[s]" that are "punishable," under various criminal statutes. As defined in the statute, racketeering activity consists not of acts for which the defendant has been convicted, but of acts for which he could be. Thus, a prior conviction requirement cannot be found in the definition of "racketeering activity." Nor can it be found in §1962, which sets out the statute's substantive provisions. Indeed, if either §1961 or §1962 did contain such a requirement, a prior conviction would also be a prerequisite, nonsensically, for a criminal prosecution, or for a civil action by the government to enjoin violations that had not yet occurred.

The Court of Appeals purported to discover its prior conviction requirement in the term "violation" in §1964(c). However, even if that term were read to refer to a criminal conviction, it would require a conviction under RICO, not of the predicate offenses. That aside, the term "violation" does not imply a criminal conviction. It refers only to a failure to adhere to legal requirements. This is its indisputable meaning elsewhere in the statute. Section 1962 renders certain conduct "unlawful"; §1963 and §1964 impose consequences, criminal and civil, for "violations" of §1962. We should not lightly infer that Congress intended the term to have wholly different meanings in neighboring subsections.

The legislative history also undercuts the reading of the court below. The clearest current in that history is the reliance on the Clayton Act model, under which private and governmental actions are entirely distinct. The only specific reference in the legislative history to prior convictions of which we are aware is an objection that the treble damages provision is too broad precisely because "there need *not* be a conviction under any of these laws for it to be racketeering." 116 CONG. REC. 35342 (1970) (emphasis added). The history is otherwise silent on this point and contains nothing to contradict the import of the language appearing in the statute. Had Congress intended to impose this novel requirement, there would have been at least some mention of it in the legislative history, even if not in the statute.

Finally, we note that a prior conviction requirement would be inconsistent with Congress' underlying policy concerns. Such a rule would severely handicap potential plaintiffs. A guilty party may escape conviction for any number of reasons—not least among them the possibility that the Government itself may choose to pursue only civil remedies. Private attorney general provisions such as §1964(c) are in part designed to fill prosecutorial gaps. This purpose would be largely defeated, and the need for treble damages as an incentive to litigate unjustified, if private suits could be maintained only against those already brought to justice.

Underlying the Court of Appeals' holding was its distress at the "extraordinary, if not outrageous," uses to which civil RICO has been put. Instead of being used against mobsters and organized criminals, it has become a tool for everyday fraud cases brought against "respected and legitimate 'enterprises.'" Yet Congress wanted to reach both "legitimate" and "illegitimate" enterprises. The former enjoy neither an inherent incapacity for criminal activity nor immunity from its consequences. The fact that §1964(c) is used against respected businesses allegedly engaged in a pattern of specifically identified criminal conduct is hardly a sufficient reason for assuming that the provision is being misconstrued.

It is true that private civil actions under the statute are being brought almost solely against such defendants, rather than against the archetypal, intimidating mobster. Yet this defect—if defect it is—is inherent in the statute as written, and its correction must lie with Congress. It is not for the judiciary to eliminate the private action in situations where Congress has provided it simply because plaintiffs are not taking advantage of it in its more difficult applications.

[Reversed.]

SELECTED STATE STATUTES

Before leaving the subject of statutory law, several widely adopted state statutes deserve brief mention.

UNIFORM COMMERCIAL CODE

The **Uniform Commercial Code** (UCC) is especially significant to businesspersons because (1) it is a dramatic illustration of one way changes in law can occur in response to shortcomings that exist in prior law; (2) it governs numerous commercial law subjects; and (3) it has been adopted with little variation by all states except Louisiana (which has adopted only Articles 1, 3, 4, and 5).

Historical Background

At the beginning of this century, the growth in interstate commercial activity was hobbled by great variation in the commercial laws of the various states. This caused substantial planning problems for merchants and raised legal expenses as a cost of doing business to unnecessarily high levels. In 1941, the National Conference of Commissioners on Uniform State Laws and the American Law Institute joined forces to draft a single "modern, comprehensive, commercial code, applicable through the country." Most states have adopted the official 1962 version of the UCC, along with amendments in 1972 and 1978.

Coverage

The UCC consists of 11 "articles", or chapters. The 9 substantive areas of law covered by the code are found in Articles 2 to 9. (Articles 1 and 10 are merely introductory and procedural.)

Article 2, Sales, consists of 104 sections that govern virtually all aspects of the law of the sale of goods. Several provisions of Article 2 are discussed in Chapter 9. Article 2A, the first new article added to the UCC since 1962, regulates leases of goods. As of this writing, 9 states have adopted Article 2A. Wider adoption is expected to come in the near future.

Article 3, Commercial Paper, includes sections governing such matters as the rights and obligations of the makers of notes and the drawers of checks and drafts and the rights and duties of holders and endorsers of all types of negotiable instruments.

Articles 4 to 8 deal with more specialized situations, such as the duties that exist between depositary and collecting banks and the resolution of problems resulting from the issuance and transfer of bills of lading and other documents of title. Article 9 covers all kinds of secured transactions, which arise when creditors seek to retain a security interest in goods physically in the possession of a debtor.

HUMOR AND THE LAW

As you have no doubt deduced from the cases presented in this and other chapters, judicial *precedent* plays an important role in the outcome of most lawsuits. Indeed, in a model of brevity, one judge resolved a case with the following opinion, which is quoted in its entirety:

Denny v. Radar Industries
184 N.W.2d 289 (Mich. App. 1970)

The appellant has attempted to distinguish the factual situation in this case from that in *Renfroe v. Higgins Rack Coating and Manufacturing Co., Inc.* (1969), 17 Mich. App. 259, 169 N.W. 2d 326. He didn't. We couldn't.

Affirmed.

Similarly succinctness supposedly occurred in a California case:

"Defendant: As God is my judge, I didn't do it. I'm not guilty."
Judge: He isn't, I am. You did. You are."

DECEPTIVE TRADE PRACTICES ACTS

Most states have **deceptive trade practices acts,** which specifically forbid specified kinds of business misconduct. The typical act, for example, prohibits merchants from "passing off" (representing and selling) their goods or services as those of another; from representing used goods as being new; and from disparaging the goods or services of their competitors by false representations of fact. Additionally, the typical statute also prohibits such practices as advertising goods or services with the intent not to sell them as advertised, and the making of false statements concerning the reasons for, or the amounts of, price reductions. Such acts will be discussed in Chapter 12.

BUSINESS ORGANIZA- TION ACTS

All states have comprehensive statutes that control the formation, operation, and dissolution of various forms of business organizations. These will be studied in Chapter 13. For now it is sufficient to make just a few observations about these laws. In the area of general partnerships, there is substantial uniformity from state to state because virtually all states have adopted versions of the Uniform Partnership Act (UPA). The UPA has successfully accomplished the uniformity for partnership law that the UCC was meant to create for commercial transactions.

There is less uniformity for limited partnership law because some states' laws are based heavily on the Uniform Limited Partnership Act (ULPA) of 1916, others on the Revised Uniform Limited Partnership Act (RULPA) of 1976, and still others have adopted portions of a 1985 amended version of RULPA. Still, the states' laws are generally similar and moving in the same direction.

There is even less uniformity, however, in the states' laws governing corporations. Here, there is no *uniform* act, only two versions of a *model* act, the Model Business Corporation Act (MBCA) and the Revised Model Business Corporation Act (RMBCA). Many states pattern their laws after one of these two model acts, but most have felt free to introduce their own variations. Furthermore, many states pattern their corporate codes not on some version of the MBCA but on the Delaware Corporate Code. Delaware is the leading corporate law jurisdiction in the nation.

Questions *and* Problems

1. Dissenting in *Taylor v. Allen*, 151 La. 82 (1921), Justice O'Neill wrote: "I have heard that lawyers in one of the Western states [say that a] precedent is a 'goose case.' The expression arose from the perplexity of a so-called 'case lawyer,' who was unprepared to advise his client whether he was liable in damages because his geese had trespassed on his neighbor's lawn. The lawyer said he had found several cases where the owners were held liable because their horses, cows, sheep, goats, or dogs had committed acts of trespass; but he could not find a 'goose case.' The distinction which he observed was that his 'goose case' was not 'on all fours.'" Explain what constitutes a "goose case." How does one avoid the problems of the perplexed lawyer in Justice O'Neill's story?

2. Maddux was injured when the car she was riding in was struck by a car driven by Donaldson, and almost immediately thereafter, by a second car driven by Bryie. When Maddux sued the two negligent drivers, the facts of the case were such that it was impossible to determine which of her injuries were caused by the first collision and which by the second collision. At the time of the suit, the Michigan common-law rule was that, in such a case, neither defendant could be held liable for any damages; accordingly, the trial court dismissed Maddux's action. She then appealed to the Supreme Court of Michigan, claiming that the rule of non-recovery was too unfair to an injured plaintiff. Do you agree with this contention? If so, what do you think a better rule would be? (*Maddux v. Donaldson*, 108 N.W.2d 33, 1961.)

3. In a number of cases, the supreme court of State X had adopted the rule that a seller of land who overstated the *value of the land* to a prospective buyer was not guilty of fraud, even if he or she knew that the true market value of the land was much lower than the figure that he or she stated to the buyer. (In these cases, the reasoning of the court was that the value of any property is merely a matter of opinion and that the buyer should realize this.) Suppose that a new case reaches the supreme court in which the buyer of land claims that the seller was guilty of fraud when he—the seller—intentionally misrepresented the *rental value* of the property (seller told buyer, an out-of-state resident who had never seen the land, that "it can readily be rented for $100 a month," a statement that proved to be false). If the supreme court felt that the seller in such a case should be made to pay damages on the theory that he *was* guilty of fraud, would the court have to overrule the prior decisions, or do you think the facts of the new case are sufficiently different to permit the court simply to apply a different rule to it? Explain your reasoning. (*Cahill v. Readon*, 273 P. 653, 1928.)

4. A student demonstrator and four labor pickets were convicted in the Hamilton County Municipal Court, Ohio, of violating a Cincinnati ordinance making it a criminal offense for three or more persons to assemble on a sidewalk "and there conduct themselves in a manner annoying to persons passing by." On appeal to the U.S. Supreme Court the five contended that the ordinance was unconstitutionally vague (that it was so vague that it violated the due process clause). Do you agree with this contention? Discuss (*Coates v. Cincinnati*, 402 U.S. 611, 1971.)

5. The City of Petersburg had maintained a cemetery

for more than 100 years when it decided to move some of the bodies onto a 1.1-acre tract adjacent to the cemetery so that a road running in front of the cemetery could be widened. The Temples owned a home directly across the street from the 1.1-acre tract. They sued to prevent the bodies from being moved onto the tract, citing a state statute which said: "No cemetery shall be hereafter established within the corporate limits of any town; nor shall any cemetery be established within 250 yards of any residence without the consent of the owner of such residence." Can the city take the proposed action? Discuss. (*Temple v. City of Petersburg*, 29 S.E.2d 357, Va. 1944.)

6. Johnson, a teen-aged boy living in North Carolina, owned a motorcycle. After the motorcycle's original headlight became very weak, he and a friend taped a five-cell flashlight to the handlebars, and that evening, with both boys on the motorcycle, they had a collision with an automobile. In ensuing litigation, the car owner pointed out that a North Carolina statute required every motorcycle to have a "headlamp," and he contended that the flashlight was not a headlamp. If you were a judge on the North Carolina Supreme Court hearing the case on appeal, what steps would you take in deciding whether the flashlight was a headlamp under the statute? What result? (*Bigelow v. Johnson*, 277 S.E.2d 347, 1981.)

7. In 1885 Congress passed a statute which provided: "[I]t shall be unlawful for any person, company, partnership, or corporation, in any manner whatsoever, to prepay the transportation, or in any way assist or encourage the importation or migration of any alien or aliens...into the United States...under contract or agreement...made previous to the importation or migration of such alien or aliens,...to perform labor or service of any kind in the United States." In 1887 the Holy Trinity Church of New York City made a contract with Warren, a pastor then living in England, under the terms of which he was employed to serve as its pastor. Pursuant to that contract, Warren immigrated to the United States and assumed his pastoral duties. The church was soon charged with violating the quoted statute. Did Congress intend the statute to cover this case? Discuss. (*Holy Trinity Church v. United States*, 143 U.S. 457, 1892.)

8. A city ordinance required that operators of coin-operated amusement machines be licensed and provided that the chief of police was to determine whether an applicant has any "connections with criminal elements." The city manager, after receiving the report of the chief of police and reports from the building inspector and the city planner, would then decide whether to issue the license. (If the application were denied, the applicant could then petition the city council for a license.) In a legal case brought by a rejected applicant, the contention was made that the licensing ordinance was *unconstitutionally vague* because of the "connections with criminal elements" language. Do you think this contention is correct? Why or why not? (*City of Mesquite v. Aladdin's Castle, Inc*, 102 S.Ct. 1070, 1982.)

CHAPTER 5

The most important single document in the United States and, arguably, the world, is the U.S. Constitution. This document is the foundation of our democratic system of government and the basis of our many freedoms. Although drafted in a simpler time, the Constitution has evolved over the past 200 years to keep pace with changes in American society. Partly through amendment, but more importantly through flexible Supreme Court interpretations, the Constitution has remained as vital and timely as it was when originally written.

CONSTITUTIONAL LAW

Few areas of the law can be studied without reference to the Constitution. For example, Chapter 2 discussed the structure of the federal court system, which is established in the Constitution, as well as the exercise of personal jurisdiction by state and federal courts, which is constrained by the Constitution's due process provisions. The Constitution governs the ability of the government to intervene in business activities; for example, Chapter 6 points out that the government's power to conduct inspections and searches of business firms is limited by the Fourth Amendment of the Constitution. The Constitution contains several protections for defendants charged with crimes, as discussed in Chapter 8. The Constitutional right to freedom of speech affects the principles of defamation law discussed in Chapter 10, and the rules of trademark and copyright law discussed in Chapter 12. Although not everyone realizes this fact, the Constitution has at least as much relevance to the operation of business enterprises as it does to the personal affairs of individuals. Our discussion of constitutional law in this chapter is fairly broad, but it will emphasize the role the Constitution plays in both empowering the government to regulate business and placing limits on the exercise of these regulatory powers.

Before turning to a discussion of the U.S. Constitution, it bears mentioning that every state in this country also has a constitution. These documents include many provisions similar to those found in the federal Constitution, such as those separating state governments into three branches and protecting fundamental liberties. Most state constitutions are much more detailed than is the U.S. Constitution. A state constitutional provision is the supreme law within that state, unless it conflicts with the U.S. Constitution or some other federal law.

The U.S. Constitution contains three general categories of provision:

1. It prescribes the basic organization of the federal government into legislative, executive, and judicial branches.

2. It delineates the authority of the federal government, in contrast with the states, by granting specific powers to the three branches of the federal government.

3. It protects certain basic rights of individuals and businesses by placing limitations on federal and state governmental power.

ORGANIZATION OF THE FEDERAL GOVERNMENT

One major function of the Constitution is to establish the basic organization of the federal government into legislative, executive, and judicial branches. The essential function of the legislative branch, Congress, is to make laws, as well as to collect revenue and appropriate funds for carrying out those laws.

The main function of the executive branch is to enforce these laws; however, the executive branch also plays the primary role in conducting foreign relations and directing our military forces. The basic task of the judicial branch is to decide how particular laws should be applied to actual disputed cases.

SEPARATION OF POWERS

As a general proposition, each branch of the federal government is supposed to exercise only those types of powers expressly given to it by the Constitution. Stated somewhat differently, one branch generally is not supposed to encroach on the powers of another branch. The doctrine of **separation of powers** is, however, a flexible one that is subject to various exceptions based on practicality.

Checks and Balances

To begin with, the Constitution expressly provides for a number of "checks and balances" to insure against any single branch of government developing an excessive degree of power. Examples include the requirement that the president sign legislation passed by Congress (the executive veto power) and the ability of Congress to override a presidential veto by a two-thirds vote in both houses.

Judicial Review

Another type of permissible interplay among the three branches of government is *judicial review*. Although this could be characterized as another form of "check and balance," the concept of judicial review is not expressed in the Constitution. During the early days of the Republic, the question of which branch had ultimate authority to determine constitutional issues was unsettled. In *Marbury v. Madison*, 5 U.S. 137 (1803), the U.S. Supreme Court assumed this power for the judicial branch of government. Because of the practicality and logic of placing this task in the hands of the federal courts and because of the stature of Chief Justice John Marshall, the author of the opinion in *Marbury*, the doctrine of judicial review is generally accepted without question today. Under the principle of judicial review, the federal courts have the final say in deciding whether the Constitution has been violated by a congressional law or executive action. It is no exaggeration to say that "the Constitution means what the Supreme Court says it means." (Although not involving a federal separation of powers question, it also should be noted that the doctrine of judicial review later expanded to include the power of the federal courts to determine whether actions of *state* courts, legislatures, and executive officials violate the U.S. Constitution.)[1]

---

[1] In a similar vein, it also has come to be an accepted principle in our law that state courts have the power to determine whether state legislative or executive actions are valid under that particular state's constitution. Moreover, state courts have power to review state legislative and executive actions for conformity to the U.S. Constitution, subject only to possible ultimate review by the U.S. Supreme Court. This power of state courts to apply the U.S. Constitution to state legislative and executive actions, is, of course, an example of concurrent state–federal subject matter jurisdiction, as discussed in Chapter 2.

Reasonable Overlap of Functions

It is sometimes necessary for one branch of government to engage in an activity that closely resembles the type of function that the Constitution has assigned to another branch of government. For example, in providing for the implementation of many of its regulatory laws, Congress has found it necessary to give judicial-like powers to government agencies that are not part of the federal judiciary. These agencies may be part of the executive branch, such as the Social Security Administration (part of the Department of Health and Human Services), or they may be relatively independent of the executive branch, such as the Securities and Exchange Commission. In any event, such an agency frequently performs an adjudicative type of function, that is, deciding whether an individual meets the requirements for Social Security disability benefits or whether a corporation has made misleading statements in connection with the issuance of stocks or bonds. Similarly, Congress sometimes has to exercise investigative powers that traditionally have been considered executive in nature. Also, the federal courts engage in a form of "lawmaking" when they interpret provisions of the Constitution and federal statutes.

There are many other examples of situations in which one branch, to effectively carry out its primary role, may find it necessary to perform tasks similar to those of another branch. Performing such a "borrowed" function is permissible under the separation of powers doctrine as long as (1) it is reasonably necessary and incidental to the primary functions of that branch of government, and (2) the power of one branch is not substantially enlarged at the expense of another branch.

Especially in recent years, the U.S. Supreme Court has not seemed to be greatly concerned about most exercises of judicial-like powers by Congress or the executive branch, as long as they are based on good reasons and are reasonably limited. However, the court has tended to scrutinize legislative–executive overlaps more closely. For example, in *Bowsher v. Synar,* 478 U.S. 714 (1986), the Supreme Court decided a legal challenge brought against the so-called Gramm-Rudman Act of 1985, which established an automatic process for reducing the federal budget deficit. Under the statute, after a rather complex process the Comptroller General essentially determined the amount to be cut from the next year's budget. The Comptroller General is an employee of Congress and thus is part of the legislative branch. The Supreme Court concluded that this aspect of the Gramm-Rudman Act violated the separation of powers doctrine because budget execution is an executive power. This was not an appropriation of funds, which is a congressional power; to be valid exercise of the legislative appropriation power, the action would have had to go through the normal voting process in both houses of Congress. The Court was of the opinion that there was too great an encroachment by Congress on the power of the executive branch. (Congress later amended the law to place the budget reduction power in the executive branch.)

Delegation of Powers

The final category of exception to the separation of powers doctrine is found in the principle that Congress may expressly delegate legislative powers to the other two branches. Congress often delegates rule-making powers, for example, to federal administrative agencies that are outside the legislative branch. For example, in the Securities Exchange Act of 1934, Congress prohibited fraudulent and deceptive practices in connection with the sale of securities and delegated to the Securities and Exchange Commission the power to make rules specifying in more detail the types of conduct that would violate this prohibition. Congress also has delegated certain rule-making powers to the federal courts, namely, the limited power to prescribe rules of procedure and evidence. Express delegations of legislative power are normally valid as long as Congress (1) indicates the basic policy objectives it is seeking to achieve and (2) provides some degree of guidance as to how the power is to be exercised.[2]

AUTHORITY OF FEDERAL AND STATE GOVERNMENTS

A second major function of the U.S. Constitution is to delineate the authority of the federal government, in contrast with that of the states. In our dual system of sovereignty, there are 51 primary governments—the federal government and the 50 state governments. When the original 13 colonies ratified the Constitution, they agreed to cede certain important sovereign powers to the federal government; as other states were added they similarly agreed. Under our system of federalism, the federal government has those powers that are specifically given to it in the Constitution—the so-called **delegated powers** (or "enumerated powers"). Those powers not granted to the federal government continue to reside with the states—the so-called **reserved powers.**

Our discussion of federal authority will focus on the power of Congress and primarily on the power of that federal legislative body to regulate business activities. Article I, section 8 of the Constitution spells out the powers of the U.S. Congress, the most important of which include the power:

> To lay and collect Taxes, Duties, Imposts and Excises, to pay the Debts and provide for the common Defense and general Welfare of the United States; ...
> To borrow Money on the Credit of the United States;
> To regulate Commerce with foreign Nations, and among the several States, and with the Indian Tribes;
> To establish an uniform Rule of Naturalization, and uniform Laws on the subject of Bankruptcies throughout the United States;
> To coin Money, regulate the Value thereof, and of foreign Coin, and fix the Standard of Weights and Measures; ...

---

[2] At the state government level, the same general principles typically are applied to the separation of powers doctrine and its exceptions.

To establish Post Offices and post Roads;

To promote the Progress of Science and useful Arts, by securing for limited Times to Authors and Inventors the exclusive right to their respective Writings and Discoveries;

To constitute Tribunals inferior to the Supreme Court; ...

To declare War, grant Letters of Marque and Reprisal, and make Rules concerning Captures on Land and Water;

To raise and support Armies, but no Appropriation of Money to that Use shall be for a longer Term than two Years;

To provide and maintain a Navy;

To make Rules for the Government and Regulation of the land and naval forces;

To provide for calling forth the Militia to execute the Laws of the Union, suppress Insurrections and repel Invasions;

To provide for organizing, arming, and disciplining the Militia, and ...

To make all Laws which shall be necessary and proper for carrying into Execution the foregoing Powers, and all other Powers vested by this Constitution in the Government of the United States, or in any Department or Officer thereof.

STATE POLICE POWER

In most circumstances, the lines of demarcation between the authority of the federal and state governments are quite clear. Most of the legislative powers delegated to the federal government under article I, section 8—such as the power to operate post offices and to maintain the various armed forces—involve such obviously federal powers that no state reasonably could claim to possess any regulatory authority over them.

By the same token, the powers reserved to the states are also relatively clear and well established. Virtually all the powers of a particular state derive from the **state police power**—a term referring to the inherent governmental power to regulate the health, safety, morality, and general welfare of its people. Statutes relating to the operation of motor vehicles, the manufacture and sale of alcoholic beverages, and the regulation of crime obviously fall within the police power, because they are directly involved with matters of health, safety, and morals. Typical state laws based on the "general welfare" component of the police power are those that regulate such matters as marriage and divorce, the inheritance of property, and landlord–tenant relationship.

The power to enact zoning laws specifying restrictions on the use of real estate also falls within the state police power, but state legislatures normally delegate this power to their cities; thus, most zoning regulations are actually found in city ordinances or the regulations of city zoning commissions. In fact, state legislatures may delegate any part of the police power they wish to local political subdivisions such as cities or counties. They also sometimes delegate very limited police powers to specialized political subdivisions of the state, such as port authorities, flood control districts, school districts, water supply and conservation districts, hospital districts, and so forth. Later, when we discuss limits that the U.S. Constitution places on state governmental powers, it should be understood that these limits are the same whether the state power is exercised directly by the state or is delegated to a local government entity.

FEDERAL POWER — THE COMMERCE CLAUSE

In examining the authority of the federal government, we are primarily concerned here with the power to regulate business. Although in many areas there is a clear delineation between the powers of the federal government on one hand and the state governments on the other, one area presents difficult problems—regulation of commercial activities. Despite the fact that the federal power to regulate commerce is very broad, the states also have a substantial amount of regulatory power over commerce. The dual nature of the power to regulate commerce has created many instances of state–federal friction. Seldom does a year go by in which the U.S. Supreme Court does not decide an important case bearing on the respective spheres of authority to regulate commerce.

Federal Regulation of Interstate Commerce

Article I, section 8 of the U.S Constitution grants to Congress the power "to regulate Commerce with foreign Nations, and among the several States." Many provisions of the Constitution were aimed at preventing various kinds of provincialism and thus at making the United States truly "united." By giving Congress the primary authority to regulate interstate commerce, the **commerce clause** was intended to make the United States a common market, with the many economic advantages of trade that is unhindered by state boundaries. Before the adoption of the Constitution, economic "Balkanization" had plagued trade relations among the Colonies under the Articles of Confederation, the Colonies having erected various barriers to free trade among themselves.

By giving Congress the power to regulate trade with foreign nations, the framers of the Constitution recognized that the nation could not join the international trading community unless it could speak with one voice in maintaining international trade relations.

Until the late 1930s, the Supreme Court interpreted the commerce clause very narrowly with respect to the power of Congress over interstate and foreign commerce. The Court took the view that Congress could regulate a commercial activity only to the extent that it actually occurred *in the course of* interstate or foreign commerce. To the extent that an activity took place within the borders of a particular state, Congress could not normally regulate it, no matter how great the activity's ultimate effect on interstate or foreign commerce might be. Thus, under this older interpretation, Congress had no constitutional power to regulate manufacturing or other productive activities within a state; for example, it could not regulate wages, hours, or working conditions of manufacturing employees.

Beginning in the late 1930s, the Supreme Court took an almost 180° turn in its interpretation of the commerce clause. Since that time, the power of Congress in this area has been interpreted very broadly. It is still true that any commercial activity that actually crosses state or national boundaries is within the scope of the commerce clause. In addition, the regulatory power of Congress today extends to any activity that has "any appreciable effect" on interstate or foreign commerce, even though the activity took place solely within a particular state.

In the increasingly interdependent national and international economy in which we find ourselves, most significant commercial activities have an "appreciable" (i.e. meaningful or significant) effect on either interstate or foreign commerce. Today, most of our federal regulatory laws have been passed by Congress under this expanded commerce clause power. Examples include the federal laws regulating securities markets, workplace safety, wages and hours, and competition (antitrust laws). Indeed, Congress often uses the commerce clause as a constitutional foundation for enacting legislation even when its primary goal is not an economic one. Examples of this include laws aimed at protecting the environment and prohibiting employment discrimination.

"Commerce" includes almost anything remotely related to an economic activity, including manufacturing, advertising, contracting, sales and sales financing, transportation, capital-raising, and so on. Because the federal regulatory power encompasses *intrastate* commercial activity that affects interstate or foreign commerce, few local businesses can escape the reach of the federal government. For example, in *Wickard v. Filburn,* 317 U.S. 111 (1942), an Ohio farmer was limited by federal law to raising 11.1 acres of wheat. Farmer Filburn ignored the limitation and planted 23 acres. He fought a penalty assessed by the government by arguing that because he used much of the wheat he grew right on his own farm and sold the rest at an elevator a few miles away, he was not engaged in interstate commerce. But the Supreme Court held that the power to regulate interstate commerce includes the power to regulate prices. The purpose of the law in question was to support agricultural prices by limiting production. If all small farmers such as Filburn were viewed as beyond the reach of the act, the supply of wheat would no doubt increase and appreciably *affect* the price of wheat selling in interstate commerce. Congressional authority extended to Filburn.

More recently, in *McLain v. Real Estate Board of New Orleans,* 444 U.S. 232 (1980), a question arose whether a number of New Orleans real estate firms and trade associations had violated the federal antitrust laws by entering into several price-fixing contracts. The lower courts dismissed the action, ruling that the defendants' actions, which involved sales of land in New Orleans, were "purely local" in nature and thus not subject to federal law. The Supreme Court reversed, finding that the indirect effects of the defendants' activities were sufficiently related to interstate commerce to justify application of federal law. This finding of sufficient effect—a "not insubstantial effect"—was based primarily on the fact that (1) significant amounts of money lent by local banks to finance real estate purchases came from out-of-state banks, and (2) most of the mortgages taken by the local banks were "physically traded" by them to financial institutions in other state.

Although there are very few businesses today whose activities are so completely local (intrastate) in nature as to be outside the power of Congress to regulate, it is important to note that Congress has not exercised all its regulatory power. The fact that an activity affects, or even directly involves, interstate or foreign commerce does not necessarily mean that Congress has chosen to regulate the activity. The power granted by the commerce clause, as interpreted by the Supreme Court, can be viewed as a reservoir of law-making power. In any given situation, Congress may or may not have drawn from that reservoir to enact legislation. The same is true of other powers granted by the Constitution.

In addition, when Congress decides to regulate a particular commercial activity, it sometimes chooses to exercise less than its full constitutional authority. For example, Congress might choose to include within a particular law only certain activities that actually cross state or national boundaries, even though it could regulate activities not crossing these boundaries because of their effect on interstate or foreign commerce. For instance, Congress has expressly exempted "intrastate offerings" of stocks and bonds from many of the document-filing requirements of the federal Securities Act of 1933, leaving the regulation of intrastate sales of new securities to the discretion of the particular state. Congress may choose to exempt certain activities in other ways, as well. Thus, the employment discrimination prohibitions found in Title VII of the 1964 Civil Rights Act apply only to employers whose businesses affect interstate commerce *and* who have 15 or more employees, thus exempting employers with a smaller number of workers. Similarly, other laws might expressly exclude from coverage businesses with assets below a certain value or transactions below a stated amount.

State Regulation of Commerce

Despite the dominant federal role, the states retain substantial authority to regulate commercial activities. A state's police power permits it to protect the health, safety, and general welfare of its citizens. This power includes the authority to regulate commercial activities within the state, even if those activities have a substantial affect on interstate or foreign commerce and even if they originated outside the state. To give effect to the primary power of the federal government in these areas, however, the courts have developed several principles that limit the power of the states. These include preemption, discrimination against interstate commerce, and unduly burdening interstate commerce. Although different, all these concepts are closely related, and more than one of them may sometimes be at issue in the same case. (There principles also apply to state laws that affect foreign commerce—that is, international trade. Unless we say otherwise in this discussion, international commerce will be included within the term *interstate commerce*.)

Federal Preemption: The concept of **federal preemption** is a general principle of constitutional law that applies to any state–federal conflict. The doctrine of preemption is relevant regardless of whether a particular federal power comes from the commerce clause or from some other provision of the

Constitution. However, we discuss the preemption doctrine in the context of the federal commerce clause power because it is in this context that most of the issues arise.

If a particular governmental power is exclusively federal, we say that there is federal preemption of this field of government activity. Federal preemption may be either express or implied, or it may result from a direct conflict between state and federal law. As we mentioned in the previous section, some federal powers in the Constitution are obviously of an exclusively federal nature, such as conducting foreign affairs, maintaining an army, and establishing a monetary system. The state governments have no power to act in such matters. In the case of other powers granted to the federal government, however, it may not be so obvious that the power is exclusively federal. When the Constitution gives the federal government a certain type of authority and a state attempts to exercise a similar or related power, the courts may have to determine whether there actually is federal preemption.

Express preemption. When a preemption question arises, we begin with one basic proposition: the **supremacy clause** found in article VI, section 1 of the Constitution makes federal law the "supreme law of the land." The supremacy clause applies regardless of the specific source of the state or local law and regardless of the specific source of the federal law. The supremacy clause means, among other things, that if the Constitution gives a power to the federal government, the federal government also has the authority to prohibit the states from exercising a similar power. For example, the Constitution specifically gives Congress the power to enact patent laws that protect the creative work of inventors. When using this power to pass patent legislation, Congress can engage in *express preemption* by specifying in the legislation that the states have no power to adopt similar laws. If Congress exercises its authority to expressly preempt the states, no state can adopt a law that provides to inventors any legal protection for their inventions that is basically the same as the protection provided by the federal patent laws.

Although Congress has this power of express preemption, it usually does not use it. In fact, when passing a law, Congress often provides expressly that states retain the power to adopt similar or related laws as long as those laws do not conflict with or hinder the objectives of the federal law.

Implied preemption. When Congress has chosen to regulate some activity but has said nothing about whether the states do or do not have power to pass related laws, a question of *implied preemption* may arise. For example, Congress has extensively regulated labor–management relations, as discussed in Chapter 18. Federal law establishes a framework within which groups of employees may fairly and democratically decide whether they want to form a union and, if so, which labor organization they wish to represent them in negotiating with the employer about wages, hours, and working conditions. The conduct of both employers and unions is closely regulated during this process. Once a group of employees decides to be represented by a particular union and the union is officially certified, the employer is under a legal obligation to bargain with the union in good faith. The objective of the regulated negotiation process is to achieve a collective bargaining agreement governing the rights and responsibilities of the employer and employees during the term of the contract. Suppose that, in State X, there has been a history of labor strife in a particular industry that is important to the state's economy. Strikes by employees and lockouts by employers have sometimes resulted, causing economic harm to the state. In response, State X's legislature passes a statute authorizing the state governor to issue an executive order ending a strike or lockout in that industry after a stated time period if the governor finds that serious harm is being done to the state's economy. Assume that, when the governor later exercises this power, a union or employer challenges the validity of the state law under which the governor acted. Because the federal labor–management relations laws say nothing about state authority to engage in similar regulation, a challenge to the state law is likely to be based on a claim of implied preemption. (The employer or union might also claim that the law places an undue burden on interstate commerce—this concept will be discussed shortly.)

When a claim of implied preemption is made, the one challenging the state law is asking the court to draw an inference about the intent of Congress—in other words, that party tries to prove that Congress implicitly intended to preempt the regulation of this general area. The challenger usually must prove two conditions before a court will conclude that implied preemption exists. First, it must be shown that the federal regulation is relatively *comprehensive*. In other words, the court must be convinced that Congress attempted to impose a fairly complete regulatory structure on this type of activity. Otherwise, it makes no sense to infer a preemptive intent on the part of Congress. This first condition is clearly met in the case of federal labor–management relations laws.

Second, it also must be shown that there is a very strong need for a uniform national regulatory policy in this area, so that individual state laws of this type are likely to interfere with the objectives of the federal regulatory effort. Most unions represent employees in several states, and many of the employers that negotiate with unions also operate in more than one state. Moreover, a group of employers may negotiate with one large union, and sometimes one large employer must negotiate with several unions. In other words, relationships between companies and unions generally transcend state boundaries, but the objective of a particular negotiation is a single contract. If these often-sensitive negotiations had to be conducted within a framework of several different sets of state regulations, it would be extremely difficult for the parties to ever achieve a collective bargaining agreement, and the collective bargaining agreement is the cornerstone of federal regulation in this area. Thus, the second condition for implied preemption also exists. Because both conditions are met, the Supreme Court has concluded that the states are preempted from adopting laws dealing with the company–union relationship.

It should be noted that, even in a situation in which there is implied federal preemption, states still may protect important state interests by passing laws that are only peripherally related to the federally regulated area and that are not likely to interfere with the federal regulatory objectives. For example, despite implied preemption, an employee may be punished under state criminal or tort law for assault and battery or property destruction even though the wrongful conduct occurred during the course of a union-sponsored strike.

Direct conflict. A much narrower form of preemption occurs when a specific state law is in *direct conflict* with a specific provision of federal law. In the labor–management relations setting, recall that there is no express federal preemption. For the sake of illustration, now let us also assume that either or both of the requirements for implied preemption was not met. What this would mean is that there is no federal preemption of this general field of regulatory activity, and the states could enact laws regulating company–union relations. However, if a particular state provision comes into direct conflict with a federal law, the state law is void to the extent of the conflict. Suppose that, even if there is no express or implied federal preemption, there is a specific federal statute that empowers the U.S. president to seek a federal court injunction ending a strike or lockout under certain carefully prescribed conditions. In such a case, the law in State X authorizing its governor to halt strikes or lockouts might very well be void because of a direct conflict with the federal law.

A state law is not void because of direct conflict just because the state provision deals with the same type of activity. Moreover, the mere fact that a state law is more stringent than a similar federal law does not make the state law void. For example, the fact that California law places stricter pollution control standards on automobiles does not mean that this state law is in conflict with federal auto emission control regulations. A state law is void because of direct conflict in only two situations. First, there is a direct conflict if it is impossible to comply with both the state and federal laws. An example of this would be a state law *requiring* wholesalers to grant quantity discounts to retailers in the state even in circumstances in which the discounts are not justified by any lower costs of selling in larger quantities. This state law would require conduct that violates the federal Robinson-Patman Act's prohibition of price discrimination.

Second, even if it is literally possible to comply with both laws, there nevertheless is a direct conflict if the state law substantially interferes with the purpose of the federal law. For example, suppose that when Congress passed the law giving the president authority to stop strikes or lockouts in certain carefully defined situations, it clearly indicated an intent to permit government interference in company–union confrontations only when national defense is threatened or when a national economic emergency exists. In such a case, the hypothetical law giving the governor of State X the power to stop strikes when economic injury to the state is threatened might be void for direct conflict because it interferes with objectives of the federal law.

It should be reemphasized that either type of direct conflict is really just a narrower form of implied preemption, with the preemption applying only to a specific state law and a specific federal law rather to an entire field of regulated activity.

One final note on the concept of preemption is worth noting. In this country, there is a presumption against preemption. Thus, a court will normally find federal preemption only if Congress or a federal agency clearly expressed that intent or if the evidence of implied preemption or direct conflict is very strong. In the European Economic Community (EEC), however, the presumption is reversed. When the EEC adopts a regulation of some kind, there is a presumption that this law was intended to preempt related laws of member nations.

The following case illustrates the concept of implied preemption in the case of a federal regulatory system aimed at encouraging the use of American ports in international trade.

XEROX CORP. v. HARRIS COUNTY

U.S. SUPREME COURT
459 U.S. 145 (1982)

Pursuant to its powers under the commerce clause, Congress established a comprehensive customs system aimed at placing certain controls on the flow of goods into and out of the country, while at the same time encouraging international trade between the United States and other countries. For many years, federal customs law has provided for a system of "customs bonded warehouses" at various U.S. ports of entry. These warehouses are owned and run by private operators but are under the continuous control and supervision of the federal customs officials at that port. Ordinarily, imported goods are subject to a federal tax known as a "duty." However, under certain conditions federal customs law permits goods to be imported duty-free if they are stored in a customs bonded warehouse. The owner of imported goods is permitted to store them in such a warehouse when they are intended for ultimate sale somewhere outside the United States—in other words, when the United States is just a stop-over for goods that are destined for sale in some other country. Such goods can remain duty-free in the customs bonded warehouse for up to five years. If they are stored for more than five years or if the owner changes its plans and markets the goods within the United States, an import duty must be paid. Congress established this system for the purpose of encouraging the use of American ports as a stop-over for goods in international trade when the owner finds it efficient to do so.

Increased use of American ports produces more economic activity in the vicinity of those ports.

Xerox Corporation manufactured parts for copying machines in Colorado and New York. These parts were then shipped to Mexico for assembly. After assembly, the copiers were imported into the United States and stored in a customs bonded warehouse in Houston, Texas, while awaiting shipment to various destinations in Latin America. The copiers were designed especially for sale in the Latin American market; the machines operated on an electric current of 50 cycles per second as is common in Central and South America, rather than the 60 cycles per second that is standard in the United States. In addition, all printing on the machines and instructions was in either Spanish or Portuguese; thus there was no question about Xerox's claim that the goods were not intended for sale in the United States. (Until 1974, Xerox had shipped its Mexican-assembled copiers to the Free Trade Zone of Panama, where they were stored tax-free. In 1974, rising anti-American sentiment in Panama caused Xerox to look for another storage

CONTINUED

facility. It decided on the Houston customs bonded warehouse because of the excellent port facilities at Houston and its proximity to Latin America.)

Beginning in 1977, Harris County (where Houston is located) assessed local property taxes on Xerox's copiers in the customs bonded warehouse. (The city and school district also levied these taxes.) The taxes were nondiscriminatory—they applied to all goods in described categories for the period of time they were physically located within the county, regardless of where the goods originated or where they came from. The county did not place a tax directly on imports or exports as the goods entered or exited but instead based the tax on the physical location of the goods within the county for the duration of their stay. Thus, the local property tax was not automatically void under the constitutional prohibition against state or local taxes on imports or exports. Xerox filed suit in a state trial court in Houston, alleging that the tax measure was unconstitutional because it was impliedly preempted by the federal regulations setting up the system of customs bonded warehouses. The trial court ruled for Xerox, but the intermediate level state appellate court reversed and upheld the tax. The Texas Supreme Court refused to review the decision, and the U.S. Supreme Court agreed to hear Xerox's appeal of the federal constitutional question.

BURGER, CHIEF JUSTICE:

Government regulated, bonded warehouses have been a link in the chain of foreign commerce since "a very early period in our history." *Fabbri v. Murphy*, 95 U.S. 191, 197 (1877). A forerunner of the present statute was the Warehousing Act of 1846, ch. 84, 9 Stat. 53 (1846). A major objective of the warehousing system was to allow importers to defer payment of duty until the goods entered the domestic market or were exported. The legislative history explains that Congress sought to reinstate:

> "the sound though long neglected maxim of Adam Smith, 'that every tax ought to be levied at the time and in the manner most convenient for the contributor to pay it;' [by providing] that the tax shall only be paid when the imports are entered for consumption..." H. R. Rep. No 411, 26th Cong., 1st Sess. 3 (1846).

The Act stimulated foreign commerce by allowing goods in transit in foreign commerce to remain in secure storage, duty free, until they resumed their journey in export. The geographic location of the country made it a convenient place for transshipment of goods within the Western Hemisphere and across both the Atlantic and the Pacific. A consequence of making the United States a center of world commerce was that:

> "...our carrying trade would be vastly increased; that shipbuilding would be stimulated; that many foreign markets would be supplied, wholly or in part, by us with merchandise now furnished from the warehouses of Europe; that the industry of our seaports would be put in greater activity; [and] that the commercial transactions of the country would be facilitated...." App. to Cong. Globe, 29th Cong., 1st Sess. 792 (1846) (remarks of Sen. Dix).

To these ends, Congress was willing to waive all duty on goods that were reexported from the warehouse, and to defer, for a prescribed period, the duty on goods destined for American consumption. This was no small sacrifice at a time when customs duties made up the greater part of federal revenues, but its objective was to stimulate business for American industry and work for Americans.

In short, Congress created secure and duty free enclaves under federal control in order to encourage merchants here and abroad to make use of American ports. The question is whether it would be compatible with the comprehensive scheme Congress enacted to effect these goals if the states were free to tax such goods while they were lodged temporarily in government regulated bonded storage in this country.

In *McGoldrick v. Gulf Oil Co.*, 309 U.S. 414 (1939), the City of New York sought to impose a sales tax on imported petroleum that was refined into fuel oil in New York and sold as ships' stores to vessels bound abroad. The crude oil was imported under bond and refined in a customs bonded manufacturing warehouse and was free from all duties. We struck down the state tax, finding it preempted by the Congressional scheme.

The Court determined that the purpose of the exemption from the tax normally laid upon importation of crude petroleum was "to encourage importation of the crude oil for [refinement into ships' stores] and thus to enable American refiners to meet foreign competition

CONTINUED

and to recover trade which has been lost by the imposition of the tax." The Court went on to note that, in furtherance of this purpose,

> "Congress provided for the segregation of the imported merchandise from the mass of goods within the state, prescribed the procedure to insure its use for the intended purpose, and by reference confirmed and adopted customs regulations prescribing that the merchandise, while in customs bonded warehouse, should be free from state taxation."

The Court concluded that

> "the purpose of the Congressional regulation of commerce would fail if the state were free to impose a tax which would lessen the competitive advantage conferred on the importer by Congress, and which might equal or exceed the remitted import duty." . . .

The analysis in *McGoldrick* applies with full force here. First, Congress sought, in the statutory scheme reviewed in *McGoldrick*, to benefit American industry by remitting duties otherwise due. The import tax on crude oil was remitted to benefit oil refiners employing labor at refineries within the United States, whose products would not be sold in domestic commerce. Here, the remission of duties benefited those shippers using American ports as transshipment centers. Second, the system of customs regulation is as pervasive for the stored goods in the present case as it was in *McGoldrick* for the refined petroleum. In both cases, the imported goods were segregated in warehouses under continual federal custody and supervision. Finally, the state tax was large enough in each case to offset substantially the very benefits Congress intended to confer by remitting the duty. In short, freedom from state taxation is as necessary to the Congressional scheme here as it was in *McGoldrick*.

Although there are factual distinctions between this case and *McGoldrick*, they are distinctions without a legal difference. We can discern no relevance to the issue of Congressional intent in the fact that the fuel oil in *McGoldrick* could be sold only as ships' stores whereas Xerox had the option to pay the duty and withdraw the copiers for domestic sale, or that in *McGoldrick* the City sought to impose a sales tax and here appellees assessed a property tax. . . .

[The state appeals court decision is reversed; the tax is unconstitutional and thus void. Because of this holding, there is no need to address the additional argument of Xerox that the tax is, in practical effect, a constitutionally prohibited tax on imports.]

Discrimination Against Interstate Commerce: Even when there is no preemption of any kind, a state cannot pass a law that discriminates against interstate commerce (or international commerce). Such discrimination interferes with the primary authority of Congress over interstate and foreign commerce, and thus violates the supremacy clause. States may not, for example, shelter their own industries from competition emanating from other states or nations.[3] Although states may act to preserve their own natural resources, they cannot do so by discriminating against out-of-state buyers. They also cannot require that business operations that could be conducted more efficiently elsewhere take place within the state. For example, a state could not require that shellfish caught off its shores be processed in-state before being shipped elsewhere for sale.

---

[3] Although it often may be unwise to do so, Congress does have the power to shield business in the United States from international competition.

A state's intent to discriminate might be explicit or it might be inferred from surrounding circumstances. For example, in *Philadelphia v. New Jersey*, 437 U.S. 617 (1978), the state legislature of New Jersey explicitly prohibited garbage from being imported into the state. Operators of several landfills in New Jersey, as well as several cities from other states that had agreements with these landfill operators for waste disposal, challenged the law. The Supreme Court held that the law unconstitutionally discriminated against interstate commerce; even a desire on the part of New Jersey to conserve landfill space was not a strong enough state interest to justify an explicit discrimination against the interstate transportation of solid waste. In its opinion the Court also distinguished the so-called quarantine cases, in which state quarantine laws had been upheld. The Court said that these laws, which forbade the transportation of diseased livestock or plants, had been held to be constitutional because they were aimed primarily at the act of moving the livestock or plants from one place to another, whether the movement was totally within the state or into it from another state.

Sometimes the circumstances may lead a court to conclude that a state intended to discriminate against interstate commerce even though the intent was not made explicit. As with any question of intent in the law, the court attempts to draw the most logical inference from surrounding circumstances. An example is *Hunt v. Washington State Apple Advertising Commission*, 432 U.S. 333 (1977), which involved a North Carolina law, unique in the 50 states, that required all apples sold in the state to have only the applicable grade under U.S. Department of Agriculture grading standards stamped on the crates; state grades were expressly prohibited. For many years all apples shipped from the state of Washington had been stamped with grades under that state's grading system. In all cases, Washington state grades were superior to the comparable federal ones. The state of Washington and its apple industry had spent decades developing the quality and national reputation of its apples. If they still wanted to sell apples in North Carolina, Washington apple growers would have to segregate apples intended for shipment there and package them differently, in addition to losing the competitive advantage of being able to use their well-known grading standards. North Carolina asserted that the law was adopted to protect consumers in the state from deception and confusion caused by multiple grading systems. The evidence was very convincing, however, that North Carolina was really engaging in economic protectionism by placing Washington apples at a disadvantage in the North Carolina market. The factors indicating an intent to discriminate against interstate commerce included (1) the complete lack of evidence that any consumers in North Carolina had ever been confused or deceived by multiple apple grading standards; (2) the fact that customers do not normally buy apples in the crates on which grades are stamped; and (3) the fact that the local North Carolina apple industry would clearly benefit from the Washington apple industry's increased costs of selling in North Carolina and its inability to use its highly reputed grading system. The law was found unconstitutional.

When a court concludes that a state has intentionally discriminated against interstate commerce, the state action is almost always void. It would be a rare case indeed in which a state could prove a sufficiently important state interest to justify such discrimination, because the interest could almost always be promoted by less restrictive means that do not discriminate in this way.

Most questions about state power over commerce involve attempts by a state to regulate the activities of business firms. However, if the state government itself actually becomes a *participant* in the market, the state has much more latitude. In fact, the Supreme Court has held that the general rule prohibiting discrimination against interstate commerce does not apply when a state or local government is a seller or buyer. For example, when a state or a city makes contracts for the purchase of goods or services, it may grant preferences to in-state companies or individuals. The same exception applies when the state is a seller. For example, in *Reeves, Inc. v. Stake,* 447 U.S. 429 (1980), the state of South Dakota owned a large cement factory, and during times of short supply state law required that a preference be given to in-state buyers over those from outside the state. The Supreme Court upheld the state's discriminatory policy.

Unduly Burdening Interstate Commerce:

Another restriction on the power of the states to regulate commercial activities is that they may not unduly burden the free flow of interstate or international commerce. The concept we just discussed, discrimination against interstate commerce, involves a question of intent, whereas the concept of unduly burdening involves a question of impact. The two concepts are closely related, often both being raised by a challenger in the same case. Some of the same information will often be relevant to both types of claims. Despite their close relationship, however, the two concepts provide separate grounds for invalidating a state regulatory measure.

If a state law challenged on this basis is shown to hinder the free flow of interstate commerce in some way, the court uses a balancing analysis to determine whether the law is constitutional. The analysis is very similar to the balancing of competing interests that takes place throughout constitutional law and, indeed, throughout the law generally. To determine whether there is an undue burdening of interstate commerce, the court balances the local interest being furthered by the state law against the degree of burden it places on interstate commerce. In general, the stronger the state interest, the greater will be the burden that can be tolerated under the Constitution. Purely economic interests of a state are certainly legitimate, but such interests typically do not weigh as heavily as a state's interest in protecting the safety and health of its citizens or protecting them against fraudulent or other wrongful practices. In addition, some economic interests are stronger than others; thus, a state law aimed at preventing the spread of a citrus fruit disease that could wipe out a major industry in the state could permissibly burden interstate commerce to a greater extent than one aimed at protecting an economic interest of less magnitude.

The *Hunt* case discussed in the previous section also illustrates the undue burdening concept. There, the local interest did not weigh very heavily in the balancing process because there was no evidence to indicate that consumers actually had been deceived or confused by multiple apple grading standards, and the regulation would not have solved such a problem if there had been one. On the other side, the evidence demonstrated that the North Carolina law would impose substantial economic inefficiency on the selling of Washington apples in North Carolina. The Washington apple industry had developed substantial economies of scale in packaging, storing, and shipping its apples, and compliance with the North Carolina law would destroy much of these scale economies. In the *Hunt* case, the Supreme Court ultimately struck down the statute because it unduly burdened interstate commerce. Even though there was ample evidence to infer intentional discrimination against interstate commerce, the Court said that it was not necessary to make a ruling on that separate contention.

Another example is *Kassell v. Consolidated Freightways Corp.*, 450 U.S. 662 (1981), which involved an Iowa law that prohibited the use of 65-foot double-trailer trucks on its highways, while allowing 55-foot single trailers and 60-foot double trailers. States around Iowa all allowed 65-foot double trailers, but Iowa claimed that the law was a safety measure. However, statistics showed no relationship between truck length and accident rates. Instead, studies showed a strong positive correlation between mileage driven and truck accident rates. Thus, the evidence of a legitimate state interest was quite weak; in fact, the law actually worked against safety interests by requiring use of smaller trucks that would have to travel more total miles to deliver the same amount of cargo. However, interstate commerce was substantially burdened because trucks with the more efficient 65-foot double trailers either had to go around the state or unload onto smaller trucks when reaching the Iowa border. The law was found unconstitutional.[4]

Finally, many of the cases involving the undue burdening concept have challenged various state and local taxes on property items used in interstate commerce. Examples include state road use taxes on trucks used in interstate transportation, and state or local property taxes on items such as railroad cars, airplanes, barges on inland waterways, and shipping containers. As we saw in the *Xerox* case, a local property tax was found unconstitutional because it was preempted by the federal law setting up a system of customs

---

[4] After the *Kassel* case, Congress stepped in to provide a degree of national uniformity to the regulation of truck-trailer lengths on interstate highways and on other "primary" highways built or maintained with any federal funds. The congressional enactment, which applies to about 42,000 miles of interstate highways and 140,000 miles of other highways, requires states to permit double-trailer rigs with each trailer having a length up to 28 feet, an approximate total rig length of 65 feet. The law also required states to permit such rigs to have a width up to 102 inches, with exceptions for particular highways specifically found to be too narrow for rigs of such width to operate safely.

bonded warehouses. Usually, however, there is no federal regulatory scheme that preempts state or local taxes on the instrumentalities of interstate commerce. In most cases, state and local government entities do have the right to tax such items located or used within their jurisdiction. It usually is only fair that the owners should pay some type of tax to contribute to the cost of police and fire protection and other services they receive within the taxing jurisdiction.

Such a tax must be carefully designed, however, to avoid being stricken down by the courts. First, it is obvious that the tax must not discriminate against interstate commerce by being higher for items used in interstate commerce than for items used only within the state. Assuming that the tax is nondiscriminatory, the Supreme Court has held that such a tax must meet three additional requirements to avoid being invalid under the undue burdening theory. The tax (1) can only be applied to property or activities that have a substantial "nexus" (i.e., connection) with the taxing jurisdiction; (2) must be reasonably related to the services provided by the taxing jurisdiction; and (3) must be "apportioned" so that the item is not subjected to multiple taxation in the various places in which it is used or located. This last condition, the requirement of "apportionment," has been an issue in a great many cases. It basically requires a formula that bases the tax on only the degree of connection the item has with the particular taxing jurisdiction. For example, a state might apportion a property tax on railroad cars by taxing only a fraction of the value of the cars that corresponds to the average fraction of a tax year the cars are located in the state.

Regarding taxation, in *Japan Line, Ltd. v. County of Los Angeles,* 441 U.S. 434 (1979), the Supreme Court held that a local property tax could not be levied on an item owned by a *foreign* company or individual and used exclusively in foreign commerce. The items in question were modular shipping containers owned by a Japanese corporation. The non-discriminatory property tax imposed by Los Angeles County was based on only the time the containers spent in that county and would have been valid if the containers were used in interstate rather than international commerce. For two reasons, however, the Supreme Court concluded that the tax unduly burdened international commerce and was thus unconstitutional. First, in the case of property owned by a foreign citizen, U.S courts have no power to require the foreign jurisdiction to apportion its own taxation of the item; consequently, permitting a state or local property tax in this country would create a risk of subjecting the property to taxation on more than its total value. Second, such a tax might interfere with the ability of the United States to "speak with one voice" in matters of international trade.

OTHER STATE LIMITATIONS

At this point, two other constitutional limitations on the discretion of states are appropriately mentioned—the full faith and credit clause, and the contract clause.

Article IV, section 1 of the Constitution provides in part that "full faith and credit shall be given in each State to the public acts, records, and judicial

HUMOR AND THE LAW

Our Constitution is a wonderful document that grants Americans as much freedom as is enjoyed by anyone in the entire world. However, inevitably persons will attempt to invoke the Constitution for purposes our Founding Fathers could never have attempted. For example, one court was constrained to rule (though not in the Pee Wee Herman case):

> [T]o accede to plaintiffs' argument would be tantamount to finding that the patrons have some kind of right to masturbate themselves and others in the seclusion of these booths. This is not a "right" which is protected by the first amendment. While one may be entitled to engage in this activity in the privacy of one's home, there is no such entitlement to do so in a public place. [As another court recently stated]: "We decline to hold that the 'right' to unobserved masturbation in a public theater is 'fundamental' or 'implicit' in the concept of ordered liberty."

Broadway Books, Inc. v. Roberts, 642 F. Supp. 486 (E.D.Tenn. 1986).

Other courts have held that police officers had no constitutionally protected right to engage in sexual relations with prostitutes while on duty (*Fugate v. Phoenix Civil Service Board*, 791 F.2d 737 (9th Cir. 1986)), and that the Constitution does not protect the "right to kick and rock a video to retrieve fifty cents." (*Friedman v. Village of Skokie*, 763 F.2d 236 (7th Cir. 1985)).

On the other hand, some of us can take comfort in another court's ruling that "it is an essential part of our national heritage that an irresponsible slob can stand on a street corner and, with impunity, heap invective on all parties in public office." *Desert Sun Publishing Co. v. Superior Court*, 158 Cal.Rptr. 519 (Cal.App. 1979).

---

proceedings of every other State." The import of the **full faith and credit clause** is quite clear: The courts of one state must recognize court judgments and other public actions of its sister states. Thus a business firm that obtains a valid judgment against a debtor in one state may enforce that judgment in the courts of any other state in which that debtor's property may be located. The requirement is, however, subject to two important limitations. First, if the court that entered the judgment originally did not have jurisdiction, the courts of other states are not obligated to (and will not) recognize the judgment. Second, if the judgment violates the public policy of the state where enforcement is sought, the courts of that state will not enforce it. For example, if a court in State A awards damages for breach of a loan contract that included a rate of interest that was valid in State A and the creditor then tries to enforce the judgment against the debtor's property in State B, where that interest rate is higher than allowed by State B's law, the courts of State B will refuse to enforce the judgment on public policy grounds.

Our Constitution's full faith and credit clause obviously has no applicability to the enforcement of American state or federal court judgments in other nations or to the enforcement in this country of court judgments from other nations. Similar principles are generally applied, however. Under customary international law, the doctrine of "comity" generally calls for the enforcement of another nation's court judgments, subject to the two exceptions for lack of jurisdiction and public policy. This doctrine and its exceptions have also been embodied in a number of bilateral and multilateral treaties to which the United States is a party.

Article I, section 10 of the Constitution provides that "no State shall ... pass any ... Law impairing the Obligation of Contracts...." The **contract clause** applies only to the states and not to the federal government and is intended to prevent states from changing the terms of *existing* contracts by passage of subsequent legislation. When a state passes a statute that might affect contractual obligations, it normally includes a "grandfather clause" specifying that the new law applies only to transactions entered into after the effectie date of the law. This not only ensures compliance with the contract clause, but also makes the law fairer. However, even if a state law docs have an effect on preexisting contractual rights and obligations, it does not violate the contract clause if the law promotes an important state government interest and interferes with contracts only to an extent that is reasonably necessary to further the state interest.

PROTECTING BASIC RIGHTS

The Constitution contains numerous provisions aimed at protecting individuals and businesses by limiting the powers of the federal and state governments to regulate our affairs. Many of our basic rights are guaranteed in the Bill of Rights—the first ten amendments to the Constitution. Other protective provisions are found in the body of the original Constitution itself and in subsequent amendments.

Before we look at several of the most important rights-protecting provisions of the Constitution, two preliminary observations are necessary. First, by its express terms, the Bill of Rights applies only to the *federal* government and not to state or local governments. Nothing in the Constitution specifically prohibits the states from infringing freedom of speech, for example. However, the U.S. Supreme Court has used the Fourteenth Amendment's due process clause as a vehicle for applying almost everything in the Bill of

Rights to state and local governments. The Fourteenth Amendment, which was passed in 1868 shortly after the Civil War, includes several provisions that expressly limit the powers of the states. As we will see later, one of these provisions—the due process clause—directly guarantees certain important rights. In addition, under the **doctrine of incorporation,** the Supreme Court has concluded that the concept of due process includes many other basic rights. Thus, the Fourteenth Amendment's due process clause implicitly incorporates almost all the protections in the Bill of Rights and applies them to state and local governments. Among the many guarantees applied to the states in this way are freedom of speech, freedom of the press, freedom of religion, right to an attorney, privilege against self-incrimination in criminal cases, and freedom from unreasonable searches and seizures.[5] Although the doctrine of incorporation has always been very controversial among constitutional scholars, it is now so firmly embedded in our law as to be beyond question.

Second, it must be emphasized that the protective provisions of the Constitution are limitations on *government;* thus, these provisions only apply to governmental actions and not to actions by individuals or business firms. Thus, the Constitution's free speech and assembly provisions do not prevent a private employer from restricting the speech of its employees or a private university from banning a political rally on its campus. However, Constitutional protections apply when a governmental body either compels the private action or substantially participates in it or when governmental power is used to enforce the private action against others. For example, there is a violation of the equal protection clause of the fourteenth Amendment when a private attorney in a criminal or civil case intentionally excludes potential jurors on the basis of race. The reason for the Constitution's applicability is that jury selection is such an integral part of a governmental process that the government is essentially a co-participant with the private attorney. Another example is found in the rule that a court—an arm of the government—will not enforce a private deed restriction that excludes those of a particular race from purchasing property in a subdivision on the basis of their race; to do so would violate the equal protection clause. However, the mere fact that a particular business or industry is subject to substantial government regulation does not turn the actions of the regulated business firms into governmental actions. For example, public utilities such as telephone and electric companies are very closely regulated by the states, but their actions are not subject to the Constitution unless the government in a particular situa-

---

[5] The only two important guarantees in the Bill of Rights that the Supreme Court has held inapplicable to the states are (1) the right to jury trial in *civil* cases and (2) the requirement that a person be indicted by a grand jury before being tried for a criminal offense. The states are free to devise their own rules regarding these two matters; in fact, state constitutional and statutory provisions guarantee these rights in most circumstances.

tion has actually compelled, substantially participated in, or enforced those actions.

Even though the Constitution does not prohibit private actions, a federal or state statute might. For example, racial discrimination by a private employer or restaurant does not violate the equal protection clause, but it does violate a federal statute—the Civil Rights Act of 1964. We will now turn to a discussion of several important Constitutional guarantees.

PRIVILEGES AND IMMUNITIES

Article IV, section 2 of the Constitution states, in part, that "the citizens of each State shall be entitled to all privileges and immunities of the several states." The basic aim of the **privileges and immunities clause** is to prohibit states from discriminating against residents of other states merely because of their residency. Thus a state cannot prohibit travel by nonresidents within its borders, nor can it deny nonresident plaintiffs access to its court system. The privileges and immunities clause is yet another provision of the Constitution intended to prevent states from erecting barriers around their borders. The fundamental individual right (and also the national interest) that the clause protects from state infringement is that of moving freely among the states without being unreasonably disadvantaged because of the state of residency.

Like other constitutional guarantees, the privileges and immunities clause is not an absolute limitation on governmental power. A state law may treat residents of other states differently if the law protects a legitimate "local" (state) interest and does not discriminate more than is necessary. For example, because state universities are substantially assisted by the taxes that state residents pay, the charging of higher tuition for nonresident students does not violate the privileges and immunities clause. The balancing of a state's local interest against the national interest in individual freedom of travel is a familiar process; the form of the analysis closely resembles the process of resolving claims that state laws unduly burden interstate commerce.

The privileges and immunities clause is one of the few constitutional protections that applies only to individuals and not to corporations. Even though the privileges and immunities clause does not apply to corporations, however, a state's discriminatory treatment of companies incorporated in other states will often have a negative impact on interstate commerce and thus is likely to violate the commerce clause unless it furthers a legitimate state interest and is reasonably limited so as to discriminate no more than necessary.

The following case involves a privileges and immunities clause challenge to a state law in Alaska, in which the Supreme Court balanced the local interest against the individual and national interest, paying careful attention to whether the law was narrowly tailored to fit the state's problem.

Hicklin v. Orbeck

U.S. Supreme Court
437 U.S. 518 (1978)

The Alaska legislature passed a statute in 1972 (known as "Alaska Hire") for the stated purpose of reducing unemployment within the state. The key provision of the statute required all employers engaged in specified lines of work to hire qualified Alaska residents in preference to nonresidents. The types of work related to construction of the Trans-Alaska pipeline after discovery of the huge North Slope oil field. To implement the law, persons who had resided in the state for a minimum of one year were furnished "resident cards" as proof of their preferred status.

Hicklin and others, the plaintiffs, were nonresidents who had worked on the Trans-Alaska pipeline for short periods until late 1975, when the law was first enforced. In 1976, when the plaintiffs were refused employment on the pipeline, they brought this action against Orbeck, the state official charged with enforcing Alaska Hire, contending that the law violated the privileges and immunities clause. The Alaska Supreme Court, by a 3–2 vote, upheld the law, and the U.S. Supreme Court granted the plaintiff's request for review.

Brennan, Justice:

...The Privileges and Immunities Clause... establishes a norm of comity that is to prevail among the States with respect to their treatment of each other's residents.... Appellants' appeal to the protection of this Clause is strongly supported by this Court's decisions holding violative of the Clause state discrimination against nonresidents seeking to ply their trade, practice their occupation, or pursue a common calling within the State. For example, in [an early case this Court]... recognized that a resident of one State is constitutionally entitled to travel to another State for purposes of employment free from discriminatory restrictions in favor of state residents imposed by the other State.

Again, [in] *Toomer v. Witsell*, 334 U.S. 385 (1948), the leading exposition of the limitations the Clause places on a State's power to bias employment opportunities in favor of its own residents, [this Court] invalidated a South Carolina statute that required nonresidents to pay a fee 100 times greater than that paid by residents for a license to shrimp commercially in the three-mile maritime belt off the coast of that state. The Court reasoned that although the Privileges and Immunities Clause "does not preclude disparity of treatment in the many situations where there are perfectly valid independent reasons for it, it does bar discrimination against citizens of other States where there is no substantial reason for the discrimination beyond the mere fact that they are citizens of other States." A "substantial reason for the discrimination" would not exist, the Court explained, "unless there is something to indicate that noncitizens constitute a peculiar source of the evil at which the statute is aimed."...

Even assuming that a State may validly attempt to alleviate its unemployment problem by requiring private employers within the State to discriminate against nonresidents — an assumption made at least dubious [by prior cases] — it is clear under the *Toomer* analysis that Alaska Hire's discrimination against non-residents cannot withstand scrutiny under the Privileges and Immunities Clause. For although the Statute may not violate the Clause if the State shows [in the words of *Toomer*] "something to indicate that noncitizens constitute a peculiar source of evil," *certainly no showing was made on this record that nonresidents were a peculiar source of the evil [that] Alaska Hire was enacted to remedy, namely, Alaska's uniquely high unemployment.* [Emphasis added.] What evidence the record does contain indicates that the major cause of Alaska's high unemployment was not the influx of nonresidents seeking employment, but rather the fact that a substantial number of Alaska's jobless residents—especially the unemployed Eskimo and Indian residents—were unable to secure employment either because of their lack of education and job training or because of their geographical remoteness from job opportunities. The employment of nonresidents threatened to deny jobs to Alaska residents only to the extent that jobs for which untrained residents were being prepared might be filled by nonresidents before the residents' training was completed.

Moreover, even if the State's showing is accepted as sufficient to indicate that nonresidents were "a peculiar source of evil," *Toomer* compels the conclusion

CONTINUED

that Alaska Hire nevertheless fails to pass constitutional muster, [because] the discrimination the Act works against nonresidents does not bear a substantial relationship to the particular "evil" they are said to present. Alaska Hire simply grants all Alaskans, regardless of their employment status, education, or training, a flat employment preference for all jobs covered by the Act. A highly skilled and educated resident who has never been unemployed is entitled to precisely the same preferential treatment as the unskilled, habitually unemployed Arctic Eskimo enrolled in a job-training program. If Alaska is to attempt to ease its unemployment problem by forcing employers within the State to discriminate against nonresidents—again, a policy which [itself] may present serious constitutional questions—the means by which it does so must be more closely tailored to aid the unemployed the Act is intended to benefit. Even if a statute granting an employment preference to unemployed residents or to residents enrolled in job-training programs might be permissible, Alaska Hire's across-the-board grant of a job preference to all Alaskan residents clearly is not. . . . [For these reasons,] Alaska Hire cannot withstand constitutional scrutiny.

Judgment reversed.

FREEDOM OF RELIGION

The First Amendment contains two clauses protecting freedom of religion. It provides that "Congress shall make no law [1] respecting an establishment of religion, or [2] prohibiting the free exercise thereof." Although the establishment and free exercise clauses overlap (and sometimes even conflict), they clearly create two separate guarantees. Both guarantees provide that the government's role is to be one of "benevolent neutrality," neither advancing nor inhibiting religion.

Establishment Clause

A large part of the metaphoric "wall" between church and state arises from the **establishment clause,** which prohibits the government from establishing a state religion and, according to the Supreme Court, from financially supporting religion, becoming actively involved in religion, or favoring one religion over another.

The most controversial manifestation of the Supreme Court's view of the establishment clause is probably the "school prayer" case, *Engel v. Vitale,* 370 U.S. 421 (1962). The New York State Board of Regents had written a nondenominational prayer to be recited by students in school on a voluntary basis. The Supreme Court found an establishment clause violation, saying, in part, that "the constitutional prohibition against laws respecting an establishment of a religion must at least mean that in this country it is no part of the business of government to compose official prayers for any group of the American people to recite as a part of a religious program carried on by any government."

An attempt to circumvent *Engel v. Vitale* by institution of a "moment of silence" in the public schools "for meditation or voluntary prayer" was declared unconstitutional in the more recent case, *Wallace v. Jaffree,* 472 U.S. 38

(1985). The legislative history of the law in question made it clear that its primary purpose was to promote religion.

When a state or federal law is challenged as violative of the establishment clause, it will be evaluated by a three-pronged test. First, the court will ask whether the law has a secular (nonreligious) purpose. If there is no such purpose, the law is invalid. Even if the law has a secular purpose, the court will ask, second, whether its *primary* purpose is to advance or inhibit religion. If the answer is in the affirmative, the law is unconstitutional. If the answer is in the negative, the court will ask, third, whether the law fosters excessive government entanglement with religion. Such entanglement might include government evaluation of religious practices, extensive government involvement in church finances and operations, or government attempts to classify what is religious and what is not. Presence of such entanglement obviously indicates in establishment clause violation.

A recent establishment clause case affecting business is *Estate of Thornton v. Caldor, Inc.*, 472 U.S. 703 (1985), which involved a Connecticut statute guaranteeing every employee who "states that a particular day of the week is observed as his Sabbath," the right not to work on his or her chosen day. Because the law gave an absolute preference to the worker's religious practice, no matter how severe the hardship to the employer, the Court held that its primary purpose was to advance religion. Federal law validly requires that employers subject to Title VII, discussed in our later chapter on employment law, make "reasonable accommodations" for the religious practices of employees. But an absolute preference is invalid.

Finally, although the trend across the country is for states to repeal so-called **blue laws**—statutes and ordinances that limit or prohibit the carrying on of specified business activities on Sunday—such laws are generally upheld in the courts on the ground that the primary purpose of such statutes is the furtherance of legitimate social or economic ends, which affect religious beliefs and practices only incidentally.

Free Exercise Clause

The general thrust of this clause is to guarantee to all persons the right of religious belief and the freedom to practice their beliefs without governmental interference. The government may not single out any particular religion for discrimination. To claim the protection of the free exercise clause, a plaintiff must normally prove that he or she is a sincere adherent of an established religion and that a fundamental tenet of that religion is at stake in the case. These requirements weed out spurious, insincere, and trivial claims.

Under the free exercise clause, plaintiffs, frequently belonging to religious minorities, have paved the way for the religious freedoms we all enjoy. For example, in *West Virginia State Board of Education v. Barnette*, 319 U.S. 624 (1943), the Supreme Court held that a board of education requirement that students salute the flag and say the pledge of allegiance was unconstitutional as applied to the plaintiff, a member of the Jehovah's Witnesses. The court said: "If there is any fixed star in our constitutional constellation, it is that no official, high or petty, can prescribe what shall be orthodox in politics, nationalism, religion, or other matters of opinion, or force citizens to confess by word or act their faith therein. If there are any circumstances which permit an exception, they do not now occur to us."

To overcome the very important interest in free exercise of religious beliefs, the government must demonstrate that an unusually important interest is at stake (denominated in various cases "compelling," "of the highest order," or "overriding") and that granting an exemption to the plaintiff will do substantial harm to that interest. The government has succeeded in cases requiring vaccinations for children against their parents' religious objections in furtherance of public health, in cases requiring medical treatment for children over their parents' objections when such treatment was necessary to save the child's life, and in cases banning the handling of poisonous snakes in religious services.

Recently, the Supreme Court reduced the government's burden where incidental effects of government programs interfere with religious practices but do not coerce individuals to act contrary to their religious beliefs. In such cases, the government need not show a "compelling justification" to prevail. Thus, in *Oregon v. Smith,* 494 U.S. 872 (1990), the Supreme Court held that a state's interest in fighting drugs validated its decision to deny unemployment compensation on grounds of "misconduct" to two men who had been fired by a private employer because they ingested peyote, a hallucinogenic drug, for sacramental purposes at a ceremony of their native American church. The balancing test approach was held inapplicable to an across-the-board criminal prohibition on a particular form of conduct.

FREEDOM OF SPEECH

No right of Americans receives greater protection than freedom of speech. As with most other constitutional guarantees, the First Amendment's **free speech clause** has been expanded to limit not only the actions of the federal government but also the actions of state and local governments. Unlike citizens in so many other countries, we may freely criticize public officials and the laws of our government.

All methods of expression are within the scope of the free speech clause, including oral and written communications, and those recorded on tape, film, and so on. Moreover, *symbolic expression* is also protected. In other words, expression by nonverbal means such as wearing black arm bands or picketing is protected from government suppression. The giving of money to political candidates, charitable organizations, or various other entities is even treated as a form of protected expression. However, a government limitation of symbolic expression is somewhat more likely to be upheld than a limitation on verbal expression, simply because the conduct that constitutes symbolic expression is somewhat more likely to interfere substantially with some important public interest. If symbolic expression does not substantially interfere with an important public interest, however, it is fully protected.

The right of association is also viewed as a component of free speech. The groups and organizations we join often provide us with one of our most effective means of expressing our beliefs and opinions. Thus, a government limitation on our ability to associate with groups of our choice is a limitation on free speech.

Not only does free speech include the right to express oneself, but it also includes the right to avoid expressing opinions that we do not agree with. For example, in *Pacific Gas & Electric Co. v. Public Utilities Commission of California,* 475 U.S. 1 (1986), the Supreme Court overturned on free speech grounds an order of the California utility regulatory agency that had required an investor-owned utility to include in its billing envelopes a leaflet expressing the views of a consumer group with which the utility disagreed. The Court held that the agency's order unconstitutionally burdened the utility's freedom not to speak, a right that is protected because all speech inherently involves choices of what to say and what to leave unsaid.

Corporate Speech

In addition to protecting the speech of individuals, the First Amendment has been interpreted to also protect the expressions of corporations. This proposition was evident in the above reference to the *Pacific Gas & Electric* case. Corporate speech, like individual speech, has informational value—it contributes to the public debate on important issues. Thus, in *First National Bank of Boston v. Bellotti,* 435 U.S. 765 (1978), the Supreme Court struck down a state statute that prohibited expenditures by business corporations for the purpose of influencing the vote on state referendum proposals, unless a particular proposal "materially affected" the business or property of the corporation. The law was passed to silence the voice of corporations in the public debate over an upcoming referendum concerning a personal income tax. Because the referendum did not deal with a corporate income tax, it did not materially affect the business or property of corporations; thus the statute prohibited corporations from issuing press releases, publishing advocacy advertisements, or otherwise speaking out on the personal income tax issue. The First National Bank of Boston wished to speak out because it felt that a personal income tax would harm the overall economic climate of the state. In overturning the law, the Supreme Court noted that "the inherent worth of the speech in terms of its capacity for informing the public does not depend upon the identity of its source, whether corporation, association, union, or individual."

Unprotected Speech

Although almost all expression is constitutionally protected, a few categories are not. If particular expression is unprotected, this simply means that the government may limit or prohibit it without violating the First Amendment.

The first category of unprotected speech is *obscenity*. A local, state, or federal law that punishes the dissemination of obscene material is constitutional if the particular material to which the law is applied in a given case meets the Supreme Court's definition of obscenity. In *Miller v. California*, 413 U.S. 15 (1973), the Supreme Court held that, for a book, movie, or other material to be considered obscene, a court must determine that (1) "the average person, applying contemporary community standards" would find that the work, taken as a whole, appeals to the prurient interest; (2) the work depicts or describes, in a patently offensive way, sexual conduct specifically defined by the applicable law; and (3) the work, taken as a whole, lacks serious literary, artistic, political, or scientific value. Under today's community standards in most places, it is very difficult if not impossible to prove that most pornographic material is obsence. When pornography involves children or when children are exposed to such material, however, there is a much higher probability that it will be within the definition of obscenity.

A second category of unprotected speech is *defamation*. Thus it is constitutionally permissible for state tort or criminal laws to be applied to libel or slander—false statements that defame a person's character.

The third category of unprotected speech is a rather amorphous one commonly referred to as *fighting words:* threats, epithets, profanity, false alarms, and the like, which by their nature are likely to lead to violence. Their minimal social value is viewed as being outweighed by the danger to civilized society. This unprotected category of speech is narrowly construed, however; to be outside the scope of constitutional protection, fighting words must contain no significant informational content, must be apparently calculated to lead to violence, and must be made under circumstances in which actual violence is a very real danger.

Unpopular Views

The fact that particular speech is unpopular, or even highly offensive to many people, does not take it out of the zone of constitutional protection. As the Supreme Court said in *Cox v. Louisiana,* 379 U.S. 536 (1965), "Mere expression of unpopular views cannot be held to be a breach of peace." In fact, sometimes the government has an obligation to provide protection for those who express unpopular positions.

Many examples of government attempts to suppress unpopular views have been found unconstitutional. For instance, speech that is critical of the government, even to the point of being very disrespectful or "unpatriotic," is normally protected. In *Texas v. Johnson,* 491 U.S. 397 (1989), the Supreme Court struck down a state law making it a criminal act to "desecrate" the American flag. The Court invalidated the conviction of a communist protestor who had burned the flag at a Republican National Convention, saying: "If there is a bedrock principle underlying the First Amendment, it is that the Government may not prohibit the expression of an idea simply because society finds the idea itself offensive or disagreeable." Indeed, in *Brandenburg v. Ohio,* 395 U.S. 444 (1969), the Supreme Court held that even speech calling for the overthrow of the government is protected by the First Amendment unless it is "directed to inciting or producing *imminent* lawless action and is *likely* to incite or produce such action." This is really just another example of the narrowness of the "fighting words" exception. Among other reasons, providing constitutional protection for the expression of views that are unpopular, distasteful, or offensive to the majority helps to guarantee that the public debate on important issues will be as fully informed and undistorted as possible. The greater number of varied ideas (even bad ones) people are exposed to, the better equipped they will be to recognize worthy ideas.

Scope of Protection

Assuming that speech is protected, a court faced with a First Amendment issue must engage in further analysis to determine the scope of protection to which the expression is entitled under the circumstances. Although powerful, the right of free expression is not absolute and occasionally must yield in limited ways to other public interests.

Commercial Speech: A court must determine whether speech is commercial or noncommercial. **Commercial speech** is intended primarily to propose a commercial transaction. Advertising is the most obvious form of commercial speech. Until the mid-1970s, the general assumption was that commercial expression was not protected. However, the Supreme Court held that it is indeed protected in *Virginia Board of Pharmacy v. Virginia Citizens Consumers Council*, 425 U.S. 748 (1976); in that case, the Court struck down a state law that banned the advertising of prices for prescription drugs. A state law prohibiting advertising by lawyers was invalidated in *Bates v. Arizona State Bar*, 433 U.S. 350 (1977). A city ordinance forbidding the posting of "for sale" signs on real estate was found to violate free speech in *Linmark Associates v. Township of Willingboro*, 431 U.S. 85 (1977), despite the fact that the city had the laudable goal of preventing "white flight" from racially integrated neighborhoods.

According to the Supreme Court, commercial speech is protectable primarily because of its informational value. Prescription drug consumers in the *Virginia Pharmacy* case could not learn, before the advertising ban was struck down, that price variations of up to 600 percent existed among competing pharmacies.

Commercial speech is only protected if it relates to a lawful activity and if it is not misleading. Thus, commercial speech that either relates to an unlawful activity or that is misleading could be listed as another category of unprotected speech. Although most commercial speech is protected by the First Amendment, it receives a lower level of protection than noncommercial speech. A restriction on commercial speech will be valid if the government can show that it is necessary to further a significant governmental interest and that the restriction is reasonably related to that interest. The following case is an important one in which the Supreme Court clarified this legal standard for restrictions on commercial speech.

BOARD OF TRUSTEES OF THE STATE UNIVERSITY OF NEW YORK v. FOX

U.S. SUPREME COURT, 492, U.S. 469 (1989)

The State University of New York (SUNY) adopted a rule (66-156) for its dormitories that banned private commercial enterprises except to provide food, legal beverages, books, vending, linen supply, laundry, and a few other specified services. American Future Systems, Inc. (AFS), sells housewares such as china and crystal to college students by demonstrating and offering products for sale to groups of ten or more prospective buyers at gatherings assembled and hosted by one of the buyers (for which the host or hostess receives some award). Fox, a student at SUNY's Cortland campus, was hosting one of these "Tupperware-type parties" when campus police asked the AFS representative to leave and arrested her when she refused to do so. Fox and other students sued, claiming that the rule violated the First Amendment. The trial court upheld the rule. The court of appeals reversed, noting that rule 66-156 was not the least restrictive means of advancing the state's interests. The Supreme Court granted certiorari and addressed the commercial speech issue in that portion of the opinion reproduced below.

SCALIA, JUSTICE:

... We have described our mode of analyzing the lawfulness of restrictions on commercial speech as follows:

At the outset, we must determine whether the expression is protected by the First Amendment. For commercial speech to come within that provision, it at least must concern lawful activity and not be misleading. Next, we ask whether the asserted governmental interest is substantial. If both inquiries yield positive answers, we must determine whether the regulation directly advances the governmental interest asserted, and whether it is not more extensive than is necessary to serve that interest. Central Hudson Gas & Electric Corp. v. Public Service Comm'n of New York, 447 U.S. 557, 566 (1980).

The Court of Appeals held, and the parties agree, that the speech here proposes a lawful transaction, is not misleading, and is therefore entitled to First Amendment protection. The Court of Appeals also held, and we agree, that the governmental interests asserted in support of the Resolution are substantial: promoting an educational rather than a commercial atmosphere on SUNY's campuses, promoting safety and security, preventing commercial exploitation of students, and preserving residential tranquility. The Court of Appeals did not decide, however, whether Resolution 66-156 directly advances these interests, and whether the regulation it imposes is more extensive than is necessary for that purpose. As noted earlier, it remanded to the District Court for those determinations. We think that remand was correct, since further factual findings had to be made. It is the terms of the remand, however, that are the major issue here— specifically, those pertaining to the last element of the *Central Hudson* analysis. The Court of Appeals in effect instructed the District Court that it could find the Resolution to be "not more extensive than is necessary" only if it is the "least restrictive measure" that could effectively protect the State's interests.

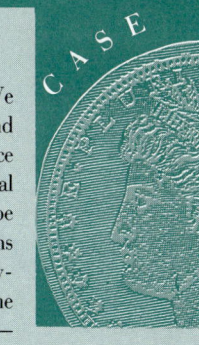

Our cases have repeatedly stated that government restrictions upon commercial speech may be no more broad or no more expansive than "necessary" to serve its substantial interests. Our jurisprudence has emphasized that "commercial speech [enjoys] a limited measure of protection, commensurate with its subordinate position in the scale of First Amendment values," and is subject to "modes of regulation that might be impermissible in the realm of noncommercial expression." The ample scope of regulatory authority suggested by such statements would be illusory if it were subject to a least-restrictive-means requirement, which imposes a heavy burden on the State....

None of our cases invalidating the regulation of commercial speech involved a provision that went only marginally beyond what would adequately have served the governmental interest. To the contrary, almost all of the restrictions disallowed under *Central Hudson's*

CONTINUED

fourth prong have been substantially excessive, disregarding "far less restrictive and more precise means." ...

On the other hand, our decisions *upholding* the regulation of commercial speech cannot be reconciled with a requirement of least restrictive means. In *Posadas*, for example, where we sustained Puerto Rico's blanket ban on promotional advertising of casino gambling to Puerto Rican residents, we did not first satisfy ourselves that the governmental goal of deterring casino gambling could not adequately have been served (as the appellant contended) "not by suppressing commercial speech that might *encourage* such gambling, but by promulgating additional speech designed to *discourage it.*" Rather, we said that it was "up to the legislature to decide" that point, so long as its judgment was reasonable. Similarly, in *Metromedia, Inc. v. San Diego*, 453 U.S., at 513, where we upheld San Diego's complete ban of offsite billboard advertising, we did not inquire whether *any* less restrictive measure (for example, controlling the size and appearance of the signs) would suffice to meet the City's concerns for traffic safety and esthetics. It was enough to conclude that the ban was "perhaps the only effective approach." ...

What our decisions require is a "fit" between the legislature's ends and the means chosen to accomplish those ends," a fit that is not necessarily perfect, but reasonable; that represents not necessarily the single best disposition but one whose scope is "in proportion to the interest served"; that employs not necessarily the least restrictive means but, as we have put it in the other contexts discussed above, a means narrowly tailored to achieve the desired objective. Within those bounds we leave it to governmental decisionmakers to judge what manner of regulation may best be employed.

We reject the contention that the test we have described is overly permissive. Here we require the government goal to be substantial, and the cost to be carefully calculated. Moreover, since the State bears the burden of justifying its restrictions, it must affirmatively establish the reasonable fit we require. By declining to impose, in addition, a least-restrictive-means requirement, we take account of the difficulty of establishing wth precision the point at which restrictions become more extensive than their objective requires, and provide the legislative and executive branches needed leeway in a field (commercial speech) "traditionally subject to governmental regulation." Far from eroding the essential protections of the First Amendment, we think this disposition strengthens them. To require a parity of constitutional protection for commercial and noncommercial speech alike could invite dilution, simply by a leveling process, of the force of the Amendment's guarantee with respect to the latter kind of speech.

[Reversed.]

Noncommercial Speech: If a court determines that particular expression is noncommercial in nature, the degree of constitutional protection is considerably greater than it is for commercial speech. Often the courts use the term *political speech* to refer to noncommercial expression. It should be understood that when the term *political speech* is used, it includes virtually all noncommercial speech—the term is not limited to discussion of political issues.

When noncommercial speech is at issue, a court first must determine whether the restriction merely limits the *time, place, or manner* of expression. (Here, *manner* essentially means *method.*) A governmental body is entitled to place reasonable limits on the time, place, or manner of speech. A time, place, or manner restriction is not based on the content of the expression. For such a restriction to be valid, the government must show that it is necessary to further a significant governmental interest and that the restriction is reasonably related to that interest. Thus, a time, place, or manner restriction on noncommercial speech must meet the same requirements as a restriction on commercial speech. In both cases, the government's burden of justifying the limitation is not extremely difficult. There are countless examples of valid time, place, or manner restrictions. For example, even though I may have a constitutional right to express any view on virtually any subject, a city government has the power to forbid me from expressing my views in the middle of a downtown intersection during rush hour or by means of a sound truck in a residential neighborhood at 3:00 a.m.

Although it may be obvious that a particular government restriction relates only to the time, place, or manner of expression and not to the content of that expression, sometimes the distinction can be difficult. Suppose, for example, that a statute passed by Congress forbids persons from carrying signs or banners within 500 feet of a foreign embassy in Washington, D.C., if those signs "hold the particular foreign government up to public opprobrium" (i.e., scorn or contempt). One might argue that this is merely a time, place, or manner restriction, because it only applies to the area within a 500-foot radius around the embassy. In *Boos v. Barry* 485 U.S. 312 (1988), however, this statute was treated as a limitation on content and not merely on time, place, or manner. There were two reasons for this conclusion, either of which would have been sufficient: (1) 500 feet was so far away that it would have placed protesters on the other side of the next block, thus completely foreclosing them from their intended audience; and (2) the statute specifically targeted the content of the signs or banners—those expressing disapproval of the foreign government. Thus, if government limits the time, place, or manner of expression in such a way that those wishing to communicate find it either impossible or extremely difficult to reach the intended audience, the restriction will be viewed as one that limits the content of expression. The same is true of a restriction that superficially seems to be a mere time, place, or manner restriction, but which, in fact, is tied to the content of the affected expressions.

The greatest degree of constitutional protection is given to *content-based* restrictions on noncommercial speech—restrictions that are based on *what* is said. When the government attempts to impose a content-based limitation on noncommercial speech, it must bear a very heavy burden of justification. The restriction must be necessary to protect a "compelling" government interest—one that is of extreme importance to society—and the restriction must be "narrowly tailored" to limit expression only to the extent needed to further the government interest. Several examples of compelling government interests are the need to preserve security and order in prisons, prevent disruptions in public schools, maintain a quiet and reflective environment at the place where election votes are cast, maintain discipline in the armed forces, efficiently and effectively manage the workforce at a government agency, protect the national security, or protect the security of a foreign embassy in the United States.

Even if a compelling interest is involved, however, the narrow tailoring requirement can be very difficult for the government to satisfy. For example, in the *Boos v. Barry* case mentioned above, the asserted government interest was protecting the security of foreign embassies in Washington, D.C., which is a compelling interest. The statute prohibiting people from negative picketing within 500 feet of embassies was found unconstitutional, however, because the government was unable to demonstrate that the restriction was essential to the security of the embassies. Although prohibiting signs with negative messages around embassies might protect foreign embassy officials from being offended, this is merely a legitimate interest and not a truly compelling one.

Although most content-based restrictions on speech violate the Constitution, one type of content-based limitation is even more likely to be void than others. A content-based restriction that is also *viewpoint discriminatory*—one that favors or disfavors a particular viewpoint—can almost never be justified by the government.

Figure 5.1 summarizes the analytical process employed to resolve questions under the free speech clause.

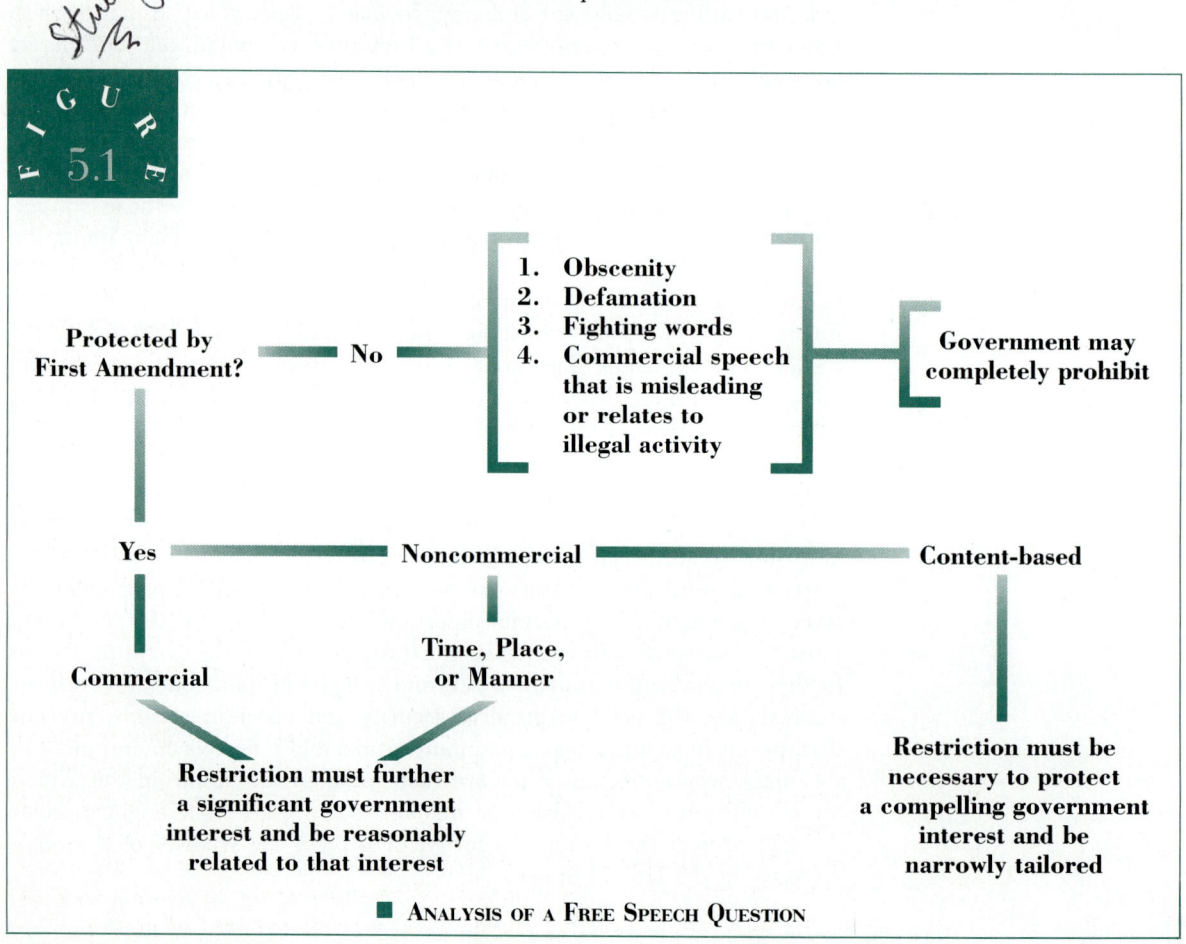

FIGURE 5.1

Protected by First Amendment? → No → 1. Obscenity 2. Defamation 3. Fighting words 4. Commercial speech that is misleading or relates to illegal activity → Government may completely prohibit

Yes → Noncommercial → Content-based

Commercial | Time, Place, or Manner

Restriction must further a significant government interest and be reasonably related to that interest

Restriction must be necessary to protect a compelling government interest and be narrowly tailored

■ ANALYSIS OF A FREE SPEECH QUESTION

EQUAL PROTECTION

The Fourteenth Amendment was passed in 1868, shortly after the Civil War. It states, in part, that "no State shall...deny to any person within its jurisdiction the equal protection of the laws." Although no provision of the Constitution explicitly mentions equal protection in connection with the *federal* government, the concept has been found to be implicit in the Fifth Amendment's due process clause, which does apply to the federal government. Thus, the guarantee of equal protection acts as a limitation on all levels of government—federal, state, and local.

The fundamental thrust of the **equal protection clause** is to prohibit the government from making arbitrary and unreasonable distinctions among persons. Because virtually every law and regulation involves distinctions and classifications—for example, applying to some industries but not to others, applying to larger companies but not to smaller ones, giving benefits to older people but not to younger ones—legal questions involving the equal protection clause arise frequently. Unfortunately, the Supreme Court's interpretations of the clause have not been as clear or consistent as we would like. The Court has definitely identified two different levels of protection under the clause and has probably identified a third. For our purposes, we will characterize the equal protection clause as providing three different levels of protection against unreasonable distinctions. We will first examine those aspects of the law under the equal protection clause that are relatively certain and then look briefly at those that are less clear.

Economic and Social Regulation

One area that is quite clear is the application of the equal protection clause to economic and social regulation. The Supreme Court realizes that legislatures must make distinctions in passing such legislation. Only the poor need welfare; the rich do not. Some industries cause pollution; others do not. Some jobs imperil the safety of workers; others do not. Therefore, the Supreme Court uses a lax standard for economic and social legislation when equal protection challenges are raised. This standard is often referred to as the *rational basis test*. The distinction or classification merely has to have a rational basis; in other words, there merely has to be a legitimate government interest (not even a strong one), and the distinction must have some rational relationship with that interest. If a state legislature, for example, has identified a problem and has made a good faith effort to solve it, the test is normally met. Only if the court can conceive of no reasonable set of facts that would justify the distinction and it is clearly a display of arbitrary power and not a matter of judgment will the distinction be invalidated on equal protection grounds.

To decide that the rational basis test applies to economic or social regulation is almost to decide the case. There is such a strong presumption of reasonableness that discrimination in such regulations are almost always upheld. Distinctions need not be drawn with "mathematical nicety" nor must a legislature attack all aspects of a problem at once. Thus, a law requiring operators of "flea markets" who leased space to persons wishing to sell automobiles to have a type of license not required of persons who leased land to regular car dealers constituted permissible discrimination. The state has a legitimate interest in preventing fraud, and it is rational to presume that fraud will be a bigger problem in a "flea market" than in a stationary car dealership that will probably still be there when a defrauded customer goes back to complain.[6] Similarly, in *Minnesota v. Clover Leaf Creamery Co.*, 449 U.S. 456 (1981), the Supreme Court upheld a state statute that banned the retail sale of milk in nonreturnable, nonrefillable plastic containers but permitted such sale in paperboard containers. The law also did not prohibit the sale of other kinds of products in plastic containers. The state legislature had identified an environmental problem—solid waste disposal—and had made a good faith effort to solve part of the problem. The legislature wanted to encourage the development of environmentally superior containers and had chosen one major industry as a basis for its experiment. Whether the law would work as intended was not the Supreme Court's business; the distinctions in the law did have a rational basis.

Strict Scrutiny

Another relatively clear area of law under the equal protection clause today involves governmental distinctions based on race or national origin. The highest level of protection applies in such cases. If a law or other government action discriminates against someone because of the person's ethnic group or ancestral origin, the courts apply what they refer to as *strict scrutiny*. The test is essentially the same one that courts apply to content-based restrictions on noncommercial speech. The government must demonstrate that the distinction is necessary to protect a compelling interest and that the distinction is narrowly tailored to discriminate no more than is absolutely needed. A governmental body can almost never meet this test, and a distinction based on race or national origin will almost always be void.[7]

Perhaps the most well-known application of the equal protection clause to a racial classification by the government was the Supreme Court's decision in *Brown v. Board of Education*, 347 U.S. 483 (1954), in which racially segregated public school systems were found to be unconstitutional. A more recent example is *Palmore v. Sidoti*, 466 U.S. 429 (1984), in which the Supreme Court invalidated the action of a state trial judge who took a child away from its mother in a custody fight, because the white mother had married a black man. The legal standard normally applied in child custody cases involves a determination of what is in the best interests of the child; the trial judge had concluded that, in many locales, prevailing societal attitudes against interracial families would make life difficult for the child. However, the Supreme Court said that attempting to shield the child from "the reality of private biases" was not a sufficient justification for a racial distinction.

---

[6] *North Dixie Theatre, Inc. v. McCullion*, 613 F. Supp. 1339 (S.D. Ohio 1985).

[7] The courts have also applied the strict scrutiny standard to government distinctions and classifications that interfere with fundamental rights such as free speech, right to privacy, and right to travel interstate. The equal protection clause has no independent significance when applied to such matters, however, because these fundamental rights are protected by other constitutional provisions.

The courts apply the strict scrutiny test only to *intentional* racial or national origin distinctions by the government. If a distinction or classification is neutral on its face but happens to have a disproportionate impact on a particular ethnic group, strict scrutiny does not apply. In such a case of *de facto* discrimination, the courts apply the rational basis test. Examples include public school districts that follow a "neighborhood school" concept, which may result in particular schools having predominantly white or predominantly black enrollments solely because of housing patterns and not because of any discriminatory act by the school district. There is no violation of the equal protection clause. (A word of caution is in order, however: If government *employment* practices are challenged for being discriminatory, *de facto* discrimination might be illegal under a Title VII of the 1964 Civil Rights Act. Although the equal protection clause of the Constitution would not apply, *de facto* employment discrimination can be illegal under this federal statute whether a government or private employer is involved. Employment discrimination is discussed in Chapter 17.)

Thus far, the only form of racially based distinction that has been upheld is *affirmative action.* Sometimes referred to as "benign" or "reverse" discrimination, affirmative action programs grant limited preferences to ethnic minorities. Affirmative action in the employment setting, by either government or private employers, is governed by Title VII of the 1964 Civil Rights Act, our most important employment discrimination law. Affirmative action occurs in several other contexts, as well; in any nonemployment situation in which an affirmative action program is instituted by a governmental body, the equal protection clause applies. Examples include programs that give limited preferences to minorities in admission to state universities or in the awarding of government contracts for the purchase of goods or services. The purposes of such programs include increasing diversity in state-supported higher education, helping minority-owned entrepreneurs become established by enabling them to break into government contract work, and assisting minorities in overcoming the effects of past discrimination in various endeavors.

Although affirmative action has proved to be the only situation in which racial or national origin distinctions have been permitted under the equal protection clause, the government must meet stringent requirements to justify them. For example, in *Richmond v. J. A. Croson Co.,* 488 U.S. 469 (1989), the Supreme Court struck down the minority business enterprise (MBE) set aside program for awarding city government contracts in Richmond, Virginia. Under this program the City of Richmond required that 30% of the dollar volume of all city construction contracts be awarded to businesses that were owned and controlled by blacks, Hispanics, Asians, or Native Alaskans. The percentage could be met by a white-owned general contractor subcontracting work to MBEs. The MBE program was challenged by a white-owned construction company that lost a small contract to install guard rails on a highway, even though its bid was slightly lower than the successful bid of the MBE. The Supreme Court held that the city did have compelling interests in both remedying the effects of past discrimination and making sure that city tax money was not spent to support an industry that engaged in discriminatory practices (i.e., discriminatory subcontracting). However, the Court held that for an MBE program to be valid, the city had to produce evidence demonstrating (1) that discrimination against MBEs in the awarding of city contracts and subcontracts had occurred in the past, (2) a reasonable estimate of the extent of that discrimination, and (3) that it had narrowly tailored the program to take race into account to the least extent possible to serve the city's compelling interest. The city had not fulfilled these requirements. In light of this decision, Richmond let its MBE program expire; thereafter, the amount of MBE participation in city construction contracts dropped to almost zero in Richmond. This result has been repeated in a number of other places. However, many other state and local government agencies are attempting to satisfy the requirements of the *Croson* case.

It should be noted that, at the federal level, Congress has much more latitude to use MBE or other affirmative action programs than do state or local government entities. Such programs enacted by Congress must merely meet a rational basis test. The reason is that in addition to placing a number of limitations on state and local governments, the Fourteenth Amendment also explicitly gave Congress extensive powers to pass legislation carrying out the remedial purposes of that amendment.

Intermediate Scrutiny

We know for sure that the rational basis test applies to classifications in economic regulations and most social legislation, and we also know that the strict scrutiny test applies to government distinctions based on race or national origin. There are a number of other types of distinctions, however, about which the law is not very clear. There appears to be a "middle tier" of protection that applies to distinctions based on important personal characteristics other than race or national origin. Sometimes courts refer to an "intermediate" level of scrutiny. It is fairly clear that this middle tier of protection applies to gender-based distinctions; in such a case, the government must prove that the classification bears a "*substantial* relationship to an *important* government interest." This test is stricter than the rational basis test but not as stringent as the strict scrutiny test.

Applying such a test, however, most gender-based distinctions will violate the equal protection clause. For example, in *Arizona v. Norris*, 463 U.S. 1073 (1983), the Supreme Court Struck down an Arizona state employees' retirement plan which paid women smaller monthly benefits than men because actuarial tables predicted that the average woman would live longer than the average man. The plan was deemed unfair to the plaintiff who could not count on living as long as the "average" woman.[8]

---

[8] If this same type of sex-discriminatory employee benefit plan is used by a *private* employer, the equal protection clause obviously does not apply. However, such a benefit plan in private employment will violate the prohibition against sex discrimination in Title VII of the 1964 Civil Rights Act.

Several other kinds of distinctions also apparently fall within this middle tier of protection, including those based on "alienage" (whether a person is a U.S. citizen or merely a legal resident), age, a child's legitimacy or illegitimacy, and a few others involving important personal characteristics. The Supreme Court has not given clear guidance, however. Sometimes it seems to recognize that an intermediate level of scrutiny is being applied; in other cases it claims to be applying only the rational basis test but reaches conclusions indicating that it actually is applying an intermediate level of scrutiny. For example, in *City of Cleburne v. Cleburne Living Center,* 473 U.S. 432 (1985), the plaintiffs wished to establish a closely supervised and highly regulated home for the mentally retarded in Cleburne, Texas. The city required a special use permit for "homes for the lunatic" and denied the plaintiff's request. The Supreme Court specifically stated that it was applying the rational basis test and concluded that there was no rational basis for prohibiting a residential-type home for the mentally retarded within the city. The Court was obviously scrutinizing the city ordinance more closely than it would if it had been an economic regulation. An economic regulation can be practically nonsensical and still pass the rational basis test. Thus, despite the Court's claim that it was merely applying the rational basis test, it was providing some type of middle-tier protection against government distinctions based on mentally retarded condition.

DUE PROCESS OF LAW

Among other clauses in the Fifth Amendment, the due process clause states that "no person shall . . . be deprived of life, liberty, or property without due process of law." This provision applies to actions of the federal government. Among the several provisions of the Fourteenth Amendment, there is also a due process clause that applies to actions of state and local governments. The two clauses are identical, both in their language and in the way they have been interpreted by the courts; thus, there is no reason for distinguishing between the two and people usually refer to the due process clause as a single provision that applies to all levels of government. The courts have interpreted the due process clause as limiting government action in two different ways: the first kind of limitation is referred to as **substantive due process;** the second is called **procedural due process.** Today, procedural due process is much more important than substantive due process.

Substantive Due Process

The substantive component of due process prohibits statutes, regulations, and other kinds of government action that are arbitrary and irrational. Until the late 1930s, the Supreme Court used substantive due process as a basis for invalidating many economic regulations; basically, if the Court disagreed with the law's underlying rationale, it found the law to be arbitrary and irrational. For example, in one leading case, a law limiting the number of hours that bakers could work was found violative of substantive due process because it unreasonably interfered with "the freedom of master and employee to contract in relation to their employment." Since the late 1930s, the

Supreme Court has taken a dramatically different view of substantive due process. Under the modern interpretation, the Court refuses to "sit as a super-legislature second-guessing the wisdom of legislation." The standard the Court applies today is essentially the same "rational basis" test that is applied to economic classifications under the equal protection clause. Thus, substantive due process is used only rarely to invalidate economic regulation.

Today, substantive due process still plays a role in several situations, although that role is rather limited:

1. Substantive due process incorporates the standards of the equal protection clause and applies them to the federal government. Thus, the different levels of protection that apply under the equal protection clause to classifications by state and local governments are applied to federal government distinctions by means of substantive due process.

2. As mentioned earlier, under the doctrine of incorporation, the protections in the Bill of Rights have been extended to the states by means of the Fourteenth Amendment's due process clause. Substantive due process is the means by which this has been accomplished.

3. Substantive due process protects against extreme instances of statutory vagueness. If a statute is so vague or incomplete that a reasonable person, even after consulting an attorney, would have to engage in sheer guesswork to determine what conduct is permitted or prohibited, the statute violates substantive due process. Sometimes the courts say that a statute must "establish a reasonably ascertainable standard for conduct" to comply with substantive due process. Claims of statutory vagueness are frequently made but are successful only in unusual cases of extreme vagueness.

4. Substantive due process protects against "irrational presumptions." As a matter of practical necessity, the law must make presumptions—presuming the existence of Fact B from proof of Fact A. Presuming one fact because another has been proved is legitimate as long as there is a logical connection between the two. Suppose, for example, that a state law makes it a crime either to steal property or to knowingly take possession of stolen property. Suppose also that, if someone is found in possession of stolen property, the law presumes that the person either stole it or else took possession of it with knowledge that it was stolen. This has been held to be a valid presumption, because the possessor of the property is in a better position than anyone else to explain how he or she acquired it, and he or she is given ample opportunity to explain the circumstances. Thus, he or she is in the best position to explain why the presumption should not be applied in this case. Another example, with an opposite result, involved a federal statute providing that if a kidnapping occurred and nothing was heard from either the kidnapper or the victim for 24 hours after the crime, it was presumed that the kidnapper had crossed state lines. This presumption caused a federal criminal statute to become applicable, thus giving investigative jurisdiction to the Federal Bureau of Investigation. This presumption was found to violate substantive due process, because of the Supreme Court's view that there was no rational connection between a 24-hour period of silence and the act of crossing state lines.

Procedural Due Process

Of much greater importance today is the procedural component of due process. When procedural due process applies, it essentially guarantees that the government will follow fair procedures before taking certain actions against individuals or companies.

Deprivation of Life, Liberty or Property: The due process clause applies only if particular government action "deprives" a person of "life, liberty, or property." This prerequisite exists whether substantive or procedural due process is at issue; however, most of the problems in determining whether this requirement has been met arise in the procedural due process context. Due process questions almost never involve governmental deprivations of "life," the obvious exception being a criminal prosecution in which the death penalty is a possibility. Thus, the question normally is whether particular government action constitutes a deprivation of "liberty" or "property." These terms are interpreted rather broadly. The term *deprivation of liberty* includes virtually any substantial restriction on the freedom of an individual or company, and the term *deprivation of property* includes virtually any substantial negative effect on any type of property interest. It can be seen from this statement that the term *deprivation* really just means a substantial adverse impact; there does not have to be total destruction of a liberty or property interest to constitute a deprivation. One example of the breadth of the term *property* is that a person can even be viewed as having a property interest in a job with a local, state, or federal government agency. If there is a statutory provision or an agency regulation that gives the employee some type of legally enforceable job security, the person has a property interest in the job and must be given procedural due process before the job can be terminated. The statute or regulation might, for example, provide that the employee can be terminated only for "good cause" or only in other described conditions. Such a guarantee creates a property interest. There are many other examples of situations in which individuals or corporations have legal rights that rise to the level of property interests.

Basic Procedural Requirements: When procedural due process applies to government action, the government must provide the affected party with (1) advance notice of the proposed action, (2) an "opportunity to be heard," that is, a hearing of some type, and (3) an impartial decision maker.[9]

---

[9] As we saw in Chapter 2, in the case of civil lawsuits, procedural due process additionally requires that the case be heard in state with which the defendant has had significant contacts.

These requirements are very flexible. The type of notice that will be sufficient may vary with the circumstances. The general rule is simply that the timing and content of the notice must be such that the affected party is reasonably apprised of the nature of the proposed action and has an adequate opportunity to prepare a response.

The requirement of a hearing is also very flexible; the fact that procedural due process applies does not mean that there has to be a full-blown court-like hearing. The hearing must be "meaningful under the circumstances" and might range from a very informal face-to-face meeting between the affected party and the decision maker all the way to a very formal trial-type hearing. The kind of hearing required in a particular case depends on how important the affected party's interest is, how important the government's interest is, and what seems to be the best way to optimize those conflicting interests under the circumstances.

The requirement of an impartial decision maker usually just means that a person having the responsibility for making the decision (either alone or as a member of a decision-making group) should not have prejudged the case and should not have a substantial monetary or emotional stake in the outcome of the decision. The mere fact that a decision maker has a particular ideology or has very strong views about the general subject of the decision does not disqualify him or her.

There are several reasons for requiring fair procedures in any decision-making process, including those in government. The most important reason is that fair procedures generally tend to produce better decisions because these procedures improve the chances that all relevant issues will be identified, all important positions will be presented and considered, and relevant information will be adequately screened and tested. Another important reason for fair procedures is making people feel as if their views count for something, thus increasing their acceptance of decisions even when those decisions go against them. It is much easier to get the compliance and cooperation necessary to carry out decisions when people accept those decisions as being legitimate.

Adjudicative–Legislative Distinction: It is also important to note that the courts have made an important distinction between *adjudicative* and *legislative* types of governmental actions. In general, procedural due process applies only to adjudicative types of governmental actions and not legislative ones. The most obvious example of such an action is a court proceeding. Many other kinds of action at all levels of government, however, fall within the definition of adjudicative. Most of the decisions made by government officials, even informal decisions, are of an adjudicative nature. The essential characteristics of an adjudicative process are that (1) it usually seeks to determine a very specific set of facts relating to the prior conduct of an individual or business (or a relatively small number of individuals or businesses), (2) it applies some already established rule or guideline to these facts, and (3) based on the application of the rule to these facts, it produces a decision and imposes legal consequences on an individual or business (or a relatively small group of them).

The most obvious example of a legislative type of action is the enactment of a statute by Congress or a state legislature. Again, however, many other kinds of action at all levels of government are legislative in character. For instance, when a federal agency adopts regulations that will apply in the future to an industry or when a city zoning board adopts a zoning plan to guide future land uses in the city, the action is basically legislative. The essential characteristics of a legislative process are that (1) if it involves fact-finding, those facts are usually of a very general nature, (2) it seeks to develop policies or rules that will apply either to the general population or to a relatively large group of individuals or businesses, and (3) it usually imposes legal consequences only for future conduct and not for prior conduct.

Like most other distinctions, the adjudicative–legislative distinction is sometimes obvious and sometimes not. Some government actions are hybrids. Actually, government decision-making processes run along a continuum from purely adjudicative to purely legislative. The more that a particular action looks like an adjudicative one, the more likely it is that a court will find that procedural due process applies. Even when a govermental body takes action that is essentially legislative in nature, it may provide notice, hearing, and other procedural safeguards if it so chooses. Thus, Congress has passed legislation requiring federal agencies to provide notice and hearing before certain kinds of agency rule-making activities—this was simply a choice made by Congress despite the fact that the due process clause of the Constitution would not require these procedures. Fair procedures can have great value even if not required by the Constitution.

The basic reasons why the courts have generally applied procedural due process guarantees to adjudicative actions but not to legislative ones are that (1) fundamental fairness usually demands more procedural safeguards when legal consequences are imposed for past conduct than when rules are developed to guide future conduct, (2) providing advance notice and an opportunity for a hearing becomes extremely difficult and expensive when very large numbers of parties are affected, as is usually the case with legislative actions, and (3) the fact that legislative actions affect a large number of parties usually means that there will be more publicity and more collective economic and political power to guard against arbitrary actions by the government.

The following case illustrates the method courts use to determine whether particular procedures are adequate to fulfill the requirements of procedural due process.

SOUTHERN OHIO COAL CO. V. DONOVAN

U.S. SIXTH CIRCUIT
COURT OF APPEALS
774 F.2d 693 (1985)

The Federal Mine Safety and Health Review Commission ("Commission"), a branch of the U.S. Department of Labor, is charged with enforcing the Federal Mine Safety and Health Act ("the Act"). One provision of the Act prohibited a mine operator from discharging a miner for asserting any of his or her safety rights under the law. The Commission implemented this provision of the statute by adopting Rule 44, which specified the detailed procedures to be followed in dealing with a miner's complaint. Under Rule 44, if a miner filed a complaint with the Secretary of Labor alleging that he had been discharged because he had complained about safety conditions, the Secretary had to commence an investigation within 15 days. If the Secretary decided that the complaint was "not frivolous," he filed an application with the Commission requesting that the company be ordered to reinstate the miner. The application simply set forth the Secretary's finding that the complaint was not frivolous, and the application was attached to a copy of the miner's original complaint. The Secretary's application was then examined "on an expedited basis" by an Administrative Law Judge (ALJ), who is a judicial-type official within the agency. The ALJ checked the application and complaint to make sure the documents were in order and, if so, ordered the company to immediately reinstate the miner to his job. The company could then request a hearing before the ALJ, who had to conduct the hearing within five days after the request. However, the question to be decided at the hearing was still limited to whether the miner's complaint was "not frivolous." If after the hearing the ALJ agreed with the Secretary that the miner's complaint was not frivolous, the reinstatement order continued. This conclusion by the ALJ could be reviewed by the Commission and ultimately by a federal court of appeals. Still, however, the issue was limited to whether the complaint was frivolous and not whether the miner actually had been discriminated against for having raised questions about safety. This ultimate question would be determined under separate procedures that would take a substantial period of time; the company was required to keep the miner on the job until final disposition of the claim.

In this case, Southern Ohio Coal Co. (SOCCO) fired a miner for the stated reason of excessive absenteeism. The miner had earlier objected to company officials about unsafe methane levels in SOCCO's mines, and when he was fired he filed a complaint alleging that SOCCO terminated him because of his prior safety objections. Under the procedures described above, the company was ordered to reinstate him. The company challenged the constitutionality of Rule 44 in federal district court. The court held that Rule 44 violated the company's procedural due process rights, and the Secretary of Labor (Donovan) appealed. (It should be noted that the action of Congress in passing the Act, as well as the action of the Commission in adopting Rule 44, were legislative actions, and procedural due process did not apply to the methods they used in making these decisions. However, Rule 44 specified procedures for taking adjudicative types of actions; thus, Rule 44's application to particular adjudicative situations was governed by the constitutional guarantee of procedural due process.)

WELLFORD, CIRCUIT JUDGE:

Whether the Commission's Rule 44 violates a mine operator's due process rights by failing to provide for a pre-deprivation hearing is at the heart of these controversies. Neither party questions that the mine operators are due some process under the Constitution when a miner claims the opportunity for immediate reinstatement. The Secretary, however, claims that a post-deprivation hearing is sufficient process in light of the (allegedly) overriding governmental interests involved. The mine operators, on the other hand, claim that a post-deprivation hearing is insufficient to protect their Constitutional rights and that a pre-deprivation hearing is mandated, because they could be compelled to make substantial payments before a decision is made initially as to the potential merit of a claim, and because they could be compelled to reinstate a person who is a danger to himself or to others.

Mathews v. Eldridge, 424 U.S. 319 (1976), requires a court to consider three factors to determine whether a

CONTINUED

particular procedure comports with the requirements of due process:

1. The private interests that will be affected by the official action in question;
2. The risk of an erroneous deprivation of such interests through the procedures involved and the probable value of additional or substitute procedural safeguards; and
3. The government's interest, including the function involved and the fiscal and administrative burdens that the additional or substitute procedural requirement would entail.

The final *Eldridge* factor is met in the instant case. Currently the Secretary is required to give the mine operator a hearing within five days of the temporary reinstatement order. What the mine operators would have this Court require is a pre-deprivation hearing—in other words, the Secretary would have to reverse the order of its procedures and hold a hearing before granting temporary reinstatement. Thus, there would be absolutely no additional fiscal or administrative burdens in granting the operators' desired predeprivation hearing.

The first and second factors, however, are not as easily answered as the third. On the first factor, the Secretary correctly notes that "[t]he usual rule has been '[w]here only property rights are involved, mere postponement of the judicial enquiry is not a denial of due process, if the opportunity given for ultimate judicial determination of liability is adequate.'" *Mitchell v. W. T. Grant Co.*, 416 U.S. 600 (1974). Were the employer permitted in all cases to provide merely economic reinstatement rather than normally being required to provide actual physical reinstatement, the Secretary's argument would be more persuasive.

The district court found "compelling" the mine operator's interest in "not being required to employ in a sensitive position a man whom it has discharged."

> Prolonged retention of a disruptive or otherwise unsatisfactory employee can adversely affect discipline and morale in the work place, foster disharmony, and ultimately impair the efficiency of an office or agency.

This factor is particularly important when, as here, the order does not expire by its own terms at any specific time after it issues. Although an operator is given an opportunity to present evidence on its own behalf within five days of the reinstatement, the hearing focuses on whether the miner's complaint was frivolously brought, not whether the complaint is meritorious.

The reliability (or unreliability) of the initial procedures leading to an imposition of temporary reinstatement is perhaps a significant weakness in the administrative scheme under scrutiny. All the Secretary need do to force the mine operator to reinstate the discharged miner is find "minimal supporting evidence" in favor of the complainant. As long as the Secretary finds that the complaint was not "frivolously brought," then the Secretary makes an application for temporary reinstatement. The application itself consists only of the miner's complaint, an affidavit setting forth the Secretary's reasons for his finding that the complaint was not frivolously brought, and proof of service on the operator. The application permits no input from the employer....

...[T]he Supreme Court's most recent pronouncement concerning due process requirements, *Cleveland Board of Education v. Loudermill*, 105 S.Ct. 1487 (1985), strongly supports the mine operator's arguments that the Secretary should provide at least some kind of *pre-deprivation* hearing:

> Some opportunity for the employee to present his side of these cases is recurringly of obvious value in reaching an accurate decision. Dismissal for cause will often involve factual disputes. Even where the facts are clear, the appropriateness or necessity of the discharge may not be; in such cases, the only meaningful opportunity to invoke the discretion of the decision maker is likely to be before the termination takes effect.

This language is equally applicable to the employer situation in which the issue presented is the issue of forced reinstatement rather than the other side of the coin, employee termination. We believe this rationale meets the second factor set out in *Mathews v. Eldridge*. While something less "than a *full* evidentiary hearing is sufficient prior to adverse administrative action," the employers here must be afforded a minimal opportunity to present their side of the dispute before temporary reinstatement is forced upon them. Since the Secretary's Rule 44 fails to insure any reasonable opportunity for at least some minimal pre-deprivation hearing, we hold that it violates the mine operator's due process rights.

[Affirmed.]

Takings Clause

The final constitutional provision we will examine is the *takings clause* of the Fifth Amendment. It applies explicitly to the federal government and, through the doctrine of incorporation, also applies to state and local governments. The takings clause states that private property shall not "be taken for public use without just compensation." The clause recognizes the ancient principle that a sovereign may take private property for public purposes. This long-recognized governmental power is referred to as the power of **eminent domain.** The takings clause, however, also places limitations on this power. Private property can be taken only for a public purpose, but this requirement is interpreted so broadly that almost any governmental objective will suffice. The most important limitation is that the government must pay "just compensation"—the fair market value—of the property it takes.

The concept of property is very broad under the takings clause. It obviously includes land, as well as the many different types of interests in land such as subsurface mineral rights, easements, and "air rights" (the right to use the air space above land). It also includes any other tangible property, such as a boat or piece of equipment, and intangible property rights such as those that exist in a company's trade secret information.

The government is required to pay the owner when there has been a "taking." It will be remembered that procedural due process applies to any government action that has a significant negative effect on a property interest. To be a taking for which compensation must be paid, however, there must be much more than just a significant negative effect on the property interest. All or most of the property's value and utility must have been appropriated by the government's action. When the government physically appropriates the ownership of property, as when it builds a highway on your land, there obviously is a taking. If you do not agree to sell the land, the government must take legal action to condemn the property and have a court determine its fair value.

Difficult questions can arise, however, when the government does something that has a substantial negative effect on the utility and value of a property interest, without actually appropriating the property. When the government engages in some physical act that greatly diminishes the utility and value of someone's property, courts sometimes view the action as a taking. For example, the government might extend an airport runway so that takeoffs and landings are now very low over an adjoining tract of land. If the government has not bought the adjoining land, either through negotiated purchase or condemnation, the property owner is likely to file suit claiming a *de facto* taking of his or her property. If the court concludes that the government's actions substantially destroyed the owner's ability to make productive use of his or her property, the court usually decides that there has been a taking for which compensation is due. Although the government's action can constitute a taking without totally destroying all possible uses of the property, one of the factors a court will consider in determining whether there has been a sufficiently large destruction of value is whether there are other comparably productive uses for the property.

The issue of whether there has been a taking can also arise when some law or regulation affects the value of property. Most of the time, a regulation that limits the uses an owner can make of his or her property or that otherwise affects its value will not constitute a taking. Courts usually view these regulations as one of the burdens a person or company must bear in return for the many benefits of living in an organized society. The most obvious example is a city zoning law that permits only single-family homes in certain areas, multifamily dwellings in other areas, retail stores elsewhere, and various categories of industry in yet other sections. Despite occasional claims by property owners that they are deprived of the greater financial return they could receive by putting their property to some other use, zoning laws almost never constitute takings. Among other reasons for this conclusion, zoning usually benefits property values on the whole because of the predictability it creates.

The Supreme Court's many cases involving application of the takings clause to regulations have not provided very clear guidance. Unfortunately, the cases in this area are of a rather *ad hoc* nature. Generally speaking, a regulation that limits use will only constitute a taking in circumstances in which a particular property owner is forced to bear an unusual financial burden that is totally out of proportion with the benefits to be received by either himself or the community. For example, in *Nollan v. California Coastal Commission*, 483 U.S. 825 (1987), the Supreme Court held that a state agency had committed a taking when it required a landowner to grant public access across a section of the owner's private beach; the requirement was imposed as a condition before the agency would permit the landowner to demolish an old structure and replace it with a house on the property. The Court found a taking because of a combination of factors: (1) the landowner was singled out for a special burden not imposed on a general community of landowners; (2) the restriction on the owner's ability to demolish and build was not really related to the condition of granting public access; and (3) the granting of access to the public resembled the actual appropriation of an easement by the government (an easement—the right to do something on someone else's land—is a property interest).

Questions and Problems

1. Blanco was arrested at his apartment complex for disorderly conduct after he refused numerous requests by neighbors, the apartment manager, and police to turn down his stereo, which he had positioned in such a manner as to direct the sound of his rock music toward the swimming pool area of the complex. He had turned the stereo's volume up loud enough to cause vibrations in nearby apartments and to force his musical preferences on many neighbors who did not share them. What is the source, if any, of the city's authority to arrest Blanco? (*Blanco v. State*, 761 S.W.2d 38, Tex. App. 1988.)

2. The Heart of Atlanta Motel (P) was a 216-room motel in downtown Atlanta, Georgia. It was not located near a state line, although it was near two interstate highways and two state highways. It did extensive advertising in other states, and 75 percent of its guests were from outside Georgia. P refused to rent rooms to blacks, a practice that Congress outlawed by passage of Title II of the Civil Rights Act of 1964. P sued, claiming that the law was unconstitutional because Congress had no authority to regulate such a motel. Discuss. (*Heart of Atlanta Motel v. United States*, 379 U.S. 241, 1964.)

3. New York passed a law requiring every drug prescription form to have two signature lines, one stating "dispense as written" and one state "subsitution permissible." If the latter line is signed, the doctor must tell the patient that the pharmacist will substitute a (generally cheaper) generic drug for the normal "name brand" drug if the FDA has determined the generic drug to be a bioequivalent substitute. Pharmacists who do not wish to dispense the generic drug challenge the law as unduly burdening interstate commerce. Should this claim prevail? (*Pharmaceutical Society of New York v. Lefkowitz*, 586 F.2d 953, 2d Cir. 1978.)

4. The Montana Fish and Game Commission adopted a regulation in 1976 that set the price of combination hunting licenses at $30 for residents and $225 for non-residents. (A combination license permitted the taking of one elk, one deer, one black bear, and a specified number of game birds.) This regulation was challenged by non-resident hunters, who contended that it violated the privileges and immunities clause of the U.S. Constitution. The State of Montana contended, among other things, that the interest of Montana residents in the wildlife within its borders was a matter of state protection and that this interest was substantial enough to justify the regulation. Do you think the U.S. Supreme Court agreed with this defense? Why or why not? (*Baldwin v. Fish and Game Commission of Montana*, 436 U.S. 371, 1978.)

5. Lee, an Amish carpenter and farmer who employed other Amish people in his business, had trouble with the Internal Revenue Service because he did not deduct for or contribute to Social Security. The Internal Revenue Service Code provides a religious exemption for self-employed individuals that Amish can take advantage of. However, there is no such exemption for employment of others. Lee claims that he should not be required to comply with the Code because religious principles prevent him and his employees from claiming Social Security benefits. Discuss the validity of Lee's claim. (*United States v. Lee*, 455 U.S. 252, 1982.)

6. The legislature of Puerto Rico passed a statute that legalized certain forms of casino gambling for the purpose of promoting tourism. The legislature was very concerned, however, that widespread casino gambling by residents of Puerto Rico would have various negative effects on the population. Thus, the legislature prohibited the operators of casinos there from directing their advertising at local residents. Within Puerto Rico and its territorial waters, casino operators were only permitted to advertise gambling on airplanes, cruise ships, or other places where only incoming travelers were likely to be; they also could advertise in the mainland United States and other places outside Puerto Rico. A casino owner wishing to advertise within Puerto Rico challenged the ad restriction on free speech grounds. (The U.S. Constitution applies in Puerto Rico.) Discuss. (*Posadas de Puerto Rico Associates v. Tourism Co. of Puerto Rico*, 478 U.S. 328, 1986.)

7. Rock Against Racism (RAR), furnishing its own sound equipment and technicians, sponsored yearly programs of rock music in a bandshell in New York City's Central Park. Because of complaints about excessive noise from neighbors, the city adopted new guidelines under which it provided the sound equipment and sound technicians for the bandshell. Although the technician generally accommodated any band's requests regarding mixing of sound, he controlled the mix and volume. RAR sued, claiming a free speech violation. RAR argued, in part, that it should be allowed to control the sound equipment, subject to an overall volume limit. Discuss. (*Ward v. Rock Against Racism*, 491 U.S. 781, 1989.)

8. For the express purpose of providing a place where teenagers can socialize with each other but not be subjected to the potentially detrimental influence of older teenagers and adults (involving alcohol, drugs, and promiscuous sex), a Dallas ordinance was passed that authorized the licensing of "Class E" dance halls, restricting admission to persons between the ages of 14 and 18 and limiting their hours of operation. Stanglin, whose roller-skating rink and Class E dance hall, shared a divided floor space, filed suit contending that the age and hour restrictions violated the minors' equal protection rights. Discuss. (*City of Dallas v. Stanglin*, 490 U.S. 19, 1989.)

9. A motorist was convicted of two traffic offenses in a municipal court in which the city's mayor served as judge, and the convictions were affirmed by the state's supreme court. He appealed this judgment to the U.S. Supreme Court. He contended that he had been denied a trial before "a disinterested and impartial judicial officer as guaranteed by the Due Process clause," in view of the fact that a major part of the village's income was derived from the fines, costs, and fees imposed by the municipal court, and the mayor also served as the city's chief executive with responsibility. Do you believe that the appellant's contention is valid? Explain. (*Ward v. Village of Monroeville,* 409 U.S. 57, 1972.)

10. Ewing enrolled in a 6-year program of study at the University of Michigan that awarded an undergraduate degree and a medical degree on successful completion of the program. To qualify for the final two years of the program a student must pass an examination known as NBME Part I. Ewing, after an undistinguished academic career, was dismissed from the university when he failed this examination with the lowest score recorded in the history of the program. He sued, seeking readmission to the program and an opportunity to retake the exam on the ground that he had a property interest in the program and that his dismissal was in violation of due process. Evidence showed that academic authorities had given careful consideration to their decision to dismiss Ewing but that all other students in the program who had failed NMBE Part I had been allowed to retake it, some as many as four times. Should Ewing's due process claim prevail? Discuss. (*Regents of the University of Michigan v. Ewing,* 474 U.S. 214, 1986.)

CHAPTER 6

In the preceding chapters we have studied the major processes by which law is made—the formulation of common-law rules by the courts, the enactment of statutes by the legislative bodies, and the interpretation of statutes by the courts. But his examination does not present the total lawmaking picture. Administrative agencies—the hundreds of boards and commissions existing at all levels of government— also "make law" by their continual promulgation of rules and regulations. The number of administrative agencies has grown so rapidly in the past

LAWMAKING BY ADMINISTRATIVE AGENCIES

40 years that the practical impact of local, state, and federal agencies on the day-to-day activities of individuals and businesses is today probably at least as great as that of legislatures and courts. Every day, boards and commissions across the country engage in such traditional functions as assessing properties for tax purposes, granting licenses and business permits, and regulating rates charged in the transportation and public utility industries—actions that affect millions of Americans. And, more recently, newer agencies such as the Environmental Protection Agency (EPA), Occupational Safety and Health Administration (OSHA), and the National Highway Traffic and Safety Administration (NHTSA) have spawned regulations having broad impact on the nation's businesses. Justice Jackson was right when he wrote in *FTC v. Ruberoid Co.*, 343 U.S. 470 (1952):

> *The rise of administrative bodies probably has been the most significant legal trend of the last century and perhaps more values today are affected by their decisions than by those of all the courts. . . . They also have begun to have important consequences on personal rights. . . . They have become a veritable fourth branch of the Government, which has deranged our three-branch legal theories as much as the concept of a fourth dimension unsettles our three-dimensional thinking.*

RISE OF THE ADMINISTRATIVE AGENCY

At the risk of oversimplification, we can say that two major factors are responsible for the dramatic growth of the administrative agency in recent years. First was a change in attitude toward government regulation of business. Until about 1880 the basic attitude of the state and federal governments toward business firms was that of "hands-off"—a philosophy frequently characterized by the *laissez-faire* label. The theory was that trade and commerce could best thrive in an environment free of government controls. By the end of the nineteenth century, however, various monopolistic practices had begun to surface. The passage of the Sherman Act in 1890 reflected the growing idea that a certain amount of government regulation of business was necessary to preserve minimum levels of competition.

A second, and perhaps even more powerful, reason for the emergence of the modern administrative agency is that as our nation grew and became more industrialized, many complex problems sprang up that did not easily lend themselves to traditional types of regulation. Some were posed by technological advances such as the greatly increased generation and distribution of electrical power and the rapid growth of the airline industry. Others resulted from changes in social and economic conditions, particularly the rise of the giant manufacturers and the new methods by which they marketed their products on a national basis. The solution of these problems required expertise and enormous amounts of time for continuous regulation, which

HUMOR AND THE LAW

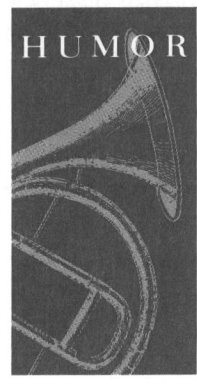

Administrative law plays a vital role in our economy, but when bureaucrats get carried away, the results would be humorous if they weren't so tragic. Researchers at the University of Colorado once counted the regulations that governed the conversion of a cow into a hamburger served at your local restaurant, and came up with a number in the neighborhood of 42,000. Are all of the regulations issued by agencies necessary? Well, just ask a comatose sea turtle. One legal magazine gave its award for "most arcane federal regulation" to the National Oceanic and Atmospheric Administration's emergency regulations providing for alternative resuscitation procedures for comatose sea turtles accidentally caught in commercial fishing operations. We certainly hope that mouth-to-mouth was not one of the alternatives. *Case and Comment* (Jan/Feb. 1981).

---

the courts and the legislatures simply did not possess. Faced with this situation, the legislative bodies sought new ways to regulate business (and to implement nonbusiness government programs, such as Social Security) that would be more workable.

THE AGENCY—AN OVERVIEW

To understand the basic workings of administrative agencies and the nature of the legal problems we will discuss later, it will be helpful to see how the typical agency is created and how it receives its powers. For this purpose, the Federal Trade Commission provides a good example.

By the turn of the century, it was apparent that some firms in interstate commerce were engaging in practices that, although not violating the Sherman Act, were nonetheless felt to be of an undesirable nature. Although persons who were injured by these practices were sometimes able to obtain relief in the courts, the relief was sporadic, and there was no single body that could maintain surveillance of these practices on a continuing basis.

Accordingly, in 1914 Congress passed the Federal Trade Commission Act, which created the *Federal Trade Commission (FTC)* and authorized it (among other things) to determine what constituted "unfair methods of competition" in interstate commerce. Not only could the commission issue regulations defining and prohibiting such practices, but additionally, it could take action against companies that it believed to be violating such regulations.

Several federal agencies are considered to be part of the executive branch, such as the Small Business Administration (SBA), OSHA, and the Federal Aviation Administration (FAA). Others are structurally independent of the executive branch; once the president's appointment of agency heads and members is confirmed by the Senate, the president has no direct control over the appointee and cannot remove him or her from office. Examples of independent regulatory agencies include the FTC, the Interstate Commerce Commission (ICC), the Securities and Exchange Commission (SEC), the National Labor Relations Board (NLRB), and the Federal Reserve Board (FRB).

LEGISLATIVE DELEGATION OF LAWMAKING POWER

The administrative agency sits somewhat uncomfortably in our tripartite (legislative–executive–judicial) system of government. An agency that is technically part of the executive branch or perhaps an "independent regulatory agency" may exert powers that entail adjudication and rule making as well as traditional executive functions such as investigation and enforcement. A constitutional problem arises because the Constitution in article I, section 1, clearly vests all legislative powers in the Congress and does not provide for delegation of those powers. Therefore, rules and regulations that have been promulgated by agencies and that have the force and effect of law have been challenged as resulting from an unconstitutional delegation of legislative power.

Only in a couple of cases decided during the 1930s, in which the Supreme Court found "delegation running riot," have such challenges succeeded. The courts are well aware of the very practical need for administrative agencies that was described earlier in this chapter. Therefore, they will uphold any agency ruling, regulation, or act that is within standards set forth in an enabling act *if* that act contains "reasonable standards" to guide the agency. What are reasonable standards? Courts have upheld as constitutional delegations of power "to promulgate regulations fixing prices of commodities," to institute rent controls on real property anywhere in the nation under specified circumstances, even "to issue such orders and regulations as he [the President] deems appropriate to stabilize prices, rents, wages and salaries." Indeed, the doctrine of unconstitutional delegation of legislative power appears moribund at the federal level, although it still has some vitality in litigation involving state agencies.[1]

---

[1] For example, in *State v. Marana Plantations, Inc.*, 252 P.2d 87 (1953), in which the power to "regulate" sanitary policies in the interests of public health" was deemed too vague.

FUNCTIONS AND POWERS

MINISTERIAL AND DISCRETIONARY POWERS

Before addressing the legal questions that are presented when agencies' rules or orders are appealed to the courts, we will briefly look at the nature of agency activities. The activities of these government boards and commissions vary widely. The functions and powers of some agencies are only **ministerial**—concerned with routinely carrying out duties imposed by law. Boards that issue and renew drivers' licenses fall within this category, as do the many Social Security offices that give information or advice to persons filing for Social Security benefits.

But most agencies also possess broad **discretionary powers**—powers that require the exercise of judgment and discretion in carrying out their duties. Again there is variety in the specific powers of these agencies. Some agencies' discretionary power is largely **investigative** in nature. Two examples are the authority granted to the Internal Revenue Service to inquire into the legality of deductions on taxpayers' returns and the authority of some commissions to make investigations for the purpose of recommending needed statutes to legislatures. Other agencies have largely **rule-making powers,** with perhaps some investigative but little **adjudicative power** (enforcement power).

"Full-fledged" federal agencies, such as the FTC and the NLRB, possess all three types of discretionary power—investigative, rule making, and adjudicative. Thus, typically, a board will conduct investigations to determine if conditions warrant the issuance of rules to require (or prohibit) certain kinds of conduct; then it will draw up the regulations and thereafter take action against individuals or firms showing evidence of violating them. In drawing up the rules the board acts quasi-legislatively, and in enforcing them it acts quasijudicially.

INVESTIGATIVE POWER

Agencies frequently hold hearings before drafting regulations, and the investigative powers they possess in connection with such hearings are largely determined by the statutes by which they are created. Normally, agencies can order the production of accounts and records relative to the problem being studied and can **subpoena** witnesses and examine them under oath. More disruptive to businesses are the powers most major agencies have to investigate whether statutes they are charged with enforcing and rules they have promulgated are being violated. The two most intrusvie forms of investigative power are the subpoena and the physical search and seizure.

Subpoena Power

In the exercise of its adjudicative powers, which are soon to be discussed, agencies may issue subpoenas compelling witnesses to appear and give testimony at an agency hearing.

In any sort of investigation, agencies also may issue subpoenas *duces tecum*, which order the production of books, papers, records, and documents. Agency authority is construed very broadly in this area. According to *United States v. Powell*,[2] an agency must demonstrate that (1) the investigation will be conducted for a legitimate purpose, (2) the inquiry is relevant to the purpose, (3) the information sought is not already possessed by the agency, and (4) the administrative steps required by law have been followed. The agency does not, however, have to prove that there is "probable cause" to believe that a violation of the law has occurred, as is usually required in criminal investigations by the police.

Once the agency has established an apparently valid purpose for the investigation, the burden shifts to the company or individual being investigated to show that the purpose is illegitimate (e.g., undertaken for harassment). The following case illustrates the difficulty that the target of a federal agency's investigation can have in attempting to block enforcement of such a subpoena.

EEOC v. PEAT, MARWICK, MITCHELL AND CO.

U.S. EIGHTH CIRCUIT COURT OF APPEALS, 775, F.2d 928 (1985)

In May 1982, the Equal Employment Opportunity Commission (EEOC) began investigating the retirement practices and policies of Peat, Marwick, Mitchell & Co. (PM) in an effort to determine whether those policies violated the Age Discrimination in Employment Act (ADEA). In accord with its statutory investigative powers, the EEOC subpoenaed from PM documents bearing on the relationship of members to the firm and documents relating to PM's retirement practices and policies.

PM refused to comply with the subpoena, so the EEOC initiated this enforcement proceeding in the district court. The district court ordered enforcement of the subpoena, and PM appealed.

FAGG, CIRCUIT JUDGE:

PM's primary argument on appeal is that the subpoena should not be enforced because the EEOC's investigation is not for a legitimate purpose authorized by Congress. The ADEA prohibits discrimination by an employer against an employee or prospective employee on the basis of age. PM contends that its partners are not employees under the ADEA but rather they fall within the definition provided for employers in the Act. Thus, according to PM, the EEOC's investigation of the relationship of PM partners as employers, to the firm and to each other and its investigation of the retirement practices and policies of the partnership is not for a legitimate purpose authorized by Congress.

EEOC maintains that it has subpoenaed the records of PM in an effort to determine whether individuals that PM clas-

CONTINUED

---

[2] 379 U.S. 48 (1964).

sifies as "partners" fall within the definition of "employees" for purposes of the ADEA.

Congress has established the EEOC as the administrative body empowered to investigate violations of the ADEA and has given the EEOC subpoena power in order to carry out its investigations. The authority to investigate violations includes the authority to investigate coverage under the statute. *Donovan v. Shaw*, 668 F.2d 985 (8th Cir. 1982). It can no longer be disputed that "a subpoena enforcement proceeding is not the proper forum in which to litigate the question of coverage under a particular federal statute." *Id.* The initial determination of the coverage question is left to the administrative agency seeking enforcement of the subpoena. Often a coverage question cannot be resolved until the administrative agency has had an opportunity to examine the subpoenaed records.

"The showing of reasonable cause required to support an application for enforcement of a subpoena duces tecum 'is satisfied . . . by the court's determination that the investigation is authorized by Congress, is for a purpose Congress can order, and the documents sought are relevant to the inquiry.'" *Donovan*, 668 F.2d at 989. *See also United States v. Powell*, 379 U.S. 48 (1964). The EEOC's investigation of PM is in an effort to determine whether PM's retirement practices and policies discriminate against individuals classified as employees for purposes of the ADEA. Thus, EEOC's investigation is for a legitimate purpose authorized by Congress. PM has not questioned the relevancy of the documents subpoenaed by the EEOC to a determination of this question.

PM also argues that the district court committed error in enforcing the subpoena because it is abusive, unreasonable, not in good faith, and violative of the constitutional rights of PM and its members. In this regard, PM argues that the EEOC has never made or attempted to make a showing that PM's partners may in fact be employees for purposes of the ADEA, or that it has reason to believe that PM's retirement practices and policies may be violative of the ADEA.

The EEOC is not required to make such a showing. As previously indicated, the EEOC must show that its investigation is for a legitimate purpose authorized by Congress and that the documents subpoenaed are relevant to its inquiry. If this demonstration is made, the EEOC is entitled to the documents subpoenaed unless PM demonstrates that judicial enforcement of the subpoena would amount to an abuse of the court's process. PM has presented no evidence of bad faith or an abuse of the court's process by the EEOC.

We affirm.

Search and Seizure

Many agencies carry out on-site inspections or searches when investigating matters under their jurisdiction. From city health inspectors checking a restaurant's kitchen to OSHA personnel investigating trenches at a construction site to federal mine safety inspectors probing underground coal mines, such investigations are a frequent and, for the investigated company, troublesome occurrence.

These searches have constitutional implications, because the warrant clause of the Fourth Amendment protects commercial buildings as well as private homes. As the Supreme Court pointed out in *Marshall v. Barlow's, Inc.*, 436 U.S. 307 (1978), the searching of businesses by the British immediately preceding the American Revolution was particularly offensive to the colonists and provided part of the rationale for the warrant requirement.

However, we are not accorded as great an expectation of privacy for our businesses as for our homes. For example, several types of businesses, including gun dealers, stone quarries, day care centers, and fishing vessels, have been held to be so "pervasively regulated" that they can have little or no reasonable expectation of privacy. This doctrine appears to be shrinking the protection that businesses have from warrantless searches and seizures, as the following case illustrates.

NEW YORK V. BURGER

U.S. SUPREME COURT, 107 S.Ct. 2636 (1987)

Burger owned a junkyard that dismantled cars and sold their parts. Pursuant to a New York statute [Sec. 415-a] authorizing warrantless inspections of such junkyards, police officers entered Burger's junkyard and asked to see his license and records. He replied that he did not have such documents, though they are required by the statute. The officers then announced their intent to search the premises; Burger did not object. The officers found stolen vehicles and parts. Burger was charged in state court with possession of stolen property and unregistered operation of a vehicle dismantler. He moved to suppress the evidence, claiming that the administrative inspection statute was unconstitutional. The trial court denied the motion, but the New York Court of Appeals reversed. The Supreme Court granted the State's application for certiorari.

BLACKMUN, JUSTICE:

The Court long has recognized that the Fourth Amendment's prohibition on unreasonable searches and seizures is applicable to commercial premises, as well as to private homes. An owner or operator of a business thus has an expectation of privacy in commercial property, which society is prepared to consider to be reasonable. An expectation of privacy in commercial premises, however, is different from, and indeed less than, a similar expectation in an individual's home. This expectation is particularly attenuated in commercial property employed in "closely regulated" industries.

[A] warrantless inspection, however, even in the context of a pervasively regulated business, will be deemed to be reasonable only so long as three criteria are met. First, there must be a "substantial government interest" that informs the regulatory scheme. Second, the warrantless inspections must be "necessary to further [the] regulatory scheme." *Donovan v. Dewey*, 452 U.S. 594, 600 (1981). Finally, "the statute's inspection program, in terms of the certainty and regularity of its application, [must] provid[e] a constitutionally adequate substitute for a warrant." *Ibid.* In other words, the regulatory statute must perform the two basic functions of a warrant: it must advise the owner of the commercial premises that the search is being made pursuant to the law and has a properly defined scope, and it must limit the discretion of the inspecting officers. To perform this first function, the statute must be "sufficiently comprehensive and defined that the owner of commercial property cannot help but be aware that his property will be subject to periodic inspections undertaken for specific purposes." *Ibid.* In addition, in defining how a statute limits the discretion of the inspectors, we have observed that it must be "carefully limited in time, place, and scope." *United States v. Biswell*, 406 U.S. 311, 315 (1972).

Searches made pursuant to Sec. 415-a, in our view, clearly fall within this established exception to the warrant requirement for administrative inspections in "closely regulated" businesses. First, the nature of the regulatory statute reveals that the operation of a junkyard, part of which is devoted to vehicle dismantling, is a "closely regulated" business in the State of New York. The provisions regulating the activity of vehicle dismantling are extensive. [The Court then described these regulations in detail.]

The New York regulatory scheme satisfies the three criteria necessary to make reasonable warrantless inspections pursuant to Sec. 415-a5. First, the State has a substantial interest in regulating the vehicle-dismantling and automobile-junkyard industry because motor vehicle theft has increased in the State and because the problem of theft is associated with this industry. In this day, automobile theft has become a significant social problem, placing enormous economic and personal burdens upon the citizens of different States.

CONTINUED

Second, regulation of the vehicle-dismantling industry reasonably serves the State's substantial interest in eradicating automobile theft. It is well established that the theft problem can be addressed effectively by controlling the receiver of, or market in, stolen property.

Moreover, the warrantless administrative inspections pursuant to Sec. 415-a5 "are necessary to further [the] regulatory scheme." *Donovan v. Dewey*, 452 U.S., at 600. We explained in *Biswell*:

> [I]f inspection is to be effective and serve as a credible deterrent, unannounced, even frequent inspections are essential. In this context, the prerequisite of a warrant could easily frustrate inspection; and if the necessary flexibility as to time, scope, and frequency is to be preserved, the protections afforded by a warrant would be negligible.

Third, Sec. 415-a5 provides a "constitutionally adequate substitute for a warrant." The statute informs the owner of a vehicle-dismantling business that inspections will be made on a regular basis. Thus, the vehicle dismantler knows that the inspections to which he is subject do not constitute discretionary acts by a government official but are conducted pursuant to statute. Section 415-a5 also sets forth the scope of the inspection and, accordingly places the operator on notice as to how to comply with the statute. In addition, it notifies the operator as to who is authorized to conduct an inspection.

Finally, the "time, place, and scope" of the inspection is limited to place appropriate restraints upon the discretion of the inspecting officers. The officers are allowed to conduct an inspection only "during [the] regular and usual business hours." The inspections can be made only of vehicle-dismantling and related industries. And the permissible scope of these searches is narrowly defined: the inspectors may examine the records, as well as "any vehicles or parts of vehicles which are subject to the record-keeping requirements of this section and which are on the premises."

The Court of Appeals, nevertheless, struck down the statute as violative of the Fourth Amendment because, in its view, the statute had no truly administrative purpose but was "designed simply to give the police an expedient means of enforcing penal sanctions for possession of stolen property." In arriving at this conclusion, the Court of Appeals failed to recognize that a State can address a major social problem *both* by way of an administrative scheme *and* through penal sanctions. Administrative statutes and penal laws may have the same *ultimate* purpose of remedying the social problem, but they have different subsidiary purposes and prescribe different methods of addressing the problem.

Nor do we think that this administrative scheme is unconstitutional simply because, in the course of enforcing it, an inspecting officer may discover evidence of crimes, besides violations of the scheme itself. The discovery of evidence of crimes in the course of an otherwise proper administrative inspection does not render that search illegal or the administrative scheme suspect.

Finally, we fail to see any constitutional significance in the fact that police officers, rather than "administrative" agents, are permitted to conduct the Sec. 415-a5 inspection. [W]e decline to impose upon the States the burden of requiring the enforcement of their regulatory statutes to be carried out by special agents.

[Reversed.]

Obviously, warrantless searches may occur in motel lobbies, bars, and other business premises open to the public. The business has no expectation of privacy there. Additionally, the "open field" doctrine allows warrantless searches of areas that are so open to plain view that no reasonable expectation of privacy can exist. For example, the Supreme Court approved a warrantless EPA search carried out by a commercial aerial photographer flying over a 2,000-acre chemical plant consisting of numerous covered buildings with outdoor manufacturing equipment and piping conduits.

Although the company had substantial ground-level security, the Court concluded that the plant was more like an open field than it was like "curtilage"—open space in the immediate vicinity of a dwelling, such as a yard. The Court noted that a commercial property owner has to expect less privacy than a homeowner so that, correspondingly, the government's latitude to conduct warrantless searches is greater.[3]

RULE MAKING

Much of the legislative-type activity of federal agencies is carried out through their rule-making function. Sometimes Congress spells out the procedures for rule-making by a particular agency in that agency's enabling statute. Sometimes the agency is left to follow the Administrative Procedure Act (APA), which the more specific statutes normally follow anyway. The APA provides a comprehensive set of procedural guidelines for a variety of agency activities. In the rule-making area, the APA provides for two basic types—informal and formal. A third type, called hybrid rule-making, has also developed.

Informal Rule Making

Sometimes Congress will authorize informal rule-making. To properly promulgate a rule under these procedures, the agency usually publishes a notice of the proposed rule in the *Federal Register*. There follows a comment period, typically of 30 days, in which any interested citizen or company may send written comments to the agency regarding the rule. Such comments might argue that the rule is unnecessary, unduly burdensome to business, does not go far enough to remedy the problem, goes too far, and the like. The agency is then supposed to digest and react to the comments, perhaps by altering or even scrapping the proposed rule. Normally the rule is modestly altered, and then published in final form in the *Federal Register*. At that point, it becomes effective. Untimately it will be codified in the *Code of Federal Regulations* along with the rules of all other federal administrative agencies.

Formal Rule Making

Formal rule-making also involves "notice and comment," but supplements these with formal hearings at which witnesses testify and are cross-examined by interested parties. Transcripts of the testimony are preserved and become part of the public record. Formal rule-making can be very expensive and time-consuming but theoretically leads to especially well-considered results.

Hybrid Rule Making

Hybrid rule-making closely resembles formal rule-making, except that there is no right to cross-examine the agency's expert witnesses, and, as we shall soon see, a different standard of review is applied by the courts if the rule-making procedure is challenged.

---

[3] *Dow Chemical Co. v. U.S.*, 426 U.S. 227 (1986).

Judicial Review of Rule Making

Naturally some parties are likely to be aggrieved by promulgation of rules that affect them adversely. Few important rules are issued without a subsequent court challenge. Courts will invalidate rules issued pursuant to an unconstitutional delegation of legislative power (as noted above, an extremely rare occurrence) and rules that are unconstitutional (perhaps because they discriminate on the basis of race in violation of equal protection principles).

Courts will also invalidate rules not issued in accordance with applicable procedural standards. For example, if an agency engaged in informal rulemaking fails to publish a proposed version of the rule in the *Federal Register* so that comments may be received, the rule will likely be invalidated if challenged. The courts will permit minor deviations from APA procedures, but major ones are risky.

Standards of Review: In issuing rules, an agency will have to make several types of decisions. One type of decision will likely turn on a pure **question of law** regarding its powers and the scope of its charge under a law passed by Congress. Courts are experts on the law. Therefore, they have the authority to substitute their interpretations for the meaning of laws passed by Congress for the interpretations made by the agency. Nonetheless, the Supreme Court has concluded that it makes sense to give deference to the expertise developed by the agency, noting:

> When a court reviews an agency's construction of the statute which it administers, it is confronted with two questions. First, always, is the question whether Congress has spoken to the precise question at issue. If the intent of Congress is clear, that is the end of the matter; for the court, as well as the agency, must give effect to the unambiguously expressed intent of Congress. If, however, the court determines Congress has not directly addressed the precise question at issue, the court does not simply impose its own construction on the statute, as would be necessary in the absence of an administrative interpretation. Rather, if the statute is silent or ambiguous with respect to the specific issue, the question for the court is whether the agency's answer is based on a permissible construction of the statute....
>
> We have long recognized that considerable weight should be accorded to an executive department's construction of a statutory scheme it is entrusted to administer, and the principles of deference to administrative interpretations.[4]

An agency issuing rules must also make decisions as to facts and policy. Two tests predominate review of these types of decisions. The "arbitrary and capricious" test assumes the correctness of an agency's decision, placing the burden on any challenger to prove that the decision was not simply erroneous but so far off the mark as to be arbitrary and capricious. The "substantial evidence" test requires that an agency's decision be based not just on a scintilla of evidence, but on such relevant evidence as a reasonable mind might accept as adequate to support a conclusion.

---

[4] *Chevron U.S.A., Inc. v. Natural Resources Defense Council*, 467 U.S. 837 (1984).

The "arbitrary and capricious" test is usually used to judge any policy decision by an agency. Findings of fact made pursuant to formal rule making are judged by the "substantial evidence" test. Factual determinations made in informal rule making are gauged by the "arbitrary and capricious" test unless an agency's authorizing act calls for use of the "substantial evidence" test. Many courts have noted that there is little practical difference in how the two tests are usually applied. Both require court deference to agency decision making, but the following case shows that such deference is not unlimited.

MOTOR VEHICLE MANUFACTURERS ASS'N v. STATE FARM MUTUAL AUTO. INS. CO.

U.S. SUPREME COURT, 463 U.S. 29 (1983)

To improve highway safety, Congress passed the National Traffic and Motor Vehicle Safety Act of 1966, which directs the Secretary of Transportation or his designated representative to issue motor vehicle safety standards. In 1967, the Secretary's representative, the National Highway Traffic Safety Administration (NHTSA) issued Standard 208, which required installation of seatbelts in all new automobiles. Because usage by consumers was quite low, NHTSA studied passive restraints in the form of automatic seatbelts and airbags, which it estimated could prevent approximately 12,000 deaths and more than 100,000 serious injuries annually. Deadlines for implementation of the passive restraint systems were repeatedly extended until, in 1977, the Secretary promulgated Modified Standard 208, which ordered a phase in on all new cars to take place between 1982 and 1984. The Secretary assumed that 60 percent of new cars would have airbags and 40 percent would have automatic seatbelts.

However, it soon became apparent that 99 percent of American cars would have detachable seatbelts. In light of this fact and of economic difficulties in the auto industry, the Secretary began in 1981 to reconsider the passive restraint requirement of Modified Standard 208 and ultimately rescinded it.

State Farm Mutual and other insurance companies sued for review of the rescission order. The federal district court and court of appeals held the rescission to be arbitrary and capricious in violation of law. The petitioner Motor Vehicle Manufacturers Association brought the case to the Supreme Court.

WHITE, JUSTICE:

Both the Motor Vehicle Safety Act and the 1974 Amendments concerning occupant crash protection standards indicate that motor vehicle safety standards are to be promulgated under the informal rulemaking procedures of §553 of the Administrative Procedure Act. The agency's action in promulgating such standards therefore may be set aside only if found to be "arbitrary, capricious, an abuse of discretion, or otherwise not in accordance with law." We believe that the rescission or modification of an occupant protection standard is subject to the same test.

The Department of Transportation argues that under this standard, a reviewing court may not set aside an agency rule that is rational, based on consideration of the relevant factors and within the scope of the authority delegated to the agency by the statute. We do not disagree with this formulation. The scope of review under the "arbitrary and capricious" standard is narrow and a court is not to substitute its judgment for that of the agency. Nevertheless, the agency must examine the relevant data and articulate a satisfactory explanation for its action including a "rational connection between the facts found and the

CONTINUED

choice made." *Burlington Truck Lines v. U.S.*, 371 U.S. 156 (1962). In reviewing that explanation, we must "consider whether the decision was based on a consideration of relevant factors and whether there has been a clear error of judgment." *Bowman Transp. Inc. v. Arkansas-Best Freight System, Inc.*, 419 U.S. 281 (1974). Normally, an agency rule would be arbitrary and capricious if the agency has relied on factors which Congress has not intended it to consider, entirely failed to consider an important aspect of the problem, offered an explanation for its decision that runs counter to the evidence before the agency, or is so implausible that it could not be ascribed to a difference in view or the product of agency expertise. The reviewing court should not attempt itself to make up for such deficiencies: "We may not supply a reasoned basis for the agency's action that the agency itself has not given." *SEC v. Chenery Corp.*, 332 U.S. 194 (1947). "We will, however, uphold a decision of less than ideal clarity if the agency's path may reasonably be discerned." *Bowman Transp.*

The ultimate question before us is whether NHTSA's rescission of the passive restraint requirement of Standard 208 was arbitrary and capricious. We conclude, as did the Court of Appeals, that it was. We also conclude, but for somewhat different reasons, that further consideration of the issue by the agency is therefore required. We deal separately with ... airbags and seatbelts.

The first and most obvious reason for finding rescission arbitrary and capricious is that NHTSA apparently gave no consideration whatever to modifying the Standard to require that airbag technology be utilized. Not one sentence of its rulemaking statement discusses the airbags-only option. [W]hat we said in *Burlington Truck Lines v. United States*, 371 U.S., at 167, is appropos here:

> There are no findings and no analysis here to justify the choice made, no indication of the basis on which the [agency] exercised its expert discretion. We are not prepared to and the Administrative Procedures Act will not permit us to accept such ... practice. ... Expert discretion is the lifeblood of the administrative process, but "unless we make the requirements for administrative action strict and demanding, expertise, the strength of modern government, can become a monster which rules with no practical limits on its discretion." *New York v. United States*, 342 U.S. 882.

We have frequently reiterated that an agency must cogently explain why it has exercised its discretion in a given manner. [T]he airbag is more than a policy alternative to the passive restraint standard; it is a technological alternative within the ambit of the existing standard. We hold only that given the judgment made in 1977 that airbags are an effective and cost-beneficial life-saving technology, the mandatory passive-restraint rule may not be abandoned without any consideration whatsoever of an airbags-only requirement.

Although the issue is closer, we also find that the agency was too quick to dismiss the safety benefits of automatic seatbelts. NHTSA's critical finding was that, in light of the industry's plans to install readily detachable passive belts, it could not reliably predict "even a 5 percentage point increase as the minimum level of expected usage increase." The Court of Appeals rejected this finding because there is "not one iota" of evidence that Modified Standard 208 will fail to increase nationwide seatbelt use by at least 13 percentage points, the level of increased usage necessary for the standard to justify its cost.

Recognizing that policymaking in a complex society must account for uncertainty ... does not imply that it is sufficient for an agency to merely recite the terms "substantial uncertainty" as a justification for its actions. The agency must explain the evidence which is available and must offer a "rational connection between the facts found and the choice made." *Burlington Truck Lines*. Generally, one aspect of that explanation would be a justification for rescinding the regulation before engaging in a search for further evidence.

The agency is correct to look at the costs as well as the benefits of Standard 208 [but i]n reaching its judgment, NHTSA should bear in mind that Congress intended safety to be the preeminent factor under the Act.

The agency also failed to articulate a basis for not requiring nondetachable belts under Standard 208. By failing to analyze the continuous seatbelt in its own right, the agency has failed to offer the rational connection between facts and judgment required to pass muster under the arbitrary and capricious standard. We agree with the Court of Appeals that NHTSA did not suggest that the emergency release mechanisms used in non-detachable belts are any less effective for emergency egress than the

CONTINUED

> buckle release system used in detachable belts.
>
> "An agency's view of what is in the public interest may change, either with or without a change in circumstances. But an agency changing its course must supply a reasoned analysis...." *Greater Boston Television Corp. v. FCC*, 444 F.2d 841 (CADC).
>
> [Remand to Court of Appeals with directions to remand to NHTSA for further consideration consistent with this opinion.]

ADJUDICATION

Most major federal agencies also exercise substantial powers of adjudication. That is, they not only issue rules and investigate to uncover violations, they may also charge alleged violators and try them to determine whether a violation has actually occurred.

Because the agency is acting as legislator, policeman, prosecutor, *and* judge and jury, care must be taken to avoid abuse. For that reason, the APA and the courts demand that fairly formal procedural requirements be followed.

Over the years, procedures have evolved such that a person or company brought before an administrative agency for adjudication of a charged violation will usually have the right to notice, the right to counsel, the right to present evidence, and the right to confront and cross-examine adverse witnesses.

A jury trial is not allowed, but the case is heard by an Administrative Law Judge (ALJ), who is the finder of fact in the first instance. Although the 1,000-plus ALJs in the federal system are employees of the agencies whose cases they hear, they cannot be disciplined except for good cause as determined by the federal Merit System Protection Board. Thus, the ALJs exercise substantial autonomy and are seldom puppets of the agency employing them.

Under the APA, all ALJ decisions are reviewable by the employing agency. The agency reviews the record developed in the hearing that was conducted by the ALJ, and reviews the ALJ's fact-findings and legal conclusions. Although the agency usually conducts a limited appellate-type review of the ALJ's findings and conclusions, it does have the power to substitute its own findings and conclusions for those of the ALJ. If the agency does so, however, it still must base it's decision on the evidence that appears in the ALJ-hearing record—it cannot disregard this record.

Adjudication is a very influential process. Not only are findings of fact required (e.g., Did the employer consult the union before deciding to move the plant?), but the ALJ and the agency must also interpret the applicable law (e.g., Is the employer required to consult the union before deciding to move the plant?). During the Reagan administration, the NLRB largely rewrote American labor policy through the process of adjudication. Although done piecemeal through several decisions involving unfair labor practice charges, the change in the law was as complete as if major rule-making had been undertaken.

The quasi-judicial powers of major federal agencies are so significant that such decisions are normally reviewed directly by the Circuit Courts of Appeal. Other types of decisions—such as the decision to issue a subpoena or to promulgate a new rule—are normally reviewed in the first instance by federal district courts. (Figure 6.1 helps illustrate the adjudicatory process of a federal agency.)

FIGURE 6.1

Nature of violation or investigation (complaint).

↓

Informal discussion with agency. Process may end if party complies or ceases and desists.

↓

Hearing before administrative law judge. Decision rendered.

↓

Appeal to full board of agency. Agency may overturn decision of administrative law judge.

↓

Appeal to court of appeals or district court. Case must fulfill three requirements: standing, ripeness, and exhaustion of administrative remedies. Court must hear case if it meets these requirements; no discretionary power.

↓

Appeal to Supreme Court if certiorari is granted.

■ ADMINISTRATIVE LAW PROCESS

Many different kinds of agency action obviously can have an effect on the liberty or property of individuals and companies. As we saw in the previous chapter, procedural due process requires that many of these actions be preceded by notice and a hearing of some type. These principles were discussed and illustrated at length. The following case involves a procedural due process challenge to an agency action. Because the agency's action was of an adjudicative type—aimed at a particular company based on specific facts—procedural due process applied. The question that remained, however, was whether the agency had provided sufficient procedural protections under the circumstances.

Gun South, Inc. v. Brady

U.S. Eleventh Circuit Court of Appeals, 877 F.2d 858 (1989)

Gun South, Inc. (GSI), is a wholesale gun dealer licensed by the Treasury Department's Bureau of Alcohol, Tobacco, and Firearms. In late 1988 and again in early 1989, GSI applied for and was granted permits to import semiautomatic rifles for sporting purposes. On January 23, 1989, GSI ordered 800 AUG-SA semiautomatic rifles and obligated itself to pay $700,000 toward a larger total purchase price. On March 21, 1989, William Bennett, the "Drug Czar," speaking for the secretary of the treasury, announced a temporary 90-day suspension on the importation of five "assault-type" weapons, including those order by GSI, so that the bureau could review its conclusion that such rifles are "generally suitable for sporting purposes." Although the bureau assured GSI that the suspension did not apply to weapons purchased under preexisting permits, the Customs Service intercepted GSI's shipment of the aforementioned rifles at the Birmingham Airport.

GSI brought this action to enjoin the government from interfering with the delivery of firearms imported under permits issued before the suspension. The district court issued such an injunction; Brady, secretary of the treasury, appealed. The appellate court's discussion of the due process issue follows.

Hatchett, Circuit Judge:

According to GSI, the Government's failure to give it notice of the suspension and an opportunity to respond prior to imposing the suspension deprived GSI of its due process rights. GSI reaches this conclusion by arguing that the Government may not deprive an individual of property without giving such individual an opportunity to be heard. Although GSI correctly argues the general rule, GSI fails to recognize that the Constitution does not always require such predeprivation procedural protection. *Hodel v. Virginia Surface Mining and Reclamation Assoc.*, 452 U.S. 264, 300 (1981) ("summary administrative action may be justified in emergency situations"). See *Barry v. Barchi*, 443 U.S. 55 (1979) (pending prompt judicial or administrative hearing to determine issue, state's board could properly temporarily suspend horse trainer's license prior to hearing); *Ewing v. Mytinger and Casselberry, Inc.*, 339 U.S. 594 (1950) (allowing seizure of misbranded articles by enforcement agency prior to hearing).

Rather than setting categories of mandatory procedural protections in all cases, the Supreme Court decides the nature and timing of the requisite process in an individual case by accommodating the relevant competing interests.

CONTINUED

The Supreme Court's balancing test essentially requires us to weigh three factors: (1) the nature of the private interest; (2) the risk of an erroneous deprivation of such interest; and (3) the government's interest in taking its action, including the burdens that any additional procedural requirement would entail. *Mathews v. Eldridge*, 424 U.S. 319, 335 (1976). Balancing these considerations, we conclude that the Bureau's summary action did not violate GSI's due process rights.

The Bureau imposed the temporary suspension to protect the public by ensuring that nearly three-quarters of a million rifles do not improperly enter the country. The protection of the public's health and safety is a paramount government interest which justifies summary administrative action:

> Protection of the health and safety of the public is a paramount governmental interest which justifies summary administrative action. Indeed, deprivation of property to protect the public health and safety is '[o]ne of the oldest examples' of permissible summary action.

Hodel, 452 U.S. at 300 (safety concerns justified summary seizure of vitamin product). The public interest in avoiding the important of possible illegal assault rifles which could contribute significantly to this country's violent crime epidemic is clearly substantial, especially given the large number of rifles approved for importation under the current outstanding permits. The Government could not protect the public interest without imposing the temporary suspension.

On the other side of the balancing equation, we consider the nature of the private interest, including the deprivation's length and finality. GSI has not suffered a permanent loss because the Government has not revoked GSI's license or its permits. The Government has merely deprived GSI of the ability to import the AUG-SA rifle for ninety days. The Government has further reassured the court that it will not revoke GSI's permits without giving GSI the right to participate in a hearing.

In addition to being a non-final, temporary deprivation, the ninety-day suspension does not affect a significant portion of GSI's imports. The rifles which GSI seeks to import during this ninety-day period are only a small percent of the number of fire-arms it plans to import under its permits this year.

Considering the final factor, we do not find that the Government's summary action presents a significant risk of an erroneous deprivation of GSI's right to import the rifles. First, GSI only loses its right to import the rifles for ninety days. Second, as discussed above, the Bureau considered ample evidence before imposing the temporary suspension, and therefore, it minimized the risk that its actions would erroneously deprive GSI of its right to import the AUG-SA rifles.

Balancing GSI's temporary non-final loss of its right to import one type of rifle against the Government's interest in preventing the unlawful importation of firearms, we conclude that the Government did not err by suspending the importation of the AUG-SA rifle prior to giving GSI an opportunity to respond. The strong public interest in the immediate action outweighs the temporary and limited impact on GSI's alleged property interest. We find support for this decision in other cases which have subordinated more substantial property interests to the Government interest in protecting the public. *See Mackey v. Montrym*, 443 U.S. 1 (1979) (although license to operate motor vehicle is substantial property interest, the substantial nature of such interest is diminished measureably by maximum duration of suspension being ninety days and availability of immediate post-suspension hearing). Furthermore, the availability of a hearing at the end of this temporary suspension provides adequate procedural protection. Thus, the summary imposition of the import suspension does not violate GSI's due process rights.

[Reversed.]

ESTOPPEL

Often businesses that deal with the government seek advice from government officials, asking such questions as the right way to fill out tax returns, the correct interpretation of a zoning ordinance, or the legality of a securities sale. What all businesspersons must keep in mind is that government officials may from time to time give erroneous advice, but that does not relieve the businesses from culpability.

The legal doctrine of **estoppel** provides in many areas that an entity that take a particular position that others rely on cannot later change that original position when to do so would injure the party that relied on it. Unfortunately, the general rule is that the doctrine of estoppel does not operate against the government. That is to say, if the government gives erroneous advice, it is not later "estopped to deny" its original position.

The leading case on this subject is *Federal Crop Insurance Corp. v. Merrill*,[5] in which a government official told farmer Merrill that reseeded spring wheat would be covered by federal crop insurance. Unfortunately, the agency's regulations, printed in the *Federal Register,* stated that insurance would not be provided for reseeded crops. Merrill, not knowing of the regulation, relied on the advice. When the crop was destroyed, however, Merrill was unable to recover insurance. The government was not "estopped to deny" its original position. It was allowed to change its position in a way that the doctrine of estoppel would probably prevent a private insurance company from doing.

The reasoning behind the government exclusion lies, in part, in the notion that federal statutes are contained in the *United States Code* and federal regulations are printed in the *Federal Register* and codified in the *Code of Federal Regulations,* and therefore all citizens are "on notice" of these rules. Still, the exclusion seems unjust to many people, so some exceptions have developed. For example, some courts will invoke estoppel against the government when an official has intentionally misled someone. Others create an exception when the government is acting in a proprietary (business-like) capacity. Today, for example, many courts might decide the 1947 *Merrill* case differently, because in that case the agency was acting more in the role of a private insurance company than like a government agency.

The doctrine's impact when lower levels of government are involved is less clear but cannot be ignored. This lesson was brought home recently when builders given the "go-ahead" by local government officials to build a 31-story building were, after substantial construction, forced to remove everything above the 19th floor because the officials had misread a zoning ordinance.[6] The court said that estoppel is not available "for the purpose of ratifying an administrative error."

---

[5] 332 U.S. 380 (1947).

[6] *Matter of Parkview Assoc. v. City of New York,* 513 N.Y.S.2d 342, *cert. denied,* 109 S.Ct. 30 (1988).

RECENT DEVELOPMENTS

The federal administrative process has been closely scrutinized from several angles in recent years. To make federal agencies more open to public view and more responsive to the needs of constituents and to fiscal and economic concerns, many changes have been made.

FREEDOM OF INFORMATION ACT

The Freedom of Information Act of 1967, with significant amendments in 1974, is codified as section 552 of the Administrative Procedure Act. Before its enactment it was extremely difficult for a private citizen to obtain and examine government-held documents. The agency from which the information was requested could deny the applicant on the grounds that he or she was not properly and directly concerned or that the requested information should not be disclosed because to do so would not be in the public interest. Under FOIA, any person may reasonably describe what information is sought and the burden of proof for withholding information is on the agency. A response is required of the agency within ten working days after receipt of a request, and denial by the agency may be appealed by means of an expeditable federal district court action. There are, of course, exemptions—nine specific areas to which the disclosure requirements do not apply. That is, if the information concerns certain matters, the agency is not required to comply with the request. The nine exemptions apply to matters that are

1. Secret in the interest of national defense or foreign policy
2. Related solely to internal personnel rules and practices of an agency
3. Exempted from disclosure by statute
4. Trade secrets and commercial or financial information obtained from a person and privileged or confidential
5. Interagency or intraagency memoranda or letters
6. Personnel and medical files, the disclosure of which would constitute an invasion of personal privacy
7. Certain investigatory records compiled for law enforcement purposes
8. Related to the regulation or supervision of financial institutions
9. Geologic and geophysical information and data, including maps concerning wells

With regard to the exemptions, Chief Judge Bazelon had this to say in *Soucie v. David*, 448 F.2d 1067 (D.C.Cir. 1971):

> The touchstone of any proceedings under the Act must be the clear legislative intent to assure public access to all governmental records whose disclosure would not significantly harm specific governmental interests. The

policy of the Act requires that the disclosure requirements be construed broadly, the exemptions narrowly.

Businesses have often complained that confidential information they were required to disclose to the government pursuant to regulatory programs might be vulnerable to disclosure to competitors through the FOIA. In 1987, regulations were issued that require federal agencies to provide early notification to businesses whenever "arguably" confidential business data in government hands is about to be released under the FOIA. Those businesses are given an opportunity to object to the disclosure. Agencies are required to explain in writing if they choose to override such an objection.

PRIVACY ACT

The Federal Privacy Act of 1974 seeks to protect individuals from unnecessary disclosures of facts about them from files held by federal agencies. Although the need of federal agencies for information is recognized through a large series of exceptions and qualifications, the general thrust of the Privacy Act is to prohibit federal agencies from disclosing information from their files about an individual without that individual's written consent. Federal agencies are specifically forbidden from selling or renting an individual's name and address, unless authorized by another law.

GOVERNMENT IN THE SUNSHINE ACT

A further effort to open up the government is provided by the 1976 Government in the Sunshine Act, codified as section 552b of the Administrative Procedure Act. The purpose of the Act is to assure that "every portion of every meeting of an agency shall be open to public observation." There are, however, exceptions to the open meeting requirement. If the meeting qualifies for one of ten specified exemptions and the agency by majority vote decides to do so, the meeting may be closed to the public. The exemptions of the Act are similar to the nine provided for in the FOIA but are not identical.

Most states have passed some form of open meetings laws. There is considerable diversity, but the common purpose is to permit the public to view the decision-making process at all stages.

REGULATORY FLEXIBILITY ACT

We are all presumed to know the law, and when final versions of rules are published in the *Federal Register,* legally speaking, we are all put on notice of their existence. Congress realized, however, that as a practical matter many persons, especially small businesses, do not closely follow proposed and final rules printed in the *Federal Register.* Therefore, Congress passed the Regulatory Flexibility Act in 1980. Among other provisions, the RFA requires most federal agencies to transmit to the Small Business Administration on a semiannual basis agendas briefly describing areas in which they may propose rules having a substantial impact on small entities (including small businesses, small governmental units, and nonprofit organizations). In this way the small businesses may be on the lookout for potential changes. Also, when any rule is promulgated that will have a significant economic impact on a substantial number of small entities, the agency proposing the rule must give notice not only through the *Federal Register* but also through publications of general notice likely to be obtained by small entities, such as trade journals.

DEREGULATION

The economic efficiency of many programs of federal regulation is easily questioned. Furthermore, the paperwork burden on many companies attempting to comply with complex federal regulatory schemes can be overwhelming. For these and other reasons, recent administrations have attempted to "deregulate" the economy.

Congress has, at times, assisted the deregulation movement, as evidenced by the Airline Deregulation Act of 1978, the CAB Sunshine Act of 1984, and the Motor Carrier Act of 1980. Various executive orders and agency interpretations have supplemented the effort. During the Reagan administration, for example, there was a noticeably less aggressive enforcement attitude in such agencies as OSHA, the Consumer Products Safety Commission (CPSC), and the EPA.

The advantages and disadvantages of deregulation will be debated for years. Proponents point to the cost savings and the general fare reductions that have occurred in the airline industry through introduction of free competition and elimination of government rate setting. Opponents point to a recent rise in injuries from products and in the workplace, the provinces of OSHA and the CPSC, and to alleged increases in various types of pollution caused by EPA inactivity. Neither increases in regulation nor decreases in regulation (as the *Motor Vehicle Manufacturers Ass'n v. State Farm Mutual Auto Ins. Co.* case shows) come without cost. To a large extent, the positions taken on the deregulation debate are determined by political philosophies and "whose ox is being gored."

Questions and Problems

1. Louisiana passed a statute to regulate commercial marine diving. Among other things, the statute created a Licensing Board, which thereafter promulgated rules and regulations relative to the qualifications of apprentice, journeyman, and master marine divers. One regulation provided that a person could be licensed as a master marine diver only if he or she had "continuously worked for a period of five years under supervision of a master marine diver." Under this regulation, the board refused to license a diver (as a master marine diver) who had had

several years' diving experience in the U.S. Navy and who had also had about eight years' commercial diving experience in Louisiana (but not under supervision of a master marine diver). The diver challenged the board's action, contending that the statute was an unconstitutional delegation of legislative authority because it permitted the board to set licensing qualifications without containing any statutory limitations on it, or any standards to which the board should look in setting its qualifications. Do you agree with this contention? Why or why not? (*Banjavich v. Louisiana Licensing Board of Marine Divers*, 111 So.2d 505, 1959.)

2. The U.S. Department of Energy (DOE) issued a subpoena for Phoenix Petroleum Company records during the course of an investigation to determine whether Phoenix had illegally sold crude oil. Phoenix moved to quash the subpoena, claiming DOE was on a "fishing expedition." DOE proved the subpoenaed items were reasonably relevant to the purpose of the investigation but admitted that it could not establish probable cause to believe a violation had taken place. Should the subpoena be quashed (i.e, invalidated) by the court? Discuss. (*U.S. v. Phoenix Petroleum Co.*, 571 F.Supp. 16, S.D. Tex. 1982.)

3. Biswell, a pawnshop operator who was federally licensed to deal in sporting weapons, was visited one afternoon by a policeman and a Federal Treasury agent who requested entry into a locked gun storeroom. They had no search warrant but showed Biswell a section of the Gun Control Act of 1968, which authorized warrantless entry of the premises of gun dealers. Biswell then allowed a search that turned up two sawed-off rifles and led to Biswell's conviction for dealing in firearms without having paid a required special occupational tax. On appeal, Biswell challenged the constitutionality of the warrantless search. Discuss. (*U.S. v. Biswell*, 406 U.S. 311, 1972.)

4. The Federal Trade Commission Act authorizes the Federal Trade Commission to determine what kinds of business practices constitute "unfair methods of competition, and deceptive or unfair practices" and to prohibit such practices. Traditionally, when such a practice has been found to exist, the FTC has simply ordered the offending company to stop the practice. In 1975, however, when the FTC ruled that Listerine ads had—for many years—falsely stated that Listerine was "effective in preventing and curing colds and sore throats," the FTC ordered the manufacturer to stop such advertising, and in addition, it ordered the manufacturer to insert in *future* advertising the statement that Listerine would *not* prevent or cure colds and sore throats. The manufacturer then asked the federal courts to rule that the FTC did not have the power, under the Federal Trade Commission Act, to issue such an order (known as "corrective advertising"). Do you think the manufacturer's argument is a good one? Why or why not? (*Warner-Lambert v. FTC*, 562 F.2d 749, 1977.)

5. A New Jersey statute provided that every taxicab owner who wished to operate in a city within the state had to obtain consent of the "governing body" of the municipality. The statute also provided that the governing body could "make and enforce" ordinances to "license and regulate" all vehicles used as taxis. Under this law a New Jersey city passed an ordinance that set a flat rate taxicab fare of $1.15 for all trips made within the city, regardless of the miles involved. A taxicab owner who wanted to charge $1.50 for some trips attacked this ordinance on the grounds that the statute did *not*, expressly or impliedly, give to cities the power to set taxi fares. (I.e., the gist of the attack was that legislatures could not delegate *rate-making* powers to municipalities.) What was the result? Discuss. (*Yellow Cab Corp. v. Clifton City Council*, 308 A.2d 60, 1973.)

6. One section of an Oklahoma law provided that no person shall "knowingly sell" alcoholic beverages to a minor. Certain penalties were provided for, in the event of violations. Another section of the law authorized the Oklahoma Beverage Control Board to promulgate rules and regulations to carry out the act. The board then adopted a rule that, in essence, provided that any liquor license could be revoked if the licensee sold liquor to a minor, even if he or she did *not* know the buyer was a minor. When the license of a liquor retailer. Wray, was revoked by the board as a result of his sale of liquor to a person whom he did not know was a minor, he contended in the Oklahoma courts that the rule of the board was invalid because it conflicted with the quoted statute. Do you agree with this argument? Discuss. (*Wray v. Oklahoma Alcoholic Beverage Control Board*, 442 P.2d 309, 1968.)

7. A Social Security Administration field representative erroneously told Hansen that she was not eligible for "mother's insurance benefits." Because of this advice, Hansen did not file a written application, which, by the terms of the law, was a prerequisite to receiving benefits. Nor did the agent follow instructions to advise potential claimants of the written filing requirement and to encourage them to file in a close case. A year or so later, Hansen filed an application and received benefits. She then sued to recover the benefits that she had missed during the period that she had relied on the erroneous advice. Will she succeed? (*Schweiker v. Hansen,* 450 U.S. 785, 1981.)

CHAPTER 7

Jill is a regional sales manager for a nationwide chain of retail consumer electronics stores. She and her assistants at company headquarters design promotional programs for stores in the region, supervise store managers' implementation of company marketing strategies, and conduct sales seminars for salespeople at these stores.

Questions continually arise about how far promotional materials and the statements of individual salespeople can go in pushing their products. These questions relate not only to what is legal, but also to what is "appropriate"

BUSINESS ETHICS, CORPORATE SOCIAL RESPONSIVENESS, AND THE LAW

or "ethical." If particular statements are legal, is there any reason at all to be concerned about them? Are there any other standards? Jill and her associates know that it usually will be illegal to brazenly lie about the quality of a product. But they also know that it is often very difficult for a buyer to prove that a seller made intentionally deceptive statements, so the legal risk is small even in such a case. Jill understands that a company's reputation, and ultimately its sales, may suffer if it becomes known for dealing dishonestly. She also knows, however, that if some forms of subtle deception are practiced with skill, most customers will never know. Although a few customers may discover the deception, the number probably will be small enough that sales will not be hurt enough to offset the gains from the practice.

Even if the legal or financial risks are not great, Jill feels that it is "wrong" to lie to a customer. When she receives a lot of pressure from her superiors to increase sales, however, she begins to ask herself various questions: "Why is it wrong, really?" "Who, after all, defines what is wrong if it isn't illegal?" "We're selling to adults; aren't they supposed to look after themselves?" "Isn't this just the free market at work, and doesn't the market operate impersonally on the assumption that all sellers and buyers pursue their own economic self-interests?" "Isn't it okay to do it if I *feel* okay about it?" "But what if I feel good about it only after some strained rationalizing?" "And ... let's face it—I don't always feel good about what happens."

When Jill tries to define what is "wrong," she finds it difficult to come up with any standards or any systematic way to develop such standards. Not only that, but she cannot even decide whether there is a rational way to analyze problems of this nature. Assuming, again, that there are no significant legal risks, Jill wonders how much latitude a salesperson should have in extolling the virtues of a product. Must every shortcoming of the item be revealed? Surely not. But why not? May the sales pitch be couched in vague, laudatory terms or must all responses be absolutely factual, precise, and to-the-point? Should the salesperson be concerned about the customer's real need for the product, or is the customer's apparent willingness to purchase the only thing that matters? Should there be any regard for the customer's particular susceptibilities to advertising? What if the advertising campaign that brought the customer into the store was full of "subliminal" messages that subconsciously persuaded him that this product would improve his love life? Jill finally decides that she does not have the time or energy to worry about such things, and that she will just be guided by the opinion of the company's attorneys about the legal risks of particular strategies and statements. Over a period of time, however, she is increasingly bothered by some of the promotional strategies that she initiates or approves. After doing some reading, she realizes that she has been grappling with age-old questions and that there is an entire field of study concerned with questions of this nature. Jill has discovered "business ethics."

HUMOR AND THE LAW

Lawyers are always accused, and often justly so, of evading justice and abusing the English language by specializing in verbosity and obfuscation. Such charges led one lawyer to suggest that had a lawyer written the Book of Genesis in the Bible, it might begin like this:

> In, at, around and/or in close proximity to the beginning, God, in conjunction with his agents, assignees and successors in interest created, devised, caused to be made, fashioned, formed, brought into being, conceived, invented and occasioned the Heaven and the Earth. And said Earth was without form and void, but not voidable; and darkness was upon the face of the deep. And the Spirit of God moved upon the face of the waters.
>
> And God stated, "Let there be light," or words essentially to that effect. And based on information and belief, there was light. Given all the facts known presently, and in the absence of any evidence to the contrary, it is reasonable to draw the inference that God's utterance was the proximate cause of the light.

Mr. Lavine continued at greater length, but you get the idea. (Lavine, *At Issue*, American Bar Association Journal, (Sept. 1983), p. 1192).

Along a similar line, it has been suggested that when an ordinary man might say "I give you this orange," an attorney would say:

> Know all men by these presents: that I hereby give, grant, bargain, sell, release, convey, transfer, and quitclaim all my right, title, interest, benefit, and use whatever in, of, and concerning this chattel, otherwise known as an orange, or citrus orantium, together with all the appurtenances thereto of skin, pulp, pip, rind, seeds, and juice, to have and to hold the said orange together with its skin, pulp, pip, rind, seeds, and juice for his own use and behoof, to himself and his heirs in fee simple forever, free from all liens, encumbrances, easements, limitations, restraints, or conditions whatsoever, any and all prior deeds, transfers or other documents whatsoever, anywhere made to the contrary notwithstanding, with full power to bite, cut, suck, or otherwise eat the said orange or to give away the same, with or without its skin, pulp, pip, rind, seeds, or juice.

(New York State Bar Association, *State Bar News*, Nov. 1977).

WHAT IS ETHICS?

In a formal sense, the term **ethics** refers to the study of **morality** by systematically exploring moral values, moral standards and obligations, moral reasoning, and moral judgments. The terms *morality* and *morals* refer to the appropriate treatment of our fellow human beings. Although some people observe a technical distinction between *ethics* and *morals,* these terms are often used interchangeably. When someone says, for example, that "Joe did not act ethically in that situation," the word *ethically* means the same thing as *morally.* In this chapter, we are not very fussy about the use of these terms. Sometimes we will use them in their technical sense, and sometimes we will not. The context will make the meaning clear.

IS BUSINESS ETHICS DIFFERENT?

Should a study of "business ethics" differ from a more general study of the subject? Questions about how we ought to interact with and treat others arise in all aspects of life. Moral issues arise in the realm of the family, social groups, neighborhoods, politics and government, interactions between nations, professional associations, and other relationships, as well as in business. The basic questions, arguments, and problem-solving methods remain the same for all these domains. The factual context will vary, of course, depending on the nature of the relationship. In studying "business" ethics, we focus on business relationships and use examples of business problems that raise ethical questions. In other words, business ethics consists of the application of moral principles to people in a business setting.

THE RELATIONSHIP BETWEEN LAW AND ETHICS

One might legitimately ask why a study of business ethics should be included as a unit in a business course about law and the legal system. The material is admittedly somewhat different from the rest of the material in this book, and one could argue that the subject represents a digression from the main focus of the course. There are, however, a number of ways in which ethics and law fit together very naturally. As a result, there are several excellent reasons for dealing with the subject in the context of law. We will first recognize and discuss some of the differences between law and ethics and then study the close relationship between the two.

DIFFERENCES BETWEEN LEGAL AND MORAL STANDARDS

As we will see shortly, legal standards often have their counterparts in the ethical domain, and vice versa. For example, lying not only may violate a fundamental moral standard but also may constitute fraud under the law of torts and under various criminal statutes. Similarly, breaking a promise not only may be unethical but also may constitute a legally impermissible breach of contract in some circumstances. There are, however, several basic differences between legal and moral standards.

First, legal standards have a different source than moral ones. Whether found in a constitution, statute, judicial decision, or administrative agency regulation, legal standards are defined and applied by governmental processes. It takes governmental power to adopt and enforce laws.

Moral standards, on the other hand, are internal; they are developed within each person. It is true that people develop their moral standards from input they receive from external sources, such as the tenets of their religion and instructions from parents, teachers, friends, and others under whose influence they fall during their formative years. People even pick up information about appropriate and inappropriate moral behavior by observing the conduct and speech of strangers. These moral perceptions are formed, modified, and reinforced over time as we go through the process of having to give rational support and justification for our conduct when it affects others. Despite external influences, people ultimately develop, apply, and modify *their own* moral standards. Legal authority may be complex, even murky, but it is always there. In the personal realm of morality, however, we simply cannot get off the hook by referring to outside authority. Our only human source of authority is our rational thought process: clear and objective thinking about the dignity, worth, and integrity of people around us and our impact on their lives. Even when one derives his or her basic moral standards from religion, thus referring to a higher authority, conformity with those standards involves an individual choice—an exercise of the will.

Second, the consequences of violating legal and moral standards are different. Violations of the law, if detected, result in concrete sanctions. When lying violates the law against fraud, for example, the guilty person may have to pay damages to the victim in a civil action and may even be prosecuted in a criminal action and forced to pay a fine to the state or serve a jail term. There are no externally imposed sanctions for violating moral standards, however. Although lying usually is clearly unethical even if it does not meet the legal definition of fraud, the violation of ethical norms by itself is not subject to any definite penalties. It is true that unethical conduct sometimes *can* result in tangible consequences such as lost business because of a damaged reputation. Mostly, however, the consequences are like the standards themselves, internal and difficult to define.

Third, even though legal standards sometimes need to be a bit vague in order to be flexible, they must be more clearly defined than moral standards. The obvious reason is that legal standards are imposed on us by society, and we can be punished for violating them; because of this, legal standards must be expressed with enough clarity to give us reasonable notice of society's expectations.

Fourth, moral standards usually require more of us than legal standards. The law tends to seek out the average in human behavior, for at least three reasons: (1) Although people's ideas about what is appropriate behavior vary, the law attempts to prescribe and enforce norms for an entire society. (2) The enforcement of laws requires the use of scarce public resources to support courts, police, and so on. As a result, for legal standards to be effective, they must survive a rough cost/benefit analysis. In other words, we should generally allocate society's scarce resources to the enforcement of legal standards only if we feel that the costs of that enforcement are outweighed by the benefits to society of upholding those standards. This is one of the reasons why our legal system often does not do a very good job of providing remedies for small claims. (3) The law must be practical. It may be unethical to break a vaguely expressed promise, for example, but a court can require someone to pay monetary damages for breaking a promise only when the promise describes obligations with reasonable certainty.

Fifth, some laws have little or nothing to do with moral behavior because they exist for other purposes. Some laws, for instance, are adopted solely for the purpose of bringing order to our affairs. There is nothing inherently moral or immoral about driving on one side of the road rather than the other. To prevent chaos, however, a society must decide one way or the other.

LEGAL/ETHICAL OVERLAP

Despite their differences, law and ethics have much in common. First, as we will see shortly, sound moral reasoning is quite similar in methodology to sound legal reasoning. In other words, the method for rationally identifying and analyzing moral issues is very much like the method for dealing with legal issues.

Second, laws are intended to serve a variety of social purposes including, in some cases, promoting moral conduct. To again use fraud as an example, the laws that prohibit intentional misrepresentations of important facts in business transaction have at least two objectives: promoting adherence to the fundamental moral obligation of honesty in our dealings with others, and enhancing economic efficiency by improving the quality of information in the market.

Third, regardless of whether a given legal principle has a substantial moral content, evidence of ethical or unethical conduct can have significant effects on the outcome of a dispute. Judges, juries, arbitrators, and other decision makers in legal proceedings cannot help but take note of such behavior. Regardless of their own ethical level, they are likely to recoil when confronted with *your* unethical behavior. Most lawsuits or other dispute resolution procedures involve some close calls on factual and legal questions. When your behavior in the relevant events has been ethically questionable, these close calls are more likely to go against you.

The now-famous dispute between Texaco and Pennzoil illustrates how the ethical background of a transaction can affect the close decisions that often must be made when legal disputes are being resolved. Pennzoil claimed that it had reached an agreement to merge with Getty Oil Co. Even after the alleged agreement had been reached, Getty secretly shopped around for another merger partner. Within a matter of days, Texaco "pulled the rug out from under" Pennzoil and acquired Getty. Pennzoil sued, claiming that Texaco had committed the tort of intentionally interfering with its contract to buy Getty. As a foundation for its claim, Pennzoil had to show that there had actually been a contract between it and Getty. The facts relevant to this question were quite ambiguous, and the question was a close one. Although the way Texaco and Getty had behaved was not too unusual in the context of mergers and acquisitions, the jury was not favorably impressed by Getty's and Texaco's apparently cavalier attitude toward commitments. Even though the commitments were somewhat vague, and even though many observers thought that the decision was wrong on legal grounds, Pennzoil won a $10.5 billion judgment against Texaco (Getty and its principals were not defendants because Texaco had agreed to indemnify these parties against any liability that might arise from Texaco's acquisition. The indemnities also did not look good to the jury; even though such clauses are common in merger transactions, the jury was persuaded that Texaco must have known that it and Getty were doing something wrong or it would not have granted the indemnities.)

ARE THERE ANY MORAL STANDARDS?

There are those who believe that it is impossible to identify any concrete rules or standards to serve as a general foundation for evaluating the morality of behavior. The existence and content of particular ethical standards are too personal and individualized to formulate generally applicable rules. Moreover, they argue that what is "ethical" depends a great deal on what is viewed as acceptable behavior in a particular culture and that norms very greatly from one culture to another. They assert that the formal study and practical application of ethics can consist only of defining and improving the *processes* by which moral issues are identified and analyzed.

Others argue that although there are no overarching moral "rules" that can be applied to all human behavior, the general standard of **utilitarianism** can serve as a guide for moral behavior. Advanced by noted philosophers such as Jeremy Bentham and John Stuart Mill, utilitarianism is an ethical theory that is committed solely to the purpose of promoting "the greatest good for the greatest number." Utilitarianism essentially permits all conduct that will serve the objective of maximizing the social utility (i.e., the social "benefit" or "good"). As an abstract theory, utilitarianism makes a lot of sense. In actual practice, however, it can be all but impossible to predict, even roughly, which specific actions are likely to provide the greatest benefit to society. Moreover, even deciding how to define "benefit" to society can be an exercise in futility because of the many possible value judgments that may be involved. What one person views as a benefit to society may be quite different from the view of another person. In large part because of these difficulties, other ethicists view utilitarianism as being just one useful component in a rational process of ethical reasoning.

Some well-known philosophers do feel that certain threshhold standards of moral behavior can be identified and applied to real problems across various circumstances and cultures. The German philosopher Immanuel Kant wrote that every person's actions should be judged morally by asking this question: "Can this action be justified by reasons that are uniformly applicable to all other persons?" In other words, he suggested as an over-aching standard of moral behavior the rule that people cannot make exceptions of themselves; one's behavior is morally defensible only if everyone else could do the same thing without interfering with the optimal functioning of an organized society. This means, among other things, that we should all treat others as we would wish to be treated, a wisdom embodied in the so-called Golden Rule. Each person should be treated as an end in himself, not as a means to an end.

We think there is merit in all of these positions and that the best approach to questions about ethical behavior includes elements of each. Process is extremely important. It is essential to employ a rational process for analyzing these kinds of questions. (We will present such a process later in this chapter.) We also think, as did Kant, that there are certain fundamental moral standards that are virtually universal. As we discuss these principles, it will become apparent that some elements of utilitarianism are included; we recognize that costs and benefits of alternative courses of action may have to be taken into account when there are extenuating circumstances or conflicting moral obligations.

THE "MORAL MINIMUM"

As we observe human interactions and learn more about human nature, study and think deeply about the effects that our own actions have on others, and perhaps study the writings of those philosophers who have pondered moral questions over the years, we may begin to discover that certain basic values and standards of conduct are truly necessary for the existence of an advanced civilization. What form do these principles take? Lawrence Kohlberg writes that the morally mature individual bases his actions on "principles chosen because of their logical comprehensiveness, their universality, and their consistency." He then adds: "These ethical principles are not concrete like the Ten Commandments but abstract universal principles dealing with justice, society's welfare, the equality of human rights, respect for the dignity of individual human beings, and with the idea that persons are ends in themselves and must be treated as such."[1]

In our search for generally applicable moral standards, let us assume that we are looking only for those guideposts that are relatively comprehensive, universal, and consistent. We can also assume that the foundation for this search is a view of each human being as unique and as deserving to be treated as we ourselves would wish to be treated. Important questions remain, however: Exactly where do we find these standards? If they can be

---

[1] Lawrence Kohlberg, "Moral Stages and Moralization: The Cognitive-Developmental Approach," in Manuel Velasquez, *Business Ethics: Concepts and Cases* (Englewood Cliffs, N.J.: Prentice-Hall, Inc., 1982), 20–23.

found, can they ever be expressed with enough certainty to provide meaningful guidance for our conduct?

The answer to the first question is that to satisfy the requirements of comprehensiveness, universality, and consistency, we must rely on the rational human thought process as our source. Any other source is likely to produce results that are too variable across cultures, beliefs, circumstances, and even across time.

One approach to the second question is to determine whether there are any standards of behavior that do not need to be defended by a rational person. In other words, from the perspective of a rational mind, are there any general categories of behavior that stand on their own moral foundation, without any need for justification? If so, they could be identified as the **moral minimum**—a set of general standards that constitute the ethical minimum necessary for the functioning of civilization. Stated somewhat differently, violation of these standards is *prima facie* (on its face) wrong. Compliance with such standards requires no defense or justification. To the contrary, a rational person would expect a defense or justification for a *failure to comply* with them. The reason for expecting such a justification is that failure to comply with these standards tends to *destroy the social and economic relationships* that cause a society to function. We suggest the following as components of the moral minimum, fully recognizing that these components sometimes will overlap and that they could be organized and labeled in a variety of ways.

HONESTY

A rational person does not have to justify telling the truth. The notion that one should correctly represent the facts is so firmly ingrained in human relations that we expect a justification for not doing so. Without reasonable expectations of honesty, we cannot maintain the personal and business relationships that create order and economic well-being. As we have seen, there are also principles in the *legal* domain that are intended to encourage **honesty,** as with legal prohibitions against fraud. The moral obligation, however, is more encompassing.

LOYALTY

In any culture there are certain voluntary relationships in which one party places a higher degree of trust and confidence in the other than one would place in a stranger. These relationships are not forced on us; we consent to them either explicitly or implicitly. Examples include an agent or employee's relationship with her principal, the corporate manager's relationship with the company's shareholders, a trustee's relationship with the beneficiary, and each partner's relationship with the others. A moral duty of **loyalty** is based on two facts: First, by virtue of the relationship, we have created in the other person a legitimate expectation that we will further his or her interests. Second, the relationship has placed us in a position where we have the ability to cause serious harm if we do not act in that person's interests. For example, these relationships often give one party some degree of control over information or assets that are valuable to the other person.

When we enter such relationships we take on an affirmative obligation to (1) fully disclose to the other person all material information that is relevant to our dealings; (2) keep confidential any information that the other party reasonably expects us to protect; (3) avoid undisclosed conflicts of interest, that is, unless we obtain the other party's consent, stay out of situations that are likely to put pressure on us to act against the other party's best interests; and (4) generally act in the best interests of the other party, even if such action is not entirely in our own best interests. Relationships based on trust and confidence cannot exist without the observance of such behavioral standards, and these kinds of relationships contribute greatly to economic efficiency and social order. The moral duty of loyalty is one of those ethical obligations that has a very close analog in the legal domain. The law identifies certin *fiduciary* relationships, such as agent–principal, in which there are legally enforceable obligations of loyalty. Again, the legal obligation is usually less demanding than the moral one.

KEEPING COMMITMENTS

Social and commercial relationships among people are quite difficult to maintain without accepting the notion that we should keep the promises we make to each other. For this reason, the rational person is not likely to feel it necessary to defend his actions in **keeping commitments.** Failing to keep them, however, normally requires justification. Sometimes there can be difficult questions about whether a commitment has been made and, if so, about its scope, but once these questions are resolved the rational mind will find little need to justify keeping a promise. Once again, we can find a narrower legal counterpart to this obligation—when a promise is part of a legally enforceable contract there are sanctions for breaking it.

DOING NO HARM

The rational person does not have to defend himself when he refrains from *intentional, reckless, or careless conduct that can cause reasonably foreseeable harm to others.* To the contrary, justification is usually expected for such conduct. Our actions have both expected and unexpected effects on others, and these effects can be positive or negative. Negative effects are those that damage some legitimate interest of another person. It is generally recognized that people have legitimate interests in their physical, economic, and emotional well-being, as well as in their property, privacy, and reputation. There obviously is overlap among these interests but, taken together, they include most of the things that are important to people. Sometimes our actions have negative consequences for others that we never could have foreseen. When, however, cautious concern for the welfare of others should lead us to anticipate that certain action or inaction may harm the legitimate interests of others, we should do what we can to avoid harm. Narrower legal counterparts for the obligation of **doing no harm** are found throughout the law of torts.

In the following case, the legal issue is whether the defendant committed the tort of fraud. After reading the court's legal analysis and conclusions, carefully consider the following questions: (1) Aside from the legal principles involved, are there any basic moral obligations that are possibly relevant? If so, what are they? (2) Is this a situation in which the extent of any relevant moral obligation is basically the same as the legal obligation? If not the same, is the moral obligation broader or narrower than the legal one? (3) If the moral and legal obligations are somewhat different in scope, can you think of any reasons why this is so?

GRENDELL v. KIEHL

SUPREME COURT OF ARKANSAS, 723, S.W.2d 830 (1987)

Don Grendell had served as an insurance agent for Loretta and Ferdinand Kiehl since 1971. The Kiehls also relied on Grendell for financial advice. One investment that Grendell promoted to the Kiehls was an oil and gas drilling venture. Grendell told the Kiehls that the investment was "a good thing" and would "make money" for them. On another occasion he "guaranteed that they would make lots of money" and "were going to get 50 barrels a day." No oil was discovered, and the Kiehls lost their investment. They sued Grendell, claiming that he had committed fraud, and they received a judgment against him for $11,329.60. Grendell appealed.

HAYS, JUSTICE:

The essential elements of an action for [fraud] are well established: (a) a false, material representation of fact made by the defendant; (b) scienter—knowledge by the defendant that the representation is false, or an assertion of fact which he does not know to be true; (c) an intention that the plaintiff should act on such representation; (d) justifiable reliance by the plaintiff on the representation; and (e) damage to the plaintiff resulting from such reliance.

... The [statement] that the oil investment was a good thing and would make money, even the inference of "50 barrels a day," fails to rise to the level of misrepresentation of fact. Even at its strongest, the proof constitutes expressions of opinion in the nature of "puffing." Admittedly, Mr. and Mrs. Kiehl were relatively inexperienced in business affairs but we cannot conclude they were incapable of recognizing the difference between an opinion that a proposed investment in an oil lease looked promising and was a "good thing," as opposed to a factual assertion that an oil well would become a producer. Nothing in the testimony suggests the Kiehls were not mindful that while some oil ventures succeed, a good many others, just as inviting at the outset, do not. Indeed, Mrs. Kiehl candidly acknowledged recognizing the risk factor in oil leases and was aware that a "dry hole" was a possibility.

Finding the dividing line between misrepresentation of fact and expression of opinion is often troubling. *Prosser and Keeton on Torts* states that [a claim for fraud] cannot be based on "misstatements of opinion, as distinguished from those of fact. The usual explanation is that an opinion is merely an assertion of one man's belief as to a fact, of which another should not be heard to complain, since opinions are matters about which many many men will be of many minds, and which is often governed by whim and caprice. [Expression of] judgment and opinion in such a case implies no knowledge."

An opinion may take the form of a statement of quality, of more or less indefinite content. One common application of the opinion rule is in the case of loose, general statements made by sellers in commending their wares. No action lies against a dealer who describes the automobile he is selling as a "dandy," a "bear cat," a "good little car," and "a sweet job," or as "the pride of our line" and the "best in the American market," or merely makes use of broad, and vague, commendatory language comparing his goods favorably with others, or praising them as "good," "proper," "sufficient" and the like.

A statement that ... a real estate investment will insure a handsome profit, that an article is the greatest bargain ever offered, and similar claims are intended and understood to be merely emphatic methods of urging a sale. These things, then, a buyer must disregard in forming a sober judgment as to his conduct in the transaction. If he succumbs to such persistent solicitation, he must take the risk of any loss attributable to a disparity

CONTINUED

between the exaggerated opinion of the purchaser and a reasonable or accurate judgment of the value of the article.

The Kiehls point out that their [long-standing] reliance on Don Grendell [in both insurance and financial matters] produced a special relationship of trust and confidence requiring the utmost in good faith and disclosure of all material facts. Even so, there was an absence of proof by the Kiehls that Grendell either knew the assurances made to them were false or made factual representations while lacking knowledge of their truthfulness.

[The court found that Grendell was not guilty of fraud. However, the evidence also showed that he had kept $3,500 of the Kiehl's money that had been deposited with him and not invested, so the court ordered him to pay back that money.]

IS THERE A DUTY TO "DO GOOD"?

The components of the moral minimum relate only to preventing harm that we may cause or correcting harm that we have actually caused. What about situations in which harm is being caused through no moral fault on our part? Do we also have a fundamental moral obligation to affirmatively "do good" by trying to prevent or correct harm that we had no part in causing?

Many people, of course, help others without even thinking about the moral implications. They give to charities, volunteer their time, and perform other altruistic acts for many complex reasons. They may do so for religious reasons, because they want to help create a better world for their children, because of the attention it brings them, or just because it makes them feel good. The questions we are raising here are whether there is a rationally based moral obligation to do such things and, if so, what are its limits. In other words, is there something resembling the moral minimum for doing good, and can it be defined in any useful way?

Many people do seem to feel a strong sense of obligation to help others. Again, the reasons why they feel this way are varied and complex. It is therefore difficult to isolate the phenomenon's purely rational element. If we study the question solely from the perspective of rational analysis, we will find less general agreement than we did in the case of the moral minimum. At least part of the reasoning process that supports the moral minimum, however, can also be used to argue in favor of a moral obligation to do good. Most rational people would not feel it necessary to defend their actions in doing good. Similarly, they usually would not expect others to defend such actions. On the other hand, does the rational mind expect a justification of *not* doing good? The answer, which is not very helpful, is that some rational minds would and some would not.

If one tries to build an argument that there is a rationally based moral obligation to do good, the argument probably should contain the following elements:

1. In many cases it can be practically impossible to assign a specific moral responsibility for the existence of needs. A family may be desperate because the breadwinner has lost a job from bad health or an economic recession, and they have no family or friends who can help. A Boy Scout troop may need volunteer adult leadership in order to fulfill its goals of teaching, guiding, and nurturing a group of youths. The existence of such needs is really no one's "fault." Even if we can identify a responsible person or group, it may be totally unrealistic to expect them to take remedial action. The needy family's breadwinner may have lost the job because the company was recklessly or dishonestly managed and went bankrupt. In this case, we can trace moral fault, but it is highly unlikely that the blameworthy person or group will correct the harm it has caused. Thus, in an organized society, the rational person should expect there to be unmet needs and should understand that his efforts to meet these needs will improve the functioning of the society of which he is a member.

2. Although we should use government as one vehicle for meeting people's needs, government cannot serve effectively as our *only* social problem solver. For example, even though government programs can do much good in providing food and shelter for the poor, such programs will usually be inadequate by themselves. Resources will always be too scarce. Government agencies sometimes can be too impersonal and too remote from the problem to provide assistance as effectively as individuals or private groups. Moreover, government bureaucracy sometimes can make it a less efficient provider of assistance than individuals and private groups.

3. Helping others is clearly in harmony with the view that we generally should treat others as we would wish to be treated in similar circumstances.

4. In circumstances in which (1) a problem or need is brought to our attention, (2) we are in a good position to help, (3) we have the ability to help, and (4) taking positive action would not require an unreasonable risk or cost, our failure to do something positive is very similar to actually *doing harm by intentional, reckless, or careless conduct.*

If one argues that there is a moral obligation to do good, one must define some limits to the obligation. In item 4, we identified some possible limits which require a bit of further explanation. *First,* we can have no obligation to meet a need that we do not know about. This statement assumes, of course, that we have not consciously tried to avoid knowledge of the situation. If there is such an obligation, it cannot be avoided by intentional ignorance. *Second,* in a given situation we may not be the appropriate person to take action. There are some cases in which our help is unwanted or may actually do more harm than good. In addition, there may be some other person, organization, or agency that is much better equipped to do the job than we are. This is not an excuse that one should look for, but sometimes good judgment suggests that we are inadequate to be useful. Of course, the fact that we are unable to solve the entire problem does not necessarily mean that we should do nothing at all. One person cannot solve the problem of world hunger or even hunger in one city, but one person can *do something*. *Third,* any rational argument that there is a moral duty to do good must incorporate the concept of costs and benefits (or "risks and utility"). A rational person would not expect someone to take positive action that would entail far greater cost or risk to the provider than benefit to the recipient. One cannot be expected to impoverish oneself or one's family in order to give to a worthy cause. (Here, of course, a moral obligation to one's family would be violated at the same time.)

Although we have so far focused on personal situations, the preceding discussion serves as a necessary foundation for our later study of corporate social responsiveness.

EXCUSING CONDITIONS

There occasionally will be circumstances that may excuse one's violation of a basic moral obligation. The particular conditions surrounding a person's action or inaction may reduce the degree of moral responsibility or even completely remove it. Breaking a promise for example, is *prima facie* wrong on moral grounds, but it may not always be absolutely wrong. **Excusing conditions** may be present. One must be careful about introducing this concept of excusing conditions into ethical analysis, however, because it so easily can be used improperly as a "cop-out." People are usually quite ready to offer "excuses" for their bad behavior, and they may have to be reminded that "reasons" are not necessarily moral excuses. When we speak of excusing conditions, we assume that they are not the result of carelessness, laziness, or conscious disregard of relevant information.

The kinds of circumstances likely to be viewed by a rational person as excusing conduct that otherwise would be morally blameworthy are those affecting a person's *knowledge* or *freedom of action*. Our status as fully responsible moral beings (or "moral agents") assumes that we act with knowledge of relevant and material information and that our freedom of action is not substantially impaired by some external force. Suppose, for instance, that Joe promises to deliver 100 laser printers to Sam by December 1. We are not likely to view Joe as morally blameworthy if he fails to deliver on time because, through no fault of Joe's, one of his main suppliers suddenly cuts him off or his own factory has to shut down for several weeks because of a strike by a labor union. His freedom of action has been impaired. Morally he is still expected, of course, to do everything legally within his power to minimize the harm caused to Sam or to come as close as he can to fulfilling the commitment. His moral responsibility is diminished, however, to the extent that his freedom of action is diminished. In a similar fashion, Joe's moral culpability is reduced to the extent that, when he made the promise, he neither knew nor had reason to know of existing facts that would make it impossible to deliver on time.

As is true of many ethical concepts, the idea of excusing conditions has a roughly similar counterpart in the law. In some situations, evidence showing that a person did not have the knowledge or freedom to have acted differently can prevent liability for breach of contract, negligence, or some other *legal* wrong. Moral excuses and legal excuses are not necessarily equivalent, but the general concepts exist in both domains. Thus, the actions or failures of one of Joe's suppliers might excuse Joe from the *moral* obligation to carry out a promise to deliver printers, but in some circumstances the law may hold that Joe had assumed the risk of such an occurrence and is *legally* responsible. In other situations, extenuating circumstances may provide a legal excuse but not a moral one. In still other cases, both kinds of excuses may exist.

MORAL DILEMMAS

On some occasions fundamental moral obligations may conflict. You know the familiar phrase for such a dilemma: "Caught between a rock and a hard place." Although **moral dilemmas** can arise in a wide variety of situations, *whistleblowing* presents a classic and often agonizing version of such an ethical conflict. The term *whistleblowing* normally refers to a situation in which an employee objects to or reports to the authorities the illegal or unethical activities of his employer. Because this kind of situation is frequently so rich in ethical questions, we will use the following hypothetical case for two purposes: as an illustration of how moral dilemmas arise and as a basis for our subsequent discussion of moral reasoning.

Suppose that Alexis works in the tax division of a large public accounting firm. One of the firm's major clients is Leviathan Corp. While working on one part of Leviathan's tax return, Alexis discovers that some expense items appear to have been overstated. No single item has been grossly inflated, and the total amount of expense overstatement is significant but not huge. Thus the risk of detection by the Internal Revenue Service probably is relatively small. Also, Alexis cannot tell for sure whether the overstatements are intentional or simply resulted from honest mistakes or incompetence. She speaks with her immediate supervisor about the matter, but the supervisor dismisses the evidence as a "nonproblem." When Alexis presses the issue a little harder, the supervisor says, "Just do your job and don't stick your nose in too far." Should Alexis take up the matter with a higher-level manager, perhaps even with the firm's top management? Suppose that she does so and receives the same kind of response at that level. What then?

Alexis owes a general moral duty of loyalty to her employer, an obligation that requires her to act in the firm's best interests. Moreover, in this case, she owes a duty of loyalty to the client. She also has made commitments, either explicitly or implicitly, to obey her superiors in the firm. Fulfilling these obligations, however, requires actions that are possibly dishonest and that may violate several conflicting moral obligations.

If Alexis refuses to overlook the problem or if she reports it to the IRS, she stands an excellent chance of losing her job. How likely is it that she will be able to find a comparable job, especially if she cannot get a good reference from her current firm, a possibility that cannot be ignored? Does she have dependents who count on her for support? If so, she probably owes them a moral obligation that could be characterized as one of loyalty or perhaps doing no harm. Is this duty strong enough to support a decision to keep quiet about something that is possibly dishonest?

Alexis owes a conflicting moral duty of honesty to the government and to taxpayers who will have to pay more to make up for the underpayments by her firm's clients. It is true that the harm to any other single taxpayer will be extremely small, but the obligation exists nonetheless.

As an accountant, she also has made commitments to other members of her profession to uphold professional standards of honesty and competence. The failures of one member of a professional or trade group taint the reputation of the entire group and thus cause harm to every other member. To overlook the expense overstatements may violate this commitment and, if detected, harm the profession and its members.

Alexis faces a moral dilemma. Is there any way out of it? Of course, there are always ways out, but there may not be a painless way out. In the next section we will look at moral reasoning to see how ethical questions can be analyzed in a rational way. Part of this discussion will focus on moral dilemmas as a part of the overall process of moral reasoning. Clear, rational thinking about moral dilemmas does not necessarily eliminate the conflict or turn a difficult situation into an easy one. On the other hand, fuzzy or irrational thinking can certainly make matters worse. In the next section, we will explore the benefits that structured, rational thinking can bring to ethical problems, including moral dilemmas.

MORAL REASONING AND DECISION MAKING

Ethical issues frequently are emotionally charged. Although it can be quite difficult to think rationally about emotional issues, it is in such situations that clear, organized thinking is most needed. One of the most important lessons one can learn from a study of ethics is that moral questions are capable of being analyzed rationally. The process of analyzing moral questions is essentially the same as rational problem solving or decision making in other situations.

IDENTIFYING ISSUES

The necessary first step in problem solving is to figure out exactly what the problems are. In other words, one must identify the issues. If one is confronted with legal, financial, or marketing issues, for example, they first should be recognized and spelled out as clearly as possible. The same is true of ethical issues. In the hypothetical case involving Alexis, the issue she must cope with immediately is *not* (1) whether it is wrong in general to cheat on one's taxes; (2) whether her superiors are bad people; (3) whether her accounting firm or Leviathan Corp. has developed an organizational structure that is insufficient to establish lines of individual accountability for wrongdoing; or (4) whether she can sue her employer for the tort of wrongful discharge if she is fired for objecting to the expense overstatements or reporting them to the IRS.

Problems have to be defined narrowly enough so that we have the ability both to analyze them adequately *and* exercise some degree of influence over the outcome. The issue that Alexis must confront at the present time is whether her most morally defensible course of action is to keep quiet and go along with her firm's possibly inappropriate behavior or to resist it by "blowing the whistle." Other issues may arise later, but for now this is all she needs to deal with from an ethical perspective.

IDENTIFYING THE GOVERNING PRINCIPLES

For every kind of issue there are governing principles or rules that guide or limit our decision. The source of these principles will vary, depending on the nature of the issue. There are legal rules, generally accepted accounting principles, marketing principles, generally accepted courses of medical treatment for particular illnesses, formulas for computing stress in the construction of bridges, and so on. In ethics we have the components of the moral minimum—the foundational moral obligations identified earlier in our discussion.

In some cases the principles will be relatively *specific*, but in others they may be quite *general*. Whether they are specific or general, different principles may be characterized by varying degrees of *certainty* or *acceptance*. In the case of some legal principles, for example, it can be difficult to determine precisely what the rule is. This uncertainty can result from conflicting court decisions, ambiguous statutory language, or other reasons. In addition, some principles are more generally accepted than others, whether the relevant field is law, medicine, accounting, engineering, ethics, or another discipline. These qualifying remarks do not diminish the importance of guiding principles. They represent the collective knowledge gained from experience and rational thought and should serve as the foundation for rational problem solving.

In ethics, the principles are fairly general. As indicated earlier, however, we think that the *prima facie* duties that constitute the moral minimum are widely accepted across time, culture, and circumstance. Their relative degree of acceptance as societal norms has varied, no doubt, at different times and in different cultures, but in general they have remained intact.

When analyzing ethical issues, it is important to identify the pertinent moral obligations as precisely as possible. What is the *nature* of the obligation? Honesty? Loyalty? Keeping commitments? Doing no harm? After identifying the nature of each moral obligation, we must make sure we understand exactly *who* owes which obligation to *whom*. In Alexis's case we have already done a pretty good job of identifying the obligations that she owes to various parties. If we are doing a complete ethical analysis of the entire situation, we also would find it necessary to identify the moral obligations owed *to* Alexis by her superiors. One can argue persuasively that they are violating their duty of doing no harm by intentionally, recklessly, or negligently engaging in conduct that may cause reasonably foreseeable harm to Alexis. Acting in behalf of the firm, essentially what they have done is ask her to participate in conduct that may be dishonest and possibly even illegal. Even if she does not get into any legal trouble, emotional trauma also can be viewed as "harm" when it is a reasonably foreseeable result of their actions.

COLLECTING, VERIFYING, AND DRAWING INFERENCES FROM INFORMATION

Issues of any kind always arise in a factual context—they do not exist in a vacuum. In our hypothetical case, the relevant information (i.e., "evidence" or "data") that initially caused Alexis to perceive a problem were the apparent inconsistencies between entries in Leviathan's general ledgers used to prepare its tax return and the figures in supporting documentation. When information raises potential ethical, legal, or other issues, we should first do what we can to verify the accuracy, reliability, and completeness of that information. If the issues are sensitive, we obviously must exercise great care in doing this. Caution and good judgment are essential.

We may find that the true facts are very different than we initially suspected, and that there is no problem at all. Of course, we may find that things are much worse than we thought. Frequently we may conclude after an initial inquiry that our information is incomplete and that we need further evidence to understand the situation. Again, in the subsequent search for additional evidence, caution is the watchword. It is usually impossible to acquire information that is so complete and so clearly accurate and reliable as to resolve all doubt. Decisions always have to be made on the basis of information that is less than perfect. When analyzing important issues and preparing to make important decisions, however, it is essential that our information be as complete and accurate as circumstances will allow.

As with any fact-finding process that serves as a foundation for problem solving, in ethical analysis we infer relevant facts from the evidence. In other words, we infer that certain things have happened. In addition to inferring facts, we use the evidence as a basis for making predictions about likely future events. Thus, from the evidence she has at her disposal. Alexis might infer that her firm condones or possibly even assists in tax cheating by clients, although more information is needed to support this inference. Alexis also may have enough information to predict that any further objection to superiors within the firm is likely to be fruitless, and that she may even be penalized in some way for making a fuss.

APPLYING THE FACTS TO THE PRINCIPLES

The remainder of the ethical problem-solving, or moral reasoning, process involves further application of the guiding principles to the facts that we have inferred from the evidence. In other words, we must determine how the identified moral obligations should apply to these particular facts. This determination should be relatively straightforward, of course, if there are no excusing conditions or moral dilemmas. Such complicating factors are present in many cases, however, and must be incorporated into the analysis.

In our hypothetical scenario, we already have identified the moral dilemmas created by several conflicting duties. The next step is to weigh and balance these obligations against one another. In doing so, we must keep in mind that this is not algebra. Despite being a rational analytic process, it is highly qualitative and involves a degree of subjectivity. The process of balancing conflicting obligations should incorporate at least the following factors.

Excusing Conditions

Are there any excusing conditions that might lessen the strength of one obligation relative to another? Remember that our moral accountability can be diminished or eliminated by genuine lack of knowledge or freedom. In Alexis's case, one can argue that her status as an employee who is acting under orders from her superiors causes her freedom of action to be considerably less than if she were in charge. No doubt this is true; the degree of her moral responsibility surely is not as great as it would be if she had more power over the firm's decisions. Is her freedom of action curtailed so much, however, that she has no moral duty at all? Certainly not—otherwise a person in a subordinate position could be morally answerable for his conduct only if he initiated and controlled the situation. In such a case, of course, either he would be acting outside his authority or else he really would not be acting as a subordinate at all. Completely relieving all subordinates of moral responsibility for their actions within the organization's chain of command has the potential to lower substantially the level of moral behavior within organizations and throughout society. Thus, Alexis should continue to have a moral duty of honesty with respect to her complicity in the firm's possible wrongdoing, although the strength of her obligation may be somewhat less than in other situations in which she is not playing a subordinate role.

Conflict Reduction

Are there ways to minimize the conflicts? As in this case, a *prima facie* moral duty usually is not eliminated by an excusing condition. Most of the time there either is no such condition or else the condition merely curtails the strength of a duty rather than doing away with it entirely. Thus, any moral dilemma that we previously identified still exists. Before getting to the point of having to make an all-or-nothing choice between conflicting duties, however, we should search for creative solutions that may diminish or remove the conflict.

Alexis might consider requesting reassignment within the firm, perhaps to another geographic location, to remove her from any direct role in the questionable activity. Reassignment may not be feasible, and even if it is feasible it may damage her future opportunities in the firm. Moreover, if the attitude of her current superiors is found throughout the organization, she may encounter similar problems in her new position. Assuming that she finds a higher level of ethical standards at her new location, Alexis still *knows* about the possible dishonesty at her previous one. If she remains silent about it, is she guilty of complicity in the questionable behavior even though she is no longer a participant? Many people would say yes. If we take the view that the duty of loyalty to her employer continues to exist, Alexis still owes the same basic duty because she has remained in the same organization. One can see that removing ourselves from direct involvement does not always eliminate a moral dilemma, although this course of action may reduce the acuteness of the conflict. Other options, which we will not pursue here, remain for Alexis.

In other situations, creative ideas for minimizing the degree of conflict between obligations will take other forms. For example, in some cases a person caught in a moral dilemma might be able to work out agreements with one or more of the parties to whom duties are owed so that the duties no longer conflict and all can be fulfilled. If we cannot make agreements that enable us to fulfill all moral duties, it may be possible to work out compromises that permit us to comply fully with one and partially with another. Such opportunities will not always exist, but it is important to give careful consideration to the possibilities.

Prioritizing

When we cannot eliminate a moral dilemma, we must choose between the obligations that we will attempt to satisfy. The choice should be made only after carefully weighing the strength and importance of the conflicting duties. In other words, we must prioritize the obligations. We already may have gone a long way toward weighing and prioritizing our duties as we considered whether excusing conditions were present and sought creative ways to minimize the conflict. We may have found that excusing conditions reduce the significance of one moral duty with respect to another. Similarly, we may have worked out agreements or discovered alternative courses of action that strengthen or weaken different obligations and, consequently, make our choice easier.

If the relative importance of particular obligations, and thus their proper place on our list of priorities, still remains unclear, we should next attempt to evaluate the *harm* that may result from violating the various moral duties. A careful evaluation of harm will take into account both *degree* and *probability*. Other factors being equal, the relative importance of a moral obligation increases proportionately with increases in (1) the degree of harm that is likely to be caused by violating the obligation and (2) the probability (or likelihood) that the harm actually will occur.

In the case of Alexis, for instance, the harm done to taxpayers by this instance of expense overstatement, or even by all similar actions by her employer's clients, is probably pretty small in relative terms. On the other hand, we should also consider cumulative effects. When one tax cheater is reported and gets caught, other cheaters may change their behavior. Thus the harm to taxpayers caused by her firm's conduct, and the harm that may be prevented by her reporting it, could be a lot greater than one might think. With regard to probability, the harm caused by even a single instance of cheating is certain to occur even if it is very small.

The potential harm that Alexis's silence may cause to her profession apparently has a very low probability of occurrence. This harm will occur only if real tax cheating actually happened, she gets into trouble for going along with it, and the profession receives bad publicity as a result. This harm not only has a low probability of occurring, but if limited to this one event, it will also be relatively minor. Again, however, we should consider whether there may be cumulative harmful effects.

If Alexis reports the expense overstatements to the IRS, there is no doubt that short-term harm will be caused to both her employer and Leviathan, especially if the overstatements are found to have been intentional. They will incur penalties, and perhaps substantial legal fees and court costs. These harms appear to be high in both degree and probability. In addition, the accounting firm and Leviathan may suffer long-term harm in the form of damaged company reputations and the various costs associated with an increased level of future oversight by the IRS. This kind of harm probably is somewhat less certain to occur, but if it does occur it could be even more substantial than the short-term damage. At the same time, we must not overlook the possibility that, if Alexis's firm and Leviathan are reported and get into legal trouble now, this event could lead them to clean up their general level of ethical behavior. Arguably, more ethical behavior in the future will reduce their chances of encountering costly legal problems. This leads us to the question of whether ethical behavior produces economic benefit to the ethical company or person. "Does ethics pay?" is an exceedingly difficult and complicated question. We will discuss it later, although we will not even pretend to answer it.

Finally, we need much more information before evaluating the degree or probability of harm that might be caused to others if Alexis loses her job after "blowing the whistle." How likely is it that she will actually lose her job? If she gets fired, how likely is it that she will be able to recover damages from her former employer in a lawsuit claiming the tort of wrongful discharge? Will she have a difficult time finding comparable employment? Do others depend on her for support?

Making a Moral Decision

Ultimately Alexis must make a decision that reflects a choice. Even inaction is a choice. There may be no choice that is totally satisfactory, and there almost certainly will not be one that is completely free of doubt or negative consequences. Whatever course she takes, her choice should be the *conscious* result of a rational process similar to the one we have described.

It is true that quick decisions sometimes have to be made. If so, we may not have the luxury to gather as much information or reflect on our choices as much as we would like. There is almost always *some* time, however, for reflection and rational thinking. When emotionally charged ethical questions arise, we are far more likely to work them out through a rational analytic process if we have already anticipated and carefully thought about general problems of this nature. This is especially true when decisions have to be made under pressure and in relatively short periods of time. If we have not already practiced rational thinking about ethical issues in our actual experiences, we should at least have taken the time to examine our own values and to think about how we would deal with particular moral questions should they arise. Without some preparation, we run a much greater risk of making rash responses under pressure.

It is true that decisions, moral or otherwise, may turn out all right even if not preceded by sound analytical reasoning. Such a result probably represents simple good fortune more than anything else. Conversely, rational thinking does not guarantee optimal results. Although carrying no guarantees, such a process can have the following benefits:

1. It increases our chances of having better and more complete information on which to base a decision.

2. It lowers the risk of completely overlooking an important issue.

3. It improves our chances of making a decision that best balances the various conflicting interest that may be present.

4. If we are later called on to defend our decision, we will be better prepared to do so. Difficult decisions that effect others are often challenged, and a decision resulting from the type of process described here is more defensible. We have our facts straighter, and our reasons for making particular choices can be presented more clearly and forcefully because they have been thought through carefully. In addition, we are able to demonstrate a good faith effort to do the right thing. Evidence of good faith is no small matter, and often can make the difference when close judgment calls are at issue.

ARE CORPORATIONS MORAL AGENTS?

There is nearly unanimous agreement that individuals are morally responsible for their actions within business organizations. Managers and employees in corporations, like other individuals in other settings, have moral obligations. These obligations can never be erased by joining anything, be it a club, fraternity, political party, or business organization. We do not, or at least should not, leave our values at the door when we enter the workplace.

There is less consensus, however, about whether a corporation itself can owe moral obligations independent of the individuals within the organization. A corporation is recognized as a **legal entity** that is capable of owning property, making contracts, being a party to legal proceedings, and so on. It can act, however, only through human beings. Thus, is a corporation a **moral agent** in addition to being a legal entity?

DOES IT MAKE ANY DIFFERENCE?

Before examining this question, it is legitimate to ask, "So what?" Does it make any difference? It is no doubt true that in many cases, we can resolve relevant moral questions in business by focusing only on the moral duties of particular individuals within the company. There are situations, however, in which it is impossible to trace decisions or actions to any given individual. So the question about corporate moral status is not a purely abstract one. Even if we recognize the question as being a real one, does the answer to it have any impact? Suppose that we conclude that corporations themselves do have moral responsibilities. If a particular corporation's actions do not violate the *law*, however, are there any meaningful consequences of a conclusion that it has "acted unethically"?

We think there can be meaningful consequences. The consequences are not nearly as obvious or immediate as they may be when the law is violated, but they are there. The behavior of corporations is a frequent subject of discussion in the media, legislatures, regulatory agencies, classrooms, living rooms, and elsewhere. If there is a general perception in society that corporations are morally accountable for their actions, this perception will have an impact on the public debate over corporate behavior. It can alter the basic structure and direction of the debate, as well as the effect this debate has on people's attitudes about corporations. Feelings that a particular corporation, as an independent moral agent, has acted unethically can affect consumers' buying decisions. Similar feelings about an entire industry, or about corporations in general, can affect the decisions of legislatures and regulatory agencies as to the need for regulation. On the other hand, a company, industry, or the business community in general is much more likely to receive the benefit of the doubt in many different ways when there are no generally negative perceptions about its ethical standards.

THE VIEW THAT CORPORATIONS ARE NOT MORAL AGENTS

The most widely advanced view that corporations cannot have moral obligations is that of philosopher John Ladd, who regards corporations as purely formal organizations analogous to programmable robots or machines.[2] Machines have neither a will nor any freedom of action. Similarly, according to Ladd, a corporation is merely an aggregation of legally binding documents such as a state charter and the corporate bylaws, organizational charts, operating procedures, and customs. The human cogs in this machine are role-players. Moreover, they are replaceable and often virtually interchangeable. Rule-governed activities and impersonal operating procedures prevent the application, or even the hint, of moral responsibility. Support for Ladd's view may be found, among other places, in Chief Justice John Marshall's description of a corporation in the famous *Dartmouth College* case:

> A corporation is an artificial being, invisible, intangible, and existing only in contemplation of law. Being the mere creature of law, it possesses only those properties which the charter of creation confers upon it, either expressly, or as incidental to its very existence. These are such as are supposed best calculated to effect the object for which it was created.[3]

---

[2] John Ladd, "Morality and the Ideal of Rationality in Formal Organizations," *Monist* 54 (1970): 488–516.

[3] Wheat. (17 U.S.) 518 (1819).

The fact that corporations are mere "artificial being(s)," or "creature(s) of law," does seem to support the argument that corporations cannot be moral agents with separate moral obligations. The lifeless pieces of paper that bring the corporation into existence and provide governing rule for its operation do not provide it with autonomy or reason. Therefore, we must look elsewhere for support if we are to argue that corporations are moral agents.

THE VIEW THAT CORPORATIONS DO HAVE MORAL RESPONSIBILITIES

We mentioned that violations of moral obligations frequently cannot be traced to a particular individual within a corporation. As a rule, most actions and inactions of relatively large corporations cannot be tallied as the sum of individual actions—the whole is truly greater than the sum of its parts. As a result, individuals tend to escape moral accountability. This fact, in itself, provides considerable support for the argument that corporations should be viewed as separate moral agents.

Organization theory explains this phenomenon in terms of **group dynamics.** Groups often behave very differently than any member would have behaved, because the dynamics of the group transcend individual reason and autonomy. People sometimes just get "caught up in the spirit of things." Examples range all the way from the lynch mob to a corporate board that makes an ethically questionable decision despite the fact that each of its individual members has high personal moral standards. We find the phenomenon not only in groups of co-equal members but also in chains of command. For example, managers at the top may set policies and give orders but deny any responsibility for conduct by their subordinates that they did not intend. Similarly, we often find those at the bottom denying responsibility because they did not make the policy and they themselves intended no harm; they were "just carrying out orders." Several complex factors seem to be responsible for the peculiarities of group dynamics in corporations:

1. Because the action is motivated by corporate purposes rather than personal reasons, participating individuals may not view their conduct as really their own. If they do not associate the action with themselves as human beings, they are not as likely to apply their own personal moral standards to it.

2. A member of a group may feel that there is "safety in numbers." As the number of individual participants in group action increases, each member's feeling of *anonymity* may also increase. Even if a person does recognize and feel somewhat responsible for the moral consequences of his group's proposed action, he nevertheless may go along with a plan because he doubts that he personally will ever be called on to defend it.

3. Formal lines of authority and accountability within the organization may be fuzzy, thus increasing the chances that no single person really feels responsible. When people do not *feel* responsible, they are less likely to *act* responsibly.

4. Communication among individuals within the decision-making group may be less than perfect, and thus different individuals or subgroups may be acting on the basis of somewhat different facts and assumptions. One individual or subgroup within the organization may not be completely aware of the total picture, leading to the classic situation of the "right hand not knowing what the left hand is doing."

5. Peer pressure can cause a member of a group to be fearful of speaking up when he sees something wrong with the group's proposed action. Many of us do not want to be perceived as "different" or as a "prude." Peer pressure can produce some really strange results. One example is found in the actions preceding the so-called "Watergate cover-up" that ultimately led to President Nixon's resignation in 1974. Later interviews with the participants revealed that, when a group of Nixon's associates was planning to burglarize and plant microphones in Democratic Party headquarters in Washington, D.C.'s Watergate Hotel in the early 1970s, all the major participants thought it was a dangerous, stupid thing to do. No one voiced this opinion at the time, however; each person thought that the others viewed the break-in as a good idea and no one wanted to risk being tagged as "not a team player." Similar things can happen in business when advertising campaigns, joint ventures, capital restructurings, mergers, new products, research and development programs, personnel policies, and countless other actions are being planned.

On balance, we believe that the arguments in favor of treating corporations as separate moral agents are stronger than those to the contrary. This conclusion is based on three facts: (1) corporations can act only through the individuals they employ; (2) group dynamics is a reality and often produces behavior very different than would have occurred had any individual in the group acted alone; and (3) it is frequently impossible to trace ethical failings to an individual in the organization, and consequently, there is no place to attach moral blame if we cannot attach it to the corporation.

DOES ETHICS PAY?

Earlier we alluded to the question of whether ethical behavior by a corporation and the people within it actually produces economic benefit for the company. Ethical behavior ought to be our ideal regardless of the economic consequences. A corporation is, however, created for the primary purpose of operating a business profitably and providing a sufficient return on the shareholders' investment to justify their continuation of that investment. So the question about economic consequences of ethical behavior is a legitimate one.

"Does ethics pay?" is a complex question that is exceptionally difficult to answer. Although there can be no doubt that ethics does pay in some ways some of the time, there is no clear-cut answer that covers all situations. In trying to work toward a general answer, we find a few relevant facts that are based on fairly concrete evidence, but we must rely on intuition and even speculation for many others.

Several possible economic benefits of ethical behavior seem likely to occur, although they are of a long-term nature and are incapable of being measured with any precision. The following are some of these possible economic benefits:

1. It seems almost certain that the maintenance of high ethical standards in a company creates an environment in which very costly violations of the law are less likely to occur.

2. As mentioned earlier, such standards also may reduce the likelihood of new government regulations that are costly to comply with. Although this potential benefit is rather speculative, we do have evidence that **bad** ethical behavior can produce *more* regulation. The Foreign Corrupt Practices Act, for example, was passed by Congress primarily in response to revelations about widespread bribery by American companies in overseas transactions.

3. It also seems reasonable to assume that a high moral tone within a company will have a positive impact on employee morale and productivity. Intuitively, it would seem that, at least for most people, working in a company that observes and requires high ethical standards will be a much more pleasant experience than working in one with low standards. Employees and managers should experience less "cognitive dissonance," a disquieting and disruptive mental state caused by conflicting beliefs. Such a state can be created, for instance, when a manager or employee believes strongly that he should be loyal to the company, obey superiors, and work hard in pursuit of the company's interests, but where prevailing moral attitudes in the company are contrary to his personal moral standards. Because happier employees usually are more productive, the company should be more productive.

4. High ethical standards are likely to generate good will with suppliers and customers. The good reputation that results from ethical behavior does not substitute for quality products, good service, and competitive prices, but it can produce many intangible benefits over time. It makes it possible, for example, to develop long-lasting business relationships based on trust. These kinds of relationships are more economically efficient than those that are based solely on lengthy legal documents, legal threats, and keeping a close watch on the other party.

Balanced against these possible economic benefits is the fact that ethical behavior can sometimes be costly, and when these costs occur they are likely to be direct, immediate, and measurable. For example, it may be quite expensive to install better pollution control equipment than the law requires because of a strong moral commitment to those who drink the water and breathe the air. Competitors may not do the same thing, and their lower costs may enable them to undersell us. Or a company may lose business in the short term because it refuses to pay a bribe or kickback. And, unfortunately, an honest company can lose a business deal to a competitor who misrepresents the facts.

It takes a long-term view to properly assess the economic impact of ethical behavior. Whenever possible, of course, business firms should approach problems with a long-term perspective regardless of whether ethical questions are involved. We believe that the long-term economic benefits of high corporate ethical standards outweigh the more direct short-term economic benefits that low ethical standards sometimes produce. We cannot prove it, however. Some studies indicate that very profitable companies *are* more likely to exhibit high standards of ethical behavior than less profitable ones. Although these studies may lend support to the argument that ethics pays, the results could also be interpreted as simply indicating that companies behave more ethically when they can *afford* to do so. Although we can engage in reasonable speculation that ethics pays, we are unable to prove that companies can become more profitable by behaving ethically.

CORPORATE SOCIAL RESPONSIVENESS

If a person accepts the notion that corporations are moral agents and thus owe separate moral obligations, another question arises. Is it appropriate for a corporation to go beyond the moral minimum and correct problems it did not cause? Should a corporation expend corporate resources "doing good" by meeting societal needs? Such actions are sometimes described by the phrase *corporate social responsibility,* but *responsiveness* describes the idea better than *responsibility*. Going further, if it is *appropriate* for a corporation to do these kinds of things, is there actually an *obligation* to do them?

We first must recognize that questions about **corporate social responsiveness** do not necessarily arise every time a corporation's management considers spending corporate funds for a socially worthwhile cause such as helping a local elementary school offer enrichment programs for gifted students. Voluntarily responding to community needs often can be justified solely on economic grounds. Such actions can provide excellent promotional opportunities for the company and enhance its reputation and goodwill in a variety of ways. Also, improving the local community may improve the company's workforce and even its property values. Essentially, social responsiveness can provide some of the same economic benefits to a corporation that we mentioned earlier in our discussion of whether complying with the moral minimum can produce such benefits. Any attempts to justify socially responsive behavior on economic grounds must focus on long-term rather than short-term benefits, because the kind of benefit derived from such behavior is necessarily indirect and imprecise. Also, we should not put any less value on a corporation's voluntary contribution to society just because management was motivated by the company's self-interest. Indeed, the motives of the managers may have been very complex and indeterminate.

Our main question here, however, is how to deal with the question on moral grounds. Is socially responsive conduct appropriate regardless of whether it pays, and are there any circumstances in which it is morally required.

AGENTS OF CAPITAL VIEW

One of the most well-known proponents of the view that corporations do not owe a moral duty to be socially responsive is Milton Friedman, a Nobel laureate in economics and an influential spokesman on the role of corporations in society. To begin with, Friedman does not view corporations as moral agents; only its managers and employees as individuals have moral status. In addition, he contends that there is no obligation to spend corporate resources correcting problems the company did not cause, and going even further, he asserts that it is not even *appropriate* for the company's managers to do so. They are **agents of capital,** that is, agents of the shareholders who own the corporation and provide its capital. As such, their only duty is to earn as much money as possible for the shareholders, within the limits of the law and customary ethical practices.

Unless specially approved by shareholder resolution, decisions concerning the use of corporate resources to do good necessarily are made by individual managers. According to Friedman, it is completely inappropriate for them to do so. Corporate managers are free to devote their own time and money to whatever pursuits they deem morally or socially appropriate, but when they divert corporate resources to such projects they breach their duty of loyalty to shareholders. Friedman finds the social responsiveness movement to be a "fundamentally subversive doctrine" that resembles theft—managers are using "someone else's money." The proper function of government is to attend to matters of the common good and social welfare. Corporate managers are not, by training or otherwise, equipped to do that, and even if they were, it would be intolerable in a democracy for unelected, unaccountable "civil servants" to be charged with the responsibility. Although government might be slow and unresponsive in addressing current social problems, the insistence that this gap be filled by corporate action is just an acknowledgment of defeat by proponents of corporate social responsiveness who "have failed to persuade a majority of their fellow citizens to be of like mind and [who] are seeking to attain by undemocratic procedures what they cannot attain by democratic procedures."[4]

Another argument along the same lines is that when a social or religious organization or a government agency attempts to meet the needs of society, it usually does so with resources that we placed under the organization's control because of the merits of its social objectives. For example, grants from the American Cancer Society to researchers seeking a cure for cancer are

---

[4] *New York Times,* Sept. 12, 1962, sect. 6, 122.

made from funds that were donated to the Society because of the knowledge that the money would be used to fight the disease. Because of scarce resources, there is a "competition among good causes." Although it is unfortunate that all such needs cannot be fully met, this competition provides a method for roughly measuring the relative importance and value to the public of particular social needs. This prioritizing of needs by the marketplace is a very imperfect process that will always leave worthy needs unsatisfied. It does, however, introduce some necessary utilitarianism into the allocation of resources by reducing the chances that too much will go to causes that benefit too few. However, resources come into a corporation solely because of its business success, unless shareholders invest with the explicit understanding that certain corporate moneys will be spent on identified good causes. Thus, when managers use corporate funds to do good, the needs they meet have not withstood the test of this "market for donated funds."

AGENTS OF SOCIETY VIEW

There are those who argue that it is both appropriate and morally obligatory for corporations to contribute to the correction of problems they did not cause. They place this duty on the corporation as a moral agent, as well as on managers whose individual and group decisions energize the company. In a speech to the Harvard Business School in 1969, Henry Ford II stated: "The terms of the contract between industry and society are changing.... Now we are being asked to serve a wider range of human values and to accept an obligation to members of the public with whom we have no commercial transactions."[5] His words were foreshadowed by those of his grandfather some two generations earlier. "For a long time people believed that the only purpose of industry is to make a profit. They were wrong. Its purpose is to serve the general welfare."[6]

This notion of a "social contract" forms the foundation for many of the arguments that corporate social responsiveness is morally required. Under this view, a corporation is the result of a contract between those forming the corporation and the society that permits its creation. Thus, the corporation has a contract-like obligation to contribute positively to society, and the corporation's managers are not just agents of the shareholders but are also **agents of society.** One noted proponent of this view, philosopher Thomas Donaldson, hypothesized the existence of a society in which individuals always work and produce alone, and never in corporate form. A society such as this, composed of rational persons, would permit the legal creation of corporations only if the benefits to the public are great enough to justify the privileges granted to corporations and to outweigh the potential drawbacks. The privileges include limited liability—only the corporate entity and its assets are liable for corporate debts, not the individual shareholders or

---

[5] Thomas Donaldson, *Corporations and Morality* (Englewood Cliffs, N.J.: Prentice-Hall, Inc., 1982), 36.
[6] Ibid.

managers. This limited liability can come at a cost to other members of society. One potential drawback is that permitting corporations to exist generally leads to much larger aggregations of resources being under the effective control of a smaller number of people. Large resource accumulations in corporations can bring both economic and political power that few, if any, individuals could ever match. Such power can create risks for society.

Supporters of the agents of society view also would use the same basic line of reasoning that one would use to argue that *individuals* have a moral obligation to do good. These arguments were discussed earlier in the chapter. Similarly, for those wishing to build a rational argument in favor of morally required corporate social responsiveness, the same limits that were applied to the individual's obligation to do good would apply to the corporation's duty to be socially responsive.

Questions and Problems

1. Robinson and Walters made an oral agreement for Walters to sell five acres of land to Robinson for $138,000. Walters definitely promised to sell and Robinson definitely promised to buy. Robinson wanted the land very badly so that he could build a home for his family in a place that provided them with a lot of space but was still relatively close to the city. Robinson felt that he had gotten a good price. Robinson made a down payment of $6,900. After they made the agreement Robinson prepared a brief written memorandum stating the basic terms of the deal. He signed it and gave a copy to Walters, but Walters never signed. Robinson paid an architect to draw plans for a new home. About this time, however, Walters called Robinson and said he had changed his mind and no longer wished to sell. Walters wanted to hold on to the land for another couple of years because he thought its value would increase substantially. Robinson was terribly upset, but Walters refused to speak with him any further about the matter. Robinson filed a lawsuit claiming breach of contract. Robinson lost in court, however. In most cases, an agreement for the sale of land is legally enforceable only if it is evidenced by a written document that is signed by the defendant and contains the agreement's essential terms, including an adequate legal description of the land. The memorandum Robinson had prepared was not sufficient for this purpose, because Walters had not signed it and there was not an adequate legal description of the property. Compare the applicable legal rules with any relevant moral standards. Are they different? If so, how are they different, and what are some likely reasons for the difference? Do the reasons make sense?

2. Sally worked as a state government relations specialist for Amalgamated Industries, a large and diversified corporation with operations in many states. She maintained contacts with members of state legislatures and their staffs, as well as with personnel in state regulatory agencies. Her job was to keep top management apprised of proposed legislation and regulations that might affect the company and to put forth the company's positions on such proposals. The job required her to travel a great deal. Her company reimbursed her for all reasonable business-related travel expenses for which she had receipts. After she had been in the position for a few months, she discovered that many hotels did various things for certain business guests whose jobs would probably bring them to that city on a regular basis. At some hotels, for example, a business guest that the hotel hoped would become a "regular" would be given $20 or $30 cash as a "discount" on the room rate. The written receipt from the hotel, which the guest would submit to his or her employer for reimbursement, did not reflect this discount. What should Sally do if she is offered money in this way? Analyze any ethical questions that are raised by these facts.

3. Frenzoil Corporation is an American oil and gas company engaging in exploration, drilling, production, refining, and wholesale distribution. In addition to doing its own refining and distribution, it also sells crude oil to other refiners, especially smaller ones. One of its tanker ships was carrying a shipment of crude oil to a customer in an African coastal nation. The three-million gallon shipment was worth $1.5 million and had to be delivered by March 29 in order to fulfill Frenzoil's commitment to its customer. The customer had to have the oil by this date so that it could meet commitments to its own customers for refined petroleum products. When Frenzoil's captain neared the port of his destination on March 28, he sought permission from the harbor master to dock and unload. The harbor master told the captain that many tankers and other ships were in the harbor and a lot of others were nearby awaiting entry. It would be very difficult for Frenzoil's tanker to dock and unload for at least the next two weeks, the harbor master said, "unless other arrangements were made." He said that one of his assistants would come aboard the tanker and talk to the captain about such arrangements. When the assistant arrived at the tanker, the captain found out that the "arrangements" included substantial bribes to the harbor master and several other officials. If these arrangements were made, the tanker could dock and unload ahead of the many other ships that were waiting. Many of these other ships were operated by companies that were much smaller than Frenzoil and that could not afford to pay a bribe of this size. The captain radioed his boss at Frenzoil, who took the matter to the company's management and attorneys. They concluded that, even though such bribes might violate federal law—the Foreign Corrupt Practices Act—the chances of the violation being detected were quite small. Some of Frenzoil's managers, however, were still bothered by the ethical implications of paying the bribes. Analyze these implications.

4. Tom Sayles worked as a deck hand on a merchant vessel, the *M. S. North Star*. While carrying cargo in the Atlantic Ocean near the north Florida coast, Tom's boss told him to dump the ship's bilge into the sea. The bilge of a ship is the place where foul water containing various wastes collects. At each port there are facilities for pumping out bilges for proper treatment and disposal of the wastes. Tom thought he remembered seeing a U.S. Coast Guard regulation prohibiting bilge-dumping in U.S. territorial waters. Even if the practice does not violate a legal regulation, Tom concluded, it obviously damages the environment. What should Tom do? Analyze the moral issues in this situation.

5. Judith Watson worked for Merritt Flynch & Co., a large New York securities firm with underwriting, brokerage, and investment advising operations throughout the United States and the world. Merritt had branches in many foreign countries. Although serving a stint at one of the foreign offices was not an absolute requirement for advancement, everyone understood that successfully handling a foreign assignment was viewed by top management as very important. Employees who aspired to be on the "fast track" for promotion through the ranks of management almost always had a foreign assignment relatively early in their careers. During her four years at Merritt, Judith had received two significant promotions. Her work had been universally praised by her superiors, who viewed her as having tremendous potential for advancement into top management.

She was offered a position at the firm's office in Naphtali, an east Asian nation. This was considered a "plum" assignment, successful completion of which could mean a great deal to a person's career. Judith accepted the assignment and began work. She soon found, however, that the business culture in Naphtali was much different than in the United States. Women were generally not well accepted in management positions in that culture. Her immediate superior in the bank's Naphtali office, Dan Moseley, gave Judith much responsibility and always treated her as a co-equal professional, except when they were in the presence of Naphtali clients. In these situations, he referred to her as his "little helper," or his "lovely assistant." Viewed in this way, Merrit's clients felt comfortable dealing with her. On one occasion during discussions with Naphtali clients, Dan treated her as a manager with significant responsibility, and the clients became very uncomfortable, silent, and cold. The deal did not go through, and in all future situations Dan treated and referred to her in ways that made clients comfortable but that infuriated Judith. She discussed the situation with him, and he was very sympathetic and understanding but said he just could not see any other way to handle it. After feeling humiliated a few more times, Judith spoke with Dan's boss, who headed the Naphtali office. He responded in about the same way that Dan had. After continuing in these circumstances for several more months, Judith became irritable and uncooperative, and her performance suffered. The ratings she received on her quarterly performance reviews declined. She really did not know what to do. Analyze the ethical implications of this situation.

CHAPTER 8

Businesses are the victims of crime. Businesses commit crimes. This sad reality necessitates a general overview of the role of criminal law in the legal environment of business. Armed robberies, bad checks, employee pilfering, and other criminal acts cost businesses billions of dollars annually. Consumers suffer as well, because these losses are manifested either in the form of higher prices or, worse, failed businesses.

Criminal acts committed by businesses also cause enormous losses to our society. Though crimes committed by

CRIMINAL LAW AND BUSINESS

businesses received little attention in the criminal law until recently, that situation has changed dramatically as we have become aware of such wrongful acts as stifling competition by fixing prices, selling stock based on contrived financial statements, using false advertising to lure customers into buying inferior products, and the like.

The strong interrelationship between criminal law and the vital interests of business is highlighted by frequent references to criminal acts in other chapters of this text. For example, there is discussion of contracts calling for criminal acts in Chapter 9, of criminal securities law violations in Chapter 15, of illegal competitive acts in Chapter 14, and of criminal violation of environmental laws in Chapter 19.

NATURE OF CRIMINAL LAW

A **crime** is a wrong committed against society. Indeed, that wrong is also defined by society, because the criminal law is one of a civilized society's primary tools for conforming the behavior of its citizens to societal norms. Even in a society with as many freedoms as America's, limits must be placed on individual and corporate actions. Today's drug epidemic is a vivid reminder of the damage that certain types of individual activity can inflict on society as a whole. Criminalizing activity is often far from the best way to address the causes of that activity or to solve the problems that arise from it. Nonetheless, criminal law is one of society's most important mechanisms for controlling individual behavior, and that will not change anytime soon.

CIVIL AND CRIMINAL LAW CONTRASTED

Most of this text discuss civil law matters. While there are many similarities between criminal law and civil law, there are also important distinctions. The civil law adjusts rights between or among individuals. The basis of the controversy may be a broken commercial promise, an injury caused by someone's careless driving, or a loss caused by a defective product. The focus is on adjusting the rights of the parties to the transaction. The criminal law, on the other hand, focuses on the individual's relationship to society. In enacting criminal statutes, a government is saying that there are certain activities so inherently contrary to the public good that they must be flatly prohibited *in the best interests of society.*

A civil lawsuit is brought by one individual or company (the plaintiff) against another (the defendant). A criminal action, on the other hand, is always brought by an agent of the government (the prosecutor or district attorney) against the alleged wrongdoer. The essence of the civil suit is an injury that the defendant's wrongful act caused to the individual plaintiff. The essence of a criminal prosecution is the injury that the defendant's wrongful act caused society. Of course, there are usually individual victims of criminal acts. The suffering of those victims is not ignored by the criminal law, but greater emphasis is placed on the implications that such conduct has for society at large.

A plaintiff in a civil suit usually requests money damages as compensation for injuries sustained by the defendant's wrongful conduct. In a criminal action, however, even a successful prosecution will not usually produce a dime for the plaintiff. Rather, the remedy sought by the prosecutor typically is punishment for the defendant, such as a fine (which usually goes to the state) and/or imprisonment.

Of course, many types of acts (such as battery) constitute both criminal wrongs and actionable torts. As illustrated in Figure 8.1, the same activity might be the subject of both a civil suit by the victim and a criminal action by the state. A critical difference in such actions lies in the burden of proof. A plaintiff in a civil action must prove the elements of recovery by only "a preponderance of the evidence." Because the consequences of a criminal conviction are generally considered much more severe, a higher standard of

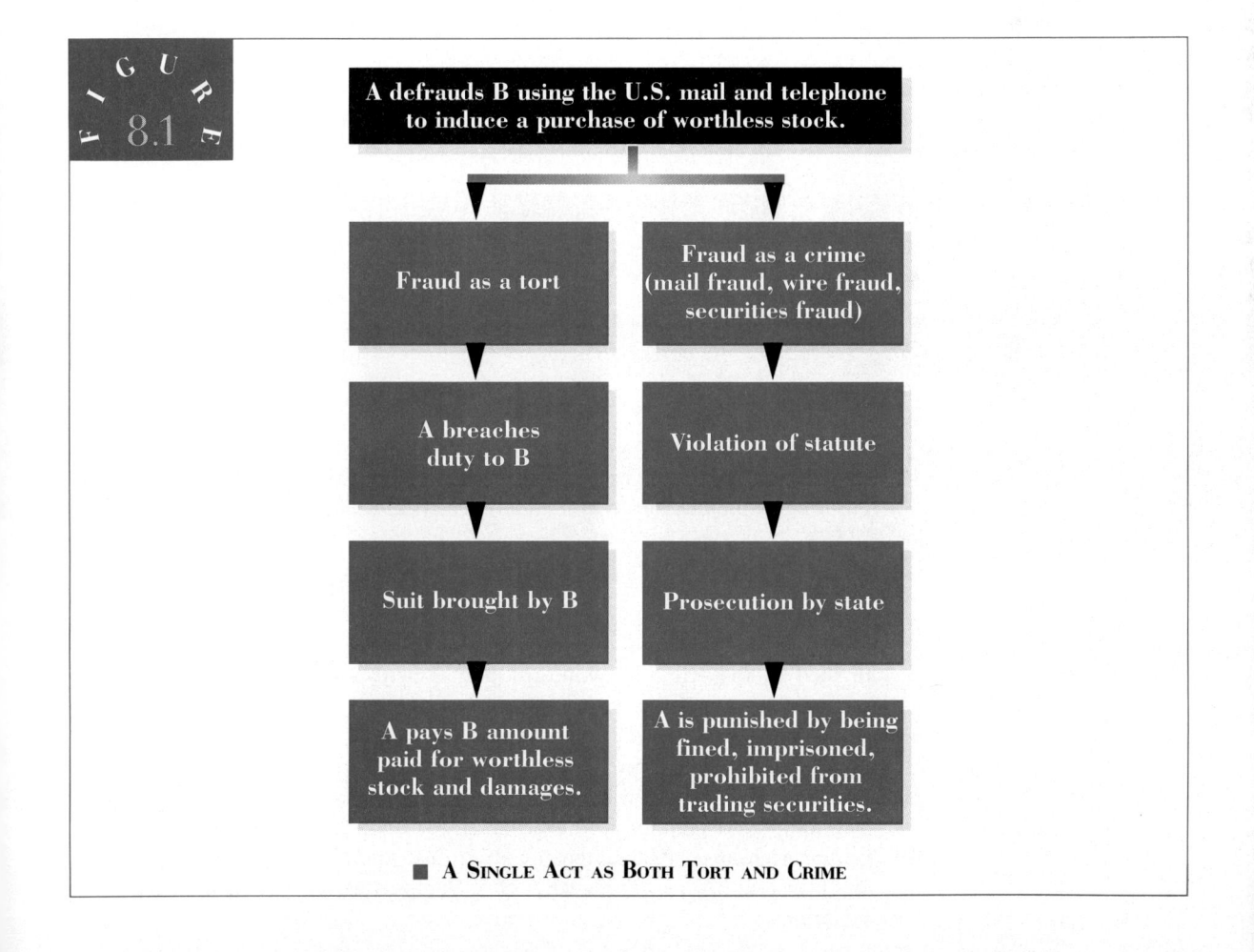

FIGURE 8.1

A defrauds B using the U.S. mail and telephone to induce a purchase of worthless stock.

- Fraud as a tort → A breaches duty to B → Suit brought by B → A pays B amount paid for worthless stock and damages.
- Fraud as a crime (mail fraud, wire fraud, securities fraud) → Violation of statute → Prosecution by state → A is punished by being fined, imprisoned, prohibited from trading securities.

■ A SINGLE ACT AS BOTH TORT AND CRIME

FIGURE 8.2

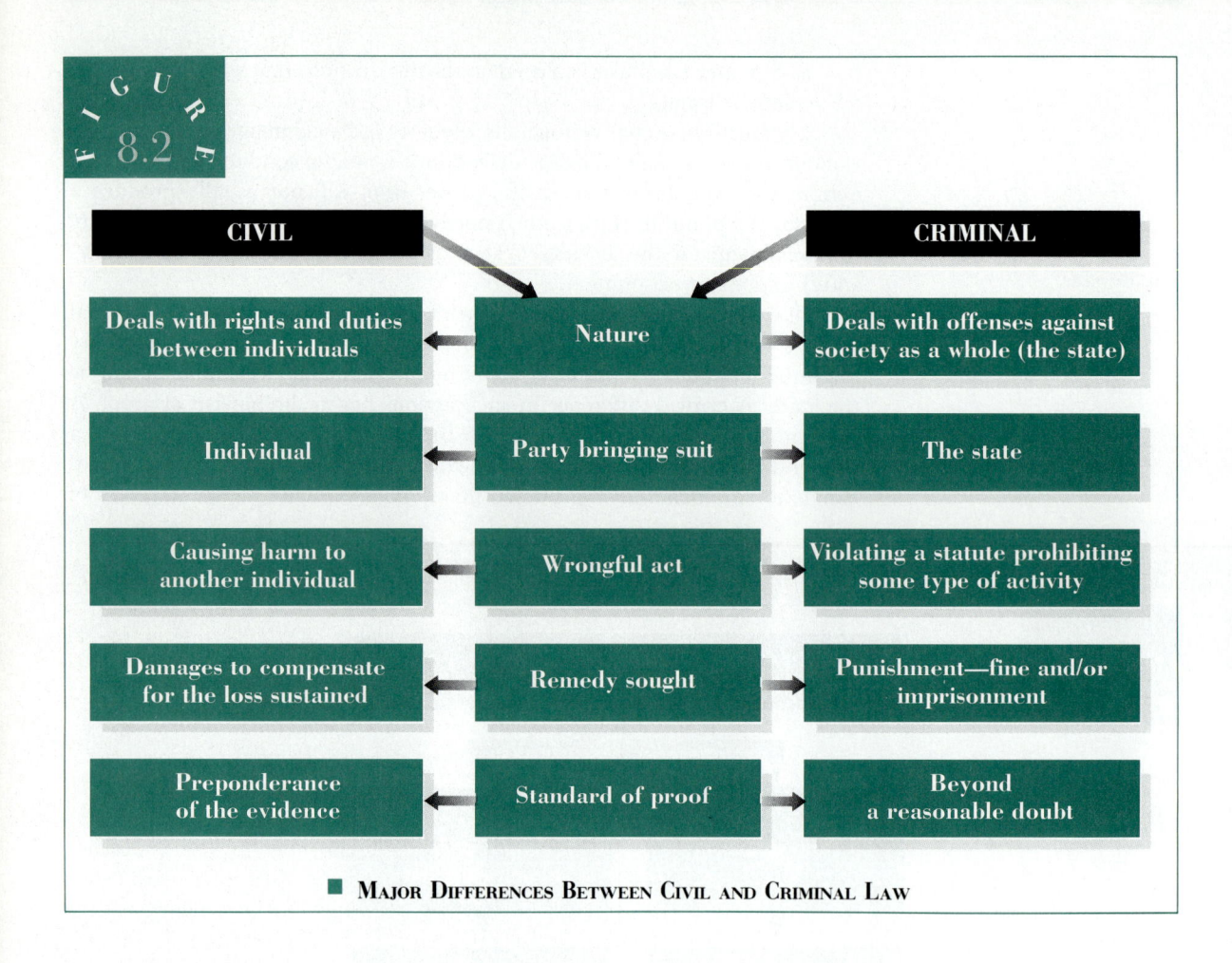

CIVIL	Nature	CRIMINAL
Deals with rights and duties between individuals	Nature	Deals with offenses against society as a whole (the state)
Individual	Party bringing suit	The state
Causing harm to another individual	Wrongful act	Violating a statute prohibiting some type of activity
Damages to compensate for the loss sustained	Remedy sought	Punishment—fine and/or imprisonment
Preponderance of the evidence	Standard of proof	Beyond a reasonable doubt

■ Major Differences Between Civil and Criminal Law

proof must be met by prosecutors. Jurors must be convinced of the defendant's guilt "beyond a reasonable doubt" before a guilty verdict is appropriate. Figure 8.2 outlines major differences between civil and criminal law.

CLASSIFICATION OF CRIMES

Degree of Seriousness

Except for the most serious crime of treason, crimes are either *felonies* or *misdemeanors*, depending on the severity of the penalty that the statute provides. The definition of **felony** varies from state to state, but it is usually defined as any crime in which the punishment is either death or imprisonment for more than one year in a state penitentiary, as in the cases of murder, robbery, or rape. **Misdemeanors** are all crimes carrying lesser penalties (such as fines or confinement in county jails)—for example, petit larceny and disorderly conduct. In the federal system, felonies are crimes for which the designated penalty is more than one year in prison; misdemeanors are crimes with lesser designated penalties. Yet another category used in some states is *petty offenses,* covering such infractions as traffic and building code violations.

The distinction between felonies and misdemeanors can be important because of various penalties often imposed on persons convicted of the former, such as loss of the right to vote, to hold public office, or to pursue various careers.

Degree of Moral Turpitude

Crimes such as murder, rape, arson, or robbery are evil in and of themselves. Such acts are called *malum in se,* meaning that they are criminal because they are inherently wicked. Other acts, such as jaywalking or speeding are *malum prohibitum,* meaning that they are crimes merely because the legislature has said that they are wrongful. Typically, greater punishments attach to crimes that involve moral turpitude.

Jurisdiction

As has already been noted, in America a federal criminal justice system is superimposed over state and local systems. These systems generally address different concerns. Murder is usually a concern only of the state in which it occurred unless, for example, it occurred on federal property, the victim was a federal official, or it occurred as part of an interstate kidnapping. Still, there are several areas of overlap and actions that might well violate both federal and state laws. For example, during the wave of bank robberies during the 1930s Depression, a federal law against bank robberies was passed so that the Federal Bureau of Investigation and federal prosecutors could supplement the efforts of state police and judicial systems.

Purpose of Punishment

Perhaps the most salient feature of the criminal justice system is the punishment that it imposes on wrongdoers. As noted earlier, the punishment is not imposed to compensate the victim. That is the province of the civil tort system. Rather, there are four primary purposes of criminal punishment. First, there is *rehabilitation* or reformation. Although published rates of recidivism (relapse into crime) indicate that this is the most difficult of the punishment goals to attain, it is important that our system at least attempt to reform wrongdoers.

A second, less ambitious, purpose of punishment is simply *restraint* or incapacitation, on the theory that a robber cannot rob and a rapist cannot rape while they are locked up. A third purpose of punishment, and a somewhat controversial one, is that of *retribution.* The concept of retribution predates the Bible's admonition of "an eye for an eye," and society's infliction of retribution on criminals still has strong popular support.

A final purpose of punishment is *deterrence.* The law seeks to persuade the wrongdoer being punished not to err again and, at the same time, to provide an example that might generally deter other potential lawbreakers. The effectiveness of various types of criminal sanctions, in deterring crime is not clear. One very cotroversial subject is the death penalty. Although most evidence makes it clear that a state will not reduce its murder rate by adopting a death penalty, advocates still justify the ultimate punishment on restraint and retribution grounds.

CONSTITUTIONAL PROTECTIONS

Once arrested, a criminal defendant has the considerable power and resources of the government lined up against him or her. The potential for abuse of that power is considerable, and one need not be a student of history to discover blatant examples of such abuses. Because our system operates on the theory that it is better that a guilty man or woman go free than that an innocent man or woman should suffer unjust punishment, we provide manifold protections for criminal defendants. Many of these protections are set forth in the Bill of Rights. Through the controversial process of "incorporation," most of these rights have been applied to the states as well. Additionally, many state constitutions contain parallel protections. The following discussion will help complete the examination of constitutional law begun in Chapter 5.

FOURTH AMENDMENT

The Fourth Amendment protects people (and, as we saw in Chapter 6, businesses) against "unreasonable searches and seizures," requiring that search warrants not be issued absent "probable cause." A search warrant will be issued by a judge if the police have produced evidence that would lead a reasonably prudent person to believe there is a substantial likelihood that the defendant is guilty of the offense the police charge. The Fourth Amendment requires that the warrant "particularly describe" the place to be searched and the persons or things to be seized.

A controversial question regards enforcement of this prohibition. What happens to evidence that the police seize without a valid warrant? In *Mapp v. Ohio*, 367 U.S. 643 (1961), the Supreme Court held that "all evidence obtained by searches and seizures in violation of the Constitution is ... inadmissible in a state court." This holding was very controversial, opponents arguing that "the crook should not go free just because the constable has erred." In recent years the increasingly conservative Supreme Court has fashioned a number of exceptions to this "exclusionary rule," weakening its impact substantially. For example, in *United States v. Leon*, 468 U.S. 189 (1984), the Court created a "good faith" exception for situations in which the police searched pursuant to an apparently valid search warrant that was later determined to have been improperly issued. The Court reasoned, in part, that the exclusionary rule was meant to deter police abuses rather than to correct errors by judges.

FIFTH AMENDMENT

The Fifth Amendment contains a number of provisions that protect criminal defendants from government abuse. For example, individuals cannot be held to answer for major federal criminal charges unless they have been indicted by a **grand jury.** A grand jury typically consists of 23 members of the community who hear evidence presented by the prosecution. If a majority concludes that there is probable cause to believe that the defendant has committed the crime alleged, the grand jury issues a "true bill." The right to indictment by grand jury is one of the few protections in the Bill of Rights that the Supreme Court has not applied to the states. However, many state constitutions have similar provisions.

The Fifth Amendments also protects defendants from **double jeopardy,** which is being tried twice for the same offense. This means that when a jury finds a defendant "not guilty," the government cannot simply reindict the defendant for the same crime and try again to convict him or her. However, it does not mean that a defendant acquitted of criminal assault and battery could not be sued civilly by his or her alleged victim. Because of the differential burden of proof, the same body of evidence that did not convince a criminal jury beyond a reasonable doubt might convince a civil jury applying a preponderance of evidence standard. The fact that a state prosecution will not bar a subsequent federal prosecution and vice versa constitutes another major exception to the double jeopardy prohibition. Thus, theoretically, a defendant who was acquitted of a federal bank robbery charge might be prosecuted by a state claiming that the same alleged robbery violated a state statute.

The Fifth Amendment mandates that no person be deprived of life, liberty, or property without **due process** of law. We know quite a bit about due process from previous chapters. One aspect of due process, for example, is that no one should be convicted of violating a statute that is unduly vague, so that a well-intentional person could not conform his or her conduct to comply with the law. *Kolender v. Lawson,* 461 U.S. 352 (1981), is a good example. In that case, a California criminal statute requiring persons on the street to provide "credible and reliable" identification and to account for their presence when requested to do so by a policeman was held to be unduly vague.

As another example, it would be a due process violation for a prosecutor intentionally to suppress material evidence favorable to the accused. *Brady v. Maryland,* 373 U.S. 83 (1963). But the Supreme Court recently held that the government's accidental destruction of evidence that *might* have supported the defendant's innocence did not violate due process. Nor was due process violated by the government's innocent failure to use the most modern, sophisticated scientific methods of examining evidence. *Arizona v. Youngblood,* 488 U.S. 51 (1988).

The most controversial part of the Fifth Amendment, as interpreted by the Supreme Court, is its protection against self-incrimination. No person "shall be compelled in any criminal case to be a witness against himself." This includes matters of document production as well as of oral testimony. The right is not available to corporations and is individual to the person charged. In a case of interest to all businesspersons, *United States v. Doe,* 465 U.S. 605 (1984), the court held that the sole owner of a corporation could not claim the privilege against self-incrimination to avoid producing records that belonged *to the corporation.* Had the business been a sole proprietorship, the owner could have claimed the privilege because the records would have been his or hers, not a separate entity's.

The most famous self-incrimination case is *Miranda v. Arizona*, 384 U.S. 436 (1966), which excluded from evidence any incriminating statements made by a defendant (and evidence to which those statements led police, called "fruit of the poisonous tree") who had not been fully warned of his constitutional right against self-incrimination (and his right to counsel). Thus, the famous "Miranda warning" was born.

As with the exclusionary rule, the current more conservative members of the Supreme Court have diluted the impact of *Miranda*. For example, in *Duckworth v. Eagan*, 492 U.S. 195 (1989), the police told a criminal suspect that "we have no way of giving you a lawyer, but one will be appointed for you, if you wish, if and when you go to court." Dissenters felt that this statement might have misled the defendant into believing, inaccurately, that he did not have the right to consult an attorney then and there in the stationhouse before being interrogated by the police. But the majority said that "*Miranda* does not require that attorneys be producible on call..." and felt that the statement was not necessarily misleading given that the defendant had already been read the standard Miranda warning, which informs defendants that they have the right to speak to a lawyer before any questions are asked.

SIXTH AMENDMENT

The Sixth Amendment contains a litany of constitutional protections for criminal defendants, including the important right to counsel that was mentioned in the previous discussion of the *Miranda* case. Generally speaking, any individual facing potential incarceration has the right to consult an attorney and to have one provided if he or she cannot afford one.

The right to counsel is made more meaningful by the defendant's Sixth Amendment rights to be informed of the nature of the accusation, to confront witnesses against him or her, and to call witnesses on his or her own behalf.

There is also the right to a "speedy and public trial." Court backlogs have threatened to make a mockery of the right to a "speedy" trial, but the federal government and most states have now passed "speedy trial" acts that place time limits on the government and give criminal cases priority over civil cases on crowded court dockets.

Importantly, there is also a right to trial by an impartial jury that applies in cases involving "serious" criminal charges. Juries, serving as the "conscience of the community," are a critical safeguard against the heavy hand of the government.

EIGHTH AMENDMENT

The Eighth Amendment contains important protections for criminal defendants. It states that "excessive bail" shall not be required. Thus, when a judge sets bail before trial, the aim should be not to punish the defendant who is presumed innocent, but simply to guarantee the defendant's appearance at trial. In recent years, Congress has increased the courts' authority to deny bail in situations in which defendants pose special harm to the public.

HUMOR AND THE LAW

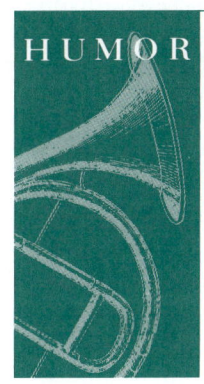

Someone once said: "No one's liberty or property is safe while the legislature is in session." If you had ever speculated that Congress occasionally spends its time on rather silly matters when it should be solving the deficit, attacking poverty, aiding education and the like, you are correct. We offer as a modest illustration the fact that Congress has made all of the following acts *federal crimes:*

1. Unauthorized use of the 4-H symbol (Title 18 United States Code Sec. 707).

2. Unauthorized use of "Smokey Bear" name or character (18 U.S.C. 711).

3. Issuing false weather reports (18 U.S.C. 2074).

4. Interstate transportation of dentures by unauthorized persons (18 U.S.C. 1821).

5. Cruelty to seamen (you'd better be nice to those Navy ROTC guys and gals) (18 U.S.C. 2191).

6. Illegal use of a cremation urn (don't even ask!) (18 U.S.C. 710).

The Eighth Amendment also bans "excessive fines" and "cruel and unusual punishment." The latter provision has been held not to bar the death penalty, even for juveniles or retarded defendants.

MISCELLA-NEOUS PROTECTIONS

Other protections for criminal defendants are scattered throughout the Constitution. For example, there is a ban on *ex post facto* laws—laws that are passed to criminalize conduct *after* the conduct has occurred. Obviously, criminal laws must also be scrutinized to ensure that they do not violate basic freedoms, such as religion and speech. The government could not, for example, make it a crime to be a Baptist. Nor, the court has held, can a state criminalize the burning of the American flag when performed as a form of political expression. *Texas v. Johnson,* 491 U.S. 397 (1989).

GENERAL ELEMENTS OF CRIMINAL RESPONSIBILITY

As a general rule, the prosecutor in a criminal case must do three things to obtain a valid conviction: (1) show that the defendant's actions violated an existing criminal statute; (2) prove beyond a reasonable doubt that the defendant did do the *acts* alleged; and (3) prove that the defendant had the requisite *intent* to violate the law. The first element is important because although many of our crimes have strong common-law roots, today almost all crimes are statutory in nature. The other two elements of act and intent deserve separate consideration.

GUILTY ACT

A basic element of a criminal conviction is the *actus reus,* a Latin term meaning "guilty act." This is a critical part of a criminal conviction because our legal system generally does not punish persons for their thoughts. Evil thoughts alone normally do not injure society and therefore do not justify bringing to bear the full power of the government's criminal justice system. This does not mean that a defendant must always successfully complete a criminal act to be guilty. Generally any act that clearly is a step in the commission of a crime will be sufficient for a conviction for *attempted* larceny, murder, and so on, if the intent requirement is also present.

The guilty act must be voluntary and generally must be an act of commission rather than mere omission. However, there are exceptions. Failure to perform a legally imposed duty will constitute a sufficient *actus reus.* An example is failure to fulfill the legally required duty to file an income tax return.

GUILTY MIND

Generally, a defendant is not guilty unless his or her guilty act is coupled with a guilty mind, that is, unless the defendant had *mens rea,* an intent to do wrong. A murder conviction, for example, requires the act of killing the victim plus the evil intent to take a life.

Because a person's actual intent can rarely be known with absolute certainty, juries may often presume a criminal intent on the part of the defendant based on the established facts. Thus a jury may presume that an armed powler apprehended at night entered the house "with the intention of committing a felony," one of the usual statutory elements of the crime of burglary. Intent is often a difficult element to prove beyond a reasonable doubt, but as Justice Oliver Wendell Holmes once stated, "even a dog distinguishes between being stumbled over and being kicked."

Many crimes are called "specific intent" crimes, in that conviction is appropriate only if the defendant had the intent to commit the exact forbidden act charged. For other crimes, "general intent" will suffice, meaning that the defendant had the general intent to commit a wrongful act even though he or she did not intend to bring about the specific result. First degree murder is typically a specific intent crime; to be guilty the defendant must have intended to take a human life. However, if a defendant became very drunk and went on a rampage, killing a man with a gun, he may be found guilty of second degree murder even though he was so drunk he did not know he had a gun. This is an example of general intent.

In the following case, which surprised many observers, the Supreme Court addressed the question of whether a good faith, but objectively unreasonable, belief could negate the intent element.

Cheek v. United States

U.S. Supreme Court, 111 S.Ct 604 (1991)

Petitioner Cheek was charged with multiple counts of willfully failing to file a federal income tax return in violation of section 7203 of the Internal Revenue code and of willfully attempting to evade his income taxes in violation of section 7201. Cheek admitted that he had not filed the returns but testifed that he had not acted willfully because he sincerely believed, based on his indoctrination by a tax protest organization and his own study, that the tax laws were being unconstitutionally enforced and that his actions were lawful. The court of appeals affirmed Cheek's conviction, rejecting his challenge to the trial judge's instructing the jury that an honest but unreasonable belief is not a defense and that Cheek's beliefs that wages are not income and that he was not a taxpayer within the meaning of the code were not objectively reasonable. Cheek appealed.

White, Justice:

The general rule that ignorance of the law or a mistake of law is no defense to criminal prosecution is deeply rooted in the American legal system. Based on the notion that the law is definite and knowable, the common law presumed that every person knew the law.

The proliferation of statutes and regulations has sometimes made it difficult for the average citizen to know and comprehend the extent of the duties and obligations imposed by the tax laws. Congress has accordingly softened the impact of the common-law presumption by making specific intent to violate the law an element of certain federal tax offenses. Thus, the Court almost 60 years ago interpreted the statutory term "willfully" as used in the federal criminal tax statutes as carving out an exception to the traditional rule. This special treatment of criminal tax offenses is largely due to the complexity of the tax laws.

Willfulness, as construed by our prior decisions in criminal tax cases, requires the Government to prove that the law imposed a duty on the defendant, that the defendant knew of this duty, and that he voluntarily and intentionally violated that duty. We deal first with the case where the issue is whether the defendant knew of the duty purportedly imposed by the provision of the statute or regulation he is accused of violating, a case in which there is no claim that the provision at issue is invalid. In such a case, if the Government proves actual knowledge of the pertinent legal duty, the prosecution, without more, has satisfied the knowledge component of the willfulness requirement. But carrying this burden requires negating a defendant's claim of ignorance of the law or a claim that because of a misunderstanding of the law, he had a good faith belief that he was not violating any of the provisions of the tax laws. This is so because one cannot be aware that the law imposes a duty upon him and yet be ignorant of it, misunderstand the law, or believe that the duty does not exist. In the end, the issue is whether, based on all the evidence, the Government has proved that the defendant was aware of the duty at issue, which cannot be true if the jury credits a good-faith misunderstanding and belief submission, whether or not the claimed belief or misunderstanding is objectively reasonable.

It was therefore error to instruct the jury to disregard evidence of Cheek's understanding that, within the meaning of the tax laws, he was not a person required to file a return or to pay income taxes and that wages are not taxable income, as incredible as such misunderstandings of and beliefs about the law might be. Of course, the more unreasonable the asserted beliefs or misunderstandings are, the more likely the jury will consider them to be nothing more than simple disagreement with known legal duties imposed by the tax laws and will find that the Government has carried its burden of proving knowledge.

[Cheek's] claims that some of the provisions of the tax code are unconstitutional are submissions of a different order. They do not arise from innocent mistakes caused by the complexity of the Internal Revenue Code. Rather, they reveal full knowledge of the provisions at issue and a studied conclusion, however wrong, that those provisions are invalid and unenforceable. Thus in this case, Cheek paid his taxes for years, but after attending various seminars and based on his own study, he concluded that the income tax laws could not constitutionally require him to pay a tax.

We do not believe that Congress contemplated that such a taxpayer,

CONTINUED

without risking criminal prosecution, could ignore that duties imposed upon him by the Internal Revenue Code and refuse to utilize the mechanisms provided by Congress to present his claims of invalidity to the courts and to abide by their decisions. There is no doubt that Cheek, from year to year, was free to pay the tax that the law purported to require, file for a refund and, if denied, present his claims of invalidity, constitutional or otherwise, to the courts. Also, without paying the tax, he could have challenged the claims of tax deficiencies in the Tax Court, with the right to appeal to a higher court if unsuccessful. Cheek took neither course in some years, and when he did was unwilling to accept the outcome. As we see it, he is in no position to claim that his good-faith belief about the validity of the Internal Revenue Code negates willfulness or provides a defense to criminal prosecution.

[T]he judgment of the Court of Appeals is vacated, and the case is remanded for further proceedings consistent with this opinion.

There are a few crimes for which negligence will suffice and no intent need be proven. Negligent vehicular homicide is an example. There are even some *strict liability* crimes, in which defendants can be found guilty absent intent or even careless behavior. These are typically misdemeanors. Examples include selling liquor to minors, violating traffic rules, and violating pure food and drug laws.

GENERAL CRIMINAL DEFENSES

DEFENSES NEGATING INTENT

Many defenses raised in a criminal case are aimed at negating the *mens rea* element by showing that the defendant did not intend to commit a crime. Several such defenses exist. We will learn in Chapter 9 that many of these concepts also provide grounds for escaping contractual obligations.

Infancy

The common-law rule was that children younger than seven years were *conclusively* presumed to be incapable of forming criminal intent. Children between seven and fourteen years were accorded the same presumption but in a *rebuttable* form. The presumption could be overcome by proof that the child understood the wrongful nature of his or her act. Many states still follow these basic notions in their criminal statutes. However, virtually all states have created juvenile courts, which treat juveniles as delinquents rather than criminals with the purpose of reforming rather than punishing them. Therefore, infancy as a criminal defense is not as important as it once was, although prosecutors usually have the option of attempting to convince a court to try a juvenile as an adult when a particularly heinous crime has been committed.

Insanity

There are several approaches, none satisfactory, to handling defendants who "plead insanity." Some states use the *M'Naghten* test, which excuses a defendant whose mental defect renders him or her incapable of appreciating the difference between right and wrong. Others excuse defendants who may appreciate the difference between right and wrong but who suffer a mental defect causing an "irresistible impulse" to commit the crime. The District of Columbia courts developed the *Durham* rule, which simply asks whether the defendant was insane at the time of the crime and, if so, whether the crime was a product of that insanity. Finally, the Model Penal Code provides that a defendant "is not responsible for criminal conduct if at the time of such conduct as a result of mental disease or defect he lacks substantial capacity either to appreciate the wrongfulness of his conduct or to conform his conduct to the requirements of the law."

Intoxication

If a person *voluntarily* becomes intoxicated (or "high" on drugs), the general rule is that this may negate specific intent but will not negate general intent, as discussed above. Voluntary intoxication is generally no defense to crimes requiring mere negligence or recklessness.

Involuntary intoxication, however, is generally treated as equivalent to insanity. Thus, if a defendant unforeseeably became intoxicated because of an unusual reaction to prescribed medication, courts would be reluctant to hold him or her responsible for crimes he or she might commit under the influence of that medication.

Duress

Occasionally, persons will be forced to commit crimes against their will. When the wrongful threat of others causes a person to commit a crime, *mens rea* is negated. Duress is generally shown when an immediate and inescapable threat of serious bodily injury or death (that is greater than the harm to be caused by the crime) forces a person to commit a crime that he or she does not wish to commit. The threat must come through no fault of the defendant's. If, for example, a defendant voluntarily joins a criminal gang, he or she has no duress defense if the gang leader forces him or her to help in one of the gang's planned crimes.

Mistake

Because ignorance of the law is no excuse, a *mistake of law* is generally no defense to a criminal charge. Thus, a defendant who has intentionally performed a specific act cannot usually defend by saying: "I didn't know that it was illegal," or even "My attorney told me that it was okay." The courts' refusal to hold an attorney's advice to be a valid defense discourages "attorney shopping." However, many courts will find that a mistake of law negates the intent element if (1) the law was not reasonably made known to the public, or (2) the defendant reasonably relied on an erroneous but official statement of the law (such as in a judicial opinion or administrative order).

A defense based on *mistake of fact* is more likely to succeed. Thus, a defendant charged with stealing a blue 12-speed bicycle might successfully defend by showing that he or she owned an identical blue 12-speed bicycle parked at the next rack and mistakenly rode off on the wrong one.

OTHER DEFENSES

Entrapment

Police undercover work is often aimed at catching criminals "in the act." If the police not only create an opportunity for a criminal act but also persuade the defendant to commit a crime that he or she would not otherwise have committed, defendant may have a good **entrapment** defense. The entrapment defense presents difficult factual questions, for the court must draw the line between an unwary innocent and an unwary criminal. The key issue is whether the defendant was *predisposed* to commit the crime. That is, the criminal idea must originate with the defendant, not with the policeman. As the Supreme Court once said, "When the criminal design originates with the [police who] implant in the mind of an innocent person the disposition to commit the alleged offense and induce its commission in order that they may prosecute," entrapment results. *Sorrells v. United States,* 287 U.S. 435 (1932).

Self-Defense

Self-defense and defense of others may justify acts of violence that otherwise would be criminal. Although the courts do not require "detached reflection in the presence of an uplifted knife," *Brown v. United States,* 256 U.S. 335 (1921), the general rule permits only that degree of force reasonable under the circumstances. Deadly force can be used if the defendant has a reasonable belief that imminent death or grievous bodily injury will otherwise result. The law does not allow one to shoot an assailant in the back once that assailant is clearly fleeing and poses no further threat. In some cases, retreat might even be required as preferable to deadly force. Nondeadly force can be used in the degree reasonably believed necessary to protect persons or property from criminal acts, although obviously, a lesser degree of force will be viewed as "reasonable" in defense of property.

Immunity

Through the process of "plea bargaining," defendants often agree to testify against other criminals in return for consideration at time of sentencing and, perhaps **immunity** from prosecution of certain potential charges. It is often said that such persons are "turning state's evidence" to help the prosecutor's case.

STATE CRIMES AFFECTING BUSINESS

So many crimes against persons and property are contained in state criminal codes that it would be impossible to list them all. Furthermore, there is such variation from state to state that it is difficult to generalize about criminal

THEFT

Many state statutes criminalize the unlawful taking of another's property under a general statute that often terms the crime "theft." Such statutes consolidate a variety of related crimes that developed separately at the common law, such as larceny, burglary, false pretenses, and embezzlement.

Larceny

At common law, **larceny** was the trespassory taking away of the personal property of another with wrongful intent permanently to deprive that person of the use of the property. Larceny is viewed as an injury to the owner's interest in possessing the goods. Shoplifting is a good example. Promising to sell someone your car, taking the money, and then refusing to turn over the car is not larceny, because there is no wrongful taking. The concept of personal property generally does not include trees or personal services but would include computer programs and trade secrets.

There are degrees of larceny. Petit larceny covers theft of smaller amounts (e.g., less than $500). Thefts of property worth more would be grand larceny. These statutory distinctions vary in amount from state to state.

Burglary

At common law, **burglary** was the trespassory breaking and entering of the dwelling house of another during the nighttime with intent to commit a felony. Over time, many of the technical requirements have been dropped. Now, most statutes would find burglary even though the building broken into was not a dwelling house and even though it occurred during the daytime. Burglary with use of a weapon is called aggravated burglary.

False Pretenses

Obtaining goods by **false pretenses** was defined by the common law as obtaining title to someone else's property by knowingly or recklessly making a false representation of existing material fact that is intended to and does defraud the victim into parting with his or her property. Technically, false pretenses is an injury to title, not mere possession. Title passes to the thief, quite unlike larceny. Examples of such conduct are the filing of false claims with insurance companies, the buying of a VCR with a check the purchaser knows will "bounce," and the taking of buyers' money for goods or services with no intent of delivering such goods or services.

Embezzlement

A wholly statutory offense, **embezzlement** is the fraudulent conversion of the property of another by one who has lawful possession of it. This crime somewhat overlaps with larceny, but the original possession by the wrongdoer is lawful. An example is an attorney who receives funds from his or her client for payment of a settlement but later decides to spend the money on her- or himself instead.

Some of the key elements of an embezzlement charge are discussed in the following case.

STATE v. JOY

SUPREME COURT OF VERMONT, 549 A.2d 1033 (1988)

Defendant Joy was president and sole shareholder of Credit Management Services (CMS), a debt collection agency that collected delinquent accounts for businesses in exchange for 40 percent of the amount collected. CMS was entitled to this percentage regardless to whether the debtor paid CMS or settled with the client directly. When CMS received a payment from a debtor, it would deposit the money with a Barre bank and within a month an invoice detailing the transaction would be sent to the client. If monies were due the client, a check would accompany the invoice. In addition, CMS maintained an account with a Montpelier bank from which it drew operating expenses.

In early 1981 CMS, suffering financial difficulties, began transferring funds from the Barre account to the Montpelier account to cover its operating expenses. In June 1981, CMS was hired by Stacey Fuel to collect several delinquent accounts. On August 14, CMS received a check from one of Stacey's debtors in the amount of $1,920.25. CMS never forwarded any of this money to Stacey, nor did it inform Stacey that the money had been received. Stacey ended its relationship with CMS in August 1982 and only later learned that CMS had filed for bankruptcy and had listed Stacey as one of its creditors.

Joy was convicted of embezzlement and appealed.

DOOLEY, JUSTICE:

In his first claim on appeal, defendant suggests that the trial court improperly refused to charge the jury that "[t]he mere fact that C.M.S Corporation failed or was unable to pay its creditors is not a sufficient showing of intent to justify conviction [of embezzlement]."

Defendant's main objection to the charge is that it failed to state that the jury could consider intent to repay as evidence that the defendant had no fraudulent intent. The elements of embezzlement are detailed in 13 V.S.A. § 2531, which states in pertinent part that:

> An officer, agent, bailee for hire, clerk or servant of a banking association or an incorporated company.... who embezzles or fraudulently converts to his own use, or takes or secretes with intent to embezzle or fraudulently convert to his own use, money or other property which comes into his possession or is under his care by virtue of such employment, notwithstanding he may have an interest in such property, shall be guilty of embezzlement....

The law is clear that intent to repay is not a defense to embezzlement under a statute like ours. See, e.g., 3 Wharton's Criminal Law § 397, at 405–07 (14th ed. 1980). Further, the proposition that defendant's intent to repay should have been considered by the jury in its determination of whether or not he possessed the necessary mens rea is inconsistent with the state of the law. A leading authority on criminal law has observed that "[g]iven a fraudulent appropriation or conversion, an embezzlement is committed even if the defendant intends at some subsequent time to return the property or to make restitution to the owner." 3 Wharton's Criminal Law § 397, at 405–06.

The rationale for this rule was stated by the Pennsylvania Supreme Court in *Commonwealth v. Bovaird*:

> Where one is charged with embezzlement or fraudulent conversion, the intention to abstract the money and appropriate it to his own use has been fully executed upon its wrongful taking; the ability and intention to indemnify the party from whom it has been withdrawn remains unexecuted, and such intention, even if conscientiously entertained, may become impossible to fulfillment. The crime is consummated when the money is intentionally and wrongfully converted, temporarily or permanently, to the defendant's own use.

Bovaird, 373 Pa. 60, 95 A.2d at 178.

The trial judge properly charged the elements of the offense of embezzlement. Regarding intent, the judge stressed that "there must be a fraudulent intent and the State must prove fraudulent intent beyond a reasonable doubt." And the court properly noted that "the intent to

CONTINUED

embezzle is a state of mind which can be shown by words or conduct."

Defendant also argues that the trial court erred by not instructing the jury that a mere inability or failure to pay creditors is not sufficient to demonstrate the fraudulent intent necessary for the crime of embezzlement. For the same reasons that intent to repay is not relevant to the existence of fraudulent intent, neither is the ability or inability to repay. Moreover, the charge urged by defendant misstates the facts of this case and mischaracterizes his relationship with Stacey.

There is no question that "[in] a debtor–creditor relation, the debtor's failure to pay the creditor does not constitute embezzlement." 3 Wharton's Criminal Law § 402, at 417. However, defendant's relationship with Stacey was not that of debtor-creditor, but rather it was one of agent and principal. We are satisfied that the facts and circumstances of this case support defendant's status as an agent of Stacey. The trial court instructed the jury that an agency relationship was critical to the offense charged and that the State was burdened with proving beyond a reasonable doubt that such relationship existed. The court also instructed that "[a] debtor–creditor relationship alone is insufficient to create an agency relationship." The evidence supports a finding of an agency relationship, and the jury so found. Moreover, on appeal, defendant does not argue that he was anything other than an agent of Stacey.

As an agent, rather than a debtor, of Stacey, defendant was obligated to hold and remit to Stacey its percentage of any amounts collected. Given the existence of an agency relationship—as found by the jury—defendant's conversion of the money credited to Stacey's account was precisely the activity prohibited by the embezzlement statute.

[Affirmed.]

Specialized Statutes

The common-law classifications and general theft statutes have been supplemented by a variety of more specific laws aimed at the same types of conduct. For example, although obtaining money or property by the giving of a bad check would constitute false pretenses or general theft, all states have specific statutes relating to the issuance of bad checks, which impose criminal liability on persons who, with intent to defraud, issue or transfer checks or other negotiable instruments knowing that they will be dishonored. Such knowledge is presumed to exist, under the typical statute, if the drawer had no account with the drawee bank when the check was issued, or if the check was refused payment because of insufficient funds in the drawer's account when it was presented to the bank for payment. Similarly, most states have separate statutes relating to a number of special offenses, such as the setting back of automobile odometers with the intent to defraud and the knowing delivery of "short weights"—the charging of buyers for quantities of goods that are greater than the quantities that were actually delivered.

ROBBERY

Robbery is stealing from a person or in his or her presence by use of force or threat of force. It is, essentially, a form of larceny but the extra element of force makes it a more serious offense. Removing someone's earring by stealth would be larceny; ripping it from the victim's earlobe would be robbery. Use of a weapon escalates the crime to aggravated robbery.

FORGERY

Forgery is the false making or altering of a legally significant instrument (such as a check, credit card, deed, passport, mortgage, or security) with the intent to defraud. Writing an insufficient funds check is not forgery, although it may constitute false pretenses or violate a state bad check law. But changing the true payee's name as written on a check to your own and cashing the check is certainly forgery.

Forgery is a crime with roots deep in the common law, but changing technologies can challenge traditional rules, as the following case illustrates.

CASE

PEOPLE v. AVILA

COLORADO COURT OF APPEALS, 770 P.2d 1330 (1988)

For fees of between $1,500 and $3,000, Avila, a lawyer, altered the driver records of two of his clients whose driver's licenses were under revocation for alcohol-related offenses. Avila would instruct his contact in the Motor Vehicle Division (MVD) Office, who had access to the data base where the driving records were maintained on computer disk, to delete the clients' records. The client would later apply for a driver's license, stating that he had no previous driver's license, which the altered computer records would verify. Avila was convicted of two counts of second degree forgery. He appealed.

VAN CISE, JUDGE:

Initially, we note that much of Avila's argument relies on the assertion that forgery cannot be committed on a computer. We reject that contention.

A forgery can be made by any number of artificial means. Indeed, "whether [the forgery] is made with the pen, with a brush . . . with any other instrument, or by any other device whatever; whether it is in characters which stand for words or in characters which stand for ideas . . . is quite immaterial. . . ." *Benson v. McMahon*, 127 U.S. 457 (1888).

Avila also contends, in essence, that there was insufficient evidence to sustain his convictions. We disagree.

The elements of second degree forgery pertinent to this case are that (1) the defendant, (2) with intent to defraud, (3) falsely alters, (4) a written instrument, (5) which is or purported to be, or which is calculated to become or to represent if completed, a "written instrument officially issued or created by a public office, public servant, or government agency." Section 18-5-103(1)(c).

Avila contends that there was no written instrument in this case so the forgery conviction cannot stand. We disagree.

Section 18-5-101(9) defines "written instrument" as follows:

"Written instrument" means any paper, document, *or other instrument containing written or printed matter or the equivalent thereof,* used for purposes of reciting, embodying, conveying, or recording information . . . which is capable of being used to the advantage of disadvantage of some person. (Emphasis supplied.)

A fair reading of the statute indicates that a computer disc is included in the definition of a "written instrument."

Next, Avila contends that, since the driving records were deleted, the evidence at trial does not support the finding that he falsely altered a written instrument. He argues that "alter" means to change,

CONTINUED

while "delete" means to cause to vanish completely. Therefore, he claims he committed no forgery. We are not persuaded.

Section 18-5-101(2) states:

> To "falsely alter" a written instrument means to change a written instrument without the authority of anyone entitled to grant such authority, *whether it be* in complete or incomplete form, *by means of erasure*, obliteration, *deletion*, insertion of new matter, transposition of matter, or any other means, so that such instrument in its thus altered form falsely appears or purports to be in all respects an authentic creation of or fully authorized by its ostensible maker. (Emphasis supplied.)

The record shows that the driving records of two of Avila's clients were deleted so that instead of containing their history of driving violations, the computer found no driving record and thus would display the message "no record found."

Under the plain language of the statute, Avila's actions constituted a false alteration within the meaning of § 18-5-101(2).

Next, Avila asserts that there is a distinction between a document falsely made and a genuine document that contains false information. Based on this distinction, he contends that the written instruments were not false but rather were genuine MVD documents which contained false information and, as such, they cannot form the basis for a forgery conviction. We disagree.

In *DeRose v. People*, 64 Colo. 332, 171 P. 359 (1918), the court held that a false statement of fact in an instrument which is genuine is not forgery. It stated:

> This writing is what it purports to be—a true and genuine instrument, although it contains false statements. It is not a false paper, and the execution of such a document does not constitute forgery.

In *DeRose*, defendant was a railroad foreman whose job was to draft and submit the time rolls for his men. He was charged with forgery because he credited one of his men with more days than the man had worked. Because the defendant was authorized to draft and submit the time roll, the court found that the document was not "falsely made." It was a genuine railroad time roll prepared by one authorized to do so, but which contained false information.

In *DeRose* the defendant had the authority to perform the general act that led to the production of the document containing the false information. In contrast, in the instant case, testimony showed that Avila's confederate at the MVD had no authority to delete driver histories. Therefore, under *DeRose*, the documents were forged.

[Affirmed.]

ARSON

At common law, **arson** was the malicious burning of the dwelling house of another. Today, the building burned need not be a dwelling house. And, as all too commonly occurs, people who burn their own house (or other building or personal property) for purposes of defrauding an insurance company are almost certainly violating a state criminal statute prohibiting such fraud.

FEDERAL CRIMES AFFECTING BUSINESS

As with state crimes, there are so many federal criminal statutes that it would be impossible to list them all. Many have been passed in response to perceived crises. In the era of the giant trusts in the late 1800s, Congress passed many antitrust laws, including some carrying criminal penalties (discussed in Chapter 14). As noted earlier, during the Depression Era epidemic of bank robberies, Congress passed a federal bank robbery law. In the wake of the Watergate scandal in the early 1970s, investigation disclosed widespread bribery of foreign officials by U.S. companies, leading to enactment of the Foreign Corrupt Practices Act (discussed in Chapter 15). After the Ivan Boesky case and other insider trading scandals in the late 1980s, Congress increased the criminal penalties for that fraudulent activity (also discussed in Chapter 15). Congress responded to the recent savings and loan scandal by enacting criminal penalties to punish several types of fraudulent activity that required a multibillion dollar taxpayer bailout of savings and loans (see the Financial Institutions Reform, Recovery, and Enforcement Act of 1989). Instead of trying to list all such federal criminal statutes, we will briefly address a few of the more general ones.

MAIL AND WIRE FRAUD

Two very general federal statutes punish **mail fraud** (use of the mails to defraud or swindle) and **wire fraud** (similar use of telephone, telegraph, radio, or television). The typical mail or wire fraud case would involve use of the mails or telephones to make false representations to sell products or securities. For example, the mail fraud law has been used to punish fraudulent representations in the use of the mails to advertise such articles as hair-growing products that proved to be worthless, to retrofit carburetors that totally failed to improve automobile fuel economy, and to issue false identification cards that the sellers knew were ordered by purchasers for the purpose of deceiving third parties. Similarly, schemes for the operation of "mail-order" schools, where degrees or diplomas are awarded "without requiring evidence of education or experience entitled thereto," and where the operators know such documents are likely to be used by purchasers to misrepresent their qualifications to prospective employers, violate these sections of the law. However, the statutes have been construed to cover a wide variety of factual situations.

For example, in *Carpenter v. United States,* 484 U.S. 19 (1987), a *Wall Street Journal* reporter tipped material nonpublic information (the contents of his columns that were about to be published) to confederates who profitably traded on it. Although the Supreme Court split 4–4 regarding the specific insider trading theory offered by the prosecution, it unanimously affirmed the defendant's conviction for mail and wire fraud. The fraudulent scheme's connection to the mails and wire services used to distribute the newspaper was deemed sufficient to support the conviction.

In the following case the Supreme Court dealt with a difficult mail fraud issue.

CASE

SCHMUCK v. UNITED STATES

U.S. SUPREME COURT,
109 S.Ct 2091
(1989)

Petitioner Schmuck, a used-car distributor, purchased used cars, rolled back their odometers, and then sold the automobiles to Wisconsin retail dealers for prices artificially inflated because of the low-mileage readings. These unwitting car dealers, relying on the altered odometer figures, then resold the cars to customers, who in turn paid prices reflecting Schmuck's fraud. To complete the resale of each car, the dealer who bought it from Schmuck would submit a title-application form to the Wisconsin Department of Transportation on behalf of his retail customer. The receipt of a Wisconsin title was a legal prerequisite for transferring title and obtaining car tags.

Schmuck was convicted on 12 counts of mail fraud. He appealed, alleging that the mailings that were the crux of the indictment—the submissions of the title-application forms by the auto dealers—were not in furtherance of the fraudulent scheme and, thus, did not satisfy the mailing element of the crime of mail fraud. The circuit court rejected Schmuck's claim but reversed on other grounds. The Supreme Court granted certiorari to resolve both issues. (The following excerpt addresses only the mail fraud issue.)

BLACKMUN, JUSTICE:

"The federal mail fraud statute does not purport to reach all frauds, but only those limited instances in which the use of the mails is a part of the execution of the fraud, leaving all other cases to be dealt with by appropriate state law." *Kann v. United States*, 323 U.S. 88, 95 (1944). To be part of the execution of the fraud, however, the use of the mails need not be an essential element of the scheme. *Pereira v. United States*, 347 U.S. 1, 8 (1954). It is sufficient for the mailing to be "incident to an essential part of the scheme," *ibid.*, or "a step in [the] plot," *Badders v. United States*, 240 U.S. 391, 394 (1916).

Schmuck argues that mail fraud can be predicated only on a mailing that affirmatively assists the perpetrator in carrying out his fraudulent scheme. The mailing element of the offense, he contends, cannot be satisfied by a mailing, such as those at issue here, that is routine and innocent in and of itself, and that, far from furthering the execution of the fraud, occurs after the fraud has come to fruition, is merely tangentially related to the fraud, and is counterproductive in that it creates a "paper trail" from which the fraud may be discovered. We disagree both with this characterization of the mailings in the present case and with this description the applicable law.

We begin by considering the scope of Schmuck's fraudulent scheme. Schmuck was charged with devising and executing a scheme to defraud Wisconsin retail automobile customers who based their decisions to purchase certain automobiles at least in part on the low-mileage readings provided by the tampered odometers. This was a fairly large-scale operation. Evidence at trial indicated that Schmuck had employed a man known only as "Fred" to turn back the odometers on about 150 different cars. Schmuck then marketed these cars to a number of dealers, several of whom he dealt with on a consistent basis over a period of about 15 years. Thus, Schmuck's was not a "one-shot" operation in which he sold a single car to an isolated dealer. His was an ongoing fraudulent venture. A rational jury could have concluded that the success of Schmuck's venture depended upon his continued harmonious relations with and good reputation among retail dealers, which in turn required the smooth flow of cars from the dealers to their Wisconsin customers.

Under these circumstances, we believe that a rational jury could have found that the title-registration mailings were part of the execution of the fraudulent scheme, a scheme which did not reach fruition until the retail dealers resold the cars and effected transfers of title. Schmuck's scheme would have come to an abrupt halt if the dealers either had lost faith in Schmuck or had not been able to resell the cars obtained from him. These resales and Schmuck's relationships with the retail dealers naturally depended on the successful passage of

CONTINUED

title among the various parties. Thus, although the registration-form mailings may not have contributed directly to the duping of either the retail dealers or the customers, they were necessary to the passage of title, which in turn was essential to the perpetuation of Schmuck's scheme. As noted earlier, a mailing that is "incident to an essential part of the scheme," *Pereira*, 347 U.S., at 8, satisfies the mailing element of the mail fraud offense. The mailings here fit this description. *See, e.g., United States v. Locklear*, 829 F. 2d 1314, 1318–1319 (CA4 1987) (retail customers obtaining title documents through the mail furthers execution of wholesaler's odometer tampering scheme).

Once the full flavor of Schmuck's scheme is appreciated, the critical distinctions between this case and the three cases in which this Court has delimited the reach of the mail fraud statute—*Kann*, *Parr*, and *Maze*—are readily apparent. In other cases, the Court has found the elements of mail fraud to be satisfied where the mailings have been routine. *See, e.g., Carpenter v. United States*, 484 U.S. 19 (1987) (mailing news-papers).

We also reject Schmuck's contention that mailings that someday may contribute to the uncovering of a fraudulent scheme cannot supply the mailing element of the mail fraud offense. The relevant question at all times is whether the mailing is part of the execution of the scheme as conceived by the perpetrator at the time, regardless of whether the mailing later, through hindsight, may prove to have been counterproductive and return to haunt the perpetrator of the fraud. The mail fraud statute includes no guarantee that the use of the mails for the purpose of executing a fraudulent scheme will be risk free. Those who use the mails to defraud proceed at their peril.

For these reasons, we agree with the Court of Appeals that the mailings in this case satisfy the mailing element of the mail fraud offenses.

TRAVEL ACT

Section 1952 of Title 18 of the *United States Code* is called the Travel Act. It punishes anyone who travels in interstate or foreign commerce or uses any facility in such commerce to (1) distribute the proceeds of illegal activity, (2) commit any crime of violence or further any unlawful activity, or (3) promote, manage, establish, carry on or facilitate any unlawful activity. Obviously, this is a very broad act that federalizes all sorts of traditionally state crimes. The "interstate commerce" element can be met by simply mailing a letter or using a telephone, for these are instrumentalities of interstate commerce. The Act has been used, for example, to convict a city electrical inspector who took bribes from private electrical contractors to overlook code violations and to facilitate departmental paperwork even though all the letters mailed by defendant stayed in one state. The mail is a facility of interstate commerce because it *can* be used to send letters from state to state.

HOBBS ACT

The Hobbs Act, 18 U.S.C. Sec. 951, punishes anyone who "in any way or degree obstructs, delays, or affects commerce or the movement of any article or commodity in commerce, by robbery or extortion...." This law punishes extortion (obtaining money or something else of value by use of violence or threat of violence) but not merely accepting bribes. The distinction between the two can be difficult to draw but has been characterized as the difference between "pay me and be assisted" (commercial bribery) and "pay me or be precluded" (extortion).

Because the law punishes those who "in any way" affect commerce, the reach of the federal statute is very broad. In one case, a county sheriff who extorted bribes to protect gamblers and prostitutes was convicted under the Hobbs Act after he solicited payments from an FBI undercover bookie operation. The court held that because the FBI operation bought furniture, paper, food, and natural gas and could have bought more had it not given money to defendant, interstate commerce was affected. *United States v. Frasch,* 818 F.2d 631 (7th Cir. 1987).

RACKETEER INFLUENCED AND CORRUPT ORGANIZATIONS ACT

In 1970 Congress passed the Racketeer Influenced and Corrupt Organizations Act (RICO) to attack organized crime, especially its infiltration into legitimate business. RICO is an unusual criminal statute in that it expressly contains parallel civil provisions. In other words, it provides for both criminal penalties and private civil suits for damages. However, RICO neither included a definition of "organized crime" nor expressly required a link between a defendant's activities and organized crime. Therefore, about nine-tenths of the civil suits and many of the criminal prosecutions brought under RICO have had no connection with professional criminals (as thought of in the common sense) but have, instead, named as defendants accounting firms, banks, law firms, manufacturing corporations, anti-abortion protestors, and a wide variety of others. Because of the importance of RICO *civil* actions to the area of securities law, RICO is examined in some detail in Chapter 15.

Fortunately, most of the criminal prosecutions brought under RICO have attacked the more traditional manifestations of organized crime. Prosecutors have secured RICO criminal convictions in cases involving marijuana smuggling, kickbacks to judges, extortion of "protection money" by police officers, loansharking, gambling, and the like. However, even in criminal prosecutions the government has occasionally pushed RICO to its limits by prosecuting actions in circumstances it is difficult to believe Congress had in mind when passing RICO. The following case is a more standard RICO criminal action.

CASE

UNITED STATES v. LeROY

U.S. SECOND CIRCUIT COURT OF APPEALS, 687 F.2d 610 (1982)

Defendant LeRoy was vice-president and later business manager of Local 214 of the Laborers International Union. During his terms, LeRoy was placed on the payroll of several contractors hiring Local 214's members. LeRoy did no work but received compensation so the contractors could "keep peace with the laborers." LeRoy also bought gasoline and had his brakes fixed and in so doing had the union pay the bills and then "reimburse" him as though he had paid them. LeRoy appeals his conviction of one count of conspiracy to violate §1962(c) of RICO, in violation of §1962(d).

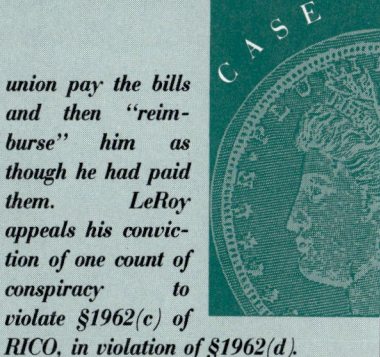

CONTINUED

MOORE, CIRCUIT JUDGE:

Pursuant to §1962(c), it is unlawful "for any person employed by or associated with any enterprise engaged in, or the activities of which affect, interstate or foreign commerce, to conduct or participate, directly or indirectly, in the conduct of such enterprise's affairs through a pattern of racketeering activity...." Unions are expressly included within the term "enterprise."

LeRoy concedes that the Government conclusively proved the existence of an enterprise affecting interstate commerce—namely Local 214. He also admits that the Government demonstrated LeRoy's, as well as his co-conspirators', association with the union. LeRoy contends, however, that the Government failed to show that he participated in the conduct of the union's affairs or that his activities constituted a "pattern" of racketeering activity.

Specifically, LeRoy alleges that the Government proved at most illegal conduct committed in furtherance of LeRoy's personal interest, but not in the conduct of the union's business. Accordingly, LeRoy argues, his actions fall beyond the purview of the statute. We find no merit to LeRoy's contention and conclude that his actions took place in the conduct of Local 214's affairs and thus, within the scope of RICO.... [W]hile RICO does not specify the degree of interrelationship between the pattern of racketeering and the conduct of the enterprise's affairs, the Act also does not require that predicate acts be in furtherance of the enterprise.

The evidence in this case demonstrates that LeRoy accepted unearned wages while he served as vice-president of Local 214 from various contractors who testified that they paid him in order to preserve union peace, in violation of the Taft-Hartley Act, and later used his position as business manager to obtain payments from the union treasury for expenses not properly incurred, in violation of the Landrum-Griffin Act. These violations of the Landrum-Griffin and Taft-Hartley Acts were the predicate offences forming the pattern of racketeering. LeRoy was able to commit these predicate offenses solely by virtue of his positions in Local 214, since the predicates acts were inextricably tied to LeRoy's role as a union official.

We also reject LeRoy's argument that the Government failed to prove that his participation in the union's affairs was "through a pattern of racketeering activity." A "pattern of racketeering activity" is established by proof of the commission of at least two "acts of racketeering" within a ten-year period. Moreover, a violation of either the Landrum-Griffin Act or the Taft-Hartley Act constitutes an act of racketeering. Since the evidence demonstrates that LeRoy violated the provisions of these acts on more than two occasions, the Government clearly proved a pattern of racketeering activity.
[Affirmed.]

COMPUTER CRIME

The explosive growth in the use of computers in the business world in the past few years has brought with it a corresponding increase in computer misuse. The *Avila* forgery case mentioned earlier in this chapter is a good example. Burgeoning computer crime and corresponding government responses justify separate discussion of the area of computer crime. Traditional (precomputer) state and federal laws applicable to such crimes as larceny are not necessarily appropriate for prosecution of cases of computer fraud and computer theft. For example, some cases held that an employee's unauthorized use of his or her employer's computer facilities in private ventures could not support a theft conviction because the employer had not been deprived of any part of value or use of the computer. Other cases have held that use of a computer is not "property" within traditional theft statutes.

Computer crimes fall mainly into three broad categories: unauthorized access, theft of information, and theft of funds. Among schemes that have been subject to prosecution are (1) stealing a competitor's computer program; (2) paying an accomplice to delete adverse information and insert favorable false information into the defendant's credit file; (3) a bank president's having his or her account computer coded so that his or her checks would be removed and held rather than posted so he or she could later remove the actual checks without their being debited; (4) a disgruntled ex-employee's inserting a "virus" into his former employer's computer to destroy its records; and (5) three computer "hackers'" foray into the forbidden recesses of computers that run BellSouth Corporation's phone network.

A recent survey found that 25 percent of businesses responding had recently experienced losses caused by computer crime that averaged between $2 million and $10 million per year. Some estimate that losses caused by computer misuse may be as high as $35 to $40 billion per year (including thefts of funds, losses of computer programs and data, losses of trade secrets, and damages to computer hardware). These estimates may not be reliable, but it is clear that a substantial amount of computer crime is never discovered, and a high percentage of that which is discovered is never reported because (1) companies do not want publicity about the inadequacy of their computer controls and (2) financial institutions such as banks and savings and loans fear that reports of large losses of funds, even when insured, are likely to cause customers to withdraw their deposits.

Whatever the actual loss caused by computer misuse, both Congress and the state legislators have passed statutes to deal specifically with computer crime.

FEDERAL LAWS

Although there have been convictions for computer crimes under general federal criminal statutes—such as those dealing with wire fraud, theft, and misappropriation—Congress has recently enacted laws specifically to deal with computer crime. The Access Device and Computer Fraud and Abuse Act of 1984, for example, outlaws (1) obtaining classified information from a computer without authorization and with intent or reason to believe that it is to be used to injure the United States; (2) obtaining from a computer without authorization information that is protected by the Right to Financial Privacy Act or contained in the consumer files of a credit reporting agency; and (3) interfering with the operation of a government computer.

The Comprehensive Crime Control Act of 1984 contained a section on the use of computers in credit card fraud and established penalties for violation. In addition, the Computer Fraud and Abuse Act of 1986 established three federal crimes for computer fraud, destruction, and password trafficking.

STATE LAWS

At least 48 states have passed laws dealing with computer crime. Most of the statutes comprehensively address the problem, outlawing (1) computer trespass (unauthorized access); (2) damage to computers or software (e.g., use of "viruses"); (3) theft or misappropriation of computer services; and (4) obtaining or disseminating information by computer in an unauthorized manner.

WHITE COLLAR CRIME

The term *white collar crime* generally encompasses nonviolent acts by individuals or corporations to obtain a personal or business advantage in a commercial context. Many of the crimes discussed earlier in this chapter are examples of white collar crime. White collar crime has become an extremely controversial subject in recent years for at least two reasons. First, there is evidence that the economic losses caused by white collar crime are at a staggering level (often estimated at more than $100 billion annually) and growing rapidly. Second, there is a perception, based on substantial fact, that criminal penalties for white collar crimes costing the public millions of dollars are often much less severe than criminal penalties imposed on the average street hood who steals a $75 pair of shoes.

Traditional criminal law did not punish corporations for crimes, reasoning that because a corporation is an artificial entity, it could not form the intent required to supply *mens rea*, and it could not be punished by incarceration. Also, American law was slow to punish corporate officials who committed crimes. One reason is illustrated by the oft-quoted sentiment of a federal judge who said that he would not "penalize a businessman trying to make a living when there are felons out on the street."

In recent years, however, the traditional views have changed rather dramatically. Potential criminal liability must now be a significant concern for both corporations and their officials.

CRIMINAL LIABILITY OF CORPORATIONS

Today, most criminal statutes include corporations in their definition of "persons" who may violate the statute. The traditional reluctance to impose criminal sanctions on corporations has been overcome by modern reasoning which suggests (1) that the *mens rea* necessary to convict a corporation can be supplied by imputing the intent of the corporation's agents who physically commit the crimes to the corporation (as has long been done in the area of tort law), and (2) that corporations can be punished by fines and by innovative punishments that might, for example, require a corporation that has been caught polluting to fund an environmental education course at a local high school.

The general rule today is that corporations can be held criminally liable for any acts performed by an employee if that employee is acting within the scope of his or her authority for the purpose of benefiting the corporation. The basic idea is that the corporation receives the benefit when the agent acts properly and must bear the responsibility when the agent errs. This is simply an application of the *respondeat superior* doctrine (let the master answer for the wrongs of the agent) that is discussed in more detail in Chapter 13. The corporation can even be held liable when the agent is violating company policy or disobeying a specific order from a superior. Some jurisdictions refuse to hold the corporation criminally liable for crimes committed by lower-level employees, but many states find the corporation responsible no matter how far down the ladder the actual wrongdoer is.

Corporations have been indicted for homicide and a wide variety of lesser offenses, including health and safety violations arising out of toxic waste disposal, failure to remove asbestos from buildings, and construction-site accidents.

On November 1, 1991, federal sentencing guidelines went into effect, significantly increasing the punishments meted out to corporations that violate federal criminal statutes. A sentencing judge now has the prerogative to place a corporation on probation to supervise it for a time to ensure that criminal activity is eradicated. Fortunately for corporations, the suggested punishment structure is mitigated substantially if the defendant company has in place an "effective program to prevent and detect violations of law." The purpose of this mitigation factor is to induce corporations to "police their own" by establishing standards of conduct for employees and using various means to enforce those standards.

CRIMINAL LIABILITY OF CORPORATE OFFICIALS

The increase in prosecutions of corporations has been matched by an increase in prosecutions of corporate officers as well. Corporate officers will definitely be held liable for criminal acts that they participate in or authorize. In addition, they will be held liable for acts that they aid and abet through any significant assistance or encouragement. Some courts find sufficient encouragement in mere acquiescence of a superior (which a subordinate may read as tacit approval) and even in failure to stop criminal activity that the official knows is occurring. In rare instances involving *strict liability* statutes, corporate officers have been held criminally liable because they failed to control the criminal acts of subordinates (even where they had no knowledge of the acts or had been assured that the acts had stopped). *United States v. Park,* 421 U.S. 658 (1975).

Indicative of the trend toward increased criminal liability are some recent cases in which corporate officials have been tried for *murder* in the deaths of employees exposed to hazardous conditions in the workplace. Additionally, federal laws have recently been enacted or beefed up to encourage criminal actions against individuals who engage in insider trading, environmental pollution, savings and loan fraud, defrauding of the Defense Department, and a host of other activities that have been in the news recently.

INTERNATIONAL CRIMINAL ENFORCEMENT

As in so many areas of endeavor, criminal activity occurring abroad affects the United States and vice versa. The purchasing in the United States of cocaine that was grown in South America is an obvious example. The interplay of Swiss bank secrecy laws and insider trading in U.S. stocks is another. The international scope of the B.C.C.I. banking scandal that came to light in 1991 is yet another.

Each of these examples highlights the inadequacy of current levels of international cooperation in such matters. But this is not to say that there is no cooperation. American law enforcement agencies do cooperate with similar foreign agencies. The U.S. Securities and Exchange Commission has worked closely with Swiss officials in an attempt to police international insider trading. Many countries have extradition treaties with the United States to facilitate the return of fugitive suspects. Although most attempts at international cooperation have occurred at a bilateral level, perhaps some day more nations will adopt the model treaties on international criminal cooperation that have been approved by the United Nations Congresses on the Prevention of Crime and the Treatment of Offenders in 1985 and 1990. These include the Model Treaty on Extradition, Model Treaty on Mutual Assistance in Criminal Matters, and the Model Treaty on the Transfer of Proceedings in Criminal Matters.

Questions and Problems

1. Minnick was arrested for murder. Federal officials gave him the Miranda warning and suspended interrogation when he requested a lawyer. He consulted with his lawyer two or three times. Then state officials sought to question Minnick, telling him that he would "have to talk" and "could not refuse." Minnick then confessed and was convicted of murder and sentenced to death when his motion to suppress the confession was overruled. Was Minnick denied his right against self-incrimination? Discuss. (*Minnick v. Mississippi,* 111 S.Ct. 13, 1991).

2. To interdict drugs, police in Florida routinely boarded buses at scheduled stops and asked passengers for permission to search their bags. Bostick was such a passenger who was approached without any basis for suspicion, questioned, and informed of this right to refuse a request to search. Bostick gave permission and cocaine was discovered. Bostick was convicted of drug trafficking when his motion to suppress the cocaine was overruled. Were Bostick's Fourth Amendment rights to protection from unreasonable searches and seizures denied? Discuss. (*Florida v. Bostick,* 111 S.Ct. 2382, 1991.)

3. Speckman was an attorney for a partnership that financed a waterslide operation. In 1980, a partner, Schwab, indicated a desire to sell his interest. Speckman told Schwab that he had a buyer and later gave Schwab a check for about $5,000. In 1983, Speckman's client Young indicated an interest in investment opportunities. Speckman recommended the waterslide operation and gave Speckman a check for $7,500 to be used to buy Schwab's interest. However, Speckman never altered the partnership records to indicate that Schwab was no longer a partner. Neither Schwab nor Young received any monetary distribution from the partnership. In essence, Speckman bought Schwab's interest, resold it to Young, but then denied Young the benefit of his investment. A jury convicted Speckman of *both* embezzlement and larceny by false pretenses in the obtaining of Young's $7,500. Discuss the appropriateness of this verdict. (*State v. Speckman,* 374 S.E.2d 419, N.C.App. 1989.)

4. Using the name "Larry Grimes," Tolliver opened an account at Pioneer Savings & Loan with $50. He applied for a TYME card for use with Pioneer's automated tellers. He later used an automated teller to deposit a $2,500 check that had been stolen from Terry McCaughey. He then made several cash withdrawals with his TYME card before the McCaughey check was returned to Pioneer with the notation that the account was closed and the signature unauthorized. Tolliver was convicted of uttering a forged check. Under the statute, the forged writing must be "uttered" or offered as genuine. Tolliver appealed, claiming that it is impossible to offer a writing as genuine to a machine, and therefore the offering or uttering took place when the machines' owners presented the check for payment to the drawee. Is Tolliver's defense valid? (*State v. Tolliver,* 440 N.W.2d 571, Wis.App. 1989.)

5. Matt was a division manager in charge of sales promotion for a tobacco company. One promotion was to give cigarettes to retailers so they could engage in "buy one, get one free" promotions. Matt concocted a scheme that involved removing complimentary tobacco products and exchanging them through sales representatives for salable merchandise. Matt would sell the merchandise and keep the money. To hide the scheme, Matt forced sales representatives to file false reports with respect to the placement of complimentary goods, which he would then mail to the company. Matt was indicted for mail fraud. Should he be convicted? (*United States v. Matt,* 838 F.2d 1356, 5th Cir. 1988.)

6. Mulder was a commissioned salesman for Englehart's wholesale furniture business. He told Bateman, a furniture maker, that he "was in with a couple of new partners" who might have some work for him. Englehart and Mulder met Bateman; Englehart paid Bateman $8,750 to build 50 entertainment centers. A few days later, defendant told Bateman that Englehart had decided to get entertainment centers elsewhere and he would have to give the money back. Bateman, believing defendant to be Englehart's partner, gave him $6,250, retaining $2,500 per an agreement with defendant to stain units defendant falsely claimed were being bought elsewhere. Defendant used the $6,250 to pay personal debts. When charged with embezzlement, Mulder claimed that, unlike a bank teller, for example, his job was not to handle Englehart's money, and therefore he had not committed embezzlement. Is this a reasonable defense? (*People v. Mulder,* 421 N.W.2d 605, Mich. App. 1988.)

7. Mathews, an administrator for the Small Business Administration, was taped by the FBI as he apparently accepted a bribe. Mathews was indicted for accepting a gratuity in exchange for an official act in violation of federal law. Mathews wished to raise an entrapment defense, but the trial judge refused to allow it unless Mathews first admitted all elements of the offense. In other words, Mathews could not plead in the alternative: "I didn't do it, but if I did I was entrapped." Should a defendant be required to admit the substantive elements of the offense or be barred from raising an entrapment defense? (*United States v. Mathews,* 485 U.S. 58, 1988.)

8. Being Director of Network Services for NYNEX Mobile Communications Co., Covino had substantial influence over selection of and compensation for construction companies working for NYNEX. Great Northeastern was a construction company that did a large proportion of its work for NYNEX. In May 1984, Covino told Brennan, Great Northeastern's president, that one of Brennan's employees had improperly billed $3,200 in phone calls to a NYNEX credit card and that it "wouldn't look good" if Covino showed the bill to his superiors. Brennan offered to pay the bill, but Covino said that he would take care of it. Not long thereafter, Covino asked Brennan to build a sun deck on Covino's home, telling him to keep "in mind the phone bill." The project evolved into a $20,000 addition. Covino asked Brennan to take a $15,000 check and then give him back that much in cash so that it would appear Covino had paid for the work. Brennan declined to assist in the coverup but did not charge for the work. Because Brennan was afraid of losing the NYNEX work, he eventually

paid over $85,000 in cash to Covino in addition to doing more work on his house. Covino was discovered and indicted for a violation of the Hobbs Act. Discuss the appropriateness of this charge. (*United States v. Covino*, 837 F.2d 65, 2d Cir. 1988.)

9. Covino, from the preceding case, was also charged with a violation of the Travel Act. It was basically alleged that he had phoned Brennan to facilitate the comission of a state crime, specifically, bribery in violation of New York law. Discuss the appropriateness of this charge.

10. Covino was *also* accused of wire fraud. The indictment stated that he had used the wires to "violate his fiduciary duty to NYNEX Communications, by concealing information, to wit, his receipt of money and property ..., which information was material to the conduct of the business of NYNEX," which was in furtherance of a scheme to defraud NYNEX by depriving it of defendant's "loyal and unbiased services." Discuss the validity of this charge.

PART II

BUSINESS AND THE LAW OF COMMERCE

CHAPTER 9

In Part III of this text, attention is turned to certain areas of business law that are heavily influenced or even dominated by governmental regulatory agencies. The fields of antitrust law, securities regulation, employment and labor law, environmental law, and consumer protection are studied. Attention is also focused on the increasing impact of legal constraints on international legal transactions. Before turning to those business-focused laws and the regulatory agencies that often implement them, however, it is essential that mention be made of a

CONTRACT AND SALES LAW

number of broader (and more traditional) fields of law that also have application to some kinds of business activities. Thus, when one considers the legal environment of business—that is, the entire "seamless web of the law" within which all businesses must operate—several of these broad fields must at least be surveyed. Not only do these fields have their own significant impact on the business world, but many of their principles are the basis on which the somewhat narrower, regulatory fields of law are built. For example, some acquaintanceship with elementary principles of *contract law* is necessary for a full appreciation of the antitrust laws, and the products liability rules of tort law are the "jumping off" point for many of the consumer protection statutes.

In the five chapters in this part, we survey a number of traditional bodies of law that have a particularly close relationship to the business world and that collectively make up the bulk of law referred to as "business law" or "commercial law." Chapter 9 covers the subjects of *contracts* and *sales law*. The following three chapters address general *tort law* as it applies to business, the products liability area of tort law, and then specific areas of business or competitive torts. Finally, Chapter 13 will survey the subjects of *agency, partnership,* and *corporations*.[1]

INTRODUCTION

A **contract** is a special kind of agreement—one that the law will enforce in the event of a breach by one of the contracting parties. Contract law is obviously important to both individuals and business firms because of its all-pervasive nature. When a person simply buys a newspaper, leaves a car at a parking lot; or purchases a ticket to an athletic event, he or she has entered into a contract of some sort. When someone borrows money, or has a painter paint a house, or insures a car, a contract has again most certainly been made—a somewhat more complex one than in the prior situations. And retailers (whether an individual running a corner store or a multimillion-dollar corporation) make contracts of an infinite variety—to buy or lease office space and equipment, to employ managers and salespersons, and to buy the goods that stock their shelves. Manufacturers, wholesalers, and financial institutions and other companies in the service industries must obviously make many of the same kinds of contracts. Even the formation of a partnership requires some kind of contract between the partners, and the

---

[1] Throughout these chapters, it must be borne in mind that space limitations permit consideration of only the basic principles of each subject.

formation of a corporation requires the making of a contract (using the term broadly) between the incorporators and the state.

GOVERNING LAW

Over the centuries, the common law courts of England and the United States created a body of **contract law** that applied to every conceivable type of contract. This body of law is a marvelous example of the product of the legal mind of man. Exquisitely complex, contract law provides a system of rules and remedies to expedite all manner of business arrangements and to compensate those who are injured when others do not live up to their bargains.

Sales law is that branch of law applicable to a large class of contracts: those calling for the sale of "goods." To tailor the common law of contracts to solve specific problems arising in transactions in goods, the legislatures of every state but Louisiana[2] have adopted article 2 of the Uniform Commercial Code (UCC).[3] Article 2 follows the general outline of contract law but contains several modifications and unique features designed for the peculiar problems that arise in sales contracts. Thus, while the common law of contracts continues to govern all other types of agreements (including especially contracts for sales of real estate and services), the UCC provisions govern contracts for the sales of *goods*—items of tangible, personal (movable) property.

This chapter explains the most important facets of the common law of contracts while, at the same time, highlighting areas where article 2 has altered the law to fit the special needs of transactions in goods. It is wise to note that the concept of "goods," for UCC purposes, includes such diverse articles as pig iron, wheat, automobiles, CD players, and designer jeans. But the UCC does not apply to transactions in services, intangible rights (such as rights assigned under a contract), or land or items attached to the land such as buildings.

Although most provisions of article 2 apply to all contracts for the sale of goods, a few apply only where one or both of the contracting parties are *merchants*. A "merchant" is a person or firm who is in the business of selling the kinds of goods that are the subject of the contract. Thus, a department store is a merchant when it sells clothes and jewelry, but not (most courts hold) when it sells one of its obsolete delivery trucks.

TYPES OF CONTRACTS

Virtually all contracts may be classified as being either bilateral or unilateral in nature. **Bilateral contracts,** by far the most common in the business

---

[2] Louisiana's civil law system has its own version of sales law.
[3] As this chapter is being revised, the Permanent Editorial Board of the UCC is considering alterations that could substantially alter certain UCC sections but only if finally promulgated and ultimately adopted by state legislatures.

world, consist of the mutual *exchange of promises* between the parties, the actual performance of the promises to occur at some later time. Thus when a manufacturer enters into an agreement in May with a supplier, calling for the supplier to deliver 1,000 steel wheels during September and for the manufacturer to pay on delivery, a bilateral contract has come into existence in May. In contrast, a **unilateral contract** is formed only when one person makes an offer that is phrased in such a way as to indicate that it can be accepted only by the *performance of a specified act* (and where the specified act is subsequently performed). An example of such an offer would be the promise by a TV station to pay $5,000 to the first person who brings to its executive offices any piece of a fallen U.S. satellite. This offer can be accepted only by the actual physical production of a portion of the designated satellite; a promise by a person listening to the station that he or she will bring in the item later does not, therefore, result in the formation of a contract.

Contracts may also be classified as being either express or implied. If the intentions of the parties are stated fully and in explicit terms (often in writing), they constitute an **express contract.** The typical real estate lease and construction contract normally fall within this category. However, if the agreement between the parties (that is, the mutual intentions of the parties) has to be inferred in large part from their conduct and from the circumstances in which the agreement took place, the agreement is an **implied contract.** It is reasonable to infer, for example, that a person who is getting his or her hair cut in a barbershop actually desires the service and, by receiving the haircut, is impliedly promising to pay a reasonable price for it.

In exceptional circumstances the law imposes a "quasi-contractual liability" on a person or firm even though no true contract (one based on the intentions of the parties) was ever formed. Often termed *implied-in-law* contracts (to distinguish them from the "implied-in-fact" contracts just discussed), quasi-contractual obligations are imposed to prevent the "unjust enrichment" of a defendant. To illustrate: Trane Co. delivered six blowers to a subcontractor on a construction site. The subcontractor had agreed to pay $13,448 but became insolvent and left the site. The general contractor, Randolph, completed the subcontractor's work, installed the blowers, and was paid for the job. Trane Co. was allowed to recover from Randolph for the value of the blowers.[4] Courts often state that the two key requirements of quasi-contract are (1) the enrichment of defendant must be unjust; and (2) plaintiff cannot be a mere "volunteer."

The following case discusses these concepts.

---

[4] *The Trane Co. v. Randolph Plumbing & Heating,* 722 P.2d 1325 (Wash. App. 1986). Note that some courts would not allow recovery in such a case because they do not allow plaintiffs (like Trane) to pursue quasi-contract if they originally looked to another (the subcontractor) for compensation.

CASE

EATON v. ENGELCKE MANUFACTURING, INC.

722 P.2d 1325
(Wash. App. 1986)

Defendant Engelcke asked plaintiff Eaton, an employee, if he could design an electronic schematic for an electronic game, "Whizball," that Engelcke wished to sell. Eaton estimated that he could design the schematic in three months at a cost of $1,200 to $1,500. Engelcke told Eaton to proceed, telling him that compensation would be figured when the project was completed. Engelcke made several design changes during the project but repeatedly promised Eaton that he would be paid. However, an agreement as to the amount of compensation was never reached. After Eaton had worked on the project during his off-duty hours for 11 months and completed 90 percent of the job, Engelcke fired him without compensation for the project. Eaton sued and was awarded $5,415 by the trial judge on the basis of implied contract and quantum meruit. Engelcke appealed.

RINGOLD, JUSTICE:

The various contentions concerning liability and damages may be resolved by a careful definition of the terms involved. An express contract is one where the intentions of the parties and the terms of the agreement are expressed by the parties in writing or orally at the time it is entered into. The law recognizes two classes of implied contracts: those implied in fact and those implied in law. A contract implied in fact is an agreement depending for its existence on some act or conduct of the party sought to be charged and arising by implication from circumstances which, according to common understanding, show a mutual intention on the part of the parties to contract with each other. The services must be rendered under such circumstances as to indicate that the person rendering them expected to be paid therefor, and that the recipient expected, or should have expected, to pay for them. A true implied contract, or contract implied in fact, does not describe a legal relationship which differs from an express contract: only the mode of proof is different. A contract implied in law or "quasi contract," on the other hand, arises from an implied duty of the parties not based on a contract, or any consent or agreement. Recovery in quasi contract is based on the prevention of unjust enrichment.

"Quantum meruit" is not a legal obligation like contract or quasi contract, but is rather a remedy, "a reasonable amount for work done." It literally means "as much as he deserved." The burden of proving an express contract is on the party asserting it, who must prove that the parties expressly agreed to each essential fact, including the price, time and manner of performance. The trial court's findings indicate that the parties did not expressly agree to these elements. Those unchallenged findings are verities on appeal, and support the conclusion that the parties did not have an express contract for the design of the schematic.

In other unchallenged findings, the court found that Eaton's services in designing the prototype were rendered at Engelcke's request. The findings demonstrate that the services were "rendered under such circumstances as to indicate that the person rendering them expected to be paid therefor, and that the recipient expected, or should have expected, to pay for them." *Johnson v. Nasi*, 309 P.2d 380 (Wash. 1957). These findings, in turn, support the court's legal conclusion that the parties had an enforceable implied in fact contract to pay Eaton the reasonable value of the services rendered.

Engelcke also challenges Eaton's recovery on the ground that Engelcke received nothing of value from Eaton. This argument mistakenly assumes that the [trial] court held Engelcke liable in quasi contract and awarded damages so as to prevent Engelcke's unjust enrichment. As previously indicated, Engelcke's liability was based on an implied in the fact contract. The proper measure of recovery is not the benefit obtained but the reasonable value of the services rendered.

The judgment is affirmed.

HUMOR AND THE LAW

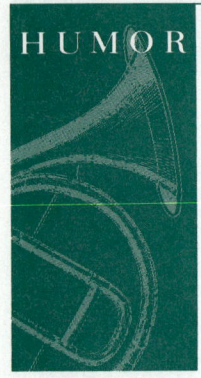

One of the most important rules of contract law is that a court should not assist in the enforcement of an illegal contract. In one famous (and possibly apocryphal) case, *Everet v. Williams*, 9 Law Quarterly Review 197 (England 1725), a suit was brought for an accounting of a partership. The complaint was framed in ambiguous terms, describing a partnership between defendant and plaintiff, who was described as "skilled in dealing in several sorts of commodities." The complaint alleged that the parties had "proceeded jointly in said dealing on Hounslow heath, where they dealt with a gentleman for a gold watch," and that the partners had "dealt with several gentlemen for divers watches, rings, swords, canes, hats, cloaks, horses, bridles, saddles, and other things, to the value of 2000 pounds and upwards." It further claimed that the partners had prevailed upon a certain gentleman to part with some of his things and that "after some small discourse with the said gentlemen," the things were acquired "at a very cheap rate." It is told that when the judges in the case realized the nature of the partnership—you may have already guessed that the plaintiff and defendant were highwaymen, the English equivalent of American stagecoach robbers—they dismissed the suit, jailed the attorneys, and ordered both plaintiff and defendant hanged. It does not always pay to be litigious!

ELEMENTS OF A CONTRACT

Because contract law is, like torts, essentially common-law in nature, it is the courts who have spelled out, on a case-by-case basis over the years, the minimum qualities that an agreemet must possess to constitute a contract. The elements normally required are an *agreement, consideration, competent parties,* and a *lawful objective.* Subject to significant exceptions we note later, contracts need not be in writing; that is, oral contracts are generally enforceable if their terms can be proven in court.

THE AGREEMENT

Offer

An agreement requires an **offer** followed by an **acceptance.** For a particular proposal to constitute a legal offer, it must be reasonably definite to what the other party is to do, and it must manifest a genuine intent to contract. Proposals that do not meet these requirements are called mere **preliminary negotiations,** the acceptance of which does not result in the formation of a contract. Suppose, for example, that X in a letter proposes to employ Y as a manager of his business for which Y would receive at the end of the first year a "fair share of the profits" and that Y sends back a letter of acceptance. In this case, X's proposal is too vague to be an offer, and thus Y's "acceptance" does not result in the formation of a contract. Similarly, a statement that "I am hoping to sell my car for $2,000" fails to constitute an offer because the language does not manifest a genuine intent to contract. An expression of one's hope, or wishes, is not the legal equivalent of a letter by a car owner to a prospective buyer in which it is said "I will sell you my car for $2,000 cash."

Similarly, advertisements are generally considered to be preliminary negotiations only, for two reasons: (1) Most ads are silent on other material matters, such as the available quantity and credit terms, and (2) sellers of goods have the right to choose with whom they deal and do not intend to commit themselves to sell to the potentially unlimited number of persons who might see and respond to an ad. Thus in most instances an ad is merely an invitation for readers to make an offer, and a request by an advertisement's reader that the goods be sold to him or her at the advertised price is not an acceptance of an offer but is, instead, an *offer to purchase* the goods. Exceptions arise when the advertisement is worded to limit the number of persons who could reasonably accept the offer—for example, where the advertisement limits the quantity of goods ("Three 1992 Mazda Pegasus autos at $30,000 each, on sale Sunday!"), or where the ad creates a special method of sale ("1 Black Lapin Stole, Beautiful, Worth $139.50 ... $1.00, First-Come, First-Served.") In these cases, an advertisement is an offer that a reader may accept, thus creating a binding contract.

Termination

Once an offer has been communicated to the offeree, it is normally terminated only by revocation, by rejection, or by "lapse of time" (the passage of an unreasonable length of time). Once any of these events has occurred, the offeree's power of acceptance has died.

A revocation is a withdrawal of the offer by the offeror. Thus if an offeree receives either a written or oral message from the offeror to the effect that the offer is no longer open, any attempted acceptance thereafter is ineffective. Normally, an offer may be revoked by the offeror at any time before an acceptance—even if the offeror had originally promised to keep the offer open for a stated period of time. Thus if A makes an offer to B on June 1, assuring B that he has ten days in which to accept, a revocation by telephone by A to B on June 3 terminates the offer. The major exception to this rule is where an "option contract" is entered into, which usually occurs only when the offeree pays the offeror a sum of money in return for the offeror's promise to keep the offer open. Thus, in the above example, if B had paid A $10 on June 1 in return for A's assurance that the offer would remain open, A's attempted revocation on June 3 would be ineffective.

The UCC creates a second exception to the general rule by treating as irrevocable a *firm offer*. Under section 2-205, an offer for the sale of goods that contains a promise that it will be held open a specified period of time *cannot* be revoked prior to that time if (1) the offeror is a merchant and (2) the offer is in writing and signed by the offeror. No comparable rule exists in the common law of contracts.

A rejection occurs when the offeree notifies the offeror that he or she does not intend to accept the offer. A rejection has no effect until it has been legally communicated to the offeror. Thus if an offeree mails a letter of rejection but changes his or her mind and accepts the offer by telephone, at which time the rejection is still in the mail, the acceptance is valid. The usual rejection is a flat "no," or any words to that effect. (One form of rejection, the counteroffer, is discussed below in connection with the acceptance.)

With the exception of offers that contain fixed deadlines by which an acceptance must occur, offers remain open for a "reasonable" period of time. Once that time has passed without an acceptance, the offer lapses. In any case in which the offeror claims that the acceptance was not made within a reasonable time, the question of reasonable time is ordinarily left to the jury and thus may vary widely from case to case, depending on the different circumstances each case presents. For example, if the offer indicates that a "quick reply" must be made, the offer may lapse after only a period of a few days. In other circumstances, in which the offeror or past dealings between the parties indicate that the offeree may reasonably expect to have a substantial time to think the offer over, an offer may not lapse for weeks or even months.

Revocations, rejections, and lapses of time are acts of the parties that terminate offers. Offers may also be terminated by "operation of law," as when either party dies or is declared insane or the subject matter of the offer is declared illegal. In such instances, the offer is revoked automatically on the occurrence of the event. Thus if X makes an offer to Y on August 1 and X dies on August 2, a mailed acceptance by Y on August 3 is ineffective even if Y is not aware of X's death. (Figure 9.1 summarizes the ways an offer may be terminated).

Acceptance

Insofar as the *acceptance* is concerned, the basic requirements are that it be both unequivocal and unconditional. Thus, replies by the offeree that "your offer is the best I have received" or "I shall give your order prompt attention" do not constitute an acceptance. (And silence—a failure by the offeree to reply to the offer—is almost never construed by the courts to be an acceptance, even where the offeror states that "I will conclude we have a contract if I do not hear from you soon.")

Definiteness

Under common law, valid offers and acceptances are expected to address the key contractual terms—the parties, the subject matter, the price, and the time of performance. However, because the drafters of article 2 realized that many sales contracts are somewhat fragmentary in nature (for instance, the time of delivery or the time of payment may be lacking), they drafted section 2-204 to "save" those contracts, as far as the law is concerned, if

FIGURE 9.1

Offeror → Offer → **Offeree**

Acceptance ← or

↓

Contract

Offer terminates due to:
1) *revocation by offeror.*
2) *rejection by offeree.*
3) *lapse of time.*
4) *operation of law.*

■ **METHODS OF TERMINATING AN OFFER**

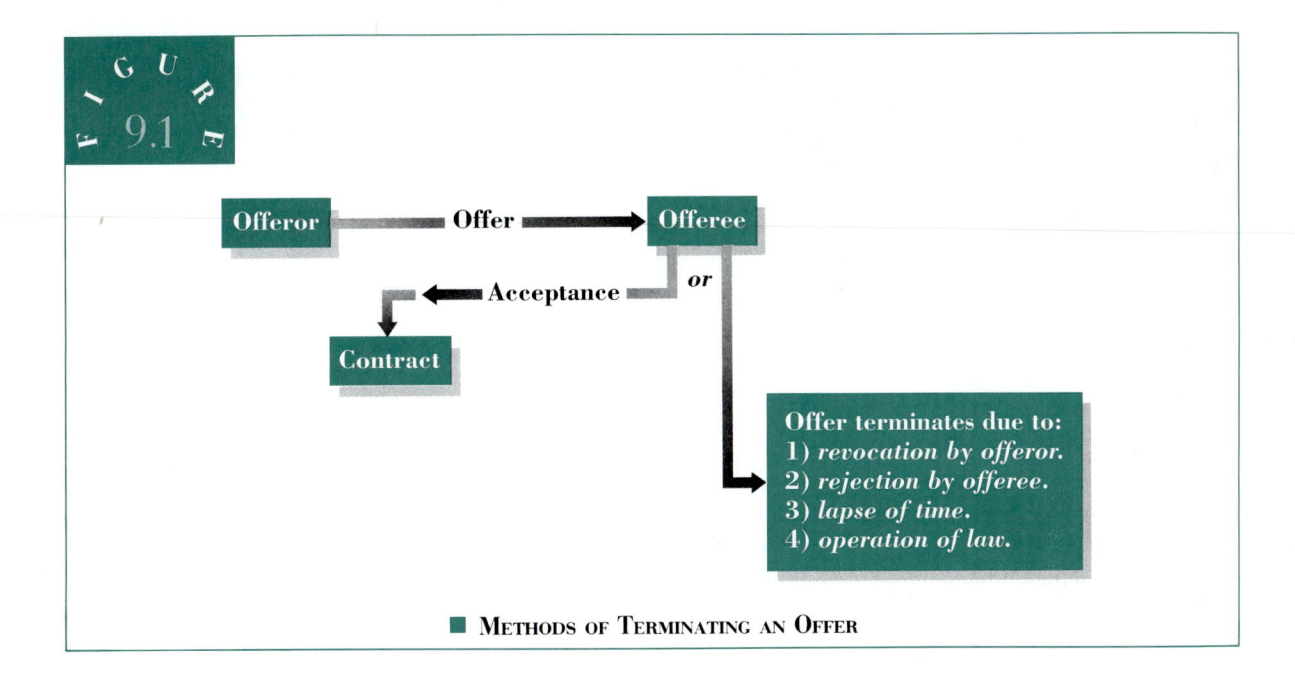

reasonably possible to do so. That section broadly states that a sales contract is enforceable even if one or more terms are left open, so long as (1) the court feels that the parties intended to make a contract, and (2) the agreement and surrounding circumstances give the court a reasonably certain basis for granting an appropriate remedy (normally, damages) in the event of a breach. The drafters then framed additional sections that would supply missing terms in varying circumstances. The following cases illustrate the operation of section 2-204:

Case 1: A sales contract is entered into that is complete except that it lacks a delivery date. The contract is valid, because a subsequent section of the UCC provides that in such an instance delivery must be made within a reasonable time after the making of the contract.

Case 2: A sales contract is entered into that is complete except that it lacks a price or provides that a price will be determined later. The contract is valid, because section 2-305 contains several rules to guide the court in determining a price in either instance.

Under common law, courts occasionally speak of the "mirror image" rule—the idea that for an agreement to arise the terms of the acceptance must reflect the terms of the offer in all particulars.

An "acceptance" by the offeree that contains a term in conflict with a term of the offer, or which adds a new condition, is a *counteroffer* rather than an acceptance. Because a counteroffer is one form of rejection, once it is made

FIGURE 9.2

Legal Ramifications of the Counteroffer

X → Offer → Y

Counteroffer— (X's offer ends. Y becomes offeror.) → X

X → Accepts → Contract
X → Rejects → No Contract

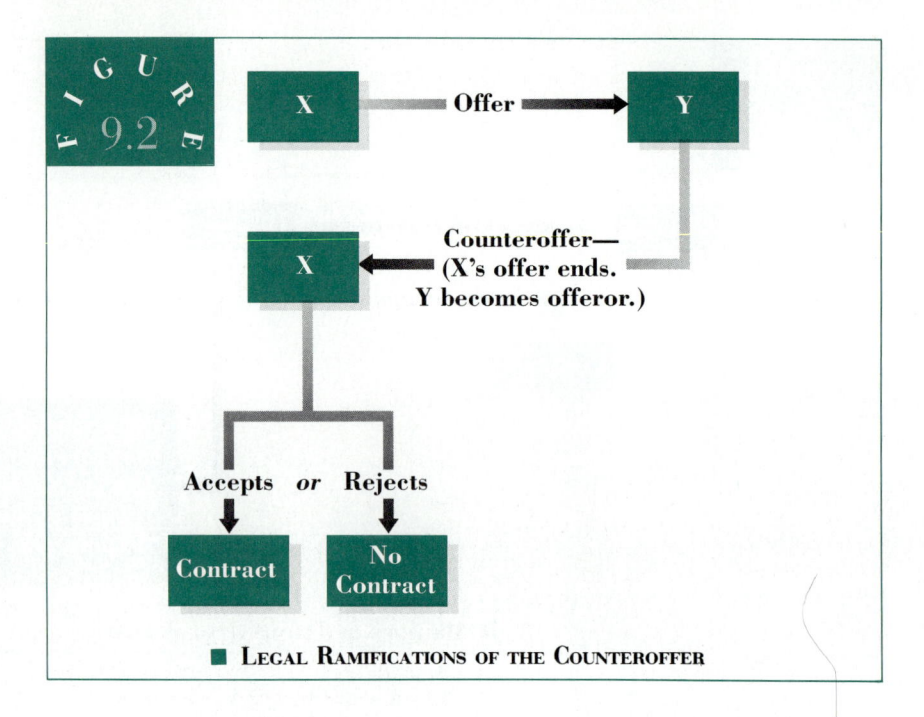

the offeror's original offer is terminated forever. To illustrate: The X Company offers certain industrial supplies to the Y Company for $15,000, and the Y Company responds by saying it will pay only $13,000. If the X Company refuses the lower price and the Y Company then replies that it is accepting the $15,000 offer, there is no contract at this point. This concept is illustrated in Figure 9.2.

The realities of the commercial world led the UCC's drafters to alter the "mirror image" rule for sales contracts. In the business world one company often uses its own order form in making an offer to buy goods, and the offeree company "accepts" the offer by using its form (such as a "Sales Acceptance" form), which frequently contains one or more terms *in addition* to those appearing in the offer. If one of the parties later wants out of the deal, he or she may argue that the offeree company's "acceptance" was legally a counteroffer and thus no contract was ever formed. Section 2-207 rejects this argument by providing that if the offeree's response indicates a definite intent to accept, the response *constitutes an acceptance* even if it contains terms additional to those found in the offer. This section then sets forth a number of rules to be used in determining whether the additional terms also become a part of the contract.

Mail Box Rule

If a valid acceptance is made and if the parties are dealing face-to-face or by telephone, the acceptance is effective immediately. If, however, the parties are negotiating by mail or by telegram, the usual rule is that the acceptance takes effect *on dispatch* if the offeree has selected a "reasonable means of communication" in replying. Thus if the offeree uses the same means of communication as that used by the offeror, or some other means that is commonly used in such situations, the acceptance is effective when sent. Example: A makes an offer by mail to B, who mails a letter of acceptance at noon of the day the offer is received. If A should call B later that same day to say that the offer is revoked, the attempted revocation is invalid because a contract was formed at noon.

The often-cited case below presents a typical question in the offer and acceptance area.

RICHARDS V. FLOWERS ET AL.

DISTRICT COURT OF APPEAL, CALIFORNIA
14 CAL. REPTR. 228 (1961)

Mrs. Richards, plaintiff, wrote defendant Flowers on January 15, 1959, as follows: "We would be interested in buying your lot on Gravatt Drive in Oakland, California, if we can deal with you directly and not run through a realtor. If you are interested, please advise us by return mail the cash price you would expect to receive."

On January 19, 1959, Flowers replied: "Thank you for your inquiry regarding my lot on Gravatt Drive. As long as your offer would be in cash I see no reason why we could not deal directly on this matter.... Considering what I paid for the lot, and the taxes which I have paid I expect to receive $4,500 for this property. Please let me know what you decide."

On January 25, 1959, Mrs. Richards sent the following telegram to Flowers: "Have agreed to buy your lot on your terms will handle transactions through local title company who will contact you greatly appreciate your sending us a copy of the contour map you referred to in your letter as we are desirous of building at once...."

On February 5, 1959, Flowers entered into an agreement to sell the property to a third party, Mr. and Mrs. Sutton. Mrs. Richards, after learning of the Sutton transaction, called on the defendant to deliver his deed to her, claiming the above correspondence constituted a contract between him and her. Flowers refused to do so, denying that his letter of January 19 constituted an offer to sell, whereupon Mr. and Mrs. Richards commenced action, asking for specific performance of the alleged contract. (The Suttons intervened in this action to protect their interest by supporting Flowers's contention that a contract was not formed between him and the plaintiffs.)

The trial court ruled that the defendant's letter of January 19 did constitute an offer to sell, but it further ruled that the plaintiff's telegram of January 25 was not a valid acceptance under a particular California statute. Accordingly, the court entered judgment for defendant and the Richards appealed. (Note: The higher court agreed with the lower court that a contract had not been formed, but on a different ground: namely, that defendant's letter of January 19 was not an offer. The higher court's reasoning is set forth below.)

SHOEMAKER, JUSTICE:

... Under the factual situation in the instant case, the interpretation of the series of communications between the parties is a matter of law and an appellate court is not bound by the trial court's determination. Respondent Flowers argues that the letter of January 19th merely invited an offer from appellants for the purchase of the property

CONTINUED

and that under no reasonable interpretation can this letter be construed as an offer. We agree with the respondent. Careful consideration of the letter does not convince us that the language therein used can reasonably be interpreted as a definite offer to sell the property to appellants. As pointed out in *Restatement of the Law, Contracts*, section 25, comment a.: "It is often difficult to draw an exact line between offers and negotiations preliminary thereto. It is common for one who wishes to make a bargain to try to induce the other party to the intended transaction to make the definite offer, he himself suggesting with more or less definiteness the nature of the contract he is willing to enter into...." Under this approach, our letter seems rather clearly to fall within the category of mere preliminary negotiations. Particularly is this true in view of the fact that the letter was written directly in response to appellants' letter inquiring if they could deal directly with respondent and requesting him to suggest a sum at which he might be willing to sell. From the record, we do not accept the argument that respondent Flowers made a binding offer to sell the property merely because he chose to answer certain inquiries by the appellants. Further, the letter appears to us inconsistent with any intent on his part to make an offer to sell. In response to appellants' question, respondent stated that he would be willing to deal directly with them rather than through a realtor as long as their "offer would be in cash." We take this language to indicate that respondent anticipated a *future offer* from appellants but was making no offer himself. [Emphasis added.]

Appellants refer to the phrase that he would "expect to receive" $4,500 and contend this constitutes an offer to sell to them at this price. However, respondent was only expressing an indication of the lowest price which he was presently willing to consider. Particularly is this true inasmuch as respondent wrote only in response to an inquiry in which this wording was used. We conclude that respondent by his communication confined himself to answering the inquiries raised by appellants, but did not extend himself further and did not make an express offer to sell the property. We have before us a case involving a mere quotation of price and not an offer to sell at that price. The cause, therefore, comes within the rule announced in such authorities as *Nebraska Seed Co. v. Harsh*, 1915, 152 N.W.310, wherein the seller had written the buyer, enclosing a sample of millet seed and saying, "I want $2.25 per cwt. for this seed f.o.b. Lowell." The buyer telegraphed his acceptance. The court, in reversing a judgment for plaintiff buyer, stated: "In our opinion the letter of defendant cannot be fairly construed into an offer to sell to the plaintiff. After describing the seed, the writer says, 'I want $2.25 per cwt. for this seed f.o.b. Lowell.' He does not say, 'I offer to sell to you.' The language used is general, ... and is not an offer by which he may be bound, if accepted, by any or all of the persons addressed"; and *Owen v. Tunison*, 1932, 158A. 926, wherein the buyer had written the seller inquiring whether he would be willing to sell certain store property for $6,000. The seller replied: "Because of improvements which have been added and an expenditure of several thousand dollars it would not be possible for me to sell it unless I was to receive $16,000.00 cash...." The court, in holding that the seller's reply did not constitute an offer, stated: "Defendant's letter ... may have been written with the intent to open negotiations that might lead to a sale. It was not a proposal to sell." It would thus seem clear that respondent's quotation of the price which he would "expect to receive" cannot be viewed as an offer capable of acceptance....

Since there was never an offer, hence never a contract between respondent Flowers and appellants, the judgment must be affirmed, and it becomes unnecessary to determine whether appellant's purported acceptance complied with the statute of frauds or whether appellants failed to qualify for specific performance in any other regard.

Judgment affirmed.

CONSIDERATION

Once an offer and an acceptance occur, the second requirement of a contract—an elusive thing called **consideration**—is ordinarily present. Consideration may initially be defined as that element that supports a promise, thereby causing the promise to be enforceable, as distinguished from the mere promise of a gift, which is not enforceable.

Assume that Company A promised to deliver 5,000 tires to Company B on July 1 in exchange for Company B's promise to pay $200,000. Assume further that Company B breached the promise, Company A sued, and Company B raised the defense that no consideration existed to support its promise. According to Justice Cardozo, consideration consists of three elements.[5] The first determination is whether the promisee (Company A) suffered a **legal detriment,** defined as doing (or promising to do) something it was not obligated to do or refraining from doing (or promising to refrain from doing) something it had a right to do. Unless Company A had a preexisting statutory or contractual obligation to deliver the 5,000 tires, it is clear that Company A did suffer a legal detriment. It promised to do something it did not otherwise have to do—to deliver 5,000 tires.

The second element of consideration is that the detriment (A's promise to deliver the 5,000 tires) must induce the promise (B's promise to pay $200,000). Unless there is some other explanation for why Company B promised to pay $200,000 to Company A, it is clear that the detriment did induce the promise in this case.

The third element of consideration is that the promise (B's promise to pay $200,000) must induce the detriment (A's promise to deliver the 5,000 tires). Again, unless some other reason appears to explain why A promised to deliver the 5,000 tires, it seems clear that it was to earn the $200,000 promised by B. All three elements of consideration are present, so the contract is enforceable.

Viewed in this light, consideration is easy to understand and, obviously, is present in most cases. Companies and individuals promise to deliver goods and services because they want the money that other companies and individuals are willing to pay for the goods and services.

Consideration may be lacking in some situations, however. To illustrate: X, a longtime employee of the Y Company, decides to retire and, on his last day of work, is told by the president that the company will pay him $100 a month thereafter as long as he lives. X promptly replies, "I accept." If the Y Company stops making payments after three months, at which time X brings action to make the company continue the payments, X will lose the case. Because X, the promisee, was not asked to do anything or to give up any rights, he suffered no legal detriment. This is simply an unenforceable promise to make a gift.

The **preexisting duty rule** may also prevent a legal detriment from occurring. Suppose that in October, S contracts to sell a piece of land to B for $50,000, with the closing—the payment of the money by B and the delivery of a deed by S—to occur the following December 1. In November, General Motors announces that an automobile assembly plant will be built in the area, greatly increasing the value of the land. When S complains about the price he is getting and threatens not to go through with the deal, B—who desperately needs the property—promises to pay $75,000 for it. In such a

---

[5] *Allegbeny College v. National Chautauqua County Bank,* 246, N.Y. 369, 159 N.E. 173 (1927).

case, B is liable to S for only $50,000. The promise to pay the extra $25,000 is unenforceable because S did not do (or promise to do) anything that he was not already bound by contract to do.

Similarly, there is no consideration if the detriment does not induce the promise. Assume M Company promises to throw some business to N Company, and in reliance N Company, unbeknownst to M Company, spends money expanding its plant. If M later refused to grant the business and N sued, the plant expansion might be a legal detriment but could not provide consideration because that was not what induced M to make its promise. This is frequently called the "bargained for" requirement. M did not bargain for a plant expansion by N.

Finally, remember that the promise must induce the detriment. In one vivid case,[6] domestic dispute resulted in a husband (D) lying on the floor and his wife about to bring an ax down on his head. P, a neighbor, put her arm in the ax's path, saving D's life, but suffering serious injury. D jumped up and promised to pay P a reward, which he later did not pay. And he did not have to. His promise (to pay the reward) did not induce the detriment (P's act of self-sacrifice) because it was not made until after the detriment was incurred. "Past consideration" usually is no consideration.

Try to analyze the following case using Justice Cardozo's three elements.

LAMPLEY v. CELEBRITY HOMES, INC.

COLORADO COURT OF APPEALS, DIVISION II
594 P.2d 605 (1979)

Linda Lampley, the plaintiff, began work at Celebrity Homes in Denver in May 1975. On July 29 of that year Celebrity announced the initiation of a profit-sharing plan. Under that plan all employees were to receive bonuses if a certain "profit goal" was reached for the 1975 fiscal year— April 1, 1975, to March 31, 1976. (Linda was working under an at-will agreement— that is, both she and Celebrity could terminate the relationship at any time.) The plaintiff's employment was terminted in January 1976. At the end of March 1976, the company announced that the profit goal had been reached, and it made its first distribution of profits in May 1976. When the plaintiff was excluded from this distribution, she brought this suit for the share allegedly due her.

In the trial court Celebrity argued that its promise to pay the bonus was a mere "gratuity" on its part, on the ground that there was no consideration on the employee's part to support its promise. The trial court rejected this contention and entered judgment for the plaintiff. Celebrity appealed.

KELLY, JUDGE:

... In further support of its claim that the plan is not a binding contract,

CONTINUED

---

[6] *Harrington v. Taylor*, 36 S.E. 2d 227 (N.C. 1945).

Celebrity contends that there was no consideration [given by the plaintiff]. Benefit to the promisor or detriment to the promisee, however slight, can constitute consideration. The plan states as its objective:

> Our goal is... to produce added employee benefits gained through a higher quality of operation. Through teamwork in our day-to-day operation, we can achieve not only higher levels of profits, but also better performance for our customers, a better quality in design of products, fair treatment of customers, subcontractors, and suppliers.

This language indicates that the plan was established as an inducement to Celebrity's employees to remain in its employ and to perform more efficient and faithful service. Such result would be of obvious benefit to Celebrity, and thus consideration was present.... [The court also implicitly found a detriment on the part of the promisee, as follows:]

Lampley, who was employed for an indefinite term, was not obligated to remain until 1976, and it can be inferred from the evidence in the record that she was induced to do so, in part at least, by the profit-sharing offer made to her by Celebrity. Thus, this case can be distinguished from [those] which hold that there can be no recovery where the company gets no more service as a result of such a promise than it would if no such promise had been made. The memorandum of the profit-sharing plan was an offer to add additional terms to the original employment contract, and Lampley's continued employment with Celebrity [until January 1976] was an acceptance of the offer and the consideration for the contract.

Judgment affirmed.

In exceptional circumstances a promise is binding on the promisor even though there is no consideration on the part of the promisee. The most common example occurs in circumstances in which the doctrine *of promissory estoppel* is applied by the courts. Under that principle, a promisor is liable on his or her promise—even though there is no consideration given by the promisee—if (1) the promisor knows or should know that the promise alone is likely to induce a specific action on the part of the promisee; (2) that the promisee, after the promise is made, does take the expected action; and (3) that such action is definite and substantial in nature.

In recent years the doctrine of promissory estoppel has been used more and more by courts to prevent unfairness. Promissory estoppel is often used as a substitute for consideration and, in cases where one party has substantially performed his duties under an agreement, as a means of circumventing the requirement that certain types of contracts be in writing. But these two categories do not exhaust the uses of the doctrine, as the following case illustrates.

HOFFMAN v. RED OWL STORES, INC.

SUPREME COURT OF WISCONSIN, 133 N.W.2d 267 (1965)

In 1960 Hoffman, the plaintiff, hoped to establish a Red Owl franchised grocery store in Wautoma, Wisconsin. During that year he and the divisional manager of Red Owl, Lukowitz, had numerous conversations in which general plans for Hoffman's becoming a franchisee were discussed. Early in 1961 Lukowitz advised Hoffman to buy a small grocery to gain experience in the grocery business before operating a Red Owl franchise in a larger community.

Acting on this suggestion, Hoffman bought a small grocery in Wautoma. Three months later Red Owl representatives found that the store was operating at a profit, at which time Hoffman told Lukowitz that he could raise $18,000 to invest in a franchise. Lukowitz then advised Hoffman to sell the store, assuring him that the company would find a larger store for him to operate elsewhere—that he would "be operating a Red Owl store in a new location by fall."

Relying on this promise, Hoffman sold the grocery and soon thereafter bought a lot in Chilton, Wisconsin (a site that the company had selected for a new store), making a $1,000 down payment on the lot. Hoffman then rented a home for his family in Chilton and, after being assured by Lukowitz that "everything was all set," made a second $1,000 payment on the lot.

In September 1961 Lukowitz told Hoffman that the only "hitch" in the plan was that he (Hoffman) would have to sell a bakery building he owned in Wautoma and that the proceeds of that sale would have to make up a part of the $18,000 he was to invest, thereby reducing the amount he would have to borrow. Hoffman sold the building for $10,000, incurring a loss thereon of $2,000.

About this time, Red Owl prepared a "Proposed Financing for an Agency Store" plan that required Hoffman to invest $24,100 rather than the original $18,000. After Hoffman came up with $24,100 by virtue of several new loans, Red Owl told him that another $2,000 would be necessary.

Hoffman refused to go along with this demand, negotiations were terminated, and the new store was never built. When Hoffman and his wife brought suit to recover damages for breach of contract, Red Owl defended on the ground that its promises were not supported by consideration on Hoffman's part (in view of the facts that no formal financing plan was ever agreed to by Hoffman and no franchise agreement obligations were undertaken by him). Hoffman contended that liability should nonetheless be imposed on the basis of promissory estoppel; the trial court agreed, entering judgment in his favor. Red Owl appealed.

CURRIE, CHIEF JUSTICE:

. . Sec. 90 of Restatement, 1 Contracts, provides: "A promise which the promisor should reasonably expect to induce action or forbearance of a definite and substantial character on the part of the promisee and which does induce such action or forbearance is binding if injustice can be avoided only by enforcement of the promise."

[The Chief Justice then observed that the Wisconsin Supreme Court had never recognized the above rule, but continued:] Many courts of other jurisdictions have seen fit over the years to adopt the principle of promissory estoppel [embodied in section 90], and the tendency in that direction continues. . . . The development of the law of promissory estoppel "is an attempt by the courts to keep the remedies abreast of increased moral consciousness of honesty and fair representations in all business dealings." *People's National Bank of Little Rock v. Linebarger Construction Co.*, 240 S.W.2d 12 (1951). . . .

Because we deem the doctrine of promissory estoppel, as stated in Section 90 of Restatement, 1 Contracts, [to be] one which supplies a needed tool which courts may employ in a proper case to prevent injustice, *we endorse and adopt it.* [Emphasis added.]

The record here discloses a number of promises and assurances given to Hoffman by Lukowitz in behalf of Red Owl, [and] upon which plaintiffs relied and acted upon to their detriment.

Foremost were the promises that for the sum of $18,000 Red Owl would estab-

CONTINUED

lish Hoffman in a store, [and] in November, 1961, [the assurance] to Hoffman that if the $24,100 figure were increased by $2,000, the deal would go through. [In return,] Hoffman was induced to sell his grocery store fixtures and inventory in June, 1961, on the promise that he would be in his new store by fall. In November, plaintiffs sold their bakery building on the urging of defendants and on the assurance that this was the last step necessary to have the deal with Red Owl go through [and on which sale, incidentally, the plaintiffs suffered the $2,000 loss earlier referred to].

We determine that there was ample evidence to sustain [the jury's finding that Hoffman relied on the promises of Red Owl], and that his reliance was in the exercise of ordinary care. . . .

[In regard to a contention by Red Owl that its promises were too vague and indefinite to be enforceable in this action, in view of the fact that the size, cost, and design of the proposed store building were never agreed on, the court disagreed, saying:] We deem it would be a mistake to regard an action grounded on promissory estoppel as the [precise] equivalent of a breach of contract action.

The third requirement [of promissory estoppel,] that the remedy can only be invoked where necessary to avoid injustice, is one that involves a policy decision by the court. Such a policy necessarily embraces an element of discretion.

We conclude that injustice would result here if plaintiffs were not granted some relief because of the failure of defendants to keep their promises which induced plaintiffs to act to their detriment. . . .

Judgment affirmed.

COMPETENT PARTIES

Most contracting parties are fully "competent," meaning that, in the eyes of the law, they have the full capacity (legal ability) to contract. But if one of the parties to a contract has only *partial* capacity (*e.g.,* a minor, an intoxicated person, or a person who is, in fact, insane), the contract is "voidable" (one that the incompetent party may subsequently set aside if he or she wishes). If one of the parties has *no* capacity (*e.g.,* a baby or a person who has been adjudicated insane), the contract is "void" (one that, in the eyes of the law, never existed at all).

The most common voidable contracts are those made by minors, who are defined by most state statutes as natural persons younger than the age of 18 years. Thus, although minors may make contracts, they also generally possess the legal right to disaffirm (cancel) any contracts as long as they do so while still minors, or within a reasonable time after they become 18 years of age. The other party to the contract has no similar right.

The general rule is that a minor may disaffirm a contract and recover *all* consideration given to the other party. Thus, if a 16 year old buys a car for $15,000 and then disaffirms on his or her 18th birthday (returning the car to the seller), the seller must give back all $15,000 even though the value of the car has greatly diminished because of accidents, use, and general depreciation. This rule is often very unfair to the adult party to the contract but serves the law's purpose of protecting minors by discouraging adults from dealing with them.

If a minor were out on his or her own, we would want him or her to be able to buy the *necessities* of life—food, clothing, shelter, and medical care. So, to encourage adults to provide these items to minors, the law creates an exception. Minors cannot completely disaffirm such contracts. But to protect minors from mistakes of judgment, they are liable not for the contract price, but only for the "reasonable value" of the goods and services they use.

Minors who induce adults to deal with them by pretending to be adults themselves are either prohibited from disaffirming or (in other states) allowed to disaffirm only if they can show that disaffirmance would cause no loss to the other party. Furthermore, on public policy grounds most states provide that certain classes of contracts (*e.g.*, contracts of marriage or enlistment, and contracts with banks and insurance companies) cannot be disaffirmed.

Another significant class of incompetent parties is intoxicated (or "high") persons. The general rule is that such persons may disaffirm on regaining sobriety only if the person can show that he or she was so intoxicated as not to understand the nature of the purported agreement at the time it was made. Thus, a question of fact is presented, because a lesser degree of intoxication is not grounds for disaffirmance. Most courts also require a showing that the nonintoxicated party will not be injured by the disaffirmance.

LEGALITY

The fourth element of a contract, a lawful purpose, is present only when the contract is in conformity with all applicable statutes and common-law rules. All states have statutes expressly prohibiting certain kinds of contracts, such as wagering agreements or the charging of interest above specified limits on loans. Contracts in violation of these statutes, being unlawful, are unenforceable. Similarly, contracts made by certain unlicensed persons, such as lawyers and real estate brokers who are required to be licensed by statute, are also generally illegal. In other instances a contract may also be illegal simply because it violates the "public policy" of that state, as defined by the state's courts on a case-by-case basis. Contracts that restrain trade unreasonably (such as an agreement by one company not to compete with another) and clauses in contracts that contains terms purporting to free a party from liability if he or she performs a service negligently (exculpatory clauses) are typical of those that are generally contrary to public policy and thus unenforceable on that ground.

Although covenants (promises) not to compete are also generally disfavored by the law, they may be lawful when they are a subsidiary or auxiliary part of a larger agreement that is, itself, lawful. For example, a seller of a small retail business may, at the demand of the buyer, include in the sale agreement a promise that he or she (the seller) will not open a competing business within a specified area for a certain length of time after the sale. Such restraints are not contrary to public policy if they are not "excessive" or "unreasonable" under the circumstances—that is, if the restraints do not afford more than a reasonable protection to the buyer. Thus in the prior example, a promise by the seller not to operate a competing business within a one-mile radius of the store being sold for a period of six months after the sale is probably binding on the seller.

Covenants not to compete are also common in employment contracts, under the terms of which the employee promises, on termination of his or her employment, not to engage in (or work for) a competing business within a designated area for a specified period of time after such termination. Such covenants, like those in contracts under which businesses are being sold, are also lawful—that is, binding on the employee—if the restraints are not excessive under the circumstances. But, as the following case shows, covenants in employment contracts that are too broad are often found to be contrary to public policy and thus not binding on the employee.

BRYCELAND v. NORTHEY

COURT OF APPEALS OF ARIZONA 772 P.2d 36 (1989)

Bryceland, doing business as Johnny B's Disc Jockey Express, is in the mobile disc jockey business, providing recorded entertainment played by a "deejay" at parties, weddings, dances, and similar functions. He has numerous competitors in the Phoenix area.

Northey and Malvin applied to become deejays for Bryceland in 1985 and 1986, respectively. They received both classroom training and on-the-job help from Bryceland. After completing their training, they signed contracts in which they promised not to compete with Johnny B's for a period of two years within a 50-mile radius of Phoenix and such other areas where they might have performed.

In February 1987, Malvin and Northey both went to work for another mobile disc jockey service owned by Northey's father. Bryceland sued to enforce the covenant not to compete. The trial judge held for Bryceland on this issue, ordering defendants not to compete within a 50-mile radius of Phoenix for two years. Northey and Malvin appealed.

KLEINSCHMIDT, JUDGE:

Restrictive covenants that tend to prevent an employee from pursuing a similar vocation after termination of employment are disfavored and are strictly construed against the employer. *Amex Distrib. Co. v. Mascari*, 150 Ariz. 510, 514, 724 P.2d 596, 600 (App. 1986). A contrasting rule applies to a covenant given in the sale of a business. As to the latter, courts are more lenient because of the need to see that goodwill is effectively transferred. *Restatement (Second) of Contracts* § 188 comment b (1981). The burden is on the employer to prove the extent of its protectable interest.

Restrictive covenants that are no broader than the employer's legitimately protectable interest will be enforced. An employer may not enforce a post-employment restriction on a former employee simply to eliminate competition *per se*. Comment b to section 188 of the Restatement provides in part:

[A postemployment restraint] must usually be justified on the ground that the employer has a legitimate interest in restraining the employee from appropriating valuable trade information and customer relationships to which he has had access in the course of his employment. Arguably the employer does not get the full value of the employment contract if he cannot confidently give the employee access to confidential information needed for [the] most efficient performance of his job. But it is often difficult to distinguish between such information and normal skills of the trade, and preventing use of one may well prevent or inhibit use of the other.

At trial, Bryceland's primary concern was that Malvin and Northey had taken classroom notes, could tell others that they were trained by Bryceland and would use their skills to serve another employer. These will not justify a restraint. A restrictive covenant is not enforceable to prevent a former employee

CONTINUED

from using the skills and talents he learns on the job in a new job.

The trial court found that there had been no appropriation and disclosure of trade secrets and customer information. Bryceland has not appealed from this finding. Thus, the interest for which Bryceland obtained protection was not its proprietary interest in confidential information.

An employer does have a protectable interest in maintaining customer relationships when an employee leaves. The law will guard this interest by means of a covenant not to compete for as long as may be necessary to replace the employee and give the replacement a chance to show that he can do the job. Each case hinges on its own particular facts. Malvin and Northey, applying this rule, contend that the restrictive covenant is unreasonable in length. In *Amex*, we said:

> In determining whether a restraint extends for a longer period of time than necessary to protect the employer, the court must determine how much time is needed for the risk of injury to be reasonably moderated. When the restraint is for the purpose of protecting customer relationships, its duration is reasonable only if it is no longer than necessary for the employer to put a new man on the job and for the new employee to have a reasonable opportunity to demonstrate his effectiveness to the customers. If a restraint on this ground is justifiable at all, it seems that a period of several months would usually be reasonable. If the selling or servicing relationship is relatively complex, a longer period may be called for.

Amex, 150 Ariz at 518, 724 P.2d at 604 (quoting Blake, *Employment Agreement Not to Compete*, 73 Harv.L.Rev. 625, 677 (1960)).

The apparent purpose of this principle is to prevent a skilled employee from leaving an employer and, based on his skill acquired from that employment, luring away the employer's clients or business while the employer is vulnerable—that is—before the employer has had a chance to replace the employee with someone qualified to do the job. Here, the evidence showed that it took approximately fourteen weeks for adequate schooling and on-the-job training of new personnel to handle the duties of a deejay, far less than the two-year restriction contained in the agreement. Bryceland did not present evidence, which the trial court accepted as true, of any protectable interest other than the time it would require to replace Malvin and Northey with trained deejays.

We also note, without deciding, that the restriction against employment by any "potential customer or client" of Bryceland may be overly broad. This language goes well beyond protecting Bryceland from Malvin and Northey taking customers away as a result of meeting the customers during the course of their appearances for Johnny B's.

We find that the restrictive covenant is unreasonable in restricting Northey and Malvin's future employment as mobile disc jockeys for a two-year period. Neither the contract itself nor other evidence in the record indicates that this unreasonable portion of the contract was severable.

[Reversed.]

RESCISSION OF CONTRACTS

In some circumstances a party to a contract may have it rescinded (set aside by a court) even if all the basic contractual elements are present. Rescission is most commonly granted where *fraud* or *mistake of fact* is shown to exist. Essentially, fraud is the intentional misrepresentation of a fact by one person to another. If X, in selling his car to Y, tells Y that the mileage on the odometer is correct when in fact X knows that the car has been driven many miles more than the odometer shows, and if Y purchases the car believing X's statement to be true, Y is entitled to rescission if he is able to prove the above facts in court. (A statement of opinion or prediction is to be distinguished from a statement of fact, however; thus X is not guilty of fraud if he tells Y that "this is the cleanest '84 Celebrity in town" or that "used car prices absolutely won't be lower in the next six months," even if both statements prove to be false.) Once fraud is established, the innocent party usually has the choice of rescinding the contract—returning the car in the case above and recovering the purchase price—or keeping what he or she has received and recovering damages from the defrauding party.

Insofar as mistake in general is concerned, a party is not entitled to rescission simply because the contract proved to be unwise, unprofitable, or made on a mistaken assumption as to future events (for instance, that the economy is going to rebound in the coming year when in fact it does not). However, rescission *is* allowed in the case of mutual, or bilateral, *mistake of fact*—that is, when both parties are mistaken as to a material, existing fact at the time of contracting. For example: B purchases S's summer home on April 10. B later learns that, unknown to either party, the home has been destroyed by fire on April 1. Because both parties entered into the contract under the mistaken assumption that the home actually existed at that time, B can have the contract set aside. A second situation where rescission is permitted arises in the case of unilateral mistake—in which one party is mistaken as to a material fact, but the other party is not. In such a case, rescission usually is allowed only if the mistaken party can prove that the other party was or should have been aware of his or her mistake when the contract was made and failed to correct the mistake.

CONTRACTS IN WRITING

As a general rule, oral contracts are as enforceable as written ones if their terms can be established in court. However, all states have adopted a statute known as the "Statute of Frauds," which requires five major kinds of contracts to be in writing (or at least to be evidenced by a writing). The most important of these are (1) contracts calling for the sale of land or an interest therein; (2) contracts that cannot be performed within one year from the time they are made; and (3) contracts under which one party promises to pay the debt of another party. Thus oral contracts falling in any of these categories are usually unenforceable in court—although judicially recognized exceptions in narrow circumstances have sometimes been made.

In the event that an oral contract in one of the above categories is entered into, followed by a written confirmation that is sent by one of the parties to the other, the contract is enforceable against the party sending the confirmation but not against the recipeint.

SALES CONTRACTS

The UCC has its own statute of frauds provision for sales of goods. Under section 2-201, the general rule is that sales contracts must be in writing if the sale price is $500 or more. Thus if the S Co. and the B Co. make an oral agreement calling for the sale of 2,000 widgets by the S Co. to the B Co. for a price of $800, either company can subsequently refuse to go through with the deal without incurring liability to the other.

Section 2-201(3), however, contains a number of exceptions to the writing requirement, the most important of which are (1) contracts in which either the seller or the buyer has fully performed before the attempted repudiation of the oral contract by the other party, and (2) contracts of special manufacture. These exceptions can be illustrated as follows:

1. *Performance by One Party:* If, after an oral contract has been made, the buyer pays the seller the price (and the seller accepts the payment), the contract is now binding on the seller. That is, if the seller should subsequently refuse to deliver the goods, the buyer can recover damages from him or her even though nothing was in writing. Similarly, if after an oral contract has been made the seller delivers the goods to the buyer and the buyer accepts them, the buyer is liable for the purchase price (even though, again, the contract was entirely an oral one).

2. *Contracts of Special Manufacture:* Another part of section 2-201(3) provides that oral contracts calling for the sale of articles of "special manufacture"—that is, goods made according to the buyer's specifications—are binding on the buyer if two conditions exist. First, the specifications of the buyer must be such as to make the goods "not suitable for sale to others in the ordinary course of the seller's business." And, second, the seller—before the buyer's attempted repudiation of the contract—must have made a "substantial beginning of [the goods'] manufacture," or have made "commitments for their procurement."

PAROL EVIDENCE RULE

With limited exceptions, the parol evidence rule provides that once a written contract is entered into, neither party will thereafter be allowed to come into court and introduce parol (oral) evidence in an effort to show that there were other terms or conditions agreed on in addition to, or different from, those of the writing. For this reason, it is extremely important that all terms and understandings be set forth whenever an agreement is reduced to writing.

THIRD PARTIES

As a general rule, contracts can be enforced only by the original contracting parties. *Beneficiaries* and *assignees,* however, are exceptions to the rule. A

beneficiary is a nonparty for whose benefit the contract was originally made. For example, if the A Company sells a truck to the B Company, with the B Company agreeing to pay the price of the truck to C (rather than to the A Company), C may maintain a court action to recover the price from the B Company in the event that it does not pay him voluntarily. An **assignee** is a person to whom contractual rights are assigned by one of the contracting parties after the contract has been made. To illustrate: The X Company contracts to remodel the kitchen in Y's home for $12,000, and the X Company thereafter assigns (transfers) the right to collect the $12,000 to a third party, Z. In this case Z, the assignee, is entitled to payment by Y, the obligor, after the X Company has completed the work. An assignee's rights are no better than the assignor's; thus in the above case if the X Company had walked off the job and never did complete it, Z could *not* recover from Y. An illustration appears in Figure 9.3.

A party may assign his or her rights under a contract without the consent of the other party with two major exceptions: when the right that is attempted to be assigned is "personal" in nature, and when the terms of the contract require consent by the other party. In addition, state and federal statutes prohibit the assignment of limited types of rights in which cases, of course, assignment cannot occur even with the consent of the other party.

The following case presents an assignment problem in a modern business setting.

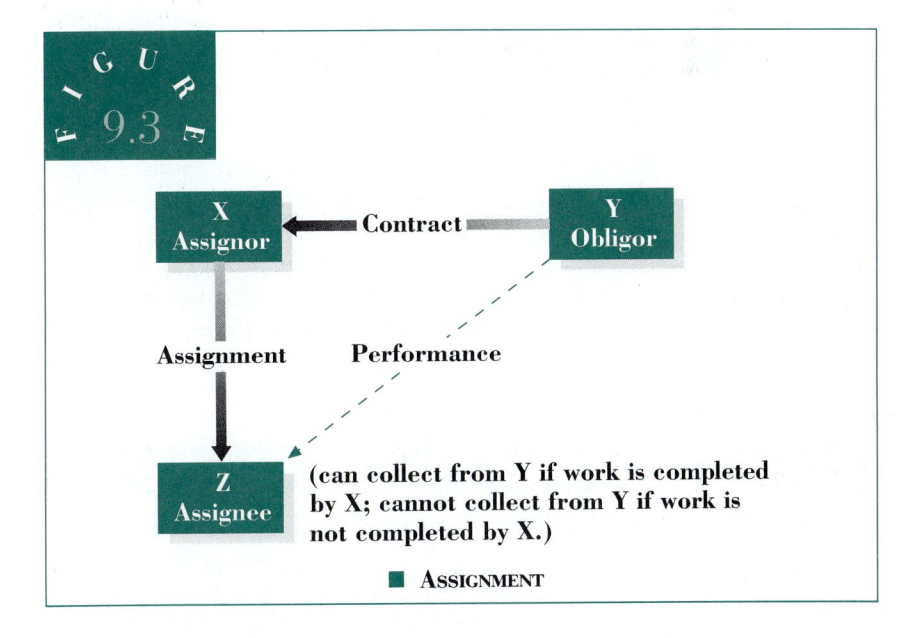

FIGURE 9.3

X Assignor ←—Contract—— Y Obligor

Assignment   Performance

Z Assignee   (can collect from Y if work is completed by X; cannot collect from Y if work is not completed by X.)

■ ASSIGNMENT

Schupach v. McDonald's Systems, Inc.

Supreme Court of Nebraska 264 N.W.2d 827 (1978)

McDonald's, the defendant, is the corporation that grants all McDonald fast-food restaurant franchises. In 1959 the defendant granted a franchise to a Mr. Copeland, giving him the right to own and operate McDonald's first store in the Omaha-Council Bluffs area. A few days later, in conformity with the negotiations leading up to the granting of the franchise, McDonald's sent a letter to Copeland giving him a "Right of First Refusal;" the right to be given first chance at owning any new stores that might be subsequently established in the area. In the next few years Copeland exercised this right and opened five additional stores in Omaha. In 1964 Copeland *sold and assigned all of his franchises to Schupach, the plaintiff, with McDonald's consent.*

When McDonald's granted a franchise in the Omaha-Council Bluffs area in 1974 to a third party without first offering it to Schupach, he brought this action for damages resulting from establishment of the new franchise, claiming that the assignment of the franchises to him also included the right of first refusal.

A number of issues were raised in this litigation. The defendant contended, among other things, that the right it gave to Copeland was personal in nature and thus was not transferable without its consent. The plaintiff alleged, however, that the right was not personal in nature or, in the alternative, that its transfer was, in fact, agreed to by defendant.

On these issues the trial court ruled that the right was personal in nature. It also ruled, however, after analyzing voluminous correspondence between the parties, that defendant had consented to the transfer. It entered judgment for the plaintiff, and the defendant appealed. (Only that part of the higher court's opinion relating to these two issues appears below.)

White, Justice:

...McDonald's was founded in 1954 by Mr. Ray Kroc. Kroc licensed and later purchased the name McDonald's [and all other rights relating thereto] from two brothers named McDonald, who were operating a hamburger restaurant in San Bernardino, California. In 1955 Kroc embarked on a plan to create a nationwide standardized system of fast-food restaurants....

At the trial, Kroc testified about the image he sought to create with McDonald's.... He wanted to create "an image people would have confidence in. An image of cleanliness. An image where the parents would be glad to have the children come and/or have them work there."

Kroc testified that careful selection of franchisees was to be the key to success for McDonald's and the establishment of this image... People were selected "who had a great deal of pride, and had an aptitude for serving the public, and had dedication."

Fred Turner, the current president of McDonald's testified [in a similar vein].... He stated that by 1957 it became apparent that McDonald's could only achieve its goal by careful selection of persons who would adhere to the company's high standards. He stated that an individual's managerial skills and abilities were a matter of prime importance in the selection process....

Summarizing, the evidence is overwhelming, [and establishes the conclusion that] the Right of First Refusal was intended to be personal in nature, and was separately a grant independent of the terms of the franchise contract itself. [It also establishes the fact that] the grant depended upon the personal confidence that McDonald's placed in the grantee, and that to permit the assignability by the grantee without permission of McDonald's would serve to destroy the basic policy of control of the quality and confidence in performance in the event any new franchises were to be granted in the locality....

[The court then reviewed the same correspondence that was studied by the trial court and ruled that McDonald's had *not* given its permission to the transfer of the right. The judgment for plaintiff was therefore reversed.]

DISCHARGE

Sooner or later all contractual obligations come to an end—that is, are "discharged." A party's obligations are most often discharged by (1) full performance on his or her part; (2) breach by the other party; or (3) the occurrence of conditions that excuse his or her performance.

The great majority of contracts are discharged by performance—both parties fully performing the acts that they have promised to do. In cases in which one party claims to have performed, while the other party contends that the performance is not completely in conformity with the contract, the question arises as to the degree of performance that the law requires of the performing party. To illustrate: C, a contractor, contracts to build a home for O, owner, according to detailed plans and specifications. The contract calls for O to make partial payments as construction progresses, with the full price being, $75,000. When C completes the job and requests the last payment of $7,500, O refuses to pay because of shortcomings in C's work. If C should sue O to recover the last payment, his success depends on whether the *doctrine of substantial performance* is applicable. Under that doctrine, a promisor or performer is entitled to the contract price (minus damages, if any) if (1) his or her performance is "substantial"—very close to 100 percent, and (2) he or she acted in good faith—that is, the defects in the performance were not intentional. Thus, in the above illustration, if the breaches on C's part were merely the failure to install insulation on one part of an attic wall and the installation of 5" drains instead of 6" drains in the basement, C will probably recover most of the $7,500. However, if C neglected to install insulation in any of the downstairs walls, his or her breach is so significant that substantial performance has not occurred, and no recovery is allowed while the shortcoming remains uncorrected.

As might be expected, when one contracting party is guilty of a material breach of contract—one so significant that substantial performance has not occurred—the other party is freed of his or her contractual duties. Additionally, the nonbreaching party is ordinarily entitled to recover damages to compensate him or her for loss that the breach has occasioned.

The UCC has its own rules governing performance of a contract for the sale of goods. Its various sections, which are subject to change by agreement of the parties, speak to the seller's responsibility to tender delivery of goods with reasonable notice to the buyer to enable him to take delivery; address the meaning of various shipping terms to make it clear where delivery is to occur and who has responsibility for the goods during shipment; and impose on the seller a "perfect tender" obligation. The "perfect tender" rule excuses a buyer from accepting goods "if the goods or the tender of delivery fail in *any* respect to conform to the contract." There are some exceptions, such as the right to "cure" an imperfect tender if the contractual time for performance has not yet expired.

The UCC also addresses the buyer's rights and obligations. For example, the buyer has an obligation to accept properly tendered conforming goods and, absent agreement to the contrary, to pay upon receiving the goods.

WARRANTIES

If goods do not perform as promised or if they are not reasonably fit for the usual purpose for which they are purchased or for the particular purpose which the buyer had in mind, the UCC's warranty provisions may provide a remedy to the disappointed buyer. These provisions are covered in some detail in Chapter 11 on products liability.

EXCUSED PERFORMANCE

In some instances, contracting parties are legally excused from performing their obligations even in the absence of a breach of contract. This most often occurs where express conditions are written into the contract that either provide (1) that the parties need not perform unless and until a specified event occurs, or (2) that the parties are freed from the obligation to perform if a specified event occurs. Clauses in the first category are called "conditions precedent," and those in the second "conditions subsequent." Thus the *failure* (non-occurrence) of a condition precedent excuses performance, and the *occurrence* of a condition subsequent has the same effect.

In limited circumstances courts will recognize implied conditions—that is, conditions recognized by the law even though they do not actually appear in the contract. Under the traditional view, for example, the courts held that, in a contract calling for the rendering of personal services, it was implied that the death or illness of the performing party would excuse performance; in a contract calling for the sale of property, it was implied that the destruction of the property (without fault on the part of the seller) before the time that possession was to be transferred would excuse performance; and in all contracts, a change of law making performance illegal would excuse performance. In these (and only these) situations, it was said that performance had become "impossible."

Today, the courts in an increasing number of states have substituted the "doctrine of commercial impracticability" for the traditional impossibility theory in cases where a party is contending that he or she is discharged by reason of the happening of some event subsequent to the time that the contract was made. Under this newer view, a number of subsequent events are recognized as grounds for the discharge of the parties *in addition to* the three events recognized under the impossibility doctrine. For example, under the UCC a contracting party is discharged under the doctrine of commercial impracticability by the occurrence of such events as (1) an unforeseen destruction of a source of supply on which the contracting party was depending for his or her performance; (2) a drastic increase in cost of performance caused by such unforeseen occurrences as war or local crop failure; and (3) any other contingency "the non-occurrence of which was a basic assumption upon which the contract was made."[7]

---

[7] Section 2-615 of the Uniform Commercial Code.

The following case discusses a bundle of doctrines—impossibility, commercial impracticability, and others—tracing their origins and rationale.

NORTHERN INDIANA PUBLIC SERVICE CO. v. CARBON COUNTY COAL CO.

SEVENTH CIRCUIT COURT OF APPEALS, 779 F.2d 265 (1986)

In 1978 Northern Indiana Public Service Company (NIPSCO), an electric utility in Indiana, contracted to buy 1.5 million tons of coal every year for 20 years, at a price of $24 a ton (subject to various provisions for escalation which by 1985 had driven the price up to $44 a ton) from Carbon County Coal Co., which operated a coal mine in Wyoming. NIPSCO's rates are regulated by the Indiana Public Service Commission, which because of complaints from consumers about higher rates, ordered NIPSCO ("the economy purchase orders") to make a good-faith effort to find and purchase electricity from other utilities who could produce it at prices lower than NIPSCO's internal generation. NIPSCO was able to buy substantial amounts of electricity from other utilities at costs below the costs of generating its own electricity using Carbon County's coal. Therefore, NIPSCO stopped accepting coal deliveries from Carbon and brought suit seeking a declaration that it was excused from its obligations under the contract. The trial court ruled against NIPSCO, and it appealed.

POSNER, JUDGE:

In the early common law a contractual undertaking unconditional in terms was not excused merely because something had happened (such as an invasion, the passage of a law, or a natural disaster) that prevented the undertaking. See *Paradine v. Jane*, Aleyn, 26, 82 Eng. Rep. 897 (K.B. 1647). Excuses had to be written into the contract; this is the origin of *force majeure* clauses. Later it came to be recognized that negotiating parties cannot anticipate all the contingencies that may arise in the performance of the contract; a legitimate judicial function in contract cases is to interpolate terms to govern remote contingencies—terms the parties would have agreed on explicitly if they had the time and foresight to make advance provision for every possible contingency in performance. Later still, it was recognized that physical impossibility was irrelevant, or at least inconclusive; a promisor might want his promise to be unconditional, not because he thought he had superhuman powers but because he could insure against the risk of nonperformance better than the promisee, or obtain a substitute performance more easily than the promisee. Thus the proper question in an "impossibility" case is not whether the promisor could not have performed his undertaking but whether his nonperformance should be excused because the parties, if they had thought about the matter, would have wanted to assign the risk of the contingency that made performance impossible or uneconomical to the promisor or to the promisee; if to the latter, the promisor is excused.

Section 2-615 of the Uniform Commercial Code takes this approach. It provides that "delay in delivery . . . by a seller . . . is not a branch of his duty under a contract for sale if performance as agreed has been made impracticable by the occurrence of a contingency the non-occurrence of which was a basic assumption on which the contract was made. . . ." Performance on schedule need not be impossible, only infeasible—provided that the event which made it infeasible was not a risk that the promisor had assumed. Notice, however, that the only type of promisor referred to is a seller; there is no suggestion that a buyer's performance might be excused by reason of impracticability. The reason is largely semantic. Ordinarily all the buyer has to do in order to perform his side of the bargain is pay, and while one can think of all sorts of reasons why, when the time came to pay, the buyer might not have the money, rarely would the seller have intended to assume the risk that the buyer might, whether through improvidence or bad luck, be unable to pay for the seller's goods or services. To deal with the rare case where the buyer or (more broadly) the

CONTINUED

paying party might have a good excuse based on some unforeseen change in circumstances, a new rubric was thought necessary, different from "impossibility" (the common law term) or "impracticability" (the Code term), and it received the name "frustration."...

The leading case on frustration remains *Krell v. Henry*, [1903] 2 K.B. 740 (C.A.). Krell rented Henry a suite of rooms for watching the coronation of Edward VII, but Edward came down with appendicitis and the coronation had to be postponed. Henry refused to pay the balance of the rent and the court held that he was excused from doing so because his purpose in renting had been frustrated by the postponement, a contingency outside the knowledge, or power to influence, of either party. The question was, to which party did the contract (implicitly) allocate the risk? Surely Henry had not intended to insure Krell against the possibility of the coronation's being postponed, since Krell could always relet the room, at the premium rental, for the coronation's new date. So Henry was excused....

Since impossibility and related doctrines are devices for shifting risk in accordance with the parties' presumed intentions, which are to minimize the costs of contract performance, one of which is the disutility created by risk, they have no place when the contract explicitly assigns a particular risk to one party or the other.... [A] fixed-price contract is an explicit assignment of the risk of market price increases to the seller and the risk of market price decreases to the buyer, and the assignment of the latter risk to the buyer is even clearer where, as in this case, the contract places a floor under price but allows for escalation. If, as is also the case here, the buyer forecasts the market incorrectly and therefore finds himself locked into a disadvantageous contract, he has only himself to blame and so cannot shift the risk back to the seller by invoking impossibility or related doctrines.... It does not matter that it is an act of government that may have made the contract less advantageous to one party. Government these days is a pervasive factor in the economy and among the risks that a fixed-price contract allocates between the parties is that of a price change induced by one of government's manifold interventions in the economy. Since "the very purpose of a fixed-price agreement is to place the risk of increased costs on the promisor (and the risk of decreased costs on the promisee)," the fact that costs decrease steeply (which is in effect what happened here—the cost of generating electricity turned out to be lower than NIPSCO thought when it signed the fixed-price contract with Carbon County) cannot allow the buyer to walk away from the contract. *In re Westinghouse Electric Corp. Uranium Contracts Litigation,* 517 F.Supp. 440, 452 (E.D.Va. 1981).

[Affirmed.]

CONTRACT INTERPRETATION

Many breach of contract lawsuits include, among other issues, a dispute as to the meaning of the contract generally or some of its specific terms. Courts attempt to determine these meanings using the processes of *interpretation* (which focuses on determining the meaning of words as used in the contract) and *construction* (which deals with the legal effect given those words).

The primary role of a court asked to interpret a contract is to determine the intent of the parties *at the time the contract was made* and to give effect to that intent. Most courts speak of an "objective" test that gauges the meaning of a contract's words by how a hypothetical "reasonably intelligent person" would understand them. However, courts often strive to determine the common intent of the contracting parties at the time they made the contract.

In relatively rare cases, the words of the contract may be the *only* evidence of the parties' intentions that a court will consider. As in statutory interpretation (see Chapter 4), there is a well-recognized *plain meaning rule*. But courts often resort to evidence outside the language of the contract, including the parties' subsequent conduct in carrying out the agreement. Courts have also developed several rules of interpretation, such as (1) the parties' *principal objective* in forming the contract must be determined and all terms construed consistently with that objective; (2) a contract will be construed to give effect to all its provisions; (3) the parties intend their contract to be legal, reasonable, and effective; (4) words and phrases are given their ordinary meaning, unless the parties indicate otherwise; (5) specific language controls general language; (6) when a contract is embodied in a printed form, any conflicting provisions added by the parties (*e.g.*, in handwritten form) will prevail over typewriting; and (7) ambiguous language is construed against the party who prepares the agreement.

The UCC has its own rules of interpretation in section 2-202, which backs away from the plain-meaning rule and focuses attention primarily on the language of the parties by assuming that the parties considered matters such as (1) course of performance (acts of the parties in carrying out the contract), (2) course of dealing (acts of the parties in carrying out previous similar contracts), and (3) usage of trade (regular practices observed in the industry) in making their agreement.

REMEDIES

If a valid, enforceable contract is made and then broken by one of the parties, the other may sue for breach of contract and select from available remedies.

DAMAGES

In virtually all breach of contract actions, the injured party is entitled to the legal remedy of **damages.** The law tries to put the successful plaintiff in the financial position that he or she would have occupied had there been no breach by the defendant. This is typically performed by ordering the defendant to pay the plaintiff a sum of money.

The plaintiff generally is entitled to recover *compensatory damages*—a sum of money equal to the actual financial loss suffered as a direct result of the breach of contract. Thus, if a seller of corn reneges on his contract and the buyer has to pay an additional $1,500 to procure the same quantity of corn elsewhere, the buyer is entitled to recover at least this difference from the seller. In any event, the plaintiff is required to prove the damages with "reasonable certainty" so that the jury is not required to speculate as to the amount of injury sustained.

In the event a breach of contract results in no financial loss to the innocent party, that person is awarded **nominal damages**—a judgment of a trifling sum, such as few cents or one dollar. This sum is awarded as a matter of principle and, additionally, permits the court to order the defendant to pay court costs.

Sometimes the parties will specify in the contract the amount of damages one party can recover in the event of a breach by the other. Such damages, called **liquidated damages,** are ordinarily given effect as long as the sum agreed on appears to have been a reasonable attempt by the parties to estimate in advance what the actual loss would be in the event of a breach. However, if the court feels that the sum was clearly excessive under the circumstances, then it is termed a "penalty" and may be ignored. In such a case the plaintiff is entitled to receive actual damages only.

The general rule is that **punitive damages** are not recoverable in cases involving mere breach of contract.

SPECIFIC PERFORMANCE, INJUNCTION, AND RESCISSION

In exceptional circumstances a plaintiff may be entitled to a **decree of specific performance**—an order requiring the defendant to perform his or her contractual obligations. Although plaintiffs would frequently prefer this remedy, the court generally will grant it only when they believe that money damages will not fully compensate the plaintiff. Thus, if S contracts to sell his farm to B for $225,000 and later refuses to convey the property a court will order him to do so if B requests such action. The theory is that each parcel of land is, of and by itself, necessarily unique—even though similar land may be available nearby.

Whereas a decree of specific performance orders a defendant to perform a promise he has made, an **injunction** orders the defendant not to do that which he has contracted not to do. For example, if A sells his business to B and promises not to compete with B within the business's trade area for a reasonable time, yet soon thereafter breaches that promise by opening a competing store, a court might well grant B's request for an injunction barring A from operating the new store.

Under certain circumstances, such as where A contracts with B and later learns that B had made fraudulent representations to induce A to enter the contract or that B has already breached the contract himself, the party in A's position can bring suit requesting the remedy of **rescission**—a court-ordered cancellation of the contract.

REMEDIES IN SALES CONTRACTS

Where the buyer breaches the contract, the seller has a number of remedies available. These remedies under section 2-703 are the rights (1) to cancel the contract, (2) to withhold delivery, (3) to stop delivery when the goods are in the hands of a carrier, (4) to resell the goods and recover damages, and (5) to retain the goods and recover damages for non-acceptance. Each of these remedies is available only under certain circumstances—for example, a seller obviously cannot withhold delivery if the buyer's breach occurs after delivery. Thus, when any breach occurs by the buyer, the seller must study sections 2-704 through 2-710 to determine which precise remedy or remedies are available.

When the seller breaches the contract, the buyer's remedies under section 2-711 are the rights (1) to cancel, (2) to "cover" (by buying the goods elsewhere) and to recover damages, (3) to recover damages for non-delivery, and (4) to obtain the actual goods from the seller, in exceptional circumstances. Again, certain conditions must be met before any of these remedies is available.

TITLE AND RISK OF LOSS

One problem that is largely unique to the sale of goods and is therefore governed by the UCC relates to the question of when in the course of a sale of goods the title thereto transfers from the seller to the buyer. After a sales contract is made, some amount of time will usually pass before the goods are actually delivered to the buyer. In exceptional cases, several events may occur during this time that raise problems relative to *title* (ownership) and *risk of loss*. A creditor of the seller, for example, may bring a legal action seeking attachment (possession) of the goods while they are in the seller's hands—an action that will normally be successful only if title had not passed to the buyer before the attachment. Or the goods may be damaged while in the hands of a trucking company en route to the buyer, thereby requiring a court to determine which party had the risk of loss at the time the damage occurred.

The rules for determining the time of passing of title and passing of risk of loss are governed by separate sections of article 2. However, the rules in most instances bring about the same results. Thus, in our discussion of the risk of loss rules below, it may be assumed that title passes at the same time as the risk of loss, with one exception to be noted.

RISK OF LOSS

Section 2-509 governs passage of risk of loss. It first provides that the parties may, by agreement, decide when risk of loss passes. In the absence of agreement, this section contains rules applicable to three basic classifications of contracts.

Classification 1: In many contracts the parties "contemplate delivery" of the goods—for example, the buyer and seller are located in different cities, and the goods will be delivered by a common carrier (such as a trucking company). In such a situation, if the contract is a "shipment contract," risk of loss normally passes to the buyer when the seller delivers the goods to the carrier. By contrast, if the contract is a "destination contract," risk of loss does not pass until the goods reach their destination—usually the buyer's place of business—and are "duly tendered" to the buyer.[8] To illustrate:

---

[8] A due tender occurs when the buyer is given notice that the goods have arrived and are available to him or her. (The next case in the chapter presents a real-life situation in which determination of the precise time of tender was necessary for the court to decide whether the risk of loss had, or had not, passed to the buyer before the goods' theft.)

(A) The S Company, in Chicago, sells 50 motors to the B Company in Phoenix. The contract price is "$25,000 f.o.b. Chicago." Because of the f.o.b. term, this is a shipment contract. Thus if the goods are damaged or lost en route to Phoenix, the B Company—having the risk at that time—must still pay for them.

(B) Same case as above, except that the contract price is "$25,000 f.o.b. Phoenix." Because of the f.o.b. term, this is a destination contract. Thus if the goods are damaged or lost en route to Phoenix, the B Company need not pay for them (and the seller has an obligation to make a second shipment).

Classification 2: In situations in which the parties do not contemplate delivery, the goods are often in the hands of a *bailee,* such as an independent warehouse, when the contract is made. At the time that the seller deposits the goods, he or she usually receives a "negotiable warehouse receipt" from the warehouseman as evidence of the transaction. The general rule in such a case is that risk of loss passes to the buyer when the buyer receives the warehouse receipt from the seller. Special rules apply if the warehouse receipt is nonnegotiable or if no receipt was issued by the warehouse.

Classification 3: In contracts not falling into the first two classifications, the usual understanding is that the buyer will pick up the goods at the seller's place of business. Where the seller is a merchant, as is usually the case, *title* passes to the buyer when he or she is notified by the seller that the goods are available for pickup, but *risk of loss* does not pass until the buyer actually takes possession of the goods. Where the seller is not a merchant, title and risk both pass to the buyer when the seller notifies him or her that the goods are available.

The case below presents a typical risk of loss question.

SCHOCK v. RONDEROS

SUPREME COURT OF NORTH DAKOTA 394 N.W.2d 697 (1986)

Schock (Buyer) negotiated to buy a mobile home that was owned by the Ronderoses (Sellers) and located on their property. On April 15, 1985, Buyer went to Sellers' home and paid them the agreed purchase price of $3,900. Buyer received a bill of sale and an assurance from Sellers that title would be delivered soon. With Sellers' permission, Buyer prepared the mobile home for removal. Buyer intended to remove the home from Sellers' property on the following Monday, April 22. Sellers had no objection to the mobile home remaining on their premises until that time. They agreed to remove a piano and davenport that were still in the home and to disconnect the electricity and natural gas.

On Friday, April 19, the mobile home was destroyed by high winds as it sat on Sellers' property. Buyer received in the mail a clear certificate of title on April 23. Buyer later filed this suit for return of the purchase price, arguing that when the home was destroyed, the risk of loss was on the Sellers. The trial judge ruled for Sellers on this claim, and Buyer appealed.

CONTINUED

ERICKSTAD, CHIEF JUSTICE:

The issue of which party in this case must bear the loss of the mobile home is determined by the risk of loss provisions of [UCC 2-509], which provide in relevant part:

> 3. In any case not within subsection 1 or 2, the risk of loss passes to the buyer on his receipt of the goods if the seller is a merchant; otherwise the risk passes to the buyer on tender of delivery.

It is undisputed that the Sellers are not merchants; therefore, the risk of loss was on them until they made a "tender of delivery" of the mobile home at which time the risk of loss passed to Buyer. The location or status of the title is not a relevant consideration in determining which party must bear the loss of the mobile home.

Pursuant to [UCC 2-503], tender of delivery requires that the seller "put and hold conforming goods at the buyer's disposition...." the trial court determined that there had been payment for and acceptance of the mobile home by Buyer. Within that conclusion is an implicit determination that there was a completed tender of delivery by Sellers.

The Sellers disconnected the electricity and natural gas to the mobile home prior to its destruction, and nothing remained for them to do as a prerequisite to Buyer's taking possession of the home other than the removal of the piano and davenport. Under the circumstances of this case, we believe that their failure to remove those items did not result in an uncompleted tender of delivery. The Sellers testified that following Buyer's payment for the home on April 15, 1985, Buyer could have removed the home from their premises at any time. They further testified that if Buyer had expressed a desire to remove the home prior to Monday, April 22, 1985, they would have removed the piano and davenport immediately so that he could have done so. The Sellers, consistent with a completed tender of delivery, acquiesced in Buyer's decision to prepare, on April 15, 1985, the mobile home for removal. As part of those preparations Buyer removed the skirting, the tie downs, and the [foundation] blocks. He also removed and took with him a set of steps to the mobile home. We believe those actions by the Buyer constituted an exercise of possession which is consistent with our conclusion that Sellers had tendered delivery of the mobile home to him on that date. Thus, we hold that on April 15, 1985, the Sellers tendered delivery of the mobile home and the risk of loss passed to Buyer.

[Affirmed.]

INTERNATIONALIZATION OF CONTRACT LAW

Virtually no area of American law has escaped the increasing influence of internationalization of business transactions. Contract law is no exception, as expert E. Allan Farnsworth recently listed "internationalization" as one of the top ten developments in contract law during the 1980s.[9] Most prominently, the United Nations promulgated (and the United States and more than 20 other nations adopted) the Convention on Contracts for the International Sale of Goods (CISG). Roughly equivalent to an international UCC, the CISG replaces most of article 2 in contracts among parties from signatory nations. The CISG is discussed in some detail in Chapter 21.

---

[9] Farnsworth, *Developments in Contract Law During the 1980's: The Top Ten,* 41 Case W. Res. L. Rev. 203 (1990)

Questions and Problems

1. P owned a crane, which it leased to Ashton Co. for use in a construction project. When Ashton completed the project, it hired D trucking company to transport the crane back to P. Before transporting the crane, D, without the permission of P or Ashton, used the crane to put into place a transformer for a utility company and was paid $6,000. When P learned of this, it sued D to recover the $6,000. D pointed out that it had no contract with P and that under the terms of the Ashton lease, P did not even have a right to demand that the crane be returned before the date D used the crane. Will P recover? Under what theory? (*Artukovich, Inc. v. Reliance Truck Co.*, 614 P.2d 327, Ariz. 1980.)

2. A corporation employed a contractor to build a barn. Later the contractor quit the job, leaving the subcontractor unpaid. A corporation officer then told the subcontractor to finish the job and promised that the corporation would pay him for his time and materials. Later the subcontractor finished the job, but the corporation refused to pay the amount that the subcontractor demanded. (It was, however, willing to pay a lesser sum.) In the ensuing lawsuit the corporation contended that no contract had ever been entered into here; the subcontractor, however, argued that the corporation had made a unilateral offer that he, the subcontractor, had accepted by the act of completing the barn. Do you agree with the corporation that no contract of any kind was entered into here? Why or why not? (*Redd v. Woodford County Swine Breeders, Inc.*, 370 N.E.2d 152, 1977.)

3. Blakeslee, who wished to buy some land owned by the Nelsons, wrote a letter to them asking if they would accept "$49,000 net" for the property. The Nelsons replied that they would "not sell for less than $56,000," whereupon Blakeslee wired back, "Accept your offer of $56,000 net." (*Blakeslee v. Nelson*, 207 N.Y.S. 676, 1925.) Does a contract now exist between the parties? Explain.

4. Dorton ordered substantial quantities of carpets from Collins & Aikman Corp. Collins & Aikman responded by sending a sales acknowledgement form. The language of the form purported to accept Dorton's offer to buy, but it also stated: "Acceptance of your order is subject to all of the terms and conditions on the face and reverse sides hereof." The acknowledgment listed several terms that were not in Dorton's offer, including the provision that disputes arising out of the contract must be submitted to arbitration. (*Dorton v. Collins & Aikman Corp.*, 453 F.2d 1161, 1972.) Was Collins & Aikman's acknowledgment an acceptance of Dorton's offer? Discuss.

5. P, a general contractor, intended to bid on a Navy contract to build housing for sailors. The deadline for submission of bids was 2:00 P.M. on August 11, 1981. The last half hour before the deadline was, as is typical in such matters, very hectic. At about 1:30 P.M., D, a potential subcontractor, telephoned P and quoted a price to supply all hollow metal doors and frames required by the Navy's specifications. The price promised was $193,121. P based its computations on this figure and was awarded the contract. Later, D refused to perform and P was forced to find another subcontractor to supply the doors and frames, paying $45,562 more than D's quoted price. P sued D for the difference. D argued (accurately) that there had been no promise by P to use D's doors even if P received the bid. Therefore, D argued that there was no consideration to support D's promise. Can P recover in this case? On what theory? (*Allen M. Campbell Co. v. Virginia Metal Indus.*, 708 F.2d 930, 4th Cir. 1983.)

6. After losing his race for the U.S. Senate, Collins did not pay the $29,526.98 he owed for campaign posters that the Williamson Printing Corporation had printed for him and that his supporters had spread around the state. Williamson sued for breach of contract. Collins defended by proving that there was no written contract. Is this a good defense? (*Collins v. Williamson Printing Corporation*, 746 S.W.2d 489, Tex.App. 1988.)

7. Northern Corporation contracted with Chugach Electric Association to quarry, transport, and install large quantities of rock ("riprap") on the upstream face of a dam on Cooper Lake in Alaska. The parties originally contemplated that the rock would be obtained from a specific quarry, but when it proved unsuitable, they amended the contract by adding to the price and allowing Northern to use alternative sites. Northern selected a site at the opposite end of the lake, intending to transport the rock across the lake on the ice during winter. The contract did not specify a means of transportation, but Chugach authorized Northern to transport the rock "across Cooper Lake to the dam site when such lake is frozen to a sufficient depth to permit heavy vehicle traffic thereon." In two successive winters, the ice was never thick enough to allow Northern to transport the rock across the ice. It lost four vehicles and two drivers in the attempt. Northern then advised Chugach that it considered the contract "terminated for impossibility of performance." Was the contract impossible to perform? If so, should Northern recover its expenses incurred in trying to perform? Discuss. (*Northern Corporation v. Chugach Electric Association,* 518 P.2d 76, Alaska 1974.)

8. In 1622, a fleet of Spanish treasure ships sank off the coast of Florida. Treasure Salvors, Inc. (TSI) located one of the wrecked ships. TSI and the state of Florida both believed that the ship's location was in an area within Florida's legal jurisdiction, so they entered into a series of annual contracts giving TSI the right to search and salvage in return for paying 25 percent of the booty located to the state. Later, a court ruled that this particular strip of the continental shelf was *not,* in fact, within Florida's legal jurisdiction. TSI sued to rescind the contract it had with Florida. Discuss the likelihood of success of TSI's suit. (*Florida v. Treasure Salvors, Inc.,* 651 F.2d 1340, 5th Cir. 1980.)

9. The City of Spokane hired Keltch to construct storm sewers. The contract form, provided by the city, stated that "Sales tax on this Contract ... will be added to the amount due...." The city's bid form instructed bidders to omit sales taxes from their proposal. The final total read: "Total Bid Price (Not Including Sales Tax) $_____." Keltch claims that these documents indicate that he is entitled to be paid for the sales tax he paid on materials he purchased for installation. The city claims that the provisions simply reflect that the city is exempt from sales tax and that it does not have to reimburse Keltch for sales tax on materials. What rule of interpretation might help resolve this dispute? (*See Universal/Land Construction Co. v. City of Spokane,* 745 P.2d 53, Wash.App. 1987.)

10. Eikon Corporation was in the medical records business, a highly competitive field. D worked in an executive capacity for Eikon and at one time had been one of its owners. In 1986, Eikon was purchased by MRS, and at that time D was hired by MRS and orally agreed not to compete with MRS in the medical records business in Houston and San Antonio (where D's work had been) for three years after his leaving MRS's employment. Not long thereafter, D quit at MRS and went to work for a competing company in the Houston area, taking some of MRS's customers with him. MRS sued to enforce the covenant-not-to-compete. Discuss MRS's chances of success. (*MRS Datascope v. Exchange Data Corp.,* 745 S.W.2d 542, Tex.App. 1988.)

CHAPTER 10

A PREFACE

Two areas of law, criminal law and contract law, developed at an early time in England. Although both were intended to eliminate, insofar as possible, various kinds of wrongful conduct, each was concerned with markedly different wrongs. The major purposes of criminal law were to define wrongs against the state—types of conduct so inherently undesirable that they were flatly prohibited—and to permit the state to punish those who committed such acts by the imposition of fines or imprisonment. The major purposes of contract law, however, were

GENERAL TORT LAW

(1) to spell out the nature of the rights and duties springing from *private agreements between individuals* and (2) in the event that one party failed to live up to these duties, to compensate the innocent party for the loss resulting from the other's breach of contract.

Although criminal law and contract law were in their initial stages of development, it became apparent that neither one afforded protection to the large numbers of persons who suffered losses resulting from other kinds of conduct equally unjustifiable from a social standpoint—acts of carelessness, deception, and the like. Faced with this situation, the courts at an early time began to recognize and define other "legal wrongs" besides crimes and breaches of contract—and began to permit persons who were injured thereby to bring civil actions to recover damages against those who committed them. Acts that came to be recognized as wrongs under these rules, which were formulated by judges over the years on a case-by-case basis, acquired the name of **torts** (the French word for "*wrongs*").

Because tort law applies to such a wide range of activities, any introductory definition of tort must necessarily be framed in general terms—as, for example, "any wrong excluding breaches of contract and crimes," or "any noncontractual civil wrong committed upon the person or property of another." Although such definitions are of little aid in illustrating the specific kinds of torts that are recognized, they do, at least, reflect the historic lines of demarcation between breaches of contract, crimes, and torts.[1]

SCOPE AND COMPLEXITY OF TORT LAW

As our society has become increasingly industrialized and complex, with many relationships existing among individuals that were perhaps unthought of 50 years ago, the legal duties owed by one member of society to others have become considerably more numerous and varied. As a result, tort law encompasses such a wide range of human conduct that the breaches of some duties have little in common with others. For example, some actions are considered tortious (wrongful) only when the actor intended to cause an injury, whereas in other actions—especially those involving negligence—the actor's intentions are immaterial. Similarly, in some tort actions the plaintiff is required to show physical injury to his or her property as a result of the defendant's misconduct, whereas in other actions such a showing is not required. In the latter situations other kinds of legal injury are recognized, such as damage to reputation or mental suffering.

---

[1] As indicated by these definitions, torts and crimes are essentially two different kinds of wrongs—the first a wrong against the individual and the second a wrong against the state. However, as we will see, in many situations a single wrongful act can constitute both a tort and a crime.

A somewhat clearer picture of the broad sweep of tort law can be gained from the realization that the rules making up this area of law must deal with such diverse matters as the care required of a surgeon in the operating room, the circumstances in which a contracting party has a legal obligation to inform the other party of facts that he or she knows that the other party does not possess, and the determination of the kinds of business information (trade secrets) that are entitled to protection against theft by competitors.

The courts clearly engage in some degree of social engineering as they shape the common law of torts. Common to all successful tort actions are the twin concepts of *interest* and *duty*. Each time a court allows tort recovery, it is saying that the plaintiff has an interest (for example, in bodily integrity, in enjoying the benefits of private property, in a good reputation) sufficiently important for the law to furnish protection and that, correspondingly, in a civilized society the defendant has a duty (for example, not to strike the plaintiff, not to steal plaintiff's property, not to falsely injure plaintiff's reputation) that was breached. As society evolves technologically, morally, philosophically, and otherwise, tort law will evolve also. For example, 100 years ago, Americans had very little privacy. However, as increased wealth has allowed us to purchase and enjoy privacy, most of us have come to value privacy very much. In recent years most courts have come to recognize privacy as an interest worth protecting and, as we shall see, have imposed a duty on others not to invade our privacy.

The law of torts is so broad and so pervasive that it cannot be treated in a single chapter. This chapter focuses on the law of negligence and on certain intentional torts. A number of torts of specific concern to business are discussed in Chapter 12. Lawsuits arising out of the sale of defective products are also primarily tort-related; they are discussed in Chapter 11. Although these three chapters are devoted almost solely to tort law, the subject will make appearances in several other chapters.[2]

This chapter begins with a treatment of negligence law and then studies several important intentional torts.

NEGLIGENCE

Negligence, to oversimplify, is carelessness. The courts long ago decided that our interests in economic well-being and personal safety are sufficiently important to be protected from the careless acts of others. Correspondingly, each of us has a duty as we live our lives and carry on our professions to exercise care not to carelessly injure others. Even though we may not intend

---

[2] For example, Chapter 13 (liability of parties in an agency relationship), and Chapter 20 (consumer transactions and the law).

HUMOR AND THE LAW

There is a rule of law known as the "no harm in asking rule." This is a great rule. The basic idea is that A may ask B: "Would you like to have sex with me?" (or words to that effect), because B might think this is a great idea. Certainly there can be no harm in asking. Magruder, *Mental and Emotional Disturbance in the Law of Torts*, 49 HARVARD LAW REVIEW 1033 (1936).

However, a corollary rule might be formulated: "No means no!" If B says "no", A should get the message. Repeated inquiries, which are often accompanied by more aggressive activities, quickly escalate into the types of outrageous and harassing actions that may well constitute the tort of intentional infliction of emotional distress. Recovery has been allowed, for example, where defendant made uninvited, unwelcome, and repeated requests for sexual favors from a married woman. Defendant went so far as to go to plaintiff's house in order to expose for the plaintiff's viewing those portions of himself that she was missing due to her refusal of his advances. See *Samms v. Eccles*, 184 P.2d 289 (Utah 1961).

Sometimes, college age males can be a little dense in this area. For example, in one case, defendant was at a tavern when he grabbed the hips of a female college student he did not know, bit her buttocks, and then laughed and exchanged "high-fives" with his friends. Although defendant claimed that he considered his actions to be a "compliment," the jury sent the message that this kind of activity is not considered "funny" anymore (if it ever was), awarding plaintiff damages in the sum of $27,500. *Brodie v. Hurth*, (Mo. 1990).

---

to injure, the harm is just as real to the victim who is struck by the careless driver, burned by the carelessly designed product, crippled by the careless surgeon, or ruined financially by embezzlement that an accountant carelessly failed to detect.

The negligence cause of action is the most important method of redress existing today for persons injured accidentally. The newspapers are filled with accounts of negligence actions involving asbestos exposure, Agent Orange, the Exxon *Valdez* oil spill in Alaska, and the like. Whether a plaintiff was injured by a careless driver, a careless product designer, a careless surgeon, or a careless accountant, the same basic elements must be proved to establish a right of recovery: (1) that defendant owed plaintiff a *duty* of due care; (2) that defendant *breached* that duty of due care; (3) that defendant's breach *proximately caused* the injury; and (4) that plaintiff suffered *injury*.

DUTY

Few concepts are more fraught with difficulty than that of "duty" in the negligence cause of action. As a general rule, it may be said that we each owe a duty to every person whom we can *reasonably foresee* might be injured by our carelessness. If we drive down the street carelessly, pedestrians and other drivers are within the class of foreseeable plaintiffs whom we might injure. That we do not know the exact names of our prospective victims is unimportant.

To quickly illustrate, in *Burke v. Pan American World Airways, Inc*,[3] the plaintiff sued the defendants allegedly responsible for a terrible plane collision in the Canary Islands, claiming that she, although in California at the time, felt as though she were being "split in two" and felt an emptiness "like a black hole" at the exact instant of the crash. The plaintiff claimed that in that instant she knew that something terrible had happened to her identical twin sister, who was, in fact, killed in the collision. The plaintiff was prepared to document the phenomenon of "extrasensory empathy" between some pairs of identical twins. Even assuming the plaintiff could establish the point, the court dismissed the suit. When a plane crashes because of an airline's negligence, its passengers are certainly foreseeable plaintiffs, as are any persons on the ground hit by falling wreckage. However, Burke's injuries were too bizarre to be reasonably foreseeable, even if she did sustain them. The defendants owed no legal duty to plaintiff.

Although foreseeability is a very important consideration in establishing the parameters of a careless actor's duty, it is not the only one. The California courts, which have extended the notion of duty about as far as any jurisdiction, have taken into account such factors as:

> ...*the foreseeability of harm to the plaintiff, the degree of certainty that the plaintiff suffered injury, the closeness of the connection between the defendant's conduct and the injury suffered, the moral blame attached to the defendant's conduct, the policy of preventing future harm, the extent of the burden to the defendant and consequences to the community of imposing a duty to exercise care with resulting liability, and the availability, cost, and prevalence of insurance for the risk involved.*[4]

Indeed, these are the factors the court used in *Soldano v. O'Daniels,* a case discussed in Chapter 1, to impose a duty not to interfere with a Good Samaritan's attempt to aid a victim in distress.

The following case is just one illustration of a court's struggle to meld foreseeability and public policy factors to produce a proper scope of duty.

---

[3] 484 F.Supp. 850 (S.D.N.Y. 1980).
[4] *Rowland v. Christian,* 70 Cal. Rptr. 97 (1968).

Otis Engineering Corp. v. Clark

TEXAS SUPREME COURT, 668 S.W.2d 307 (1983)

Matheson, an employee of defendant Otis Engineering Corporation, had a history of being intoxicated on the job. One night he was particularly intoxicated, and his fellow employees believed he should be removed from the machines. Roy, Matheson's supervisor, suggested that Matheson go home, escorted him to the company parking lot, and asked him if he could make it home. Matheson answered that he could, but 30 minutes later and some 3 miles away he caused an accident killing the wives of plaintiffs Larry and Clifford Clark.

The Clarks sued Otis in a wrongful death action, but the trial court dismissed the suit, holding that Otis could not be liable because Matheson was not acting within the scope of his employment at the time of the accident. The intermediate court of appeals reversed, and Otis appealed to the Texas Supreme Court.

KILGARLIN, JUSTICE:

The Clarks contend that under the facts in this case Otis sent home, in the middle of his shift, an employee whom it knew to be intoxicated. They aver this was an affirmative act which imposed a duty on Otis to act in a non-negligent manner.

In order to establish tort liability, a plaintiff must initially prove the existence and breach of a duty owed to him by the defendant. As a general rule, one person is under no duty to control the conduct of another, *Restatement (Second) of Torts* §315 (1965), even if he has the practical ability to exercise such control. Yet, certain relationships do impose, as a matter of law, certain duties upon parties. For instance, the master–servant relationship may give rise to a duty on the part of the master to control the conduct of his servants outside the scope of employment. This duty, however, is a narrow one. Ordinarily, the employer is liable only for the off-duty torts of his employees which are committed on the employer's premises or with the employer's chattels.

Though the decisional law of this State has yet to address the precise issues presented by this case, factors which should be considered in determining whether the law should impose a duty are the risk, foreseeability, and likelihood of injury weighed against the social utility of the actor's conduct, the magnitude of the burden of guarding against the injury and consequences of placing that burden on the employer.

While a person is generally under no legal duty to come to the aid of another in distress, he is under a duty to avoid any affirmative act which might worsen the situation. One who voluntarily enters an affirmative course of action affecting the interests of another is regarded as assuming a duty to act and must do so with reasonable care.

Otis contends that, at worst, its conduct amounted to nonfeasance and under established law it owed no duty to the Clarks' respective wives. Traditional tort analysis has long drawn a distinction between action and inaction in defining the scope of duty. However, although courts have been slow to recognize liability for nonfeasance, "[d]uring the last century, liability for 'nonfeasance' has been extended still further to a limited group of relations, in which custom, public sentiment and views of social policy have led the courts to find a duty of affirmative action." W. Prosser, *The Law of Torts* at 339. Be that as it may, we do not view this as a case of employer nonfeasance.

What we must decide is if changing social standards and increasing complexities of human relationships in today's society justify imposing a duty upon an employer to act reasonably when he exercises control over his servants. Even though courts have been reluctant to hold an employer liable for the off-duty torts of an employee, "[a]s between an entirely innocent plaintiff and a defendant who admittedly has departed from the social standard of conduct, if only toward one individual, who should bear the loss?" W. Prosser, *supra*, at 257. Dean Prosser additionally observed that "[t]here is nothing sacred about 'duty,' which is nothing more than a word, and a very indefinite one with which we state our conclusion."

During this year, we have taken a step toward changing our concept of duty in premises cases. In *Corbin v. Safeway*

CONTINUED

Stores Inc., 648 S.W.2d 292 (Tex. 1983), we held that a store owner has a duty to guard against slips and falls if he has actual or constructive knowledge of a dangerous condition and it is foreseeable a fall would occur. Following *Corbin*, why should we be reluctant to impose a duty on Otis? As Dean Prosser has observed, "[c]hanging social conditions lead constantly to the recognition of new duties. No better general statement can be made than the courts will find a duty where, in general, reasonable men would recognize and agree that it exists."

Therefore, the standard of duty that we now adopt for this and all other cases currently in the judicial process, is: when, because of an employee's incapacity, an employer exercises control over the employee, the employer has a duty to take such action as a reasonably prudent employer under the same or similar circumstances would take to prevent the employee from causing an unreasonable risk of harm to others. The duty of the employer is not an absolute duty to insure safety, but requires only reasonable care.

Therefore, the trier of fact in this case should be left free to decide whether Otis acted as a reasonable and prudent employer considering the following factors: the availability of the nurses' aid station [on the plant premises], a possible phone call to Mrs. Matheson, having another employee drive Matheson home, and the foreseeable consequences of Matheson's driving upon a public street in his stuperous condition.

[Affirm judgment of court of appeals and remand to trial court.]

Duty of Landowners

A recurring problem in establishing the nature of a duty exists regarding the responsibility of owners or occupiers of land. How much of a duty they owe to visitors to their land has traditionally turned on whether the visitor was a trespasser (one who enters the land with no right to do so), a licensee (one who has a right to come onto the property for self-benefit, such as a door-to-door salesman or a neighbor dropping in uninvited), or an invitee (one invited by the owner or occupier or who enters for the benefit of the owner or occupier, such as a customer at a store). Under this traditional approach (which is still the majority view), trespassers could sue only for intentional torts, licensees could sue also for hidden dangers they should have been warned about, and invitees could sue under the ordinary rules of negligence. Several recent cases have rejected this tripartite approach, not differentiating between plaintiffs and treating all defendants in this context under the general rules of negligence "governed by the test of reasonable care under all the circumstances in the maintenance and operation of their property." *Oulette v. Blanchard*, 364 A.2d 631 (N.H. 1976).

BREACH

To be liable for negligence, a defendant must *breach* an existing duty. A breach occurs when defendant fails to exercise the same care as a "reasonable person under similar circumstances" would have exercised. This hypothetical "reasonable person" or "reasonable man" standard can be fairly strict because of a jury's tendency, confronted with a seriously injured plaintiff, to use 20-20 hindsight:

> [The reasonable man] is one who invariably looks where he is going and is careful to examine the immediate foreground before he executes a leap or bound; who neither star-gazes nor is lost in meditation when approaching trap doors or the margin of a dock; ... who never mounts a moving omnibus, and does not alight from any car while the train is still in motion ... and who informs himself of the history and habits of a dog before administering a caress.[5]

All the Circumstances

Whether or not a defendant's conduct met the "reasonable person" standard of care should be examined in light of all the circumstances of the case. Emergency conditions, for example, may be considered. Normally it would be a clear breach of due care to abandon a moving vehicle, but if a cab driver does so because a robber in his or her back seat has pulled a gun, a jury might determine that, under all the circumstances, there was no breach of due care to render the cab company liable to a pedestrian who was struck by the driverless cab.[6] An unexpected bee sting might cause a bus driver unavoidably to lose control of a bus, though he was a most careful driver.[7]

The custom of others in the community or of other companies in the industry may also shed light on the proper standard of due care. If the defendant has acted in the same manner as most others in the same situation, it is difficult to conclude that a reasonable person standard was breached. However, custom is not always binding. In one famous case, barges were lost at sea because the tugs towing them had no radio sets to listen to weather reports that would have warned them to take shelter from an approaching storm. That few tug companies used the radio set was not proof that the "reasonable person" standard was met, because "a whole calling may have unduly lagged in the adoption of new and available devices."[8]

Conduct of Others

Traditionally the courts allowed us to assume that other members of society would act carefully and lawfully. In other words, we had no duty to anticipate the negligent or criminal acts of others. However, increasingly courts and juries are concluding that such acts can and must be anticipated in certain circumstances. Thus, operators of a motel located in a high crime area that has itself been the scene of criminal acts in the past may be held to have breached a duty of due care by not providing adequate security for guests who are victimized by crime.[9] Though some courts refuse to impose a

---

[5] A. P. Herbert, *Uncommon Law: Fardell v. Potts*. Reprinted by permission of Lady Herbert.
[6] *Cordas v. Peerless Transp. Co.*, 27 N.Y.S.2d 198 (N.Y. 1941).
[7] *Schultz v. Cheney School District*, 371 P.2d 59 (Wash. 1962).
[8] *The T. J. Hooper*, 60 F.2d 737 (2d Cir. 1932).
[9] *Garzilli v. Howard Johnson's Motor Lodges, Inc.*, 419 F.Supp. 1210 (E.D.N.Y. 1976) (the "Connie Francis case").

duty in such circumstances, providing adequate security is increasingly a concern for motel owners, common carriers, store owners, concert promoters, and even universities.

Negligence *Per Se*

Although the standard of care to which a defendant will be held in a negligence case is usually formulated by the jury's assessment of what a reasonable person would have done, in some cases the conduct is measured in accordance with legislative imposed standards. One example is a "dramshop" act, which many states have passed making it illegal to sell liquor to an intoxicated person. Another is the 65-mile-per-hour speed limit.

Most courts have held that if a defendant violates such a statute, it is negligence *per se*.[10] That is, if the plaintiff can show that he or she is within the class of persons that the statute was meant to protect and the harm sustained was the type the statute was meant to prevent, the issue of breach of due care is conclusively resolved against the defendant. The jury can be instructed that the defendant has breached the duty of due care. Lack of damages or proximate causation still might prevent recovery.

In one case, a small girl was abducted from the street in front of the building in which she lived, taken across the street to an open, vacant apartment, and assaulted. The girl sued the owners of the apartment building in which the assault occurred for not having locks on the doors, in violation of a city ordinance, and thereby providing a tempting location for the crime. Emphasizing that the ordinance was intended to provide security against crime by requiring all vacant apartments to be secured, the court found negligence *per se* in its violation.[11]

Many courts do not go quite so far, holding only that violation of a statute is one factor the jury can consider among all others in deciding whether the defendant breached the duty of due care.

PROXIMATE CAUSE

After proving existence and breach of a duty of due care, the plaintiff in a negligence action must demonstrate that the breach proximately caused the plaintiff's alleged injuries. There are many different labels and many different approaches to the proximate cause concept. Fundamentally, **proximate cause** means direct cause—that there is a direct causal connection between the defendant's act of carelessness and the plaintiff's injury—but it is more complicated than that.

"Legal cause," according to many courts, has two requirements. First, *causation in fact* must be shown. Some courts stress that defendant's carelessness must be a *substantial factor* in bringing about the injury and without which no harm would have occurred. In other words, can we say that "but

---

[10] And, of course, if a plaintiff violates such a statute it is comparative negligence *per se*. This is a concept we shall address directly under the topic of "defenses."
[11] *Nixon v. Mr. Property Management Co.*, 690 S.W.2d 546 (Tex. 1985).

for" the defendant's act the injuries would not have happened? For example, assume that Jill is driving her car at 40 miles per hour on a street where the speed limit is 30 miles per hour when a small child darts into the street from between two cars and is hit by Jill's car. Assume further that the child was so close to Jill's car when he darted into the street that even had Jill been driving 30 miles per hour, or even 20, she could not have avoided striking the child. In such a case we cannot say that "but for" Jill's speeding the accident would not have happened. Jill's careless speeding was not a proximate cause of the accident, and Jill would not be liable.

"But for" causation is insufficient in and of itself, however. Almost every act has consequences that ripple through society, and every incident has several causes. Perhaps "but for" your carelessly running a stop sign, ambulance driver A would never have met nurse B and had child C who at the age of 14 years murdered D. May D's family sue you? Obviously not. For policy reasons, we must limit the liability stemming from our actions in some fashion.

Most courts return to the notion of *foreseeability* in establishing the second element of legal causation. Factual causation ("but for") plus foreseeability will establish proximate or legal causation. Because foreseeability is an important factor in the establishment of both duty and proximate cause, court discussions of the two concepts tend to overlap.

The most famous tort case of all time is perhaps *Palsgraf v. Long Island R.R.*,[12] in which railway employees carelessly pushed a passenger who was trying to board a train. This caused him to drop a package he was carrying which, in turned out, contained fireworks that exploded beneath the wheels of the train. The force of the concussion knocked over a scale at the far end of the train station, injuring Mrs. Palsgraf. Injury to the boarding passenger and his property was a foreseeable result of the negligence of the railroad employees. They owed a duty of care to him and any injuries to him would have been proximately caused by their actions. However, the court found the injury to Mrs. Palsgraf unforeseeable. The duty owed to the boarding passenger did not protect her.

The *Palsgraf* dissent argued that every person owes to the world a duty to refrain from careless acts and that we should be liable for all injuries flowing directly from our negligence, regardless of foreseeability. The dissenters felt the wrongdoer should be liable for all "proximate consequence," even when they consist of injuries to persons outside the foreseeable radius of danger.

Generally speaking, the "foreseeability" test of *Palsgraf* holds sway in our law today, but the "direct consequences" view of the dissent is frequently applied in various circumstances. For example, if we carelessly injure a person who turns out to be a hemophiliac, who then bleeds to death when most persons would not have, we are still liable for the death. Courts say that we must take our victims as we find them. Although it might not be

---

[12] 162 N.E. 99 (N.Y. 1928).

reasonably foreseeable to us that our victim would be a hemophiliac, his death is a direct result of our carelessness.

Independent Intervening Cause

Especially in terms of foreseeability, the concept of **independent intervening cause** is important. Such a cause is one that emanates from a third party or source to disrupt the causal connection between the defendant's careless act and the plaintiff's injury. Assume that Sue is driving down the street when she comes to an intersection that is blocked by an accident caused by Joe's having run a stop sign. Sue turns her car around and while driving away is hit by a tree that is blown down by a strong wind. Sue can argue that "but for" Joe's carelessness the intersection would not have been blocked and she would have been several miles away from the tree at the time it fell over. But should we hold Joe liable for Sue's injury? No, because the tree's falling is an independent, intervening cause that breaks up the causal chain between Joe's careless driving and Sue's injury. The key, again, is foreseeability. An intervening cause that can reasonably be foreseen by the defendant is usually insufficient to break the causal chain. The following case applies these principles of causation.

HOYEM v. MANHATTAN BEACH CITY SCHOOL DISTRICT

SUPREME COURT OF CALIFORNIA, 585 P.2d 851 (1978)

Michael Hoyem, a 10-year-old boy, attended a school in defendant Manhattan Beach City School District. One day during summer school he left early and was struck and seriously injured by a motorcycle at a public intersection nearby. Michael and his mother sued the school district for negligence, based on its alleged failure to properly supervise Michael. The trial court dismissed the suit, and plaintiffs appealed.

TOBRINER, JUSTICE:

In this case we must determine whether, under California law, a school district may ever be held liable when, as a result of school authorities' negligent supervision of students on school premises, a pupil leaves the school grounds during school hours and is subsequently injured by a motorist.

[The court first held that California law imposes on school authorities a duty to supervise students and to enforce rules and regulations necessary for their protection. Therefore, the mere fact that an injury occurred off school premises would not mean, as a matter of law, that the school owed no duty to the injured student.]

[Defendant] also claims that as a matter of law negligent on-campus supervision *cannot* be the proximate cause of an off-campus injury. Proximate cause, however, is generally a question of fact for the jury, and, as we explain, on the basis of the allegations in the instant case the trial court could not properly hold as a matter of law that defendant's alleged negligent supervision on the campus did not proximately cause plaintiff's off-campus injury.

CONTINUED

Defendant does not contend that the trial court could conclude that its alleged negligence was not an actual or "but for" cause of the accident as a matter of law. Plaintiff alleges that if defendant had provided adequate supervision, Michael would never have left the school premises and would not have sustained his subsequent injuries. On the basis of this pleading, the issue of actual causation is clearly a question of fact for the jury.

Defendant [does contend] that it should not be expected to foresee that students will take advantage of a lapse in supervision to leave the school premises and therefore that any off campus injury is unforeseeable as a matter of law. At least since the days of Huck Finn and Tom Sawyer, however, adults have been well aware that children are often tempted to wander off from school, and a jury might well conclude that defendants could have reasonably foreseen that this temptation might be especially strong during summer session when a student's friends might not be in school. Indeed, the duty to supervise school children is imposed in large part in recognition of the fact that without such supervision students will not always conduct themselves safely or in accordance with school rules. Thus, we cannot say that Michael's departure from school was unforeseeable as a matter of law.

Defendant furthermore argues that the conduct of the motorcyclist who hit the plaintiff represents a "superceding cause" which cuts off any liability that the school district might bear for the accident.

As we explained in *Akins v. County of Sonoma*, 430 P.2d 57 (Cal. 1967).

> where [an] injury was brought about by a later cause of independent origin... [the question of proximate cause] revolves, around a determination of whether the later cause of independent origin, commonly referred to as an intervening cause, was forseeable by the defendant or, if not foreseeable, whether it caused injury of a type which was foreseeable. If either of these questions is answered in the affirmative, then the defendant is not relieved of liability towards the plaintiff; if, however, it is determined that the intervening cause was not foreseeable and that the results which it caused were not foreseeable, then the intervening cause becomes a supervening cause and the defendant is relieved from liability for the plaintiff's injuries.

In the instant case, we certainly cannot say that the risk of a student's injury at the hands of a negligent motorist is, as a matter of law, not a foreseeable risk created by a school district's failure to exercise due care in supervising its pupils.

[Reversed and remanded for a jury trial.]

INJURY

As the final element of a negligence cause of action, the plaintiff must prove injury. Negligence recovery is allowed primarily for injury to person or property. Recovery for economic loss not related to personal injury or property damage is generally not allowed, although there are several exceptions for special situations.[13]

Courts have also been reluctant to allow recovery for emotional distress on grounds that such injuries are too intangible and too easily faked. Over the years, most courts have changed their views as psychiatric testimony regarding the actual existence of emotional distress has become more dependable.

---

[13] For example, some courts hold accounting firms liable for injuries caused by negligent auditing when third parties (such as creditors) foreseeably rely on financial documents the firms prepared for their clients. *H. Rosenblum, Inc. v. Adler*, 461 A.2d 138 (N.J. 1983).

At first, courts allowed recovery for negligently caused emotional distress when the plaintiff also sustained a physical injury in the accident. It was easier to believe that the plaintiff suffered emotional distress if there were accompanying physical injuries. Later courts also awarded recovery to plaintiffs who were not physically injured but were in the "zone of danger." Thus, a pedestrian who was narrowly missed by an automobile that ran down a fellow pedestrian could sue the careless driver for emotional damages.

Because application of the "zone of danger" test leads sometimes to rather arbitrary distinctions, many courts have taken an additional step by allowing "bystander recovery." Thus, according to the leading case,[14] a parent who sees or hears an accident killing the parent's child can recover for emotional distress although not within the zone of danger. Three factors to be weighed in deciding whether to allow recovery are: (1) whether the plaintiff was located near the scene of the accident; (2) whether the emotional shock resulted from a contemporaneous perception of the accident, as opposed to hearing about it later; and (3) whether the plaintiff and the victim were closely related. Many courts have rejected bystander recovery, which obviously entails an extension of the concept of duty. But the modern trend is to recognize that if an actor's carelessness causes an injury that kills or seriously injures someone, the victim's loved ones are almost certain to suffer emotional trauma.

Punitive damages, also known as exemplary damages, are not recoverable in mere negligence cases. These are monetary damages, over and above the sums necessary to compensate for the plaintiff's injuries, which are assessed against the defendant to punish for wrongdoing and to deter defendant and others from engaging in such wrongful conduct. A defendant in a negligence action is guilty of mere carelessness, so punitive damages are viewed as inappropriate. However, punitive damages are generally available to plaintiffs injured by the intentional torts that we discuss later in the chapter.

DEFENSES

Even if the plaintiff establishes all four elements of a negligence cause of action, the defendant may avert or reduce recovery by establishing certain defenses.

Contributory Fault

If the plaintiff is guilty of fault that contributed to the accident, a defense may exist. Under the old system of **contributory negligence,** a plaintiff who was guilty of carelessness that contributed in any material way to the accident was barred from recovery altogether. Even if the jury concluded that the plaintiff was 1 percent at fault and the defendant 99 percent, the plaintiff could recover nothing, no matter how serious the injuries were.

---

[14] *Dillon v. Legg*, 69 Cal. Rptr. 72 (1958).

Because of the harshness of the contributory negligence system, most jurisdictions have replaced it with a system of **comparative negligence.** Comparative negligence or comparative fault systems vary widely from jurisdiction to jurisdiction, so it is difficult to generalize. Some states have "pure" comparative negligence systems under which, no matter how great a share of the fault is attributable to the plaintiff, the plaintiff still is entitled to recover the portion of damages caused by the defendant's carelessness. For example, let's assume that in a case arising out of an auto collision between P and D, a jury assesses P's damages at $100,000 and finds P 40 percent at fault and D 60 percent at fault. Rather than being barred from recovery as in a contributory negligence system, P would recover $60,000—that portion of the damages caused by D's fault. Indeed, in a pure system, even if P is found 99 percent at fault and D 1 percent, P would still recover $1,000. That P is many times more at fault than D does not bar recovery for that portion of the loss caused by D's carelessness.

Most jurisdictions have not adopted a pure comparative negligence system. Many allow a plaintiff to recover whatever percentage of damages were caused by the defendant, unless the plaintiff's share of the fault is assessed at 51 percent or higher. If the plaintiff's fault exceeds 50 percent, recovery is barred altogether on the theory that the plaintiff should recover nothing if he or she is more at fault than the defendant. Other states set 49 percent as the cap, not allowing recovery to a plaintiff found 50 percent or more at fault.

Statute of Limitations

In negligence, as in other causes of action, every state has a **statute of limitations** within which the suit must be filed or forever barred. A typical tort statute of limitations is two years. Thus, a plaintiff injured by defendant's negligence must file suit within two years of the occurrence. Occasionally a plaintiff may not even know of the injury until more than two years after the occurrence, for example, when carelessly designed drugs with side effects that will not show up for years are sold. Most states have applied tolling devices that provide that in such a case the statute of limitations is tolled; that is, will not begin to run, until the plaintiff knows or should know of the injury. In response to the medical malpractice and products liability "crises," several states have passed statutes of "repose" that bar certain actions after, say 15 years, whether the injuries sustained were discoverable or not during that period.

NO FAULT SYSTEMS

Negligence has been eliminated as a basis for lawsuits in at least two contexts that should be mentioned here. Every state has a *workers' compensation* system that allows injured employees to recover benefits from their employers when injured on the job. The employee can recover regardless of the presence of employer fault but forfeits the right to sue the employer even if the employer has been careless. Most jurisdictions, however, allow an employee covered by workers' compensation to sue his or her employer in tort if injured by the employer's gross negligence (for example, if the employer has allowed several employees to be injured by the same defective machine without replacing it) or intentional tort. Workers compensation plays a role in the *Caudle v. Betts* case in the next section and is discussed in more detail in Chapter 16.

Several states have enacted "no fault" automobile statutes. The thrust of these statutes is to reduce litigation by allowing persons who suffer only minor injuries in car accidents to recover only from their own insurance company. Although these laws vary widely from jurisdiction to jurisdiction, in most the plaintiffs' losses must exceed a certain statutory threshhold before resort to litigation is allowed.

MAJOR INTENTIONAL TORTS

ASSAULT AND BATTERY

Assault and battery are similar torts that may be treated together. Although modern courts and statutes frequently use the two terms interchangeably, technically a **battery** is a rude, inordinate contact with the person of another. An **assault,** basically, is any act that creates an apprehension of an imminent battery. That we can sue for assault and battery protects our personal dignity from intrusions of the mind (assault) and body (battery). The courts long ago concluded that we have a legitimate interest in being protected from offensive bodily contacts and fear of them. Indeed, assault and battery also constitute crimes.

Elements

One way to formulate the basic elements of the torts of assault and battery is to require the plaintiff to prove (1) the defendant's affirmative conduct, (2) intent, and (3) the plaintiff's injury.

Affirmative Conduct and Intent: If Sue is carefully driving down the street and is hit by a car that runs a red light and as a result Sue's car is pushed into a pedestrian, Sue has not committed assault or battery. Although the pedestrian has sustained both apprehension (assuming she saw the accident as it happened) and rude contact, Sue committed no affirmative act that caused the injuries. The driver of the car that ran the red light did commit an affirmative act that was tortious, but that act was negligence, not assault or battery. However, if, while driving down the street, Sue spotted an enemy and deliberately ran down that person in a crosswalk, an assault and battery would have occurred.

The intent required for both assault and battery is the intent either to create an offensive contact to the plaintiff's body or the apprehension of it in the plaintiff. Furthermore, a person is presumed to intend the natural consequences of his or her actions. Thus, if A points an unloaded gun at B and utters threats to use it, an assault occurs if B did not know the gun was unloaded even if A's intent is simply to play a harmless prank. The natural consequences of A's act of pointing the gun is to create an apprehension in B.

Under the *doctrine of transferred intent,* if Sam shoots at Bill, but Bill ducks and the bullet hits Carlos, Carlos has an assault (assuming he saw the incident happening) and battery claim against Sam even if he is Sam's best friend and Sam would not intentionally hurt him for the world. The law transfers the intent Sam had to injure Bill to Carlos.

Injury: If plaintiff seeks to establish an assault, the injury sustained must be in the nature of an apprehension of imminent bodily contact of an offensive nature. A threat of future contact or a threat by a defendant far away is insufficient. Threats or even attempts at violence that the intended victim does not know about until much later do not create the requisite apprehension, as where D shoots at and misses P from so far away that P never realizes the shot was fired. Usually the plaintiff's reactions are judged by what would have caused apprehension in a reasonable person, but if the defendant knows that the plaintiff is an unusually sensitive person and threatens contacts that the plaintiff finds offensive although most persons would not, an assault occurs.

If the plaintiff sues for battery, the injury that must be demonstrated is an offensive contact. Being struck with a fist, a knife, or a bullet obviously satisfies the requirement. So does being spat on, poisoned, and having one's clothes ripped or cane knocked away.

The following case illustrates the tort of battery in an employment context, thereby raising also some important workers' compensation issues.

CAUDLE v. BETTS

SUPREME COURT OF LOUISIANA, 512 So.2d 389 (1987)

Plaintiff Ruben Caudle was a salesman at Betts Lincoln-Mercury, Inc. Shortly before an office Christmas party on December 23, 1983, other employees engaged in horseplay with an electric automobile condenser after discovering that it could be charged by touching one end to a car's spark plug wire and turning the engine over. Once charged, the condenser would deliver a slight electric shock when touched at both ends. Several employees played catch with the charged condenser. Peter Betts, president of the corporation, shocked the back of Caudle's neck with the charged condenser and chased Caudle with it until Caudle escaped by locking himself in an office. After the incident, Caudle suffered headaches and passed out 30 to 40 times in the following months. The condition finally required occipital nerve surgery, leaving a slight numbness on the right side of the plaintiff's head.

Caudle sued Betts individually and Betts Lincoln-Mercury, Inc., for battery, seeking damages for, among other things, pain and suffering, past medical expenses, and loss of earnings. The trial court held that the injury to the plaintiff was not an intentional injury and, therefore, that workers' compensation benefits were the plaintiff's sole remedy. The appellate court affirmed the dismissal of the plaintiff's tort suit, and plaintiff appealed to the Louisiana Supreme Court.

CONTINUED

Dennis, Justice:

The Louisiana Worker's Compensation Act provides for compensation if an employee receives personal injury by accident arising out of and in the course of his employment. As a general rule, the rights and remedies granted to an employee therein are exclusive of all rights and remedies against his employer, any officer or principal of the employer, or any co-employee. However, an exception to this rule provides that nothing therein shall affect the liability of an employer, principal, officer, or co-employee resulting from an "intentional act." ... [I]n drawing a line between intentional and unintentional acts the legislative aim was to make use of the well established division between intentional torts and negligence.

A harmful or offensive contact with a person, resulting from an act intended to cause the plaintiff to suffer such a contact, is a battery.... The intention need not be malicious nor need it be an intention to inflict actual damage. It is sufficient if the actor intends to inflict either a harmful or offensive contact without the other's consent.

The original purpose of the courts in providing the action for battery undoubtedly was to keep the peace by affording a substitute for private retribution. F. Stone, Louisiana Civil Law Treatise, Tort Doctrine, Sec. 125 (1977). The element of personal indignity always has been given considerable weight. Consequently, the defendant is liable not only for contacts that do actual physical harm, but also for those relatively trivial ones which are merely offensive and insulting. W. Prosser and W. Keeton, The Law of Torts, Sec. 9 (5th ed. 1984).

The intent with which tort liability is concerned is not necessarily a hostile intent, or a desire to do any harm.... Rather it is an intent to bring about a result that will invade the interests of another in a way that the law forbids. The defendant may be liable although intending nothing more than a good-natured practical joke, or honestly believing that the act would not injure the plaintiff, or even though seeking the plaintiff's own good. [*Id.*]

Bodily harm is generally considered to be any physical impairment of the condition of a person's body, or physical pain or illness. Restatement (Second) of Torts, American Law Institute, Sec. 15 (1965). The defendant's liability for the resulting harm extends, as in most other cases of intentional torts, to consequences which the defendant did not intend, and could not reasonably have foreseen, upon the obvious basis that it is better for unexpected losses to fall upon the intentional wrongdoer than upon the innocent victim....

Applying these precepts to the facts found and affirmed by the lower courts, we conclude that the plaintiff employee proved that a battery had been committed on him by another employee and that he is entitled to recovery for all injuries resulting there from including his occipital nerve impairment. It is undisputed that when Mr. Betts shocked the employee, Mr. Caudle, with the condenser, he intended the contact to be offensive and at least slightly painful or harmful. The fact that he did so as a practical joke and did not intend to inflict actual damage does not render him immune from liability. Further, as between the innocent employee victim and the wrongdoer, it is better for unexpected losses to fall upon the intentional wrongdoer. Mr. Caudle is entitled to recover for all consequences of the battery, even those that Mr. Betts did not intend and could not have foreseen.

[Reversed and remanded.]

Defenses

In addition to the statute of limitations, which typically is two years in such cases, the two primary defenses to assault and battery are **consent** and **self-defense.** A plaintiff who has consented to offensive contacts and the threat of them cannot sue for assault and battery. Thus, a boxer who steps into the ring or the quarterback who steps onto the football field consents to the normal contacts that go with the rules of the game. However, if a football player is forearmed from behind by an opposing player after the play was over, he might have a good battery claim because his consent does not extend to this contact outside the rules of the game any more than it would extend to being shot by an opponent.[15]

Consent cannot be procured by fraud, nor can it be ill-informed. Thus, if M procures F's consent to sexual intercourse by hiding the fact that he has herpes, her consent to the intercourse does not constitute consent to the harmful contact with the disease. She may sue for battery.[16] Doctors performing surgery must be very careful to fully inform their patients regarding the contacts that will take place during the surgery to avoid liability for battery. Consent to an appendectomy does not extend to removal of some of the reproductive organs even though it may be the doctor's best medical judgment that they should be removed.

Self-defense creates a well-recognized privilege to assault and battery. In Chapter 8 we described how the courts restrict one to that degree of force considered reasonable in the circumstances of a crime. The same rule applies in the circumstances of a tort.

DEFAMATION

Long ago the courts decided that we have a legitimate interest in preserving our good reputation in the community. Those who damage our reputation by spreading falsehoods commit the tort of **defamation** and may be liable in damages. Although defamation has historic common-law roots, its development in recent years has been strongly influenced by a series of Supreme Court decisions that have molded the tort in accordance with First Amendment principles.

Libel versus Slander

Defamation takes two basic forms. **Libel** is written defamation; **slander** is oral. Television and radio broadcasts have generally been categorized as libel. The distinction is important because, traditionally, libel, perhaps because of its more permanent form, was considered more damaging than slander. At common law, a person who proved libel was able to recover damages without any proof of special damages; that is, the very proof that something potentially damaging to the reputation was circulated in public led the court to presume injury. The jury could assess damages without evidence of any specific loss.

Slander, however, required proof of special damages. Generally, a plaintiff had to prove some sort of economic loss stemming from the damage to reputation. Once that was proved, plaintiff could recover for all sorts of injuries, including humiliation, loss of friendship, and the like. However, in four special categories known as slander *per se*, no special damages needed to be proved. These categories were imputation of serious crime, of loathsome

---

[15] *Hackbart v. Cincinnati Bengals,* 601 F.2d 516 (10th Cir. 1979).
[16] *Long v. Adams,* 333 S.E.2d 852 (Ga. App. 1985).

disease, of incompetence in the plaintiff's profession, and of unchastity in women.

However, as we shall see, the Supreme Court's First Amendment decisions have had an impact on this traditional distinction.

Elements

In a defamation case, the plaintiff must generally establish four elements to prevail: (1) that a matter defamatory of the plaintiff, (2) and untrue, (3) was communicated by the defendant, (4) to the plaintiff's injury. Questions of the defendant's fault, as we shall see, also arise.

Matter Defamatory of Plaintiff: To be defamatory, a statement must be of such a nature as to tend to lower the plaintiff's esteem in the eyes of others. An infinite variety of statements has been held defamatory, but if defendant falsely tells other that the plaintiff is a thief, a bankrupt, a nazi, a communist, or a homosexual, it is likely that the plaintiff's esteem in the eyes of others will be lowered. Although most defamation actions are brought by individuals, they can also be brought by corporations and other organizations.

The defamatory statement must be one that the readers or hearers will associate with the plaintiff. Although not mentioned by name, a person who is obviously referred to in a disparaging way in a "novel" that is closely based on reality may have a claim against the author. So may a member of a small group when the defendant defames the entire group (e.g., "All the male clerks at this store have AIDS") although the plaintiff is not mentioned by name. When larger groups are referred to (e.g., "All Republicans are fascists"), the courts hesitate to allow recovery.

Untrue: To be defamatory, a statement must not only tend to lower the plaintiff's esteem in the eyes of others, it must be untrue. The question may be: Who has the burden of proving truthfulness or falsity? The common law presumed that everyone was a good person; therefore, if the plaintiff proved that a statement tending to defame him or her had been published by defendant, the burden of proof was on the defendant to prove the truthfulness of the statement. Truth, in other words, was an absolute *defense* to a defamation claim.

A recent Supreme Court case redistributed this burden of proof, at least in some cases, on First Amendment grounds. In *Philadelphia Newspaper, Inc. v. Hepps,*[17] the Court held that if the plaintiff is a public figure (such as a famous actress or athlete), a public official (such as a governor), or a "limited" public figure (a private citizen caught up in a public controversy,

---

[17] 475 U.S. 767 (1986).

such as a businessman whose name appears in a newspaper article about the Mafia), free speech concerns require that the plaintiff be given the burden of proof to demonstrate falsity. The common-law presumption that defamatory speech is false was rejected, at least when the defendant is a member of the media. The implications for a nonmedia defendant or a case involving a private plaintiff not involved in any public controversy are unclear.

Communication: To be defamatory, a statement must be "published" or communicated by the defendant—that is, overheard or read by a third party. If Joe and Kim are standing alone in a field miles from anyone else, Joe can say all the nasty things he wants to Kim without committing defamation. Kim's reputation in the community cannot be hurt if no one else hears the statements. If Kim goes back into town and repeats the statements for others, it is Kim doing the communicating, not Joe.[18]

Injury: As noted earlier, the traditional common-law rule presumed damages in libel and the four special types of slander. If a false statement tending to lower the plaintiff's esteem in the eyes of others appeared in a local newspaper, it was sensible to presume that persons read it and that their impressions of plaintiff were adversely affected. Injury was presumed, and it made no difference that the defendant did not intend to injure the plaintiff.

The Supreme Court has indicated that this presumption of injury is inconsistent with the First Amendment, at least when the media are reporting about public officials, public figures, or about private figures involved in public controversies. In these cases, at least, plaintiffs must introduce some evidence to show that the defamatory publication injured their reputations.

Defenses

Several noteworthy defenses are available in defamation cases.

Statute of Limitations: In most jurisdiction the statute of limitations for defamation cases is one year, only half the two-year statute of limitations typically found for other types of tort claims.

Absolute Privilege: To encourage certain types of activity, the courts have created an absolute privilege for the potential defendant in several contexts. That is, even if the plaintiff could prove all the elements of defamation discussed above, no liability would attach. The two most important of these are the privileges for judicial and legislative proceedings. To encourage judges to judge, witnesses to testify, lawyers to advocate, and legislators to aggressively debate the issues, all are protected absolutely when involved in

---

[18] This is not to rule out a possible, but probably weak, claim for intentional infliction of emotional distress in this scenario.

their respective activities. Note, however, that the absolute privilege is narrow in scope. An attorney who wrote a book about a case after the trial was over or a legislator making statements not while debating a bill but while campaigning would not be protected.

Qualified Privileges: There are also several qualified privileges when the defendant will be protected if he or she acted in *good faith;* that is, malice must be proved as a prerequisite for recovery. The primary example of this is when the plaintiff is a public figure or public official. Others include, according to some jurisdictions, communications to those who can act in the public interest (for example, complaints to a school board about a teacher) and fair comment on matters of public interest by news commentators.

Many states have provided a business-related good faith privilege for those who traffic in commercially useful information such as credit reports and employee references. Thus, in many jurisdictions, a job applicant's former employer is protected if he tells the applicant's prospective employer that "We think she stole from us." The plaintiff would have to prove malice to prevail. Note, however, that *Dun & Bradstreet, Inc. v. Greenmoss Builders,* 472 U.S. 749 (1985) makes it clear that this privilege is not constitutionally mandated.

Opinion: Under the First Amendment, there is no such thing as a false idea. We are all entitled to our opinions. Thus, "I think Joe is a jerk" is not actionable. Neither is "I just don't trust Joe; he looks sneaky to me." However, when an editorial writer stated that a plaintiff had lied under oath, the Supreme Court rejected a defense of opinion because the statement was "sufficiently factual to be susceptible of being proved true or false." *Milkovich v. Loran Journal Co.,* 105 S.Ct. 2695 (1990).

Injurious Falsehood

Closely allied to defamation (and perhaps equally as closely connected to the business torts discussed in Chapter 12) is the tort of **injurious falsehood,** also known as "disparagement," "slander of goods," and "trade libel." The elements are generally the same as for traditional defamation, but the subject matter relates not to an individual's reputation, but to the plaintiff's title to property or to the quality or conduct of the plaintiff's business. The tort is aimed at protecting economic interests and would allow suit against a defendant who, for example, falsely stated that the plaintiff's business was no longer in existence.

FALSE IMPRISONMENT

The privilege to come and go as we please is important in our society. The courts protect that interest by recognizing the right to sue for the tort of **false imprisonment** when persons are unlawfully confined or restrained without their consent. If the defendant purports to arrest the plaintiff as well, the nearly identical claim of **false arrest** is applicable.

Elements

To prove a false imprisonment claim, plaintiff must usually prove that defendant (1) confined or restrained the plaintiff, (2) with intent, (3) without the plaintiff's consent, (4) thereby injuring the plaintiff.

Confinement: False imprisonment can occur when the plaintiff is confined in a room, a building, a car, or even a boat. It can even occur in the wide open spaces if the plaintiff is held in one spot against his or her will by force or threat. If the defendant blocks one exit to a room but another is available to the plaintiff, the confinement requirement is not met.

Intent: If someone accidentally locks another in a room, perhaps negligence is involved, but not false imprisonment. False imprisonment requires a wrongful intent on the defendant's part. As with assault and battery, an intent to injure will suffice, as well as an intent to confine. If the defendant stands outside the plaintiff's house with a gun, issuing threats of bodily injury should the plaintiff emerge, the intent requirement is met. Although the defendant would like nothing better than for the plaintiff to come out of the house, the natural consequence of the defendant's actions is to force the plaintiff to remain in the house.

Without Consent: The same force and threats of force that create an assault may force a person to remain in one place against his or her will. A large man could easily intimidate a small person into staying involuntarily in one place. However, if the plaintiff stays in one place as an accommodation or to clear up an accusation with police, there is no involuntary confinement. If, for example, a store clerk told a customer only "We believe you have stolen from the cash register and have called the police," and the customer voluntarily stayed in the store to give his or her side of the story—there would be no false imprisonment.

Injury: The injury necessary for a valid false imprisonment claim arises automatically from the confinement, even if it is brief. A restraint of hours or days is not required for the necessary injury to occur. However, because the injury is somewhat mental in nature, it will not occur if the plaintiff is unaware of the confinement. Thus, if the plaintiff sleeps through a confinement, there would be no cognizable injury. But if the plaintiff knows of the confinement, actual and punitive damages are available.

Defenses

In addition to the statute of limitations (typically two years), the defendant's best chance in a false imprisonment case is to prove legal right. Obviously, police officers in possession of probable cause have the right to detain or confine suspects.

Many false imprisonment claims involve shopkeepers. Shoplifting, unfortunately, is a problem of epidemic proportions in the United States. When a shopkeeper detains a suspected shoplifter and presses charges, any number of things can prevent a conviction from being obtained, including prosecutorial or police error, or the failure of a witness to appear. At common law, even a well-founded belief by a shopkeeper that a theft had occurred frequently would not prevent the success of a later false imprisonment claim if, for whatever reason no criminal conviction was obtained. However, many state legislatures have acted to protect shopkeepers with legislation such as that discussed in the following case. Additionally, some states have updated their protective statutes to reflect usage of modern technology, as the following case illustrates.

ESTES v. JACK ECKERD CORPORATION

COURT OF APPEALS OF GEORGIA, 360 S.E.2d 649 (1987)

As she left Eckerd's store after purchasing some items, the plaintiff Estes activated an antishoplifting device's buzzer. Posters warned customers that such devices were in use. Estes was approached by a store manager who told her that he had to look in her shopping bag because the alarm had gone off. His inspection of the bag and the plaintiff's receipt indicated that Estes had paid for all the items, but the sales clerk had not deactivated a special tag on a bottle of shampoo. Estes was soon released. The parties' version of events differed on whether the store manager had treated Estes in a rude and derogatory fashion. The jury apparently believed that he had not, returning a verdict for the defendant on Estes' false imprisonment claim. Estes appealed.

BEASLEY, JUDGE:

False imprisonment is "the unlawful detention of the person of another, for any length of time, whereby such person is deprived of his personal liberty." By OCGA 51-7-60, the [legislature] provided a qualified immunity to merchants from tort liability for false arrest or false imprisonment. No recovery is permitted where plaintiff's conduct is such "as to cause a man of reasonable prudence to believe" that the plaintiff was shoplifting or where the manner of detention or arrest and the length of the detention was reasonable under all the circumstances.

Later, OCGA 51-7-61 was added to provide that where a store used an antishoplifting or inventory control device "the automatic activation of the device as a result of a person exiting the establishment or a protected area within the establishment *shall* constitute reasonable cause for the detention of the person so exiting by the owner or operator ... or employee.... Each detention shall be made only in a reasonable manner and only for a reasonable period of time sufficient for any inquiry into the circumstances surrounding the activation of the device." [Emphasis added.] This applies only when a warning notice is conspicuously posted.

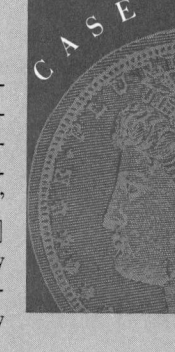

In response to Eckerd's position that the statute acts as an absolute bar to Mrs. Estes' recovery, she asserts that immunity is granted only if Eckerd used all reasonable care and due diligence in the use of the device and did not cause harm to her through its negligence.

"False imprisonment is an intentional tort, not a tort of negligence." *Williams v. Smith*, 348 S.E.2d 50 (Ga.App. 1986).... The present case is governed by OCGA 51-7-61, not by 51-7-60.... A Louisiana court considered a similar Louisiana antishoplifting device statute ... [and] reasoned that ... the legislature's clear intention was "to afford to the merchant a right, within statutory limitations, to detain a person when the electronic device has been triggered." The conclusion was that the

CONTINUED

essential question under such a statute was "not whether 'reasonable cause' exists, but whether the method and extent of plaintiff's detention was reasonable under the circumstances. . . ."

The reasoning of the Louisiana court is persuasive and substantiates our construction of the language of the Georgia statute, which is mandatory, inasmuch as it states that "automatic activation of the device . . . shall constitute reasonable cause. . . ." That is, it makes no difference to "reasonable cause" whether or not negligence on the part of Eckerd's employee in failing to deactivate the special tag on the bottle of shampoo set the device off. What matters is whether the method and time of detention were reasonable within the statutory limitations. Defendant's right to detain is lawful once the device is activated.

Having determined that the defendant's alleged precursor negligence is immaterial when an antishoplifting device has been automatically activated, the only issue under OCGA 51-7-61 is whether the detention was made in a reasonable manner, as she does not contend that it was not for a reasonable period of time, and if proper notice was posted as required. The latter is undisputed as there were at least two warning signs prominently displayed in the store near the entrance and exit.

While the testimony of Estes and Eckerd's manager was conflicting as to what he said when he approached her, there is no dispute that he searched her bag without any objection on her part, and that the episode lasted only five to ten mintues. Clearly there was no restraint by force or fear here. . . . We find the evidence sufficient to support the jury's apparent conclusion tht Mrs. Estes was not detained unreasonably.

[Affirmed.]

TRESPASS

We work hard for our money, and when we spend it on property we should have the right to use that property without interference from others. When others infringe on our right to use real property—land and those things attached to it, such as houses—the tort of **trespass** to real property is committed. The tort has a convoluted common-law history that protects property owners from innocent as well as mean-spirited invasions of the right to use real property.

Elements

Generally speaking, to prevail in a trespass case the plaintiff must establish the following elements: (1) affirmative conduct by the defendant; (2) with intent to enter onto realty in the possession of another; and (3) resulting in actual entry.

Affirmative Conduct: If Joe is driving down the street when Alan runs a stop sign with his car, smashes into Joe, and pushes Joe up onto Ed's lawn, no trespass has been committed by Joe. He invaded Ed's real property but not through any affirmative act of his own.

Intent: Unlike most other intentional torts, the intent element of a trespass cause of action requires only that the plaintiff demonstrate that the defendant intended to enter the place he did, which place belonged to the plaintiff. No intent to do harm is required. Thus, if Cindy walks across Ann's land believing that she is walking across her own or across land belonging to her friend Sally who has given her permission to cross it, Cindy commits a trespass actionable by Ann. Cindy's good faith is no defense. However, if Mark has a heart attack and dies instantly while driving down the street, and his car runs onto Ed's lawn, the affirmative conduct element is arguably not met and certainly the intent element is missing. The same may be said of a person who, driving too fast on slick streets, loses control of the car and winds up on someone's lawn. The intent element is missing.

Actual Entry: Entry is required for completion of the tort, but *usually* no real injury. Damage is presumed from the fact of entry, even if the only injury is trampled blades of grass. A judgment in the form of nominal damages of a dollar or so would still be warranted. According to most courts, the invasion need only be slight, including throwing a rock onto the plaintiff's property, shooting a bullet over it, or tunneling under it. Some courts refuse to recognize injury where the invasion is truly minor, such as where A's tree limb grows so far that it extends over B's property line.

The court must sometimes balance competing interests. For example, in *Bradley v. American Smelting and Refining Co.*, 709 P.2d 782 (Wash. 1985), the defendant operated a copper smelter that emitted particulate matter, including arsenic, cadmium, and other metals. Although undetectable by human senses and not harmful to health, this matter did sometimes settle on the plaintiff's property. The court felt constrained to create an exception to the general rule that any entry constitutes an injury, stating:

> When [airborne] particles or substance accumulates on the land and does not pass away, then a trespass has occurred. While at common law any trespass entitled a landowner to recover nominal and punitive damages for the invasion of his property, such a rule is not appropriate under the circumstances before us. No useful purpose would be served by sanctioning actions in trespass by every landowner within a hundred miles of a manufacturing plant. Manufacturers would be harassed and the litigious few would cause the escalation of costs to the detriment of the many. . . . The plaintiff who cannot show actual and substantial damages should be subject to dismissal.

The trespassory entry is an affront to the use of the property. Therefore, the cause of action is normally recognized as belonging to the possessor of the land. Thus, if T were renting a farm from L, and X trespassed on the farm, T would normally have the right to sue for trespass rather than L.

Defenses

In addition to the typical two-year statute of limitations (which is extended if the trespass is a continuing one, as when the trespasser has erected a small building on the plaintiff's property), the main defenses to a trespass cause of action are *consent* and *legal right*. Thus, a tenant has the landlord's consent, pursuant to a lease, to remain on the landlord's property. However, if the tenant stays beyond the term of the lease and refuses to leave, a trespass is committed because consent has expired.

A legal right might arise from, for example, an *easement*, which is a right to use someone's property for a limited purpose. Thus, if M's land is between N's land and a major highway, N might negotiate an easement from M, paying M a sum of money in exchange for the limited right to travel over M's land going to and from the highway.

OTHER INTENTIONAL TORTS

INVASION OF PRIVACY

Slowly over the past 75 years or so, the courts have begun to recognize privacy as an interest worthy of legal protection. Today, many jurisdictions have recognized one or more of the following varieties of tort that come under the umbrella of **invasion of privacy.**

Intrusion

Intrusion occurs whenever a defendant intrudes into an area where a plaintiff has a reasonable expectation of privacy. The invasion must be highly offensive to a reasonable person to be actionable. Secretly placing a microphone under the plaintiff's bed to overhear the goings on would be actionable. So might an employer's secretly searching an employee's locker (where the employee provided his or her own lock and therefore had a justifable expectation of privacy) without reasonable grounds for doing so.[19]

Disclosure of Embarrasing Private Facts

Where no justification exists, it may be actionable to disclose to the public facts that plaintiff finds embarrasing or offensive. Because they are "true," the disclosures do not constitute defamation; they may be more akin to blackmail. However, a newsworthiness defense exists, at least for the media. In one case, a woman sued for the embarrassment she was caused by a newspaper's disclosing that her husband was killed in a fire in a motel while accompanied by another woman. The court held that fires are newsworthy events, and the newspaper could not be liable for accurately reporting the names of the victims.[20]

False Light

Very similar to the tort of defamation, the action for "false-light" privacy renders liable a defendant who makes statements or does acts that place the plaintiff in a false light in the public eye. Although usually these statements

---

[19] *K-Mart Corp. Store No. 7441 v. Trotti*, 677 S.W.2d 632 (Tex. App. 1984).
[20] *Fry v. Ionia Sentinel Standard*, 300 N.W.2d 687 (Mich. App. 1980).

or actions would injure the plaintiff's reputation and also be actionable as defamation, occasionally they might involve statements that the plaintiff had performed many wonderful things which in fact he had not. Rather than suing for injury to reputation as in defamation suits, a false-light plaintiff seeks compensation for shame, embarrassment, mental anguish, or humiliation. An attraction of this tort is that it frequently has a two-year statute of limitations, longer than the one-year statutes typical for defamation.

Appropriation of Name or Likeness

This final type of privacy tort protects the economic interests that persons have in the potential exploitation of their names and faces. Thus, if a company uses the name or picture of a famous actress in its advertising campaign without her permission, it has appropriated her name or likeness to her economic detriment. The company should have acquired her consent and paid her for such use. After singer Bette Midler refused to sing for a company's TV commercial, it hired one of her back-up singers and asked her to sound as much like Midler as possible. Many listeners thought they were hearing the real Bette Midler, which formed the basis for a successful appropriation suit by Midler.[21]

Several employer–employee disputes have involved claims of invasion of privacy, as the following case illustrates.

YOUNG v. JACKSON

SUPREME COURT OF MISSISSIPPI 572 So.2d 378, 1990

The plaintiff, Young, worked at a nuclear power station operated by the defendant, Mississippi Power & Light Co. One day while Young, wearing protective gear, was working in an area highly contaminated by radioactivity, she lost consciousness and was transported to the hospital. Co-worker and defendant Jackson called and visited her at the hospital to inquire about her status. The substance of what happened is disputed. Young claimed that Jackson told her that government safety officials were inquiring about the incident and she needed to tell what happened. Young further claimed that she told Jackson that it was not a safety matter but stemmed from a partial hysterectomy she recently had. The operation was very upsetting to Young, who felt like "half a woman now." Young testified that she made Jackson promise to keep the information secret because she had not even told her husband. Jackson, however, testified that Young volunteered the information about her hysterectomy, telling him not to worry about any radiation.

Word spread quickly throughout the plant that Young had collapsed and been taken to the hospital. Rumors spread that Young was a victim of radiation and other employees might

CONTINUED

---

[21] *Midler v. Ford Motor Co.*, 849 F.2d 460 (9th Cir. 1988).

be also. In this setting, Jackson told his boss about the hysterectomy and Jackson's boss called employees together and told them there was no reason to worry about radiation because Young had passed out because of the aftereffects of her recent partial hysterectomy.

Later, Young filed this action against the defendants claiming invasion of privacy. The trial court granted the defendants' motion for summary judgment and Young appealed.

ROBERTSON, JUSTICE:

The positive law of this state affords each person a substantial zone of freedom which, at his election, he may keep private. The zone surrounds person and place and without his consent may not be invaded by other persons. We have made no effort to identify the outer limits of a person's right of privacy and certainly make none here. Suffice it to say that where, as here, the invasion is by private parties, we have recognized a right of action in at least three contexts: (1) the portrayal of Plaintiff in a false light; (2) appropriation of Plaintiff's likeness and unpermitted use; and (3) public disclosure of private facts. It is this latter theorum that Betty Young invokes and we accept its more precise statement in Restatement (Second) of Torts Sec. 652D (1977): "One who gives publicity to a matter concerning the private life of another is subject to liability to the other for invasions of his privacy, if the matter publicized is of a kind that (a) would be highly offensive to a reasonable person, and (b) is not of legitimate concern to the public."

No doubt an objective test obtains. A person may not be held liable for public disclosure of facts about another unless he should reasonably have foreseen that the person would be likely offended. It requires little awareness of personal prejudice and human nature to know that, generally speaking, no aspects of life [are] more personal and private than those having to do with one's sexual organs and reproductive system. It may be the fact that many women who have undergone a hysterectomy do not keep that fact secret, but this is not the test. We do not regard it unreasonable that a woman would consider the fact a private matter, nor unforeseeable that she would so consider it.

Without further ado, we hold that the fact that she has undergone a hysterectomy is a fact that a woman ordinarily has the right to keep private if she wishes and that public disclosure of that fact by unauthorized persons and without her consent may be actionable.

The [trial court] did not hold Young stated no claim but rather that, in the present state of the record, Defendants' qualified privilege defense prevailed as a matter of law. The defense of qualified privilege has long been accepted in our law of defamation, but we have had no occasion to consider it in an invasion of privacy context. The settings are certainly analogous. We hold that actions for invasion of privacy are subject to the defense of privilege the same as defamation actions. Turning to the contours of the qualified privilege defense as it has evolved in the law of defamation, we can improve little on this Court's early statement:

> A communication made in good faith and on a subject-matter in which the person making it has an interest or in reference to which he has a duty, is privileged if made to a person or persons having a corresponding interest or duty, even though it contains matter which without this privilege would be slanderous. There are certain occasions on which a man is entitled to state what he believes to be the truth about another, and in doing so public policy requires that he shall be protected, provided he makes the statement honestly and not for any indirect or wrong motive. Such occasions are called occasions of qualified privilege, for the reason that the protection is not absolute, but depends entirely upon the honesty of purpose with which the statement is made. Among such statements is one made on a subject-matter in which the person making it, and the person to whom it is made, have a legitimate common interest. The underlying principle is public policy.

Louisiana Oil Corp. v. Renno, 157 So. 705 (Miss. 1934).

Specifically, this Court has recognized that a public policy reason of the sort contemplate[d] exists in the context of the employer/employee relationship. Today's case arises in such an employer/employee context, and the statements concerning Young's hysterectomy were made against the backdrop of that relationship. The work at [the nuclear power station] was disrupted by rumors concerning Young's accident. Young's co-workers were concerned for her welfare, but for their own as well. Disclosing the true facts of Young's operation could reasonably have been seen likely to allay the fears of her co-workers of excessive levels of radiation in the areas in which they worked.

[Affirmed.]

INTENTIONAL INFLICTION OF MENTAL DISTRESS

As noted earlier, because emotional injuries are difficult to prove and to value, courts have traditionally been reluctant to allow recovery for them. But just as they are now allowed in suitable cases of negligence, they are also allowed when intentionally caused. The turning point may have been cases such as *Wilkinson v. Downtin*,[22] in which, as a practical joke, the defendant called the plaintiff, a woman whose mental state was somewhat suspect anyway, and told her that her husband had been in a serious accident. This so upset the plaintiff that she had to be hospitalized. Recovery for her emotional distress was allowed.

The requisite elements of proof for the tort of **intentional infliction of mental distress** are generally formulated as follows. First, that the defendant is guilty of extreme and outrageous conduct. Mere insults are usually insufficient, as are profanity and other abuses of a relatively minor nature. Second, the defendant must have intended to cause the plaintiff severe emotional distress. Again, the defendant will be presumed to intend the natural consequences of his or her actions. And a defendant who is aware of a particular plaintiff's susceptibilities to mental distress will be judged accordingly. Finally, the plaintiff must actually suffer such severe distress. Physical consequences are not required, but their presence does assist in establishing proof of severe emotional anguish.

Today, such suits frequently involve attempts by collection agencies to force debtors to pay bills. Thus, in *Turman v. Central Billing, Inc.*, 568 P.2d 1382 (1977), the collection agency was held liable to Turman, who was blind, when it badgered her in trying to collect a small debt assigned to it for collection, even after it knew that she and the creditor had come to a satisfactory settlement. This harassment, which resulted in the plaintiff's hospitalization for anxiety and severe stress, was carried out by repeated phone calls—sometimes twice a day—in which the defendant's agent "shouted" at her, used profanity, told her several times that her husband would lose his job and house if she did not pay, and called her "scum" and a "deadbeat."

This tort cannot be used to evade First Amendment restrictions on recovery for defamation. When the Reverend Jerry Falwell sued *Hustler* magazine over an extremely rude parody, showing that it had caused him emotional distress, the Supreme Court held that freedom of expression considerations barred recovery.[23]

FRAUD

The essence of the tort of *fraud* is the intentional misleading of one person by another, which results in a loss to the deceived party. Because many kinds of fraudulent conduct occur when the sole purpose of the wrongdoer is to cause the innocent party to enter a contract that that person otherwise would not make, addition consideration of this subject was undertaken in Chapter 9.

---

[22] [1897] 2 Q.B.D. 57.
[23] *Hustler Magazine v. Falwell*, 108 S.Ct. 876 (1988).

CONVERSION AND TRESPASS TO PERSONAL PROPERTY

The tort of **conversion** renders actionable certain invasions of personal property interests, just as trespass protects real property interests. Conversion remedies invasions so serious that they justify forcing the defendant to compensate the plaintiff for the reasonable value of the item involved. An example would be the defendant's theft of the plaintiff's automobile. A tort that generally covers more minor invasions of personal property rights is frequently called trespass to personal property. This tort would remedy, for example, the defendant's minor vandalism of the plaintiff's car.

NUISANCE

Like trespass to real property, the tort of **nuisance** protects the enjoyment of such property. Frequently nuisance is used to compensate an intangible disruption of the enjoyment of property, as when the plaintiff is injured by the defendant's invasion through light (erection of tall light poles), vibrations (blasting with dynamite), or smells (pig farming). The courts will consider such factors as the type of neighborhood, the nature of the wrong, its proximity to the plaintiff, its frequency or continuity, and the nature and extent of the injury in deciding whether an actionable nuisance exists.

SPECIAL PROBLEMS

BUSINESS TORTS

Some torts, such as the theft of trade secrets and the unjustified interference with business contracts, are so peculiarly related to the commercial world that they are called *business torts*. Because of the special issues that these kinds of torts present—and also because of their obvious importance to businesspersons—they are considered at length in Chapter 12.

EMPLOYERS'S LIABILITY

Ordinarily, the application of the principles of tort law results in the imposition of liability on the wrongdoer alone. There is one major exception, however, which springs from the principles comprising our master–servant law and our law of agency.

Under these principles, an employer is uniformly held liable for the torts of employees if the employees are acting "within the scope of their employment" at the time of the injury. Thus, if T, a truckdriver employed by the D Furniture Company, negligently injures P while delivering a piece of furniture to a customer's home, P has a cause of action against both T and the D Company, as illustrated in Figure 10.1.

Ordinarily, in such a case, P brings just one action against both defendants; if he is successful in proving the facts as alleged, he obtains a "joint and several" judgment against T and the D Company. This means that if he is awarded a judgment of $4,000, he can enforce the judgment against the assets of either party, or of both, until that sum is recovered. (The "scope of employment" problem is covered further in Chapter 13.)

FIGURE 10.1

```
ABC employs John Doe to drive
its delivery truck.
          │
          ▼
Mr. Doe wrongfully causes an accident
in which Mr. Smith is injured.
          │
          ▼
      Mr. Smith sues.
       ╱         ╲
      ▼           ▼
John Doe      ABC because John Doe
for causing   is ABC's employee and
the harm.     was within the scope of
              employment when
              the harm was done.
```

■ EMPLOYER'S LIABILITY FOR EMPLOYEE'S TORT

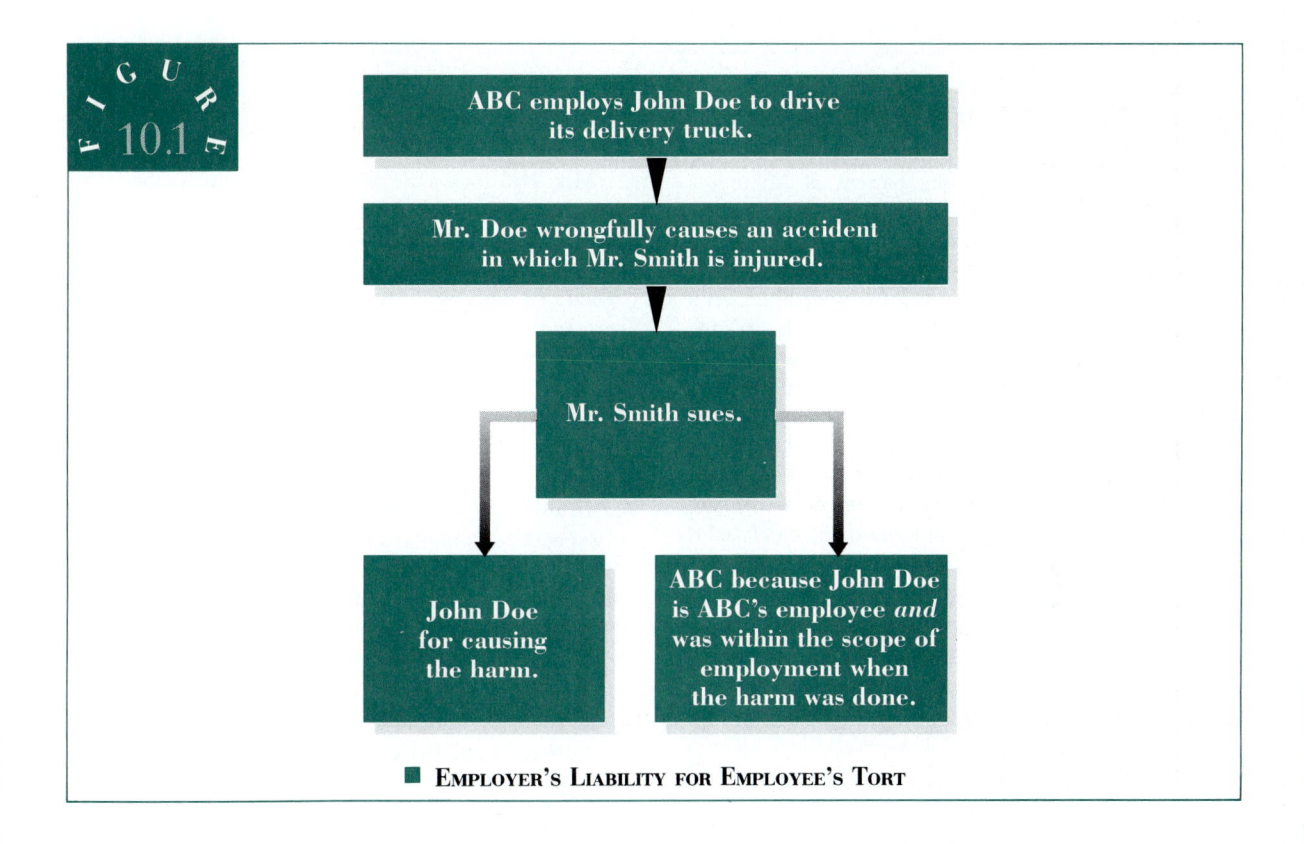

JOINT AND SEVERAL LIABILITY

When two defendants' actions together contribute to a plaintiff's injury, they are frequently held jointly and severally liable. The "joint" portion of this liability means that each defendant may be held responsible for the entire loss caused to the plaintiff. Thus, theoretically one defendant who is only 10 percent at fault might have to pay also for the 90 percent fault of another defendant, especially if the latter defendant is judgment-proof. The relatively harsh result that this can have for "deep pocket" defendants is a major cause of criticism of our present tort system. Several states have enacted limits on joint and several liability in certain types of cases.

STATUTORY REFORMS

Increases in the number of tort suits filed, the size of judgments, and consequently, insurance rates have become a major topic of discussion in both the federal and state legislatures. As this chapter is written both state and federal legislative reforms to limit tort recoveries are being debated and passed across the country. Although the ultimate impact of this wave of legislation cannot yet be gauged, it thus far has concentrated on such matters as medical malpractice and products liability suits, punitive damages, damages for emotional distress, joint and several liability, and statutes of limitation.

Questions and Problems

1. For two years Lee was the patient of Milano, a psychiatrist. Lee was diagnosed as having an adjustment reaction to adolescence. He related many fantasies to Milano about being a hero or an important villain or using a knife to threaten those who frightened him. At a session he showed a knife to Milano. Lee also related certain alleged sexual experiences with Kim, his next door neighbor. He was emotionally involved, possessive, and had fired a BB gun at a car occupied by Kim and her boyfriend as they drove away on a date. Later, Lee murdered Kim with a knife. Kim's family sued Milano in negligence for not having warned them of the danger from Lee. Should Milano be liable? Discuss. (*McIntosh v. Milano*, 403 A.2d 500, N.J. 1979.)

2. D sent its employee, Wells, into an industrial tank to clean it. The tank contained nitrogen gas and lacked oxygen to breathe. Wells was not wearing protective gear and was overcome by the gas. He became incoherent and delirious. Wells was transported to a nearby hospital where P, a nurse, attended to him. While in a state of delirium, Wells bit off a portion of P's right middle finger. P sued D in negligence. Assuming that P can prove that D's carelessness in safety procedures proximately caused Wells' delerium, should she recover? Discuss. (*Widlowski v. Durkee Foods*, 562 N.E.2d 967, Ill. 1990).

3. Charles and Carolyn needed to repair and clean a well on their property. Charles entered the well and placed a gasoline-powered pump directly above it to remove water. This was a bad idea because all the carbon monoxide from the engine seeped into the well. When Charles did not respond to Carolyn's calls, she asked her neighbor Bob for help. Bob entered the well to help Charles but was overcome by fumes himself and died. Bob's family sued Carolyn and Charles' estate for negligence. Should the family recover? Discuss. (*Lowrey v. Horvath*, 689 S.W.2d 625, Mo. 1985.)

4. Two children, Lisa and Deborah, were standing alongside a highway when Lisa was struck by Burd's carelessly driven car. Deborah was barely missed. JoAnne, the girls' mother, saw the whole incident from her front porch. When Lisa, Deborah, and JoAnne sue Burd for the emotional distress caused by his careless driving, who will be allowed to recover? (*Sinn v. Burd*, 404 A.2d 672, Pa. 1979.)

5. Mrs. Hill took a clock to the defendant's office, and there she found Sapp in charge, sitting behind a 4-foot counter that separated him from the public. She handed him the clock. Having had a few drinks and feeling "good and amiable," Sapp said: "If you will come back here and let me love and pet you, I will fix your clock." He then reached forward in an effort to grasp Mrs. Hill's arm, but she jumped back out of the way, and no physical contact occurred. She later sued for assault. Should she prevail? (*Western Union Telegraph Co. v. Hill*, 150 So. 709, Ala. 1933.)

6. In a review of the plaintiff's restaurant, the defendant newspaper columnist referred to the sauce on the duck as "yellow death on duck" and the poached trout as something that should be renamed "trout à la green plague." The plaintiff sued for defamation, proving that most persons very much liked both dishes. Does the plaintiff have a strong defamation claim? Discuss. (*Mashburn v. Collins*, 355 So.2d 879, La. 1977.)

7. National Bond Co. sent two of its employees to repossess Whithorn's car when Whithorn got behind in his payments. The two repossessors located Whithorn while he was driving his car. They asked him to stop, which he did, but he refused to abandon the car to them. They called a wrecker and ordered the driver to hook Whithorn's car and move it down the street while Whithorn was still in it. Whithorn started the car and tried to escape, but the wrecker lifted the car off the road and progressed 75 to 100 feet before Whithorn managed to stall the wrecker. Whithorn claimed that this incident amounted to a false imprisonment and sued National Bond Co. Does Whithorn have a valid claim? Discuss. (*National Bond Co. v. Whithorn*, 123 S.W.2d 263, Ky. 1939.)

8. The defendant is a crop duster who became confused and flew over the plaintiff's land, spraying poison on the plaintiff's crop. The defendant thought he was spraying the land he had been hired to spray, which was adjacent to the plaintiff's land. The plaintiff sued defendant in trespass. Does the plaintiff have a good claim? Discuss. (*Schronk v. Gilliam*, 380 S.W.2d 743, Tex. Civ. App. 1964.)

9. In 1955, the plaintiff was 17 years old. He was convicted of being involved in a hit-and-run accident that

killed a Las Vegas policeman. In 1978, in an article about police officers who had died in the line of duty, the defendant newspaper mentioned the plaintiff's 1955 conviction and his conviction two years later for possession of marijuana. The plaintiff sued the newspaper for disclosure of embarrassing private facts. Should the plaintiff prevail? Discuss. (*Montesano v. Donrey Media Group*, 668 P.2d 1081, Nev. 1983.)

10. The defendant credit company called the plaintiff and, to obtain the address of her son for collection purposes, told her that her grandchild had been in a car accident and the defendant needed her son's address. When this turned out to be false, the plaintiff sued for infliction of emotional distress. Does she have a good claim? Discuss. (*Ford Motor Credit Co. v. Sheehan*, 373 So.2d 956, Fla. App. 1979.)

Yes, she could show mental harm.

11
CHAPTER

In recent years, courts have found themselves plagued with the problem of manufacturer liability, specifically the extent to which a manufacturer should be liable to a consumer who is injured by its product. To address this problem, various rules and legal theories for determining liability have been developed, and these make up the expanding area of law known as products liability. Since the 1960s, products liability has become one of the most rapidly changing areas in the history of common law, its bias having undergone a dramatic shift away from

PRODUCTS
LIABILITY

the seller to favor, instead, the consumer. The pendulum has taken such a sudden swing that sellers' liability has emerged as one of the most controversial subjects in the business world today.

Under products liability law and sales law, three legal theories may be available to an injured consumer seeking redress: (1) warranty, (2) negligence, and (3) strict liability. The first is a contract theory and is governed by the UCC; the other two are tort theories. The elements of negligence have been discussed in Chapter 10 and are applied here in the context of products liability. The principles of strict liability are taken from section 402A of the American Law Institute's *Restatement (Second) of Torts*. Unlike the UCC, the *Restatement* is not a statute, but a model code of law whose recommendations have been adopted by courts or legislatures in many states. Like the UCC, the strict liability theory applies primarily to transactions involving goods and not to those involving real estate or services.

WARRANTY

A **warranty** is an assurance or guarantee that goods will conform to certain standards. If the standards are not met, the buyer can recover damages from the seller, under a breach of warranty theory.

Such has not always been the case, for although suits involving warranties date as far back as fourteenth century England, a recovery theory was slow in developing. *Caveat emptor* ("let the buyer beware") governed the state of law until recent times—here in America, until the beginning of the twentieth century. The concept of *caveat emptor* allowed the seller to escape liability altogether, in the absence of fraud.

With the growth of business and industry came a clear need to move away from laissez-faire values and to place legal strictures on sales transactions. Chains of distribution were widening the distance between manufacturers and ultimate consumers, and an increasing sophistication in product design made inspection for defects more difficult. As a result, courts came to recognize the existence of three types of warranties, discussed in the following pages: express warranties, implied warranties, and warranties of title.

EXPRESS WARRANTIES

Express warranties are those that originate from the words or actions of the seller. To create an express warranty, the seller does not have to use the word *warranty* or *guarantee*, and the buyer does not have to show that the seller intended to make a warranty. Under section 2-313 of the UCC, a seller can create an express warranty in three different ways: (1) by an affirmation of fact or a promise relating to the goods, (2) by a description of the goods, or (3) by providing a sample or model of the goods. Such representations by the seller create contractual obligations to the extent that they become "part of the basis of the bargain."

Affirmation of Fact or Promise

By making an affirmation of fact or a promise relating to the goods, the seller tacitly guarantees that the goods will conform to the specifics he or she sets forth. For example, the seller might claim. "This boat is equipped with a two-year-old, 100-horsepower engine that was overhauled last month." The statement contains several affirmations of fact: (1) the boat is equipped with an engine, (2) the engine is two years old, (3) it generates 100 horsepower, and (4) it was overhauled last month. The seller might further state, "I assure you that this boat will not stall when run in choppy water." His affirmations concern past and present conditions; his promise, by contrast, relates to future events. Both affirmations and promises may create express warranties.

A seller's *commendation* or *expression of opinion* does not constitute an express warranty; neither does a statement that relates only to the *value* of the goods. Thus, the seller could claim that his boat was a "first-class vessel, worth $25,000 at retail" without creating a warranty. The law is not so rigid as to disallow "puffing" of products; it assumes that a consumer can distinguish between sales talk and fact.

But at times the distinction between fact and opinion is not easy to make. Consider, for example, the following statement: "The steering mechanism on this boat has been thoroughly engineered." The claim is rather vague, and as a descriptive phrase, "thoroughly engineered" may not be appreciably different from "first class." Yet the reference to engineering may create an impression of technologic excellence in the mind of an unsophisticated buyer and thus create a wrong impression.

In such cases, the courts tend to consider a number of factors, principally the buyer's frame of reference. If the buyer has limited knowledge of the goods involved, the statement from the seller is apt to be an affirmation of fact. If, however, the buyer is more knowledgeable than the seller, vague statements will be treated as mere expressions of opinion.

These additional generalizations can be made about the creation of express warranties: Statements that are specific and absolute are more readily construed as warranties than indefinite ones. Terms put in writing are more likely to create warranties than those given orally. A warranty is more likely to be found if the statement is objectively *verifiable* (e.g., "This machine is one year old."). The nature and seriousness of the defect may also have a bearing on the determination.

Description of Goods

A descriptive word or phrase used in a sale of goods may create an express warranty that the goods will conform to the description. The word *pitted* or *seedless* on a box of prunes or raisins warrants that the fruit will have no seeds. Recognized trade terms may also constitute descriptions. For example, the term *Scotchguard*, used in connection with furniture upholstery, describes fabric that has been treated to make it water and stain-resistant. Goods described by trade terms are warranted to possess those characteristics generally associated with the terms in the trade or business involved.

Sample or Model

If the seller provides to the buyer a sample or model of the goods to be sold, a warranty arises that the goods will conform to the sample or model. A sample is a single item taken from the mass to be sold, whereas a model is used to represent the goods. In a sale of wheat, a sample of one bushel might be drawn from the thousand bushels to be sold. But when the item being sold has not yet been manufactured or is too difficult to transport, a model might be used instead.

Although the UCC makes no distinction between express warranties arising out of sales by sample or by model, a sample is more likely to create such a warranty than a model. Because a sample is actually taken from the inventory to be sold, it is usually easier for the buyer to prove that a sample was intended to establish a standard of quality for the sale.

Basis of the Bargain

Under section 2-313, an express warranty is created only if the affirmation or promise, description, model, or sample is "part of the basis of the bargain." Courts have applied this phrase to two types of circumstances: First is the case in which the seller makes a statement about the goods, and circumstances indicate that both parties intended the statement to be a part of the agreement. This would certainly be true if the statement appeared in the sales contract itself and would apply also when it is reasonably clear that the statement played a material part in the buyer's decision to purchase the goods. The second type of case involves statements of fact contained in a brochure, provided to the buyer by the seller. Under pre-Code law, the burden of proof was generally on the buyer to show that he or she had read the statement and relied on it. If reliance could not be shown, the buyer could not recover on the breach of warranty theory. By contrast, under the "basis of the bargain" language, courts *assume* that the statement became a part of the contract unless the seller can show "good reason" for the contrary (section 2-313, comment 8).

A different question arises when, *after* the sale has been made, the buyer requests a promise from the seller that the goods meet certain standards. If given, does this promise become "part of the basis of the bargain"? Before the enactment of the UCC, the answer probably would have been *no;* today it is probably *yes.* Under section 2-209(1), the seller's postsale promise is a modification of the contract and becomes an integral part of the agreement, even without additional consideration from the buyer.

A similar problem occurs sometimes in a sales negotiation, during which the seller makes statements that fail to appear in the written contract. Buyers who attempt to base a claim for breach of warranty on a recollection of oral statements are often thwarted by the *parol evidence rule* of UCC section 2-202. Under this rule, if the court finds that the written form was intended as the final expression of the parties' agreement, any oral statement in contradiction of the written terms will not be admissible as evidence.

The following case illustrates how a company's advertising may expand the scope of an express warranty.

COMMUNITY TELEVISION SERVICES, INC. v. DRESSER INDUSTRIES, INC.

U.S. COURT OF APPEALS, 8TH CIRCUIT, 586 F.2d 637 (1978)

In 1965, two television stations in South Dakota created a separate corporation, Community Television Services, Inc. (Community), for the purpose of constructing and operating a 2,000-foot tower that would broadcast signals for both stations. Community contracted with Dresser Industries, Inc. (Dresser), who designed, manufactured, and erected the tower for a price of $385,000. The tower was completed in 1969, and Community used it until 1975. During this time, Community regularly inspected and properly maintained the tower. On January 10 and 11, 1975, a severe winter blizzard occurred in the area where the tower was located. During the early morning hours of January 11, as the storm reached its height with wind speeds of up to 80 miles per hour near the top of the tower, the structure collapsed.

Dresser denied responsibility, and Community sued in federal district court for breach of an express warranty. The verdict and judgment in the trial court were in favor of Community, the plaintiff, for damages of $1,274,631.60, and Dresser, the defendant, appealed.

LAY, CIRCUIT JUDGE:

...Expert witnesses called by both sides differed in their opinions as to the cause of the collapse. Community's experts testified that they had eliminated metallurgical or mechanical failure or abnormal wind loading as the cause of collapse. They theorized that the cause was high winds setting up a phenomenon known as mechanical resonance. They concluded that because of the resonance, the tower members "were inadequate to support the load that they sustained." On the other hand, Dresser's experts testified that a combination of ice, snow and wind subjected the tower to a total force greater than the ultimate capacity of its structural elements. They theorized that a substantial accumulation of ice on the upper fourth of the tower enlarged the tower members to a greater load than their designed wind loading capacity. Community attempted to refute Dresser's ice theory by calling several witnesses who testified that they did not see any such ice on or near the area where the tower collapsed. In turn, Dresser countered Community's theory through expert testimony that relatively constant winds were necessary for resonance to begin, and the winds were gusty and varied in speed and direction at the time of collapse. Furthermore, Dresser argued that the warranty did not guarantee against mechanical resonance, and experts testified that its prevention was beyond the current state of the art.

The specifications incorporated in the sale contract included a specified "Design Wind Load," which set forth the tower's capacity to withstand wind velocity as measured in pounds of pressure per square foot against the flat surface of its members. The specification reads: "The tower shall be designed to resist a uniform wind load per drawing T-5172, sheet S-1, 60 psf on flats." The trial court instructed the jury that this specification constituted an express warranty that the structure would withstand wind exerting pressure of 60 pounds per square foot on the flat surfaces of the tower. Dresser's advertising materials and the testimony of experts at trial revealed that the wind velocity necessary to create 60 pounds of pressure on the flat surfaces of the tower would be approximately 120 miles per hour. The evidence showed that the wind loading specifications referred, at least in engineering parlance, to "a force caused by the wind that is introduced parallel to the ground ... [which] would be tending to blow the structure over."

Dresser argues that the trial court erred in failing to direct a verdict on the express warranty claim or grant it judgment notwithstanding the verdict, because expert testimony that the tower met the design specification was uncontradicted. Community's own experts stated unequivocally that in their opinion the tower conformed in a mathematical

CONTINUED

or analytical sense to the 60 pounds per square foot wind loading specification. If the warranty may be restricted to the technical specification set forth in the written contract, we would find Dresser's argument convincing. However, we agree with Community that the warranty was amplified, in advertising materials Dresser gave to Community prior to purchase of the tower, to promise more than mere compliance with technical measurements. In an advertising catalog, Dresser made the following supplementary affirmation:

> Wind force creates the most critical loads to which a tower is normally subjected. When ice forms on tower members thereby increasing the surface area resisting the passage of wind, the load is increased.
>
> Properly designed towers will safely withstand the maximum wind velocities and ice loads to which they are likely to be subjected. Dresser-Ideco can make wind and ice load recommendations to you for your area based on U.S. Weather Bureau data.
>
> In the winter, loaded with ice and hammered repeatedly with gale force winds, these towers absorb some of the roughest punishment that towers take anywhere in the country... yet continue to give dependable, uninterrupted service.

Although we agree with Dresser that a seller cannot be held to be the insurer of its product, Dresser nevertheless provided the catalog to Community to induce purchase of its product, and in the absence of clear affirmative proof to the contrary, the above affirmation must be considered part of the "basis of the bargain." Standing alone, the statements provide a warranty that Dresser's tower would be properly designed so as to safely withstand the maximum wind velocities and ice loads to which it would likely be subjected. Dresser did not indicate that this broad affirmation was superseded or cancelled by the technical specification in the contract. When the affirmation is read in tandem with the contract, as part of the "fabric" of the agreement of the parties, it enlarges the warranty created by the technical wind loading specification, giving evidence of its full intent and scope.

We find that the statements in the advertising catalog, which supplement the wind loading specification, could reasonably have been found by the jury to be an affirmation of fact or a promise concerning the actual durability or performance of the tower during the wind and ice storms to which it was likely to be subjected.

Although Dresser's defense was that the tower collapsed by reason of excessive loading due to ice on the tower members, no disclaimer or limitation of the warranty that a properly designed tower would safely withstand the maximum wind and ice loads to which it was likely to be subjected appeared in the advertising materials or the contract. Under the *integrated* warranty given, a purchaser could reasonably assume that the tower, if properly designed for its location, would withstand maximum wind speeds to which it was likely to be subjected, even if ice accumulated on the tower members. While the blizzard was a severe one, the evidence does not support the conclusion that the wind alone, or the combination of wind and ice which Dresser claimed caused the collapse, was not within the range of storm conditions to be reasonably contemplated for the tower's location. Breach of a warranty created by standards describing the specific capacity of goods is proved when the product is shown by direct or circumstantial evidence to have failed to perform reasonably and safely the function for which it was intended by the manufacturer. In view of the affirmation made in the catalog, there was sufficient evidence for the jury to reasonably find that the tower was not as durable as it was warranted to be.

[Affirmed.]

HUMOR AND THE LAW

Many products liability cases involve foreign substances in items of food or drink. Few are more repulsive than *Pillars v. Reynolds Tobacco*, 78 So. 365 (Miss. 1918). Today, the case would be an "open and shut" victory for plaintiff on a strict liability or breach of implied warranty theory. In 1918, however, plaintiff's only theory was negligence. He nonetheless won a suit over his plug of "Brown Mule Chewing Tobacco". The court described the fact as follows:

> It seems that [plaintiff] consumed one plug of his purchase, which measured up to representations, that it was tobacco unmixed with human flesh, but when [plaintiff] tackled the second plug it made him sick, but, not suspecting the tobacco, he tried another chew, and still another, until he bit into some foreign substance, which crumbled like dry bread, and caused him to foam at the mouth, while he was getting "sicker and sicker." Finally, his teeth struck something hard; he could not bite through it. After an examination he discovered a human toe, with flesh and nail intact. We refrain from detailing the further harrowing and nauseating details.

The court ruled for plaintiff on the negligence issue, noting:

> We can imagine no reason why, with ordinary care, human toes could not be left out of chewing tobacco, and if toes are found in chewing tobacco, it seems to us that someone has been very careless.

IMPLIED WARRANTIES

An implied warranty is created through the mere act of selling and is imposed on the seller by law. Its purpose is to protect buyers who suffer economic and commercial losses when products fail to serve their needs. Unlike with express warranties, specific representations about a product have not actually been made. The consumer has been guided, instead, by the belief that his or her purchase is suitable for its intended use. In sections 2-314 and 2-315, the UCC names two types of implied warranties: the implied warranty of merchantability and the implied warranty of fitness for a particular purpose.

Merchantability

The law injects into the sales contract a warranty that the goods are "merchantable," if the seller is a *merchant with respect to the type of goods being sold*. (When a student sells his or her 1980 VW to a neighbor, no implied warranty of his or her merchantability exists because the student is not a merchant in automobiles.)

"Merchantable" means essentially that the goods are *fit for the ordinary purpose for which such goods are used*. The warranty of merchantability requires, for example, that shoes have their heels attached well enough that they will not break off under normal use. The warranty does not require, however, that ordinary walking shoes be suitable for mountain climbing. To be merchantable, goods must also serve their ordinary purpose *safely*. A refrigerator that keeps food cold but that gives an electric shock when the handle is touched is not merchantable. This is not to say that the seller becomes an insurer against accident or malfunction; the purchaser is expected to maintain his or her goods against the attrition of use.

The **implied warranty of merchantability** also does not guarantee that goods will be of the highest quality available. They are required to be only of *average or medium grade,* in addition to being adequately packaged and labeled. A growing minority of jurisdictions finds that the implied warranty of merchantability applies to sales of *used* goods; most limit the warranty to sale of new goods.

When applied to food, the implied warranty of merchantability can be related to *wholesomeness*. A tainted pork chop, for instance, is not merchantable. A number of cases decided before enactment of the UCC held that food purchased at a restaurant, hotel, or other such establishment carried no warranty because the sale involved a service rather than a product. The UCC, however, explicitly states that the implied warranty of merchantability extends to food sold at service establishments such as restaurants and hotels, whether the food is consumed on or off the premises.

Many cases alleging a breach of the implied warranty of merchantability have involved objects in food that caused harm to the consumer. Exceptional examples range from a mouse in a bottled soft drink to a screw in a slice of bread. In such cases the courts traditionally have distinguished between "foreign" and "natural" objects. They usually find that if the object is foreign to the mass (such as the mouse or screw mentioned above), the warranty of merchantability has been breached. If, however, the object is natural (such as a bone in a piece of fish), no breach of warranty has occurred.

A growing number of courts have rejected this approach and have based their decisions instead on the "reasonable expectation" of the consumer. The controlling factor in this approach is whether a consumer can reasonably expect the object in question to be in the food. A piece of chicken may be expected to contain a bone but not when in a chicken sandwich; an olive may be expected to contain a pit but not when a hole at the end indicates that it has been pitted. Bones and olive pits will not render food unmerchantable under the "foreign–natural object" test *but may do so under the "reasonable expectation" test*. Thus, the results of a legal suit may vary considerably, depending on which approach is used. A famous case in this area follows.

Webster v. Blue Ship Tea Room, Inc.

Supreme Judicial Court of Massachusetts, 198 N.E.2d 309 (1964)

Plaintiff, Webster, who was born and brought up in New England, ordered a cup of fish chowder while dining at the defendant's "quaint" Boston restaurant. She choked on a fish bone contained in the soup, necessitating two esophagoscopies at the Massachusetts General Hospital. The plaintiff sued for breach of the implied warranty of merchantability. A jury returned a verdict for the plaintiff. The defendant appealed the trial judge's refusal to direct a verdict for the defendant.

Reardon, Justice:

We must decide whether a fish bone lurking in a fish chowder, about the ingredients of which there is no other complaint, constitutes a breach of implied warranty under applicable provisions of the Uniform Commercial Code. As the [trial] judge put it, "Was the fish chowder fit to be eaten and wholesome? Nobody is claiming that the fish itself wasn't wholesome. But the bone of contention here—I don't mean that for a pun—but was this fish bone a foreign substance that made the fish chowder unwholesome or not fit to be eaten?"

The plaintiff has vigorously reminded us of the high standards imposed by this court where the sale of good is involved.

The defendant asserts that here was a native New Englander eating fish chowder in a "quaint" Boston dining place where she had been before; that "[f]ish chowder, as it is served and enjoyed by New Englanders, is a hearty dish, originally designed to satisfy the appetites of our seamen and fishermen"; that "[t]his court knows well that we are not talking of some insipid broth as is customarily served to convalescents." We are asked to rule in such fashion that no chef is forced "to reduce the pieces of fish in the chowder to miniscule size in an effort to ascertain if they contained any pieces of bone." In so ruling, we are told (in the defendant's brief), "the court will not only uphold its reputation for legal knowledge and acumen, but will, as loyal sons of Massachusetts, save our world-reknowned fish chowder from degenerating into an insipid broth containing the mere essence of its former stature as a culinary masterpiece."

Chowder is an ancient fish dish preexisting even "the appetites of our seamen and fishermen." It was perhaps the common ancestor of the "more refined cream soups, purees, and bisques." Berolzheimer, The American Woman's Cook Book (Publisher's Guild, Inc., New York, 1941) p. 176. The all embracing Fannie Farmer states in a portion of her recipe, fish chowder is made with a "fish skinned, but head and tail left on. Cut off head and tail and remove fish from backbone. Cut fish in 2-inches pieces and set aside. Put head, tail, and backbone broken in pieces, in stewpan; add 2 cups cold water and bring slowly to boiling point."

Thus, we consider a dish which for many years, if well made, has been made generally as outlined above. It is not too much to say that a person sitting down in New England to consume a good New England fish chowder embarks on a gustatory adventure which may entail the removal of some fish bones from his bowl as he proceeds. We are not inclined to tamper with age old recipes by any amendment reflecting the plaintiff's view of the effect of the Uniform Commercial Code on them. We are aware of the heavy body of case law involving foreign substances in food, but we sense a strong distinction between them and those relative to unwholesomeness of the food itself, e.g., tainted mackeral, and a fishbone in fish chowder. We consider that the joys of life in New England include the ready availability of fresh fish chowder. We should be prepared to cope with the hazards of fish bones, the occasional presence of which in chowders is, it seems to us, to be anticipated, and which, in the light of a hallowed tradition, do not impair their fitness or merchantability.

Judgment for the defendant.

Fitness for a Particular Purpose

In section 2-315, the UCC provides: "Where the seller at the time of contracting has reason to know any particular purpose for which the goods are required and that the buyer is relying on the seller's skill or judgment to furnish suitable goods, there is... an implied warranty that the goods shall be fit for such purpose" (hence the name **implied warranty of fitness for a particular purpose,** sometimes referred to as "warranty of fitness"). Note that the seller is not required to be a merchant, although merchants are defendants in most cases.

Often the liability incurred by the seller under the implied warranty of fitness is greater than one incurred under the implied warranty of merchantability—a difference that can be best illustrated by a simple example: Suppose a buyer purchases an electric clock and discovers that its hands do not glow in the dark. The packaging carries no reference to visibility of the dial; neither does the instruction card. No breach of the implied warranty of merchantability exists here, for visibility of the dial under all conditions is not within the realm of a clock's "ordinary purpose." Yet, the seller *may* be liable to the buyer for breach of the implied warranty of fitness for a particular purpose if he or she knew that the buyer had a particular reason to need a clock with a lighted dial.[1]

A close examination of facts is required to ascertain whether a warranty of fitness exists, because such a warranty arises only if the following conditions exist:

1. The seller had "reason to know" of the particular purpose for which the goods were purchased. This requirement is obviously met if the seller was *actually informed* of the intended purpose, but such knowledge does not have to be proven. The requirement is also met if the circumstances dictate that the seller, as a reasonable person, *should have known* that the buyer was purchasing the goods for a particular purpose.

2. The seller also had reason to know that the buyer was relying on the seller's skill or judgment to furnish suitable goods. That is, the buyer must have relied on the seller's recommendation and the seller must have known or should have known of this dependence. If the buyer shows initiative by presenting brand names or introducing other specifications, recovery will be less likely:

3. Items 1 and 2 above must have existed at the time of contracting. If the seller learns the relevant facts only after the sale contract is made, a warranty does not exist.

These elements are applied in the following unique case.

---

[1] Some confusion exists because courts are split as to whether the "particular purpose" must be something other than the ordinary purpose for which the goods are used for the implied warranty of fitness to arise. Assume that Sally tells the salesman at the ABC Shoe Store that she wants some running shoes for jogging. He selects shoes clearly labeled as running shoes, which turn out to be unsuitable. Some courts would find that there was a breach of the implied warranty of fitness. Others would hold that because running was the ordinary purpose for which the shoes were intended, only an implied warranty of merchantability arose.

CASE

DEMPSEY v. ROSENTHAL

CIVIL COURT, CITY OF NEW YORK, 448 N.Y.S.2d 441 (1983)

Plaintiff bought a poodle, Mr. Dunphy, from defendant for $541.25. Five days later, an inspection by a veterinarian disclosed that Mr. Dunphy had one undescended testicle. The plaintiff returned the dog and demanded a refund. The defendant refused. The plaintiff brought this suit in small claims court, claiming breach of the implied warranties of merchantability and fitness.

SAXE, JUDGE:

[The judge first found that Mr. Dunphy's condition breached the implied warranty of merchantability because a dog with an undescended testicle would not pass without complaint in the trade. Although fertile, the dog could pass the condition on to future generations. The judge then turned to the matter of implied warranty of fitness.]

The next issue to be resolved here is whether warranty of fitness for a particular purpose has been breached. [The UCC] makes it clear that the warranty of fitness for a particular purpose is narrow, more specific, and more precise than the warranty of merchantability which involves fitness for the *ordinary* purposes for which such goods are used. The following are the conditions that are not required by the implied warranty of merchantability but that must be present if a plaintiff is to recover on the basis of the implied warranty of fitness for a particular purpose:

1. The seller must have reason to know the buyer's particular purpose.
2. The seller must have reason to know that the buyer is relying on the seller's skill or judgment to furnish appropriate goods.
3. The buyer must, in fact, rely upon the seller's skill or judgment.

Nevertheless, I find that the warranty of fitness for a particular purpose has also been breached. Ms. Dempsey testified that she specified to [defendant's] salesperson that she wanted a dog that was suitable for breeding purposes. Although this is disputed by the defendant, the credible testimony supports Ms. Dempsey's version of the event. Further, it is reasonable for a seller of a pedigree dog to assume that the buyer intends to breed it. But, it is undisputed by the experts here (for both sides) that Mr. Dunphy, with only one descended testicle, was as capable of siring a litter as a male dog with two viable and descended testicles. This, the defendant contends, compels a finding in its favor. I disagree.

While it is true that Mr. Dunphy's fertility level may be unaffected, his stud value, because of this hereditary condition (which is likely to be passed on to future generations) is severely diminished.

The fact that Mr. Dunphy's testicle later descended and assumed the proper position is not relevant. "The parties were entitled to get what they bargained for at the time that they bargained for it. The right of the buyer to rescind must be determined as of the time the election to rescind was exercised. The parties' rights are not to be determined by subsequent events." *White Devon Farm v. Stahl*, 389 N.Y.S.2d 724 (Sup.Ct.N.Y.Co. 1976). *White Devon Farm* involved the "tale of a stud who was a dud." The court there held that the warranty of fitness for a particular purpose was breached despite the fact that the horse's fertility later rose and the stallion sired 27 live foals.

A judgment for the claimant in the amount of $541.25 shall be entered by the clerk.

WARRANTIES IN LEASES

Article 2A of the UCC contains warranty provisions for *leases* of goods. Except for "finance leases," article 2A's rules regarding imposition and disclaimer of express and implied warranty liability are generally the same as those of article 2 that we have just discussed.

WARRANTIES OF TITLE

In most sales of goods, a warranty as to the validity of the seller's title automatically exists. Section 2-312 of the UCC imposes two basic types of **warranty of title.** The first is a warranty that *the title conveyed shall be good and its transfer rightful.* This warranty is obviously breached if the seller has stolen the goods from some third party and therefore has no title at all. Other breaches, however, are not so obvious. Suppose that A buys goods from B and then is approached by C who claims to be the rightful owner. Inquiries reveal that there is some basis for C's claim and that the matter can be resolved only through a lawsuit. Will A have to become involved in a lawsuit initiated by C to determine if she bought a good title from B? Or has B breached his warranty of title by conveying a "questionable" title? The answer is that A has the option of returning the goods to B and getting her money back or defending against C's claim. If A takes the latter route and wins the lawsuit, she can recover her legal expenses from B. If A loses the lawsuit, she can recover from B not only her legal expenses, but also the value of the goods lost to C. A breach of the warranty of title exists if C's claim places a "substantial shadow" on the title, even if it ultimately might be proved invalid.

The second type of title warranty is that *the goods shall be delivered free from any security interest or other lien or encumbrance of which the buyer at the time of contracting has no knowledge.* This warranty will be breached, for instance, if B sells mortgaged goods to A without telling A of the mortgage.

Warranties of title accompany a sale of goods unless the seller indicates by specific language that no such assurances are being made or unless the circumstances indicate as much (for example, in a public sale of goods seized by the sheriff to satisfy a debt, rightful transfers of title are generally not guaranteed).

An additional obligation—not, strictly speaking, a warranty of title—is imposed on some sellers by section 2-312: Unless otherwise agreed, a seller who is a merchant in the type of goods involved is deemed to warrant *that the goods sold do not infringe on the patent, copyright, or trademarks of a third party.* If a claim of infringement is made by a third party against the buyer, the seller is responsible—unless, of course, the goods were manufactured according to the *buyer's specifications.*

CONFLICTING AND OVERLAPPING WARRANTIES

Two or more warranties sometimes exist in a single sales transaction. For example, a machine might be warranted to perform certain functions and to last for a specified time. In addition to these express warranties, an implied warranty of merchantability or of fitness for a particular purpose, or both, might exist.

When more than one warranty is created in a given transaction, the buyer does not have to choose among them. The warranties are *cumulative,* such that the buyer can take advantage of *any* or *all* of them. According to section 2-317, courts should interpret the warranties as being "consistent" whenever such an interpretation is reasonable. In the unusual event that two warranties are in conflict and cannot both be given effect, the court must attempt to determine the intent of the parties as to which warranty should prevail. Several rules offer guidance in determining intention:

1. Exact or technical specifications take precedence over inconsistent samples or models or general language of description.

2. A sample drawn from the goods to be sold takes precedence over inconsistent general language or description.

3. An express warranty, regardless of how it was created, takes precedence over the implied warranty of merchantability if the two are inconsistent. (An express warranty does not take precedence over the implied warranty of fitness for a particular purpose, although it is difficult to imagine a situation in which the two would be inconsistent.)

These rules are not absolute and can be disregarded by the court if they produce an unreasonable result. The following case illustrates a situation in which a seller's express promise conflicted with a claimed implied warranty.

CASE

MOHASCO INDUSTRIES, INC. v. ANDERSON HALVERSON CORP.

SUPREME COURT OF NEVADA, 520 P.2d 234 (1974)

Anderson Halverson Corp., owner of the Stardust Hotel in Las Vegas, Nevada, ordered carpeting to be manufactued by Mohasco and installed in the hotel lobby and casino showroom of the Stardust. After installation the buyer refused to pay, claiming that the carpet "shaded" excessively, giving it a mottled effect and the appearance of being water stained. Mohasco, the plaintiff, sued Anderson Halverson, the defendant, to recover the price of $18,242.50. The trial court held in favor of the defendant, and the plaintiff appealed.

THOMPSON, JUSTICE:

... One Fritz Eden, an interior decorator selected and hired by Stardust, designed a pattern for the carpet to be used in the hotel lobby and casino showroom. A sample run of the chosen pattern was taken to the hotel by Eden, and was approved. Eden then specified the material and grade of carpet which the Stardust also approved. The Stardust then issued a detailed purchase order designating the type and length of yarn, weight per square yard, type of weave, color and pattern. No affirmation of fact or promise was made by any representative of ... the seller to ... the buyer. The carpet which was manufactured, delivered and installed was consistent with the sample and precisely conformed to the detailed purchase order. There were no manufacturing defects in the carpet.

Upon installation, however, the carpet did shade and, apparently, to a much greater extent than the Stardust or its representative had anticipated. It is clear from the testimony that "shading" is an inherent characteristic of all pile carpeting. When the tufts of the carpet are bent in different angles, the light reflection causes portions of the carpet to

CONTINUED

appear in different shades of the same color. The only explanation in the record for the "excessive shading" was that Fritz Eden, the decorator for Stardust, decided not to specify the more expensive "twist yarn." That type yarn causes the tufts to stick straight up (or at least tends to do so) thus aiding in the elimination of excessive shading.

The trial court found that the sale of the carpet was a sale by sample which was made a part of the basis of the bargain and created an express warranty that the carpet delivered for installation would conform to the sample. Moreover, [the trial court found] that the *express warranty was breached by the seller*, thus precluding its claim for relief. [Emphasis added.] . . .

That finding is clearly erroneous. The installed carpet conformed precisely to the description of the goods contained in the purchase order. Moreover, it conformed precisely to the sample which the buyer approved. Whether the sale be deemed a sale by description or by sample, in either event the express warranty of conformity was met. The seller delivered the very carpet which the buyer selected and ordered.

Although there is substantial evidence to support the trial court's finding that the installed carpet shaded excessively, that consequence may not be equated with a breach of an express warranty since the seller delivered and installed the very item which the buyer selected and ordered. Had the buyer, through its interior decorator, selected the more expensive carpet with "twist yarn," perhaps this controversy would not have arisen. The buyer, not the seller, must bear the consequence of that mistake.

[The court then turned to the implied warranty of merchantability question, as follows:] As already noted, the judgment below rests upon an erroneous finding that the seller breached an express warranty that the whole of the carpet would conform to the sample which the buyer had approved. The buyer suggests, however, that the judgment should be sustained in any event since it is otherwise clear that the seller breached the implied warrant[y] of merchantability. . . . We turn to consider this contention.

Unless excluded, or modified, a warranty of merchantability is implied in a contract if the seller is a merchant with respect to the goods in question. We have not, heretofore, had occasion to consider the impact, if any, of the implied warranty of merchantability upon a case where the goods are sold by sample or description and the buyer's specifications are so complete that it is reasonable to conclude that he had relied upon himself and not the seller with regard to the merchantability of the goods. . . .

It is apparent that in a case where the sample or description of the goods may, for some reason, result in an undesirable product, the seller is placed in a dilemma. In Hawkland, A Transactional Guide to the Uniform Commercial Code, Sec. 1.190206, at 65, the following example is given. Suppose a buyer provides his seller with minute specifications of the material, design and method of construction to be utilized in preparation of an order of shoes, and the seller delivers to the buyer shoes which exactly conform to the specifications. If the blueprints are in fact designs of defective shoes, the buyer should not be able to complain that the shoes are defective. For such an order might put the seller in the dilemma of being forced to breach either the express warranty of description or the implied warranty of merchantability.

The matter at hand is similar to the example just given. Although the carpet was not defective, it did shade excessively and was, in the view of the buyer, an undesirable product. Yet, it was the product which the buyer specified and ordered. The manufacturer-seller was not at liberty to add "twist yarn" and charge a higher price. The buyer relied upon its decorator, Fritz Eden, and the seller performed as directed. . . . *[W]e hold that the implied warranty of merchantability is limited by an express warranty of conformity to a precise description supplied by the buyer, and if the latter warranty is not breached, neither is the former.* [Emphasis added.] . . .

The judgment for [the buyer] is reversed, and since there is no dispute concerning the amount of the plaintiff's claim, the cause is remanded to the district court to enter judgment for the plaintiff against the said defendant for $18,242.50, together with appropriate interest and costs.

DISCLAIMERS (EXCLUDING AND LIMITING WARRANTIES)

As we have seen, a sales transaction can give rise to three types of warranties: express warranties, implied warranties, and warranties of title. But the creation of these warranties is by no means automatic. The UCC allows a seller to disavow the existence of warranties or to limit the circumstances in which liability will apply by including a **disclaimer** in the sales contract. Theoretically, disclaimers can be justified on the grounds that their use advances freedom of contract, permitting parties to bargain over contract terms and to allocate the risk of loss. Yet in reality, the arrangement tends to be one-sided: consumers usually are in no bargaining position and often do not read disclaimers when making a purchase. For this reason, courts may find a particular disclaimer *unconscionable* under UCC section 2-302.

Disclaimers of Express Warranties

A seller who wishes to avoid liability on an express warranty obviously should not do anything to create a warranty in the first place (a highly impractical measure to take in making sales!). An alternative would be to include a disclaimer in the contract. However, if a warranty has actually become part of the contract, an attempt to disclaim liability will usually not be effective. Section 2-316(1) states that a disclaimer will be disregarded if it is inconsistent with the words or conduct that created the express warranty. Suppose that an express warranty has been created by a statement of the seller, by the use of a sample, or by a written description of the goods. Liability could not then be disclaimed by specifying: "These goods are sold without warranties." Such a statement would almost always be inconsistent with the words or conduct that created the warranty. In short, *it is extremely difficult for a seller to disclaim an express warranty which has become part of the contract.*

Disclaimers of Implied Warranties

Because the existence of an implied warranty depends on circumstances rather than on the precise words used by the seller, such a warranty is relatively easy to disclaim. The UCC permits disclaimers of implied warranties through (1) the use of language specified in section 2-316 of the Code, (2) the buyer's examination of the goods, or (3) custom and usage.

Disclaimer by Language:

In the case of the *warranty of merchantability*, the language used by the seller to disclaim liability does not have to be in writing. If written, however, the disclaimer must be "conspicuous" enough to be noticed by any reasonable person involved in the purchase. (A disclaimer printed in larger type or in a different color than the remainder of the document will probably be considered conspicuous.) In addition, the word *merchantability* must be used—unless the seller uses a phrase such as "with all faults" or "as is," language that serves to disclaim *both* or *either* of the implied warranties.

In the case of the *warranty of fitness for a particular purpose*, the disclaimer must be in writing and must be conspicuous. Yet the statement itself can be a general one, such as, "There are no warranties extending beyond the description on the face hereof."

Disclaimer by Examination: If before making a contract, the buyer fully examines the goods (or a sample or model of them) or deliberately refuses to examine them at all, no implied warranty exists for *reasonably apparent* defects. Yet if the buyer has no opportunity to examine the goods before contracting, the seller becomes liable for such defects.

When defects are hidden, the seller is always liable, unless it can be proved that the buyer had knowledge of the defects before contracting. When deciding whether a defect is "reasonably apparent" or "hidden," a court will take into account the buyer's knowledge or skill. Such a factor obviously has a bearing on what an examination should have revealed to the buyer.

For example, in *Dempsey v Rosenthal*, Mr. Dunphy's defective condition—the undescended testicle—was not readily observable. A manual manipulation of the scrotal area would have been the only means to verify the condition. The court found that Ms. Dempsey, the buyer, did not know this and should not be charged with knowledge of the fact. The type of examination that would be undertaken by the average buyer of a male puppy would not disclose the defective condition, so recovery was not barred by the inspection provisions of UCC 2-316.

Disclaimer by Custom or Usage: Implied warranties are sometimes excluded or modified by *trade usage* (industry-wide custom) or by a custom that has been established between the contracting parties. An industry-wide custom will have no effect, however, on a buyer who is not a member of the particular industry and is unaware of the custom.

Limitation on Damages: In contract cases, punitive damages traditionally have not been available to plaintiffs. For this reason, express and implied warranty suits usually involve two types of damages: basis-of-the-bargain damages (the value of the goods warranted less the value received) and consequential damages (personal and property damages proximately caused by the warranty breach, along with any indirect economic loss foreseeable by the defendant).[2] The buyer injured by a breached warranty also has the option to rescind the contract.

The Code allows limitations to be placed by the seller on damages that may be recovered by a breach of warranty. For example, recovery may be limited to *liquidated damages*—that is, a specified amount to be paid in the event of a breach. A limitation may also be placed on the type of remedy available, guaranteeing, for example, only the replacement of the product without charge.

---

[2] In addition to damages, the buyer has an option to rescind the contract when a warranty has been breached.

However, such limitations will not be given effect if they are *unconscionable*. For example, UCC 2-719(3) provides that "[l]imitation of consequential damages for injury to the person in the case of consumer goods is prima facie unconscionable...." Furthermore, comment #1 to 2-719 provides that "it is of the very essence of a sales contract that at least minimum adequate remedies be available...." Even a clause that appears not to be unconscionable may be ignored if "because of circumstances [it] fails in its purpose or operates to deprive either party of the substantial value of the bargain."

CASE

GREAT DANE TRAILER V. MALVERN PULPWOOD

SUPREME COURT OF ARKANSAS 785 S.W.2d 13, 1990

The plaintiff, Malvern Pulpwood, Inc., bought two drop-deck, 65,000-pound weight-rated pulpwood trailers from the defendant, Great Dane Trailer Sales, Inc. Great Dane issued warranties on the trailers that were limited to the repair or replacement of defective parts, and remedies were limited by the exclusion of consequential and incidental damages. The drop-deck trailers exhibited serious defects, as did their replacements, two straight-decked trailers. Malvern Pulpwood sued for breach of the implied warranties of merchantability and fitness. Great Dane defended on the basis of the "repair or replacement" warranty and disclaimer. Great Dane appeals after a jury verdict in Malvern's favor for $40,000.

GLAZE, JUSTICE

Under [UCC] 2-719, parties to an agreement may limit the buyer's remedies to the repair and replacement of nonconforming goods or parts and to make the remedy agreed upon the sole remedy, unless circumstances cause the exclusive or limited remedy to fail of its essential purpose. When there is substantial evidence tending to show that a particular piece of machinery obviously cannot be repaired or its parts replaced so that it is made free of defects, a jury verdict, which implicitly concludes that a limitation of the remedy to the repair and replacement of nonconforming parts deprived the purchaser of the substantial value of the bargain, should be sustained. Such a limited remedy fails whenever the warrantor, given the opportunity to do so, fails to correct the defect within a reasonable period.

In connection with the sale of two drop-deck trailers sold to Malvern Pulpwood. Great Dane offered the following warranty:

Great Dane Trailers, Inc.'s sole obligation under this warranty shall be limited to the repair or replacement, at its option, of any defective part of said trailer which is the result of defective materials and/or defective workmanship of parts furnished and installed by Great Dane Trailers, Inc. This warranty will expire sixty (60) months from date of delivery to the purchaser, and repairs under this warranty shall be at repair facilities designated by Great Dane Trailers, Inc. Transportation expenses to the repair facility are to be borne by the purchasers. THE EXPRESS WARRANTY HEREIN IS IN LIEU OF ANY AND ALL OTHER WARRANTIES, EXPRESSED OR IMPLIED, NO IMPLIED WARRANTY OF MERCHANTABILITY IS MADE AND THERE ARE NO WARRANTIES WHICH EXTEND BEYOND THE DESCRIPTION ON THE FACE HEREOF.

Although the foregoing five-year warranty was given to repair or replace the

65,000 pound GVWC rated drop-deck trailers, we believe the evidence sufficiently shows the limitation failed of its essential purpose. The drop-deck trailers were described as ten-year trailers with a five-year warranty. Both drop-deck trailers "broke" in the same spot within one year from the time Malvern Pulpwood acquired them. Malvern Pulpwood offered testimony that Great Dane's repair job was sloppy and renderd the trailers unsafe. One witness, a welder, stated he did not believe the repairs would fix the trailers; he said that any time steel is welded, the steel would not be as strong as it was before. Great Dane finally replaced the drop-deck trailers with straight-deck trailers. Nevertheless, the replacements, too, broke in the same spot as the drop-deck trailers. [W]e have no doubts that substantial evidence existed to support Malvern Pulpwood's claims that Great Dane failed to correct the trailers' defect within a reasonable period and that the limitation failed of its essential purpose.

[Affirmed.]

DEFENSES

Privity Defense

Privity is a legal term for the direct relationship between buyer and seller. **Privity of contract** means relationship of contract: If Manufacturer A sells a yacht to Retailer B who in turn sells it to Consumer C, there is privity of contract between A and B between B and C but *not* between A and C. Because a warranty arises from the formation of a contract, privity of contract between the plaintiff and the defendant used to be required for the plaintiff suing for breach of warranty. Warranties did not "run with the goods" to subsequent purchasers and users. Thus, C could sue B but not A.

The privity requirement was not a major hindrance in the early days of our country, when consumers bought most of their goods directly from artisans or local manufacturers. Today, however, when goods travel through chains of distribution, a privity requirement imposes an intolerable burden on consumers. Therefore, it has been greatly relaxed today *and is in the process of being eliminated.* All parties in the chain of distribution (manufacturers, wholesalers, and retailers) are now usually responsible to the last buyer for failure of the goods to live up to the standards of any warranties, especially for personal injuries.

Innocent Bystanders: A final problem with the privity requirement is that defects in goods often injure persons other than the purchaser; yet the privity requirement prevented nonpurchasers (e.g., innocent bystanders or persons who borrowed the product from the buyer) from suing anyone in the chain of distribution for breached warranties.

Section 2-318 of the UCC has somewhat alleviated this problem by extending warranty protection to (1) members of the buyer's family, (2) members of the buyer's household, and (3) guests in the buyer's home, "if it is reasonable to expect that such person may use, consume or be affected by the goods, and [such person] is injured [physically] by the breach of the warranty." As the language indicates, the extended protection applies only when defective goods have caused a *physical injury to the individual.*

In recent years the drafters of the UCC have proposed alternative versions of section 2-318 to further relax the privity requirement—primarily by granting protection to *any* injured person who could reasonably have been expected to use, consume, or be affected by the goods. Although only 15 or so states have enacted these versions of section 2-318 to date, the trend in most jurisdictions is toward a loosening of the privity requirement in breach of warranty actions.

Plaintiff Misconduct Defenses

When a plaintiff's carelessness contributes to a products-related accident, the defendant can use that carelessness as a defense to warranty claims in most jurisdictions. Because the plaintiff's carelessness defenses to warranty claims are generally the same as such defenses to a strict liability claim, which we are about to discuss, we defer discussion of the matter to the strict liability section.

Statute of Limitations and Notice Requirements

Under UCC 2-725, an action for breach of contract for sale of goods must be commenced within four years after the cause of action accrues. A traditional tort statute of limitations begins to run only when the right to sue is or should be discovered (and typically lasts two years). The UCC has a similar rule where a warranty *explicitly* extends to future performance of the goods and discovery of the breach must await the time of such performance. In such cases, the statute of limitations does not begin to run until the breach is or should be discovered. However, for all other suits under article 2, the UCC statute of limitations begins to run when the goods are tendered for delivery. Thus, if the defect is not discovered for four years, the suit may well be time-barred before the defect is discovered. Many potential plaintiffs lose the right to sue by allowing the seller to attempt to effect repairs until after the four-year limit has expired. Furthermore, the Code provides that by agreement the parties may reduce the period of limitation to not less than one year but may not extend it. Thus, the statute of limitations often bars warranty suits.

Some warranty actions are barred by a plaintiff's failure to comply with UCC 2-607(3), which imposes on the buyer a duty to notify the seller of a breach within a reasonable time after he or she discovers or should discover any breach, or be barred from remedy. The purpose of such a requirement is to minimize litigation by giving the seller a chance to effect repairs or otherwise satisfy the buyer. Courts have generally been reluctant to allow this provision to bar recovery by consumers who suffered personal injuries caused by a breach of warranty. Courts are inclined to construe a "reasonable time" as being a longer period in a personal injury case than in a suit brought for economic loss by a commercial purchaser. The courts are split as to whether a person who bought an item from a retailer must give notice not only to that retailer but also to the manufacturer to be allowed to sue the manufacturer.

NEGLIGENCE

Because the elements of negligence have been discussed at length in Chapter 10, our purpose here is simply to apply them to the area of products liability. Remember that in an action based on negligence, the defendant must have owed a duty to the plaintiff, and this duty must have been breached. Where a sales transaction is involved, the seller's duty to use reasonable care arises from the mere act of placing goods on the market. The economic benefit derived from a sale generates a responsibility to consumers, for the act of selling directly affects the interests of those who have no choice but to rely on the integrity of sellers. Privity of contract is no longer required in the usual negligence suit.

The manufacturer's liability for negligence is often predicated on negligent design or manufacture; in addition, *both* manufacturer and seller may be liable for failure to inspect or failure to adequately warn.

If the seller is a retailer, distributor, or wholesaler, he or she usually has no duty to inspect new goods, barring knowledge of defects. A duty to inspect does exist, however, when the seller is involved in the installation of goods (new or used) or in their preparation for eventual sale. Liability is imposed to the extent that defects are *reasonably apparent*. By the same token, a manufacturer is charged with taking reasonable measures to discover flaws created during the production process.

A *duty to warn* arises when a product's design (or its intended use) subjects the user to hazard or risk of injury. The danger in question need only be reasonably foreseeable—discoverable only within the limits of existing technology. Warnings given must be adequate in their specifics and must extend to all individuals whose harm is reasonably foreseeable. There is no duty to warn of obvious dangers—no duty, for example, to warn about fire on a box of matches.

Negligent manufacture is often cited in cases in which defects are the result of oversight, human or mechanical error, or lack of judgment. For example, production line employees might not be properly trained, or materials selected for construction might not have sufficient strength to resist the stresses of normal use.

In contrast, actions based on charges of *negligent design* hold the manufacturer responsible for more than the exercise of care in production. In addition to warning about risks and hazards inherent in a design, the manufacturer is expected to design a product with optimal safety as the ideal, compromised only when the costs of improving design exceed the benefits derived therefrom. Under the rule adopted by most states, there is a duty to design products so that accidents are unlikely to occur and so that injuries suffered will be minimal if an accident does occur. To illustrate: say X is driving a car that explodes when struck in the rear by Y, who has negligently maneuvered his truck. X may recover from Y for initial injuries and may possibly recover from the car's manufacturer for additional injuries resulting from the impact if, for example, the gas tank were located vulnerably close to the rear bumper.

Of course, it would be unreasonable to expect cars to be accident-proof in all situations. (If this were the law, some courts have observed, manufacturers would produce nothing but tanks.) In evaluating the adequacy of design standards, courts have considered such factors as the state of existing technology, the expectation of the ordinary consumer, the danger of a product in relation to its social use, and compliance with government safety standards.

To conclude, the negligence theory became viable as an avenue of recovery to injured plaintiffs when the privity requirement was finally abandoned. This theory offers some advantages over the warranty theory, for example, the buyer does not have to prove that a warranty existed, the buyer does not have to notify the seller within a reasonable time after discovering the defect, and disclaimers in the sales contract usually do not allow the seller to escape liability resulting from his or her negligence.

Yet certain disadvantages exist as well. A plaintiff must prove negligent conduct on the part of the manufacturer or seller, and proof of negligence is at times almost impossible to establish. Only in relatively rare cases have courts inferred negligence pursuant to the doctrine of **res ipsa loquitur** ("the thing speaks for itself").[3]

A second impediment to recovery under the negligence theory is that any type of plaintiff misconduct, even simple plaintiff carelessness, will reduce or bar recovery.

Third, most jurisdictions hold that the UCC provides the only avenue for product liability recovery for mere *economic* loss (generally defined as all losses other than personal injury and tangible damage to property other than the product itself). For example, the majority rule is that if a piece of equipment contains an electrical defect that causes it to be destroyed in a fire resulting in no other loss, warranty provides the buyer's only avenue for recovery. Suit on a negligence theory (and, as we are about to see, a strict liability theory) is precluded in most states.

STRICT LIABILITY

Most courts and legislatures have concluded in recent years that the warranty and negligence theories do not afford consumers as much protection as they ought, in fairness, to have. Many warranty claims are barred, for

---

[3] The doctrine of *res ipsa loquitur* may presume negligence from the fact that the accident did indeed occur. A plaintiff who can show that (1) the defendant controlled the product and (2) the defect would not normally occur absent negligence can benefit from *res ipsa loquitur's* presumption of negligence. The presumption would be applicable, for example, if a product exploded immediately on being removed from a container that was sealed at the defendant's factory.

example, by disclaimers or because of the statute of limitations or failure to give notice of breach within a reasonable time. Many negligence suits fail because the plaintiff is not able to prove specific acts of negligence on the part of the manufacturer.

Recognizing these deficiencies, most jurisdictions have adopted the theory of **strict liability** by which manufacturers and sellers are held liable irrespective of fault. (See Figure 11.1 for a comparison of strict liability with negligence.) Today, strict liability is the most common basis for imposition of product liability for personal injuries.

Justification for the strict liability theory lies in the notion that merchants and manufacturers are better able to bear losses than injured consumers and that, in many cases, losses will be transferred to the buying public in the form of higher prices on products. Thus, society at large assumes the cost of damages suffered by a few—an arrangement that is perhaps more equitable in that it offers relief for those injured by defective products.

Proponents of strict liability argue, in addition, that eliminating the need to prove negligence in a tort action will make manufacturers and sellers more mindful of accident prevention.

Finally, there is an economic basis for adopting this liability theory: Because negligence is often difficult to prove, litigation beomes excessively costly. From an overall economic standpoint, then, it can make sense to abandon proof of negligence in a products liability action.

ELEMENTS OF STRICT LIABILITY

The elements of strict liability are recorded in section 402 of the American Law Institute's *Restatement (Second) of Torts*, a summary and clarification of American common-law principles. Section 402A reads:

> **1.** One who sells any product in a defective condition unreasonably dangerous to the user or consumer or to his property is subject to liability for physical harm thereby caused to the ultimate user or consumer, or to his property, if
>
> **a.** the seller is engaged in the business of selling such a product, and
>
> **b.** it is expected to and does reach the user or consumer without substantial change in the condition in which it is sold.
>
> **2.** The rule stated in Subsection (1) applies although
>
> **a.** the seller has exercised all possible care in the preparation and sale of his product, and
>
> **b.** the user or consumer has not bought the product from or entered into any contractual relation with the seller.

Two points regarding section 402A merit special emphasis. First subsection (1)(a) limits application of the strict liability theory to those engaged in the business of selling the products in question. Second, subsection (2) makes it clear that negligence and privity are not issues under the strict liability theory.

FIGURE 11.1

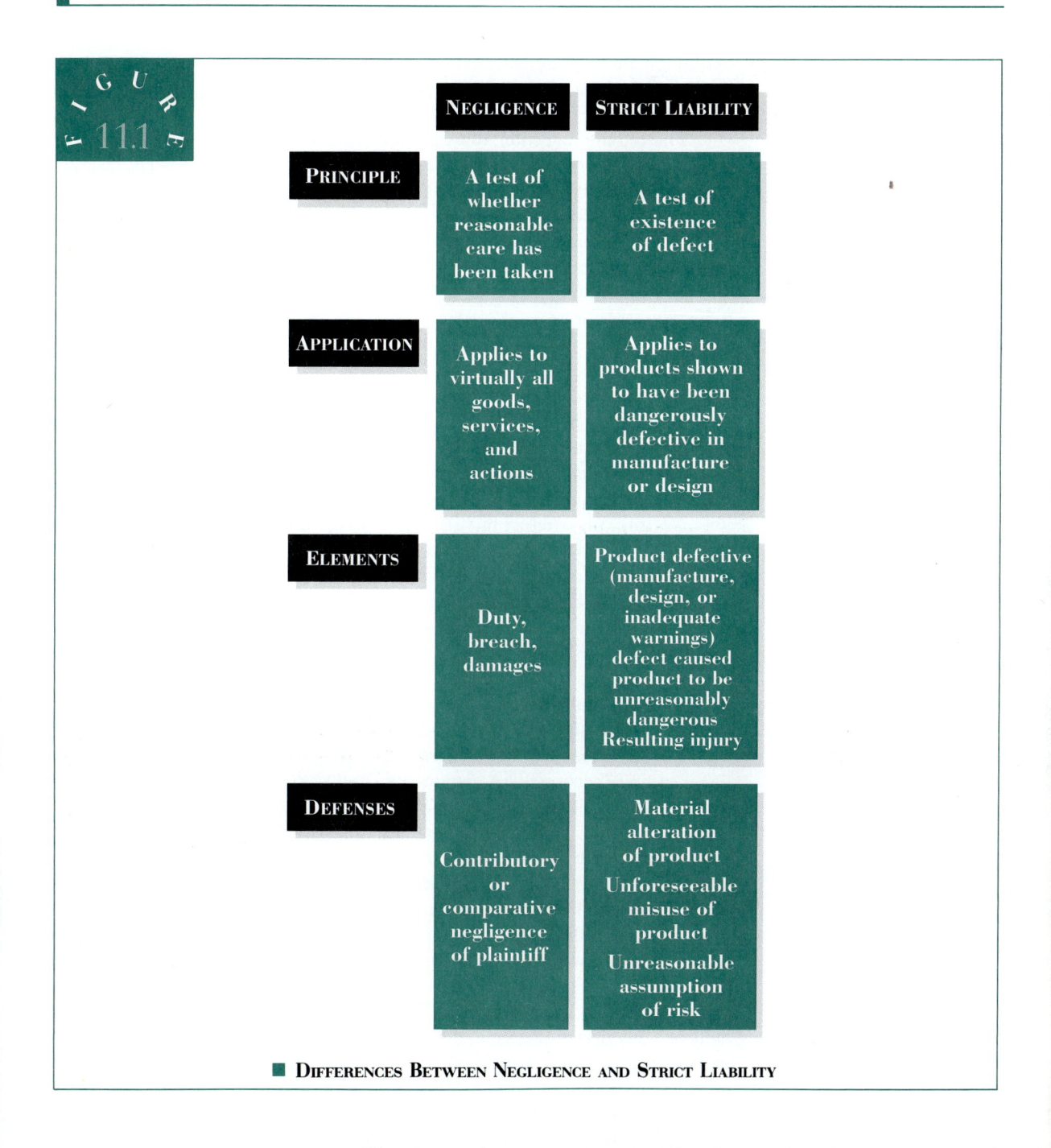

	NEGLIGENCE	STRICT LIABILITY
PRINCIPLE	A test of whether reasonable care has been taken	A test of existence of defect
APPLICATION	Applies to virtually all goods, services, and actions	Applies to products shown to have been dangerously defective in manufacture or design
ELEMENTS	Duty, breach, damages	Product defective (manufacture, design, or inadequate warnings) defect caused product to be unreasonably dangerous Resulting injury
DEFENSES	Contributory or comparative negligence of plaintiff	Material alteration of product Unforeseeable misuse of product Unreasonable assumption of risk

■ DIFFERENCES BETWEEN NEGLIGENCE AND STRICT LIABILITY

Thus in certain respects, strict liability may be viewed as an extension of the implied warranty of merchantability, where the warranty theory was applied to foreign objects in food and drink. (Recall our discussion of the "reasonable expectation" and "foreign–natural object" tests.) Taken further, strict liability is applied in cases involving virtually all kinds of goods.

Although there is, in fact, some overlapping here with the warranty theory, actions based on strict liability are nevertheless considered to be actions in tort rather than under warranty.

The crux of a section 402A action is the sale of a *defective product* that is *unreasonably dangerous* to the *user* or *consumer* or to his or her property. Section 402A covers only sales of products, not services. A product is defective if it is unreasonably dangerous because of a flaw in the product or a weakness in its design or because adequate warning of risks and hazards related to the design has not been given.

A strict liability action differs from a negligence action in that the plaintiff need not prove the defect resulted from the defendant's failure to use reasonable care. Although in failure-to-warn cases the manufacturer will almost always be found negligent, the same cannot be said of resellers. New products packaged with inadequate warnings may be resold without subjecting middlemen and retailers to liability under the negligence theory; yet these very resellers could be held liable under section 402A because no fault is required under the strict liability theory.

Defective conditions may result not only from flaws or harmful ingredients within the product but also from foreign objects in its composition and defects in its container. In this regard, a product is not defective "when it is safe for normal handling or consumption." For example, beer consumed only occasionally and in moderate amounts is probably not harmful. If an adult drinks too much beer at a party and then becomes ill, the seller is probably not liable.

To be safe, a product should be properly packaged and otherwise treated so that it will not deteriorate or be rendered dangerous within a reasonable period of time under normal conditions.

The question of what constitutes an "unreasonably" dangerous product is taken up in section 402A, comments i and k. Presumably, certain products are reasonably dangerous or "unavoidably unsafe"—that is to say, existing technology and scientific knowledge are insufficient to produce a completely safe result. An example often cited is that of the rabies vaccine, which has dangerous side effects but which is the only existing treatment against a deadly disease. Drugs sold under prescription and experimental treatments also fall within this category. Unavoidably unsafe products must be accompanied by instructions and warnings, so that the user can decide whether to undergo the risks involved. If the harmful consequences of using a product generally exceed the benefits and if safer alternatives are available, a product will be considered unreasonably unsafe. In defining what is meant by "unreasonably unsafe," section 402A also considers the expectations of the ordinary consumer, stating: "The articles sold must be dangerous to an extent beyond that which would be contemplated by the ordinary consumer who purchases it, with the ordinary knowledge common to the community as to its characteristics. . . . Good butter is not unreasonably dangerous merely because, if such be the case, it deposits cholesterol in the arteries and leads to heart attacks; but bad butter, contaminated with poisonous fish oil, is unreasonably dangerous."

Another stipulation in section 402A is that products must be in a defective condition when they leave the seller. The burden of proof lies with the plaintiff to show that the product was defective at the time of sale. Subsequent alteration or further processing may operate to relieve the seller of liability.

In addition, the plaintiff's injury must occur as a result of a defect in the product itself, rather than from conditions surrounding its use or consumption. For example, if a killer bee stings a longshoreman unloading crates of tropical fruit, the fruit company is not necessarily liable under section 402A—first, because there is no proof that the bee was a stowaway in the fruit, and second, because there is no defect inherent in the fruit itself.

Among the most problematic strict liability cases are those based on a product's defective warning. The following case is illustrative.

BRUNE v. BROWN FORMAN CORPORATION

TEXAS COURT OF APPEALS 758 S.W.2d 827 (1988)

Marie Brinkmeyer, an 18-year-old college freshman, bought a bottle of tequila manufactured by the defendant/appellee, Brown Forman. She drank straight shots of it with some friends until she was escorted to her room. She died that night, allegedly as a direct result of acute alcohol poisoning. Her mother, the plaintiff/appellant Brune, brought this strict liability action on behalf of Brinkmeyer's estate. She alleged that the tequila was an unreasonably dangerous product in that it lacked a warning and/or instructions for its safe use because many teenagers are unaware that the mere ingestion of the drug in excess quantity can cause an overdose resulting in death. The trial court granted summary judgment to Brown Forman. Brune appealed.

UTTER, JUSTICE:

The question raised on appeal is: whether the risk of death from acute alcohol poisoning is a matter of common knowledge to the community such that there was no duty on the manufacturer to warn of the danger as a matter of law.

If a manufacturer knows or should know of potential harm to a user because of the nature of its product, the manufacturer is required to give an adequate warning of such dangers and provide instructions for the safe use of the product. Therefore, in order to prevent the product from being unreasonably dangerous, the seller may be required to give directions or warnings on the container as to its use. This includes the duty to warn against foreseeable misuse.

Appellee submitted no summary judgment proof and argues that there was no duty to warn as a matter of law, because the dangers inherent in its product were within the ordinary knowledge common to the community.

Comment h [to the Restatement (Second) of Torts Sec. 402A] states that:

A product is not in a defective condition when it is safe for normal handling and consumption. If the injury results from . . . abnormal consumption, as where a child eats too much candy and is made ill, the seller is not liable. Where, however, he has reason to anticipate that danger may result from a particular use, as where a drug is sold which is safe only in limited doses, he may be required to give adequate warning of the danger, and a product sold without such warning is in a defective condition.

CONTINUED

A close look at comment h, reveals that in a situation where the manufacturer can anticipate a danger from a particular use, such as death resulting from acute alcohol poisoning, he may be required to give adequate warning of that danger. Nowhere does comment h state that there is no duty to warn under any circumstances involved. If fact, appellee may have had reason to anticipate that danger may result from this particular use.

Likewise, comments i and j do not preclude a cause of action based on a duty to warn. In pertinent part, comment i states:

> Many products cannot possibly be made entirely safe for all consumption, and any food or drug necessarily involves some risk of harm, if only from overconsumption. *The article sold must be dangerous to an extent beyond that which would be contemplated by the ordinary consumer who purchases it, with the ordinary knowledge common to the community as to its characteristics.* Good whiskey is not unreasonably dangerous merely because it will make some people drunk and is especially dangerous to alcoholics.

Lastly, comment j states in relevant part: Directions or warnings. In order to prevent the product from being [in a defective condition] unreasonably dangerous [to the user or consumer], the seller may be required to give directions or warning, on the container, as to its use. . . . *In the case of poisonous drugs, or those unduly dangerous for other reasons, warning as to use may be required.*

But a seller is not required to warn with respect to products, or ingredients in them, which are only dangerous, or potentially so, when consumer in excessive quantity, or over a long period of time, *when the danger, or potentiality of danger, is generally known and recognized.* Again the dangers of alcoholic beverages are an example, as are those of foods containing such substances as saturated fats, which may over a period of time have a deleterious effect upon the human heart.

Appellee interprets comment j to mean that the dangers of excessive alcohol consumption are well known to the public. Comment j, however, does not say that the dangers of acute ethyl ingestion resulting in death are necessarily generally known. Rather, it says that *when* the danger is generally known, no warning is required.

Although there is no question that drinking alcoholic beverages will cause intoxication and possibly even cause illness is a matter of common knowledge, we are not prepared to hold, as a matter of law, that the general public is aware that the consumption of an excessive amount of alcohol can result in death.

Appellant offered evidence which showed that, prior to the time of her death, Brinkmeyer had little exposure to the use of alcohol. Brinkmeyer's mother stated that she had warned Brinkmeyer of the dangers of impaired physical capacity which can result from the consumption of alcohol, but that she had not warned her daughter that alcohol was lethal because she had no knowledge of that fact. In addition, appellant submitted documents showing that the United States Congress has been considering legislation on whether to require warning labels on bottles of alcohol and that the government of Mexico has already instituted such legislation. Appellant further showed that warning labels are presently used in the United States on "Everclear" grain alcohol bottles.

Since we find genuine issues of material fact to exist in this case, we will REVERSE the summary judgment and REMAND for further proceedings.

LIMITATIONS AND DEFENSES

As we have already observed, the advantages of the strict liability theory are heavily stacked in favor of the consumer. The focus is no longer on the conduct of the defendant but on the product itself—a far more tangible target. However, the strict liability theory is not an answer to every plaintiff's prayer. Various limitations and defenses operate against him or her, a number of which are effective in some states but not in others.

Limitations

First is the requirement that the product undergo no material change in condition after leaving the defendant's hands. Second, the plaintiff may find it difficult to prove that a product left the hands of the seller in a defective condition. Where the technology involved in production is complex, witnesses who can testify to defective manufacture may not be available. For this reason, failure-to-warn cases are more common than those alleging errors in the production process.

Although strict liability makes recovery easier in certain respects, the requirement that a defective product be "unreasonably dangerous" precludes recovery in many instances. Damages resulting from the failure of a product to perform its ordinary purpose, for example, would not be covered under section 402A. As a result, some states have eliminated the "unreasonably dangerous" requirement.

In addition, section 402A limits recovery to users and consumers (including family members, guests, and employees of the purchaser; and individuals who prepare a product for consumption, who repair a product, and who passively enjoy the benefit of a product, as in the case of passengers on an airplane). Recovery is not always allowed to injured bystanders or others who are brought into contact with the defective product; courts differ on this point, depending on the state. Most states have extended application of the theory to anyone suffering reasonably foreseeable injury because of the defect (such as the driver of a car struck from behind by another vehicle whose brakes were defectively manufactured).

Finally, damage limitations exist. Plaintiffs can usually recover only for property damages and personal injuries but, as in negligence cases, not for basis-of-the-bargain damages. Recovery for mere economic losses is usually disallowed as inconsistent with the UCC's scheme for warranty recovery. Punitive damages are available in *some* jurisdictions if the defendant evinces utter disregard for the safety of consumers and users of the product. Finally, as we shall discuss in more detail later in the chapter, many states have recently imposed statutory limitations on recoveries in products liability cases in an attempt to stem the "products liability revolution."

Privity Defense

Most states, but not all, follow the section 402A(2)(b) position abolishing the privity requirement. In some states the middleman is protected from section 402A liability by requirements that the manufacturer be included in the plaintiff's suit whenever possible or that the manufacturer be sued instead of the middleman.

Sophisticated Purchaser Defense

Some courts recognize a **sophisticated purchaser defense** in strict liability cases based on a defective warning. For example, in one case[4] the defendant sold sand to a foundry firm. The plaintiff, an employee of the buyer, allegedly contracted cancer from long-term inhalation of silica dust contained in the

---

[4] *Smith v. Walter C. Best, Inc.,* 927 F.2d 736 (3d Cir. 1990).

sand. Because the buyer was knowledgeable as to the risks of silica sand, the court granted summary judgment to the defendant seller, allowing it to rely on the knowledgeable intermediate purchaser to supply appropriate warnings. The defense succeeds because most courts treat a duty to warn claim, even under strict liability, according to negligence standards.

Plaintiff Misconduct Defenses

In negligence cases, of course, a plaintiff's carelessness is simply compared with the defendant's in most jurisdictions. The plaintiff's own carelessness can reduce or even bar recovery. In strict liability claims (and, in most jurisdictions, express and implied warranty claims), "plaintiff carelessness" is not treated as a single concept. Rather, several types of plaintiff misconduct are recognized, with differing effects on liability.

One category is *simple plaintiff carelessness*, often described as the failure to detect or guard against a defect in a product. Although some jurisdictions compare such plaintiff carelessness with the defendant's fault under a comparative negligence statute, others conclude that consumers are entitled to assume that products are defect-free. Unwilling to impose an obligation on consumers to go about assuming that products they use might be defective, these latter jurisdictions hold that simple plaintiff carelessness is no defense at all to strict liability (or warranty) claims.

Another category of plaintiff misconduct is **product misuse,** which occurs when a plaintiff uses a product for a purpose for which it was not designed. For example, a consumer might use a pop bottle as a hammer or a lawn mower as a hedge trimmer. In some jurisdictions, unforeseeable product misuse indicates that the product is not defective and constitutes a complete defense to strict liability (and warranty) claims; in other jurisdictions, it is merely evidence of plaintiff misconduct to be compared with defendant's fault. However, when the plaintiff's misuse is foreseeable to the defendant (*e.g.,* that the purchaser of a sports car might exceed the speed limit), many jurisdictions impose on the defendant a duty to warn against the misuse, or perhaps even to install safety devices to guard against the misuse. Therefore, foreseeable misuse typically is no defense.

A final category of plaintiff misconduct is **assumption of risk,** which occurs when a plaintiff, having discovered a defect in the product and fully appreciating its danger, voluntarily uses the product anyway. In one strict liability case,[5] the plaintiff (a professional carpenter) was using the defendant's portable saw when he noticed that the "bumper" for the saw's protective blade guard had fallen off, causing the lower guard to obstruct the front of the blade, preventing it from beginning to cut. Although he had two similar saws on the job site, the plaintiff continued to use the defective one, manually retracting the blade guard before each cut. Six hours later, the plaintiff started the saw and then reached over with his left hand to retract the guard with its lift lever. Unfortunately, he missed the lever and hit the blade, amputating 3/8 inch of his finger. This was held to be an assumption of the risk by the plaintiff. In some jurisdictions, assumption of the risk is a

---

[5] *Sargia v. Skil Corp.,* No. 84 Civ. 7107 (S.D.N.Y. 1985).

complete bar to recovery; in others, it is evidence of the plaintiff's fault to be compared with that of defendant under a comparative fault statute.

There is great variation among the states regarding *application of these* plaintiff misconduct defenses. The following case illustrates one court's thinking regarding a common issue.

SMITH v. GOODYEAR TIRE & RUBBER CO.

U.S. DISTRICT COURT,
DISTRICT OF VERMONT,
600 F.SUPP. 1561
(1985)

The plaintiff, Smith, was injured in an automobile accident. He brought this action alleging negligence on the part of the driver, Young, in whose car Smith was riding at the time of the accident, and alleging a strict liability claim against the defendant tire manufacturer, the Goodyear Tire & Rubber Company.

The defendants raised a "seat belt defense," asserting that their liability is reduced or completely erased because Smith was not wearing a seat belt although one was available to him and that wearing it would have reduced, if not eliminated, his injuries. The plaintiff moved to strike this defense. The following is the trial judge's ruling on the plaintiff's motion.

COFFRIN, CHIEF JUDGE:

Courts are divided on the issue of whether evidence regarding the nonuse of automobile seatbelts should be admissible in comparative negligence cases. Plaintiff relies heavily in his brief on the fact that regulations adopted pursuant to Vermont statutes, although they do require that pleasure cars be equipped with seat belts in their front seats, do not require that the seat belts be used. Plaintiff also points out that Vermont courts have never imposed such a duty.

Plaintiff asserts that courts' reluctance to "find a duty to buckle up" stems from a concern that requiring seat belt use would lead to a flood of litigation in which defendants would argue that, as a matter of law, any plaintiff who fails not only to use his seat belt but also to install an air bag in his car, to adjust his head rest, or, indeed, "to drive a Mack Truck" would be more vulnerable to injury and, thus, guilty of contributing to his own injury.

We are unpersuaded by such reasoning. First, admitting such evidence would not create a duty but would merely allow the jury to consider the information on the question of negligence. Second, the test of negligence would continue to be whether the person acted *reasonably under the circumstances presented.* We do not presume to decide whether or not Plaintiff's failure to fasten his seat belt in the instant case was reasonable. We do believe, however, that the arguments on both sides of the issue are such that a reasonable jury could decide either way. As stated by a New York court,

[T]he seat belt affords the automobile occupant an unusual and ordinarily unavailable means by which he or she may minimize his or her damages prior to the accident. [T]he burden of buckling an available seat belt may, under the facts of the particular case, be found by the jury to be less than the likelihood of injury when multiplied by its accompanying severity. *Spier v. Barker*, 323 N.E.2d 164, 168 (Ct.App. 1974).

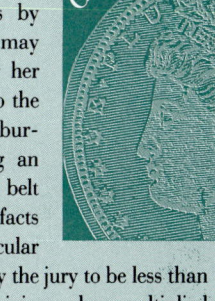

We hold that the jury should be given the task of making this assessment.

... Comment (c) to §402A explains that the justification for this special doctrine of liability is "that the seller, by marketing his product for use and consumption, has undertaken and assumed a special responsibility...." Comment (n) goes on to say that contributory negligence "is not a defense to strict liability when such negligence consists merely in a failure to discover the defect in the product, or to guard against the possibility of its existence." Instead, the Comment states, Plaintiff will be barred from recovery only if he "discovers the defect and is aware of the danger, and nevertheless proceeds unreasonably to make use of the product."

Even if Goodyear cannot prove the latter, however, we decline to follow the rigid requirements of Comment (n), and

CONTINUED

hold that Goodyear should be able to introduce evidence of Plaintiff's failure to use his seat belt as a defense to strict liability. Because Vermont follows the doctrine of comparative negligence, it need not be swayed by the "all or nothing" considerations present in the Comment to the Restatement or in contributory negligence jurisdictions. The purpose behind the strict liability doctrine is to hold certain sellers to a higher standard of care due to their assumption of a special responsibility. Our holding does not thwart that purpose, since Plaintiff still would not have to prove negligence on the part of Goodyear. Although we would be reluctant to completely excuse defendants simply because *some* of a plaintiff's injuries might have resulted from his own actions, it also does not seem fair to allow a negligent plaintiff, who may have contributed to as much as fifty percent of his injuries, to pay for none of them and to recover as much as a plaintiff who had taken all precautions reasonable under the circumstances.

There is a split of authority among other states on this issue. For the reasons stated above, we choose to follow the reasoning of many other comparative fault jurisdictions, and hold that juries may consider evidence of plaintiffs' negligence in assessing damages as to strict liability claims as well as to negligence claims.

Plaintiff's motion is Denied.

In conclusion, the strict liability doctrine favors plaintiffs in that it possesses several advantages namely (1) few defenses against liability can be raised by the defendant; (2) disclaimers are ineffectual; (3) privity is not required; and (4) buyers must prove only that goods were *dangerous defective* when they left the seller's hands and that this defect caused the buyer's injury.

However, disadvantages to the plaintiff include (1) applicability of section 402A only against sellers who are merchants, and (2) availability of damages only for physical injuries to person and property and not for economic injuries.

FEDERAL CONSUMER LEGISLATION

Over the years Congress has enacted a number of federal regulatory laws dealing with the safety and quality of goods. For the most part these laws have focused solely on protecting ultimate consumers from physical harm, and until recently, they were enacted piece-meal and were rather narrow in scope. Examples include the Food, Drug and Cosmetic Act (1938), the Flammable Fabrics Act (1953), the Refrigerator Safety Act (1956), the Hazardous Substances Act (1960), and the Poison Prevention Packaging Act (1970).

CONSUMER PRODUCT SAFETY ACT

In 1972 Congress enacted the **Consumer Product Safety Act**—the first law to deal with the safety of consumer products in general—and created a federal agency, the Consumer Product Safety Commission (CPSC), to administer it.[6]

---

[6] Some consumer products are not covered by the Consumer Product Safety Act because they come under the aegis of other federal laws. The most important of these are food, drugs, and cosmetics, which are regulated by the Food and Drug Administration under the Food, Drug, and Cosmetic Act. Automobiles are also excluded because of coverage by other legislation.

This agency possesses broad powers and performs many functions, ranging from safety research and testing to preparing safety rules and standards for more than 10,000 products. It has the power to ban or recall products and to require special labeling in certain circumstances. It can levy civil penalties on those who violate the Act and criminal penalties on those who willfully violate it. Yet despite the extensive range of its power, the CPSC has been criticized for not issuing sufficient standards to ensure the integrity of consumer products.

In 1990, Congress raised the civil penalties for Consumer Product Safety Act violations from $2,000 to $5,000, required manufacturers to report repeated and serious problems with products to the agency, and made other changes to strengthen the CPSC.

MAGNUSON-MOSS WARRANTY ACT

In 1975 Congress passed the **Magnuson-Moss Warranty Act.** Like the federal legislation discussed above, this statute is consumer-oriented. It applies only to purchases by ultimate consumers for personal, family, or household purposes and not to transactions in commercial or industrial settings. The Warranty Act, which is usually enforced by the Federal Trade Commission (FTC), does not regulate the safety or quality of consumer goods. Instead it prevents deceptive warranty practices, makes consumer warranties easier to understand, and provides an effective means of enforcing warranty obligations. The federal Warranty Act is limited to consumer transactions, and it modifies the UCC warranty rules in some respects; in nonconsumer transactions, the UCC rules continue in effect.

The type of warranty to which the Warranty Act applies is much more narrowly defined than is an express warranty under the UCC. Specifically, it is (1) any *written* affirmation of fact made by a supplier to a purchaser relating to the quality or performance of a product and affirming that the product is defect-free or that it will meet a specified level of performance over a period of time; or (2) a written undertaking to "refund, repair, replace, or take other action" if a product fails to meet written specifications. Obviously express warranties that are not in writing, such as those created by verbal description or by sample, will continue to be governed solely by the UCC, even though a consumer transaction is involved.

The Warranty Act does not *require* anyone to give a warranty on consumer goods. It applies only if the seller *voluntarily chooses* to make an express written warranty (perhaps in an effort to render a product more competitive). When a written warranty is provided for a product costing $10 or more, it must be labeled as either "full" or "limited." When the cost of goods exceeds $15, the warranty must be contained in a single document, must be written in clear language, and must make a number of disclosures, including (1) a description of items covered and those excluded, along with specific service guarantees; (2) instructions on how to proceed in the event of product failure; (3) the identity of those to whom the warranty is extended; and) (4) limitations on the warranty period.

Under a full warranty, the warrantor must assume certain minimum duties and obligations.[7] For instance, he or she must agree to *repair or replace* any malfunctioning or defective product within a "reasonable" time and without charge. If the warrantor makes a reasonable number of attempts to remedy the defect and is unable to do so, the consumer can choose to receive a *cash refund* or *replacement* of the product without charge. No *time limitation* can be placed on a full warranty; and consequential damages (such as for personal injury or property damage) can be disclaimed only if the limitation is *conspicuous*.

A written warranty that does not meet the minimum requirements must be designated conspicuously as a *limited warranty*. It may cover, for example, parts but not labor, or it may levy shipping and handling fees. If a time limit (such as 24 months) is all that prevents the warranty from being a full one, it can be designated as a "full 24-month warranty."

Because its purpose is to regulate *written* warranties, the Warranty Act generally does not concern the implied warranties of merchantability and fitness for a particular purpose. These are governed by the UCC; and as we have seen, the UCC allows implied warranties to be disclaimed. However, drafters of the Warranty Act saw fit to limit the use of disclaimers where written warranties are involved, because of certain abusive practices prevalent at the time: Sellers were providing limited express warranties in bold print and then disclaiming implied warranties, thus leaving the consumer with few rights while appearing to offer substantial protection.

For this reason, the Magnuson-Moss Act *prohibits a disclaimer of implied warranties* (1) when an express written warranty is given, whether full or limited, or (2) when a service contract is made with the consumer within 90 days after the sale.[8] If the written warranty specifies a *time* limitation, however, implied warranties may be suspended by a disclaimer effective *after* the written warranty expires.

The Warranty Act is usually enforced by the FTC, but the Attorney General or an injured consumer can also initiate an action if informal procedures for settling disputes prove ineffective. Sellers are authorized to dictate the informal procedures by which a particular dispute is to be settled. If these procedures follow FTC guidelines, the consumer cannot resort to court action until all established means have been exhausted.

LEGISLATIVE LIMITATIONS ON PRODUCTS LIABILITY REVOLUTION

From 1960 until the mid-1980s, the general trend in products liability law was strongly pro-plaintiff. New theories allowed new classes of injured per-

---

[7] Only the person who actually makes the written warranty—no one else in the chain of distribution—is responsible under the Warranty Act.

[8] Under a *service contract* the seller agrees to service and repair a product for a set period of time in return for a fixed fee.

sons to sue defendants that had never before been vulnerable to suit. Injured consumers have been well served, and it is certainly arguable that products liability litigation has been the most influential factor in bringing about improved product designs and safety practices that have saved thousands of lives.

Recent years, however, have seen a countervailing pressure to reform products liability law in order to roll back the "products liability revolution." Damage awards have increased insurance premiums, raised the prices of some products, induced some companies to cease manufacturing certain products, and arguably, caused American business to suffer a competitive disadvantage abroad. The expense of designing eminently safe products, coupled with insurance rates much higher than those in Europe, has added significantly to the costs of production. The apparent "explosion" of products liability has raised a storm of protest among manufacturers and sellers, and at present, almost every state has enacted or is considering tort reform.

Some states have already placed ceilings on damage awards in product liability suits. Others have enacted provisions that prohibit advances in technology from being used, with the benefit of hindsight, against manufacturers. More than one-third of the states have enacted **statutes of repose.** These provide a time period after which the manufacturer is not liable for injuries caused by a product, the statute of limitations notwithstanding. The periods range from 5 to 12 years and begin when a product is sold to an ultimate consumer (one who does not purchase for resale). The purpose of these provisions is to protect manufacturers from liability in situations where defects do not manifest themselves until many years after the product is sold.

State reform legislation has not been entirely anticonsumer, however. Under a recent California law, companies and managers commit a crime if they fail to notify regulators about known safety defects in their products. Substantial fines and the possibility of prison terms provide enforcement.

FEDERAL PRODUCTS LIABILITY LEGISLATION

There is substantial variation in the details of products liability law among the 50 state jurisdictions. A manufacturer seeking to market its products on a nationwide basis faces a formidable task in conforming its actions to these varying standards. Although some maintain that optimal products liability law will eventually develop at the state level, the advantages of a comprehensive federal law are obvious.

Several products liability reform measures have been introduced in Congress in recent years, although none has passed. Most bills have sought not only to produce national uniformity but also to limit product liability recoveries through a number of means. At this writing (Summer 1992), the leading federal bill (not yet near passage) has the following major provisions: (1) distributors will be liable only for their own negligence and not for simply selling a manufacturer's product; (2) a statute of repose (no suit can be brought involving a product sold more than 25 years earlier) and a narrow statute of limitations (plaintiffs must sue within two years of when they discovered or should have discovered a defect); (3) punitive damages could be awarded only if defendant acted with "conscious, flagrant" indifference to public safety; (4) joint and several liability would be restricted to economic damages; (5) workers' compensation recoveries would be subtracted from awards; (6) no suit could be brought by a plaintiff whose injuries resulted primarily from his or her own drug or alcohol use; and (7) nontrial resolution of suits would be encouraged by allowing either party to request alternative dispute resolution and by making possible an award of attorney fees from the opposing party if a settlement offer was rejected and the amount not improved at trial. Although such a bill, if enacted into law, would not satisfy the interests of labor and consumer groups, it would bring uniformity to the area of products liability and afford some relief to manufacturers from the high costs they have come to bear under the strict liability theory.

Questions and Problems

1. In August 1980, ITT loaned money to McGinn in return for a security interest in a Caterpillar hydraulic excavator. ITT properly perfected its security interest. In the summer of 1981, ITT learned that McGinn was having financial problems and had discussions with him, the contents of which are disputed. The excavator was sold by McGinn at auction through Vilsmeier in October 1981. Before the auction, Vilsmeier announced that the excavator was being sold free and clear of any liens or security interests. Arnold bought the equipment. In October 1983, however, Arnold surrendered the excavator to ITT on advice of counsel in light of ITT's security interest in the machine. Arnold sued Vilsmeier for breach of warranty of title. The trial judge directed a verdict for Arnold. Vilsmeier claimed that this was improper, for it prevented him from attempting to prove that ITT had waived its security interest in its conversation with McGinn. Did the trial judge err? (*Frank Arnold Contractors, Inc. v. Vilsmeier Auction Co.*, 806 F.2d 462, 3d Cir. 1986.)

2. Walcott & Steele, Inc., sold seed to Carpenter. State law required the package label to give the percentage of germination. The label on the seed bought by Carpenter carried the required statement, but the seed did not perform at the listed percentage. Carpenter sued for breach of an express warranty, which he claimed was created by the statement regarding percentage of germination. Did Carpenter prevail? Discuss. (*Walcott & Steele, Inc. v. Carpenter*, 436 S.W.2d 820, 1969.)

3. Kassab, a cattle breeder, purchased feed that had been manufactured by Central Soya. The feed was intended for breeding cattle, but Central had accidentally included an ingredient that should be used only for beef cattle. After eating the feed, Kassab's cattle grew and prospered. Kassab was upset, however, when he discovered that the mistakenly included ingredient had caused his entire herd of prize breeding cattle to become sterile. He sued Central for breach of the implied warranty of merchantability. Central claimed that there was no such breach because the feed had made the cattle gain weight exactly as it was supposed to do. Is Central's contention correct? Explain. (*Kassab v. Central Soya*, 246 A.2d 848, 1968.)

4. Henningsen bought a new automobile from Bloomfield Motors, Inc. Only ten days after the purchase, when the Chrysler had only 468 miles on the odometer, something under the hood cracked and the car veered 90 degrees into a brick wall. Henningsen's wife was seriously injured. When Henningsen sued Bloomfield and Chrysler on an implied warranty of merchantability theory, they raised as a defense a clause in the purchase contract that provided that the manufacturer's "obligation under this warranty [is] limited to making good at its factory any part or parts thereof which shall, within 90 days after delivery of such vehicle to the original purchaser or before such vehicle has been driven 4,000 miles, whichever event shall first occur, be returned to it with transportation charges prepaid and which its examination shall disclose to its satisfaction to have been thus defective; this warranty being expressly in lieu of all other warranties expressed or implied." Does this disclaimer bar the plaintiff's suit? Discuss. (*Henningsen v. Bloomfield Motors, Inc.*, 161 A.2d 69, N.J. 1960.)

5. Johnson, the plaintiff, raised hogs. He needed ventilating fans for his hog barn. He told the supplier's representative of his needs: When asked, the plaintiff told the representative that there were no unusual humidity or dust problems in the hog barn, but this was not accurate. The plaintiff was advised to purchase certain fans with "open" motors not sealed off from outside air. He bought them, but they malfunctioned because of clogging from humidity and feed dust. Many hogs died; the plaintiff sued the supplier and the manufacturer, among others, for breach of the implied warranty of fitness for a particular purpose. Should the plaintiff prevail? Discuss. (*Johnson v. Lappo Lumber Co.*, 181 N.W.2d 316, Mich. App. 1970.)

6. The defendant manufactures the Rohm .38 caliber revolver, often called a "Saturday Night Special." One of defendant's guns was used in a robbery, causing the death of the clerk at the grocery store being robbed. The gun functioned as it was intended; a bullet was fired with deadly force when the trigger was intentionally pulled. The clerk's family sued the defendant in strictly liability, arguing that the danger of such guns greatly outweighs their utility. The plaintiffs cited evidence that in the United States (1) handgun use results in 22,000 deaths every year; (2) medical care for gunshot victims costs $500 million per year; (3) although handguns constitute only 30 percent of all guns sold, they account for 90 percent of the cases of firearm misuse; (4) a handgun is six times more likely to be used to kill a friend or relative than to repel a burglar; and (5) a person who uses a handgun in self-defense is eight times more likely to be killed than one who quiety acquiesces. How should the judge rule? Discuss. (*Patterson v. Rohm Gesellschaft*, 608 F.Supp. 1206, N.D.Tex., 1985.)

7. Daniell felt overburdened and wished to commit suicide. Seeking a place from which she could not escape, she climbed into the trunk of a 1973 Ford LTD and latched it. Later she changed her mind about suicide but could not escape because the trunk contained no internal release mechanism. She was locked in the trunk for nine days and suffered injuries before a passerby heard her cries for help. She sued Ford on the grounds of strict liability, claiming that the trunk was defective because it had no internal release mechanism. Is this a good claim? By what standard should the claim be judged? (*Daniell v. Ford Motor Corp.*, 581 F.Supp. 728, D.N.M. 1984.)

8. Laaperi bought a smoke detector from Sears and installed it in his bedroom. The detector was designed to be powered by AC (electric) current. Six months later a fire broke out in the Laaperi home, killing three of Laaperi's children. The smoke detector did not sound an alarm on the night of the fire, because the fire started in a short circuit in an electric cord. The smoke detector was connected to the circuit, which shorted and cut off. Laaperi sued Sears claiming that it had breached a duty to warn him that the very short circuit that might ignite a fire in his home could, at the same time, incapacitate the smoke detector. Is this a viable theory? Discuss. (*Laaperi v. Sears, Roebuck & Co., Inc.*, 787 F.2d 726, 1st Cir. 1986.)

9. The Hauters, the plaintiffs, purchased a "Golfing Gizmo" for their son from the defendants. The device was designed to provide driving practice for novice golfers. On the package it said, "Completely safe ball will not hit player." But the Hauter's son, while using it as directed, was hit in the head by the ball and severely injured. The plaintiffs sued for breach of express and implied warranties, but the defendants argued that their only obligation was to provide a device that was safe when the ball was hit "properly" and that a drawing on the package depicted a golfer hitting the ball "properly." Is this a good defense? Discuss. (*Hauter v Zogarts*, 534 P.2d 377, Cal. 1975.)

10. Welch, the plaintiff, bought a new Dodge station wagon from Fitzgerald-Hicks Dodge, Inc. (FHD). During the next six months the car required a large number of repairs—"repairs too numerous to list," in the words of the higher court. Although most repairs were satisfactory, the major continuing problem was a "shimmying" that could be felt when the car was driven. After many unsuccessful attempts by FHD to remedy that problem, the plaintiff left the car with FHD with a letter stating that he was revoking his acceptance. The plaintiff then brought this action against FHD and Chrysler Corporation, the manufacturer, to recover the purchase price. Among the numerous issues at trial was the major question as to whether the shimmy caused the car to be unmerchantable. On that point the plaintiff introduced evidence that the shimmy, while reduced, was still noticeable and bothersome; the defendants, however, contended that, taken as a whole, the car was of such a nature that it would "pass without objection within the automobile industry." The jury found the car to be unmerchantable; on appeal, one of the questions was whether the jury's finding of unmerchantability was supported by the evidence (in view of evidence that all other aspects of the car were, by that time, satisfactory). Do you think the jury's verdict should be upheld? Discuss. (*Welch v. Fitzgerald-Hicks Dodge, Inc.*, 430 A.2d 144, 1981.)

CHAPTER 12

Certain kinds of business interests and rights have been recognized and protected by common-law rules since very early times. Many of these interests receive supplemental, and sometimes primary, protection from state, and especially federal, statutes. In this chapter we examine some of the most common wrongful invasions of these interests, that is, **business torts**, *including (1) interference with existing and prospective contractual and business relationships, (2) trademark infringement, (3) misuse of trade secrets, (4) patent infringement,*

BUSINESS TORTS

(5) copyright infringement, and (6) unfair competition.

INTERFERENCE WITH BUSINESS RELATIONSHIPS

Beginning with an 1853 English case in which an opera singer was induced by the defendant theater owner to breach her contract to sing at the plaintiff's theater and appear at the defendant's instead,[1] courts have recognized the general principle that a third party who wrongfully interferes with an existing contract has committed a tort. Most courts have stretched the concept to hold defendants liable for interfering with contracts that do not yet exist but are reasonably certain to be entered into, and with business relationships in general.

A typical case of tortious **interference with business relationships** involved a salesman who followed customers away from his former employer's premises and convinced them to rescind their contracts with that business and to purchase less expensive property from him. Although the customers had the right under federal law to rescind their contracts with the former employer within three days, the salesman was found civilly liable. Although there was arguably no interference with a binding contract, there was interference with prospective advantage flowing from an advantageous business relationship.[2]

ELEMENTS OF THE TORT

In a tortious interference case, the plaintiff must prove (1) the defendant acted intentionally to interfere with a known contract[3] or business relationship (or with one that was reasonably certain to occur); (2) absence of justification or privilege for the defendant's actions; and (3) damage to the plaintiff as a result.

Because defendants are presumed to intend the natural consequences of their actions, the intent element is typically satisfied if the defendant knows the facts that give rise to the plaintiff's contractual rights against another. Wrongful conduct that is intentional and without just cause or excuse gives rise to a finding of implied malice, which is sufficient for liability (as opposed to *actual* malice, which is typically required for an award of punitive damages). Thus, if D Stamp Co. knows that X Grocery Store offers P's stamps as an inducement to customers, that such arrangements are typically based on long-term written contracts, and that a store can economically offer only one

---

[1] *Lumley v. Gye*, 2 El & Bl 216.
[2] *Azar v. Lehigh Corp.*, 364 So.2d 860 (Fla. App. 1978).
[3] Most jurisdictions do not even require that the contract be binding. Thus, a defense such as duress or statute of frauds that might protect one of the parties from a breach of contract action will not usually protect a nonparty in a tortious interference suit.

company's stamps at any one time, D becomes tortiously liable if it proceeds to convince X to begin offering D's stamps.[4]

In one of the most controversial cases in recent legal history, Pennzoil sued Texaco for intentional interference with contract rights when Texaco bought control of Getty Oil after Pennzoil believed it had a contract to acquire Getty. A jury awarded Pennzoil the largest judgment in American legal history—$11.1 billion in compensatory and punitive damages. (That judgment was affirmed on appeal and later settled out of court when Texaco paid $3 billion to Pennzoil.)

DEFENSE OF PRIVILEGE OR JUSTIFICATION

Persons acting with evil motives or improper means to interfere with contracts or business relationships will likely be held liable. For example, as part of a campaign to terrorize Vietnamese-American fishermen competing with native Texas fishermen in Galveston Bay, the Ku Klux Klan told one man who leased his docks to the Vietnamese: "Watch your boats—they're easy to burn" and sent a card to a woman who also leased her docks that said: "You have been paid a 'friendly visit'; do you want the next one to be a 'real one'?" Clearly this outrageous and unjustifiable action constituted tortious interference with the dock leasing contracts.[5]

However, in cases such as the grocery store stamp case mentioned above, defendants are likely to argue that their actions constitute examples of good old American free enterprise and should not be the basis of tort liability. Indeed, liability for this tort often turns on a weighing of a plaintiff's interest in having a contract performed or a business expectation fulfilled versus a defendant's interest in competing for that business or in protecting its own economic interests. The law recognizes that no defendant will be liable for tortious interference if its actions are privileged or justified, but these defenses are difficult to delineate precisely.

Justification for a defendant's interference may be found if it is aimed at protecting a third person's legitimate interests, such as when an independent construction inspector hired by a city recommended that the city terminate the plaintiff's construction contract for poor workmanship,[6] or at protecting the public interest in general.

Furthermore, the defendant can claim justification for interference to protect its own existing contractual or property interests. For example, assume that X gets a new car franchise from D, an auto manufacturer. Later X makes a contract with P, a motorcycle wholesaler, under the terms of which P is permitted to sell motorcycles in a limited area in X's showroom. D subsequently causes X to break the contract with P because of complaints from new car buyers about dirt and noise associated with P's operation. D's interest in the proper conduct of the new car dealership would likely justify its actions, providing a defense to any tortious interference claim P

---

[4] *Top Value Enterprises v. Carlson Marketing,* 703 S.W.2d 806 (Tex. App. 1986).
[5] *Vietnamese Fishermen's Ass'n v. Knights of the Ku Klux Klan,* 518 F.Supp. 993 (N.D.Tex. 1981).
[6] *Soils v. City of Laredo,* 751 S.W.2d 132 (Tex. App. 1988).

might bring. Thus, P's only recourse would be a breach of contract action against X.

Although the defendant may act to protect **existing** economic interests, it is usually improper to induce a third party to breach an existing contract with the plaintiff solely to gain new customers. In other words, a party's interest in seeing an *existing* contract performed usually outweighs a competitor's right to competition, although many criticize this rule as inconsistent with the principles of free enterprise. However, if a plaintiff's interest has not been reduced to a binding contract but is merely prospective in nature or embodied in a terminable-at-will contract, the **privilege of competition** generally provides a defense so long as defendant vies for the plaintiff's business with the third party by honest means within the bounds of "fair play."

Even if the means of interference used are proper, such as simply opening up a competing business, the tort will be established if the purpose was improper. In one famous case,[7] the defendant opened up a competing barbershop not to make money, but as part of a malicious scheme to injure the plaintiff by destroying his barbershop's business. "To call such conduct competition is a perversion of terms," the court said in allowing recovery for interference with business conduct.

The shadowy outlines of the competition privilege are discussed in the following case.

EDWARD VANTINE STUDIOS, INC. v. FRATERNAL COMPOSITE SERVICE

IOWA COURT OF APPEALS 373 N.W.2d 512 (1985)

The plaintiff, Vantine, and the defendant, Fraternal, are involved in the business of photographing composites of college fraternities and sororities. The plaintiff's booking agent completed signed contracts with several such organizations at Iowa State University for the 1982–1983 school year. In the summers of 1981 and 1982, the defendant's sales manager had visited several Iowa State fraternities and sororities but signed no contracts. In the summer of 1982, he tried again. Although he was told that the houses had existing contracts with the plaintiff, the sales manager suggested that the legality of the contracts be investigated. He ultimately signed contracts with 12 houses that had initially contracted with the plaintiff. All but one of the contracts contained an indemnification provision stating that the defendant would pay any legal costs of fees incurred by the organization in breaking the contracts already held with the plaintiff.

The sororities and fraternities expressed dissatisfaction with the plaintiff's previous services. The defendant capitalized on these complaints by offering a lower price and an earlier delivery date. Although the

CONTINUED

---

[7] *Tuttle v. Buck,* 119 N.W. 946 (Minn. 1909).

officers who decided to terminate the plaintiff's contract in favor of the defendant's testified that they were not subjected to any undue pressure, they also stated that they would not have terminated the plaintiff's contract except for the insertion of the indemnification clause in the defendant's contract.

The plaintiff sued for tortious interference with existing contracts. The trial court found the defendant liable and awarded the plaintiff $5,016 in actual damages and $10,000 in punitive damages. The defendant appealed.

Hayden, Judge:

There can be little question but that defendant intentionally interfered with plaintiff's contracts. Defendant concedes its awareness of those contracts during the course of its attempts to obtain its own contracts with the twelve houses. Defendant advised the houses to investigate the validity of their contracts with plaintiff and then suggested or at least agreed to insert a clause in its own contracts to indemnify the houses for any legal costs or fees incurred by reason of their breach of their contracts with plaintiff. This is certainly an intentional course of conduct which induced the houses not to perform their contracts with plaintiff.

We also believe and agree with the trial court that defendant's interference was improper to the extent that it agreed to indemnify the houses for any legal costs or fees resulting from their breach of plaintiff's contracts. We concede defendant's point that the business of photographing composites for college fraternities and sororities is very competitive and that the various individual companies in that business will seek to expand their own share of the market, very often at the expense of their competitors. We do not, however, believe that this competitive factor gives defendant free reign [sic] to use whatever inducements it can think of to lure potential customers away from already existing valid and binding contracts. We adopt the trial court's language on this point:

> If the contracts had been terminated by reason of better price, better service, or better quality alone, . . . the Court would not have determined that there was a tortious interference with the contracts. It may have caused some claim or cause of action between [plaintiff] and the breaching fraternity or sorority, but it would not have created an actionable tort against Defendant. The Defendant, however, by the insertion, or the encouragement of the insertion, of the indemnity clause has crossed over the line of legitimate competition. It has committed a tort by such activity.

Representatives from five of the fraternities involved testified that they would not have breached their agreements with plaintiff and contracted without the indemnity clause agreed to by defendant. The importance of this clause to defendant is thus obvious. Our acceptance of such a tactic would render the notion of sanctity of contract a nullity and would indicate that a contract could be breached with impunity merely by having the party inducing the breach assume the financial consequences of such breach.

[The court affirmed the judgment for compensatory damages but reversed the award of punitive damages on grounds that the defendant's actions did not rise to the level of legal "malice" required in Iowa for such an award.]

Note: Why did the plaintiff in this case sue its competitor for tortious interference rather than the sororities and fraternities for breach of contract? Two main reasons are obvious. First, the plaintiff wishes to maintain business relations with these organizations and does not wish to alienate them unnecessarily by suing them. Second, punitive damages are virtually never available in a breach of contract action but are often recovered in an intentional tort suit such as this one (although the initial award in this case was not upheld).

MANAGER'S PRIVILEGE

When a corporation breaches a contract, the other party will frequently not only sue the corporation for breach of contract but also sue the corporate officers who made the decision to breach on a tortious interference claim. The corporate officers are usually protected from liability by a doctrine called the "manager's privilege" if their decision to have the corporation breach the contract was based solely or essentially on the best interests of the corporation. Such would be the case when it would be far more advisable for a corporation to pay damages resulting from a breach of contract than to live up to a contract that might be financially disastrous. However, if the officer is acting primarily to further his or her own personal interests, tort liability will be imposed.

TRADEMARK INFRINGEMENT

A **trademark** is any distinctive word, symbol, device, or design adopted for the purpose of identifying the origin of goods being offered for sale. A trademark benefits consumers by acting as a symbol enabling them to identify goods or services that have been satisfactory in the past and to reject those that have been unsatisfactory. A trademark also motivates businesses to maintain or improve quality of their goods or services over time to reap the benefits of a well-earned public trust in a mark. The tort of infringement, therefore, occurs when a competitor of the owner of the trademark uses a mark so similar to the owned trademark that purchasers of the competitor's goods are misled as to the origin of the goods that they are purchasing. In other words, a deception is accomplished that permits the competitor (typically a manufacturer) to "cash in" on the reputation and goodwill of the trademark owner (who is, typically, another manufacturer).

Although the early trademark rules were exclusively common law in nature, the basis of most of our trademark law today is the Lanham Act—a federal statute passed in 1946.

The act also governs other marks, such as **service marks**—used to identify the origin of services (for example, "Budget," as applied to the car rental business) and certification marks—used by persons who do not own the marks but who are authorized to indicate that their products are approved by the owner of such marks (for example, the "Good Housekeeping Seal of Approval"). We will limit our discussion here to consideration of only those principles of law having special applicability to the tort of trademark infringement.

REGISTRATION

Under the Lanham Act, as amended in 1988, a person who owns a trademark that is affixed to or applies to his or her goods ("vendible commodities") may register that mark on the Principal Register either by showing that the mark has already been used in commerce or indicating a "bona fide intent" to use the mark at a future date, followed by actual use within three years. Entry on the Principal Register is constructive notice effective as of the date of filing, of the registrant's exclusive right to use the trademark throughout the entire country. This grant of a nationwide priority, with few exceptions, gives the registrant a right superior to everyone's except that of a person who used the mark before the filing date, a person who filed an application before that date, and foreign applicants who can claim a priority date under special rules.

The term of the registration is ten years and may be renewed in ten-year increments by registrants who show that they are still genuinely using the mark.

Certain kinds of marks are generally not registrable—the most important of which are those that are merely descriptive or geographic in nature or are persons' surnames. Thus a term that merely described a general kind of good, which is called a **generic term** (such as aspirin), cannot be registered under any circumstances. And other descriptive terms ("tender" steak), geographical terms ("Nebraska" butter), and surnames ("Henderson" hats) cannot be registered unless they have acquired a "secondary meaning" (a concept discussed later).

In *Zatrains, Inc., v. Oak Grove Smokehouse, Inc.*, 698 F.2d 786 (1983), in which a primary question was whether Zatrains' trademark of "FISH FRI" batters was so descriptive of batters generally that it could not be protected against use of the mark "FISH FRY" batters by the defendant Oak Grove, the court illustrated the applicable principles, as follows:

> *Courts and commentators have traditionally divided potential trademarks into four categories. A potential trademark may be classified as (1) generic, (2) descriptive, (3) suggestive, or (4) arbitrary or fanciful. These categories, like the tones in a spectrum, tend to blur at the edges and merge together....*
>
> *A* generic *term is the name of a particular genus or class of which an individual article or service is but a member. A generic term connotes the basic nature of articles or services rather than the more individualized characteristics of a particular product. Generic terms can never attain trademark protection. Furthermore, if at any time a registered trademark becomes generic as to a particular product or service, the mark's registration is subject to cancellation [under the Lanham Act]. Such terms as aspirin and cellophane have been held generic and therefore unprotectable as trademarks.*
>
> *A* descriptive *term identifies a characteristic or quality of an article or service, such as its color, odor, function, dimensions, or ingredients. Descriptive terms ordinarily are not protectable as trademarks; they may become valid marks, however, by acquiring a secondary meaning in the minds of the consuming public....[An] example of a descriptive mark would be..."Vision Center" in reference to a business offering optical goods and services....*
>
> *A* suggestive *term suggests, rather than describes, some particular characteristic of the goods or services to which it applies and requires the consumer to exercise the imagination in order to draw a conclusion as to the nature of the goods and services. A suggestive mark is protected without the necessity for proof of secondary meaning. The term "Coppertone" has been held suggestive in regard to sun tanning products.*

Arbitrary or fanciful *terms bear no relationship to the products or services to which they are applied. Like suggestive terms, [these] marks are protectable without proof of secondary meaning. The term "Kodak" is properly classified as a fanciful term for photographic supplies, and "Ivory" is an arbitrary term as applied to soap.*[8]

SECONDARY MEANING CONCEPT

If a trademark appears unregistrable because it is essentially descriptive or geographic or is a surname, the mark may still be registered if the owner can prove that an appreciable number of purchasers within the applicable market do, in fact, associate the mark with the owner (as distinguished from the term's more general meaning). In such a case the mark is said to have acquired a **secondary meaning**—a name that is a misnomer, in view of the fact that such proof indicates the mark has, in fact, a strong meaning.[9] Waltham (watches) and Bavarian (beer) are examples of geographic names registered under the secondary meaning concept, and Safeway (food products) is a descriptive name that achieved registration under the same concept.

ELEMENT OF CONFUSION

In most infringement actions the plaintiff mark owner has the burden of proving that the defendant's mark is so similar to the plaintiff's that defendant's use will produce a "likelihood of confusion" in buyers' minds as to the true origin of the goods or services. Whether such likelihood exists is a question of fact in any particular case and is determined by such factors as similarity of design of the marks, similarity of product, proof of confusion among actual buyers, and marketing surveys of prospective purchasers showing an appreciable misassociation of the defendant's mark with the plaintiff's product. On the basis of these factors, for example, Rotary De-Rooting was held to be a mark so similar to Roto-Rooter that the owner of Roto-Rooter was successful in recovering damages from the owner of Rotary De-Rooting.[10] But if the products are substantially dissimilar, even identical marks may not cause confusion. Thus, where a clothing manufacturer had purchased the right to use the mark "Here's Johnny," a court held that the use of that mark by a manufacturer of portable toilets was not likely to cause purchasers of the toilets to associate them with the producer of the suits.[11]

When the trademark at issue is a design on a book, difficult First Amendment questions may arise, as the next case demonstrates.

---

[8] On this aspect of the case, the court held that FISH FRI was essentially descriptive (but, on the basis of other evidence, nonetheless protectable under the secondary meaning concept).

[9] With the exception of generic marks, marks that do not acquire a secondary meaning (or that cannot be registered on the Principal Register for any other reason) can gain some protection by being registered on a Supplemental Register.

[10] *Roto-Rooter Corp. v. O'Neal,* 513 F.2d 44 (5th Cir. 1975).

[11] *Carson v. Here's Johnny Portable Toilets, Inc.,* 698 F.2d 831 (6th Cir. 1983). Although the plaintiff suit manufacturer was unsuccessful in the infringement aspect of the case, the plaintiff, Johnny Carson, was granted an injunction restraining the defendant company from further use of the mark on the invasion of privacy theory.

CHAPTER 12 BUSINESS TORTS

CASE

Cliffs Notes, Inc. v. Bantam Doubleday Dell Publishing Group

U.S. Second Circuit Court of Appeals, 886 F.2d 490 (1989)

The plaintiff-appellee publishes "Cliffs Notes," a series of study guides that are condensed versions, with brief analyses, of various short stories, plays, and books. The defendant-appellant Bantam Doubleday Dell Publishing Group, working with the often satirical Spy magazine, publishes "Spy Notes," a one-time parody both of modern novels (such as Tama Janowitz's Slaves of New York, Bret Ellis's Less Than Zero, and Jay McInerney's Bright Lights Big City) and of Cliffs Notes.

Spy magazine's editors believed that a study guide would provide an ideal vehicle for a parody of modern novels, because the "flat, straightforward, academic style" of Cliffs Notes would contrast sharply with the "cool, ironic, sophisticated, urbane novels." Spy Notes, like Cliffs Notes, lists on the cover the works it condenses (i.e., the three aforementioned novels). It also replicates the distinctive yellow color, black diagonal stripes, and black lettering of Cliffs Notes, a design that is the subject of appellee's registered trademark.

However, Spy Notes contains (1) humorous content rather than serious condensation and analysis; (2) the words "A Satire" in bright red lettering five times on the front and four times on the back; (3) colors (red, white, and blue) not used on Cliffs Notes, (4) wry notations not found on Cliffs Notes (e.g., "Even Funnier than the Originals"). Spy Notes also is priced substantially higher than Cliffs Notes ($7.95 versus $3.50) and includes "The Spy Novel-O-Matic Fiction-Writing Device," which supposedly can be used by "young, world-weary urban authors" to create 16,765,056 different plot possibilities.

After Spy Notes had been bound but before it was shipped to bookstores, the appellee sued for trademark infringement under the Lanham Act, claiming that Spy Notes would give consumers the false impression that it was the appellee's product. The trial judge, applying the standards of Polaroid Corp. v. Polarad Elec. Corp., 287 F.2d 492 (2d Cir.), cert. denied, 368 U.S. 820 (1961), found a "profound likelihood of confusion" and granted the appellee's request for a preliminary injunction barring distribution of Spy Notes. The defendants appealed.

Feinberg, Circuit Judge:

We start with the proposition that parody is a form of artistic expression, protected by the First Amendment.

At the same time, "[t]rademark protection is not lost simply because the allegedly infringing use is in connection with a work of artistic expression." *Silverman v. CBS Inc.*, 870 F.2d 40, 49 (2d Cir.), cert. denied, 109 S.Ct. 3219 (1989). Books are "sold in the commercial marketplace like other more utilitarian products, making the danger of consumer deception a legitimate concern that warrants some government regulation." *Rogers v. Grimaldi*, 875 F.2d 994, 997 (2d Cir. 1989).

Conflict between these two policies is inevitable in the context of parody, because the keystone of parody is imitation. It is hard to imagine, for example, a successful parody of Time magazine that did not reproduce Time's trademarked red border. A parody must convey two simultaneous—and contradictory—messages: that it is the original, but also that it is *not* the original and is instead a parody. To the extent that it does only the former but not the latter, it is not only a poor parody but also vulnerable under trademark law, since the customer will be confused.

Thus, the principal issue before the district court was how to strike the balance between the two competing considerations of allowing artistic expression and preventing consumer confusion.

We believe that the overall balancing approach of *Rogers* and its emphasis on construing the Lanham Act "narrowly" when First Amendment values are involved are both relevant in this case. That is to say, in deciding the reach of the Lanham Act in any case where an expressive work is alleged to infringe a trademark, it is appropriate to weigh the public interest in free expression against the public interest in avoiding consumer

CONTINUED

confusion. This approach takes into account the ultimate test in trademark law, namely, the likelihood of confusion "'as to the source of the goods in question.'" *Universal City Studios, Inc. v. Nintendo Co.*, 746 F.2d 112, 115 (2d Cir. 1984). At the same time, a balancing approach allows greater latitude for works such as parodies, in which expression, and not commercial exploitation of another's trademark, is the primary intent, and in which there is a need to evoke the original work being parodied.

To apply the *Rogers* approach in this case, we begin by noting the strong public interest in avoiding consumer confusion over Spy Notes. As we put it in *Rogers*, the purchaser of a book, "like the purchaser of a can of peas, has a right not to be misled as to the source of the product." But, taking into account that somewhat more risk of confusion is to be tolerated when a trademark holder seeks to enjoin artistic expression such as a parody, the degree of risk of confusion between Spy Notes and Cliffs Notes does not outweigh the well-established public interest in parody. In other words, we do not believe that there is a likelihood that an ordinarily prudent purchaser would think that Spy Notes is actually a study guide produced by appellee, as opposed to a parody of Cliffs Notes.

First, the district court apparently thought that the parody here had to make an obvious joke out of the cover of the original in order to be regarded as a parody. We do not see why this is so. It is true that some of the covers of the parodies brought to our attention, unlike that of Spy Notes, contain obvious visual gags. But parody may be sophisticated as well as slapstick; a literary work is a parody if, taken as a whole, it pokes fun at its subject. Spy Notes surely does that, and there are sufficient reasons to conclude that most consumers will realize it is a parody. For example, a substantial portion of the potential audience for Spy Notes—i.e., college students or college-educated adults—overlaps with that for Cliffs Notes. Spy magazine, like Cliffs Notes, is widely read on some college campuses, although presumably for different reasons. As a result, the name "Spy" in the title, the notation "A Spy Book" emblazoned on the cover of Spy Notes and the use of a prepack marketing device prominently displaying the "Spy" name should alert the buyer that Spy Notes is a parody of some sort, or, at least, that it is not the same product as Cliffs Notes.

Furthermore, while the cover of Spy Notes certainly conjures up the cover of Cliffs Notes, the two differ in many respects. In addition to the differences listed in the following paragraphs, which indicate that Spy Notes is a parody of Cliffs Notes, the cover of Spy Notes contains red, blue and white, colors that do not appear on the cover of Cliffs Notes. Also, the Spy Notes cover shows a clay sculpture of New York City rather than a clay sculpture of a bare cliff.

In addition, a Cliffs Notes book is not likely to be bought as an impulse purchase. A prospective reader of Cliffs Notes probably has a specific book in mind when going to the bookstore for a study guide. And, even if a consumer did go to a store looking for a Cliffs Notes summary of any of the three books condensed in Spy Notes, that purchaser would not find one. Appellee does not produce Cliffs Notes for these novels, and has no plans to do so.

The label "A Satire" is also prominently used five times on the cover (and four on the back) of Spy Notes. Moreover, even for those few readers who might be slightly confused by the cover, the most likely reaction would be to open the book. Both the title page and the copyright notice page indicate that the book is written by the editors of Spy magazine and published by appellant. The copyright notice page states, "Spy Notes is a parody of Cliffs Notes." Furthermore, the reader would encounter the Spy Novel-O-Matic Fiction-Writing Device, which is an immediate tip-off that something non-serious is afoot.

Finally, with few exceptions, most Cliffs Notes are summaries of the traditional "great books," rather than contemporary works or those somewhat outside the mainstream. As indicated above, the Spy editors certainly thought that the three novels were obviously not in the former category and that the purchaser would be aware of the humor of having Cliffs Notes summarize them. Moreover, the books that Spy Notes summarizes are characterized by their spare, stripped-down prose, and uncomplicated plots. The idea of condensing them at all is something of a parody. Thus, the consumer would likely be put on notice from the first that Spy Notes was not Cliffs Notes.

The district court's ruling unjustifiably imposes the drastic remedy of a prepublication injunction upon the cover of a literary parody. Accordingly, for the reasons set forth above, we vacate the injunction against appellant.

REMEDIES

Where likelihood of confusion is established, the plaintiff's usual remedies under the Lanham Act or common-law principles are the *injunction* and *damages*. The injunction is an order prohibiting the defendant's further use of the mark, and damages is a recovery of money to compensate the plaintiff for the monetary injury (if any) that he or she has sustained as a result of the infringement.

Because of a tremendous increase in the trafficking of counterfeit designer goods, Congress passed the Trademark Counterfeiting Act of 1984 which provides escalating *criminal* penalties for multiple offenders. For example, a second offender, if an individual, can be fined up to $1,000,000 and/or imprisoned for up to 15 years.

ANTIDILUTION STATUTES

Approximately half the states have extended trademark protection beyond situations where a "likelihood of confusion" exists by enacting **antidilution** statutes, which remedy dilution of the distinctive quality of a mark or injury to business reputation even where the parties do not compete and there is no real likelihood that consumers will believe that the plaintiff (trademark owner) is the sponsor of the defendant's products.

Consider the strong TIFFANY trademark, connoting luxury and excellence in products. If someone were to open a bar called TIFFANY, it is unlikely that the public would believe that the owners of the TIFFANY trademark were also responsible for the bar—there would be no likelihood of confusion. However, use of the name TIFFANY on the bar may injure the holder of the TIFFANY trademark in two ways: (1) it lessens the distinctiveness of the mark if it can be used on all manner of products and services (for bars, bicycles, feminine hygiene products, etc.) and (2) it undermines the positive image of the mark if it is no longer restricted to luxury-type products. *Tiffany v. Boston Club*, 231 F. Supp. 836 (D.Mass. 1964). State antidilution laws protect distinctive marks from these types of injuries.

MISUSE OF TRADE SECRETS

It is an information age, and nothing is more important to most businesses than information. By means of industrial sabotage and the hiring of competitors' employees, companies annually acquire from competitors an estimated 20 billion dollars worth of confidential information. Patent law is often available to protect information, but trade secret law must be considered equally important. Trade secret law can protect a wider range of information at a cheaper cost and do so perpetually, which may be preferable to the 17-year limit to patent protection. "The maintenance of commercial ethics

HUMOR AND THE LAW

The folks at the trademark office must be a sensitive lot. They recently refused to grant a trademark to a distinctive red-white-and-blue condom, on grounds that mixing such a product with a patriotic theme was "offensive." On similar grounds, the mark "Bubby Trap" for a brassiere (*In re Riverbank Canning Co.*, 37 U.S.P.Q. 268 (Com'r 1938)) and a fried chicken establishment's motto—"Only a breast in the mouth is better than a leg in the hand" (*Bromberg v. Carmel Self Service, Inc.*, 198 U.S.P.Q. 176 (T.T.A.B. 1978)) were denied protected status.

Fortunately, trademark law is not an area totally devoid of humor. When a maker of jeans for "Larger Women" began marketing them with a smiling pig and the word "Lardashe" printed on the seat of the pants, the court held that this was an obvious parody of the popular Jordache brand, and refused to enjoin sales on grounds of trademark infringement. *Jordache Enterprises, Inc. v. Hogg Wyld. Inc.*, 828 F.2d 1482 (10th Cir. 1987).

---

and the encouragement of innovation are the broadly stated policies behind trade secret law."[12]

A **trade secret** is "any formula, pattern, device or compilation of information which is used in one's business, and which gives him an opportunity to obtain an advantage over competitors who do not know or use it."[13] Examples of protectable trade secrets include customer lists, manufacturing processes, chemical formulas, cookie recipes, operating and pricing policies, marketing techniques, raw materials sources, and computer software.

ELEMENTS OF THE TORT

After Manville Corporation spent nine million dollars over seven years to perfect a new method of insulation, one of its competitors hired six key Manville employees and was able to enter the market in less than two years. Manville later prevailed in a lawsuit against the competitor because simple concepts of fairness suggest that a company that has acquired information or developed processes as a result of its own efforts—information or processes

---

[12] *Kewanee Oil Co. v. Bicron Corp.*, 416 U.S. 460 (1973).
[13] *Restatement of Torts* §757 comment b (1939).

not generally known to others—ought to be protected from the wrongful use of such information or processes by its competitors. The common law and the statutes of almost 20 states that have adopted the Uniform Trade Secrets Act provide such protection.

To successfully bring a misappropriation of trade secrets claim, a plaintiff must prove (1) existence and ownership of a trade secret; (2) the defendant's acquisition of the trade secret by wrongful or improper means; and (3) use or disclosure of the trade secret to the injury of the plaintiff.

In any trade secrets case, two issues are paramount: (1) whether the processes or information which the plaintiff is seeking to protect against the defendant's continued use are "secret" in the eyes of the law, and (2) if so, whether the defendant acquired the information by "wrongful means."

SECRECY REQUIREMENT

A prototypical trade secret is the formula for Coca-Cola. A Coca-Cola company executive testified by affidavit in *Coca-Cola Bottling Co. v. Coca-Cola Co.*, 227 U.S.P.Q. 18 (D.Del. 1985) that

> *The written version of the secret formula is kept in a security vault at the Trust Company Bank in Atlanta, and that vault can only be opened by a resolution from the Company's Board of Directors. It is the Company's policy that only two persons in the Company shall know the formula at any one time, and that only those persons may actually oversee the actual preparation of [the product]. The Company refuses to allow the identity of those persons to be disclosed or to allow those persons to fly on the same airplaine at the same time.*

Coca-Cola knows how to meet the "secrecy" requirement.

Perhaps the extreme measures adopted by Coca-Cola need not be exercised in every case. Nonetheless, to be protected, information must be kept reasonably (not absolutely) secret by its owner. In deciding whether specified information is, in fact, secret, courts generally consider (1) the extent to which the information is known outside the business; (2) the extent to which it is known by employees of the business; (3) the extent of security measures taken by the firm; (4) the value of the information to its owner; (5) the amount of effort or money expended to create the information; and (6) the ease or difficulty with which the information could be properly acquired or duplicated by others. *Restatement (Second) of Torts*, §757, comment b. Thus, if a defendant has acquired information that was freely circulated by the plaintiff company among its employees, customers, or suppliers, the secrecy requirement is not met. In contrast, protection will be afforded when a company gives secret information only to a small number of employees on a "need to know" basis, under clear instructions not to disclose it to others. If an employee breaches this trust by passing it to a competitor, it remains a trade secret and the competitor's use of it subjects the competitor to tort liability.

WRONGFUL ACQUISITION REQUIREMENT

Even if information qualifies as a trade secret, its use by a competitor is normally lawful if the competitor has discovered the secret by means that are "not improper." Thus if X Company discovers a manufacturing process by independent research, or even by means of "reverse engineering"—disassembling a product of Y Company that it has lawfully purchased—the subsequent use of the process by X Company is generally lawful under trade secret rules (which is one reason that patent protection is usually desirable).

Historically, acquisition was considered to be improper only when it was illegal (e.g., acquisition by trespass, theft, or wiretapping) or involved breach of a confidential relationship (e.g., bribery of an employee of the owners). One high-profile example came to light in 1982 when the FBI arrested employees of Hitachi Ltd., on the basis of evidence that it had paid more than $600,000 for stolen data concerning a new IBM computer. More recently, courts have broadened the improper means concept to include methods that "fall below the generally accepted standards of commercial morality, even though not illegal."[14]

The following case illustrates a difficult trade secret question that should be of interest to any would-be inventors.

CASE

SMITH v. SNAP-ON TOOLS CORP.

U.S. FIFTH CIRCUIT COURT OF APPEALS, 833 F.2d 578 (1987)

Smith made a ratchet by combining parts of two existing tools. Hoping to see his ratchet made available for sale, he brought it to the attention of Snap-On Tools, Inc., by showing the ratchet to an independent Snap-On dealer and then submitting a tool suggestion form to Snap-On's Wisconsin headquarters. Snap-On began making and selling the ratchet without paying anything to Smith. Smith sued, claiming that Snap-On had misappropriated a trade secret. The trial court, applying Wisconsin law, ruled for Smith but did not give him as large a judgment as he desired. Both sides appealed.

RUBIN, CIRCUIT JUDGE:

Wisconsin law prescribes two essential elements in a cause of action for misappropriation of trade secrets: an actual trade secret and a breach of confidence. The essence of the tort of trade secret misappropriation is the inequitable use of the secret. Even when a trade secret exists, a person who learns the secret legitimately, without any duty of confidentiality, is free to use it.

Wisconsin therefore follows trade secret law as set out in Sec. 757 of the Restate-

CONTINUED

---

[14] *E.I. duPont de Nemours & Co., Inc. v. Christopher.* 431 F.2d 1012 (5th Cir. 1970), in which duPont recovered damages from a company that had acquired its secret method of producing methanol by means of aerial photographs of a duPont plant under construction. Apparently companies need not use antiaircraft guns to keep their secrets; only "reasonable" efforts are required.

ment of Torts. Under the Restatement, "[o]ne who discloses or uses another's trade secret, without a privilege to do so, is liable to the other if . . . his disclosure or use constitutes a breach of confidence reposed in him by the other in disclosing the secret to him." As the comment to this provision states, the proprietor of a trade secret may not unilaterally create a confidential relationship without the knowledge or consent of the party to whom he discloses the secret. No particular form of notice is necessary, however; the question is whether the receipient of the information knew or should have known that the disclosure was made in confidence.

Smith concedes that he never explicitly requested that his disclosure to Snap-On be held in confidence. Nonetheless, he argues, Snap-On knew or should have known that the disclosure was confidential. According to Smith, a "special relationship" existed between himself and Snap-On, based on the fact that he, as a relatively unsophisticated individual, submitted his invention to Snap-On, a large corporation. Under the circumstances, Smith contends, the manufacturer should have known that he, as the inventor, expected compensation even if he did not request it.

The district court accepted this argument . . . , [but t]his does not reflect Wisconsin law. The Supreme Court of Wisconsin has held [in *RTE Corp. v. Coatings, Inc.*, 267 N.W.2d 226 (1978)] that, when parties are dealing at arm's length, one party's disclosure of an alleged trade secret to another does not automatically create a confidential relationship. Although [*RTE*] involved two corporations, we see no reason to believe that it would have applied a different rule if the inventor had been an individual rather than a corporation.

Under certain circumstances, courts have found liability for misappropriation of trade secrets in cases involving implied confidentiality between an inventor and a manufacturer. When a manufacturer has actively solicited disclosure from an inventor, then made use of the disclosed material, the manufacturer may be liable for use or disclosure of the secret in the absence of any expressed understanding as to confidentiality. In this case, however, Smith disclosed the invention on his initiative, without any prompting from Snap-On. Alternatively, courts have imposed liability when the disclosing inventor did not specifically request confidentiality from the manufacturer, but did make clear that the disclosure was intended as part of a course of negotiations aimed at creating a licensing agreement or entering into a similar business transaction. These cases are also distinguishable because Smith did not indicate that he wanted any pecuniary recompense for his suggestion. . . . When Smith sent Snap-On a tool suggestion report describing the ratchet, he did not in any way indicate that he wanted compensation, and indeed wrote on the suggestion form, "I would like to be able to buy a nice new shiney [sic] one from the Snap-On truck." In none of his dealings with Snap-On over the next two years did Smith ever request confidentiality or indicate that he expected or desired any commercial arrangement based on his submission of the ratchet suggestion to Snap-On.

In February 1978, more than two years after Smith showed the ratchet to Clark, Smith's lawyer sent a letter to the supervisor of Snap-On's Product Management Division in which he asked that Smith receive compensation. Reliance on confidentiality, however, must exist at the time the disclosure is made. An attempt to establish a special relationship long after an initial disclosure comes too late.

Because there was no confidential relationship between Smith and Snap-On, Snap-On violated no obligation to Smith by manufacturing the ratchet.

We therefore reverse.

PATENT INFRINGEMENT

To encourage creation and disclosure of inventions, the Constitution authorizes the federal government to grant **patents** to inventors ("patentees"). In exchange for disclosing the invention, the inventor patentee receives a

17-year (14 years in the case of design patents) exclusive right to make, use, or sell the patented item. The 17-year patent is nonrenewable; after expiration of the period the item goes into the public domain and may be made, used, or sold by anyone.

SUBJECT MATTER

Items that may be patented include (1) processes, (2) machines, (3) manufactures (e.g., products), (4) compositions of matter (e.g., new arrangements of elements as in metal alloys), and (5) any improvement on the first four categories. In addition, design patents for ornamental designs have been granted, as have patents on computer software and new varieties of asexually reproducing plants that have been modified by humans and do not naturally occur in nature. In *Diamond v. Chakrabarty*,[15] the Supreme Court even found a new life form (a laboratory-created bacterium for "eating" oil spills) to be patentable.

However, one cannot patent (1) printed matter, (2) naturally occurring substances, (3) methods of doing business, (4) ideas (e.g., $E = MC^2$), or (5) scientific principles (e.g., chemical formulas). This list is nonexclusive, but the idea is that the patentee must create, not find; invent, not merely discover.

PATENTABILITY

If it fits into a proper subject matter category, an item may be patented if it meets three main tests: utility, novelty, and nonobviousness. An item has *utility* if it produces a direct benefit to mankind. It does not if it is dangerous, immoral, or merely a matter of curiosity. The *novelty* test is met if the item is distinctive from what was present in the prior state of the art. Prior patents, public use or sale, and written descriptions of the item can destroy novelty. *Nonobviousness* is also decided in light of the prior state of the art. If the item could easily have been produced by someone with normal skill in the area or if it is an obvious next step from prior inventions, the nonobviousness test is not met. If a product is immediately a tremendous success or if it fills a long-felt need in the marketplace, there is a presumption of nonobviousness.

In practice, these tests are somewhat vague. For that reason, although the Patent Office grants about 60 percent of the patent applications, when these applications are challenged by alleged infringers, about 60 percent of issued patents are invalidated by the courts.

PATENT PROCEDURE

A patent application must be filed in the name of the inventor at the U.S. Patent and Trademark Office in Arlington, Virginia. A person is not entitled to a patent unless the application is filed within one year after the initial public use or sale of the invention. Many inventors have lost all patent rights by failing to file in a timely fashion. The application must include a *specifica-*

---

[15] 447 U.S. 303 (1980).

tion (a precise description of the item so that one skilled in the art could make use of it), and *claims* (a description of precisely what makes the item patentable—e.g., useful, novel, and nonobvious). The Patent Office will study the application and search for previous patents on the same item. If the application is denied, it may be amended, and frequently substantial negotiation occurs between the applicant and the Patent Office. Decisions can be appealed administratively and, ultimately, to the courts.

Patent procedure is time-consuming and expensive. It is also very complicated, and an inventor would be wise to hire an attorney who specializes in patent law.

Once the application is filed, the patentee can place "Patent Pending" on his or her products for which the patent is sought. This has no legal effect because the patent is not effective until issued by the Patent Office. However, it puts others on notice of the claim, and if the patent is ultimately granted they can be sued for infringements occurring during the patent pending stage.

OWNERSHIP

The patentee can sell his or her title to the patent to a third party. The patentee can also retain the title but grant a license under which a third party can use the patented item in exchange for payment of a royalty to the patentee. Assignments of title must be filed in the Patent Office.

Employees should be aware of the **shop right doctrine.** If an employee is hired for creative or inventive work and invents something on company time while using company resources, the patent belongs to the company. The company will file the application in the employee's name, but the company will own it. Even if the employee was not hired for creative or inventive work, if he or she invents something on company time using company resources, the company will be granted a nonexclusive license to use the patented item without payment of a royalty. Of course, many employers have their employees sign agreements to assign title to all patents generated on company time to the employer.

INFRINGE-MENT

A person infringes a valid patent by using a device which (1) literally meets each of the limitations of the patent's claim, or (2) under the "doctrine of equivalents," does the "same work in substantially the same way and accomplish[es] substantially the same result" as the patented device, even though the infringing device differs in name, form, or shape.[16]

DEFENSES

An alleged misuser may raise a number of defenses. First, of course, the misuser may claim that his or her device does not meet the doctrine of

---

[16] *Autogyro Co. of America v. United States,* 384 F.2d 391 (Ct. Cl. 1967).

equivalents. Second, the misuser may challenge the validity of the patent by arguing that it flunks one or more of the tests of novelty, utility, and nonobviousness or that it is not the type of subject matter that may be properly patented. Third, the misuser may claim that the patentee *forfeited* the patent by not filing an application within one year after the invention was in public use, or should have the patent revoked because he or she breached the *duty of candor,* a duty the law imposes to disclose everything the patentee knows about previous inventions and other facts that might bear on patentability. Finally, the infringer might argue that the patent should be revoked because of *patent misuse,* which occurs when the patentee abuses the patent, frequently in violation of antitrust laws, to gain more rights than the patent legally confers.

REMEDIES

A patentee who successfully sues for infringement can obtain an injunction, damages of no less than a reasonable royalty rate (and perhaps trebled in the court's discretion when the plaintiff was damaged to a greater extent than the demonstrated royalty rate), and in exceptional cases, attorneys' fees.

The following case contains a recent Supreme Court discussion of the basic philosophy underlying federal patent policy.

BONITO BOATS, INC. v. THUNDER CRAFT BOATS, INC.

U.S. SUPREME COURT, 109 S.CT. 971 (1989)

In September 1976, Bonito Boats, Inc. (petitioner), a Florida corporation, developed a hull design for a fiberglass recreational boat that it marketed under the trade name Bonito Boat Model 5VBR. Designing the hull required substantial effort, including preparation of engineering drawings, creation of a hardwood model, and production of a fiberglass mold from the model. The 5VBR was favorably received by the boating public. Bonito never filed a patent application.

In May 1983, the Florida legislature enacted a statute that makes it "unlawful for any person to use the direct molding process to duplicate for the purpose of sale [or to sell] any manufactured vessel hull or component part of a vessel made by another without the written permission of that other person."

In 1984, Bonito filed this suit alleging that Thunder Craft Boats (respondent) had violated the Florida statute by using the direction molding process to duplicate the Bonito 5VBR fiberglass hull and had sold such duplicates.

The trial court, the Florida Court of Appeals, and the Florida Supreme Court all concluded that the Florida law was invalid under the supremacy clause of the Constitution in that it impermissibly interfered with the scheme established by the federal patent laws. Bonito brought the matter to the U.S. Supreme Court.

O'CONNOR, JUSTICE:

From their inception, the federal patent laws have embodied a careful balance

CONTINUED

between the need to promote innovation and the recognition that imitation and refinement through imitation are both necessary to invention itself and the very lifeblood of a competitive economy. Thomas Jefferson was the first Secretary of State, and the driving force behind early federal patent policy. For Jefferson, a central tenet of the patent system in a free market economy was that "a machine of which we were possessed, might be applied by every man to any use of which it is susceptible." 13 Writings of Thomas Jefferson 335 (Memorial ed. 1904).

Today's patent statute is remarkably similar to the law as known to Jefferson in 1793. Protection is offered to "[w]hoever invents or discovers any new and useful process, machine, manufacture, or composition of matter, or any new and useful improvement thereof." 35 U.S.C. § 101. Since 1842, Congress has also made protection available for "any new, original and ornamental design for an article of manufacture." 35 U.S.C. § 171. To qualify for protection, a design must present an aesthetically pleasing appearance that is not dictated by function alone, and must satisfy the other criteria of patentability. The novelty requirement of patentability is presently expressed in 35 U.S.C. §§ 102(a) and (b), which provide:

A person shall be entitled to a patent unless—

(a) the invention was known or used by others in this country, or patented or described in a printed publication in this or a foreign country, before the invention thereof by the applicant for patent, or

(b) the invention was patented or described in a printed publication in this or a foreign country or in public use or on sale in this country more than one year prior to the date of application for patent in the United States....

Sections 102(a) and (b) operate in tandem to exclude from consideration for patent protection knowledge which is already available to the public. They express a congressional determination that the creation of a monopoly in such information would not only serve no socially useful purpose, but would in fact injure the public by removing existing knowledge from public use. From the Patent Act of 1790 to the present day, the public sale of an unpatented article has acted as a complete bar to federal protection of the idea embodied in the article thus placed in public commerce.

The federal patent scheme creates a limited opportunity to obtain a property right in an idea. Once an inventor has decided to lift the veil of secrecy from his work, he must choose between the protection of a federal patent, or the dedication of his idea to the public at large.

The applicant whose invention satisfies the requirements of novelty, nonobviousness, and utility, and who is willing to reveal to the public the substance of his discovery and "the best mode ... of carrying out his invention," 35 U.S.C. § 112, is granted "the right to exclude others from making, using, or selling the invention throughout the United States," for a period of 17 years. 35 U.S.C. § 154. The federal patent system thus embodies a carefully crafted bargain for encouraging the creation and disclosure of new, useful, and nonobvious advances in technology and design in return for the exclusive right to practice the invention for a period of years. "[The inventor] may keep his invention secret and reap its fruits indefinitely. In consideration of its disclosure and the consequent benefit to the community, the patent is granted. An exclusive enjoyment is guaranteed him for seventeen years, but upon expiration of that period, the knowledge of the invention inures to the people, who are thus enabled without restriction to practice it and profit by its use." *United States v. Dubilier Condenser Corp.*, 289 U.S. 178, 186–187 (1933).

The attractiveness of such a bargain, and its effectiveness in inducing creative effort and disclosure of the results of that effort, depend almost entirely on a backdrop of free competition in the exploitation of unpatented designs and innovations. The novelty and nonobviousness requirements of patentability embody a congressional understanding, implicit in the Patent Clause itself, that free exploitation of ideas will be the rule, to which the protection of a federal patent is the exception. Moreover, the ultimate goal of the patent system is to bring new designs and technologies into the public domain through disclosure. State law protection for techniques and designs whose disclosure has already been induced by market rewards may conflict with the very purpose of the patent laws by decreasing the range of ideas available as the building blocks of further innovation.

Thus our past decisions have made clear that state regulation of intellectual property must yield to the extent that it clashes with the balance struck by Congress in our patent laws.

We believe that the Florida statute at issue in this case so substantially impedes the public use of the otherwise unprotected design and utilitarian ideas embodies in unpatended boat hulls as to run afoul of the teaching of our decisions in [earlier cases].

...[T]he Bonito 5VBR fiberglass hull has been freely exposed to the public for a period in excess of six years. For purposes of federal law, it stands in the same stead as an item for which a patent has expired or been denied: it is unpatented and unpatentable. Whether because of a determination of unpatentability or other commercial concerns, petitioner chose to expose its hull design to the public in the marketplace, eschewing the bargain held out by the federal patent system of disclosure in exchange for exclusive use. Yet, the Florida statute allows petitioner to reassert a substantial property right in the idea, thereby constricting the spectrum of useful public knowledge. Moreover, it does so without the careful protections of high standards of innovation and limited monopoly contained in the federal scheme. We think it clear that such protection conflicts with the federal policy "that all ideas in general circulation be dedicated to the common good unless they are protected by a valid patent." *Lear, Inc. v. Adkins*, 395 U.S. 653, 668 (1969).

We therefore agree...that the Florida statute is preempted by the Supremacy Clause.

[Affirmed.]

COPYRIGHT INFRINGEMENT

To reward and stimulate intellectual endeavors, federal **copyright** law grants authors protection for the *expression* of their ideas, although not for the ideas themselves. Under the Copyright Act of 1976, all copyrightable works created after January 1, 1978, receive protection for the life of the author plus 50 years after his or her death. If the work is anonymous or a work for hire, the copyright lasts for the shorter of 75 years from its first publication or 100 years from its creation.

During that period, the owner of the copyright has exclusive right to produce the work in any medium, to control derivative works, to distribute copies of the work, to perform the work in public, and to display the work in public.

SUBJECT MATTER

Copyrights protect literary works (books, newspapers, magazines), works of a musical, dramatic, graphic, choreographic, or audiovisual nature, and sound recordings. This list is nonexclusive; the law is meant to protect any "original works of authorship." In 1990, Congress (1) gave visual artists such as painters and sculptors the legal right to prevent distorting changes or destruction of their work; (2) explicitly aided architects by extending copyright protection to the constructed design of buildings; and (3) granted copyright owners of computer programs the right to prohibit rental, lending, or leasing of their software, subject to certain exemptions (e.g., the renter is a nonprofit school).

COPYRIGHTABILITY

There are three basic elements of copyrightability. First, the work must be *fixed* in some *tangible medium of expression*. When a book is written, a song is recorded, a picture is painted, or a choreography is filmed, this requirement is met. Until tangibly fixed, a mere idea is unprotected.

The work must be *creative* to at least some degree. Creativity, not "sweat-of-the-brow" effort, is the key, as the Supreme Court emphasized in *Feist Publications v. Rural Telephone Service Co.*, 111 S.Ct. 1282 (1991), when it held that a simple compilation of names and addresses in a telephone directory was not copyrightable. The court stressed the fact/expression dichotomy; facts are not copyrightable, but their expression in a compilation might be but not simply as a reward for hard work. The compilation must show some creativity to be protected. The Court held that a simple alphabetic listing is "devoid of even the slightest creativity."

Most important, the work must be *original*. This does not require novelty, only that the work not be copied from someone else. A person who had never seen the novel *Moby Dick* but wrote a nearly identical book independently could successfully copyright it.

The copyrightability of computer codes is a difficult issue. Most courts have held that the literal elements of a computer code, including its source and object code and the structure, sequence, and organization of software, may be copyrighted. But it is not clear exactly how far operating instructions embedded in a microchip or added in a sequence of transistors may be protected. One case found an infringement based on similarities between the structure and organization of the plaintiff's and defendant's computer program even though there was no literal, side-by-side similarity.[17] Another case protected the sequencing and flow of a computer screen display but denied copyright protection to an unadorned two-column listing display.[18]

COPYRIGHT PROCEDURE

Securing a copyright is much easier than securing a patent and has recently become even easier. Copyright law has an important international dimension. Books, songs, movies, and other copyrightable material quickly travel from continent to continent in today's world. There are two major copyright treaties. Until 1989, the United States belonged only to the Universal Copyright Convention, administered by UNESCO. Effective in 1989, however, the United States also joined the Berne Convention, administered by the U.N. World Intellectual Property Organization.

---

[17] *Whelan Assoc. v. Jaslow Dental Laboratory,* 797 F.2d 1222 (3d Cir. 1986).
[18] *Manufacturers Technologies v. Cams, Inc.,* 706 F.Supp. 984 (D.Conn. 1984).

The process of obtaining a copyright is virtually self-executing. Until 1989, copyright protection for a published work was obtained if each copy of the work contained (1) a copyright notice (e.g., the word "copyright," the abbreviation "Copr.," or the symbol ©), (2) the date of first publication, and (3) the name of the copyright holder. This relatively simple process is now even easier. For works first published after the March 1, 1989, effective date of the Berne Convention, the copyright notice is no longer a requirement. Before March 1989, a person who observed a published work that did not contain a copyright notice could feel assured that the work was in the public domain. For works published after that date, however, this is not necessarily the case.

Copyright registration, although permissive, is still a good idea, because (1) it will protect the author in countries that have not signed the Berne Convention, and (2) it enables plaintiffs to recover statutory damages and an award of attorneys fees in an infringement action even if actual damages cannot be proven. Registration is accomplished by sending a completed application form with a $20 check to the Register of Copyrights in Washington, D.C., along with one deposit copy of an unpublished work or two copies of a published work.

INFRINGEMENT

If a plaintiff proves (even by circumstantial evidence) that a defendant had *access* to the plaintiff's work and that the defendant's work bears a *substantial similarity* to the plaintiff's copyrighted work (or a part of it), a claim for infringement is established. The plaintiff need not prove intent; an innocent infringement is actionable. For example, in *Bright Tunes Music Corp. v. Harrisongs Music, Ltd*,[19] the judge did not believe that former Beatle George Harrison intentionally copied an earlier song, "He's So Fine," when he composed "My Sweet Lord." Nonetheless, Harrison had access to the earlier song (which was widely played on popular radio), and his song was substantially similar. Harrison was held to have infringed the owner's copyright.

FAIR USE DOCTRINE

An important, but rather vague, part of copyright law is the *fair use doctrine*. Section 107 of the Copyright Act of 1976 states:

> *[T]he fair use of a copyrighted work, including such use by reproduction in copies or phono-records or by any other means specified by [§ 106], for purposes such as criticism, comment, newsreporting, teaching (including multiple copies for classroom use), scholarship, or research, is not an infringement of copyright. In determining whether the use made of a work in any particular case is a fair use the factors to be considered shall include—*

1. the purpose and character of the use, including whether such use is of a commercial nature or is for nonprofit educational purposes;

---

[19] 420 F. Supp. 177 (S.D.N.Y. 1977).

2. the nature of the copyrighted work;

3. the amount and substantiality of the portion used in relation to the copyrighted work as a whole; and

4. the effect of the use upon the potential market for or value of the copyrighted work.

Although the applications of this doctrine are controversial, the Copyright Office has issued supplemental guidelines dealing with photocopies: obviously copies used for literary criticism, classroom teaching, and parody fare better than those used for commercial purposes.

The following controversial case illustrates the fair use doctrine.

BASIC BOOKS, INC. v. KINKO'S GRAPHICS CORP.

758 F. Supp. 1522
U.S. District Court,
Southern District of
New York (1991)

The plaintiffs (major publishing houses) sued the defendant, Kinko's, alleging copyright infringement when Kinko's copied excerpts from books whose rights are held by the plaintiffs without permission and without payment of required fees and sold the copies for a profit at book stores serving New York University and Columbia University students. Kinko's admits that it copied the excerpts in suit without permission, compiled them into course "packets," and sold them to college students. Twelve instances of copyright infringement are alleged. To illustrate, six of these instances were contained in "Packet #1: 'Work and Community,'" which included 388 pages of copied work taken from 25 books, some in print and some out-of-print.

Kinko's raised several defenses, including "fair use." After trial, the district judge entered the following opinion.

MOTLEY, DISTRICT JUDGE:

Coined as an "equitable rule of reason," the fair use doctrine has existed for as long as the copyright law. Justice Story set forth the meaning of fair use to which we adhere today. "In short, we must often... look at the nature and objects of the selections made, the quantity and value of the materials used, and the degree in which the use may prejudice the sale, or diminish the profits, or supersede the objects, of the original work." *Folsum v. Marsh,* 9 F.Cas. 342 (C.C.D.Mass. 1841).

This case is distinctive in many respects from those which have come before it. It involves multiple copying. The copying was conducted by a commercial enterprise which claims an educational purpose for the materials. The copying was just that—copying—and did not "transform" the works in suit, that is, interpret them or add any value to the material copied, as would a biographer's or critic's use of a copyrighted quotation or excerpt.

A. The 4 Factors of Fair Use.

1. Purpose and Character of the Use.

Transformative use. The Supreme Court has held that "commercial use of copyrighted material is presumptively an unfair exploitation of the monopoly privilege that belongs to the owner of the copyright." *Sony Corp. v. Universal City Studios,* 464 U.S. 417, 451 (1984). Additionally, the Supreme Court has found that "the distinction between 'productive' and 'unproductive' uses may be helpful in calibrating the balance [of interests.]" *Id.*

It has been argued that the essence of "character and purpose" is the transformative value, that is, productive use,

CONTINUED

of the secondary work compared to the original. "The use...must employ the quoted matter in a different manner or for a different purpose from the original. A quotation of copyrighted material that merely republishes the original is unlikely to pass the test." Leval, *Toward a Fair Use Standard*, 103 Harv.L.Rev. 1105, 1111 (1990). Kinko's work cannot be categorized as anything other than a mere repackaging.

Commercial use. The use of the Kinko's packets, in the hands of the students, was no doubt educational. However, the use in the hands of Kinko's employees is commercial. Kinko's claims that its copying was educational and, therefore, qualifies as a fair use. Kinko's fails to persuade us of this distinction. Kinko's has not disputed that it receives a profit component from the revenue it collects for its anthologies. The amount of that profit is unclear; however, we need only find that Kinko's had the intention of making profits.

While financial gain "will not preclude [the] use from being a fair use," *New York Times Co. v. Roxbury Data Interface*, 434 F.Supp. 217, 221 (D.N.J. 1977), consideration of the commercial use is an important one. "The crux of the profit/nonprofit distinction is not whether the sole motive of the use is monetary gain but whether the user stands to profit from exploitation of the copyrighted material without paying the customary price." *Harper & Row v. Nation Enterprises*, 471 U.S. 539, 562 (1985). This is precisely the concern here and why this factor weighs so heavily in favor of plaintiffs.

2. *The Nature of the Copyrighted Work.*

Courts generally hold that "the scope of fair use is greater with respect to factual than non-factual works." *New Era Publications v. Carol Publishing Group*, 904 F.2d 152, 157 (2d Cir. 1990). Factual works, such as biographies, reviews, criticism and commentary, are believed to have a greater public value and, therefore, uses of them may be better tolerated by the copyright law. Fictional works, on the other hand, are often based closely on the author''s subjective impressions and, therefore, require more protection. These are general rules of thumb. The books infringed in [this] suit were factual in nature. This factor weighs in favor of defendant.

3. *The Amount and Substantiality of the Portion Used.*

"There are no absolute rules as to how much of a copyrighted work may be copied and still be considered a fair use." *Maxtone-Graham v. Burtchaell*, 803 F.2d 1253 (2d Cir. 1987). This third factor considers not only the percentage of the original used but also the "substantiality" of that portion to the whole of the work; that is, courts must evaluate the qualitative aspects as well as the quantity of material copied.

This court finds and concludes that the portions copied were critical parts of the books copied, since that is the likely reason the college professors used them in their classes. While it may be impossible to determine that the quoted material was "essentially the heart of" the copyrighted material, it may be inferred that they were important parts.

This factor, amount and substantiality of the portions appropriated, weighs against defendant. In this case, the passages copied ranged from 14 to 110 pages, representing from 5.2% to 25.1% of the works. In one case Kinko's copied 110 pages of someone's work and sold it to 132 students. Even for an out-of-print book, this amount is grossly out of line with accepted fair use principles.

In almost every case, defendant copied at least an entire chapter of a plaintiff's book. This is substantial because they are obviously meant to stand alone, that is, as a complete representation of the concept explored in the chapter. This indicates that these excerpts are not material supplemental to the assigned course material but *the* assignment. Therefore, the excerpts, in addition to being quantitatively substantial, are qualitatively significant.

4. *The Effect of the Use on Potential Markets for or Value of the Copyrighted Work.*

The fourth factor, market effect, also fails the defendant. This factor has been held to be "undoubtedly the single most important element of fair use." *Harper & Row*, 471 U.S. at 566. "To negate fair use one need only show that if the challenged use 'should become widespread, it would adversely affect the *potential* market for the copyrighted work.'" *Id.* at 568 (quoting *Sony Corp.*).

Kinko's confirms that it has 200 stores nationwide, servicing hundreds of colleges and universities which enroll thousands of students. The potential for

CONTINUED

widespread copyright infringement by defendant and other commercial copiers is great.

This court has found that plaintiffs derive a significant part of their income from textbook sales and permissions. This court further finds that Kinko's copying unfavorably impacts upon plaintiffs' sales of their books and collections of permission fees. This impact is more powerfully felt by authors and copyright owners of the out-of-print books, for whom permissions fees constitute a significant source of income. This factor weighs heavily against defendant.

Therefore, this court will assess statutory damages in the amount of $50,000 for nine of the 12 infringements, and $20,000 for three of the infringements [because the copying was less] for a total of $510,000 [plus costs and attorney's fees.]

REMEDIES

A successful plaintiff in a copyright infringement action usually receives actual damages plus the defendant's profits to the extent they were not calculated into the damage award. If the plaintiffs have registered their copyright, they may elect between actual damages or "statutory damages" in an amount the court finds "just," with the normal range being between $500 and $20,000 for any one work involved in the case, and up to $100,000 if the infringement was willful. In cases where the plaintiff has difficulty proving actual damages, the right to opt for statutory damages can be quite important, as the *Kinko's* case illustrated.

Copyright infringement can also constitute a federal misdemeanor punishable by fines of up to $10,000 and/or one year in jail.

INTERNATIONAL PROTECTION OF INTELLECTUAL PROPERTY

As international commerce increases, companies must give added attention to protection of their intellectual property in the international arena. Some attention is given to this topic in Chapter 21. For purposes of this chapter, a few points will suffice.

Regarding trademarks, most nations have their own system of registration of trademarks. An American company seeking to sell its goods abroad must consider the specific laws of the various nations in which it intends to sell. Of particular concern is that failure to register may be deemed an abandonment of the mark in that nation. There is some international cooperation in the area. The World Intellectual Property Organization in Geneva administers the Vienna Trademark Registration Treaty, which the United States has signed. It also administers the Madrid Agreement, signed by most

European countries. These treaties permit some international filing of trademarks.

American courts have broadly construed the Lanham Act to protect U.S. trademarks abroad. For example, in one case an American bought watch parts in the United States. In Mexico, he assembled the parts into watches, affixed the BULOVA trademark, and sold the watches. The owner of the BULOVA trademark sued in the United States. The Supreme Court held that American courts, pursuant to the Lanham Act, had jurisdiction to punish the defendant.[20]

We have already noted that international copyright protection is founded on two international treaties. Now that the United States is a party to both the Universal Copyright Convention and the Berne Convention, Americans holding copyrights are entitled to the maximum level of international protection. Unfortunately, the theoretical level of protection is often substantially higher than the actual level of enforcement of the rules in other countries.

Regarding patents, the United States and several Latin American countries are signatories of the Convention for the Protection of Inventions, Patents, Designs and Industrial Methods. The United States has also signed the Patent Cooperation Treaty, forming along with the other members a union called the International Patent Cooperation Union that provides one international filing of an application. The International Bureau of the World Intellectual Property Organization administers this system. As is pointed out in Chapter 21, inducing lesser developed nations to respect patents, as well as trademarks and copyrights, is a difficult matter.

UNFAIR COMPETITION

The term **unfair competition** is an imprecise one. In its broadest sense, it covers all tortious business conduct. In its most common usage, however, the term refers only to those business practices that are based on *deception*. In addition to trademark infringement, unfair competition includes any deceptive use by one person of the copyright or patent rights of another. It also embraces many other common-law torts, such as falsely inducing consumers to believe a product is endorsed by another, and "palming off." Palming off refers to any word or deed causing purchasers to be misled as to a product's source. It thus includes not only trademark infringement but all other means of source deception as well.

---

[20] *Steele v. Bulova Watch Co.*, 344 U.S. 280 (1952).

STATE DECEPTIVE TRADE PRACTICES ACTS

A consumer who is misled by false advertising or other deceptive practices may have the right to sue under a common-law fraud theory or perhaps a breach of express warranty theory if the advertising involved a product. These theories are discussed in other chapters.[21] However, additional consumer protection legislation, passed at both the state and federal levels, also addresses such activity.

Misleading advertising is often prohibited by state **deceptive trade practices acts.**[22] Other types of unfair competition that are usually prohibited by such statutes are the advertising of goods or services with the intent not to sell them on the advertised terms, representing goods as new when they are used or second-hand, and disparagement—making false statements of fact about competitors' goods or services.

LANHAM ACT

The federal government has also passed various acts that prohibit unfair competition, such as misleading advertising. In Chapter 20, for example, we will examine the Federal Trade Commission Act's ban on "unfair or deceptive acts or practices." In this chapter, our focus in on section 43(a) of the Lanham Act, which outlaws "any false description or representation." Although this section is frequently used to allow trademark owners to sue competitors for trademark infringement, it has also created a general federal law of unfair competition, which is frequently applied to deceptive advertising. Designed in large part to protect consumers from being misled, the cause of action is given primarily to the competitors of the deceptive advertiser.

Illicit Acts

Section 43(a) of the Lanham Act has supported suits against companies that (1) used pictures of the plaintiff's product to advertise their own inferior brand; (2) used a confusingly similar color and shape of drug capsule that could mislead consumers into thinking that they were buying the plaintiff's nontrademarked brand; (3) printed "$2.99 as advertised on TV" when only the plaintiff had run such ads; (4) claimed that their pain reliever worked faster than the plaintiff's when it did not; and (5) displayed a rock star's picture on an album creating the impression that he or she was a featured performer when, in fact, he or she was not.

As in all advertising, some "puffing" is permitted by the Lanham Act. For example, when a computerized chess game was advertised as "like having Karpov as your opponent," mere puffing was found.[23]

---

[21] Express warranties are discussed in Chapter 11. Fraud was mentioned in Chapters 9 and 10.
[22] In states having such statutes, the wrongs are thus statutory torts (rather than common-law torts).
[23] *Data Cash Systems, Inc. v. JS&A Group, Inc.*, 223 U.S.P.Q. 865 (N.D.Ill. 1984).

Enforcement

Most courts have not allowed deceived consumers to bring section 43(a) claims. Instead, suit is usually brought by competitors who, while redressing their own injuries, seek to end false advertising that also injures consumers. These competitors have been termed *vicarious avengers* of the consumer interest. A competitor's motive for bringing such a suit is easily seen in the following case.

ALPO PETFOODS, INC. v. RALSTON PURINA CO.

913 F.2d 958
(District of Columbia Circuit Court of Appeals 1990)

Two leading dog food producers sued each other for false advertising under section 43(a) of the Lanham Act. ALPO Petfoods sued Ralston Purina for claiming that its Puppy Chow products can lessen the severity of canine hip dysplasia (CHD), a crippling joint condition. Ralston attacked ALPO's claims that ALPO Puppy Food contains "the formula preferred by responding vets two to one over the leading puppy food." After a 61-day bench trial, the district judge decided that both companies had violated section 43(a). He enjoined both from making these or similar claims and awarded ALPO $10.4 million in damages. Only Ralston appealed.

Thomas, Circuit Judge:

[T]o prevail in a false advertising suit under section 43(a), a plaintiff must prove that the defendant's ads were false or misleading, actually or likely deceptive, material in their effects on buying decisions, connected with interstate commerce, and actually or likely injurious to the plaintiff.

In reviewing the district court's findings on the elements of ALPO's section 43(a) claim, we have no authority to weigh the evidence anew. The district court heard weeks of conflicting expert testimony on the basis for and effectiveness of Ralston's CHD-related advertising. In finding that advertising false, deceptive, material, and injurious, the court cited specific experts' testimony, sometimes crediting that testimony over other evidence.

Ralston's claims had a weak empirical basis. The hypothesis behind Ralston's CHD-related product change and advertising was the "anion gap theory" of Dr. Richard Kealy, a Ralston nutritionist. This theory holds that the smaller the difference between the chlorine content and the combined sodium and potassium content of a dog's diet, the more snugly the dog's hip joints will tend to fit. [A series of four short-term studies from 1980 to 1984 arguably supported the theory, although none was statistically significant at the 5 percent level. The first long-term study, undertaken in 1985, produced results that] undermined Ralston's CHD-related claims so much that Dr. Kealy ended the study, which he had projected would last for almost three years, after only thirty-three weeks.

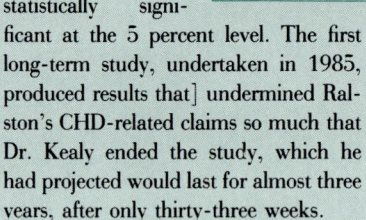

We have reviewed the record, and we cannot say that this evidence and other evidence supporting the court's view of Ralston's CHD-related claims were incoherent, facially implausible, or contradicted by extrinsic proof. Accordingly, we affirm the district court's determination that ALPO satisfactorily carried its burdens of proof and persuasion on each element of its false advertising case.

Ralston [also] attacks the monetary remedy [of] $10.4 million in favor of ALPO. [T]he [trial] court actually awarded Ralston's profits [during the time of the false advertising] to ALPO. We doubt the wisdom of an approach to

CONTINUED

damages that permits courts to award profits for their sheer deterrent effect. Since this case lacks the elements required to support the court's award of Ralston's profits, we vacate the $10.4 million judgment in favor of ALPO. On remand, the court should award ALPO its actual damages, bearing in mind the requiremet that any amount awarded have support in the record. In a false advertising case such as this one, actual damages can include: [1] profits lost by the plaintiff on sales actually diverted to the false advertisers; [2] profits lost by the plaintiff on sales made at prices reduced as a demonstrated result of the false advertising; [3] the costs of any completed advertising that actually and reasonably responds to the defendant's offending ads; and [4] quantifiable harm to the plaintiff's good will, to the extent that completed corrective advertising has not repaired that harm.

[The Lanham Act] also authorizes the court to "enter judgment, according to the circumstances of the case, for any sum above the amount found as actual damages, not exceeding three times the amount." This provision gives the court discretion to enhance damages, as long as the ultimate award qualifies as "compensation and not [as] a penalty." Given this express statutory restriction, if the district court decides to enhance damages, it should explain why the enhanced award is compensatory and not punitive.

[Affirmed as to liability; reversed as to damages and remanded.]

Commercial Defamation

Through passage of the Trademark Revision Act of 1988, Congress established a cause of action for commercial defamation, thereby increasing the volume of this type of litigation. The Lanham Act now bans false descriptions or representations about the "nature, characteristics [or] qualities of *any person's* goods, services or commercial activities." (Emphasis added.) Therefore, if Company A runs an ad comparing its products to those of Company B, and in so doing misleadingly describes the characteristics of Company B's products, Company B will be able to recover damages, perhaps including treble damages. For First Amendment reasons, the Act contains express protection for two broad types of activities: (1) political speech, consumer or editorial comment, and satire, and (2) "innocent infringement" (thereby insulating news media that innocently disseminate false advertising).

Questions and Problems

1. The plaintiff Walner, purchased an ice cream parlor franchise from the defendant, Baskin-Robbins, Inc. The franchise agreement contained language requiring the defendant's approval before the franchise could be sold. Two years later Walner contracted to sell the franchise to Garapet at a substantial profit, but Baskin-Robbins refused to grant permission for the sale. Walner sued for tortious interference with his right to contract with Garapet. Discuss. (*Walner v. Baskin-Robbins Ice Cream Co.*, 514 F.Supp. 1028, N.D.Tex. 1981.)

2. A trademark applicant wishes to mark the word "Bundt" in connection with one of its cake pans. Is this term suitable for trademark registration? Discuss. (*In re*

Northland Aluminum Products, Inc., 777 F.2d 1556, Fed. Cir. 1985.)

3. Miller Brewing Company purchased the trademark *Lite* and used this name on its labels for beer that was lower in calories than its regular beer. When a competitor, G. Heileman Brewing Company, started marketing a reduced-calorie beer that it labeled as "light beer," Miller brought a trademark infringement action against Heileman. At the trial, Heileman introduced evidence that the term *light* beer had been used for many years in the beer industry to refer to beers having certain flavors, bodies, or reduced alcoholic contents. On that basis, Heileman contended that *light* was, essentially, a generic term and thus could not be the proper subject of a trademark. The trial court rejected this argument and issued an injunction prohibiting further use of "light" by Heileman. On appeal, do you think the court should accept Heilemn argument? Discuss why or why not. (*Miller Brewing Company v. G. Heileman Brewing Company*, 561 F.2d 75, 1977.)

4. Mead Data Central developed and trademarked LEXIS, a computerized legal research service. Toyota Motor Sales planned to begin selling cars trademarked LEXUS. Discuss Mead Data's possible theories for blocking sale of the cars. (*Mead Data Central, Inc. v. Toyota Motor Sales*, 875 F.2d 1026, 2d Cir. 1989.)

5. The plaintiff bakery filmed one of the defendant bakery's delivery drivers in a grocery store taking the plaintiff's fresh bread out of the plaintiff's wrappers and replacing it with stale loaves. What theory should the plaintiff pursue? Is this a good claim? (*Basque French Bakery v. Toscana Baking Co.*, No. 2937220-0, California Superior Court, Apr. 23, 1984.)

6. In response to complaints by customers of his sons' cycle shop, P developed a device to remedy a stall-out problem occurring when Yamaha racing cycles were run in mud or water. The device closed off the rear air intake, replacing it with an air snorkel located at a higher level under the seat cover. This device was used by P's sons when they raced and P installed it on the cycles his sons sold. When Yamaha representatives visited the business, P's sons showed them the device. Yamaha soon began using the device on all its cycles. At some point thereafter, P sued Yamaha for trade secret infringement. Will this claim succeed? (*Sheets v. Yamaha*, 657 F.Supp. 319, E.D.La. 1987.)

7. By combining plastic support blocks on pontoons, spaced I-beams, and separate bouyant chambers, Rivet created a machine that could carry heavy loads across stump-filled marshes for extended periods. All three devices had been used before but never in combination. Rivet's machine, which he patended, was significantly more efficient than any previous machine. Later, a former employee began making a smiliar machine. In a patent infringement suit, the defendant claimed Rivet's patent was invalid because the invention lacked novelty and nonobviousness. Discuss. (*Kori v. Wilco Marsh-Buggies and Draglines, Inc.*, 708 F.2d 151, 5th Cir. 1983.)

8. Johnson Controls, Inc., developed a system of computer programs to control wastewater treatment plants. The "JC-5000S" program is customized for each location and carries a registered copyright. Former employees of Johnson, working for competitor Phoenix Control Systems, Inc., developed a similar program to do similar things. The Phoenix program did not copy the literal elements of Johnson's program (including the source and object code); however, it did copy the structure, sequence, and organization of the JC-5000S. Is such copying sufficient to constitute copyright infringement? (*Johnson Controls v. Phoenix Control Systems, Inc.*, 886 F.2d 1173, 9th Cir. 1989.)

9. Conventional wisdom is that John Dillinger, Public Enemy No. 1, died in a hail of bullets outside Chicago's Biograph Theater on July 22, 1934. Nash wrote two books arguing that Dillinger lived until at least 1979, because the FBI shot the wrong man at the theater. CBS televised an episode of the detective series "Simon and Simon" titled *The Dillinger Print*, which contained a plot featuring Nash's theories. One of the characters (A.J.) even purported to read from a book a description of several physical discrepancies between Dillinger and the corpse described in the 1934 autopsy. Nash cited the same discrepancies in his book. Nash sued CBS for copyright infringement. CBS admitted both access to Nash's books and copying of the books' factual material but argued that copyright law did not protect Nash this far and raised a "fair use" defense? Should Nash prevail? Discuss. (*Nash v. CBS, Inc.*, 899 F.2d 1437, 7th Cir. 1990.)

10. In 1979 U-Haul rented almost all the "self-move" household goods trailers in the United States and 60 percent of the "self-move" trucks. In that year Jartran entered the market and did so well that U-Haul's revenues for 1981 were $49 million less than it had predicted before it knew Jartran would be a competitor. Jartran's success could be traced to a $6 million ad campaign that featured comparison of the one-way rental rates charged by U-Haul and Jartran. Unfortunately, the ads were quite misleading. For example, they compared U-Haul's regular rates to special promotional rates by Jartran without disclosing that these were not the rates Jartran would normally charge. Jartran also published ads showing a Jartran truck and a U-Haul truck with the comparative sizes of the vehicles adjusted to make the U-Haul truck appear smaller and less attractive than it truly was. U-Haul sued Jartran under section 43(a) of the Lanham Act. What result? Discuss. (*U-Haul International, Inc. v. Jartran, Inc.*, 793 F.2d 1034, 9th Cir. 1986.)

CHAPTER 13

AGENCY

In this chapter we first look at the general principles of law that are applicable to a special relationship that pervades many activities in the business world, the agency relationship. We then discuss the basic rules of law applicable to partnerships and corporations, the two forms of business organization through which most of the nation's business is carried on. In a legal context the term agency ordinarily describes a relationship in which two parties—the principal and the agent—agree that one will act as a representative of the other.

AGENCY AND BUSINESS ORGANIZATIONS

The **principal** is the person who wishes to accomplish something, and the **agent** is the one employed to act in the principal's behalf to achieve it.

At one time or another, almost everyone has come into contact with the agency relationship. Anyone who has purchased merchandise at a retail store almost certainly has dealt with an agent—the salesclerk. Similarly, anyone who has ever held a job probably has served in some type of representative capacity for the employer.

The usefulness of the agency relationship in the business world is obvious. With few exceptions, no single individual—even the sole proprietor who owns and operates a business himself or herself alone—is capable of performing every act required to run a business enterprise. Similarly, even the smallest partnership must usually employ one or more persons in addition to the partners to carry on the necessary business activities. (And, as seen later, each partner is generally considered to be an agent of the partnership when carrying on routine partnership business.) Additionally, the one form of business organization through which most of the nation's large-scale business activities are carried on, the corporation, can, by definition, act *only* through agents. Thus most business transactions in this country are, in fact, handled by agents of one kind or another.

The term *agency* is often used loosely to describe many different types of relationships in which one party acts in a representative capacity for another. *Principal* and *agent* are also sometimes used loosely to denote the parties to various types of arrangements. However, throughout our discussion these terms are used narrowly to describe a particular type of relationship. The *principal–agent relationship*, as we use it, means a relationship in which the parties have agreed that the agent is to represent the principal in negotiating and transacting business: that is, *the agent is employed to make contracts or enter similar business transactions on behalf of the principal.*

Two other closely related relationships are those of *employer–employee* and *employer–independent contractor*. (Instead of *employer–employee*, some courts and writers still use the older term *master–servant*.) In these arrangements the subordinate usually has been employed to perform *physical work* for his or her superior, and the matter in dispute often concerns *tort liability*. A subordinate is an employee if the employer has the right to control the details of the job. A subordinate is an independent contractor if the person (or company) is hired to accomplish an end result, with control of the methods for accomplishing it being in the hands of the subordinate. Of course, a person may be hired to represent the employer in commercial dealings and also to perform physical tasks. In such a case he or she is an agent with respect to the authority to transact business and either a servant or an independent contractor with respect to the performance of physical tasks.

CREATION OF THE AGENCY RELATIONSHIP

The agency relationship is *consensual*—that is, based on the agreement of the parties. Many times it is created by a legally enforceable employment contract between the principal and the agent. A legally binding contract is not essential, however. Any words or actions on the parts of the principal and the agent that indicate that the agent is authorized to contract on behalf of the principal and that the agent consents to the arrangement are generally sufficient to create an agency relationship.

In fact, no formalities are required for the creation of an agency relationship in most circumstances. For example, it is not usually necessary to spell out the agent's authority in writing; oral authority is ordinarily sufficient. Exceptions do exist, however. The most common one occurs when an agent is granted authority to sell *real estate*. In most states an agent can make a contract for the sale of real estate that will bind the principal only if the agent's authority is stated in writing.

DUTIES OF PRINCIPAL AND AGENT

Duties Owed by Principal to Agent

The primary duty owed by the principal to the agent is simply that of complying with the terms of the employment contract, if one exists. Failure of the principal to do so will render him or her liable to the agent for damages; if the breach is material, it will also justify the agent in refusing to act for the principal any further. In addition, the principal has a duty to reimburse the agent for any expenses (and to indemnify the agent for any liabilities) reasonably incurred by the agent in advancing the interests of the principal.

Duties Owed by Agent to Principal

The primary obligations of the agent are the duty of obedience, the duty to use reasonable care, and the duty of loyalty. The duty of obedience requires the agent to obey instructions of the principal (as long as they are legal). The major exception of this obligation is where an *emergency* occurs. In such a situation, if the principal's instructions are not in his or her own best interests, the agent is justified in taking reasonable steps to protect the principal even if it means deviating from the prior instructions—again, subject only to the limitation that the deviations are lawful.

The "reasonable care" requirement, as the name implies, obligates the agent to act in a nonnegligent manner at all times while representing the principal. The duty of loyalty, perhaps the most important obligation of the agent, prohibits the agent from appropriating business opportunities that might be of interest to the principal or competing with the principal in the type of business he or she is conducting for the principal. Loyalty also requires that the agent avoid any existing or potential conflicts of interest. For example, if B is hired to sell goods for R, B may not sell them to himself unless R's consent is obtained. In similar fashion, the agent may not further the interests of any third party in his or her dealings for the principal. The agent also should not work for two parties on opposite sides in a transaction unless both parties agree to it. Lastly, the duty of loyalty prohibits the agent who may have acquired *confidential information* about the principal's business during the course of the agency from disclosing such information to any third party without the principal's consent. The duties of the principal and agent are illustrated in Figure 13.1.

FIGURE 13.1

AGENCY AGREEMENT

PRINCIPAL → AGENT

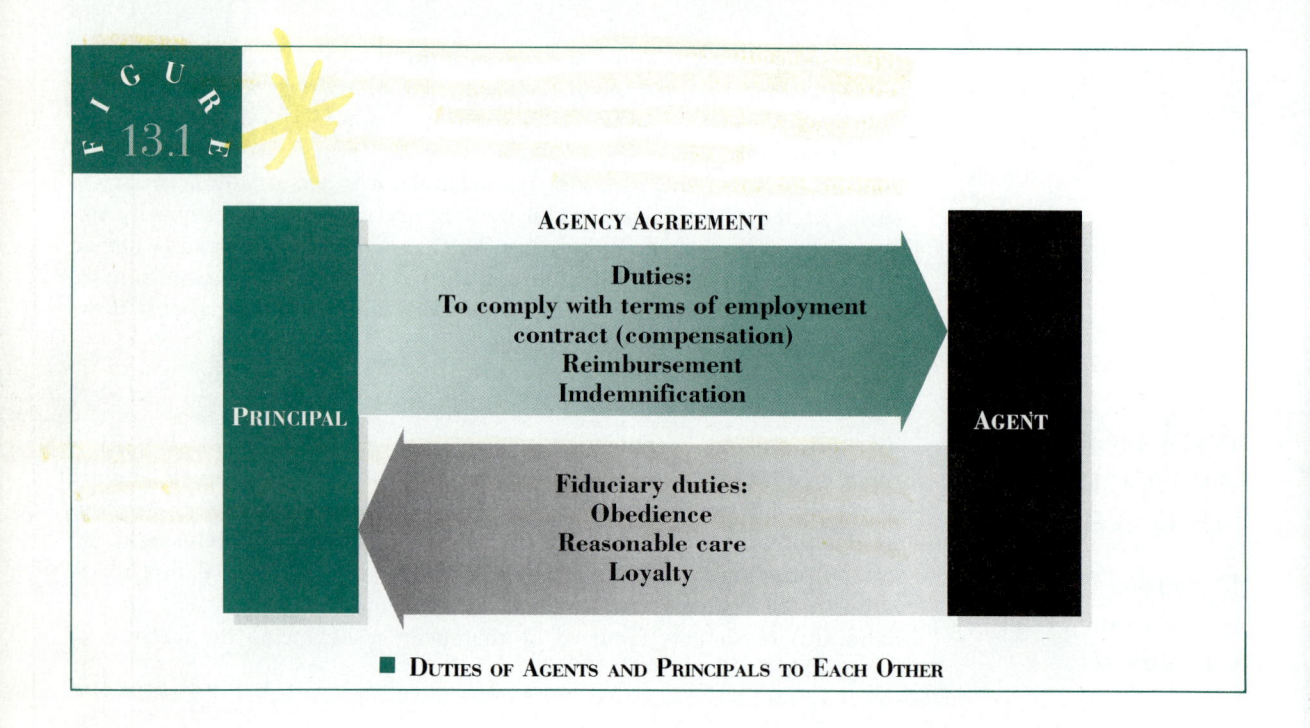

Duties:
To comply with terms of employment contract (compensation)
Reimbursement
Imdemnification

Fiduciary duties:
Obedience
Reasonable care
Loyalty

■ Duties of Agents and Principals to Each Other

LIABILITY OF THE PRINCIPAL TO THIRD PARTIES

Contractual Liability

The principal is liable on contracts negotiated by the agent only if the agent possesses some kind of *authority* to make them. Authority is classified as either "actual" or "apparent" in nature.

Actual authority is the authority that the agent has, in fact, been given by the principal. This authority is of two types: express and implied. Express authority is that which is directly granted by the principal in his or her instructions to the agent. Implied authority is that authority that an agent possesses in addition to his or her express authority and essentially refers to the authority of an agent to do any act reasonably necessary to carry out the main job that was granted to the agent. To illustrate: O, the owner of a retail store, hires M to act as manager of the store and gives M express authority to act in certain ways, for example, to purchase inventory and to make sales. In addition, M will have implied authority to handle matters that are incidental to the main purpose of the agency, such as authority to employ a plumber to repair leaks and to employ a reasonable number of salesclerks.

The term *apparent authority* is a contradiction in terms, because it refers to authority that third parties may *assume* the agent possesses, even though, in fact, actual authority is lacking. Apparent authority normally exists only when the principal, *by his or her own conduct*, has led third parties to believe that the agent has authority to engage in a particular transaction. To illustrate: S is a salesman for X, and over a long period of time X has given possession of goods to S that X has wanted S to sell and that S had, in fact, customarily sold. S, while making his rounds, receives a call from X who tells

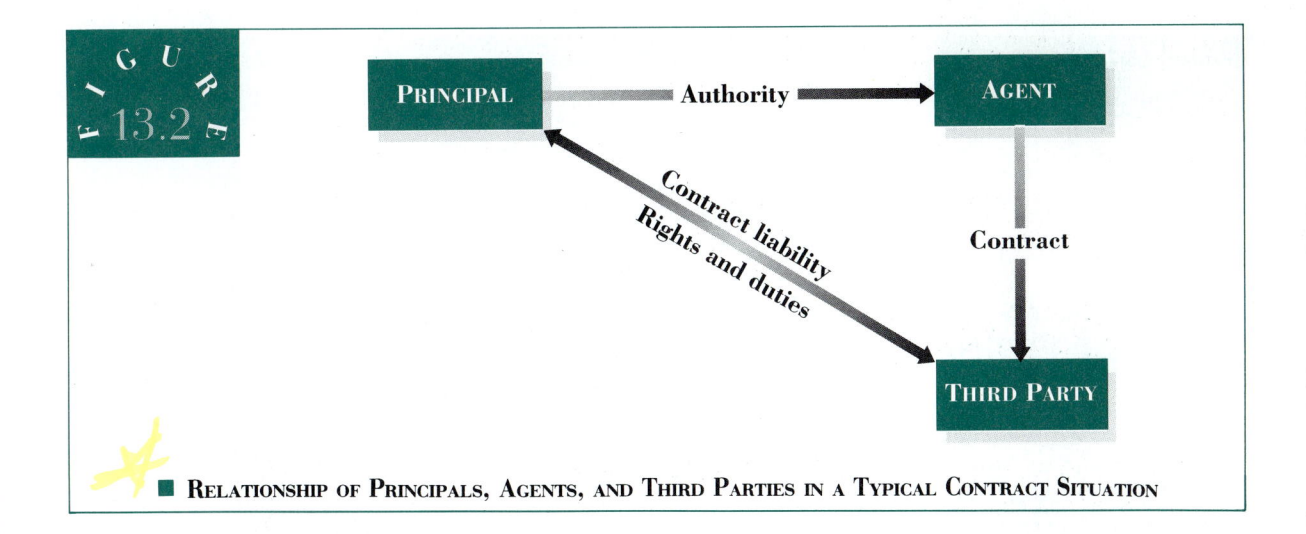

FIGURE 13.2 ■ RELATIONSHIP OF PRINCIPALS, AGENTS, AND THIRD PARTIES IN A TYPICAL CONTRACT SITUATION

[Diagram: Principal —Authority→ Agent; Agent —Contract→ Third Party; Third Party ↔ Principal (Contract liability / Rights and duties)]

S not to sell the remaining goods he has in his possession. Contrary to instructions, S sells the goods to T, a third party who had purchased such goods from S before and who had no knowledge of X's withdrawal of authority. In such a case, X is bound by the sale to T.

If a contract is made that the agent has absolutely no authority to make, the principal is not liable on such contract unless he or she subsequently *ratifies* it. A ratification occurs where the principal, with full knowledge of the terms of the contract, indicates to the third party, expressly or impliedly, that he or she will fulfill the contract even though there was no initial obligation to do so. Figure 13.2 illustrates the rule that a principal is bound by the authorized contracts made by the agent.

Tort Liability

When a tort is committed by an *independent contractor*, the employer normally cannot be held responsible for the damages. When a tort is committed by an *employee*, however, the employer frequently can be held liable. Unless the employer itself was negligent or actually authorized the employee's tort, an injured third party must prove that the employee was "acting within the scope of his or her employment" at the time that the tort occurred. In most instances this rule—the rule of **respondeat superior**—is easy to apply. For example, if an employee who is driving across town to negotiate a contract on behalf of his or her employer negligently runs into another motorist's car, the employee is clearly within the scope of his or her employment and the employer is, therefore, liable to the injured motorist. However, an off-duty employee who assaults a third party during the course of a purely personal dispute is obviously outside the scope of his or her employment.

Many real-life cases fall between these extremes, presenting situations in which the scope of employment rule is considerably more difficult to apply. The case below is typical of those in this category.

CLOVER v. SNOWBIRD SKI RESORT

SUPREME COURT OF UTAH 808 P.2d 1037 (1991)

The defendant, Snowbird Corporation, operated a ski resort with two restaurants—the Plaza located at the base of the mountain and the Mid-Gad located half-way to the top. Snowbird's employee, Chris Zulliger, was a chef at the Plaza and was instructed to make periodic trips to the Mid-Gad to monitor its operations. Zulliger had made several such trips. On December 5, 1985, Zulliger was scheduled to begin work at the Plaza at 3 P.M. Before beginning work, he had planned to go skiing. Snowbird preferred that its employees know how to ski because it made it easier for them to get to and from work. As part of the compensation for his employment, Zulliger received season ski passes. On the morning of the accident, Zulliger was asked to inspect the operation of Mid-Gad before beginning work at the Plaza.

Zulliger stopped at the Mid-Gad in the middle of his first run. He inspected the kitchen and then skied four runs before heading down the mountain to begin work. On his final run, Zulliger jumped off the crest on the side of an intermediate run. This was dangerous because it was impossible for skiers above the crest to see skiers below it. A sign instructed skiers to ski slowly at this point. Zulliger, however, skied over the crest at a significant speed and collided with the plaintiff, Clover, who was hit in the head and severely injured.

Clover sued Zulliger and Snowbird. The trial court dismissed Clover's claim against Snowbird, ruling that, as a matter of law, Zulliger was not acting within the scope of his employment at the time of the collision. Clover appealed.

HALL, CHIEF JUSTICE:

Under the doctrine of respondeat superior, employers are held vicariously liable for the torts their employees commit when the employees are acting within the scope of their employment. In *Birkner v. Salt Lake County*, 771 P.2d 1053 (Utah 1989), we stated that acts within the scope of employment are "those acts which are so closely connected with what the servant is employed to do, and so fairly and reasonably incidental to it, that they may be regarded as methods, even though quite improper ones, of carrying out the objectives of the employment." The question of whether an employee is acting within the scope of employment is a question of fact.

In *Birkner*, we observed that the Utah cases that have addressed the issue of whether an employee's actions, as a matter of law, are within or without the scope of employment have focused on three criteria. "First, an employee's conduct must be of the general kind the employee is employed to perform. ... In other words, the employee must be about the employer's business and the duties assigned by the employer, as opposed to being wholly involved in a personal endeavor." Second, the employee's conduct must occur substantially within the hours and ordinary spatial boundaries of the employment. "Third, the employee's conduct must be motivated, at least in part, by the purpose of serving the employer's interest." Under specific factual situations, such as when the employee's conduct serves a dual purpose or when the employee takes a personal detour in the course of carrying out his employer's directions, this court has occasionally used variations of this approach. These variations, however, are not departures from the criteria advanced in *Birkner*. Rather, they are methods of applying the criteria in specific factual situations.

In applying the *Birkner* criteria to the facts in the instant case, it is important to note that if Zulliger had returned to the Plaza Restaurant immediately after he inspected the operations at the Mid-Gad Restaurant, there would be ample evidence to support the conclusion that on his return trip Zulliger's action were within the scope of his employment. There is evidence that it was part of Zulliger's job to monitor the operations at the Mid-Gad and that he was directed to monitor the operations on the day of

CONTINUED

the accident. There is also evidence that Snowbird intended Zulliger to use the ski lifts and the ski runs on his trips to the Mid-Gad. It is clear, therefore, that Zulliger's actions could be considered to "be of the general kind that the employee is employed to perform." It is also clear that there would be evidence that Zulliger's actions occurred within the hours and normal spatial boundaries of his employment. Furthermore, throughout the trip he would have been on his employer's premises. Finally, it is clear that Zulliger's actions in monitoring the operations at the Mid-Gad, per his employer's instructions, could be considered "motivated, at least in part, by the purpose of serving the employer's interest."

The difficulty, of course, arises from the fact that Zulliger did not return to the Plaza after he finished inspecting the facilities at the Mid-Gad. Rather, he skied four more runs and rode the lift to the top of the mountain before he began his return to the base. Snowbird claims that this fact shows that Zulliger's primary purpose for skiing on the day of the accident was for his own pleasure and that therefore, as a matter of law, he was not acting within the scope of his employment.

There is ample evidence that there was a predominant business purpose for Zulliger's trip to the Mid-Gad. Therefore, this case is better analyzed under our decisions dealing with situations where an employee has taken a personal detour in the process of carrying out his duties. In situations where the detour was such a substantial diversion from the employee's duties that it constituted an abandonment of employment, we held that the employee, as a matter of law, was acting outside the scope of employment. However, in situations where reasonable minds could differ on whether the detour constituted a slight deviation from the employee's duties or an abandonment of employment, we have left the question for the jury.

Under the circumstances of the instant case, it is entirely possible for a jury to reasonably believe that at the time of the accident, Zulliger has resumed his employment and that Zulliger's deviation was not substantial enought to constitute a total abandoment of employment. First, a jury could reasonably believe that by beginning his return to the base of the mountain to begin his duties as a chef and to report to [his boss] concerning his observations at the Mid-Gad, Zulliger had resumed his employment.

Second, a jury could reasonably believe that Zulliger's actions in taking four ski runs and returning to the top of the mountain do not constitute a complete abandonment of employment. It is important to note that by taking these ski runs, Zulliger was not disregarding his employer's directions.

These two factors, along with other circumstances—such as, throughout the day Zulliger was on Snowbird's property, there was no specific time set for inspecting the restaurant, and the act of skiing was the method used by Snowbird employees to travel among the different locations of the resort—constitute sufficient evidence for a jury to conclude that Zulliger, at the time of the accident, was acting within the scope of his employment.

[Reversed and remanded for jury trial.]

LIABILITY OF THE AGENT OR EMPLOYEE TO THIRD PARTIES

There are a number of situations in which the agent or employee may incur personal liability to the third party. We note the most important of these here.

HUMOR AND THE LAW

Fiduciary duty cases sometimes illustrate how low man (or woman) can sink in the pursuit of personal gain.

In one case, an employer promised his servant a $20,000 payment upon the employer's death. Employees, of course, owe a fiduciary duty to their employers. This employee breached his duty by wooing the employer's wife while the employer lay on his death bed. In light of the employee's treachery, the estate resisted payment of the $20,000. The court held that the breach of fiduciary duty (and common decency) by the employee disqualified him from recovering on the breached promise. *Bright v. Ganas,* 189 A. 427 (Md. 1937).

Perhaps worse was the case of two partners. Partner #1 was diagnosed as having a serious case of cancer. Before the doctors informed her of this, Partner #2, who did know of the malignancy, induced Partner #1 to sign an agreement providing "that in the event of the decease of either of the partners, all of the partnership assets shall ipso factor immediately become the sole and exclusive property of the surviving partner." Given the fiduciary duty existing between partners, the court had no difficulty in determining that the agreement was voidable because of the crucial information that Partner #1 had hidden from Partner #2. *Alexander v. Sims,* 249 S.W.2d 832 (Ark. 1952). How low can people go?

Liability Arising out of Contracts

By making a contract, the agent impliedly warrants (guarantees) that he or she has the principal's authority to make the contract. If it turns out that such authority is totally lacking, the third party may sue the agent for damages for breach of the implied warranty of authority.

In some instances an agent acts for an undisclosed principal—that is, the agent contracts in his or her own name with the third party, the latter having no idea of a principal's existence. If the principal in such a case subsequently refuses to go through with the contract, the third party may enforce the contract against the agent personally.

An agent also incurs personal liability in the case where the purported principal is nonexistent. To illustrate: X, a member of an unincorporated church, makes a contract in the name of the church with Y. Because the unincorporated church (the purported principal) is not a legally recognized person capable of making a contract, X is personally liable on the contract in case the church refuses to live up to its terms voluntarily.

Tort Liability

The agent or employee always has personal liability for torts committed against third parties. If the agent is completely outside the scope of his or her employment at the time of the tort, the agent is solely liable. However, if the agent *is* acting within the scope of the employment at the time of the tort (in which case the third party normally sues both the agent and principal), the third party recovers a "joint and several" judgment. To illustrate: if the third party's damages are $5,000, he or she recovers a judgment in that amount against the agent personally, a judgment in that amount against the principal personally, and a similar judgment against the agent and principal jointly. If neither the principal nor the agent subsequently pays the judgment voluntarily, the third party, armed with such a judgment, may have the court attach any of the nonexempt assets of the principal, the agent, or both that are within the jurisdiction of the court and have these sold by court order to recover the $5,000 due. If the principal ends up paying the $5,000, he or she has a right to recover such sum from the agent, but, in practice, attempts to recover are often abandoned because of the agent's financial inability to make reimbursement.

TERMINATION OF THE AGENCY

The various ways in which an agency may be terminated fall into two general categories: by act of the parties, and by operation of law. We will note only the most important of these.

Termination by Act of the Parties

If an agent is employed to accomplish a particular object, such as the sale of a tract of land owned by the principal, the agency is terminated when the sale and all incidental formalities have been completed. Similarly, if the principal and agent originally agreed that the arrangement will end at a certain time, the arrival of that time obviously terminates their relationship. If nothing has been said as to the duration of the agency and if nothing occurs to terminate it, the relationship is deemed to last for a period of time that is reasonable under the circumstances.

Another common termination is by mutual agreement. It is a basic rule of agency law that the parties can mutually cancel their contract at any time, regardless of what they may have agreed to originally. And, because the agency relationship is consensual in nature, the relationship can also be terminated (with rare exception) unilaterally—by the principal alone or by the agent alone. If no binding employment contract had existed between the two of them, the party terminating the agency usually does not incur any liability to the other by this action. However, if a binding employment contract had existed, the party terminating the relationship is liable for damages on the breach of contract theory, unless his or her termination was legally justified.

Termination by Operation of Law

The death or insanity of either principal or agent terminates most agencies immediately. Additionally, the bankruptcy of the principal will terminate the agency in most circumstances, although the bankruptcy of the agent does not terminate it *unless* the nature of the agency is such that the bankruptcy impairs the agent's ability to act for the principal.

If a change of law makes the agency or performance of the authorized act illegal, the general rule is that the agent's authority to act is extinguished when he or she learns of the change. Similarly, if the subject matter of an agency is destroyed, the agency is terminated. To illustrate: X employs Y to sell grain belonging to X that is being stored in a particular storage elevator; the destruction by fire of the elevator and the grain will normally extinguish Y's authority.

PARTNERSHIPS

Although partnership law was a common-law subject at one time, the basic source of partnership law today in almost all states is the Uniform Partnership Act (UPA). Accordingly, all partnership principles discussed below are based on that act. Our discussion throughout focuses on general partnerships (those in which all partners have unlimited liability for partnership obligations), as distinguished from limited partnerships.

NATURE AND FORMATION

Section 6 of the UPA defines a **partnership** as "an association of two or more persons to carry on as co-owners a business for profit." Under this definition, "person" includes not only individuals but also corporations and other partnerships. The "co-owner" requirement distinguishes partners from those persons who are merely agents or servants of a business enterprise. Lastly, the "profit" requirement excludes nonprofit associations, such as churches and fraternal lodges.

Insofar as the legal nature of the partnership is concerned, the UPA partially rejects the common-law view that a partnership is not a separate legal enterprise apart from the partners themselves by allowing a partnership to own property in its own name. Additionally, most states permit partnerships to sue and be sued in their own names.

Any "association" to carry on a business requires either an express or implied *agreement* between the parties. Usually there is a formal, written agreement setting forth all important aspects of the relationship. However, an implied partnership agreement is sufficient; thus, if two persons manage a business jointly and share profits and losses, a partnership exists in the eyes of the law, even though such persons may not have intended to become partners and do not consider themselves to be partners. Even persons who are not partners may be treated as "partners by estoppel" if they hold themselves out (or allow themselves to be held out by others) as partners.

The following case addresses both the existence of a partnership and the concept of partnership by estoppel.

In re Indvik

U.S. Bankruptcy Court, Northern District of Iowa 118 B.R. 993 (1990)

Lowell and Eldon Indvik have a joint ownership interest in farm land bought from their parents. Lowell characterized their relationship as "just brothers farming together." Both brothers filed for individual bankruptcy and claimed certain farm equipment as exempt property. During the proceedings a question arose as to whether the brothers were partners. Much of the equipment used to farm would be exempt from creditors as individual property if they were not partners. However, if they were partners, the equipment would be nonexempt partnership property. The following is an excerpt from the bankruptcy judge's ruling on the creditors' objections to the claimed exemptions.

EDMONDS, BANKRUPTCY JUDGE:

Iowa law defines a partnership as "an association of two or more persons to carry on as co-owners a business for profit." The creation of a partnership under Iowa law requires (1) an association with an intent by the parties to associate as partners, (2) a business, (3) earning of profits, and (4) co-ownership of profits, property and control. The intention to associate as partners is the crucial test. "Evidence of an intent to associate may include a partnership name, a partnership bank account, partnership tax returns, and a division of profits and losses." *In re Waters*, 90 B.R. 946 (Bankr.N.D.Iowa 1988).

The burden of proof is on the objecting creditors to show the items initially claimed exempt are partnership property. There is evidence on both sides of the issue. There was no written partnership agreement nor did the brothers file federal or state partnership tax returns. Lowell testified that the brothers had no intention of becoming partners but merely used the "Indvik Brothers" name out of convenience. The brothers did, however, agree to share profits and losses equally. Each of the brothers signed a document entitled "Authority of Partnership to Open Deposit Account and to Procure Loans." In that document, Indvik Brothers was described as the trade name which was to be used by the partnership of Eldon and Lowell Indvik. Subsequent loan documents with Forest City Bank & Trust were executed using "Indvik Brothers" as the name of the artificial entity borrowing money. An agricultural security agreement executed November 9, 1983 identifies the document as a partnership financial statement. If the brothers did not believe themselves to be partners, they should have disavowed such documents in dealing with the bank.

Based on the evidence, the court concludes that Indvik Brothers was a partnership, and the personal property initially claimed as exempt by Eldon and Lowell Indvik was partnership property.

Even if the court were to find that a partnership did not exist, the court would conclude that the brothers are estopped from denying the existence of the partnership. A person may be estopped to deny a partnership when he holds himself out as a partner or permits someone else to do so and thus induces a third party to extend credit or otherwise act to his detriment. Loan documents submitted to Forest City Bank & Trust indicated the existence of a partnership. Although the documents submitted to FmHA were less conclusive, they nonetheless bore "Indvik Brothers" as the name of the borrower.

As a partner, neither Lowell Indvik nor Eldon Indvik may claim as exempt their partners' rights in specific partnership property

[Creditors' objections sustained.]

PARTNERSHIP PROPERTY

Under the UPA, partnerships may own property in their own names, as we have noted. This is not only a recommended practice but also, in fact, a very common one. However, property held in the names of the individual partners may also be partnership property in the eyes of the law. For example, if X and Y are partners and the title to an acre of land is in X's name, that land may legally be partnership property and thus subject to claims of partnership creditors if the property was purchased with partnership assets. And, while mere use of a partner's property for partnership purposes does not alone cause it to become partnership property, such use coupled with such factors as (1) the payment of taxes by the partnership, or (2) the carrying of the property on partnership books as an asset will cause a court to rule that the property is partnership property.

OPERATING THE BUSINESS

Relations Between the Partners

Partnership agreements often provide that a particular partner will be the "managing partner," exercising control over the daily operations of the business. In the absence of such agreement, all partners have equal rights in the conduct and management of the business.

Partners have certain rights in partnership property, but these are subject to several limitations. First, the partnership agreement may provide that only one partner may use or control a particular piece of partnership property. Second, in the absence of such agreement, all partners have equal rights to use partnership property, but only for partnership purposes; thus one partner is not entitled to exclusive use or possession without consent of all other partners. And last, a partner's right to possess and control partnership property cannot be transferred to a third party without the consent of all partners.

An individual partner's right to profits of the enterprise is usually specified in the partnership agreement. If not, profits are divided equally. The same rules are applicable to division of losses.

Each partner maintains a **fiduciary relationship** with the partnership and with every other partner in matters pertaining to the partnership. This relationship is much the same as the one existing between principal and agent. (The analogy is particularly appropriate because each partner is an agent of the partnership.) Because such a relationship requires the highest standards of loyalty, good faith, and integrity, a partner who acts in his or her own self-interest and to the detriment of the partnership is accountable to it for any profits made from the endeavor.

In addition to the broad right to have other partners act with loyalty and in good faith, each partner has the right to inspect and copy partnership books. Each partner also has the right to institute a legal proceeding, called an "accounting," under certain circumstances—for example, if he or she has been wrongfully excluded from partnership business or property or if one of the other partners has derived a personal benefit from a partnership transaction without his or her consent.

Relations with Third Parties, Generally

In partnership transactions with third parties, the law of agency governs the liabilities of the partnership, the partners, and the third party. Technically, the partnership is the principal and each partner an agent with respect to partnership affairs. Thus the partnership is liable to third parties for a partner's transactions that are contractual in nature if the partner has express, implied, or apparent authority to make such transactions.

Under the UPA, a partner possesses the implied authority to engage in transactions that are for the "carrying on of the partnership business in the usual way"—that is, transactions that are customarily carried on by partners in similar firms. Under this rule, partners usually have the implied power to borrow money on behalf of the partnership, to hire needed employees, and to purchase items reasonably necessary to the operation of the business. Additionally, partners have implied authority to sell goods and real estate belonging to the partnership if sales of such items are within the ordinary course of the business. (For example, a partner in a firm that buys and sells land has implied authority to sell a parcel of real estate owned by the partnership, while a partner in a grocery business would *not* have the implied authority to do so.)

As in agency law generally, the partnership is liable to third parties harmed by the tort or other wrongful act of a partner only if the tort was committed while the partner was acting in the ordinary course or scope of the partnership business. However, even if a partner's tort did not involve partnership business, any other partner participating in, directing, or authorizing the wrongful act is personally liable along with the one actually committing it.

In the following case, the court applies basic agency concepts contained in the UPA to the plaintiff's claim against a partnership on a real estate contract signed by a single partner.

CASE

OWENS
v.
PALOS VERDES MONACO

COURT OF APPEALS OF CALIFORNIA, 191 CAL. RPTR. 381 (1983)

Seymour Owens, Albert Fink, and Manny Borinstein were in the business of acquiring, holding, and developing real estate on the Palos Verdes peninsula in California. They bought 250 acres, divided it into four tracts, and formed four separate partnerships to own and develop the tracts. Borinstein died, and the surviving partners agreed that Borinstein's widow, Pearl, would become a partner but would hold the interests in the four partnerships in trust for her daughter Joan. Several years later, Kajima International, Inc., became interested in buying one of these tracts of land. The tract in question, 57 acres, was held by a partnership called Monaco Land Holders (MLH). A representative of Kajima contacted a real estate brokerage firm in the Palos Verdes area. The brokerage firm contacted Owens, one of the three partners in MLH and the other partnerships.

CONTINUED

Owens told the broker to show the 57-acre tract to the Kajima representative, to "pursue the sale," and "keep him [Owens] informed." After Kajima's representative had seen the land and conferred with his superiors, Kajima made a written offer to buy. This offer was delivered by the broker to both Owens and Fink. They rejected the offer and Owens told the broker that "Al Fink will be handling this from now on; just keep me apprised of what's going on." A second offer was made and was again delivered to both Owens and Fink. Fink met with Owens and they decided to reject this offer, as well. At this time, and later, Pearl Borinstein was kept informed about the negotiations and indicated that she would go along with any proposal that met with Owens' approval.

Over the next several months, the broker tried to put together a deal that would be agreeable to both sides. Three different meetings were held to negotiate the sale. Present at all three meetings were the broker and several representatives of Kajima, including a vice-president and another high-ranking officer. At the first two meetings, MLH was represented by Fink and Joan Borinstein (Pearl's daughter). Owens was informed about each of the meetings in advance, but each time he indicated that if Fink was going to be present, there was no need for him (Owens) to be there. At the third meeting, when the sale was finally concluded and the written contract was signed, only Fink was present in behalf of MLH, although Owens, Pearl, and Joan had all been notified of the meeting. Thus, Fink was the only partner signing the contract for the partnership. At this meeting, a question was raised because only one partner was signing, and Fink assured the buyers that he had authority to act for the partnership.

About two weeks after this third meeting, Owens indicated that he was unhappy with the terms of the sale contract and did not want the sale to go forward. The buyer insisted on completing the sale, and Owens filed suit against both the partnership and Kajima. In the suit, Owens sought a declaratory judgment that the contract was invalid and an injunction prohibiting the partnership from transferring title to the 57-acre tract to Kajima. Kajima filed a counterclaim against the partnership, Owens, and the other partners, seeking a decree of specific performance that would require the contract to be carried out by transferring title to Kajima. (Because initially there was some confusion as to whether the 57-acre tract was owned by MLH or by one of the other partnerships, Palos Verdes Monaco, both partnerships were named as parties to the lawsuit. Consequently, the name of Palos Verdes Monaco appears in the title of the case. After the suit was filed, it was determined that MLH owned this particular tract.) The trial court ruled that the contract was valid because Fink had authority to sign in behalf of the partnership, denied Owens' request for an injunction, and granted Kajima's request for specific performance of the contract. Owens, the partnership, and the other partners appealed.

FEINERMAN, PRESIDING JUSTICE:

The seminal issue in this appeal is whether Fink's signature alone was sufficient to bind MLH to the terms of the April 1 agreement. The resolution of that question depends upon the conclusion we reach regarding Fink's authority to act for the partnership....

In our view of the matter, the provisions of [the Uniform Partnership Act, §9] are dispositive of the issue of Fink's authority to bind the partnership....

Section 9 provides in pertinent part as follows:

(1) *Every partner is an agent of the partnership for the purpose of its business, and the act of every partner, including the execution in the partnership name of any instrument, for apparently carrying on in the usual way the business of the partnership of which he is a member binds the partnership*, unless the partner so acting has in fact no authority to act for the partnership in the particular matter, and the person with whom he is dealing has knowledge of the fact that he has no such authority. [Emphasis added by the court.]

(2) An act of a partner which is not apparently for carrying on the business of the partnership in the usual way does not bind the partnership unless authorized by the other partners....

The Supreme Court in analyzing section 9 in *Ellis v. Mihelis* (1963) 384 P.2d 7,

CONTINUED

stated: "These provisions distinguish between acts of a partner which bind the partnership because of his status as a partner without any express authority being required and acts binding on the partnership only after express authorization by all partners. Under the express terms of subdivision (1) of the section all acts of a partner which are apparently within the usual course of the particular business bind the partnership. The effect of the provision is that the status of a partner, without more, serves as a complete authority with respect to such acts, obviating the necessity of any express authority, either oral or written, from the other members of the firm. It necessarily follows that insofar as a partner limits his conduct to matters apparently within the partnership business, he can bind the other partners without obtaining their written consent. Subdivision (2), however, provides that there must be express authority for acts of a partner which do not appear to be in the usual course of the business...."

In the case before us, Fink's signature alone was sufficient to bind the partnership if the sale of the subject property was an act "for apparently carrying on in the usual way the business of the partnership." The apparent scope of the partnership business depends primarily on the conduct of the partnership and its partners and what they cause third persons to believe about the authority of the partners....

The trial court found that "[t]he sale of the land to Kajima was apparently in the ordinary course of the selling partnership's business.... Fink was the only partner who ever attended meetings with representatives of Kajima regarding this transaction up to and including April 1, 1977. Fink conducted the negotiations on behalf of the sellers. In the context of the negotiations for the sale of the land, Fink's role as sale negotiator for the sellers, and Owen's statements [to the broker] that Fink would handle the deal on behalf of the sellers, statements which were reported to Kajima, [reasonably led] Kajima to believe that Fink had authority to sell the land."

The conduct of the partnership and its partners in this case was sufficient to sustain the findings that the partnership was in the business of selling property and that Fink, a partner, was authorized to act for the partnership.

[The partners also] argue that sale of the subject property cannot be considered to be within the apparent scope of the partnership business because sale of said property would make it impossible to carry on the partnership business. Section 9, subdivision (3) specifies certain acts which are not within the scope of the usual course of business. It provides: "Unless authorized by the other partners or unless they have abandoned the business, one or more but less than all the partners have no authority to: ... (c) Do any other act which would make it impossible to carry on the ordinary business of a partnership."...

A number of reported decisions, including *Petrikis v. Hanges* (1952) 245 P.2d 39, hold that the sale of a partnership's only asset is beyond the scope of usual partnership business and thus cannot be effected by a single partner. In *Petrikis*, the seller of real property, Mr. Petrikis, sold the partnership's only asset, a cocktail lounge, without written authority from his partners. The Court of Appeal held that Petrikis had not bound the partnership because he had acted beyond the scope of usual business in selling the partnership's only asset. *Petrikis* is distinguishable from the present case in that... Petrikis's partnership was in the business of running a bar, not the business of holding a bar in anticipation of its eventual sale. In the present case, MLH had a singular purpose. It existed solely to hold and sell a piece of real property. The business of MLH was selling its land. Thus, the sale was in the ordinary course of MLH's business....

[The judgment of the trial court that the contract was valid and ordering its enforcement is affirmed.]

Partners' Liability to Third-Party Creditors

One of the cardinal characteristics of the partnership form of business is that the individual partners are *personally liable* for the obligations of the partnership. But this liability is of a secondary nature, because a creditor having a contract claim against a partnership must first look to partnership property for satisfaction of the claim. In most jurisdictions, a partnership-tort creditor can reach the assets of individual partners without exhausting partnership *assets.* Creditors of individual partners have priority as to the partner's assets while partnership creditors have priority as to partnership assets, unless the debtor is in bankruptcy, in which case both have equal priority.

TERMINATION

Complete termination of the partnership as a business organization is comprised of two elements: dissolution and winding up. *Dissolution* does not of itself bring the partnership business to a close; it is, rather, the "beginning of the end." Essentially, the word *dissolution* designates that point in time when the object of the partners changes from that of continuing the organization in its present form to discontinuing it. The partnership is not terminated at that time, but its object has become termination.

The second element of termination, commonly referred to as *winding up*, involves the actual process of settling partnership affairs after dissolution. After both dissolution and winding up have occurred, the partnership as an organization will have terminated.

Dissolution

The events that cause dissolution can be divided into four categories: (1) act of the parties not in violation of their agreement, (2) act of the parties in violation of their agreement, (3) operation of law, and (4) court decree. In many circumstances dissolution of a partnership can be brought about by the partners themselves without violating their partnership agreement and without the necessity of any formal legal proceedings. For example, the agreement may provide that the partnership will exist for only a specified period of time; on expiration of this period, the partnership will obviously dissolve. Similarly, the articles of partnership may provide that the arrangement is for some expressly indicated purpose or undertaking; once that purpose is achieved, dissolution occurs. Additionally, any partnership, regardless of the terms of the original agreement, can be dissolved at any time by agreement of all the parties.

Irrespective of the terms of the partnership agreement, any partner can at any time withdraw from the partnership and cause its dissolution. That is, partners always have the *power* to dissolve. If the partnership is "at will," they also have the *right*. However, if they do not have the right because withdrawal violates the partnership agreement (*e.g.,* they withdraw in the second year of an agreed ten-year partnership), withdrawing partners are liable to copartners for any damages resulting from the wrongful dissolution.

Dissolution by operation of law occurs when the business becomes illegal or on the death or bankruptcy of any partner. A number of situations are set forth in section 32 of the UPA in which dissolution of a partnership can be accomplished by the issuance of a formal court decree. They can be divided into two broad categories: (1) situations in which a partner can obtain a dissolution, and (2) situations in which a third party can obtain such a decree.

Once a dissolution has occurred, the authority of individual partners to act on behalf of the partnership usually ceases, except for acts necessary to complete unfinished transactions or those appropriate for winding up partnership affairs.

Winding Up

Winding up is the second and final step after dissolution in the termination of a partnership. When dissolution has occurred and the business is to be terminated, the winding up process entails such activities as liquidating partnership property (turning it into cash), collecting outstanding accounts, paying outstanding debts, and any other actions required to bring partnership accounts to a close. After all partnership assets have been liquidated, they are distributed to those having claims against the partnership. The order in which they are distributed is of little importance if the partnership assets are sufficient to pay all claims in full. But if the assets are insufficient to completely satisfy all claims, claims are paid in the following order: (1) claims of outside creditors of the partnership; (2) claims of individual partners for repayment of loans they have made to the partnership; and (3) claims of individual partners for return of contributions they have made to the partnership's working capital. If any assets remain after satisfying these claims, they are distributed as profits to the partners in the proportion in which profits were to be shared.

Limited Partnerships

Our discussion thus far has strictly pertained to general partnerships, and we are about to discuss corporations. A form of business organization that combines features of both general partnerships and corporations is the **limited partnership,** which is simply a partnership with at least one general partner and at least one limited partner. A limited partner receives the limited liability of a corporate shareholder (*i.e.,* his or her liability is limited to the amount invested in the partnership) in exchange for giving up the right to actively engage in control of the day-to-day operations of the venture.

The limited partnership is an attractive vehicle for many investors because it combines partnership "pass through" taxation with corporate limited liability for investors. This is especially true because many states' statutes now allow limited partners to engage in substantial business-related activity without being deemed to engage in such a level of control as to forfeit their limited liability status. Every limited partnership must have at least one general partner that will have unlimited liability for partnership obligations; however, that general partner may be a corporate entity that can, in turn, shield its owners from general liability.

Generally speaking, the law of limited partnerships is similar to the law of general partnerships. Indeed, the UPA is a "gap filler" that provides the law for any subject not specifically addressed by limited partnership statutes.

CORPORATIONS

All states have general corporation laws that govern all aspects of corporate life. About half the states have patterned their statutes on the **Model Business Corporation Act,** and the laws of the remaining states are sufficiently similar that they can be discussed with some degree of generalization.

NATURE

The most important characteristic of the **corporation** is its recognition as a **legal entity**—an artificial being or person separate from its stockholders and managers. As a result of this concept, the corporation can own property, make contracts, and sue and be sued in court in its own name. And an especially important consequence of the separate entity concept is the fact that the corporation alone is responsible for its debts. In other words, the stockholders (unlike the partners in a partnership) are generally *not personally liable* for corporate debts. Thus if a corporation fails, the most that the stockholders will ordinarily lose is the amount they have invested in it.

FORMATION

The first step in the formative process is preparation of **articles of incorporation** by the promoters—the persons forming the corporation. The articles normally must include the name of the corporation, its duration, the purposes for which it is formed, the financial structure, and provisions for regulating the internal affairs of the corporation. The basic steps in forming a corporation are illustrated in Figure 13.3.

If all requirements for incorporation specified in Figure 13.3 have been followed to the letter, it is said that a **de jure** corporation exists. The existence of such a corporation cannot be challenged by either the state or any other party so long as the corporation acts lawfully in the conduct of its

FIGURE 13.3

Planning and structuring

INCORPORATION

Prepare articles of incorporation

File articles with state

Charter issued

Organizational meeting

First board of directors meeting

Corporation ready to do business

■ BASIC STEPS IN CORPORATE FORMATION

business. Occasionally, however, there occurs some deviation from the procedures required for incorporation. If the deviation is relatively insignificant and no harm is caused to the public interest, the corporation still has *de jure* status. However, if the deviation is so important that there is not a substantial compliance with the mandatory incorporation procedures, there will not be a *de jure* corporation. There might, however, be what is commonly called **de facto** corporation, a corporation in fact. The status and powers of a *de facto* corporation are the same as a *de jure* corporation, with one limited exception: the state can challenge its validity, but no other party can do so. If a corporation has neither *de jure* nor *de facto* status, the validity of its existence can be challenged by the state or by any other interested party, such as a creditor seeking to hold a shareholder *personally liable* for a corporate debt.

FINANCING THE CORPORATION

The principal method of initially financing a corporation is by the issuance of **securities,** which are sold to investors. Shares of capital stock sold to investors (**shareholders**) are called *equity securities,* and bonds sold to investors are called *debt securities.* Shareholders are owners of the corporation, and bondholders are corporation creditors. Whatever kinds of shares or bonds are issued, the corporation must comply with registration laws of the state applicable to such issues, and often with all regulations of the Securities and Exchange Commission—a federal agency regulating securities sold in interstate commerce or through the mails.

CORPORATE MANAGEMENT

The structure of corporate control can be viewed as pyramidal in nature, with the shareholders forming the broad base of the pyramid. The shareholders exercise their control, for the most part, by selecting the individuals who serve on the board of directors. The board, in turn, usually selects corporate officers and other managerial employees at the top of the pyramid; these people oversee the day-to-day operations of the firm. The relationships within this structure are illustrated in Figure 13.4.

The most important shareholder functions are (1) election and removal of directors, (2) amendment of articles and bylaws, and (3) approval of certain extraordinary corporate matters. Of these functions, the election of directors is probably the most important.

Shareholders as such are not agents of the corporation and therefore cannot bind the corporation by acting individually; their powers must be exercised collectively, such as at shareholders' meetings. Action at a shareholders' meeting is, of course, taken by voting; the number of votes a shareholder has is determined by the number of shares he or she owns.

Insofar as directors are concerned, the methods of choosing them—and their functions—are dictated by state statute and the corporate articles of incorporation. Even though the corporation is generally bound by the actions of the board, the directors are not agents of the corporation. The primary reason for this is the fact that they do not have *individual* power to bind the corporation; instead, they can only act as a body. The management powers

FIGURE 13.4

OFFICERS — Carry out policies and make routine decisions

↑ Delegation

BOARD OF DIRECTORS — Determines corporate policies and supervises their execution.

SHAREHOLDERS — Elect and remove directors. Amend articles and bylaws. Approve certain extraordinary corporate matters.

■ Relationship of Shareholders, Directors, and Officers in Running the Corporation

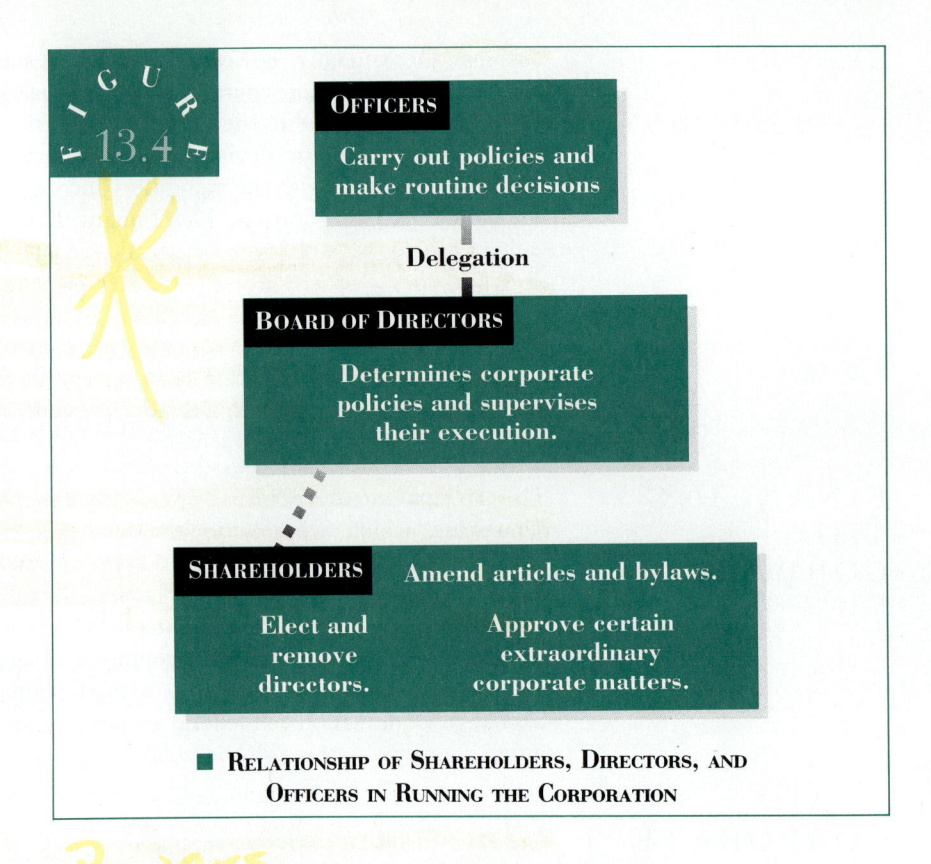

Powers of the board of directors usually include the following:

1. Setting of basic corporation policy in such areas as product lines, services, prices, wages, and labor–management relations.

2. Decisions relating to financing the corporation, such as the issuance of shares or bonds.

3. Determination of whether (and how large) a dividend is to be paid to shareholders at a particular time.

4. Selection, supervision, and removal of corporate officers and other managerial employees.

5. Decisions relating to compensation of managerial employees, pension plans, and similar matters.

RIGHTS AND LIABILITIES OF SHAREHOLDERS

The primary rights of shareholders are (1) the right to vote (except for special shares without voting rights), (2) the right to dividends, (3) the preemptive right, and (4) the right to inspect corporate records. The rules applicable to dividends and the preemptive right are so numerous that they can be sketched but briefly here.

Rights

The laws of the states differ substantially with respect to the circumstances in which dividends can legally be paid. Generally, however, the following limitations are imposed:

1. Dividends cannot be paid if the corporation is insolvent, or if the payment itself will cause the corporation to become insolvent. **Insolvency** is defined either as (a) the inability of the corporation to pay its debts as they become due, or (b) the possession of insufficient assets to meet all outstanding liabilities.

2. Dividends can ordinarily be paid only from a particular source. Some states allow dividends to be paid only from "current net earnings," for example, while many states permit dividends to be paid from any existing "surplus." In effect, this latter view means that the payment of a dividend in a particular year cannot be made if it is to come out of the original capital investment in the corporation (even if "net earnings" for that year are, in fact, equal to or greater than the amount of the contemplated dividend).

Shareholders do not have an absolute right to receive dividends. Whether a dividend is to be paid ("declared") in a given situation and how large it is to be are largely left to the discretion of the board of directors.

To protect existing shareholders' proportionate interests in the corporation, the courts have traditionally recognized the preemptive right concept. When a corporation issues new stock, the common-law preemptive right gives each shareholder an opportunity to purchase the number of new shares that will maintain his or her proportionate interst in the corporation. In general, the courts have not recognized preemptive rights in the sale of "treasury stock" (stock that was originally issued by the corporation and subsequently reacquired by it) and in shares of stock issued for consideration other than money.

Liabilities

As has been seen, shareholders are usually not personally liable for the debts of the corporation; they may lose their investment in the corporation if it is a failure, but usually their liability ends there. However, if a court believes that the shareholders of a corporation have abused the corporate form, they may *pierce the corporate veil* to impose personal liability on behalf of creditors. The corporate veil of a large, publicly traded corporation would never be pierced. But the corporate veils of small, closely held corporations are pierced from time to time. Obviously, any time a creditor's judgment against a corporation is unsatisfied by corporate funds, that creditor will consider asking the court to pierce the corporate veil so that shareholders' individual assets will be available for recovery. Although there is substantial state-to-state variation, the following case illustrates one court's approach to deciding when to pierce.

CASTLEBERRY v. BRANSCUM

Supreme Court of Texas 721 S.W.2d 270 (1987)

The plaintiff, Castleberry, and the defendants, Branscum and Byboth, were equal shareholders in Texan Transfer, Inc. (TTI). TTI delivered new furniture for Freed's Furniture Co. Branscum also operated Elite Moving as a sole proprietorship; it moved household goods, sometimes using TTI's trucks and employees. A dispute arose when Castleberry learned of Elite Moving's existence, and the three men agreed that TTI would buy Castleberry's stock for $42,000. One thousand dollars was to be paid right away and the rest in later installments. Branscum and Byboth were not personally obligated to pay. TTI soon had financial trouble and never paid more than the original $1,000. TTI's assets were sold to pay corporate liabilities, and thereafter Branscum and Byboth formed Custom Carriers, Inc., which obtained the contract to deliver Freed's furniture that had been held by TTI. Castleberry sued TTI and Branscum and Byboth personally. The trial court pierced the corporate veil in accordance with a jury finding, imposing liability on Branscum and Byboth personally. The appellate court reversed. Castleberry appealed.

Spears, Justice:

The corporate form normally insulates shareholders, officers, and directors from liability for corporate obligations; but when these individuals abuse the corporate privilege, courts will disregard the corporate fiction and hold them individually liable.

We disregard the corporate fiction, even though corporate formalities have been observed and corporate and individual property have been kept separately, when the corporate form has been used as part of a basically unfair device to achieve an inequitable result. Specifically, we disregard the corporate fiction:

(1) when the fiction is used as a means of perpetuating fraud;
(2) where a corporation is organized and operated as a mere tool or business conduit of another corporation;
(3) where the corporate fiction is resorted to as a means of evading an existing legal obligation;
(4) where the corporate fiction is employed to achieve or perpetrate monopoly;
(5) where the corporate fiction is used to circumvent a statute; and
(6) where the corporate fiction is relied upon as a protection of crime or to justify wrong.

The basis used here to disregard the corporate fiction, a sham to perpetrate a fraud, . . . is sometimes confused with intentional fraud; however, "[n]either fraud nor an intent to defraud need be shown as a prerequisite to disregarding the corporate entity; it is sufficient if recognizing the separate corporate existence would bring about an inequitable result." *Fletcher*, Cyclopedia Corporations Sec. 41.30 at 30 (Supp. 1985).

Because disregarding the corporate fiction is an equitable doctrine, Texas takes a flexible fact-specific approach focusing on equity. [In this case, Castleberry testified that after he found out about Branscum's formation of Elite Moving, Branscum stated that he would see to it that Castleberry never got anything out of Texan Transfer.] Castleberry testified that after the buyout, Elite Moving began to take over more and more of Texan Transfer's business. Texan Transfer supposedly loaned Elite Moving its trucks, but Branscum admitted that the companies had no written rental agreement and that no mileage records were kept to show how much Elite Moving owed Texan Transfer. Branscum also conceded that Texan Transfer could do Elite Moving's work.

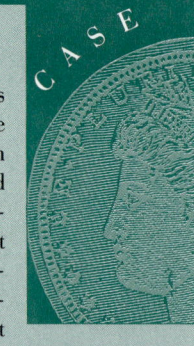

For the eighteen months prior to the buy-out agreement, Texas Transfer had a net income of $65,479. After the agreement in 1981, Texan Transfer's annual net income fell to $2,814 and in 1982 it lost more than $16,000. In contrast, the newly formed Elite Moving declared an income in 1982 of $195,765.

Sometime after Castleberry filed suit in April 1982, Branscum told Sue Campbell, then his wife, that Castleberry "would never get a dime, that he would file bankruptcy before Castleberry got any money out of the company. . . ." At trial, Byboth conceded that Custom Carriers was formed because of this lawsuit.

We hold that this is some evidence of a sham to perpetrate a fraud. A jury could find that Byboth and Branscum manipulated a closely-held corporation, Texan Transfer, and formed competing businesses to ensure that Castleberry did not get paid. Castleberry had little

CONTINUED

choice but to sell his shares back to the corporation.

In determining if there is an abuse of corporate privilege, courts must look through the form of complex transactions to the substance. The variety of shams is infinite, but many fit this case's pattern: a closely held corporation owes unwanted obligations; it siphons off corporate revenues, sells off much of the corporate assets, or does other acts to hinder the on-going business and its ability to pay off its debts; a new business then starts up that is basically a continuation of the old business with many of the same shareholders, officers and directors.

[The court of appeals' judgement is reversed; the trial court judgment is affirmed.]

CORPORATE MANAGERS

Rights

Corporate managers—directors and officers—possess several well-defined rights. Directors have the right to receive notice of board meetings and to attend and participate in them. They also have the right to inspect all corporate records (a right that is absolute, in most states), and the right to be indemnified (reimbursed) by the corporation for personal expenses or losses that they have incurred while acting on behalf of the corporation in good faith and in a reasonable manner. The right of officers and other employees are essentially spelled out in their employment contracts.

Liabilities

Those who manage the corporate enterprise owe to the corporation and its shareholders a number of basic duties that can be classified under the headings of *obedience, diligence, and loyalty*. A corporate manager incurs personal liability for the failure to fulfill any of these duties. In addition to these fundamental duties, certain special liabilities are imposed by federal security laws. Unlike the previous section on the *rights* of corporate managers, where some distinctions were made between rights of directors and other managers, the *duties* and *liabilities* of all who manage the corporation are essentially the same.

"Obedience" refers to the general duty of all managers to see that the corporation obeys the law and confines its operations to those activities that are within the limits of its corporate powers. "Diligence," as the name implies, refers to the duty of managers to exercise due care—the duty not to be negligent—at all times in carrying on the corporation's business. And, as in agency law, the duty of "loyalty" springs from the fiduciary relationship that exists between the managers and the corporation. In general, loyalty demands that the managers act in good faith and with the highest regard for the corporation's interests as opposed to their personal interests. More specifically, a director or other manager must not use corporate funds for his or her own purposes, must not use confidential information for personal gain, and must not withhold information from the corporation that would be relevant to it in making business decisions.

The following case involves a claim that the corporate directors had been negligent in their management of the business.

Shlensky v. Wrigley

Appellate Court of Illinois 237 N.E.2d 776 (1968)

Shlensky, the plaintiff, is a minority shareholder in Chicago National League Ball Club, Inc. The corporation owns and operates the major league professional baseball team known as the Chicago Cubs. The individual defendants are directors of the Cubs. Defendant Philip K. Wrigley is also president of the corporation and owner of approximately 80 percent of the corporation's shares.

Shlensky filed suit in behalf of the corporation (a derivative suit), claiming that it had been damaged by the failure of the directors to have lights installed in Wrigley Field, the Cubs' home park. No trial was held, however, because the trial court dismissed his complaint on the ground that it did not set forth a claim that the law would recognize even if his version of the facts were correct. Shlensky appealed.

Sullivan, Justice:

... Plaintiff alleges that since night baseball was first played in 1935 nineteen of the twenty major league teams have scheduled night games. In 1966, out of a total of 1,620 games in the major leagues, 932 were played at night. Plaintiff alleges that every member of the major leagues, other than the Cubs, scheduled substantially all of its home games in 1966 at night, exclusive of opening days, Saturdays, Sundays, holidays and days prohibited by league rules. Allegedly this has been done for the specific purpose of maximizing attendance and thereby maximizing revenue and income.

The Cubs, in the years 1961–65, sustained operating losses from its direct baseball operations. Plaintiff attributes those losses to inadequate attendance at Cubs' home games. He concludes that if the directors continue to refuse to install lights at Wrigley Field and schedule night baseball games, the Cubs will continue to sustain comparable losses and its financial condition will continue to deteriorate.

Plaintiff alleges that, except for the year 1963, attendance at Cubs' home games has been substantially below that at their road games, many of which were played at night.

Plaintiff compares attendance at Cubs' games with that of the Chicago White Sox, an American League club, whose weekday games were generally played at night. The weekend attendance figures for the two teams was similar; however, the White Sox week-night games drew many more patrons than did the Cubs' weekday games. ...

Plaintiff further alleges that defendant Wrigley has refused to install lights, not because of interest in the welfare of the corporation but because of his personal opinions "that baseball is a 'daytime sport' and that the installation of lights and night baseball games will have a deteriorating effect upon the surrounding neighborhood." It is alleged that he has admitted that he is not interested in whether the Cubs would benefit financially from such action because of his concern for the neighborhood, and that he would be willing for the team to play night games if a new stadium were built in Chicago. ...

Plaintiff ... argues that the directors are acting for reasons unrelated to the financial interest and welfare of the Cubs. However, we are not satisfied that the motives assigned to Philip K. Wrigley, and through him to the other directors, are contrary to the best interests of the corporation and the stockholders. For example, it appears to us that the effect on the surrounding neighborhood might well be considered by a director who was considering the patrons who would or would not attend the games if the park were in a poor neighborhood. Furthermore, the long run interest of the corporation in its property value at Wrigley Field might demand all efforts to keep the neighborhood from deteriorating. By these thoughts we do not mean to say that we have decided that the decision of the directors was a correct one. That is beyond our jurisdiction and ability. We are merely saying that the decision is one [for the] directors [to make]. ...

Finally, we do not agree with plaintiff's contention that failure to follow the example of the other major league clubs in scheduling night games constituted negligence. Plaintiff made no allegation that these teams' night schedules were profitable or that the purpose for which night baseball had been undertaken was fulfilled. Furthermore, it cannot be said that directors, even those of corporations

CONTINUED

> that are losing money, must follow the lead of the other corporations in the field. Directors are elected for their business capabilities and judgment and the courts cannot require them to forego their judgment because of the decisions of directors of other companies. Courts may not decide these questions in the absence of a clear showing of dereliction of duty on the part of the specific directors, and mere failure to "follow the crowd" is not such a dereliction.
>
> For the foregoing reasons, the order of dismissal entered by the trial court is affirmed.

Note: Because of the *business judgment rule*—the courts' reluctance to second guess the honest business decisions of directors—applied in *Shlensky v. Wrigley*, it is relatively rare for directors to be held liable for their decisions absent bad faith or dishonesty. However, in one particular context—decisions to sell the company—the courts have shown more willingness to impose liability. In *Smith v. Van Gorkom*, 488 A.2d 858 (Del. 1985), for example, directors were held potentially liable for an honest, but hurried and ill-studied, decision to sell the company. The standards currently applied in decisions of this type are summarized in Chapter 15's discussion of tender offers.

TERMINATION

A primary characteristic of the corporation is that it can have a perpetual existence. (Although a few states do place time limits on the duration of the certificate of incorporation, this is of no real consequence because renewal is usually only a formality.) This is not to say, however, that a corporation *must* exist forever. A number of different circumstances can bring about an end to its existence.

In discussing the termination of a corporation, a distinction must be made between "liquidation" and "dissolution." *Liquidation* is the conversion of the corporation's assets to cash and the distribution of these funds to creditors and shareholders. *Dissolution* is the actual termination of the corporation's existence as an artificial person—its "legal death." A liquidation can occur without an actual dissolution, as when the corporation sells its assets to another company. Although the shareholders might then choose to dissolve the corporation, it would not be required that they do so. The remainder of our discussion will be devoted primarily to the various circumstances that bring about dissolution, with a final mention of the process of winding up corporate affairs after dissolution.

Voluntary Dissolution

A corporation can voluntarily terminate its own existence. Dissolution can be accomplished by the incorporators in some unusual circumstances, but the shareholders are ordinarily the only ones with such power. The board of directors does *not* have the power to dissolve the corporation.

If the corporation has never gotten off the ground, it can be voluntarily dissolved by the *incorporators*. This can occur when the corporation has not done any business and no shares have been issued. In such a situation, the incorporators dissolve the corporation by filing "articles of dissolution" with the appropriate state official, who then issues a "certificate of dissolution."

Shareholders may discontinue the corporation's existence for any reason, at any time. The most common reason for voluntary dissolution is that the enterprise has proved unprofitable.

The procedures for voluntary dissolution vary somewhat from state to state, but their general outline is basically the same. The process is usually initiated by resolution of the board of directors. A meeting of the shareholders is then called, at which time the matter is voted on. The vote required for approval varies among the states in the same manner as for mergers and consolidations, from a simple majority to four-fifths, with a *two-thirds* vote being a common requirement. After shareholder approval, articles of dissolution are filed and the certificate of dissolution is issued.

Dissenting shareholders can challenge the dissolution in court. However, a court will issue an injunction prohibiting dissolution only if these shareholders are able to prove that the controlling shareholders dissolved the corporation in *bad faith*, with the intent of defrauding the minority.

Involuntary Dissolution

In some circumstances, a *court action* can be instituted for the purpose of dissolving the corporation. A legal proceeding of this nature can be brought by a shareholder or by the state. Dissolution ordered by a court in such a proceeding is often referred to as an "involuntary" dissolution. The laws of the various states generally provide that one or more shareholders can file a lawsuit requesting that the court dissolve the corporation. Those situations in which a *shareholder* can obtain dissolution by court order are:

Oppression of minority shareholders. In most states, oppression of minority shareholders by those in control is a ground for judicial dissolution. Oppressive conduct generally includes any act by which controlling shareholders seek to take unfair advantage of the minority. One example is the purchase of corporate assets by controlling shareholders, who then lease them back to the corporation for exorbitant rental fees.

Deadlock. Most states authorize dissolution by the court if it is proved that the corporation is unable to function because of a management deadlock. This is not a common occurrence and ordinarily could only happen in a closely held corporation. For there to be an unbreakable management deadlock, of course, there would have to be equal ownership interests by two separate factions and a board of directors with an even number of members split into equal, opposing groups.

Mismanagement. Courts are generally reluctant to interfere with decisions made by corporate managers. However, a court may order dissolution of the corporation if it is being so grossly mismanaged that its assets are actually being wasted.

Because a corporation derives its right to exist from the state where it is incorporated, it seems natural that the *state* should also be able to take away that right. This power can be exercised, however, only in certain circumstances. The grounds for dissolution by the state (which are remarkably similar in the various jurisdictions) are discussed below.

Failure to comply with administrative requirements. All states insist that corporations comply with various administrative requirements. With respect to some of these duties, noncompliance may be cause for dissolution at the instance of the state. The most common examples are (1) failure to file required annual reports with the secretary of state, (2) failure to pay franchise fees or other state taxes, and (3) failure to appoint or maintain a registered agent. Many states acknowledge the relative insignificance of such omissions by providing for easy reinstatement on compliance and payment of any penalties owed.

Ultra vires acts. The performance of acts that are beyond the corporation's powers constitutes a reason for dissolution. This principle is of little practical importance today, however, because most articles of incorporation now grant such broad powers that *ultra vires* act occur infrequently.

Dormancy. If a corporation never commences business after it is formed, or if it becomes dormant by abandoning its operations, the state can seek its dissolution in court. But the absence of corporate activity does not automatically bring about dissolution; it simply gives the state a basis for obtaining court-ordered dissolution.

Antitrust violations. In many jurisdictions, a corporation's violation of the state (not federal) antitrust laws is a cause for dissolution.

Fraudulent formation. Several states provide for dissolution where the corporation obtained its certificate of incorporation by misrepresenting material facts.

Winding Up

When voluntary dissolution occurs, the corporation's directors become **trustees** who hold corporate assets for the benefit of creditors and shareholders. They usually are allowed to wind up corporate affairs without court supervision. The directors in this situation do, however, have four basic duties:

1. They must not undertake any new business. Their authority is limited to the fulfillment of existing corporate obligations.

2. They must make a reasonable attempt to collect debts owed to the corporation.

3. After liquidation of corporate assets, they must pay creditors insofar as these assets are sufficient to do so.

4. When the claims of corporate creditors have been satisfied, they must distribute any remaining funds to shareholders. This distribution is required to be in the proportion of shareholders' respective interests and in accordance with any special rights enjoyed by preferred shareholders.

The directors can be held personally responsible for the breach of any of these winding up duties. However, if they are unwilling to serve as trustees in liquidating the corporation, a "receiver" will be appointed and supervised by a court for the purpose of winding up corporate affairs. The court can also take such action if a creditor or shareholder shows cause why the directors should not be allowed to perform this function.

In any case where dissolution is involuntary, the liquidation of corporate assets and other winding up activities are always performed by a court-appointed receiver.

SPECIAL DUTIES IN CLOSELY HELD CORPORATIONS

Most, but not all, of the corporate rules discussed above apply equally to all sizes of corporations. However, rules written for an IBM or a General Motors may not easily fit the family-owned or otherwise closely held corporation, which, in truth, is more similar to a partnership than it is to a large corporation. Given that reality, many states' legislatures have passed special codes for closely held corporations, granting them the flexibility to operate much like partnerships, without losing the limited liability feature of corporate status. The following case illustrates the special problems of the closely held corporation.

HAGSHENAS v. GAYLORD

APPELLATE COURT OF ILLINOIS 557 N.E.2d 316 (1990)

Robert and Virginia Gaylord owned 50 percent of the stock of Imperial Travel; Bruce Hagshenas owned the other 50 percent. These three, and Bruce's wife, Barbara, were officers and directors and were active in running Imperial's business, which had sales revenues of $2 million in the 10 months ending July 31, 1982.

Unfortunately, the parties became involved in disputes over several matters, including mail procedure, company records, access to an office, Bruce's purchase of a pickup for the business, and, more seriously, whether one or more of the four were skimming cash out of the business.

On April 29, 1982, Bruce filed this suit seeking dissolution of Imperial based on dissension and corporate deadlock. The trial court entered certain preliminary orders designed to keep the business operating pending a full trial. On October 2, 1982, Bruce and Barbara resigned from Imperial as officers and directors. The next day they bought a new travel agency and soon acquired many of Imperial's former employees and clients. The Gaylords asked the trial judge for a preliminary injunction to stop Bruce from competing with Imperial. That motion was granted. The trial court eventually found that Bruce had breached his fiduciary duty to the Gaylords and entered judgment for them. Bruce appealed.

CONTINUED

Dunn, Justice:

Bruce argues the court erred in finding he owed a fiduciary duty to the Gaylords after he resigned as a director and officer of Imperial. He contends he was free to compete with Imperial once he resigned. Ordinarily, after a director or officer resigns from a corporation, he or she owes no fiduciary duty to that corporation. The Gaylords contend, however, that Bruce continued to owe a fiduciary duty similar to that of a partner since he continued to own half the stock of Imperial, a company that was essentially a close corporation.

In general, a mere owner of stock in a company does not owe a fiduciary duty to that company. The Business Corporation Act [Illinois' general corporate code] provides that "[a] holder of or subscriber to shares of a corporation shall be under no obligation to the corporation or its creditors with respect to such shares other than the obligation to pay the corporation the full consideration for which said shares were issued or to be issued." In contrast to the Business Corporation Act, the Close Corporation Act provides that, where the articles of incorporation provide that the business of the corporation shall be managed by the shareholders of the corporation rather than by a board of directors, shareholders shall be deemed to be directors for purposes of the Business Corporation Act, and shareholders shall be subject to all liabilities of directors. Bruce asserts that Imperial was not organized under the Close Corporation Act and does not fall under the Close Corporation Act definitions. We accept the assertion that Imperial is not a close corporation under the Close Corporation Act, and we do not apply this act to this case.

We believe that, though Imperial was not organized or registered as a close corporation under the Close Corporation Act, for all practical purposes it acted as a close corporation. In *Galler v. Galler*, 203 N.E.2d 477 (1964), the [Illinois] supreme court defined a close corporation as "one in which the stock is held in a few hands, or in a few families, and wherein it is not at all, or only rarely, dealt in by buying and selling." Imperial meets this test.

[The court then summarized three cases holding that shareholders in a closely held corporation owe a fiduciary duty toward each other similar to that of partners.]

In this case the facts demonstrate that, though Imperial was purchased as a corporation, it clearly was an enterprise closely resembling a partnership. Hagshenas and the Gaylords were not only equal 50% shareholders; they were the directors and officers of the company; they oversaw the day-to-day operations. A partner owes a duty to exercise the highest degree of honesty and good faith in the dealings and in handling of business assets, thereby prohibiting enhancement of personal interests at the expense of the interests of the enterprise.

We find Bruce, as a 50% shareholder in this closely held corporation, owed a fiduciary duty similar to a partner to Imperial and its shareholders. He violated his fiduciary duty when he opened a competing business and hired away all of Imperial's employees.

In finding Bruce owed a fiduciary duty as a 50% shareholder in this closely held corporation, we recognize a significant difference between a shareholders of a closely held corporation and a shareholder of public stock. Unlike the holders of public stock, who can sell their stock when disagreements over management arise, shareholders in a small corporation do not usually have an available market to sell their shares. We find it implicit that people who enter into a small business enterprise, as in this case, place their trust and confidence in each other.

[Affirmed on this issue.]

Questions and Problems

1. Warren was a supervisor for TD Corporation. At lunch, he told Detmar (who previously had had no trouble with Warren): "I don't like Texans. I ain't never met a Texan I could get along with." Detmar replied: "Well, there is a million Texans and only one of you," whereupon Warren hit Detmar in the head with a claw hammer. Detmar sued TD Corporation. Is it liable for Warren's tort? Discuss. (*Tierra Drilling Corp. v. Detmar*, 666 S.W.2d 661, Tex. App., 1984).

2. Bruton lent a D-8 Caterpillar rent-free to David Eck-

vall, who wanted to clear some land owned by Eckvall. It was agreed that Eckvall would provide an operator and pay for fuel and routine maintenance. Nothing was said about major repairs. While Eckvall was using the Cat, it broke down. Without contacting Bruton, he took it to Automatic Welding & Supply (AWS), where extensive repairs were made at a cost of $2,340. When the repairs were almost completed, Bruton happened to come into the AWS shop on other business and saw his Cat. He spoke to an AWS mechanic and learned of the scope of the repairs, but nothing was said about cost. After the repairs were completed, the Cat was returned to Eckvall's property where he used it for some time thereafter. AWS billed Bruton for the repairs. Bruton denied liability, and AWS sued. (*Bruton v. Automatic Welding & Supply*, 513 P.2d 1122, 1973.) Is Bruton responsible for the $2,340 under any principles of agency law? Discuss.

3. In 1959, Bert Bell, Commissioner of the National Football League (NFL), entered into an agreement with representatives of the NFL Players Association, which provided for certain pension benefits for players who had retired from the NFL before 1959. The bylaws of the NFL required any such agreement to be approved by the owners of at least 10 of the 12 NFL teams. During negotiations leading to the agreement, Bell stated that he would resign if the agreement were not approved. The agreement was not approved and the pension benefits were not paid. Those players who would have received benefits under the agreement sued both the NFL and the players association, claiming that the NFL was bound by the agreement because Bell had acted with apparent authority. (*Soar v. National Football League Players Ass'n*, 438 F.Supp. 337, 1975.) Under basic agency law principles, do you think the players should have won their lawsuit? Discuss.

4. Anderson, Richards, and Williams formed a partnership for the purpose of producing rock music concerts. The three partners initially contributed $2,000, $4,000, and $3,000, respectively, to the partnership for use as working capital. The partnership agreement made no provision for the division of profits. At the end of the first year, the partnership had made a profit of $4,500. What is each partner's share of the profits? Explain.

5. X, Y, and Z were partners in an automobile dealership. Their partnership agreement provided for continuation of the business in the event of the death of any partner. X died, and Y and Z agree with X's widow that she would receive a lump sum payment of $50,000 and a 25 percent share of the business's profits as compensation for X's share in the partnership. It was agreed, however, that she would not be required to perform any duties for the business and would take no part in management. Is X's widow a partner of Y and Z? Explain.

6. Wrights Beauty College, Inc. (WBC), had a right of first refusal if any shareholders wished to sell their shares. In other words, a shareholder would have to offer the shares to WBC before selling to a third party. Bostic owned substantial WBC shares and worked for WBC. When he was fired, Bostic was interested in selling his shares. He was, therefore, interested in determining how much they were worth. He asked to inspect WBC documents to make this determination, but WBC denied him access to most of the documents, claiming that he did not have a "proper purpose." Bostic sued to enforce his alleged right to inspect. Will he prevail? Discuss. (*Wrights Beauty College, Inc. v. Bostic*, 576 N.E.2d *626*, Ind. App., 1991.)

7. Russell and Carol Nugent were sole shareholders, officers, and directors of Russell Nugent Roofing, Inc. In 1985, the business's name was changed to On Top Roofing, Inc. In 1987, On Top ceased doing business and RNR, Inc. was incorporated, only to go out of business in 1988 and be replaced by RLN Construction, Inc. By the time of trial in 1990, Nugent testified that he was doing business as Russell Nugent, Inc. Russell and Carol were sole owners, officers, and directors of all five corporations. The plaintiff, a roofing supplier that had sold on credit to On Top Roofing, sought to pierce the corporate veil and hold Russell personally liable for the On Top Roofing's unpaid bills. Should the court pierce? Discuss. (*K.C. Roofing Center v. On Top Roofing, Inc.*, 807 S.W.2d *545,* Mo. App., 1991.)

8. The president of Hessler, Inc., made a contract with an employee, Farrell, in which retirement benefits were promised to him. In the past, the president had been allowed to manage the company's affairs more or less independently of the board; he also owned approximately 80 percent of the corporation's stock. When Farrell retired, the corporation refused to pay the benefits, and Farrell sued. The corporation claimed that the agreement made with Farrell by the president was invalid because it had not been approved by the board of directors. (*Hessler, Inc. v. Farrell*, 226 A.2d 708, 1967.) Is the corporation correct? Discuss.

PART III

BUSINESS AND THE REGULATORY ENVIRONMENT

TRANSITIONAL NOTE

INTRODUCTION TO GOVERNMENT REGULATION OF BUSINESS

The remainder of this text is devoted primarily to government regulation of business. Before we explore specific areas of law dealing with government regulation, however, we review some of the underlying rationales for this regulatory activity.

THE MARKET ECONOMY

The U.S. Economy is essentially capitalistic. In other words, it is based primarily on the concept of free enterprise and private ownership of the means of production. Under this system, the purchasing decisions of consumers ultimately provide the fuel on which the market operates. The interplay of supply and demand causes the market itself to regulate economic behavior. The market determines price and output, as well as the optimal level of innovation, quality, service, and so on. In ordinary circumstances, the market achieves an efficient allocation of resources. Even if the market-based economy does not always allocate resources with maximum efficiency, in this country it is preferred over a government-administered economy for another reason: It obviously harmonizes more closely with fundamental notions of free choice.

REASONS FOR GOVERNMENT INTERVENTION IN THE MARKETPLACE

Although the American economy continues to be predominantly market-based, today there is a significant degree of government involvement. Most economists who believe strongly in the validity of a market-based economy also believe that some government interference in the functioning of markets is necessary. They often disagree, however, as to *when* government involvement is needed, *what form* it should take, and *to what degree* it is required.

Some resource allocations do not fit within the market system and consequently are not viewed as business activities. Such services as national defense, police and fire protection, and public streets and highways are so-called **public goods,** which are provided by the government and paid for with tax revenues. It is impossible, or at least impractical, to charge consumers according to their use of these types of items.

In most situations, however, the market is capable of allocating resources. But there are sometimes imperfections in the way the market functions. Such imperfections, often called *market failure,* provide one of the most commonly asserted justifications for government involvement. In addition, even when the market works well it cannot accomplish all of society's goals.

We now look at several of the most important reasons for government regulation of business activities in the marketplace, some of which are interrelated and sometimes overlapping.

EXTERNALI-TIES

In a few situations, **externalities** prevent the market from functioning properly. Some types of cost associated with producing a product may be involuntarily borne by persons other than the producer or customer. Because these costs, or externalities, are not accounted for in the price of the product, the market cannot properly regulate them and government must do so.

A prime example of externalities is found in the harm done by air and water pollution. If a manufacturer pollutes while producing a product, this pollution imposes costs on society in the form of health problems, diminished property values, decreased recreational opportunities, and esthetic sacrifices. Although these are part of the costs of producing the product, they are paid for by many people who may not buy the product. Because the costs of pollution are not passed on to consumers of the product, they do not affect the demand for that product and the producer is not likely to take the initiative to control them. The market provides insufficient incentives for the producer to stop polluting, and *environmental protection laws* are necessary. The cost of complying with these laws is then borne by the producer, who passes them on to the customers who benefit from the product.

The costs of on-the-job injuries and occupational diseases provide another example of externalities. At least part of the costs to workers and their families resulting from these injuries and diseases will not find their way into the cost of the employer's product without government action. *Workers' compensation laws* requiring the payment of benefits to injured employees place some of these costs on the employer (producer) and thus put them into the cost of the product. *Occuptional safety and health laws* requiring safe working conditions aim both to prevent injuries and also to put a significant portion of the costs of improving workplace safety back under the control of the market by imposing them on the employer.

INADEQUATE INFORMATION

A market can function correctly only when sellers and buyers have adequate information about the economic decisions they make. This information is never perfect in real-life markets, of course, but it usually is sufficient to enable the market to work.

In several situations, the purpose of government regulation may be to improve the quantity or quality of information that is made available to buyers. For example, in capital markets, most of the information relating to the value of securities is solely in the hands of the company issuing the stocks or bonds and may not be readily accessible to many investors. In addition, such information may be too voluminous and complex to be assimilated by all but the most sophisticated investors. Without government regulation, these investors must rely on the company issuing the securities to select, interpret, and divulge information. One of the main purposes of our *securities regulation laws* is to require companies that issue securities to publicly disclose particular types of information in particular ways, thus improving the investor's ability to make knowledgeable decisions.

Two other example of government regulation intended to improve the quantity or quality of information in the marketplace are the laws (1) prohibiting deceptive advertising, and (2) requiring lenders to disclose all credit charges and rates in a uniform way.

MARKET POWER

A market certainly is capable of functioning when one or more firms possess substantial economic power, but it often will not work as well as it otherwise might—a market ordinarily can perform at something close to an optimal level of efficiency only if economic power is relatively dispersed among a number of firms. In addition, market functioning sometimes can be impaired when there are great differences between the power possessed by sellers and that possessed by buyers.

The primary objective of *antitrust laws* is to prevent a firm, or several firms acting together, from using economic power to impede the functioning of the market.

In labor markets (markets for the sale of workers' labor to employers) there is a natural disparity between the economic power of the average employer and that of the average employee. *Labor relations laws* were enacted to equalize the economic power of employers and employees and thereby to promote industrial peace and stability by requiring employers to recognize and bargain with organized groups of employees (labor unions).

NATURAL MONOPOLIES

In unusual circumstances, the production of a good or provision of a service may be a **natural monopoly.** At least two reasons can work either together or separately to produce a natural monopoly: (1) the capital investment required for production may be so great, and economies of scale so important, that only one firm in a particular geographic area can earn a sufficient rate of return, or (2) production of the good or service may be subject to certain inherent physical limitations that make competition among two or more firms either impossible or impractical.

Public utilities, involved in activities such as electrical generation or natural gas delivery, are generally viewed as natural monopolies. In the case of a public utility, both of the above reasons are applicable. Capital costs are prohibitive, and the physical limitations of cables, pipelines, and so on, make competition in a given area impractical.

If a firm operates as a natural monopoly, it has a degree of market power approaching the maximum. Market principles do not work, so government must provide a substiitute for the discipline of the market. Government can either (1) treat the item as something akin to a public good and take over the production process itself, or (2) leave production in private hands but closely regulate pricing and output decisions. The second alternative is the most common response, as evidenced by the rate-setting activities of state public utility commissions.

ACHIEVING OTHER SOCIETAL GOALS

Some forms of government regulation may be prompted by a desire to achieve societal goals not directly related to market efficiency. In the case of some of the regulatory laws already mentioned, certain noneconomic objectives may have worked alongside the economic ones.

The operation of a market, whether efficient or inefficient, can lead to temporary individual hardships. Particular government activities affecting business may have the purpose of relieving some of these hardships. When natural market forces drive a firm out of business, laws such as those relating to *bankruptcy, unemployment compensation,* and *insurance for bank deposits* can soften the blow to individuals.

Finally, there are some cases in which government regulation in a given industry may be based in part on the desires and lobbying efforts of firms in the industry to be relieved from some of the rigors of competition. A highly competitive market presents a challenge to its participants, and operating under the close supervision of a government agency may be less demanding than operating in an open market. Some authorities feel that this was true in the transportation industry. Rates charged by interstate trucking firms were regulated for years by the Interstate Commerce Commission rather than by market forces. When Congress acted to deregulate rate-setting in interstate trucking and return this function to the market itself, many trucking firms strongly opposed the deregulation.

The chapters that follow look at several of the most important areas of the law concerned with government regulation of business activities. In Part III of the text, Chapter 14 deals with antitrust law; Chapter 15 with securities regulation; and Chapters 16, 17, and 18 with laws regulating the employment relationship. The final chapters then focus more broadly on some of business's duties toward larger segments of society. Chapter 19 discusses environmental protection; Chapter 20 examines consumer protection; and finally, Chapter 21 deals with the increasingly important area of international business.

14

CHAPTER

INTRODUCTION

An economy such as that of the United States, which depends primarily on the operation of market forces, cannot function properly without competition. Although the word competition is subject to various shades of meaning, it most often refers to a condition of economic rivalry among firms. That is, firms should be engaged in a contest for customers, the outcome of that contest depending on each firm's ability to satisfy customer wants.

The primary purpose of antitrust law is to promote competition. In the various types of markets, competition can take

ANTITRUST LAW

OBJECTIVES OF ANTITRUST LAW

somewhat different forms. In the case of many kinds of products, for example, price is a very important factor in customers' buying decisions (that is, "price elasticity" is high), and much of the competitive rivalry among sellers may focus on price. On the other hand, in some markets price may not be quite as important to most customers as good service, availability of many product options, convenience, or other factors. In such markets, competition among sellers is likely to emphasize these nonprice attributes to a greater extent. Not only does the form of competition vary somewhat among markets, but the intensity of competition also is less in some markets than in others. The job of antitrust law is to encourage competition in its various forms and to preserve it to the extent feasible in a given market.

Most economists feel that a competitive, market-based economy produces a number of beneficial results such as efficient allocation of scarce resources, lower prices, higher quality, greater innovation, and economic freedom. In the view of some authorities, there is another reason for having a strong antitrust policy in the United States—more competition in an economic sense may diminish the amount of power that large firms have over the political process and over the lives of large numbers of people.

Has antitrust law achieved its goals? This question cannot be answered with certainty because it is practically impossible to measure the effects of antitrust law on the American economy. There are many markets (so-called **oligopolies**) in which most of the sales are made by a few large companies. Many of these firms are very efficient; some are not. Many do not abuse their power; some do. In some of these markets, competition appears to be quite vigorous, but in others it is rather stagnant. Moreover, in many of these markets concentration of power in a few firms is an inevitable result of extremely large capital requirements and economies of scale. However, the *degree* of economic concentration is clearly not always inevitable.

Thus, it is not surprising to find substantial disagreement among authorities concerning the wisdom and effect of antitrust law. Some say the law has not been enforced aggressively enough, while others say that it has been applied too aggressively to the wrong things. Many points of criticism and support have been raised over the years. Only two conclusions are relatively certain: (1) Although the interpretation of some of the antitrust rules will vary over time, the fundamental principles are probably going to remain with us; and (2) antitrust law will always be controversial. With that, we will study the law itself.

FEDERAL ANTITRUST STATUTES

The first, and still the most important, of the federal antitrust laws is the Sherman Act, passed by Congress in 1890. Section 1 of this act prohibits "contracts, combinations, and conspiracies in restraint of trade." The focus of section 1 is collusion among firms that are supposed to be acting independently when making basic business decisions. Section 2 prohibits "monopolization, attempts to monopolize, and conspiracies to monopolize." The prohibition of monopolization, which is the most important part of section 2, focuses on single-firm domination of a market.

In 1914, Congress enacted the Clayton Act with two main purposes in mind: (1) to make the prohibitions against certain anticompetitive practices more specific, and (2) to make it easier to challenge certain practices, such as mergers, when the evidence shows only probable future anticompetitive effects and not actual present effects. Section 2 of the act prohibits price discrimination; Section 3 prohibits some tying and exclusive dealing agreements; and Section 7 forbids anticompetitive mergers. In any of these cases, the law is violated only if the evidence demonstrates an actual or highly probable anticompetitive effect of a substantial nature. Section 8 of the Clayton Act prohibits *interlocking directorates* between certain large corporations that are in direct competition with each other. An interlocking directorate occurs when the same individual serves on the board of directors of two corporations.

Also in 1914, Congress passed the Federal Trade Commission Act (FTC Act). In addition to creating the Federal Trade Commission (FTC) as an enforcement agency, the act also prohibited "unfair methods of competition" in section 5. Any conduct that violates one of the other antitrust laws, plus a few other types of conduct, constitutes an unfair method of competition. In 1938, Congress added another phrase to section 5 prohibiting "unfair or deceptive acts or practices." Thus the first part of the statute deals with antitrust matters, and the second part deals with various forms of consumer deception such as false advertising.

In 1936 Congress passed the Robinson-Patman Act, which amended section 2 of the Clayton Act in an effort to make the law against price discrimination more effective.

Even though antitrust law is based on statutory enactments, most of the language in those statutes is so broad that court interpretations account for most of the lawmaking process. Also, our attention in this chapter is focused only on *federal* antitrust law. Most states have their own antitrust laws, which usually apply to the same basic practices that are forbidden by federal law.

COVERAGE AND EXEMPTIONS

Coverage

Like many other federal statutes that are based on the commerce clause of the U.S. Constitution, the federal antitrust laws apply to business activities that either directly involve or substantially affect interstate commerce. Business activities occurring in foreign commerce, such as imports and exports, are also covered by U.S. antitrust law if there is a substantial effect on an American market.

Exemptions

The actions of the federal government are exempt from the antitrust laws, as are most actions of state governments so long as they are acting pursuant to legitimate and clearly expressed state regulatory interests. In this regard, actions of cities and other local governments are treated as state action if the local government is essentially just carrying out some aspect of state regulatory policy. Actions by foreign governments also are not within the scope of the antitrust laws.

HUMOR AND THE LAW

Antitrust law can be complex and confusing. However, nothing in the law matches the Internal Revenue Code for bewildering detail. Judge Learned Hand once wrote that the words of the tax law "dance before my eyes in a meaningless procession: cross-reference to cross-reference, exception to exception—couched in abstract terms that offer no handle to seize hold of—leave in my mind only a confused sense of some vitally important (but successfully concealed) purport which it is my duty to extract, but which is within my power, if at all, only after the most inordinate expenditure of time. I know that these monsters are the result of fabulous industry and ingenuity, plugging up this hole and casting out that net, against all possible evasion; yet at times I cannot help recalling a saying of William James about certain passages of Hegel: that they were no doubt written with a passion of rationality, but that one cannot help but wondering whether to the reader they have any significance save that the words are strung together with syntactical correctness." Hand, *Thomas Walter Swan*, 57 YALE LAW JOURNAL 167 (1947).

Want an example? Consider Internal Revenue Code Sec. 509(a): "For purposes of paragraph (3), an organization described in paragraph (2) shall be deemed to include an organization described in section 501(c) (4), (5), or (6) which would be described in paragraph (2) if it were an organization described in section 501 (c) (3)."

If particular activities of a firm are subject to special regulation by a federal agency, such as the Securities Exchange Commission or the Commodity Futures Trading Commission, any possible anticompetitive consequences of those activities will usually not be scrutinized under the antitrust laws if the responsible agency has approved the activities after carefully considering the impact on competition.

In addition, the formation and ordinary activities (collective bargaining and strikes, for instance) of labor unions are exempt. Similarly, the actions of firms are exempt to the extent that they form a legitimate part of the union–company collective bargaining agreement and do not affect parties outside the union–company relationship. Finally, the joint activities of two kinds of selling cooperatives are exempt from the antitrust laws: (1) those formed by agricultural or livestock producers, and (2) export groups, so long as the limitation on export competition among members of the group does not adversely affect a domestic U.S. market.

ENFORCEMENT

Enforcement of the federal antitrust laws can take one or more of several different forms. The Antitrust Division of the U.S. Department of Justice, which operates under the attorney general as part of the executive branch, can institute civil lawsuits and criminal prosecutions in federal district court. In a civil suit, if the Justice Department proves a violation of the Sherman, Clayton, or Robinson-Patman acts, the remedy it normally obtains from the court is an injunction. The injunction will order the cessation of particular illegal actions and may even require substantial modification of a firm's everyday business practices to lessen the likelihood of future violations. Many times the terms of an injunction are the result of an agreed settlement between the Justice Department and the defendant. In such cases, the injunction issue by the court after approving the terms of the settlement is called a *consent decree*. A firm or individual violating the terms of an injunction will be held in contempt of court.

If the case falls under the Sherman Act and involves a flagrant violation, such as blatant price fixing among competitors, the Justice Department may file a criminal prosecution in federal court. Upon conviction (which is a felony), the maximum penalty in a criminal case is a $10 million fine for corporations, and a $350,000 fine and three years' imprisonment for individuals.

The FTC also has authority to enforce the Clayton, Robinson-Patman, and FTC acts. Even though it technically has no power to enforce the Sherman Act, any conduct that would violate the Sherman Act will also constitute an "unfair method of competition" under section 5 of the FTC Act. FTC enforcement, which is civil in nature, consists of a hearing before an administrative law judge of the agency, with subsequent review by the five-member FTC. If a violation is found, the FTC will issue a "cease and desist order," which is essentially the same as an injunction. Violation of an FTC order is punishable by a penalty of up to $10,000 for each day of noncompliance.

A private party can file a civil lawsuit in federal court claiming a violation of the Sherman, Clayton, or Robinson-Patman acts. The plaintiff sometimes can obtain an injunction in such a suit, but the remedy normally sought in *treble damages*. This means that if the plaintiff proves it was damaged by the defendant's violation, the law automatically multiplies the plaintiff's money damages by three. However, only an injunction is available against a municipality (city); neither single nor treble damages can be recovered. Also, only single (not treble) damages are available in the case of a violation by a government-certified research and development joint venture.

In the following pages, we look first at that portion of the law concerned primarily with industry structure, namely, the law of *monopolization* and *mergers*. We then turn to the antitrust laws that focus on particular kinds of conduct in our discussion of *horizontal restraints of trade, vertical restraints of trade,* and *price discrimination*.

MONOPOLIZATION

In trying to formulate a working definition of **monopoly** under section 2 of the Sherman Act, as a practical matter the courts could not simply adopt the classical economic model of monopoly: one seller, very high entry barriers to the market, and no close substitutes for the product. Instead, they defined a monopoly in more pragmatic terms as "a firm having such an overwhelming degree of market power that it is able to control prices or exclude competition."

The center of this definition is **market power.** Essentially, market power is the ability of a firm to behave differently than it could behave in a perfectly competitive market. Stated differently, market power is the ability to exercise some degree of control over the price of its product, that is, to raise its price without losing most of its customers. In virtually every market, there will be firms with *some* control over the price they charge, although the degree of control varies greatly from case to case.

The concept of market power is critical to any study of competition under the antitrust laws, because competition usually cannot be harmed unless one firm, or a group of firms acting together, possesses some degree of market power. With respect to other issues in antitrust law, degrees of market power that are less than monopolistic can be very important. However, in deciding whether there is a monopoly under section 2 of the Sherman Act, courts look for an *overwhelming* degree of market power. This exists when one firm dominates a market to such an extent that it does not have to worry much about the response of competitors.

MEASURING MARKET POWER

Traditionally, the enforcement agencies and courts have looked primarily at the *structure* of a market when trying to draw inferences about degrees of market power. The most important structural factor is usually the firm's **market share.** In other words, what percentage share of the relevant market does the firm have? The courts have not developed hard and fast rules as to what market share definitely does or does not demonstrate overwhelming market power. However, the cases indicate that a market share of less than 50 percent will never be enough, and a share of 75 percent will frequently (but not always) be enough. Although other indicators of market power are always important, they become critical when the share is within this range.

Other structural factors include the following:

1. The *relative size of other firms* in the market can be important. If M has, say, 60 percent of the market, M generally will have less market power if there are at least one or two other very large firms with perhaps 20 or 30 percent shares than if the remainder of the market is occupied by a large number of very small firms. The reason is that if the other firms are themselves quite large, even though smaller than M, they are more likely to have economies of scale and costs similar to M. Thus, although oligopoly may not be the most desirable market structure, it is usually much better than monopoly.

2. The *size and power of customers* is also relevant, because the existence of large, powerful buyers can put a damper on the market power of a potentially monopolistic seller.

3. The market's **entry barriers** are quite important. Entry barriers are conditions that make entry into the market by a new competitor significantly more costly and risky. If a market has low entry barriers and a powerful firm in the market earns very high returns by using its power to charge high prices, the high returns will attract new competition to the market that will diminish the dominant firm's power. High entry barriers, on the other hand, provide substantial insulation for the powerful firm so that it can fully exploit its market power. Examples of entry barriers include excess production capacity in the market, higher costs of capital for potential competitors than for the dominant firm, strong customer preferences for brands produced by the dominant firm, important technology or know-how that is protected by patents or by trade secret law, complex distribution channels, and so forth. Entry barriers are not necessarily good or bad; they are just conditions that may be relevant. It also should be noted that some entry barriers are inevitable, whereas some can be intentionally erected by a dominant firm. Although the importance of entry barriers has long been recognized, in recent years some authorities have come to view them as even more important to the question of market power than the internal composition of the market.

4. In addition to market share and other structural factors, the *dynamics* of the market can also be relevant to the question of how much power a firm has. For instance, it the market is characterized by rapidly developing technology or if total market demand is expanding rapidly, it will be much harder for a firm to hold on to its dominant position for very long.

DEFINING THE RELEVANT MARKET

Before seeking to determine whether a firm has overwhelming power, it is necessary to define the relevant market. Essentially, the process of market definition involves an attempt to identify a category of business transactions that accurately reflects the operation of competitive forces. A market can be thought of as the context within which competitive forces can be measured with reasonable accuracy. Any market must be defined in terms of two elements: (1) a particular product or service, or some grouping of products or services, and (2) a geographic area.

Product Market

Suppose that M Company is charged with monopolizing the market for the sale of zippers in the United States. Most of M's zippers are sold to clothing manufacturers, but some are sold to fabric stores and other retail outlets for resale to consumers. M produces 90 percent of the zippers sold in the United States. If "zippers" is the proper market definition, M's market share almost certainly demonstrates overwhelming market power. M argues, however, that zippers actually face stiff competition from buttons, snaps, hooks, and Velcro, and that the 90 percent figure does not accurately portray M's power. If buttons, snaps, hooks, and Velcro are included in the market definition, let us suppose that M's share of this larger "clothing fastener" market will be only 23 percent, a figure that certainly does not indicate overwhelming power.

The approach that most courts have taken to such a problem is to look first at the **cross elasticity of demand** among the products in question. The term describes the concept of interchangeability. If there is a substantial degree of cross elasticity of demand between two or more products, they usually will be treated as occupying the same product market. In other words, if the evidence indicates that a substantial portion of customers view two products as being reasonable substitutes for one another, a court is likely to treat the products as being part of a single market.

The evidence in such a case, like so many others, will usually not be very "neat." It probably will show that zippers are preferred by most customers for particular uses and that these customers are willing to pay significantly more for zippers than other fasteners for these uses. Buttons are probably preferred for certain other uses, snaps for others, and Velcro for still others. For some uses, two or more types of fasteners may be viewed as basically equivalent, and customers may choose solely on the basis of price. Courts necessarily must employ some fairly rough approximations in such cases. Thus, if the evidence convinces a court that a substantial body of customers views two or more products as reasonably interchangeable for a substantial number of important uses, they probably will be included in a single product market. It is also possible, of course, that the evidence will justify a conclusion that fasteners for one particular use constitute a separate market, and that one or more other markets exist for other uses. This conclusion is likely only if the use is quite distinctive from other uses and the volume of business for this use is very substantial.

Another factor that sometimes is relevant to the process of product market definition is **cross elasticity of supply.** This refers to the relative ease or difficulty with which producers of related products may respond to increases in demand. Suppose, for example, that many customers view buttons and zippers as basically interchangeable for certain important uses. Thus, there may be a high degree of cross elasticity of *demand*. However, all button manufacturers are operating at close to their production capacity, and the building of additional button-making facilities is very costly and time-consuming. Therefore, if M raises the price of zippers substantially and many customers would consider switching to buttons, button manufacturers cannot absorb the additional demand. These zipper customers will have to keep buying zippers at a higher cost. Button makers will not build additional capacity unless they think that zipper prices will remain high for the foreseeable future, so they could count on the additional demand for buttons for a long enough time to justify the investment in new button-making capacity. Thus, even though *demand* cross elasticity may be relatively high, there is low *supply* cross elasticity, and courts will probably treat zippers and buttons as two separate markets. It is also true that high cross elasticity of supply can support a conclusion that two products should be in the same market even though there is currently a low degree of demand cross elasticity. Suppose, for example, that most customers view zippers and Velcro as not being interchangeable for a particular use. However, if a price increase for zippers causes many customers to look for a substitute, and if Velcro manufacturers could modify their product easily and inexpensively so that it would be a reasonable zipper substitute for this particular use, zippers and Velcro may be treated as one market.

Geographic Market

Depending on the situation, the relevant geographic market can be local, regional, national, or international. It represents the area within which buyers can reasonably be expected to seek alternative sources of supply. Retail geographic markets tend to be smaller than wholesale markets, which tend to be smaller than manufacturing markets, although there are many exceptions to this generalization. The factor that usually determines the size of a geographic market is the relative cost of searching for and shipping products from more distant geographic locations. When we speak of relative cost, we mean relative to the cost of the product itself. Buyers obviously will spend more time and money searching for better deals and shipping from more distant places when the desired purchase is 100 million computer chips than when it is a loaf of bread.

INTENT TO MONOPOLIZE

If a firm has overwhelming market power and thus is a monopolist, is there automatically a violation of section 2 of the Sherman Act? Or must something else be proved? The answer is that the evidence must also demonstrate that the dominant firm had an intent to monopolize, that is, that it willfully acquired or maintained its monopoly power. This obviously means that there can be legal monopolies. For example, a monopoly is legal if it exists solely because of lawful patents or trade secrets, or because economies of scale are so large that the market will support only one profitable firm.

As in other areas of law, intent is inferred from conduct. In the case of monopolization, courts usually will infer an intent to monopolize only if the dominant firm has engaged in *predatory* conduct, that is, conduct aimed at inflicting economic harm on one or more other firms for reasons that are not related to greater efficiency or better performance. There are two very general categories of predatory behavior: predatory pricing and nonprice predation.

Predatory pricing is usually found where the dominant firm has persistently sold at prices below its average variable cost. Such pricing is viewed as predatory because it cannot be justified by a legitimate profit motive;

while these prices are being charged, it is a money-losing proposition for the dominant firm. Instead, predatory pricing can only pay off for the dominant firm if it permits that firm to maintain its monopoly position so that it can later recover its losses by charging very high prices and earning monopoly profits. Predatory pricing can be used to drive another firm out of the market, although this is so costly for the dominant firm and has such uncertain long-term payoffs for that firm that it may not happen very often. Strategic predatory pricing can also be used on a periodic basic to discourage other firms from entering the market or to send a clear signal to smaller firms in the market and they had better not engage in aggressive price competition. Predatory pricing for these purposes is probably more common than for the purpose of actually driving a competitor out.

Nonprice predation is probably more common than any kind of predatory pricing because it does not cost the dominant firm as much. Most forms of nonprice predation are aimed at increasing the costs of competitors or increasing entry barriers for potential competitors. A few examples are (1) tying up customers with long-term contracts that are not justified by cost savings, so that it is much more difficult for existing and potential competitors to engage in a fair contest for those customers; (2) taking away key employees from a smaller competitor; (3) falsely disparaging the products of smaller competitors; (4) forcing smaller firms into completely unjustified lawsuits and administrative proceedings because the costs of such proceedings hurt the smaller firms more than the dominant firm; and (5) various forms of sabotage. Some kinds of nonprice predation may violate other laws as well, but many kinds do not.

The following case illustrates a form of nonprice predation that the U.S. Supreme Court found sufficient to fulfill the intent requirement of section 2.

ASPEN SKIING CO. v. ASPEN HIGHLANDS SKIING CORP.

U.S. SUPREME COURT, 472 U.S. 585 (1985)

The plaintiff, Aspen Highlands Skiing Corp. (Highlands), and the defendant, Aspen Skiing Co. (Ski Co.), were involved in the business of operating downhill skiing facilities in the Aspen, Colorado, area. There are four major mountain facilities in the area, and most customers prefer a ticket that permits them to use all four facilities. Because of this customer preference, the companies operating the facilities at the four mountains had for several years cooperated in offering an "all-Aspen" ticket that would permit customers to use any of the four facilities. Although the four facilities were originally developed by separate firms, over a period of years Ski Co. acquired ownership of three of these facilities. The fourth was owned and operated by Highlands. After several years of cooperating to the extent necessary to offer an all-Aspen ticket because of strong customer demand for such a ticket, Ski Co. stopped the practice and began offering only a

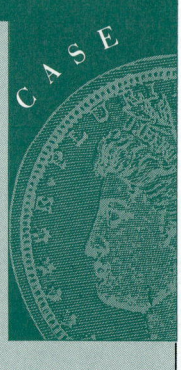

CONTINUED

ticket that permitted access to its three facilities. Highlands suffered substantial economic damage as a result, because there was not a great demand for a ticket to just its one mountain. The skiing school operated by Highlands, which was generally recognized as the best in the area, also lost a great deal of business because of the termination of the all-Aspen ticket program.

Highlands sued Ski Co., alleging illegal monopolization in violation of section 2 of the Sherman Act. Based on a jury verdict, the trial court found that Aspen Ski Co. had a monopoly in the market for downhill skiing facilities in the Aspen area and that its refusal to deal with Highlands demonstrated the requisite intent to monopolize. Highlands was awarded a judgment of $7.5 million (after trebling). The court of appeals affirmed. The only issue presented to the Supreme Court was whether the evidence was sufficient for an inference of intent to monoplize.

STEVENS, JUSTICE:

Ski Co. contends that even a firm with monopoly power has no duty to engage in joint marketing with a competitor, that a violation of §2 cannot be established without evidence of substantial exclusionary conduct, and that none of its activities can be characterized as exclusionary.... Ski Co. is surely correct in [stating] that even a firm with monopoly power has no general duty to engage in a joint marketing program with a competitor.... [In general, a firm is free to choose those with whom it wishes to deal, and this proposition also applies is most situations to a monopolist. In the case of a monopolist, however, this freedom is qualified somewhat, because a monopolist's refusal to deal may constitute evidence of unlawful exclusionary intent when it apparently was not motivated by efficiency concerns or other legitimate business justifications.]

In the actual case that we must decide, the monopolist did not merely reject a novel offer to participate in a cooperative venture that had been proposed by a competitor. Rather, the monopolist elected to make an important change in a pattern of distribution that had originated in a competitive market and had persisted for several years. The all-Aspen, 6-day ticket with revenues allocated on the basis of usage was first developed when three independent companies operated three different ski mountains in the Aspen area. It continued to provide a desirable option for skiers when the market was enlarged to include four mountains, and when the character of the market was changed by Ski Co.'s acquisition of monopoly power. Moreover, since the record discloses that interchangeable tickets are used in other multi-mountain areas which apparently are competitive, it seems appropriate to infer that such tickets satisfy consumer demand in free competitive markets....

Perhaps most significantly, however, Ski Co. did not persuade the jury that its conduct was justified by any normal business purpose. Ski Co. was apparently willing to forgo daily ticket sales.... [The evidence supports the jury's conclusion] that Ski Co. elected to forgo these short-run benefits because it was more interested in reducing competition in the Aspen market over the long run by harming its smaller competitor.... That conclusion is strongly supported by Ski Co.'s failure to offer any efficiency justification whatever for its pattern of conduct.... Ski Co. claimed that usage could not be properly monitored. The evidence, however, established that Ski Co. itself monitored the use of the 3-area passes based on a count taken by lift operators, and distributed the revenues among its own mountains on that basis. Ski Co. contended that coupons were administratively cumbersome, and that the survey takers had been disruptive and their work inaccurate. Coupons, however, were no more burdensome than the credit cards accepted at Ski Co. ticket windows. Moreover, in other markets Ski Co. itself participated in interchangeable lift tickets using coupons. As for the survey, its own manager testified that the problems were much over-emphasized by Ski Co. officials, and were mostly resolved as they arose. Ski Co.'s explanation for its rejection of Highlands' offer to hire—at Highlands' own expense—a reputable national accounting firm to audit usage of the 4-area tickets at Highlands' mountain, was that there was no way to "control" the audit....

Thus the evidence supports an inference that Ski Co. was not motivated by efficiency concerns and that it was willing to sacrifice short-run benefits and customer good will in exchange for a perceived long-run impact on its smaller rival.... Affirmed.

COMMENT

Although the all-Aspen four-mountain ticket program had been a legitimate joint venture because it resulted in a product for which there was strong demand and which could not have been offered by a single firm, the participants in such an arrangement would have to maintain independent control of their own pricing and be careful not to let the joint venture limit competition any more than necessary to achieve its legitimate goals. If the participants cooperated in pricing more than necessary to make the joint venture work, they could be guilty of violating the prohibition in section 1 of the Sherman Act against "contracts, combinations, or conspiracies in restraint of trade."

MERGERS

BASIC PRINCIPLES

A **merger** between two companies clearly is a "combination" that could be scrutinized under section 1 of the Sherman Act, which prohibits "contracts, combinations, and conspiracies in restraint of trade." In the early years after Congress passed the Sherman Act, however, the Supreme Court interpreted section 1 in such a narrow way, at least as applied to mergers, that a merger could be illegal only if it occurred between two direct competitors with very large market shares. Because Congress intended antitrust law to reach some other mergers as well, in 1914 it enacted section 7 of the Clayton Act. The statute was amended substantially by the Cellar-Kefauver Act of 1950, further demonstrating an intent to prevent mergers when the evidence indicates either actual harm to competition or a substantial probability of such harm in the future. Another amendment in 1976 requires the participants in most mergers of any significant size to give both the Justice Department and the FTC advance notice of a merger so that these agencies can assess its possible effects before it occurs.

Section 7 prohibits one company from acquiring the stock or assets of another company if the acquisition is likely to diminish competition in a substantial way. Total or partial acquisitions are covered. Obviously, however, a stock acquisition cannot raise any concerns about harming competition unless the acquiring company obtains a large enough stake in the acquired company either to control it or at least to have substantial influence over its board of directors. Similarly, an acquisition of assets cannot harm competition unless the assets are very important to competition in the particular market, such as major manufacturing facilities, airline routes, critical patented technology, and so on.

So long as there is an acquisition of assets or shares of stock, the exact form of the transaction does not matter. It may be a "friendly" merger or consolidation negotiated between the boards of the two firms and then approved by shareholders, a "hostile" stock acquisition by means of a public tender offer, a series of stock purchases either on the open market or through negotiations with individual shareholders, or any other form.

In attempting to assess a merger's actual or probable effects on competition, a court will first define the relevant market or markets. This is done in exactly the same way as in a monopoly case. As we will see in our discussion of the different types of mergers, the question of market power is also very important in merger cases. It is important to note, however, that a merger does not have to result in market power that is even close to being monopolistic in order to be ruled illegal. Although substantial market power is necessary for substantial anticompetitive effects, that power does not have to be overwhelming for such effects to occur.

Another important point about the law in this area is that periodic political changes in Washington affect the enforcement and interpretation of section 7 to a greater extent than the other antitrust laws. Although such changes affect antitrust law in general, private lawsuits are much less important as an enforcement tool in the case of mergers than in other areas of antitrust. Most challenges to mergers are made by either the Justice Department or the FTC, rather than by private plaintiffs. Thus, when the current political climate is relatively conservative and probusiness, the enforcement attitude toward mergers is likely to be quite lenient. On the other hand, when an administration is in power that distrusts large concentrations of economic power and does not really believe that most mergers contribute to economic efficiency, more mergers are usually challenged under section 7. In recent times, the attitude toward mergers was rather strict between the mid-1950s and early 1970s. It was somewhat less strict during the remainder of the 1970s and was quite lenient during the 1980s.

TYPES OF MERGERS

Mergers traditionally have been classified as horizontal, vertical, or conglomerate. A *horizontal merger* occurs if the two firms are competitors, and a *vertical merger* occurs if one of the firms sells something that the other firm buys. Any other is a *conglomerate merger*. Although these classifications are useful to describe very broadly some relevant differences in the various factual settings in which mergers occur, the same basic test applies to all mergers: Does the merger substantially diminish competition, or is it quite likely to do so in the future? Moreover, a merger may sometimes fit more than one category. For instance, in *Brown Shoe Co. v. United States*, 370 U.S. 294 (1962), the challenged merger had both horizontal and vertical aspects because each of the merging firms, Brown Shoe Co. and Kinney Shoe Co., was both a manufacturer *and* a retailer of shoes.

Horizontal Mergers

A merger between competitors poses the greatest danger to competition because the market has one less competitor. In assessing the impact of a **horizontal merger,** the courts usually emphasize the same general kinds of evidence that are important in measuring market power in a monopoly case.

Market Share: The *combined market share* of the merging firms is often the first thing the courts look at. During earlier periods when the attitude toward mergers was very strict, a number of them were challenged and ruled illegal when the combined market shares were under 10 percent and other evidence indicated a definite trend toward concentration of economic power in the relevant market. Today, however, a horizontal merger is not likely to get much attention under section 7 unless the combined market share exceeds 30 percent.

Market Concentration: The *overall concentration of the market* is also important. In general, the more concentrated the market is at the time of the merger, the more likely it is that a questionable merger will be held illegal. Suppose, for example, that a merger occurs between two firms having market shares of 20 percent and 15 percent, and the remainder of the market consists of three other firms with shares of 25 percent, 20 percent, and 20 percent. This merger would be somewhat more likely to violate section 7 than it would if the remainder of the market consisted of, say, six other firms with shares of approximately 11 percent each.

Acquisition by Leading Firm: In addition, if a single firm already dominates a market rather completely and there are no other firms that can come close to its resources and scale economies, *any* acquisition of a competitor by the *dominant firm* runs a great risk of being held illegal.

Entry Barriers: If the market is characterized by high entry barriers, a borderline merger is much more likely to be ruled illegal, and vice versa. Indeed, as we mentioned in the discussion of monopoly, an increasing number of authorities have begun to view a market's entry barriers as being at least as important to the market power question as the market's internal composition. One practical difficulty with this view, however, is that entry barriers usually are much more difficult to measure with any kind of precision than the market's internal structure.

Increased Risk of Collusion: Another relevant factor could be the existence of evidence indicating that collusion among competitors had been a problem in this market in the past and that by further reducing the number of competitors this merger could make collusion even easier in the future. In general, the lower the number of competitors, the easier it is for them to put together and maintain a price-fixing conspiracy or other collusive anticompetitive arrangement.

Other Factors: Other factors can also be important to the evaluation of horizontal mergers. For example, a firm with 15 or 20 percent of a market ordinarily could acquire a firm with a 2 or 3 percent share without much fear of legal challenge. Suppose, however, that the smaller firm had recently developed patented technology of major significance to future competition in the market, or that it had traditionally been a very efficient "maverick" and frequently had led the way in vigorous price competition. In such a case, the

Vertical Mergers

acquisition would run a significantly higher risk of being challenged successfully under section 7.

Although a **vertical merger** is much less likely to harm competition than a horizontal one, it is possible for such a merger to diminish competition. Essentially, a vertical merger creates **vertical integration,** which occurs when one firm operates at more than one level of the distribution chain for a product. (Obviously, a firm can also become vertically integrated, without a merger, by creating new facilities to operate at another level.) Suppose that S Company is an important producer of a key component or ingredient used by B Company in manufacturing an end product and that S acquires B. S would be using the merger to vertically integrate "downstream." If B had acquired S, B would be vertically integrating "upstream."

The Debate: There has been a long-standing debate about the merits of vertical integration. Some experts have viewed vertical integration as being primarily a vehicle for greater efficiency. Others have viewed it as being primarily a tool for locking up markets and supply sources, raising entry barriers, and making collusion easier. Still others have viewed vertical integration as something of a "mixed bag" of economic effects that is exceptionally difficult to sort out. Currently, the prevailing attitude among a majority of economists and enforcement officials toward vertical integration is basically a favorable one. Not everyone shares that view, however, and the pendulum of expert opinion could swing in the other direction at some point in the future.

Efficiency Argument: Undoubtedly, vertical integration can create efficiencies, primarily by saving transaction costs. If the vertically integrated firm ("S–B") is managed properly, it usually should be able to transfer goods and services from one level to another more cheaply than if it were two separate firms operating at the two levels. Being part of one company ideally should permit better coordination and planning. Having an assured source of supply for B and an assured market for S should permit better inventory control. This, in turn, should produce lower carrying costs by avoiding excess inventory and lower delay-related costs by reducing instances of shortage. Vertical integration also can reduce the various kinds of selling costs between S and B, such as those associated with promotion, sales personnel, and contract drafting and monitoring. Opponents of vertical integration reply that, even if these efficiencies are created, the cost savings are not going to be passed along to consumers unless competition in the downstream market is vigorous. They also argue that many of the same efficiencies can be achieved through relatively long-term contracts without creating the same degree of risk for competition.

Entry Barriers: Some observers argue that vertical integration can increase entry barriers and thus insulate firms in the market from new competition. The reason, they say, is that a firm thinking about entering a market in which the major competitors are vertically integrated will have to come into the market at two levels simultaneously, which is more costly and difficult. Those favoring vertical integration, however, reply that new entry into such a market is more difficult simply because the vertically integrated firms in the market are more efficient and that it is more difficult to compete against efficient firms with low costs.

Making Collusion Easier: Some critics of vertical integration also claim that it can make collusion easier for the vertically integrated firms, especially those at the "upstream" level (in our example, S's level). This can happen, they claim, because removing the layer of independent buyers from the downstream level does away with an important set of "watchdogs" on the upstream firms. Those with a favorable view of vertical integration often admit that this is a possibility, but point out that it is likely to happen only if there are very few firms at both levels and if most of these large firms are already vertically integrated. Besides, they say, antitrust enforcers can just watch out for the collusion and take action if they find it.

Current Law: Because of today's generally favorable attitude toward vertical integration, a vertical merger will usually be legal. A successful challenge to such a merger is likely only if most of the firms in the market are already vertically integrated, this vertically combined market is a highly concentrated oligopoly, and both S and B have large market shares. It is mainly the fear of collusion being made easier in this kind of situation that creates the risk of a successful legal challenge.

Conglomerate Mergers

Mergers without horizontal or vertical characteristics are usually called **conglomerate mergers.** Although several grounds for striking down conglomerate mergers have been used in the past, such a merger creates very little legal risk today. About the only situation in which such a risk exists now is in the following circumstances: (1) X enters the widget market in the western United States by acquiring Y, a major producer of widgets in that area. (2) That market was already a highly concentrated oligopoly. (3) For a substantial period of time before the merger, X had a special incentive to enter the market and the resources to do it. Other potential new entrants did not have similar incentives. This special incentive may have existed because the widget market was an unusually attractive extension of X's product line, or perhaps because X already sold widgets elsewhere and this was an ideal geographic expansion. In either case, X could get into the market and compete more easily and cheaply than other new firms because of the product or geographic relationship. (4) The western widget market had high entry barriers that discouraged other firms from entering, but that were not so high as to discourage X because of its large resources and special incentive. (5) Prior to the merger, the major firms in the western widget market knew that X was a probable future entrant.

In this situation, the presence of X "on the edge" of the western widget market prior to the merger was probably having a beneficial effect by causing widget makers in the market to keep their prices lower than they would have otherwise, in the hope of discouraging X from actually entering. When X enters, this beneficial "edge effect" is removed. If X had entered by building new facilities, or by acquiring a very small firm in the market and expanding it into a major competitor, X's entry would have positive effects that would offset the removal of its former "edge effect." But when X enters by acquiring a firm that is already a major player, there is nothing positive to counteract the negative, and the merger may be illegal.

FAILING COMPANY DEFENSE

Even if a merger is one that normally would violate section 7 of the Clayton Act, proof of the *failing company defense* prevents a violation. This defense exists if one of the merging firms probably will not be able to meet its financial obligations in the near future; (2) it appears unlikely that the failing firm will be able to reorganize successfully under Chapter 11 of the Bankruptcy Code and emerge as a viable company; and (3) the failing firm has made a good faith, but unsuccessful, effort to obtain a merger offer from another firm that would pose less danger to competition than does the merger being challenged.

MERGER GUIDELINES

The Justice Department's Antitrust Division first issued Merger Guidelines in 1968. The guidelines, which are also followed by the FTC, were completely rewritten in 1982, and again revised slightly in 1984. These guidelines are not binding law but do provide business with a valuable planning tool by specifying the circumstances in which the two agencies can ordinarily be expected to challenge a merger.

One of the key innovations of the current guidelines is the use of the Herfindahl-Hirschman Index (HHI) for measuring the relative level of economic concentration in a market. This index involves squaring the market share of each firm in the market and then adding the squares. Thus, a market with 10 firms of equal size would have an HHI of 1,000. The guidelines consider a market with an HHI less than 1,000 to be unconcentrated, between 1,000 and 1,800 to be moderately concentrated, and greater than 1,800 to be concentrated. The greater the level of concentration in the relevant market, the more likely it is that a merger will be challenged and that it will be ruled illegal.

The following Supreme Court decision is from a case involving a horizontal merger between two relatively large competitors. It is an important decision because, among other things, it illustrates how evidence of surrounding economic circumstances may convince a court that such a merger is legal.

UNITED STATES v. GENERAL DYNAMICS CORP.

U.S. SUPREME COURT, 415 U.S. 486 (1974)

Material Service Corp. owned Freeman Coal Mining Co. In 1954 Material Service began purchasing the stock of United Electric Coal Co., and by 1959 had acquired effective control of United. General Dynamics Corp. then acquired Material Service Corp. Subsequently, the government sued General Dynamics, claiming that the merger of Freeman and United violated section 7 of the Clayton Act.

Freeman and United together accounted for about 23 percent of total coal production in the state of Illinois. If the geographic market was defined more broadly as the Eastern Interior Coal Province, one of the country's four major coal distribution areas, the combined share would have been about 12 percent. The district court found that the merger did not violate section 7, and the government appealed to the Supreme Court. The Supreme Court pointed out that such market share figures could possibly lead to a ruling of illegality except for the existence of other important factors. These other economic factors caused the court to approve the merger without deciding how the geographic market should be defined or whether the resulting market shares were large enough for illegality.

STEWART, JUSTICE:

... Much of the District Court's opinion was devoted to a descritpion of the changes that have affected the coal industry since World War II. ... To a growing extent since 1954, the electric utility industry has become the mainstay of coal consumption. While electric utilities consumed only 15.76% of the coal produced nationally in 1947, their share of total consumption increased every year thereafter, and in 1968 amounted to more than 59% of all the coal consumed throughout the Nation.

To an increasing degree, nearly all coal sold to utilities is transferred under long-term requirements contracts, under which coal producers promise to meet utilities' coal consumption requirements for a fixed period of time, and at predetermined prices. ...

Because of these fundamental changes in the structure of the market for coal, the District Court was justified in viewing the statistics relied on by the Government as insufficient to sustain its case. Evidence of past production does not, as a matter of logic, necessarily give a proper picture of a company's future ability to compete. In most situations, of course, the unstated assumption is that a company that has maintained a certain share of a market in the recent past will be in a position to do so in the immediate future. ...

In the coal market, however, statistical evidence of coal *production* was of considerably less significance. The bulk of the coal produced is delivered under long-term requirements contracts, and such sales thus do not represent the exercise of competitive power but rather the obligation to fulfill previously negotiated contracts at a previously fixed price. The focus of competition in a given time-frame is not on the disposition of coal already produced but on the procurement of new long-term supply contracts. In this situation, a company's past ability to produce is of limited significance, since it is in a position to offer for sale neither its past production nor the bulk of the coal it is presently capable of producing, which is typically already committed under a long-term supply contract. A more significant indicator of a company's power effectively to compete with other companies lies in the state of a company's uncommitted reserves of recoverable coal. ...

The testimony and exhibits in the District Court revealed that United Electric's coal reserve prospects were "unpromising." United's relative position of strength in reserves was considerably weaker than its past and current ability to produce. While United ranked fifth among Illinois coal producers in terms of annual production, it was 10th in reserve holdings, and controlled less than 1% of the reserves held by coal producers in Illinois, Indiana, and western Kentucky. Many of the reserves held by United had already been depleted, at the time of trial, forcing the closing of some of United's midwest mines. Even more significantly, the District Court found

CONTINUED

that of the 52,033,304 tons of currently mineable reserves in Illinois, Indiana, and Kentucky controlled by United, only four million tons had not already been committed under long-term contracts. United was found to be facing the future with relatively depleted resources at its disposal, and with the vast majority of those resources already committed under contracts allowing no further adjustment in price. In addition, the District Court found that "United Electric has neither the possibility of acquiring more [reserves] nor the ability to develop deep coal reserves," and thus was not in a position to increase its reserves to replace those already depleted or committed.

Viewed in terms of present and future reserve prospects—and thus in terms of probable future ability to compete—rather than in terms of past production, the District Court held that United Electric was a far less significant factor in the coal market than the Government contended or the production statistics seemed to indicate. While the company had been and remained a "highly profitable" and efficient producer of relatively large amounts of coal, its current and future power to compete for subsequent long-term contracts was severely limited by its scarce uncommitted resources. Irrespective of the company's size when viewed as a producer, its weakness as a competitor was properly analyzed by the District Court and fully substantiated that court's conclusion that [the merger] would not "substantially... lessen competition...."

Affirmed.

HORIZONTAL RESTRAINTS OF TRADE

In studying the law pertaining to monopolies and mergers, we were concerned primarily with market structure and only secondarily with specific instances of conduct. We now turn our attention to particular types of business behavior. Market structure continues to be relevant here, but its role is a secondary one.

Our first inquiry into the behavioral side of antitrust is **horizontal restraints of trade**—arrangements between two or more competitors that suppress or limit competition. The applicable statute is section 1 of the Sherman Act, which, as stated earlier, prohibits "contracts, combinations, or conspiracies in restraint of trade."

THE REQUIREMENT OF COLLUSION

Section 1 of the Sherman Act can be applied only if there was **collusion** between two or more independent entities. Many different terms are used to describe the concept: joint action, concerted action, agreement, combination, conspiracy, and others. As is true of all things that must be proved in the law, the collusion requirement is sometimes obvious and sometimes not. An example of a case in which the requirement obviously was present is *National Society of Professional Engineers v. United States*, 435 U.S. 679 (1978), in which the Court held illegal an ethical rule of the society that prohibited competitive bidding by its 69,000 members. The collusion requirement was so obviously satisfied that it was not even an issue. In such a case, even if the association has been incorporated and thus is a separate entity, its rules and other actions are in reality the collective actions of its members who explicitly or implicitly granted their approval. The reason is that each member continued to be an independent business.

If collusion is not obvious, courts normally have to rely on circumstantial evidence to decide the question. Evidence of any *communications* among the parties can be very important, but such evidence may or may not be strong enough to permit the fact-finder to conclude that collusion has taken place. If there is no such evidence, or if it is not sufficient to prove collusion, there must at least be evidence demonstrating that the parties had an *opportunity to conspire*. To establish a circumstantial case of collusion, it usually is also necessary to prove *uniformity of action* among the defendants. Thus, a court is quite unlikely to find that collusion occurred unless the defendants acted in a very similar fashion in pricing, refusing to deal with another party such as a customer or supplier, or other important matter.

It is not enough, however, merely to prove that the firms did about the same thing at about the same time, because there can be many legitimate reasons for such an occurrence. This is especially true in a market with a relatively small number of firms. In an oligopoly, for example, it sometimes is inevitable that several companies will make similar pricing moves within a relatively short time span primarily because they all know what the others are doing and the actions of each one are quite important. In other situations, there also may be reasonable explanations for uniformity; for instance, the same external factor such as a supply shortage may have affected all firms simultaneously. If there is substantial uniformity, however, without any legitimate explanation, the situation is suspicious and the firms' parallel conduct is fairly strong evidence of collusion. Also, the greater the *degree* of uniformity, the more strongly this evidence points toward collusion.

THE RULE OF REASON

Assuming that collusion has been proved, the defendants' action violates section 1 only if it "restrains trade." What this means is that their conduct must have suppressed or limited competition. Relatively early in the history of the Sherman Act, in *Standard Oil Co. v. United States,* 221 U.S. 1 (1911), the Supreme Court held that section 1 does not forbid *all* arrangements that limit competition. If the statute had been interpreted in a literal, all-inclusive fashion, it could have produced strange and inefficient results such as prohibiting the formation of partnerships because they involve the combination of individuals who might otherwise be competitors. Instead, the Court adopted the so-called **rule of reason,** under which arrangements are illegal only if they "unreasonably" restrict competition.

The next question, of course, is how do the courts decide whether a particular arrangement is reasonable or unreasonable? In essence, the rule of reason involves an examination of the *purpose* and the *effect* of the conduct being challenged.

Purpose

The firms will always claim that their purpose was legitimate—that is, not anticompetitive. They may insist, for example, that their motive was to promote ethical conduct in their industry, prevent fraudulent practices by their suppliers or customers, encourage product standardization or safety, or any one of many other lawful purposes. The court will examine all pertinent evidence before deciding whether the defendants are to be believed, or whether their predominant motive was to restrict competition. If the court concludes that their primary motive was to limit competition, the arrangement is illegal if there is a likelihood of even a small restriction on competition. If, however, the court decides that their primary motive was a legitimate one, the court will find a violation of section 1 only if the evidence indicates that competition will be diminished in a substantial way. There is actually something of a rough sliding scale. The greater the apparent bad effect on competition, the less weight the court will give to any legitimate motive.

Effect on Competition

Perhaps the most important factor in the analysis of an arrangement's effect on competition is the collective *market power* of the group. Market power is evaluated in the same way here as in the more structurally oriented situations of monopoly and merger. A group's aggregate market power does not have to be overwhelming for an arrangement to violate the rule of reason, but if the group's purpose was apparently all right, its power must be substantial enough to convince a court that serious anticompetitive effects are likely to result.

Another factor that often plays a part in the court's analysis is the existence of a *less restrictive alternative*. Thus, if the evidence establishes that the firms could have achieved their claimed objectives by using some other arrangement that would have posed less danger to competition, a court is somewhat more likely to find a violation of section 1. The existence of a less restrictive alternative does not automatically cause their arrangement to be illegal, but it does tip the scales a bit in that direction, for two reasons. First, it demonstrates that the firms caused a greater negative effect on competition than they really had to. Second, such evidence may even cause a court to view their alleged motive with more suspicion.

If evidence of market power and other relevant factors indicates that a substantial negative effect on competition is possible, the legality of the arrangement sometimes can be saved by clear evidence that it also will have *offsetting procompetitive effects*. These are just positives to offset the negatives, and usually involve some aspect of the arrangement that will improve the efficiency of the market. The court will engage in a rough balancing of these effects against the anticompetitive ones and decide which seem to predominate. Examples of procompetitive effects include creating a new kind of market that otherwise would not exist, stimulating competition by bringing more transaction into the market, improving the quality or quantity of information available to buyers and sellers, and so on.

The following landmark Supreme Court case illustrates most of these aspects of rule-of-reason analysis. You will be able to see the Court examining (1) motives; (2) market power (although it does not use this term); (3) the fact that the scope of the arrangement seemed to be limited so that it was not any more restrictive than it had to be; and (4) what the judges viewed as offsetting procompetitive effects brought about by taking quite a few transactions from a few large dealers and bringing them into the organized market where information was more accurate and up-to-date and trading more open and competitive.

CHICAGO BOARD OF TRADE v. UNITED STATES

U.S. Supreme Court, 246 U.S. 231 (1918)

In the late 1800s and early 1900s, Chicago was the leading grain market in the world, and the Board of Trade was the commercial center through which most of the trading in grain was done. Its 1,600 members included brokers, commission merchants, dealers, millers, manufacturers of grain products, and grain elevator owners. Grain transactions usually took one of three forms: (1) spot sales—sales of grain already in Chicago in railroad cars or elevators ready for immediate delivery; (2) future sales—agreements for delivery of grain at a later time; (3) sales "to arrive"—agreements for delivery of grain that was already in transit to Chicago or which was to be shipped almost immediately from other parts of the Midwest.

On each business day, sessions of the Board of Trade were held at which all bids and sales were publicly made. Spot sales and future sales were made during the regular session between 9:30 A.M. and 1:15 P.M. Special sessions, referred to as the "Call," were held immediately after the close of the regular session. During the Call, which usually lasted about 30 minutes, members of the Board of Trade engaged only in "to arrive" transactions. These transactions usually involved purchases from farmers or small dealers in one of the midwestern states. Participation in the Call session was limited to members, but they could trade on behalf of nonmembers if they wished. Members also could make any of the three types of transaction privately with each other at any place, either during or after board sessions. Members could engage privately in any type of transaction at any time with nonmembers, but not on the board's premises.

With respect to "to arrive" transactions, a particular market price would be established by the public trading during the short Call session. Until 1906, however, members were not bound by that price during the remainder of the day. In that year the Board of Trade adopted what was known as the "Call rule." The rule, which applied only to "to arrive" transactions, required members to use the market price established at the public Call session when they bought grain in private transactions between the end of that session and 9:30 the next morning.

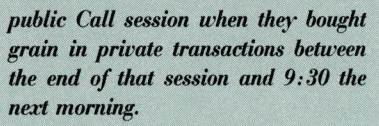

The government filed suit in federal district court, claiming that the Call rule violated section 1 of the Sherman Act. The board contended that the purpose and effect of the rule was to bring more of the "to arrive" transactions into the public market at the Call session. By bringing more of these transactions into the public market, the board felt that four or five large grain warehouse owners in Chicago would no longer have such a controlling grip over "to arrive" transactions. The district court, however, ruled that evidence relating to the history and purpose of the rule was irrelevant and issued an injunction against the operation of the rule. The Board of Trade then appealed to the U.S. Supreme Court.

CONTINUED

Brandeis, Justice:

... Every agreement concerning trade, every regulation of trade, restrains. To bind, to restrain, is of their very essence. The true test of legality is whether the restraint imposed is such as merely regulates and perhaps thereby promotes competition or whether it is such as may suppress or even destroy competition. To determine that question the court must ordinarily consider the facts peculiar to the business to which the restraint is applied; its condition before and after the restraint was imposed: the nature of the restraint and its effect, actual or probable. The history of the restraint, the evil believed to exist, the reason for adopting the particular remedy, the purpose or end sought to be attained, are all relevant facts. This is not because a good intention will save an otherwise objectionable regulation or the reverse; but because knowledge of intent may help the court to interpret facts and to predict consequences. The District Court erred, therefore, in striking from the [Board's] answer allegations concerning evidence on that subject. But the evidence admitted makes it clear that the rule was a reasonable regulation of business consistent with the provisions of the AntiTrust Law.

First: The nature of the rule: The restriction was upon the period of price-making. It required members to desist from further price-making after the close of the Call until 9:30 A.M. the next business day: but there was no restriction upon the sending out of bids after close of the Call. Thus it required members who desired to buy grain "to arrive" to make up their minds before the close of the Call how much they were willing to pay during the interval before the next session of the Board. The rule made it to their interest to attend the Call; and if they did not fill their wants by purchases there, to make the final bid high enough to enable them to purchase from country dealers.

Second: The scope of the rule: It is restricted in operation to grain "to arrive." It applies only to a small part of the grain shipped from day to day to Chicago, and to an even smaller part of the day's sales: members were left free to purchase grain already in Chicago from anyone at any price throughout the day. It applies only during a small part of the business day; members were left free to purchase during the sessions of the Board grain "to arrive," at any price, from members anywhere and from nonmembers anywhere except on the premises of the Board. It applied only to grain shipped to Chicago: members were left free to purchase at any price throughout the day from either members or nonmembers, grain "to arrive" at any other market. Country dealers and farmers had available in practically every part of the territory called tributary to Chicago some other market for grain "to arrive." Thus Missouri, Kansas, Nebraska, and parts of Illinois are also tributary to St. Louis; Nebraska and Iowa, to Omaha; Minnesota, Iowa, South and North Dakota, to Minneapolis or Duluth; Wisconsin and parts of Iowa and of Illinois, to Milwaukee; Ohio, Indiana and parts of Illinois, to Cincinnati; Indiana and parts of Illinois, to Louisville.

Third: The effects of the rule: As it applies to only a small part of the grain shipped to Chicago and to that only during a part of the business day and does not apply at all to grain shipped to other markets, the rule had no appreciable effect on general market prices; nor did it materially affect the total volume of grain coming to Chicago. But within the narrow limits of its operation the rule helped to improve market conditions thus:

(a) It created a public market for grain "to arrive." Before its adoption, bids were made privately. Men had to buy and sell without adequate knowledge of actual market conditions. This was advantageous to all concerned, but particularly so to country dealers and farmers.

(b) It brought into the regular market hours of the Board sessions more of the trading in grain "to arrive."

(c) It brought buyers and sellers into more direct relations; because on the Call they gathered together for a free and open interchange of bids and offers.

(d) It distributed the business in grain "to arrive" among a far larger number of Chicago receivers and commission merchants than had been the case there before.

(e) It increased the number of country dealers engaging in this branch of the business; supplied them more regularly with bids from Chicago; and also increased the number of bids received by them from competing markets.

(f) It eliminated risks necessarily incident to a private market, and thus enabled country dealers to do business on a smaller margin. In that way the rule made it possible for them to pay more

CONTINUED

> to farmers without raising the price to consumers.
>
> (g) It enabled country dealers to sell some grain "to arrive" which they would otherwise have been obliged either to ship to Chicago commission merchants or to sell for "future delivery."
>
> (h) It enabled those grain merchants of Chicago who sell to millers and exporters to trade on a smaller margin and, by paying more for grain or selling it for less, to make the Chicago market more attractive for both shippers and buyers of grain....
>
> The decree of the District Court is reversed with directions to dismiss the [government's complaint].

THE PER SE RULE

Also relatively early in the history of the Sherman Act, the Supreme Court recognized that certain types of practices are obviously anticompetitive and do not really have any redeeming social virtues. In such a case, the **per se rule** applies. This means that, once the particular type of activity is identified as one that falls within a *per se* category, it is automatically illegal and the inquiry ends. Of the various horizontal restraints of trade, price fixing, market division, and boycotts are *per se* illegal. It is very important to understand, however, that the *per se* rule has its greatest impact in situations where the challenged activity can be easily labeled as price fixing, market division, or a boycott. If there is a close question whether the arrangement should be characterized in this way, the court must analyze its purpose and effect in order to decide how to label it. This analysis is basically the same as in a rule-of-reason case.

Price Fixing

Price fixing among competitors is *per se* illegal. This activity occurs when two or more competitors agree obviously to charge a specific price, or to set a price floor, but many other arrangements can also constitute price fixing because they substantially interfere with the price-setting function of the market. Some examples include agreements or understandings among competitors to (1) not submit competitive bids; (2) rotate the privilege of being low bidder on contracts; (3) artificially manipulate supply or demand in a way that affects price substantially; (4) not advertise prices; (5) not grant certain discounts; (6) maintain uniformity on a particular term that constitutes a component of price, such as shipping or credit charges; (7) keep prices within a particular range; and even (8) maintain a *ceiling* on prices.

Many other joint arrangements may have an arguable effect on the market's pricing mechanism. If the court is convinced that the parties' main purpose is to suppress price competition, it will probably call the arrangement price fixing and find it illegal. As mentioned earlier, however, if there is significant doubt about the question, a court will probably engage in a rule-of-reason type analysis, regardless of whether it uses that phrase.

Market Division

Market division among competitors is also *per se* illegal, assuming that such division is found to be the primary objective of a particular arrangement. The same rule can be applied to market division agreements involving *potential* competitors making decisions about entering new markets. Market division arrangements can take at least three forms: (1) in a *territorial* market division, the firms agree to refrain from competing with each other in designated geographic areas; (2) in a *customer allocation* arrangement, the firms assign particular customers or classes of customers to each seller and agree not to solicit customers of another seller; (3) in a *product line* division, the firms agree to limit their activities to particular types of products or services so as to avoid competing with each other.

Boycotts

A firm ordinarily has freedom to choose those with whom it will transact business. However, when two or more parties agree not to deal with some other party, antitrust problems arise. When the agreeing parties are competitors and their primary purpose apparently is to curtail competition, the resulting **boycott** is *per se* illegal. Two or more firms will violate section 1, for example, if they agree to quit selling to a customer because the latter is trying to integrate upstream and become their competitor. Likewise, a group of firms would be engaged in an illegal boycott if they agreed to stop selling to certain customers unless those customers quit buying from a competitor of those in the agreeing group. A similar violation would occur if the group agreed not to buy from a supplier unless that supplier refrained from selling to a competitor or potential competitor of the group. Boycotts are sometimes used to drive a firm out of a market, keep it from entering in the first place, or discipline a firm by "showing it who's boss" and thus convincing it to stop competing so aggressively.

Although labeling problems occur with respect to all of the *per se* categories, they seem to be especially troublesome in the case of boycotts. The reason is that there are many group activities that have legitimate reasons for existing, but that also may have the tendency to *exclude* other firms. Suppose for example, that many of the automotive repair businesses in Missouri, Kansas, and Oklahoma form an organization called the Midwest Auto Repair Association (MARA). The stated purposes of the group are to promote the auto repair business in various ways and encourage high ethical standards in the industry. Like any organization, MARA establishes rules for membership that might require such things as full-time participation in the auto repair business, a fee to cover the organization's costs, fewer than a specified number of verified customer complaints during a given period of time, and so on. Jones does not meet one of the requirements and is either denied membership initially or is forced out later. He claims that he has been the victim of a boycott.

There are many other examples. Similar problems can arise if a group of firms in the same industry tries to establish uniform product standards for the purpose of either safety or reducing customer confusion and dissatisfaction.

One firm's product does not meet the standard and thus does not receive the approval of the group. The firm claims a boycott.

Yet another example arises when a group of firms pools their resources to develop a facility such as a research laboratory. This can be legitimate when the great cost, risk, and uncertain pay-off associated with constructing a major facility or engaging in a particular undertaking is too much for a single firm. (This last example describes a "joint venture," which is discussed shortly.) A competitor is not permitted to join the venture and claims a boycott.

When confronted with such claims, courts first look at the group's apparent *purpose*. If the primary purpose was to exclude others and achieve some restriction on competition, it will be *per se* illegal as a boycott. If the main purpose appears to have been a legitimate one, the court engages in a rule-of-reason type of analysis. The court will try to determine just how important it is for a firm to participate. (This is just another kind of inquiry into a group's collective market power.) If exclusion really does *not* harm a firm's ability to compete in the relevant market, the arrangement is legal. On the other hand, if participation *is* very important to a firm's ability to compete, the rules or restrictions that have the result of excluding others must be *reasonable*. To be reasonable, they must (1) have a logical relationship to the group's legitimate objectives, and (2) not exclude others any more than a necessary to accomplish those objectives.

TRADE ASSOCIATIONS

A trade association is a loosely knit organization of firms with mutual interests. Its membership usually includes firms within the same industry but sometimes also includes suppliers or customers of these firms, and perhaps others with an interest in the field, such as consultants. The mere existence of a trade association presents no antitrust problems—most industries have some type of trade association. Moreover, the activities of these associations usually are legitimate and socially useful. Associations in some industries have been instrumental, for example, in setting product safety standards, maintaining ethical norms, providing arbitration or other procedures for resolving disputes between members, forming group self-insurance pools, and so on.

The problem with trade associations is that they can present very tempting opportunities for illegal group activities such as price fixing, market divisions, boycotts, or other arrangements that stifle competition. Members must be vigilant to ensure that the association's activities do not harm competition, and have all proposals reviewed by attorneys with antitrust expertise. If a firm believes that action about to be taken by the group is legally questionable, the firm should voice its dissent and not participate.

JOINT VENTURES

Although the term **joint venture** has no precise meaning, it has been likened to a partnership for a limited purpose. The joint research lab used earlier as an illustration is a type of joint venture. When two or more firms collaborate for some reason, their joint undertaking may or may not be a joint venture.

The basic characteristics of a legitimate joint venture are (1) a partial pooling of resources by two or more firms, (2) a limited degree of integration of some aspect of the firms' operations, and (3) an intent to accomplish a defined business objective that could not be accomplished as efficiently (or at all) by a single firm. Situations in which joint ventures are commonly accepted as legitimate include those in which extremely large economies of scale, very high risks, or unusually extended long-term payoffs are involved, or where the nature of the product is such that it cannot be produced or marketed efficiently without collaboration between two or more firms.

Joint ventures usually do not violate the antitrust laws, but they can do so on occasion. Section 1 of the Sherman Act is the primarily applicable statute, and joint ventures are normally judged under the rule of reason. If formation of the joint venture involves an asset or stock acquisition, section 7 of the Clayton Act also can be applied, although the legal standards for joint ventures are basically the same under both statutes.

The risk of illegality obviously is greater when actual or potential competitors are involved. In addition, certain kinds of activities are more likely to limit competition than those involving other kinds of activities. A joint venture might involve matters ranging along a continuum from basic research to applied research, product development, production, promotion and other marketing activities, selling, and finally, distribution. The risk of harm to competition, and thus the degree of scrutiny under the antitrust laws, increases as the activity moves along the continuum away from research. Joint ventures involving activities farther along the continuum, such as production, can be valid, but their justification must be stronger.

Assuming that the basic objectives of the joint venture are legitimate, three basic types of antitrust questions can still be raised. First, the formation of a joint venture occasionally may create dangers to competition that probably will not be outweighed by increased efficiency or other positive effects. This may happen if the venture is just *too big*—that is, if it is larger than really necessary to accomplish its legitimate objectives. Second, even if the venture is not too large, it may include some *ancillary restriction* that limits competition among the participants more than necessary. For example, participants might agree to exchange certain kinds of information which, if misused, could make it fairly easy to engage in horizontal price fixing. This restriction would require a very strong justification. Third, the joint venture may harm outsiders who are excluded from participation. This situation is analyzed as described earlier in the discussion of various group activities that tend to exclude others.

VERTICAL RESTRAINTS OF TRADE

When firms operating at different levels of the distribution chain enter some arrangement that may harm competition, we call it a **vertical restraint of trade.**

RESALE PRICE MAINTENANCE

Resale price maintenance (RPM), which is also called *vertical price fixing*, occurs when a seller and buyer agree on the price at which the buyer will resell to its own customers. RPM usually is a method by which a manufacturer or other supplier limits price competition among its dealers or distributors in the market for resale of the product. Competition among such dealers for sales of the manufacturer's product is called **intraband competition,** in contrast with the **interbrand competition** that occurs between different manufacturers' brands.

RPM has always been controversial. Many economists and legal scholars believe that RPM and other forms of restriction on intrabrand competition are usually employed to increase efficiency. They claim that these limits on intrabrand competition can be used by a manufacturer to make sure that its dealers invest in the facilities, trained personnel, and promotional activities necessary to stimulate sales and properly serve customers. If one dealer makes such an investment and thereby stimulates demand for the manufacturer's product, but another dealer does not, the latter has lower costs and can underprice the former. The first dealer will then be discouraged and will stop making such investments. Because of some dealers' **free riding,** the argument goes, many (or most) of the manufacturer's dealers will not do those things necessary to compete vigorously with other brands. If the manufacturer uses RPM to put a floor below its dealers' resale prices, however, some argue that this will solve the problem by reducing dealers' incentives to take a free ride on the investment of other dealers. The incentive is gone because they cannot use their lower costs to underprice and take customers from another dealer. Those arguing that the law should treat RPM very leniently also claim that, because any potential harm to compettition is only intrabrand, customers are protected so long as competition among different brands remains active.

Other experts have serious doubts about the "free rider" justification for RPM. They argue that free rider problems are really not that common, and that many cases of resale price maintenance have involved products like toothpaste or blue jeans, for which there is not much need for the kinds of costly facilities or services that are susceptible to free riding. They also claim that, even if free rider problems are common, other means are available for solving them that do not cause similar harm to price competition. Such means include contractual commitments from dealers to provide the necessary facilities, personnel, promotion, and services. Opponents of RPM claim that the true reason for the practice often may be the manufacturer's desire to keep dealers' prices up and relieve them from intrabrand competition so that they do not pressure the manufacturer to lower its prices to them. They also sometimes argue that RPM can be used as a device to carry out a horizontal price-fixing conspiracy among dealers.

Legal Standards

The statute applicable to RPM is section 1 of the Sherman Act. From the early days of the Sherman Act, RPM was viewed as *per se* illegal. In 1937, Congress passed legislation that delegated to state legislatures the power to determine the status of RPM in their particular states. Most states passed so-called Fair Trade laws that permitted RPM on branded merchandise within their borders if meaningful competition existed among different brands of the same product. Congress strengthened the power of the states to permit this practice in 1945. Gradually, however, the notion of permitting RPM fell out of favor. Many states repealed their Fair Trade laws, and many state supreme courts held that the statutes violated provisions in their state constitutions. Most of the remaining Fair Trade statutes fell into disuse, either because ambiguous interpretations created uncertainty, or simply because it was difficult for an interstate seller to use RPM legally when it was illegal in so many places. In 1975, Congress repealed the federal law that permitted states to enact Fair Trade laws. Thus, RPM became *per se* illegal everywhere in the nation once again.

Although resale price maintenance is *per se* illegal, there continues to be a vigorous debate about whether it should be. Until the early 1980s, the U.S. Justice Department aggressively prosecuted cases of RPM, and the federal courts generally took a very harsh view of the practice. (Until 1975, the Justice Department and courts dealt with RPM only if it occurred in a state where it was illegal.) Since the early 1980s, the law against RPM has not been enforced as aggressively, and the courts have begun to interpret the law so as to make it somewhat more difficult for either the Justice Department or private parties to prove RPM. These attitudes and interpretations could easily change again in the future, as they have several times in the past.

Proving a Vertical Agreement

Most of the difficult issues in RPM cases have involved the question of whether there actually has been an "agreement" to set resale prices. "Suggested" resale prices at the retail level are quite common. They do not constitute RPM unless there is evidence that there really has been an agreement (either voluntary or coerced) that gives the manufacturer or other supplier effective control over the dealer's resale prices. This point also illustrates the fact that there can be an illegal RPM "agreement" even if one party has coerced the other into participating; section 1 of the Sherman Act does not require that the agreement be completely voluntary.

One of the most difficult issues in this area involves the extent to which a seller lawfully may use a *refusal to deal* in an attempt to control buyers' resale prices. In *United States v. Colgate & Co.*, 250 U.S. 300 (1919), the Supreme Court stated that a "unilateral refusal to deal" cannot violate section 1 of the Sherman Act even if controlling resale prices is the seller's ultimate goal. In other words, so long as a seller acts entirely on its own ("unilaterally") it can refuse to sell to anyone it chooses, regardless of the motive. The problem, of course, is distinguishing between unilateral action by the seller and action that is part of an RPM arrangement between the seller and others. Suppose that M, a manufacturer, either initially refuses to sell to R, a retailer, or later terminates an existing supplier–customer relationship with R. (When RPM is claimed, the second situation is the most common.) To create a genuine fact issue for the jury, R must present evidence indicating that (1) there was an agreement to fix resale prices at R's level, and (2) M refused to deal with R because R would not go along with the arrangement. The agreement to limit price competition at R's level could be between M and wholesalers who act as intermediaries between M and R, between M and other retailers who compete with R, or even between M and R if the evidence shows that R previously had been part of an RPM arrangement with M and then tried to get out of it.

VERTICAL NONPRICE RESTRICTIONS

Nature and Effects

Vertical restrictions may relate to matters other than price. The **vertical nonprice restrictions (VNRs)** that can cause some concern under section 1 of the Sherman Act generally are those involving some type of market division. VNRs take many forms, depending on several factors. These factors include the relative bargaining power of the manufacturer and its dealers or distributors and the nature of the product and the markets in which it sells.

One type of VNR is the *territorial exclusive,* in which M, the manufacturer, guarantees its dealers that they will have the exclusive right to market M's product in their respective geographic areas. To honor this arrangement with each dealer, M obviously must keep all dealers from reselling outside their own areas. Because this restriction places a contractual limitation on M's freedom, M will not use exclusive territories in its distribution system unless it has relatively less bargaining power than its dealers. More often M will use **territorial and customer restrictions,** without any promise of exclusive territories. Such an arrangement requires dealers or distributors to resell only within their respective territories or only to particular customers, but does not guarantee them exclusive rights to sell in those areas or to those customers. A similar provision that restricts dealers somewhat less is the *area of primary responsibility,* which does not absolutely prohibit a dealer from reselling outside its designated territory but requires only that the territory be thoroughly served before sales can be made outside the area. Another fairly common provision is the *location requirement,* which requires a dealer to sell only from a specified location. In most cases, a location requirement has the same effect as a territorial restriction.

Like RPM, all forms of VNRs have the common characteristic of limiting *intrabrand* competition. Also like RPM, there is a long-standing debate about the competitive benefits and dangers of VNRs. Today, and commonly during the past, the prevailing attitude toward these restrictions has been more favorable than the attitude toward RPM. Generally, the feeling has been that VNRs are more likely than RPM (1) to be based on legitimate motives and (2) to help *intrabrand* competition more than they hurt *intrabrand* competition. A significant number of authorities think, however, that the law should not treat VNRs and RPM any differently because they are usually employed for the same purposes, have basically the same effects, and can be difficult to distinguish in practice.

Legal Standards

The legal status of VNRs has varied over the years. Until 1967, they were analyzed under the rule of reason. In that year, a decision of the U.S.

Supreme Court caused some kinds of nonprice restriction on dealers to be *per se* illegal. This decision was overruled by the Court in 1977, and since then the rule of reason has been applied to all forms of VNRs.

In the case of VNRs, the question of motive is usually not as important as it can be when the rule of reason is applied to horizontal restrictions. Courts generally accept as legitimate M's objective of using a VNR to limit intrabrand competition, so long as there apparently is some business justification for the limitaion. Under the rule of reason, M's market share will be the most important factor. If it is below 10 percent, the restriction will be legal without further inquiry. If the share is between 10 and 30 percent, courts will look at other factors, but the restriction usually will be legal. When M's market share is above 30 percent, these other factors become even more important and there is a greater risk of illegality. Other factors that could increase the chances of illegality in a close case include (1) evidence that *interbrand* competition in this particular market is not very strong, and that *intrabrand* competition is especially important; (2) evidence that most other manufacturers in this market also use such restrictions to limit intrabrand competition among their dealers; and (3) evidence that M selected a form of VNR that limits intrabrand competition much more than is really necessary under the circumstances.

The following case is the one in which the U.S. Supreme Court switched from the *per se* rule back to the rule of reason of judging VNRs. The Court's discussion outlines and adopts some of the arguments made by those who feel that VNRs usually produce more economic benefits than harms.

CASE

Continental T.V., Inc. v. G.T.E. Sylvania, Inc.

U.S. Supreme Court, 433 U.S. 36 (1977)

Sylvania manufactured and sold television sets through its Home Entertainment Products Division. Before 1962, like most other television manufacturers, Sylvania sold televisions to independent or company-owned wholesale distributors who then resold them to a large and diverse group of retailers. Prompted by a decline in its market share to a relatively insignificant 1 to 2 percent of national television sales, Sylvania conducted an intensive reassessment of its marketing strategy and in 1962 adopted the franchise plan challenged here. Sylvania phased out its wholesale distributors and began to sell its televisions directly to a smaller and more select group of franchised retailers. The main purpose of the change was to decrease the number of competing Sylvania retailers in the hope of attracting the more aggressive and competent retailers, which Sylvania felt was necessary to improve its market position.

Thus, Sylvania limited the number of franchises granted for any given area and required each retail dealer to sell Sylvania products only from the location or locations specified in the franchise agreement. These retailers were not prohibited from selling the products of competing manufacturers. A franchise did not

CONTINUED

constitute an exclusive territory, and Sylvania retained sole discretion to increase the number of retailers in an area in light of the success or failure of existing retailers in developing their market. The revised marketing strategy apparently was successful, and by 1965 Sylvania's share of national television sales increased to 5 percent, making it the eighth largest manufacturer of televisions.

In 1965 Sylvania proposed to franchise an additional retailer in San Francisco. This proposal upset Continental T.V., an existing Sylvania dealer in the city. Continental then proposed to open a new store in Sacramento. Sylvania denied Continental's request because it felt that Sacramento presently was being adequately served. Continental then began selling Sylvania televisions in Sacramento in defiance of Sylvania, and the manufacturer stopped selling to Continental.

Continental filed a treble damage suit against Sylvania, claiming that the restrictions on dealer location violated section 1 of the Sherman Act. In federal district court Continental received a jury verdict against Sylvania for approximately $600,000 and a judgment for $1.8 million. In ruling for Continental, the district court applied the Supreme Court's 1967 decision in United States v. Arnold, Schwinn & Co., *which had held vertical nonprice restrictions to be* per se *illegal. When Sylvania appealed to the court of appeals, that court reversed and ordered a retrial because it thought that the* Schwinn *case was inapplicable to the present situation. Continental then appealed to the U.S.* Supreme Court. The Supreme Court felt that the Schwinn *case was indeed applicable to the facts of the present case, but wished to decide whether* Schwinn *should still be the law. Thus, the issue for the Supreme Court was whether to follow its earlier decision in the* Schwinn *case and apply the* per se *rule, or to overrule that case and apply the rule of reason to vertical nonprice restrictions.*

POWELL, JUSTICE:

... Since its announcement, Schwinn has been the subject of continuing controversy and confusion, both in the scholarly journals and in the federal courts. The great weight of scholarly opinion has been critical of the decision, and a number of the federal courts confronted with analogous vertical restrictions have sought to limit its reach. In our view, the experience of the past 10 years should be brought to bear on this subject of considerable commercial importance. ...

Per se rules of illegality are appropriate only when they relate to conduct that is manifestly anti-competitive. As the Court explained in Northern Pac. R. Co. v. United States, 356 U.S. 1, 5, 78 S.Ct. 514, 518, 2 L.Ed.2d 545 (1958), "there are certain agreements or practices which because of their pernicious effect on competition and lack of any redeeming virtue are conclusively presumed to be unreasonable and therefore illegal without elaborate inquiry as to the precise harm they have caused or the business excuse for their use."

In essence, the issue before us is whether Schwinn's per se rule can be justified under the demanding standards of Northern Pac. R. Co. ...

The market impact of vertical restrictions is complex because of their potential for a simultaneous reduction of intrabrand competition and stimulation of interbrand competition. ...

Vertical restrictions reduce intrabrand competition by limiting the number of sellers of a particular product competing for the business of a given group of buyers. Location restrictions have this effect because of practical constraints on the effective marketing area of retail outlets. Although intrabrand competition may be reduced, the ability of retailers to exploit the resulting market may be limited both by the ability of consumers to travel to other franchised locations and, perhaps more importantly, to purchase the competing products of other manufacturers. ...

Vertical restrictions promote interbrand competition by allowing the manufacturer to achieve certain efficiencies in the distribution of his products. These "redeeming virtues" are implicit in every decision sustaining vertical restrictions under the rule of reason. Economists have identified a number of ways in which manufacturers can use such restrictions to compete more effectively against other manufacturers. For example, new manufacturers and manufacturers entering new markets can use the restrictions in order to induce competent and aggressive retailers to make the kind of investment of capital and labor that is often required in the distribution of products unknown to the consumer. Established manufacturers can use them to induce retailers to engage in promotional activities or to provide service

CONTINUED

and repair facilities necessary to the efficient marketing of their products. Service and repair are vital for many products, such as automobiles and major household appliances. The availability and quality of such services affect a manufacturer's good will and the competitiveness of his product. Because of market imperfections such as the so-called "free rider" effect, these services might not be provided by retailers in a purely competitive situation, despite the fact that each retailer's benefit would be greater if all provided the services than if none did. . . .

Certainly, there has been no showing in this case, either generally or with respect to Sylvania's agreements, that vertical restrictions have or are likely to have a "pernicious effect on competition" or that they "lack . . . any redeeming virtue." Accordingly, we conclude that the *per se* rule stated in *Schwinn* must be overruled. In so holding we do not foreclose the possibility that particular applications of vertical restrictions might justify *per se* prohibition under *Northern Pac. R. Co.* But we do make clear that departure from the rule of reason standard must be based upon demonstrable economic effect. . . .

In sum, we conclude that the appropriate decision is to return to the rule of reason that governed vertical restrictions prior to *Schwinn.* When anti-competitive effects are shown to result from particular vertical restrictions they can be adequately policed under the rule of reason, the standard traditionally applied for the majority of anti-competitive practices challenged under § 1 of the Act. Accordingly, the decision of the Court of Appeals is affirmed.

COMMENT

On retrial, the district court found that Sylvania's vertical restrictions were valid under the rule of reason. This holding was based primarily on (1) Sylvania's legitimate business justification, (2) Sylvania's small market share, and (3) the court's feeling that Sylvania had chosen the "least restrictive alternative"—in other words, that the location clause was less restrictive of competition than other methods Sylvania might have used to accomplish its objectives.

TYING AGREEMENTS

Nature and Effects

When one party agrees to supply (sell, lease, etc.) a product or service only on the condition that the customer also take another product or service, a **tying agreement** has been made. The desired item is the *tying* product, and the item the customer is required to take is the *tied* product. Tying agreements are scrutinized under both section 1 of the Sherman Act and section 3 of the Clayton Act. Section 3 of the Clayton Act applies only to the tying of two tangible commodities. Section 1 of the Sherman Act applies to all tying arrangements, including those in which either or both products are not a tangible commodity (such as a service, an intangible property right, or land). Today tying agreements are analyzed the same way under the two statutes, so section 3 of the Clayton Act is largely redundant.

An early landmark case provides a clear example of tying. In *IBM v. United States,* 298 U.S. 131 (1936), IBM was found guilty of illegal tying by requiring all customers leasing its tabulating machines to also purchase their tabulating cards from IBM.

The main concern about tying is that a supplier may use power in one market (the market for the *tying* product) to distort competition in another market (the market for the *tied* product). Such distortion can occur, it is argued, because the supplier's sales of the tied product are not based on the independent competitive merits of that product.

Several different motivations may lead a supplier to use tying arrangements. In some cases, the supplier may be trying to use the power it has in the tying market to expand its power in the tied market. Such a practice is sometimes referred to as *leveraging*. There is quite a bit of debate among experts as to the extent to which power actually can be leveraged from one market to another.

A supplier also might use tying in an attempt to *protect its goodwill*. This could be the motive, for example, where the supplier sells or leases product X, and where product Y must be used in conjunction with X. The supplier may be concerned that some customers might use inferior versions of Y that will cause X to perform poorly, and thus hurt the reputation of X. In such a case, the supplier might require buyers to buy the supplier's own version of Y along with X. The general feeling under the antitrust laws, however, has been that the supplier should accomplish its objective by requiring the customer to use any version of Y that meets specifications set by the supplier, unless the use of specifications is very difficult.

Another possible motive for tying is to *discriminate among customers* according to the intensity with which they use the supplier's product. Suppose that M manufactures a machine used by food processing companies to inject salt into foods during processing. If M feels that customers who use the machine more may be willing to pay more for it, M may try to charge them based on intensity of use so as to maximize its total revenues. Direct metering may be very difficult. Sometimes, howver, intensity of use is directly proportional to the amount of a second product the customer uses in connection with M's product. In the case of the salt-dispensing machine, intensity of use can be measured by the amount of salt used by the customer. Thus, M may try to measure intensity by requiring customers of its machines also to buy its salt. Through the salt sales, M's total revenue will be greater in transactions with high-intensity users.

Legal Standards

Tying can occur only if two separate products are involved. Often this is obvious, but sometimes it is not, as for example in the case of various options on new automobiles. Generally, a transaction will be viewed as including two separate products if the evidence demonstrates that there really are two separate markets in which the different items are commonly demanded. However, even if there are two separate markets, courts usually will treat a transaction as involving only one product if packaging two items is significantly more efficient than selling them separately.

If there are two separate products, tying is illegal only if the supplier has *substantial power in the market for the tying product*. The reason for this requirement is the generally accepted proposition that tying cannot cause any substantial harm in the *tied* market unless the supplier has quite a bit of power in the *tying* market. Market power is measured in the same way here as in other cases. Today, a supplier probably has to have at least a 30 percent share of the tying market to be viewed as having substantial power in that market. Other factors, such as entry barriers, are also very important. According to the courts, there is a second requirement for tying to be illegal, namely, that the supplier's tying arrangements must generate a substantial amount of business in the *tied* market. This requirement is so easy to establish, however, that it is practically always present.

EXCLUSIVE DEALING

Nature and Effects

The most common form of **exclusive dealing** agreement is one in which the customer makes a commitment that it will purchase a particular product or service only from the supplier (and, implicitly or explicitly, *not* from the supplier's competitors). Many times these arrangements are called "requirements contracts" because the parties often speak in terms of the buyer's commitment to purchase its "requirements" of a product from the seller. The primary concern caused by this type of arrangement is that there may be fewer and less frequent opportunities for the seller's competitors to compete for those customers who are parties to the exclusive dealing. Widespread use of such agreements in a market may also increase entry barriers for potential competitors.

Another kind of exclusive dealing that occurs less often is one in which the seller agress to sell only to a particular buyer (and, thus, not sell to the buyer's competitors). This is sometimes called an "output" contract, because the seller obligates itself to sell all of its output of a product to the buyer. Output contracts usually raise no competitive concerns but occasionally might unreasonably prevent the buyer's competitors from acquiring products needed to compete.

Legal Standards

Today, exclusive dealing is likely to be illegal under section 1 of the Sherman Act or section 3 of the Clayton Act only if a dominant share—probably more than 30 percent—of the relevant market is locked away from competitors. Thus, the practice creates a real legal risk only when a leading or dominant firm in a market makes widespread use of it.

PRICE DISCRIMINATION

Although the original version of section 2 of the Clayton Act contained a prohibition of **price discrimination,** it proved ineffective because of certain major loopholes. In 1936 Congress enacted the Robinson-Patman Act in an effort to make the law against price discrimination more effective. Congress's main purpose in passing this law was to protect small businesses from having to pay higher prices than larger companies.

Basic Elements

The interstate commerce requirement in the Robinson-Patman Act is more difficult to prove than in any other of the antitrust laws. It is not enough that the seller or buyer is an interstate company or that the transaction affects interstate commerce—at least one of the relevant sales must actually cross state lines. Only a few states have laws prohibiting intrastate price discrimination within their borders. It should also be noted that many nations, including the United States, have *antidumping laws* that prohibit a foreign producer from selling goods in the country at a lower price than in that producer's home country.

Assuming that the interstate commerce requirement is met, the following must be proved to establish a violation of the Robinson-Patman Act. (1) The seller must have charged *different prices* to two or more different customers. (2) The transaction must have involved *tangible commodities,* not services, land, or intangibles. (3) The transactions must have been *sales,* rather than consignments, leases, or some other form of transaction. (4) The goods sold in the transactions being compared must have been *of like grade and quality,* which means that the product sold to different customers at different prices must have been essentially the same. Trivial differences are ignored. (5) The evidence must demonstrate a likelihood of *substantial harm to competition.* Generally speaking, isolated or sporadic instances of price discrimination will not violate the Act because it usually will be impossible to prove competitive injury. Such injury normally can be proved only where the discrimination was recurring and systematic. To prove injury to one of the seller's competitors, it is usually necessary to show that the discriminatorily lower prices to favored customers were *predatory* (below cost). To prove injury to one of the favored customer's competitors, it is usually necessary to show that the disfavored buyer actually lost substantial business to the favored buyer because of the discrimination.

Defenses

When the basic elements of a Robinson-Patman Act violation are proved, the seller is guilty unless it can prove one of three available defenses. The first is *cost justification.* There is no violation if the seller's different prices are simply a reflection of differences in the costs of "manufacture, sale, or delivery." Thus the seller wins if it proves that the higher prices to one buyer or group of buyers are directly attributable to the higher costs of providing the goods to that buyer or group. The second defense is *meeting competition.* A seller does not violate the act if a lower price to one buyer "was made in good faith to meet an equally low price of a competitor." Suppose S generally charges $10 for a product but learns that its competitor is offering the product to a certain customer for $9. S can legally meet the $9 price to that customer even while keeping its price to other buyers at $10. Another version of the meeting competition defense permits a seller to charge different prices in different geographic markets in order to meet different prevailing market prices in those different areas. The third defense is *changing conditions.* The seller is permitted to change prices in response to changing conditions that affect the marketability of the goods, such as imminent deterioration of perishable commodities or obsolescence of seasonal goods.

Questions and Problems

1. Alcoa was charged with monopolizing the U.S. market for aluminum ingot. Aluminum ingot is sold in blocks or bars to fabricators, who use it to make aluminum sheets, conduit, wiring, and other end products. Alcoa produced 90 percent of the "virgin" aluminum ingot sold in the United States. Some of its ingot production, however, was actually fabricated by Alcoa into end products before being sold. Another factor in the market was "secondary" ingot, or aluminum ingot made from recycled aluminum. Secondary ingot was acceptable for many of the same uses as virgin ingot, but not for all of them. If the product market was defined to include all of Alcoa's virgin ingot production, including that part which Alcoa itself fabricated before selling, but not to include secondary ingot, Alcoa's market share would be about 90 percent. If the market definition also included secondary ingot, Alcoa's share would be 64 percent. If the market definition included secondary ingot, but did not include that part of Alcoa's ingot which it fabricated before selling, Alcoa's share would be 33 percent. Discuss how the product market should be defined. (*United State v. Aluminum Co. of America*, 148 F.2d 416, 2d Cir. 1945.)

2. Suppose that in a particular three-state region there are only two granite quarries from which granite suitable for cemetery monuments can be obtained. This type of granite is not available anywhere else in this region, and transportation costs are too high for granite to be shipped in from outside the region. Ace owns one quarry and Beta owns the other. Ace produces 60 percent of the region's total granite production from its quarry, and Beta produces the other 40 percent. Ace does not fabricate any of its granite but sells it in large blocks to firms who make cemetry monuments. Beta is also a cemetery monument maker and uses all of its granite production to manufacture monuments. It sells none to other monument manufacturers. Ace is charged by the Justice Department with monopolizing the sale of granite in this three-state region. Discuss how the product and geographic market should be defined and whether Ace is likely to be found in violation of section 2 of the Sherman Act.

3. Martex Co. produces a special type of scalpel used by surgeons. The scalpel effectively cauterizes the incision as the surgeon operates, thus eliminating much of the bleeding problem in surgery. Although Martex was not able to obtain a patent on the scalpel when it was developed several years ago, there still is only one other manufacturer of this type of scalpel. Of the total sales of the cauterizing scalpel, Martex accounts for 85 percent. The scalpel is used by most surgeons for major surgical procedures, and Martex sales represent 70 percent of the total sales of all types of scalpels. Whenever Martex sells these scalpels to surgeons or hospitals, it does so under a contract requiring the buyer to return the scalpel to Martex when it is worn out. Martex uses the worn-out scalpels in its research laboratory for experimentation, with the objective of improving the product. Discuss whether Martex may have violated section 2 of the Sherman Act.

4. The nation's second largest can producer acquired the nation's third largest producer of glass containers. Cans and bottles did not compete for all end uses, but for some uses they did compete. For example, there was clear rivalry between cans and bottles for the business of soft drink and beer producers. Both industries were relatively concentrated: the top two can manufacturers had 70 percent of can sales; the top three bottle manufacturers had 55 percent of bottle sales. If cans and bottles were viewed as a single market, the two firms would have, respectively, 22 percent and 3 percent of that market. Discuss whether this merger would violate section 7 of the Clayton Act. (*United States v. Continental Can Co.*, 378 U.S. 441, 1964.)

5. General Motors, Ford, and Chrysler, in that order, were the largest automobile producers in America. Together they accounted for 90 percent of domestic production. The domestic spark plug market was dominated by Champion (40 percent), AC (30 percent—wholly owned by General Motors), and Autolite (15 percent). The remainder of the spark plug market was accounted for by very small producers.

The independent spark plug makers (primarily Champion and Autolite) sold spark plugs to the automakers (primarily Ford and Chrysler) at cost or below. These original equipment (OE) plugs were sold so cheaply because auto mechanics almost aways replace worn out plugs with the same brand that had been original equipment (called the OE tie). Thus, it was essential to get into the OE market in order to get into the market for replacement plugs—the aftermarket. Large profits were made in this aftermarket.

Ford, whose purchases of OE plugs from the independent spark plug makers amounted to 10 percent of all the spark plugs produced domestically, wanted to gain entry into the profitable spark plug aftermarket. It did so by purchasing Autolite's only spark plug factory, as well as its trademark and distribution facilities. Discuss whether this merger might violate section 7 of the Clayton Act. (*Ford Motor Co. v. United States*, 405 U.S. 562, 1972.)

6. Theatre Enterprises, Inc., owned and operated the Crest Theatre in a suburban shopping center located about 6 miles from downtown Baltimore. At that time, the downtown area was still the most important shopping district. As a result, a downtown movie theatre generally had about ten times the drawing power of a suburban theatre like the Crest. Before and after the opening of the Crest, Theatre Enterprises sought to obtain first-run films from several major film distributors. It approached each distributor individually and was turned down on every occasion. As a result, the Crest was able to show first-run films only after the downtown theatres had shown them. Other than these delayed first-runs, Crest was left with "subsequent runs" (films that had been re-released). Theatre Enterprises sued the distributors, claiming that they had violated section 1 of the Sherman Act by engaging in a group refusal to deal. There was no direct evidence of agreement among the distributors. Discuss whether and under what circumstances Theatre Enterprises could prevail. (*Theatre Enterprises, Inc. v. Paramount Film Distributing Corp.*, 346 U.S. 537, 1954.)

7. During a period of time in which demand for refined sugar was falling because of increasing consumer preferences for artificial sweeteners, several sugar refiners began offering price discounts to some of their larger customers in an effort to stimulate sales and decrease inventories. These discounts were generally in the form of secret rebates. Before long, most other sugar refiners and their customers learned about these rebates. Claiming that these discriminatory rebates were "demoralizing the industry at a time when market conditions were already bad" and that customers were "losing faith in the integrity of the sugar industry," these other refiners urged those granting rebates to stop the practice. The rebating refiners argued, however, that their practices were completely legitimate because "everybody knows it's cheaper to sell to large customers." The nonrebating refiners then put pressure on sugar cane and sugar beet growers and within a short time the rebating refiners were unable to buy cane and beets for making sugar. Within a month the rebating refiners all stopped that practice of favoring certain customers. The Justice Department filed suit in federal district court, claiming that the "nonrebating" sugar refiners and the growers had violated section 1 of the Sherman Act. Discuss whether section 1 has been violated.

8. Many retail department stores provide delivery service for large items purchased by their customers. In the New York City area, the presidents of three stores were talking privately about delivery problems at a Chamber of Commerce luncheon. One of them mentioned that the costs involved in maintaining delivery trucks, forklifts, and other equipment and employees were becoming too great to justify the service. The other two agreed, but all of them were concerned about the business they might lose if they discontinued delivery service. They decided to contact other department stores in the metropolitan area to find out what their feelings were. After a series of discussions among the presidents of 18 of the 20 largest department stores in the area, they came up with the following alternative proposals:

a. They could all simultaneously stop providing delivery service.

b. They could jointly select and deal with an existing independent delivery service. The group would investigate existing services, invite them to submit bids, and ultimately select one and jointly contract with it.

Upon hearing of these proposals, the U.S. Department of Justice initiated an investigation. The department was interested in whether any of these proposals might violate section 1 of the Sherman Act. Discuss the legality of proposals a and b.

9. Chemco is a manufacturer of various agricultural chemicals such as herbicides and insecticides. Most of these products were sold to wholesale distributors who then resold either to retail dealers or directly to farmers. During a 20-day period in late 1980, Chemco received individual complaints from five of its distributors in the Pacific Coast region of the country. These distributors complained that a sixth distributor, Ace, had been significantly undercutting their prices and hurting their sales. Chemco made no promises to them, but a month later it announced to all of its distributors across the nation that it was implementing a new policy. Chemco's new policy was that, in the future, it would sell only to those distributors who would indicate in advance their intent to abide by Chemco's schedule of suggested resale prices. Most distributors responded affirmatively to Chemco's new policy. Those few who did not respond affirmatively were discontinued as Chemco distributors. One of those who did not respond affirmatively and who was discontinued was Ace. Discuss whether Chemco and its distributors may have violated section 1 of the Sherman Act.

10. Sarco, Inc., a manufacturer of various types of electronic equipment and devices used for industrial and medical purposes, sold its products to franchised dealers who then resold to their customers. Many of the products were complicated and relatively expensive. As a result, dealers needed to be carefully selected and trained so that they would be knowledgeable about the products and could offer essential consultation and demonstration services to potential customers. In addition, it was necessary that dealers be able to expertly perform repairs on the products. Sarco, which accounted for between 10 and 18 percent of national sales in its various product lines, granted each dealer an exclusive territory and required each to sell only in that territory. Sarco's distribution system was challenged under section 1 of the Sherman Act. Discuss whether the system is likely to be legal or illegal under section 1 of the Sherman Act.

CHAPTER 15

The great stock market crash of 1929 was one of the most dramatic turning points in American economic history. That event not only ushered in the Great Depression but also heralded the creation of modern securities regulation. Securities regulation is one of the most complicated areas of the law; attorneys who practice in the securities field are among the most specialized and well-paid of all lawyers. Although this vast, everchanging subject may be intimidating to the novice, few persons in business can afford to remain ignorant of its effects on the way

SECURITIES
REGULATION

business is done in this country.

Many aspects of securities regulation are highly visible. Most Americans are familiar with the hustle and bustle of the New York Stock Exchange. More than 45 million Americans own stock, many in major corporations such as General Motors and IBM. Through securities regulation, the federal government, and to a lesser degree the states, regulate trading on the stock exchanges, protect the interests of shareholders, and attempt to ensure that the collapse of 1929 is never repeated.

In this chapter, some of the more important aspects of the law of securities regulation are surveyed.

INTRODUCTION TO SECURITIES REGULATION

As explained in Chapter 13, there are various forms of business organizations including partnerships and corporations. There are sufficient advantages to incorporating, especially for very large businesses, that three million corporations exist in the United States. The corporate form allows for accumulation of capital investment from many shareholders. These investors do not directly own the assets of the business; rather, they own part of the corporate entity, as evidenced by shares of stock. Shares of stock constitute the most familiar type of security regulated by federal and state governments.

A security such as a stock or a bond has no intrinsic value—its value lies in the ownership interest that it represents. The value of that ownership interest may be difficult to discover and easy to misrepresent. Securities may be produced in nearly limitless supply at virtually no cost by anyone with access to a printing press. For all these reasons, fraud, manipulation, and deceit have been frequent companions of the security. Government regulation of securities dates back to at least 1285, when King Edward I of England attempted to gain some control over the capital markets by licensing brokers located in London.

Securities regulation in the United States was almost nonexistent until 1911, when Kansas enacted securities laws. Other states soon followed suit, but without federal laws, companies could evade regulation by operating across state lines.

The 1920s were an especially active time for the issuance and trading of securities. The securities business was then characterized by price manipulation, deceitful practices, selling on excessive credit, and the abuse of secret information by corporate insiders. Of the $50 billion of new securities offered for sale in the United States in the 1920s, about one-half were worthless. The public and the national economy were devastated when stock market prices fell 89 percent between 1929 and 1933, a situation that finally produced federal action.

FEDERAL LEGISLATION

The first federal securities law was the *Securities Act of 1933* (the 1933 Act), which regulated the initial issuance of securities by companies. Fraudulent and deceptive practices were outlawed, and registration was required before a new security could be offered or sold, unless that security was entitled to an exemption from registration.

A year later, Congress passed the *Securities Exchange Act of 1934* (the 1934 Act), which extended federal regulation to trading in securities already issued and outstanding, required registration of securities brokers and dealers, and created the Securities and Exchange Commission (SEC), the federal agency that enforces the federal securities laws through its extensive powers.

In 1935, Congress passed the *Public Utility Holding Company Act* in response to manipulative and monopolistic practices in the public utilities industry. The SEC in its early years was largely concerned with correcting abuses in the financing and operating of large public utilities. Because the commission has been very successful in this area, separate enforcement of the Public Utility Holding Company Act is no longer a major SEC priority.

The next securities law passed by Congress was the *Trust Indenture Act of 1939*, which helped protect persons investing in bonds, debentures, notes, and other debt securities by imposing qualification requirements on trustees of such instruments. A year later, the *Investment Company Act of 1940* imposed additional requirements on companies engaged primarily in the business of investing, reinvesting, and trading securities. For example, that act prohibits anyone found guilty of securities fraud from being associated with investment companies and bans transactions between such companies and their officers without prior SEC approval. The *Investment Advisers Act of 1940* required persons or firms who engaged in the business of advising others about investments for compensation to register with the SEC, as brokers and dealers are required to register under the 1934 Act.

The *Securities Investor Protection Act of 1970* amended the 1934 Act in response to a rash of failures in the late 1960s in the broker–dealer business. The act creates the Securities Investor Protection Corporation (SIPC), which manages a fund to protect investors from the failure of broker–dealers in the same manner as the Federal Deposit Insurance Corporation protects the customers of banks.

In 1977 Congress passed the *Foreign Corrupt Practices Act* (FCPA) in response to questionable foreign political payments by U.S. companies that were disclosed in the wake of the Watergate scandal. This act has two aspects. First, it bans bribery of foreign political parties officials, and candidates for the purpose of obtaining or retaining business and attaches strong criminal penalties to violation. Concern that fear of violating the FCPA was hindering U.S. businesses in their attempts to compete internationally led to a 1988 amendment in which Congress emphasized an exception that allows so-called grease payments to lower-level officials to expedite the processing of permits, licenses, and the like. It also provides an affirmative defense for payments that are legal under the *written* law of the foreign country and

HUMOR AND THE LAW

Dave Barry, one of America's funniest men and author of "Claw Your Way to the Top: How to Become the Head of a Major Corporation in Roughly a Week," defined *insider information* in this way: "Let's say you're working in your company's headquarters and you notice that the entire first floor is on fire. If you call your stockbroker and tell him to sell your stock, that would be insider trading. Legally you must wait until the flames are clearly visible to people on public sidewalks." Funny! And not a bad example, either.

---

allows the payment of legitimate expenses (e.g., travel expenses of a foreign official) associated with promotional activities.

The second part of the FCPA establishes stringent accounting requirements for bigger companies so that such illegal activities cannot be easily concealed. These accounting rules are not especially clear, and in 1988 Congress amended the FCPA to make it clear that penalties should not be imposed for insignificant or technical infractions or inadvertent conduct.

Although not a securities act in a strict sense, the *Racketeer Influenced and Corrupt Organizations Act of 1970* (RICO) affects the securities business. The basics of RICO were explained in Chapter 8. Because one of RICO's "predicate acts" is securities fraud, many lawsuits complaining primarily of securities law violations have been parlayed into RICO claims by aggressive prosecutors and inventive civil plaintiffs.

Of these acts, the 1933 Act and the 1934 Act remain the most important.

WHAT IS A SECURITY?

Securities are commonly thought of as the stock issued by corporations. The shares of common and preferred stock issued by corporations constitute a major type of security. These are *equity securities* which evidence an ownership interest in the corporation. Holders of equity securities are normally entitled to vote on important corporate matters and to receive dividends as their share of the corporate profits. The other major type of security is the *debt security*, such as the bond, note, or debenture. Holders of debt securities are creditors rather than owners. They have no voice in corporate affairs but are entitled to receive regular interest payments according to the terms of the bond or note.

Because the inventive human mind has devised an inordinate variety of investment interests, securities regulation goes beyond items that are clearly labeled "stocks" or "bonds." Section 2(1) of the 1933 Act broadly defines "security" to include

> any note, stock, treasury stock, bond, debenture, evidence of indebtedness, certificate of interest or participation in any profit-sharing agreement,... investment contract, voting-trust certificate, fractional undivided interest in oil, gas or other mineral rights, or, in general, any interest or instrument commonly known as a 'security.'...

This broad definition has, of necessity, been liberally construed by the courts. Interests in limited partnerships, condominiums, farm animals with accompanying agreements for their care, franchises, whiskey warehouse receipts, and many other varied items have been deemed to be securities.

The inclusion of the term *investment contract* in the 1933 Act's definition of security has produced much litigation. Some very interesting investment opportunities have been held to constitute investment contracts, as the following case illustrates.

SMITH v. GROSS

U.S. NINTH CIRCUIT COURT OF APPEALS
604 F.2d 292 (1979)

Gross used a promotional newsletter to solicit buyer–investors to raise earthworms to help him reach his quota of selling earthworms to fishermen. Buyers were promised that the seller's instructions would enable them to have a profitable worm farm, that the time required was similar to that of a garden, that the worms doubled in quantity every 60 days, and that Gross would buy back all bait-size worms produced by buyers at $2.25 per pound.

The Smiths invested but later sued claiming that contrary to Gross's representations, the worms multiplied at a maximum of eight rather than 64 times per year and that the promised profits could be achieved only if the multiplication rate were as fast as represented and Gross repurchased the Smiths' production at $2.25 per pound, which was much higher than the true market value. Gross could pay that amount only by selling the worms to new worm farmers at inflated prices.

The Smiths claimed that Gross made false representations, which violated the federal securities laws. The federal district court dismissed the action for want of subject matter jurisdiction after concluding that no "security" was involved in the case. The Smiths appealed.

PER CURIAM:

... The Smiths contend that the transactions between the parties involved an investment contract type of security. In *SEC v. W. J. Howey Co.*, 328 U.S. 293, 301 (1946), the Supreme Court set out the conditions for an investment contract: "[t]he test is whether the scheme involves [1] an investment of money [2] in a common enterprise [3] with profits to come solely from the efforts of others." This court in *SEC v. Glenn W. Turner Enterprises, Inc.*, 474 F.2d 476, 482 (9th Cir.), *cert. denied*, 414 U.S. 821 (1973), held that, despite the Supreme Court's use of the word "solely," the third element of the *Howey* test is "whether the efforts made by those other than the investor are the undeniably significant ones, those essential managerial efforts which affect the failure or success of the enterprise." The *Turner* court defined a common enterprise as "one in which the fortunes of the investor are interwoven with and dependent upon the efforts and success of

CONTINUED

those seeking the investment or of third parties."

We find this case virtually identical with *Miller v. Central Chinchilla Group, Inc.*, 494 F.2d 414 (8th Cir. 1974). In *Miller* the defendants entered into contracts under which they sold chinchillas to the plaintiffs with the promise to repurchase the offspring. The plaintiffs were told that it was simple to breed chinchillas according to the defendants' instructions and that the venture would be highly profitable. The plaintiffs alleged that the chinchillas were difficult to raise and had a high mortality rate, and that the defendants could return the promised profits only if they repurchased the offspring and sold them to other prospective chinchilla raisers at an inflated price.

The *Miller* court focused on two features in holding there was an investment contract: (1) the defendants persuaded the plaintiffs to invest by representing that the efforts required of them would be very minimal; and (2) that if the plaintiffs diligently exerted themselves, they still would not gain the promised profits because those profits could be achieved only if the defendants secured additional investors at the inflated prices. Both of these features are present in the instant case. We find *Miller* to be persuasive and consistent with *Turner*. . . .

There was a common enterprise as required by *Turner*. The Smiths alleged that, although they were free under the terms of the contract to sell their production anywhere they wished, they could have received the promised profits only if the defendants repurchased above the market price, and that the defendants could have repurchased above the market price only if the defendants secured additional investors at inflated prices. Thus, the fortune of the Smiths was interwoven with and dependent upon the efforts and success of the defendants.

We also find that here, as in *Miller* the third element of an investment contract set forth in *Turner*—that the efforts of those other than the investor are the undeniably significant ones—was present here. The *Miller* court noted that the plaintiffs there had been assured by the sellers that the effort neeeded to raise chinchillas was minimal. The significant effort necessary for success in the endeavor was that of the seller in procuring new investors who would purchase the chinchillas at inflated prices. Here, the Smiths alleged that they were promised that the effort necessary to raise worms was minimal and they alleged that they could not receive the promised income unless the defendants purchased their harvest.

We find the analysis in *Miller* persuasive and hold that the Smiths alleged facts that, if true, were sufficient to establish an investment contract. . . .

The judgment of the district court is reversed.

1933 ACT: REGULATING THE ISSUANCE OF SECURITIES

A major portion of federal securities regulation concerns the issuance of securities by companies. Congressional investigations after the 1929 stock market crash disclosed that enthusiasm for investment opportunities in the 1920s was often so great that large offerings of stock would be gobbled up by an investing public that knew virtually nothing about the selling company. The goal of the 1933 Act is to protect the investing public. The 1933 Act is a disclosure statute frequently called the "Truth in Securities" law. The Act requires full disclosure by companies wishing to issue and sell stock to the public. By requiring such companies to file a registration statement with the SEC and to use an offering circular called a **prospectus** when attempting to sell securities, the law attempts to enable the investor to make an informed decision. The SEC, which is charged with enforcement of the law, does not attempt to pass on the value of the securities offered nor to advise investors to purchase or not purchase the securities of particular companies.

The 1933 Act also protects investors by prohibiting fraud and deceit in the distribution of shares, even those that the law does not require to be registered.

REGISTRATION PROCESS

Elements of the Process

Securities are distributed much like any product. The corporation selling securities to raise capital, the *issuer*, is analogous to the manufacturer of goods. *Underwriters* act as wholesalers, *dealers* act as retailers, and the *investor* is a consumer. By regulating the activities of the issuer, underwriter, and dealer, the 1933 Act seeks to ensure that the investor has access to adequate information before purchasing a particular security.

The keystones to the disclosure process are the registration statement and the prospectus, the contents of which are discussed presently. Section 5(a) of the 1933 Act makes it unlawful to sell or deliver any security without first filing with the SEC a registration statement that has become effective. Section 5(b)(1) makes it unlawful to sell a security by means of a prospectus that does not meet statutory standards. Section 5(b)(2) makes it unlawful to sell securities that are not accompanied or preceded by a prospectus. Finally, section 5(c) makes it illegal even to *offer* to sell or buy securities before a registration statement is filed.

SEC Approval

The registration statement filed with the SEC is not automatically effective. Rather, the staff of the SEC may review the statement for omissions and inaccuracies. Some reviews may be more thorough than others. Because of budgetary cutbacks and staff reductions, the SEC in recent years has had to give cursory reviews to many registration statements, reserving the full review process primarily for statements filed by new issuers selling to the public for the first time. Indeed, today most registration statements are not reviewed at all.

Section 8(a) of the 1933 Act provides that if the SEC is silent, the registration statement automatically becomes effective on the twentieth day after its filing. The registration process may be analyzed in terms of its three major time periods. The first stage of the process is the period before the registration statement is filed (the "pre-filing" period). The second stage lasts from the filing of the statement until it becomes effective (the "waiting" period). The final stage is, of course, after the statement becomes effective (the "post-effective" period).

Pre-Filing Period: To prevent circumvention of the provisions of section 5, an issuer is strictly limited during the pre-filing period. The issuer may not sell or even offer to sell a security before the registration statement is filed. The term *offer* is broadly construed and encompasses not only formal sales campaigns, but any type of activity meant to "pre-condition" the market. A simple speech by a corporate executive or a press release about how well the company is doing may be improper if it "just happens" to be soon followed by the filing of a registration statement.

The only activities permitted during the prefiling period, other than normal advertising and communications with shareholders by an issuer, are preliminary negotiations between the issuer and underwriters. This is necessary because a large distribution of securities may require that an entire syndicate of underwriters be assembled.

Waiting Period: The purpose of the waiting period is to slow the distribution process so that the dealers and the public have time to familiarize themselves with the information disclosed in the registration process. Although no sales may be consummated during this period, certain types of offers are allowed, and underwriters may now make arrangements with dealers for their assistance in distribution.

In addition to oral offers, certain types of written offers are permissible during the waiting period. For example, an issuer may place in *The Wall Street Journal* a short announcement known as a tombstone ad because it is usually surrounded by a black border. Under SEC Rule 134, the announcement may contain only a few limited items, such as (1) the kind of security, (2) the amount, (3) by whom purchase orders will be executed, and (4) the location at which a prospectus may be obtained. The announcement must state that no offer to purchase can actually be accepted during the waiting period and that an indication of interest is not binding on a prospective investor.

Offers may also be made by use of a preliminary prospectus, which contains information from the registration statement then under review. These are called "red herring" prospectuses, because SEC Rule 430 requires that a special legend be printed in red ink on each one labeling it a preliminary prospectus, stating that a registration statement has been filed but is not yet effective, that no final sale can be made during the waiting period, and that it does not constitute an offer to sell.

Post-Effective Period: Once the registration statement becomes effective, sales of securities may be completed. However, the law still imposes requirements aimed at encouraging dissemination of information. With some exceptions, the issuer, underwriter, and dealer must provide a copy of the final prospectus with every written offer, supplemental sales literature, written confirmation of sale, or delivery of securities. The prospectus must be used as long as the distribution is taking place; if this period extends beyond nine months, section 10(a)(3) requires that the prospectus be updated to reflect more recent information on the status of the issuer. In addition, the issuer must update the prospectus whenever important new developments occur; otherwise the information can become stale and misleading, resulting in liability for fraud under section 17(a) of the 1933 Act.

Shelf Registration

Originally, an issuer was required to file a new registration statement every time it sought to initiate a new distribution of stock. However, Rule 415 now establishes a system known as **shelf registration.** Under this system a company is allowed to file one registration statement announcing its long-term plans for sales of securities. Then, whenever the company thinks market conditions and its own financial needs require the sale of securities, it can issue the additional securities without going through the registration process described above to achieve SEC approval because it already has a registration statement and a prospectus "on the shelf." If periodically updated, the registration statement will remain continuously effective. Rule 415 enhances the ability of corporations to raise capital on short notice, but its use has been restricted primarily to the larger, more reliable corporations.

DISCLOSURE REQUIREMENTS

The information disclosure requirements of the 1933 Act and the 1934 Act were for a long time separate, often overlapping, and sometimes conflicting. In recent years, the SEC has made an effort to coordinate the requirements for information disclosure contained in the two acts. The filing requirements of the 1934 Act must be mentioned here because they now bear significantly on the disclosure requirements of the 1933 Act regarding the registration statement and prospectus.

Registration and Reporting

Section 12 of the 1934 Act requires all companies whose securities are traded on the national stock exchanges (such as the New York Stock Exchange) and any other companies with more than $5 million in assets and more than 500 shareholders to register their securities with the SEC. These companies are referred to as registered or reporting companies. There are about 10,000 such companies. The required registration statement must contain extensive information about such areas as the organization, financial structure, and nature of the business, the structure of present classes of stock, the directors and officers and their remuneration, important contracts, balance sheets, and profit-and-loss statements for the three preceding fiscal years.

Section 13 requires that the registration statement be continually updated with annual reports (called 10-Ks) and quarterly reports (10-Qs). In addition, if important facts change between quarterly reports, the company should amend the registration statement by use of an 8-K report.

Integration of Registration Requirements

Despite all the information made public under the 1934 Act, even reporting companies traditionally had to go through the expensive registration process under the 1933 Act, which required disclosure of information already made public in the 1934 Act reports. Because of complaints about duplication and needless expense, the SEC changed the rules in 1982 to make disclosure requirements uniform under the 1933 and 1934 acts and to use the periodic reports of the 1934 Act to satisfy many of the disclosure requirements of the 1933 Act registration statements by a process of incorporation by reference. The core of this procedure is a three-tiered registration structure that creates three distinct categories of registration statement, depending on the issuer's financial size and reporting history. The largest, most dependable companies can file very basic prospectuses that incorporate by reference all the information contained in previously filed 1934 Act reports. Medium-sized companies with less reliable reporting histories are allowed some incorporation by reference, and the remaining companies must file full-blown prospectuses with no incorporation by reference.

Section 10 of the 1933 Act, as supplemented by various rules issued by the SEC, controls the content of the prospectus. The most important information in the registration statement regarding the financial structure, organization, operations, and officers and directors of the issuer must be summarized in the prospectus (unless incorporation by reference is allowed under the new system).

Materiality

Exactly which details must be included in the registration statement and prospectus is a matter governed not only by statutes and rules but also by the concept of **materiality.** The most important element in the disclosure provisions of both the 1933 and 1934 acts is that all matters that are important or material to an investor's decision should be disclosed. Materiality is an elusive concept, but the Supreme Court has described information as material "if there is a substantial likelihood that a reasonable shareholder would consider it important" in making an investment decision.[1] This is usually limited to matters having a significant bearing on the economic and financial performance of the company.

Examples of material facts include an erratic pattern of earnings, an intention to enter into a new line of business, adverse competitive conditions, litigation with the government that might lead to imposition of a financially damaging fine, and a substantial disparity between the price at which the shares are being offered to the public and the cost of the shares owned by officers, directors, and promoters. The following case illustrates one application of the concept of materiality in the context of the 1933 Act disclosure requirements.

---

[1] *TSC Industries, Inc. v. Northway, Inc.*, 426 U.S. 438, 449 (1976).

CASE

IN RE DOMAN HELICOPTERS, INC.

SECURITIES AND EXCHANGE COMMISSION, 41 S.E.C. 431 (1963)

Doman Helicopters, Inc., was formed in 1945 but never was able to do business on a profitable basis. Except for one experimental model sold in 1950, two prototypes delivered to the Army in 1956 and 1957 (both subsequently repurchased by Doman), and one helicopter on loan to its Italian licensee, by 1962 Doman had never manufactured or sold any helicopters. Instead, it had continually flirted with bankruptcy. By September 30, 1961, its accumulated losses totaled more than $5.7 million. On January 31, 1962, Doman's current liabilities were $292,446 while its assets were only $13,178.

On April 19, 1962, Doman filed a Form S-1 registration statement proposing to offer publicly 681,971 shares, some to current shareholders, some to creditors, and some to the public. The contemplated price was $1.50 per share. Doman's future plans were predicated on development of a proposed helicopter, the D-10B.

The SEC commenced a proceeding under section 8(d) of the 1933 Act to determine whether a stop order should issue suspending the effectiveness of Doman's registration statement. The focus of the investigation was on deficiencies in the prospectus.

THE COMMISSION:

...1. Status and Prospectus of the Model D-10B. The prospectus describes the D-10B as though it were an existing and operational helicopter possessing superiority in specified respects [economy of operation, range, payload per dollar invested] over other helicopters offered on the market.... There is no adequate factual foundation for the[se] statements, and they were false and misleading.

The D-10B has never been flown or tested or even assembled in prototype form, crucial facts which are nowhere disclosed in the registration statement.

2. The Doman Hingeless Rotor System. The prospectus makes the following claims for the so-called "Doman Hingeless Rotor System": "In comparison with other devices, this system provides greater inherent stability in forward flight, less vibration in any flight attitude or maneuver, long life for the rotor and blade assembly, relatively low initial and maintenance costs and exceptional permissible range of the center of gravity of the fuselage and its cargo."...

These representations present in their totality a misleading picture of uniqueness and substantiated superiority of the Doman rotor system. That system has been used only on a few converted or prototype models. No production model using the Doman rotor system has ever been subjected to normal day to day usage by a user or customer. In such circumstances the unqualified claims as to superior durability and lower maintenance costs were not warranted, and it was deceptive to describe the system as "fully developed and proven."...

3. Efforts to Secure Defense Contracts. The prospectus makes only a passing reference to the fact that registrant unsuccessfully attempted to secure a military market for its helicopters. It does not disclose the nature of those attempts or of the action of the Department of Defense with respect to them. Registrant had from 1951 to 1962 made strenuous and persistent efforts to interest that Department in its proposals and devices. The Department made a number of tests with the two prototype helicopters that it purchased from the registrant and made an extensive study of the Doman rotor system. It found "no significant advantages in the Doman rotor system over other types," and those findings were reaffirmed upon successive reviews following objections raised by registrant. ... Irrespective of the correctness of the Department's conclusions, they constitute a determination by the technical staff and responsible authorities of the largest single purchaser of helicopters that for their purposes registrant's rotor system had no special merit. Such determination was a significant adverse factor, and the failure to disclose it rendered the prospectus misleading.

4. Application of Proceeds. The prospectus stated that the proceeds of the offering would be used to develop the D-10B, but failed to state the order of priority in which the proceeds would be applied as required by Instruction 2 to

CONTINUED

Item 3 of Form S-1. The prospectus did not adequately disclose that except to the extent that the creditors to whom part of the offering is to be made elected to take stock in exchange for their debt claims, $292,466 of the proceeds from the public offering would first have to be applied to the liquidation of registrant's outstanding indebtedness, thereby reducing and perhaps exhausting the funds that the prospectus stated would be allocated to the D-10B. It also failed to disclose that approximately $13,000 of the estimated proceeds would have to be used to pay the accrued salaries of certain officers and directors, and that a large portion of the proceeds would have to be used to meet current expenses, which were being incurred at the rate of $11,000 per month, and would be used for that purpose even if the proceeds of the offering were insufficient to permit registrant to go forward with its D-10B program.

5. Dilution Aspects of Offering. The prospectus fails to disclose the dilution aspects of the offering. As of January 31, 1962, registrant's shares had a book value of minus 30 cents per share. If all the shares that the registrant proposes to offer to its existing stockholders and to its creditors were in fact sold at the proposed offering prices, that book value would increase to 55 cents per share. Purchasers paying $1.50 per share would therefore suffer an immediate dilution of 95 cents per share, the benefit of which will inure entirely to the present stockholders. It was pertinent to an informed appraisal by the persons to whom the securities being offered may be sold that this dilution be described in the prospectus....

A stop order will issue.

EXEMPTIONS

In certain situations where there is less need for regulation, sections 3 and 4 of the 1933 Act provide exemptions from section 5's registration requirements (although not from the antifraud provisions of the 1933 and 1934 acts).

Perhaps the most important exemption is that for "transactions by any person other than an issuer, underwriter, or dealer" provided by section 4(1). This simply means that once the issue is sold to the investing public, the public may trade, and the dealers may handle most transactions, without any worry about registration or prospectus delivery requirements. Thus, the 1933 Act does not generally apply to so-called secondary trading, which is regulated by the 1934 Act.

Section 3(a) exempts from registration the securities of governments (state and federal), charitable organizations, banks, savings and loans, and common carriers, which are regulated under other federal laws.

Small Issues

There are also exemptions for small issues and small issuers. Section 4(2) exempts "transactions by an issuer not involving any public offering," an exemption used primarily in connection with (1) bank loans, (2) privately negotiated sales of securities to large institutional investors (private placements), and (3) the promotion of business ventures by a few closely related persons. Section 3(b) authorizes the SEC to exempt securities if it finds that registration "is not necessary in the public interest and for the protection of investors by reason of the small amount involved [a $5 million ceiling] or the limited character of the public offering."

Regulation D: The SEC's Regulation D fleshes out the 3(b) exemption in Rules 504 and 505 and the 4(2) exemption in Rule 506. Rule 504 exempts from registration any offering in a 12-month period totalling less than $1 million (reduced by amounts sold in reliance on other exemptions). This exemption is aimed at smaller businesses and is not available to 1934 Act reporting companies.

Rule 505 allows a company, including reporting companies, to sell up to $5 million in securities (reduced by amounts sold in reliance on other exemptions) in any 12-month period without registering, provided the sales are to no more than 35 unaccredited investors. **Accredited investors** are persons and institutions—such as pension funds, banks, corporate insiders, and millionaires—who because of their very nature are unlikely to need government protection in making investment decisions. The number of sales to accredited investors is not limited, although no general advertising or soliciting is allowed.

Rule 506 allows all companies to sell an unlimited amount of securities in an issuance where sales are limited to 35 unaccredited investors, if the issuer makes a determination that all purchasers are "sophisticated" and therefore capable of protecting themselves without the assistance of a registration statement and prospectus. Accredited investors are assumed to be sophisticated, and an unsophisticated purchaser may act through a sophisticated purchaser representative. As with Rule 505, no general advertising or soliciting is allowed, which is why these are often called "private placement" offerings. Typically, an issuer, rather than offering shares to the open market, will place them through private direct negotiations with an institutional investor, such as an insurance company.

Local Offerings

A final important exemption is section 3(a)(11)'s exemption for intrastate offerings, which applies where a selling company doing business in a state offers and sells securities only to residents of the same state and intends to use the proceeds there. An issuer, according to Rule 147, is doing business within a state if (1) it derives 80 percent or more of its revenue from operations within the state, (2) at least 80 percent of its assets are located within the state, (3) at least 80 percent of the net proceeds of the issuance will be used within the state, and (4) the issuer's principal office is located there. Offer of the shares for sale to a single nonresident will void the exemption. Federal regulation is deemed unnecessary because of the availability of state regulation and the close proximity of purchaser to seller.

Institutional Investors

Buyers of private placement securities under Rule 506 have traditionally been hindered in attempts to resell them. To encourage trading in the private placement markets by large institutional investors, in 1990 the SEC adopted Rule 144A, which exempts a sale of securities so long as (1) they are not of the same class as those listed on an exchange or quoted on NASDAQ—the National Association of Securities Dealers Automated Quotation system; (2) the buyer is a qualified institutional buyer (QIB); and (3) the seller and prospective purchaser may request basic financial information from an issuer. A QIB must in the aggregate own and invest at least $100 million, ensuring that QIBs are large institutions that can take care of themselves. Rule 144A functionally allows large investors to trade among themselves without worrying about registration and disclosure requirements.

ENFORCEMENT AND CIVIL LIABILITIES

Government Action

The SEC has numerous powers to enforce compliance with the provisions of the 1933 Act. For example, if the SEC believes that a registration statement is incomplete or inaccurate, section 8(b) authorizes issuance of a "refusal order," which prevents the statement from becoming effective until SEC objections are satisfied. If inaccuracies are discovered after the effective date, the SEC may issue a "stop order" pursuant to section 8(d), as was done in the *Doman Helicopters* case, to suspend the effectiveness of the statement. Section 8(e) authorizes the SEC to conduct an "examination" to fully investigate whether a stop order should issue.

More generally, section 19(b) gives the SEC power of subpoena to aid investigations of any potential violation of the 1933 Act. Section 20(b) allows the SEC to go into federal district court to seek an injunction whenever it appears that any person is violating the 1933 Act.

The 1933 Act even contains criminal provisions. Section 24 provides that any person who willfully violates any provision of the act or any SEC rule or any person who willfully makes an untrue statement or omits a material fact in a registration statement is subject to a fine of not more than $10,000, imprisonment of not more than five years, or both.

Private Suit

The 1933 Act provides remedies for violation of its provisions in the form of lawsuits that may be brought by injured investors.

Section 11: An investor who is injured after buying securities with reliance on a rosy picture falsely painted in a prospectus will probably not be satisfied with the SEC's injunction remedy or even criminal prosecution. The investor will desire to recoup losses through a civil action for damages, and the 1933 Act has express provision for such lawsuits. Section 11 states that if "any part of the registration statement, when such part became effective, contained an untrue statement of a material fact or omitted to state a material fact required to be stated therein or necessary to make the statements therein not misleading, any person acquiring such security" may file a civil action. Potential defendants in such an action include every person who signed the registration statement (which includes the issuer, its principal executive officers, chief financial officer, principal accounting officers, and most of the board of directors), every person who was a director or identified as about to become a director, every accountant, every appraiser or other expert who is named as having helped prepare it, and every underwriter.

The section 11 cause of action is loosely patterned after a common-law fraud action but is modified to greatly ease a plaintiff's burdens in seeking recovery. For example, the common-law fraud elements of privity of contract and reliance are not necessary in a section 11 claim so long as plaintiff can trace the purchased shares back to the defective offering and show they were not previously issued shares of the same company being publicly traded at the same time.

If plaintiff proves the registration statement contained misstatements or omissions of material facts, the law presumes that these caused plaintiff's damages, and the burden of proof shifts to defendants to prove that other factors were the true cause of plaintiff's losses.

Furthermore, section 11 does not require proof of fraudulent intent. Proof of misstatement or omission shifts the burden of proof to defendants to establish that they were guilty of neither fraudulent intent nor negligence in preparing the registration statement. Individual defendants must establish that they used "due diligence" in preparing the registration statement. The amount of diligence that is due from a defendant depends on his or her position as an "insider" (with full access to key information) or an "outsider," and a defendant is generally allowed to rely on "expertised" portions of the statement—those portions prepared by experts such as independent auditors. The due diligence defense is not available to the issuing company, which is strictly liable for inaccuracies in the registration statement.

Section 12: Complementing section 11 are section 12(1), which allows an investor to recover when offers or sales are made in violation of section 5 (that is, without the filing of a registration statement, by use of a defective prospectus, or where securities are delivered without an accompanying prospectus), and section 12(2), which allows recovery by investors injured by misrepresentations made outside a prospectus (such as in an oral sales pitch or in literature accompanying an unregistered offering). The elements of recovery and defenses in section 12 suits are roughly the same as under section 11, although the range of potential defendants is limited to "sellers" of securities—those who actually pass title or those who "solicit" transactions, such as brokers and dealers.

1934 ACT: REGULATING THE TRADING OF SECURITIES

Although the 1933 Act regulates primarily the initial issuance of securities, the 1934 Act regulates the subsequent trading of those securities. An array of complex problems comes within the purview of the 1934 Act. The general registration and reporting requirements of the 1934 Act have already been discussed. Attention is now turned to several other major concerns of the act.

INSIDER TRADING

Knowledge of the inner workings of a corporation can be very valuable in making investment decisions. For example, if a corporate vice-president learned that his company's scientists had just been granted an important patent that will open up a new sales field, he would have a distinct and arguably unfair trading advantage over the general investing public. Insider trading was a widespread phenomenon in the 1920s, yet the common law provided little protection from such abusive practices.

Section 16(b)

One response to the insider trading problem is section 16 of the 1934 Act, which applies to three categories of persons: officers, directors, and owners of more than 10 percent of the shares of any one class of stock of a 1934 reporting company. Thus, the provision applies only to persons reasonably assumed to have influence in and therefore access to inside information of large, publicly traded companies. Subsection (1) of section 16 requires that these three categories of "insider" file three types of reports with the SEC. The two most important are an initial report revealing the holdings when a director or officer takes office or when a stockholder first obtains a 10 percent holding, and an additional report each month thereafter in which a change in holdings occurs. Because many insiders had been lax in filing such reports, in 1991 the SEC added a requirement that in their proxy statements sent to shareholders, issuers list any insiders who did not comply with section 16(a).

Subsection (b) of section 16 provides that any profits realized (or losses avoided) by such an insider in connection with a purchase and sale (or sale and purchase) within a six-month period is an illegal "short-swing" profit. Any such profit may be recovered on the issuer's behalf. The striking thing about section 16(b) is the near absolute nature of the liability it imposes. Thus, assume that Sherry, a director of ABC Co., buys ABC shares on January 1. If she sells any ABC shares (not necessarily the same ones she bought on January 1) within six months thereafter at a higher price than she purchased, she is liable to forfeit her profit *even if* she did not use any inside information. A classic section 16(b) case follows.

CASE

SMOLOWE v. DELENDO CORPORATION

U.S. COURT OF APPEALS, SECOND CIRCUIT 136 F.2d 231 (1943)

Litigation over a tax claim disrupted Delendo Corp.'s negotiations for sale of its assets to Schenley Distillers. Four years later, negotiations were reopened and the sale was completed on April 30, 1940. In the six months before the sale, defendants Seskis and Kaplan—both officers, directors, and major shareholders of Delendo—bought Delendo shares, which they then sold at substantial profits in the Schenley deal. Plaintiff shareholders of Delendo sued to recover those profits for the benefit of the corporation, apparently claiming that Seskis and Kaplan had inside information that the tax problem with the government was being negotiated away, thus clearing the way for the profitable sale of assets.

The defendants claimed they did not use inside information in making their purchases, thus raising the issue of whether such use is a necessary element of recovery in a section 16(b) claim. The trial court ruled for the plaintiffs; the defendants appealed.

CLARK, CIRCUIT JUDGE:

The primary purpose of the Securities Exchange Act . . . was to insure a fair and honest market, that is, one which would reflect an evaluation of securities in the light of all available and pertinent data. Furthermore, the Congressional hearings indicate that Sec. 16(b), specifically, was designed to protect the "outsider" stockholders against at least short-swing speculation by insiders with advance information. It is apparent too, from the language of Sec. 16(b) itself, as well as from the Congressional hearings, that the only remedy which its framers deemed effective for this reform was the imposition of a liability based upon an objective measure of proof. This is graphically stated in the testimony of Mr. Corcoran, chief spokesman for the drafters and proponents of the Act, in Hearings before the Committee on Banking and Currency: "You hold the director, irrespective of any intention or expectation to sell the security within six months after, because it will be absolutely impossible to prove the existence of such intention or expectation, and you have to have this crude rule of thumb, because you cannot undertake the burden of having to prove that the director intended, at the time he bought, to get out on a short swing."

A subjective standard of proof, requiring a showing of an actual unfair use of inside information, would render senseless the provisions of the legislation limiting the liability period to six months, making an intention to profit during the period immaterial, and exempting transactions wherein there is a bona fide acquisition of stock in connection with a previously contracted debt. . . . And its total effect would be to render the statute little more of an incentive to insiders to refrain from profiteering at the expense of the outside stockholders than are the common law rules of liability; it would impose a more stringent statute of limitations upon the party aggrieved at the same time that it allowed the wrongdoer to share in the spoils of recovery. Had Congress intended that only profits from an actual misuse of inside information should be recoverable, it would have been simple enough to say so.

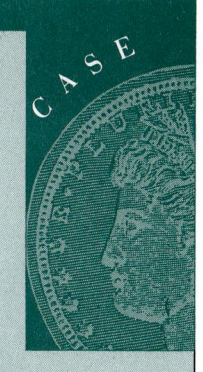

The present case would seem to be of the type which the statute was designed to include. Here it is conceded that the defendants did not make unfair use of information they possessed as officers at the time of the transactions. When these began they had no offer from Schenley. But they knew they were pressing the tax suit; and they, of course, knew of the corporate offer to settle it which reestablished the offer to purchase and led to the favorable sale. It is naive to suppose that their knowledge of their own plans as officers did not give them most valuable inside knowledge as to what would probably happen to the stock in which they were dealing. It is difficult to find this use "unfair" in the sense of illegal; it is certainly an advantage and a temptation within the general scope of the legislature's intended prohibition.

Affirmed.

Section 10(b)

Another provison of the 1934 Act that regulates insider trading, as well as many other facets of securities trading, is section 10(b). This provision makes it unlawful to "use or employ, in connection with the purchase or sale of any security, ... any manipulative or deceptive device or contrivance in contravention of such rules and regulations as the Commission may prescribe...."

Pursuant to section 10(b), the SEC has issued the most famous of all its rules, Rule 10b-5, quoted in full:

> It shall be unlawful for any person, directly or indirectly, by the use of any means or instrumentality of interstate commerce, or of the mails, or of any facility of any national securities exchange,
> (1) to employ any device, scheme or artifice to defraud,
> (2) to make any untrue statement of a material fact or to omit to state a material fact necessary in order to make the statements made, in the light of the circumstances under which they were made, not misleading, or
> (3) to engage in any act, practice, or course of business which operates or would operate as a fraud or deceit upon any person, in connection with the purchase or sale of any security.

General Provisions: One important category of Rule 10b-5 cases involves insider trading. Although a section 10(b) case is more difficult to prove, its coverage is broader than section 16(b)'s. The broad purpose of section 10(b) and Rule 10b-5 is to protect the investing public by preventing fraud and equalizing access to material information. Section 10(b) applies to any purchase or sale by any person of any security—there are no exceptions. Thus, small close corporations (the shares of which are not offered to the public for sale but are typically held by just a few, perhaps members of a single family) are covered as well as the largest public corporations. Transactions covered include those occurring on the stock exchanges, in over-the-counter sales through stockbrokers, or even in privately negotiated sales. Any person connected with the transaction is regulated, not only insiders as in section 16(b).

Unlike section 16(b), section 10(b) requires proof of actual use of inside information to establish a violation. There is no automatic presumption. Furthermore, the information must be material, and it must be nonpublic.

Enforcement: A willful violation of any provision of the 1934 Act, including those banning insider trading, subjects the violator to the criminal provisions of section 32, which carry penalties of imprisonment up to 10 years and/or a fine of up to $1 million for individuals and $2.5 million for partnerships or corporations.

The SEC refers criminal cases to the Department of Justice for prosecution. But the SEC itself can take steps against inside traders. It can hold disciplinary proceedings if a regulated broker, dealer, or underwriter is involved. It can go to federal district court to obtain an injunction to halt illegal practices and perhaps an order rescinding the fraudulent sale. In 1988, the SEC was authorized to seek civil fines against securities firms that "knowingly and recklessly" fail to properly supervise their employees who engage in insider trading. Additionally, the SEC is authorized in civil insider trading cases to seek relief in the form of disgorgement of illicit profits and assessment of a civil penalty of up to three times the profit gained or loss avoided. Pursuant to these provisions, infamous arbitrageur Ivan Boesky consented to disgorge insider trading profits of $50 million and to pay a civil fine of $100 million.

In 1990, the SEC was further authorized to issue its own "cease and desist" orders to persons engaged in illicit activity and to seek *civil* fines in court ranging up to $100,000 for each violation by individuals and $500,000 for each violation by organizations. Although the insider trading scandals of the 1980s largely prompted this new legislation, these new SEC powers apply to virtually any violation of any federal securities law.

In addition to government civil and criminal actions, a private civil lawsuit for damages may be brought by victims of fraud, such as insider trading, against the perpetrators. Although the 1934 Act does not explicitly provide for such a right of action, the courts have implied one since 1946.[2] Private lawsuits brought under section 10(b) and Rule 10b-5 in the 1960s and 1970s dramatically altered the law of securities regulation in the United States.

Potential Defendants:

The key to insider trading liability is the "disclose or abstain" rule, which requires that certain persons either disclose material nonpublic information that they possess or abstain from trading in the relevant company's stock until that information becomes public. The disclose or abstain rule promotes fairness in securities trading by equalizing *access* to important information affecting the value of securities. Equal information is not the goal, only equal access. Although the goal cannot be perfectly achieved, small investors will likely be more willing to enter the market if they know the SEC is actively promoting equal access.

Four major categories of persons owe a duty to disclose or abstain. First, such a duty clearly applies to corporate "insiders," a term defined more broadly than in the section 16 provisions to include any corporate employee with access to material inside informtion, not just officers and directors.

A second major category of potential insider trading defendant are "temporary insider." These are persons who receive confidential corporate information for a corporate purpose and with the expectation that it will be kept confidential but then use it in insider trading. Classic examples are attorneys, accountants, and investment bankers hired temporarily by a corporation. For example, if an attorney is hired to help Corporation A merge with Corporation B and the attorney realizes that this will be a very

---

[2] *Kardon v. National Gypsum Co.*, 69 F. Supp. 512 (E.D.Pa. 1946).

favorable arrangement for Corporation A, he or she may be tempted to trade in its stock. That would be illegal so long as the information is nonpublic.

A third category of potential insider trading defendant consists of "misappropriators"—noninsiders who steal confidential inside information. The "disclose or abstain" obligation must rest on a *duty* to someone. Insiders, their tippees, and temporary insiders all owe a duty to the corporation in whose shares they trade. It can be a little more elusive to determine the duty owed by a misappropriator. The misappropriation theory was used by the lower courts to criminally convict a *Wall Street Journal* reporter who secretly leaked information about articles the newspaper was about to publish to confederates who traded profitably on the information. In *Carpenter v. United States*, 484 U.S. 19 (1987), the Supreme Court addressed the misappropriation theory and split 4–4 in a vote on its validity, although the Court affirmed the conviction on the basis of the federal wire fraud statute.

Fourth, a "tippee" of any of the first three categories also owes a duty to disclose or abstain. Unless tippees are covered, a corporate president could tip his or her spouse and then enjoy the fruits of the spouse's trading. The Supreme Court has held that a tippee cannot be liable for insider trading unless he or she knows that the tipper breached a duty in passing along the information.[3] Such a breach occurs if the information is passed for a personal benefit (whether monetary or otherwise) rather than for a corporate purpose.

The "misappropriation" category of insider trading is the most controversial and is illustrated in the following case.

S.E.C. v. CHERIF

U.S. Court of Appeals, Seventh Circuit 933 F.2d 403 (1991)

Defendant Cherif worked for the First National Bank of Chicago until he was terminated in late 1987. He had a magnetic identification card that allowed him to enter the bank after normal business hours. He was supposed to surrender the card on termination. Instead, Cherif persuaded a bank secretary with whom he was romantically involved to type a fake memorandum that led to this card being reactivated. During the year after his termination, Cherif used this card 30 times to enter the bank on nights and weekends. He went to the Special Finance Department of the bank, which assisted in tender offers, corporate restructurings, and leveraged buyouts. He discovered confidential information about upcoming deals that had not been publicly announced. He then would buy stock in the companies involved in the proposed deals, selling his shares after the price rose following public announcement. Cherif profited more than $200,000.

The SEC brought this civil enforcement

CONTINUED

---

[3] *Dirks v. SEC*, 463 U.S. 646 (1983).

action against Cherif claiming, **inter alia,** *that he had violated section 10(b) and Rule 10b-5. The trial court held that Cherif had committed such violations. Cherif appealed.*

CUMMINGS, CIRCUIT JUDGE:

The "classical" theory [of insider trading] brings corporation insiders and tippees of those insiders within the ambit of Rule 10b-5. Under the classical theory, a person violates the rule when he or she buys or sells securities on the basis of material, non-public information and at the same time is an insider of the corporation whose securities are traded, or a tippee who knows or should know of the insider's breach. The theory is that an insider owes a fiduciary duty to the corporation's shareholders not to trade on inside information for his personal benefit. A tippee of an insider owes a fiduciary duty which is derivative of the duty owed by the insider.

The misappropriation theory extends the reach of Rule 10b-5 to outsiders who would not ordinarily be deemed fiduciaries of the corporate entities in whose stock they trade. The misappropriation theory focuses not on the insider's fiduciary duty to the issuing company or its shareholders but on whether the insider breached a fiduciary duty to any lawful possessor of material non-public information.

[I]n *SEC v. Materia,* 745 F.2d 197 (2d Cir. 1984), the employee of a financial printer was held liable under Rule 10b-5 for trading upon information the printing company had acquired in confidence from its clients. The Second Circuit found that Materia had perpetrated a fraud upon this employer by misappropriating information entrusted to the printing company. ("By purloining and trading on confidences entrusted to [the printer], it cannot be gainsaid that Materia undermined his employer's integrity.").

There is a common sense notion of fraud behind the misappropriation theory. As the court [in *SEC v. Clark,* 915 F.2d 439 (9th Cir. 1990)] put it: "[B]y becoming part of a fiduciary or similar relationship, an individual is implicitly stating that she will not divulge or use to her own advantage information entrusted to her in the utmost confidence. She deceives the other party by playing the role of the trustworthy employee or agent; she defrauds it by actually using the stolen information to its detriment."

The only possible barrier to application of the misappropriation theory to Cherif's case is, as Cherif points out, the fact that his employment with First Chicago ended before he stole and traded upon inside information. Cherif argues that no fiduciary duty existed between him and his employer at any time after December 1987, when he began to obtain information about upcoming transactions from the Specialized Finance Department.

As an initial matter, Cherif misconstrues the nature of his duty to First Chicago. He argues that the terms of the bank's "integrity policy" [which explicitly identified its "internal policies" as confidential information which "should not be utilized for personal gain"] only prevented him from using information specifically about future transactions obtained while he was on the job. He also believes that the use of such inside information was restricted only to the term of his employment.

Notwithstanding the contractual agreement, Cherif was bound by a broader common law duty. The common law duty obligates an employee to protect any confidential information entrusted to him by his employer during his employment. In addition, an employee is obligated to continue to protect such information after his termination.

Cherif betrayed a trust in a way that a mere thief does not. He used property and information belonging to First Chicago, and made available to him only through his fiduciary relationship, against the bank's own interests. His actions were fraudulent in the common understanding of the word because they deprived some person of something by "trick, deceit, chicane or overreaching." *McNally v. United States,* 483 U.S. 350 (1987). Cherif may have eroded client confidence in First Chicago, by suggesting the company's susceptibility to treachery from within. We have little difficulty concluding that his course of conduct was fraudulent within the meaning of Rule 10b-5.

Affirmed.

Note: Cherif was also *criminally* convicted of mail and wire fraud in connection with these transactions. *United States v. Cherif,* 943 F.2d 692 (7th Cir. 1991).

FALSE OR INADEQUATE CORPORATE DISCLOSURES

A second major category of section 10(b) cases relates to disclosures of information about corporations. Already noted are the registration and reporting requirements of the 1934 Act. The registration forms—the 10-Ks, 10-Qs, and 8-Ks—are all designed to promote full disclosure of information important to the investing public. When a corporation or some person fraudulently misstates or fails to disclose material information, a section 10(b) violation may occur.[4]

An investor who is injured because he or she bought or sold shares on the basis of inaccurate or incomplete corporate information may bring a private cause of action under the antifraud provisions of section 10(b). The requirements of a valid claim in such a lawsuit are patterned after those of common-law fraud: (1) a misrepresentation of material fact, (2) made by defendant with knowledge of the falsity, (3) an intent to induce the plaintiff to rely, (4) actual reliance by the plaintiff, (5) privity of contract between the plaintiff and the defendant, and (6) damage sustained. Modification of some of these common-law elements has been a source of controversy in this type of section 10(b) case.

Privity

Privity of contract has been largely eliminated as a requirement of a section 10(b) cause of action in the corporate disclosure setting. An injured shareholder is normally allowed to sue those persons responsible for false statements whether or not the stockholder purchase shares from or sold shares to the defendants.

Intent

Actual intent to defraud arising from knowledge of the falsity of a statement is a traditional element of common-law fraud. To advance the remedial purposes of the 1934 Act, many lower courts formerly interpreted section 10(b) to virtually eliminate the requirement of intent by holding defendants liable although they were guilty of nothing more than simple negligence.

The Supreme Court overruled these cases, however, in *Ernst & Ernst v. Hochfelder*, 425 U.S. 185 (1976). There the Court held that the defendant accounting firm was not liable for a section 10(b) violation "in the absence of any allegation of scienter—intent to deceive, manipulate, or defraud."

The question has subsequently arisen as to whether a defendant should be liable if guilty of "recklessness," which means being highly negligent or so careless as to exhibit a complete disregard for possible damage to others. Most lower courts have concluded that reckless conduct is sufficient for imposition of liability, although the Supreme Court has not spoken on the issue.

---

[4] False or misleading statements in documents filed with the SEC may also lead to liability under section 18(a) of the 1934 Act.

Reliance

In a common-law fraud case, the plaintiff must normally prove that the defendant's fraudulent statement was relied on in making the sale or purchase. To advance the broadly remedial purposes of the 1934 Act, some adjustments have been made to the traditional reliance requirement.

A misleading corporate disclosure can occur either when a material fact is concealed or when it is misrepresented. Because it is impractical to require an investor to prove reliance on a fact that was concealed from him or her, the Supreme Court has eliminated the reliance requirement in concealment cases. In *Affiliated Ute Citizens v. United States*, 406 U.S. 128 (1972), the plaintiffs, mixed-blood Ute Indians, sold shares in the Ute Development Corporation through the defendants, bank officials. The defendants failed to disclose to the plaintiffs their own interest in the transactions or the fact that shares were trading at higher prices among whites. The Court held:

> Under the circumstances of this case, involving primarily a failure to disclose, positive proof of reliance is not a prerequisite to recovery. All that is necessary is that the facts withheld be material in the sense that a reasonable investor might have considered them important in the making of this decision. This obligation to disclose and this withholding of a material fact establish the requisite element of causation in fact.

In cases of active misrepresentation, proof of reliance is practicable; nonetheless, there have been some important modifications of the reliance requirements even in misrepresentation cases, due partly to the impersonal nature of transactions that occur through the stock exchanges. The leading case follows.

BASIC, INC. v. LEVINSON

U.S. SUPREME COURT, 485 U.S. 224 (1988)

In 1965, Combustion Engineering, Inc., expressed an interest in acquiring Basic, Inc. That interest was reawakened by regulatory developments in late 1976. Beginning in September 1976, Combustion representatives had meetings and phone calls with Basic officers and directors about a possible merger. During 1977 and 1978, Basic made three public statements denying that it was engaged in merger negotiations. On December 18, 1978, Basic was asked by the New York Stock Exchange to suspend trading in its shares. It issued a press release stating that it had been "approached" about a merger. On December 19, Basic's board accepted Combustion's offer, and this was publicly announced on December 20.

Former Basic shareholders (respondents), who sold their stock after Basic's first denial that it was engaged in merger talks (October 21, 1977) and before the suspension of trading, sued Basic and its directors (petitioners). The respondents claim that petitioners' misleading statements caused them to miss the opportunity to sell at the higher merger price, in violation of section 10(b) of the 1934 Securities Act.

The district court (1) granted class action status to the respondents, adopting a presumption that they had relied on

CONTINUED

petitioners' public statements thereby satisfying the "common question of fact or law" requirement of the Federal Rules of Civil Procedure; and (2) granted summary judgment to petitioners on the merits, holding that petitioners had no obligation to disclose the ongoing merger negotiations.

The circuit court affirmed on the class action issue, adopting the district court's "fraud on the market" theory, but reversed on the merits, finding that a duty to disclose the merger talks might have existed. Petitioners appealed.

BLACKMUN, JUSTICE:

[The Supreme Court first rejected the circuit court's resolution of the merits of the case. Unlike the circuit court, which held that almost any misleading statement about merger negotiations could be material, the Supreme Court held that materiality must depend on a balancing of (1) the indicated probability that the merger will occur, and (2) the anticipated magnitude of the merger in light of the totality of the company's activities. It then catalogued various factors, such as board resolutions and instructions to investment bankers (which might show probability that the merger would occur) and the size of the corporations involved and of the premium over market price being discussed (which might show magnitude of the event), for lower courts to consider in applying its subjective, fact-specific approach.]

We turn to the question of reliance and the fraud-on-the-market theory. Succinctly put:

The fraud-on-the-market theory is based on the hypothesis that, in an open and developed securities market, the price of a company's stock is determined by the available material information regarding the company and its business. . . . Misleading statements will therefore defraud purchasers of stock even if the purchasers do not directly rely on the misstatements. . . . The causal connection between the defendants' fraud and the plaintiffs' purchase of stock in such a case is no less significant than in a case of direct reliance on misrepresentations. *Peil v. Speiser*, 806 F.2d 1154, 1160–1161 (CA3 1986).

We agree that reliance is an element of a rule 10b-5 cause of action. See *Ernst & Ernst v. Hochfelder*, 425 U.S. [185], at 206 [(1976)]. Reliance provides the requisite causal connection between a defendant's misrepresentation and a plaintiff's injury. . . . There is, however, more than one way to demonstrate the casual connection. . . .

The modern securities markets, literally involving millions of shares changing hands daily, differ from the face-to-face transactions contemplated by early fraud cases [that required a showing of privity], and our understanding of Rule 10b-5's reliance requirement must encompass these differences.

In face-to-face transactions, the inquiry into an investor's reliance upon information is into the subjective pricing of that information by that investor. With the presence of a market, the market is interposed between the seller and buyer and, ideally, transmits information to the investor in the processed form of a market price. Thus the market is performing a substantial part of the valuation process performed by the investor in a face-to-face transaction. The market is acting as the unpaid agent of the investor, informing him that given all the information available to it, the value of the stock is worth the market price. *In re LTV Securities Litigation*, 88 F.R.d. 134, 143 (N.D. Tex. 1980).

. . . Requiring a plaintiff to show a speculative state of facts, *i.e.*, how he would have acted if omitted material information had been disclosed, . . . or if the misrepresentation had not been made . . . would place an unnecessarily unrealistic evidentiary burden on the Rule 10b-5 plaintiff who has traded on an impersonal market.

The presumption of reliance employed in this case is consistent with, and, by facilitating Rule 10b-5 litigation, supports the congressional policy embodied in the 1934 Act. In drafting that Act, Congress expressly relied on the premise that securities markets are affected by information, and enacted legislation to facilitate an investor's reliance on the integrity of those markets. . . .

The presumption is also supported by common sense and probability. Recent empirical studies have tended to confirm Congress' premise that the market price of shares traded on well-developed markets reflects all publicly available information, and, hence, any material

CONTINUED

> misrepresentation. It has been noted that "it is hard to imagine that there ever is a buyer or seller who does not rely on market integrity. Who would knowingly roll the dice in a crooked crap game?" *Schlanger v. Four Phase Systems, Inc.*, 555 F.Supp. 535, 538 (SDNY 1982)....
>
> Any showing that severs the link between the alleged misrepresentation and either the price received (or paid) by the plaintiff, or his decision to trade at a fair market price, will be sufficient to rebut the presumption of reliance.
>
> [Court of Appeals' judgment is vacated and remanded.]

Although the outer limit of permissible 10b-5 actions is not completely settled, the Supreme Court has attempted to confine the actions to situations involving deceit and manipulation. Simple corporate mismanagement or breaches of fiduciary duty by corporate officials, not involving deceit, are not actionable under Rule 10b-5.[5]

PROXY REGULATION

Although most corporate decisions are made by the officers and directors, shareholders do occasionally vote on matters of importance. At the annual shareholders meeting, that state incorporation laws require be held, the shareholders elect directors to the board of directors. Their approval may also be required for certain extraordinary matters, such as amendments to corporate bylaws or articles of incorporation, mergers, or sales of major assets.

Valid shareholder approval requires at least a majority vote (and sometimes a two-thirds or three-fourths approval) of a quorum of shares eligible to vote. However, in a large corporation with thousands of shareholders, it is very unusual for more than a small percentage of shareholders to appear at the annual meeting. To obtain a quorum, corporate management is usually required to solicit *proxies* from the shareholders. A **proxy** is an authorization to vote shares owned by someone else. At a typical corporation's annual meeting, incumbent management will solicit and receive proxies from a sufficient number of shareholders to vote itself into control for another year.

Section 14(a) of the 1934 Act prohibits solicitation of proxies for any shares registered under the act in contravention of rules promulgated by the SEC. The rules that the SEC has issued have three broad goals: full disclosure, fraud prevention, and increased shareholder participation.

Full Disclosure

State laws have not always required corporate management to be responsive to the informational needs and desires of shareholders. The SEC, knowing that most major corporations solicit proxies at least annually, requires

---
[5] *Santa Fe Industries v. Green*, 430 U.S. 462 (1977).

in Rule 14a-3 that no soliciting occur unless each person solicited is furnished with a written proxy statement containing the information specified in Schedule 14A.

Schedule 14A contains more than 20 items, some of which are applicable only if specified matters, such as merger approval, are involved. In the typical solicitation by management relating to election of directors, the proxy statement must be accompanied by an annual report to contain, *inter alia,* comparative financial statements for the last two fiscal years, a summary of operations, a brief description of the business done by the issuer and its subsidiaries, and identification of the issuer's directors and executive officers and their principal occupations. This information must be clearly presented.

Proxy Contests

Normally, incumbent management will face no organized opposition in the election of directors at the annual meeting. But if the corporation is floundering financially, perhaps a group of "insurgent" shareholders will attempt to elect its own slate of candidates to the board of directors. Or perhaps the insurgents have lined up a merger with or tendered their shares to another corporation, which intends to fire incumbent management, and incumbent management has negotiated a proposed defensive merger with yet another company, which would be willing to retain the incumbents in their present positions. In these and other situations, proxy contests arise over the control of the corporation. Incumbent management and insurgent shareholders vie for sufficient proxies to prevail in the shareholders' vote. Federal regulations specify the procedure for such contests and punish any fraud that may occur.

Before solicitation, Rule 14a-11 requires insurgents to file an informational statement with the SEC and exchanges disclosing the participants in the insurgent group—those persons soliciting the proxies, financing the effort, or serving as attorneys and accountants for the group. Schedule 14B sets out the information that must be disclosed about the participants, including their employment history, past criminal violations, and stock holdings. At the time of solicitation, the insurgents must provide the shareholders with their own proxy statement similar to that which management is required to provide.

Antifraud: Proxy contests sometimes become quite heated. To prevent fraud, Rule 14a-9 prohibits the use of false or misleading statements to solicit proxies. The term *solicitation* is broadly defined to cover both statements seeking proxies and communications urging shareholders to refuse to give proxies. Thus, if incumbent management falsely states or omits to state a material fact in urging shareholders not to grant proxies to an insurgent group, a violation of Rule 14a-9 and section 14(a) occurs. A private cause of action is available to remedy such a violation.

TENDER OFFERS

A final important area of federal securities law regulates a method of taking control of a corporation, called a **tender offer.** In a typical tender offer, one corporation (the "offeror") will publicly offer to purchase a controlling interest (more than 50 percent of the shares) in another corporation (the "target"). The target's shareholders are invited to tender their shares to the offeror in return for cash or the offeror's equity or debt securities (or a combination) in an amount usually well above the prior market price of the target's stock.

Because of the easy availability of credit then and lack of government regulation, the tender offer gained widespread usage in the 1960s. One variety, termed the *Saturday Night Special,* featured a "take-it-or-leave-it" offer to the target's shareholders with a very short time for them to make up their minds. Afraid of losing an opportunity to sell their shares at above the market price, shareholders frequently would tender their shares without time to learn anything about the offeror or to evaluate the possibility of a higher offer from a different source.

Federal Legislation

Comprehensive federal regulation of tender offers began with the passage of the Williams Act in 1968. That act amended sections 13 and 14 of the 1934 Act with the basic purpose of increasing both the amount of information flowing to target shareholders and the time available to use that information.

Filing Requirements: Section 13(d) of the 1934 Act requires that any person or group acquiring more than 5 percent of the shares of any corporation must file a Schedule 13D within ten days with the SEC. That schedule requires disclosure of the background of the person or group, their source of funds, their purpose, the number of shares owned, relevant contracts or other arrangements with the target, and any plans for change of the target's affairs.

Procedural Rules: Section 14(d) and Rule 14d-2 provide that a tender offer is commenced on the date of public announcement of the offer. On that date, Rule 14d-3 requires the offeror to file with the SEC a Schedule 14D-1, which requires informational disclosures similar to those Schedule 13D.

The target's management may support a tender offer; perhaps the management even negotiated it. But tender offers frequently are "hostile," and the offeror intends to replace the target's management with its own people. Even if the target's management opposes the offer, section 14(d) and Rule 14d-5 require the target's management to mail the tender offer to the target's shareholders or to promptly provide the offeror with a shareholder list so it can do the mailing itself.

Target management must file with the SEC a Schedule 14D-9. This document (1) discloses whether the officers and directors intend to hold their shares or to tender, (2) describes any contractual arrangements management may have with the offeror (for instance, the offeror sometimes can obtain management's support through monetary incentives), and (3) discloses any concrete negotiations with a "white knight"—a company willing to make a competing tender offer that is more advantageous to incumbent management.

Substantive Rules: Substantively, section 14(d) and Rule 14e-1 provide that a tender offer must be held open for a minimum of 20 business days, so the target's shareholders will have an opportunity to fully evaluate the offer. No more Saturday Night Specials will occur. If more shares are tendered than the offeror wishes to purchase, the offeror must purchase from each shareholder on a *pro rata* basis. This requirement promotes equal treatment of shareholders.

What if an offeror initiates the tender offer at $40 per share, seeking to purchase 51 percent of the target's shares, but only 25 percent are tendered? The offeror may choose to extend the offering period and amend the offer to $50 per share. This higher price must be given to all tendering shareholders, including those who were willing to sell at the lower price.

The final important provision of the Williams Act is section 14(e), the prohibition of fraud or manipulation in either supporting or opposing a tender offer.

Remedies: Violations of sections 13(d), 14(d), and 14(e) may be remedied by civil actions for injunctive relief. Injured shareholders who, relying on fraudulent statements, either tendered when they would not have done so had they known the truth or failed to tender when they would have had they not been defrauded, also can sue for damages under Section 14(e).

Defensive Tactics

A recent controversy has focused on the latitude that should be accorded target management in opposing hostile tender offers. Normally, a court is hesitant to review the business judgments of a corporation's management. However, in recent years target managements have often taken extreme measures to fend off tender offers. For example, they have spent corporate cash and borrowed large sums of money to make the corporation less attractive and to prevent an offeror from using the target's own assets to help pay off debts incurred in the takeover. They have moved the corporation to states with laws that tend to make tender offers more difficult to consummate successfully. They have acquired competitors of the offeror in an attempt to create an antitrust impediment to the takeover. They have launched "Pac-Man" counter tender offers for control of the offeror. They have sold the corporation's "crown jewel" (the subsidiary that attracted the offer in the first place). They have granted "lock-up options" (opportunities to purchase part of the company at bargain prices) to "white knights" (friendly third-party bidders) to assure their victory over the hostile offerors. They have issued "poison pills" (shares of stock that, for example carry the right, effective in the event of a change of control, to buy the corporation's shares for 50 cents on the dollar, thereby dramatically diluting the position of the offeror). They have even threatened "corporate suicide" (liquidation and dissolution).

Legal challenges to these defensive tactics have taken two major forms. One basis for attack is the argument based on state corporation law, that target managers are breaching their fiduciary duties to shareholders by using defensive tactics to save their jobs at the expense of the shareholders' opportunity to sell at a profit. For many years, such challenges were uniformly unsuccessful as the courts repeatedly held that defensive actions taken by target managements were protected by the "business judgment rule"—the courts' determination to defer to the expertise of the board of directors.

In recent years, however, the courts have been less willing to apply the business judgment rule automatically to protect target management, in light of the conflict-of-interest situation that exists when target managers face a hostile tender offer that has the potential for great profits for the shareholders but loss of jobs for the managers.

Two important rules have developed in Delaware, the leading corporate law jurisdiction. First, in *Unocal Corp. v. Mesa Petroleum Co.*, 493 A.2d 946 (Del. 1985), the Delaware Supreme Court held that a target management's defensive tactics must be reasonable in relation to the threat posed. If a hostile bidder's tender offer is coercive or clearly inadequate, target management will be given substantial leeway to defeat it. However, if the bid is not coercive and at a fair price that target shareholders can take or leave at their own discretion, target management "does not have unbridled discretion to defeat any perceived threat by any draconian means available."

Second, once target managers have decided that the corporation is for sale—for example, they respond to a hostile bid by bringing in a white knight to make a competing bid or they make their own bid through a management-sponsored leveraged buy-out (an attempt by target management to buy out the public investors by using huge amounts of credit secured by the corporation's own assets)—they become "auctioneers" with a responsibility to obtain the highest possible price for the shareholders. *Revlon, Inc. v. MacAndrews & Forbes Holdings, Inc.*, 506 A.2d 173 (Del. 1986) holds that use of lock-up options to sell crown jewels to a white knight may unduly favor that white knight, thereby impermissibly stifling the bidding contest.

In *Paramount Communications, Inc. v. Time, Inc.*, 571 A.2d 1140 (Del. 1990), the Delaware Supreme Court's interpretation of these rules gave additional leeway to a target board by holding that directors "are not obliged to abandon a deliberately conceived corporate plan for a short-term shareholder profit [in the form of a tender offer] unless there is clearly no basis to sustain the corporate strategy." Time approved a target board's use of a poison pill to "just say no" to a hostile bid that would have disrupted the target's long-term strategic plan to merge with another corporation.

A second basis for attacking defensive tactics is to argue that they are "manipulative" in violation of second 14(e) of the federal Williams Act. The Supreme Court dealt a serious blow to this argument in the following case.

Schreiber v. Burlington

U.S. Supreme Court, 472 U.S. 1 (1985)

On December 21, 1982, Burlington Northern, Inc. made a hostile tender offer for 25 million shares of El Paso Gas Co. at $24 per share. Although El Paso's management initially opposed the offer, its shareholders fully subscribed it. Burlington did not accept the tendered shares, however. Instead, after negotiations with El Paso's management, Burlington rescinded the December tender offer, purchased 4 million shares from El Paso, substituted a new tender offer for only 21 million shares at $24 each, and recognized certain contractual arrangements between El Paso and its management that guaranteed the managers substantial compensation upon a change of control ("golden parachutes"). More than 40 million shares were tendered in response to the second tender offer.

Rescission of the first offer diminished payment to those shareholders who had tendered during the first offer. Not only were fewer shares purchased, but the shareholders who retendered were subjected to substantial proration. Petitioner Schreiber sued on behalf of similarly situated shareholders, alleging that Burlington, El Paso, and members of El Paso's board had violated §14(e). She claimed that withdrawal of the first tender offer coupled with substitution of the second was a "manipulative" distortion of the market for El Paso stock.

The trial court dismissed the suit for failure to state a claim. The U.S. Court of Appeals for the Third Circuit affirmed. Schreiber petitioned to the Supreme Court.

Burger, Chief Justice:

We are asked in this case to interpret §14(e) of the Securities Exchange Act. The starting point is the language of the statute. Section 14(e) provides:

> It shall be unlawful for any person to make any untrue statement of a material fact or omit to state any material fact necessary in order to make the statements made, in the light of the circumstances under which they are made, not misleading, or to engage in any fraudulent, deceptive or manipulative acts or practices, in connection with any tender offer or request or invitation for tenders, or any solicitation of security holders in opposition to or in favor of any such offer, request, or invitation. The Commission shall, for the purposes of this subsection, by rules and regulations define, and prescribe means reasonably designed to prevent, such acts and practices as are fraudulent, deceptive, or manipulative.

Petitioner reads the phrase "fraudulent, deceptive or manipulative acts or practices" to include acts which, although fully disclosed, "artificially" affect the price of the takeover target's stock. Petitioner's interpretation relies on the belief that §14(e) is directed at purposes broader than providing full and true information to investors.

Petitioner's reading of the term "manipulative" conflicts with the normal meaning of the term. We have held in the context of an alleged violation of §10(b) of the Securities Exchange Act:

> Use of the word 'manipulative' is especially significant. It is and was virtually a term of art when used in connection with the securities markets. It connotes intentional or willful conduct designed to deceive or defraud investors by controlling or artificially affecting the price of securities. *Ernst & Ernst v. Hochfelder*, 425 U.S. 185, 199 (1976) (emphasis added).

The meaning the Court has given the term "manipulative" is consistent with the use of the term at common law, and with its traditional dictionary definition.

Our conclusion that "manipulative" acts under §14(e) require misrepresentation or nondisclosure is buttressed by the purpose and legislative history of the provision. "The purpose of the Williams Act is to insure that public shareholders who are confronted by a cash tender offer for their stock will not be required to respond without adequate information." *Rondeau v. Mosinee Paper Corp.*, 422 U.S. 49, 58 (1975).

The expressed legislative intent was to preserve a neutral setting in which the contenders could fully present their arguments. The Senate sponsor [said]:

> We have taken extreme care to avoid

CONTINUED

tipping the scales either in favor of management or in favor of the person making the takeover bids. S. 510 is designed solely to require full and fair disclosure for the benefit of investors. The bill will at the same time provide the offeror and management equal opportunity to present their case.

Congress' consistent emphasis on disclosure persuades us that it intended takeover contests to be addressed to shareholders. In pursuit of this goal, Congress, consistent with the core mechanism of the Securities Exchange Act, created sweeping disclosure requirements and narrow substantive safeguards. The same Congress that placed such emphasis on shareholder choice would not at the same time have required judges to oversee tender offers for substantive fairness. It is even less likely that a Congress implementing that intention would express it only through the use of a single word placed in the middle of a provision otherwise devoted to disclosure.

We hold that the term "manipulative" as used in §14(e) requires misrepresentation or nondisclosure. Without misrepresentation or nondisclosure, §14(e) has not been violated.

Applying the definition to this case, we hold that the actions of respondents were not manipulative. The amended complaint fails to allege that the cancellation of the first tender offer was accompanied by any misrepresentation, nondisclosure or deception. The District Court correctly found, "All activity of the defendants that could have conceivably affected the price of El Paso shares was done openly."

Petitioner also alleges that El Paso management and Burlington entered into certain undisclosed and deceptive agreements during the making of the second tender offer. The substance of the allegations is that, in return for certain undisclosed benefits, El Paso managers agreed to support the second tender offer. But both courts noted that petitioner's complaint seeks redress only for injuries related to the cancellation of the first tender offer. Since the deceptive and misleading acts alleged by the petitioner all occurred with reference to the making of the second tender offer—when the injuries suffered by petitioner had already been sustained—these acts bear no possible causal relationship to petitioner's alleged injuries.

Affirmed.

STATE REGULATION

Because every state has its own system of securities regulation, corporations must always be cognizant of these rules also. The Commissioners on Uniform State Laws have produced the Uniform Securities Act, which has been used as a pattern for many states' laws. Still, because many large states have not followed this act and many have amended it to varying degrees, there is a lack of uniformity that complicates the marketing of securities. Perhaps the Revised Uniform Securities Act, promulgated in late 1985, will lead to more uniformity. It will likely change some of the present state practices described below.

REGISTRATION

Most states have laws that, like the 1933 Securities Act, regulate the original distribution of securities. A corporation that intends to market its shares nationwide must comply with not only the 1933 Act but also approximately 40 separate state registration laws. There are three basic systems of state registration. Some states use *registration by notification,* which requires the filing of certain material and then a waiting period before the securities may be sold, similar to the procedure under the 1933 Act.

Registration by qualification is used by some states. This process goes beyond the simple disclosure philosophy of the 1933 Act and actually involves merit review of the securities by state officials. Typically, states using merit review refuse to allow sales of securities that do not meet a "fair, just and equitable" standard. The standard may not be met, for example, if the organizers and promoters of the corporation intend to sell to the public at per share prices much greater than they themselves paid.

The third type is *registration by coordination,* which results in automatic state approval whenever a security's registration has become effective under the 1933 Act at the federal level.

Some states allow registration by more than one method.

EXEMPTIONS

State registration laws contain exemptions, as does the 1933 Act. There is an ongoing effort to coordinate state and federal exemptions to produce uniformity. A uniform system of exemptions would greatly simplify matters for a corporation planning a widespread distribution of securities, but the chances of achieving complete uniformity appear slim.

OTHER PROVISIONS

Many state securities laws also contain antifraud provisions similar to those in the 1933 and 1934 federal laws. In states without such laws, the courts have extended the common law of fraud to prohibit deceitful securities practices.

Some states also have qualification and registration provisions governing the activities of securities brokers and dealers, which are usually similar to federal registration provisions in the 1934 Act.

Many states also regulate tender offers in a manner that burdens offerors and therefore discourages such transactions. The Supreme Court held one such state act to be constitutional in *CTS Corp. v. Dynamics Corp.,* 481 U.S. 69 (1987).

INTERNATIONAL IMPLICATIONS

Each year, Americans buy tens of billions of dollars worth of foreign securities, and foreign investors purchase tens of billions of dollars of U.S. securities. Many American investors watch the London and Tokyo stock markets almost as closely as they monitor the NYSE. Because our economy increasingly intersects with those of other nations, international concerns affect virtually every sphere of U.S. securities law.

REGISTRATION EXEMPTIONS

Earlier we listed the important domestic exemptions to the registration requirements of the 1933 Act. To encourage foreign issuers to raise equity in American markets, in 1990 the SEC added a foreign exemption—Regulation S. Generally speaking, Regulation S provides that section 5's registration requirement does not apply to sales or resales of securities if two requirements are met. First, the sale must be an "offshore transaction," defined as one in which no offer is made to a person in the United States, *and* either (1) at the time the buy order is originated the buyer is outside the United States, or (2) the transaction is executed through the facilities of a designated offshore securities market. Second, there can be no "directed selling efforts" in the United States. Issuers must take additional precautions to assure that the shares, once purchased outside the United States, are not quickly resold in the United States as a means of circumventing the registration requirements.

ANTIFRAUD

Regulation S provides an exemption only from registration, not from antifraud rules. Therefore, section 10(b) and Rule 10b-5 continue to apply whenever (1) fraudulent conduct occurs in the United States (even if the impact is on American or foreign investors in other countries), or (2) fraudulent conduct occurs abroad, having significant effects in the United States. To illustrate the "conduct test": Foreign investors who bought the issuer's shares abroad were allowed to sue an American accounting firm for a fraud involving allegedly fraudulent certified financial statements that occurred primarily in Ireland, because, in large part, the audit was directed primarily by the firm's American office where engagement partner responsibility lay (even though the field work was performed mostly in Ireland).[6] To illustrate the "effects test": American investors were allowed to sue in the United States the directors of a Canadian corporation who allegedly authorized the sale of the company's stock in Canada at an unfairly low price, thus affecting the value of the company's shares that were traded on the American Stock Exchange.[7]

INSIDER TRADING

As noted in Chapter 8, many of the insider trading schemes occurring in the United States in the 1980s were aided by the bank secrecy laws of Switzerland and other countries. In recent years, with pressure from the United States, many of these nations have become more cooperative in divulging information, thereby allowing the SEC to prosecute more successfully foreign citizens who are inside traders as well as U.S. citizens who attempt to cover their tracks with use of foreign bank accounts.

---

[6] *Dept. of Economic Development v. Arthur Andersen & Co.*, 683 F. Supp. 1463 (S.D.N.Y. 1988).
[7] *Schoenbaum v. Firstbrook*, 405 F.2d 200 (2d Cir. 1969).

TENDER OFFERS

As foreign investors from Japan, Europe, and elsewhere have bought American companies through tender offers, some Americans have become uneasy with the implications of these purchases. Therefore, Congress passed the Exon-Florio Amendment to a 1988 Trade Bill. Exon-Florio authorizes the President or his delegates to prevent or even reverse such a takeover if it threatens national security.

QUESTIONS and PROBLEMS

1. Co-op City was a massive, government-subsidized housing complex, operated as a nonprofit corporation. To acquire an apartment, eligible prospective tenants had to buy 18 shares of Co-op stock for each room at $25 per share. The purchase was in effect a recoverable deposit. The shares could not be transferred to a nontenant, did not carry votes as to management of the co-op, and had to be offered to the co-op for sale at the initial selling price whenever the tenant moved out. When rental rates went up, some tenants sued claiming inadequate disclosure under the federal securities law. Discuss whether these "shares of stock," as they were labeled, constituted securities under federal law. (*United Housing Foundation, Inc. v. Forman*, 421 U.S. 837, 1975.)

2. Wherehouse Entertainment, Inc., offered convertible subordinated debentures, stressing that purchasers would have the right to redeem the bonds in the event of certain triggering events that might endanger the value of the debentures, *unless* the transaction was approved by a "majority of the Independent Directors." Eighteen months later, Wherehouse entered into a merger, which triggered the right to tender. Plaintiff purchasers attempted to redeem the bonds but were rejected on grounds that the board had nullifed the right to tender by approving the merger. The plaintiffs sued under sections 11 and 12(2) of the 1933 Act and section 10(b) of the 1934 Act, alleging that the right to redeem, presented as a valuable feature in the offering materials, was in fact illusory. The defendant claimed that every individual statement that it had made in selling the debentures was literally true. The plaintiffs argued that even if that were the case, the defendant gave the misleading overall impression that exercise of the right to redeem would be the norm and waiver by directors would be the exception. Can statements that are literally true still be materially misleading in cumulative effect? Discuss. (*McMahan & Co. v. Wherehouse Entertainment, Inc.*, 900 F.2d 576, 2d Cir. 1990.)

3. After the terrible industrial accident in Bhopal, India, caused by a leak of methyl isocyanate (MIC) at a Union Carbide plant, Union Carbide shareholders sued the corporation under section 10(b), claiming that Union Carbide had made material omissions in several of its annual reports, quarterly reports, and similar documents. Basically, the plaintiffs claimed that Union Carbide failed to describe the manufacture, storage, risks, and personnel requirements attendant to MIC and that Union Carbide failed to disclose the financial implications of a possible MIC accident. Should this information have been disclosed? Discuss. (*In re Union Carbide Class Action Securities Litigation*, 648 F. Supp. 1322, S.D.N.Y. 1986.)

4. Lee bought the stock of Pal's Finer foods but became unhappy with the purchase and filed suit under section 12(2) of the 1933 Act against Pal's former owners, their lawyer, and their accountants, Diodate. Diodate filed a motion for summary judgment, claiming that he was merely the seller's accountant and not a "seller" himself within the meaning of the statute. Lee submitted an affidavit swearing that Diodate participated in the stock sale and recommended that Lee buy the stock. Should the court grant Diodate's motion? Discuss. (*Lee v. Spicola*, FED.SEC.L.REP. (CCH) @94,120, M.D. Fla. 1988.)

5. Claiming the intrastate exemption of section 3(a)(11) of the 1933 Act, McDonald Investment Company did not register its offering of shares with the SEC. McDonald is a Minnesota corporation with its only offices in that state. It sold shares only to Minnesota residents. However, the funds were raised to lend to real estate developers in Arizona. Discuss the availability of the

exemption. (*SEC v. McDonald Investment Co.*, 343 F. Supp. 343, D. Minn. 1972.)

6. Moore, a psychiatrist, was treating the wife of an officer of Posi-Seal. Another company was planning to acquire Posi-Seal. At a treatment session with the wife that the Posi-Seal officer attended to facilitate the treatment process, Moore learned of the planned acquisition. Before public announcement of the acquisition, Moore bought 9,000 shares of Posi-Seal stock. He sold them after the acquisition at a profit of $26,933.74. Discuss whether Moore has violated §10(b)'s ban on insider trading. (*SEC v. Morgan F. Moore*, No. N-86-88-PCD D.Conn. 1986.)

7. Lund was CEO of Verit Industries. Horowitz was on Verit's board and was CEO of P&F Co. Lund and Horowitz were friends. P&F began negotiating a particular deal, and Horowitz called Lund to ask him if Verit would be interested in providing capital and being an investor in the acquisition. Lund said that Verit would not be interested. However, he soon bought 10,000 shares of P&F stock in his own name at $1.25 per share—his only purchase of P&F stock in ten years. Soon the P&F deal was completed and announced to the public. Lund sold his shares for a $12,500 profit. The SEC charged that Lund that violated Rule 10b-5's insider trading prohibition. Did he? (*SEC v. Lund*, 570 F. Supp. 1397, C.D. Cal. 1983.)

8. A registered broker–dealer's sales force repeatedly made false and misleading statements in an effort to sell Lawn-A-Mat common stock. After several complaints were ignored, the SEC sought an injunction to halt the illicit practices. One respondent was the sales supervisor, who was informed of the misdeeds but did not take affirmative steps to prevent a recurrence of the deceit. One issue that arose was whether the SEC would have to prove scienter to obtain an injunction against practices that allegedly violated Rule 10b-5. Discuss (*Aaron v. SEC*, 446 U.S. 680, 1980.)

9. Hamm bought 1,000 shares of Playboy stock at $17/share in September 1979. On April 13, 1981, Playboy announced that it was in danger of losing the operating licenses for its three London gambling casinos, which provided a substantial portion of Playboy's operating revenue. The market price of Playboy stock dropped after these disclosures, and Hamm sued under section 10(b), claiming that Playboy had known as early as 1979 that its licenses were in danger but had not revealed this in its quarterly and annual reports. Playboy defended by pointing out that Hamm had not read those reports anyway. Is this a good defense? Discuss. (*HSL, Inc. v. Daniels*, FED.SEC.L.REP. (CCH), @99,577, N.D. Ill. 1983.)

10. VAC, a Delaware corporations, was the world's largest maker of cutting tools and quality hand tools. Its management and ownership were dominated by the Thomas family. Throughout its history, VAC pursued long-term profit maximization, often investing large amounts of capital at the expense of short-term profit. VAC has been quite successful. Newell Co. has also been successful, primarily by acquiring other companies. Ninety percent of Newell's sales and profits were generated by past acquisitions, often achieved through tender offers. Newell slowly accumulated 11 percent of VAC's stock and then made a tender offer for 10 percent more. The VAC board, dominated by outside directors, authorized a repurchase by VAC of its own shares that would increase the holdings of the Thomas family to more than 50 percent, effectively blocking any attempted takeover. Is the repurchase consistent with the fiduciary duties of the VAC board? Discuss. (*Newell Co. v. Vermont American Corp.*, 725 F. Supp. 351, N.D. Ill. 1989.)

CHAPTER 16

As in most other areas of law, the legal principles governing the employer–employee relationship were developed by the courts as part of the common law until this century. The law of agency was the primary area of law relevant to employment, although the laws of contracts and torts also had some bearing. The law of agency,

which was discussed in Chapter 13, continues to consist mainly of judge-made principles and still plays an important role in determining the extent of an employee's duties to the employer and in deciding when an

EMPLOYMENT LAW: PROTECTION OF EMPLOYEE SECURITY AND WELFARE

employer is liable to third parties for an employee's actions. The laws of contracts and torts, discussed in Chapters 9 and 10, also continue to consist mostly of common-law principles and have significant applicability to employment.

As traditionally applied, these areas of law provided very little protection for the security, safety, or welfare of employees. The twentieth century, however, witnessed the development of a growing body of state and federal legislation aimed at recognizing and guarding a variety of employee rights. Several of the most important of these enactments are discussed in this chapter, including those dealing with employee privacy, compensation for job-related accidents and diseases, improvement of workplace safety, wage and hour standards, and unemployment compensation. In addition, in relatively recent times state and federal courts have taken the initiative to increase the protection of employees' rights by expanding common-law tort and contract concepts. One very important example discussed at the beginning of this chapter is the set of newly developed judge-made rules limiting the ability of employers to fire employees for reasons that offend basic notions of public policy.

The next chapter examines the complex legal framework that has developed in modern times for protecting employees against discrimination on the basis of race, color, sex, religion, national origin, age, and handicap. The third employment law chapter then deals with labor–management relations, that is, government regulation of the relationship between companies and unions.

THE EMPLOYEE–INDEPENDENT CONTRACTOR DISTINCTION

In general, the various laws discussed in this and the next two chapters apply to employees, not to independent contractors. A person is an employee when an employer has the right to control the method and manner of doing a particular job. An independent contractor is hired to accomplish a result and is not subject to the employer's control as to the details of performing the work. In most situations the distinction is obvious: For example, a stenographer or factory worker almost always is an employee; a construction contractor hired to erect a building is clearly an independent contractor. When the distinction is not so clear, various factors are taken into account. Some facts that would increase the likelihood of a person being an independent contractor are: (1) the person has his or her own independent business or profession; (2) the person uses his or her own tools, equipment, or workplace to perform the task; (3) the person is paid by the job, not by the hour, week, or month; (4) the person has irregular hours of work; and (5) the person is performing a task that is not part of the employer's regular business. None of these factors automatically makes someone an independent

THE EMPLOYMENT RELATIONSHIP AND JOB SECURITY

contractor; each must be weighed along with all the other evidence relating to the question of control.

Most people are almost totally dependent economically on their jobs. To many of these individuals their jobs also are the source of significant satisfaction, socialization, and self-esteem. As a result, one of the most traumatic events in the average person's life is to lose a job. When a worker is fired, or is forced to quit by being put into an intolerable situation (called a "constructive discharge"), and he or she has evidence that the employer's action were unjustified, the question whether legal recourse is available becomes very important. Suppose, for example, that Sally has information indicating that her employer has been violating federal or state water pollution laws. She then takes the matter up with her boss, or informs the authorities, or both, and is promptly fired because of her "whistle blowing." Or, suppose that Sally is fired because she filed a workers' compensation claim after having been injured on the job, or because she cooperated with authorities in their investigation of another employee's charge of racial discrimination. In these and other situations in which the employer's actions were arguably unjustified, does Sally have a legal remedy? (Throughout the following discussion, the terms *fired* or *discharged* include both actual and constructive discharges.)

CONTRACTUAL PROTECTIONS

An employee who has an individual employment contract with the employer enjoys whatever job security protections are included in the contract. If the employee is fired before the expiration of the time specified in the contract, he or she may sue the employer for breach of contract. Likewise, if the contract provides that the employee may be fired or otherwise penalized only if particular procedures are followed, only for particular reasons, or only for "good cause," the employee has legal protection when the employer violates such a provision. It is very rare, however, for an individual to have an employment contract for a specified term.

If an employee does not have a formal employment contract, certain words or actions of the employer sometimes create specific contractual guarantees to an employee. For example, an employer's personnel policies expressed in a handbook or otherwise communicated to employees may sometimes indicate that employees will be discharged only after particular procedures are followed, or only for particular reasons. If the employer's language apparently expresses a definite commitment and there is no disclaimer of contractual intent, several courts have found that an enforceable obligation to follow the stated policy may be created. Although employees have won a few cases of this type, the legal basis for such a claim against the

HUMOR AND THE LAW

Workers' compensation claims and other matters arising out of on-the-job injuries often turn on the testimony of the injured party. Sometimes this testimony is more helpful than other times. Judge Jerry Buchmeyer, who writes a regular column in the *Texas Bar Journal* collected this example:

Q. Okay, What has [the co-worker who saw the accident] told you?

A. He told me that when it hit me, when the electricity hit me, it froze me up there. He in turn ran over to the machine ... He hit the down button. The first time he hit it, it knocked him back about 10 feet, so he told me. Then he came back again. And I assumed that he hit something right, you know, and it pulled me down, it let the man lift down, which pulled me away from the wire. They drug me out of the bucket, [and] Mr. Sistruck got me out of the bucket, he gave me *artificial insemination,* you know, mouth-to-mouth, whatever.

Q. Resuscitation?

A. Yes, resuscitation."

---

employer is too uncertain and unpredictable to provide really meaningful protection. From the employer's perspective, it usually is a good management practice to express personnel policies clearly, but the company's managers and attorneys should consciously decide whether contractual obligations are intended and spell out those intentions one way or the other.

If an employee is a member of a unionized work force, the collective bargaining contract negotiated between the employer and union normally provides certain job security protections. For example, most such contracts include a clause prohibiting the employer from firing or otherwise disciplining a worker except for "good cause," and require binding arbitration of disputes about whether the employer's action was valid under the contract. Examples of "good cause" include excessive absenteeism, intoxication, fighting, insubordination, and continuing substandard performance. Only about one-sixth of American workers enjoy this form of contractual protection. The subject of labor–management relations law, which is applicable to a unionized employee group, is dealt with at length in Chapter 18.

SPECIAL PROTECTION FOR PUBLIC EMPLOYEES

Most federal, state, and local government employees ("public" employees) are covered by federal or state "civil service" laws. After a public employee has satisfactory completed a specified probationary period, these laws generally permit the employing agency to fire the worker only for good cause and only after following required procedures. Approximately 17 percent of U.S. workers are employed by federal, state, or local governments.

In addition, hiring, firing, and other employment actions by government agencies are governed by the U.S. Constitution. Thus if a public employee, under a statute or regulation, is guaranteed certain job security protections, the employee's entitlement is a "property" interest that is protected by due process. Due process, in turn, guarantees that discharge or other adverse employment action will be preceded by reasonable notice and a hearing that is appropriate under the circumstances.

Regardless of whether a public employee has a sufficient legal entitlement to job guarantees to have a property interest, the equal protection and free speech clauses of the Constitution will apply to the government agency's employment actions. In applying the free speech clause of the expression of a government employee, however, any harm to legitimate government interests will be balanced against the employee's right of expression. Such interests include the need for the agency to maintain an efficient work force, protect general employee morale, and effectively carry out the overall mission of the agency.

EMPLOYMENT-AT-WILL

From the above discussion, one can see that about two-thirds of all employees in the nation, or about five-sixths of those working for private (nongovernmental) employers, have no general legal protection for their job security. Under traditional common-law principles, these employees work under an **"employment-at-will"** arrangement. In other words, at any time and without advance notice the employer has the legal right to fire them for no reason or for a bad reason. It is interesting to note that, among the world's industrialized nations, the United States stands virtually alone in permitting employers to discharge workers without justification.

Although the employment-at-will doctrine continues to be the general rule in this country, in recent years legislative enactments and judicial decisions have eroded the doctrine somewhat by creating certain exceptions to it.

It is important to understand that caution is required when a legislature or court is deciding whether to create an exception to the employment-at-will doctrine. Both fairness to the individual and furtherance of the public interest necessitate the establishment of exceptions in certain circumstances. Going too far in this direction, however, can stifle the employer's ability to maintain an efficient work force by shielding the disgruntled or shirking employee, and everyone pays for this inefficiency through higher prices and lower quality.

EXCEPTIONS TO THE EMPLOYMENT-AT-WILL DOCTRINE

A number of federal and state statutes provide limited protection against unjustified discharges in particular circumstances. Several federal laws regulating the employment relationship, for example, also include specific protections against employer retaliation. The Fair Labor Standards Act (FLSA), discussed later in this chapter, generally guarantees a minimum wage and overtime pay and regulates the use of child labor. FLSA also contains a provision prohibiting an employer from discharging or otherwise

Specialized Statutory Exceptions

penalizing an employee because the employee either instituted or testified in any legal proceeding under the statute.

Somewhat broader protection against employer retaliation is found in Title VII of the 1964 Civil Rights Act, which prohibits discrimination in employment based on race, color, sex, religion, or national origin, and in the Age Discrimination in Employment Act of 1967. These laws are discussed in detail in Chapter 17. The provisions in each of these statutes prohibit employer retaliation against the employee in the same situations as in FLSA, but go further by protecting an employee who merely objected to a practice (such as race or age discrimination) that is unlawful under the statute or who cooperated in any way with the investigation or prosecution of such an unlawful practice.

Similarly broad protection against retaliation is found in the federal Occupational Safety and Health Act. This law, which is aimed generally at maintaining safe working conditions, is discussed later in this chapter.

At the state level, several states include antiretaliation sections in their workers' compensation statutes. These laws, which provide compensation for on-the-job injuries, are also discussed later in this chapter. Legislation in some states forbids employers from penalizing employees who take time off to serve on juries.

Broader Statutory Exceptions

Several states, including California, Connecticut, Maine, Michigan, New Jersey, and New York, have recently passed statutes protecting employees against retaliation for **whistle blowing.** These statutes generally apply to situations in which the employee was discharged for complaining about the employer's violation or suspected violation of a law or regulation. Some of these statutes apply only if the employee first gave company management an opportunity to deal with the problem internally, while others apply whether the employee initially complained to management or to law enforcement authorities. A number of other states have whistle-blower protection statutes that apply only to state or local government employees.

Judicially Created Exceptions

Relatively recent state court decisions have made inroads on the employment-at-will doctrine to a greater extent than state legislation. Within the past few years courts in most states have created exceptions as part of the evolutionary common-law process. These state court decisions have been based on two separate but related theories: (1) public policy and (2) an implied covenant of good faith and fair dealing.

Public Policy: Most of the courts that have fashioned exceptions to employment-at-will have based their decisions on public policy grounds. In other words, these courts have ruled that an employee should be able to recover damages for the tort of "wrongful discharge" (or "retaliatory discharge") when the employer's conduct is contrary to a clearly established public policy. Defining public policy is not always an easy task, however. Most courts are fully aware that a vague, expansive public policy concept will provide very little guidance to employers or employees. Without reasonable guidance, employers will find it very difficult to maintain an effective personnel management system because of the fear that every discharge might lead to an expensive lawsuit.

As a result, most courts have concluded that the public policy claimed to have been violated by the employer must be clearly stated in a federal or state statute, constitutional provision, or widely recognized and accepted judicial decision. In those states permitting an employee to assert a claim for wrongful discharge based on public policy, a fired employee is likely to have a good claim in the following situations:[1]

1. The employer may not discharge a worker for refusing to commit an act that is *illegal* under a statute, constitutional provision, or prior judicial decision. For example, courts have found employers liable for firing employees who refused to participate in an illegal price-fixing scheme, commit perjury, mislabel food products, falsify a pollution control test, sign a false defamatory statement about a coemployee, perform a medical procedure for which the nurse–employee was not licensed, or pump a ship's bilges into the water.

2. Generally, an employee has a good wrongful discharge claim if he or she has been fired for *exercising a statutory right* or *performing a legal duty*. For example, an employer has been held liable for damages to an employee who was fired for exercising the right to sign a union authorization card. Similarly, employers have been held liable for discharging employees because they filed workers' compensation claims or served on juries, even if there was no specific antiretaliation statute in that state covering the situation.

3. An employer often will be held liable to an employee who was fired for *whistle blowing*—objecting to or disclosing the employer's violations of the law. The employee normally has a valid claim if he or she (1) acted in good faith (sincerely) and (2) had reasonable cause to believe that the employer was violating the law, even if later investigation reveals that the employer actually did not act illegally. On the question of whether an employee must first give company management an opportunity to correct the problem before complaining to the authorities, the courts are split. Most of them, however, recognize the wrongful discharge claim regardless of where the employee first lodged an objection.

Courts usually have stressed that an employee is not protected from discharge just because he or she acted out of strong, and even admirable,

---

[1] This categorization is adapted from William Daughtery, "Another Exception under the Employment-at-Will Doctrine," *American Business Law Journal* 24 (1986), 243–268.

convictions if a purely private matter is involved that does not affect the public interest. For example, one court concluded that there was no wrongful discharge claim where the employee was fired for refusing to follow a particular research program. As a matter of personal conscience, the employee felt that the research was not proper, but there was nothing illegal, immoral, or hazardous about it. Two Illinois cases also provide an illustrative contrast. In one, the court found that no violation of public policy had occurred when a company's chief financial officer was fired for a continuing disagreement with the company's president about accounting methods. There was no plausible claim that the president's methods were deceptive or violated securities or tax laws or generally accepted accounting principles. In the other case, the court held that the employee did have a claim for wrongful discharge when he had been fired for complaining about the company's use of accounting methods that substantially overstated income and assets in a way that very likely would violate tax laws and the disclosure provisions of federal securities laws.

On relatively rare occasions, courts have ruled a discharge to be wrongful because of the court's own perceptions of what is appropriate public policy, without any meaningful guidelines from another source. For example, one court found in favor of an employee who had been fired for refusing to lobby in favor of no-fault insurance reform that was contrary to his private views. Another ruled for an employee who was fired for being a police informer. Although these two cases involve facts that demonstrate unreasonableness and poor personnel practices on the part of the employers, the courts' decisions may not be very wise in the long run. As mentioned earlier, recognizing the tort of wrongful discharge without any meaningful guidelines poses the very real danger of crippling the employer's ability to manage its employees in an effective manner.

Implied Covenant of Good Faith and Fair Dealing:

A few courts have recognized an exception to the employment-at-will doctrine by implying a covenant (promise) of good faith and fair dealing in every employment arrangement. This approach will often produce the same results as the public policy approach, but it can provide protection to employees in a few situations in which the public policy concept would not. For example, in one case in which the court implied a covenant of good faith, the employer was held liable to an employee who had been fired for the purpose of cutting off the employee's right to commissions that would have accrued shortly thereafter. If the court had used the public policy approach, it probably would not have been able to find a clearly established public policy violated by the employer's actions.

The following case illustrates an unfortunate situation that led one state supreme court to consider and adopt the public policy exception to employment-at-will.

CASE

WAGENSELLER v. SCOTTSDALE MEMORIAL HOSPITAL

ARIZONA SUPREME COURT, 710 P.2d 1025 (1985)

Catherine Wagenseller worked as an emergency room nurse for the Scottsdale Memorial Hospital. She had originally been recruited personally by the emergency department's manager, Kay Smith, and for four years maintained a superior work record and enjoyed excellent professional and personal relationships with Smith and others in the department. She was an "at-will" employee, with no contractual or other job guarantees.

Wagenseller, Smith, and several others from the emergency department, as well as a number of employees from other area hospitals, went on an eight-day camping and rafting trip down the Colorado River. While on the trip, Wagenseller became very uncomfortable because of the behavior of Smith and a few others. This behavior included heavy drinking, group nude bathing and other public nudity, and a lot of unnecessary closeness while rafting. In addition, Smith and others staged a parody of the song "Moon River," which ended with members of the group "mooning" the audience. Wagenseller declined to participate in any of these activities. Smith and others also performed the "Moon River" skit twice at the hospital after the group's return from the river, but Wagenseller declined to participate there as well.

After the trip, relations between Wagenseller and Smith deteriorated. Smith began harassing Wagenseller, using abusive language and embarrassing her in the presence of other staff. These problems continued, and Wagenseller was fired about five months after the camping trip. Wagenseller appealed her dismissal to the hospital's administrative and personnel department, but the dismissal was upheld. She then filed suit for damages against Smith, the hospital, and several of its personnel administrators. In the suit, she alleged that her termination violated public policy and therefore constituted the tort of wrongful discharge. Although Wagenseller's claims had been substantiated by the pretrial statements of several others, the trial court refused to recognize any exception to the employment-at-will doctrine and granted the defendants' motions for summary judgment. The appeals court reversed part of the judgment, but still did not grant Wagenseller the relief she sought, so she appealed to the Arizona Supreme Court.

FELDMAN, JUSTICE:

... Under the traditional employment-at-will doctrine, an employee without an employment contract for a definite term can be fired for cause, without cause, or for "bad" cause.... In recent years there has been apparent dissatisfaction with the absolutist formulation of the common law at-will rule.... The trend has been to modify the at-will rule by creating exceptions to its operation.... The most widely accepted approach is the "public policy" exception, which permits recovery upon a finding that the employer's conduct undermined some important public policy.... A majority of the states have now either recognized a cause of action based on the public policy exception or have indicated their willingness to consider it, given appropriate facts. The key to an employee's claim in all of these cases is the proper definition of a public policy that has been violated by the employer's actions.

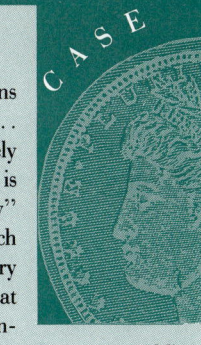

Before deciding whether to adopt the public policy exception, we first consider what kind of discharge would violate the rule. The majority of courts required, as a threshold showing, a "clear mandate" of public policy. The leading case recognizing a public policy exception to the at-will doctrine is *Palmateer v. International Harvester Co.*, 421 N.E.2d 876, 878 (Ill. 1981), which holds that an employee stated a cause of action for wrongful discharge when he claimed he was fired for supplying information to police investigating alleged criminal violations by a co-employee. Addressing the issue of what constitutes "clearly mandated public policy," the court stated:

> There is no precise definition of the term. In general, it can be said that public policy concerns what is right and just and what affects the citizens of the State collectively. It is to be found in the State's constitution and

CONTINUED

statutes and, when they are silent, in its judicial decisions. Although there is no precise line of demarcation dividing matters that are the subject of public policies from matters purely personal, a survey of cases in other States involving retaliatory discharges shows that a matter must strike at the heart of a citizen's social rights, duties, and responsibilities before the tort will be allowed.

... It is difficult to justify this court's further adherence to a rule which permits an employer to fire someone for a cause that is morally wrong.... Certainly, a court would be hard-pressed to find a rationale to hold that an employer could with impunity fire an employee who refused to commit perjury.

... We therefore adopt the public policy exception to the at-will termination rule. We hold that an employer may fire for good cause or for no cause. He may not fire for bad cause—that which violates public policy....

... In the case before us, Wagenseller refused to participate in activities which arguably would have violated our indecent exposure statute. This statute provides that a person commits indecent exposure by exposing certain described parts of the body when someone else is present and when the defendant is "reckless about whether such other person, as a reasonable person, would be offended or alarmed by the act."... While this statute may not embody a policy which "strikes at the heart of a citizen's social rights, duties, and responsibilities" as clearly and forcefully as some other statutes, such as a statute prohibiting perjury, we believe that it was enacted to preserve and protect the commonly recognized right of public privacy and decency. The law does, therefore, recognize bodily privacy as a "citizen's social right."... We are compelled to conclude that termination of employment for refusal to participate in the public exposure of one's buttocks is a termination contrary to the policy of this state....

[The trial court's action granting summary judgment against Wagenseller was in error. The decision is reversed and remanded to the trial court for a trial where Wagenseller will have a full opportunity to prove her allegations.]

PROTECTION OF EMPLOYEE PRIVACY

LIE DETECTOR TESTING

Employers have extremely important interests in learning certain kinds of background information about people who are applying for jobs. Incompetent, dishonest, or violent employees can cause untold harm to an employer. A company may need to know about a job applicant's past work record, criminal record, and general character when legitimately attempting to protect itself against lawsuits and against a damaged reputation, as well as to protect its customers and its other employees from physical harm. Employers also have a valid interest in obtaining information from existing employees when theft or other wrongdoing has occurred at the workplace.

During the past several decades, more and more employers used the lie detector (polygraph) examination in an effort to get accurate information from employees and job applicants. Because of mounting evidence that these examinations are not very reliable, and that thousands of employees and applicants were being harmed each year by erroneous results, Congress passed the Employee Polygraph Protection Act of 1988. This law prohibits most uses of the polygraph by private employers, subject only to a few limited exceptions. The most important exception permits a private employer to require an employee to take a lie detector test as part of an ongoing investigation of theft, sabotage, or other property loss, if this employee had custody of the property and if there is other independent evidence creating a reasonable suspicion that this employee was involved in the incident. The law also does not prohibit federal, state, or local government agencies from requiring their employees and job applicants to take lie detector tests, mainly because the Constitution applies to government employers. The constitutional right of privacy protects against many unreasonable uses of the polygraph by government employers but clearly does not protect employees to the extent that the federal polygraph statute does.

EMPLOYEE DRUG TESTING

Employees who are impaired by drugs or alcohol endanger the public and their fellow workers, and cost their employers millions of dollars annually as a result of accidents, absenteeism, higher health insurance claims, low productivity, and poor workmanship. Employers have legitimate interests in minimizing these costs; maintaining a safe, secure, and productive workplace; and protecting themselves against liability to those injured by actions of impaired employees. Both co-workers and members of the public have a legitimate claim to protection against the unsafe conduct or defective products resulting from employees' drug or alcohol use.

Employees subjected to drug testing, on the other hand, have important interests in preventing harm to their reputations and economic security resulting from inaccurate test results and avoiding unwarranted intrusions into their personal lives. Drug tests are not always accurate, and the analysis of urine, blood, or hair specimens often reveals a lot of private information about the subject that has nothing to do with the use of illicit drugs. It is certainly true that alcohol use causes the same kinds of workplace problems as drug use, but alcohol-impaired employees often can be identified more easily without the risk of erroneous test results or the disclosure of irrelevant private information that may be revealed in drug testing. Most of the difficult legal issues, therefore, have involved employers testing for controlled substances other than alcohol.

Most employers take some kind of action against an employee who refuses a test or who tests positive for illicit drugs. This action can range from required enrollment in a rehabilitation program to immediate discharge. Similarly, job applicants who refuse testing or test positive are virtually assured of not getting the job. As a result, legal action by employees challenging drug-testing programs is becoming increasingly common. The legal system has not yet had sufficient time, however, to develop a coherent, uniform set of principles to balance the various interests that are involved. Although the law pertaining to employee drug testing is still in a formative stage, it is possible to make some generalizations.

If the employer is a federal, state, or local government agency, the Constitution provides a measure of protection for the legitimate privacy interests of employees. The Constitution also applies if the government requires a private employer to do drug testing. For example, the U.S.

Department of Transportation issued regulations in 1988 requiring random drug testing of both public and private employees in safety-sensitive or security-related positions in several industries, including mass transit, trucking, rail transportation, and aviation. Also, the Department of Defense adopted regulations that same year requiring companies having contracts with that agency to establish drug-testing programs covering employees who work in certain sensitive positions. In these kinds of situations, government involvement causes the protections of the Constitution to apply even though the testing is done by private employers.

The most obviously applicable constitutional provision is the Fourth Amendment prohibition of *unreasonable searches and seizures.* The taking of a urine, blood, or hair specimen is a "search and seizure." Generally, people and their belongings can be searched only if there is "probable cause" to believe that they possess evidence of a violation of the law. Recently, in *National Treasury Employees Union v. Von Raab,* 489 U.S. 656 (1989) (involving testing by a government agency) and *Skinner v. Railway Labor Executives Ass'n,* 489 U.S. 602 (1989) (involving government-required testing by private employers), the U.S. Supreme Court held that drug testing sometimes is constitutionally permissible even without any evidence that a particular employee is a drug user. The Court said that, in the case of employees whose work creates significant safety, health, or security risks, testing may be done on a random or mass basis so long as the testing program is conducted in a reasonable manner overall. To be reasonable, the program must include ample safeguards to ensure accuracy and privacy. The *Von Raab* case is presented at the end of this section.

The Constitution does not apply to drug testing by private employers unless the testing is required by the government. Tort law does apply, however, if an employer conducts a test or uses the results in such a way that a tort is committed. If the employer intentionally reveals private information from the test to others who have no legitimate interest in receiving it, the employer may be liable to the employee for the tort of invasion of privacy. If the test produces a false positive result and the employer reveals it to others without a legitimate interest in knowing it, the employer may be liable for defamation. In some cases, carelessness in the administration of the test or use of the results may cause the employer to be liable for the tort of negligence.

A few states have passed statutes specifically regulating the design and implementation of drug-testing programs by private employers. The objective of these statutes is to increase the likelihood that results will be accurate and that employee privacy will be protected to the fullest extent possible.

In the case of unionized workers, the implementation of a drug-testing program is a so-called mandatory subject of collective bargaining. This means that the employer cannot make such a decision on its own but must submit the question to the process of collective bargaining with the union. If the company and the union cannot agree, either or both may use economic weapons such as lockouts or strikes to put pressure on the other side.

Following is the *Von Rabb* case, in which the U.S. Supreme Court established several important principles concerning the validity of drug-testing programs under the Fourth Amendment to the Constitution.

NATIONAL TREASURY EMPLOYEES UNION v. VON RAAB

U.S. SUPREME COURT, 489 U.S. 656

The U.S. Customs Service, a bureau of the Department of the Treasury, is the federal agency responsible for processing persons, carriers, cargo, and mail into the United States, collecting revenue from imports, and enforcing customs and related laws. An important responsibility of the Service is the interdiction and seizure of contraband, including illegal drugs. In the routine discharge of their duties, many Customs employees have direct contact with those who traffic in drugs for profit. In 1986, after extensive research and consultation with experts in the field, Von Raab, Commissioner of the Customs Service, announced implementation of a drug-testing program. Drug tests were made a condition of promotion to or employment in a position that requires either (1) direct involvement in drug interdiction or enforcement of drug-related laws, (2) the carrying of firearms, or (3) the handling of "classified" materials that could fall into the hands of smugglers if the employee is susceptible to bribery or blackmail because of his own drug use.

Petitioners, a union of federal employees and a union official, filed suit in federal district court alleging that the drug-testing program violated the Fourth Amendment. The district court agreed and found the program unconstitutional because it called for the testing of employees without any evidence of "individualized suspicion" of drug use. The court of appeals reversed, and the union appealed to the U.S. Supreme Court.

KENNEDY, JUSTICE:

... In *Skinner v. Railway Labor Executives Ass'n*, decided today, we held that [government-required urine tests] .... are "searches." ... While we have often emphasized, and reiterated today, that a search must be supported, as a general matter, by a warrant issued upon probable cause, our decision in *Railway Labor Executives* reaffirms the longstanding principle that neither a warrant nor probable cause, nor, indeed, any measure of individualized suspicion, is an indispensable component of reasonableness in every circumstance. As we note in *Railway Labor Executives,* our cases establish that where a Fourth Amendment intrusion serves special governmental needs, beyond the normal need for law enforcement, it is necessary to balance the individual's privacy expectations against the Government's interests to determine whether it is impractical to require a warrant or some level of individualized suspicion in the particular context.

It is clear that the Customs Service's drug testing program is not designed to serve the ordinary needs of law enforcement.... The purposes of the program are to deter drug use among those eligible for promotion to sensitive positions within the Service and to prevent the promotion of drug users to those positions. These substantial interests, no less than the Government's concern for safe rail transportation at issue in *Railway Labor Executives,* present a special need that may justify departure from the ordinary warrant and probable cause requirements. ...

[The Court first concluded that the Customs Service should not be required to obtain a warrant from a federal judge or magistrate before conducting the "search" (i.e., taking a urine sample) because the rules specifying who is to be tested are clear and are known to employees, and applying the rules requires no exercise of discretion by a representative of the Customs Service. There is thus nothing for a judge or magistrate to review for the purpose of preventing

CONTINUED

abuse of governmental discretion in a particular case.]

Even where it is reasonable to dispense with the warrant requirement in the particular circumstances, a search ordinarily must be based on probable cause. However, the probable-cause standard is peculiarly related to criminal investigations. In particular, the traditional probable-cause standard may be unhelpful in analyzing the reasonableness of routine administrative functions, especially where the Government seeks to prevent the development of hazardous conditions.... We think the Government's need to conduct the suspicionless searches required by the Customs program outweighs the privacy interests of employees engaged directly in drug interdiction, and of those who otherwise are required to carry firearms.

The Customs Service is our Nation's first line of defense against one of the greatest problems affecting the health and welfare of our population... [the] smuggling of illicit narcotics.... Many of the Service's employees are often exposed to this criminal element and to the controlled substances they seek to smuggle into the country. The physical safety to these employees may be threatened, and many may be tempted not only by bribes from the traffickers with whom they deal, but also by their own access to vast sources of valuable contraband seized and controlled by the Service. ... It is readily apparent that the Government has a compelling interest in ensuring that front-line interdiction personnel are physically fit, and have unimpeachable integrity and judgment. ... This national interest in self protection [from drug smuggling] could be irreparably damaged if those charged with safeguarding it were, because of their own drug use, unsympathetic to their mission of interdicting narcotics.... The public interest demands effective measures to bar drug users from positions directly involving the interdiction of illegal drugs.

The public interest likewise demands effective measures to prevent the promotion of drug users to positions that require the employee to carry a firearm, even if the employee is not engaged directly in the interdiction of drugs. ... We agree with the Government that the public should not bear the risk that employees who may suffer from impaired perception and judgment will be promoted to positions where they may need to employ deadly force....

Against these valid public interests we must weigh the interference with individual liberty that results from requiring these classes of employees to undergo a urine test.... It is plain that certain forms of public employment may diminish privacy expectations even with respect to personal searches. Employees of the United States Mint, for example, should expect to be subject to certain routine personal searches when they leave the workplace every day....

We think Customs employees who are directly involved in the interdiction of illegal drugs or who are required to carry firearms in the line of duty likewise have a diminished expectation of privacy in respect to the intrusions occasioned by a urine test. Unlike most private citizens or government employees in general, employees involved in drug interdiction reasonably should expect effective inquiry into their fitness and probity.

Much the same is true of employees who are required to carry firearms....

The procedures prescribed by the Customs Service for the collection and analysis of the requisite samples do not carry the grave potential for arbitrary and oppressive interference with the privacy and personal security of individuals that the Fourth Amendment was designed to prevent. Indeed, these procedures significantly minimize the program's intrusion on privacy interests. Only employees who have been tentatively accepted for promotion or transfer to one of the three categories of covered positions are tested, and applicants know at the outset that a drug test is a requirement of those positions. Employees are also notified in advance of the scheduled sample collection. ... There is no direct observation of the act of urination, as the employee may provide a specimen in the privacy of a stall.

Further, urine samples may be examined only for specific drugs. The use of samples to test for any other substances is prohibited. And... the combination of EMIT and GC/MS tests required by the Service is highly accurate, assuming proper storage, handling, and measurement techniques. Finally, an employee need not disclose personal medical information to the Government unless his test result is positive, and even then any such information is reported to a licensed physician. Taken together, these procedures significantly minimize the intrusiveness of the Service's drug screening program....

In sum, we believe the Government has demonstrated that its compelling in-

CONTINUED

terests in safeguarding our borders and the public safety outweigh the privacy expectations of employees who seek to be promoted to positions that directly involve the interdiction of illegal drugs or that require the incumbent to carry a firearm. We hold that the testing of these employees is reasonable under the Fourth Amendment.

[The Court then concluded that the third category of employee required to submit to drug testing, those who "handled classified material," might be too broad to withstand constitutional scrutiny. The Court remanded the case on this point so that the court of appeals could determine whether this category was indeed too broad.] . . .

We hold that the suspicionless testing of employees who apply for promotion to positions directly involving the interdiction of illegal drugs, or to positions which require the incumbent to carry a firearm, is reasonable.

OTHER PRIVACY ISSUES

Issues of employee privacy arise in many other situations, as well. For example, tests or questionnaires designed to assess personality or to obtain a psychological profile are used by some companies as a means of screening job applicants or trouble-shooting among current employees. The use of such pen-and-paper tests has increased markedly since Congress banned most employment-related uses of the lie detector. Individual employees and employee groups sometimes claim that these tests are unreliable and constitute unwarranted intrusions into workers' private lives. Although some bills have been introduced in Congress and a few state legislatures to regulate the use of these tests, no significant regulation has resulted. As long as such tests and their results are used properly, there is little risk of employer liability under basic tort law principles. Some states do have statutes prohibiting certain questions from being asked of job applicants, such as those relating to arrests for minor crimes when no conviction has resulted. In addition, some of the employment discrimination laws discussed in the next chapter prohibit certain types of questions, such as those relating to religion. Regardless of legal questions, however, an employer should use tests or questionnaires only when there is an excellent justification for doing so, and the instrument should be designed to intrude into the lives of individuals to no greater extent than is absolutely necessary. Even if there are no legal problems, misuse of these measuring devices can generate ill will and bad publicity.

Other current privacy issues in the workplace involve attempts by companies to monitor employees in various ways. Some employers, for instance, monitor employees' telephone conversations and computer communications, use devices to count computer keystrokes, or watch employees' activities by means of closed-circuit television. Although there also have been complaints among employees and their organizations about such monitoring activities, thus far there has been no specific legal response. Again, regardless of any legal risk for employers, good personnel management calls for use of monitoring techniques only when there are compelling reasons for doing so, as well as design of the monitoring program in the least intrusive way possible.

WORKERS' COMPENSATION LEGISLATION

On-the-job injuries and work-related diseases have always been with us. These problems, with their enormous social costs and individual tragedies, became much more acute in the latter nineteenth and early twentieth centuries, in part because of rapid industrialization. In addition, there was a growing recognition that society must deal more adequately with a variety of problems facing the workforce.

By this time the principle was already well established in common law that an employer was legally responsible for the injury or death of employees resulting from the employer's negligence (for example, knowingly permitting an unsafe condition in the workplace). An employee seeking compensation for injuries was faced with bringing a lawsuit against an employer who usually had far greater resources. Moreover, the employee was required to prove that the employer had actually been negligent in some particular way, often a difficult task. The common law also recognized several defenses of the employer that often defeated the employee's claim even if it was proved that the employer had been negligent.

The harshness with which the law treated the disabled employee led to demands for change. Between 1900 and 1910 many states passed statutes modifying the employer's defenses against a claim of negligence. Nonetheless, the employee was still faced with the burden of a lawsuit in which the employer's negligence must be proved. Other legal remedies were urged, and in 1911 the first significant workers' compensation statute was enacted in the United States. Today, all states have enacted such legislation. Similar workers' compensation laws are found in many other nations.

The basic thrust of modern workers' compensation legislation is to provide payments to injured employees for medical expenses and lost income regardless of whether the employer or anyone else was at fault. The costs of paying these benefits, or the premiums for insurance to pay them, are borne by the employer. The payments or premiums are viewed as costs of production and, to the extent permitted by the marketplace, are passed on to the employer's customers in the price of the goods or services sold. Thus, the financial risk of on-the-job injury or work-related disease is at least partly spread across the society that benefited from the injured employee's labor.

The remainder of this section examines the basic provisions of state workers' compensation statutes and then briefly discusses several federal statutes that have been enacted by Congress to deal with particular groups of employees.

CHAPTER 16 EMPLOYMENT LAW: PROTECTION OF EMPLOYEE SECURITY AND WELFARE

GENERAL COVERAGE OF WORKERS' COMPENSATION LAWS

Practically all industrial employment is covered by workers' compensation. In about two-thirds of the states, the workers' compensation laws apply regardless of the number of employees a firm has. In the other states, employers with fewer than a specified number of employees (usually three to five) are exempt. Many states exclude farm laborers and domestic servants, although a number of states have recently included such employees.

In addition to covering most private employment, the workers' compensation statutes of almost all states cover state and local government employees. Federal government employees, as well as maritime, railroad, and airline employers, are protected by federal legislation that will be discussed later.

The nationwide trend during the 1970s and 1980s was to bring more and more employees into state workers' compensation systems, primarily by reducing the number of exemptions from coverage and by changing from elective to compulsory systems. By the late 1980s slightly over 90 percent of all civilian employees paid on a wage or salary basis were covered by workers' compensation.

HOW WORKERS' COMPENSATION LAWS OPERATE

Assume that Roger, an employee in an aluminum fabricating plant, injures his hand while working. If Roger is covered by workers' compensation he usually cannot sue his employer or a co-worker for damages resulting from the injury.[2] Instead, he notifies his employer of his claim within a prescribed period of time. In many cases, the employer (or the employer's insurance carrier) will simply pay the employee the amount prescribed by state law, and the claim will be settled. On the other hand, if the employer or insurance company feels there is a question about the nature or severity of the injury, or perhaps whether it was job-related at all, a settlement may not be forthcoming. In such a case, the employee must file a formal claim with the designated state agency. In a few states, such claims are filed directly in a court, but in most states they are filed with an administrative agency. These agencies are given various names, such as Industrial Accident Board or Workers' Compensation Commission. Either party can appeal if dissatisfied with the initial ruling. In most states the appeal is from the agency to a court. In those few states in which a court makes the initial ruling, the appeal is to a higher court.

A No-Fault System

As mentioned previously, workers' compensation is a no-fault system. If the agency (or the court) decides that the injury was job-related, compensation is awarded regardless of whether the employer, employee, or anyone else was at fault. The employee does not have to prove that the employer was negligent, and there are virtually no defenses. The major exception is that workers'

---

[2] In the rare case in which the employee can prove that the employer or a co-worker *intentionally* caused the injury, the employee is permitted to sue for damages. A few states also permit a lawsuit in the case of *gross negligence*, which is the failure to exercise even a slight degree of care.

compensation does not cover intentionally self-inflicted injuries. There may, of course, be a controversy as to the nature or extent of the injury, but such a controversy is resolved by the agency or court as are other factual disputes—on the basis of the evidence.

Claims against Outsiders

Even though workers' compensation laws ordinarily do not permit an injured employee to sue the employer or another employee for negligence, such a suit can be brought against an outsider who caused the injury. For example, if the employee's injury is caused by a defectively made machine that the employer had purchased, the employee will be able to sue the machine's manufacturer on the basis of negligence or strict tort liability. Similarly, suppose that the employer had hired an independent contractor to renovate its business premises, and the job had been done negligently. If, because of this negligence, a newly installed light fixture falls on an employee, he or she usually can sue the independent contractor. In cases where an outsider is responsible, damages collected from the outsider generally are deducted from the amount for which the employer or its insurance carrier are responsible under workers' compensation law. Or, the employer or insurance carrier may initially pay the employee's workers' compensation claim and then sue the outsider. Any money recovered from the outsider above the amount of the workers' compensation claim would have to be paid over to the employee.

Course of Employment

The typical workers' compensation statute provides coverage for "personal injury caused by accidents arising out of and in the course of employment." Under such a standard, many injuries are clearly job-related and thus covered without question. An employee working in a factory who suffers a back injury while carrying a heavy load as part of his job duties is obviously covered by workers' compensation. Employees usually are also covered while engaging in actions that are reasonably incidental to job duties. For example, an employee on a lunch break who slips and falls in the employer's cafeteria would be covered. Similarly, an employee who uses shower facilities provided by the employer at the workplace will be covered for an injury from a fall while showering.

Sometimes, however, a difficult course-of-employment question can be presented. Suppose that an employee is injured while attending an employer-sponsored activity such as a company picnic. If attendance was required explicitly or if the evidence indicates that attendance was implicitly required because failure to attend such functions could adversely affect an employee's career, an injury suffered at the picnic would be covered. The question whether the activity was implicitly required is often a very close one.

An employee whose job requires travel will normally be able to receive workers' compensation benefits for almost any injury related to the various risks involved in traveling. Automobile accidents while traveling for the employer clearly woulld be included. In addition, injuries sustained while stopping to help a stranded motorist or to direct traffic at the scene of an accident, for example, would be covered. An employee is usually not covered, however, while merely commuting between home and work.

When an employee's job responsibilities require him or her to be away from home on a 24-hour basis, the course of employment is expanded to include virtually all reasonable activities. For example, if Jones's employer sends her to another city on business for two weeks, Jones obviously would be covered by workers' compensation while traveling and also while actually doing the employer's business in the other city. In addition, Jones would be within the course of employment while staying in the hotel, going out to dinner, or attending a concert during the evening in the other city. Any such voluntary activity that is reasonable and does not greatly increase the employee's risk of injury is normally covered by workers' compensation in the away-from-home situation. However, if Jones went skydiving or drove a car in a demolition derby during her off hours in the other city, any resulting injury probably would not be covered by workers' compensation because the activity greatly increased her risk of injury.

In the common situation in which an employee's injury occurs while he or she is on the employer's premises, the agencies and courts generally have shown a tendency in recent years to rule in the employee's favor when the course of employment question is a close one. However, an agency or court will only go so far—the injury must have at least some reasonable relation to the employee's work. For instance, an injury incurred by an employee while fighting, playing a practical joke, or otherwise clearly departing from job duties will not be covered unless the evidence demonstrates that the employer or a supervisor knew that such activities were customary and did not take adequate steps to stop them. The following case illustrates the usual approach of courts when they have to decide whether (and under what circumstances) an employee's departure from duties should cause a denial of workers' compensation benefits.

CASE

SEGLER
v.
THE INDUSTRIAL COMMISSION,

SUPREME COURT OF ILLINOIS 406 N.E.2d 542 (1980)

Gary Selger was employed by Caterpillar Tractor Co. as a "punch-out monitor" in one of its factories. Approximately 20 to 25 feet from his work station, there was a large industrial oven, through which passed a conveyor-roller system. Block-like 30-inch-high flasks, which contained molds, were fixed at regular intervals on the conveyor. They were transported on the conveyor into the oven. Selger testified that, to reach his work area, he was regularly required to pass through the spaces between the flasks.

One morning, the conveyor system was not operating, but the oven was warm. Selger, having previously observed one employee put food into the oven, placed a frozen pot pie on a

CONTINUED

shelf inside the oven. Approximately 30 minutes later, as he reached into the oven to retrieve the pie, the conveyor system was started. The flask nearest the oven struck and moved Segler's right foot, placing him in a position between one flask and the oven. A vertically protruding pin, approximately 1 1/2 inches in diameter and 3 1/2 inches high, affixed to the advancing flask, struck Segler's left hip, forcing him against the oven. Thus wedged, Segler was injured as the flask pin tore through his left, then his right, hip and buttocks.

Segler (claimant) filed a claim for workers' compensation benefits with the Illinois Industrial Commission. The Commission denied Segler's claim, ruling that his injury had not arisen out of and in the course of his employment. Segler appealed to the Circuit Court of Peoria County, which affirmed the Commission's decision. Segler then appealed to the Illinois Supreme Court.

MORAN, JUSTICE:

...An injury is compensable under workmen's compensation only if it arose out of and in the course of employment. To "arise out of" employment, an injury must have its origin in some risk connected or incidental to the employee's duties so that there is a causal connection between the injury and the employment. An injury is "in the course of" employment when it occurs within the period of employment, at a place where the employee can reasonably be expected to be in the performance of his duties, and while he is performing those duties or doing something incidental thereto. Acts of personal comfort are generally held to be incidental to employment duties and, thus, are in the course of employment. However, if the employee voluntarily and in an unexpected manner exposes himself to a risk outside any reasonable exercise of his duties, any injury incurred as a result will not be within the course of employment.

In the present case, the claimant was not in the reasonable exercise of his duties at the time the injury occurred. He was performing no job task in that area, and his actions cannot be thought of as beneficial to the employer. Instead, the claimant voluntarily undertook a course of action solely for his own benefit, thereby exposing himself to a risk greater than that to which he would have been exposed had he been pursuing his assigned duties at his designated work area 25 feet away. His actions were, in fact, unnecessary, inherently dangerous and unreasonable.

Despite the fact that an employee chooses an unreasonable and unnecessary risk, the employer may, nonetheless, be held liable if he has knowledge of or has acquiesced in such a practice or custom. In the present case, however, there is no basis for finding that the employer had knowledge of or acquiesced in such an act. The claimant himself testified that, during the 1 1/2 years he had worked in this area, he had seen only one person place food in the oven.

The claimant argues that his injuries are compensable since he was regularly required to pass over the conveyor in order to get to and from his work area and since his act of placing a pot pie in the oven exposed him to no greater risk than that to which he was daily exposed. At the time of injury, however, claimant was not going to and from his work station and was, in fact, between the oven and a flask, not between two fixed flasks, his customary point of crossing the conveyor.

We have often stated the rule that it is within the unique province of the Commission to draw inferences from facts presented and to determine whether the injury was the result of unreasonable, unexpected and unnecessary risks to which an employee voluntarily exposed himself. We find that, under the instant circumstances, the Commission could find that the claimant's conduct constituted an unreasonable risk and, consequently, that the injury did not arise out of or in the course of employment. Such a conclusion is not against the manifest weight of the evidence.

Judgment affirmed.

OCCUPATIONAL DISEASES

Workers' compensation laws originally made no provision for job-related diseases. Today, however, all states provide coverage for them. Thus, an employee who has incurred a disease "arising out of and in the course of employment" may recover essentially the same benefits as one who has suffered an on-the-job injury. Most such diseases result from prolonged exposure to certain substances in the workplace. Examples include silicosis from silicon, asbestosis from asbestos, and radiation disability from radioactive materials.[3] Loss of hearing from prolonged noise exposure is another example.

In recent years the issue of job-related *stress* has been especially troublesome for courts and workers' compensation commissions. Sometimes the continual physical or psychological stress of an occupation actually disables a worker by causing an emotional breakdown or physical illness such as a heart attack or an ulcer. When there is clear proof that job stress was the primary cause of the disabling condition, should the condition be treated as a compensable injury or disease? The commissions and courts have said yes when stress is proved to have caused an identifiable *physical* ailment. When the stress has caused a purely psychological or emotional disability, commissions and courts in a majority of states have held that the disability is covered by workers' compensation, but in a number of states they have held that it is not covered.

INSURANCE REQUIREMENTS

In all states, an employer who is subject to the workers' compensation law is required to insure against employees' claims for benefits. Ordinarily the employer meets this requirement by purchasing insurance from a private insurance carrier. In a small number of states, however, employers must pay premiums to a state-administered insurance fund rather than to a private carrier.

In almost all states, employers are permitted the option of self-insuring. In other words, under state supervision an employer can set up a reserve fund to cover claims and regularly contribute to it instead of paying insurance premiums. Generally, only a large company with many employees is capable of self-insuring. However, most states now permit smaller employers to join together in a group self-insurance pool.

BENEFITS

The benefits payable as the result of a job-related injury or disease are of four types: income replacement, medical, death, and rehabilitation.

An injured employee who misses work and consequently loses income is entitled to cash **income replacement** benefits to partially replace the lost income. In all states a waiting period must elapse before income replacement benefits are payable. In other words, the employee must be out of work for a

---

[3] Coal miners suffering from black lung disease as a result of prolonged exposure to coal dust are covered by separate federal legislation, the Black Lung Act.

certain period of time before there is a right to this type of compensation. The typical waiting period ranges from three to seven days. However, if the disability continues for more than a specified time (from one to six weeks in various states), benefits are made retroactive to the actual date of injury.

The benefits payable, and the method of calculation, depend on the extent (total or partial) and the duration (permanent or temporary) of the disability. Most of the benefits paid are for either temporary total or permanent partial disability. For example, an employee who breaks a leg and cannot work for three months has a temporary total disability. Income replacement benefits in such a case will be a certain percentage (usually 66 2/3, but ranging from 60 to 90) of the employee's current average weekly wages. In many states, the amount of the payment is subject to minimum and maximum limits. This weekly amount is paid for the duration of the disability. Of course, total disability sometimes is permanent, such as a paralyzing or brain-damaging injury. In such cases, most state laws provide for permanent payment of the specified weekly amount. In some states, however, a time limit is placed on payments for permanent total disability (such as 500 weeks in Indiana).

An injury that causes only a partial inability to continue at one's job may also be of either a temporary or permanent nature. The loss, or loss of use, of a member of the body is one type of injury resulting in permanent partial disability. Most states provide specified lump-sum compensation for so-called *scheduled injuries*. In other words, the law includes a schedule, or list, of body members and a set amount of compensation for the loss of that particular member. In addition to the scheduled amount, most state laws also would provide this employee with benefits for temporary total disability during recovery.

In times of rapidly increasing health care costs, **medical benefits** are one of the most important workers' compensation benefits received by an injured employee. If an injury or disease is compensable, all medical expenses are usually paid without dollar or time limits.

When an industrial accident or occupational disease causes death, the laws of all states provide for **death benefits** to be paid to the worker's spouse and children. The amount usually varies with the number of dependents and is a stated percentage of the employee's average weekly wages. In most states these payments are subject to minimum and maximum limitations. Death benefits to a spouse ordinarily terminate on remarriage, and benefits for children cease when they reach a certain age. Several states also impose a maximum time limit (such as 450 weeks) on the payment of death benefits regardless of a spouse's remarriage or the age of children.

Rehabilitation benefits are also an important part of state workers' compensation laws. In addition to helping ease the financial burden of job-related injuries and diseases, workers' compensation also should attempt to return the worker to productivity as soon as possible. In furtherance of this objective, almost all states require that at least some financial assistance be provided for rehabilitative therapy and training.

FEDERAL WORKERS' COMPENSATION LAWS

In response to the particular needs of certain groups of employees, Congress has enacted several pieces of legislation dealing with the injured worker.

The Federal Employees' Compensation Act (FECA) provides a comprehensive workers' compensation system for civilian employees of the federal government. The provisions of FECA are very much like those of the typical state workers' compensation statute.

The Longshoremen's and Harbor Workers' Compensation Act (Longshore Act) provides a compensation system for dock workers. It, too, is similar to most state workers' compensation laws.

The job-injury law for employees of interstate railroads and airlines is the Federal Employers' Liability Act (FELA). FELA is quite different from other workers' compensation laws in that it does not provide for a no-fault system. Instead, the employer is liable for an employee's injury only if the employer was negligent. The employer's common-law defenses against a claim of negligence, however, have been almost completely abrogated. The only substantive defense remaining under the FELA is *comparative negligence*. In other words, if a jury concludes that the employee's own negligence contributed a certain percentage to the injury, the amount of damages is reduced by that percentage. Another federal law, the Jones Act, applies the rules of FELA to workers on seagoing vessels.

AN APPRAISAL OF WORKERS' COMPENSATION

The objectives of workers' compensation laws have been achieved only in part during the first 80 years of their existence. In many states the benefits payable to an injured employee traditionally have been set unrealistically low. In addition, certain classes of employers and employees usually were excluded from coverage. As a result, the federal government in 1970 created the National Commission on State Workmen's Compensation Laws to study the problem and make recommendations. In 1972 the Commission issued its report, in which it concluded that state workers' compensation legislation is theoretically sound in its "no-fault" approach to work-related injuries and diseases, but that in most states a number of changes were necessary for the system to achieve its goals. The Commission was particularly concerned about incomplete coverage and inadequate compensation. In 1976 a task force of representatives from several federal government agencies was similarly critical of existing state laws.

Although these groups recommended change, they both felt that a unified federal system of workers' compensation was *not* the answer. Legislation has been introduced in Congress on several occasions that would involve the federal government in setting minimum standards for state workers' compensation laws, but these bills have never received sufficient support to come even close to passage. In the late 1970s and the 1980s, many state legislatures obviously have noticed the criticisms directed at workers' compensation laws, and have significantly liberalized their provisions in favor of the injured employee.

From the employer's perspective, however, liberalization of workers' compensation substantially increases the cost of doing business. The lack of uniformity in coverage and benefits contributes to the large differences in business costs among the various states. Moreover, when U.S. companies face competition from overseas manufacturers who do not incur these same costs, they are unable to pass on a sizable portion of these costs to consumers. The pressure then increases to move manufacturing operations to overseas locations, or to buy more component parts overseas. The obvious answer seems to be a major effort to *prevent* workplace injuries and diseases. As we will see in the next section, this effort has begun, but the level of success it has achieved in questionable.

THE OCCUPATIONAL SAFETY AND HEALTH ACT

With regard to job-related accidents and diseases, the goal of society should be *prevention,* not just compensation. Workers' compensation laws have had little effect on the accident and disease rate. By the late 1960s, when workers' compensation laws had been on the books for 50 years or more, about 14,500 persons were killed annually as a result of industrial accidents. Approximately 2.2 million workers were disabled on the job each year, causing an annual loss of 250 million employee work days. An estimated 390,000 workers each year developed occupational diseases. Moreover, the rate of industrial accidents and diseases continued to increase at an alarming rate.

Most states had industrial safety laws as early as 1920. These laws obviously were ineffective. Congress had enacted specialized safety legislation before 1970. For example, the Coal Mine Safety Act was passed in 1952 and was superseded in 1969 by the Coal Mine Health and Safety Act. The Maritime Safety Act was made law in 1958 to improve working conditions of maritime employees. In 1966, Congress passed the Metal and Nonmetallic Mine Safety Act. In 1969 legislation was adopted to establish safety standards on federally funded construction projects. The Federal Railway Act of 1970 contained several provisions aimed at employee safety.

These specialized statutes paved the way for a more comprehensive response to the job safety problem—the Occupational Safety and Health Act (OSHA) of 1970, in which Congress attempted to promote health and safety across all segments of American industry.

OSHA covers almost all private employers. It also applies to the federal government as an employer, but not to state and local governments.

SPECIFIC SAFETY STANDARDS

OSHA places the responsibility for developing detailed occupational safety and health standards on the Secretary of Labor. The Secretary carries out this responsibility through the Occupational Safety and Health Administration (also called OSHA, or sometimes the OSH Administration), which is part of the U.S. Department of Labor.[4] These standards usually are *affirmative* rather than *prohibitive*. In other words, OSHA standards ordinarily do not prohibit particular actions. Instead, they affirmatively require the maintenance of safe conditions, or the adoption and use of one or more practices, methods, or operations necessary to make the workplace safer.

When OSHA was passed, many safety standards had already been developed by private standard-setting organizations, industry trade associations, and other government agencies. The Labor Department adopted many of these preexisting standards as its own in order to bring them under the uniform interpretative and enforcement procedures of OSHA. For example, a number of OSHA standards have come from the American National Standards Institute and the American Society for Testing and Materials. One of OSHA's most important standards, dealing with electrical wiring in the workplace, was taken primarily from the National Electrical Code. This code had been developed previously by the National Fire Protection Association. An example of standards developed under prior federal legislation and subsequently adopted by the Labor Department are the safety rules for federally financed construction projects.

The Labor Department also has developed, and continues to develop, many new standards. In doing so, it continues to rely partly on private standard-setting organizations, but today it relies substantially on the recommendations of the National Institute for Occupational Safety and Health (NIOSH). This agency, which operates as part of the Department of Health and Human Services, was created by Congress to conduct studies and research for the development of recommended safety and health standards. Before considering a new standard, the Labor Department also will consult frequently with one or more advisory committees. These committees consist of representatives from management, labor, the public, and the occupational safety and health professions, appointed by the Secretary of Labor and the Secretary of Health and Human Services. It also must be kept in mind that the adoption of standards under OSHA is a type of government agency rule making. As a result, such adoption normally must be preceded by notice to affected parties, a public hearing, and opportunity for public comment.

A few examples of standards developed under OSHA include rules mandating eye goggles for employees operating saws, sanders, and similar equipment; maximum noise levels; protective guards on various kinds of factory machines; maximum levels of exposure to toxic substances such as lead and asbestos; and safety nets, scaffolds, temporary floors, or other safety devices for employees working more than 25 feet above the ground.

GENERAL DUTY CLAUSE

OSHA contains a provision, often referred to as the "general duty clause," which defines an employer's basic obligation to its employees when no specific standards are applicable. Under the general duty clause, an employer is

---

[4] In referring to the Labor Department in this discussion of OSHA, we usually are referring to the Labor Department's Occupational Safety and Health Administration.

required to provide every employee with a workplace that is free from recognized hazards that are actually causing or are likely to cause death or serious physical harm. In speaking of "recognized" hazards, OSHA is referring to conditions that generally would be considered hazardous in the industry involved, or that an employer knew or should have known were hazardous.

In *REA Express, Inc. v. Brennan,* 495 F.2d 822 (2d Cir. 1974), an early precedent-setting case, an employer was ruled to have violated the clause by permitting untrained employees to attempt electrical repairs on a wet concrete floor without protective equipment. In other cases, violations have been found where an employer failed to brace a free-standing wall on a construction site, operated a freight elevator with its rear shaftway doors open, and transported farmworkers in a standing position amid unsecured cargo in the back of a truck.

RIGHTS AND RESPONSIBILITIES OF EMPLOYEES

The law not only imposes a duty on the employer to keep the workplace safe and follow OSHA standards, but it also requires the *employee* to comply with prescribed safety and health rules. An employee's willful failure to comply is grounds for dismissal.

In addition to this duty of compliance, an employee also has the right to avoid unreasonably dangerous situations. When the employee (1) acts in good faith, (2) has a reasonable basis for believing that an assigned task poses a substantial risk of serious injury or death, and (3) has a reasonable belief that disobeying the employer is the only available alternative, the employee may refuse to perform the task. Under these conditions, the employee is protected by OSHA from being dismissed or otherwise penalized by the employer.

RECORD-KEEPING AND NOTICE REQUIREMENTS

Employers with more than ten employees are required to keep detailed records of most types of job-related injuries and illnesses. In a special log supplied by the Labor Department, an *injury* must be recorded within six days after the employer learns of it if the injury resulted in (1) death, (2) one or more lost workdays, (3) restriction of work or motion, (4) loss of consciousness, (5) transfer to another job, or (6) medical treatment other than first aid. A job-related *illness* must be recorded regardless of its severity. Records relating to a particular injury or illness must be retained for at least five years after the date of the occurrence, and must be made available for inspection by the Labor Department or the relevant state agency. Annual summaries of this data must be posted where notices to employees are customarily posted.

If an on-the-job accident occurs that results in the death of an employee or the hospitalization of five or more employees, all employers (regardless of size) must immediately report the accident in detail to the nearest office of the Labor Department's OSH Administration.

CHAPTER 16 EMPLOYMENT LAW: PROTECTION OF EMPLOYEE SECURITY AND WELFARE

INSPECTIONS

In addition to developing standards, the Labor Department's OSH Administration also has responsibility for enforcing OSHA. Unannounced inspections of workplaces are conducted by the agency's compliance officers.[5] In *Marshall v. Barlow's, Inc.*, 436 U.S. 307 (1978), the Supreme Court dealt with the question whether such an inspection requires a search warrant under the Fourth Amendment to the Constitution. The Court held that a warrant is required if the employer demands it. This requirement has had little effect on OSHA enforcement for two reasons. First, only about 2.5 percent of employers have been demanding a search warrant. Second, the warrant is much easier to obtain than it is in a criminal investigation. A federal court or magistrate will issue a warrant for OSHA purposes if it appears either (1) that there was a reasonable, *uniformly applied* basis for selecting that particular workplace for inspection or (2) that the Labor Department is acting pursuant to an employee complaint. The reasonable basis could include a history of violations by the employer, or a high accident or disease rate in the particular industry. In the case of employee complaints, the Labor Department must have reasonable grounds to believe that a violation of the law or a danger to health and safety exists.

The employer or its representative, plus a representative of the employees, are entitled to accompany the compliance officer during an inspection. Employees also may be interviewed privately. They may not be discriminated against in any way for having originally filed a complaint or for subsequently cooperating with a compliance officer. After the inspection a closing conference is held, in which the compliance officer and employer discuss workplace conditions and any possible violations.

Citations

If the inspection discloses violations of OSHA, the Labor Department will usually issue and mail a written citation to the employer. A copy of the citation must be posted at the workplace near the site of the violation. The citation describes the nature of the alleged violation and fixes a reasonable time for correction ("abatement") of the condition. If a penalty is assessed, it must be stated in the citation. Penalties may be as much as $1,000 for each violation. Whether a penalty is assessed, and its amount, are determined by the seriousness of the violation as well as the employer's size, good faith, and history of compliance. Repeated or willful violations can result in penalties of as much as $10,000 each. In addition, the employer can be criminally prosecuted for a willful violation that caused death. If the citation is contested by the employer, an employee, or a union, it will be reviewed by the Occupational Safety and Health Review Commission, an independent

---

[5] Any person giving unauthorized advance notice of an OSHA inspection may be punished by a fine of up to $1,000, imprisonment for up to six months, or both.

judicial-type administrative agency created solely for this purpose. The decision of the Review Commission may be appealed to a federal court of appeals.

STATE ENFORCEMENT PLANS

One of the primary reasons for OSHA's enactment was that the states had not taken adequate steps to promote job safety and health. In addition to providing for a uniform federal safety and health program, OSHA also encourages individual states to develop new measures. Under section 18 of OSHA, a state may submit a safety and health regulatory plan to the Labor Department. If the department concludes that the state plan contains standards and enforcement procedures that are at least as effective as OSHA's, it will approve the plan. In a state with an approved plan, the Labor Department relinquishes jurisdiction to state authorities. However, the department will continue to monitor the state's activities and will revoke its approval if enforcement procedures prove to be inadequate. Almost one-half of the states now have approved plans, although the degree of implementation varies greatly among these states. Only a few states, such as California, have put their plans fully into operation.

APPRAISAL OF OSHA

During the first few years after OSHA's passage, its implementation and enforcement by the Labor Department were severely criticized. A number of OSHA standards, often consisting of dozens of pages each, concerned matters that were quite trivial. OSHA seemed more concerned with things such as bathroom locations, design of toilet seats, and the details of how ladders should be built than with major workplace hazards.

In the late 1970s and early 1980s, the Labor Department began to focus its enforcement efforts on more important hazards and on particular high-risk industries. The department has simplified many of its standards and repealed a number of orders. In some cases, performance-oriented standards have replaced earlier, more complex ones. Paperwork requirements have been reduced somewhat, particularly for small businesses.

In the view of many observers, OSHA and its enforcement have become more sensible and realistic as a result of these changes. OSHA continues to be a controversial law, however. Today, unions and others representing employee interests often claim that the Labor Department's enforcement of OSHA is underfunded and not aggressive enough. However, many employers continue to view OSHA as overly intrusive into their affairs. Perhaps the most disturbing fact is that, after adjustments for business cycles, on-the-job injury and disease rates have not been affected dramatically by OSHA. Some observers feel that a completely different approach is needed to the workplace safety problem, such as "injury taxes" or other measures that would provide goals and incentives but leave the details to individual employers. OSHA seems to represent another one of those situations in which a serious social problem clearly exists, but the attempted solution still needs much refinement.

THE FAIR LABOR STANDARDS ACT

Before the Great Depression of the 1930s, the federal government had not been significantly involved in the regulation of basic labor standards. As a safety measure Congress in 1907 had set a maximum 16-hour day for certain interstate railroad workers, but wage and hour legislation had otherwise been left to the states. During the late 1800s and early 1900s, a substantial number of states enacted legislation setting minimum wages and maximum hours for women and children because they were viewed as having insufficient bargaining power for self-protection. Several states also had maximum hour statutes for workers in certain hazardous occupations.

In 1933, with national unemployment at 25 percent, Congress attempted to limit hours of work so as to spread available employment over a larger segment of the population. This legislation, the National Industrial Recovery Act (NIRA), also contained other provisions aimed at relieving the depressed state of the economy. In 1935, however, the statute was declared unconstitutional by the Supreme Court, partly because it delegated too much legislative power to the executive branch without sufficient guidelines.

In 1938 Congress passed our present federal wage and hour law, the Fair Labor Standards Act (FLSA). It is a law that, in essence, establishes a floor for wage rates and requires that employees be paid a premium for overtime work. FLSA also contains protective child labor provisions.

GENERAL COVERAGE OF FLSA

The coverage of FLSA is extremely broad. In the case of a private employer, an employee ordinarily will be covered by the Act if any aspect of the employer's business enterprise has any involvement with interstate commerce. Moreover, all civilian employees of the federal government and all state and local government workers are covered by FLSA. As we will see in the next section, however, FLSA rules on "overtime" are somewhat different for state and local government workers than for other types of employees.

The Act specifically exempts some employees from its minimum wage and overtime provisions. Employees with substantial managerial or supervisory responsibilities are excluded from FLSA. In addition, outside salespeople and professional employees such as lawyers and accountants are not covered by the Act. These types of employees would rarely benefit from the minimum wage provisions, and the nature of their work is often such that it cannot fit a normal workweek schedule for overtime purposes. Moreover, they normally have more opportunities to protect themselves economically than many other types of employees.

Employees who are members of a union having a collective bargaining agreement with the employer are not covered by FLSA's overtime provisions if the agreement provides for certain maximum hours over a six-month or one-year period. In this latter situation, Congress viewed the overtime provisions of FLSA as unnecessary.

FLSA also exempts the employees of certain small retail stores and small farms, many of which could not bear the cost of compliance. To encourage their employment in specially designed programs, learners, apprentices, and handicapped workers may sometimes be paid less than the minimum wage if specific government approval has been obtained. Also to encourage their employment, full-time students working in retail or service establishments, agriculture, or institutions of higher education may be paid subminimum wages with special government permission.

Many states also have minimum wage and overtime laws. The primary function of these laws is to provide some degree of protection for those employees not covered by FLSA, such as workers in small retail stores.

Minimum Wage and Overtime

The first minimum wage was set at 25 cents per hour in 1938. Since 1991 the minimum wage has been $4.25 an hour. Covered employees must be paid at least this amount for the first 40 hours worked in a week. If more than 40 hours are worked in a given week, the employee must be paid at least one and one-half times his or her regular wage rate for each hour more than 40. Thus, an employee who regularly makes $6.00 an hour is entitled to $9.00 an hour for time worked past 40 hours.[6] In the case of state and local government workers, however, FLSA permits their employers to grant future time off ("comp time") at a time-and-a-half rate instead of overtime pay.

Some employees are not paid on an hourly basis. For instance, a worker's pay might be based on a piecework rate, a weekly, biweekly, or monthly salary, or a salary plus commission. Regardless of the basis, a covered employee must receive at least the minimum wage for each hour worked in a week. Thus, at the present minimum of $4.25 an hour, a salaried employee or pieceworker must receive at least $170 for a 40-hour week. Overtime for such workers is computed as one and one-half times the average hourly pay during a given week. In the case of pieceworkers, however, the law provides a second method for figuring overtime if the employee and employer agree to it beforehand. This method involves payment of one and one-half times the piece rate during overtime hours.

To give needed flexibility to employers, the standard 40-hour workweek does not have to begin on Monday—an employer might, for example, choose to keep the payroll records on a Wednesday through Tuesday basis. For minimum wage and overtime purposes the workweek must, however, consist of seven consecutive 24-hour periods. With certain very narrow exceptions, there can be no averaging of two or more workweeks.

Except for its minimum wage and overtime provisions, FLSA does not attempt to regulate the terms of employment relationships. For example, it does not require an employer to give vacations or holidays, whether paid or unpaid. It has no provisions concerning rest periods during the day, pre-

---

[6] If a covered employee makes less than the minimum wage, the overtime to which he or she is entitled is one and one-half times the minimum wage.

mium pay rates for holidays or weekends, pay raises, or fringe benefits. In addition, there is no prohibition against compulsory overtime. No limit is placed on the hours an employee may work, unless the employee is younger than 16 years of age. All these matters are left to be determined by agreement between employer and employee or employer and labor union.

CHILD LABOR PROVISIONS

As previously mentioned, many of the pre-FLSA labor laws enacted by various states were aimed at protecting children. Today, most states still have child labor laws serving primarily to fill gaps in FLSA coverage. The child labor provisions of FLSA are designed to protect the educational opportunities of children and to prohibit their employment under conditions detrimental to their health and well-being. In furtherance of these goals, FLSA regulates the hours children may work and prohibits their employment in designated hazardous occupations. These provisions are summarized as follows:

1. A person 18 years of age or older may work at any job without restrictions on hours.

2. A person 16 or 17 years of age may work without restrictions on hours but not in occupations defined as hazardous. Examples of hazardous occupations include mining, logging, roofing, excavation, operating many types of power-driven machines or saws, and work involving exposure to radioactive substances.

3. A person 14 or 15 years of age may work only certain hours, and may not work in a hazardous occupation. Someone of this age may not work during school hours and may work no more than three hours on a school day, 18 hours in a school week, eight hours on a nonschool day, or 40 hours in a nonschool week. Work may not begin before 7 A.M. or end after 7 P.M., except that evening hours are extended to 9 P.M. in the summer. These restrictions are relaxed slightly for 14 and 15 year olds in an approved Work Experience and Career Exploration Program.

4. Although 14 is the minimum age for most work, children younger than this age may deliver newspapers, work in entertainment, work for their parents, and with some restrictions work in agriculture.

ADMINISTRATION AND ENFORCEMENT

FLSA is administered and enforced by the Labor Department's Wage and Hour Division. The Division requires complete employment and payroll records to be maintained, although these required records usually are no more extensive than good personnel practices would dictate. On an informal basis, the Division often advises employers as to changes in their business practices that would bring them into compliance with the law.

Willful violations of FLSA may be prosecuted criminally, resulting in large fines and, for a second offense, imprisonment. Those violating the law's child labor provisions, whether willfully or not, can be forced to pay a penalty of $1,000 per violation. The Division may supervise the payment of back wages under a settlement between the parties. In addition, the Division may bring suit in federal district court for an injunction restraining an employer from violating the law. A lawsuit against the employer for back wages may be brought by either the employee or the Division. If the court finds a violation and orders back wages to be paid, it may also order the employer to pay an additional amount equal to the back wages. This additional amount is referred to in FLSA as "liquidated damages." Actually, however, these damages are more in the nature of punishment because the court may reduce or refuse to award this amount if it concludes that the employer attempted in good faith to comply with the law.

The following case provides an illustration of one of the many situations in which an employer's practice of having employees on call can create a difficult overtime pay issue under FLSA.

NORTON v. WORTHEN VAN SERVICE, INC.

U.S. COURT OF APPEALS, 10TH CIRCUIT 839 F.2d 653 (1988)

Worthen Van operates a van service throughout Wyoming and adjoining states, transporting railroad crews to and from their trains. When the railroad needs a crew transported, a dispatcher telephones a driver who is responsible for quickly arriving at the Worthen facility. Drivers generally work shifts of eight to 12 hours a day. During these shifts, drivers must be near enough to the employer's premises to be able to respond to calls within 15 to 20 minutes. However, drivers are compensated for their waiting time only if they receive a call to transport railroad crews within two hours of their last call. If a driver fails to respond promptly to a dispatcher's call, he is disciplined by the company. A driver may be fired if he is disciplined three times.

Norton and several others who were either employees or former employees, filed suit against Worthen seeking back wages, overtime compensation, and liquidated damages under FLSA. The main basis for their claim was that all of their waiting time was working time for purposes of calculating overtime. The federal district court ruled for the employer, because the court concluded that the time spent on call was used primarily for the benefit of the employees, because they could leave the employer's premises and pursue personal matters that did not interfere with their ability to quickly return to work. The plaintiffs appealed.

MOORE, CIRCUIT JUDGE:

... Plaintiffs argue that this final finding by the trial court is clearly eroneous and urge us to decide that waiting while on call constitutes an integral part of their job. The employees argue that the unpredictability of assignments and the short response time which they are allowed preclude their using this waiting period for their own purposes. Rather, they argue, the period between assignments is predominantly for Worthen Van's benefit, and employees should therefore receive compensation for the time they spend waiting. Plaintiffs also argue that Worthen Van strongly encourages drivers on call to remain at work between runs. Because of this policy, according to the plaintiffs, drivers have waited on or very near the Worthen Van premises for up to seven hours without getting paid.

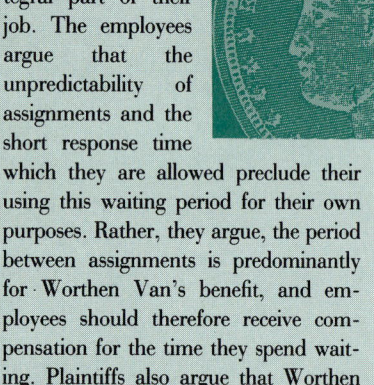

Whether periods of waiting for work should be compensable under the FLSA is to be determined by the facts and circumstances of each case. The FLSA

CONTINUED

simply defines "employ" as "to suffer or permit to work," and does not further define the relevant terms. Case law has focused on how close an on-call employee must remain to the employer's premises or a work-related vehicle to be considered working. In *Armour v. Wantock*, 323 U.S. 126 (1944), plaintiffs had to remain on call on the employer's premises for fifteen hours after their regular shifts as auxiliary firemen. The Supreme Court affirmed a lower court holding that the time spent eating and sleeping did not constitute work time, but that all waiting or on-call time should be compensated under the FLSA because "time spent lying in wait for threats to the safety of the employer's property may be treated by the parties as a benefit to the employer." That same day, the Court in *Skidmore v. Swift & Co.*, 323 U.S. 134 (1944), awarded compensation to auxiliary firemen for their on-call shifts, during which they had to remain on or very near the employer's premises. According to the Court, resolution of the matter involved determining the degree to which the employee could engage in personal activity while subject to being called. "Facts may show that the employee was engaged to wait, or they may show that he waited to be engaged."

The progeny of *Armour* and *Skidmore* further elucidate when waiting to work should be compensable. In *Allen v. United States*, 1 Cl. Ct. 649 (1983), aff'd, 723 F.2d 69 (Fed. Cir. 1983), the court determined that federal marshals should not receive compensation under the FLSA for being on call after their regular work day. In reaching this conclusion, the court emphasized that on-call federal marshals were free to pursue their individual pursuits subject only to the requirement that they remain sober and within range of their electronic beepers. Similarly, in *Pilkenton v. Appalachian Regional Hospitals*, 336 F. Supp. 334 (W.D. Va. 1971), the court held that plaintiff laboratory technicians should not receive compensation for being on call because their freedom during these periods was circumscribed only by the requirements that they leave a phone number and arrive at the hospital within twenty minutes of receiving the call.

These opinions indicate that plaintiffs should not recover for the time they are on call. The firemen in *Armour* had to remain on the employer's premises, and in *Skidmore*, plaintiffs only had the choice of remaining in the firehall or staying within immediate hailing distance. Subsequent case law follows *Armour* and *Skidmore* by compensating employees who are required to remain either on the employer's premises, in the immediate vicinity, or by a work-related vehicle. The Worthen Van employees, on the other hand, have more of an opportunity to pursue personal business between assignments, even if being on call does limit their activity. Testimony showed that drivers spent their time between assignments at the homes of friends, at church, at laundromats, at restaurants, at pool halls, and at a local gymnasium. Several plaintiffs testified that they pursued hobbies, such as working on guns or physical fitness, while waiting to be called by a dispatcher. Furthermore, a simple paging device, which the drivers are free to purchase and to use, would have allayed the necessity of remaining by a phone.

We also believe Worthen Van made a significant effort to allow its drivers to use their waiting time effectively. Although on several occasions drivers were told by dispatchers to wait at the employer's premises, in each instance the head dispatcher sat down with the driver and the ordering dispatcher and reiterated the "Worthen Van policy" that on-call drivers may wait anywhere so long as they can be reached. Drivers also had the option to "go unavailable" for a certain period of time during which they would not be called, or to drop to the bottom of the driving list, making it far more unlikely they would be called. Even though a condition of the plaintiffs' employment required a restriction on their personal activities, we believe the trial court correctly concluded this restriction did not constitute working time. Accordingly, the judgment of the district court is affirmed.

COMMENT

Although the time during which an employee is required to stay on the employer's premises usually will be treated as working time under FLSA, this is not true if the employee actually *lives* on the employer's premises. In such a case, the time spent by the employer in living quarters on the employer's property is not automatically viewed as working time. A combination of other factors, such as being on call, restricted to the premises, and subject to frequent interruptions for the employer's benefit, would have to be proved in order for time in living quarters to be treated as working time.

OTHER FEDERAL LABOR STANDARDS LAWS

Several other federal laws focus on minimum labor standards for employers who contract with the federal government. The Davis-Bacon Act, passed in 1931, determines wage rates for federally financed or assisted construction. It does not set a minimum wage, but requires employers involved in such construction to pay its employees at least the prevailing rate for similar work in that locality. The prevailing rate is determined by the Labor Department, and will never be set below FLSA's minimum wage. Overtime under Davis-Bacon is required for hours over 40 per week *or* eight per day. A noncomplying employer can have its federal construction contract terminated, and will be liable for any of the government's additional costs in getting someone else to complete the project.

Two other enactments containing almost identical provisions apply to employers making other types of contracts with the federal government. The Walsh-Healey Act of 1936 applies to employers contracting to furnish goods and supplies to the government. The Service Contract Act of 1965 applies to employers contracting to provide services for the government. The "prevailing rate" under the Service Contract Act is determined by the Labor Department for the particular locality, as it is under the Davis-Bacon Act. Under Walsh-Healey, however, the prevailing rate is set by the Labor Department for entire industries. Overtime under the Walsh-Healey and Service Contract Acts is required for hours over 40 per week *or* eight per day, as it is under the Davis-Bacon Act.

UNEMPLOYMENT COMPENSATION

The extremely high unemployment levels of the Depression era spawned a federal attempt to provide partial income replacement for unemployed workers. The Social Security Act of 1935 included provisions imposing a three percent tax on the payroll of most employers to finance the payment of unemployment compensation.

Since 1935, operation of the unemployment compensation system has been taken over almost completely by the individual states. In the original enactment, Congress stated that employers would be excused from 90 percent of the tax (2.7 of the 3 percent) in any state that adopted a federally approved compensation plan. All states have done so. Each state must levy a tax to finance its own system, and most states adopted taxes equal to the amount that could be credited against the federal tax. Today, an employer's basic unemployment tax liability is 0.8 percent to the federal government and 5.4 percent to the state. This tax is payable, however, only on the first $7,000 of each employee's wages. In addition, a particular employer's actual tax may be somewhat lower or higher than this basic rate because the "experience rating" of the employer will cause an adjustment of its tax rate. In other words, an employer with a record of maintaining a relatively stable workforce will pay a smaller unemployment tax than one with a poorer record. Such a system encourages employers to strive for less turnover among their employees. On the other hand, it also tends to worsen fluctuations in the business cycle, because unemployment taxes are generally higher when the overall economy is doing poorly and lower when it is doing well.

Each state has its own rules for determining when an employee is entitled to benefits. For instance, there are statutory formulas to ensure that an employee has been employed on a reasonably regular basis for a period of time before the present unemployment. In addition, most states permit an individual to file a claim for unemployment compensation only after he or she has been unemployed for a certain period of time, usually one week. To be eligible for benefits, a person also must register with the state employment agency, which will assist in finding new employment. A person who refuses to accept reasonably suitable work is disqualified from receiving unemployment benefits. In addition, benefits usually will not be paid to someone who has been fired for good cause or who quit work without good cause. For example, courts have held that an employee has good cause for quitting, and is therefore entitled to benefits, when he or she quits to take care of a seriously ill or injured family member or quits because of extreme heat and dust in the workplace. However, courts have held that an employee does not have good cause for quitting, and is therefore not entitled to benefits, when he or she quits because of dissatisfaction with pay or because of a reasonable request by the employer to change working hours. In most states, a striking employee is not permitted to collect unemployment compensation. Those who are *unable* to work are not eligible for these payments, because other more appropriate benefits are available. Unemployment compensation is intended essentially for workers who have been "laid off" or have had to quit through no fault of their own.

Benefits are computed in various ways in different states. They usually are based on some stated fraction of average wages during a recent period, subject to minimum and maximum amounts. In most states benefits can be received for a maximum of 26 weeks. If the general level of unemployment reaches a prescribed level, however, benefits ordinarily are available for an additional period, usually 13 weeks. One-half of the benefits paid during this extended period are financed by the federal government.

Although most types of employment are covered by state unemployment compensation statutes, there are some exemptions. Many states, for example, exempt employees of small farms, the federal government, and churches. The employment of immediate family members and full-time students also is usually exempted.

QUESTIONS and PROBLEMS

1. Stilphen and Bell, co-workers at Northrop Corp., went to a party together from work in Bell's car, leaving Stilphen's car in the Northrop parking lot. According to Stilphen, Bell became extremely drunk at the party and Stilphen drove Bell's car and Bell back to the Northrop parking lot. Stilphen apparently was also drunk but not to the same degree as Bell. At the parking lot, Stilphen refused to return Bell's car keys because Bell was too drunk to drive and offered to take Bell home. Bell became enraged and insisted on driving himself home. The two argued and then began fighting. A Northrop security guard broke up the fight and reported the incident to company management. After an investigation, Northrop fired both men for being intoxicated and fighting on company property. Stilphen filed suit against Northrop for wrongful discharge, claiming that he had been fired for trying to keep a drunk driver off the road. He argued that the state of Illinois had a strong public policy of preventing intoxicated persons from driving and that Northrop's actions were contrary to that policy. Should Stilphen win his lawsuit? Discuss. (*Stilphen v. Northrop Corp.*, 515 N.E.2d 154, Ill. App. 1987.)

2. The Chattanooga Police Department instituted mandatory departmentwide drug testing by urinalysis. Of the 360 officers in the department, only two tested positive, both for marijuana. The evidence showed, however, that if the department had observed these two officers and closely monitored their personnel records, the department would have had a reasonable suspicion of their marijuana use sufficient to justify testing them. The next year the department initiated a new round of mandatory tests for the entire police department based on the following information: (a) the fact that two officers had tested positive the previous year; (b) a statement by one of these two officers that it is possible for a person being tested to switch a clean sample of urine; (c) unsubstantiated rumors that there had been some switched samples the previous year; (d) a tip from the FBI that one officer in the department had been in contact with a drug dealer; and (e) a statement that "several" officers used marijuana, made to the chief of police by an officer who had admitted marijuana use and was terminated. This new round of testing, which also was mandatory and departmentwide, was challenged by several officers. They filed suit claiming that the testing program was an unreasonable "search" in violation of the Fourth Amendment to the Constitution. The police department argued, among other things, that the court was bound by prior judicial decisions unholding mandatory mass testing of air traffic controllers and nuclear power plant employees without individualized suspicion. Based on these facts, should the police officers win? Discuss. (*Penny v. City of Chattanooga*, 846 F.2d 1563, 6th Cir. 1988.)

3. Chennault worked as a mechanic for Chicago Extruded Metals. One day after work, Chennault was taking a shower in the washroom provided by the employer for this purpose. As he dried himself he saw a cockroach going up the wall nearby. He climbed on a bench and attempted to swat the roach with his towel. As he did so, Chennault slipped off the bench and fell, causing substantial injury to his leg. (a) Assume that you are Chennault's supervisor. After getting medical aid for Chennault, what is the next thing you should do regarding his injury? (b) If Chennault files a claim for workers' compensation benefits, is he legally entitled to receive payment? Discuss. (*Chicago Extruded Metals v. Industrial Commission*, 395 N.E.2d 569, Ill. 1979.)

4. Shearer worked as a carpenter for 17 years for Republic Steel Co. During that time he was almost continually exposed to steel, cement, and blast furnace dust, as well as various types of noxious fumes. Shearer developed chronic bronchitis and emphysema, finally becoming totally disabled. He filed a claim for workers' compensation benefits, and his employer contended that benefits were not payable because (a) he had not suffered an "injury," and (b) there was no way to pinpoint which substance irritated his lungs. Would Shearer receive payment? Discuss. (*Republic Steel v. Industrial Commission*, 399 N.E.2d 1268, Ohio 1980.)

5. McKeever worked as an attorney for the legal department of New Jersey Bell Telephone Co. While driving home from work one day he was killed in an automobile accident. His family filed a claim for workers' compensation death benefits. During the legal proceedings involving the claim, it was shown that (a) the workload of a corporate attorney like McKeever was so heavy that at-home work was essential to get the job done; (b) McKeever had work in his briefcase with him at the time of his death; (c) the employer encouraged employees like McKeever to take work home and knew that they often did so; and (d) the employer benefited from McKeever's

"off-duty" legal work. Is this workers' compensation claim a valid one? Discuss. (*McKeever v. New Jersey Bell Telephone Co.*, Workmen's Comp. Law Rep. (CCH) ¶2,566, N.J. Super. Ct. App. Div. 1981.)

6. Greencastle Manufacturing Co. operated several mechanical power presses. An earlier OSHA citation had notified Greencastle that its presses must be equipped with guards on every operation. After that citation, an OSHA compliance officer observed a company press being operated without a guard. Under OSHA, the penalty is greater for a "repeated" violation. Greencastle argued that the second violation was not a repeated one for several reasons. First, the previous citation had been issued for another press, which used different dies and presented different problems in designing guard devices. Second, Greencastle had sought the Labor Department's assistance without success when it had difficulty in designing a guard for the press. Third, employees who had complained about the risk involved in removing scrap from a moving press without a guard had been instructed by Greencastle to stop the presses when necessary to remove scrap. Should Greencastle be held liable for a repeated violation? Discuss. (*Greencastle Mfg. Co.*, 1980 O.S.H.D. ¶24,301.)

7. An employee of Davey Tree Expert Co. was electrocuted when the limb of a tree that he was trimming fell against a high-voltage power line. Electrocution caused by limbs touching high-voltage lines is a recognized hazard in the industry. The method used by the employee to trim the tree—notching the limb and pulling it to make it fall parallel to the wires—is an accepted practice in the tree trimming business. (a) Identify the hazard in this case. (b) Should Davey Tree Expert Co. be found guilty of violating OSHA's general duty clause? (c) Should the infeasibility of either insulating or de-energizing the power lines be taken into account in determining whether Davey violated the general duty clause? Discuss. (*Davey Tree Expert Co.*, 11 O.S.H.C. 1898, 1984.)

8. Adcock worked 47 1/2 hours per week on a fixed salary for Hendersonville Bowling Center. About 15 percent of his time was spent doing routine maintenance work. The remainder of his time was devoted to general managerial duties, including hiring, firing, promoting, and supervising other employees. He was subject to call at irregular hours for emergencies and was allowed flexibility in taking time off for personal needs. All his work was subject only to very general supervision by the owner. A suit was brought in Adcock's behalf by the Labor Department, claiming that Adcock was covered by FLSA and should be paid overtime. The employer contended that Adcock was an executive, or managerial, employee and thus was not covered by FLSA. Is Adcock covered by FLSA? Discuss. (*Marshall v. Hendersonville Bowling Center*, 483 F. Supp. 510, M.D. Tenn. 1980.)

9. From 1982 to 1986 David Kelly was employed by Hines-Rinaldi Funeral Home to perform light housekeeping duties during the hours of 9:00 P.M. to 12:00 midnight and 6:30 A.M. to 8:30 A.M., six days per week. During the night hours between midnight and 6:30 A.M., Kelly occupied an apartment on the premises of the funeral home. This arrangement benefited both parties, because a zoning ordinance required that someone live on the premises of the funeral home and Kelly paid nothing for the apartment. Kelly was usually required to stay on the premises between midnight and 6:30 A.M., but during this time his only duties were to answer the phone, and to go out and pick up a corpse if required. If the telephone was unanswered in the funeral home after three rings, it was answered in one of three other residences where it rang simultaneously. If the call involved a request to pick up a corpse, whoever answered the call would then call an assistant to help with the pickup. During the most recent 20-month period, there had been an average of 3.35 telephone calls and 2.2 trips to pick up corpses per month. The average time spent per trip was 49.7 minutes. By 1986 Kelly's salary was $235 per week. After Kelly's employment for the funeral home ended, he filed a claim under FLSA in which he asserted that the hours between midnight and 6:30 A.M. were working time. If these hours were considered working time, Kelly's workweek would have been 69 hours, and he would have been entitled to overtime pay for 29 hours per week during the time he was employed. Should the midnight to 6:30 A.M. hours have been treated as working time? Discuss. (*Kelly v. Hines-Rinalldi Funeral Home, Inc.*, 847 F.2d 147, 4th Cir. 1988.)

10. Trussel worked as a stenographer, receptionist, and bookkeeper for a law firm. Although much of her work was acceptable and she tried hard, some of her work contained misspellings, visible erasures, and mathematical errors. She was discharged. Was she terminated for good cause, thus disqualifying her for unemployment compensation? Discuss. (*Seavy and Jensen v. Industrial Commission*, 523 P.2d 157, Colo. App. 1974.)

CHAPTER 17

THE CONCEPT OF EQUAL OPPORTUNITY

The law of employment discrimination is but one part of a larger body of law often referred to as civil rights law. The objective of civil rights law is to guarantee equal treatment for all of the nation's residents. This goal of equal opportunity extends to housing, education, public accommodations (such as restaurants, hotels, theaters, and transportation), and credit, as well as to employment.

The fundamental premise of employment discrimination law is that there cannot be true equality among this country's residents unless there is equal

EMPLOYMENT LAW: PROTECTION AGAINST DISCRIMINATION

economic opportunity. It does very little good to have equal access to quality housing and public accommodations, for example, if one has little chance of ever being able to afford them.

Economic opportunity in the United States traditionally has not been equal—the evidence of this fact is simply too strong to deny. Even after employment discrimination of various types has been declared illegal by Congress and many state legislatures, striking imbalances still remain in our nation's workforce. For example, the unemployment rate for blacks generally is far higher than the rate for whites. There are very large disparities between the income of the average black or Hispanic family's income and that of the average white family. About one-half of American Indians live below the poverty level, and their rate of unemployment is extremely high. Substantial income differences continue to exist between men and women. There also is ample evidence of economic imbalance with respect to older workers and persons with disabilities.

There are many different causes for the economic disadvantages borne by certain groups within our society. Some of the disparities can be attributed to different pressures, goals, and expectations within different groups. Such cultural differences sometimes have historical origins with little or no relation to actual discrimination. In some cases disadvantages are traceable to differences in language, education, training, and even geographic location. However, these are not the only reasons. We know from experience that there has been and still is discrimination. Some of it has been conscious, and some has been the unconscious result of stereotypes, unrecognized bias, and sheer habit. Although there is no way to tell exactly how much of the traditional imbalance in employment opportunity has resulted from conscious and unconscious discrimination, logic and common experience indicate that discrimination has played a part.

The discussion in this chapter is divided as follows. First, we study the law as it applies to discrimination based on race, color, national origin, sex, and religion. These categories are grouped together because they are all included within Title VII of the 1964 Civil Rights Act, which is our most comprehensive law against employment discrimination. In two separate sections, we then discuss the law prohibiting discrimination on the basis of age and discrimination against persons with disabilities.

RACE, COLOR, NATIONAL ORIGIN, SEX, AND RELIGION

OVERVIEW OF THE SOURCES OF LAW

The most important law prohibiting employment discrimination on the basis of race, color, national origin, sex, and religion is Title VII of the 1964 Civil Rights Act. Because of its central role, most of our discussion will focus on

Title VII. It is not, however, the only law that is relevant to these types of discrimination. A brief description of other relevant laws follows.

Section 1981

Shortly after the Civil War, Congress passed the Civil Rights Act of 1866. One of the key provisions of this statute is now codified as Title 42, Section 1981, of the U.S. Code, and is often referred to simply as "Section 1981." Section 1981 states, in essence, that "All persons shall have the same right to make and enforce contracts as is enjoyed by white citizens." Thus, Section 1981 prohibits discrimination on the basis of race or color in contractual relationships. This prohibition against racial discrimination in contracting includes employment. For various reasons, this old civil rights law was virtually ignored until the late 1960s, when it began to be used extensively as a weapon to fight ethnic employment discrimination. According to interpretations by the Supreme Court in recent years, Section 1981 applies only to employment discrimination that is based on a person's ethnic group, such as black, Hispanic, Asian-American, and so on; it does not apply to discrimination based on sex, religion, age, or disability. In addition, the Supreme Court has concluded that Section 1981 applies only to intentional discrimination.

Although the protection provided by Section 1981 is largely duplicated by Title VII, there are some differences that make the older law important. The most important is that, unlike the relatively short statute of limitations under Title VII (usually 180 days), for a Section 1981 claim the court uses the statute of limitations for tort cases in the state where the case is heard. This is typically two years.

Equal Pay Act

In the area of sex discrimination, the Equal Pay Act can sometimes be important. This statute was passed in 1963, one year before Title VII. Essentially, the Equal Pay Act prohibits discrimination in rates of compensation based on a person's sex. The law applies only to gender-based discrimination, and only when it relates to compensation. The Equal Pay Act prohibits pay differentials between men and women who are performing jobs that require "equal skill, effort, and responsibility," and are doing the jobs "under similar working conditions." Trivial differences between two jobs do not prevent them from being considered equal—What is required is that the jobs be *substantially* the same in terms of skill, effort, and responsibility. On the other hand, if the two jobs are reallly different, an employee being paid less cannot successfully claim a violation of the Equal Pay Act by contending that the jobs are of "comparable worth"—that is, of equivalent value to the employer. Differential pay rates violate the Equal Pay Act only when they are proved to be *based on sex*, rather than on some legitimate factor other than sex.

The protection afforded by the Equal Pay Act is also largely duplicated by Title VII.[1] Almost any conduct that violates the Equal Pay Act will also violate Title VII. Somewhat like section 1981, however, the Equal Pay Act has an advantage for the plaintiff in the form of a much longer statute of limitations than is found in Title VII. The Equal Pay Act uses the statute of limitations from the Fair Labor Standards Act (the minimum wage and overtime law), which is usually two years and can even be three years if a willful violation is shown.[2]

Constitution

Employment practices, policies, and decisions by local, state, or federal government agencies constitute "government action," and thus are subject to the U.S. Constitution. In particular, government employment decisions based on race, color, or national origin will almost always violate the equal protection clause of the Fourteenth Amendment. Decisions based on sex will usually violate the same clause. Government employment decisions based on religion will violate both the First Amendment guarantee of freedom of religion and the equal protection clause. (In addition, government agency employment practices based on age or condition of disability must be supported by very sound reasons or they will violate the equal protection clause.) In general, a government agency's employment practices can be found to violate the equal protection clause only if the practices are intentionally discriminatory.

Because Title VII of the 1964 Civil Rights Act and our other employment discrimination laws generally apply to government employers as well as to private companies, the Constitution's applicability to discrimination by government employers is largely redundant. In a few situations that are beyond the scope of this discussion, however, these constitutional guarantees can have independent significance.

Federal Government Contracting

An "executive order" in existence since 1965 prohibits employment discrimination by companies that have substantial contracts with the federal government. Discrimination on the basis of race, color, national origin, sex, or religion is forbidden. Although this executive order duplicates the protection of Title VII, it is nevertheless important because it creates an additional enforcement tool—a company that violates the order commits a breach of its contract with the federal government and can be barred from receiving future contracts.

---

[1] Apparently, one of the main reasons that Congress left the Equal Pay Act standing when it passed the more comprehensive Title VII one year later was that the general prohibition against sex discrimination in Title VII was not added to that bill until very late in the legislative process.

[2] Until recently, both Section 1981 and the Equal Pay Act included another feature that many individuals would view as an advantage over Title VII—the right to a jury trial. Since late 1991, however, Title VII also permits jury trials for claims of intentional discrimination on the basis of race, color, national origin, sex, or religion.

State Laws

Today, most states have statutes prohibiting discrimination in employment and other activities. Many cities also have municipal ordinances prohibiting discrimination in various settings, including employment. In general, these employment discrimination laws are patterned after Title VII of the 1964 Civil Rights Act. In some states or municipalities, however, these laws may prohibit forms of discrimination not forbidden by federal law. For example, Title VII's prohibition against sex discrimination does not include discrimination against homosexuals; the laws of some states or cities do prohibit this type of employment discrimination, however.

TITLE VII OF THE 1964 CIVIL RIGHTS ACT

The Civil Rights Act of 1964 is a comprehensive federal enactment prohibiting discrimination in various settings, including housing, public accommodations, and education. Title VII of the act deals specifically with discrimination in employment. Title VII prohibits employment discrimination against individuals because of their race, color, national origin, sex, or religion. Our discussion of Title VII includes substantial amendments made by Congress in 1972, 1978, and 1991.

Coverage, Enforcement

Title VII applies to all private employers that have at least 15 employees and whose business affects interstate or foreign commerce. The commerce requirement of Title VII is satisfied by activities having an exceedingly slight and indirect impact on interstate or foreign commerce. It is a requirement that usually is present. The law also applies to the employment practices of federal, state, and local government agencies. In addition, labor unions and employment agencies are subject to Title VII.

Title VII is administered by the Equal Employment Opportunity Commission (EEOC). As part of its enforcement authority, EEOC issues both legally binding regulations and advisory guidelines concerning the details of compliance with Title VII. When EEOC receives a complaint of employment discrimination, it will not take action until state enforcement authorities have first had an opportunity to resolve the problem. As mentioned earlier, most states have their own employment discrimination laws, with state agencies to enforce those laws. In a state with an employment discrimination law and an enforcement agency, EEOC will not take action unless the state agency has been notified of the complaint and has had at least 60 days to handle it. Even after the expiration of this 60-day period, EEOC will not become involved if the state agency has successfully resolved the matter or is still actively pursuing it.

When EEOC does become involved, either because of a specific complaint or because the agency otherwise has reason to believe that Title VII may have been violated, it conducts an investigation to determine whether there really is evidence of discrimination. If EEOC determines that enough evidence exists to indicate that a Title VII violation may have occurred, the agency is required to attempt *conciliation*—it cannot immediately file charges. Instead, the law requires that EEOC first attempt to deal with the questionable employment practices by obtaining the employer's agreement to change them. When conciliation efforts have failed, EEOC is empowered to enforce Title VII by filing suit in federal district court.

In general, an individual claiming discrimination has only 180 days after the last alleged discriminatory act to file a complaint with a state discrimination agency or EEOC. The individual is permitted to file suit personally in federal court, but only after EEOC has had a specified period of time to resolve the matter or has decided not to pursue it. If EEOC decides that it will not pursue a complaint further, it usually sends a "right to sue letter" to the complainant, which permits the individual to file a lawsuit even though the time for EEOC to act has not expired.

Although enforcement of Title VII by an individual, a state agency, or EEOC usually is based on an individual complaint relating to a specific instance of discrimination, lawsuits under Title VII sometimes are based on charges that the employer engaged in a general "pattern or practice" of discrimination over an extended period of time. A pattern or practice of discrimination may be alleged in a "class action," in which one or a small number of persons file suit in behalf of themselves and a much larger group of persons who may have been affected by the same overall pattern or practice. A pattern or practice case also can be filed by EEOC on its own initiative, without there having been any complaint by an individual or a group. In either a class action or an EEOC case, if the court concludes that there was an illegal pattern or practice of discrimination, there is then a presumption that all persons within the affected group were affected by discrimination. Any such person can subsequently assert a claim, the burden resting on the employer to prove that this particular employee was *not* harmed by the discriminatory pattern or practice. Although pattern or practice cases are not very common, several important ones against large companies have been successful over the years.

Remedies

When a court determines that Title VII has been violated, a variety of remedies are available. The court may issue an injunction prohibiting further violations and ordering specific types of action. For example, an injunction may require the defendant to hire or rehire ("reinstatement") individuals who have been discriminated against, with retroactive seniority when appropriate. The defendant also can be ordered to pay retroactive wages ("back pay"). If the evidence proves that illegally discriminatory practices have produce a substantial imbalance in the company's workforce, the court may require the firm to implement an *affirmative action* program aimed specifically at increasing the number of minority or women employees.

Until recently, reinstatement and back pay were essentially the only remedies available to an individual in a Title VII case. Although a plaintiff could recover actual and punitive damages in a case of intentional race discrimination under Section 1981, which was discussed earlier, these remedies were not available under Title VII. In addition, a jury trial was available under Section 1981 for intentional race discrimination, but not for any type of Title VII claim.

In the Civil Rights Act of 1991, however, which included significant amendments to Title VII, the right to a jury trial and the ability to recover actual and punitive damages were expanded. Now, a plaintiff who claims *intentional* discrimination because of race, color, national origin, sex, or religion can receive a jury trial, assuming that the claim survives the summary judgment stage. If the claim of intentional discrimination is proved, the plaintiff can recover actual and punitive damages. The previously available remedy of reinstatement continues to be available in an appropriate case. To recover damages, of course, the plaintiff must prove them—the amount of actual damages depends on the evidence of economic and psychological harm to the plaintiff, and the amount of punitive damages depends on several factors including the degree of intent and bad faith on the employer's part.

In a case of intentional discrimination based on race or color, there is no absolute cap on the amount of damages. However, the Civil Rights Act of 1991 includes caps on the combined total of actual and punitive damages for claims of intentional discrimination based on national origin, sex, or religion.[3] The upper limits are $50,000 in the case of an employer–defendant with 100 or fewer employees; $100,000 for employers with 101 to 200 employees; $200,000 for employers with 201 to 500 employees; and $300,000 for employers with more than 500 employees.

It is important to emphasize that jury trials and damage remedies have been added to Title VII only for intentional discrimination cases. As we will see later, a Title VII violation can be proved by showing either intentional discrimination or a "neutral" employment practice that has a substantial discriminatory impact. In discriminatory impact cases, where there is no proof of discriminatory intent, the remedies in Title VII have not been changed—there is no jury trial and remedies are generally limited to reinstatement and back pay.[4]

Who Is Protected?

Although the meaning and scope of the terms *race, color, national origin, sex,* and *religion* frequently are clear, this is not always the case. Difficult questions can sometimes arise as to *whom* Congress intended to protect, and under what circumstances.

Race, Color, and National Origin:

Although the civil rights movement that culminated in the 1964 Civil Rights Act focused primarily on the

---

[3] As we will see shortly, the dividing line between discrimination on the basis of race or color, and discrimination on the basis of national origin, is not always clear.

[4] In a case in which there is both a jury trial on a damage claim for intentional discrimination and a discriminatory impact claim heard by the trial judge without a jury, these different aspects of the case will have to be split. Any factual issues common to both types of claim will be determined by the jury.

treatment of blacks, Title VII's prohibition of racial discrimination in employment is very broad. Title VII obviously protects blacks, but it also protects many other classes from unequal treatment. For example, Hispanics, American Indians, and Asian-Americans clearly are within the scope of Title VII. Essentially, the concept of race under Title VII includes any group that is ethnically distinctive. The term *color* in Title VII is redundant in almost all cases, adding nothing to the term *race*. One of the few situations in which the term *color* might have independent meaning in the law could occur if, say, a lighter-skinned manager discriminated against a darker-skinned employee of the same ethnic group. This would probably violate Title VII if it could be proved.

The question of whether Title VII protects whites against racial discrimination has been a troublesome one. In *McDonald v. Santa Fe Trail Transportation Co.*, 427 U.S. 273 (1976), the Supreme Court ruled that whites are within the scope of Title VII's protection. In that case three employees, one black and two white, were caught stealing from the employer. Although there was absolutely no basis other than race for distinguishing between the employees, the employer fired only the two white employees. The Court held that the employer's action against the white employees violated Title VII. This was true despite the fact that there was an obvious justification for the firing, and that there would not have been a Title VII violation if the employer had fired all three employees.

The fact that whites are also protected against racial discrimination has obvious implications for affirmative action programs granting various employment preferences to minorities, discussed later in this chapter.

Because the concept of race is so broad, the term *national origin* usually is not very important in Title VII. Discrimination because of someone's ancestry or place of origin often will also constitute discrimination because of the distinctive ethnic group to which the person belongs. In such a situation, the employer's conduct would be within the definition of racial discrimination. However, national origin is a concept that occasionally can have significance. If an employer treats an employee or job applicant differently because of which nation the person or his ancestors come from, but the discrimination has no apparent connection with any distinctive ethnic group, national origin discrimination has occurred. Suppose, for example, that an American manager discriminates against an employee or job applicant because the person was born in England and has an English accent. This could hardly be called racial discrimination, because there is no distinctive ethnicity involved; it would, however, be national origin discrimination.

The U.S. Supreme Court has held that the prohibition against national origin discrimination does not prohibit employment discrimination based solely on the lack of United States citizenship. In other words, an employer may follow a policy of hiring only U.S. citizens without violating Title VII. The employer cannot, however, give unequal treatment to different noncitizens based on their country of origin. Furthermore, discrimination based

HUMOR AND THE LAW

American employment law clearly protects the religious beliefs of individuals to a reasonable degree in most contexts. However, one court held, and sensibly so, that an employee could in fact be discharged because of his religious beliefs. His job? He was a grade school bus driver. His beliefs? He professed a belief in the religious sacrifice of small children. *Hollon v. Pierce*, 64 Cal.Rptr. 808 (Cal.App. 1968).

---

on the lack of U.S. citizenship cannot be used as a cloak to disguise discrimination that in reality is based on race or national origin.[5]

In addition to protecting the employee or job applicant from discrimination based on his or her race, color, or national origin, Title VII also protects that individual from employment discrimination based on the race, color, or national origin of his or her family members or friends.

Sex: Title VII's prohibition of sex discrimination is aimed primarily at employment discrimination against women. It also includes men, however, because it prohibits any type of discrimination based on a person's gender. Thus, in *Diaz v. Pan American World Airways*, 442 F.2d 385 (5th Cir. 1971), the court held that an airline's "women only" policy for hiring flight attendants violated Title VII. The definition of sex discrimination does not go any further than gender-based actions, however—it does *not* include discrimination based on sexual preferences or practices.

Religion: The term *religion*, as used in Title VII, obviously includes well-recognized faiths such as Jewish, Catholic, and the various Protestant denominations. However, the courts have adopted the same definition that has been used in connection with First Amendment religious freedom, and as a result, the term is a rather broad one also including unorthodox beliefs. The Supreme Court, in *United States v. Seeger*, 380 U.S. 163 (1965), said that a

---

[5] Different rules may apply if *federal, state, or local government* action results in discrimination based on lack of U.S. citizenship. The employment practices, as well as other actions, of government entities are subject to the constitutional guarantee of equal protection. This guarantee applies to both citizens and noncitizens within this country. Therefore, a government policy causing employment discrimination is valid only if it has a reasonable basis. For example, the Supreme Court has held that states have a reasonable basis for refusing to permit noncitizens to work as state police officers or public school teachers, but that they do not have a reasonable basis for refusing to grant licenses to noncitizen lawyers and engineers.

particular belief qualifies as being "religious" if it is a "sincere and meaningful belief occupying in the life of its possessor a place parallel to that filled by the God of those admittedly qualified." Regarding unorthodox beliefs, there is no protection if a court is convinced that the purported belief is not sincerely and genuinely held, but is just adopted for some ulterior motive.

Title VII's prohibition of employment discrimination based on religion includes both religious *beliefs* and religious *practices*. Congress recognized, however, that an employer's ability to operate its business efficiently could be hindered severely by having to accommodate every religious practice of every employee. As a result, Title VII only requires an employer to make *reasonable accommodation* for employees' religious practices. Section 701(j) of Title VII contains a provision stating that an employer may refuse to make a requested adjustment for an employee's religion if the employer "demonstrates that he is unable to reasonably accommodate to an employee's religious observance or practice without undue hardship on the conduct of the employer's business." For example, a school board was held to have violated Title VII when it refused to grant a teacher a one-week leave of absence to attend a religious convocation. Attendance at the convocation was required by the teacher's religion, and a reasonably competent substitute teacher was available to handle his classroom duties.

The leading case on the extent of the employer's duty to reasonably accommodate an employee's religious practices is *Trans World Airlines v. Hardison*, 432 U.S. 63 (1977). In that case the employee, Hardison, worked as a clerk in the "stores department," which provided parts and supplies for TWA's maintenance and overhaul base in Kansas City. It was essential that this department operate 24 hours a day, seven days a week, and whenever an employee was not on duty (because of sickness or vacation, for example), a supervisor or an employee from another department had to be used to cover the job. Hardison and other employees at the TWA base worked under a seniority system that was part of the company's collective bargaining contract with the union. Under the seniority system, employees bid on particular shift assignments. The most senior employees had first choice for job and shift assignments, and the most junior employees were required to work when the union steward was unable to find enough people willing to work at a particular time or in a particular job to fill TWA's needs.

Hardison became an adherent of the religion known as the Worldwide Church of God, one principle of which was that a person must observe the Sabbath by refraining from working between sunset on Friday and sunset on Saturday. When Hardison informed the manage of the stores department of this particular religious conviction, the manager agreed that the union steward should seek a job swap for Hardison or a change of days off. It was also agreed that the manager would try to find Hardison another job that would be more compatible with his religious beliefs. For a time, Hardison was able to observe his Sabbath regularly because he had sufficient seniority to keep from working Saturdays most weeks. However, he then transferred from one building to another so that he could work the day shift instead of the night shift. The two buildings had separate seniority lists, so Hardison was close to the bottom of the list after he transferred.

After his transfer, Hardison was asked to work Saturdays when a fellow employee went on vacation. TWA agreed to permit the union to seek a change of work assignments for Hardison, but the union was not willing to violate the seniority provisions of the collective bargaining agreement, and Hardison had insufficient seniority to bid for a shift having Saturdays off. Hardison's proposal that he work only four days a week was rejected by the company. His job was essential and on weekends he was the only available person on his shift to perform it. To leave the position empty would have impaired supply shop functions, which were critical to airline operations. To fill Hardison's position with a supervisor or an employee from another area would have understaffed another operation, and to employ someone not regularly assigned to work Saturdays would have required TWA to pay premium wages. When an accommodation was not reached, Hardison refused to report for work on Saturdays. After a hearing, he was discharged.

The U.S. Supreme Court ruled that TWA had not violated Title VII. The Court stated that the duty to make a reasonable accommodation does not require an employer to violate a contractual seniority system or to discriminate against other employees. Moreover, the Court held that an employer is not required to incur more than a *"de minimis"* (trivial) cost in its attempt to make reasonable accommodation. Finally, the Court noted that TWA had in fact made a reasonable accommodation for employees in Hardison's situation by reducing weekend shifts to minimum crews and allowing voluntary trading of shifts.

PROVING DISCRIMINATION UNDER TITLE VII

Illegal discrimination can be proved in either of two ways. First, the plaintiff (EEOC, state agency, or individual claimant) may show that the defendant had engaged in *intentional* discrimination—sometimes referred to as "disparate treatment." Second, the plaintiff may show that some employment practice or policy of the defendant has had a discriminatory *effect*—sometimes referred to as "disparate impact." The two methods of proving illegal discrimination will now be considered in detail.

Intentional Discrimination

In general, any employment decision or practice that treats individuals unequally *because* of race, color, religion, sex, or national origin violates Title VII. Illegal discrimination might occur, for example, in connection with firing, refusing to hire, refusing to train or promote, granting unequal compensation or fringe benefits, or practicing any type of segregation or classification of employees or applicants that tends to deprive them of employment opportunities.

A violation of Title VII may be proved by showing that the employer *intended* to discriminate for a prohibited reason. As is true in any situation in which intent is an important legal issue, it may be proved by direct evidence of an explicit motivation, or it may be proved by circumstantial evidence. If an employer maintained a "whites only" or "males only" policy for a particular job, for example, there obviously would be intentional discrimination in violation of Title VII. In such a case, there would be no need to ask a court to draw a subtle inference from circumstantial evidence. Such explicit discrimination violates Title VII with little or no further inquiry.[6]

Most of the time, however, discrimination is not explicit, especially today when most people know it is illegal. When there is no direct evidence of explicit discriminatory intent, a plaintiff must use circumstantial evidence. Such evidence might relate to the background of the questioned employment practice or decision, communications and patterns of conduct by managers within the company, and any other evidence that tends to shed light on the motivations of company decision makers.

Prima Facie Case: In an intentional discrimination case based on circumstantial evidence, the courts apply the same basic concepts to the fact-finding process that they apply in any other kind of case. The courts have, however, developed a distinctive and somewhat more structured method for analyzing the evidence in a Title VII case than in other kinds of cases. The plaintiff first must produce enough evidence to establish a ***prima facie* case** of discriminatory intent. This basically means that the plaintiff must introduce enough evidence to at least create a genuine issue of disputed fact on the question of discriminatory intent. If the plaintiff fails to do so, he or she will lose the case regardless of whether the employer comes forward with any evidence.[7]

Suppose, for example, that an individual job applicant is rejected and has reason to believe that the employer's refusal to hire was motivated by unlawful racial discrimination. Even though there was no explicit discriminatory motive on the employer's part, a *prima facie* case of intentional discrimination can be established by showing the following: (1) The applicant is within a "protected class." This usually means a member of an ethnic minority, but could be a white; in a sex discrimination case, this usually means a woman but could be a man; (2) the applicant applied for a job for which the employer was seeking applicants; (3) the applicant was qualified to perform the job; (4) the applicant was not hired; and (5) the employer either filled the position with a person from a different ethnic group (or gender group in a sex discrimination case), or continued trying to fill it.[8]

---

[6] As we will see later in the chapter, the only possible "out" for an employer that has used an explicitly discriminatory employment practice is the "bona fide occupational qualification" defense. This defense is not available at all in cases of race or color discrimination; although available in cases of sex, religion, or national origin discrimination, it is very difficult for the employer to prove.

[7] Recalling the discussion of litigation in Chapter 3, the plaintiff's failure to establish a *prima facie* case means that defendant can prevail at the summary judgment or directed verdict stage.

[8] Here we are using race and sex discrimination claims as examples, because they are the most common. The same principles would apply, however, to a claim of religious or national origin discrimination.

If the claim of discrimination is based on a discharge rather than a refusal to hire, a *prima facie* case can be established by showing that (1) the plaintiff is within a "protected class"; (2) the plaintiff was performing the job satisfactorily; (3) the plaintiff was discharged; and (4) the plaintiff's work was then assigned to someone who is within a different ethnic group (or gender group if sex discrimination is alleged). In the case of employment decisions other than hiring or firing, the requirements of a *prima facie* case are modified to fit the circumstances; to reiterate, the overall requirement is that the plaintiff produce enough credible evidence to create a genuine fact issue of discriminatory intent.

Employer's Rebuttal: When the plaintiff in such a case introduces evidence sufficient to create a *prima facie* case, the burden then shifts to the employer to bring forth evidence of a *legitimate, nondiscriminatory reason* for plaintiff's rejection. It is important to emphasize that the employer is not required to *prove* anything, but is required only to produce some plausible evidence of the nondiscriminatory reason. To overcome plaintiff's *prima facie* case, the employer can introduce evidence relating to matters such as the applicant's past experience and work record, letters of recommendation, or the superior qualifications of the person actually hired. An example is found in *Peters v. Jefferson Chemical Co.*, 516 F.2d 447 (5th Cir. 1975), in which the employer successfully rebutted the female plaintiff's *prima facie* case by showing that she had not been hired as a laboratory chemist because she had not done laboratory work for several years. The court did not require the employer to prove that her skills were actually inadequate, but accepted the employer's assumption that laboratory skills diminish from nonuse over a substantial period of time. In another case, *Boyd v. Madison County Mutual Insurance Co.*, 653 F.2d 1173 (7th Cir. 1981), a male employee established a *prima facie* case of sex discrimination against the employer by showing that the employer had a policy of awarding attendance bonuses only to clerical employees, all of whom were women. The employer was able to successfully rebut the *prima facie* case by demonstrating that there had been a serious absenteeism problem with clerical staff and that the bonus policy was aimed at correcting that problem.

In a case based on an allegedly discriminatory discharge, the employer might overcome plaintiff's *prima facie* case by showing evidence of plaintiff's poor performance, absenteeism, insubordination, and so on.

The types of reasons that are sufficient to rebut plaintiff's *prima facie* case may vary from one kind of job to another. For instance, some jobs require skills that are quite subjective and extremely difficult to measure. Many executive and professional jobs are of such a nature, requiring traits such as creativity, initiative, ability to delegate and supervise, communicative skills, and a facility for persuasion. With regard to jobs that are inherently subjective, an employer usually will be permitted to use subjective justifications for the action taken. Thus, an attorney could be rejected because of "poor reputation," so long as the employer actually had some evidence of this fact.

On the other hand, a court ordinarily will not accept an employer's purely subjective evaluation of an individual when the job in question requires little skill or responsibility or when it requires skills that can be objectively measured.

Pretext: If the plaintiff establishes a *prima facie* Title VII violation and the employer fails to come forth with acceptable evidence of a legitimate, nondiscriminatory reason, the plaintiff wins. If the employer does produce such evidence, the plaintiff will lose unless he or she can then convince the court that the employer's asserted reason was really just a "pretext"—that is, a cover-up for intentional discrimination. The plaintiff might be able to show, for example, that the employer's "legitimate reason" was applied discriminatorily. In *Corley v. Jackson Police Dept.*, 566 F.2d 994 (5th Cir. 1978), the employer proved that the plaintiffs, black police officers, had been fired for accepting bribes. Although this clearly was a legitimate reason for firing them, the plaintiffs proved that white officers who also had been accused of the same conduct by an informant were not investigated as thoroughly and were not fired. The court held that the employer's reason was a pretext for racial discrimination and that Title VII had been violated.

Mixed Motive Cases: Let us assume that the employee has established a *prima facie* case of intentional discrimination, the employer has produced plausible evidence of a legitimate nondiscriminatory reason, and the employee has produced some evidence of pretext. In most cases, after weighing the evidence, the trial judge will then find that the employer's action was based on either an illegal reason or a legitimate one and will rule accordingly. Suppose, however, that the court finds that the employer acted on the basis of a dual motive. In other words, the evidence convinces the court that the employer treated the employee in a particular way because of *both* illegitimate discrimination *and* a legitimate reason such as difficulty in getting along with subordinate staff.

One of the 1991 amendments to Title VII made it clear that in a mixed case, there is a violation of Title VII so long as illegal discrimination was a substantial contributing factor to the discharge or other employment action. However, if the employer is then able to prove that it would have made the same decision regardless of the illegal reason (that is, that the legitimate reason by itself would have led to the same decision by the employer), the employee will not be entitled to reinstatement or damages. When the employer is able to prove this, the only remedy available to the plaintiff for the Title VII violation is an injunction prohibiting similar discrimination in the future and an award of attorney's fees and court costs. On the other hand, if the employer is unable to convince the court that it would have done the same thing based on the legitimate reason alone, the plaintiff is entitled to the full spectrum of remedies, including reinstatement and damages.

Examples of Intentional Discrimination

Other examples of employment practices that may constitute intentional discrimination are examined below. These are only examples, however; discriminatory treatment can take an almost endless variety of forms.

Segregation: Any type of employee segregation by an employer will violate Title VII if the segregation is proved to have been based on race, color, religion, sex, or national origin. Maintaining separate rest rooms or eating places for black and white employees has been ruled illegal, as has employer sponsorship of racially segregated social activities for employees. In *Rogers v. EEOC,* 454 F.2d 234 (5th Cir. 1971), the court held that the employer had violated Title VII by its practice of assigning Hispanic customers to Hispanic employees and white customers to white employees.

Harassment or Intimidation: Harassment or intimidation of employees because of their race, color, sex, religion, or national origin violates Title VII. The protection of Title VII extends to working conditions, and outlaws an atmosphere that is thoroughly infected with abusive language and conduct targeted at employees for the prohibited reasons. For example, racial slurs and epithets in the workplace may amount to a violation of Title VII when they are frequent enough and offensive enough to seriously affect the working environment. Thus, in *Vance v. Southern Bell Telephone & Telegraph Co.,* 863 F.2d 1503 (11th Cir. 1989), the court held that two incidents in which a noose was found hung over an employee's work station were sufficiently severe to create a jury question on a claim of racial harassment. Generally speaking, an employer will be liable for harassment or intimidation if the conduct is either committed by a manager or supervisor, or if management either encourages the conduct or knows about it and fails to take adequate corrective steps.

One form of harassment or intimidation—sexual harassment—represents a special case of intentional discrimination, and will be discussed separately at the end of the section on intentional discrimination.

Appearance Requirements: Discrimination can exist in unequal appearance standards. In one case, an employer was found to have violated Title VII by prohibiting black employees from having beards or mustaches, but permitting them for whites. Other types of grooming standards, such as those relating to dress or hair length, are also illegal if applied differently on the basis of race, color, religion, or national origin.

However, courts have held that different grooming policies for male and female employees do not violate Title VII if these different standards are reasonable and are not more burdensome on one sex than on the other. The different standards must be enforced for both sexes and cannot significantly affect the job opportunities of either sex. Thus, an employer could require different uniforms for male and female employees if the requirement is reasonable and does not adversely affect either group.

Employment Rules Concerning Family: Discrimination against a woman because of pregnancy or childbirth is viewed as discrimination based on sex. Consequently, employer actions such as discharging women who become pregnant, or requiring them to take an involuntary leave of absence, are illegal unless it can be shown in a particular case that pregnancy significantly interferes with job performance. Similarly, it is a violation of Title

VII to treat pregnancy different than other disabilities or conditions with respect to sick leave, health insurance, or other benefits provided by the employer. For a few years after the enactment of Title VII, there was some doubt about whether an employer violated the statute by treating women employees differently because of pregnancy. These doubts were laid to rest when Congress passed the Pregnancy Discrimination Act of 1978, which amended Title VII to make it clear that pregnancy-related discrimination is unlawful sex discrimination.

In *Phillips v. Martin Marietta Corp.*, 400 U.S. 452 (1971), the Supreme Court struck down the employer's policy of refusing to hire women with preschool-aged children, but not having such a rule for men. Employers may lawfully impose rules relating to family matters, but only if these rules are applied equally to both sexes. For example, an employer could require its employees to be single, but could not legally have this rule for only its women employees.

Compensation and Benefits: It is illegal to base compensation or benefits on race, color, religion, sex, or national origin. A very difficult question is raised, however, when an employer establishes a pension plan providing for lifetime payments after retirement. Can the employer require female employees to pay more into the plan while they are working or accept smaller monthly payments after retirement because women, on the average, live longer than men? In the following case, the Supreme Court provides an answer.

LOS ANGELES DEPARTMENT OF WATER & POWER V. MANHART

U.S. SUPREME COURT
435 U.S. 702 (1978)

The Los Angeles Department of Water & Power provided retirement, disability, and death benefit programs for its employees. On retirement each employee was eligible for a monthly benefit computed as a fraction of salary multiplied by years of service. These benefits were funded by contributions from employees and the employer, plus income generated by contributed funds.

Based on a study of mortality tables and its own experience, the employer determined that its 2,000 female employees, on the average, would live a few years longer than its 10,000 male employees. Thus, the cost of a pension for the average retired female would be greater than for the average retired male. Consequently, the employer required female employees to make monthly contributions that were 14.84 percent higher than the contributions required of comparable male employees.

Manhart, a female employee, filed a class action suit in behalf of herself and other female employees of the department, claiming that this differential contribution requirement constituted sex discrimination in violation of Title VII. The federal district court and the Court of Appeals both ruled in favor of the employees, and the employer appealed to the U.S. Supreme Court.

CONTINUED

STEVENS, JUSTICE:

... There are both real and fictional differences between women and men. It is true that the average man is taller than the average woman; it is not true that the average woman driver is more accident prone than the average man. Before the Civil Rights Act of 1964 was enacted, an employer could fashion his personnel policies on the basis of assumptions about the differences between men and women, whether or not the assumptions were valid.

It is now well recognized that employment decisions cannot be predicated on mere "stereotype" impressions about the characteristics of males or females.... This case does not, however, involve a fictional difference between men and women. It involves a generalization that the parties accept as unquestionably true: Women, as a class, do live longer than men. The Department treated its women employees differently from its men employees because the two classes are in fact different. It is equally true, however, that all individuals in the respective classes do not share the characteristic that differentiates the average class representatives. Many women do not live as long as the average man and many men outlive the average woman. The question, therefore, is whether the existence or nonexistence of "discrimination" is to be determined by comparison of class characteristics or individual characteristics.

The statute makes it unlawful "to discriminate against any *individual* with respect to his compensation, terms, conditions, or privileges of employment, because of such *individual's* race, color, religion, sex, or national origin." [Emphasis added.] The statute's focus on the individual is unambiguous. It precludes treatment of individuals as simply components of a racial, religious, sexual, or national class.... Even a true generalization about the class is an insufficient reason for disqualifying an individual to whom the generalization does not apply....

It is true, of course, that while contributions are being collected from the employees, the Department cannot know which individuals will predecease the average woman. Therefore, unless women as a class are assessed an extra charge, they will be subsidized, to some extent, by the class of male employees. It follows, according to the Department, that fairness to its class of male employees justifies the extra assessment against all of its female employees.

But the question of fairness to various classes affected by the statute is essentially a matter of policy for the legislature to address. Congress has decided that classifications based on sex, like those based on national origin or race, are unlawful....

Finally, there is no reason to believe that Congress intended a special definition of discrimination in the context of employee group insurance coverage. It is true that insurance is concerned with events that are individually unpredictable, but that is characteristic of many employment decisions. Individual risks, like individual performance, may not be predicted by resort to classifications proscribed by Title VII. Indeed, the fact that this case involves a group insurance program highlights a basic flaw in the Department's fairness argument. For when insurance risks are grouped, the better risks always subsidize the poorer risks. Healthy persons subsidize medical benefits for the less healthy; unmarried workers subsidize the pensions of married workers; persons who eat, drink, or smoke to excess may subsidize pension benefits for persons whose habits are more temperate. Treating different classes of risks as though they were the same for purposes of group insurance is a common practice that has never been considered inherently unfair. To insure the flabby and the fit as though they were equivalent risks may be more common than treating men and women alike; but nothing more than habit makes one "subsidy" seem less fair than the other....

An employment practice that requires 2,000 individuals to contribute more money into a fund than 10,000 other employees simply because each of them is a woman, rather than a man,... constitutes discrimination and is unlawful....

[Although the Supreme Court agreed with the lower courts that Title VII had been violated, it disagreed with them on the question of whether the employer should have to repay all the excess contributions that had been paid by women in the past. The lower courts had ruled that repayment was required. The Supreme Court held that the practice must be stopped, but that the employer did not have to repay all prior excess contributions. The reason was that many pension plans had been structured like this one for many years on the assumption that using standard mortality tables was valid. To suddenly make this pension fund, and others across the country, *retroactively* liable could cause financial havoc and endanger their ability to pay benefits to innocent retirees.]

Sexual Harassment—A Special Case of Intentional Discrimination

Although sexual harassment is a form of sex discrimination under Title VII, a special set of rules applies. The process that is typical in other kinds of intentional discrimination cases (*prima facie* case, legitimate nondiscriminatory reason, pretext) does not fit most sexual harassment cases very well, and most courts do not use it. Instead, they apply the following rules.

The courts and EEOC have recognized two general types of sexual harassment. The two varieties, which may sometimes overlap, are referred to as *quid pro quo* and *hostile environment* sexual harassment. It should be noted that, although illegal sexual harassment can be committed by a woman against a man, almost all of the cases involve harassment directed by a man against a woman.

Quid Pro Quo Harassment: The term *quid pro quo* means "something for something," and refers to the situation in which continued employment, a favorable review, promotion, a raise, or some other job benefit or opportunity is conditioned on an employee's positive response to sexual advances. ***Quid pro quo* sexual harassment** occurs when the following facts are established:

1. The employer, or someone for whose actions the employer is responsible, requested sexual favors from an employee.

2. The request was *unwelcome*. The requirement that the sexual requests be unwelcome can be proved by evidence of refusals, avoidance, and so on. It is important to emphasize, however, that the evidence may prove that the requests were unwelcome even if the employee ultimately gave in and engaged in the requested sexual activity. In such a cse, the evidence would have to convince the court that the employee gave in only because of fear, coercion, or threats.

3. The request was a "term or condition of employment," or was reasonably seen by the employee as a term or condition of employment. This means that the evidence must show that the request for sex was made part of the job, or that a reasonable employee would interpret the request as being part of the job. Stated somewhat differently, the circumstances must have been such that it was reasonable to infer that a positive response by the employee would produce tangible job benefits and a negative response would produce the opposite. This requirement could be proved by explicit statements, implicit suggestions, or conduct showing a connection between the employee's response and job benefits.

Normally, *quid pro quo* harassment can be accomplished only by someone with managerial or supervisory authority over the employee. Although the Supreme Court has not so held, the EEOC and a number of federal courts of appeal and district courts have held that an employer is absolutely liable for *quid pro quo* harassment by one of its managers or supervisors. This liability probably exists regardless of whether the employer knew or had reason to know of the harassment, regardless of whether the employer had a policy against sexual harassment, and regardless of what the employer did when it found out about the harassment.

Hostile Environment Harassment: Claims of hostile environment sexual harassment are more common than *quid pro quo* claims. This type of harassment can occur in several ways, and can be proved even if there is no evidence of a connection between tangible job benefits and the employee's response. **Hostile environment sexual harassment** occurs when the following facts are established:

1. The employer, or someone for whose actions the employer is responsible, requested sexual favors, made sexual advances, or engaged in other verbal or physical conduct of a sexual nature.

2. The sexual requests, language, or conduct was unwelcome.

3. The conduct was sufficiently severe or pervasive to alter the employee's working conditions by creating a hostile, intimidating, and offensive environment. Although it is conceivable that a single incident could fulfill this requirement, in most cases the evidence must show a persistent pattern of conduct over time.

Unlike the *quid pro quo* variety, hostile environment sexual harassment can be committed either by supervisors or by co-workers who have no managerial authority.

The question of when a company can be held liable for hostile environment sexual harassment is more complicated and uncertain than it is in a *quid pro quo* case. The rules make distinctions among the conduct and knowledge of high-level management (at a policy-making level), lower level supervisors, and employees without any managerial or supervisory authority.

1. The employer definitely will be liable if someone in high-level management actually commits, participates in, or encourages the harassment.

2. The employer definitely will be liable if someone in high-level management knows or reasonably should know about the harassment and fails to take adequate steps to stop it. This is true whether the harassment was actually committed by a supervisor or by an employee without any supervisory authority.

3. If the harassment is committed by an employee without any managerial or supervisory authority, the company cannot ever be held liable unless a person at some supervisory or managerial level knows about the harassment and fails to take adequate corrective steps.

4. The question is somewhat more difficult when the harassment is committed by a lower-level supervisor, and no one in high-level management knows or has reason to know about it. In *Meritor Savings Bank v. Vinson,* 477 U.S. 57 (1986), the U.S. Supreme Court indicated that the company probably would be liable in this situation if it did not have a strongly worded policy against sexual harassment that had been adequately communicated to employees. To be adequate, the policy also has to include a reasonable procedure by which an employee can complain about sexual harassment; the procedure must specify a way for an employee to go around an immediate supervisor if the supervisor is the offending party. If the company has such a policy and complaint procedure, but the employee did not make a complaint within the company before filing a formal Title VII claim, the company probably is not liable for the supervisor's harassment.

The following case involves an employee's allegation of hostile environment harassment by a co-worker without any supervisory or managerial authority. The court applies some of the principles we have just discussed, and also formulates some important new concepts for this rapidly evolving area of law.

ELLISON v. BRADY

U.S. COURT OF APPEALS, NINTH CIRCUIT 924 F.2d 872 (1991)

Kerry Ellison worked as a revenue agent for the Internal Revenue Service in San Mateo, California. During her initial training in 1984 she met Sterling Gray, another trainee, who was also assigned to the San Mateo office. The two co-workers never became friends, and they did not work closely together. Revenue agents in the San Mateo office often went to lunch in groups. In June 1986 when no one else was in the office, Gray asked Ellison to lunch. She accepted. Ellison claimed that after the June lunch Gray started to pester her with unnecessary questions and hang around her desk. On October 9, 1986, Gray asked Ellison out for a drink after work. She declined, but she suggested that they have lunch the following week. She did not want to have lunch alone with him, and she tried to stay away from the office during lunch time. One day during the following week, Gray uncharacteristically dressed in a three-piece suit and asked Ellison out for lunch. Again, she did not accept.

On October 22, 1986, Gray handed Ellison a note he wrote on a telephone message slip, which read: "I cried over you last night and I'm totally drained today. I have never been in such constant term oil [sic]. Thank you for talking with me. I could not stand to feel your hatred for another day." When Ellison realized that Gray wrote the note, she became shocked and frightened and left the room. Gray followed her into the hallway and demanded that she talk to him, but she left the building. Ellison later showed the note to Bonnie Miller, who supervised both Ellison and Gray. Miller said that "this is sexual harassment." Ellison asked Miller not to do anything about it. She wanted to try to handle it herself. Ellison asked a male co-worker to talk to Gray and to tell him that she was not interested in him and to leave her alone. The next day, Thursday, Gray called in sick.

Ellison did not work on Friday, and on the following Monday, she started four weeks of training in St. Louis. Gray mailed Ellison a card and a typed, single-spaced, three-page letter, which she described this letter as "twenty times, a hundred times weirder" than the prior note. Gray wrote, in part: "I know that you are worth knowing with or without sex.... Leaving aside the hassles and disasters of recent weeks. I have enjoyed you so much over these past few months. Watching you. Experiencing you from 0 so far away. Admiring your style and elan.... Don't you think it odd that two people who have never even talked together, alone, are striking off such intense sparks.... I will [write] another letter in the near future." Explaining her reaction, Ellison stated: "I just thought he was crazy. I thought he was nuts. I didn't know what he would do next. I was frightened."

CONTINUED

She immediately telephoned Miller. Ellison told her supervisor that she was frightened. She requested that Miller transfer either her or Gray because she would not be comfortable working in the same office with him. Miller asked Ellison to send a copy of the card and letter to San Mateo. Miller then telephoned her supervisor, Joe Benton, and discussed the problem. That same day Miller had a counseling session with Gray. She informed him that he was entitled to union representation. During this meeting, she told Gray to leave Ellison alone. She also reminded Gray many times over the next few weeks that he must not contact Ellison in any way. Gray subsequently transferred to the San Francisco office on November 24, 1986. Ellison returned from St. Louis in late November and did not discuss the matter further with Miller. After three weeks in San Francisco, Gray filed union grievances requesting a return to the San Mateo office. The IRS and the union settled the grievances in Gray's favor, agreeing to allow him to transfer back to the San Mateo office provided that he spend four more months in San Francisco and promise not to bother Ellison.

On January 28, 1987, Ellison first learned of Gray's request in a letter from Miller explaining that Gray would return to the San Mateo office. The letter indicated that management decided to resolve Ellison's problem with a six-month separation, and that it would take additional action if the problem recurred.

After receiving the letter, Ellison was "frantic." She filed a formal complaint with the IRS. She also obtained permission to transfer to San Francisco temporarily when Gray returned. Gray wrote Ellison another letter, which still sought to maintain the idea that he and Ellison had some type of relationship. The IRS employee investigating the allegation agreed with Ellison's supervisor that Gray's conduct constituted sexual harassment. In its final decision, however, the Treasury Department (of which the IRS is a unit) rejected Ellison's complaint because it believed that the complaint did not describe a pattern or practice of sexual harassment. The EEOC also ruled against Ellison because it concluded that the IRS took adequate action to prevent the repetition of Gray's conduct. Ellison filed a complaint in federal district court against Brady, Secretary of the Treasury, alleging a Title VII violation. The district court granted the defendant's motion for summary judgment on the ground that Ellison had failed to state a case of sexual harassment caused by a hostile working environment; it characterized Gray's conduct as "isolated and genuinely trivial." Ellison appealed.

Beezer, Circuit Judge:

In *Meritor Savings Bank v. Vinson*, 477 U.S. 57 (1986), the Supreme Court held that sexual harassment constitutes sex discrimination in violation of Title VII. Courts have recognized different forms of sexual harassment. In "quid pro quo" cases, employers condition employment benefits on sexual favors. In "hostile environment" cases, employees work in offensive or abusive environments. This case, like *Meritor*, involves a hostile environment claim. . . .

The Supreme Court in *Meritor* held that Mechelle Vinson's working conditions constituted a hostile environment in violation of Title VII's prohibition of sex discrimination. Vinson's supervisor made repeated demands for sexual favors, usually at work, both during and after business hours. Vinson initially refused her employer's sexual advances, but eventually acceded because she feared losing her job. They had intercourse over forty times. She additionally testified that he "fondled her in front of other employees, followed her into the women's restroom when she went there alone, exposed himself to her, and even forcibly raped her on several occasions." The Court had no difficulty finding this environment hostile. . . .

[A] hostile environment exists when an employee can show (1) that he or she was subjected to sexual advances, requests for sexual favors, or other verbal or physical conduct of a sexual nature, (2) that this conduct was unwelcome, and (3) that the conduct was sufficiently severe or pervasive to alter the conditions of the victim's employment and create an abusive working environment. Here, the [defendant] argues that Gray's conduct was not of a sexual nature. The three-page letter, however, makes several references to sex and constitutes verbal conduct of a sexual nature. We need not and do not decide whether a party can state a cause of action for a sexually discriminatory working environment under Title VII when the conduct in question is not sexual. . . .

CONTINUED

To state a claim under Title VII, sexual harassment "must be sufficiently severe or pervasive to alter the conditions of the victim's employment and create an abusive working environment." . . . [The court then reviewed the facts of two cases from other circuits, the *Scott* case and the *Rabidue* case, that found no sexually hostile environment despite much evidence of sexual language and conduct, offensive posters, and even some physical contact. The courts in those cases apparently would find a hostile environment only in circumstances in which the plaintiff has suffered serious psychological effects.] We do not agree with the standards set forth in *Scott* and *Rabidue*, and we choose not to follow those decisions. . . . Surely, employees need not endure sexual harassment until their psychological well-being is seriously affected to the extent that they suffer anxiety and debilitation. . . . Although an isolated epithet by itself fails to support a cause of action for a hostile environment, Title VII's protection of employees from sex discrimination comes into play long before the point where victims of sexual harassment require psychiatric assistance. . . .

We . . . believe that Gray's conduct was sufficiently severe and pervasive to alter the conditions of Ellison's employment and create an abusive working environment. We first note that, . . . although a single act can be enough . . . repeated incidents create a stronger claim of hostile environment, with the strength of the claim depending on the number of incidents and the intensity of each incident. . . .

Next, we believe that in evaluating the severity and pervasiveness of sexual harassment, we should focus on the perspective of the victim. Courts "should consider the victim's perspective and not stereotyped notions of acceptable behavior." . . . Conduct that many men consider unobjectionable may offend many women. A male supervisor might believe, for example, that it is legitimate for him to tell a female subordinate that she has a 'great figure' or 'nice legs.' The female subordinate, however, may find such comments offensive; men and women are vulnerable in different ways and offended by different behavior. Men tend to view some forms of sexual harassment as "harmless social interactions to which only overly-sensitive women would object"; the characteristically male view depicts sexual harassment as comparatively harmless amusement.

We realize that there is a broad range of viewpoints among women as a group, but we believe that many women share common concerns which men do not necessarily share. For example, because women are disproportionately victims of rape and sexual assault, women have a stronger incentive to be concerned with sexual behavior. Women who are victims of mild forms of sexual harassment may understandably worry whether a harasser's conduct is merely a prelude to violent sexual assault. Men, who are rarely victims of sexual assault, may view sexual conduct in a vacuum without a full appreciation of the social setting or the underlying threat of violence that a woman may perceive. One writer explains: "Their greater physical and social vulnerability to sexual coercion can make women wary of sexual encounters. Moreover, American women have been raised in a society where rape and sex-related violence have reached unprecedented levels, and a vast pornography industry creates continuous images of sexual coercion, objectification and violence. . . . Because of the inequality and coercion with which it is so frequently associated in the minds of women, the appearance of sexuality in an unexpected context or a setting of ostensible equality can be an anguishing experience."

In order to shield employers from having to accommodate the idiosyncratic concerns of the rare hyper-sensitive employee, we hold that a female plaintiff states a prima facie case of hostile environment sexual harassment when she alleges conduct which a reasonable woman would consider sufficiently severe or pervasive to alter the conditions of employment and create an abusive working environment. . . . Of course, where male employees allege that coworkers engage in conduct which creates a hostile environment, the appropriate victim's perspective would be that of a reasonable man. . . .

We note that the reasonable victim standard we adopt today classifies conduct as unlawful sexual harassment even when harassers do not realize that their conduct creates a hostile working environment. . . . To avoid liability under Title VII, employers may have to educate and sensitize their workforce to eliminate conduct which a reasonable victim would consider unlawful sexual harassment. . . . If sexual comments or sexual advances are in fact welcomed by the recipient, they, of course, do not constitute sexual harassment. Title VII's prohibition of sex discrimination in employment does not require a totally desexualized work place. . . .

We cannot say as a matter of law

CONTINUED

that Ellison's reaction was idiosyncratic or hyper-sensitive. We believe that a reasonable woman could have had a similar reaction. After receiving the first bizarre note from Gray, a person she barely knew, Ellison asked a co-worker to tell Gray to leave her alone. Despite her request, Gray sent her a long, passionate, disturbing letter. He told her he had been "watching" and "experiencing" her; he made repeated references to sex; he said he would write again. Ellison had no way of knowing what Gray would do next. A reasonable woman could consider Gray's conduct, as alleged by Ellison, sufficiently severe and pervasive to alter a condition of employment and create an abusive working environment....

We next must determine what remedial actions by employers shield them from liability under Title VII for sexual harassment by co-workers. [The question is, when management knows or has reason to know of the harassment, has it taken adequate steps to stop the harassment? Because the district court in this case granted a summary judgment against Ellison on the hostile environment issue, the court did not deal with the question of whether the employer took adequate steps upon learning of Gray's conduct. Before remanding the case to the district court for a trial on both the hostile environment question and the employer liability question, the Court of Appeals provided some general guidelines for the district court to follow in determining whether an employer has taken sufficient steps to avoid liability:] Employers have a duty to "express strong disapproval" of sexual harassment, and to "develop appropriate sanctions" [that are] ... "reasonably calculated to end the harassment." ... In *Barrett v. Omaha National Bank*, 726 F.2d 424 (8th Cir. 1984), the Eighth Circuit held that an employer properly remedied a hostile working environment by fully investigating, reprimanding a harasser for grossly inappropriate conduct, placing the offender on probation for ninety days, and warning the offender that any further misconduct would result in discharge....

An employer's remedy should persuade individual harassers to discontinue unlawful conduct. We do not think that all harassment warrants dismissal; rather, remedies should be "assessed proportionately to the seriousness of the offense." Employers should impose sufficient penalties to assure a workplace free from sexual harassment.... [The Court of Appeals then noted some possible inadequacies in the employer's response to Gray's conduct: First, the employer had not indicated that he would be punished if he continued the behavior. Second, the employer had not disciplined Gray; neither the counseling nor the temporary transfer were disciplinary actions. Third, it was not appropriate for the employer to permit Gray to come back to the San Mateo office *if* his mere presence would continue to create a sexually hostile environment. Fourth, if Gray's mere presence would continue to create a hostile environment, it is not appropriate to transfer Ellison; the employer's response should not have negative consequences for the *victim*. The Court of Appeals concluded that there was a genuine fact issue as to the sufficiency of the employer's response.]

We reverse the district court's decision that Ellison did not allege a case of sexual harassment due to a hostile working environment, and we remand for [a trial on this question and on the question of whether the employer took sufficient remedial steps to avoid liability for a Title VII violation.]

Discriminatory Impact

We have seen that a violation of Title VII can be proved by showing that the employer intended to discriminate. This proof is accomplished either by proving an explicit discriminatory intent or by establishing a *prima facie* case from which discriminatory intent can be inferred.

Another way to prove that an employer has violated Title VII is to show that a particular employment rule or practice, although apparently neutral on its face, actually has an unequal impact on a protected group. Examples include height and weight requirements having the effect of excluding a disproportionate number of women or a standardized test having the effect of excluding a disproportionate number of persons from a particular ethnic group. In such a case, the plaintiff is not required to show that the defendant had an intent to discriminate.

Prima Facie Case: The individual plaintiff, or EEOC acting in the individual's behalf, must initially prove that the employment practice in question has a substantial adverse impact on the protected group of which the individual is a member. This can be accomplished by the use of several different types of evidence. It could be shown, for example, that the employment practice has caused the employer to hire 40 percent of the whites who had applied but only 20 percent of black applicants. Or, in another siutation, discriminatory impact might be proved by showing that some action of the employer had the effect of eliminating 75 percent of all women from possible consideration, even though women comprise approximately one-half of the total population. Another method for proving discriminatory impact is to do a statistical comparison of the composition of the employer's workforce with the composition of the relevant labor pool. For example, if the plaintiff alleges that a job criterion or selection method has a discriminatory impact on blacks, the plaintiff might attempt to show that the percentage of blacks working for the employer is much smaller than the percentage of qualified blacks in the available labor market. When a statistical disparity is used to prove discriminatory impact, the plaintiff must produce evidence linking the particular practice being challenged to the statistical imbalance in the employer's workforce. If several employment practices are being challenged on the grounds that they have an aggregate discriminatory impact, the plaintiff will be permitted to lump them together if it is not feasible to single out a specific practice and show its impact alone.

It is important to realize, however, that the method used to prove discriminatory impact must be tailored to fit the particular employment practice being challenged and the particular group allegedly being affected. Thus, a court usually would not accept a comparison of the employer's minority hiring rate with general population statistics when the job in question required special qualifications. For example, if the job required a degree in mechanical engineering, the employer's experience in filling that job would need to be compared with the available population of mechanical engineers. The geographic area in which the statistical comparison should be made will also differ from one case to another. Suppose, for instance, that a plaintiff is trying to establish discriminatory impact in the case of an employer in San Francisco. If the job in question involves unskilled or semiskilled labor, general population statistics for the San Francisco–Oakland Bay area would probably be appropriate for comparison. However, if the job requires such special training and qualifications that the employer normally would have to recruit over a wider geographic area, the appropriate base for statistical comparison would be the population of qualified individuals in that larger area, such as the United States.

Four-fifths rule: EEOC has adopted Uniform Guidelines on Employment Selection Procedures, which indicate that a particular method for selecting employees has a discriminatory impact if it results in a selection rate that is less than four-fifths (80 percent) of the selection rate for the group with the highest rate. For example, suppose that 100 white applicants for a job are screened by a particular selection method, such as a standardized test. If 50 of them pass it and are hired, the selection rate for that group is 50 percent. If 60 applicants from a particular ethnic minority are screened by the same selection method and 12 of them pass it and are hired, the selection rate for that group is 20 percent. Because 20 percent is less than four-fifths of 50 percent, the test would be viewed by EEOC as having a discriminatory impact. If 24 of the 60 minority applicants had passed the test, the selection rate for that group would be 40 percent. Because 40 percent is four-fifths of 50 percent, the test then would not be viewed as having a discriminatory impact based on this standard alone. EEOC recognizes that numerical selection rate is not the only way to measure discriminatory impact, however, and may use other methods when it feels they are more appropriate. Although the courts are not bound by EEOC guidelines, the Supreme Court has indicated that they should consider the guidelines and give them substantial weight. Several courts have relied on the guidelines' four-fifths rule, at least partly, in deciding whether challenged selection methods have a substantial discriminatory impact.

If the plaintiff proves discriminatory impact, a *prima facie* case of illegal discrimination has been established, and the burden then shifts to the employer.

Employer's Rebuttal: As we have seen, an employer may rebut a *prima facie* case of discriminatory intent merely by producing some plausible evidence of a nondiscriminatory reason for the employer's action. When the plaintiff has established a *prima facie* case by proving discriminatory *impact*, however, the employer's task of rebuttal is somewhat more difficult. In an impact case, the employer has to *prove* (not just introduce some plausible evidence) "business necessity." To meet this burden, the employer must prove that (1) the challenged employment practice was necessary to achieve an important business objective, and (2) the practice actually achieves this objective.

Alternatives: If the employer proves business necessity, the only way for the plaintiff to win is by proving that the employer reasonably could have achieved its business objective by some other employment practice that would not have had such a discriminatory impact. The alternative must be workable and not a great deal more costly than the challenged practice.

The theories of discriminatory intent and discriminatory impact are not mutually exclusive—in a given case there might be evidence sufficient to create a *prima facie* case of intent and also evidence of discriminatory impact.

In such a case, the plaintiff can use both methods to prove discrimination. The following case illustrates a situation in which both discriminatory intent and impact were shown. This case also demonstrates that using the so-called old boy network method of personal contacts for hiring can often lead to Title VII problems.

GRANT v. BETHLEHEM STEEL CORP.

U.S. COURT OF APPEALS, SECOND CIRCUIT 635 F.2d 1007 (1980)

Bethlehem Steel Corporation's Fabricating Steel Construction Division was engaged in the construction of steel framework for skyscrapers, bridges, and other structures. The employees on these construction projects, who were called ironworkers, worked together in groups of three to six. Each group worked under the leadership of a foreman. No special education or training was required for the job of ironworker. To be a foreman, an ironworker needed safety consciousness, leadership qualities, and productiveness.

Before enactment of Title VII, there had been a long history of racial discrimination in the hiring of ironworkers in the New York City area. Several factors, including Title VII, a shortage of ironworkers, and community pressure, led to the admission of blacks into the ironworker trade by the 1960s. Black and other minority ironworkers did not, however, advance to become foremen. On ten representative projects in the 1970s, Bethlehem employed blacks in 10 percent of its 1,018 ironworker jobs but hired only one black for 126 foreman jobs.

The method used for selection of foremen on Bethlehem's steel projects was rather haphazard. On each steel construction project Bethlehem employed a project superintendent, who chose the foreman for the project. The superintendents, all of whom were white, were given uncontrolled discretion to hire whom they pleased. These superintendents hired by word of mouth on the basis of wholly subjective criteria. No foremen's jobs were posted, and no list of eligible foremen was kept. Instead, on hearing informally of an upcoming Bethlehem project (the superintendent would learn this fact as much as eight months to a year in advance), the superintendent would communicate with persons in the trade he knew or who were recommended to him by others and line them up as prospective foremen for the project. Others interests in the job of foreman would rarely have the chance to apply for the job on any given project, because only persons solicited by the superintendent would know of the project in advance. By the time the project became known generally and notice of it was posted in the union hiring hall, there would usually no longer be any foreman openings available.

Three individuals, Grant, Ellis, and Martinez, attempted on several occasions to obtain foreman jobs with Bethlehem but were unsuccessful. Grant and Ellis were black, and Martinez was a dark-skinned Puerto Rican. All were in their forties and fifties and had many years of wide-ranging experience in ironwork, spotless work records, and excellent reputations. In addition, Ellis had worked as a foreman for two other companies, Martinez had been a foreman on one previous project for Bethlehem, and Grant had been supervisor on several projects for other companies outside the United States.

Their repeated efforts to become foremen for Bethlehem were frustrated primarily by two Bethlehem superintendents, Deaver and Driggers. Both had been Bethlehem superintendents in New York for many years and had never hired a black or Puerto Rican foreman. They both hired foremen by word of mouth from among friends and those recommended by other foremen, union officials, or superintendents. Neither of them ever kept any list of ironworkers qualified to become foremen. They defended their subjective hiring practices by pointing

CONTINUED

to the dangers of ironwork and asserting that no objective method of evaluation would have let them effectively determine an individual's competence to handle the heavy responsibility of the position.

Grant, Ellis, and Martinez, plaintiffs, brought a class action suit in federal district court against Bethlehem, Deaver, and Driggers, contending that the hiring practices in question were discriminatory both in treatment (intent) and impact. The district court ruled that the defendants had not violated Title VII, and the plaintiffs appealed.

Mansfield, Circuit Judge

... [Plaintiffs] assert that friendship and nepotism rather than assessment of ability formed the basis for the superintendents' selections, and that since blacks tended to be excluded from the all-white superintendents' friendship, they were also unlawfully excluded from jobs as foremen. In support of these allegations, [plaintiffs] point out that the supervisors often went to considerable length to solicit people whom they knew for foreman positions, sometimes calling them on the phone or personally going to ask them to work. One superintendent, Driggers, hired his two sons as foremen, notwithstanding that they had less ironwork experience than the three named plaintiffs and had not served as foremen before. On another occasion, Superintendent Deaver hired a foreman whom he knew had a drinking problem. One member of the gang which this man supervised suffered a fatal accident because he was not following safety regulations. Similarly, Deaver rehired a foreman who had lost a gang member on his last project when a column for which he was responsible fell; the same foreman lost a derrick on the new project, and left work with a nervous breakdown. [Plaintiffs] urge that concern for workers' safety could not have been the primary motive behind these hirings. ...

[W]e find insufficient the district court's grounds for holding that plaintiffs failed to make out a prima facie case of discriminatory treatment. ...

The Supreme Court's holding in *Furnco Construction Co. v. Waters*, 438 U.S. 567 (1978), does not dictate a different result. There the Court held that employers had a responsibility only to offer blacks the same employment opportunities as whites, not to solicit blacks or otherwise devise hiring methods that would maximize black employment. Here blacks were not offered the same employment opportunities as whites. The district court stated that "if Bethlehem had taken affirmative steps to find qualified blacks, one or more additional black foremen would have been appointed," but concluded that Bethlehem's failure to take such steps could not be illegal, given the logic of *Furnco*. Contrary to the district court's conclusion, we believe that the failure to solicit qualified blacks as foremen constitutes a form of unacceptable discrimination in this case, since whites were here being solicited at the same time, even though the whites made no applications for the foreman's jobs for which they were hired. ...

[Plaintiffs] made out a strong prima facie case of discriminatory treatment under Title VII. ...

Nor can we accept the district court's conclusion that [plaintiffs] failed to make out a prima facie case of discriminatory impact under Title VII. The undisputed statistics point strongly toward discrimination. After a "long history of discrimination against blacks in the hiring of ironworkers" Bethlehem during the 1970–75 period employed 1,018 ironworkers, of whom 102 were black or Puerto Rican. During the same period it appointed 126 whites as foremen and only 1 black. ...

Prior foreman experience is a factor properly considered in weighing the defense of business necessity. But without an inquiry into the nature and extent of the experience insofar as it may indicate superior competence on the part of the ironworkers, it cannot be categorized as [absolutely necessary] for appointment as foremen. An incompetent foreman should not be repeatedly hired over a qualified ironworker without foreman experience merely because the former had the good fortune to have been hired once as a foreman. Here, [plaintiffs] produced creditable evidence that the superintendents selected some foremen on the basis of friendship without knowledge of or inquiry into their prior safety history. Some of these foremen, as noted above, possessed bad safety records that would have excluded them from rehiring in a strictly merit-based hiring system. No business necessity dictated that these men be rehired without superintendents assuming any responsibility to consider qualified blacks for the job.

The record, moreover, shows that fully 50% of the foremen hired on the 10 sample projects had worked for Bethlehem less than a year before being made foremen. Each of the named

CONTINUED

plaintiffs, who were qualified to be foremen, had longer Bethlehem tenure. Many of these other foremen did not have the extensive experience gained by [plaintiffs] as ironworkers and foremen in outstanding companies other than Bethlehem. [Plaintiffs] adduced evidence that Bethlehem supervisors hired their sons, friends, and persons whom they trusted, often despite these men's relatively slight experience as Bethlehem ironworkers, even though persons with Bethlehem foreman experience (including [plaintiff] Martinez) were available for the job....

[On the question of discriminatory impact, defendants also argue] that it was incorrect to view the entire Bethlehem ironworker force as the pool of qualified candidates for foreman positions. The presence of 10% blacks in the ironworkers' labor force, the argument goes, does not suggest that 10% participation in the foreman ranks should follow. Before 1972 there were few minority workers in the union, and most blacks who belonged to the union in 1975 had been members a relatively short time. Those blacks who belonged to the workforce during the early 1970s took up a comparatively larger segment of the apprentice and trainee pools. The legacy of admitted past discrimination gave blacks less average experience per man than whites. The ratio of qualified blacks to qualified whites in the workforce, [defendants] concluded, was therefore substantially smaller than the overall percentage of blacks in the workforce.

This background, though partially true, does not justify the assumption that there were *no* appreciable blacks in the workforce with the ability to be good foremen. Though the union had few black members in the early 1970s, many black "permit" workers were working on iron work projects during that period, and some even earlier. Some black workers, including the three named plaintiffs, had more experience at Bethlehem and elsewhere than at least several of the whites hired as foremen. Moreover, as all parties have recognized, experience is only one of several factors to be considered when selecting foremen. It defies common sense to suggest that only one black was sufficiently experienced and competent to merit selection as a foreman during this period when 126 foreman jobs were filled. It would not have created any substantial difficulty for supervisors to maintain a pool of "eligibles" to be notified of foreman openings, from whom they would choose the foreman for new projects. Such a pool would undoubtedly have contained some qualified blacks....

For all of these reasons we hold that [plaintiffs] have made out a prima facie case of not only discriminatory treatment but discriminatory impact as well. We remand the case to permit [defendants] to introduce additional evidence that their discriminatory conduct may have been justified by business necessity, and for any rebuttal testimony by the plaintiffs. As the evidence thus far introduced is insufficient to meet the burden on the defendants, if no additional defensive evidence is offered the sole remaining issue would be backpay damages.

[Reversed and remanded.]

Examples of Discriminatory Impact

We now look at several specific types of employment practices that have given rise to claims of discriminatory impact.

Physical Requirements: Many jobs do, in fact, require certain physical characteristics such as strength or agility. In setting minimum qualifications for such a job, the employer must be very careful to design the standard as narrowly as possible. If substantial strength is required for a particular factory job, for instance, it may be convenient (and tempting) for the employer simply to require all applicants for the job to be at least six feet tall and 180 pounds. Such a requirement would, however, have a disproportionate impact on certain groups, such as women, Hispanics, and Asian-Americans.

In *Dothard v. Rawlinson,* 433 U.S. 321 (1977), the Supreme Court held that Title VII had been violated by a requirement that state prison guards in Alabama be at least five feet, two inches tall and weigh 120 pounds. Statistics showed that the requirement would exclude over 40 percent of the female population but less than 1 percent of males. The Court permitted the use of generalized national statistics for purposes of comparison because there was no reason to suppose that physical height and weight characteristics of Alabama men and women differed significantly from those of the national population. The Court observed that general population statistics were appropriate for the additional reason that, in this case, data concerning actual applicants might not be very valuable. The reason, in the words of the Court, was that "the application process might itself not adequately reflect the actual potential applicant pool, since otherwise qualified people might be discouraged from applying because of a self-recognized inability to meet the very standards being challenged as discriminatory." The Court then observed that strength might indeed be a legitimate qualification for the job, but that the employer could not rebut the plaintiff's *prima facie* case because there was no evidence showing a correlation between the size requirement and the amount of strength actually required for the job. In other words, the employer needed to determine how much strength is needed for the particular job and design a test to measure whether individual applicants actually possessed it.

In other cases, courts have recognized that various jobs require certain physical attributes or skills. Even if an employment rule requiring a particular attribute or skill has a discriminatory impact, the employer can prevail by showing that the attribute or skill is necessary for the job and that a valid, objective method was used to test applicants for the requirement.

Educational Requirements and Nonphysical Skills:

Minimum educational requirements, such as a high school diploma or college degree, frequently have a disproportionately adverse impact on racial minorities. Such requirements ordinarily violate Title VII in the case of unskilled or semiskilled jobs. The reason is that employers usually are unable to show that general educational achievement is necessary for the performance of these types of jobs.

In *Griggs v. Duke Power Co.,* 401 U.S. 424 (1971), the Supreme Court struck down the employer's practice of requiring a high school diploma as a prerequisite for all its jobs. Evidence showed that in North Carolina, where the employer was located and from which almost all its employees came, high school diplomas were possessed by about three times as many whites as blacks. The employer was unable to show that the diploma was really necessary for most of its jobs—it had adopted the requirement because of the feeling that the overall quality of its workforce would be improved as a result.

In contrast, courts usually have approved minimum educational requirements for jobs involving substantial responsibility, skill, or independent judgment. Such requirements have been upheld in cases involving police officers, teachers, airline flight engineers, and laboratory technicians, even without any actual demonstration by the employer that the particular educational achievement was essential to that job.

Specific nonphysical skills, like specific physical skills, legally can be required for a job despite discriminatory impact if the employer can show that the particular skill is essential for the job. For example, proficiency in English or some other language can be required if the job demands it.

Testing: Employers frequently require job applicants to perform satisfactorily on standardized tests designed to measure intelligence, aptitude, personality, achievement, or specific skills. Such tests are recognized as being valuable aids in the process of selecting the best qualified people for a variety of jobs. One of the main advantages of these tests is their relative objectivity. Section 703(h) of Title VII states that it is permissible "for an employer to give and to act upon the results of any professionally developed ability test provided that such test, its administration or action upon the results is not designed, intended, or used to discriminate because of race, color, religion, sex, or national origin."

However, the courts have interpreted this provision in such a way that standardized tests are treated essentially like other employment practices. That is, even if there is no evidence of discriminatory motive surrounding the test, it nevertheless can violate Title VII by having a discriminatory impact. If the test is shown to have a discriminatory impact, the employer must be prepared to rebut the *prima facie* case by proving that the test is legitimately job-related.

In *Griggs v. Duke Power Co.*, the employer, in addition to requiring a high school diploma, also required job applicants to pass two standardized tests. One was the Wonderlic Personnel Test, which purported to measure general intelligence, and the other was the Bennett Mechanical Comprehension Test. Use of these tests was shown to have had a discriminatory impact on blacks, and the employer was unable to establish any correlation between success on the tests and job performance. As a result, the Supreme Court ruled that the employer's testing violated Title VII. The Court stated: "Nothing in the Act precludes the use of testing or measuring procedures; obviously they are useful. What Congress has forbidden is giving these devices and mechanisms controlling force unless they are demonstrably a reasonable measure of job performance. Congress has not commanded that the less qualified be preferred over the better qualified simply because of minority origins. Far from disparaging job qualifications as such, Congress has made such qualifications the controlling factor, so that race, religion, nationality, and sex become irrelevant. *What Congress has commanded is that any tests used must measure the person for the job and not the person in the abstract.*" [Emphasis added.]

The Validation requirement: When a test is shown to have a discriminatory impact, EEOC's Guidelines require the employer to "validate" the test. In other words, the employer has the burden of showing, through the use of professional validation studies, that the test is "predictive of or significantly correlated with important elements of work behavior which comprise or are relevant to the job or jobs for which candidates are being evaluated." Even if an employer's use of a particular test has not yet been shown to have a discriminatory impact, the employer may protect itself against a challenge by having the test professionally validated.

In specifying the methods by which tests can be validated, the Guidelines rely on the validation standards established by the American Psychological Association. Validation can be accomplished by one of three methods. (1) *Criterion-related validity* is the statistical relationship between test scores and actual job performance. The employer must thoroughly analyze the job and develop objective standards for measuring job performance. For example, a weighted combination of production rate, error rate, and absenteeism might be appropriate for a particular job. For criterion validity, it has been held that a correlation between test scores and job performance of +0.3 is sufficient (+1.0 is perfect). (2) *Content validity* establishes that the test actually measures the ability to perform specific job functions. Thus a typing test would be content valid for a secretary. (3) *Construct validity* indicates that the test identifies one or more psychological traits required for successful job performance. A test that measures patience would be construct valid for a kindergarten teacher. This method is the least often used because of its difficulty.

Seniority Systems:

Senority is the length of service of an employee. Many employers use senority as the basis for determining matters such as which employees are laid off first when jobs are reduced and which ones have the first opportunity to transfer to vacant jobs (as in *TWA v. Hardison*). Some seniority systems are implemented unilaterally by employers, but most are found in collective bargaining agreements negotiated between employers and labor unions.

Seniority systems are almost universally recognized as providing a logical, objective method for making certain types of personnel decisions. The operation of such a system, however, may sometimes have an adverse impact on minorities and women. The reason for this is that equal employment opportunity is still a relatively new concept and, as a result, minority and women employees on the average have substantially less seniority than white male employees. When a lay-off occurs, it usually has a disproportionately greater impact on minorities and women when those with less seniority are laid off first.

However, because of the feeling that seniority is a legitimate, and even essential, employment practice, Congress gave it special treatment in Title VII. Section 703(h), which dealt with testing, also contains a provision stating that operation of a seniority system does not violate Title VII unless the employer *intended* to discriminate. In other words, discriminatory impact by itself is not enough to make a seniority system illegal; there must be proof of an intent to discriminate.

A question left unanswered by the statutory language was whether a seniority system would violate Title VII by causing the effects of past discrimination to be perpetuated. The Supreme Court, in *International Brotherhood of Teamsters v. United States,* 431 U.S. 324 (1977), ruled that a genuine seniority system, implemented and operated without any discriminatory intent, does not violate Title VII merely by continuing the effects of discriminatory practices that had occurred *before* enactment of Title VII. On the other hand, the Court said that such a seniority system is illegal insofar as it continues the effects of previous discriminatory practices that had occurred *after* enactment of Title VII. Thus, employees showing that they had been illegally discriminated against after the effective date of Title VII could be granted retroactive seniority.

Other Practices: Various other employment practices have created issues of discriminatory impact under Title VII. For example, the practice of refusing to hire individuals with criminal records has been challenged because it affects a disproportionately high percentage of minority applicants. The courts have held that such a practice violates Title VII if it is general in nature and does not take into account the type of job or type of criminal offense. However, a rule excluding those with serious criminal records does not violate Title VII with respect to jobs involving trust (such as a bank teller) or significantly responsibility.

In another case, an employer's policy against beards was found to have a discriminatory impact on black men, because they are more prone than white men to suffer skin irritation from shaving. The court ruled, however, that the employer had rebutted the *prima facie* case of discrimination by showing business necessity. The basis for this conclusion was that the employer, a supermarket chain, had a real need to present an image of neatness to the public.

Hiring preferences for military veterans have a discriminatory impact on women because the majority of veterans are men. With respect to federal, state, and local government employers, however, Title VII expressly exempts such preferences.

Bona fide Occupational Qualification

Section 703(e) of Title VII provides that it is not illegal to discriminate on the basis of religion, sex, or national origin in situations in which religion, sex, or national origin is a "bona fide occupational qualification" (BFOQ). Race or color cannot be a BFOQ. Employers generally raise the BFOQ defense only when they are attempting to justify an explicit discriminatory employment policy. Congress intended the BFOQ provision to be a very limited exception that would apply only to rare situations. EEOC and the courts have followed this intent by recognizing the exception very infrequently.

Most of the situations in which BFOQ has been an issue have involved sex discrimination. Stereotypes or traditional assumptions about which jobs are appropriate for men or women do not establish the BFOQ exception. A basic principle of Title VII is that the individual should decide whether the job is appropriate, assuming that person is qualified to perform it. Thus, men cannot automatically be barred from jobs such as airline flight attendants or secretaries, and women cannot be barred from mining, construction, or other jobs requiring lifting, night work, and so forth. Even the fact that the employer's customers strongly prefer employees to be of one sex or the other does not create the BFOQ exception.

In a few circumstances, however, gender is an essential element of the job. For example, the BFOQ defense has been permitted when one sex or the other is necessary for authenticity, as in the case of models or actors. In addition, being a woman has been held to be a BFOQ for employment as a salesperson in the ladies' undergarments department of a department store and as a nurse in the labor and delivery section of an obstetrical hospital. Being a man has been held to be a BFOQ for employment as a security guard, where the job involved searching male employees, and also as an attendant in a men's restroom.

The following case applies the BFOQ defense to a difficult problem faced by both employers and employees—exposure of women workers to substances that create risks of harm to fetuses.

CASE

UNITED AUTOMOBILE, AEROSPACE, & AGRICULTURAL WORKERS UNION v. JOHNSON CONTROLS, INC.

U.S. SUPREME COURT
111 S.Ct. 1196
(1991)

Johnson Controls, Inc., manufactures batteries. In the manufacturing process, the element lead is a primary ingredient. Occupational exposure to lead entails health risks, including the risk of harm to any fetus carried by a female employee. Lead exposure to men also carries some risk for their unborn children, but not to the same extent as in the case of exposure to women. Before the Civil Rights Act of 1964 became law, Johnson Controls did not employ any woman in a battery-manufacturing job. In 1977 it adopted a policy of fully informing its female employees of the fetal risks associated exposure to lead, permitting them to make a voluntary decision about whether they wished to work in a job that would expose them to lead. In 1982, the company changed its policy to one of exclusion. Under this policy, women were absolutely excluded from jobs involving significant lead exposure unless they presented medical documentation of sterility.

Several employees and the union filed a class action in federal district court, alleging that the company's fetal protection policy constituted sex discrimination in violation of Title VII. Among the individual plaintiffs were Mary Craig, who had chosen to be sterilized in order to avoid losing her job; Elsie Nason, a 50-year-old divorcee who had suffered a loss in compensation when she was transferred out of a job where she was exposed to lead; and Donald Penney, a male employee who had been denied a request for a leave of absence for the purpose of lowering his lead level because he intended to become a father. The district court treated the fetal protection policy as a

CONTINUED

neutral employment practice having a discriminatory impact on women. The court concluded that the plaintiffs had established a prima facie case of discriminatory impact, but that the company had established business necessity and the plaintiffs had failed to demonstrate reasonable alternatives that would not have such a discriminatory impact. It granted summary judgment for the company. The U.S. Court of Appeals affirmed. The plaintiffs appealed to the U.S. Supreme Court. In their appeal, they claimed that the fetal protection policy was not a gender-neutral practice, but was explicitly discriminatory on the basis of sex. Because it was explicit gender discrimination, they contended that the defendant could prevail only by proving the BFOQ defense, which is much more difficult than showing business necessity in an impact case.

BLACKMUN, JUSTICE:

The bias in Johnson Controls' policy is obvious. Fertile men, but not fertile women, are given a choice as to whether they wish to risk their reproductive health for a particular job. The policy excludes women with childbearing capacity from lead-exposed jobs and so creates a facial [i.e., explicit] classification based on gender....

[Johnson Controls] does not seek to protect the unconceived children of all its employees. Despite evidence in the record about the debilitating effect of lead exposure on the male reproduction system, Johnson Controls is concerned only with the harms that may befall the unborn offspring of its female employees.... Johnson Controls' fetal-protection policy is [explicit] sex discrimination forbidden under Title VII unless respondent can establish that sex is a "bona fide occupational qualification."

Under section 703(e)(1) of Title VII, an employer may discriminate on the basis of "religion, sex, or national origin in those certain instances where religion, sex, or national origin is a bona fide occupational qualification reasonably necessary to the normal operation of that particular business or enterprise."... The BFOQ defense is written narrowly, and this Court has read it narrowly. We have read the BFOQ language of section 4(f) of the Age Discrimination in Employment Act of 1967 (ADEA), which tracks the BFOQ provision in Title VII, just as narrowly.... The wording of the BFOQ defense contains several terms of restriction that indicate that the exception reaches only special situations. The statute thus limits the situations in which discrimination is permissible to "certain instances" where sex discrimination is "reasonably necessary" to the "normal operation" of the "particular" business. Each one of these terms— certain, normal, particular—prevents the use of general subjective standards and favors an objective, verifiable requirement. But the most telling term is "occupational"; this indicates that these objective, verifiable requirements must concern job-related skills and aptitudes....

Johnson Controls argues that its fetal-protection policy falls within the so-called safety exception to the BFOQ. Our cases have stressed that discrimination on the basis of sex because of safety concerns is allowed only in narrow circumstances. In *Dothard v. Rawlinson*, this Court indicated that danger to a woman herself does not justify discrimination. We there allowed the employer to hire only male guards in contact areas of maximum-security male penitentiaries only because more was at stake than the "individual woman's decision to weigh and accept the risks of employment." We found sex to be a BFOQ inasmuch as the employment of a female guard would create real risks of safety to others if violence broke out because the guard was a woman. Sex discrimination was tolerated because sex was related to the guard's ability to do the job—maintaining prison security. We also required in *Dothard* a high correlation between sex and ability to perform job functions and refused to allow employers to use sex as a proxy for strength although it might be a fairly accurate one. Similarly, some courts have approved airlines' layoffs of pregnant flight attendants at different points during the first five months of pregnancy on the ground that the employer's policy was necessary to ensure the safety of passengers. In two of these cases, the courts pointedly indicated that fetal, as opposed to passenger, safety was best left to the mother.

We considered safety to third parties in *Western Airlines, Inc. v. Criswell*, 472 U.S. 400 (1985), in the context of the ADEA. We focused upon "the nature of the flight engineer's tasks," and the "actual capabilities of persons over age 60" in relation to those tasks. Our safety concerns were not independent of the individual's ability to perform the assigned tasks, but rather involved the possibility that, because of age-

CONTINUED

connected debility, a flight engineer might not properly assist the pilot, and might thereby cause a safety emergency. Furthermore, although we considered the safety of third parties in *Dothard* and *Criswell*, those third parties were indispensable to the particular business at issue. In *Dothard*, the third parties were the inmates; in *Criswell*, the third parties were the passengers on the plane. We stressed that in order to qualify as a BFOQ, a job qualification must relate to the "essence," or to the "central mission of the employer's business." . . .

Third-party safety considerations properly entered into the BFOQ analysis in *Dothard* and *Criswell* because they went to the core of the employee's job performance. Moreover, that performance involved the central purpose of the enterprise. The essence of a correctional counselor's job is to maintain prison security; the central mission of the airline's business was the safe transportation of its passengers. . . . The unconceived fetuses of Johnson Controls' female employees, however, are neither customers nor third parties whose safety is essential to the business of battery manufacturing. No one can disregard the possibility of injury to future children; the BFOQ, however, is not so broad that it transforms this deep social concern into an essential aspect of batterymaking.

Our case law, therefore, makes clear that the safety exception is limited to instances in which sex or pregnancy actually interferes with the employee's ability to perform the job. . . . Women as capable of doing their jobs as their male counterparts may not be forced to choose between having a child and having a job. . . .

Pregnant women who are able to work must be permitted to work on the same conditions as other employees. . . . [E]mployers may not require a pregnant woman to stop working at any time during her pregnancy unless she is unable to do her work. Employment late in pregnancy often imposes risks on the unborn child, but Congress indicated that the employer may take into account only the woman's ability to get her job done. . . . Congress made clear that the decision to become pregnant or to work while being either pregnant or capable of becoming pregnant was reserved for each individual woman to make for herself. . . .

We have no difficulty concluding that Johnson Controls cannot establish a BFOQ. Fertile women, as far as appears in the record, participate in the manufacture of batteries as efficiently as anyone else. Johnson Controls' professed moral and ethical concerns about the welfare of the next generation do not suffice to establish a BFOQ of female sterility. Decisions about the welfare of future children must be left to the parents who conceive, bear, support, and raise them rather than to the employers who hire those parents. . . .

A word about tort liability and the increased cost of fertile women in the workplace is perhaps necessary. One of the [concurring] judges in this case expressed concern about an employer's tort liability and concluded that liability for a potential injury to a fetus is a social cost that Title VII does not require a company to ignore. . . . More than 40 States currently recognize a right to recover for a prenatal injury based either on negligence or on wrongful death. According to Johnson Controls, however, the company complies with the lead [exposure] standard developed by OSHA [i.e., the Occupational Safety & Health Administration within the Labor Department] and warns its female employees about the damaging effects of lead. . . . Without negligence, it would be difficult for a court to find liability on the part of the employer [in a case alleging injury to a fetus]. If . . . Title VII bans sex-specific fetal-protection policies, the employer fully informs the woman of the risk, and the employer has not acted negligently, the basis for holding an employer liable [under general tort principles] seems remote at best. [Without ruling on the question because it was not presented, the Supreme Court then noted that Title VII's prohibition of gender-specific fetal protection policies might preclude a tort claim for injury to a fetus on the constitutional theory of federal preemption.] . . . We, of course, are not presented with, nor do we decide, a case in which costs would be so prohibitive as to threaten the survival of the employer's business. We merely reiterate our prior holdings that [an] incremental cost of hiring women cannot justify discriminating against them. . . .

It is no more appropriate for the courts than it is for individual employers to decide whether a woman's reproductive role is more important to herself and her family than her economic role. Congress has left this choice to the woman as hers to make. The judgment of the Court of Appeals is reversed and the case is remanded.

Affirmative Action and Reverse Discrimination

The primary strategy in the legal battle against employment discrimination has been simply to prohibit discriminatory practices and to strike them down when they are discovered. Another important weapon, however, has been **affirmative action**—actually giving preferences to minorities and women in the hiring process. In many cases, affirmative action programs include goals and timetables for increasing the percentage of minorities and women in the employer's workforce. The basic purpose of affirmative action is to rectify previous discrimination.

Affirmative action has been used by some courts as a remedy in specific cases of discrimination. In other words, after concluding that an employer had practiced discrimination, some courts have both ordered the cessation of the practice and required the employer to implement an affirmative action program. In addition, some employers, either on their own or in connection with union collective bargaining agreements, have instituted voluntary affirmative action programs.

Since their inception, affirmative action programs have raised difficult legal questions. By granting preferences to minorities and women, these programs discriminate in some degree against white men. White men are protected against race and sex discrimination by Title VII: Does so-called **reverse discrimination,** brought about by affirmative action programs, violate Title VII or other discrimination laws?

In *United Steelworkers of America v. Weber*, 443 U.S. 193 (1979), the Supreme Court ruled that *voluntary* affirmative action programs are permissible under Title VII in certain circumstances. In several other cases, lower courts have upheld *mandatory* affirmative action programs in similar circumstances. As a limited exception to the basic prohibition against discrimination, reverse discrimination brought about by affirmative action programs is legal under the following conditions.

1. There must be a formal, systematic program—the employer cannot discriminate against nonminorities on an isolated, *ad hoc* basis.

2. Any such program must be temporary—it must operate only until its reasonable minority hiring goals are reached.

3. The program cannot completely bar the hiring or promotion of nonminority workers.

4. The program cannot result in the actual firing of nonminority workers.

5. The program cannot force the employer to hire or promote unqualified workers.

6. If the program is ordered by a court or legislature, it must be based on evidence that there actually had been discrimination by the employer in the past. If the program is voluntary, it can be based either on evidence of past discrimination or merely on evidence that in the past there had been an underutilization of minorities or women by the employer.

7. In general, an affirmative action plan cannot override preexisting employee rights that have been established by a valid seniority system.

AGE DISCRIMINATION

Although Title VII of the 1964 Civil Rights Act does not prohibit age discrimination, Congress passed separate legislation dealing with this problem in 1967 and broadened its coverage in 1974, 1978, and 1986. The Age Discrimination in Employment Act (ADEA) prohibits all forms of employment discrimination based on age if the victim of the discrimination is 40 years of age or older.

Like Title VII, ADEA applies to discrimination by employers, employment agencies, and labor organizations, as well as federal, state, and local government agencies. An employer is covered by ADEA if its business affects interstate commerce and it has at least 20 employees (as opposed to 15 under Title VII). The types of employment actions that constitute discrimination, and the methods for proving discrimination under ADEA, are virtually identical to the standards applied under Title VII. Thus, a violation of the ADEA can be proved by showing either discriminatory intent or impact. The process of establishing a *prima facie* case of intent or impact, the employer's rebuttal, and other aspects are the same under the age discrimination law as under Title VII. When an individual seeks to establish a *prima facie* case of discriminatory *intent* under ADEA, he must prove that the other person who was favored over the plaintiff was younger than the plaintiff; however, he does not have to prove that the favored person was below the age of 40.

ADEA also contains a *bona fide* occupational qualification defense that is practically identical to Title VII's BFOQ defense. It is interpreted narrowly and applied only in unusual cases. In *Western Airlines, Inc. v. Criswell*, 472 U.S. 400 (1985), the Supreme Court affirmed the lower court's decision that Western Airlines' policy of mandatory retirement for flight engineers at age 60 violated ADEA. Because a flight engineer is a member of the cockpit crew, Western argued that being younger than 60 is a *bona fide* occupational qualification. The Supreme Court held that an employer must meet two requirements to established the BFOQ defense under ADEA. First, the employer must prove that the age requirement is reasonably necessary to the essence of the employer's business (such as the safe transportation of passengers). Second, the employer must have a factual basis for believing either (1) that all or substantially all of the employees over a particular age are unable to safely and efficiently perform the necessary taks, or (2) that it would be impractical to make such a determination on an individual basis. Western's evidence did not fulfill either alternative of the second requirement.

Also like Title VII, ADEA permits employers to use *bona fide* seniority systems for various employment decisions, even if age discrimination results. Such a system cannot require mandatory retirement, however, unless the employer can prove that age is a BFOQ. In addition, an employer may lawfully offer employees older than a certain age a package of voluntary retirement incentives. Eligible employees must, however, be given complete information, adequate time to decide, and a completely voluntary choice.

ADEA is subject to two limited exceptions. First, business executives with significant policy-making responsibilities can be forced to retire at age 65 if they have vested retirement benefits exceeding an amount specified in the statute. Second, the age discrimination law allows states (or cities, if the particular state permits cities to exercise such authority) to legislate hiring and retirement ages for law enforcement officers and firefighters.

ADEA can be enforced by either EEOC, a state agency, or an individual victim of age discrimination. Like Title VII, ADEA requires an individual first to file a complaint with EEOC or the appropriate state agency within 180 days after the alleged discrimination occurred and to await agency action for a stated period of time before filing a lawsuit in federal court. A jury trial is permitted under ADEA, and a plaintiff is able to recover monetary damages and obtain a reinstatement order in appropriate circumstances. Punitive damages also can be received in cases of flagrant intentional discrimination.

DISCRIMINATION AGAINST PEOPLE WITH DISABILITIES

In the Rehabilitation Act of 1973, Congress prohibited discrimination in employment against people with disabilities. However, that law applied only to the employment practices of federal government agencies, businesses having contracts with the federal government, and organizations or programs receiving federal funding. The Rehabilitation Act continues to apply to these three groups of employers.

In 1990, Congress passed the Americans With Disabilities Act (ADA), which provides comprehensive protection against discrimination to persons with disabilities. The ADA includes provisions dealing not only with discrimination in employment, but also with problems of discrimination and access in public transportation, public accommodations, and communications. Title I of ADA, dealing with employment, is the only part relevant to our discussion in this chapter. By the time the ADA is fully effective in 1993, Title I will apply to all private employers whose business affects interstate commerce and who have 15 or more employees, as well as to state and local government employers. Like Title VII, ADA also applies to employment agencies and labor unions.

The ADA borrows many basic concepts and definitions from the Rehabilitation Act, such as the definition of disability.[9] Most of the following discussion of concepts in the ADA also applies to the Rehabilitation Act. The ADA adopts most of the procedures and methods of proving discrimination, however, from Title VII of the 1964 Civil Rights Act.

---

[9] Where the Rehabilitation Act uses the term *handicapped,* the ADA instead speaks of a "person with a disability."

DISABILITY

The ADA prohibits persons with disabilities against discrimination in hiring, promotion, training programs, pay, benefits, or other aspects of employment. Under the law, a person can be viewed as having a disability in either of three situations.

Physical or Mental Impairment

First, a person has a disability if he or she has a "physical or mental impairment that substantially affects one or more of the major life activities" of that person. Major life activities include functions such as caring for one's self, performing manual tasks, walking, seeing, hearing, speaking, breathing, learning, participating in social relationships and activities, and others. The law does not attempt to include an exhaustive list of disabilities. However, conditions that obviously would constitute "physical or mental impairments substantially affecting a major life activity" include orthopedic, visual, speech, and hearing impairments, cerebral palsy, muscular dystrophy, multiple sclerosis, infection with the HIV virus, cancer, diseases of the heart or other major organs, diabetes, seizure disorders (formerly called epilepsy), mental retardation, emotional illness, serious learning disabilities, drug addiction, and alcoholism. In fact, most kinds of serious physical or mental conditions fall within the definition.

Although alcoholism and drug addiction constitute disabilities, the ADA expressly provides that a *current user* of alcohol or illegal drugs is not protected by the law. Thus, an employer is free to make adverse employment decisions of various kinds based on current alcohol or illegal drug usage.

Finally, the ADA also contains a list of conditions referred to as "behavioral," which are expressly excluded from the definition of disability. These include homosexuality, bisexuality, transvestism, pedophilia, transsexualism, gender identity disorders, exhibitionism, voyeurism, compulsive gambling, kleptomania, pyromania, and several others.

Record of Impairment

The second circumstance in which the ADA considers a person to have a disability occurs when he or she has a "record" of a physical or mental impairment that substantially affects a major life activity. Thus, even if a person does not actually have a serious physical or mental impairment, he is protected against discrimination because a medical record mistakenly indicates that he has such an impairment. In addition, the person is protected from discrimination because of a past record of an impairment that has now been cured. This part of the definition recognizes the difficulty of correcting mistaken records or overcoming the stigma of a past affliction.

Regarded as Having an Impairment

The third circumstance in which the ADA protects a person against employment discrimination occurs when the person is "regarded" as having a physical or mental impairment that substantially affects a major life activity. Thus, if a person has a condition that does *not* substantially affect a major life activity, but an employer treats him as if he does, the ADA prohibits the employer from discriminating. This part of the definition is intended to deal with the devastating effects of stereotypes, myths, and fears about various conditions. For example, people often regard severe burn victims or others having disfigurements as being impaired even when they are not. Although the "regarded" category of protection against discrimination is aimed at a somewhat different problem than the "record" category, the two may sometimes overlap. Thus, in some circumstances a person who formerly had an impairment but who no longer does because the condition is either cured or completely under control might fall within either the second or third category.

QUALIFIED

As with other employment discrimination laws, a person within the ADA's definition of disabled is protected against discrimination only if he or she is *qualified* to do the job in question. In determining whether a disabled person is qualified, the law focuses on the "essential functions" of the job. In other words, if a disabled applicant is rejected because of failure to meet a particular requirement, that requirement must relate to an essential function of the job. If the requirement relates to only a minor or marginal part of the job, the person is qualified.

For example, if a person with a seizure disorder is unable to obtain a driver's license, he would not be qualified for a job as a truck driver. Suppose, however, that this person applies for a job as a guidance counselor at a youth home or camp, and the employer wants counselors to be able to drive in case of medical or other emergencies. Also assume that there are always several counselors on duty, and that there really just needs to be one on hand at any given time who can drive. If the applicant meets all of the job requirements except a driver's license, she is qualified to do the job because the license is not an essential function.

Another aspect of the "essential functions" concept is that it emphasizes the end result that the employer wants to achieve, rather than the precise means of achieving it. Suppose that a job applicant with very limited mobility in one arm applies for a position in the shipping department of a company, where he must lift and carry boxes and other packages weighing up to 50 pounds. One of the company's hiring criteria for the job is that a person be able to lift and carry these kinds of items with both arms. If the applicant can demonstrate that he is able to perform the job satisfactorily with only one arm, he is qualified. In this case, a legitimate job criterion would be the ability to lift and carry 50 pounds, but the ability to do it with both hands would not be a permissible requirement.

Even if a disabled person is qualified to do a particular job, an employer is still permitted to hire or promote the best qualified person available. The central question is the reason for the employer's decision. If the reason for a hiring or promotion decision is that the person hired is *better* qualified than a disabled person who was not hired, the employer is within its rights. Moreover, if two persons—one having a disability and the other not—are *equally* qualified, the ADA does not mandate that the employer hire or promote the person with a disability. This is largely just a theoretical statement, however; in a real situation there is usually *something* that separates two candidates. As a practical matter, the employer should be prepared with a justification for whichever decision is made.

Reasonable Accommodation

Assume that a person with a disability is not qualified to do a job as it is now designed and structured, but could do it as well as anyone else if certain changes are made. Does the employer have to make those changes? The answer is that the ADA requires the employer to make a "reasonable accommodation" for the person's disability. If a person would be qualified if a reasonable accommodation is made, then the ADA deems the person to be qualified. The ADA does not define reasonable accommodation, but does provide some illustrations of actions by an employer that might be required in order to meet this obligation.

First, the duty of reasonable accommodation may include actions that make existing facilities more accessible to persons with disabilities. Examples might include cut-outs in curbs, ramps, handrails, lower elevator buttons, and so on.

Second, the duty of reasonable accommodation may include job restructuring, part-time or modified work schedules, or reassignment to a vacant position. Job restructuring refers to making modifications in a job so that a disabled person can perform its essential functions. Restructuring might encompass the removal of nonessential functions, reorganizing and reallocating assignments, or redesigning procedures. Examples of accommodation through schedule adjustment could include the use of part-time work schedules or, in some cases, more unpaid leave. Reassignment to a vacant position is a possible accommodation only in the case of a current employee who develops difficulties with a job because of a disability, but who could probably perform well in another job that is now vacant.

Third, the duty of reasonable accommodation may include acquiring or modifying equipment or devices. Examples include adaptive computer hardware and software, electronic visual aids, braille devices, talking calculators, brailled materials, telephone handset amplifiers, telecommunication devices for hearing-impaired persons, mechanical page turners, raised or lowered furniture, and so on. Acquisition of personal items that are not specifically job-related, such as hearing aids and eyeglasses, is *not* the employer's obligation.

Fourth, the duty of reasonable accommodation may include a wide variety of other actions by the employer. Sometimes, for example, the obligation may include providing a reader, interpreter, or attendant.

An employer is under an obligation to make a reasonable accommodation only if it knows of the need for such action. Most of the time, the obligation exists only if the disabled person requests that an accommodation be made. However, if a current employee is having difficulty with a job because of a disability, the employer may be under a duty to discuss possible accommodations with the employee. Other than these two situations, it is neither required nor even proper for the employer to bring up a question of accommodation. Although stereotypes may lead an employer to believe that an accommodation will be necessary, it is often the case that nothing is needed.

Although a person with a contagious disease can be classified as having a disability under the ADA, the risk of passing the disease to others is a legitimate factor in determining whether he is qualified to do a particular job. If, according to the judgment of medical authorities, the particular disease carries a significant risk of transmission to co-workers, customers, or others, the person with this disease is not qualified unless the risk can be removed by some reasonable accommodation.

On the same general subject, the ADA includes a special provision for jobs that involve food handling. The Department of Health and Human Services, acting through its subunit, the Public Health Service, is required to develop and annually update a list of communicable diseases that may be transmitted by the handling of food. The Public Health Service is also required to give wide publicity to the list and otherwise engage in an effort to educate the public about which illnesses present risks in food handling and which do not. It is permissible for an employer to refuse to assign an employee with a listed communicable disease to a food-handling position, or to remove him from such a position. The employer has no legal obligation to the worker in this situation, unless transferring him to a nonfood-handling position is an option that would constitute a reasonable accommodation. Of course, even if a nonfood-handling job is available, a transfer would not be a reasonable accommodation if there is still a significant risk of transmitting the disease to others in that other position.

Undue Hardship

An important limitation on the employer's duty to make a reasonable accommodation is the principle that the employer is not required to take action that imposes an *undue hardship* on the business.[10]

In general, "undue hardship" refers to actions by the employer that involve substantial expense, difficulty, disruption, or fundamental changes in operations. Unfortunately, a question of undue hardship unavoidably must

---

[10] It will be remembered that, under Title VII of the 1964 Civil Rights Act, an employer is required to make reasonable accommodation for an employee's religious beliefs or practices, unless such an accommodation would impose an undue hardship on the employer's business. In the religion context, the "undue hardship" limitation has been interpreted to mean that the employer cannot be required to incur more than a *de minimis* (trivial) cost. This is not the case in the ADA; to accommodate a person's disability, an employer sometimes may be required to incur more than just a trivial cost. Thus, the reasonable accommodation obligation may require considerably more of the employer under the ADA than under the religious discrimination provisions of Title VII.

be decided on a case-by-case basis. The determination of whether a particular accommodation would impose an undue hardship on the employer's business should incorporate several factors. First, the cost of the proposed action must be considered. Second, the nature and degree of effect on the company's operations are legitimate considerations. Third, the particular characteristics of the company must be taken into account. These characteristics include the number of employees, financial resources, and financial condition of the particular facility, and of the parent company if the facility is part of a larger enterprise. Fourth, it is relevant to take into account the overall benefit to be produced by the accommodation, in addition to the benefit to a particular disabled worker. For example, the cost of a particular accommodation is more likely to be treated as reasonable (and not an undue hardship) if the action probably will benefit not only this disabled worker, but also other disabled employees, clients, or customers. Fifth, other relevant information may be considered in particular circumstances. For example, the availability of outside funding (e.g., from government or foundations) for barrier removal or other accommodation may reduce cost to such an extent that it is not an undue hardship.

PROVING DISCRIMINATION

As mentioned earlier, the ADA borrows many of is procedures from Title VII of the 1964 Civil Rights Act. Thus, a violation of the ADA may be established either by proving intentional discrimination or by demonstrating that a particular employment practice or policy has a discriminatory impact on the disabled. The process of analyzing evidence, including the requirement that the employee establish a *prima facie* case, the employer's opportunity for rebuttal, and the employee's proof of pretext will be the same as under Title VII, with appropriate modifications in the process to fit the circumstances.

Tests, requirements, or criteria that have a discriminatory impact on persons with disabilities must be closely related to essential functions of the job, must be truly necessary for obtaining qualified workers, and must not negatively affect disabled persons more than necessary.

Finally, the ADA generally prohibits an employer from requiring job applicants to take preoffer medical examinations. The employer is permitted to evaluate, apply its selection criteria to applicants, select someone in a nondiscriminatory fashion, and make a conditional job offer. This offer can be conditioned on the applicant's submission to a medical examination. The results of this examination can be used by the employer to determine whether the individual is qualified to do the job but cannot, of course, be used to discriminate on the basis of disability. The reasoning behind prohibiting preoffer medical examinations, but permitting them after a conditional offer has been made, is simply to increase the chances that an employer will focus first on a person's qualifications.

Questions and Problems

1. Five employees of Omni Georgia were fired and replaced by Orientals of Korean origin. The fired employees were all of U.S. origin; some were white and some were black. The supervisor who made the hiring and firing decisions was an Oriental of Japanese origin. The fired employees sued the employer, claiming that Title VII had been violated. No evidence was presented as to the actual motive for the firings and replacements. Has Title VII been violated? Discuss. (*Bullard v. Omni Georgia,* 640 F.2d 632, 5th Cir. 1981.)

2. An employee belonged to the Black Muslim faith. She was required by her religion to wear dresses that substantially covered her legs and arms, and that had a high neckline. Her supervisor told her that such attention-getting clothing was inappropriate and she must change her style of dress or be dismissed. Other female employees were permitted to wear miniskirts, which were fashionable at the time and which were considered by the employer to be more "business-like." EEOC contended that the employer had violated Title VII. Discuss whether this contention is correct. (CCH EEOC Decisions §6,283, 1973.)

3. Young, an atheist, was employed as a teller at a branch office of Southwestern Savings & Loan. All Southwestern employees were required to attend a monthly staff meeting at the main office devoted to various business matters. These meetings were always opened with a short religious talk and a prayer, both nondenominational in nature. Young, who felt that her freedom of conscience was violated by the religious portion of the meetings, stopped attending the meetings altogether. She did not, however, register any protest with anyone at Southwestern, nor did she tell them why she had stopped attending the staff meetings. After a few months her absence was noted, and she revealed her objection to the religious portion of the meetings to her supervisor, who informed her that attendance was required and that she could simply "close her ears" during the brief opening devotionals. At the close of business that day Young checked in her cash drawer, turned in her keys, and informed her supervisor that she was leaving Southwestern. Pressed for a reason, she stated that she could not attend the "prayer meetings." She refused to submit a letter of resignation, however, and stated that she was "being fired." Does Young have a Title VII claim against Southwestern for religious discrimination? Discuss. Is the fact that Southwestern had a policy (unknown to Young and her supervisor) permitting employees who objected to miss the religious portion of the meetings relevant to a Title VII claim? (*Young v. Southwestern Savings & Loan Ass'n,* 509 F.2d 140, 5th Cir. 1975.)

4. Margaret Hasselman worked as a lobby attendant in an office building managed by Sage Realty. She was required by her employer to wear a "revealing and provocative" uniform which caused her to be subjected to repeated and abusive sexual harassment by various people. She finally refused to wear the uniform and was fired. EEOC filed suit against the employer. Did the employer's actions violate Title VII? Discuss. (*EEOC v. Sage Realty Corp.,* 507 F.Supp. 599, S.D.N.Y. 1981.)

5. The New York City Transit Authority, which operated the subway system and certain bus lines, had a rule excluding from employment any person who regularly used narcotics. The Authority interpreted this rule as also applying to users of methadone, including those receiving methadone maintenance treatment for curing heroin addiction. Most of the Transit Authority's employees worked in jobs that were highly safety-sensitive and required maximum alertness and competence. These jobs included operating buses and subway cars; maintaining the buses, subway cars, tracks, and tunnels; operating cranes; and handling high-voltage equipment. A substantial number of other jobs involved the handling of large sums of money. Several former and prospective employees, all on methadone programs, sued the Authority for allegedly violating Title VII. Plaintiffs introduced evidence showing that (1) 81 percent of the employees who were referred to the Authority's medical director for suspected drug use were black or Hispanic, and (2) 63 percent of the persons in New York City participating in publicly operated methadone maintenance programs were black or Hispanic. Discuss whether the Transit Authority violated Title VII. (*New York City Transit Authority v. Beazer,* 440 U.S. 568, 1979.)

6. To be eligible for promotion to the position of welfare eligibility supervisor in the Connecticut Department of Income Maintenance, candidates were required to pass a standardized written examination. Only those passing the test formed the eligibility pool from which individuals were selected for promotion. The passing rate of blacks was approximately 54 percent; that of whites was

about 79 percent. Selection for promotion from the eligibility pool was based on past work performance, supervisors' recommendations, and seniority. In addition, in the final step of the process an affirmative action program was employed to ensure substantial representation of minority candidates at the supervisory level. Several black employees who failed the test filed suit claiming that the test had a discriminatory impact on their group. The State of Connecticut responded by arguing that the test should not be considered alone and that plaintiffs had not established a *prima facie* case of discrimination, because the *total* selection process did not have a discriminatory impact. Have plaintiffs established a *prima facie* violation of Title VII, thus requiring the defendant to formally validate the test? Discuss. (*Connecticut v. Teal*, 457 U.S. 440, 1982.)

7. Fernandez, a female employee of Wynn Oil Co., had worked in various positions for the company during a seven-year period. She sought a promotion to the position of director of international marketing, which would have required her to work with Latin American customers and distributors. The cultural preferences and mores of these customers and distributors were such that a man would be preferable for the job. It was shown, for example, that a woman in the position would "have great difficulty in conducting business in South America from a hotel room." She was not given the promotion and later sued Wynn, claiming that the employer had practiced sex discrimination in violation of Title VII. Wynn claimed that sex was BFOQ for this job. Who is right? Discuss. (*Fernandez v. Wynn Oil Co.*, 653 F.2d 1273, 9th Cir. 1981.)

8. Weeks, a woman, had worked for the telephone company in Georgia for 19 years before asking that she be given the job of switchman. Her request was denied, and she was told that women were not eligible for the job because it was strenuous and required the employee to be on 24-hour call. A state statute in Georgia prohibited women from being employed in a job that would require them to lift more than 30 pounds. Weeks claimed that her employer had illegally discriminated on the basis of her sex, and the employer contended that sex was a BFOQ for this job. Was there a violation of Title VII? Discuss. (*Weeks v. Southern Bell Telephone & Telegraph Co.*, 408 F.2d 228, 5th Cir. 1969.)

9. Lehman, a white man, and Tidwell, a black man, worked as temporary, part-time employees for Yellow Freight System, an interstate trucking company. Their duties primarily involved driving trucks in Indiana. Yellow Freight usually filled open positions for regular truck drivers from among those who had worked as temporary drivers. When such a position became open at the employer's Muncie, Indiana, terminal, both Lehman and Tidwell applied for the job. Lehman had the appropriate driver's license plus substantial truck driving experience, whereas Tidwell did not have the required license and his only truck driving experience was that which he received during his one month as a temporary for Yellow Freight. McDonald, manager of the Muncie terminal, hired Tidwell and rejected Lehman. The employer had to train Tidwell after hiring him. Yellow Freight had a formal affirmative action plan for its nationwide operation, but McDonald knew practically nothing about the plan and paid no attention to it. Instead, he took his own affirmative action by explicitly preferring minorities in this and several other instances. Lehman sued Yellow Freight, claiming he had been discriminated against because he was white. Did McDonald's actions violate Title VII? Discuss. (*Lehman v. Yellow Freight System, Inc.*, 651 F.2d 520, 75h Cir. 1981.)

10. Coates was a field engineer in the Danville, Virginia, office of NCR. Field engineers maintained and repaired NCR equipment under maintenance agreements with customers. During the early 1970s NCR was phasing out the manufacture of electromechanical office equipment in favor of electronic equipment. This change required the retraining of field engineers to service the electronic equipment. Younger men were generally selected for this training over the older employees. It was felt that the younger employees, who usually had lower productivity, could be more easily spared from field operations for retraining than could the older employees. Even when older employees were selected for retraining, the heavy demands made on their time in the field often made scheduling impossible. In 1974, principally because of an economic downturn, the Danville manager was directed to recommend several field engineers for discharge. Ability to service the new electronic equipment was to be a principal criteria in deciding whom to recommend for discharge. The Danville manager therefore used training level as a criterion, and discharged two employees—Coates, who was 50 years old, another who was 40. Neither had been trained on the new electronic equipment. Coates filed suit alleging a violation of ADEA. Discuss whether Coates should win. (*Coates v. National Cash Register Co.*, 433 F.Supp. 655, W.D. Va. 1977.)

CHAPTER 18

In most types of relationships harmony is a highly desirable goal. In the relationship between employer and employee, substantial harmony is critical to efficient production. On the other hand, one must realize that a certain amount of tension is an inevitable part of this association. Although employer and employee share the common goal of making the business enterprise an economic success, they also have conflicting interests. The employer is a buyer of labor, the employee a seller. The employer wants to obtain labor at the lowest possible

THE AMERICAN LABOR MOVEMENT

EMPLOYMENT LAW: LABOR-MANAGEMENT RELATIONS

cost; the employee wants to receive the highest possible price and best possible conditions.

In the average situation, the employer has much greater bargaining power than the employee. In purely economic terms, the employer is much more important to the individual employee than the employee is to the employer. Consequently, the tendency of employees has been to unite in an attempt to increase their bargaining power. By dealing with the employer as a group, employees usually have been able to negotiate higher wages and better hours and working conditions than any single employee could have obtained. All or a substantial part of the employer's workforce usually is quite important economically to the employer. This increased power has given employee groups, or unions, the ability to use various economic weapons. Strikes—work stop-pages by unions—have been particularly effective. Picketing the employer's premises—walking in highly visible places with signs and placards—sometimes has been useful in obtaining public sympathy and assistance from other employee unions. Attempts by unions to persuade the public to boycott—stop buying—the employer's products usually have not been very successful, but on a few occasions these attempts have resulted in significant economic pressure on the employer.

Employers have not been without weapons in these confrontations. In some situations, employers have successfully countered union demands by "lockout"—temporarily barring employees from the workplace. Hiring replacements for striking workers has been successfully accomplished by employers in some labor disputes. The present legal status of these economic weapons is discussed later in the chapter.

During the early stages of the American labor movement, employers frequently used the courts to stifle employee organizations. Until the mid-1800s, the **criminal conspiracy doctrine** was effectively used. The combination of employees was viewed as being a criminal offense in and of itself, without regard to any particular actions taken by the union. After courts began to view unions as legal organizations in the mid-1800s, employers pursued other routes. In many cases they were able to file civil suits and obtain *injunctions* against particular union activities, such as strikes and pickets. If union members violated the court's injunction, they could be fined and jailed for contempt of court. In 1890 employers obtained a new weapon when Congress passed the Sherman Act. Although the Sherman Act was aimed primarily at anticompetitive activities by *business firms*, employers were able to use the Sherman Act against unions by convincing many courts that union activities were "combinations in restraint of trade" and thus in violation of the Act.

Many of the labor disputes of the late 1800s and early 1900s caused significant disruptions of commercial activity. Several disputes, such as the Pullman Strike in 1893, resulted in violence. These incidents served to highlight the fact that the peaceful, expeditious resolution of labor disputes should be a high national priority. Public opinion regarding organized labor continued to be deeply divided; but regardless of their personal views of the issue, more people began to recognize the need for some kind of new approach to the labor problem. Moreover, with the Great Depression of the 1930s came a close reexamination of our economic system, including the place of organized labor in the system.

Thus, during the late nineteenth century and first three decades of the twentieth century, the stage was gradually set for major legislative action. During this same era, organized labor grew in number and political power, creating further pressure on government policy makers to provide solutions. The most important statutory enactments resulting from the rise of organized labor are now examined.

FEDERAL LEGISLATION

LEGISLATION BEFORE 1935

Clayton Act

Enacted in 1914, the Clayton Act essentially is an antitrust law dealing with mergers and several other anticompetitive business practices. In Section 6 of the Act, however, Congress provided an exemption from the antitrust laws for the organization and normal activities of labor unions.

Under this exemption, labor unions can organize, collectively bargain with an employer, and use economic weapons such as strikes and pickets without violating the Sherman Act or other antitrust law. The exemption, however, is not absolute. A labor union can violate the Sherman Act if it joins with someone outside organized labor (such as the employer) to suppress free trade in a manner that is not closely related to legitimate union objectives. For example, there is no antitrust exemption for an agreement between union and employer to the effect that the employer will not buy goods from another company that employs nonunion workers.

Railway Labor Act

Because of its obvious impact on interstate commerce, its importance to the general public, and its history of labor strife, the railroad industry was the object of the first significant piece of federal labor legislation. The Railway Labor Act, passed 1926 and amended several times through the years, is still the basic statute governing labor–management relations in the rail industry. Its coverage was extended to airlines in 1936. Although there are major differences, in many respects this Act is similar to the National Labor Relations Act, discussed later.

Norris-La Guardia Act

In 1932 Congress passed the Norris-La Guardia Act, which clearly recognized the legitimacy of labor unions and effectively removed the power of federal courts to issue injunctions against most union activities. The act did not actually require employers to recognize and bargain with unions, but it did free the unions to use economic weapons to bring about such recognition and bargaining. Because of the Norris-La Guardia Act, federal courts today grant injunctions in labor disputes only under unusual and compelling circumstances, such as when violence is involved.[1]

Another important section of Norris-La Guardia prohibited "yellow dog" contracts, in which the employer obtained the agreement of individual employees that they would not join a labor union. This legal prohibition of yellow dog contracts is still in effect.

THE NATIONAL LABOR RELATIONS ACT AND ITS AMENDMENTS

The first truly comprehensive federal legislation in the area of labor–management relations was the National Labor Relations Act of 1935 (NLRA or Wagner Act). This Act (1) established methods for selecting the labor union that would represent a particular group of employees, (2) required the employer to bargain with that union, (3) prescribed certain fundamental rights of employees, (4) prohibited several specified "unfair labor practices" by employers, and (5) created the National Labor Relations Board (NLRB) to administer and enforce the NLRA.

The Original National Labor Relations Act

After passage of the NLRA, labor unions enjoyed tremendous gains in membership and power. Total union membership in this country increased from approximately three million to 15 million from 1935 to 1947. During the years immediately after World War II, many people began to feel that unions had acquired too much power, and there was some evidence to support this view. A number of critical industries suffered crippling strikes during periods of high consumer demand after the war. The public became less supportive of labor unions because of these strikes and also because of practices such as "secondary boycotts" (discussed later) which many viewed as unfair. The apparent power of particular individuals in organized labor—the so-called labor bosses—also contributed to the increasing public distrust of unions.

The Taft-Hartley Amendments

Factors such as these led Congress in 1947 to enact the Labor–Management Relations Act, usually called the Taft-Hartley Act. The Taft-Hartley Act, which amended the NLRA, attempted to place employer and union power more in balance by (1) prohibiting particular unfair labor practices by *unions;* (2) outlawing the "closed shop," an agreement between union and employer that the employer will require all employees to join the union as a condition of their employment; (3) creating the Federal Mediation and Conciliation Service for the purpose of assisting employers and unions to reach compromises; (4) giving employers and unions (and sometimes individual employees) the power of file lawsuits to enforce collective bargaining agreements; and (5) giving the President authority to intervene in industry-

---

[1] *State* courts also are generally prohibited from enjoining nonviolent union activities under the principle of *federal preemption*. This prohibition is discussed shortly.

HUMOR AND THE LAW

Many judges are frustrated poets, playwrights, and authors. Even a mundane labor relations case led one judge, in an attempt to reconcile two key precedents—*Clements Wire and Mfg. Co. v. NLRB* and *Robbins Tire and Rubber Co. v. NLRB*, to pen the following decision which we quote, in part:

Anderson Greenwood & Co. v. NLRB 604 F.2d 322 (5th Cir. 1979)

Our decision in Robbins Tire,
Interpreting Congresses' reported desires,
Exposed workers to their bosses' ire.
The High Court, avoiding this sticky quagmire,
And fearing employers would threaten to fire,
Sent our holding to the funeral pyre.
Then along came Clements Wire,
Soon after its venerable sire.
To elections, Wire extended Tire,
Leaving app'llees arguments higher and drier.
Now to colors our focus must shift,
To Green wood and stores that are Red.
We hope this attempt at a rhyme, perhaps two,
Has not left this audience feeling too blue.

---

wide labor disputes when, in the President's opinion, the occurrence or continuance of the dispute would "imperil the national health or safety." In the last situation the President may appoint a board of inquiry to study the dispute and make a written report that identifies the positions of employer and union. After receiving this report, the President has authority to ask a federal district court for an injunction prohibiting a lockout by the employer or a strike by the union for a period of 80 days. (This injunction is sometimes called a "back to work order," and the period of time an "80-day cooling-off period.") If no settlement has been reached by the end of 80 days, the lockout or strike can continue unless Congress stops it by emergency legislation.

The Landrum-Griffin Amendments

During the 1950s there was increasing concern about the internal operations of many unions. The primary focus of this concern was evidence of a lack of democratic processes within a number of unions and actual corruption on the part of some union leaders. To protect rank-and-file employees from exploitation by union officials, Congress in 1959 passed the Labor–Management Reporting and Disclosure Act. Generally referred to as the Landrum-Griffin Act, this legislation amended the NLRA by (1) establishing a so-called bill of rights for union members, (2) requiring public financial disclosure by unions and union leaders, and (3) regulating the procedures for election of union officials by members.

When federal labor relations law is discussed in the remainder of this chapter, the general term NLRA refers to the original NLRA plus the Taft-Hartley and Landrum-Griffin amendments, as well as several other minor amendments.

THE LIMITED ROLE OF STATE LAW

Both the federal and state governments exercise regulatory authority over many matters, such as securities trading and anticompetitive business practices. In the case of labor–management relations, however, the Supreme Court has ruled that there is such a great need for a truly uniform national labor policy that **federal preemption** should be the rule. In other words, labor relations law is almost exclusively the province of Congress, the federal courts, and the NLRB. State legislatures, agencies, and courts have almost no jurisdiction over these matters.

There are, however, a few limited exceptions. For example, state courts or agencies may exercise jurisdiction over particular activities or businesses when the NLRA does not apply or when the NLRB has refused to take jurisdiction because of an insubstantial effect on interstate commerce. Also, state courts are permitted to hear a few types of cases arising from labor disputes, such as lawsuits against those who have committed or threatened violence in these disputes.

THE NATIONAL LABOR RELATIONS BOARD

The NLRA is administered and enforced by the NLRB. This agency is divided into two divisions, the Board itself and the General Counsel. The NLRB consists of five members appointed by the President for five-year terms. The General Counsel is appointed by the President for a four-year term. Most of the work of the General Counsel's division is performed by 31 regional field offices located throughout the country, each headed by a Regional Director.

The NLRB and the General Counsel perform distinct but interrelated functions in carrying out the two principal activities required by the NLRA: deciding whether employer or union conduct constitutes an unfair labor practice, and determining whether a particular union is the appropriate representative for a group of employees.

Unfair labor practice cases begin when an employer, employee, or union files a charge with one of the regional offices. The charge will be investigated, and if it has merit the Regional Director will file a formal complaint. A trial-like hearing on the complaint will then be conducted before one of the NLRB's Administrative Law Judges (ALJ); attorneys from the regional office act as prosecutors. The ALJ's decision on what the facts are, what the applicable law is, and what remedy should be ordered are then reviewed by the NLRB itself. If the NLRB determines that an unfair labor practice has been committed, it issues an administrative order. Depending on the nature of the case, this order may require the respondent (that is, the one charged) to (1) "cease and desist" particular illegal activities; (2) engage in genuine, good-faith bargaining with the other party to the labor dispute; (3) rehire illegally discharged employees, and in some cases pay them back wages; or (4) take any other steps deemed necessary to effectively correct the unfair labor practice.

A decision of the NLRB in favor of the respondent usually goes no further. A decision against the respondent, however, is frequently reviewed by a U.S. Court of Appeals. If the court upholds the NLRB's decision, the court will order compliance. Failure to comply with this court order can result in a fine, a jail term for contempt of court, or both. Review of the NLBR's decision by a U.S. Court of Appeals can take place in either of two ways: the respondent may appeal directly to the court, or the NLRB may initiate the review process by asking the court for an enforcement order. In either case, the Court of Appeals' decision will be reviewed by the Supreme Court only in those few instances in which the high court grants a writ of *certiorari*.

The other major regulatory function required by the NLRA—supervising the selection of an employee representative (union)—also begins at the regional office level. In fact, the representation decisions made at this level are usually final. In a few limited situations, however, a decision made by the Regional Director in a representation proceeding can be appealed to the board, with subsequent appeal to a U.S. Court of Appeals.

After studying the scope of the NLRA, the NLRA's regulation of the representative selection process is examined as well, followed by particular types of conduct that may constitute unfair labor practices.

SCOPE OF THE NLRA

GENERAL COVERAGE

In general, the NLRA is the governing law whenever (1) there is a "labor dispute" (2) involving an employer whose business activity either *involves* or *affects* interstate commerce.

The term *labor dispute* is a very broad one, defined in section 2 (9) of the NLRA as "any controversy concerning terms, tenure or conditions of employment, or concerning the association or representation of persons in negotiating, fixing, maintaining, changing, or seeking to arrange terms or conditions of employment...."

The test for interstate commerce is also very broad. By including within the NLRA's coverage any business whose activities even *affect* interstate commerce, Congress has exercised the maximum authority granted to it by the Constitution's commerce clause. However, when administering and enforcing the NLRA, the NLRB does not always use its jurisdiction to the fullest extent. When a particular business has only a minimal effect on interstate commerce, the NLRB has the legal discretion to refuse to take jurisdiction. For a number of years, the NLRB has followed certain objective standards in determining whether to exercise jurisdiction over a labor dispute. For example, the NLRB will assert its authority over a labor dispute involving a retail business only if the total enterprise affects interstate commerce *and* has gross sales business of at least $500,000 annually. (Other dollar amounts are used for nonretail businesses, office buildings, newspapers, public utilities, transportation firms, hotels, and other categories.)

EXEMPTIONS

The NLRA expressly exempts *federal, state, and local government employment*. Federal government employees do, however, have limited organizational and collective bargaining rights under an executive order first issued by President Kennedy in 1962. In some states, the employees of state and local governments have been given certain organizational and collective bargaining rights by state statute.

Railroads and *airlines* are not within the NLRA because their labor relations are governed by the Railway Labor Act. *Agriculture employees* and *domestic servants* also are excluded as they are from many other federal and state employment laws. *Independent contractors* are similarly not included in the NLRA and most other employment legislation.

Supervisory employees—those who spend the bulk of their time directing the work of subordinate employees—are not covered by NLRA. *Managerial employees*—those who formulate policy and make management decisions—also are excluded. These two classes of employees obviously are closely related, and a particular employee may perform both functions. Both exemptions grow out of the idea that an employer is entitled to the undivided loyalty of its own representatives. In any event, one whose primary duties are either supervisory, managerial, or both, is not covered by NLRA. An individual also will be excluded from NLRA's coverage if he or she is a so-called "confidential employee"—one who works closely with a manager on labor relations matters. An example is the secretary to the company's vice president in charge of labor relations.

Although professional employees are covered by the NLRA, the nature of their duties usually requires the exercise of significant professional discretion. Such exercises of discretion, however, do not necessarily make them "managerial employees," as illustrated by the following case.

NORANDA ALUMINUM, INC. v. NATIONAL LABOR RELATIONS BOARD

U.S. COURT OF APPEALS, 8TH CIRCUIT, 751 F.2d 268 (1984)

The United Steelworkers of America (the Union) petitioned the NLRB (the Board) to represent a group of occupational nurses at Noranda Aluminum, Inc. The Board determined that the nurses were not managerial employees and were therefore covered by the National Labor Relations Act (NLRA). In addition, the Board ruled that the nurses constituted an appropriate bargaining unit and ordered Noranda to bargain with the Union as their representative. Noranda asked the court of appeals to review the order, and the Board asked the court to enforce the order. Noranda's primary contention was that the nurses were managerial employees not within the coverage of the NLRA.

HENLEY, SENIOR CIRCUIT JUDGE:

...Managerial employees are not covered by the National Labor Relations Act. The Supreme Court has held that such employees are impliedly excluded from the Act's coverage since their interests are closely identified with those of management. Managerial employees are defined as those who formulate and effectuate management policies by expressing and making operative the decision of their employer. The question whether a certain group of employees is managerial is answered on a case-by-case basis by examining their actual job responsibilities, authority, and relationship to management. An employee is managerial only if he represents management interests by taking or recommending discretionary actions that effectively control or implement employer policy.

We believe that the Board acted permissibly in concluding that the employees are not managerial. The nurses' primary responsibilities are treating employees' injuries and illnesses, administering routine physical examinations to applicants and employees, and maintaining logs and records. They work under the direction of a nursing services supervisor and a part-time physician, who leaves standing orders for the treatment of common ailments. They have no independent authority to purchase medical supplies or equipment, but must instead have requisitions approved by the supervisor. In one instance, Noranda management did solicit their recommendations prior to purchasing an EKG machine and a breathalyzer, but the nurses did not make the final decision to purchase the equipment. There was also one occasion in which one of the nurses suggested intoxication in a work-related employee injury case. The nurse's suggestion was subsequently adopted by the company. However, this alone does not make the nurses managerial employees since they do not have the authority to implement changes without approval....

It does appear that the nurses have some authority to reject an applicant who, in the nurses' judgment, does not meet Noranda's health standards. They also determine whether an employee's injuries and illnesses are work-related and whether an employee is well enough to return to work. An employee who is kept off work by a nurse is entitled to receive medical leave payments. However, if the nurses determine that the employees are unable to perform their jobs, they are usually kept off work only until the company physician can examine them. Such duties notwithstanding, we believe that the Board could properly find that the nurses' discretion is limited to applying their professional medical skills to the job criteria established by the company and that such activities are incidental to their professional responsibilities. An employee is not managerial if her decision making is limited to the routine discharge of professional responsibilities. Only if an employee's activities fall outside the scope of the duties routinely performed by similarly situated professionals will he be found aligned with management.

We also note that the nurses do not participate in setting Noranda's labor relations policy. They attend industrial relations department meetings only when the nursing services supervisor is unavailable and this happens infrequently.

CONTINUED

Noranda asserts that the nurses' self-organization would create an impermissible conflict of interest between their job responsibilities and their loyalty to the Union. It points to the nurses' responsibilities in regard to determining sick leave and in administering the breathalyzer. Noranda states that these decisions have sometimes resulted in the filing of grievances which in some instances have required arbitration proceedings to resolve. Apparently, the nurses are sometimes required to testify at these proceedings. It also points out that the nurses have access to employee personnel and medical records and argues that the nurses might be pressured to disclose this information to the Union.

While there is some potential for a conflict of interest, we do not believe this possibility should suffice to exclude the employees from coverage under the Act. Here the employees with the alleged conflict are carefully supervised. Therefore, if a question should arise about improper action on the part of one of the nurses, Noranda has the means to correct the situation. Furthermore, there is no evidence to suggest that the nurses would actually engage in such misconduct. We can agree with the Board that Noranda's speculation should not be used to deny the nurses their collective bargaining rights. Employees whose decision making is limited to the routine discharge of professional duties in projects to which they have been assigned cannot be excluded from coverage even if union membership arguably may involve some divided loyalty....

In sum, while we might not have reached the same conclusions as the Board did were we deciding the matter de novo [that is, at the outset], we believe the Board's findings are rationally based. In close cases, it is the Board's responsibility to determine whether the line should be drawn between managerial and non-managerial employees. Our role is limited to ascertaining whether its decision is supported by substantial evidence. We accord great respect to the expertise of the Board when its conclusions are rationally based on articulated facts and consistent with the Act. We enforce the Board's order.

SELECTING THE BARGAINING REPRESENTATIVE

The basic thrust of the NLRA is to permit employees to combine, select a representative for the group (a labor union), and bargain with the employer. The employer, in turn, is required to recognize and bargain with the representative. With bargaining power being relatively equal on both sides (or at least not drastically unequal), peaceful relations and essential fairness are more likely to result.

INITIAL ORGANIZING

The organizational effort sometimes begins with several employees who feel they could benefit from collective bargaining. If there appears to be widespread interest, the next step may be to contact an established labor union, whose agents would then proceed with the organizational effort. Or the original group of employees may have contacted the union at an earlier stage, with union agents taking the initial step of determining and generating interest. In some cases, an agent of the union may have actually originated the movement by contacting employees before the employees themselves had taken any steps toward organizing.

A group of employees do not have to become part of an established union—they can form their own labor organization. Because there are already so many labor unions in existence, the formation of a completely new one today is the exception rather than the rule. Most of the existing unions are affiliated with national or international labor organizations, such as the International Longshoremen's Association. In addition, many of the national organizations have formed a loose federation with one another (the AFL-CIO).

In any event, a group of employees may choose a union and the employer may voluntarily recognize it without any formal involvement by the NLRB. For several reasons, however, this usually is not the case. More often than not, a union is chosen by means of a formal election supervised by one of the regional NLRB offices. An employer may want such an election because it doubts that most of its employees wish to join a union. Or the employer may be so opposed to the idea that it would require a formal election in any event. In some cases an employer may desire an election because two or more rival unions demand recognition. In most situations, though, it is the union that requests a supervised election. This may be because the employer has refused to recognize the union, or it may be because the union wants the protection afforded by such an election. If a union is selected by employees as their official bargaining representative in a supervised election, the union becomes *certified* and is protected from challenge by a rival union for at least one year.

THE REPRESENTATION ELECTION

Petition

The first step in the representation election procedure is the filing of a petition with the NLRB's Regional Director. The employer is permitted to petition for an election if a union has demanded recognition by the employer. However, if the demanding union is already the certified representative of employees and the employer wishes to test the union's status by election, the employer must also demonstrate that there is good reason to believe that a majority of employees no longer support the union.

A union, or a group of employees, may petition for an election only if they produce evidence of substantial employee interest in being represented by the particular union. To establish this substantial interest, the union must submit written documentation signed by at least 30 percent of the employees in the group to be represented. This documentation often takes the form of signed "authorization cards," on which each employee expresses a desire to be represented by the union. Signed applications for union membership or similar evidence can also be used. After one union has met the substantial interest requirement, another union may also have its name placed on the election ballot merely by showing that at least one employee in the group supports this rival union.

Before ordering an election, the NLRB will first decide whether the employer and employees are within the NLRB's jurisdiction under NLRA. If jurisdiction is present and the employer and union agree on all issues relating to the election, the NLRB may proceed to hold an election without further inquiry. On the other hand, if there is disagreement over any issue—such as the appropriateness of the bargaining unit, which employees are eligible to vote, or the time and place of the election—the NLRB will conduct a hearing to resolve the disputed issues.

Appropriate Bargaining Unit

An employer is required to bargain with a union only if the union represents the majority of employees in a unit that is "appropriate for the purposes of collective bargaining." Thus, if there is any question at all on this matter, the NLRB will not hold an election until it has been determined that the group of employees involved is an "appropriate bargaining unit."

The NLRA specifically states that professional employees cannot be included in a unit of nonprofessional employees unless a majority of the professional employees approve their inclusion in the unit. The law also prohibits security guards who protect property or safety on the employer's premises from being included in a unit with other employees.

Aside from these restrictions, the NLRB has wide discretion in deciding whether a particular employee group is an appropriate unit. The most important factor in this decision is *mutuality of interest*. In other words, is there substantial similarity of skills, wages, hours, and other working conditions among members of the group so that their interests are basically the same?

Even when mutuality of interest supports a conclusion that a group of employees is an appropriate bargaining unit, the NLRB may permit a portion of the group to be excluded and to form their own separate bargaining unit. Suppose that the employer operates a large chain of retail department stores. If the employees at one store, or at several stores in a particular area, wish to form a bargaining unit separate from the employees at other stores, the NLRB will often permit them to do so. Similarly, the NLRB might permit separate units of sales and nonsales employees if a majority of employees in one of these groups so desire. (From this discussion, it is obvious that an employer may have to deal with more than one union.)

In the *Noranda Aluminum* case that was presented earlier in the chapter, the court also dealt with the appropriate bargaining unit question. After concluding that the occupational nurses were covered by NLRA, the court ruled that the NLRB acted properly in permitting the nurses to form their own bargaining unit. The company argued that the nurses should be included in a larger bargaining unit with all of the firm's professional employees. The court stated that the nurses possessed sufficient common interests to form a unit and that, in any event, the NLRB's responsibility was to identify *an* appropriate bargaining unit, not *the* most appropriate unit.

Circumstances Precluding an Election

Even if the basic requirements for an election are met, there are certain circumstances in whch the NLRB will not permit the election to be held.

Prior Election: If a valid representation election has been held for this bargaining unit during the proceding 12 months, the NLRB will not allow another election. This is true regardless of whether a union was actually chosen and certified in the previous election. For the sake of workplace stability, there obviously must be a limit to how often elections can be held. In addition, if a union was certified in the previous election, this 12-month period provides it with a reasonable opportunity to negotiate a collective bargaining agreement with the employer.

Existing Agreement: If a valid collective bargaining agreement already exists, the employer and union who made the contract usually cannot petition for a representation election during the term of the agreement. However, a collective-bargaining agreement operates as a bar to an election petition by a *rival union* for a maximum of three years. Thus, if the contract between employer and one union is for a term of four years, another union may petition for an election after three years.

Exceptions do exist to the so-called "contract-bar rule." An existing contract does not bar an election if the contract (1) contains no stated duration, *or* (2) is so skeletal in nature that it covers only one or two of the many subjects that are normally included in such agreements.

Pending Unfair Labor Practice Charge: The NLRB usually will not permit an election while an unresolved unfair labor practice charge is pending, if that charge is related in some way to the employee organizing effort. An example would be a charge that the employer had discriminated against particular employees because of their union organizing efforts. In these situations, the NLRB feels that the air should be cleared, so to speak, before an election is held. Of course, an employer cannot use this rule to continually prevent union certification by committing unfair labor practices. If the union clearly demonstrates majority support and the NLRB feels that the employer's conduct will continue to prevent a free election atmosphere, the NLRB will certify the union without an election.

Election Procedures

Within seven days after the NLRB has ordered an election to be held, the employer must submit an accurate list of employees who are eligible to vote. The NLRB makes this list available to any union that will be on the ballot. Under most circumstances, an employee is eligible to vote even if he or she is striking at the time. An employer's noncompliance with the eligibility list requirement can invalidate an employer victory in the election. The election normally is held about 30 days after the NLRB orders it, usually at the employer's premises with agents of the NLRB present to supervise. Voting is by secret ballot in enclosed booths. After the election the NLRB will canvass the results. If one of the choices on the ballot (that is, a particular union or "no union") receives a majority and there were no significant irregularities in the proceedings, the NLRB certifies the results.

THE REQUIREMENT OF LABORATORY CONDITIONS

After the NLRB orders an election, a compaign usually occurs in which the union attempts to persuade employees to select it as their bargaining representative. The employer also has the right to participate in this campaign, but must be very careful in doing so. The reason is that every employee *knows* the employer has the power to terminate his or her employment. Employees may feel this power to be particularly present at this time, before they obtain the protection of unionization. And many of them may not know that it is illegal for the employer to take action against them because of their attempt to unionize. Thus the workplace environment immediately before a representation election is a sensitive one. Words or conduct of the employer at this time can very easily damage the employees' complete freedom of thought, word, and action necessary to a fair, accurate election. The NLRB and federal courts have ruled that so-called "laboratory conditions" must be maintained before a representation election. This phrase essentially means that the preelection atmosphere has to be untainted by fear—employees must be given an opportunity to objectively evaluate the pros and cons of joining a union and exercise a completely free choice.

Consequences of Disturbing Laboratory Conditions

Actions by the employer before a representation election may sometimes amount to an unfair labor practice. For example, the employer commits an unfair labor practice by the discriminating in some way against an employee because of the employee's support of a union. Conversely, an attempt by the employer to support or dominate the union unduly, thus destroying its effectiveness as a true representative of employees, is also an unfair labor practice. Such practices can occur in many different circumstances, including the preelection campaign. Unfair labor practices are studied in more detail later in the chapter.

Laboratory conditions may be disturbed even without the occurrence of unfair labor practices. If laboratory conditions have been upset and the subsequent election results in a "no-union" vote, the NLRB will invalidate the election and order a new one. And, of course, if unfair labor practices have occurred, other remedies also can be ordered.

Examples

There are many examples of situations in which the NLRB has set aside elections because laboratory conditions have been disturbed. In one case, a new election was ordered because the employer had injected racial prejudice into the election campaign. In another, the NLRB invalidated an election because during the campaign the employer had distributed to employees an outdated and misleading government publication about the reemployment rights of striking workers. Several cases have arisen in which *third parties*, such as newspapers or other business firms, have upset laboratory conditions by threatening that employees will be blacklisted by other companies if they join a union, or by making unsubstantiated claims that plant closings will result from unionization. In a situation such as this, the employer can sometimes prevent a disruption of laboratory conditions by promptly publishing or distributing to employees a statement disclaiming any connection with the third-party threats or allegations.

Employer Free Speech Rights

During an election campigan the employer does, however, have the right to present its views to employees about the pending election. Although an employer is not permitted to make threats or other coercive statements, it can lawfully state that it will be firm in dealing with the union if one is selected. Statements by the employer that it will exercise particular legal rights usually are permissible, as well. For instance, in one case a court concluded that an employer had acted properly during a union organizing effort when it told employees that they "may be replaced" if they went on strike. (As we will see later, replacement of striking employees is indeed an employer's legal right in many circumstances.)

When making predictions about possible *economic* consequences of unionization, the employer similarly must be careful to avoid statements that would be viewed as threatening or coercive. Minor misstatements of fact about economic consequences usually will not cause a disruption of laboratory conditions. However, if the misstatement of fact involves a matter of fundamental concern to employees, it might be viewed as threatening or coercive and as grounds for setting aside the election. For example, it would be proper for the employer to predict that unionization will cause the company's labor costs to rise so much that it may have to close the plant *only* if there is some objective evidence to back up the statement. The employer's misrepresentation about something as fundamental as a plant closing would probably be viewed as threatening or coercive and, consequently, as tainting the preelection atmosphere sufficiently to invalidate the election.

Assuming that the content of employer statements is proper, the employer is permitted to present its views to "captive audiences." In other words, the employer may legally assemble employees on company property during working hours for the purpose of presenting antiunion views. The employer is not required to give the union an equal opportunity to speak to such a captive audience. During the 24 hours immediately preceding an election, however, a cooling-off period is in effect, when the employer's right to present antiunion views is more limited. Captive audience speeches cannot be made in this period. The only way the employer can legally speak to a group of employees is for the speech to be made on the employees' own time and for attendance to be voluntary. This cooling-off period does not prohibit the employer or its representative, such as a supervisor, from making very brief statements urging a "no union" vote to individual employees at their work stations. It also does not prohibit the employer's distribution of antiunion literature or presentation of antiunion advertisements over the news media. (These cases assume that the content of the employer's statements is proper.)

As strange as it may seem, the employer's granting of employee benefits may even be improper if the action is taken shortly before an election, the benefits are substantial, and the overall circumstances indicate that employee freedom of choice was hindered by the action. In the following case, such conduct disrupted preelection laboratory conditions and also constituted an unfair labor practice.

NATIONAL LABOR RELATIONS BOARD v. EXCHANGE PARTS CO.

U.S. SUPREME COURT
375 U.S. 405 (1964)

Exchange Parts Co. rebuilds automobile parts at a factory in Fort Worth, Texas. On November 9, 1959, the International Brotherhood of Boilermakers, Iron Shipbuilders, Blacksmiths, Forgers and Helpers told the company that the union was conducting an organizational campaign at the factory and that a majority of the employees supported the union. On November 16 the union petitioned the NLRB (Board) for an election. After conducting hearings, the NLRB on February 19, 1960, ordered that an election be held.

On February 25 the company held a dinner for employees, at which Vice-President McDonald told them that they could decide whether a previously announced extra day of vacation in 1960 would be a "floating holiday" or would be taken on their birthdays. The employees voted for the latter. McDonald also referred to the forthcoming representation election as one in which the employees would "determine whether they wished to hand over their right to speak and act for themselves." He stated that the union had distorted some of the facts and pointed out the benefits obtained by the employees without a union.

On March 4 Exchange Parts sent its employees a letter that spoke of "the Empty Promises of the Union" and "the fact that it is the Company that puts things in your envelope...." After mentioning a number of benefits, the letter said: "The Union can't put any of those things in your envelope— only the Company can do that." Further on, the letter stated: "It didn't take a Union to get any of those things and ... it won't take a Union to get additional improvements in the future." Accompanying the letter was a detailed statement of the benefits granted by the company since 1949 and an estimate of the monetary value of such benefits to the employees. Included in the statement of benefits for 1960 were the birthday holiday, a new system for computing overtime during holiday weeks, which had the effect of increasing wages for those weeks, and a new vacation schedule, which enabled employees to extend their vacations by sandwiching them between two weekends.

The election was held on March 18, and the union lost. Subsequently, the NLRB ruled that the company's actions were done with the specific intent to induce employees to vote against the union, thus disrupting laboratory conditions and also amounting to an unfair labor practice. The NLRB sought enforcement of its ruling in the court of appeals. The court of appeals refused, and the NLRB appealed the decision to the U.S. Supreme Court.

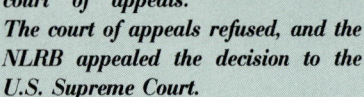

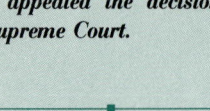

HARLAN, JUSTICE:

... Section 8(a)(1) [of the NLRA] makes it an unfair labor practice for an employer "to interfere with, restrain, or coerce employees in the exercise of [their rights to form and participate in labor organizations]." ... We think that Court of Appeals was mistaken in concluding that the conferral of employee benefits while a representation election is pending, for the purpose of inducing employees to vote against the union, does not "interfere with" the protected right to organize. ...

In *Medo Photo Supply Corp. v. N.L.R.B.*, 321 U.S. 678, 686, this Court said: "The action of employees with respect to the choice of their bargaining agents may be induced by favors bestowed by the employer as well as by his threats or domination." Although in that case there was already a designated bargaining agent and the offer of

CONTINUED

"favors" was in response to a suggestion of the employees that they would leave the union if favors were bestowed, the principles which dictated the result there are fully applicable here. The danger inherent in well-timed increases in benefits is the suggestion of a *fist inside the velvet glove.* [Emphasis added.] Employees are not likely to miss the inference that the source of benefit now conferred is also the source from which future benefits must flow and which may dry up if it is not obliged. . . .

We cannot agree with the Court of Appeals that enforcement of the Board's order will have the "ironic" result of "discouraging benefits for labor." The beneficence of an employer is likely to be ephemeral if prompted by a threat of unionization which is subsequently removed. Insulating the right of collective organization from calculated good will of this sort deprives employees of little that has lasting value.

Reversed. [The Board's order should be enforced.]

The Union's Campaign

Individual prounion employees and professional union representatives will, of course, present arguments in support of unionization during the campaign. Although most of the cases involving the disruption of laboratory conditions have involved employer statements and conduct, union supporters also are prohibited from upsetting these conditions. For example, representation elections won by the union were invalidated in one case in which the union provided free insurance coverage or other benefits to employees who joined the union before the election, and in another case in which union supporters threatened that violence would result from a union loss.

Subject to certain limitations, union supporters are subject to the employer's rules regarding use of company time and property for prounion campaigning. Although the employer cannot completely prohibit such campaigning, the following restrictions may be imposed.

1. An employer may restrict employees from campaigning during their actual working time. They cannot, however, be prohibited from these activities during lunch and break periods and other free times. However, an employee who works one shift can be prohibited from campaigning on company property during another shift when he or she is completely off duty because such an employee is likely to "get in the way" on another shift.

2. Employer rules may reasonably restrict the *places* where campaigning occurs to prevent interference with company operations. For example, distribution of handbills, union authorization cards, and other written materials can be restricted to nonworking areas such as the parking lot or company cafeteria, because the resulting litter might cause a safety problem in working areas. Other forms of campaigning, such as verbal solicitation and message buttons, can be prohibited in working areas only if there is evidence that safety or company operations would be adversely affected by solicitation. For instance, the employer can lawfully prohibit any type of campaigning in areas of a retail establishment that are open to customers. Similarly, campaigning could also be prohibited in areas where dangerous machinery was in operation or other work requiring intense concentration was being done.

3. An employer can absolutely prohibit solicitation on company property by *nonemployees*, except in the rare situation (such as a remote logging camp, a seagoing vessel, or a resort hotel) where there is no other available means for union agents to contact employees.

4. All these situations assume that the employer's rules are nondiscriminatory. A rule that otherwise would be valid is not permitted if it discriminates against prounion solicitation. For example, a rule that prohibits worktime union campaigning by employees, but permits other types of worktime solicitation (for charities, athletic events, and the like), will be invalid.

Decertification

As we have seen, the status of a certified union cannot be challenged during the 12-month period after it was selected as bargaining representative. Its status also cannot be challenged by the employer or employees during the existence of a valid collective bargaining agreement. After expiration of the 12-month period or the collective bargaining agreement, the representative status of the union can be challenged, but there is a strong presumption that the union continues to enjoy majority employee support.

If the employer can overcome this presumption by demonstrating that it has reasonable grounds for a good-faith belief that the union has lost its majority support, the employer may legally withdraw its recognition of the union and refuse to bargain with it. This is very difficult for the employer to accomplish, and such action often results in an unfair labor practice proceeding in which the employer is found guilty of violating the duty to bargain in good faith.

Employees or a rival union may overcome the presumption of continued majority support only by filing a petition with the NLRB for a *decertification election*. The NLRB will call such an election if there is a demonstration (by signed cards or similar means) that at least 30 percent of the employees in the unit wish to have an election to test the union's majority support. If called by the NLRB, the election is conducted in much the same way and according to the same rules as an initial representation election.

THE COLLECTIVE BARGAINING PROCESS

After a group of employees has selected a union as its representative, the process of bargaining with the employer will begin. The objective of this bargaining is to reach an agreement with the employer covering the various aspects of the employment relationship.

THE EXCLUSIVE REPRESENTATIVE CONCEPT

The principle of *majority rule* is a basic element of collective bargaining. When a particular group of employees is an appropriate bargaining unit under the NLRA, and when a majority of the employees in that unit has chosen a particular union as the unit's representative, that union is the *exclusive* representative for *all* employees in the unit. In other words, those employees who did not support the union are bound by the collective bargaining agreement ultimately made between employer and union. This is true even for employees who do not formally join the union. There can be no contract negotiation between the employer and any individual or splinter group within the employee unit.

Similarly, a group of employees who take action on their own, without authorization by a majority of the employee unit, is not protected from employer discipline. Thus, an employer usually can legally fire or otherwise penalize employees who engage in a so-called **wildcat strike**—a work stoppage that has not been formally approved by a majority vote.

The union's status as exclusive bargaining representative carries with it a legal duty of *fair representation*. Because each employee is bound by decisions of the majority, the union must be fair to all. The duty of fair representation obviously would be breached if the union treated employees differently on the basis of race, color, religion, sex, or national origin.[2] It also could be violated in other ways, such as the failure of a union steward[3] to properly process an employee's grievance against the employer because of personal animosity between them or because the employee had not joined the union. An affected employee may sue the union for damages for violating this duty.

SUBJECTS OF COLLECTIVE BARGAINING

The various subjects that may arise in the negotiation of a collective bargaining agreement will be either mandatory, illegal, or permissive.

Mandatory Subjects

In Section 8(d), the NLRA *requires* employer and union to engage in collective bargaining on "wages, hours, and other terms and conditions of employment." Examples of matters that the courts have found to be mandatory subjects include (1) wage rates, (2) group insurance coverage, (3) profit-sharing and stock-purchase plans for employees, (4) retirement plans, (5) availability and prices of food sold on the employer's premises, (6) paid vacations, holidays, sick leave, and break periods, (7) job classifications and types of work to be performed by employees in each classification, (8) seniority rules governing the order of employee layoffs and other matters, (9) rules relating to hours of work, shift rotations, and overtime, (10) safety rules and practices, (11) procedures for resolving employee grievances against the

---

[2] Such conduct usually would also violate Title VII of the 1964 Civil Rights Act.

[3] A union steward is an employee who also serves as the union's agent in a particular department or other section of the company.

employer, and (12) replacement of current employees with those of an independent contractor to do the same work.

The fact that a particular matter is a mandatory collective bargaining subject does not mean that the employer and union are required to include it in their contract. What is means is that if any action is to be taken concerning a mandatory subject, the employer cannot make an independent decision about it, but must negotiate the question with the union. There are, however, some exceptions to this rule. First, if the employer has done something a particular way for a long period of time and the union has not objected or insisted on bargaining about it, the employer can simply continue as before. Bargaining would be required only if a change from prior practice is proposed by employer or union. Second, in the collective bargaining agreement the union may expressly give the employer the right to unilaterally decide particular matters.

Illegal Subjects

Although the types of provisions to be negotiated and possibly included in a collective bargaining agreement are generally left up to the employer and union, there are a few items that are prohibited. Closed shop and hot cargo provisions, both of which are discussed later, are examples of illegal subjects that cannot be included in the collective bargaining agreement or even injected into the bargaining process.

Permissive Subjects

If a topic is neither mandatory nor illegal, it is permissive. A permissive subject is one that can be negotiated and included in the collective bargaining agreement if the parties wish. Neither party, however, has the right to insist that such a topic be a subject of bargaining.

Most permissive subjects involve either (1) matters of company policy that do not directly involve the employment relationship, or (2) internal union matters. In the first category would be decisions relating to corporate organization, plant locations or closing, financing, product design, marketing practices, and so forth. The union cannot demand that collective bargaining include management prerogatives like these. In the second category would be matters such as the amount or method of collection of employee contributions to the union strike fund, or the method of submitting a new collective bargaining agreement to employees for a ratification vote. The employer cannot demand that bargaining include such union prerogatives.

Even though an employer cannot be forced to bargain with the union about management decisions that do not directly involve labor relations, the company can be required to bargain about the *effects* of such decisions on employees. For example, decisions relating to the closing of a plant or sale of substantial assets can be (and usually are) made unilaterally by the employer. But issues concerning possible retraining the transfer of displaced employees, severance pay, and the like are mandatory subjects of collective bargaining. The case that follows illustrates this concept.

First National Maintenance Corp. v. National Labor Relations Board

U.S. Supreme Court
452 U.S. 666 (1981)

First National Maintenance Corp. (FNM) is in the business of providing cleaning, maintenance, and related services for commercial customers in the New York City area. It contracts with each customer and then hires employees to perform services at the customer's place of business. These employees work only at one customer's premises, and are not transferred between different locations. From the customer FNM receives reimbursement of its labor costs plus an agreed management fee.

In April 1976, FNM made such an agreement with Greenpark Care Center, a nursing home in Brooklyn. FNM employed approximately 35 workers at Greenpark. During the spring and early summer of 1977, the business relationship between FNM and Greenpark broke down because of a dispute over the amount of FNM's management fee. FNM had agreed to lower it from the original $500 per month to $250, but then found this to be insufficient and sought to have the $500 fee reinstated. Greenpark refused and on June 30 FNM gave 30 days notice (as permitted in the contract) that it was terminating the agreement.

However, during this same general period, the National Union of Hospital and Health Care Employees was conducting an organizational campaign among FNM's Greenpark employees. A representation election had been held on March 31, 1977, at which the union was selected as bargaining representative. During early July the union's vice-president wrote to FNM seeking to initiate the collective bargaining process. FNM did not respond, and on July 28 FNM notified its Greenpark employees that they would be discharged on July 31. The union tried to get FNM to negotiate with it about the matter but FNM refused.

Subsequently, the NLRB ruled that FNM had committed an unfair labor practice and ordered it to bargain with the union about its decision to terminate the Greenpark operation and the consequences of that decision. The NLRB also required FNM to pay these employees from the date of the discharge until the situation was resolved. If bargaining resulted in resumption of the Greenpark operation, discharged employees were to be given their job back; otherwise, they had to be offered similar jobs at other FNM operations. The court of appeals ordered enforcement of the NLRB's ruling, and FNM appealed to the U.S. Supreme Court.

BLACKMUN, JUSTICE:

... [The Court compared this case with two of its previous decisions. In *Textile Workers v. Darlington Mills*, 380 U.S. 263 (1965), the Court ruled that "an employer has the absolute right to terminate his entire business for any reason he pleases" without bargaining. The other case, *Fibreboard Paper Products Corp. v. NLRB*, 379 U.S. 203 (1964), involved an employer's decision to subcontract for maintenance work previously done by its own employees. The Court in that case noted that the primary motivation for the decision was a desire to reduce labor costs, a matter that is "peculiarly suitable for resolution within the collective bargaining framework." In ruling that Fibreboard's decision was a mandatory bargaining subject, the Court also said:

> The Company's decision to contract out the maintenance work did not alter the Company's basic operation. The maintenance work still had to be performed in the plant. No capital investment was contemplated; the Company merely replaced existing employees with those of an independent contractor to do the same work under similar conditions of employment. Therefore, to require the employer to bargain about the matter would not significantly abridge his freedom to manage the business.

In the present case, the Court observed that FNM's decision was not one to close down its entire business as in *Darlington* but also was different from the decision in *Fibreboard*. FNM's decision was motivated by economic concerns *other* than labor costs.] ...

CONTINUED

In order to illustrate the limits of our holding, we turn again to the specific facts of this case. First, we note that when petitioner decided to terminate its Greenpark contract, it had no intention to replace the discharged employees or to move that operation elsewhere. Petitioner's sole purpose was to reduce its economic loss, and the union made no claim of anti-union animus. In addition, petitioner's dispute with Greenpark was solely over the size of the management fee Greenpark was willing to pay. The union had no control or authority over that fee. The most that the union could have offered would have been advice and concessions that Greenpark, the third party upon whom rested the success or failure of the contract, had no duty even to consider. These facts in particular distinguish this case from the subcontracting issue presented in *Fibreboard*. Finally, while petitioner's business enterprise did not involve the investment of large amounts of capital in single locations, we do not believe that the absence of significant investment or withdrawal of capital is crucial. The decision to halt work at this specific location represented a significant change in petitioner's operations, a change not unlike opening a new line of business, or going out of business entirely. . . .

[Reversed. FNM cannot be required to bargain over its termination decision. It can, however, be required to negotiate with the union about possible alternatives for the employees other than discharge.]

COMMENT

Thus, a decision to terminate or substantially reduce operations at a particular facility usually will not be a mandatory subject of collective bargaining, and the employer legally can make the decision on its own, without consulting or negotiating with the union. In 1988, however, Congress passed a so-called "plant closing" law that places some new restrictions on employers. Generally, the law applies to employers who have at least 100 employees and requires the employer to notify employees at least 60 days before a "plant closing" or "mass layoff." A plant closing occurs if the employer shuts down a facility at a particular location or a unit within that facility and the shut-down causes an "employment loss" for at least 50 employees. An "employment loss" means that these employees either (1) lose their jobs permanently, (2) are laid off for at least six months, or (3) have their working hours cut by at least 50 percent for at least six months. A "mass layoff," which occurs when no facility or unit is shut down, occurs if there is an "employment loss" for either (1) 50 or more employees, if those employees account for at least one-third of the company's work force of employees, or (2) 500 or more employees regardless of the work force percentage they represent. The idea behind the law is that, even though company's have the right to make such decisions, fairness requires that employees know about it far enough in advance to plan and prepare.

THE DUTY TO BARGAIN IN GOOD FAITH

When negotiating a collective bargaining agreement or some modification of it, the employer and union are required to *bargain in good faith* about mandatory subjects. This duty essentially requires each party to take an active part in trying to reach agreement with the other by making honest, reasonable propositions concerning mandatory subjects of bargaining. They are not legally required to make an agreement—that negotiations reach an impasse on mandatory subjects does not necessarily mean that the parties have not bargained in good faith. On the other hand, bargaining to an impasse, or breaking off negotiations because of an inability to reach an agreement on a *nonmandatory* (permissive) subject of collective bargaining is a violation of the duty to bargain in good faith and constitutes an unfair labor practice.

Good or bad faith is a question of subjective intent, but judgments about someone's intent must be based on outward indications—words and conduct. For example, bad faith would be inferred when an employer offers terms that are so unreasonable that no responsible employee representative could ever accept them. Other examples of action that would show a lack of good faith would be a persistent "take-it-or-leave-it" attitude or obvious delaying tactics.

In addition to placing the general duty of good-faith bargaining on the parties, Section 8(d) of the NLRA also spells out certain procedural aspects of the duty when a collective bargaining agreement already exists. Specifically, when either the employer or union wishes to terminate or modify an existing agreement, it must proceed as follows:

1. It must give written notice of this intention to the other party at least (a) 60 days before the expiration date of the contract or (b) 60 days before the time it proposes to terminate or modify, if the contract contains no expiration date.

2. It must offer to meet and confer with the other party for the purpose of negotiating a new contract or a contract containing the proposed modifications.

3. It must notify the Federal Mediation and Conciliation Service and any appropriate state mediation agency within 30 days after the first notice, unless an agreement has been reached by that time.

4. It must continue to comply with the terms of the existing contract, without resorting to a strike or lockout, for a period of at least 60 days after the first notice or until the expiration date of the contract, whichever occurs later.

GRIEVANCE PROCEDURES AND ARBITRATION

The types of terms in a collective bargaining agreement will vary substantially from one situation to another. Most of the terms relate to the kinds of topics mentioned earlier as mandatory bargaining subjects. Of special importance to the effectiveness of the collective bargaining process are those contractual provisions relating to the resolution of disputes.

Grievance Procedures

Two examples will illustrate the significance of dispute resolution procedures.

1. The employer begins assigning certain work to supervisors, and several employees claim that this action violates job classification provisions of the collective bargaining agreement. The primary concern of the employees and the union is the actual or potential loss of jobs for union members.

2. The employer alleges that an employee has violated a specific work-rule (smoking in a no-smoking area or failure to follow a safety rule, for example) or has otherwise acted improperly (such as being insubordinate to a supervisor or absent without excuse). The employer then proposes to discharge the employee or perhaps levy some lesser penalty, such as placing a written reprimand in the employee's personnel file. The employee disputes the alleged facts, claims that he or she was not properly notified of the rule, or perhaps asserts that the proposed penalty is not permitted for the alleged offense under the terms of the collective bargaining agreement. Regarding the last possibility, most collective bargaining agreements provide that the employer can fire an employee only for "good cause." One of the most common factual disputes is whether particular conduct by the employee amounts to good cause for discharge.

A key feature of the average collective bargaining agreement is a set of formal procedures for the handling of "grievances." The typical grievance procedure requires an affected employee to file a formal written grievance (complaint) with the union's local office or with a designated union agent. The union then takes the grievance to the employer. Procedures usually call for initial consultation between lower level representatives of the employer (such as a department supervisor) and the union (such as a union steward). If they cannot reach agreement on how the dispute should be resolved, the question will go to higher level representatives. This process sometimes involves several different levels within both the employer's and union's organizational structures.

Arbitration

When the last step is completed without any resolution of the dispute, grievance procedures generally require the employer and union to use binding *arbitration*. The collective bargaining agreement may have included detailed procedures for selecting an arbitrator and conducting the arbitration proceeding. In many agreements, however, it is simply provided that arbitration will be conducted according to the rules of an established organization such as the American Arbitration Association (AAA), or a government agency such as the Federal Mediation and Conciliation Service (FMCS).[4] In some cases the agreement may adopt the procedures of AAA or FMCS with particular modifications.

The employer and union may agree on an individual from an AAA or FMCS list to serve as arbitrator, or each may pick one and these two will then choose the arbitrator. In some cases the employer and union will each choose a person, these two will pick a third, and all three will form an arbitration panel. Sometimes a company and a union with a large volume of grievances will contract with a person to serve as arbitrator in all their disputes during a stated time period. Whatever the selection method, arbitrators most often are either practicing attorneys or professors of law, economics, industrial relations, or business. There are even a few fulltime professional labor arbitrators.

The arbitrator conducts a hearing that is much less formal than a trial. Testimony and other evidence are presented, but formal rules of evidence are not strictly adhered to. On the basis of this hearing, the arbitrator determines what the facts are and how the collective bargaining agreement should apply to the dispute. A relatively short written opinion usually is prepared, giving the basic facts and the arbitrator's decision. The judgment of an arbitrator is called an award.

When the collective bargaining agreement calls for arbitration, a grievance must be handled in this way if it is "arbitrable." An arbitrable grievance is simply a dispute that is within the scope of the collective bargaining agreement and involves the interpretation or application of that agreement.

The NLRB and the courts usually will refuse to hear a case that properly belongs in arbitration. (This is true even if the conduct on which the grievance is based might also be an unfair labor practice.) However, if one party refuses to submit an arbitrable grievance to arbitration, the other party can file a lawsuit in state or federal court for breach of the collective bargaining agreement. The remedy will be a court order requiring arbitration. If arbitration has been used but one party refuses to comply with the arbitrator's award, the other party can go to court and obtain an order enforcing the award. And finally, where a grievance has been arbitrated and one party is dissatisfied with the arbitrator's decision, that party's right to appeal to a court is extremely limited. There generally can be a successful appeal only if the arbitrator has (1) acted in bad faith by not considering the evidence or by conspiring with one of the parties, (2) decided a question or made an award that was outside the scope of the power given to the arbitrator by the collective bargaining agreement, or (3) made a decision that upholds an illegal provision in the agreement or otherwise violates the law or public policy.

We now will see an illustrative arbitration decision.

---

[4] This federal government agency primarily serves the *mediation* function—attempting to bring the parties to an agreement in collective bargaining. It also has a set of arbitration rules and a roster of private individuals willing to serve as arbitrators, much the same as AAA.

CASE

In re Great Atlantic & Pacific Tea Co. and Amalgamated Food Employees Union

71 Lab. Arb. 805 (1978)

The employee, who was identified only as M, had worked as a stocker and checker for the company's A&P supermarkets in the Pittsburgh area since 1950. After many years without any recorded problems, a series of complaints were made against him by various people. In 1973 he pushed another employee to the floor and threatened to beat him up. The company tried to fire him, but in arbitration the discharge was reduced to a suspension. In 1976 and 1977 a number of complaints were made against M, including threatening a supervisor in the presence of customers, arguing with a sales manager, insults, alteration of time records, and arguing with a customer. In 1977 the company again reduced the penalty to a suspension.

In 1978, M had two altercations with customers. In one instance a customer asked for a sale coupon and M said, "All of you Kennedy Township housewives are the same." The customer responded, "Have a nice day anyhow," and M said, "I will if you don't come back!" Another time, he referred to a customer's children as "brats." During this same period, M had difficulties with another checker. He also told the company's district manager that "he would never come down to the level of the customer," and "I am my own man, and I won't come down to their level or yours!" The company again fired M, he filed a grievance with the union, and the dispute went to arbitration. The collective bargaining agreement permitted discharge only for "good and sufficient cause."

NERNBERG, ARBITRATOR:

...I am not unmindful of the fact that M has served the Company for twenty-eight years, and much of this time has been spent as a satisfactory, productive, and at times, exemplary employee. On the other hand, I cannot overlook the fact that the grievant has been given one chance after another by Management and by two other Arbitrators. I cannot conceive of a place where work could be found for M where he could function without further altercations developing. Unfortunately for M, we must impose "capital punishment," that is as the term is used in labor and industry; he must be terminated. This is obviously a harsh measure and one which should not be taken lightly, but with all the evidence considered, there is no alternative.

UNFAIR LABOR PRACTICES

On several occasions we have referred to the fact that certain types of conduct by the employer or union are illegal under the NLRA as "unfair labor practices." Essentially, the law relating to unfair labor practices represents a further attempt to encourage industrial peace—in this case by prohibiting unreasonable abuses of the power that the parties may sometimes possess.

We have already seen that the disruption of laboratory conditions before a representation election may involve conduct of such a threatening or coercive nature as to also constitute an unfair labor practice. One unfair labor practice, the failure to bargain in good faith, was studied in some detail. Now we take a look at other such practices. Section 8(a) of the NLRA deals with unfair labor practices of the employer, and Section 8(b) with those of the union.

EMPLOYER UNFAIR LABOR PRACTICES

Coercion and Discrimination

As seen in the *Exchange Parts* case, Section 8(a)(1) makes it illegal for an employer "to interfere with, restrain, or coerce employees" in connection with their right to participate (or refuse to participate) in a labor union. Section 8(a)(3) makes it illegal to discriminate against employees for the purpose of encouraging or discouraging union membership. In a few instances, particular conduct violates only one of these provisions, but in most situations conduct that violates one of them also violates the other. Generally speaking, almost any type of employer action can be either legal or illegal under these provisions, depending on whether surrounding circumstances indicate legitimate business reasons or antiunion motivation. Several illustrations follow.

Lockouts: A lockout is a temporary barring of employees from the workplace in anticipation of a strike. This economic countermeasure by the employer is legal if there are special circumstances indicating that the timing of a possible strike might be especially harmful to the employer. For example, in *American Ship Building Co. v. NLRB,* 380 U.S. 300 (1965), collective bargaining for a new contract had reached a stalemate and the employer feared that the union would intentionally delay a strike until the busy season. The employer used a temporary lockout before the busy season began so as to control the timing of the work stoppage. In this way, the employer hoped to exert sufficient economic pressure to bring about further compromise on the union's part. The Supreme Court ruled that no unfair labor practice had been committed. However, if there had not been this clear evidence of special economic justification, or if the union had been on the brink of losing its majority support and the lockout effectively destroyed it, the employer's action probably would have been illegal.

Threatening Behavior: Threatening employer behavior may violate section 8(a) in many different settings. For instance, surveillance of employees through the use of spies or informers is illegal if it relates to any aspect of employees' organizational rights (such as initial organization, election, pending strike, or picketing). Outright threats of discharge or other disciplinary measures against employees because of their union activity are blatantly illegal. More subtle threats may also violate Section 8(a). Interrogation of employees about their union membership or activities will be scrutinized very closely by the NLRB and the courts. Such interrogation can be used legally to obtain information in which the employer has a legitimate interest. For example, the employer can lawfully question employees to determine whether a union has majority support, whether union campaigning has been taking place on company time, or whether employees generally support a threatened strike. The employer must be careful, however, to maintain an atmosphere that is nonthreatening and noncoercive. In this regard, when questioning employees it is wise for the employer to emphasize that there is no intent to penalize anyone.

Employee Discipline: To efficiently run its business the employer must be free to discharge or otherwise discipline its employees for poor performance or improper conduct. This power cannot be used, though, to restrain union activity. There generally is no problem for the employer if the disciplined employee has not shown active support for the union. However, when discipline is exercised against a worker who has been somewhat active in union-related matters, the employer must be prepared to document legitimate reasons for the discipline. If the employer is not able to substantiate these legitimate reasons, the NLRB is likely to infer an antiunion motivation. Even if there is evidence of justification for the discipline (tardiness or poor performance, for example), there may still be an unfair labor practice if other employees not so active in the union have not received similar penalties for similar conduct.

Treatment of Strikers: When employees go on strike, how the employer can treat them depends on the nature of the strike. If the strike itself is an illegal one, such as a wildcat strike, striking employees can be fired with no right to reinstatement. If the strike is legal, strikers cannot be fired. The employer can, however, hire replacements to keep its business going. When the strike ends, or even when a single striker wants to come back to work, does the employer have to grant reinstatement? The answer hinges on the reason for the strike. If employees had gone on strike to protest conduct of the employer that had amounted to an unfair labor practice, the employer must grant full reinstatement even if the replacements have to be fired to make room. Failure to do so constitutes another unfair labor practice.

On the other hand, the employer's reinstatement duties are more limited where the strike was an economic one. An economic strike is one staged for any purpose other than protesting an unfair labor practice, such as supporting the union's demand for recognition or pressuring the employer to accept particular terms during collective bargaining. In this situation, strikers are entitled to reinstatement if replacements had been expressly hired only for the duration of the strike. However, if the replacements were hired as permanent employees, the employer does not have to fire them to reinstate strikers. Here the duty of the employer is simply to notify the striker whenever the same or a similar job becomes open and to give the striker a priority over new applicants. This duty does not exist at all if the striker has already obtained regular, comparable employment elsewhere.

As a practical matter, the union often bargains for and obtains the employer's agreement to reinstate economic strikers, and the employer is bound by such an agreement.

Domination or Assistance

To assure that the union truly represents employees and is not just an arm of the employer, Section 8(a)(2) prohibits the employer from dominating or assisting the union. Several examples illustrate the nature of this provision.

1. The employer cannot provide signiificant financial support, materials, facilities, or services to the union.

2. The employer cannot actively solicit members for a union. Thus, during the organizational stage an employer who favors one union over another can go no further than to generally indicate its preference.

3. The employer cannot assist in drafting the union's constitution or bylaws.

A line necessarily must be drawn between domination or assistance and minor instances of cooperation. It is not illegal, for example, to permit the union to post notices on a company bulletin board, to withhold union dues from employees' paychecks and turn them over to the union (but only with respect to employees who consent), or to permit a union official to come onto company property to speak with employees. Of course, a lengthy series of minor favors might sometimes add up to evidence of domination.

UNION UNFAIR LABOR PRACTICES

Section 8(b) of the NLRA itemizes the types of labor union conduct that are condemned as unfair labor practices. The most important of these are examined below, as are some situations in which particular union conduct may be legal or illegal on other grounds.

Coercion

Much like the employer, the union is prohibited from engaging in restraint or coercion of employees in connection with their decision whether to participate in a union. Because unions have less inherent power over employees than does the employer, union conduct is not nearly so likely to constitute restraint or coercion. There are, however, certain situations in which a union's conduct unduly impinges on employee's rights.

It obviously is illegal for a union to threaten or commit acts of violence in order to pressure employees into cooperating. Moreover, the union cannot threaten or actually engage in economic coercion. For instance, it is an unfair labor practice for a union agent to threaten that those employees who don't join the union will ultimately lose their jobs. Also illegal is the union's waiver of dues or fees for those who join before a representation election.[5]

Picketing the employer's premises generally is legal if it is peaceful and for a lawful purpose. It becomes an illegal activity if it involves actual or threatened violence, or if it is used to coerce employees or the employer to do something else that is unlawful. Mass picketing ("belly-to-back" picketing) in which employees walking the picket line are so numerous and situated

---

[5] In addition to being coercive and thus constituting an unfair labor practice, this action clearly would also disturb preelection laboratory conditions.

so closely as to practically form a wall is illegal. Similarly illegal is the blocking of any entrance by picketers.

Discrimination

It is an unfair labor practice for a union to discriminate or induce the employer to discriminate against employees because of their non-membership or inactivity in the union. However, this prohibition obviously does not prevent a union from requiring *reasonable* membership rules, initiation fees, and dues.

In certain industries, such as construction, the building trades, and maritime shipping, it is customary for the union to operate a hiring hall—a job referral or clearinghouse service for workers. A union may lawfully operate a hiring hall, and even obtain an employer's agreement to get employees there, so long as the union does not discriminate on the basis of union membership.

Most unions attempt to obtain some type of "union security clause" in the collective bargaining agreement. These clauses take various forms. A "closed shop" clause requires individuals to be union members before they can be hired by the employer. Closed shop provisions are unfair labor practices by both the employer and union because they discriminate on the basis of union membership and also constitute undue employer assistance of the union.

Although somewhat similar to a closed shop clause, a "union shop" or "agency shop" clause is generally permitted by the NLRA. This type of provision does not require union membership as a prerequisite to employment, but obligates the employer to require employees to begin paying union dues within 30 days after being hired and to continue paying them thereafter.[6]

Even when a union security clause specifies that employees are required to join the union within 30 days after starting work, the courts have held that employees actually can only be required to pay union dues. They cannot be required to become full union members. By having to pay dues, however, they are prevented from taking a free ride on the benefits won by the union. In *Communications Workers of America v. Beck,* 108 S.Ct. 2641 (1988), the U.S. Supreme Court recently dealt with the question of whether the union can use the money from dues paid by nonmember employees for the same purposes as dues paid by members. The Court concluded that the union cannot use nonmembers' dues for social, charitable, or political purposes, but can use them for activities relating directly to the collective bargaining process such as contract negotiation, administration, and grievance resolution.

In the area of union security arrangements, Congress has specifically delegated power to the states. Section 14(b) of the NLRA expressly permits state legislatures to enact "right-to-work" laws. These laws, which have been

---

[6] In the construction and building trades industry, a union shop or agency shop clause can require employees to join or pay dues within *seven days* after they are hired.

passed in 19 states, prohibit even union shop or agency shop clauses. Thus, the 30-day union shop or agency shop agreement is legal only in those states without right-to-work laws.

Recognitional Picketing

We have seen that picketing can be unlawful if it is violent or coercive. In addition, picketing generally is not viewed by the NLRA as the proper method to induce an employer to initially recognize and bargain with the union.

First, so-called "recognitional" picketing by any union is absolutely prohibited if there has been a valid representation election during the past 12 months. *Second,* even if there has been no election during that time, a union cannot use picketing in an attempt to secure recognition if the employer has already lawfully recognized another union and the incumbent union's status cannot be seriously challenged. *Third,* even if recognitional picketing is otherwise lawful, the union must petition the NLRB for a representation election within 30 days after picketing begins. The union's failure to do so within this 30-day period causes the recognitional picketing to be an unfair labor practice.

Featherbedding

It is an unfair labor practice for a union to engage in **featherbedding**—forcing an employer to pay for work that is not actually performed. This provision does not prohibit paid meal breaks, holidays, vacations, and so forth. It also does not prohibit the union from resisting automation or even bargaining for wasteful job procedures. Only blatant instances of "make work"—creating positions and requiring pay where there is no work to be done—are illegal.

Strikes

A strike is one of the most powerful weapons of organized labor. Subject to certain limitations, it is a legitimate method of exerting economic pressure on the employer.

A strike is legal only if it consists of a complete work stoppage by the participating majority. It is an unfair labor practice for a union to engage in either a work "slowdown" or an "on-again, off-again" work stoppage.

It also is an unfair labor practice to use a strike to achieve an illegal objective, such as pressuring the employer to agree to a closed shop, featherbedding, or other illegal contract term.

Sometimes an employer may be able to obtain a "no-strike" clause in return for some concession by the employer. These promises not to strike are enforceable against the union while the agreement is in effect. A strike in violation of such a clause is not an unfair labor practice, but merely a breach of contract. Thus, the appropriate method of resolution is arbitration or a lawsuit seeking an injunction or damages, rather than a NLRB hearing.

We have previously seen that wildcat strikes are not permissible. Such a strike, unauthorized by the majority, does not cause the union to be liable for an unfair labor practice—the result of its illegality is that the strikers have no protection from discharge.

Even when a strike is majority-authorized, an employee who wishes not to strike is legally free to continue coming to work. Although the union may not prohibit an employee from crossing a picket line or otherwise defying a majority-authorized strike, the union may levy a reasonable fine against the employee if that employee is a member of the union and does not formally resign from membership before defying the strike.

Secondary Boycotts

A general principle in the NLRA is that labor disputes should be "kept in the family." In other words, the union should not purposely draw innocent third parties into the dispute. No kind of economic pressure should be used by a union against a *secondary party*—one with whom the union does not have a labor dispute.

Hot Cargo Agreements:

A common form of secondary boycott is the so-called "hot cargo" agreement. Such an arrangement includes almost any type of union–employer agreement that the employer will not do business with a third party. For example, suppose that the Teamsters' Union represents the truck drivers of Convoy Trucking Co. The union is trying to organize and represent employees at Southern Paper Co., or perhaps merely supports the organizing effort of some other union at Southern. If the Teamsters' Union obtains convoy's agreement not to transport Southern's products, the union and employer both have committed an unfair labor practice. If the union had used a strike, picket, or other pressure in an attempt to obtain the agreement but Convoy had refused to go along, only the union would be guilty.[7]

Other Secondary Boycotts:

A similar type of secondary boycott by a union is one that directly pressures a third party in order to indirectly pressure the employer. In such a case the union ordinarily is the only party guilty of an unfair labor practice. Suppose that the Retail Clerks' Association and the Giant Food Mart grocery chain are at an impasse in their negotiation of a new collective bargaining agreement. It is normal, and usually quite legal, for the union to strike and to picket against Giant. However, if the union pickets the factory of a vegetable canning company or uses other kinds of pressure in an attempt to persuade the canning company's employees not to handle goods to be sold to Giant, the union commits an unfair labor practice.

Requests That Other Not Cross Picket Line:

There are three situations that come rather close to an illegal secondary boycott but that are, in fact, legal. First, when a union is lawfully picketing the employer in a

---

[7] The construction and clothing industries have limited exemptions from the rule against hot cargo agreements. Stated very generally, a union and an employer in either of these industries may lawfully agree that the employer cannot subcontract work to any other employer who has not signed a collective bargaining agreement with the union.

primary labor dispute with that employer, it is permissible for picketing employees to ask others not to cross the picket line. These others might be fellow employees *or even employees of another employer* who have come to make pickups or deliveries, to do repair work, or for other reasons. They have the legal right to choose whether or not to cross the picket line, and if they refuse to cross it there is no secondary boycott or other unfair labor practice.

The Ally Doctrine:
A secondary boycott is legal if the secondary employer is an "ally" of the employer with whom the union has a labor dispute. This occurs, for instance, where the secondary employer has been assisting the primary employer in the labor dispute, such as performing work that normally would be done by striking employees.

Secondary Informational Activities:
The NLRA expressly provides that there is not an illegal secondary boycott when the union merely informs the public that a product which is produced by an employer with whom the union has a labor dispute (i.e., the "primary employer") is being distributed by another employer (i.e., the "secondary employer"). The exception states that it applies only to informational activities "other than picketing" (such as passing out handbills). However, in *NLRB v. Fruit Packers,* 377 U.S. 58 (1964) (the *"Tree Fruits"* case), the Supreme Court concluded that peaceful picketing legally could be used to communicate such a message. The Court interpreted the ban on secondary boycotts as not prohibiting the so-called "product picketing," because of the likelihood that a more restrictive interpretation would violate the constitutional guarantee of free speech.

Picketing or other forms of secondary informational activity legally can be directed at the secondary employer's *customers,* but not at that employer's *employees.* For example, a union engaged in a labor dispute with Acme Milk company can peacefully picket in front of a supermarket with signs asking customers not to buy Acme milk because "it is produced by nonunion labor," "Acme pays substandard wages," and so on. The union also could legally advertise in the media, pass out handbills, or use other publicity in an effort to obtain a consumer boycott. There is not an illegal secondary boycott if supermarket customers respond by refusing to buy Acme milk or even by not going into the store. However, if union requests are directed at the supermarket's employees, or if the union's activities cause a work stoppage or interruption of deliveries at the supermarket, there is an illegal secondary boycott.

The exact language of the statutory exception for publicizing the fact that a particular product is produced by the primary employer applies only to situations in which the secondary employer actually distributes the primary employer's product. Until recently, it was unclear whether such communications directed at the customers of a secondary employer also might be permissible in some other situations. In the *DeBartolo* case that follows, the U.S. Supreme Court concludes that certain kinds of publicity lawfully may be directed at customers of a secondary employer even though that employer does not distribute the primary employer's product. As it had done earlier in the *Tree Fruits* case, the Supreme Court felt that the secondary boycott provision of NLRA should be interpreted more permissively in order to avoid a potential conflict with the constitutional guarantee of free speech. This recent decision may substantially increase the ability of unions to exert secondary pressure without committing an unfair labor practice.

CASE

EDWARD J. DEBARTOLO CORP. v. FLORIDA GULF COAST BLDG. & CONSTR. TRADES COUNCIL

U.S. SUPREME COURT
108 S.Ct. 1392
(1988)

DeBartolo Corp., which owned a shopping mall in Tampa, Florida, made an agreement with H. J. Wilson Co. that Wilson would construct a new department store at the mall. Wilson contracted with H. J. High Construction Co. to build the store. The Trade Council, a construction workers' union, was concerned that High would hire subcontractors who would pay substandard wages.

As a consequence, the union sought to influence Wilson and High by distributing handbills asking mall customers not to shop at any of the 85 stores in the mall "until the Mall's owner publicly promises that all construction at the Mall will be done using contractors who pay their employees fair wages and fringe benefits." The handbill's message was that "the payment of substandard wages not only diminishes the working person's ability to purchase with earned, rather than borrowed, dollars, but it also undercuts the wage standard of the entire community." The handbills made clear that the union was seeking only a customer boycott against the other mall tenants and not a secondary strike by their employees. At all four mall entrances, the union peacefully distributed these handbills for three weeks without any picketing or patrolling.

After DeBartolo failed to convince the union to alter the language of the handbills to state that its dispute did not involve DeBartolo or any mall tenants other than Wilson and to limit handbill distribution to the immediate vicinity of Wilson's construction site, DeBartolo filed a complaint with the NLRB alleging that the union's activity was an illegal secondary boycott. The NLRB agreed with DeBartolo that an unlawful secondary boycott had occurred, and the union appealed. The U.S. Court of Appeals concluded that the secondary boycott provision should be interpreted to not prohibit this kind of activity in order to avoid a conflict with the Constitution's free speech clause, and denied enforcement of the NLRB's order. The U.S. Supreme Court then granted DeBartolo's petition for writ of certiorari.

WHITE, JUSTICE

... The Board held that the union's handbilling was prohibited by §8(b)(4)(ii)(B), which provides:

> It shall be an unfair labor practice for a labor organization or its agents . . . to threaten, coerce, or restrain any person . . . for the purpose of forcing or requiring any person to cease using, selling, handling, transporting, or otherwise dealing in the products of any other person. . . .

. . . The Board reasoned that "appealing to the public not to patronize secondary employers is an attempt to inflict economic harm on the secondary employers by causing them to lose business," and "such appeals constitute economic retaliation and are therefore a form of coercion." The Court of Appeals . . . denied enforcement of the Board's order.

CONTINUED

Because there would be serious doubts about whether §8(b)(4) could constitutionally ban peaceful handbilling not involving nonspeech elements, such as patrolling, the court stated that the statute should be interpreted to prohibit such activity only if the congressional intent to do so was extremely clear. The language of the section, the court held, revealed no such intent, and the legislative history indicated that Congress, by using the phrase "threaten, coerce, or restrain," was concerned with secondary picketing and strikes rather than appeals to consumers not involving picketing. The court also concluded that the publicity proviso which exempts from the secondary boycott prohibition communications directed to the customers of a secondary employer who distributes the primary employer's product did not manifest congressional intent to ban all speech not coming within its terms because it was "drafted as an interpretive, explanatory section" and not as an exception to an otherwise-all-encompassing prohibition on publicity....

The statutory interpretation by the Board would normally be entitled to deference unless that construction were clearly contrary to the intent of Congress. Another rule of statutory construction, however, is pertinent here: where an otherwise acceptable construction of a statute would raise serious constitutional problems, the Court will construe the statute to avoid such problems unless such construction is plainly contrary to the intent of Congress....

We agree with the Court of Appeals.... The handbills involved here truthfully revealed the existence of a labor dispute and urged potential customers of the mall to follow a wholly legal course of action, namely, not to patronize the retailers doing business in the mall. The handbilling was peaceful. No picketing or patrolling was involved. On its face, this was expressive activity arguing that substandard wages should be opposed by abstaining from shopping in a mall where such wages were paid. Had the union simply been leafletting the public generally, including those entering every shopping mall in town, pursuant to an annual educational effort against substandard pay, there is little doubt that legislative proscription of such leaflets would pose a substantial issue of validity under the First Amendment. The same may well be true in this case, although here the handbills called attention to a specific situation in the mall allegedly involving the payment of unacceptably low wages by a construction contractor....

Contrary to the Board's decision, our decision in *Tree Fruits* makes untenable the notion that *all* kinds of handbilling, picketing, or other appeals to a secondary employer to cease doing business with the employer involved in the labor dispute is "coercion" within the meaning of the statute if it has some impact on the neutral. In that case, the union picketed a secondary employer, a retailer, asking the public not to buy a product produced by the primary employer. We held that the impact of this picketing was not coercion within the meaning of the statute even though, if the appeal succeeded, the retailer would lose revenue.

NLRB v. Retail Store Employees, 447 U.S. 607 (1980) ("*Safeco*"), in turn, held that consumer picketing urging a general boycott of a secondary employer aimed at causing him to sever relations with the union's real antagonist was coercive and forbidden by the statute. It is urged that *Safeco* rules this case because the union sought a general boycott of all tenants in the mall. But "picketing is qualitatively different from other modes of communication" and *Safeco* noted that the picketing there actually threatened the neutral with ruin or substantial loss. As Justice Stevens pointed out ... in *Safeco*, picketing is "a mixture of conduct and communication" and the conduct element "often provides the most persuasive deterrent to third persons about to enter a business establishment." Handbills containing the same message, he observed, are "much less effective than labor picketing" because they "depend entirely on the persuasive force of the idea." ...

In *Tree Fruits*, we could not discern with the "requisite clarity" that Congress intended to proscribe all peaceful consumer picketing at secondary sites. There is even less reason to find in the language of §8(b)(4)(ii), standing alone, any clear indication that handbilling, without picketing, "coerces" secondary employers. The loss of customers because they read a handbill urging them not to patronize a business, and not because they are intimidated by a line of picketers, is the result of mere persuasion, and the neutral who reacts is doing no more than what its customers honestly want it to do....

The Board's reading of §8(b)(4) would make an unfair labor practice out of any kind of publicity or communication to the public urging a consumer boycott of employers other than those the proviso

CONTINUED

specifically exempts. On the facts of this case, newspaper, radio, and television appeals not to patronize the mall would be prohibited; and it would be an unfair labor practice for unions in their own meetings to urge their members not to shop in the mall. Nor could a union's handbills simply urge not shopping at a department store because it is using a nonunion contractor, although the union could safely ask the store's customers not to buy there because it is selling mattresses not carrying the union label. It is difficult, to say the least, to fathom why Congress would consider appeals urging a boycott of a distributor of a non-union product to be more deserving of protection than non-picketing persuasion of customers of other neutral employers such as that involved in this case.

Neither do we find any clear indication in the relevant legislative history that Congress intended the statute to proscribe peaceful handbilling, unaccompanied by picketing, urging a consumer boycott of a neutral employer.... In our view, interpreting §8(b)(4) as not reaching the handbilling involved in this case is not foreclosed either by the language of the section or its legislative history. That construction makes unnecessary passing on the serious constitutional questions that would be raised by the Board's understanding of the statute. Accordingly, the judgment of the Court of Appeals is affirmed.

Questions and Problems

1. A group of buyers for Bell Aerospace Co. sought to form a bargaining unit under the NLRA. These buyers had authority to select suppliers, negotiate purchase prices, and commit the company's credit, but did not deal with management policy regarding any aspect of labor relations. The NLRB granted a union's petition for a representation election among these employees, an election was held, and the union won. The company refused to recognize the union, an unfair labor practice charge was filed, and the case ultimately went to the Supreme Court. Discuss how the Court would rule on the question whether these employees could form a bargaining unit under the NLRA. (*NLRB v. Bell Aerospace Co.*, 416 U.S. 167, 1974.)

2. You are the assistant plant manager for Essex Co. The plant manager gave you instructions to prepare a rule regarding employee solicitation on company property. His concern was that some employees were "talking and passing stuff around when they should be working." After thinking about it, you have decided to post signs that say either "No solicitation during working time" or "No solicitation during working hours." You are not sure whether the wording makes any difference. Discuss which of these two choices is more likely to be legal.

3. Serv-Air, Inc. had a "no-solicitation" rule for employees, which was properly restricted as to time and place. However, the company occasionally permitted solicitation on the premises for contributions to buy flowers for widows of deceased employees. During a union organizing campaign, the no-solicitation rule was applied and the union contended that the occasional exception granted by the company for flowers caused the rule to be invalid. The union thus claimed that the rule could not be applied to campaigning before a representation election. Is the union correct? Discuss. (*Serv-Air, Inc. v. NLRB*, 395 F.2d 557, 10th Cir. 1968.)

4. Contract negotiations between the union and Mackay Co. were not going well, and the union staged a strike in support of its demands. Mackay hired regular, full-time replacements for the strikers. When the strikers realized that their strike would not succeed, they offered to return to work. Five of the replacements wanted to continue working, so Mackay reinstated all but five of the strikers. The five who were not replaced had been among the most active in supporting the union and its strike. Did Mackay commit an unfair labor practice in its treatment of the strikers? Discuss. (*NLRB v. Mackay Radio & Telegraph Co.*, 304 U.S. 333, 1938.)

5. Truitt Manufacturing Co. and the union were negotiating for a new collective bargaining agreement. The union demanded a wage increase of ten cents an hour, but the employer offered only two and one-half cents.

Truitt stated that its average wage was already more than its competitors, and that an increase of more than two and one-half cents would break the company. The union asked to see the company's financial records to substantiate its claims. The company declined on the grounds that its financial records were confidential and not something to be bargained about. The union charged that Truitt had committed an unfair labor practice by not bargaining in good faith. Is the union correct? Discuss. (*Truitt Manufacturing Co. v. NLRB*, 351, U.S. 149, 1956.)

6. Oil Transport Co. (OTC) is a carrier engaged in transporting goods by truck. The Texas Railroad Commission had regulatory powers over the rates OTC could charge shippers within Texas. In 1979, the Commission decided that because of an increase in truck fuel costs, OTC and other carriers subject to its jurisdiction should be allowed to pass on these increased costs to shippers in the form of a "fuel adjustment charge." The commission's order provided that the amount of increased revenues thereby authorized was "to accrue and be paid only to the purchaser of fuel, with no portion thereof to be expended for any other costs incurred by carriers." OTC's collective bargaining agreement with the Union of Transportation Employees provided that drivers' pay would be based on a percentage of revenue from freight rates, and expressly stated that "fuel surcharges will be used in computation of pay." OTC refused to include the fuel adjustment charge in computing drivers' pay, claiming that the Commission's order prohibited OTC from doing so. One of OTC's drivers filed a grievance, which ultimately was submitted to arbitration. After an arbitration proceeding, the arbitrator directed OTC to include the amount of the fuel adjustment charge authorized by the Commission. OTC refused to comply with the arbitrator's award, and the union filed suit in federal court to enforce the award. One of the legal grounds for denying enforcement of an arbitrator's award is that enforcement by a court would violate public policy, and OTC defended by contending that the award in question conflicted with established public policy as declared by the Commission. Discuss whether the court should have enforced the award. (*Union of Transportation Employees, v. Oil Transport Co.*, 591 F.Supp. 439, N.D. Tex. 1984.)

7. Jefferson Standard Broadcasting Company was involved in negotiating a new contract with the union. The major issue in the dispute was whether to include an arbitration clause in the new contract as in the old one. While negotiations were going on, several employees who were still on the payroll (there was no strike) distributed handbills to the public during their off-duty hours. These handbills severely criticized the quality of programming on the employer's television station, but said nothing about a union, collective bargaining, or the disputed arbitration provision. The employer fired these employees, and the union charged that this action was an unfair labor practice. Is the union correct? Discuss. (*NLRB v. International Brotherhood of Electrical Workers, Local 1229*, 346 U.S. 464, 1953.)

8. You are assistant personnel director for Remco Metals Co. Remco and the union have reached an impasse in their bargaining for a new collective bargaining agreement, and the employees have gone on strike. During negotiations the union demanded an increase of 75 cents an hour, from $7.10 to $7.85. Remco would not agree to go higher than $7.25. After the strike began, you and your boss, the personnel director, discussed how to go about hiring replacements. The personnel director suggested that it might be wise to hire replacements at about $7.75 an hour to ensure that the company could attract good workers under these tension-filled circumstances. These replacements would also have all the benefits that striking employees had previously had. The personnel director supposed that "some of the strikers might even come back as replacements." This idea disturbs you, and you are trying to decide how to respond. What advice should you give your boss? Discuss.

9. A maritime shipping company was engaged in a labor dispute with the union. At this time, one of the company's ships was being serviced at a drydock owned by another firm. The union tried to picket the employer's ship, but the drydock company denied the union access to the individual berth where the particular ship was located. The union then picketed the main entrance to the drydock repair facility. The owner of this facility claimed that the union was engaging in an illegal secondary boycott of the drydock. Is the drydock owner correct? Discuss. (*Sailors' Union of the Pacific [Moore Dry Dock Co.]*, 92 N.L.R.B. 547, 1950.)

10. A building stone supplier and the union were involved in a labor dispute, and a strike was called. The company ordinarily delivered stone to construction companies on its own trucks. During the strike, however, these construction companies (the supplier's customers) made arrangements with independent trucking companies to make deliveries and deducted the delivery cost from the purchase price of the stone. Striking employees of the stone supplier picketed both the customers and the trucking companies. An unfair labor practice charge was filed agaisnt the union for allegedly engaging in a secondary boycott of these other firms. What should the ruling be in this case? Discuss. (*Laborers Local 859 v. NLRB*. 446 F.2d 1319, D.C. Cir. 1971.)

CHAPTER 19

Concern for the environment is growing both domestically and internationally. As Americans have gradually become more aware of the adverse impact that human consumption of resources and human technology can have on the land, sea, and air, their support for more comprehensive governmental regulation of environmental matters has grown. Well-known incidents such as the accident at the Three Mile Island nuclear facility, the contamination by dioxins of Times Beach, Missouri, the indiscriminate dumping of hazardous wastes in Love Canal, New York, and

ENVIRONMENTAL PROTECTION LAW

the Alaskan oil spill caused by the Exxon *Valdez* have intensified public concern. Problems such as acid rain, depletion of the ozone layer, and the "greenhouse effect" are creating similar concerns on an international scale.

In recent years these concerns have led to a strengthening of state and local regulation of pollution, to the creation of a mammoth array of federal pollution regulations, and to some initial efforts at international cooperation in pollution control. For businesses, these rules and regulations are decidedly a mixed blessing. On the one hand, the owners, officers, and employees of businesses are individuals who need a clean, safe environment as much as anyone else. On the other hand, many of these laws impose additional burdens on what many consider to be an already overregulated economy.

The thousands of rules and regulations issued by the Environmental Protection Agency (EPA), for example, have become a part of the legal environment of business with which industry must become familiar. Many small firms have gone out of business because they could not meet various antipollution requirements imposed by the EPA. Others, both large and small, have found that compliance has become an extremely costly budget item. As we shall see in this chapter, two obvious manifestations of the heightened level of environmental regulation lie in (a) the increasing use of *criminal* sanctions against environmental offenders (134 criminal indictments for violations of federal environmental laws were brought in fiscal 1990 alone) and (b) regulations that require persons who did not actually pollute to pay for the cleanup of pollution caused by others (for example, landowners may be liable for millions of dollars to clean up pollution caused entirely by previous owners of the land).

Nothing could be more important than the saving of our planet's environment. However, the many governmental regulations outlined in this chapter places a tremendous burden on industry, much of which is passed on to the consuming public. During the coming years there will be continuing debate as to the proper balancing of environmental versus economic interests both domestically and internationally. However, there is no doubt that environmental regulation will continue to be a consideration of enormous importance in most domestic and multinational businesses. Modern managers must view the environment and its legal regulation as a challenge, as an opportunity, and as a factor that must be continuously considered as decisions are made. New rules and regulations will create costs that must be managed. They will terminate some lines of business but open up others.

In this chapter we examine several of the known causes of pollution and the major remedial measures designed to prevent further deterioration of the environment. We also briefly address the matter of *indoor* air pollution. And we will explore the fledgling international efforts to preserve the global environment by multinational cooperation. Initially, however, we will look at common-law remedies that have long been available at the state level to remedy certain types of pollution.

COMMON LAW AND POLLUTION

Common-law remedies founded on the law of torts are totally inadequate to provide a comprehensive method of regulating air, land, and water pollution in the United States. However, as a remedial or loss-shifting device, common-law torts may be useful to individual plaintiffs who may have suffered some environmental harm. A farmer's water supply may be contaminated by industrial discharge of pollutants into a stream. Homeowners near a sanitary landfill may be exposed to noxious fumes from the constant trash fires used by the landfill to dispose of burnable refuse. Or homeowners may suffer property damage when caustic fumes from a chemical plant blanket their property, killing vegetation and causing housepaint to peel and crack. In each case the individual plaintiff may seek injunctions to prohibit further damage from the pollutants and, in appropriate cases, recover money damages. The common-law tort remedies available include nuisance, negligence, trespass, and strict liability.

NUISANCE

When property is used in such a manner that it inflicts harm on others, there may be a cause of action in tort for **nuisance** against the owner. If the harm is widespread, affecting the common rights of a substantial segment of a community, it is considered a *public* nuisance. Because fishing rights belong to the public, a discharge of pollutants into a navigable stream that killed fish would be a public nuisance. If an individual's right to quiet enjoyment of his or her land is disturbed by unreasonable and unwarranted use of property by another property owner, a *private* nuisance has occurred. Most public nuisances are abated through action by public officials charged with controlling the facility that is causing the harm. An action to abate a private nuisance is usually brought by the party affected against the party whose conduct gives rise to the nuisance.

In the case of either public or private nuisances, courts are often called on to balance the interests of plaintiffs and defendants. No court would eagerly close an offending industrial plant that employs an entire community. Similarly, residents near a large airport may be expected to endure some inconvenience caused by noise and vibration. A homeowner who buys near an existing airport or industrial facility may not find the courts sympathetic when a complaint is registered, but this is not invariably the case. To properly balance the interests of the community, courts often cannot simply rule in favor of the party who arrived first.

For example, in *Spur Industries, Inc. v. Del E. Webb Development Co.*,[1] a major developer bought 20,000 acres of farm land near Phoenix to develop Sun City, a retirement village. Nearby were cattle feedlots, later purchased

---

[1] 494 P.2d 700 (Ariz. 1972).

and expanded by Spur Industries. As the developer completed houses and Spur expanded, only 500 feet separated the two operations. Prevailing winds blew flies and odors from the cattle pens over the homesites, thus making it difficult to sell the sites most affected. The developer filed a nuisance suit against Spur, asking that Spur be enjoined from operating its cattle feedlots in the vicinity of the housing development. In an attempt to reasonably balance the parties' competing interests, the court permanently enjoined Spur from operating the feedlots but further held that Spur should be awarded damages, a reasonable amount of the cost of moving or shutting down, because the developer had brought people to the nuisance, thus causing Spur damage.

NEGLIGENCE, TRESPASS, AND STRICT LIABILITY

The tort of **negligence** involves the breach by the defendant of a duty owed to the plaintiff to use reasonable care to avoid injury to the plaintiff's person or property. If the operator of a plant negligently maintained its equipment so that harmful pollutants were discharged into a waterway, neighbors injured by the pollution would probably have a valid negligence claim against the careless plant operator.[2]

An intentional entering onto another's land without permission is a **trespass.** So too, causing particles to be borne onto another's land may be a trespass if the owner of the source of the particles has reason to believe that the activity would cause damaging deposits. For example, a physical and obvious trespass occurs when cement dust from a plant is deposited, layer on layer, on the property of nearby residents. Of course, if the particles deposited are undetectable by human senses and not harmful to health, although undeniably real, a court, in balancing the interests of society, will likely dismiss any trespass action.[3]

In certain cases in which the threat or damage is caused by abnormally or inherently dangerous activities, the theory of **strict liability** may be used to recover damages or to halt the activity. The spraying of crops with toxic chemicals and the storage of explosive or other hazardous materials are examples of activities that may result in a defendant being held strictly liable. In such cases, a defendant's reasonable care is no defense. The inherent danger of the activity and resulting damages are sufficient to justify plaintiff's recovery.

Although much attention is focused on the federal regulations that we are about to discuss, the role of these state common-law causes of action must not be overlooked. Even in situations addressed by federal laws, they provide a tremendously important supplement. For example, litigation over the costs of cleaning up hazardous waste sites is usually based on the federal "Superfund" statute to be discussed later. However, the New Jersey Supreme

---

[2] The concept of negligence was fully discussed in Chapter 10.

[3] See *Bradley v. American Smelting and Refining Co.,* 709 P.2d 782 (Wash. 1985), in Chapter 10.

Court, for example, has ruled that a company that pollutes a property can be held strictly liable for cleanup and other costs, giving an important remedy to the purchasers of such sites.[4]

These common law theories are of ancient origin but have been adapted to the environmental context in "toxic tort" litigation in recent years. In addressing the "enhanced risk" doctrine and the "medical monitoring" doctrine, the following case illustrates the modern evolution of the doctrine of negligence made necessary by the peculiar problems caused by exposure to environmental hazards.

IN RE PAOLI RAILROAD YARD PCB LITIGATION

U.S. COURT OF APPEALS, THIRD CIRCUIT 916 F.2d 829 (1990)

The plaintiffs are 38 persons who have either worked in or lived adjacent to the Paoli railyard, an electric railcar maintenance facility in Philadelphia. Their primary claim is that they have contracted a variety of illnesses as the result of exposure to polychlorinated biphenyls (PCBs). PCBs are toxic substances that, as the result of decades of PCB use in the Paoli railcar transformers, can be found in extremely high concentration at the railyard and in the surrounding air and soil. Defendants include Monsanto (maker of PCBs), General Electric (maker of transformers), Amtrak (owner of the site since 1976), and Conrail (operator of the site).

The district court excluded much of the plaintiffs' proffered testimony and thereafter granted summary judgment to the defendants. The trial court also rejected as a matter of law the plaintiffs' claim based on the "medical monitoring doctrine." The plaintiffs appealed.

BECKER, CIRCUIT JUDGE:

[The court held that the trial judge had improperly excluded plaintiffs' expert testimony and therefore concluded that summary judgment had been inappropriately granted. In the following excerpt, the court addressed the plaintiffs' "medical monitoring" theory.]

We turn ... to the viability of certain plaintiffs' "medical monitoring" claims, by which plaintiffs sought to recover the costs of periodic medical examinations that they contend are medically necessary to protect against the exacerbation of latent diseases brought about by exposure to PCBs. [Pennsylvania state courts have not] decided whether a demonstrated need for medical monitoring creates a valid cause of action.

Therefore, sitting in diversity, we must predict whether the Pennsylvania Supreme Court would recognize a claim for medical monitoring under the substantive law of Pennsylvania and, if so, what its elements are.

Medical monitoring is one of a growing number of non-traditional torts that have developed in the common law to compensate plaintiffs who have been exposed to various toxic substances. Often, the diseases or injuries caused by this exposure are latent. This latency leads to problems when the claims are analyzed under traditional common law tort doctrine because, traditionally, injury needed to be manifest before it could be compensable.

Nonetheless, in an effort to accommodate a society with an increasing aware-

CONTINUED

---

[4] *T&E Indus. v. Safety Light Corp.*, 587 A.2d 1249 (N.J. 1991).

ness of the danger and potential injury caused by the widespread use of toxic substances, courts have begun to recognize claims like medical monitoring, which can allow plaintiffs some relief even absent present manifestations of physical injury. More specifically, in the toxic tort context, courts have allowed plaintiffs to recover for emotional distress suffered because of the fear of contracting a toxic exposure disease, the increased risk of future harm, and the reasonable costs of medical monitoring or surveillance. . . .

It is easy to confuse the distinctions between these various non-traditional torts. However, the torts just mentioned involve fundamentally different kinds of injury and compensation. Thus, an action for medical monitoring seeks to recover only the quantifiable costs of periodic medical examinations necessary to detect the onset of physical harm, whereas an enhanced risk claim seeks compensation for the anticipated harm itself, proportionately reduced to reflect the chance that it will not occur. We think that this distinction is particularly important because . . . in *Martin v. Johns-Manville Corp.*, 494 A.2d 1088 (Pa. 1985), the [Pennsylvania Supreme Court] made clear that a plaintiff in an enhanced risk suit must prove that future consequences of an injury are reasonably probable, not just possible.

Martin does not lead us to believe that Pennsylvania would not recognize a claim for medical monitoring, however. First, the injury that the court was worried about finding with reasonable probability in *Martin* is different from the injury involved here. The injury in an enhanced risk claim is the anticipated harm itself. The injury in a medical monitoring claim is the cost of the medical care that will, one hopes, detect that injury. The former is inherently speculative because courts are forced to anticipate the probability of future injury. The latter is much less speculative because the issue for the jury is the less conjectural question of whether the plaintiff needs medical surveillance. Second, the Pennsylvania Supreme Court's concerns about the degree of certainty required can easily be accommodated by requiring that a jury be able reasonably to determine that medical monitoring is probably, not just possibly, necessary.

[We predict] that the Supreme Court of Pennsylvania would recognize a cause of action for medical monitoring established by proving that:

1. Plaintiff was significantly exposed to a proven hazardous substance through the negligent actions of the defendant.
2. As a proximate result of exposure, plaintiff suffers a significantly increased risk of contracting a serious latent disease.
3. That increased risk makes periodic diagnostic medical examinations reasonably necessary.
4. Monitoring and testing procedures exist which make the early detection and treatment of the disease possible and beneficial.

. . . The policy reasons for recognizing this tort are obvious. Medical monitoring claims acknowledge that, in a toxic age, significant harm can be done to an individual by a tortfeasor, notwithstanding latent manifestation of that harm. Moreover, as we have explained, recognizing this tort does not require courts to speculate about the probability of future injury. It merely requires courts to ascertain the probability that the far less costly remedy of medical supervision is appropriate. Allowing plaintiffs to recover the cost of this care deters irresponsible discharge of toxic chemicals by defendants and encourages plaintiffs to detect and treat their injuries as soon as possible. These are conventional goals of the tort system as it has long existed in Pennsylvania. [Reversed.]

REGULATION BY STATE LEGISLATURES

In addition to the common law role played by the courts, all state governments (and many subordinate governmental units) have passed laws dealing with the quality of the environment. These laws deal with all types of pollution—water, air, solid waste, noise, and others. Often states laws are patterned after federal laws. For example, several states have "mini-Superfunds" for hazardous waste site clean-up patterned after the federal Superfund law discussed later in this chapter. One popular type of state statute is the "bottle bill" designed to regulate the dumping of cans and

HUMOR AND THE LAW

Our category is "Stupid Lawyer Questions." The following questions, mostly collected by Judge Jerry Buchmeyer who writes a regular column in the *Texas Bar Journal* were all actually asked by lawyers in depositions and/or trials:

Q. Do you know how far pregnant you are right now?
A. I will be three months Nov. 8th.
Q. Apparently, then, the date of conception was Aug. 8th?
A. Yes.
Q. What were you and your husband doing at that time?

Q. And approximately when was that statement made?
A. About two weeks before she went to the hospital.

Q. Before her final death?
A. Yes

Q. And, Doctor, as a result of your examination of the plaintiff in this case, was the young lady pregnant?
A. The young lady was pregnant, but not as a result of my examination.

Q. Now, tell me, doctor, isn't it true that when a person dies in his sleep, in most cases he just passes quietly away and doesn't know anything about it until the next morning?

Q. What happened then?
A. He told me, he says 'I have to kill you because you can identify me.'
Q. Did he kill you?

---

bottles. Additionally, many federal laws that are discussed presently provide a substantial state role in the establishing and enforcing of pollution standards.

NATIONAL ENVIRONMENTAL POLICY ACT

Although all states and many localities have significant environmental rules and regulations, federal regulations clearly dominate the regulatory landscape. Recognizing that a national environmental policy was needed, Congress enacted the **National Environmental Policy Act** (NEPA) in 1969 to "encourage productive and enjoyable harmony between man and his environment and biosphere and stimulate the health and welfare of man; to enrich the understanding of the ecological systems and natural resources important to the Nation; and to establish a Council on Environmental Quality." NEPA is a major step toward making each generation responsible to succeeding ones for the quality of the environment.

ENVIRONMENTAL IMPACT STATEMENTS

NEPA requires that an **environmental impact statement** (EIS) be prepared by the appropriate agency whenever proposed major federal action will *significantly* affect the quality of the human environment. This requirement affects private enterprise as well because an EIS will be required if federal funds have been committed to a particular private venture. For example, a contractor building a federal highway or a naval base may have to help provide a detailed statement describing the environmental impact of the proposed action, unavoidable adverse effects, acceptable alternatives to the proposed project, and any irreversible and irretrievable commitments of resources involved.

Preparation of an EIS can be a costly and time-consuming task, even though regulations now limit the length to 150 pages (except in unusual circumstances.) NEPA requires that the statement be clear, to the point, and in simple English. It also requires that all key points and conclusions be set forth in a summary of no more than 15 pages. No matter how well prepared, an EIS is merely a prediction as to future environmental consequences of a proposed federal action. The proposed agency action, evaluated in light of the EIS, can be successfully challenged in court only if it can be shown to be "arbitrary and capricious."

Litigation over EISs often substantially delays and increases the costs of federal projects. Although very few federal projects have ever been halted by court actions based on NEPA, it is likely that many environmentally unsound projects have been abandoned or never begun because of EIS requirements. The EIS requirement remains controversial because it is impossible to quantify whether the environmental benefits of this process outweigh the additional time and expense incurred.

ENVIRONMENTAL PROTECTION AGENCY

In 1970 the EPA was created, consolidating into one agency, the power to regulate various aspects of the environment that previously had been scattered across several federal agencies and departments. The EPA establishes and enforces environmental protection standards, conducts research on pollution, provides assistance to state and local antipollution programs through grants and technical advice, and generally assists the Council on Environmental Quality (CEQ). The CEQ was established to facilitate implementation of NEPA by issuing guidelines for the preparation of impact statements and generally to assist and advise the president on environmental matters. In its guidelines, CEQ has required that the EISs discussed above be prepared as early in the decision-making process as possible and that other agencies and the public be given a chance to comment and criticize before any final decision is made to go ahead with major federal action.

Consolidation of diverse functions under the EPA has provided a center of control for the continuing war on pollution. How it works can be illustrated by studying the major areas of concern.

WATER POLLUTION CONTROL

As in other areas of environmental concern, federal regulation of water pollution is based on a series of measures passed over the years. For example, the **River and Harbors Act of 1890** prohibited the dumping of refuse into all navigable waters, and the **1899 Rivers and Harbors Appropriations Act** made it unlawful for ships and manufacturing establishments to discharge refuse into any navigable waterway of the United States or into any tributary of a navigable waterway. Efforts to clean up the nation's waterways began in earnest with passage of the **Federal Water Pollution Control Act** in 1948, which has been repeatedly amended over the years.

CLEAN WATER ACT

The **Clean Water Act** (passed in 1971 and subsequently amended) is the major federal law governing water pollution. It provided a comprehensive plan to eliminate water pollution, setting standards and guidelines on an industry-by-industry basis for controlling water pollution from industrial sources. The types of discharges with which the law is concerned are as varied as the industries to be controlled. Thermal pollution from heat-generating plants and particulates and toxic wastes from manufacturing activities are subject to regulation and continual monitoring to assure that prescribed standards are being met. In general, industry is expected to control and eliminate its discharge of pollutants as soon as possible through the "best available technology (BAT) economically achievable."

The law placed primary responsibility on the states but provided for federal aid to local governments and small businesses to help them in their efforts to comply with the law's requirements. It also provided a licensing and permit system, at both state and federal levels, for discharging into waterways and a more workable enforcement program.

Citizen Suits

The Clean Water Act also allows citizens or organizations whose interests are affected by water pollution to sue violators of standards established under the law. Similar provisions are contained in several other environmental laws. The following case addresses a major issue raised by these "citizen suit" provisions. The factual summary sheds additional light on the working mechanism of the Clean Water Act.

CASE

GWALTNEY OF SMITHFIELD V. CHESAPEAKE BAY FOUNDATION, INC.

U.S. Supreme Court
484 U.S. 49 (1987)

The Clean Water Act was enacted in 1972 "to restore and maintain the chemical, physical, and biological integrity of the Nation's water." The act establishes the National Pollutant Discharge Elimination System (NPDES), under which the EPA, or a state that has its own program conforming to federal standards, may issue permits authorizing the discharge of pollutants in accordance with specified conditions. If the holder of such permit violates its conditions, he or she is subject not only to federal and state action, but also to civil suits by private citizens, which are authorized against any person "alleged to be in violation of" the conditions of a federal or state NPDES permit. Section 505(a)(1).

Between 1981 and 1984, petitioner Gwaltney violated the conditions of its permits by discharging pollutants. These violations are chronicled in the Discharge Monitoring Reports (DMRs) that the permit (and the act) require the petitioner to maintain. Although the petitioner was improving its equipment to minimize problems, in February 1984 Chesapeake Bay Foundation and Natural Resources Defense Council ("respondents"), two nonprofit organizations, sent notice to Gwaltney, the EPA, and Virginia regulators indicating their intention to commence a citizen suit under the act. The suit requested declaratory and injunctive relief, imposition of civil penalties, and attorneys' fees and costs.

Gwaltney's new equipment solved its problems; the permit was not violated after May 15, 1984. Respondents filed their suit in June 1984, alleging that Gwaltney "has violated [and] will continue to violate" its NPDES permit. Gwaltney moved to dismiss on grounds that the court lacked subject matter jurisdiction because a citizen's complaint brought under section 505(a) must allege a violation occurring at the time the complaint is filed. The trial court denied that motion. Gwaltney appealed, and the Fourth Circuit Court of Appeals affirmed. Gwaltney appealed to the Supreme Court.

MARSHALL, JUSTICE:

The most natural reading of "to be in violation" is a requirement that citizen-plaintiffs allege a state of either continuous or intermittent violation—that is, a reasonable likelihood that a past polluter will continue to pollute in the future. Congress could have phrased its requirement in language that looked only to the past ("to have violated"), but it did not choose this readily available option.

Our reading of the "to be in violation" language of Sec. 505(a) is bolstered by the language and structure of the rest of the citizen suit provisions in Sec. 505 of the Act. These provisions together make plain that the interest of the citizen suit is primarily forward-looking.

One of the most striking indicia of the prospective orientation of the citizen suit is the pervasive use of the present tense throughout Sec. 505.

Any other conclusion would render incomprehensible Sec. 505's notice provision, which requires citizens to give 60 days notice of their intent to sue to the alleged violator as well as to the Administrator and the State. If the Administrator or the State commences enforcement action within that 60 day period, the citizen suit is barred, presumably because governmental action has rendered it unnecessary. It follows logically that the purpose of notice to the alleged violator is to give it an opportunity to bring itself into complete compliance with the Act and thus likewise render unnecessary a citizen suit.

Adopting respondents' interpretation of Sec. 505's jurisdictional grant would create a second and even more disturbing anomaly. The bar on citizen suits when governmental enforcement action is underway suggests that the citizen suit is meant to supplement rather than to supplant governmental action. The legislative history of the Act reinforces this view of the role of the citizen suit. The Senate Report noted that "[t]he Committee intends the great volume of enforcement actions [to] be brought by the State," and that citizen suits are proper only "if the Federal, State, and local

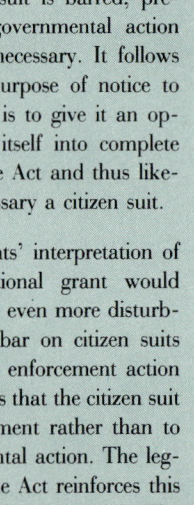

CONTINUED

agencies fail to exercise their enforcement responsibility." Respondents' interpretation of the scope of the citizen suit would change the nature of the citizens' role from interstitial to potentially intrusive. We cannot agree that Congress intended such a result.

The legislative history of the Act provides additional support for our reading of Sec. 505. Members of Congress frequently characterized the citizen suit provisions as "abatement" provisions or as injunctive measures. Moreover, both the Senate and House Reports explicitly connected Sec. 505 to the citizen suit provisions authorized by the Clean Air Act, which are wholly injunctive in nature.

Our conclusion that Sec. 505 does not permit citizen suits for wholly past violations does not necessarily dispose of the lawsuit. Section 505 confers jurisdiction over citizen suits when the citizen-plaintiffs make a good-faith allegation of continuous or intermittent violation. The statute does not require that a defendant "be in violation" of the Act at the commencement of suit; rather, the statute requires that a defendant be "*alleged* to be in violation."

Because the court below declined to decide whether respondents' complaint contained a good-faith allegation of ongoing violation by the petitioner,... we remand the case for consideration of this question.

NOTE

Between 1984 and 1988, some 806 notices of intent to sue under the Clean Water Act were filed, primarily by such groups at the National Resources Defense Fund, the Sierra Club Legal Defense Fund, and the Friends of the Earth. Only a tiny percentage of such suits are preempted by governmental enforcement action, and most lead to negotiations and court-approved settlements and consent decrees. Such citizen suits have become quite controversial. Supporters believe that they are a beneficial supplement to actions brought by overworked agencies such as EPA and its state counterparts. Critics believe that the suits have become so numerous (and arguably driven by provisions allowing for recovery of attorneys' fees) that they do not bring about cost-effective results and subvert consistency and fairness in national enforcement.

WATER QUALITY ACT OF 1987

In the **Water Quality Act of 1987,** Congress amended the Clean Water Act by emphasizing a state–federal program to control "non–point source" pollution. Whereas "point sources" such as municipal or industrial discharge pipes account for much water pollution, Congress determined that non–point source pollution such as oil and grease runoff from city streets, pesticide runoff from farmland, and runoff from mining areas must be addressed. The states were charged with developing programs to improve water quality by combatting this pollution, which is so difficult to track.

The 1987 Act also clamped down on toxic water pollution and empowered the EPA to assess administrative penalties for water pollution. The penalties were placed on a sliding scale. For more serious offenses (considering the nature, circumstances, extent and gravity of the violation, and the violator's ability to pay, history of violations, degree of culpability, and savings resulting from the violation), the EPA must provide relatively formal hearings but can assess larger penalties. Smaller penalties are assessed for minor violations after less formal procedures.

Responding to concerns about abuses of citizen suits, the 1987 Act also gave the EPA more supervision of settlement agreements in such cases, and a greater ability to preclude such suits administratively.

OIL SPILLS

All too frequently, vessels from small coastal barges to huge supertankers accidentally discharge their cargoes into the sea near the coast. The ecologic effect on fish, shellfish, and waterfowl and on the public and private shorelines and beaches may be immense. Consequently, the Clean Water Act imposes severe sanctions on those responsible for such pollution. The owner or operator of a grounded oil-carrying vessel can be liable for up to $250,000 of the cost of cleaning up its spilled oil; if the oil spill is the result of willful negligence or misconduct, the owner or operator of the vessel can be held liable to the U.S. government for the full cost of cleaning up the shore. Operators of onshore and offshore facilities are also held liable for spillage and pollution, under ordinary conditions, to the extent of $50 million and, where willful negligence and misconduct are involved, to the full extent of the cost of cleanup and removal, including the restoration or replacement of natural resources damaged or destroyed by the discharge of oil or hazardous substances.

After the Exxon *Valdez* oil spill in Alaska, the Exxon company was charged with a variety of criminal offenses and sued by all manner of private and governmental officials. A wide variety of laws and regulations dealing with water pollution and wildlife were allegedly violated. Exxon settled state and federal litigation by agreeing to pay $900 million over 11 years (in civil penalties), plus $100 million for restoration of the injured area to be split between the United States and Alaska and $25 million in criminal fines. The settlement did not affect about $59 billion in private civil suits then pending against Exxon.

ADDITIONAL REGULATIONS

Of related concern are the **Marine Protection, Research, and Sanctuaries Act,** which regulates the discharge and introduction of pollutants into coastal waterways and marine areas, and the **Safe Drinking Water Act** of 1974, which gave the states primary responsibility for enforcing national standards for drinking water. Under the act, the EPA has set maximum drinking-water contaminant levels of certain chemicals, pesticides, and microbiologic pollutants.

AIR POLLUTION CONTROL

CLEAN AIR ACT

The **Clean Air Act** of 1970 empowered the EPA to set standards to attain certain primary ambient (outside) air quality standards designed by Congress to protect public health. Because achieving the standards is costly, the

EPA's role is to balance the economic, technologic, and social factors that must be considered in attaining the clean air goals that have been set.

Several programs formed the essential elements of the Clean Air Act. Foremost was the setting of primary (health) and secondary (welfare) ambient air quality standards. Because the Clean Air Act's approach involved a federal–state partnership, another program required the states to draft state implementation plans (SIPs) for achieving ambient air quality standards. When approved by the EPA, such plans permitted the states to enforce air quality standards within their borders. Operators of air pollution sources could be required to monitor, sample, and keep appropriate records, all of which were subject to on-premises inspection by the EPA. When a proper SIP was not prepared, the burden fell to the EPA to adopt a Federal Implementation Plan (FIP).

To reduce emissions in accordance with prescribed schedules, the act also set **new source performance standards** (NSPSs)—emission standards for various categories of large industrial facilities. Major polluters must use the best acceptable control devices, those with proven capabilities to reduce emissions. To ease the burden on industry, the EPA adopted the "**bubble concept,**" under which a large plant with multiple emission points (stacks) does not have to meet standards for each one. The plant instead is under a "bubble" with a single allowable emission level. Plant management can manage each point source within the bubble to meet the sum total of emission limits by the most economical means.

Finally, the act addressed automobile pollution by developing emission standards and fuel additive regulations. Use of unleaded gasoline and catalytic converters has resulted in substantial progress. However, industry continues to complain that the standards are too burdensome, and environmentalists still claim that the rules are too lax and are ineffectually enforced.

1990 AMENDMENTS

Although measurable progress was made in many areas pursuant to the 1970 Clean Air Act, it is undeniable that serious air pollution problems remain. Therefore, in 1990, Congress enacted significant amendments to the act. With predicted costs for implementation between $20 billion and $100 billion annually, the 1990 amendments emphasized four critical areas.

First, the amendments addressed ozone, carbon monoxide, and particulate matter—where there had been significant failures to attain established standards. For example, the amendments established five categories for ozone nonattainment, ranging from marginal to extreme, with attainment deadlines stretching from 1993 to 2010, and increasingly stringent control requirements tied to the degree of nonattainment.

A second key area is air toxics. A list of 189 hazardous substances or groups of substances was added to a previous list of eight air pollutants. The EPA is to target categories of major sources of such pollutants. For each source, the EPA is required to establish emission control standards based on **maximum achievable control technology** (MACT).

The third major area is **acid rain.** With a phased-in timetable, the amendments require a reduction in emissions of sulfur dioxide by electric utility steam generating units by 10 milllion tons from 1980 levels. After full implementation, the national cap for such emissions will be 8.9 million tons annually, with the EPA issuing freely transferable "allowances" within that total to existing generating units. Holders who do not use their allowances may sell them or carry them forward for future use.

Fourth, in addressing automobile pollution, the law set emission standards that might add as much as $500 to the cost of a new car. Among other provisions, the 1990 amendments prohibited the sale of leaded gasoline for highway use after December 31, 1995, and prohibited the manufacture of an engine that requires leaded gasoline after 1992.

The amendments mean increased expenses and record-keeping for giant corporations and many small businesses as well. As many as 50,000 points of pollution may be required to obtain permits under the amendments. Those who fail to comply face the stiffest penalties yet. For example, previously, violations were generally misdemeanors, but now they are felonies with criminal penalties that may run up to $1 million per violation. Additionally, the EPA Administrator may assess civil administrative penalties up to $25,000 a day per violation, and the role of litigation by citizens and private organizations in the enforcement process has been expanded. For example, as we saw earlier, in *Gwaltney of Smithfield Ltd. v. Chesapeake Bay Foundation*,[5] the Supreme Court held that citizens could sue only for ongoing violations of the Clean Water Act, a holding applied to the Clean Air Act as well. The 1990 amendments specifically permit citizens of file complaints over *past* violations that have been repeated.

Another form of citizen input comes in the permit process. All large pollution sources (except vehicles) must obtain permits from state pollution authorities specifying that their emissions do not violate Clean Air Act limits. Those permits are subject to EPA review, and if the EPA does not object to a permit, citizens may petition the agency to do so and may comment on permits and request public hearings during the approval process. Some 34,000 facilities will be covered by the permit program.

Proponents stress that the long-term benefits to the environment and public health may well outweigh the burdens that the act places on industry and on consumers who purchase its products.

In the area of air pollution, as well as most others, major environmental programs have been established in a sequential fashion. That is, rather than having a master comprehensive plan, major initiatives have been amended and then amended again to address new problems or old problems that have proved to be intractable. The difficulties of such an approach are illustrated in the following recent case.

---

[5] 484 U.S. 49 (1987).

CASE

COALITION FOR CLEAN AIR v. EPA

U.S. DISTRICT COURT, CENTRAL DISTRICT OF CALIFORNIA 762 F.SUPP. 1399 (1991)

Before the Clean Air Act was amended in 1990, California's State Implementation Plan (SIP) for the South Coast Air Basin was rejected, and the EPA acquired the obligation to prepare a federal implementation plan (FIP). The plaintiffs brought this suit to force the EPA to prepare a FIP. EPA recognized its obligation to do so, and a settlement agreement was entered into that, as later amended, granted the EPA until February 28, 1991, to produce such a plan. However, when the 1990 amendments to the Clean Air Act were passed, the EPA moved to vacate the settlement agreement and dismiss the plaintiffs' action.

HUPP, DISTRICT JUDGE:

The question is whether Congress, in enacting the 1990 amendments to the Clean Air Act, intended to require that a Federal Implementation Plan (FIP) prepared under the new criteria in the amended Act be promulgated by EPA before [EPA rejects for noncompliance] a State Implementation Plan (SIP) hereafter to be prepared under the new criteria.

The [1990] Amendments change numerous standards which States must meet, set forth new schedules for the submission of SIP's, and continue the provision that if the State fails to submit a plan, or a state SIP is disapproved, the EPA shall prepare an FIP (now, within 2 years of disapproval), or may instead approve a State proposed revision to the SIP. Thus, the method of enforcement (a federal plan if the state does not come up with an acceptable one) is preserved from the former Act, but EPA has more time, opportunity, and flexibility to develop its own plan or approve state modifications. The difficulty presented by this motion is that Congress did not expressly say whether it intended to start the SIP process over again or not, and it is, therefore, in question whether it is Congress' intent in this circumstance that EPA must follow through on the presently pending FIP, even though the State has not had an opportunity to develop its own plan under the new criteria and schedules.

It must be said that the statute is ambiguous. Amended Sec. 110 provides in part that: "The Administrator shall promulgate a Federal Implementation Plan at any time within 2 years after the Administrator—...(B) disapproves a State implementation plan in whole or in part."

The question, then, is which rejected SIP is the revised Sec. 110 now referring to—the one which was rejected in 1988 or the new one which must be submitted under the new criteria and on the new time schedule? The answer is not provided by a reading, literal or otherwise, of Sec. 110. However, the structure of the amended Act, with revamped criteria and timing for SIPs, is clear. It includes an obvious policy that the States are encouraged to take the lead, with the potential FIP being the stick that drives them. [It refers to the new SIP.] There is an additional reason to believe that revised Sec. 110 refers to the new SIP to be prepared by the States under the revised criteria. If the Act were interpreted otherwise, there would be the anomaly that the rejected SIP prepared by the State under the former criteria is to be replaced by an FIP prepared under new criteria that the State has never had an opportunity to address. In view of Congressional policy to have States take the lead in preparation of plans, such an interpretation seems unlikely. From this, it is logical to conclude that the SIP referred to in Sec. 110 is the new SIP required of the States and referred to in other amendments to the Act. The court so concludes.

The motion [to vacate the settlement agreement and dismiss the action] is granted.

SOLID WASTE AND ITS DISPOSAL

The disposal of millions of tons of solid waste produced annually in this country presents a problem of staggering proportions. Periodic garbage pick-ups at residences or small businesses or weekly trips to the county or municipal sanitary landfill solve the problem for most people. However, less than 10 percent of solid waste is classified as residential, commercial or institutional. The greater portion is classified as agricultural or mineral. Agriculture alone contributes more than 50 percent. Undisposed of, the waste creates enormous health and pollution problems; inadequate disposal methods often create greater hazards. If burned, solid waste pollutes the air. If dumped into waterway, lakes, or streams, the Clean Water Act is violated. Consequently, federal statutes have been enacted to combat the problem.

SOLID WASTE DISPOSAL ACT/ RESOURCE CONSERVATION RECOVERY ACT

The primary goal of the **Solid Waste Disposal Act** of 1965 and the 1976 amendment known as the **Resource Conservation and Recovery Act** (RCRA) is more efficient management of waste and its disposal through financial and technical assistance to state and local agencies in the development and implementation of new methods of waste disposal. The RCRA defined **hazardous waste** as a solid waste, or combination of solid wastes, which because of its quantity, concentration, physical, chemical, or infectious characteristics may

(A) cause, or significantly contribute to an increase in mortality or an increase in serious irreversible, or incapacitating reversible, illness; or
(B) pose a substantial present or potential hazard to human health or the environment when improperly treated, stored, transported, or disposed of, or otherwise managed.

RCRA also established an Office of Solid Waste within the EPA to regulate the generation and transportation of solid waste (both toxic and nontoxic), as well as its disposal, thus providing "cradle-to-grave" regulation. Although RCRA focuses primarily on the regulation and granting of permits for ongoing hazardous waste activities, it does have a corrective action program for site cleanup. The EPA is authorized to sue to force the cleanup of existing waste disposal sites presenting imminent hazards to the public health.

These acts generally treat toxic wastes more harshly than nontoxic wastes. But where is the line drawn? The **Hazardous and Solid Waste Amendments** (to RCRA) of 1984 required the EPA to expand the list of constituents characterized as toxic. In 1990, the EPA issued its rules, adding 25 organic chemicals to a preexisting list of eight metals and six pesticides regulated for toxicity. Nearly 20,000 small (and large) businesses generating solid waste containing these substances must now comply with rules regarding hazardous waste, and a substantial number of landfills must now be treated as hazardous waste facilities, greatly expanding the costs of required disposal and cleanup. The 1984 amendments also created a comprehensive program for regulating underground storage tanks, such as gasoline tanks at service stations.

COMPREHENSIVE ENVIRONMENTAL RESPONSE, COMPENSATION, AND LIABILITY ACT OF 1980 (CERCLA/SUPERFUND)

Although RCRA provides cradle-to-grave regulation of active hazardous waste sites, in the wake of the Love Canal incident referred to earlier, Congress passed the **Comprehensive Environmental Response, Compensation, and Liability Act of 1980** (CERCLA), better known as the **Superfund** legislation, to clean up abandoned or inactive sites. CERCLA initially established a $1.6 billion Hazardous Substance Response Trust Fund to cover the cost of "timely government responses to releases of hazardous substances into the environment."

Addressing a much broader range of hazardous substances than RCRA, CERCLA holds the polluter, rather than society, responsible for the costs of cleaning up designated hazardous waste sites, instructing the EPA to list the nation's worst toxic waste sites, identify responsible parties, and sue them for cleanup costs, if necessary. **Potentially responsible parties** ("PRPs") were initially enumerated: (1) present owners and operators of facilities, (2) any person who at the time of disposal, owned or operated such a facility; (3) generators of hazardous substances who arrange for disposal or treatment at another's facility; or (4) transporters of hazardous substances. These parties are strictly liable for cost of removal and remediation, response costs incurred by others, and damages to natural resources owned or controlled by any government. Due care and compliance with existing laws are no defense. Once determined to be responsible, a PRP may have to bear the *entire* cost of cleanup because liability is joint and several. In other words, if the government proves that owner A, prior owner B, and transporter C are all PRPs, and B and C are insolvent, A may have to pay for the entire cleanup. Furthermore, CERCLA is retroactive, covering both disposal acts committed and response costs incurred before the law was passed. Thus, potential CERCLA liability can be staggering.

The act also allowed a category of exceptions, including owners of property incident to a security interest ("security interest exception") and owners of land contaminated by the acts or omissions of third parties who are not contractually related to the owner ("third-party defense").[6] The third-party defense is unavailable if the polluter is an employee or agent of the responsible party or one in a direct or indirect contractual relationship with him or her.

Under the original version of CERCLA, completely innocent current owners of hazardous dumps faced liability for cleanup. In 1986, Congress

---

[6] CERCLA also allows a PRP to avoid liability when pollution is caused by an act of God or of war.

passed the **Superfund Amendments and Reauthorization Act** (SARA), which provided an "innocent landowner" defense for those who could not only establish the third party defense but also show (1) they had no reason to know of the contamination of the property when they purchased and (2) they had made all appropriate inquiry into the previous ownership and uses of the property consistent with good commercial and customary practice. SARA also replaced the original CERCLA trust fund with the $8.5 billion **Hazardous Substance Superfund** (Superfund) financed by general revenue appropriations, certain environmental taxes, and monies recovered under CERCLA on behalf of the Superfund, and CERCLA-authorized penalties and punitive damages. SARA authorized civil penalties of up to $25,000 per day for willful failure to comply with EPA regulations.

Although in the earlier years, the costs of Superfund fell primarily on large corporations, in recent years, those corporations have spread the pain by suing small businesses and even municipalities for contribution specifically authorized by CERCLA. For example, two large corporations who had settled an EPA action by agreeing to pay for a $9 million cleanup of a landfill, sued a tiny pizzeria (among several other small businesses), surmising that it might have included cleanser, insecticide cans, or other items containing traces of toxins in its garbage sent to the landfill. Small companies often settle such cases out of court because the cost of defending would be so high.[7]

The financial threat that CERCLA poses to industries that generate toxic wastes and companies that dispose of them is obvious. Additionally, CERCLA poses substantial hidden liabilities for a wide range of entities, including the pizzeria mentioned above; real estate buyers, lessees, and landlords; purchasers of corporations with unknown environmental liabilities; and indirect owners and operators such as lenders or parent corporations. For example, a lender might under certain circumstances be liable to cleanup a borrower's waste site at an expense far in excess of the amount of the loan. Furthermore, several courts have held that despite traditional notions of limited liability for corporations, parent corporations may be liable for pollution caused by subsidiaries over which the parents exert substantial influence,[8] and that when two corporations merge the acquiring corporation may well be responsible for pollution caused long before by the acquired corporation.[9]

One of the most liberal applications of CERCLA liability came in the following case addressing the "security interest" exception.

---

[7] Tomsho, *Big Corporations Hit by Superfund Cases Find Way to Share Bill*, Wall St. J., Apr. 2, 1991, at A1, col. 6.

[8] E.g., *United States v. Kayser-Roth Corp.*, 910 F.2d 24 (1st Cir. 1990).

[9] E.g., *Anspec Co. v. Johnson Controls, Inc.*, 922 F.2d 1240 (6th Cir. 1991).

UNITED STATES v. FLEET FACTORS CORP.

U.S. COURT OF APPEALS, 11TH CIRCUIT 901 F.2d 1550 (1990)

Fleet Factors Corporation ("Fleet") was a creditor of Swainsboro Print Works ("SPW"), holding as collateral a security interest in SPW's textile facility, all its equipment, inventory, and fixtures. After SPW was adjudicated as bankrupt, a trustee assumed title and control of SPW's plant. In May 1982, Fleet foreclosed on its security interest in some of SPW's inventory and equipment and contracted with Baldwin to auction the collateral. Baldwin sold the material "as is," removal of the items being the responsibility of the purchasers. In August 1982, Fleet allegedly contracted with Nix to remove the unsold equipment in consideration for leaving the premises "broom clean." Nix testified in deposition that he understood he had been given a "free hand" by Fleet to do whatever was necessary to remove the machinery and equipment. He left the facility by the end of 1983.

On January 20, 1984, the EPA inspected the facility and found 700 fifty-five-gallon drums containing toxic chemicals and 44 truckloads of material containing asbestos. The EPA spent $400,000 in responding to this environmental threat. On July 7, 1987, the facility was conveyed to Emanuel County, Georgia, at a foreclosure sale resulting from SPW's failure to pay taxes. Fleet never had foreclosed its security interest on the SPW facility itself.

The government sued the two principal officers of SPW and Fleet to recover the cost. The government claimed that Fleet was liable either as a present owner and operator of the facility under 42 U.S.C. Sec. 9607(a)(1) of CERCLA or as the owner or operator of the facility at the time the wastes were disposed of under section 9607(a)(2). The trial judge rejected the government's first claim but found a sufficient issue as to the second to deny Fleet's motion for summary judgment. Each party appealed.

KRAVITCH, CIRCUIT JUDGE:

A. Fleet's Liability Under Section 9607(a)(1). CERCLA holds the owner or operator of a facility containing hazardous waste strictly liable to the United States for expenses incurred in responding to the environmental and health hazards posed by the waste in that facility. This provision of the statute targets those individuals presently "owning or operating such facilities." ... On July 9, 1987, the date this litigation was commenced, the owner of the SPW facility was Emanuel County, Georgia. Under CERCLA, however, a state or local government that has involuntarily acquired title to a facility is generally not held liable as the owner or operator of the facility. Rather, the statute provides that "[its owner or operator is] any person who owned, operated or otherwise controlled activities at such facilities immediately beforehand."

Essentially, the parties disagree as to the interpretation of the phrase "immediately beforehand." ... We agree with Fleet that the plain meaning of the phrase "immediately beforehand" means without intervening ownership, operation, and control. Fleet, therefore, cannot be held liable under section 9607(a)(1) because it neither owned, operated, or controlled SPW immediately prior to Emanuel County's acquisition of the facility. It is undisputed that from December 1981, when SPW was adjudicated as bankrupt, until the July 1987 foreclosure sale, the bankrupt estate and trustee were the owners of the facility. Similarly, the evidence is clear that neither. Fleet nor any of its putative agents had anything to do with the facility after December 1983.

B. Fleet's Liability Under Section 9607(a)(2). CERCLA also imposes liability on "any person who at the time of disposal of any hazardous substance owned or operated any...facility at which such hazardous substances were disposed of..." CERCLA excludes from the definition of "owner or operator" any "person, who, without participating in the management of a... facility, holds indicia of ownership primarily to protect his security interest in the...facility." 42 U.S.C. Sec. 9601(20)(A) Fleet has the burden of establishing its entitlement to this ["security interest"] exemption. There is no dispute that Fleet held an "indicia

CONTINUED

of ownership" in the facility through its deed of trust to SPW, and that this interest was held primarily to protect its security interest in the facility. The critical issue is whether Fleet participated in management sufficiently to incur liability under the statute.

In *U.S. v. Mirabile*, 15 Envtl. L.Rep. 20992 (E.D.Pa.1985), the district court granted summary judgment to the defendant creditors because their participation in the affairs of the facility was "limited to participation in financial decisions." The court below, relying on *Mirabile*, similarly interpreted the statutory language to permit secured creditors to "provide financial assistance and general, and even isolated instances of specific management advice to its debtors without risking CERCLA liability if the secured creditor does not participate in the day-to-day management of the business facility either before or after the business ceases operation."

Although we agree with the district court's resolution of the summary judgment motion, we find its construction of the statutory exemption too permissive toward secured creditors who are involved with toxic waste facilities. In order to achieve the "overwhelmingly remedial" goal of the CERCLA statutory scheme, ambiguous statutory terms should be construed to favor liability for the cost incurred by the government in responding to the hazards at such facilities.

Under the standard we adopt today, a secured creditor may incur section 9607(a)(2) liability, without being an operator, by participating in the financial management of a facility to a degree indicating a capacity to influence the corporation's treatment of hazardous wastes. It is not necessary for the secured creditor actually to involve itself in the day-to-day operations of the facility in order to be liable—although such conduct will certainly lead to the loss of the protection of the statutory exemption. Nor is it necessary for the secured creditor to participate in the management decisions relating to hazardous waste. Rather, a secured creditor will be liable if its involvement with the management of the facility is sufficiently broad to support the inference that it could affect hazardous waste disposal decisions if it so chose. We, therefore, specifically reject the formulation suggested by the district court in *Mirabile*.

Our ruling today should encourage potential creditors to thoroughly investigate the waste treatment systems and policies of potential debtors. If the treatment systems seem inadequate, the risk of CERCLA liability will be weighed into the terms of the loan agreement. Creditors, therefore, will incur no greater risk than they bargained for; and debtors, aware that inadequate hazardous waste treatment will have a significant adverse impact on their loan terms, will have powerful incentives to improve their handling of hazardous wastes.

Similarly, creditors' awareness that they are potentially liable under CERCLA will encourage them to monitor the hazardous waste treatment systems and policies of their debtors and insist upon compliance with acceptable treatment standards as a prerequisite to continued and future financial support. Once a secured creditor's involvement with a facility becomes sufficiently broad that it can anticipate losing its exemption from CERCLA liability, it will have a strong incentive to address hazardous waste problems at the facility rather than studiously avoiding the investigation and amelioration of the hazard.

We agree with the court below that the government has alleged sufficient facts to hold Fleet liable under section 9607(a)(2). Fleet's involvement with SPW, according to the government, increased substantially after SPW ceased printing operations at the Georgia plant on February 27, 1981 and began to wind down its affairs. Fleet required SPW to seek its approval before shipping its goods to customers established the price for excess inventory, dictated when and to whom the finished goods should be shipped, determined when employees should be laid off, supervised the activity of the office administrator at the site, received and processed SPW's employment and tax forms, controlled access to the facility, and contracted with Baldwin to dispose of the fixtures and equipment at SPW. These facts, if proved, are sufficient to remove Fleet from the protection of the secured creditor exemption. The district court's finding to the contrary is erroneous.

With respect to Fleet's involvement at the facility from the time it contracted with Baldwin in May 1982 until Nix left the facility in December 1983, we share the district court's conclusion that Fleet's alleged conduct brought it outside the statutory exemption for secured creditors. Indeed, Fleet's involvement would pass the threshold for operator liability under section 9607(a)(2).

[Affirmed and remanded for further proceedings consistent with this opinion.]

NOTE

The *Fleet Factors* result was so potentially dangerous for lenders that the EPA issued rules granting them some protection from unlimited liability.[10] However, it is clear that potential Superfund liability under CERCLA is very broad and quite dangerous for many segments of American business. For example, in 1991, the EPA thought it was being generous to a bank, which had foreclosed on a property that turned out to contain hazardous waste that had polluted a bay, by agreeing to limit the bank's liability to (1) pay to clean up the foreclosed property and (2) contribute $350,000 toward cleaning up the bay (which was expected to cost millions). As is often noted, Superfund is intended to cleanup hazardous waste dumps, not to be fair. For that reason, CERCLA will continue to cause litigation, to generate attempts at legislative reform, and to be extremely controversial. As of mid 1992, the EPA has targeted 1,235 hazardous waste sites as among the nation's worst, had begun cleanups at 28 percent of them, but had finalized cleanup of only 6 percent at an average cost of $24 million.

REGULATION OF TOXIC SUBSTANCES

In addition to the identifiable pollutants that are controlled at the source by the EPA, a more serious threat may be posed by the thousands of chemicals and compounds that are manufactured for commercial and generally beneficial use. These include herbicides, pesticides, and fertilizers, some of which may be highly toxic as single elements or which may become toxic when combined with other elements. It is now apparent that toxic substances, initially applied to serve some useful purpose, are working their way into the environment, often with potentially dangerous results to humans exposed to those substances. An infamous example occurred at Times Beach, Missouri, where deadly dioxins deposited years before may have caused severe health problems for local residents.

TOXIC SUBSTANCES CONTROL ACT

In 1976 Congress enacted the **Toxic Substances Control Act** (TSCA) to create a review and control mechanism for the process of bringing chemical substances into the markeplace. The EPA is required to develop a comprehensive inventory of existing chemicals by calling on manufacturers to report the amount of each chemical substance they produce. TSCA imposes testing requirements on manufacturers and requires notice to the EPA when a new substance is being considered for development and production. The main purpose of the act is to prohibit the introduction of substances that would present an uncontrollable risk. Additionally, TSCA provides for testing,

---

[10] Some courts are limiting CERCLA liability by restricting application of "joint and several" liability. U.S. v. Alcan, 964 F.2d 252 (3d Cir. 1992).

warnings, and instructions leading to the safe use of toxic chemicals with minimal effects on humans and the environment. Enforcement procedures permit the EPA to issue an order to prohibit the manufacture of high-risk substances. Pursuant to the TSCA, the EPA has developed specific standards for PCBs, asbestos, chlorofluorocarbons, dioxins, and other substances.

Unlike some other environmental laws (the Clean Air Act, for example), the TSCA orders the EPA to consider the economic and social impact of its decisions as well as the environmental effects. Therefore, more than some environmental regulations, the TSCA seeks to avoid unnecessary burdens on the economy.

PESTICIDE REGULATION

Obviously pests such as insects and mice cause significant crop damage and health problems. For that reason, chemicals that can kill or inhibit the reproduction of such pests are quite valuable for the health and economic welfare of Americans. Unfortunately, the widespread and long-term use of such substances can itself endanger the environment, injuring wildlife and human health. For that reason, Congress passed the **Federal Environmental Pesticide Control Act** in 1972, amending an earlier 1947 law, the **Federal Insecticide, Fungicide, and Rodenticide Act** (FIFRA). These acts together require that pesticides be registered with the EPA before they can be sold. Applicants for registration must provide comprehensive safety testing information to the EPA, which will approve the application only if the pesticide is properly labeled, lives up to its claims, and does not cause "unreasonable adverse effects on the environment." Such substances, when applied to crops that provide food for animals or people, may be used only within established limits. It is under this legislation that the EPA substantially banned the well-known insecticide DDT.

NOISE POLLUTION

The **Noise Control Act of 1972,** the first major federal assault on excessive noise emanating from sources to which the public is exposed on a continual basis, empowers the EPA to establish noise emission standards for specific products in cooperation with agencies otherwise concerned with them and to limit noise emissions from those products that can be categorized as noise producers. The act specifically targets transportation vehicles and equipment, machinery, appliances, and other commercial products. The act subjects federal facilities to state and local noise standards and expressly reserves the right to control environmental noise in the states through licensing and regulation or restriction of excessively noisy products.

The thrust of the Noise Control Act is to reduce environmental noise in an effort to prevent what are recognized as long-range effects (hearing problems) on public health and welfare. Violations of the prohibitions of the act are punishable by fines, imprisonment, or both.

Many states and localities have their own noise pollution rules and regulations.

INDOOR POLLUTION

Until recently, indoor pollution was given relatively little attention by environmentalists, businesses, and regulators. Recently, however, many experts have concluded that indoor air is many times more hazardous than outdoor air. Because Americans spend a very high percentage of their time indoors, a serious problem is pressented by such indoor pollutants.

Among the most serious indoor pollutants are radon gas (a colorless, odorless gas that often percolates from the soil into homes and other buildings), asbestos (natural fibers often used as insulation and for other construction purposes), and formaldehyde (a chemical also often found in insulation and other construction materials). The tendency of these substances and others to cause cancer or other diseases is widely accepted.[11]

Despite the dangers presented by these and other substances, as of this writing there is no comprehensive federal policy on indoor air quality. Nor have the states taken any uniform action. For example, the federal government's efforts at regulating radon have not yet moved past the research and study phase. Hit-and-miss attempts have led to substantial amounts being spent to clean up asbestos, especially in schools, and to the demise of the formaldehyde insulation industry. Nonetheless, the regulatory efforts have been incomplete. Therefore, the substantial dangers posed by indoor air pollution will undoubtedly lead to additional state and federal regulation in the near future.

Litigation in the area of indoor pollution is also in its infancy, but increased activity will likely be seen in coming years. In *Pinkerton v Georgia Pacific Corp.*,[12] for example, $16.2 million was recovered to compensate for sensitivity reactions in the plaintiffs caused by indoor formaldehyde exposure caused by the defendant's negligence.

INTERNATIONAL LEGAL ASPECTS OF POLLUTION

The various forms of pollution do not respect national borders. Therefore, pollution has a critical international dimension that cannot be overlooked. International law and international organizations now play an increasingly

---

[11] *See* F. CROSS, LEGAL RESPONSES TO INDOOR AIR POLLUTION (Quorum Books 1990).
[12] No. CV 186-4651CC (Mo. Cir. Ct. 1990).

important role in solving important environmental problems. Unfortunately, as in nonenvironmental areas, their weaknesses prevent truly effective action. Nonetheless, important strides have been made.

INTERNATIONAL ORGANIZATIONS

Naturally, a look at international organizations must begin with the United Nations. Unfortunately, the United Nation has no executive-type environmental agency. Its strongest arm is **UNEP** (United National Environment Programme), which has helped formulate international treaties on pollution but has a limited budget and therefore can neither fund major projects nor comprehensively enforce international law.

The **International Court of Justice** plays at least a minor role in enforcing customary international law on transnational pollution. For example, in the *Corfu Channel Case*,[13] that body ruled that countries have an obligation not to allow their territory to be used for acts (including polluting acts) contrary to the rights of other states. An International Joint Commission established a similar "good neighbor" principle in a pollution dispute between the United States and Canada in the *Trail Smelter Arbitration*,[14] which involved claims by citizens of the State of Washington against smelters located in the British Columbia province, ruling that "under the principles of international law, . . . no state has the right to use or permit the use of its territory in such a manner as to cause injury by fumes in or to the territory of another or the properties or persons therein, when the case is of serious consequence and the injury is established by clear and convincing evidence."

INTERNATIONAL CONVENTIONS

The international community has in recent years attacked various aspects of the pollution problem through conventions and conferences. For example, as a starting point, **Principle 21 of the Stockholm Conference** (1972) provides that

> *States have, in accordance with the Charter of the United Nations and the principles of international law, the sovereign right to exploit their own resources pursuant to their own environmental policies, and the responsibility to ensure that activities within their own jurisdiction or control do not cause damage to the environment of other States or of areas beyond the limits of national jurisdiction.*

Pursuant to that principle, several important conventions have been formulated. To attack the problem of "garbage imperialism" (the exporting of waste by developed countries for disposal in underdeveloped countries), the **Basel Convention** (1989) sought to prohibit transboundary movement of hazardous wastes absent written consent by all countries involved. Another requirement is that the receiving country have an environmentally sound way to dispose of the waste.

---

[13] *Greece v. Italy*, 1949 I.C.J. 18.
[14] *United States v. Canada*, 3 R. Int'l. Arb. Awards 1907 (1949).

Water pollution in the form of oil spills by tankers has been addressed several times, including through the **Protocol of 1984 to Amend the International Convention on Civil Liability for Oil Pollution Damage** and the **Protocol of 1984 to Amend the International Fund for Compensation for Oil Pollution Damage.** The goal of these conventions was to create international standards of liability and an internationally enforced insurance scheme.

The endangering of species has been addressed in the **1973 Convention on International Trade in Endangered Species and Wild Fauna and Flora** and the **1979 Convention on Conservation of Migratory Species of Wild Animals.** These conventions address such matters as the illicit international trade in ivory, exotic birds, and rhinoceros horns.

The matter of ozone depletion is of primary importance in the international legal community because of the potential for worldwide adverse effects. Recently the **Montreal Protocol** called for industrialized nations to completely phase out the use of ozone-depleting chloroflourocarbons (CFCs) by the year 2000. It also provided a $100 million "financial mechanism" trust fund to enable developing countries to reduce their reliance on CFCs and to fund the attempt to find nonpolluting substitutes.

The June 1992 **U.N. Conference on the Environment and Development** ("Earth Summit") in Brazil resulted in some progress in several areas of international concern, although the progress may have been overshadowed by the U.S. decision to be the only country of 172 attending to refuse to sign the Convention on Biological Diversity.

LIMITATIONS

Unfortunately, although most of these conventions look good on paper and all are important symbolic steps, most suffer in varying degrees from limitations that are common to all international legal measures. Most of the conventions were signed by substantially more nations than ultimately ratified them. Most do not apply to nations that did not ratify. Most lack methods of enforcement and suffer from vagueness in terminology. Still, international cooperation is essential to saving the planet, and every effective step in the right direction should be appreciated and supported.

THE ENVIRONMENT, INDUSTRY, AND SOCIETY

At least two things should be clear from this chapter. First, businesses are faced with a myriad of environmental rules and regulations, some extremely costly and difficult to implement. To cover them fully would require a discussion hundreds of pages long. We have scarcely touched on the thousands of state and local antipollution ordinances and have not mentioned several matters of intense federal concern, such as the controversies over saving endangered species, preserving national parks, and drilling for oil and gas offshore. Nor have we mentioned some very important federal laws, including the **Hazardous Materials Transportation Act** (promoting safe movement of "hazardous materials" through our nation's transportation system), the **Emergency Planning and Community Right-to-Know Act** (aimed at forcing communities to prepare for a Bhopal-type spill of hazardous chemicals in the United States), or the Occupational Safety and Health Administration's numerous rules to protect workers from chemical injury, including the **Worker Right-to-Know Rule** (under which chemical manufacturers and employers using hazardous chemicals must communicate their hazards to affected employees).

Second, it should be obvious that striking a balance among competing interests—protection of the environment, economic health of business, long-term health of citizens—is exceedingly difficult. For that reason, the national debate on our priorities in this area and the best way to meet them will continue long into the future.

Questions and Problems

1. Defendant Atlantic Cement operated a large cement plant near Albany, New York. Neighboring landowners brought an equitable action seeking damages and an injunction. Their complaint alleged that they had suffered, and would continue to suffer, property damage caused by dirt, smoke, and vibration from the cement plant. The trial court found that the cement plant was a nuisance and awarded temporary damages but refused to issue an injunction. The record disclosed that Atlantic Cement had more than $45 million invested in the plant and provided employment for some 300 employees. In awarding temporary damages to landowners, the trial court further granted the right to bring later suits for future damages. Is this a reasonable resolution of this suit? Discuss. (*Boomer v. Atlantic Cement Co.*, 257 N.E.2d 870, N.Y. App., 1970).

2. In 1974 the Secretary of Defense announced the closing of an Army Depot near Lexington, Kentucky. The closing would eliminate 18 military and 2,630 civilian jobs in the area. The Army prepared an environmental assessment that concluded that a formal EIS would not be needed because the closing would cause no significant impact on the human environment. A nongovernmental research institution concluded that the area would suffer only minimal short-term unemployment after the closing. In litigation that followed, the question arose whether the impact on employment would constitute "a major Federal action significantly affecting the quality of the human environment," necessitating the filing of an EIS. What did Congress intend when it passed NEPA? Discuss. (*Breckinridge v. Rumsfeld,* 537 F.2d 864, 6th Cir. 1976).

3. T&E bought property once owned by U.S.R. Corp., which had processed radium there. In 1981, the EPA placed the property on its CERCLA National Priorities List. T&E closed the facility and sued all the successor corporations of U.S.R. Corp., alleging, among others, a state law claim of strict liability for an abnormally dangerous activity. The defendants claimed that strict liability could be imposed only if defendants knew *at the time of performance* that their activity was in fact abnormally dangerous. Are they right? Discuss. (*T&E Industries v. Safety Light Corp.*, 587 A.2d 1249, N.J. Sup. Ct., 1991).

4. In facts similar to the previous case, Anspec Co. bought land from Ultraspherics, later selling the land to a third party and leasing it back from him. After Anspec had bought the property, Ultraspherics merged into Hoover Group, which was designated as the corporation to survive the merger. Hoover assumed all assets and liabilities of Ultraspherics. Johnson Controls is the sole shareholder of Hoover Group and of Ultraspherics' parent corporation, Hoover Universal. Before Anspec bought the property, Ultraspherics had disposed of hazardous waste on the site. The Michigan Department of Natural Resources notified Anspec of the contamination, and Anspec spent substantial amounts in response. Anspec sought reimbursement of these costs under CERCLA. Johnson Controls, Hoover Universal, and Hoover Group all moved to dismiss on grounds that they had not owned, occupied, or stored chemicals on the property. Is this a good defense? Discuss. (*The Anspec Co., Inc. v. Johnson Controls, Inc.,* 922 F.2d 1240, 6th Cir. 1991).

5. The plaintiff, Anthony, leased office space from the defendant, Commonwealth Enterprises, but a fire in the building caused exposure and release of asbestos material into the offices. The air was polluted, and asbestos dust contamination on the plaintiff's property made its use, movement, or removal hazardous. When the defendant refused to decontaminate the asbestos, the plaintiff hired consultants for the job. The plaintiff then sued the defendant under CERCLA for reimbursement of the costs incurred. Should the plaintiff recover? Discuss. (*Anthony v. Blech,* 760 F.Supp 832, C.D. Cal. 1991).

6. Arco and other oil companies were assessed monetary penalties under the Water Pollution Control Act Amendments of 1972 (later renamed the Clean Water Act). The penalties included the cost of cleaning up oil discharges. It appeared that Arco had spilled oil accidentally, reported the spill to appropriate authorities, and then cleaned the spill up at its own expense. Arco argued that imposition of the penalties on an "accidental, reporting self-cleaner" such as itself was a criminal penalty that denied due process. Is imposition of the fine unconstitutional? Discuss. (*United States v. Atlantic Richfield Co.,* 429 F.Supp. 830, E.D. Pa., 1977).

7. When OSHA set standards for cotton dust permissible in the air in plants preparing and manufacturing cotton, it set the level according to what would be economically feasible for the industry. The cotton industry challenged the standards on grounds that the costs imposed were excessive in relation to the health benefits gained. Does the failure to undertake a cost-benefit analysis render the standards invalid? Discuss. (*American Textile Manufacturers Institute v. Donovan,* 452 U.S. 490, 1981).

8. Union Electric Co., an electrical utility company servicing St. Louis and much of Missouri, was informed that sulfur dioxide emissions from its coal-fired generating plants violated the Missouri plant sulfur dioxide restrictions. Union claimed that it had encountered economic and technologic difficulties that made compliance with the emission limitations impossible. For example, it claimed that low-sulfur coal had become too scarce and expensive; that the installation of sulfur dioxide removal equipment would cost more than $500 million; and that to operate and maintain such equipment would cost more than $120 million a year. Should the EPA grant Union a variance if to do so would permit the company to operate? Discuss. (*Union Electric Co. v. EPA,* 427 U.S. 246, 1975).

9. An employee of Standard Oil of Kentucky accidentally left open a shut-off valve, causing a large quantity of aviation gasoline to flow in to the St. Johns River in Florida. The Rivers and Harbors Act of 1899 provides, in part, that "It shall not be lawful to throw, discharge, or deposit ... any refuse matter of any kind or description whatever other than that flowing from streets and sewers and passing therefrom in a liquid state, into any navigable water of the United States." Should commercially valuable gasoline be considered refuse for purposes of the Act, thus making Standard Oil guilty of a violation? Discuss. (*United States v. Standard Oil Co.,* 384 U.S. 224, 1966).

10. The EPA limited the rights of Quivera Mining Co. and Homestake Mining Co. to discharge pollutants into Arroyo del Puerto and San Mateo Creek. Because these were nearly dry "gullies," the companies challenged the EPA's order, pointing out that the Clean Water Act authorizes the EPA to regulate discharges only into "navigable waters." Was the EPA within its jurisdiction? Discuss. (*Quivera Mining Co. v. EPA,* 765 F.2d 126, 10th Cir. 1985).

CHAPTER 20

During recent years the creditor–debtor relationship has undergone a significant shift in emphasis from protection of the creditor to protection of the debtor in the consumer transaction, *in which a consumer borrows to purchase a product or purchases on credit. Consumer protection law is designed to protect the buyer–debtor from such*

things as **usury** *(lending money at interest rates higher than the law allows),* **excessive garnishments,** *and* **hidden costs** *in credit transactions. This is not to say that the creditor, or seller, is completely at the mercy of the buyer,*

CONSUMER TRANSACTIONS AND THE LAW

or debtor. However, the rights of the seller–creditor are defined by the numerous laws on the subject. Therefore, a knowledge of the basic provisions of consumer protection statutes is essential to the businessperson wanting to operate a commercially successful venture and, at the same time, conduct consumer transactions within the law.

The law of consumer transactions is primarily statutory. Consumers derive their rights and incur their obligations from the many state and federal statutes available for their benefit. Some laws protect consumers from false advertising and other deceptive practices. A number of statutes protect consumers in the financial dealings associated with borrowing or buying. Others afford protection in the purchasing process and set guidelines for the degree of performance and satisfaction it is reasonable to expect from a purchase. Finally, some statutes and a large body of case law relate to product safety. They provide a measure of protection against unsafe products and allow recovery for damages or injury caused by such products. Table 20.1 is a guide to some of the more important statutes. This information is important to all business students so that they may know their rights as consumers and their obligations as businesspersons.

The final portion of this chapter discusses bankruptcy law, an increasingly important area of the law for both individuals and businesses, debtors and creditors.

DECEPTIVE TRADE PRACTICES

A consumer who is misled by false advertising or other deceptive practices may have the right to sue under a common-law fraud theory or perhaps a breach of express warranty theory if the advertising involved a product. These theories have been discussed in earlier chapters.[1] However, two federal statutes help protect consumers from such deceptive practices without involving the consumers as plaintiffs. These are §5 of the Federal Trade Commission Act and §43(a) of the Lanham Act.

FEDERAL TRADE COMMISSION ACT

Section 5(a)(1) of the FTC Act declares invalid (1) unfair methods of competition and (2) unfair or deceptive acts or practices. Both must at least "affect" interstate commerce for federal jurisdiction to exist. Unfair methods of competition substantially duplicate the antitrust violations that were

---

[1] Fraud was covered in Chapter 9; products liability warranty claims were discussed in Chapter 11, along with the Magnuson-Moss Act and the Consumer Products Safety Act, which also protect consumers from dangerous products. Indeed, in Chapter 6 the *Sun and Sand Imports* case illustrated the CPSC in action to protect consumers from potentially dangerous products. Trademark law also naturally protects consumers. It was discussed in Chapter 12, along with regulation of deceptive advertising under the Lanham Act. Obviously, the law is a web of regulations with lots of overlap.

TABLE 20.1 Current Consumer Protection Statutes

POPULAR NAME	PURPOSE	REFERENCES
Child Protection and Toy Safety	Requires special labeling and child-proof devices	15 U.S.C.A. §§1261 et seq.
Cigarette Labeling and Advertising	Surgeon general's warning of possible health hazard	15 U.S.C.A. §§1331 et seq.
Consumer Credit Protection	Comprehensive protection, all phases of credit transactions	15 U.S.C.A. §§1601 et seq.
Consumer Leasing Act	Improves disclosure of true costs in leasing transactions	15 U.S.C.A. §§1667
Consumer Product Safety	Protects consumer against defective or dangerous products	15 U.S.C.A. §§2051 et seq.
Equal Credit Opportunity	Prohibits discrimination in extending credit	15 U.S.C.A. §1691
Fair Credit and Charge Card Disclosure	Allows consumers to comparison shop for credit	15 U.S.C.A. §1610
Fair Credit Reporting	Protects consumer's credit reputation	15 U.S.C.A. §1681
Fair Debt Collection Practices	Prohibits abuses by debt collectors	15 U.S.C.A. §1692
Fair Packaging and Labeling	Requires accurate name, weight, quantity	15 U.S.C.A. §§1451 et seq.
Federal Trade Commission	Prohibits unfair or deceptive trade practices	15 U.S.C.A. §45
Flammable Fabrics	Eliminates or controls manufacture and marketing of dangerous fabrics	15 U.S.C.A. §§1191 et seq.
Food, Drug, and Cosmetic	Prohibits marketing of impure, adulterated products	21 U.S.C.A §§301 et seq.
Fur Products Labeling	Prohibits misbranding of fur products	15 U.S.C.A. §69
Home Equity Loan Consumer Protection Act	Protects consumers who use homes as collateral	15 U.S.C.A. §1637a
Interstate Land Sales Act	Protects against land sale abuses	15 U.S.C.A. §1701
Lanham Act	Prohibits deceptive acts or practices in product sales	15 U.S.C.A. §43(a)
Magnuson-Moss Warranty	Governs content of warranties	15 U.S.C.A. §§2301 et seq.
National Traffic and Motor Vehicle Safety	Promotes traffic and auto safety	15 U.S.C.A. §§1381 et seq.
Real Estate Settlement Procedures	Requires disclosure of home buying costs	HUD Reg. X
Truth in Lending	Requires complete disclosure of credit terms	15 U.S.C.A. §§1601 et seq.
Uniform Commercial Code	Law of sales—unconscionable contracts	§2-302
Uniform Consumer Credit Code	Similar to federal Truth in Lending	9 states have adopted[a]

[a] Colorado, Idaho, Indiana, Iowa, Kansas, Maine, Oklahoma, Utah, and Wyoming have adopted substantial parts of some version of the Uniform Consumer Credit Code (UCCC).

covered earlier.[2] Our major concern in this chapter on consumer protection relates to the prohibition against "unfair or deceptive acts or practices."

Illicit Acts

Deceptive advertising is the main target of FTC concern in the realm of "unfair or deceptive acts or practices." With assistance from the courts, the FTC has prohibited and often punished (1) deceptive price advertising (e.g., advertising a sale as 20 percent off a "suggested retail price" when in fact the goods are hardly ever sold at that price); (2) affirmative product claims that cannot be substantiated (e.g. claiming without evidence that a mouthwash helps fight the common cold); (3) deceptive advertising demonstrations (e.g., claiming that a shaving cream moisturizes so well that sandpaper can easily be shaved, yet demonstrating this by passing a razor through loose sand scattered on plexiglass); (4) product endorsements by celebrities who do not really use the product; (5) failure to indicate the origin of foreign goods; (6) use of "no cholesterol" labels on food that, although literally true, still misled consumers into thinking that the products were also low in fat; (7) production of "infomercials"—half-hour television commercials designed to look like consumer programs rather than paid advertisements; and (8) product claims that tend to deceive, such as giving the name "Fresh Choice" to an orange juice made from concentrate.

The FTC's reach under §5 extends beyond deceptive advertising to other deceptive practices, including (1) "bait and switch" tactics (e.g., advertising a low-quality good at a low price to induce consumers to come to the store and then pressuring them to buy a higher-priced model); (2) deceptive debt collection practices (e.g., sending letters to delinquent creditors that promised that a suit would be filed if no payments were made when, in fact, a determination to sue had not been made); and (3) unfair door-to-door selling—the FTC has promulgated a rule allowing consumers three days to rescind purchases made in their homes from door-to-door salesmen.[3]

Enforcement

The FTC issues various rules, regulations, and guidelines regarding deceptive or unfair acts and practices. If the FTC discovers a potential violation, it can institute proceedings by filing a formal administrative complaint against the offender. The charge is normally heard before an FTC administrative law judge (ALJ), whose decision is reviewed by the FTC. The FTC's decisions may be reviewed by the courts.

Normally the FTC issues a "cease and desist" order to recalcitrant violators, ordering them to stop the deceptive acts or practices. Violation of such an order can precipitate fines of up to $10,000 per day. If the FTC has a strong case, an offender may agree to a "consent" order in which the FTC

---

[2] Antitrust law is discussed in Chapter 14.
[3] A similar provision under the Uniform Consumer Credit Code is discussed later in this chapter.

promises no further prosecution if the offender agrees to "go and sin no more."

In addition to obtaining injunctive orders from courts to support its cease and desist orders, the FTC is empowered to seek redress for consumers, perhaps in the form of refunds or cancellation of unfair contracts.

In the advertising cases, the FTC has occasionally ordered "corrective advertising" by a company that has long deceived the public. In such a case, the company must spend its own money to inform the public that its prior claims were untrue. "Multiproduct orders" are more frequently issued. Such an order is typically used against a company that has flagrantly engaged in falsely advertising a few of its products and is aimed at *all* the company's products. The rationale for such an order is that a company that has engaged flagrantly in the false advertising of some of its products is likely to do the same with others of its products.

Although the FTC Act is aimed primarily at false advertising, it has been applied to other types of behavior, as the following case illustrates.

ORKIN EXTERMINATING CO., INC. v. FTC

U.S. ELEVENTH CIRCUIT COURT OF APPEALS, 849 F.2d 1354 (1988)

In a series of promotions between 1968 and 1975, the defendant, Orkin, made guarantees of lifetime *termite control in exchange for timely payment of an annual fee that* would not be raised *unless the homeowner structurally modified the covered house. In 1978, Orkin decided that it could no longer afford to live up to this guarantee, so it substantially raised the annual fee on 207,000 contracts, pleading "inflation" as an excuse. Many customers complained, leading Orkin to roll back increases on 21,500 contracts. Those who did not complain or who did not have the documentation that Orkin required did not receive a rollback, however. Pursuant to its section 5 authority to block behavior constituting "unfair or deceptive" acts, the FTC ordered Orkin to rescind the price increases as to all the contracts. Orkin sought review of this order.*

CLARK, CIRCUIT JUDGE:

Section 5 declares that "unfair or deceptive acts or practices in or affecting commerce" are unlawful, 15 U.S.C. § 45(a)(1); it also empowers the Commission to prevent certain entities from engaging in behavior that constitutes "unfair or deceptive acts or practices." 15 U.S.C. § 45(a)(2)

Orkin contends that a "mere breach of contract," which does not involve some sort of deceptive or fraudulent behavior, is outside the ambit of section 5. In support of this proposition, Orkin cites cases that have interpreted state statutes similar to the FTCA, commonly referred to as "little" section 5 laws, to require "something more" than a simple breach of contract before a given course of conduct can be found "unfair or deceptive."

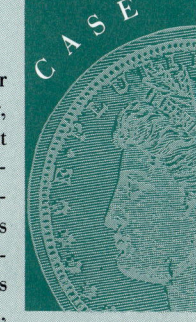

In 1980, the Commission promulgated a policy statement containing an abstract definition of "unfairness" which focuses upon unjustified customer injury. Under the standard enunciated in this policy statement.

[t]o justify a finding of unfairness the injury must satisfy three tests. It must be substantial; it must not be

CONTINUED

outweighed by any countervailing benefits to consumers or competition that the practice produces; and it must be an injury that consumers themselves could not reasonably have avoided.

The first prong of the unfairness standard requires a finding of substantial injury to consumers. In finding that Orkin's conduct has caused the requisite harm, the Commission said,

> The harm resulting from Orkin's conduct consists of increased costs for services previously bargained for and includes the intangible loss of the certainty of the fixed price term in the contract.

108 F.T.C. at 362. The Commission's finding of "substantial" injury is supported by the undisputed fact that Orkin's breach of its pre-1975 contracts generated, during a four-year period, more than $7,000,000 in revenues from renewal fees to which the Company was not entitled. As the Commission noted, although the actual injury to individual customers may be small on an annual basis, this does not mean that such injury is not "substantial."

As for the second prong of the unfairness standard, the Commission noted that "conduct can create a mixture of both beneficial and adverse consequences." But because "[t]he increase in the fee was not accompanied by an increase in the level of service provided or an enhancement of its quality," the Commission concluded that no consumer benefit had resulted from Orkin's conduct. The Commission also rejected various arguments that an order requiring Orkin to roll back its fee increases "would have adverse effects on its entire customer base and on many of its competitors." On appeal, Orkin has not challenged the Commission's conclusions regarding consumer benefits and benefits to competition.

With regard to the third prong of the unfairness standard, the Commission concluded that consumers could not have reasonably avoided the harm caused by Orkin's conduct. The Commission's focus on a consumer's ability to reasonably avoid injury "stems from the Commission's general reliance on free and informed consumer choice as the best regulator of the market." As the Commission explained, "Consumers may act to avoid injury before it occurs if they have reason to anticipate the impending harm and the means to avoid it, or they may seek to mitigate the damage afterward if they are aware of potential avenues toward that end." 108 F.T.C. at 366.

The Commission determined that "neither anticipatory avoidance nor subsequent mitigation was reasonably possible for Orkin's pre-1975 customers." *Id.* at 366. Anticipatory avoidance through consumer choice was impossible because these contracts give no indication that the company would raise the renewal fees as a result of inflation, or for any other reason.

As for mitigation of consumer injury, the Commission concluded that the company's "accommodation program" could not constitute an avenue for avoiding injury because relief from Orkin's conduct was available only to those customers who complained about the increases in the renewal fees.

There remains, however, the question whether this case represents a significant departure from prior Commission precedent. We note what has been written in a recent law review article:

> Some of the oldest "unfairness" decisions involve sellers' refusals to live up to the terms of their contract. The Commission has often challenged sellers for traditional breaches of contract: failure to fill orders, delivery of inferior merchandise, refusal to return goods taken for repair, or refusal to return promised deposits. Recent trade regulation rules have focused on similar issues. These actions have attracted little controversy. Breach of contract has long been condemned as a matter of law economics, and public policy.

Craswell, 1981 Wis.L.Rev. at 128–29.

An adoption of Orkin's position would mean that the Commission could never proscribe widespread breaches of retail consumer contracts unless there was evidence of deception or fraud. The statutory scheme at issue here "necessarily gives the Commission an influential role in interpreting section 5 and in applying it to facts of particular cases arising out of *unprecedented situations.*" *F.T.C. v. Colgate-Palmolive Co.*, 380 U.S. 374, 385, (1965).

This case may be "unprecedented" to the extent it concerns non-deceptive contract breaches. But given the extraordinary level of consumer injury which Orkin has caused and the fact that deceptiveness is often not a component of the unfairness inquiry, we think the limitation of the Commission's section 5 authority urged by Orkin would be

CONTINUED

inconsistent with the broad mandate conferred upon the Commission by Congress. Thus, because the Commission's decision fully and clearly comports with the standard set forth in its Policy Statement, we conclude that the Commission acted with its section 5 authority.

Orkin's final argument is that the Commission erred in declining to consider evidence that it relied, in good faith, upon advice of counsel when it decided to increase its annual renewal fees. Orkin's reliance upon counsel—a fact we assume—is irrelevant to an action brought pursuant to section 5. The unfairness standard, focusing as it does upon consumer injury, does not take into account the mental state of the party accused of a section 5 violation. "The purpose of the Federal Trade Commission Act is to protect the public, not punish the wrong doer...." *Regina Corp. v. F.T.C.*, 322 F.2d 765, 768 (3d Cir. 1963).

[The FTC's injunction order is upheld.]

LANHAM ACT

The Lanham Act is another important federal act that outlaws "any false description or representation" in connection with any person's goods, services, or commercial activities. The pertinent provisions of section 43(a) of the Lanham Act have been discussed in Chapter 12 and will not be repeated here.

CONSUMER CREDIT PROTECTION ACT

It is a fairly easy matter for the average householder to obtain and use any number of credit cards. The cash purchase of major appliances and automobiles is now a rare occurrence. The proliferation of credit has required legislation to define the rights and obligations of those who deal in it.

Congress enacted the Consumer Credit Protection Act (CCPA) in 1968 in response to unscrupulous and predatory practices on the part of creditors extending credit in consumer transactions. Congress was concerned with consumer credit disclosure methods, credit advertising, garnishment methods, questionable procedures used by some credit reporting agencies, and certain debt collection practices (a problem recognized in a 1977 amendment to the act).

TRUTH IN LENDING

Before the **truth-in-lending** portion of the CCPA was passed in 1969, it was very difficult for consumers to understand what they were being charged for borrowing money or buying on time. Some lenders or sellers on credit would quote a "discount," others would refer to an "add on," and still others to various fees plus "simple interest." Some would quote monthly rates, whereas others quoted annual rates. The purpose of the Truth in Lending Act (TILA) is not to limit interest rates but to mandate disclosure of the true cost

Coverage

TILA as amended, applies to credit transactions involving personal, family, or household purposes. Loans for commercial or agricultural purposes are not covered. And because Congress assumed that borrowers of large sums can protect themselves, TILA only applies to consumer loans not exceeding $25,000. Unlike many other consumer protection statutes, however, TILA also applies to credit secured by real property or a dwelling, such as a mortgage loan. There is no ceiling amount for this type of transaction; TILA applies even if the amount involved exceeds $25,000.

Only natural persons are protected by TILA's provisions. Debtors such as corporations or other organizations are not protected. All creditors who in the ordinary course of business lend money or sell on credit must comply with TILA provisions. TILA would not, however, apply to one consumer's loan to another.

Disclosure

TILA is primary a disclosure act. It is clarified by Regulation Z, a set of rules promulgated by the Federal Reserve Board. TILA's two key disclosure requirements relate to the **annualized percentage rate (APR),** which is the yearly cost of credit calculated on a uniform basis, and the *finance charge,* which is any additional amount the consumer pays as a result of buying on credit instead of paying cash. Examples of a finance charge would include application and processing charges such as a loan origination fee charged by mortgage lenders, investigation or credit reporting fees, and premiums for required credit insurance.

All disclosures must be written, clear, and conspicuous. The APR and finance charge must be more conspicuous than the other required disclosures.

Specific disclosure requirements are keyed to the type of transaction. On the one hand is an *open-end* (revolving) transaction, such as a gasoline credit card or VISA and MasterCard. On the other hand are all transactions other than open-end, usually characterized as closed-end (installment) sales or loans with a fixed number of payments. If repeated transactions are reasonably expected by the creditor, the open-end requirements apply.

In an open-end transaction, there are two types of required disclosure—an initial disclosure and periodic supplementary disclosures. The initial disclosure, which should be made before the first transaction, is general in nature, covering important terms of the credit plan rather than specific transactions. Required initial disclosures include (1) a statement of when finance charges begin to accrue, including any "free-ride" period; (2) the APR; (3) in a variable rate plan, conditions under which the interest rate may increase; (4) an explanation of the method used to determine the balance on which the finance charge may be computed and of how the amount of finance charge will be determined; (5) conditions under which the creditor may acquire a security interest in the debtor's property; and (6) a statement of the debtor's billing rights.

Creditors in open-end transactions must also make periodic disclosures at the end of each billing cycle. These disclosures are geared to the specific transactions that have occurred, and include such things as (1) the account balance at the beginning of the cycle; (2) identification of each transaction with descriptions of date, amount, and creditor; (3) the periodic rates that may be used to compute the finance charge and corresponding APR; (4) amounts of other charges; (5) account balance as of the closing date of the cycle; (6) any free-ride period; and (7) an address to be used for notice of billing errors. These disclosures are contained in the monthly statements credit card holders receive.

Disclosures in a closed-end transaction are somewhat different. They must be made before consummation of the transaction in question. An important concept is the "federal box." The written disclosures should, by use of lines, a separate sheet of paper, boldface type, or the like, call attention to the required TILA disclosures. If the creditor puts too much information in the "federal box," thus detracting from attention given the required federal disclosures, a TILA violation occurs just the same as if insufficient information is disclosed.

Among the required disclosures in a closed-end transaction are (1) the creditor's identity; (2) the amount financed and how it is computed; (3) the finance charge and APR (and circumstances under which it may be increased); (4) number, amounts, and timing of payments; (5) total dollar value of all payments; and (6) effect of prepayment.

Substantive Provisions

Although TILA is primarily a disclosure statute, it does shape some credit practices through substantive provisions. For example, it provides a three-day right of rescission for consumers who use their residence to secure credit in a nonpurchase money transaction. The rule does not apply to the first mortgage, issued when a house is purchased. But assume a homeowner contracts to buy a new air conditioner on credit. If the credit purchase is secured by the retailer's receiving a second mortgage on the residence, the right of rescission would apply. Absent an emergency, the seller should not deliver goods or perform services during that three-day period.

TILA also contains certain rules regarding how credit may be advertised. Again, the purpose is to create uniform, clear statements that will allow for comparison shopping. Furthermore, TILA contains numerous provisions regarding use of credit cards, even when no finance charge exists. One such provision is the $50 maximum ceiling for credit card holder liability, which is discussed later in this chapter.

Enforcement

Various federal agencies, most importantly the FTC, enforce the civil provisions of TILA, and the Department of Justice can bring criminal charges for TILA violations. The maximum criminal penalty is one year in jail and/or a $5,000 fine for *each* violation.

Consumers are accorded a private right of action under TILA and may recover their actual damages *plus* two times the finance charge (not to be less than $100 nor more than $1,000) and attorneys' fees. Suit should be brought within one year of a disclosure violation. The statute of limitations in a case involving a house being used as collateral is three years from the date of violation. TILA also contains a limited good-faith defense, which is applied in the following case.

HENDLEY V. CAMERON-BROWN CO.

U.S. ELEVENTH CIRCUIT COURT OF APPEALS, 840 F.2d 831 (1988)

On April 1, 1984, the Hendleys and the Blacks (appellants) obtained discounted variable rate mortgage loans from Cameron-Brown Co. (appellee) to finance the purchase of their homes. The loans featured an annual adjustment of the interest rate. The annual interest rate was based on an "index plus margin" formula that was determined by adding to the margin, then at 2.79 percent, the current index (subject to a 2 percent annual cap and an overall cap of 5.75 percent for the lifetime of the loan). Appellants claim they were told that the interest rate would adjust annually in the same direction as the index.

At the end of the first year, appellee informed appellants that the interest rate for the second year would increase from 9.875 percent to 11.875 percent. Appellee claims that this increase was based on the "index plus margin" formula checked by the 2 percent cap.

Objecting to this increase, appellants filed this suit claiming that appellee had violated TILA's disclosure requirements. Because the index actually declined in the second year from 10.53 percent to 9.61 percent, appellants maintain that the increase is inconsistent with the disclosure statement's language that the interest rate would be adjusted annually in the same direction as the index. Appellants argue that appellee failed to disclose the initial index and that the initial interest rate was discounted (lower than it would have been if it had been calculated by using the "index plus margin" formula).

The trial court granted summary judgment to appellee, finding that it had "technically complied" with TILA and that any deficiencies were protected by its "good-faith" effort at complying with relatively new rules. Appellants appealed.

VANCE, CIRCUIT JUDGE:

Congress enacted the Truth In Lending Act to ensure meaningful disclosures in consumer credit transactions. The Federal Reserve Board ("Board") promulgated Regulation Z to execute the purposes of the Truth In Lending Act. The Board established the disclosure requirements for variable rate loans in 12 C.F.R. § 226.18(f). This provision provides:

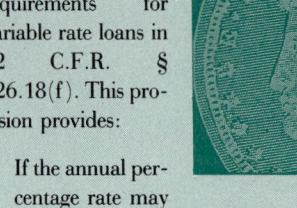

> If the annual percentage rate may increase after consummation, the following disclosures [are required]:
> (1) The circumstances under which the rate may increase.
> (2) Any limitations on the increase.
> (3) The effect of an increase.
> (4) An example of the payment terms that would result from an increase.

We hold that appellee did not comply with the first requirement by fully disclosing the "circumstances under which the rate may increase." The disclosure statement provided that "the interest rate may increase during the term of this transaction if the index increases." This, however, was not the only circumstance which could cause an increase in the interest rate. As the district court stated, "The problem is that the statement fails to note that the initial interest rate is discounted, creating the possibility of an increase even when the index does not

CONTINUED

rise." Due to the initial discounted interest rate, the annual interest rate could increase if the index remained constant, or even if the index declined. Absent this information, the disclosure failed to meet regulatory standards.

Appellee argues that at the time these transactions occurred the Board had recently amended its official staff interpretation of regulation § 226.18(f) to explain its application to discounted variable rate loans. The amended interpretation required the disclosure to "reflect a composite annual percentage rate based on the initial rate for as long as it is charged and, for the remainder of the term, the rate that would have been applied using the index or formula at the time of consummation." Appellee maintains that this amended interpretation was only optionally effective on April 1, 1984, and that due to the "dramatic change in the disclosure requirements" appellee was not required to go beyond the requirements of the existing interpretation. Regardless of the effective date of the amended interpretation, however, the regulation's requirements did not change and we believe that appellee failed to comply with the clear disclosure requirements of the regulations.

Appellee also argues that even if the disclosure were improper, it is insulated from liability under 15 U.S.C. § 1640(f) because it acted in good faith in accordance with the Board's official interpretation of regulation § 226.18(f). Section 1640(f) provides:

> No provision of this section, section 1607(b), section 1607(c), section 1607(e), or section 1611 of this title imposing any liability shall apply to any act done or omitted in good faith in conformity with any rule, regulation, or interpretation thereof by the Board or in conformity with any interpretation or approval by an official or employee of the Federal Reserve System duly authorized by the Board to issue such interpretations or approvals under such procedures as the Board may prescribe therefor, notwithstanding that after such act or omission has occurred, such rule, regulations, interpretation, or approval is amended, rescinded, or determined by judicial or other authority to be invalid for any reason.

Section 1640(f) "does not protect a creditor who *fails* to conform with a regulation or interpretation through an honest, good faith mistake." *Cox v. First Nat'l Bank of Cincinnati*, 751 F.2d 815, 825 (6th Cir. 1985). So a creditor's honest and reasonable but mistaken interpretation is not protected. Appellee's belief that the regulation did not require further disclosure based on its mistaken interpretation of the regulation and reliance on an inapplicable interpretation does not protect it from liability. As a matter of law, the section 1640(f) good faith defense is not available.

[Reversed.]

HOME EQUITY LOAN CONSUMER PROTECTION ACT

Consumers occasionally use their homes as security when applying for open-end credit. The consequences for the homeowner who defaults on such a loan are obviously quite significant. Therefore, in an amendment to TILA, Congress passed the Home Equity Loan Consumer Protection Act of 1988 (HELCPA). Basically, this act requires lenders to provide an application-stage disclosure statement in addition to a consumer education pamphlet whenever a consumer puts up his or her "principal dwelling" (defined, unusually, to include second or vacation homes) as security for open-end credit. In addition to a broad range of disclosure requirements, HELCPA also contains several substantive provisions, including (1) restrictions on the creditor's ability to change unilaterally the plan's terms; (2) limitations on grounds for terminating the loan and requiring immediate repayment of the balance ("acceleration"); and (3) requirements that an external, publicly available index or formula be used if the home equity plan allows for rate changes.

RESTRICTIONS ON GARNISHMENT

Garnishment can be defined as the legal proceedings of a judgment creditor to require a third person owing money to the debtor or holding property belonging to the debtor to turn over to the court or sheriff the property or money for the satisfaction of the judgment. Congressional hearings leading to the enactment of the CCPA revealed that the unrestricted garnishment of wages encouraged predatory extension of credit, that employers were often quick to discharge an employee whose wages were garnished, and that the laws of the states on the subject were so different they effectively destroyed the uniformity of the bankruptcy laws and defeated their purpose. Consequently, the CCPA section on garnishment set limits on the extent to which the wages of an individual could be garnished. In general, wages cannot be garnished in any workweek in excess of 25 percent of the individual's disposable (after-tax) earnings or the amount by which the disposable earnings for that workweek exceed 30 times the federal minimum hourly wage, whichever is less. Such restrictions do not apply in the case of a court order for the support of any person (wife or child, for example), any order of a court of bankruptcy under Chapter 13, Adjustment of Debts of an Individual with Regular Income, of the Federal Bankruptcy Act, or any debt due for state or federal taxes.

Of particular interest to students is that in the 1991 Federal Unemployment Benefits Bill, Congress authorized a 10 percent garnishment of wages of persons who are more than 180 days behind in repayment of student loans.

FAIR CREDIT REPORTING ACT

The section of the CCPA known as the Fair Credit Reporting Act is directed at consumer reporting agencies. It is an effort by Congress to ensure that the elaborate mechanism developed for investigating and evaluating the credit worthiness, credit standing, credit capacity, character, and general reputation of consumers is fair with respect to the confidentiality, accuracy, relevance, and proper use of the reported information. Too often in the past, the consumer was denied credit because of misleading or inaccurate information supplied to a prospective creditor by a consumer reporting agency.[4] The effect could be devastating, particularly as it affected the consumer's credit standing and general reputation in the business community.

The information on individual consumers is derived from many sources, including creditors and court and other official records, and, in many cases, from facts consumers supply themselves. Information accumulated in a **consumer report** and disseminated to users can and often does include such items as judgments, liens, bankruptcies, arrest records, and employment history. In addition, the Fair Credit Reporting Act covers the **investigative reports** made by credit reporting agencies. Often used by prospective employers or by insurance companies, investigative reports are more personal in nature than consumer reports and can contain information on the subject's

---

[4] This is not an agency of the government. Such agencies are persons or businesses that regularly assemble credit information and provide it to others for a fee.

personal habits, marital status (past and present), education, political affiliation, and so on.

With regard to both consumer reports and investigative reports, the law requires that, on request and proper identification, consumers are entitled to know the nature and substance of all information about them (except medical information) in the agency's file, the sources of the information, and the identity of those who have received the report from the credit reporting agency. Those entitled to receive consumer reports include business that may want to extend credit to the consumer, prospective employers or insurers, and government licensing agencies that may be concerned with the financial responsibility of the consumer. Access to the information can also be gained by court order. In addition, an investigative report cannot be prepared on an individual consumer unless that person is first notified and given the right to request information on the nature and scope of the pending investigation.

An important provision of the act requires that all information in consumer reports be current and that consumer reporting agencies maintain reasonable procedures designed to avoid violations of certain other provisions. This is obvious effort to reduce the incidence of carelessly prepared reports having inaccurate information.

Finally, civil penalties for a *negligent* violation of the act include the actual damages to the consumer and, in a successful action, court costs and reasonable attorneys' fees. In case of *willful* noncompliance, punitive damages may also be awarded to the successful plaintiff–consumer. Administrative enforcement of the act is a function of the FTC because violations are considered unfair or deceptive acts or practices.

CASE

COMEAUX v. BROWN & WILLIAMSON TOBACCO CO.

U.S. COURT OF APPEALS, NINTH CIRCUIT 915 F.2d 1264 (1990)

The defendant, B&W, offered the plaintiff, Comeaux, a job. Comeaux accepted, gave notice to his then-current employer, and moved to Fremont, California, where the job was. While Comeaux made these arrangements, B&W ran a credit check on Comeaux without telling him that it was going to do so or that the results could affect his employment. The credit report from Trans Union Credit Information Co. revealed that Comeaux had a poor credit history. B&W then told Comeaux that it would not hire him. Comeaux sued B&W, inter alia, *for breach of contract. In February 1988, soon after the lawsuit was filed, B&W ran a second credit check on Comeaux, not because it was considering hiring him but to prepare for the litigation. When Comeaux learned of this, he amended his complaint to add a claim for violation of the FCRA.

The trial judge granted B&W summary judgment on all claims. Comeaux appealed. [The following portion of the court's opinion addresses only the FCRA claim.]

CONTINUED

SNEED, CIRCUIT JUDGE:

The FCRA provides for civil and criminal penalties for those who do not comply with the Act. Sections 1681n and 1681o, respectively, make consumer reporting agencies and users liable for willful or negligent noncompliance with "any requirement" imposed under the Act. Section 1681q provides a criminal penalty for "knowingly and willfully obtain[ing] information on a consumer from a consumer reporting agency under false pretenses." Noncompliance with 1681q thereby forms a basis for civil liability under 1681n.

B&W told Trans Union that it wanted the February 1988 credit report on Comeaux "for employment purposes." The record before us establishes that this statement was false, even though B&W claimed at one stage in the litigation that it was true. Thus, B&W requested the report under false pretenses, thereby violating section 1681q and providing Comeaux with a cause of action under section 1681n or 1681o.

B&W argues, however, that its receipt and use of the February 1988 credit report is not governed by the FCRA, which only regulates "consumer reports." It claims that the report was not a consumer report because it sought the report for a *non-consumer* purpose. The term "consumer report" is defined in section 1681a(d). [Its] plain language reveals that a credit report will be construed as a "consumer report" under the FCRA if the credit bureau providing the information *expects* the user to use the report for a purpose permissible under the FCRA, without regard to the ultimate purpose to which the report is *actually* put. B&W's construction of the statute [which the district court adopted] would render meaningless the FCRA's goal of allowing the release of credit reports for certain purposes only.

If a consumer reporting agency provides a report based on a reasonable expectation that the report will be put to a use permissible under the FCRA, then that report is a "consumer report" under the FCRA and the ultimate use to which the report is actually put is irrelevant to the question of whether the FCRA governs the report's use and the user's conduct.

[The district court's summary judgment order on the FCRA claim is REVERSED.]

CREDIT CARDS

The widespread use of credit cards, issued by all manner of companies, created much legal controversy when a card fell into the wrong hands through loss or theft. Many companies provided their credit cards indiscriminately to any person who might want one and to many who had not requested them. It became a major problem to determine who was to assume the liability for unauthorized credit card purchases: the person to whom the card was issued, the unauthorized user, the merchant who made the sale, or the credit card issuer. Congress addressed the problem in CCPA provisions that prohibit the issuance of credit cards except in response to a request or application and that place limits on the liability of a cardholder for its unauthorized use. In general, if a cardholder loses a credit card and it is used by someone without authority to do so, the cardholder is liable if (1) the liability does not exceed $50; (2) the card is an accepted card; (3) the issuer has given notice to the cardholder as to the potential liability; (4) the issuer has provided the cardholder with a self-addressed, prestamped notification to be mailed, by the cardholder in the event of loss or theft; (5) the unauthorized use occurs before the cardholder has notified the issuer that an unauthorized use of the card has occurred; and (6) the card issuer has provided a method whereby the user of the card can be identified by the merchant, either by photograph or signature, as the authorized user.

The above provisions are for the protection of a lawful cardholder. Unauthorized use of a credit card can result in severe penalties. If the unauthorized transaction involves goods or services, or both, having a retail value of $5,000 or more, the penalty can be a fine of up to $10,000 or imprisonment for up to five years, or both.

CASE

TOWERS WORLD AIRWAYS v. PHH AVIATION SYSTEMS

U.S. COURT OF APPEALS, SECOND CIRCUIT 933 F.2d 174 (1991)

In February 1988, the plaintiff, PHH, issued a credit card to the defendants, Towers World Airways, to buy fuel and other aircraft-related goods and services for a corporate jet leased by Towers from PHH. World Jet Corporation, a subsidiary of United Air Fleet, was responsible for maintaining the aircraft. An officer of Towers designated Schley, an employee of World Jet, as the chief pilot of the leased jet and gave him permission to make purchases with the PPH credit card at least in connection with **noncharter flights, which were used exclusively by Towers executives.** Notwithstanding United Air Fleet's promise to pay the cost of fuel on chartered flights, Schley used the credit card to charge $89,025.87 to Towers in connection with such flights before the card's cancellation.

Towers filed suit seeking a declaratory judgment absolving it of liability for all improperly charged amounts. PHH counterclaimed for recovery of the $89,025.87 in unpaid charges. The district court granted PHH summary judgment on Towers' claims and entered judgment for PHH on its counterclaim against Towers for the full amount. Claiming that its liability is limited to $50, Towers appealed.

NEWMAN, CIRCUIT JUDGE:

The [1970 amendments to TILA] enacted a scheme for limiting the liability of cardholders for all charges by third parties made without "actual, implied or apparent authority" and "from which the cardholder receives no benefit." Where an unauthorized use has occurred, the cardholder can be held liable only up to a limit of $50 for the amount charged on the card, if certain conditions are satisfied.

By defining "unauthorized use" as that lacking in "actual, implied, or apparent authority," Congress apparently contemplated, and courts have accepted, primary reliance on background principles of agency law in determining the liability of cardholders for charges incurred by third-party card bearers. [Because of conflicting testimony as to what Towers' agent told Schley,] we cannot affirm the grant of summary judgment on the theory that Schley possessed express or implied authority.

Unlike express or implied authority, however, apparent authority exists entirely apart from the principal's manifestations of consent to the agent. Rather, the cardholder, as principal, creates apparent authority through words or conduct that, reasonably interpreted by a third party from whom the card bearer makes purchases, indicate that the card user acts with the cardholder's consent. Though a cardholder's relinquishment of possession may create in another the appearance of authority to use the card, the statute clearly precludes a finding of apparent authority where the transfer of the card was without the cardholder's consent, as in cases involving theft, loss, or fraud.

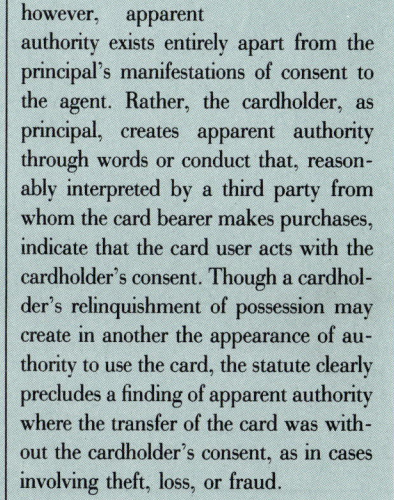

Because the statute provides no guidance as to uses arising from the *voluntary* transfer of credit cards, the general principles of agency law govern disputes over whether a resulting use was unauthorized. These disputes frequently involve, as in this case, a cardholder's claim that the card bearer was given permission to use a card for only a limited purpose and that subsequent charges exceeded

CONTINUED

the consent originally given by the cardholder. Acknowledging the absence of express or implied authority for the additional charges, several state courts have ... declined to apply the Truth-in-Lending Act to limit the cardholder's liability, reasoning that the cardholder's voluntary relinquishment of the card for one purpose gives the bearer apparent authority to make additional charges.

Though we agree that a cardholder, in lending or giving his card for one purpose, acts in a way that significantly contributes to the appearance of authority, at least as perceived by the third-party merchant, to make other purchases, we need not decide whether voluntary relinquishment for one purpose creates in every case apparent authority to incur other charges. In the pending case, the appearance of authority for Schley to purchase fuel on chartered flights was established not only by Towers' consent to Schley's unrestricted access to the PHH card but by only conduct and circumstances as well.

Nothing about the PHH card or the circumstances surrounding the purchases gave fuel sellers reason to distinguish the clearly authorized fuel purchases made in connection with non-charter flights from the purchases for chartered flights. It was the industry custom to entrust credit cards used to make airplane-related purchases to the pilot of the plan. By designating Schley as the pilot and subsequently giving him the card, Towers thereby imbued him with more apparent authority than might arise from voluntary relinquishment of a credit card in other contexts. In addition, with Towers' blessing Schley had used the card, which was inscribed with the registration number of the Gulfstream jet, to purchase fuel on non-charter flights for the same plane. The only differences between these uses expressly authorized and those new claimed to be unauthorized—the identity of the passengers—was insufficient to provide notice to those who sold the fuel that Schley lacked authority for the charter flight purchases.

Towers contends that, despite its own failure to have the card cancelled, once PPH, as the card issuer, learned, either through Towers or a third party, that Schley lacked authority to make certain charges, any such transaction that Schley entered into becomes an unauthorized use even if fuel sellers reasonably perceived that Schley had apparent authority to charge fuel purchases. Whether notifying the card issuer that some uses (or users) of a card are unauthorized makes them so has divided those courts that have considered the issue.

The rule of agency law contained in section 166 of the *Restatement* would permit the principal to qualify the authority of an agent to make purchases from a merchant by giving the merchant notice of the limitation. But to whatever extent a cardholder can limit the authority of a card user by giving notice to a merchant, we do not believe he can accomplish a similar limitation by giving notice to a card issuer. In four-party arrangements of this sort, it is totally unrealistic to burden the card issuer with the obligation to convey to numerous merchants whatever limitations the cardholder has placed on the card user's authority.

Because the disputed charges were not unauthorized, PHH was entitled to recover their full value from Towers under their credit agreement. [Affirmed.]

FAIR CREDIT AND CHARGE CARD DISCLOSURE ACT

Concerned over high interest rates charged credit card borrowers, Congress considered enacting a ceiling on such charges, but ultimately decided that competition was the best regulation. Therefore, to enable consumers to better comparison shop, Congress enacted the Fair Credit and Charge Card Disclosure Act (FCCCDA) of 1988 (an amendment to TILA), which requires disclosure of certain key items of information at the solicitation and application stages for credit and charge card accounts.

The amount of disclosure required varies with the type of solicitation. Direct mail applications and solicitations must disclose more information, for

HUMOR AND THE LAW

Consumer disputes over trivial matters often erupt into litigation. Anyone who wishes to pay the filing fee may initiate a lawsuit. Fortunately, courts have various tools at their disposal to justify dismissal or meritless claims. Truly insignificant claims are often dismissed on grounds of the doctrine *de minimis non curat lex*—"the law does not concern itself with trifles." This is a handy doctrine to know, especially because it allows you to understand the following limerick, quoted by a judge in an indecent exposure case:

> There was a defendant named Rex
> With a miniscule organ of sex.
> When jailed for exposure
> He said with composure,
> De minimis non curat lex.

U.S. v. Irving, No. 76–151 (E.D.Cal. 1977)

---

example, than solicitations made by telephone or through ads contained in magazines. A complete catalogue of the required disclosures would be too lengthy to repeat here. However, among the key disclosures that must be made in connection with a direct mail solicitation for a *credit card* are (1) each periodic rate of finance charge expressed as an annual percentage rate; (2) if the plan includes a variable rate of interest, the fact that the rate may vary, how the rate is determined, and the APR in effect within 30 days before the time of the mailing; (3) any annual or other periodic fee imposed for issuance of the credit card; (4) any transaction fee imposed in connection with purchase transactions; and (5) any minimum or fixed finance charge that could be imposed during a billing cycle. These and other "core disclosures" must be placed in a prominent location either on or with the application or solicitation.

Less onerous disclosures are required for applications or solicitations for a "charge card," defined as "a card, plate, or other single credit device that may be used from time to time to obtain credit which is *not* subject to a finance charge." The act also requires disclosure of any fees charged to renew a credit or charge card account. Atypically, it preempts rather than supplements state laws in the area.

FAIR DEBT COLLECTION PRACTICES ACT

The Fair Debt Collection Practices Act has as its purpose the elimination of abusive debt collection practices by debt collectors and the protection of individual debtors against debt collection abuses. The following excerpt from *Duty v. General Finance Co.*, 273 S.W.2d 64 (Tex. 1954), illustrates some of the tactics used by an overzealous debt collector. It is important to note that each and every tactic employed by the General Finance Company debt collector is now prohibited by the Fair Debt Collection Practices Act.

> *The harassment alleged may be summarized as follows: Daily telephone calls to both Mr. & Mrs. Duty which extended to great length; threatening to blacklist them with the Merchants' Retail Credit Association; accusing them of being deadbeats; talking to them in a harsh, insinuating, loud voice; stating to their neighbors and employers that they were deadbeats; asking Mrs. Duty what she was doing with her money; accusing her of spending money in other ways than in payments on the loan transaction; threatening to cause both plaintiffs to lose their jobs unless they made the payments demanded; calling each of the plaintiffs at the respective places of their employment several times daily; threatening to garnish their wages; berating plaintiffs to their fellow employees; requesting their employers to require them to pay; calling on them at their work; flooding them with a barrage of demand letters, duncards, special delivery letters, and telegrams both at their homes and their places of work; sending them cards bearing this opening statement. "Dear Customer: We made you a loan because we thought that you were honest"; sending telegrams and special delivery letters to them at approximately midnight, causing them to be awakened from their sleep; calling a neighbor in the disguise of a sick brother of one of the plaintiffs, and on another occasion as a stepson; calling Mr. Duty's mother at her place of employment in Wichita Falls long distance, collect; leaving red cards in their door, with insulting notes on the back and thinly-veiled threats; calling Mr. Duty's brother long distance, collect, in Albuquerque, New Mexico, at his residence at a cost to him in excess of $11, and haranguing him about the alleged balance owed by plaintiffs.*

The debt collector's communications with others and with the debtor in an effort to locate the debtor are governed by a provision of the act. The debt collector is prohibited from making false representations or misleading the debtor about the nature of the collection process. The collector cannot solicit or take from any person a check postdated by more than five days without notice of the intent to deposit the check. On occasion, debt collectors have encouraged the debtor to write a postdated check for the amount of the debt knowing that the debtor had insufficient funds to cover the check. A threat to deposit the postdated check was often enough to compel the debtor to seek the funds necessary to pay the collector and thereby avoid criminal prosecution for issuing a bad check. The act further provides that written notice of the amount of the debt and the name of the creditor be sent to the customer together with a statement that, unless the consumer disputes the validity of the debt within 30 days, the debt collector can assume it is a valid obligation. If the consumer owes multiple debts and makes a single payment, the debt collector cannot apply the payment to any debt that is disputed by the consumer.[5]

---

[5] This provision may be contrary to a commonly accepted principle of contract law: Where a debtor owes multiple debts and fails to specify to which debt the payment is to be applied, the creditor can make the choice.

The Fair Debt Collection Practices Act protects the consumer–debtor and places significant burdens on the debt collector. Compliance with the act is enforced by the Federal Trade Commission, because violations are considered to be unfair or deceptive trade practices. A debt collector who fails to comply with the provisions of the act may incur civil liability to the extent of actual damages sustained by the plaintiff, additional punitive damages not to exceed $1,000, and court costs and reasonable attorneys' fees.

FAIR CREDIT BILLING

Before the Fair Credit Billing Act, the burden of resolving a billing dispute rested mainly on the customer–debtor. This is no longer true. The Fair Credit Billing Act requires that creditors maintain procedures whereby consumers can complain about billing errors and obtain satisfaction within a specified period, not later than two billing cycles or 90 days. The consumer must give the creditor notice of the billing error with a statement explaining the reasons for questioning the item or items felt to be in error. The creditor must then either make appropriate corrections in the consumer's account or conduct an investigation into the matter. If, after the investigation, the creditor feels that the statement is accurate, it must so notify the debtor and explain why it believes the original statement of account to be correct. The act also requires that payments be credited promptly and that any overpayment be refunded (on request by the debtor) or credited to the debtor's account.

EQUAL CREDIT OPPORTUNITY

The Equal Credit Opportunity Act (ECOA), as amended, quite simply prohibits discrimination based on race, color, religion, national origin, sex, marital status, or age in connection with extensions of credit. The applicant must, however, have contractual capacity; minors, for example, cannot insist on credit under the act. The enactment is the result of complaints by married persons that credit frequently was denied unless both parties to the marriage obligated themselves. Each party can now separately and voluntarily apply for and obtain credit accounts, and state laws prohibiting separate credit no longer apply. The act also directs the Board of Governors of the Federal Reserve System to establish a Consumer Advisory Council to provide advice and consultation on consumer credit and other matters. The following case offers an interesting application of the ECOA.

CASE

UNITED STATES v. AMERICAN FUTURE SYSTEMS, INC.

U.S. THIRD CIRCUIT COURT OF APPEALS, 743 F.2d 169 (1984)

American Future Systems, Inc. (AFS), sells china, cookware, crystal, and tableware, 95 percent of the time on credit. AFS markets its wares through three separate programs. Its summer program targets as preferred customers single white women between the ages of 18 and 21 years who live at home. AFS hopes parents will co-sign the order but will extend credit and automatically ship goods to the buyer even without a co-signature. Nonpreferred customers, almost always young black women, are extended credit only after a satisfactory credit check. If the buyer does not pass the check, goods will not be shipped. AFS sales employees are urged to sell only in areas believed to be all or predominantly white and work under commission arrangements that encourage sales to whites.

AFS's winter program has two aspects. Its preferred sales targets are single white women in their final three years of college. They are given immediate credit and the ordered goods are shipped to them immediately, regardless of age, credit histories, or any other normal indicia of creditworthiness. Nonpreferred customers for the winter program include all minorities, men, married persons, and freshmen in college. AFS will not ship goods to these customers until they have made three successive monthly payments. Although these customers are led to believe they are being treated the same as other AFS customers, AFS has made a marketing judgment to prefer white women.

The Department of Justice sued AFS, its president, and an affiliated company, claiming violation of the ECOA. AFS defended, claiming that minority customers are, as a group, less creditworthy than their white counterparts. AFS could produce no reliable evidence to support this position, so the trial court found both the winter and summer programs to violate the ECOA. AFS appealed as to the winter program only.

HIGGINBOTHAM, CIRCUIT JUDGE:

The Equal Credit Opportunity Act proscribes discrimination in the extension of credit. Section 1691(a) of the ECOA states that

> [i]t shall be unlawful for any creditor to discriminate against any applicant, with respect to any aspect of a credit transaction—(1) on the basis of race, color, religion, national origin, sex or marital status, or age (provided the applicant has the capacity to contract).

The ECOA does provide, however, for special purpose credit programs responsible to special social needs of a class of persons. Section 1691(c)(3) carves out this exception:

> It is not a violation of this section for a creditor to refuse to extend credit offered pursuant to...any special purpose credit program offered by a profit-making organization to meet special social needs which meets standards prescribed in regulations by the [Federal Reserve] Board.

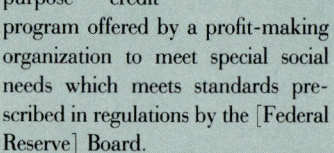

The district court made a finding which shows that the class of persons between the ages of 18 and 21 are in special need of credit assistance. [The court then found that AFS's program met the three conditions for this exception in that (1) there was a "special social need" for credit for this age group, (2) the program was in writing, and (3) the preferred class "probably would not receive such credit or probably would receive it on less favorable terms" absent the program.]

Notwithstanding a credit program having satisfied these three requirements, a program once established cannot discriminate on prohibited bases such as race, sex or marital status.

Congressman Annunzio, who recommended key amendments which broadened the types of discrimination prohibited by the ECOA, elaborated on the purpose of the ECOA:

> The essential concept of nondiscrimination in the extension of credits is that each individual has a right when he applies for credit to be evaluated as an individual: to be evaluated

CONTINUED

on his individual creditworthiness, rather than based on some generalization or stereotype about people who are similar to him in race, color, national origin, religion, age, sex, or marital status. Bias is not creditworthiness. Impression is not creditworthiness. An individual's ability and willingness to repay an extension of credit is creditworthiness.

Thus the specific issue before us is whether the ECOA permits [preferred treatment to single white woman] where the district court expressly found that each person in the group of individuals between the ages of 18 and 21 shares the same credit disability....

There is a particular irony in AFS's approach where it singles out white women as a "disadvantaged" group and gives them a special advantage that it unhesitatingly denies to black and other minority women.

Despite all of the disadvantages that women have had, historically and at present, the significant disadvantages suffered by white women have been far less than those disadvantages black women, Native American women (Indians), Hispanic and other minority American women have had to endure for centuries. Yet, the paradox of AFS's plan is that it perpetuates the past disparities between white and minority women and rather than helping all women it aids only white women and slams the door of equal credit opportunity in the faces of minority women.

We do not believe that it was the intention of Congress to accentuate the disparities among disadvantaged groups by helping those women who have been the *least* deprived while denying equal opportunity to those women who have been the most deprived.

[Affirmed.]

Supplementing the ECOA is the Women's Business Ownership Act of 1988, aimed at eliminating discrimination in the extension of credit to businesses owned and controlled by women.

UNIFORM CONSUMER CREDIT CODE

Federal legislation does not necessarily preclude similar state legislation. For example, section 1610 of the Consumer Credit Protection Act generally preempts only state laws that are *less* protective of debtors. State laws that are *more* protective probably are not precluded.[6] This principle—that state laws are enforceable even though they may regulate an area already covered by federal statutes—is illustrated by the Uniform Consumer Credit Code (UCCC).

The UCCC has been promulgated by the National Conference of Commissioners on Uniform State Laws in two versions—one in 1968 and one in 1974. Nine states have adopted substantial parts of one form or another of the UCCC. Many other states have similar provisions. However, there is great variation from state to state, even among the UCCC adopters. Therefore, our discussion of the UCCC's features must be somewhat general.

---

[6] For example, state laws that prohibit garnishments or provide for more limited garnishments than are allowed under the federal statute are effective and enforceable despite the federal regulations on the same subject.

The UCCC is much like the Federal Consumer Credit Protection Act. It covers consumer credit sales, loans, garnishment, and insurance provided in relation to a consumer credit sale. Its truth-in-lending provisions require full disclosure to the consumer of all aspects of the credit transaction and further require that charges to the consumer be computed and disclosed as an annual percentage rate. The code does not prescribe any specific rates for credit service charges, but it sets maximums based on unpaid balances—36 percent per year on $300 or less in non-open-end accounts, 21 percent per year for balances of $300 to $1,000, and 15 percent for unpaid balances in excess of $1,000. Because the law permits higher charges for smaller transaction, it forbids creditors from breaking large transactions down into smaller ones to take advantage of higher credit charges.

HOME SOLICITATION SALES

The UCCC covers door-to-door solicitation in some detail, because this is a troublesome area for consumers. Consumers tend to be more vulnerable to high-pressure selling tactics in their homes; after signing an agreement to purchase, they often regret the decision. The UCCC therefore permits the rescission of a credit sale solicited and finalized in the customer's home if the customer gives written notice to the seller within 72 hours after signing the agreement to purchase.[7] The cancellation notice is effective when deposited in a mailbox and can take any form so long as it clearly expresses the buyer's intention to void the home solicitation sale. Sellers are required to provide a statement informing buyers of their right to cancel, including the mailing address for the written cancellation notice.

CASE

COLE v. LOVETT

U.S. DISTRICT COURT, SOUTHERN DISTRICT OF MISSISSIPPI 672 F.SUPP 947 (1987)

On Tuesday, November 9, 1982, at approximately 6:00 P.M. the plaintiffs, Norman and Judy Cole, were visited by two representatives of Capitol Roofing, Tony Stepp and Ken Smith. That same evening the plaintiffs signed a contract for the installation of vinyl siding on their home. At that time, Stepp provided several documents for the Coles to sign but did not allow them to read them, representing that they were work papers, credit applications, and insurance papers. The Coles received only a single carbon copy of the work order contract and a copy of a disclosure statement. Shortly after Stepp and Smith left, the plaintiffs changed their minds and decided to obtain more estimates. The next morning Judy called Stepp and

CONTINUED

---

[7] Many of the states that have not adopted the UCCC do have statutes governing door-to-door solicitation, and many municipalities have ordinances regulating solicitors, peddlers, and transient merchants. The latter regulations are known as Green River ordinances. See *Green River v. Fuller Brush Co.*, 65 F.2d 112 (1933).

informed him of this decision, but Stepp replied that the papers had already been processed, the workers would be out at the end of the week, and there was nothing he could do.

When she returned home from work that day, Judy discovered Capitol's workers installing siding. She did not tell them to leave, because she thought she had no choice. As soon as the work was completed, Capitol Roofing assigned the contract to defendant UCM. Problems resulted with the siding but repeated calls to Capitol brought no satisfaction. After having made 11 monthly payments to UCM on the $4900 bill, the plaintiffs consulted a lawyer who, by letter of December 19, 1984, informed both Capitol and UCM that the Coles desired to exercise their right of rescission under both the Truth in Lending Act (TILA) and the Mississippi Home Sales Solicitation Act (MHSSA). On receiving no response, the plaintiffs sued J. L. Lovett d/b/a Capitol Roofing to rescind. UCM counterclaimed for the remaining sum due on the contract. After hearing the evidence, the trial judge rendered the following opinion.

LEE, DISTRICT, JUDGE:

[The judge first found that the plaintiffs were entitled to rescind the contract for TILA violations. For example, Capitol had failed to disclose the security interest it was acquiring in the plaintiffs' home, a violation of 12 C.F.R. Sec. 226.23(a)(1) (which grants a right to rescind in any "credit transaction in which a security interest is or will be retained or acquired in the consumer's principal dwelling") and failed to furnish plaintiffs with adequate notice of their right to rescind as required by 12 C.F.R. Sec. 226.23(a) and (b). The judge found that the violations were not mere clerical errors; therefore, the plaintiffs were entitled to cancellation of the finance charges on the transaction and to have the security interest in their home voided.]

In addition to their TILA claims, plaintiffs have alleged violations of the MHSSA. Like TILA, the MHSSA imposes notice and disclosure requirements upon a seller in a transaction which is a "home solicitation sale." A home solicitation sale is defined as "a consumer credit sale of goods or services in which the seller engages in a personal solicitation of the sale at a residence of the buyer and the buyer's agreement or offer to purchase is there given to the seller. . . ." Miss. Code Ann. Sec. 75-66-1. This section excludes from coverage sales which are initiated by the buyer.

In the present case, there was substantial disagreement between the parties as to the manner in which the initial contact between Capitol Roofing and the Coles occurred. Stepp testified that in November 1982 Capitol Roofing had installed siding on the home of Wanda Collins, a neighbor of the Coles. He claimed that while the crew was working at the Collins home, Judy Cole approached a member of the installation crew and, as a result of a conversation between them, the applicator told Ken Smith to see if the Coles wanted siding. According to Stepp's version, the sales call was at the insistence of Judy Cole. The Coles' testimony that their first contact with anyone from Capitol Roofing occurred when Smith and Stepp came to their home on November 9 was corroborated by Wanda Collins, who explained that she had suggested to Stepp that Judy Cole might be interested in purchasing siding . . . and Stepp promised Wanda Collins a $100 commission on any referrals by her which resulted in sales. The court finds the sales call . . . was not at the Coles' request. Consequently, this transaction constituted a "home solicitation sale" within the meaning of MHSSA.

MHSSA provides the buyer a right to cancel a home solicitation sale until midnight of the third business day following the day on which the buyer signs an agreement or offer to purchase. With limited exceptions, none of which are applicable here, the seller is required to obtain the buyer's signature on a statement, executed simultaneously with the agreement to purchase, which must conspicuously inform the buyer of his rights under the Act. Until the seller has complied with the notice provisons of the Act, the buyer may cancel the home solicitation sale by notifying the seller "in any manner and by any means of his intention to cancel." . . . As the court has concluded that the transaction constituted a home solicitation sale, and as Capitol Roofing never informed the Coles of their right to cancel under the Mississippi Act, the Coles properly and timely exercised their right to cancel by letter from their attorney to defendants dated December 19, 1984.

The obligations of the parties to a home solicitation sale upon cancellation are set forth [in the act] which requires the seller, within ten days of cancellation of a home solicitation sale to tender to the

CONTINUED

buyer "any payments made by the buyer and any note or other evidence of indebtedness." If the seller complies with this obligation, he is allowed to retain a cancellation fee of five percent of the cash price, not to exceed any cash down payment. Until the seller complies, "the buyer may retain possession of the goods delivered to him by the seller or has a lien on the goods in his possession or control for any recovery to which he is entitled." Section 75-66-9 provides in pertinent part that:

(1) . . . within a reasonable time after a home solicitation sale has been cancelled or an offer to purchase revoked, the buyer upon demand must tender to the seller any goods delivered by the seller pursuant to the sale. . . . If the seller fails to demand possession of goods within a reasonable time after cancellation or revocation, the goods become the property of the buyer, without obligation to pay for them. For the purposes of this section forty (40) days is presumed to be a reasonable time. . . .

(3) If the seller has performed any services pursuant to a home solicitation sale prior to its cancellation, the seller is entitled to no compensation except the cancellation fee provided in this chapter.

. . . Hence, as a result of defendants' noncompliance with the requirements of MHSSA, they are required to cancel the deed of trust and to return to plaintiffs payments made in the amount of $1703.57. The Coles are also entitled to cancellation of the underlying contract. Finally, as a result of Capitol Roofing's failure to demand possession of the siding within a reasonable time after cancellation, the siding became the property of the Coles and they are relieved of any further obligation to pay for it.

As one court has observed,

If this result appears to deal harshly with merchants who have fully performed under their contracts, it seems clear to this court that the message which the legislature has attempted to convey by the [law] is "Caveat Vendor." Merchants, put on notice by the statute, can easily and inexpensively protect themselves, . . . by including a right to cancel provision and an accompanying notice of cancellation as a matter of course in all contracts signed outside their trade premises.

Weatherall Aluminum Products Company v. Scott, 139 Cal. Rptr. 329, 331 (1977).

[It is so ordered.]

DEBTOR DEFAULT

Generally, if a consumer defaults on payments, creditors can repossess the property the consumer has purchased and sell it to satisfy the unpaid debt. If the sale earns too little to discharge the debt, the creditor can normally sue the debtor and obtain a deficiency judgment. However, the 1968 UCCC distinguishes between debts incurred in the purchase of goods for $1,000 or less and debts exceeding $1,000. If the goods purchased were worth $1,000 or less, the creditor must *either* repossess the goods *or* sue the debtor for the unpaid balance. If the creditor chooses to repossess, the debtor is not personally liable for the unpaid balance. Only if the original sale exceeded $1,000 can the creditor repossess *and* seek a deficiency judgment if repossession fails to cover the unpaid balance.

With regard to garnishment, the UCCC prevents any prejudgment attachment of the debtor's unpaid earnings and limits the garnishment to 25 percent of net income or to that portion of the income in excess of 40 times the federal minimum hourly wage. The UCCC also prohibits an employer from discharging an employee whose wages are garnished to pay a judgment arising from a consumer credit sale, lease, or loan.

Although the UCCC has been adopted by nine states, the law as adopted can vary considerably from state to state. It is generally true of the so-called uniform laws that a state can make significant changes so the law reflects local attitudes or conforms to local policy in the particular matter covered.

REAL ESTATE SETTLEMENT PROCEDURES ACT

The purchase of a residence is the largest single transaction most consumers ever make. It can be a traumatic experience for the novice who finds that, in addition to the down payment, substantial sums of money will be required on settlement, or closing day. Items to be paid for may include attorney's fees; title insurance; various inspections, surveys, and appraisals; agent's or broker's services; taxes and insurance; and many other miscellaneous items. Congress found that because of the variation in the kinds of items included in the settlement costs and the amount charged for each, significant reforms were needed in the real estate settlement process. The purpose of the Real Estate Settlement Procedures Act (RESPA), enacted in 1974 and subsequently amended, is to ensure that buyers of residential property are given timely information on the nature and costs of the settlement process and that they are protected against obvious abuses. The act requires that effective advance disclosure be made to home buyers and sellers. It prohibits kickbacks or referral fees and, in general, affords considerable protection by letting the home buyer know what it is going to cost to buy a given home.

RESPA applies to all federally related mortgage loans and is administered and enforced by the Secretary of Housing and Urban Development.[8] The secretary has issued comprehensive regulations, known as Regulation X, to prescribe procedures for curbing questionable practices in real estate transactions. Various forms have been devised and are in use, and a special information booklet has been developed for the lender to distribute to the borrower at the time a loan application is made. The lender is also required to provide the borrower with "good-faith estimates" of the dollar amount or range of each settlement service charge that the borrower is likely to incur. Generally speaking, RESPA places the burden on the lender to provide the borrower good advance information about the costs of purchasing a home—the basic cost and the substantial sums needed on settlement day.

---

[8] Most, if not all, mortgage loans on residential property are federally related. The deposits or accounts of the lending institution may be insured by an agency of the federal government or the lender may be regulated by a federal agency.

ADDITIONAL CONSUMER PROTECTION MEASURES

Federal legislation primarily ensures fair treatment for consumers seeking credit, borrowing money, or contemplating the purchase of a residence or automobile. For the most part, the statutes studied in this chapter have been remedial in nature. Their purpose is to correct what Congress has determined to be persistent abuses. Many other statutes, however, are designed to protect the consumer's safety and well-being. These laws concern general health and welfare and alert the consumer to the possibility of harm from the use or misuse of certain products.

PACKAGING AND LABELING

The Public Health Cigarette Smoking Act of 1969, popularly known as the Cigarette Labeling and Advertising Act, establishes a comprehensive federal program to deal with labeling and advertising the ill effects of smoking on health. The act bans completely advertising of cigarettes and little cigars on any medium of electronic communication subject to the jurisdiction of the Federal Communications Commission. It also requires that every cigarette package, every cigarette advertisement, and every billboard carrying such an advertisement carry one of four warning labels. These labels warn consumers about the various adverse health effects of smoking.

In *Cipollone v. Liggett Group,* 60 U.S.L.W. 4703 (1992), the Supreme Court held that compliance with federal labeling laws preempts state law products liability claims by smokers or their families against cigarette makers based on a failure-to-warn theory. However, the Court held that claims are not preempted if based on breach of express warranty, fraudulent misrepresentation by way of false statements and concealment of material facts in advertising, or conspiracy to misrepresent or conceal material facts concerning health hazards by cigarette companies.

The Wholesome Poultry Products Act and the Wholesome Meat Act are also examples of the protective statute. Each establishes procedures to ensure that only wholesome products are distributed to consumers and that they are properly labeled and packaged.

The Nutrition Labeling and Education Act of 1990 (NLEA) required that particular nutrition information—regarding amounts of cholesterol, sodium, sugar, and protein, for example—be included in most food labeling. It also authorized the Food and Drug Administration to regulate the labeling of claims that can be made for foods regarding the characteristics (e.g., "low salt," "reduced fat") and disease prevention or other health benefits (e.g., "fiber prevents cancer").

The Federal Food, Drug, and Cosmetic Act establishes extensive controls over various products and regulates their development, premarket testing, labeling, and packaging.

In the Fair Packaging and Labeling Act, Congress has stated that informed consumers are essential to the fair and efficient functioning of a free-market economy and that packages and labels should enable consumers to obtain accurate information about the quantity of the contents and should facilitate value comparisons. The act therefore establishes comprehensive requirements for the identification of commodities and provides that net quantities must be conspicuously displayed in a uniform location on the principal panel of the product. The main purpose of the act, set forth in some detail, is the prevention of unfair or deceptive packaging and labeling and general misbranding of consumer commodities.

An important amendment, the Poison Prevention Packaging Act of 1970, resulted in the mandatory development and use of childproof devices on household substances that could harm young children if mishandled or ingested. Other statutes for children are the Flammable Fabrics Act and the Child Protection and Toy Safety Act. The Consumer Product Safety Commission is responsible for administering many of the statutes relating to product safety.

BANKRUPTCY—RELIEF FOR THE OVEREXTENDED CONSUMER

In England, before 1861, it was not unusual for a debtor to be thrown in prison until the debts were paid. Many early American colonists were debtors who had experienced debtor's prison and were not enthusiastic about that kind of treatment. Their views are reflected in the U.S. Constitution in a provision recognizing the problems of debtors. Article I, section 8, clause 4 provides that "The Congress shall have the power . . . to establish . . . uniform laws on the subject of bankruptcies throughout the United States." This notwithstanding, the handling of insolvency matters was effectively left to the states until 1898 when Congress passed the first comprehensive bankruptcy act. This has been substantially revised in 1938 and, more recently, in 1978.[9]

The purpose of the bankruptcy law is to permit the debtor to make a fresh start free of the prior debts he or she was unable to pay, in part or entirely. A good-faith creditor who, as a result of the debtor's discharge in bankruptcy, now finds that all or a portion of the debt is uncollectible, may question the fairness of the procedure. The merchant's so-called bad debts are in effect a cost of doing business, losses that must be passed on to the consumer in the form of higher prices.

The number of bankruptcies has exploded in recent years, quadrupling over the past decade or so to more than a million a year. Causes of this dramatic increase include the liberalizing effect of the Bankruptcy Reform Act of 1978, a seemingly diminished stigma attached to those who seek

---

[9] This act, the Bankruptcy Reform Act of 1978, has been amended several times. This discussion includes those changes.

shelter in bankruptcy court, easy lending policies of banks that allowed (some might say induced) many borrowers to put themselves into a precarious financial situation, and the aggressive practices of big corporations in using bankruptcy court in a tactical fashion when confronting financial crises (such as Texaco's attempt to cope with the $11 billion judgment rendered against it in litigation by Pennzoil Co., and Johns-Manville's attempt to control its exposure in thousands of suits filed by workers exposed to asbestos).

BANKRUPTCY PROCEEDINGS TODAY

The 1978 Act recognizes the uniqueness of bankruptcy proceedings by creating a separate system of federal bankruptcy courts. Each federal district within the United States contains such a court. Bankruptcy judges are appointed by the president for 14-year terms. The bankruptcy law provides for three different proceedings: (1) liquidation; (2) reorganization; and (3) adjustment of the debts of an individual with regular income.[10] The liquidation proceeding, often referred to as "straight bankruptcy," is the most common type. Brief mention is also made of the other two types.

Liquidation Proceedings

Stated very generally, the object of a **liquidation** proceeding under Chapter 7 of the Bankruptcy Act is to sell the debtor's assets, pay off creditors insofar as possible, and legally discharge the debtor from further responsibility. A liquidation proceeding will be either a voluntary case commenced by the debtor or an involuntary case commenced by creditors. The filing of a voluntary case automatically subjects the debtor and any property to the jurisdiction and supervision of the Bankruptcy Court.

Any debtor, whether an individual, a partnership, or a corporation, may file a petition for voluntary bankruptcy, with the following exceptions: (1) banks; (2) savings and loan associations; (3) credit unions; (4) insurance companies; (5) railroads; and (6) governmental bodies.[11] These exempted organizations are covered by special statutes, and their liquidation is supervised by particular regulatory agencies. A debtor does not have to be insolvent to file a petition for voluntary bankruptcy, but it is usually insolvency that prompts such a petition. Insolvency is defined as the financial condition of a debtor whose debts exceed the fair market value of assets.

In an involuntary case, filed by creditors, if the debtor has 12 or more creditors, at least three must join in filing the case. If there are fewer than 12 creditors, the involuntary case may be filed by one or more of them. Regardless of the number of creditors, those filing the petition must have noncontingent unsecured claims against the debtor totaling at least $5,000.

---

[10] The Family Farmer Bankruptcy Act of 1986 added a separate chapter in the Bankruptcy Code that provides adjustments of debts for family farmers. Enacted during what was perceived as a temporary crisis, this chapter will be automatically repealed on October 1, 1993, unless extended.

[11] The city of Bridgeport, CN, made headlines in 1991 by filing for bankruptcy under Chapter 9, a type of proceeding that cannot be started involuntarily and does not involve creation of a bankruptcy estate.

The Trustee: After the debtor becomes subject to the bankruptcy proceeding, the U.S. Trustee must appoint an *interim trustee* to take over the debtor's property or business. Within a relatively short time thereafter, a *permanent trustee* is usually elected by the creditors, but if they do not do so, the interim trustee receives permanent status.

The trustee is an individual or corporation who, under the court's supervision, administers and represents the debtor's estate. (The property that makes up the debtor's estate is discussed later.) The basic duties of the trustee are to

1. Investigate the financial affairs of the debtor
2. Collect assets and claims owned by the debtor
3. Temporarily operate the debtor's business if necessary
4. Reduce the debtor's assets to cash
5. Receive and examine the claims of creditors, and challenge in bankruptcy court any claim that the trustee feels to be questionable
6. Oppose the debtor's discharge from obligations when the trustee feels there are legal reasons why the debtor should not be discharged
7. Render a detailed accounting to the court of all assets received and the disposition made of them
8. Make a final report to the court when administration of the debtor's estate is completed

In the capacity of representative of the debtor's estate, the trustee may bring actions to set aside the debtor's transfers of assets that may have been fraudulent, including property that had been transferred to a third party within one year before filing the bankruptcy petition. If, for example, a debtor had "sold" an automobile or boat to a brother for ten dollars in contemplation of bankruptcy, it can be presumed that he or she did so to remove the property from the estate. Such a transfer is considered an attempt to defraud creditors, and the trustee may therefore reclaim the property for inclusion in the bankrupt's estate.

Creditors' Meetings: Within a reasonable time after commencement of the case, the U.S. Trustee must call a meeting of creditors. The debtor will have already supplied the court with a list of creditors, so that they may be notified of the meeting. The creditors will usually elect the trustee. At least 20 percent of the total amount of unsecured claims that have been filed and allowed must be represented at the meeting. A trustee is elected by receiving the votes of creditors holding a majority, in amount, of the unsecured claims represented at the meeting. The other major item of business at the first creditors' meeting is an examination of the debtor. The debtor, under oath, will be questioned by the creditors and the trustee concerning the debtor's assets and matters relevant to whether the debtor will be entitled to a discharge.

Duties of the Debtor: The bankruptcy law imposes the following duties on the debtor:

1. Within a reasonable time after commencement of the proceedings, file with the court a list of creditors, a schedule of assets and liabilities, a schedule of income and expenses, and a statement of financial affairs.

2. File with the court a statement of intention with respect to the retention or surrender of any property of the estate that secures consumer debt, specifying that such property shall be claimed as exempt, redeemed, or the debt reaffirmed thereon, and perform these intentions within 45 days after filing the notice.

3. Cooperate and respond truthfully during the examination conducted at the first creditors' meeting

4. Surrender to the trustee all property to be included in the debtor's estate, as well as all documents, books, and records pertaining to this property

5. Cooperate with the trustee in whatever way necessary to enable the trustee to perform his or her duties

6. Appear at the hearing conducted by the court concerning whether the debtor should be discharged

A debtor who fails to fulfill any of these duties may be denied a discharge from liabilities.

Debtor's Estate: The property owned by the debtor that becomes subject to the bankruptcy proceeding, ultimately to be sold by the trustee, is the *debtor's estate*. This includes all tangible and intangible property interests of any kind, unless specifically exempted. For example, the estate could consist of consumer goods, inventory, equipment, any of the various types of interests in real estate, patent rights, trademarks, copyrights, accounts receivable, and various contract rights.

Exemptions: A debtor who is an individual (rather than a partnership or corporation) may claim certain exemptions for certain types of property not to be included in the debtor's estate. The debtor may keep such property and still receive a discharge from liabilities at the close of the proceedings. Every state has exemption statutes setting forth the types of property that are exempt from seizure under a writ of execution. Before passage of the 1978 bankruptcy law, the debtor's exempt property in a federal bankruptcy case was determined solely by the exemption statutes of the state where he or she lived. The 1978 Code however, included for the first time a list of federal exemptions that are available to the debtor in bankruptcy regardless of the state of domicile.

Under the 1978 Code the debtor may claim the following exemptions (and *each* spouse may claim them in a joint case): (1) the debtor's interest in a homestead used as a residence, up to a value of $7,500; (2) the debtor's interest in a motor vehicle, up to $1,200; (3) the debtor's interest, up to $200 *per item*, in household furnishings, appliances, wearing apparel, animals, crops, or musical instruments that are owned primarily for personal, family, or household (nonbusiness) uses, subject to a total of $4,000 for all such items; (4) the debtor's interest in jewelry, up to a total of $500, which is owned primarily for personal, family, or household uses; (5) the debtor's interest in any kind of property, up to a limit of $400; (6) any unused portion of the $7,500 homestead exemption, subject to a limit of $3,750; (7) the debtor's interest in implements, tools, or professional books used in his or her trade; (8) any unmatured life insurance policies owned by the debtor (except for credit life policies); (9) professionally prescribed health aids; (10) the debtor's right to receive various government benefits, such as unemployment compensation, social security, and veteran's benefits; (11) the debtor's right to receive various private benefits, such as alimony, child support, and pension payments, to the extent reasonably necessary for support of the debtor or the debtor's dependents; and (12) the right to receive damage awards for bodily injury.

The 1978 Code has not achieved uniformity of exemptions because it permits the debtor to choose either the federal exemptions or those of the state where the debtor lives. That is, the debtor may choose one or the other, as a whole; there cannot be a selection of some exemptions from the federal law and some from a state law. And because some state exemption laws are more liberal than the federal, especially those placing no dollar limit on the homestead exemption, disparate state exemption laws will continue to be important in federal bankruptcy cases. Congress also provided that any state legislature can prohibit debtors in that state from using the federal exemptions in a bankruptcy case. Most states have done so.

Claims against the Debtor: As a general rule, any legal obligation of the debtor gives rise to a claim against the estate in the bankruptcy proceeding. Subject to certain specific limitations, any claim filed with the bankruptcy court is allowed unless it is contested by an interested party, such as the trustee, debtor, or another creditor. If challenged, the court will rule on the claim's validity after pertinent evidence is presented at a hearing held for that purpose. In this regard, claims against the debtor's estate will be subject to any defenses that the debtor could have asserted had there been no bankruptcy. The fact that a claim is allowed does not mean that the particular creditor will be paid in full.

Distribution of the Debtor's Estate: A secured creditor—that is, one having a security interest or lien in a specific item of property—can proceed directly against that property for satisfaction of the claim. This is true even though the debtor is or is about to become subject to a bankruptcy proceeding. In a sense, then, secured creditors have priority over all classes of unsecured creditors.

When the trustee has gathered all the assets of the debtor's estate and reduced them to cash, these proceeds are distributed to unsecured creditors. There are certain unsecured claims that are given priority in this distribution. These claims are paid in full in the order of their priority, assuming there are sufficient proceeds available. The following seven classes of debts are listed in order of priority. Each class must be fully paid before the next is entitled to anything. If the available funds are insufficient to satisfy all creditors within a class, payment to creditors in that class is made in proportion to the amount of their claims.

1. First to be paid are all costs and expenses involved in the administration of the bankruptcy proceeding, such as the trustee's fee and accountants' and attorneys' fees.

2. If the proceeding is an involuntary one, the second priority is any expense incurred in the ordinary course of the debtor's business or financial affairs after commencement of the case but before appointment of the trustee.

3. Next is any claim for wages, salaries, or commissions earned by an individual within 90 days before the filing of the petition or the cessation of the debtor's business, whichever occurs first. This priority is limited to $2,000 per individual.

4. The fourth priority is any claim for contributions to an employee benefit plan arising from services performed within 180 days before filing or business cessation. Again the limit is $2,000 per individual. However, a particular individual cannot receive more than $2,000 under the third and fourth priorities combined.

5. Fifth are claims of grain producers or U.S. fishermen against a debtor who owns or operates a grain or fish storage facility for the produce or its proceeds, limited to $2,000 for each such individual.

6. Next are claims of individuals, up to $900 per person, for deposits made on consumer goods or services that were not received.

7. Claims of governmental units for various kinds of taxes, subject to time limits that differ depending on the type of tax, are the last priority.

If all priority claims are paid and funds still remain, other unsecured creditors (called *general creditors*) are paid in proportion to the amounts of their claims. Any portion of a priority claim that was beyond the limits of the priority is treated as a general claim. An example would be the amount by which an individual's wage claim exceeded $2,000.

Discharge: After the debtor's estate has been liquidated and distributed to creditors, the bankruptcy court will conduct a hearing to determine whether the debtor should be discharged from liability for remaining obligations. Under certain circumstances the court will refuse to grant the debtor a discharge. These are as follows:

1. Only an individual can receive a discharge. For a corporation to receive a discharge, it must go through a reorganization proceeding or be dissolved in accordance with state corporation statutes.

2. A debtor will be denied a discharge if he or she had previously received such a discharge within six years before the present bankruptcy petition was filed.

3. The debtor will be denied a discharge if he or she has committed any of the following acts: (a) intentionally concealed or transferred assets for the purpose of evading creditors, within one year before the filing of the petition or during the bankruptcy proceedings; (b) concealed, destroyed, falsified, or failed to keep business or financial records unless there was reasonable justification for such action or failure; (c) failed to adequately explain any loss of assets; (d) refused to obey a lawful court order or to answer a material court-approved question in connection with the bankruptcy case; or (e) made any fraudulent statement or claim in connection with the bankruptcy case.

4. If a discharge has been granted, the court may revoke it within one year if it is discovered that the debtor had not acted honestly in connection with the bankruptcy proceeding.

Nondischargeable Claims: Even if the debtor is granted a general discharge from obligations, there nevertheless are a few types of claims for which he or she will continue to be liable. Examples of these nondischargeable debts are taxes (under certain conditions), liability for a willful and malicious tort, claims for alimony and child support, obligations for student loans, and certain debts compiled by credit card abuse occurring shortly before bankruptcy was filed.

Reaffirming a Debt that Has Been Discharged: Before the 1978 Code, a debtor could renew his or her obligation on a debt that had been discharged in bankruptcy simply be expressing a willingness to be bound. This reaffirmation required no new consideration by the creditor, but some states did require it to be in writing. The new code, however, places significant restraints on the making of a reaffirmation. Specifically, a reaffirmation is not valid unless the bankruptcy court conducted a hearing at which the debtor was fully informed of the consequences of his or her action, and the agreement to reaffirm was made before the debtor's discharge. In addition, the debtor can rescind the reaffirmation within 60 days after it was made.

Business Reorganization

If it is felt that **reorganization** and continuance of a business is feasible and preferable to liquidation, a petition for reorganization may be filed under Chapter 11 of the 1978 Code. A reorganization case can be either voluntary or involuntary, and the requirements for filing an involuntary case are the same as for a liquidation proceeding. In general, the types of debtors exempted from reorganization proceedings are the same as those exempted from liquidation proceedings. Although Chapter 11 has been used primarily by businesses (whether owned by individuals, partnerships, or corporations), the Supreme Court ruled in 1991 that individuals may also reorganize their personal finances under its provisions.[12]

Policy Issues in Reorganizations: The attempt by bankruptcy laws to achieve equity among debtors and creditors has always raised questions of ethics and public policy. The fact that the 1978 Code no longer requires that a debtor be insolvent to file a voluntary case has made these ethical questions even more important: If it is in the best interest of society to provide relief to an insolvent debtor, how far should public policy go in protecting a solvent, but financially beleaguered debtor?

Bankruptcy reorganization is today being successfully used by major corporations to defer prepetition debts to improve cash flow for postpetition operating costs, to alter obligations under burdensome labor contracts and underfunded pension plans, and to block products liability litigation. The Texaco and Johns-Manville cases were mentioned earlier. Such efforts were given a boost in *NLRB v. Bildisco*,[13] when the Supreme Court held that collective bargaining agreements, like other contracts, can be cancelled by the debtor-in-possession when cancellation is in the best interests of a successful reorganization. Although Congress later limited this "union-busting" bankruptcy reorganization, corporations have been very aggressive in using reorganizations for strategic purposes. Recently, corporation have devised "prepackaged bankruptcies" wherein, instead of seeking Chapter 11 protection to gain time to devise a plan for repaying debts, the debtor has already devised its plan and gotten the approval of 50 percent of the creditors holding two-thirds of the debt—before filing.

Adjustment of Debts

Because there is some stigma attaching to a bankrupt, Chapter 13 of the 1973 Code, **Adjustment of Debts** of an Individual with Regular Income, provides a method by which an individual can pay his or her debts from future income over an extended period of time. It is intended for use mainly by an individual whose primary income is from salary, wages, or commissions—an employee. The debtor must be an individual; partnerships and corporations cannot file an adjustment case.

---

[12] *Toibb v. Radloff*, 111 S. Ct. 2197 (1991).
[13] 465 U.S. 513 (1984).

There is no such thing as an involuntary adjustment case; only the debtor can file the petition. The U.S. Trustee will always appoint a trustee in such cases to receive and distribute the debtor's income on a periodic basis.

The debtor alone prepares and files an adjustment plan with the court. The plan designates the portion of the debtor's future income that is turned over to the trustee for distribution to creditors, describes how creditors are to be paid, and indicates the period of time during which payment is accomplished. The court must confirm the plan if it is proposed in good faith and all secured creditors have accepted it.

At any time before or after confirmation of the plan, the debtor has the privilege of converting the adjustment proceeding to a liquidation case. The bankruptcy court may convert the adjustment proceeding to a liquidation case or dismiss the case altogether if the debtor fails to perform according to the plan. However, if the debtor does perform, he or she will ordinarily be granted a discharge on completion of the payments provided for in the plan. There is no discharge from the types of claims that cannot be discharged in a liquidation case.

QUESTIONS and PROBLEMS

1. Removatron International makes and sells an epilator machine designed to remove unwanted hair permanently without the side effects associated with electrolysis. The machine uses a pair of tweezers to remove the hair; while the tweezers grasp the hair but before it is removed, the machine emits radio frequency energy that travels down the tweezers and along the hair. Removatron advertises in beauty industry trade magazines. Removatron's ads state that hair removal can be "permanent" and that unwanted hair will no longer be a problem, that the machine has been "clinically tested and endorsed," and that it is approved by the FCC. When the FTC challenged these ads, evidence showed that the machines cost $4,000 and treatment costs $35/hour. During the sales process, purchasers are informed that the machine will not work for everyone and that permanent removal will be obtained only after several treatments. The FCC does not approve the product but only approved the machine to emit radio waves at a particular frequency. No controlled scientific studies have been performed to test the effectiveness and safety of the machine. Should the FTC be allowed to block Removatron's ads in their current form? How should a cease and desist order be structured? (*Removatron International Corp. v. FTC*, 884 F.2d 1489, 1st Cir. 1989.)

2. Litton Industries advertised that a survey of "independent microwave oven service technicians" indicated that 76 percent of the surveyed population "recommend Litton." Evidence showed that in conducting its survey, Litton used only its own service agency lists, although it had lists of its competitors; Litton knew at least 100 agencies were excluded from the survey; Litton surveyed only one technician at each agency; Litton knew its list contained some dealers who sold Litton microwaves and therefore had reason to favor them and certainly were not "independent"; Litton knew many of those surveyed had insufficient experience with other brands to respond accurately. In a section 5 action, the FTC entered a "multiproducts" order, prohibiting Litton from misusing survey information with all its products, not just microwaves. Should the court uphold this order? (*Litton Industries, Inc. v. FTC*, 676 F.2d 364, 9th Cir. 1982.)

3. An ambulance company charges its customers an additional $5.00 when they do not pay by cash or check at the time services are rendered. Does this arrangement constitute a "finance charge" that must be disclosed under the Truth in Lending Act? Discuss. (*Hahn v. Hank's Ambulance Service, Inc.*, 787 F.2d 543, 11th Cir. 1986.)

4. Maurice had an American Express card. Later, his wife Virginia was granted a supplementary card. When Maurice died, Virginia's card was cancelled under American Express's general policy of automatically terminating supplemental cards on the death of the basic cardholder. The cancellation had nothing to do with Virginia's creditworthiness or ability to pay. Virginia did reapply for a card and was granted it. Still, she sued American Express for violation of the ECOA. Discuss. (*Miller v. American Express Co.*, 688 F.2d 1235, 9th Cir. 1982.)

5. The odometer of a motorcycle purchased by the plaintiff indicated that it had been driven 875 miles. The actual mileage was 14,000. Plaintiff sought damages claiming that the defendant failed to disclose the actual mileage or that the true mileage was unknown; that the defendant altered the odometer intending to defraud; or that the defendant repaired the odometer, failed to adjust it to zero, and failed to so notify the purchaser of the repair. Such allegations, if proven, would constitute violations of the Motor Vehicle Information and Cost Savings Act. Defendant moved to dismiss, claiming that the act did not apply to motorcycles and, if it did, it was unconstitutionally vague. The act provided that notice of any alteration in mileage must be attached to the left door frame of the vehicle. Motorcycles, claimed the defendant, do not have door frames. Is this a good defense? Discuss. (*Grambo v. Loomis Cycle Sales, Inc.*, 404 F. Supp. 1073. N.D. Ind. 1975.)

6. In October, 1974, Sheehan purchased a Ford automobile that was financed by Ford Credit on a retail installment contract. Later Sheehan moved to various locations and became delinquent on his account. When Ford Credit was unable to locate Sheehan it assigned the delinquent account to a central recovery office for collection or repossession. A short time later Sheehan's mother, who resided in Rhode Island, received a phone call from a woman who identified herself as an employee of the Mercy Hospital in San Francisco. (The call actually emanated from Ford Credit's office in Dearborn, Michigan.) She advised Sheehan's mother that one or both of Sheehan's children had been involved in a serious automobile accident and that she, the caller, was attempting to locate Sheehan. The mother supplied the caller with Sheehan's home and business addresses and phone numbers. The following day Sheehan's car was repossessed and subsequent inquiry revealed that the call referred to above was a ruse and that Sheehan's children had not been injured. Are consumers protected against such practices? (*Ford Motor Credit Company v. Frances C. Sheehan*, 373 So.2d 956, Fla. 1979.)

7. A consumer who tried to obtain information from a credit reporting agency on the nature and substance of items in his file was denied such information and forced to return to the credit reporting agency's office several times. The consumer was finally given some of the information held by the agency, but several items were withheld. Discuss this situation with regard to the Fair Credit Reporting Act. (*Millstone v. O'Hanlon Reports, Inc.*, 383 F. Supp. 269, 1974.)

8. Betty Jones had a VISA and Master Charge account with the defendant bank. On her request, the bank issued cards on those accounts to her husband also. On November 11, 1977, Jones informed the bank by two separate letters that she would no longer honor charges made by her husband on the two accounts, whereupon the bank immediately revoked both accounts and requested the return of the cards. Despite numerous notices and requests for surrender of the cards, both Jones and her husband retained the cards and continued to make charges against the accounts. Not until March 9, 1978, did Jones relinquish her credit cards. Is Jones responsible for the balance owing on the account, which includes sums charged by her husband after November 11, 1977? Discuss. (*Walker Bank & Trust Co. v. Jones*, 672 P.2d 73, Utah 1983.)

9. The plaintiff was responsible for one-half of her daughters' medical bills; her ex-husband (Julius) was responsible for the rest. When Julius did not pay two bills—one of $100 for their daughter and one of $35 for Julius's next wife—the defendant credit bureau sent a notice to the plaintiff. A second notice stated in capital letters: "48 Hour Notice, Notice is Hereby Given That This Item Has Already Been Referred For Collection Action, We will At Any Time After 48 Hours Take Action As Necessary and Appropriate To Secure Payment in Full, Pay This Amount Now If Action Is to Be Averted." The plaintiff never paid any amount, including the $50 that she conceded owing, because she did not get a breakdown on the $135 bill. The defendant admits that it was mistaken regarding the $35 amount, which the plaintiff was not responsible for. Defendant's president admits that it never sues for amounts less than $150 but limits its collection actions to letters and telephone calls. The plaintiff sued, claiming violation of the FDCPA. Is this a valid claim? Discuss. (*Pipiles v. Credit Bureau of Lockport*, 886 F.2d 22, 2d Cir. 1989.)

10. D liked P's work when he remodeled D's bedroom, so D called P when he wanted his kitchen remodeled. After some discussion, a contract prepared by P was signed in D's home. It did not provide that D could cancel within three days; D was not provided with a form "notice of cancellation." D was unhappy with P's work on the kitchen and refused to pay. P sued. D counterclaimed, arguing that P breached the state's home solicitation act. May D rescind the contract? Discuss. (*Langston v. Brewer,* 649 S.W.2d *827,* Tex. App. 1983.)

CHAPTER 21

INTRODUCTION

As early as 1816 in The Schooner Exchange v. McFadden,[1] Chief Justice Marshall wrote: "The world [is] composed of distinct sovereignties . . . . whose mutual benefit is promoted by intercourse with each other, and by an exchange of those good offices which humanity dictates and its wants require." As long as nations have existed, there has been commercial activity among them. That activity is generally very beneficial to all the parties involved, and in our modern world the amount of international commercial activity is exploding.

[1] Cranch 116 (1812).

THE LEGAL ENVIRONMENT OF INTERNATIONAL BUSINESS

For example, worldwide exports of goods exceed $2 trillion annually. The United States alone exports more than $200 billion in goods per year. (Unfortunately for our trade balance, we import a substantially greater amount annually than that.) Many of the largest U.S. corporations derive more than half their profits from sales outside the country. On the flip side of the coin, more than 70 percent of U.S. manufacturers face direct foreign competition for sales in the United States.

Direct U.S. investment[2] in foreign countries exceeds $475 billion. In turn, foreigners have directly invested about $300 billion in the United States. More than 3 million Americans are employed by companies directly owned by foreign investors. This is only one aspect of the situation, because foreign entities also own more than a trillion dollars of U.S. securities.[3] Increasingly, U.S. companies are forming joint ventures with foreign companies to do business overseas. Conversely, many foreign companies are entering U.S. markets through similar means.

All in all, an already small world is growing smaller. Every day, investors in the United States watch the Tokyo stock market, for its fluctuations will affect the U.S. stock markets. The collapse of the Soviet Union and the tearing down of the Berlin Wall are cause for celebration in the United States not only because they portend democracy but also because of the commercial opportunities opening for U.S. businesses in Eastern Europe. Just as dramtically, the events of Tiananmen Square in China in 1989 quickly put a damper on the interests of foreign investors.

Just as each company or investor hoping to do business abroad must be concerned with the events occurring in other countries, so must they be concerned with the *legal* aspects of international transactions. The laws of the countries in which they intend to do business, as well as **international law,** must be considered in each and every transaction.

Legal problems are pervasive and inescapable. Can a U.S. company selling its goods in South Korea expect protection from trademark infringement by local companies?[4] Must a Japanese company operating its plant on American soil comply with U.S. laws when making its employment decisions?[5] Does a European company wishing to purchase an American

---

[2] "Direct investment" means that the investor not only invests money but also takes an active role in the foreign enterprise.

[3] The purchasing of securities of a foreign business (but not actively taking a part in its operation) is often called "portfolio investment."

[4] Under American pressure, South Korea has strengthened its trademark laws, but these laws often are underenforced.

[5] Generally, Japanese companies must follow U.S. antidiscrimination laws, but they are allowed to prefer Japanese nationals for top management positions. U.S. courts have not been completely consistent in interpreting laws in this area. The Supreme Court did rule that U.S. antidiscrimination laws embodied in Title VII do not apply extraterritorially to regulate the employment practices of U.S. firms that employ American citizens abroad, *EEOC v. Arab American Oil Co.,* III S. Ct. 1227 (1991), but Congress quickly passed legislation to reverse this result.

company face any barriers that a potential U.S. purchaser would not face?[6] An endless variety of legal questions shape international commerce.

This chapter provides an introduction to the basic aspects of international legal rules as they bear most directly on persons and business organizations engaged in commercial transactions across national borders. It does not pursue in any detail many related and very important fields such as *public* international law, which regulates legal and political relationships among sovereign states.

CLASSIFYING INTERNATIONAL TRADE

Today we classify within the term *international trade* any movement of goods, services, or capital across national boundaries. In its normal use, the term includes three major components:

1. *Export* of goods, services, or commodities from one country to another

2. *Import* of goods, services, or commodities into one country from another

3. Of increasing importance since the end of the Second World War, *foreign direct investment*, such as the acquisition of interests in capital facilities in one country by investors from another

Each of these components of international trade is distinct from the other; each raises particular legal and business issues; and each has been met with a distinct legal response intended to facilitate, harmonize, and regulate this aspect of global commercial and economic relations. With the growth in complexity of modern trade, the competition among nations as expressed in trade policy, and the shrinking presence of centrally planned economies in socialist bloc and Third World countries, the three main facets of international trade noted above have come to demonstrate, to varying degrees, three different sources of regulations:

1. Procedures developed by the *international trading community*, intended to ease trading relations and foster the resolution of disputes

2. Regulations developed by *national governments* designed to protect national trading interests and to make them more competitive in international markets

3. Laws and standards for international trade relations established by *international governmental organizations* such as the United Nations and the Organization for Economic Cooperation and Development, intended to harmonize trading community and national principles, to eliminate trade abuses, and to develop a greater participation in world trade, especially on the part of those nations that form the Third World

---

[6] In 1988, the Omnibus Trade and Competitiveness Act authorized the president to block purchases of U.S. firms by foreign buyers when the takeover would threaten national security.

This chapter looks at some of the major features of each of these components of the international trade framework.

INTERNATIONAL SALES CONTRACT

Although foreign direct investment has become an increasingly important factor in world trade in the past 30 years, most international business transactions still relate to the transfer of goods across national frontiers. This type of transaction—an export from the seller's perspective and an import from the buyer's point of view—is fundamentally a contract of sale, much like its domestic cousin in its essential features. However, special factors such as the great distances involved, accompanying insurance considerations, and differences in legal systems present special problems. An overriding factor in the formation of the international sales contract is that the parties do not, in the normal situation, know each other well; this ignorance can lead to uneasiness over the creditworthiness of the buyer and the dependability of the seller, and anxiety about the enforcement of the obligations of the parties if there should be a breach of contract.

In response to these and other concerns, international private sector traders have over time devised a series of specialized but fairly standard techniques and legal devices that take the form of a series of "side" contracts that supplement the basic sales contract.

FINANCING THE TRANSACTION: THE LETTER OF CREDIT

Because of the presumed lack of knowledge on the part of the seller as to the creditworthiness of the buyer, the export trade has developed a reliance on the **letter of credit** financing device.[7] Basically, the letter of credit is an irrevocable assurance by the bank of the importer/buyer that funds for the payment for the goods sold by the exporter/seller are available beyond the control of the buyer and that these can be obtained by the seller on provision of documentary proof that the goods have been shipped and that other contractual obligations of the seller have been fulfilled and are thus beyond the arbitrary control of the seller.

The documents that the seller must produce to be paid can include (1) inland and ocean **bills of lading** to establish receipt of the goods by the shipper and to serve as "documents of title" for the merchandise; (2) commercial invoices and packing lists to attest to the contents of bulk and packaged materials; (3) an **export license** and shipper's export declaration to show compliance with any applicable export controls; and (4) any **import**

---

[7] Standardization in the use and implications of the letter of credit device has been advanced by the publication of *Uniform Customs and Practice for Documentary Credits*, Publication No. 400, (Paris: The International Chamber of Commerce, 1984).

licenses, consular invoices, or **certificates of origin** necessary to comply with the import laws of the receiving country.

Because the buyer's bank is typically a foreign bank, the seller may have no more confidence in it than in the buyer itself. It is not unusual, then, for the seller to involve its own bank in the transactions to transmit the funds or to confirm or guarantee the performance of the buyer's bank that is issuing the letter of credit. In these circumstances, the seller's bank may undertake only to accept the transfer of funds from the buyer's bank and to credit these to the account of the seller (an "advising" bank); it may go further, however, and contract to guarantee this payment to the seller (a "standby" or "confirming" bank). In either event, an additional layer of contractual obligation will appear, this time between the seller and its bank and, further, between the seller's bank and the buyer's bank.

The letter of credit is essentially a means to make the seller comfortable that the goods will be paid for and to assure the buyer that the purchase money will not be released to the seller until proper, conforming goods are suitably shipped. Strict compliance with the letter of credit is generally required, as the following case illustrates.

BOARD OF TRADE OF SAN FRANCISCO v. SWISS CREDIT BANK

U.S. NINTH CIRCUIT COURT OF APPEALS, 728 F.2d 1241 (1984)

Swiss Credit Bank (SCB) refused to honor a letter of credit issued in favor of the plaintiff's assignor (Antex Industries) for the sale of 92,000 microchips to Electronic Arrays for use in electronic computers. When the letter was presented to the bank, it was accompanied by an air waybill showing that the goods had been air-freighted to their destination. The letter of credit stipulated that a "full set clean on board bills or lading," evidencing ocean shipment of the microchips, was to have been presented. The trial court refused to order SCB to honor the letter of credit, and Antex appealed.

BOOCHEVER, CIRCUIT JUDGE:

...SCB dishonored the letter of credit because of Antex's failure to comply with its terms. [It is conceded] for the purposes of this appeal that the letter of credit required marine shipment and that Antex's air shipment was nonconforming. [It is maintained], however, that the dishonor was improper, because the manner of shipment was not material.

This court's earlier decision in the case precludes [the] argument that Antex's noncompliance with the terms of the letter of credit was not a material defect.... As we noted in the prior decision, strict compliance with the letter's terms was required:

> The Bank notes that strict compliance with the terms of the letter of credit is required.... In this case the shipment was by air, not ocean; and if the Bank's interpretation of the letter of credit is correct, the refusal to pay was not wrongful.

Even if we were not bound by the prior decision, we would reach the same

CONTINUED

result. The issuer of a letter of credit should not be placed in the position of having to determine whether an unauthorized method of shipment is material. In this instance, whether air shipment would have been considered hazardous by the parties or apt to cause damage to sensitive electronic equipment is not the type of evaluation that should be required in a transaction where promptness and certainty are of the essence. Absent a waiver, an issuer may insist on strict compliance with the terms of a letter of credit. In fact, the parties here agreed to be bound by the Uniform Customs and Practice or Documentary Credits (1974 Revision) International Chamber of Commerce (Brochure No. 290), which requires strict compliance with all terms of the letter of credit.

We conclude that SCB was justified in dishonoring the letter of credit because of Antex's failure to comply with its terms. The district court's judgment is affirmed.

The complexity of these multilayered arrangements is greatly reduced by the frequency with which they are used and their corresponding familiarity in the international trading community. It may help to chart the usual financing techniques of a typical international sales transaction in goods (see below).

TRADE TERMS

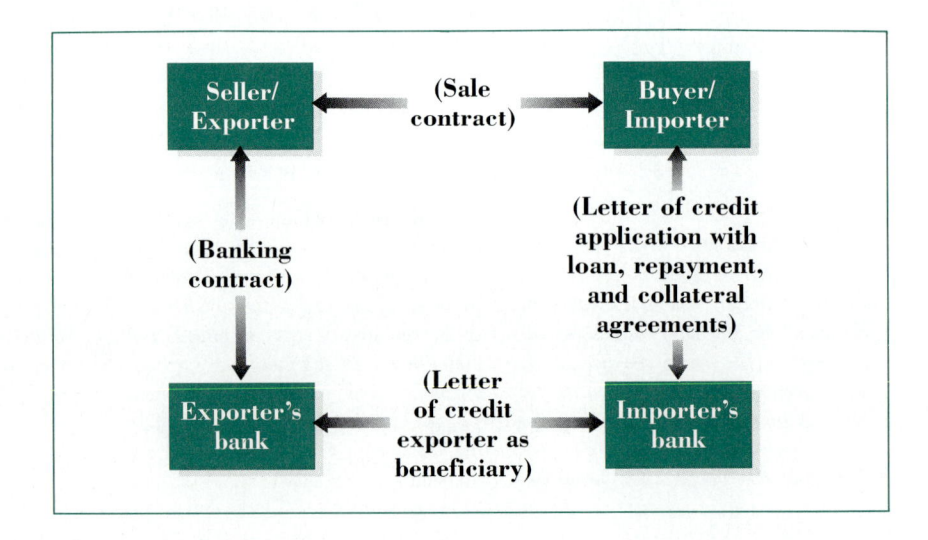

Financing is, of course, only a means to an end, and a myriad of other factors—almost all of them bearing directly on the ultimate price paid for the goods—will be resolved in the terms of the international sales contract. The parties may wish to provide for a fixed rate of currency exchange or to specify the currency of payment for the contract; they may elect to identify the "official" language of the sales contract or to provide that two or more languages each represent the agreed terms of the transaction; they may choose the applicable law and identi the court that will have jurisdiction in the event of a subsequent disagreement; or they may decide to refer any contract disputes to binding or nonbinding arbitration. Clauses such as these, although very important, may or may not appear in the final contract, depending on a host of subtle factors, including the current economic and political climate, the degree of mutual trust and familiarity between the parties, and the extent to which they share common linguistic, cultural, business, or legal tradition. For instance, an American exporter will have, in most cases, fewer questions about the conditions of commerce with a long-time Canadian business associate than, for instance, with a first-time trading partner in Sri Lanka or Liechtenstein.

Various commonly accepted **trade terms,** addressing matters of universal concern such as factors of distance, language barriers, and general unfamiliarity between the parties, have evolved over time within the international trading community.[8] These terms are often used to allocate responsibility between the parties. For example, *CIF* stands for "cost, insurance, and freight," meaning that the seller's quoted price is inclusive of the cost of goods, shipping charges, and a marine insurance policy providing at least minimum coverage. This implies that the seller will bear the risk of loss during transit from the factory to the port of shipment; thereafter the risk shifts to the buyer who pays for the marine insurance policy that is usually arranged by the seller.

The term *FAS* (Fee Alongside) implies that the risk of loss will pass from the seller/exporter when the goods are delivered alongside a vessel, usually designated by the buyer. Risk of damage in the onloading operation rests on the buyer. "FOB" (Free On Board) contemplates delivery of the goods by seller, usually on a designated vessel where shipment has been arranged by the buyer; risk of loss passes at the ship's rail. "CAF" (Cost and Freight) is similar to CIF, but the buyer arranges for insurance during carriage. *Ex* terms (e.g., "exfactory") can be used to designate a place of delivery from seller to buyer that is other than the location of the carrier—for instance, at the factory, or perhaps, at the ultimate destination of the goods.

---

[8] Attempts have been made to further standardize these trade terms by the publication of uniform trade term definitions. This work was undertaken in the Revised American Foreign Trade Definitions (RAFTD) of 1941 and subsequently by the International Chamber of Commerce (ICC) in the 1953 publication of "International Commercial Terms" (Incoterms), which has been periodically revised since that time. The Uniform Commercial Code also sets forth definitions of some of these terms, and these are, in states which have adopted the UCC, binding as law although subject to express modification by agreement of the parties. The 1980 U.N. Convention on the International Sale of Goods will displace inconsistent UCC provisions in circumstances where the Convention applies.

CONVENTION ON CONTRACTS

In an attempt to add uniformity and certainty to the terms of international sales of goods contracts, several countries have ratified the 1980 United Nations Convention on Contracts for the International Sale of Goods (CISG). The CISG became part of American law on January 1, 1988, and has been ratified by China, Finland, France, Italy, Mexico, and several other countries. It is predicted that most of America's major trading partners will soon ratify the CISG.

Assume that Country A and Country B have both ratified the CISG. If a purchaser with a place of business in A makes a contract to buy goods from a company with a place of business in B, the CISG's provisions will automatically govern the contract unless the parties "opt out" of its coverage. The CISG does not apply to consumer sales and has no provisions governing the validity of contracts, ownership claims of third parties, or liability claims for death or personal injury. However, it does have provisions governing most other issues that could arise in a contractual setting. The parties may provide their own variations, but the CISG augments contractual terms and provides the rules for situations the parties did not contemplate or address in their agreement.

The CISG could be loosely termed an international Uniform Commercial Code. It addresses most of the same subjects as article 2 of the UCC, such as definiteness and revocability of offers, timeliness of acceptances, risk of loss, excuse from performance, and remedies. However, the CISG differs from the UCC in several respects. For example, article 11 of the Convention largely abolishes the statute of frauds requirement of a written contract. Article 16 states that an offer cannot be revoked if it was reasonable for the offeree to rely on it as being irrevocable and the offeree has acted in reliance thereon. Article 35 alters the UCC's "perfect tender" rule. A seller must deliver goods fit for ordinary use or the buyer's particular purpose that is known to the seller. A buyer may reject goods only if there is a "fundamental breach." Article 50 addresses buyers' remedies, providing that a buyer may require a seller to perform in accordance with the promise or fix an additional time for the seller to perform. This latter option is not contained in the UCC but is derived from German law. A complete discussion of the CISG's provisions is beyond the scope of this chapter, but be assured that lawyers who specialize in international law are acquainting themselves with them. A single set of rules should greatly assist businesspersons in planning and executing international sales transactions.

CONVENTION ON NOTES

The CISG's attempt to add uniformity to international sales law may soon be supplemented by the U.N. Convention on International Bills of Exchange and International Promissory Notes. Approved by the U.N. General Assembly on December 9, 1988, and now open for ratification, the Convention creates a new type of international negotiable instrument and represents an attempt to provide the same uniformity for international commercial paper transactions that article 3 of the UCC provides for interstate transactions.

RESOLVING INTERNATIONAL TRADE DISPUTES

No contract—including one for an international business transaction—can be so tightly drawn that it is totally impervious to later disagreement; similarly, unforeseen changes in circumstances may make performance of the contract impossible or, perhaps, more difficult or expensive than originally contemplated by the parties. An international trader should, therefore, have a clear understanding of the means available to resolve such disputes if they should arise.

Judicial litigation is rarely the best means to resolve any business dispute: The costs associated with it (attorney's fees, court costs, and general expenses) will often offset any profit expected from the transaction. These factors are compounded in transnational litigation.

Difficulties often arise, in the first instance, in identifying a court with proper jurisdiction over the subject matter of the action or the parties to the transaction. In many types of litigation the question will arise as to which state has the authority to assert its law over the transaction and the parties.

DOMESTIC COURT JURISDICTION

In business litigation, and in other types of litigation touching the international sphere, the rules of jurisdiction are evolving but are as yet unclear. The as yet unadopted American Law Institute *Restatement of the Foreign Relations Law of the United State (Revised)* may be a good indicator of the direction in which the law is heading. Rather than using the traditional categories of subject matter jurisdiction and personal jurisdiction, the proposed revision to this Restatement establishes three categories: (1) *jurisdiction to prescribe,* that is, the authority of a state to make its law applicable to persons or activities; (2) *jurisdiction to adjudicate,* that is, the authority of a state to subject particular persons or things to its judicial process; and (3) *jurisdiction to enforce,* that is the authority to use the resources of government to induce or compel compliance with its law.

Attempts by the United States to impose its legal regulations on activities occurring abroad has caused substantial resentment in foes and allies alike in recent years. The revised Restatement's section 402 would recognize a nation's *jurisdiction to prescribe* with respect to

> (1) (a) conduct, a substantial part of which takes place within its territory; (b) the status of persons, or interests in things, present within its territory; (c) conduct outside its territory which has or is intended to have a substantial effect within its territory;
> (2) the activities, status, interests or relations of its nationals outside as well as within its territory; or
> (3) certain conduct outside its territory by persons not its nationals which is directed against the security of the state [example: terrorism] or a limited class of other state interests.

Thus, links of territoriality and nationality are ordinarily necessary to the power to prescribe law, although they are not sufficient in all cases. Furthermore, these criteria are expressly limited by section 403, which states that even when they are present, jurisdiction to prescribe should not be exercised when it would be "unreasonable" as determined by an evaluation of all relevant factors, including (1) the extent to which the activity takes place in the regulating state and has a substantial, direct, and foreseeable effect there; (2) the connections, such as nationality, residence, or economic activity, between the regulating state and the persons responsible for the activity to be regulated or between the state and those whom the law is designed to protect; (3) the character of the activity to be regulated, the extent to which other states regulate it, and its general acceptability; (4) the existence of justified expectations that might be injured; (5) the importance of the regulation to the international political, legal, or economic system; (6) the extent to which such regulation is consistent with the traditions of the international system; (7) the extent to which another state may have an interest in regulating the activity; and (8) the likelihood of conflict with regulation by other states. A state should defer to another state whose interest in regulating the same conduct is clearly greater.

The *Timberlane* case, which soon follows, illustrates a court's independent formulation of a "reasonableness" approach.

Reasonableness also is the hallmark of the revised Restatement's approach to *jurisdiction to adjudicate*. According to proposed section 421, personal jurisdiction is to be exercised only if reasonable. Such exercise will generally be deemed reasonable if an individual defendant is present (other than transitorily) in the territory of the state, *or* is a domiciliary, resident, or national of the state, *or* regularly carries on business there, *or* has consented to the exercise of jurisdiction. Additionally, exercise of jurisdiction to adjudicate will be reasonable if the person had carried on activity in the state that created the liability in question or had carried on outside the state an activity having a substantial, direct, or foreseeable effect within the state that created the liability in question.

Finally, under section 431 of the proposed revised Restatement, *jurisdiction to enforce* will be present only where a state had the power to prescribe, in accordance with sections 402 and 403, and the power to adjudicate as to the particular defendant. Enforcement measures must be proportional to the gravity of the violation and may be used against persons located outside the territory of the enforcing state only if such persons are given fair notice and an opportunity to be heard.

The following case illustrates one court's approach to the thorny jurisdictional problems that arise in the international setting.

TIMBERLANE LUMBER CO. v. BANK OF AMERICA

U.S. NINTH CIRCUIT COURT OF APPEALS, 549 F.2d 597 (1976)

Timberlane Lumber Company, an American corporation with subsidiary corporations in Honduras, brought a Sherman Act antitrust suit against the Bank of America and several Honduran citizens alleging that the defendants had conspired to shut down the plaintiff's milling operations in Honduras so that the Bank (and its Honduran affiliates and customers) could monopolize Honduran lumber exports to the United States. Timberlane filed suit in a federal court in California, arguing that the illegal activities of the defendants in Honduras had effects in the United States sufficient to vest the American court with personal jurisdiction over the foreign defendants. The district court dismissed the action for lack of jurisdiction, and the plaintiff appealed.

CHOY, CIRCUIT JUDGE:

... There is no doubt that American antitrust laws extend over some conduct in other nations. ...

That American law covers some conduct beyond this nation's borders does not mean that it embraces all, however. Extraterritorial application is understandably a matter of concern for the other countries involved. Those nations have sometimes resented and protested, as excessive intrusions into their own spheres, broad assertions of authority by American courts. ... Our courts have recognized this concern and have, at times, responded to it, even if not always enough to satisfy all the foreign critics. ... In any event, it is evident that at some point the interests of the United States are too weak and the foreign harmony incentive for restraint too strong to justify an extraterritorial assertion of jurisidiction.

What that point is or how it is determined is not defined by international law. ...

Even among American courts and commentators, however, there is no consensus on how far the jurisdiction should extend. The district court here concluded that a "direct and substantial effect" on United States foreign commerce was a prerequisite, without stating whether other factors were relevant or considered. ...

Few cases have discussed the nature of the effect required for jurisdiction, perhaps because most of the litigated cases have involved relatively obvious offenses and rather significant and apparent effects on competition within the United States. ... It is probably in part because the standard has not often been put to a real test that it seems so poorly defined. ...

Implicit in [the] observation ... in several of the cases and commentaries employing the "effects" test, is the suggestion that factors other than simply the effect on the United States are weighed, and rightly so. As former Attorney General (then Professor) Katzenbach observed, the effect on American commerce is not, by itself, sufficient information on which to base a decision that the United States is the nation primarily interested in the activity causing the effect. "[A]nything that affects the external trade and commerce of the United States also affects the trade and commerce of other nations, and may have far greater consequences for others than for the United States." Katzenbach, *Conflicts on an Unruly Horse,* 65 Yale L.J. 1087, 1150 (1956).

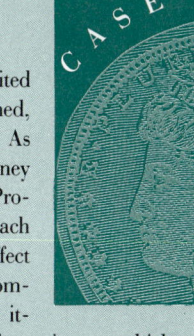

The effects test by itself is incomplete because it fails to consider other nations' interests. Nor does it expressly take into account the full nature of the relationship between the actors and this country. Whether the alleged offender is an American citizen, for instance, may make a big difference; applying American laws to American citizens raises fewer problems than application to foreigners. ...

American courts have, in fact, often displayed a regard for comity and the preogratives of other nations and considered their interests as well as other parts of the factual circumstances, even when professing to apply an effects test. To some degree, the requirement for a "substantial" effect may silently incorporate these additional considerations, with "substantial" as a

CONTINUED

flexible standard that varies with other factors. . . .

[T]he antitrust laws require in the first instance that there be effect—actual or intended—on American foreign commerce before the federal courts may legitimately exercise subject matter jurisdiction under those statutes. . . .

[Also], there is the additional question which is unique to the international setting of whether the interests of, and links to, the United States—including the magnitude of the effect on American foreign commerce—are sufficiently strong, vis-à-vis those of other nations, to justify an assertion of extraterritorial authority.

It is this final issue which is both obscured by undue reliance on the "substantiality" test and complicated to resolve. An effect on United States commerce, although necessary to the exercise of jurisdiction under the antitrust laws, is alone not a sufficient basis on which to determine whether American authority *should* be asserted in a given case as a matter of international comity and fairness. In some cases, the application of the direct and substantial test in the international context might open the door too widely by sanctioning jurisdiction over an action when these considerations would indicate dismissal. At other times, it may fail in the other direction, dismissing a case for which comity and fairness do not require forebearance, thus closing the jurisdictional door too tightly—for the Sherman Act does reach some restraints which do not have both a direct and substantial effect on the foreign commerce of the United States. A more comprehensive inquiry is necessary. . . .

What we prefer is an evaluation and balancing of the relevant consideration in each case—in the words of Kingman Brewster, a "jurisdictional rule of reason." . . .

The elements to be weighed include the degree of conflict with foreign law or policy, the nationality or allegiance of the parties and the locations or principal places of business of corporations, the extent to which enforcement by either state can be expected to achieve compliance, the relative significance of effects on the United States as compared with those elsewhere, the extent to which there is explicit purpose to harm or affect American commerce, the foreseeability of such effect, and the relative importance to the violations charged of conduct within the United States as compared with conduct abroad. A court evaluating these factors should identify the potential degree of conflict if American authority is asserted. A difference in law or policy is one likely sore spot, though one which may not always be present. Nationality is another; though foreign governments may have some concern for the treatment of American citizens and business residing there, they primarily care about their own nationals. Having assessed the conflict, the court should then determine whether in the face of it the contacts and interests of the United States are sufficient to support the exercise of extraterritorial jurisdiction.

The comity question is . . . complicated. [Author's note: Generally speaking, "comity" is respect for another nation's sovereignty.] From Timberlane's complaint it is evident that there are grounds for concern as to at least a few of the defendants, for some are identified as foreign citizens. . . . Moreover, it is clear that most of the activity took place in Honduras, though the conspiracy may have been directed from San Francisco, and that the most direct economic effect was probably on Honduras. However, there has been no indication of any conflict with the law or policy of the Honduran government, nor any comprehensive analysis of the relative connections and interests of Honduras and the United States. Under these circumstances, the dismissal by the district court cannot be sustained on jurisdictional grounds.

We, therefore, vacate the dismissal and remand the Timberlane action. [In other words, it is not obvious that Honduran sovereignty will be offended by permitting this case to proceed, so this by itself is not reason enough to dismiss the case. The case is remanded to the district court for full consideration of the various factors discussed.]

FOREIGN SOVEREIGN IMMUNITIES ACT

Even in circumstances in which the court would be willing to assert its jurisdiction over the defendant under the effects or the reasonableness tests, it may be barred from doing so because of a personal immunity of the defendant. This bar is most often encountered when the defendant is a foreign state or state agency, a circumstance more frequently present today

CHAPTER 21 THE LEGAL ENVIRONMENT OF INTERNATIONAL BUSINESS 705

when many nations—especially those with centrally planned economies—are engaging directly in trading activities. The Foreign Sovereign Immunities Act (FSIA), passed by Congress in 1976, modifies the absolute sovereign immunity that the common law had recognized but continues to limit a plaintiff's ability to recover a judgment from a foreign state or state agency. The act basically permits suits against foreign sovereigns when the claim arises from

1. Commercial activity of the foreign sovereign in the United States

2. Activities in the United States related to the sovereign's commercial undertakings outside this country

3. Commercial actions of the foreign sovereign outside the United States that have direct effects within this nation

The act imposes additional limitations on the seizure of property of a foreign sovereign to satisfy any judgment that the plaintiff might ultimately obtain. The following case is one of the Supreme Court's most recent applications of the FSIA.

ARGENTINE REPUBLIC V. AMERADA HESS SHIPPING CORPORATION

U.S. SUPREME COURT, 488 U.S. 428 (1989)

A crude oil tanker chartered by one Liberian corporation to another (respondents United Carriers, Inc. and Amerada Hess Corp.) was severely damaged when it was attacked in international waters by Argentine military aircraft during the war between Great Britain and Argentina over the Falkland Islands (Malvinas).

Respondents brought this suit in federal district court, claiming subject matter jurisdiction under (1) the Alien Tort Statute (ATS) (which grants district courts jurisdiction in civil actions by an alien for a tort committed in violation of the law of nations or a treaty of the United States), (2) general admiralty and maritime jurisdiction of the federal courts, and (3) "the principle of universal jurisdiction recognized under international law."

The district court dismissed the suit for lack of subject matter jurisdiction, holding that the action was barred by the Foreign Sovereign Immunity Act (FSIA). The court of appeals reversed. Petitioner brought the suit to the Supreme Court.

REHNQUIST, CHIEF JUSTICE:

...In the FSIA, Congress added... Section 1604 [which] provides that "[s]ubject to existing international agreements to which the United States [was] a party at the time of the enactment of this Act, a foreign state shall be immune from the jurisdiction of the courts of the United States and of the States except as provided in Section 1605–1607 of this chapter." The FSIA also added Sec. 1330(a) to Title 28 [which] provides that "[t]he district courts shall have original jurisdiction without regard to amount in controversy of any nonjury civil action against a foreign state...as to any claim for relief in personam in respect to which the foreign state is not entitled to immunity under section 1607 of this title or under any applicable international agreement."

We think that the text and structure of the FSIA demonstrate Congress'

CONTINUED

intention that the FSIA be the sole basis for obtaining jurisdiction over a foreign state in our courts. Section 1604 and section 1330(a) [of Title 28] work in tandem: 1604 bars federal and state courts from exercising jurisdiction when a foreign state *is* entitled to immunity, and 1330(a) confers jurisdiction on district courts to hear suits brought by United States citizens and by aliens when a foreign state is not entitled to immunity. As we [have] said, the FSIA "must be applied by the district courts in every action against a foreign sovereign, since subject-matter jurisdiction in any such action depends on the existence of one of the specified exceptions to foreign sovereign immunity." *Verlinden B. V. v. Central Bank of Nigeria*, 461 U.S. 480, 493 (1983).

...Having determined that the FSIA provides the sole basis for obtaining jurisdiction over a foreign state in federal court, we turn to whether any of the exceptions enumerated in the Act apply here. These exceptions [found in section 1605] include cases involving the waiver of immunity, commercial activities occurring in the United States or causing a direct effect in this country. property expropriated in violation of international law, real estate, inherited, or gift property located in the United States, and maritime liens. We agree with the District Court that none of the FSIA's exceptions applies on these facts.

Respondents assert that the FSIA exception for noncommercial torts is most in point... [That provision] is limited by its terms, however, to those cases in which the damage to or loss of property occurs *in the United States*. Congress' primary purpose is enacting [this provision] was to eliminate a foreign state's immunity for traffic accidents and other torts committed in the United States, for which liability is imposed under domestic tort law. In this case, the injury to respondents' ship occurred on the high seas some 5,000 miles off the nearest shore of the United States.

We hold that the FSIA provides the sole basis for obtaining jurisdiction over a foreign state in the courts of this country, and that none of the enumerated exceptions to the Act applies to the facts of this case. The judgment of the Court of Appeals in therefore *reversed*.

ACT OF STATE DOCTRINE

Closely related in effect to the doctrine of sovereign immunity is the **act of state doctrine.** This doctrine is based on the concept that it is beyond the sensible exercise of judicial powers for a court in this country to sit in judgment on the actions of another sovereign nation taken in its own territory. Any redress of grievances caused by such actions should be obtained by the United States government dealing directly with the other sovereign. Thus, in *Banco Nacional de Cuba v. Sabbatino*, 376 U.S. 398 (1964), a case challenging Cuba's expropriation of a Cuban corporation that was largely owned by U.S. residents, the Supreme Court held

> [T]he Judicial Branch will not examine the validity of a taking of property within its own territory by a foreign sovereign government, extant and recognized by this country at the time of the suit, in the absence of treaty or other unambiguous agreement regarding controlling legal principles, even if the complaint alleges that the taking violates customary international law.

Also related to sovereign immunity is the doctrine of **sovereign compulsion,** under which American courts will refuse to hold a defendant liable for actions that it was compelled to take under the law of a recognized foreign sovereign.

The following case illustrates some of the difficult questions that can arise in application of the act of state doctrine.

W. S. KIRKPATRICK & CO. V. ENVIRONMENTAL TECTONICS CORPORATION

U.S. SUPREME COURT, 110 S.Ct. 701 (1990)

Petitioner W. S. Kirkpatrick & Co. pleaded guilty to a violation of the Foreign Corrupt Practices Act for having paid a bribe to a Nigerian official to obtain a contract with the Republic of Nigeria. Respondent Environmental Tectonics Corporation, an unsuccessful bidder on the contract, then brought this suit claiming that petitioner had violated the Racketeer Influenced Corrupt Organizations Act (RICO) among others. Despite having received a lettter from the Department of State indicating its view that this case posed no "unique embarrassment" to execution of American foreign policy, the trial court granted summary judgment to the petitioner on grounds that the act of state doctrine barred the claim. The court of appeals reversed, concluding that no embarrassment of the executive in its conduct of foreign affairs was evident. Petitioner appealed.

SCALIA, JUSTICE:

This Court's description of the jurisprudential foundation for the act of state doctrine has undergone some evolution over the years. We once viewed the doctrine as an expression of international law, resting upon "the highest considerations of international comity and expediency," *Oetjen v. Central Leather Co.*, 246 U.S. 297, 303–304 (1918). We have more recently described it, however, as a consequence of domestic separation of powers, reflecting "the strong sense of the Judicial Branch that its engagement in the task of passing on the validity of foreign acts of state may hinder" the conduct of foreign affairs. *Banco Nacional de Cuba v. Sabbatino*, 376 U.S. 398, 423 (1964). Some Justices have suggested possible exceptions to application of the doctrine where one or both of the foregoing policies would seemingly not be served: an exception, for example, for acts of state that consist of commercial transactions, since neither modern international comity nor the current position of our Executive Branch accorded sovereign immunity to such acts.... or an exception for cases in which the Executive Branch has represented that it has no objection to denying validity to the foreign sovereign act, since then the courts would be impeding no foreign policy goals.

The parties have argued about the applicability of these possible exceptions, and, more generally, about whether the purposes of the act of state doctrine would be furthered by its application in this case. We find it unnecessary, however, to pursue those inquiries, since the factual predicate for application of the act of state doctrine does not exist. Nothing in the present suit requires the court to declare invalid, and thus ineffective as "a rule of decision for the courts of this country," *Ricaud v. American Metal Co.*, 246 U.S. 304, 310 (1918), the official act of a foreign sovereign.

In every case in which we have held the act of state doctrine applicable, the relief sought or the defense interposed would have required a court in the United States to declare invalid the official act of a foreign sovereign performed within its own territory.... In the present case, by contrast, neither the claim nor any asserted defense requires a determination that Nigeria's contract with Kirkpatrick International was, or was not, effective.

The short of the matter is this: Courts in the United States have the power, and ordinarily the obligation, to decide cases and controversies properly presented to them. The act of state doctrine does not establish an exception for cases and controversies that may embarrass foreign governments, but merely requires that, in the process of deciding, the acts of foreign sovereigns taken within their own jurisdiction shall be deemed valid. That doctrine has no application to the present case because the validity of no foreign sovereign act is at issue.

[Affirmed.]

INTERNATIONAL LITIGATION: OTHER CONCERNS

In the domestic setting, it can be quite troublesome to obtain service of summons over a proper defendant, obtain evidence to support the claim through oral depositions, written interrogatories, and document production, and ultimately enforce the judgment against a recalcitrant defendant. In the international context, such tasks can be overwhelming. To reduce these barriers to the civil prosecution of a valid claim, several international agreements have been reached that are intended generally to increase international cooperation in these respects.

The Hague Convention on Service Abroad of Judicial and Extrajudicial Documents in Civil or Commercial Matters provides that each signatory state will maintain a Central Authority to process judicial documents, such as complaints, and expedite their transmission. The Hague Convention on the Taking of Evidence Abroad in Civil or Commercial Matters of 1970 seeks to reduce the barriers raised by national laws to obtaining evidence for use in court and to streamline the discovery process in international litigation. The Convention creates Central Authorities in each signatory nation through which discovery requests ("Letters of Request") are channeled; it permits consuls to conduct some discovery procedures regarding their own nationals; and, finally, it allows the use of court-appointed commissioners for discovery purposes in limited circumstances. The United States is a signatory of both Conventions.

What happens if an American company, for example, receives a judgment against a foreign defendant in a foreign country's court and wishes to enforce that judgment against the defendant's property located in the United States. Will U.S. courts recognize such foreign judgments? Enforcement of foreign judgments is a matter of state law, which varies somewhat from jurisdiction to jurisdiction. Guidance is provided by the Restatement (Third) of the Foreign Relations Law of the United States, which provides that final money judgments of the courts of a foreign state will generally be enforced in the United States. However, a U.S. court is prohibited from enforcing a judgment that (1) was rendered by a judicial system that does not provide impartial tribunals or due process of law, or (2) was rendered by a court lacking personal jurisdiction over the defendant under its own law or international law. Furthermore an American court has discretion to refrain from enforcing a foreign judgment on several grounds, including: the rendering court did not have subject matter jurisdiction, the defendant did not receive notice of the proceedings in time to defend, the judgment was obtained by fraud, or the judgment is based on a cause of action repugnant to American public policy.

ARBITRATION

In view of the special difficulties encountered in international court litigation, it is not surprising that the international business community has actively sought alternative methods of commercial dispute resolution. Quite popular is **arbitration,** a process whereby parties to a transaction agree (either within the terms of their basic agreement or subsequently) to submit any future (or existing) disputes to an impartial third party (or panel) for nonjudicial resolution. The decision of the arbitrator—termed an *award*—may, depending on the agreement of the parties, be binding or nonbinding.

Binding arbitration within the international trading context has a long and colorful history and today is the preferred alternative to litigation in international commercial circles. The advantages of arbitration are many, including: (1) it is less expensive and more speedy than court procedures; (2) it is more private than litigation; and (3) the parties may choose knowledgeable experts (rather than generalist judges and untrained juries) to decide the matter based on commercial realities.

Arbitration is not, however, without its disadvantages. Arbitral panels generally do not have the power to compel the attendance of witnesses or the production of other information relevant to the case. The informality of the procedure can lead to an undesired degree of "looseness" in the process; and, because arbitrators are generally not bound by the strict letter of the law, final outcomes may be difficult to forecast.

Several organizations have sought to facilitate this means of dispute resolution by providing standard arbitral rules and procedures. Chief among these organizations are the International Chamber of Commerce (headquartered in Paris), the U.N. Commission on International Trade Law (UNCITRAL), the American Arbitration Association, the International Centre for Settlement of Investment Disputes (ICSID—created by the 1965 Convention on the Settlement of Investment Disputes Between States and Nationals of Other States), the Inter-American Commercial Arbitration Commission, and the London Court of Arbitration.

So well accepted is the use of arbitration in international commercial disputes that most nations readily enforce such awards. In the United States, such enforcement is a matter of federal law. As with foreign court judgments, guidance is provided by the Restatement (Third) of Foreign Relations, which provides that awards pursuant to valid written arbitral agreements will generally be enforced, although a court may deny recognition on such grounds as: (1) the agreement to arbitrate was not valid under applicable law; (2) the losing party was not given an opportunity to present its case; (3) the award deals with matters outside the terms of the agreement to arbitrate; or (4) recognition of the award would be contrary to public policy. The Restatement's rules are based on the U.N. Convention on the Recognition and Enforcement of Foreign Arbitral Awards (known as the New York Convention). Almost 80 nations are parties to this Convention, reflecting the widespread acceptance of arbitration in the international sphere. The following case is illustrative.

MITSUBISHI MOTORS CORP. v. SOLER CHRYSLER-PLYMOUTH, INC.

U.S. SUPREME COURT, 473 U.S. 614 (1985)

Petitioner Mitsubishi, a Japanese corporation that manufactures automobiles, is the product of a joint venture between Chrysler International, S.A. (CISA), a Swiss corporation, and another Japanese corporation, aimed at distributing automobiles manufactured by the petitioner through Chrysler dealers outside the continental United States. Respondent Soler, a Puerto Rican corporation, entered into distribution and sales agreements with CISA. These agreements contained a clause providing for arbitration by the Japan Commercial Arbitration Association of all disputes arising out of certain articles of the agreement or for the breach thereof. Disagreements did arise, and petitioner filed suit in federal district court in Puerto Rico under the federal Arbitration Act and the Convention on the Recognition and Enforcement of Foreign Arbitral Awards, seeking an order to compel arbitration of the dispute in accordance with the arbitration clause. Respondent filed a counterclaim alleging antitrust violations by petitioner and CISA. The district court ordered arbitration of almost all issues. On appeal, the circuit court affirmed, except as to the antitrust issues, which it held to be inappropriate for arbitration.

BLANKMUN, JUSTICE:

By agreeing to arbitrate a statutory claim, a party does not forgo the substantive rights afforded by the statute; it only submits to their resolution in an arbitral, rather than a judicial, forum. It trades the procedures and opportunity for review of the courtroom for the simplicity, informality, and expedition of arbitration. We must assume that if Congress intended the substantive protection against waiver of the right to a judicial forum, that intention will be deducible from text or legislative history.... Having made the bargain to arbitrate, the party should be held to it unless Congress itself has evinced an intention to preclude a waiver of judicial remedies for the statutory rights at issue....

We now turn to consider whether Soler's antitrust claims are nonarbitrable even though it agreed to arbitrate them. In holding that they are not, the Court of Appeals followed the decision of the Second Circuit in *American Safety Equipment Corp. v. J. P. McGuire & Co.*, 391 F.2d 821 (1968) [finding] that "the pervasive public interest in enforcement of the antitrust laws, and the nature of the claims that arise in such cases, combine to make ... antitrust claims ... inappropriate for arbitration." We find it unnecessary to assess the legitimacy of the *American Safety* doctrine as applied to agreements to arbitrate arising from domestic transactions. As in *Scherk v. Alberto-Culver Co.*, 417 U.S. 506 (1974), we conclude that concerns of international comity, respect for the capacities of foreign and transnational tribunals, and sensitivity to the need of the international commercial system for predictability in the resolution of disputes require that we enforce the parties' agreement, even assuming that a contrary result would be forthcoming in a domestic context.

Even before *Scherk*, this Court had recognized the utility of forum-selection clauses in international transactions. In *The Bremen v. Zapata Off-Shore Co.*, 407 U.S. 1 (1972), an Amercian oil company, seeking to evade a contractual choice of an English forum and, by implication, English law, filed a suit in admiralty in a United States District Court against the German corporation which and contracted to tow its rig to a location in the Adriatic Sea. Notwithstanding the possibility that the English court would enforce provisions in the towage contract exculpating the German party which an American court would refuse to enforce, this Court gave effect to the choice-of-forum clause. It observed:

> The expansion of American business and industry will hardly be encouraged if, notwithstanding solemn contracts, we insist on a parochial concept that all disputes must be resolved under our laws and in our courts.... We cannot have trade

CONTINUED

and commerce in world markets and international waters exclusively on our terms, governed by our laws, and resolved in our courts.

... In *Scherk*, ... this Court [enforced] the arbitration agreement even while assuming for purposes of the decision that the controversy would be non-arbitrable had it arisen out of a domestic transaction. Again, the Court emphasized:

A contractual provison specifying in advance the forum in which disputes shall be litigated and the law to be applied is ... an almost indispensable precondition to achievement of the orderliness and predictability essential to any international business transaction.

A parochial refusal by the courts of one country to enforce an international arbitration agreement would not only frustrate these purposes, but would invite unseemly and mutually destructive jockeying by the parties to secure tactical litigation advantages.... [It would] damage the fabric of international commerce and trade, and imperil the willingness and ability of businessmen to enter into international commercial agreements.

... There is no reason to assume at the outset of the dispute that international arbitration will not provide an adequate mechanism. To be sure, the international arbitral tribunal owes no prior allegiance to the legal norms of particular states; hence, it has no direct obligation to vindicate their statutory dictates. The tribunal, however, is bound to effectuate the intentions of the parties. Where the parties have agreed that the arbitral body is to decide a defined set of claims which includes, as in these cases, those arising from the application of American antitrust law, the tribunal therefore should be bound to decide that dispute in accord with the national law giving rise to the claim. And as long as the prospective litigant effectively may vindicate its statutory cause of action in the arbitral forum, the statute will continue to serve both its remedial and deterrent function. ...

As international trade has expanded in recent decades, so too has the use of international arbitration to resolve disputes arising in the course of that trade. The controversies that international arbitral institutions are called upon to resolve have increased in diversity as well as in complexity. Yet the potential of these tribunals for efficient disposition of legal disagreements arising from commercial relations has not yet been tested. If they are to take a central place in the international legal order, national courts will need to "shake off the old judicial hostility to arbitration." *Kulukundis Shipping Co. v. Amtorg Trading Corp.*, 126 F.2d 978 (CA2 1942), and also their customary and understandable unwillingness to cede jurisdiction of a claim arising under the domestic law to a foreign or transnational tribunal. To this extent, at least, it will be necessary for national courts to subordinate domestic notions of arbitrability to the international policy favoring commercial arbitration.

Accordingly, we "require this representative of the American business community to honor its bargain," ... by holding this agreement to arbitrate "enforce[able] in accord with the explicit provisions of the Arbitration Act." *Scherk*, 417 U.S., at 520.

The judgment of the Court of Appeals is affirmed in part and reversed in part.

NATIONAL REGULATIONS OF THE EXPORT/IMPORT PROCESS

The impact of export trade transcends, of course, the private interests of the parties to the international sales contract. Concerns at the national level touch on defense and security matters (especially in the export of high technology with military applications) and the depletion of national stocks of critical materials. Moreover, the volume and direction of flow of export sales are inextricably bound up in the general economic posture of a nation and thus bear directly on its overall pattern of foreign relations. Not surprisingly, almost all nations have responded to these factors by adopting broad regulatory schemes to control exports. The implementation of these programs will directly affect the international trader and the methods used in that trade.

In the United States, the power to regulate international trade is vested in the Congress under the provisions of the commerce clause of the federal Constitution. Congress has used this power repeatedly since the early days of the Republic and the trail of congressional legislation dealing with import and export matters continues into the present day. The Export Administration Act of 1979 is perhaps the most important piece of federal legislation impacting American export traders today.

EXPORT ADMINISTRATION ACT

This act is a comprehensive scheme to regulate exports from the United States and, together with the regulations adopted pursuant to it, extends its controls in some instances to the re-export of certain American goods to third countries. The act grants discretionary authority to the Office of Export Administration (OEA) of the Department of Commerce to impose export controls for three basic reasons: (1) national security (to prevent "dual use" products that might have military applications from reaching our enemies; (2) foreign policy (for example, to prevent goods from reaching countries that practice terrorism or apartheid); and (3) short supply of the goods in the United States.

In general terms, the act provides for three broad types of required export licenses:

1. A general license authorizing exports—this type of license covers the vast bulk of American exports and is normally issued by the OEA without a formal application by the exporter. (There is also a qualified general license authorizing multiple imports.)

2. A validated license relating to a specific export

3. A distribution license permitting export of unlimited quantities of certain commodities under an international marketing program without additional approval from OEA

The Export Administration Regulations (found in the *Code of Federal Regulations*) round out, define, and implement the provisions of the 1979 act. They contain a Commodity Control List, which will assist the exporter in identifying circumstances when a validated export license must be obtained and when a general license will not suffice. In most instances, this decision is a function of what commodity is going to which country. Some few nations (North Korea and Cuba, among others) are virtually closed to American exports. These regulations also contain provisions relating to the export of technical data (as opposed to commodities, which are treated as a separate and distinct category for licensing purposes). The general license "GTDR" controls the export of technical data both in terms of destination and the degree of "public accessibility" to the information; a more liberal license, the general license "GTDA," allows technical data exports to virtually any destination if the data meet the regulations' standard of public availability. A 1985 amendment to the Export Administration Act also provides for a comprehensive operations license to govern exports from American corporations to offshore affiliates and subsidiaries. This type of license will have frequent use within transnational corporate systems.

Although the Export Administration Act is the major source of export regulation in the United States, it is by no means the only one.[9] Export control provisions are also found in the Nuclear Non-Proliferation Act (1978) and Atomic Energy Act (1954), which govern the export of nuclear materials. The Arms Export Control Act, the Trading with the Enemy Act, and the International Emergency Economic Power Act also contain important export restrictions.

In addition, the United States is a member of the Coordinating Committee for Multilateral Export Controls (COCOM) along with Japan and most NATO members. This is an international group that cooperates in the control of exports of strategic goods to sensitive destinations. COCOM has no authority to enforce its own policies but relies on regulations of its member states. During the 1980s, the United States was much more sensitive to export of technology than were other COCOM members. The culmination in 1992 of the European Economic Community (EEC) (to be discussed soon) and the disintegration of the Soviet Union are combining to pressure the United States to reduce its attempts to impose its technology export controls extraterritorially. However, in the aftermath of Operation Desert Storm and the information it brought regarding Iraq's ability to obtain western weapons technology, this area is receiving new attention.

EXPORT INCENTIVES

U.S. export policy and legislation is not, however, totally negative. Important legislation has long been on the books to encourage increased export trade by manufacturers and suppliers in this country.

As early as 1918, Congress adopted the Webb-Pomerene Act to promote American export trade by granting limited exemptions to exporters from the application of U.S. antitrust laws, principally the Sherman and Clayton acts. Congress acted in the belief that American traders could better compete in foreign markets if they were permitted to form associations capturing the benefits of economies of scale and greater efficiency; such associations, however, involved a danger of criminal or civil liability under American antitrust laws. The Webb-Pomerene Act, therefore, relieved export associations of this

---

[9] Note, too, the impact of other federal legislation on the conduct of international business. For instance, the Foreign Corrupt Practices Act controls bribery and other undesirable acts abroad. This act is considered separately in Chapter 15.

risk but conditioned the exemption in important respects. Principally, such an association is prohibited by the act from entering into any agreement that "artificially or intentionally" depresses commodity prices within the United States or that "substantially lessens competition within the United States, or otherwise restrains trade therein." Further, the benefits of the act (obtained by registration of the association with the Federal Trade Commission) are limited to associations formed for the export of commodities; transactions for services or technology are not protected. As a result of these limitations and lingering anxiety about possible antitrust liability, comparatively few Webb-Pomerene associations are registered with the FTC.

Export Trading Company Act

The Failure of the 1918 legislation to promote greater American export trade, coupled with increasing U.S. trade deficits in the mid and late 1970s[10] created a sense of urgency in Congress to devise new and more effective means to encourage increased exports from this country, especially by small- and medium-sized companies historically underrepresented in international trade transactions. The legislative response was the Export Trading Company Act of 1982.

At the heart of this Act is the provision that

> *no criminal or civil action may be brought under the antitrust laws [of the United States] against a person to whom a certificate of review is issued [by the Secretary of Commerce] which is based on conduct which is specified in, and complies with the terms of, a certificate ... which ... was in effect when the conduct occurred.*

This exemption is available to individual persons resident in the United States, partnerships or corporations created under state or federal law, and significantly for antitrust purposes, "any association or combination, by contract or other arrangement" between or among any of these.

The act's scope is comprehensive. It extends its antitrust protection to activities related to the export of goods and mechandise and (going beyond the reach of the Webb-Pomerene Act) to services. This latter category is defined to include services that are the subject of the transaction (as in transborder management agreements) and includes accounting, architectural, data processing, business, communications, consulting, and legal services. Also eligible for exemption from possible antitrust liabilities are "export trade services," that is, international market research, product research and design, transportation, warehousing, insurance, and the like.

The Export Trading Company Act also contains important provisions that modify statutory impediments that separate the banking community

---

[10] The United States never experienced a trade deficit—an excess of imports over exports—until 1971. Between 1971 and 1976, however, the American trade deficit rose to $5 billion, largely because of massive oil imports that amounted to $77 billion in 1981 alone. The deficit then exploded, reaching $170 billion in 1986. (U.S. Bureau of the Census, *Highlights of U.S. Export and Import Trade*, FT1990, Feb. 1987.)

from participation in international trade. Title II of the act (termed the *Bank Export Services Act*) permits banks to invest in export trading companies up to the statutory limit of 5 percent of their consolidated capital and surplus; further, they are also allowed to own such companies outright. These provisions are intended to marshal substantial capital to promote international trade. The absence of such funding has hobbled export trade in the past because many small- and medium-sized banks were reluctant to finance "speculative foreign ventures" over which they had little or no control.

REGULATING IMPORTS

Compared with the elaborate nature of export controls and incentives, the regulation of imports into the United States is relatively straightforward. The application of these import control laws can, however, be quite complex.

Under the import–export clause of the federal Constitution, the power to levy import customs and duties rests exclusively with the federal government. Using federal power in this regard, the government has established a comprehensive system of tariff schedules that apply to goods entering the United States—the Tariff Schedules of the United States (TSUS). The TSUS will be applied by federal customs officials first to classify the entering goods and then to determine the applicable tariff rate to the goods so classified. The federal government sets the actual rate, but does so subject to bilateral or multilateral restraints that it has assumed. For example, a treaty with another nation may stipulate the tariff level or, more generally, the applicable tariff may have been negotiated within the framework of a multinational commitment, example, the General Agreement on Tariffs and Trade (GATT). In either event, the tariff generally must be paid before the goods are admitted into this country.

An important exception to this principle is the use of a foreign trade zone (FTZ). Established by federal law, these zones are fenced-off, policed warehouses and industrial parks usually located near American ports of entry. Goods entering the port from abroad may be taken into the FTZ and stored there without paying any applicable tariff and with a minimum of formality and procedure. As long as the goods are warehoused within the FTZ, no duty is payable and the goods may be further processed, assembled, or finished. Only when the merchandise leaves the confines of the FTZ will the duty be imposed, frequently at a reduced rate. The FTZ has shown itself to be an effective device for encouraging additional international trade in the United States.

While import licenses are generally not required for imports into the United States, certain goods may be denied entry altogether. Bans on importation may be applied against undesirable imports such as narcotics, pornographic material, or printed materials advocating the violent overthrow of the United States. Import bans may be applied to prevent entry of automobiles that do not meet vehicle safety regulations or against other products not meeting standards established to protect public health and safety. Products violating the patent, trademark, and copyright laws of the

United States may also be excluded. Moreover, certain goods may be subjected to tariff increases to offset foreign government subsides that unfairly reduce their U.S. market price or to counteract a foreign producer's deliberate attempt to destabilize or destroy the product's domestic production in the United States. These "countervailing" and "antidumping" measures are considered again in this chapter with regard to the GATT.

Trade and Tariff Act

One method of increasing the access of U.S. companies to foreign markets is retaliation against countries that treat U.S. companies unfairly. A series of acts over the years have authorized and encouraged the president to take such retaliatory action. In recent years Congress has been specifically concerned with the difficulty U.S. companies have had gaining access to markets in Asia, especially Japan. At various times Congress has authorized, and even mandated, the President to respond to unfair trade practices by use of higher tariffs, import quotas, or withdrawal from existing trade agreements with offending parties. Prying open new markets for U.S. companies without unduly antagonizing existing trading partners requires the striking of a delicate balance.

Protection from Unfair Competition

Various provisions of federal law protect U.S. companies from unfair practices by foreign competitors selling in this country. The primary protective provision is section 337 of the Tariff Act of 1930, which protects "domestic industries" from "substantial injury" stemming from "unfair methods of competition and unfair acts in the important of articles into the United States, or in their sale. . . ." Section 337 has been invoked most often in cases of alleged patent infringement, but it also protects U.S. businesses from copyright and trademark infringement, false advertising, trade secret misappropriation, palming off (misleading consumers into thinking they are buying another company's goods), and even "dumping."

Section 337 is activated by a domestic company's complaint to the U.S. International Trade Commission, an independent federal regulatory commission. The commission follows the Administrative Procedure Act in investigating the complaint and determining whether there has been a violation. The President has 60 days to review the commission's decision. Remedies can include cease and desist orders, temporary exclusion orders, and even permanent exclusion orders.

Because American businesses were losing as much as $40 billion annually from foreign infringement of U.S. patents and other intellectual property rights, in 1988 Congress directed the President to identify countries that do not protect copyrights and patents and to initiate expedited unfair trade investigations in egregious cases unless to do so would harm national economic interests.

HUMOR AND THE LAW

Lawyers appreciate humor, generally speaking. Two of the oldest jokes told among lawyers go like this:

*A young attorney is assigned to try a case in a distant town. Unexpectedly prevailing, the attorney sent a telegram to the home office, saying: "Justice was done." The senior partners telegrammed back: "Appeal at once!"

*An earnest young attorney gave an earnest if somewhat ineffectual two-hour closing statement to the jury, whereupon the wily and more experienced opposing counsel stood up and said: "Ladies and gentlemen of the jury, I shall follow the example of my young friend, and submit this case to you *without argument*."

Of course these days many jokes are at the expense of lawyers. Our favorite goes like this:

*A famous evangelist dies and goes to heaven. As St. Peter shows the evangelist to this rather humble abode, he notices a male attorney making passionate love to a beautiful young woman. The evangelist can't help but protest: "Wait a minute! You give me this humble shack with no television and no companionship of any type, while that lawyer makes love to a beautiful woman. What is going on here?" St. Peter simply replied: "Who are you to question that woman's punishment?"

ORGANIZING FOR INTERNATIONAL TRADE

The massive devastation of the Second World War had among its many casualties the international trade infrastructure, which had been growing slowly but perceptibly since the middle of the nineteenth century. One of the major tasks of reconstruction following 1945 was the recreation of a framework for international trade. Negotiations focusing on trade, money, and finance led to establishment of the current international economic institutions, including the GATT, the International Monetary Fund, and the International Bank for Reconstruction and Development. More recently, regional trade agreements have become a prominent means of facilitating international trade.

THE GATT

The United Nations Conference on Trade and Employment met in Havana in late 1947 and was attended by more than 50 countries. Although the conference was unsuccessful in creating a proposed International Trade Organization, it led almost two dozen countries to conclude the GATT (General Agreement on Tariffs and Trade), the essential purpose of which was to achieve a significant reduction of the general level of national tariffs and, further, to provide an institutional framework within which future tariff conflicts be resolved. The GATT has, since its creation, shown itself to be of enduring significance in international economic and trade relations. According to its supporters, the GATT trading system has achieved unprecedented trade expansion and world prosperity. (Its detractors note that GATT provisions are often breached by participating countries.)

The GATT achieves its overall objective of liberalized international trade by addressing a series of key issues regarding import restrictions. It requires that each signatory state extend "most favored nation" tariff rates to goods from other signatory nations and, further, obligates participating nations to afford "national treatment" to the imported goods from other signatory countries. Article III of the agreement provides

> *The products of the territory of any contracting party imported into the territory of any other contracting party shall be accorded treatment no less favorable than that accorded to like products of national origin in respect of all laws, regulations and requirements affecting their internal sale, offering for sale, purchase, transportation, distribution or use.*

The GATT prohibits discrimination by participating states through quantitative trade restrictions by providing that import quotas, if adopted at all by a state, shall be applied equally to all nations that are parties to the agreement. An even more ambitious objective of the GATT is the elimination of all prohibitions or restrictions (other than duties, taxes, or other charges) on imports and exports among the member nations.

In large measure, the GATT implements its goals of free trade through a series of published tariff schedules developed through an intricate negotiation process within the framework of the organization and that, once published, are binding on each of the participating states. In recognition of inevitable trade anomalies and to secure the willing participation and cooperation of member states in its tariff reduction program, the GATT provides special circumstances when unilateral exceptions to the schedules of tariffs may be made. The most well known of these relate to antidumping duties and countervailing subsidies.

If the products of one country are "dumped" into another at prices below their fair market value in the exporting country in an effort to disrupt or destroy the domestic production of those goods in the receiving nation, the GATT contemplates that the government of the receiving country may impose an "antidumping duty" in an effort to equalize the domestic price in those goods with the prevailing fair market price in the exporting country.

Similarly, when the production of certain goods in the exporting state is heavily subsidized by the government of that nation (leading to a reduced export price for that product), the GATT permits the receiving state to impose a "countervailing duty" to bring the market price up to a competitive level.

In its formative years, the GATT concentrated almost exclusively on measures to reduce tariff barriers to increase international trade. More recently, it has turned its attention to the reduction of nontariff barriers, such as unreasonably restrictive local standards and inaccessible national distribution systems, to further increase the volume of trade among nations.

During the rounds of negotiation, nations bargain to advance their positions. The United States, for example, seeks to induce Europe and Japan to lower subsidies for their farmers who compete with American agriculture and to induce Third World nations to refrain from pirating U.S. trademarks, copyrights, and patents. Many nations seek to induce Japan to open its economy to foreign sellers and urge the United States to reduce its protection for textiles. For their part, underdeveloped nations seek freer access to advanced technology and to markets for their agricultural products.

IMF AND THE IBRD

The International Monetary Fund (IMF), like the GATT, is intended to coordinate the activities of governments regarding international trade functions and does not primarily address the individual international trader. Growing out of discussions held at Bretton Woods, New Hampshire, late in the Second World War, the IMF was designed to speed international financial and economic reconstruction by providing an institutional structure within which intergovernmental loans would be used to stabilize currency exchange rates and, through a system of credits (termed *Special Drawing Rights* or *SDRs*), to enable member countries to borrow from the fund or from each other as a means of stabilizing their national currencies with the international monetary system.

Affiliated with the International Monetary Fund is the International Bank for Reconstruction and Development (IBRD), which was founded to "assist in the reconstruction and development of territories of members by facilitating the investment of capital for productive purposes" and to "promote private foreign investment by means of guarantees or participations in loans and other investments made by private investors." The IBRD, located in Washington, D.C., is permitted under its charter to guarantee, participate in, or make loans to member states and to any business, industrial, or agricultural enterprise in the territories of a member state. The availability through the IMF and IBRD of massive amounts of financial credit was particularly significant in Western Europe during the immediate postwar years and has had, in addition, a very significant role in the industrial development of Asia and Africa in the past several decades.

REGIONAL TRADE AGREEMENTS

The multilateral approach to trade negotiation embodied in GATT is complemented by various regional trading arrangements. Latin American countries, Pacific Rim countries, and various other regional groupings have acted in concerted fashion to enhance trade and investment among their members. Two such regional agreements are of particular importance to American businesses.

United States–Canada Free Trade Act

The United States and Canada have the world's largest trading partnership. Trade between the two countries rose from $74 billion in 1980 to more than $150 billion by 1988. To further enhance this already productive relationship, the two countries entered into the Free Trade Act (FTA), which took effect on January 1, 1989, and, over a 10-year period, is intended to phase out virtually all remaining tariffs.

The FTA will not result in the complete integration that exists among American states or Canadian provinces. However, it will curtail trade barriers and ensure that any still existing serve legitimate purposes, such as protection of health, environment, or national security. Approximately 80 percent of all goods were already crossing the border between the two countries duty-free. The FTA will reduce tariffs on most other items and will significantly relax foreign investment restrictions (especially those existing in Canada) to facilitate direct investment between businesses of the two nations. The FTA also aims to facilitate fair competition, to establish effective dispute-resolution procedures, and to lay the foundation for further bilateral and multilateral trade cooperation.

United States–Mexico Free Trade

As this edition is written, the United States is negotiating with Mexico to obtain a free-trade relationship along the lines of that developed with Canada. Such efforts are aimed at creating a unified continental market in North American similar to that in Europe discussed in the next section.

European Economic Community

By the Treaty of Rome in 1958, six European countries (Belgium, France, Italy, Luxembourg, The Netherlands, and West Germany) formed the EEC. Eventually joined by six other nations (Denmark, Ireland, the United Kingdom, Greece, Portugal, and Spain), the EEC seeks economic integration and the creation of a single internal European market.[11] The Single Euorpean Act of 1987 set December 31, 1992, as the target date for completion of implementing legislation.

EEC members are motivated not only by the hope of gaining an economic advantage by combining their markets, but also by a desire to bind Western Europe more tightly in a political and social sense. A basic principle

---

[11] Greenland joined the EEC but later withdrew. Turkey has asked to become a member, and it is expected that Austria will also apply for membership.

of the EEC is creation of a Community Law, which will preempt national law wherever national law might conflict. The EEC is not likely to create a "United States of Europe." After all, there are still 12 separate governments and nine different languages. However, by harmonizing economic regulations in the various states and breaking down trade barriers, the EEC will probably become a very stong economic entity that all trading competitors, including U.S. businesses, will have to reckon with.

As of this writing, the EEC has already transferred to Community institutions the power to set tariff policies and abolish customs duties among member states, harmonized the system for designation and codification of goods, empowered the Community to counteract anticompetitive practices and to defend itself politically, and issued 300 very precise directives concerning industrial products, metrology, textiles, electricity, labeling, advertising, sale of hazardous materials, and the like—all aimed at expediting trade among Community members.

OTHER WAYS OF DOING BUSINESS

Thus far, we have spoken of international trade mainly in terms of direct sales from a seller in one country to a buyer in another. However, there are many other forms of international transactions. Take the case of an American corporation wishing to export its goods. Rather than sending its own employees to the foreign markets to drum up business at the retail or wholesale level, it might hire an **agent** in that foreign country to act on its behalf. Such agents would typically have authority to contract on behalf of the American sellers. Complications would likely arise from the differences between agency law and customs in the United States and those of the foreign country.

Or the American company might choose to do business through a **licensee** in the foreign country. That licensee would pay a fee to the American company for the right to sell the company's goods. Such licensees, of course, will want exclusive rights to sell the American company's products, if possible. Legal problems here may result from the antitrust laws of the United States and the foreign country. An increasingly popular form of such licensing arrangement is the franchising of trademarks, tradenames, and copyrights. Many American service industries, such as fast food chains and convenience store chains, are expanding to foreign markets through use of this device.

Or an American seller may wish to have a foreign subsidiary corporation formed in the foreign nations in which it seeks to do business. This process is complicated by the many restrictions that most countries, especially in the underdeveloped world, place on such corporations. Such restrictions may take the form of **currency controls,** which make it difficult to take profits out of the country. Or the most country may require a certain percentage of host country ownership of the American company's subsidiary or require that it enter into a joint venture with the host government or a local company.

India, for example has endeavored to "Indianize" foreign companies operating there. In the wake of the terrible 1984 Bhopal, India, gas leak that killed 2,700 and injured perhaps 200,000, the Union Carbide Corporation has *claimed* that its subsidiary—Union Carbide India Ltd.—was so "Indianized" that Union Carbide could not have shut the plant down out of safety concerns had it wanted to. All 9,000 employees of the company were Indian, and quasi-governmental Indian financial institutions owned 25 percent of its stock. Union Carbide itself retained only 50.9 percent of the subsidiary's stock. In many lesser developed countries, foreign corporations are limited to 49 percent ownership; local entities must retain control.

The following case illustrates legal issues that may arise with use of one of these methods of doing business abroad—the franchise.

DAYAN v. McDONALD'S CORPORATION

APPELLATE COURT OF ILLINOIS 466 N.E.2d 958, 1984

In 1971, Dayan and McDonald's Corp. signed a master license agreement (MLA), granting Dayan a 30-year franchise right to use the McDonald's patents, trademarks, and tradenames in Paris. The agreement bound Dayan to meet McDonald's Quality, Service, and Cleanliness (QSC) standards, because his departure from them would impede the successful operation of McDonald's restaurants in other parts of the world. If Dayan defaulted, McDonald's had the right to terminate the agreement. McDonald's issued operating licenses to Dayan for 14 restaurants.

However, McDonald's was never satisfied with Dayan's compliance with QSC standards. In 1976, McDonald's told Dayan that his substandard operation could no longer be tolerated and that he would have six months to bring his restaurants into compliance with the QSC standards. When Dayan failed to do so, McDonald's sued in Paris to terminate the MLA. Dayan then brought this action in Illinois to enjoin the termination.

The trial judge, after 65 days of testimony, refused to issue the injunction, ruling that McDonald's properly terminated the MLA because of Dayan's breach of its QSC provisions. Dayan appealed.

BUCKLEY, PRESIDING JUSTICE:

[Several] cases reflect judicial concern over longstanding abuses in franchise relationships, particularly contract provisions giving the franchisor broad unilateral powers of termination at will. Taken collectively, they stand for the proposition that the implied covenant of good faith restricts franchisor discretion in terminating a franchise agreement to those cases where good cause exists.

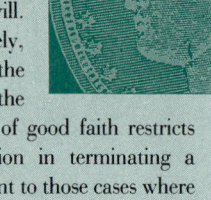

After finding good cause for termination existed, the trial court found that McDonald's sole motive for termination was Dayan's failure to maintain QSC standards.

Our review of the evidence admits of no doubt; the trial court properly resolved this issue in favor of McDonald's. To characterize the condition of Dayan's restaurants as being in substantial noncompliance with McDonald's QSC standards is to engage in profound

CONTINUED

understatement. Throughout trial the various witnesses struggled to find the appropriate words to describe the ineffably unsanitary conditions observed in these restaurants, as did the trial court in its memorandum opinion. Terms describing the uncleanliness—such as "indescribable," "extremely defective sanitary conditions," "filthy, grimy, cruddy," "deplorable," "significantly unsanitary," "contaminated," "insanitary," "very dirty," "very, very dirty," "disgusting," "abundance of filth," "pig pens"—tell only part of the story. The accuracy of these epithets is supported by voluminous, detailed testimonial evidence which consumed many weeks of trial and thousands of pages of transcript and is also corroborated by over 1,000 photographs admitted in evidence at trial. The conditions of filth were so widespread and reported by so many persons that any attempt to catalog them all would only unduly lengthen this opinion.

[Dayan's complaint that McDonald's did not provide a trained, French-speaking operations man] rings false. As the trial court correctly realized:

"It does not take a McDonald's trained French speaking operational man to know that grease dripping from the vents must be stopped and not merely collected in a cup hung from the ceiling, that dogs are not permitted to defecate where food is stored, that insecticide is not blended with chicken breading, that past-dated products should be discarded, that a potato peeler should be somewhat cleaner than a tire-vulcanizer and that shortening should not look like crankcase oil."

[Affirmed.]

REGULATING THE TRANSNATIONAL CORPORATION

The rise of huge and powerful transnational corporations (TNCs) is one of the defining elements of the post-World War II global economic environment. TNCs such as IBM, Exxon, and Toyota can have a tremendous impact on the economy, culture, and environment of developing host countries. In the early 1970s, a series of economic, political, and legal factors focused international attention on the role and impact of these TNCs in global economic relationships.

TNCs are naturally interested in gaining free entry to foreign economies and protecting the investments they make there. For their part, developing countries are concerned with avoiding repetition of the consequences of earlier colonialism. They wish to have their local laws and autonomy respected and to protect their resources, culture, environment, and workers. They wish to be fairly treated and assisted to develop and not merely exploited.

For the past two decades efforts at balancing these competing interests have been ongoing in a number of spheres. Several bilateral treaties have been signed between developed and developing nations, wherein the former promised certain concessions to obtain the latters' protection of TNC investments. Some regional pacts have also been signed.

Perhaps most importantly, the United Nations has played a major role. Completion of the U.N. Code of Conduct on Transnational Corporations may finally be at hand. The code specifies that treatment of TNCs by host countries should be fair and equitable. Specific standards on matters of nationalization and compensation, national regulation, transfer of payments, and settlements of disputes are all set forth.

Additional guiding principles include an International Code of Marketing of Breast-Milk Substitutes (under the jurisdiction of the World Health Organization), Guidelines of Consumer Protection (adopted by the U.N. General Assembly), and Criteria for Sustainable Development (aimed at discouraging overexploitation by TNCs).

Questions and Problems

1. Schlunk, an American whose parents were killed in an accident, filed suit in the United States against a German company, Volkswagen AG (VWAG), and its wholly owned U.S. subsidiary, Volkswagen of America (VWOA). Schlunk did not attempt to serve VWAG in West Germany. Instead, he argued that service on VWOA in the United States constituted adequate service on VWAG. VWAG took the view that it could be served only at its West German headquarters pursuant to the provisions of the Hague Convention on the Service of Process. Which view seems to be the better one? (*Volkswagenwerk Aktiengesellschaft v. Schlunk,* 108 S. Ct. 2104, 1988.)

2. Defendants are two corporations owned by the Republic of France. They design, manufacture, and market aircraft, including the "Rallye." The plaintiffs were injured when a Rallye crashed in Iowa; they filed a breach of warranty suit in federal court in Iowa. The plaintiffs made various discovery requests under the Federal Rules of Civil Procedure. The defendants complied with initial requests but later took the position that because they were French corporations, "and the discovery sought can only be found in a foreign state, namely France," the Hague Convention on the Taking of Evidence Abroad in Civil or Commercial Matters provided the exclusive means of pretrial discovery. Should this be the case? (*Societe Nationale Industrielle Aerospacetiale v. U.S. District Court,* 482 U.S. 522, 1987.)

3. In *Board of Trade of San Francisco v. Swiss Credit Bank,* the court held that the shipper's use of aircraft to transport goods did not strictly comply with the provision of the letter of credit stipulating ocean shipment. Does the manner of shipment make any difference if, in fact, they arrive on time and undamaged? What if the commercial invoices presented to the bank by the seller do not use the same unit of measurement for the goods as used in the letter of credit? The court in *Atari, Inc. v. Harris Trust and Savings Bank,* 599 F. Supp. 592 (N.D. Ill. 1984) said that this was not a basis on which to dishonor the letter of credit. How strict, then, is the doctrine of strict compliance?

4. It is normally important to an exporter that the letter of credit issued in payment for the goods be "irrevocable" so that the buyer/importer cannot cancel the letter after the seller has shipped under the contract. Must the term *irrevocable* be used in the letter of credit to make it so? Will words having the same significance make the letter "irrevocable"? If the letter of credit states that it "shall remain in force for a period of six (6) months," is it an irrevocable letter of credit for that period of time? *Conoco, Inc. v. Norwest Bank Mason City,* 767 F.2d 470 (8th Cir. 1985) held that such language made the letter of credit an irrevocable one.

5. Lamb grows tobacco in Kentucky. He sells to Phillip Morris and B.A.T. (defendants) and in so doing competes with foreign tobacco growers. Lamb filed an antitrust action against the defendants, claiming that their subsidiaries in Venezuela agreed to make periodic contributions to the favorite charity of the Venezuelan president's wife, in exchange for price controls on Venezuelan tobacco, elimination of controls on retail cigarette prices in Venezuela, and other concessions. The trial court dismissed the antitrust claim, holding that the act of state doctrine blocked their prosecution. Was the trial court correct? Discuss. (*Lamb v. Phillip Morris, Inc.*, 915 F.2d 1024, 6th Cir. 1990.)

6. In deciding a dispute over the ownership of a trademark originally owned by a company formed in pre-World War II Germany, a New York federal court had to decide whether to give effect to a judgment rendered by a court in post-World War II East Germany. The judge determined that the defendant had not received advanced notice of the opinion rendered by the Supreme Court of East Germany, that defendant had not participated in the proceedings, that East German courts did not have before them much of the essential proof needed to decide the case, and that the East German court's opinion lacked a "reasoned objective approach" and was "thoroughly saturated with a combination of communist propaganda, diatribes against the 'capitalist oriented' decision of the West German courts, and the absence of judicial restraint." Should the East German court's decision be given effect? Discuss. (*Carl Zeiss Stiftung v. VEB Carl Zeiss Jena*, 433 F.2d 686, 2d Cir. 1970.)

7. Geosource, Inc., of Houston, Texas, owned Sensor, a Netherland business organization. Sensor made a contract, governed by the law of The Netherlands, to deliver 2,400 strings of geophones to C.E.P. by September 1982, with the ultimate destination identified as the U.S.S.R. In June 1982, pursuant to the Export Administration Act of 1979, President Reagan prohibited the shipment to the U.S.S.R of equipment manufactured in foreign countries under license from U.S. firms. The purpose of the embargo was to sanction the imposition of martial law in Poland. Sensor notified C.E.P. that as a subsidiary of a U.S. company, it was bound to follow this ban and could therefore not fulfill its contract. C.E.P. sued in District Court at The Hague, Netherlands. To what extent should the court be bound to follow U.S. political policies? (*Compagnie Europeenne Des Petroles v. Sensor Nederland*, 22 ILM 66, District Court at The Hague, 1983.)

8. The possibility of damage is not the only risk that passes to the buyer at ship's rail in a C.I.F. contract. In *Badhwar v. Colorado Fuel & Iron Corp.*, 138 F. Supp. 595 (S.D.N.Y. 1955), goods shipped under a C.I.F. contract from California to Bombay were delayed en route almost six months because of a labor strike on the West Coast, causing damage to the Indian buyer. Neither buyer nor seller was responsible for the delay or the consequent loss to the buyer. The court nonetheless held that the risk of this loss had passed to the buyer when the goods cleared ship's rail in California. Does fault play no role in allocating the risk of loss? What if a seller is responsible for delay or damage after the goods are unloaded? Will this make any difference in a C.I.F. contract?

9. Nelson was hired in the United States to be a monitoring systems engineer for a hospital in Saudi Arabia. During the course of his duties, Nelson claims that he was detained and tortured by agents of the Saudi government in Saudi Arabia in retaliation for reporting safety violations at the hospital. Nelson sued Saudi Arabia, the hospital where he worked, and Royspec, a corporation owned and controlled by the Saudi government, claiming subject matter jurisdiction under the FSIA. The trial court dismissed for lack of such jurisdiction. Did the trial court err? Discuss. (*Nelson v. Saudi Arabia*, 923 F.2d 1528, 11th Cir. 1991.)

10. Chuidian, a Philippine citizen, has various business interests in California. In 1985, a Philippine government agency (Guarantee Corporation) sued Chuidian, who counterclaimed. The suit was settled out of court with the Philippine National Bank (Bank), a state-owned bank, issuing an irrevocable letter of credit to Chuidian on behalf of the Guarantee Corporation. Soon thereafter, the Philippine government of President Ferdinand Marcos was overthrown and replaced by a government led by Corazon Aquino. The new regime formed a Presidential Commission on Good Government for the purpose of recovering "ill-gotten wealth" accumulated by Marcos and his associates. Daza was appointed a member of the commission. Because the commission suspected that Marcos and Chuidian had entered into a fraudulent settlement of the aforementioned litigation to pay off Chuidian for not revealing certain facts about Marcos's involvement in Chuidian's business enterprises, Daza instructed the Bank not to make payment on the letter of credit issued to Chuidian. Chuidian filed suit against the Bank and added Daza as a defendant. The trial court granted Daza's motion to dismiss on grounds of sovereign immunity. Did the trial court err? Discuss. (*Chuidian v. Philippine Nat'l Bank*, 912 F.2d 1095, 9th Cir. 1990.)

THE CONSTITUTION OF THE UNITED STATES OF AMERICA

We the People of the United States, in Order to form a more perfect Union, establish Justice, insure domestic Tranquility, provide for the common defence, promote the general Welfare, and secure the Blessings of Liberty to ourselves and our Posterity, do ordain and establish this Constitution for the United States of America.

ARTICLE I

Section 1

All legislative Powers herein granted shall be vested in a Congress of the United States, which shall consist of a Senate and House of Representatives.

Section 2

The House of Representatives shall be composed of Members chosen every second Year by the People of the several States, and the Electors in each State shall have the Qualifications requisite for Electors of the most numerous Branch of the State Legislature.

No Person shall be a Representative who shall not have attained to the Age of twenty five Years, and been seven Years of Citizen of the United States, and who shall not, when elected, be an Inhabitant of that State in which he shall be chosen.

Representatives and direct Taxes shall be apportioned among the several States which may be included within this Union, according to their respective Numbers, which shall be determined by adding to the whole Number of free Persons, including those bound to Service for a Term of Years, and excluding Indians not taxed, three fifths of all other Persons. The actual Enumeration shall be made within three Years after the first Meeting of the Congress of the United States, and within every subsequent Term of ten Years, in such Manner as they shall by Law direct. The number of Representatives shall not exceed one for every thirty Thousand, but each State shall have at Least one Representative; and until such enumeration shall be made, the State of New Hampshire shall be entitled to chuse three, Massachusetts eight, Rhode Island and Providence Plantations one, Connecticut five, New York six, New Jersey four, Pennsylvania eight, Delaware one, Maryland six, Virginia ten, North Carolina five, South Carolina five, and Georgia three.

When vacancies happen in the Representation from any State, the Executive Authority thereof shall issue Writs of Election to fill such vacancies.

The House of Representatives shall chuse their Speaker and other Officers; and shall have the sole Power of Impeachment.

Section 3

The Senate of the United States shall be composed of two Senators from each State, chosen by the Legislature thereof, for six Years; and each Senator shall have one Vote.

Immediately after they shall be assembled in Consequence of the first Election, they shall be divided as equally as may be into three Classes. The Seats of the Senators of the first Class shall be vacated at the Expiration of the second Year, of the second Class at the Expiration of the fourth Year, and of the third Class at the Expiration of the sixth Year, so that one third may be chosen every second Year; and if Vacancies happen by Resignation, or otherwise, during the Recess of the Legislature of any State, the Executive thereof may make temporary Appointments until the next Meeting of the Legislature, which shall then fill such Vacancies.

No Person shall be a Senator who shall not have attained to the Age of thirty Years, and been nine Years a Citizen of the United States, and who shall not, when elected, be an Inhabitant of that State for which he shall be chosen.

The Vice President of the United States shall be President of the Senate, but shall have no Vote, unless they be equally divided.

The Senate shall chuse their other Officers, and also a President pro tempore, in the Absence of the Vice President, or when he shall exercise the Office of President of the United States.

The Senate shall have the sole power to try all Impeachments. When sitting for that Purpose, they shall be on Oath or Affirmation. When the President of the United States is tried, the Chief Justice shall preside: And no Person shall be convicted without the Concurrence of two thirds of the Members present.

Judgment in Cases of Impeachment shall not extend further than to removal from Office, and disqualification to hold and enjoy any Office of honor, Trust or Profit under the United States: but the Party convicted shall nevertheless be liable and subject to Indictment, Trial, Judgment and Punishment, according to Law.

Section 4

The Times, Places and Manner of holding Elections for Senators and Representatives, shall be prescribed in each State by the Legislature thereof: but the Congress may at any time by Law make or alter such Regulations, except as to the Places of chusing Senators.

The Congress shall assemble at least once in every Year, and such Meeting shall be on the first Monday in December, unless they shall by Law appoint a different Day.

Section 5

Each House shall be the Judge of the Elections, Returns and Qualifications of its own Members, and a Majority of each shall constitute a Quorum to do Business; but a smaller Number may adjourn from day to day, and may be authorized to compel the Attendance of absent Members, in such Manner, and under such Penalties as each House may provide.

Each House may determine the Rules of its Proceedings, punish its Members for disorderly Behaviour, and, with the Concurrence of two thirds, expel a Member.

Each House shall keep a Journal of its Proceedings, and from time to time publish the same, excepting such Parts as may in their Judgment require Secrecy; and the Yeas and Nays of the Members of either House on any question shall, at the Desire of one fifth of those Present, be entered on the Journal.

Neither House, during the Session of Congress, shall, without the Consent of the other, adjourn for more than three days, nor to any other Place than that in which the two Houses shall be sitting.

Section 6

The Senators and Representatives shall receive a Compensation for their Services, to be ascertained by Law, and paid out of the Treasury of the United States. They shall in all Cases, except Treason, Felony and Breach of the Peace, be privileged from Arrest during their Attendance at the Session of their respective Houses, and in going to and returning from the same; and for any Speech or Debate in either House, they shall not be questioned in any other Place.

No Senator or Representative shall, during the Time for which he was elected, be appointed to any civil Office under the Authority of the United States, which shall have been created, or the Emoluments whereof shall have been encreased during such time; and no Person holding any Office under the United States, shall be a Member of either House during his Continuance in Office.

Section 7

All Bills for raising Revenue shall originate in the House of Representatives; but the Senate may propose or concur with Amendments as on other bills.

Every Bill which shall have passed the House of Representatives and the Senate, shall, before it become a Law, be presented to the President of the United States; If he approve he shall sign it, but if not he shall return it, with his Objections to that House in which it shall have originated, who shall enter the Objections at large on their Journal, and proceed to reconsider it. If after such Reconsideration two thirds of that House shall agree to pass the Bill, it shall be sent, together with the Objections, to the other House, by which it shall likewise be reconsidered, and if approved by two thirds of that House, it shall become a Law. But in all such Cases the votes of both Houses shall be determined by Yeas and Nays, and the Names of the Persons voting for and against the Bill shall be entered on the Journal of each House respectively. If any Bill shall not be returned by the President within ten Days (Sundays excepted) after it shall have been presented to him, the Same shall be a Law, in like Manner as if he had signed it, unless the Congress by their Adjournment prevent its Return, in which Case it shall not be a Law.

Every Order, Resolution, or Vote to which the Concurrence of the Senate and House of Representatives may be necessary (except on a question of Adjournment) shall be presented to the President of the United States; and before the Same shall take Effect, shall be approved by him, or being disapproved by him, shall be repassed by two thirds of the Senate and House of Representatives, according to the Rules and Limitations prescribed in the Case of a Bill.

Section 8

The Congress shall have Power to lay and collect Taxes, Duties, Imposts and Excises, to pay the Debts and provide for the common Defence and general Welfare of the United States; but all Duties, Imposts and Excises shall be uniform throughout the United States;

To borrow Money on the credit of the United States;

To regulate Commerce with foreign Nations, and among the several States, and with the Indian Tribes;

To establish an uniform Rule of Naturalization, and uniform Laws on the subject of Bankruptcies throughout the United States;

To coin Money, regulate the Value thereof, and of foreign Coin, and fix the Standard of Weights and Measures;

To provide for the Punishment of counterfeiting the Securities and current Coin of the United States;

To establish Post Offices and post Roads;

To promote the Progress of Science and useful Arts, by securing for limited Times to Authors and Inventors the exclusive Right to their respective Writings and Discoveries;

To constitute Tribunals inferior to the supreme Court;

To define and punish Piracies and Felonies committed on the high Seas, and Offenses against the Law of Nations;

To declare War, grant Letters of Marque and Reprisal, and make Rules concerning Captures on Land and Water;

To raise and support Armies, but no Appropriation of Money to that Use shall be for a longer Term than two Years;

To provide and maintain a Navy;

To make Rules for the Government and Regulation of the land and naval Forces;

To provide for calling forth the Militia to execute the Laws of the Union, suppress Insurrections and repel Invasions;

To provide for organizing, arming, and disciplining, the Militia, and for governing such Part of them as may be employed in the Service of the United States, reserving to the States respectively, the Appointment of the Officers, and the Authority of training the Militia according to the discipline prescribed by Congress;

To exercise exclusive Legislation in all Cases whatsoever, over such District (not exceeding ten Miles square) as may, by Cession of particular States, and the Acceptance of Congress, become the Seat of the Government of the United States, and to exercise like Authority over all Places purchased by the Consent of the Legislature of the State in which the Same shall be, for the Erection of Forts, Magazines, Arsenals, dock-Yards, and other needful Building;—And

To make all Laws which shall be necessary and proper for carrying into Execution the foregoing Powers, and all other Powers vested by this Constitution in the Government of the United States, or in any Department or Officer thereof.

Section 9

The Migration or Importation of such Persons as any of the States now existing shall think proper to admit, shall not be prohibited by the Congress prior to the Year one thousand eight hundred and eight, but a Tax or Duty may be imposed on such Importation, not exceeding ten dollars for each Person.

The Privilege of the Writ of Habeas Corpus shall not be suspended, unless when in Cases of Rebellion or Invasion the public Safety may require it.

No Bill of Attainder or ex post facto Law shall be passed.

No Capitation, or other direct, Tax shall be laid unless in Proportion to the Census or Enumeration herein before directed to be taken.

No Tax or Duty shall be laid on Articles exported from any State.

No Preference shall be given by any Regulation of Commerce or Revenue to the Ports of one State over those of another: nor shall Vessels bound to, or from, one State, be obliged to enter, clear, or pay Duties in another.

No Money shall be drawn from the Treasury, but in Consequence of Appropriations made by Laws; and a regular Statement and Account of the Receipts and Expenditures of all public Money shall be published from time to time.

No Title of Nobility shall be granted by the United States: And no Person holding any Office of Profit or Trust under them, shall, without the consent of the Congress, accept of any present, Emolument, Office, or Title, of any kind whatever, from any King, Prince, or foreign State.

Section 10

No State shall enter into any Treaty, Alliance, or Confederation; grant Letters of Marque and Reprisal; coin Money; emit Bills of Credit; make any Thing but gold and silver Coin a Tender in Payment of Debts; pass any Bill of Attainder, ex post facto Law, or Law impairing the Obligation of Contracts, or grant any Title of Nobility.

No State shall, without the Consent of the Congress, lay any Imposts or Duties on Imports or Exports, except what may be absolutely necessary for executing its inspection Laws: and the net Produce of all Duties and Imposts, laid by any State on Imports or Exports, shall be for the Use of the Treasury of the United States; and all such Laws shall be subject to the Revision and Controul of the Congress.

No State shall, without the Consent of Congress, lay any Duty of Tonnage, keep Troops, or Ships of War in time of Peace, enter into any Agreement or Compact with another State, or with a foreign Power, or engage in War, unless actually invaded, or in such imminent Danger as will not admit of delay.

ARTICLE II

Section 1

The executive Power shall be vested in a President of the United States of America. He shall hold his Office during the Term of four Years, and, together with the Vice President. But if there should remain two or more as follows:

Each State shall appoint, in such Manner as the Legislature thereof may direct, a Number of Electors, equal to the whole Number of Senators and Representatives to which the State may be entitled in the Congress: but no Senator or Representative, or Person holding an Office of Trust or Profit under the United States, shall be appointed an Elector.

The Electors shall meet in their respective States, and vote by Ballot for two Persons, of whom one at least shall not be an Inhabitant of the same State with themselves. And they shall make a List of all the Persons voted for, and of the Number of Votes for each; which List they shall sign and certify, and transmit sealed to the Seat of the Government of the United States, directed to the President of the Senate. The President of the Senate shall, in the Presence of the Senate and House of Representatives, open all the Certificates, and the Votes shall then be counted. The Person having the greatest Number of Votes shall be the President, if such Number be a Majority of the whole Number of Electors appointed; and if there be more than one who have such Majority, and have an equal Number of Votes, then the House of Representatives shall immediately chuse by Ballot one of them for President; and if no Person have a Majority, then from the five highest on the List the said House shall in like Manner chuse the President. But in chusing the President, the Votes shall be taken by States, the Representation from each State having one Vote; A quorum for this Purpose shall consist of a Member or Members from two thirds of the States, and a Majority of all the States shall be necessary to a Choice. In every Case, after the Choice of the President, the Person having the greatest Number of Votes of the Electors shall be the Vice President. But if there should remain two or more who have equal Votes, the Senate shall chuse from them by Ballot the Vice President.

The Congress may determine the Time of chusing the Electors, and the Day on which they shall give their Votes; which Day shall be the same throughout the United States.

No Person except a natural born Citizen, or a Citizen of the United States, at the time of the Adoption of this Constitution, shall be eligible to the Office of President; neither shall any Person be eligible to that Office who shall not have attained to the Age of thirty five Years, and been fourteen Years a Resident within the United States.

In Case of the Removal of the President from Office, or of his Death, Resignation, or Inability to discharge the Powers and Duties of the said Office, the Same shall devolve on the Vice President, and the Congress may by Law provide for the Case of Removal, Death, Resignation or Inability, both of the President and Vice President, declaring what Officer shall then act as President, and such Officer shall act accordingly, until the Disability be removed, or a President shall be elected.

The President shall, at stated Times, receive for his Services, a Compensation, which shall neither be encreased nor diminished during the Period for which he shall have been elected, and he shall not receive within that Period any other Emolument from the United States, or any of them.

Before he enter on the Execution of his Office, he shall take the following Oath or Affirmation:—"I do solemnly swear (or affirm) that I will faithfully execute the Office of President of the United States, and will to the best of my Ability, preserve, protect and defend the Constitution of the United States."

Section 2

The President shall be Commander in Chief of the Army and Navy of the United States, and of the Militia of the several States, when called into the actual Service of the United States; he may require the Opinion, in writing, of the principal Officer in each of the executive Departments, upon any Subject relating to the Duties of their respective Offices, and he shall have Power to grant Reprieves and Pardons for Offences against the United States, except in Cases of Impeachment.

He shall have Power, by and with the Advice and Consent of the Senate, to make Treaties, providing two thirds of the Senators present concur; and he shall nominate, and by and with the Advice and Consent of the Senate, shall appoint Ambassadors, other public Ministers and Consuls, Judges of the supreme Court, and all other Officers of the United States, whose Appointments are not herein otherwise provided for, and which shall be established by Law: but the Congress may by Law vest the Appointment of such inferior Officers, as they think proper, in the President alone, in the courts of Law, or in the Heads of Departments.

The President shall have Power to fill up all Vacancies that may happen during the Recess of the Senate, by granting Commissions which shall expire at the End of their next Session.

Section 3

He shall from time to time give to the Congress Information of the State of the Union, and recommend to their Consideration such Measures as he shall judge necessary and expedient; he may, on extraordinary Occasions, convene both Houses, or either of them, and in Case of Disagreement between them, with Respect to the Time of Adjournment, he may adjourn them to such Time as he shall think proper, he shall receive Ambassadors and other public Ministers; he shall take Care that the Laws be faithfully executed, and shall Commission all the Officers of the United States.

Section 4

The President, Vice President and all civil Officers of the United States, shall be removed from Office on Impeachment for, and Conviction of, Treason, Bribery, or other high Crimes and Misdemeanors.

ARTICLE III

Section 1

The Judicial Power of the United States, shall be vested in one supreme Court, and in such inferior Courts as the Congress may from time to time ordain and establish. The Judges, both of the supreme and inferior Courts, shall hold their Offices during good Behaviour, and shall, at stated Times, receive for their Services, a Compensation, which shall not be diminished during their Continuance in Office.

Section 2

The judicial Power shall extend to all Cases, in Law and Equity, arising under this Constitution, the Laws of the United States, and Treaties made, or which shall be made, under their Authority;—to all Cases affecting Ambassadors, other public Ministers and Consuls;—to all Cases of admirality and maritime Jurisdiction;—to Controversies to which the United States shall be a Party;—to Controversies between two or more States;—between a State and Citizens of another State;—between Citizens of different States;—between Citizens of the same State claiming Lands under Grants of different States, and between a State, or the Citizens thereof, and foreign States, Citizens or Subjects.

In all Cases affecting Ambassadors, other public Ministers and Consuls, and those in which a State shall be Party, the supreme Court shall have original Jurisdiction. In all the other Cases before mentioned, the supreme Court shall have appellate Jurisdiction, both as to Law and Fact, with such Exceptions, and under such Regulations as the Congress shall make.

The Trial of all Crimes, except in Cases of Impeachment, shall be by Jury; and such Trial shall be held in the State where the said Crimes shall have been committed; but when not committed within any State, the Trial shall be at such Place or Places as the Congress may by Law have directed.

Section 3

Treason against the United States, shall consist only in levying War against them, or in adhering to their Enemies, giving them Aid and Comfort. No Person shall be convicted of Treason unless on the Testimony of two Witnesses to the same overt Act, or on Confession in open Court.

The Congress shall have Power to declare the Punishment of Treason, but no Attainder of Treason shall work Corruption of Blood, or Forfeiture except during the Life of the Person attained.

ARTICLE IV

Section 1

Full Faith and Credit shall be given in each State to the public Acts, Records, and judicial Proceedings of every other State. And the Congress may be general Laws prescribe the Manner in which such Acts, Records and Proceedings shall be proved, and the Effect thereof.

Section 2

The Citizens of each State shall be entitled to all Privileges and Immunities of Citizens in the several States.

A Person charged in any State with Treason, Felony, or other Crime, who shall flee from Justice, and be found in another State, shall on Demand of the executive Authority of the State from which he fled, be delivered up, to be removed to the State having Jurisdiction of the Crime.

No Person held to Service or Labour in one State, under the Laws thereof, escaping into another, shall, in Consequence of any Law or Regulation therein, be discharged from such Service or Labour, but shall be delivered up on Claim of the Party to whom such Service or Labour may be due.

Section 3

New States may be admitted by the Congress into this Union; but no new State shall be formed or erected within the Jurisdiction of any other State; nor any State be formed by the Junction of two or more States, or Parts of States, without the Consent of the Legislatures of the States concerned as well as of the Congress.

The Congress shall have Power to dispose of and make all needful Rules and Regulations respecting the Territory or other Property belonging to the United States; and nothing in this Constitution shall be so construed as to Prejudice any Claims of the United States, or of any particular State.

Section 4

The United States shall guarantee to every State in this Union a Republican Form of Government, and shall protect each of them against Invasion; and on Application of the Legislature, or of the Executive (when the Legislature cannot be convened) against domestic Violence.

ARTICLE V

The Congress, whenever two thirds of both Houses shall deem it necessary, shall propose Amendments to this Constitution, or, on the Application of the Legislatures of two thirds of the several States, shall call a Convention for proposing Amendments, which, in either Case, shall be valid to all Intents and Purposes, as Part of this Constitution, when ratified by the Legislatures of three fourths of the several States, or by Conventions in three fourths thereof, as the one or the other Mode of Ratification may be proposed by the Congress; Provided that no Amendment which may be made prior to the Year One thousand eight hundred and eight shall in any Manner affect the first and fourth Clauses in the Ninth Section of the first Article; and that no State, without its Consent, shall be deprived of its equal Suffrage in the Senate.

ARTICLE VI

All Debts contracted and Engagements entered into, before the Adoption of this Constitution, shall be as valid against the United States under this Constitution, as under the Confederation.

This Constitution, and the Laws of the United States which shall be made in Pursuance thereof; and all Treaties made, or which shall be made, under the Authority of the United States, shall be the supreme Law of the Land; and the Judges in every State shall be bound thereby, any Thing in the Constitution or Laws of any State to the Contrary notwithstanding.

The Senators and Representatives before mentioned, and the Members of the several State Legislatures, and all executive and judicial Officers, both of the United States and of the several States, shall be bound by Oath or Affirmation, to support this Constitution; but no religious Test shall ever be required as a Qualification to any Office or public Trust under the United States.

ARTICLE VII

The Ratification of the Conventions of nine States, shall be sufficient for the Establishment of this Constitution between the States so ratifying the Same.

AMENDMENT I {1791}

Congress shall make no law respecting an establishment of religion, or prohibiting the free exercise thereof; or abridging the freedom of speech, or of the press; or the right of the people peaceably to assemble, and to petition the Government for a redress of grievances.

AMENDMENT II {1791}

A well regulated Militia, being necessary to the security for a free State, the right of the people to keep and bear Arms, shall not be infringed.

AMENDMENT III {1791}

No Soldier shall, in time of peace be quartered in any house, without the consent of the Owner, nor in time of war, but in a manner to be prescribed by law.

AMENDMENT IV {1791}

The right of the people to be secure in their persons, houses, papers, and effects, against unreasonable searches and seizures, shall not be violated, and no Warrants shall issue, but upon probable cause, supported by Oath or affirmation, and particularly describing the place to be searched, and the persons or things to be seized.

AMENDMENT V {1791}

No person shall be held to answer for a capital, or otherwise infamous crime, unless on a presentment or indictment of a Grand Jury, except in cases arising in the land or naval forces, or in the Militia, when in actual service in time of War or public danger; nor shall any person be subject for the same offense to be twice put in jeopardy of life or limb; nor shall be compelled in any criminal case to be a witness against himself, nor be deprived of life, liberty, or property, without due process of law; nor shall private property be taken for public use, without just compensation.

AMENDMENT VI {1791}

In all criminal prosecutions, the accused shall enjoy the right to a speedy and public trial, by an impartial jury of the State and district wherein the crime shall have been committed, which district shall have been previously ascertained by law, and to be informed of the nature and cause of the accusation; to be confronted with the Witnesses against him; to have compulsory process for obtaining witnesses in his favor, and to have the Assistance of counsel for his defence.

AMENDMENT VII {1791}

In Suits at common law, where the value in controversy shall exceed twenty dollars, the right of trial by jury shall be preserved, and no fact tried by a jury, shall be otherwise reexamined in any Court of the United States, than according to the rules of the common law.

AMENDMENT VIII {1791}

Excessive bail shall not be required, no excessive fines imposed, nor cruel and unusual punishment inflicted.

AMENDMENT IX {1791}

The enumeration in the Constitution, of certain rights, shall not be construed to deny or disparage others retained by the people.

AMENDMENT X {1791}

The powers not delegated to the United States by the Constitution, nor prohibited by it to the States, are reserved to the States respectively, or to the people.

AMENDMENT XI {1798}

The Judicial power of the United States shall not be construed to extend to any suit in law or equity, commenced or prosecuted against one of the United States by Citizens of another State, or by Citizens or Subjects of any Foreign State.

AMENDMENT XII {1804}

The Electors shall meet in their respective states and vote by ballot for President and Vice-President, one of whom, at least, shall not be an inhabitant of the same state with themselves; they shall name in their ballots the person voted for as President, and in distinct ballots the person voted for as Vice-President, and they shall make distinct lists of all persons voted for as President, and of all persons voted for as Vice-President, and of the number of votes for each, which lists they shall sign and certify, and transmit sealed to the seat of the government of the United States, directed to the President of the Senate;—The President of the Senate shall, in the presence of the Senate and House of Representatives, open all the certificates and the votes shall then be counted;—The person having the greatest number of votes for President, shall be the President, if such number be a majority of the whole number of Electors appointed; and if no person have such majority, then from the persons having the highest numbers not exceeding three on the list of those voted for as President, the House of Representatives shall choose immediately, by ballot, the President. But in choosing the President, the votes shall be taken by states, the representation from each state having one vote; a quorum for this purpose shall consist of a member or members from two-thirds of the states, and a majority of all the states shall be necessary to a choice. And if the House of Representatives shall not choose a President whenever the right of choice shall devolve upon them, before the fourth day of March next following, then the Vice-President shall act as President, as in the case of the death or other constitutional disability of the President. The person having the greatest number of votes as Vice-President, shall be the Vice-President, if such number be a majority of the whole number of Electors appointed, and if no person have a majority, then from the two highest numbers on the list, the Senate shall choose the Vice-President; a quorum for the purpose shall consist of two-thirds of the whole number of Senators, and a majority of the whole number shall be necessary to a choice. But no person constitutionally ineligible to the office of President shall be eligible to that of the Vice-President of the United States.

AMENDMENT XIII {1865}

Section 1

Neither slavery nor involuntary servitude, except as a punishment for crime whereof the party shall have been duly convicted, shall exist within the United States, or any place subject to their jurisdiction.

Section 2

Congress shall have power to enforce this article by appropriate legislation.

AMENDMENT XIV {1868}

Section 1

All persons born or naturalized in the United States, and subject to the jurisdiction thereof, are citizens of the United States and of the State wherein they reside. No State shall make or enforce any law which shall abridge the privileges or immunities of citizens of the United States; nor shall any State deprive any person of life, liberty, or property, without due process of law; nor deny to any person within its jurisdiction the equal protection of the laws.

Section 2

Representatives shall be appointed among the several States according to their respective numbers, counting the whole number of persons in each State, excluding Indians not taxed. But when the right to vote at any election for the choice of electors for President and Vice President of the United States, Representatives in Congress, the Executive and Judicial officers of a State, or the members of the Legislature thereof, is denied to any of the male inhabitants of such State, being twenty-one years of age, and citizens of the United States, or in any way abridged, except for participation in rebellion, or other crime, the basis of representation therein shall be reduced in the proportion which the number of such male citizens shall bear to the whole number of male citizens twenty-one years of age in such State.

Section 3

No person shall be a Senator or Representative in Congress, or elector of President and Vice President, or hold any office, civil or military, under the United States, or under any State, who, having previously taken an oath, as a member of Congress, or as an officer of the United States, or as a member of any State legislature, or as an executive or judicial officer of any State, to support the Constitution of the United States, shall have engaged in insurrection or rebellion against the same, or given aid or comfort to the enemies thereof. But Congress may by a vote of two-thirds of each House, remove such disability.

Section 4

The validity of the public debt of the United States, authorized by law, including debts incurred for payment of pensions and bounties for services in suppressing insurrection or rebellion, shall not be questioned. But neither the United States nor any State shall assume or pay any debt or obligation incurred in aid of insurrection or rebellion against the United States, or any claim for the loss or emancipation of any slave; but all such debts, obligations and claims shall be held illegal and void.

Section 5

The Congress shall have power to enforce, by appropriate legislation, the provisions of this article.

AMENDMENT XV {1870}

Section 1

The right of citizens of the United States to vote shall not be denied or abridged by the United States or by any State on account of race, color, or previous condition of servitude.

Section 2

The Congress shall have power to enforce this article by appropriate legislation.

AMENDMENT XVI {1913}

The Congress shall have power to lay and collect taxes on incomes, from whatever source derived, without apportionment among the several States, and without regard to any census or enumeration.

AMENDMENT XVII {1913}

The Senate of the United States shall be composed of two Senators from each State, elected by the people thereof, for six years; and each Senator shall have one vote. The electors in each State shall have the qualifications requisite for electors of the most numerous branch of the State legislatures.

When vacancies happen in the representation of any State in the Senate, the executive authority of each State shall issue writs of election to fill such vacancies; *Provided*, That the legislature of any State may empower the executive thereof to make temporary appointments until the people fill in the vacancies by election as the legislature may direct.

This amendment shall not be so construed as to affect the election or term of any Senator chosen before it becomes valid as part of the Constitution.

AMENDMENT XVIII {1919}

Section 1

After one year from the ratification of this article the manufacture, sale, or transportation of intoxicating liquors within, the importation thereof into, or the exportation thereof from the United States and all territory subject to the jurisdiction thereof for beverage purposes is hereby prohibited.

Section 2

The Congress and the several States shall have concurrent power to enforce this article by appropriate legislation.

Section 3

This article shall be inoperative unless it shall have been ratified as an amendment to the Constitution by the legislature of the several States, as provided in the Constitution, within seven years from the date of the submission hereof to the States by the Congress.

AMENDMENT XIX {1920}

The right of citizens of the United States to vote shall not be denied or abridged by the United States or by any State on account of sex.

Congress shall have power to enforce this article by appropriate legislation.

AMENDMENT XX {1933}

Section 1

The terms of the President and Vice President shall end at noon on the 20th day of January, and the terms of Senators and Representatives at noon on the 3d day of January, of the years in which such terms would have ended if this article had not been ratified; and the terms of their successors shall then begin.

Section 2

The Congress shall assemble at least once in every year, and such meeting shall begin at noon on the 3d day of January, unless they shall by law appoint a different day.

Section 3

If, at the time fixed for the beginning of the term of the President, the President elect shall have died, the Vice President elect shall become President. If a President shall not have been chosen before the time fixed for the beginning of his term, or if the President elect shall have failed to qualify, then the Vice President elect shall act as President until a President shall have qualified; and the Congress may by law provide for the case wherein neither a President elect nor a Vice President elect shall have qualified, declaring who shall then act as President, or the manner in which one who is to act shall be selected, and such person shall act accordingly until a President or Vice President shall have qualified.

Section 4

The Congress may be law provide for the case of the death of any of the persons from whom the House of Representatives may choose a President whenever the right of choice shall have devolved upon them, and for the case of the death of any of the persons from whom the Senate may choose a Vice President whenever the right of choice shall have devolved upon them.

Section 5

Section 1 and 2 shall take effect on the 15th day of October following the ratification of this article.

Section 6

This article shall be inoperative unless it shall have been ratified as an amendment to the Constitution by the legislatures of three-fourths of the several States within seven years from the date of its submission.

AMENDMENT XXI {1933}

Section 1

The eighteenth article of amendment to the Constitution of the United States is hereby repealed.

Section 2

The transportation or importation into any State, Territory, or possession of the United States for delivery or use therein of intoxicating liquors, in violation of the laws thereof, is hereby prohibited.

Section 3

This article shall be inoperative unless it shall have been ratified as an amendment to the Constitution by conventions in the several States, as provided in the Constitution, within seven years from the date of the submission hereof to the States by the Congress.

AMENDMENT XXII {1951}

Section 1

No person shall be elected to the office of the President more than twice, and no person who has held the office of President, or acted as President, for more than two years of a term to which some other person was elected President shall be elected to the office of the President more than once. But this Article shall not apply to any person holding the office of President when this Article was proposed by the Congress, and shall not prevent any person who may be holding the office of President, or acting as President, during the term within which this Article becomes operative from holding the office of President or acting as President during the remainder of such term.

Section 2

This article shall be inoperative unless it shall have been ratified as an amendment to the Constitution by the legislatures of three-fourths of the several States within seven years from the date of its submission to the States by the Congress.

AMENDMENT XXIII {1961}

Section 1

The District constituting the seat of Government of the United States shall appoint in such manner as the Congress may direct:

A number of electors of President and Vice President equal to the whole number of Senators and Representatives in Congress to which the District would be entitled if it were a State, but in no event more than the least populous State; they shall be in addition to those appointed by the States, but they shall be considered, for the purposes of the election of President and Vice President, to be electors appointed by a State; and they shall meet in the District and perform such duties as provided by the twelfth article of amendment.

Section 2

The Congress shall have power to enforce this article by appropriate legislation.

AMENDMENT XXIV {1964}

Section 1

The right of citizens of the United States to vote in any primary or other election for President or Vice President, for electors for President or Vice President, or for Senator or Representative in Congress, shall not be denied or abridged by the United States or any State by reason of failure to pay any poll tax or other tax.

Section 2

The Congress shall have power to enforce this article by appropriate legislation.

AMENDMENT XXV {1967}

Section 1

In case of the removal of the President from office or of his death or resignation, the Vice President shall become President.

Section 2

Whenever there is a vacancy in the office of the Vice President, the President shall nominate a Vice President who shall take office upon confirmation by a majority vote of both Houses of Congress.

Section 3

Whenever the President transmits to the President pro tempore of the Senate and the Speaker of the House of Representatives his written declaration that he is unable to discharge the powers and duties of his office, and until he transmits to them a written declaration to the contrary, such powers and duties shall be discharged by the Vice President as Acting President.

Section 4

Whenever the Vice President and a majority of either the principal officers of the executive departments or of such other body as Congress may by law provide, transmit to the President pro tempore of the Senate and the Speaker of the House of Representatives their written declaration that the President is unable to discharge the powers and duties of his office, the Vice President shall immediately assume the powers and duties of the office as Acting President.

Thereafter, when the President transmits to the President pro tempore of the Senate and the Speaker of the House of Representatives his written declaration that no inability exists, he shall resume the powers and duties of his office unless the Vice President and a majority of either the principal officers of the executive department or of such other body as Congress may by law provide, transmit within four days to the President pro tempore of the Senate and the Speaker of the House of Representatives their written declaration that the President is unable to discharge the powers and duties of his office. Thereupon Congress shall decide the issue, assembling within forty-eight hours for that purpose if not in session. If the Congress, within twenty-one days after receipt of the latter written declaration, or, if Congress is not in session, within twenty-one days after Congress is required to assemble, determines by two-thirds vote of both Houses that the President is unable to discharge the powers and duties of his office, the Vice President shall continue to discharge the same as Acting President; otherwise, the President shall resume the powers and duties of his office.

AMENDMENT XXVI {1971}

Section 1

The right of citizens of the United States, who are eighteen years of age or older, to vote shall not be denied or abridge by the United States or by any State on account of age.

Section 2

The Congress shall have power to enforce this article by apropriate legislation.

APPENDIX B

SHERMAN ACT (AS AMENDED) (EXCERPTS)

Section 1. Every contract, combination in the form of trust or otherwise, or conspiracy, in restraint of trade or commerce among the several States, or with foreign nations, is delcared to be illegal. Every person who shall make any contract or engage in any combination or conspiracy hereby declared to be illegal shall be deemed guilty of a felony, and, on conviction thereof, shall be punished by fine not exceeding one million dollars if a corporation, or, if any other person, one hundred thousand dollars or by imprisonment not exceeding three years, or by both said punishments, in the discretion of the court.

Section 2. Every person who shall monopolize,, or attempt to monopolize, or combine or conspire with any other person or persons, to monopolize any part of the trade or commerce among the several States, or with foreign nations, shall be deemed guilty of a felony, and, on conviction thereof, shall be punished by fine not exceeding one million dollars if a corporation, or, if any other person, one hundred thousand dollars or by imprisonment not exceeding three years, or by both said punishments, in the discretion of the court.

CLAYTON ACT (AS AMENDED) (EXCERPTS)

Section 3. It shall be unlawful for any person engaged in commerce, in the course of such commerce, to lease or make a sale or contract for sale of goods, wares, merchandise, machinery, supplies, or other commodities, whether patented or unpatented, for use, consumption, or resale within the United States or any Territory thereof or the District of Columbia or any insular possession or other place under the jurisdiction of the United States, or fix a price charged therefor, or discount from, or rebate upon, such price, on the condition, agreement, or understanding that the lessee or purchaser thereof shall not use or deal in the goods, wares, merchandise, machinery, supplies, or other commodities of a competitor or competitors of the lessor of seller, where the effect of such lease, sale, or contract for sale or such condition, agreement, or understanding may be to substantially lessen competition or tend to create a monopoly in any line of commerce.

Section 4. Any person who shall be injured in his business or property by reason of anything forbidden in the antitrust laws may sue therefor in any district court of the United States in the district in which the defendant resides or is found or has an agent, without respect to the amount in controversy, and shall recover threefold the damages by him sustained, and the cost of suit, including a reasonable attorney's fee....

Section 6. The labor of a human being is not a commodity or article of commerce. Nothing contained in the antitrust laws shall be construed to forbid the existence and operation of labor, agricultural, or horticultural organizations, instituted for the purposes of mutual help, and not having capital stock or conducted for profit, or to forbid or restrain individual members of such organizations from lawfully carrying out the legitimate objects thereof; nor shall such organizations, or the members thereof, be held or construed to be illegal combinations or conspiracies in restraint of trade, under the antitrust laws.

Section 7. No person engaged in commerce or in any activity affecting commerce shall acquire, directly or indirectly, the whole or any part of the stock or other share capital and no person subject to the jurisdiction of the Federal Trade Commission shall acquire the whole or any part of the assets of another person engaged also in commerce or in any activity affecting commerce, where in any line of commerce in any section of the country, the effect of such acquisition may be substantially to lessen competition, or to tend to create a monopoly.

No person shall acquire, directly or indirectly, the whole or any part of the stock or other share capital and no person subject to the jurisdiction of the Federal Trade Commission shall acquire the whole or any part of the assets of one or more persons engaged in commerce or in any activity affecting commerce, where in any line of commerce in any section of the country, the effect of such acquisition, of such stocks or assets, or of the use of such stock by the voting or granting of proxies or otherwise, may be substantially to lessen competition, or to tend to create a monopoly.

This section shall not apply to persons purchasing such stock solely for investment and not using the same by voting or otherwise to bring about, or in attempting to bring about, the substantial lessening of competition....

Section 8.... [N]o person at the same time shall be a director in any two or more corporations, any one of which has capital, surplus, and undivided profits aggregating more than $1,000,000, engaged in whole or in part in commerce,... if such corporations are or shall have been theretofore, by virtue of their business and location of operation, competitors, so that the elimination of competition by agreement between them would constitute a violation of any of the provisions of any of the antitrust laws....

APPENDIX D

ROBINSON-PATMAN ACT (EXCERPTS)

Section 2. (a) It shall be unlawful for any person engaged in commerce, in the course of such commerce, either directly or indirectly to discriminate in price between different purchasers of commodities of like grade and quality, where either or any of the purchases involved in such discrimination are in commerce, where such commodities are sold for use, consumption, or resale within the United States or any Territory thereof or the District of Columbia or any insular possession or other place under the jurisdiction of the United States, and where the effect of such discrimination may be substantially to lessen competition or tend to create a monopoly in any line of commerce, or to injure, destroy, or prevent competition with any person who either grants or knowingly receives the benefit of such discrimination, or with customers of either of them: *Provided,* That nothing herein contained shall prevent differentials which make only due allowance for differences in the cost of manufacture, sale, or delivery resulting from the differing methods or quantities in which such commodities are to such purchasers sold or delivered: *Provided, however,* That the Federal Trade Commission may, after due investigation and hearing to all interested parties, fix and establish quantity limits, and revise the same as it finds necessary, as to particular commodities or classes of commodities, where it finds that available purchasers in greater quantities are so few as to render differentials on account thereof unjustly discriminatory or promotive of monopoly in any line of commerce; and the foregoing shall then not be construed to permit differentials based on differences in quantities greater than those so fixed and established: *And provided further,* That nothing herein contained shall prevent persons engaged in selling goods, wares, or merchandise in commerce from selecting their own customers in bona fide transactions and not in restraint of trade: *And provided further,* That nothing herein contained shall prevent price changes from time to time where in response to changing conditions affecting the market for or the marketability of the goods concerned, such as but not limited to actual or imminent deterioration of perishable goods, obsolescence of seasonal goods, distress sales under court process, or sales in good faith in discontinuance of business in the goods concerned.

(b) Upon proof being made, at any hearing on a complaint under this section, that there has been discrimination in price or services or facilities furnished, the burden of rebutting the prima-facie case thus made by showing justification shall be upon the person charged with a violation of this section, and unless justification shall be affirmatively shown, the Commission is authorized to issue an order terminating the discrimination: *Provided, however,* That nothing herein contained shall prevent a seller rebutting the prima-facie case thus made by showing that his lower price or the furnishing of services or facilities to any purchaser or purchasers was made in good faith to meet an equally low price of a competitor, or the services or facilities furnished by a competitor.

(c) It shall be unlawful for any person engaged in commerce, in the course of such commerce, to pay or grant, or to receive or accept, anything of value as a commission, brokerage, or other compensation, or any allowance or discount in lieu thereof, except for services rendered in connection with the sale or purchase of goods, wares, or merchandise, either to the other party to such transaction or to an agent, representative, or other intermediary therein where such intermediary is acting in fact for or in behalf, or is subject to the direct or indirect control, of any party to such transaction other than the person by whom such compensation is so granted or paid.

(d) It shall be unlawful for any person engaged in commerce to pay or contract for the payment of any thing of value to or for the benefit of a customer of such person in the course of such commerce as compensation or in consideration for any services or facilities furnished by or through such customer in connection with the processing, handling, sale, or offering for sale of any products or commodities manufactured, sold, or offered for sale by such person, unless such payment or consideration is available on proportionally equal terms to all other customers competing in the distribution of such products or commodities.

(e) It shall be unlawful for any person to discriminate in favor of one purchaser against another purchaser or purchasers of a commodity bought for resale, with or without processing, by contracting to furnish or furnishing, or by contributing to the furnishing of, any services or facilities connected with the processing, handling, sale or offering for sale of such commodity so purchased upon terms not accorded to all purchasers on proportionally equal terms.

(f) It shall be unlawful for any person engaged in commerce, in the course of such commerce, knowingly to induce or receive a discrimination in price which is prohibited by this section.

APPENDIX E

FEDERAL TRADE COMMISSION ACT (AS AMENDED) (EXCERPTS)

Section 5. (a) (1) Unfair methods of competition in or affecting commerce, and unfair or deceptive acts or practices in or affecting commerce, are hereby declared unlawful....

APPENDIX F

TITLE VII OF THE 1964 CIVIL RIGHTS ACT (AS AMENDED) (EXCERPTS)

Section 701.... (j) The term "religion" includes all aspects of religious observance and practice, as well as belief, unless an employer demonstrates that he is unable to reasonably accommodate to an employee's or prospective employee's religious observance or practice without undue hardship on the conduct of the employer's business....

(k) The terms "because of sex" or "on the basis of sex" include, but are not limited to, because of or on the basis of pregnancy, childbirth, or related medical conditions; and women affected by pregnancy, childbirth, or related medical conditions shall be treated the same for all employment-related purposes, including receipt of benefits under fringe benefit programs, as other persons not so affected but similar in their ability or inability to work, and nothing in Section 703(h) of this title shall be interpreted to permit otherwise. This subsection shall not require an employer to pay for health insurance benefits for abortion, except where the life of the mother would be endangered if the fetus were carried to term, or except where medical complications have arisen from an abortion: *Provided,* That nothing herein shall preclude an employer from providing abortion benefits or otherwise affect bargaining agreements in regard to abortion....

Section 703. (a) It shall be an unlawful employment practice for an employer—

(1) to fail or refuse to hire or to discharge any individual, or otherwise to discriminate against any individual with respect to his compensation, terms, conditions, or privileges of employment, because of such individual's race, color, religion, sex, or national origin or

(2) to limit, segregate, or classify his employees or applicants for employment in any way which would deprive or tend to deprive any individual of employment opportunities or otherwise adversely affect his status as an employee, because of such individual's race, color, religion, sex, or national origin.

(b) It shall be an unlawful employment practice for an employment agency to fail or refuse to refer for employment, or otherwise to discriminate against, any individual because of his race, color, religion, sex, or national origin, or to classify or refer for employment any individual on the basis of his race, color, religion, sex, or national origin.

(c) It shall be an unlawful employment practice for a labor organization—

(1) to exclude or to expel from its membership, or otherwise to discriminate against, any individual because of his race, color, religion, sex, or national origin;

(2) to limit, segregate, or classify its membership or applicants for membership, or to classify or fail or refuse to refer for employment any individual, in

any way which would deprive or tend to deprive any individual of employment opportunities, or would limit such employment opportunities or otherwise adversely affect his status as an employee or as an applicant for employment, because of such individual's race, color, religion, sex, or national origin; or

(3) to cause or attempt to cause any employer to discriminate against an individual in violation of this section.

(d) It shall be an unlawful employment practice for any employer, labor organization, or joint labor-management committee controlling apprenticeship or other training or retraining, including on-the-job training programs to discriminate against any individual because of his race, color, religion, sex, or national origin in admission to, or employment in, any program established to provide apprenticeship or other training.

(e) Notwithstanding any other provision of this subchapter, (1) it shall not be an unlawful employment practice for an employer to hire and employ employees, for an employment agency to classify, or refer for employment any individual, for a labor organization to classify its membership or to classify or refer for employment any individual, or for an employer, labor organization, or joint labor-management committee controlling apprenticeship or other training or retraining programs to admit or employ any individual in any such program, on the basis of his religion, sex, or national origin in those certain instances where religion, sex, or national origin is a bona fide occupational qualification reasonably necessary to the normal operation of that particular business or enterprise, and (2) it shall not be an unlawful employment practice for a school, college, university, or other educational institution or institution of learning to hire and employ employees of a particular religion if such school, college, university, or other educational institution or institution of learning is, in whole or in substantial part, owned, supported, controlled, or managed by a particular religion or by a particular religious corporation, association, or society, or if the curriculum of such school, college, university, or other educational institution or institution of learning is directed toward the propagation of a particular religion.

(f) As used in this subchapter, the phrase "unlawful employment practice" shall not be deemed to include any action or measure taken by an employer, labor organization, joint labor-management committee, or employment agency with respect to an individual who is a member of the Communist Party of the United States or of any other organization required to register as a Communist-action or Communist-front organization by final order of the Subversive Activities Control Board pursuant to the Subversive Activties Control Act of 1950 [50 U.S.C. 781 et seq.].

(g) Notwithstanding any other provision of this subchapter, it shall be an unlawful employment practice for an employer to fail or refuse to hire and employ any individual for any position, for an employer to discharge any individual from any position, or for an employment agency to fail or refuse to refer any individual for employment in any position, or for a labor organization to fail or refuse to refer any individual for employment in any position if—

(1) the occupancy of such position, or access to the premises in or upon which any part of the duties of such position is performed or is to be performed, is subject to any requirement imposed in the interest of the national security of the United States under any security program in effect pursuant to or administered under any statute of the United States or any Executive order of the President; and

(2) such individual has not fulfilled or has ceased to fulfill that requirement.

(h) Notwithstanding any other provision of this subchapter, it shall not be an unlawful employment practice for an employer to apply different standards of compensation, or different terms, conditions, or privileges of employment pursuant to a bona fide seniority or merit system, or a system which measures earnings by quantity or quality of production or to employees who work in different locations, provided that such differences are not the result of an intention to discriminate because of race, color, religion, sex, or national origin, nor shall it be an unlawful employment practice for an employer to give and to act upon the results of any professionally developed ability test provided that such test, its administration or action upon the results is not designed, intended or used to discriminate because of race, color, religion, sex, or national origin. It shall not be an unlawful employment practice under this subchapter for any employer to differentiate upon the basis of sex in determining the amount of the wages or compensation paid or to be paid to employees of such employer if such differentiation is authorized by the provisions of section 206(d) of title 29.

(i) Nothing contained in this subchapter shall apply to any business or enterprise on or near an Indian reservation with respect to any publicly announced employment practice of such business or enterprise under which a preferential treatment is given to any individual because he is an Indian living on or near a reservation.

(j) Nothing contained in this subchapter shall be interpreted to require any employer, employment agency, labor organization, or joint labor-management committee subject to this subchapter to grant preferential treatment to any individual or to any group because of the race, color, religion, sex, or national origin of such individual or group on account of an imbalance which may exist with respect to the total number or percentage of persons of any race, color, religion, sex, or national origin employed by any employer, referred or classified for employment by any employment agency or labor organization, admitted to membership or classified by any labor organization, or admitted to, or employed in, any apprenticeship or other training program, in comparison with the total number or percentage of persons of such race, color, religion, sex, or national origin in any community, State, section, or other area, or in the available work force in any community, State, section, or other area.

Section 704. (a) It shall be an unlawful employment practice for an employer to discriminate against any of his employees or applicants for employment, for an employment agency, or joint labor-management committee controlling apprenticeship or other training or retaining, including on-the-job training programs, to discriminate against any individual, or for a labor organization to discriminate against any member thereof or applicant for membership, because he has opposed any practice made an unlawful employment practice by this subchapter, or because he has made a charge, testified, assisted, or participated in any manner in an investigation, proceeding, or hearing under this subchapter.

(b) It shall be an unlawful employment practice for an employer, labor organization, employment agency, or joint labor-management committee controlling apprenticeship or other training or retraining, including on-the-job training programs, to print or publish or cause to be printed or published any notice or advertisement relating to employment by such an employer or membership in or any classification or referral for employment by such a labor organization, or relating to any classification or referral for employment by such an employment agency, or relating to admission to, or employment in, any program established to provide apprenticeship or other training by such a joint labor-management committee, indicating any preference, limitation, specification, or discrimination, based on race, color, religion, sex, or national origin, except that such a notice or advertisement may indicate a preference, limitation, specification, or discrimination based on religion, sex, or national origin when religion, sex, or national origin is a bona fide occupational qualification for employment.

APPENDIX G

NATIONAL LABOR RELATIONS ACT (AS AMENDED) (EXCERPTS)

Section 7. Employees shall have the right to self-organization, to form, join, or assist labor organizations, to bargain collectively through representatives of their own choosing, and to engage in other concerted activities for the purpose of collective bargaining or other mutual aid or protection, and shall also have the right to refrain from any or all of such activities except to the extent that such right may be affected by an agreement requiring membership in a labor organization as a condition of employment as authorized in section 8 (a)(3).

Section 8. (a) It shall be an unfair labor practice for an employer—

(1) to interfere with, restrain, or coerce employees in the exercise of the rights guaranteed in section 7;

(2) to dominate or interfere with the formation or administration of any labor organization or contribute financial or other support to it: *Provided,* That subject to rules and regulations made and published by the Board pursuant to section 6, an employer shall not be prohibited from permitting employees to confer with him during working hours without loss of time or pay;

(3) by discrimination in regard to hire or tenure of employment or any term or condition of employment to encourage or discourage membership in any labor organization: *Provided,* That nothing in this Act, or in any other statute of he United States, shall preclude an employer from making an agreement with a labor organization (not established, maintained, or assisted by any action defined in section 8(a) of this Act as an unfair labor practice) to require as a condition of employment membership therein on or after the thirtieth day following the beginning of such employment or the effective date of such agreement, whichever is the later, (i) if such labor organization is the representative of the employees as provided in section 9(a), in the appropriate collective-bargaining unit covered by such agreement when made, and (ii) unless following an election held as provided in section 9(e) within one year preceding the effective date of such agreement, the Board shall have certified that at least a majority of the employees eligible to vote in such election has voted to rescind the authority of such labor organization to make such an agreement: *Provided further,* That no employer shall justify any discrimination against an employee for nonmembership in a labor organization (A) if he has reasonable grounds for believing that such membership was not available to the employee on the same terms and conditions generally applicable to other members, or (B) if he has reasonable grounds for believing that membership was denied or terminated for reasons other than the failure of the employee to tender the periodic dues and the initiation fees uniformly required as a condition of acquiring or retaining membership;

(4) to discharge or otherwise discriminate against an employee because he has filed charge or given testimony under this Act;

(5) to refuse to bargain collectively with the representatives of his employees, subject to the provisions of section 9(a).

(b) It shall be an unfair labor practice for a labor organization or its agents—

(1) to restrain or coerce (A) employees in the exercise of the rights guaranteed in section 7: *Provided*, That this paragraph shall not impair the right of a labor organization to prescribe its own rules with respect to the acquisition or retention of membership therein; or (B) an employer in the selection of his representatives for the purposes of collective bargaining or the adjustment of grievances;

(2) to cause or attempt to cause an employer to discriminate against an employee in violation of subsection (a)(3) or to discriminate against an employee with respect to whom membership in such organization has been denied or terminated on some ground other than his failure to tender the periodic dues and the initiation fees uniformly required as a condition of acquiring or retaining membership;

(3) to refuse to bargain collectively with an employer, provided it is the representative of his employees subject to the provisions of section 9(a);

(4)(i) to engage in, or to induce or encourage any individual employed by any person engaged in commerce or in an industry affecting commerce to engage in, a strike or a refusal in the course of his employment to use, manufacture, process, transport, or otherwise handle or work on any goods, articles, materials, or commodities or to perform any services; or (ii) to threaten, coerce, or restrain any person engaged in commerce or in an industry affecting commerce, where in either case an object thereof is:

(A) forcing or requiring any employer or self-employed person to join any labor or employer organization or to enter into any agreement which is prohibited by section 8(e);

(B) forcing or requiring any person to cease using, selling, handling, transporting, or otherwise dealing in the products of any other producer, processor, or manufacturer, to cease doing business with any other person, or forcing or requiring any other employer to recognize or bargain with a labor organization as the representative of his employees unless such labor organization has been certified as the representative of such employees under the provisions of section 9: *Provided*, That nothing contained in this clause (B) shall be construed to make unlawful, where not otherwise unlawful, any primary strike or primary picketing;

(C) forcing or requiring any employer to recognize or bargain with a particular labor organization as the representative of his employees if another labor organization has been certified as the representative of such employees under the provisions of section 9;

(D) forcing or requiring any employer to assign particular work to employees in a particular labor organization or in a particular trade, craft, or class rather than to employees in another labor organization or in another trade, craft, or class, unless such employer is failing to conform to an order or certification of the Board determining the bargaining representative for employees performing such work: *Provided*, That nothing contained in this subsection (b) shall be construed to make unlawful a refusal by any person to enter upon the premises of any employer (other than his own employer), if the employees of such employer are engaged in a strike ratified or approved by a representative of such employees whom such employer is required to recognize under this Act: *Provided further*, That for the purposes of this paragraph (4) only, nothing contained in such paragraph shall be construed to prohibit publicity, other than picketing, for the purpose of truthfully advising the public, including consumers and members of a labor organization, that a product or products are produced by an employer with whom the labor organization has a primary dispute and are distributed by another employer, as long as such publicity does not have an effect of inducing any individual employed by any person other than the primary employer in the course of his employment to refuse to pick up, deliver, or transport any goods, or not to perform any services, at the establishment of the employer engaged in such distribution;

(5) to require of employees covered by an agreement authorized under subsection (a)(3) the payment, as a condition precedent to becoming a member of such organization, of a fee in an amount which the Board finds excessive or discriminatory under all the circumstances. In making such a finding, the Board shall consider, among other relevant factors, the practices and customs of labor organizations in the particular industry, and the wages currently paid to the employees affected;

(6) to cause of attempt to cause an employer to pay or deliver or agree to pay or deliver any money or other thing of value, in the nature of an exaction, for services which are not performed or not to be performed; and

(7) to picket or cause to be picketed, or threaten to picket or cause to be picketed, any employer where an

object thereof is forcing or requiring an employer to recognize or bargain with a labor organization as the representative of this employees, or forcing or requiring the employees of an employer to accept or select such labor organization as their collective bargaining representative, unless such labor organization is currently certified as the representative of such employees:

(A) where the employer has lawfully recognized in accordance with this Act any other labor organization and a question concerning representation may not appropriately be raised under section 9(c) of this Act,

(B) where within the preceding twelve months a valid election under section 9(c) of this Act has been conducted, or

(C) where such picketing has been conducted without a petition under section 9(c) being filed within a reasonable period of time not to exceed thirty days from the commencement of such picketing: *Provided,* That when such a petition has been filed the Board shall forthwith, without regard to the provisions of section 9(c)(1) or the absence of a showing of a substantial interest on the part of the labor organization, direct an election in such unit as the Board finds to be appropriate and shall certify the results thereof: *Provided further,* That nothing in this subparagraph (C) shall be construed to prohibit any picketing or other publicity for the purpose of truthfully advising the public (including consumers) that an employer does not employ members of, or have a contract with, a labor organization, unless an effect of such picketing is to induce any individual employed by any other person in the course of his employment, not to pick up, deliver or transport any goods or not to perform any services.

Nothing in this paragraph (7) shall be construed to permit any act which would otherwise be an unfair labor practice under this section 8(b).

(c) The expressing of any views, argument, or opinion, or the dissemination thereof, whether in written, printed, graphic, or visual form, shall not constitute or be evidence of an unfair labor practice under any of the provisions of this Act, if such expression contains no threat of reprisal or force or promise of benefit.

(d) For the purposes of this section, to bargain collectively is the performance of the mutual obligation of the employer and the representative of the employees to meet at reasonable times and confer in good faith with respect to wages, hours, and other terms and conditions of employment, or the negotiation of an agreement, or any question arising thereunder, and the execution of a written contract incorporating any agreement reached if requested by either party, but such obligation does not compel either party to agree to a proposal or require the making of a concession: *Provided,* That where there is in effect a collective-bargaining contract covering employees in an industry affecting commerce, the duty to bargain collectively shall also mean that no party to such contract shall terminate or modify such contract, unless the party desiring such termination of modification—

(1) serves a written notice upon the other party to the contract of the proposed termination or modification sixty days prior to the expiration date thereof, or in the event such contract contains no expiration date, sixty days prior to the time it is proposed to make such termination or modification;

(2) offers to meet and confer with the other party for the purpose of negotiating a new contract or a contract containing the proposed modifications;

(3) notifies the Federal Mediation and Conciliation Service within thirty days after such notice of the existence of a dispute, and simultaneously therewith notifies any State or Territorial agency establish to mediate and conciliate disputes within the State or Territory where the dispute occurred, provided no agreement has been reached by that time; and

(4) continues in full force and effect, without resorting to strike or lockout, all the terms and conditions of the existing contract for a period of sixty days after such notice is given or until the expiration date of such contract, whichever occurs later:

The duties imposed upon employers, employees, and labor organizations by paragraph (2), (3), and (4) shall become inapplicable upon an intervening certification of the Board, under which the labor organization or individual, which is a party to the contract, has been superseded as or ceased to be the representative of the employees subject to the provisions of section 9(a), and the duties so imposed shall not be construed as requiring either party to discuss or agree to any modification of the terms and conditions contained in a contract for a fixed period, if such modification is to become effective before such terms and conditions can be reopened under the provisions of the contract. Any employee who engages in a strike within any notice period specified in this subsection, or who engages in any strike within the appropriate period specified in subsection (g) of this section shall lose his status as an employee of the employer engaged in the particular labor dispute, for the purposes of section 8, 9, and 10 of this Act, as amended, but such loss of status for such employee shall terminate if and when he is reemployed by such employer. Whenever the collective bargaining involves employees of a health care institution, the provisions of this section 8(d) shall be modified as follows:

(A) The notice of section 8(d)(1) shall be ninety days; the notice of section 8(d)(3) shall be sixty days; and the contract period of section 8(d)(4) shall be ninety days;

(B) Where the bargaining is for an initial agreement following certification or recognition, at least thirty days' notice of the existence of a dispute shall be given by the labor organization to the agencies set forth in section 8(d)(3).

(C) After notice is given to the Federal Mediation and Conciliation Service under either clause (A) or (B) of this sentence, the Service shall promptly communicate with the parties and use its best efforts, by mediation and conciliation, to bring them to agreement. The parties shall participate fully and promptly in such meetings as may be undertaken by the Service for the purpose of aiding in a settlement of the dispute.

(e) It shall be an unfair labor practice for any labor organization and any employer to enter into any contract or agreement, express or implied, whereby such employer ceases or refrains or agrees to cease to refrain from handling, using, selling, transporting or otherwise dealing in any of the products of any other employer, or to cease doing business with any other person, and any contract or agreement entered into heretofore or hereafter containing such an agreement shall be to such extent unenforceable and void: *Provided,* That nothing in this subsection (e) shall apply to an agreement between a labor organization and an employer in the construction industry relating to the contracting or subcontracting of work to be done at the site of the construction, alteration, painting, or repair of a building, structure, or other work: *Provided further,* That for the purposes of this subsection (e) and section 8(b)(4)(B) the terms "any employer", "any person engaged in commerce or in industry affecting commerce", and "any person" when used in relation to the terms "any other producer, processor, or manufacturer", "any other employer", or "any other person" shall not include persons in the relation of a jobber, manufacturer, contractor, or subcontractor working on the goods or premises of the jobber or manufacturer or performing parts of an integrated process of production in the apparel and clothing industry: *Provided further,* That nothing in this Act shall prohibit the enforcement of any agreement which is within the foregoing exception.

(f) It shall not be an unfair labor practice under subsections (a) and (b) of this section for an employer engaged primarily in the building and construction industry to make an agreement covering employees engaged (or who, upon their employment, will be engaged) in the building and construction industry with a labor organization of which building and construction employees are members (not established, maintained, or assisted by any action defined in section 8(a) of this Act as an unfair labor practice) because (1) the majority status of such labor organization has not been established under the provisions of section 9 of this Act prior to the making of such agreement, or (2) such agreement requires as a condition of employment, membership in such labor organization after the seventh day following the beginning of such employment or the effective date of the agreement, whichever is later, or (3) such agreement requires the employer to notify such labor organization of opportunities for employment with such employer, or gives such labor organization an opprotunity to refer qualified applicants for such employment, or (4) such agreement specifies minimum training or experience qualifications for employment or provides for priority in opportunities for employment based upon length of service with such employer, in the industry or in the particular geographical area: *Provided,* That nothing in this subsection shall set aside the final proviso to section 8(a)(3) of this Act: *Provided further,* That any agreement which would be invalid, but for clause (1) of this subsection, shall not be a bar to a petition filed pursuant to section 9(c) or 9(e).

(g) A labor organization before engaging in any strike, picketing, or other concerted refusal to work at any health care institution shall, not less than ten days prior to such action, notify the institution in writing and the Federal Mediation and Conciliation Service of that intention, except that in the case of bargaining for an initial agreement following certification or recognition the notice required by this subsection shall not be given until the expiration of the period specified in clasue (B) of the last sentence of section 8(d) of this Act. The notice shall state the date and time that such action will commence. The notice, once given, may be extended by the written agreement of both parties.

Section 9. (a) Representatives designated or selected for the purposes of collective bargaining by the majority of the employees in a unit appropriate for such purposes, shall be the exclusive representatives of all the employees in such unit for the purposes of collective bargaining in respect to rates of pay, wages, hours of employment, or other conditions of employment: *Provided,* That any individual employee or a group of employees shall have the right at any time to present grievances to their employer and to have such grievances adjusted, without the intervention of the bargaining representative, as long as the adjustment is not inconsistent with the terms of a collective-bargaining contract or agreement then in effect: *Provided further,* That the bargaining representative has been given opportunity to be present at such adjustment.

(b) The Board shall decide in each case whether, in order to assure to employees the fullest freedom in exercising the rights guaranteed by this Act, the unit appropriate for the purposes of collective bargaining shall be the employer unit, craft unit, plant unit, or subdivision thereof: *Provided,* That the Board shall not (1) decide that any unit is appropriate for such purposes if such unit includes both professional employees and employees who are not professional employees unless a majority of such professional employees vote for inclusion in such unit; or (2) decide that any craft unit is inappropriate for such purposes on the ground that a different unit has been established by a prior Board determination, unless a majority of the employees in the proposed craft unit vote against separate representation or (3) decide that any unit is appropriate for such purposes if it includes, together with other employees, any individual employed as a guard to enforce against employees and other persons rules to protect property of the employer or to protect the safety of persons on the employer's premises; but no labor organization shall be certified as the representative of employees in a bargaining unit of guards if such organization admits to membership, or is affiliated directly or indirectly with an organization which admits to membership, employees other than guards.

(c)(1) Whenever a petition shall have been filed, in accordance with such regulations as may be prescribed by the Board—

(A) by an employee or group of employees or an individual or labor organization acting in their behalf alleging that a substantial number of employees (i) wish to be represented for collective bargaining and that their employer declines to recognize their representative as the representative defined in section 9(a), or (ii) assert that the individual or labor organization, which has been certified or is being currently recognized by their employer as the bargaining representative, is no longer a representative as defined in section 9(a); or

(B) by an employee, alleging that one or more individuals or labor organizations have presented to him a claim to be recognized as the representative defined in section 9(a);

the Board shall investigate such petition and if it has reasonable cause to believe that a question of representation affecting commerce exists shall provide for an appropriate hearing upon due notice. Such hearing may be conducted by an officer or employee of the regional office, who shall not make any recommendations with respect thereto. If the Board finds upon the record of such hearing that such a question of representation exists, it shall direct an election by secret ballot and shall certify the results thereof.

(2) In determining whether or not a question of representation affecting commerce exists, the same regulations and rules of decision shall apply irrespective of the identity of the persons filing the petition or the kind of relief sought and in no case shall the Board deny a labor organization a place on the ballot by reason of an order with respect to such labor organization or its predecessor not issued in conformity with section 10(c).

(3) No election shall be directed in any bargaining unit or any subdivision within which, in the preceding twelve-month period, a valid election shall have been held. Employees engaged in an economic strike who are not entitled to reinstatement shall be eligible to vote under such regulations as the Board shall find are consistent with the purposes and provisions of this Act in any election conducted within twelve months after the commencement of the strike. In any election where none of the choices on the ballot receives a majority, a run-off shall be conducted, the ballot providing for a selection between the two choices receiving the largest and second largest number of valid votes cast in the election.

(4) Nothing in this section shall be construed to prohibit the waiving of hearings by stipulation for the purpose of a consent election in conformity with regulations and rules of decision of the Board.

(5) In determining whether a unit is appropriate for the purposes specified in subsection (b) the extent to which the employees have organized shall not be controlling.

(d) Whenever an order of the Board made pursuant to section 10(c) is based in whole or in part upon facts certified following an investigation pursuant to subsection (c) of this section and there is a petition for the enforcement or review of such order, such certification and the record of such investigation shall be included in the transcript of the entire record required to be filed under section 10(e) or 10(f), and thereupon the decree of the court enforcing, modifying, or setting aside in whole or in part the order of the Board shall be made and entered upon the pleadings, testimony, and proceedings set forth in such transcript.

(e)(1) Upon the filing with the Board, by 30 per centum or more of the employees in a bargaining unit covered by an agreement between their employer and a labor organization made pursuant to section 8(a)(3), of a petition alleging they desire that such authority be rescinded, the Board shall take a secret ballot of the employees in such unit and certify the results thereof to such labor organization and to the employer.

(2) No election shall be conducted pursuant to this subsection in any bargaining unit or any subdivision within which, in the preceding twelve-month period, a valid election shall have been held.

Section 14.... (b) Nothing in this Act shall be construed as authorizing the execution or application of agreements requiring membership in a labor organization as a condition of employment in any State or Territory in which such execution or application is prohibited by State or Territorial law.

GLOSSARY

abuse of discretion The failure of a judge or administrator to use sound or reasonable judgment in arriving at a decision.

acceptance In contract law, the agreement of the offeree to the proposal or offer of the offeror.

action at law A suit in which the plaintiff is seeking a legal remedy (such as damages), as distinguished from an equitable remedy (such as an injunction).

action in equity A civil suit in which the plaintiff is seeking an equitable remedy, such as an injunction or decree of specific performance.

actual authority The express and implied authority of an agent.

adjudication The legal process of resolving a dispute.

adjudicatory power In administrative agency law, the right of an administrative agency to initiate actions as both prosecutor and judge against those thought to be in violation of the law (including agency rules and regulations) under the jurisdiction of the administrative agency—referred to as the quasi-judicial function of an agency.

administrative agency A board, commission, agency, or service authorized by a legislative enactment to implement specific laws on either the local, state, or national level.

administrative law Public law administered and/or formulated by a government unit such as a board, agency, or commission to govern the conduct of an individual, association, or corporation.

affirmative action In employment law, any voluntary or required program or action designed to remedy discriminatory practices in hiring, training, and promoting of protected class members. Such programs attempt to eliminate existing and continuing discrimination, to remedy lingering effects of past discrimination, and to create procedures to prevent future discrimination.

Age Discrimination in Employment Act (ADEA) A 1967 congressional prohibiting all forms of employment discrimination based on age. Workers between the ages of 40 and 70 are protected from employer discrimination not based on a bona fide occupational qualification.

agency A relationship created by contract, agreement, or law between a principal and an agent whereby the principal is bound by the authorized actions of the agent.

agency shop or union shop provision A union security clause which requires an employer to discharge any employee who does not join a union or at least pay union dues within a specified time after hiring. Such a clause is permitted by the NLRA if employees are given at least 30 days after hiring to join the union or pay dues.

agent One who is authorized to act for another, called a *principal*, whose acts bind the principal to his or her actions.

airfreight International transportation by air from point of export of goods or merchandise subject to an international sales contract.

ally doctrine In labor-management law, the doctrine which permits a secondary boycott of an employer who is assisting the employer with whom the union has a labor dispute.

annual percentage rate The total of the items making up the finance charge, or cost of borrowing money or buying on credit, expressed as a yearly percentage rate that the consumer can use to "shop around" for the best credit terms.

answer In pleadings, the defendant's response to the plaintiff's complaint or petition.

apparent authority Authority created by the words or conduct of the principal that leads a third person to believe the agent has such authority.

appellant The party who appeals a decision of a lower court, usually that of a trial court.

appellee The party against whom an appeal is made (sometimes referred to as a *respondent*—a person who defends on an appeal).

arbitration The submission of a dispute to a third party or parties for settlement.

articles of incorporation A legal document, meeting the legal requirements of a given state, filed with a designated state official as an application for a certificate of incorporation.

articles of partnership The agreement of the partners that forms and governs the operation of the partnership.

assault The intentional movement or exhibition of force that would place a reasonable person in fear of physical attack or harm.

assault and battery Any intentional physical contact by a person on another without consent or privilege.

assignee The one to whom an assignment has been made.

assignment The transfer of rights or a property interest to a third person, who can receive no greater rights than those possessed by the transferor.

assignor The one who makes an assignment.

assumption of risk A person's full awareness and understanding of the risk connected with a particular activity, followed by that person's voluntary involvement in the activity. If the person is injured in the activity and sues a defendant for negligence, the defendant can use the plaintiff's assumption of risk as a defense. Also, assumption of risk is one of the few defenses that can be asserted in response to a strict liability claim involving injury caused by an allegedly defective product. However, assumption of risk can no longer be used as a defense against a workers' compensation claim.

award In arbitration proceedings, the decision or determination rendered by an arbitrator on a controversy submitted for settlement. In general usage, to grant, assign, or give by sentence or judicial determination. For example, the court *awards* an injunction; the arbitration *award* is equitable.

back to work order An injunction requested by the President under the Taft-Hartley Act prohibiting a lockout by the employer or a strike by the union for an 80-day period. If at the end of 80 days no settlement is reached, the lockout or strike can continue unless prohibited by emergency congressional legislation.

bankruptcy A court procedure by which a person who is unable to pay his or her debts may be declared bankrupt, have nonexempt assets distributed to his or her creditors, and thereupon be given a release from any further payment of the balance due on most of these debts.

battery The wrongful intentional physical contact by a person (or object under control of that person) on another.

beneficiary A person for whose benefit a will, trust, insurance policy, or contract is made.

benefit test A test through which the law determines whether a promise has consideration by seeing if the promisor has received an advantage, profit, or privilege in return for his or her promise.

bilateral contract A contract formed by the mutual exchange of promises of the offeror and the offeree.

bilateral mistake A mistake in which both parties to a contract are in error as to the terms of or performance expected under the contract. Also called mutual mistake.

bill of lading A document used in international sales contracts to evidence the shipper's receipt of the goods, the issuance of a contract of insurance during the period of transportation, and to serve as evidence of title (ownership) of the goods.

blue sky laws Laws enacted for the protection of investors that regulate the sales of stocks and bonds, and that also regulate other activities of investment companies related to such sales.

board of directors A body composed of persons elected by the corporation's shareholders and entrusted with the responsibility of managing the corporation.

bona fide occupational qualification (bfoq) An exception to otherwise illegal discrimination on the basis of religion, sex, or national origin. Where an essential element of a job requires certain qualifications (e.g., a drama role or a church position) to be present, Title VII permits such qualifications to be used as criteria for employment. Such cases are rather rare, however.

boycott In antitrust law, an agreement between two or more parties to not deal with a third party. When the purpose is to exclude a firm or firms from a market, such an agreement is per se illegal under Section 1 of the Sherman Act. In labor law, action by a union to prevent others from doing business with the employer. A primary boycott, directed at the employer with whom the union has a labor dispute, is usually legal. A secondary boycott, aimed at an employer with whom the union does not have a labor dispute, is usually an unfair labor practice.

breach of duty Failure to fulfill a legal obligation.

burden of proof The duty of a party to prove or disprove certain facts.

business necessity A legal defense to a *prima facie* case of discriminatory impact. The defendant must prove (1) the challenged employment practice is necessary to achieve a legitimate business objective, (2) the practice actually achieves such an objective, and (3) there is no other reasonably available method for accomplishing the objective without discriminatory effects.

bylaws The internal rules made to regulate and govern the actions and affairs of a corporation.

capacity The legal ability to perform an act—especially an act from which legal consequences flow, such as the making of a contract.

career tenure In effect, the guarantee of lifetime employment or for as long as the tenured person can function adequately.

case law Essentially synonymous with "common law."

cause of action A person's right to seek a remedy when his or her rights have been breached or violated.

caveat emptor In sales law, "let the buyer beware."

Celler-Kefauver Act A 1950 congressional enactment amending Section 7 of the Clayton Act. The act prohibits a firm from acquiring all or part of the stock or assets of another firm where, in any line of commerce in any section of the country, the effect of such acquisition may be substantially to lessen competition.

certificate of incorporation A document of a state that grants permission to do business in that state in the corporate form—sometimes called a *charter*.

certificate of origin A certificate issued to establish the national origin of goods, frequently used in international sales contracts to comply with the laws of the importing country which ban or otherwise limit imports from specified countries.

certification The process by which a union is selected by employees as their official bargaining representative. Certification via supervised elections protects the union from rival union challenges for a period of one year.

challenge for cause In jury selection, an objection to a prospective juror hearing a particular case, stating a reason that questions the impartiality of the juror.

circumstantial context In the process of statutory interpretation, a court's examination of the problem or problems that caused the enactment of the statute.

civil law As compared to criminal law, rules for establishing rights and duties between individuals whereby an individual can seek personal redress for a wrong committed by another individual. As compared to common law, codified rules reduced to formal written propositions as the law of a state or country. The written code serves as the basis of all decisions.

Civil Rights Act A comprehensive 1964 congressional enactment that prohibits discrimination in housing, public accommodations, education, and employment.

civil rights law That body of statutory and constitutional law defining and enforcing the privileges and freedoms belonging to every person in the United States. The objective of civil rights law is to secure equality of opportunity for all persons.

class action A legal proceeding initiated by one or more members of a similarly situated group or class of persons on behalf of themselves and other group members.

Clayton Act A 1914 congressional enactment to generally prohibit price discrimination by a seller of goods, exclusive dealing and tying of a seller's products, mergers and consolidations of corporations that result in a substantial lessening of competition or tend to create a monopoly, and certain interlocking directorates. The act also provides an exemption from the antitrust laws for the organization and normal activities of labor unions.

closed shop A union security clause requiring an employer to hire and retain only union members. Such a provision is an unfair labor practice.

collective bargaining agreement An agreement between an employer and a labor union regulating the terms and conditions of employment. Such an agreement becomes a binding labor contract when formally adopted by both the employer and a majority of employees in an appropriate bargaining unit.

commerce clause A clause contained in Article I, Section 8, of the U.S. Constitution, which permits Congress to control trade among the several states (and with foreign nations).

commercial contract A contract between two or more persons (merchants) engaged in trade or commerce.

common carrier A carrier that holds itself out for hire to the general public to transport goods.

common law Rules that have been developed from custom or judicial decisions without the aid of written legislation, and subsequently used as a basis for later decisions by a court—also referred to as judge-made or case law.

common stock A class of stock that carries no rights or priorities over other classes of stock as to payment of dividends or distribution of corporate assets upon dissolution.

community property A system of marital property ownership recognized in eight states under which property acquired after marriage (except by gift or inheritance) is co-owned by the husband and wife, regardless of which person acquired it.

comparative negligence The rule used in negligence cases in many states that provides for computing both the plaintiff's and the defendant's negligence, with the plaintiff's damages being reduced by a percentage representing the degree of his or her contributing fault. If the plaintiff's negligence is found to be greater than the defendant's, the plaintiff will receive nothing and will be subject to a counterclaim by the defendant.

compensatory damages A monetary sum awarded for the actual loss a person has sustained for a wrong committed by another person.

competition The condition of economic and noneconomic rivalry among firms for consumers' business.

complaint In an action at law, the initial pleading filed by the plaintiff in a court with proper jurisdiction. In an action inequity, it is frequently referred to as a *petition*.

concurrent jurisdiction Where more than one court of a different name or classification has the power to hear a particular controversy.

conflict of laws The body of rules specifying the circumstances in which a state or federal court sitting in one state shall, in deciding a case before it, apply the rules of another state (rather than the rules of the state in which the court is sitting).

conglomerate merger A merger between two companies which are not competitors and do not occupy a supplier-customer relationship.

conscious parallelism Uniformity of action by firms who apparently know their actions are uniform. Does not prove conspiracy under Section 1 of the Sherman Act, but is an extremely important factor in determining whether a conspiracy existed.

consent decree A court injunction, the terms of which are arrived at by agreement of the parties.

consent order An administrative agency order, the terms of which are arrived at by agreement between the agency and the charged party.

consideration In contract law, a detriment to the promisee or benefit to the promisor, bargained for and given in exchange for a promise.

constitutional law Those provisions of the state and federal constitutions that prescribe the structure and functions of the respective governments and the basic rights of and limitations upon these governments, as well as the courts' interpretation of these provisions.

consumer products Goods that are used or bought primarily for personal, family, or household purposes.

Consumer Product Safety Act A congressional enactment that created the Consumer Product Safety Commission, which has the responsibility of establishing and enforcing rules and standards to insure that products covered under the Act are safe for consumers' use.

consumerism The movement that has led to increased protection for the consumer and substantial burdens on the manufacturer and merchant.

contract An agreement that establishes enforceable legal relationships between two or more persons.

contract-bar rule Provision of the National Labor Relations Act prohibiting an election petition by a rival union while a valid collective bargaining agreement is in force, up to a maximum of three years. The parties to the agreement are similarly barred while the agreement is in force, but there is no maximum time. An existing contract does not bar an election if it (1) contains no stated duration *or* (2) is so skeletal in nature that it covers few subjects normally found in such agreements.

contract, combination, or conspiracy Express or tacit agreement required for a violation of the Sherman Act.

contributory negligence The fault (negligence) of a plaintiff, the result of which contributed to or added to his or her injury (used as a defense by a defendant against whom the plaintiff has filed a negligence action).

corporate stock Shares of stock, each representing an ownership interest in the business, issued by a corporation for the purpose of raising capital.

corporation An association of persons created by statute as a legal entity (artificial person) with authority to act and to have liability separate and apart from its owners.

corrective advertising Statements in advertising, placed by a firm acting under orders from an administrative agency (usually the Federal Trade Commission), which correct erroneous or misleading statements about its product that have appeared in earlier advertisements.

counterclaim A pleading by the defendant in a civil suit against the plaintiff, the purpose being to defeat or sue the plaintiff so as to gain a judgment favorable to the defendant.

counteroffer A proposal made by an offeree in response to the offer extended him or her, the terms varying appreciably from the terms of the offer. Such a proposal by the offeree constitutes a rejection of the offer.

course of employment The legal standard requiring that injuries covered by workers' compensation statutes be job-related or reasonably incidental to job duties. The injury must have at least some reasonable relation to an employee's work.

crime Any wrongful action by an individual or persons for which a statute prescribes redress in the form of a death penalty, imprisonment, fine, or removal from an office of public trust.

criminal conspiracy doctrine The legal view held until the mid-1800s that any combination of employees for effecting actions against an employer was illegal *per se*. Employers used this doctrine to stifle employee unions until the courts began to view unions as legal entities.

criminal law The law of crimes.

cross-elasticity of demand The extent to which the quantity of a commodity demanded responds to changes in price of a related commodity. Used to help courts define the relevant market.

cross-elasticity of supply The extent to which the quantity of a commodity supplied to the market responds to changes in the price of a related commodity. Utilized to help courts define the relevant market.

cumulative voting Where permitted, the procedure by which a shareholder is entitled to take his or her total number of shares, multiply that total by the number of directors to be elected, and cast the multiplied total for any director or directors to be elected.

damages The monetary loss suffered by a party as a result of a wrong.

Davis-Bacon Act A 1931 congressional enactment regulating wage rates for federally financed or assisted construction projects.

debenture In securities regulation law, a debt security; a written promise by a corporation to repay borrowed money. Usually refers to a corporate bond or promissory note that is not secured by specific assets of the firm (i.e., is not secured by a mortgage on corporate assets).

debtor A person who owes payment of a debt and/or performance on an obligation.

decedent A person who has died.

deceit A false statement, usually intentional, that causes another person harm.

deed The document representing ownership of real property.

de facto corporation A corporation not formed in substantial compliance with the laws of a given state but which has sufficiently complied to be a corporation in fact, not right. Only the state can challenge the corporation's existence.

default The failure to perform a legal obligation.

defendant The party who defends the initial action brought against him or her by the plaintiff.

defense Any matter which is advanced or put forth by a defendant as a reason in law or fact why the plaintiff is not entitled to recover the relief he seeks.

defined benefit pension plan A pension plan which specifies the amount of or method for computing benefits the employer contributes to the plan for each employee.

defined contribution pension plan A pension plan which specifically states either the amount of or the method for computing employer contributions to a company pension plan.

de jure corporation A corporation formed in substantial compliance with the laws of a given state; a corporation by right.

delegated powers The constitutional right of the federal government to pass laws concerning certain subjects and fields, thereby keeping the states from passing laws in these areas (sometimes referred to as *enumerated powers*).

delegation In contract law, the transfer of the power or right to represent or act for another; usually referred to as the delegation of duties to a third party, as compared to the assignment of rights to a third party.

delegation of authority In administrative law, a grant of authority from a legislative body to an administrative agency.

demurrer A pleading by a defendant in the form of a motion denying that plaintiff's complaint or petition states a cause of action.

de novo To start completely new. A trial *de novo* is a completely new trial requiring the same degree of proof as if the case were being heard for the first time.

detriment test A test through which the law determines whether a promise has consideration by seeing if the promisee, by entering into the contract, has thereby given up a legal right.

directed verdict A verdict that the jury is instructed (or directed) by the court to return in accordance with a motion by one of the parties that reasonable persons could not differ as to the result.

disaffirmance The legal avoidance, or setting aside, of an obligation.

discharge in bankruptcy A release granted by a bankruptcy court to a debtor who has gone through proper bankruptcy proceedings; the release frees the person from any further liability on provable claims filed during the proceedings.

disclaimer A provision in a sales contract which attempts to prevent the creation of a warranty.

discretionary powers The right of an administrative agency to exercise judgement and discretion in carrying out the law, as opposed to ministerial powers (the routine day-to-day duty to enforce the law).

discrimination Any failure to treat all persons equally, where no reasonable distinction can be made between those favored and those not favored.

discriminatory impact A legal test employed to determine violations of Title VII in the Civil Rights Act. Any employment rule or practice, although neutral on its face, which has an unequal impact on a protected class is considered discriminatory and in violation of Title VII. If the plaintiff proves such a discriminatory impact exists, a *prima facie* case of illegal discrimination is established, and the employer then bears the burden of proving business necessity.

disparagement of goods Making malicious and false statements of fact as to the quality or performance of another's goods.

diversity of citizenship An action in which the plaintiff and defendant are citizens of different states.

domestic corporation A corporation chartered or incorporated in the state in which the corporation is doing business.

due process The right of every person not to be deprived of life, liberty, or property without a fair hearing and/or just compensation.

duress The overcoming of a person's free will through the use of threat, force, or actions whereby the person is forced to do something he or she otherwise would not do.

duty to speak A legal obligation of one party to divulge information to another party.

economic duress The overcoming of a person's free will by means of a threat or other action involving the wrongful use of economic pressure, whereby the person is forced to do something he or she otherwise would not do.

edge effect The effect upon competition caused by the presence of a potential entrant having the ability and incentive to compete with established firms in the market, where that market is highly concentrated and the firms presently in the market perceive the presence of the potential entrant.

eminent domain The power of the government to take private property for public use by paying just compensation.

Employee Retirement Income Security Act (ERISA) A 1974 congressional enactment regulating the funding, managing, and membership rules of private pension and welfare plans. Provisions for protecting employee benefits and fairly allocating those benefits are also detailed in the act.

environmental impact statement The statement required by federal law that describes the effect of proposed major federal action on the quality of the human environment.

Environmental Protection Agency The federal agency charged with the responsibility or establishing and enforcing environmental standards and for continuing research on pollution and measures to eliminate or control it.

Equal Employment Opportunity Commission (EEOC) An independent federal administrative agency comprised of five presidentially appointed members responsible for enforcing Title VII of the 1964 Civil Rights Act and several other employment discrimination laws. The EEOC has authority to issue legally binding regulations, and to bring suit in federal court to enforce these laws.

Equal Pay Act A 1963 congressional amendment to the Fair Labor Standards Act prohibiting an employer from paying an employee of one sex less than an employee of the opposite sex where the two perform jobs (1) requiring "equal skill, effort, and responsibility," and (2) "under similar working conditions."

equal protection of laws A constitutional guaranty that no state government shall enact a law that is not uniform in its operation, that treats persons unfairly, or that gives persons unequal treatment by reason of race, religion, national origin, or sex.

equitable action An action brought in a court seeking an equitable remedy, such as an injunction or decree of specific performance.

exclusive dealing An agreement which commits a buyer to purchase a certain product only from one seller. These agreements, often called *requirements contracts,* can foreclose markets to competitors. Section 1 of the Sherman Act and Section 3 of the Clayton Act are applied in analyzing these actions.

executed contract A contract wholly performed by both parties to the contract, as opposed to an executory contract, which is wholly unperformed by both parties.

execution of a judgment The process by which a judgment creditor obtains a writ directing the sheriff or other officer to seize nonexempt property of the debtor and sell it to satisfy the judgment.

executive order An order by the president of the United States or governor of a state that has the force of law.

ex parte On one side only. For example, an *ex parte* proceeding is held on the application of one party only, without notice to the other party; and an *ex parte* order is made at the request of one party when the other party fails to show up in court, when the other party's presence is not needed, or when there is no other party.

experience rating The standard by which an employer's actual tax for unemployment insurance is determined. Employers with a record of stable employment pay less unemployment tax than ones with a record of higher employee turnover.

export license A license issued under government authority as permission for identified goods to be exported from the country issuing the license.

express authority Authority specifically given by the principal to the agent.

express contract A contract formed from the words (oral and/or in writing) of the parties, as opposed to an implied contract, which is formed from the conduct of the parties.

express warranty In sales law, a guarantee or assurance as to the quality or performance of goods that arises from the words or conduct of the seller.

externalities Third-party costs associated with producing a product that cannot be totally reflected in the product's price. Pollution is an externality borne by everyone in modern industrial societies.

Fair Labor Standards Act (FLSA) A 1938 congressional enactment regulating minimum wages, overtime, and child labor. Small businesses, managerial and professional employees, and state and local government workers are exempted from its minimum wage and overtime provisions. The FLSA is administered and enforced by the Labor Department's Wage and Hour Division.

false imprisonment The wrongful detention or restraint of one person by another.

fault Breach of a legal duty, sometimes used in lieu of the term *negligence*. The UCC definition is "wrongful act, omission, or breach."

featherbedding The union practice of forcing an employer to hire an employee for a job when there is no work to be done. An unfair labor practice.

Federal Communications Commission (FCC) A seven-member commission established in 1934 by congresssional enactment of the Federal Communications Act. The commission is empowered to regulate all interstate communication by telephone, telegraph, radio, and television.

Federal Employers' Liability Act (FELA) A 1906 congressional enactment, reenacted in 1908 and amended in 1939, providing workers' compensation for employees of interstate railroads and airlines. It is not a no-fault system; employers are liable for an employee's injury only if the employer is negligent. The primary defense is comparative negligence.

Federal Employment Compensation Act (FECA) A congressional enactment providing a comprehensive workers' compensation system for civilian employees of the federal government. Similar to typical state workers' compensation laws.

federal law Rules of law derived from the U.S. Constitution, federal statutes and administrative agencies, and from cases interpreting and applying these rules.

federal preemption A legal principle which grants the Congress, the federal courts, and federal agencies exclusive authority in certain matters of law where the need for a uniform national body of law is great. Labor relations law, for example, is almost exclusively the domain of the federal government.

federal question A question presented by a case in which one party, usually the plaintiff, is asserting a right (or counterclaim, in the case of the defendant) which is based upon a federal rule of law—e.g., a provision of the U.S. Constitution, an act of Congress, or ruling of a federal administrative agency.

Federal Trade Commission (FTC) A five-member commission established in 1914 by congressional enactment of the Federal Trade Commission Act. The commission enforces prohibitions against unfair methods of competition and unfair or deceptive acts or practices in commerce; it also enforces numerous federal laws (particularly federal consumer protection acts, such as "Truth in Lending" and "Fair Packaging and Labeling").

Federal Trade Commission Act A 1914 congressional enactment prohibiting unfair methods of competition and unfair or deceptive acts or practices in commerce.

fellow-servant rule Common-law defense that an employer is not responsible for injuries to an employee if they were caused by the negligence of a fellow employee.

felony A serious crime resulting in either punishment by death or imprisonment in a state or federal penitentiary, or where a given statute declares a wrong to be a felony without regard to a specific punishment.

fiduciary A position of trust in relation to another person or to his or her property.

finding of fact The process whereby from testimony and evidence a judge, agency, or examiner determines that certain matters, events, or act took place upon which conclusions of law can be based.

firm offer In sales law, an irrevocable offer dealing with the sale of goods made by a merchant offeror in a signed writing and giving assurance to the offeree that the offer will remain open. This offer is irrevocable without consideration for the stated period of time, or if no period is stated, for a reasonable period, neither period to exceed three months.

forebearance The refraining from doing something that a person has a legal right to do.

foreign corporation A corporation chartered or incorporated in one state but doing business in a different state.

four-fifths rule An EEOC guideline for determinining when a standardized employment test has a discriminatory impact or effect. If using the test causes the selection rate for any protected class to be less than 80 percent of that for the group with the highest rate, then the test is considered to have a discriminatory impact.

franchise (1) A business conducted under someone else's trademark or tradename. The owner of the business, which may be a sole proprietorship, partnership, corporation, or other form of organization, is usually referred to as the *franchisee*. The owner of the trademark or tradename, who contractually permits use of the mark or name, in return for a fee and usually subject to various restrictions, is orindarily referred to as the *franchisor*. The permission to use the mark or name, which is part of the franchising agreement, is called a *trademark license*. (2) The term can also be used to refer to a privilege granted by a governmental body, such as the exclusive right granted to someone by a city to provide cable TV service in that city.

fraud An intentional or reckless misrepresentation of a material fact that causes anyone relying on it injury or damage.

garnishee A person who holds money owed to or property of a debtor subject to a garnishment action.

garnishment The legal proceeding of a judgment creditor to require a third person owing money to the debtor or holding property belonging to the debtor to turn over to the court or sheriff the property or money owed for the satisfaction of the judgment. State and federal laws generally permit only a limited amount of a debtor's wages to be garnished.

general duty clause An OSHA provision requiring employers to provide every employee a workplace free from recognized hazards causing or likely to cause death or serious bodily injury.

general intent In antitrust law, legal inference that a firm's actual conduct contributes to the acquisition or continuation of its market power. Usually proved by evidence of conduct that raises entry barriers.

good faith Honesty in fact on the part of a person in negotiating a contract, or in the carrying on of some other transaction.

goods Tangible and movable personal property (except for money used as a medium of exchange). Typical examples are automobiles, books, and furniture.

Green River ordinances State and municipal laws that regulate door-to-door sales on private premises. So called after the Green River, Wyoming, case in which such laws were held to be valid and enforceable.

group boycott In antitrust law, the express or implied agreement of two or more persons of firms to refuse to deal (buy, sell, etc.) with a third party. Such an agreement is usually illegal.

horizontal merger A merger of two competing firms at the same level in the production or distribution of a product.

horizontal price fixing Price fixing among competitors. *Per se* illegal under Section 1 of the Sherman Act.

hot cargo agreement A form of secondary boycott whereby a union and an employer agree not to do business with a third party for the purpose of coercing that party in a separate, unrelated labor dispute. Such an agreement is in violation of the NLRA.

implied authority Authority inferred for an agent to carry out his or her express authority and/or authority inferred from the position held by the agent to fulfill his or her agency duties.

implied contract A contract in which the parties' manifestation of assent or agreement is inferred, in whole or in part, from their conduct, as opposed to an express contract formed by the parties' words.

import license A license issued under government authority as permission for identified goods to be imported into the country issuing the license.

incorporation The act or process of forming or creating a corporation.

inference of discriminatory intent The legal presumption of the court that a Title VII violation exists even though there is no explicit intent to discriminate. If a plaintiff proves certain facts which make it logical to conclude an employer *intended* to discriminate, the court will find a *prima facie* case of discriminatory intent is present. The employer then has the burden of producing evidence that shows a legitimate, nondiscriminatory reason for its action.

injunction A decree issued by a court hearing an equity action either prohibiting a person from performing a certain act or acts or requiring the person to perform a certain act or acts.

inland freight Domestic transportation of goods from the point of manufacture or production to point of export.

insider trading The buying or selling of corporate securities of a particular firm by persons having business knowledge about such firm that is not available to the general public, with the expectation of making a personal profit in such transactions.

insolvency In bankruptcy law, the financial condition of a debtor when his or her assets at fair market value are less than his or her debts and liabilities.

intent requirement Judicial requirement that an alleged monopolist exhibit an *intent* to obtain or preserve a monopoly position. Such intent must be proved to exist in addition to overwhelming market power before Section 2 of the Sherman Act is violated.

interstate commerce The carrying on of commercial activities or the commercial transportation of person or property between points lying in different states.

Interstate Commerce Commission (ICC) An eleven-member commission established in 1887 by congressional enactment of the Interstate Commerce Act regulating the licensing and rates of common carriers in interstate commerce.

investigative power In administrative agency law, the right of an administrative agency by statute to hold hearings, subpoena witnesses, examine persons under oath, and require that records be submitted to it in order to determine violations and to do research for future rule making.

involuntary bankruptcy Bankruptcy of a person upon petition of a certain number of creditors whose claims are statutorily sufficient in amount. [Note: This was changed by new Bankruptcy Law in 1979. Deletion makes it accurate.]

joint venture A pooling of resources by two or more firms to achieve a common objective.

judgment notwithstanding the verdict (judgment n.o.v.) The entry of a judgment by a trial judge in favor of one party even though the jury returned a verdict in favor of the other party.

judicial review The process by which the courts oversee and determine the legitimacy or validity of executive, legislative, or administrative agency action.

judicial self-restraint The philosophy that controversies must be settled, insofar as possible, in conformity with previously established principles and decisions.

jurisdiction of a court The right, by law, of a specific court to hear designated controversies.

justice The application of rules to arrive at what is recognized as a fair and reasonable result; also a title given to a judge.

laissez-faire doctrine The doctrine whereby business is permitted to operate without interference by government.

Landrum-Griffin Act A 1959 congressional amendment of the 1935 NLRA which established a bill of rights for union members, required public financial disclosures by unions and union leaders, and regulated election procedures for union officials by union members.

law Enforceable rules governing the relationship of individuals and persons, their relationship to each other, and their relationship to an organized society.

law merchant Rules and regulations developed by merchants and traders that governed their transactions before being absorbed by common law. These rules and regulations were developed and enforced by "fair courts" established by the merchants themselves.

legal entity An association recognized by law as having the legal rights and duties of a person.

legal environment A broad, imprecise term referring generally to those judicial, legislative, and administrative processes and rules that have particular application to the business world.

legal impossibility of performance An event that takes place after a contract is made, rendering performance under the contract, in the eyes of the law, something that cannot be done. Also referred to as objective impossibility, it legally discharges a party's obligation; it can be compared to subjective impossibility, which makes the contractual obligation more difficult to perform but does not discharge it.

legal rate of interest The rate of interest applied by statute where there is an agreement for interest to be paid but none is stated, or where the law implies a duty to pay interest irrespective of agreement. In the latter case, this may be referred to as a *judgment rate,* a rate of interest applied to judgment until paid by the defendant.

legislative history The history of the legislative enactment used by the court as a means of interpreting the terms of a statute. It consists primarily of legislative committee reports and the transcripts of committee hearings and floor debates.

letter of credit An agreement by the bank of a party to a sales contract (the buyer) to pay funds to the other party (the seller of goods) upon the presentation of stipulated documents. A letter of credit may be *revocable* (subject to withdrawal) or *irrevocable* (not subject to cancellation prior to a stated date). Used extensively in international trade.

lex mercatoria A body of principles governing commercial practices, first appearing in the Middle Ages, and based upon the international custom and practice of merchants. It is the predecessor of the U.S. Uniform Commercial Code and the commercial codes of several modern civil law nations in Europe.

libel Written defamation of one's character or reputation.

limited partnership A partnership created under statute with at least one limited and one general partner. The limited partner's liability to third persons is restricted to his or her capital contributions.

liquidation damages In employment law, the additional amount of damages which an employer may be required to pay when the court finds it in willful violation of the FLSA provisions.

lobbying contract A contract made by one person with another under the terms of which the former agrees to represent the latter's interest before legislative or administrative bodies by attempting to influence their votes or decisions on legislative, quasi-legislative, or related proceedings.

lockout The withholding of employment by an employer as a means of coercing concessions from or resisting demands of employees.

long-arm statutes Laws that permit a plaintiff to bring a certain action and recover a judgment in a court in his or her home state against a defendant who resides in another state.

Magnuson-Moss Warranty Act A congressional enactment designed to prevent deceptive warranty practices, make warranties easier to understand, and create procedures for consumer enforcement of warranties. The act applies only to written warranties given in a consumer sales transaction and can be enforced by the Federal Trade Commission, Attorney General, or an aggrieved party.

marginal cost The cost of producing an additional unit of a product. In antitrust law, sales below marginal cost in some circumstances are viewed by courts as predatory.

market (1) An area over which buyers and sellers negotiate the exchange of a well-defined commodity. (2) From the point of view of the consumer, the firms from which he can buy a well-defined product. (3) From the point of view of a producer, the buyers to whom it can sell a well-defined product. Market definition is crucial in determining the relevant market share of firms under antitrust scrutiny.

market division arrangements Any concerted action among actual or potential competitors to divide *geographic* markets, to assign particular *customers,* or to market particular *products* among themselves so as to avoid or limit competition. Such market divisions are treated as *per se* violations of Section 1 of the Sherman Act.

market power The ability of a firm to behave in some way other than it could in a perfectly competitive market.

master In employment law, one who appoints or designates another to perform physical tasks or activities for him or her and under his or her control as to the manner of performance (sometimes designated employer).

maximum rate of interest A statutory limit on the amount of interest that can be charged on a given transaction.

mechanic's lien A statutory lien against real property for labor, services, or materials used in improving the real property.

merchant In sales law, a person who customarily deals in goods of the kind that are involved in a transaction, or who otherwise by occupation holds himself of herself out as having knowledge or skill peculiar to the goods involved in the transaction.

merger The purchase of either the physical assets or the controlling share ownership of one company by another. As a business combination, a merger can come under antitrust review if the Justice Department or the FTC have reason to believe it might lessen competition.

ministerial power In administrative agency law, the routine day-to-day administration of the law, as opposed to discretionary powers, which involve the power to exercise judgment in the rendering of decisions.

minor An infant; any person under the age of majority. In most states the age of majority is eighteen years; in some it is twenty-one.

misdemeanor Any crime less serious than a felony, resulting in a fine and/or confinement in a jail other than a state or federal penitentiary.

Model Business Corporation Act Uniform rules governing the incorporation and operation of corporations for profit recommended by the American Bar Association for enactment by the various states.

monopoly According to the economic model, a market having only one seller, high barriers to entry, and no close substitutes for the product being sold. The courts generally define a monopolist as a firm possessing such an overwhelming degree of market power that it is able to control prices or exclude competition.

National Labor Relations Act (NLRA) A 1935 congressional enactment regulating labor-management relations. This act (1) established methods for selecting a labor union that would represent a particular group of employees, (2) required the employer to bargain with that union, (3) prescribed certain fundamental employee rights, (4) prohibited several "unfair labor practices" by employers, and (5) created the National Labor Relations Board to administer and enforce the NLRA. Also known as the Wagner Act.

natural monopoly Unusual market structure resulting from unique characteristics of the product or service offered. Some goods (e.g., electricity) or services (e.g., local telephone system) require large capital outlays and/or require uniformity in delivery systems so that only one firm can efficiently provide them at a profit.

negligence The failure to exercise reasonable care required under the circumstances, which failure is the proximate or direct cause of damage or injury to another.

nolo contendere A plea by a defendant in a criminal prosecution that without admitting guilt subjects him to conviction but does not preclude him from denying the truth of charges in collateral legal proceedings.

nominal damages A monetary award by a court where there is a breach of duty or contract but where no financial loss has occurred or been proven.

Norris-La Guardia Act A 1932 congressional enactment (1) generally prohibiting federal courts from enjoining union activities in nonviolent labor disputes and (2) prohibiting yellow-dog contracts.

notice A fact that a person actually knows, or one he or she should know exists, based on all facts and circumstances.

nuisance Action by a defendant that impinges upon or interferes with the rights of others. The remedy for plaintiff is an injunction compelling abatement.

occupational disease A disease arising from, or incidental to, the usual and ordinary course of a person's employment.

Occupational Safety and Health Act (OSHA) A 1970 congressional enactment creating the Occupational Safety and Health Administration as part of the Labor Department, and requiring that agency to develop and enforce occupational safety and health standards for American industries.

ocean freight International transportation by sea from port to export of goods subject to an international sales contract.

offer In contract law, a proposal made by an offeror which manifests a present intent to be legally bound and expresses the proposed terms with reasonable definiteness.

offeree The person to whom an offer is made.

offeror A person who makes a proposal to another, with the view in mind that if it is accepted, it will create a legally enforceable agreement between the parties.

oligopoly A market structure in which a small number of firms dominate the industry.

open shop Any business in which union and nonunion workers can be employed indiscriminately. See right-to-work laws.

output contract An enforceable agreement for the sale of all the goods produced by a seller (the exact amount of which is not set or known at the time of the agreement) or all those produced at a given plant of the seller during the term of the contract; a contract in which the seller agrees to sell and buyer agrees to buy all or up to a stated amount that the seller produces.

parens patriae suit A legal proceeding instituted in behalf of the citizens of a state by the state attorney general.

pari delicto Parties equally at fault.

partnership An association of two or more persons who by agreement as co-owners carry on a business for profit.

peremptory challenge The right to exclude a prospective juror without having to state a reason or cause.

performance Carrying out of an obligation or promise according to the terms agreed to or specified. In contract law, complete performance by both parties discharges the contract.

performance-oriented standards OSHA standards which state broad safety goals and leave the method of achieving those goals to individual employers.

per se rule Antitrust doctrine wherein certain types of group business behavior are inherently anticompetitive and are therefore automatically illegal. Horizontal price fixing and boycotts are examples of *per se* illegal activities.

personal property All property not classified as real property; "movables." May be tangible (e.g., cars and gasoline) or intangible (e.g., shares of corporate stock and other contractual rights).

picketing Posting of striking workers at entrances to a place of work affected by a strike for the purposes of discouraging nonstrikers from working, and publicizing the labor dispute. Such assembly must be conducted in a peaceful manner and must not disturb the public peace.

plain meaning rule The rule under which a court applies a particular statute literally, where it feels the wording of the statute is so clear as to require no interpretation (that is, no resort to outside factors).

plaintiff The party who initiates an action at law and who seeks a specified remedy.

police power The inherent power of a government to regulate matters affecting the health, safety, morals, and general welfare of its citizens; usually used to refer to such power possessed by the state governments, as distinguished from the federal police power.

precedent A rule of a previously decided case that serves as authority for a decision in a current controversy—the basis of the principle of *stare decisis*.

preemption The federal regulation of an area of law which is so complete that any state statutes or other regulations affecting that area are, as to such area, completely void.

preliminary negotiations In contract law, usually an invitation to a party to make an offer—not the offer itself but only an inquiry.

preponderance of the evidence The greater weight and degree of the credible evidence; this is the burden of proof in most civil lawsuits.

price discrimination Under the Robinson-Patman Act, the practice of charging different prices to different buyers for goods of like grade and quality.

price fixing Any action or agreement which tampers with the free market pricing mechanism of a product or service.

prima facie At first sight (Latin); on the face of it; a fact that will be considered as true unless disproved.

principal One who agrees with another (called an *agent*) that that person will act on his or her behalf.

private corporation A corporation formed by individuals, as compared to one formed by the government.

private law Rules that govern the rights and duties of an individual, association, or corporation to another.

privity of contract Relationship of contract; a relationship that exists between two parties by virtue of their having entered into a contract.

procedural law The rules for carrying on a lawsuit (pleading, evidence, jurisdiction), as opposed to substantive law.

promisee The person who has the legal right to demand performance of the promisor's obligation. In a bilateral contract both the offeror and the offeree are promisees. In a unilateral contract only the offeree is the promisee.

promisor The person who obligates himself or herself to do something. In a bilateral contract both offeror and offeree are promisors. In a unilateral contract only the offeror is the promisor.

prospectus A document put out by a corporation that sets forth the nature and purposes of an issue of stock, bonds, or other securities being offered for sale, usually including additional financial data about the issuing corporation.

protected class (group) In civil rights law, any group of persons accorded specific legal protection from economic and social discrimination.

proximate cause The foreseeable or direct connection between the breach of duty and an injury resulting from that breach.

proxy An authorization by one person to act for another (used primarily by an individual who wants another to vote in his or her place at a shareholders' meeting because he or she cannot attend).

public corporation A corporation formed by the government, as distinguished from one formed by private parties.

public goods Those goods or services which cannot be provided by market mechanisms of price, demand, and supply. National defense, police and fire protection, and interstate highways are examples of such goods which are impractical to provide and price according to individual usage.

public law Rules that deal with either the operation of government or the relationship between a government and its people.

public policy Any conduct, act, or objective that the law recognizes as being in the best interest of society at a given time. Any act or conduct contrary to the recognized standard is illegal, even if there is no statute expressly governing such act or conduct.

punitive damages A monetary sum awarded as a punishment for certain wrong committed by one person against another. The plaintiff must prove his or her actual out-of-pocket losses directly flowing from the wrong before punitive damages will be awarded.

qualified pension plan Any pension plan which meets Internal Revenue Service requirements for tax-exempt status.

quasi-contract A contract imposed upon the parties by law to prevent unjust enrichment, even though the parties did not intend to enter into a contract (sometimes referred to as an *implied-in-law contract*).

quasi-judicial The case-hearing function of an administrative agency.

quasi-legislative The rule-making power of an administrative agency.

quid pro quo Something given or received for something else.

ratification The affirmance of a previous act.

rational basis test The usual test applied by the courts in determining the constitutionality of a statute that is challenged on the ground that it violates the equal protection clause; under this test, if the classification of subject-matter in the statute is found to be reasonably related to the purposes of the statute, the statute is not a violation of the equal protection clause.

real property Land and most things attached to the land, such as buildings and vegetation.

receiver A person appointed and supervised by the court to temporarily manage a business or other assets for the benefit of creditors or others who ultimately may be entitled to the assets. The business or other property is said to be placed in *receivership*.

reciprocity Business practice whereby one firm buys from another only if the other buys from it. May be voluntary or coerced, and can violate Section 1 of the Sherman Act. Also, a merger creating a probability of reciprocity may violate Section 7 of the Clayton Act.

registration statement A document setting forth certain corporate financial and ownership data, including a prospectus, that is generally required by the S.E.C. to be filed with it before the corporation can offer its securities for sale.

regulatory law Essentially, the state and federal rules emanating from Congress, state legislatures, and administrative bodies that impose duties and restrictions upon business firms.

Rehabilitation Act A 1973 congressional enactment prohibiting federal agencies, employers having federal contracts exceeding $2,500, and federally subsidized programs from discriminating against qualified handicapped job applicants and employees.

rejection In contract law, a refusal by the offeree of proposal or offer of the offeror, such refusal being known to the offeror.

release The voluntary relinquishing of a right, lien, interest, or any other obligation.

relevant market In antitrust law, the geographic market area and/or product or products determined by a court or government unit to measure whether an antitrust violation has taken place.

remedy Generally, the means by which a right is enforced or a wrong is prevented; in a narrower sense, a court order addressed to the defendant, in proper circumstances, requiring the defendant to do a particular act requested by plaintiff (e.g., payment of damages) or to refrain from a particular act (e.g., prohibition of specified conduct on the part of defendant by the issuance of an injunction).

replevin A legal remedy that permits recovery of possession of chattels (personal property).

repossession The taking back or regaining of possession of property, usually on the default of a debtor. Repossession can take place peaceably (without breach of the peace) or by judicial process.

requirement contract An enforceable agreement for a supply of goods, the exact amount of which is not set or known at the time of the agreement but which is intended to satisfy the needs of a buyer during the term of the contract; a contract in which the seller agrees to sell and the buyer agrees to buy all (or up to a stated amount) of the goods that the buyer needs.

res In law a thing or things; property (corpus) made subject to a trust.

res ipsa loquitur The thing speaks for itself. In an action for negligence the plaintiff may allege that the act causing the injury or damage would not have happened but for the negligence of the defendant.

rescission In contract law, the cancellation of a contract by a court, the effect being as if the contract had never been made.

reserved powers The constitutional rights of states to pass laws under powers that are not specifically delegated to the federal government.

respondeat superior The doctrine under which a master or employer can be held liable for the actions of his or her subordinate.

restraint of trade Any contract, agreement, or combination which eliminates or restricts competition (usually held to be against public policy and therefore illegal).

reverse discrimination The unequal treatment of nonminorities arising from affirmative action programs. Subject to certain conditions, the courts permit such discrimination where court-ordered affirmative action is aimed at eliminating specific discriminatory practices or where affirmative action is strictly voluntary and temporary in nature.

revocation In contract law, the withdrawing of an offer by the offeror.

right-to-work laws Laws passed by state legislatures prohibiting closed shop, union shop, and agency shop clauses. Businesses in such states are free to hire union and nonunion employees.

Robinson-Patman Act A 1936 congressional enactment that substantially amended Section 2 of the Clayton Act, basically making it illegal for a seller in interstate commerce to so discriminate in price that the result would be competitive injury and prohibiting illegal brokerage fees, allowances, and discounts.

rule-making power The statutory right of an administrative agency to issue rules and regulations governing both the conduct and the activities of those within the agency's jurisdiction (referred to as an agency's *quasi-legislative function*).

rule of reason Antitrust doctrine adopted in *Standard Oil and American Tobacco* cases (1911) in judging Section 1 Sherman Act cases. Any business action or agreement whose *purpose* or *effect* is found to be substantially anticompetitive will unreasonably restrain trade and thus be illegal.

sale Passage of a title from a seller to a buyer for a price.

sanction A penalty used as a means of coercing obedience with the law or with rules and regulations.

scope of employment The range of activities of a servant for which the master is liable to third persons. These actions may be expressly directed by the master or incidental to or foreseeable in the performance of employment duties.

secondary party The drawer or indorser of an instrument.

secured party The lender, seller or other person in whose favor there is a security interest.

securities In securities regulation law, primarily stocks and bonds; also includes such items as debentures, investment contracts, and certificates of interest or participation in profit-sharing agreements.

Securities Act of 1933 A federal statute establishing requirements for the registration of securities sold in interstate commerce or through the mails (prior to sale). The statute basically requires that pertinent financial information be disclosed to both the Securities and Exchange Commission and to the prospective purchaser. A misleading failure to make such disclosure renders directors, officers, accountants, and underwriters severally and jointly liable.

Securities and Exchange Commission A federal agency given the responsibility to administer and enforce federal securities laws.

Securities Exchange Act of 1934 A federal statute designed to strengthen the Securities Act of 1933 and expand regulation in the securities business. This Act deals with regulation of national stock exchanges and over-the-counter markets. Numerous provisions were enacted to prevent unfair practices in trading of stock, to control bank credit used for speculation, to compel publicity as to the affairs of corporations listed on these exchanges, and to prohibit the use of inside information. This act created the Securities and Exchange Commission (SEC).

security A type of instrument (bond or share of stock) that is issued in a bearer or registered form and that is most often bought, sold, or traded on recognized exchanges or markets. Securities are used in corporate financing by a corporation to acquire capital and by purchasers as investments.

separation of powers The result of the U.S. Constitution, which created and balanced the powers of three branches of government (executive, legislative, and judicial) by giving each separate duties and jurisdictions.

servant In employment law, one who performs physical tasks or activities for and under the control of a master (sometimes designated an *employee* of the master).

shareholder The owner of one or more shares of capital stock in a corporation.

shareholder agreement A binding agreement made prior to a meeting by a group of shareholders as to the manner in which they will cast their votes on certain issues.

shares of capital stock Instruments in the form of equity securities representing an ownership interest in a corporation.

Sherman Antitrust Act An 1890 congressional enactment that (1) made illegal every contract, combination in the form of trust or otherwise, or conspiracy in restraint of trade or commerce among the several states, and (2) made it illegal for any person to monopolize, or attempt to monopolize, or combine or conspire with any other person or persons to monopolize any part of the trade or commerce among the several states.

Simplified Employee Pension Plan A pension plan created by the Revenue Act of 1978 which allows employers to contribute up to 15 percent of an employee's income or $30,000 whichever is less, to an individual retirement account (IRA). Such a plan permits employees to change employers without losing previous pension benefits.

slander Oral defamation of one's character or reputation.

sole proprietorship A person engaged in business for himself or herself without creating any form of business organization.

sovereign immunity The doctrine that bars a person from suing a government body without its consent.

specific intent In antitrust law, the intent of a firm to achieve a monopoly position. Evidence of predatory actions such as below-cost pricing, stealing trade secrets, etc., can prove specific intent.

specific performance A decree issued by a court of equity that compels a person to perform his or her part of the contract where damages are inadequate as a remedy and the subject matter of the contract is unique.

standing The right to sue.

stare decisis Literally "stand by the decision"—a principle by which once a decision has been made by a court, it serves as a precedent or a basis for future decisions of similar cases.

Statute of Frauds The requirement that certain types of contracts be in writing (or that there be written evidence of the existence of the oral contract) in order for the contract to be enforceable in a lawsuit.

statute of limitations A law that sets forth a maximum time period, from the happening of an event, for a legal action to be properly filed in or taken to court. The statute bars the use of the courts for recovery if such action is not filed during the specified time.

statutory interpretation The process by which a court discovers or decides the meaning of a statute as it applies to a particular case.

statutory law Enforceable rules enacted by a legislative body.

stock Equity securities that evidence an ownership interest in a corporation; shares of ownership in a corporation.

strict liability A legal theory under which a person can be held liable for damage or injury even if not at fault or negligent. Basically, any seller of a defective product that is unreasonably dangerous is liable for any damage or injury caused by the product, provided that the seller is a merchant and the product has not been modified or substantially changed since leaving the seller's possession. This rule applies even if there is no sale of the product and even if the seller exercised due care.

strike A cessation of work by employees for the purpose of coercing their employer to accede to some demand. A strike is legal only if it consists of a complete work stoppage by a participating majority of employees for a legally-recognized labor objective.

Subchapter S corporation A corporation with only one class of stock held by twenty-five or fewer individual stockholders who all agree in writing that the corporation will be taxed in the same manner as a partnership.

subsidiary corporation A corporation that is controlled by another corporation (called a *parent corporation*) through the ownership of a controlling amount of voting stock.

substantial performance The doctrine that a person who performs his or her contract in all major respects and in good faith, with only slight deviation, has adequately performed the contract and can therefore recover the contract price less any damages resulting from the slight deviation.

substantive law The basic rights and duties of parties as provided for in any field of law, as opposed to procedural law, under which these rights and duties are determined in a lawsuit.

summary judgment A court's judgment for one party in a lawsuit, before trial, on the ground that there are no disputed issues of fact which would necessitate a trial. The court's conclusion is based upon the motion of that party, the pleadings, affidavits, and depositions or other documentary evidence.

summons A writ by a court that is served on the defendant, notifying that person of the cause of action claimed by the plaintiff and of the requirement to answer.

Taft-Hartley Act A 1947 congressional amendment of the 1935 NLRA which (1) prohibited certain "unfair labor practices" by unions, (2) outlawed closed shop agreements, (3) established the Federal Mediation and Conciliation Service for the purpose of assisting employees and unions reach compromises, (4) granted employers and unions the power to file lawsuits to enforce collective bargaining agreements, and (5) gave the president authority to intervene in industry-wide disputes when, in the president's opinion, the occurrence or continuance of the dispute would "imperil the national health or safety." This act is also known as the Labor-Management Relations Act.

tender An offer by a contracting party to pay money, or deliver goods, or perform any other act required of him or her under the contract.

tender offer In securities regulation law, an offer to buy a certain amount of a corporation's stock at a specified price per share; usually made with the intention of obtaining the controlling interest in the corporation.

testator (female, testatrix) A person who makes a will.

textual context The court's reading of a statute in its entirety rather than a single section or part; a principle of statutory interpretation.

title A person's right of ownership in property. The extent of this right is dependent on the type of title held.

Title VII That part of the 1964 Civil Rights Act which prohibits employment discrimination against individuals because of their race, color, religion, sex, or national origin. Employers, employment agencies, labor unions, and governmental units are subject to Title VII provisions if they (1) have fifteen or more employees and (2) engage in an activity affecting interstate or foreign commerce. Violation of Title VII can be proved by showing an explicit or implicit *intent* to discriminate or by showing that an employer's actions result in a discriminatory *impact* on a protected class.

title warranty In sales law, an assurance or guarantee given by the seller, expressly or impliedly, to the buyer that he or she has good title and the right to transfer that title, and that the goods are free from undisclosed security interests.

tort A noncontractual wrong committed by one against another. To be considered a tort, the wrong must be a breach of a legal duty directly resulting in harm.

tortfeasor A person who commits a noncontractual wrong (sometimes referred to as a *wrongdoer*).

tort of conversion One's unlawful interference with the right of another to possess or use his or her personal property.

trademark A distinctive mark, sign, or motto that a business can reserve by law for its exclusive use in identifying itself or its product.

trade term A standardized term of trade which serves as a shorthand expression of the agreement of the parties to a sales contract to allocate responsibilities, costs, and risks of damage to or loss of the goods.

transferee A person to whom a transfer is made.

transferor A person who makes a transfer.

transnational corporation A corporation created or headquartered in one country having a network of foreign affiliated (subsidiary) corporation which it controls through equity ownership or management devices.

treasury stock Shares of stock that were originally issued by a corporation and that subsequently were reacquired by it.

trespass In realty and personalty, the wrongful invasion of the property rights of another.

trial-type hearing The adjudicatory process by which administrative law judges determine the validity of administrative action. Similar in nature to a federal, nonjury civil trial.

trust Two or more companies that have a monopoly. In the law of property, a relationship whereby a settlor transfers legal ownership of property to a trustee to be held and managed for a beneficiary who has equitable title to the property.

trustee One who administers a trust.

trustee in bankruptcy A person elected or appointed to administer the estate of the bankrupt person.

tying agreement Any arrangement in which one party agrees to supply a product or service only on the condition that the customer also take another product or service. Such activity is scrutinized under Section 1 of the Sherman Act and Section 3 of the Clayton Act.

ultra vires Any acts or actions of a corporation that are held to be unauthorized and beyond the scope of the corporate business as determined by law or by the article of incorporation.

unconscionable contract A contract or a clause within a contract which is so grossly unfair that a court will refuse to enforce it.

undisclosed principal In agency law, a principal whose identity and existence are unknown by third parties, leading them to believe that the agent is acting solely for himself or herself.

undue influence The overcoming of a person's free will by misusing a position of confidence or relationship, thereby taking advantage of that person to affect his or her decisions or actions.

unenforceable contract Generally a valid contract that cannot be enforced in a court of law because of a special rule of law or a failure to meet an additional legal requirement (such as a writing).

Uniform Commercial Code (UCC) Uniform rules dealing with the sales of goods, commercial paper, secured transactions in personal property, and certain aspects of banking, documents of title, and investment securities. Recommended by the National Conference of Commissioners on Uniform State Laws for enactment by the various states, it has been adopted by forty-nine states (and Louisiana has adopted parts of it).

Uniform Limited Partnership Act (ULPA) Uniform rules governing the organization and operation of limited partnerships recommended by the National Conference of Commissioners on Uniform State Laws for enactment by the various states. A Revised Uniform

Limited Partnership Act (RULPA) was drafted in 1976. The RULPA has been adopted by 30 states; 19 states still follow the ULPA.

Uniform Partnership Act (UPA) Uniform rules governing the partnership operation, particularly in the absence of an agreement, recommended by the National Conference of Commissioners on Uniform State Laws for enactment by the various states.

unilateral contract An offer or promise of the offeror which can become binding only by the completed performance of the offeree; an act for a promise, whereby the offeree's act is not only his or her acceptance but also the completed performance under the contract.

unilateral mistake A mistake in which only one party to a contract is in error as to the terms or performance expected under the contract.

usage of trade Any practice or method repeated with such regularity in a vocation or business that it becomes the legal basis for expected performance in future events within that vocation or business.

usury An interest charge exceeding the maximum amount permitted by statute.

U.S. Code The full and complete compilation of all federal statutes.

validation requirement An EEOC guidelines requiring an employer to prove that an otherwise illegally discriminatory employment test is legal. The employer must show the test predicts important work behavior relevant to the job or jobs for which applicants are being evaluated.

valid contract A contract that meets the four basic requirements for enforceability by the parties to it.

venue A designation of the right of the defendant to be tried in a proper court within a specific geographic area.

vertical integration Operation of a firm at more than one level in the chain of production and distribution of a product.

vertical merger A merger of two firms, one of which is a supplier or customer of the other.

vertical price fixing Price fixing between supplier and customer, relating to the price at which the customer will resell. *Per se* illegal under Section 1 of the Sherman Act.

vertical restraints of trade Any actions or arrangements made by firms operating at different levels of the distribution chain that harm competition. Vertical price fixing, tying and exclusive dealing arrangements, and reciprocity are examples of such restraints.

vesting right The legally enforceable right to certain pension benefits earned by an employee participating in a private pension plan. Such rights accrue even if there is no right to collect such benefits until a later date. ERISA regulates how private pensions may vest pension benefits to their employees.

vicarious liability The liability of a person, not himself or herself at fault, for the actions of others.

voidable contract A contract from which one or both parties can, if they choose, legally withdraw without liability.

voidable transfer In bankruptcy law, a transfer by a bankrupt debtor that can be set aside by a trustee in bankruptcy.

void contract A contract without legal effect.

voir dire The examination of prospective jurors by lawyers in a particular case to determine their fitness (i.e., to discover whether they have an interest in the outcome of the suit, a bias or prejudice against a party, or are otherwise unlikely to exercise the objectivity necessary in jury deliberations).

voluntary bankruptcy Bankruptcy based upon petition of the debtor.

waiver The voluntary giving up of a legal right.

warranty An assurance or guaranty, expressly or impliedly made, that certain actions or rights can take place, that information given is correct, or that performance will conform to certain standards.

warranty deed A deed with covenants, express or implied, that the title to real property is good and complete.

warranty of fitness for a particular purpose In sales law, an implied warranty imposed by law on a seller, who has reason to know of the buyer's intended use of the goods (where the buyer relies on the seller's skill and judgment), that the goods are suitable for the buyer's intended use.

warranty of merchantability In sales law, an implied warranty imposed by law upon a merchant seller of goods that the goods are fit for the oridinary purposes for which goods of that kind are used.

watered stock Shares of stock issued by a corporation for a consideration less than the par value or stated value of the stock.

wildcat strike A work stoppage initiated by a group of workers without the approval of a majority of employees in the bargaining unit. Such a strike is illegal and participating employees have no legal protection against discharge.

will A document by which a person directs the disposition of his or her property (estate) upon his or her death.

workers' compensation laws State statutory provisions calling for payments to employees for accidental injuries or diseases arising out of and in the course of employment. These payments, for medical expenses and lost income, are made regardless of whether anyone is at fault.

writ of certiorari What the appellant seeks by application to a higher court. An order issued by an appellate court directing a lower court to remit to it the record and proceedings of a particular case so that the actions of the lower court may be reviewed.

yellow-dog contract A contract by which an employer requires an employee to promise that he will not join a union, and that he can be discharged if he later joins a union. Such an agreement is illegal.

CASE INDEX

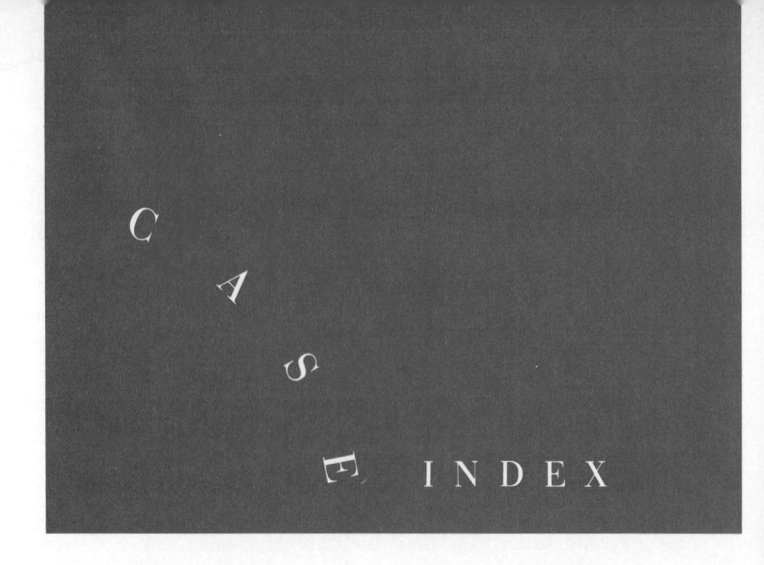

Cases appearing in boldface are summarized in the text.

Aaron v. SEC, 503
Action Repair, Inc. v. American Broadcasting Co., 86–87
Affiliated Ute Citizens v. United States, 491
Air Crash Disaster at Gander Newfoundland, *in re*, 46
Akins v. County of Sonoma, 302
Alexander v. Sims, 400
Allegheny College v. National Chautauqua County Bank, 267
Allen M. Campbell Co. v. Virginia Metal Indus., 288
Allen v. United States, 537
ALPO Petfoods, Inc. v. Ralston Purina Co., 388–389
American Safety Equipment Corp. v. J.P. McGuire & Co., 710
American Ship Building Co. v. NLRB, 615
American Textile Manufacturers Institute v. Donovan, 653
Amex Distrib. Co. v. Mascari, 273–274
Anderson Greenwood & Co. v. NLRB, 593
Anspec Co., Inc. v. Johnson Controls, Inc., 644, 652–653
Anthony v. Blech, 653
Argentine Republic v. Amerada Hess Shipping Corporation, 705–706
Arizona v. Norris, 154
Arizona v. Youngblood, 229
Armour v. Wantock, 537
Artukovich, Inc. v. Reliance Truck Co., 288
Aspen Skiing Co. v. Aspen Highlands Skiing Corp., 438–439
Atari, Inc. v. Harris Trust and Savings Bank, 724
Autogyro Co. of America v. United States, 377
Azar v. Lehigh Corp., 362

Badders v. United States, 243
Badhwar v. Colorado Fuel & Iron Corp., 725

Baldwin v. Fish and Game Commission of Montana, 164
Banco Nacional de Cuba v. Sabbatino, 706, 707
Banjavich v. Louisiana Licensing Board of Marine Divers, 187–188
Barrett v. Omaha National Bank, 565
Barry v. Barchi, 182
Basic Books, Inc. v. Kinko's Graphics Corp., 383–385
Basics, Inc. v. Levinson, 491–493
Basque French Bakery v. Toscana Baking Co., 390
Bates v. Arizona State Bar, 18, 146
Beebe-Owen v. Western Ohio Pizza, Inc., 69–71
Benson v. McMahon, 240
Bigelow v. Johnson, 115
Birkner v. Salt Lake County, 398
Blackburn v. Goettel-Blanton, 87
Blakeslee v. Nelson, 288
Blanco v. State, 163
Board of Trade of San Francisco v. Swiss Credit Bank, 697–698, 724
Board of Trustees of the State University of New York v. Fox, 147–148
Bonito Boats, Inc. v. Thunder, 378–380
Boomer v. Atlantic Cement Co., 652
Boos v. Barry, 149–150
Bowman Transp. Inc. v. Arkansas-Best Freight System, Inc., 179
Bowsher v. Synar, 120
Boyce Motor Lines, Inc. v. United States, 103, 104
Boyd v. Madison County Mutual Insurance Co., 555
Bradley v. American Smelting and Refining Co., 315, 630
Brady v. Maryland, 229
Brandenburg v. Ohio, 145
Breckinridge v. Rumsfeld, 652
The Bremen v. Zapata Off-Shore Co., 710
Bright Tunes Music Corp. v. Harrisongs Musics, Ltd., 382
Bright v. Ganas, 400

774

Broadway Books, Inc. v. Roberts, 136
Brockton Sav. Bank v. Peat, Marwick & Mitchell, 86
Brodie v. Hurth, 294
Bromberg v. Carmel Self Service, Inc., 372
Brown Shoe Co. v. United States, 441
Brown v. Board of Education, 152
Brown v. United States, 236
Brune v. Brown Forman Corporation, 349–350
Bruton v. Automatic Welding & Supply, 422
Bryceland v. Northey, 273–274
Bullard v. Omni Georgia, 586
Burke v. Pan American World Airways, Inc., 295
Burlington Truck Lines v. United States, 179
Burnham v. Superior Court of California, 46

Cahill v. Readon, 114
Carl Zeiss Stiftung v. VEB Carl Zeiss Jena, 725
Carpenter v. United States, 242, 244, 488
Carson v. Here's Johnny Portable Toilets, Inc., 368
Castelberry v. Branscum, 414–415
Caudle v. Betts, 305, 306–307
Celotex Corp. v. Catrell, 60
Central Hudson Gas & Electric Corp. v. Public Service Comm'n of New York, 147–148
Cheek v. United States, 233–234
Chevron U.S.A., Inc. v. Natural Resources Defense Council, 177
Chicadee, *re*, 101
Chicago Board of Trade v. United States, 450–452
Chicago Extruded Metals v. Industrial Commission, 540
Chuidian v. Philippine Nat'l Bank, 725
Cipollone v. Liggett Group, 680
City of Cleburne v. Cleburne Living Center, 155
City of Dallas v. Stanglin, 164
City of Mesquite v. Aladdin's Castle, Inc., 115
Clements Wire and Mfg. Co. v. NLRB, 593
Cleveland Board of Education v. Loudermill, 161
Cliff's Notes, Inc. v. Bantam Doubleday Publishing Group, 369–370
Clover v. Snowbird Ski Resort, 398–399
Coalition for Clean Air v. EPA, 641
Coates v. Cincinnati, 114
Coates v. National Cash Register Co., 587
Coca-Cola Bottling Co. v. Coca-Cola Co., 373
Cole v. Lovett, 676–678
Collins v. Williamson Printing Corporation, 288
Comeaux v. Brown & Williamson Tobacco Co., 667–668
Commonwealth v. Bovaird, 238
Communications Workers of America v. Beck, 618
Communications Workers of America v. Western Electric, 19
Community Television Services, Inc. v. Dresser Industries, Inc., 329–330
Compagnie Europeenne Des Petroles v. Sensor Nederland, 725
Connecticut v. Teal, 586–587
Conoco, Inc. v. Norwest Bank Mason City, 724
Continental T.V., Inc. v. Sylvania, Inc., 459–461
Corbin v. Safeway Stores Inc., 296–297
Cordas v. Peerless Transp. Co., 298
Corfu Channel Case, 650
Corley v. Jackson Police Dept., 556

Cox v. First Nat'l Bank of Cincinnati, 665
Cox v. Louisiana, 145
CSXT, Inc. v. Pitz, 46
CTS Corp. v. Dynamics Corp., 500

Daniell v. Ford Motor Corp., 359
Darrin v. Gould, 21
Dartmouth College case, 213
Data Cash Systems, Inc. v. JS&A Group, Inc., 387
Davey Tree Expert Co., 541
Dayan v. McDonald's Corporation, 722–723
Dempsey v. Rosenthal, 335
Dempsey v. Rosenthal, 340
Denault v. Holloway Builders, Inc., 87
Denny v. Radar Industries, 113
Dept. of Economic Development v. Arthur Andersen & Co., 501
DeRose v. People, 241
Desert Sun Publishing Co. v. Superior Court, 136
Diamond v. Chakrabarty, 376
Diaz v. Pan American World Airways, 551
Dillon v. Legg, 303
Doman Helicopters, Inc., *in re*, 479–480, 482
Donovan v. Dewey, 174, 175
Donovan v. Shaw, 173
Dorton v. Collins & Aikman Corp., 288
Dothard v. Rawlinson, 571, 576, 577
Dow Chemical Co. v. U.S., 176
Duckworth v. Eagan, 230
Dun & Bradstreet, Inc. v. Greenmoss Builders, 311
Durant v. Black River Electric Cooperative, 47
Duty v. General Finance Co., 671–672

E.I. duPont de Nemours & Co., Inc. v. Christopher, 374
Eaton v. Engelcke Manufacturing, Inc., 259
Edward J. DeBartolo Corp. v. Florida Gulf Coast Bldg. & Constr. Trades Council, 621–624
Edward Vantine Studios, Inc. v. Fraternal Composite Service, 364–365
Edwards v. Clinton Valley Center, 93–94
EEOC v. Arab American Oil Co., 694
EEOC v. Peat, Marwick, Mitchell and Co., 172–173
EEOC v. Sage Realty Corp., 586
Ellis v. Mihelis, 406
Ellison v. Brady, 562–565
Engel v. Vitale, 141
Ernst & Ernst v. Hochfelder, 490, 498
Estate of Thornton v. Caldor, Inc., 142
Estes v. Jack Eckerd Corporation, 313–314
Everett v. Williams, 260
Ewing v. Mytinger and Casselberry, Inc., 182

Fabbri v. Murphy, 130
Federal Crop Insurance Corp. v. Merrill, 184
Feist Publications v. Rural Telephone Service Co., 381
Fernandez v. Wynn Oil Co., 587
Fibreboard Paper Products Corp. v. NLRB, 609–610
First National Bank of Boston v. Bellotti, 144

First National Maintenance Corp. v. National Labor Relations Board, 609–610
Flagiello v. Pennsylvania Hospital, 95–97
Florida v. Bostick, 250
Florida v. Treasure Salvors, Inc., 289
Folsum v. Marsh, 383
Fontenot v. Upjohn Co., 87
Ford Motor Co. v. Sheehan, 323
Ford Motor Co. v. United States, 465–466
Ford Motor Credit Company v. Frances C. Sheehan, 690
Frank Arnold Contractors, Inc. v. Vilsmeier Auction Co., 358
Franklin v. State of Oregon, 52
Friedman v. Village of Skokie, 136
Fry v. Ionia Sentinel Standard, 316
FTC v. Colgate-Palmolive Co., 660
FTC v. Ruberoid Co., 168
Fugate v. Phoenix Civil Service Board, 136
Furnco Construction Co. v. Waters, 569

Galler v. Galler, 421
Garzilli v. Howard Johnson's Motor Lodges, Inc., 298
Gear Corp. v. Foundry Allied Industries, Inc., 57–58
Grambo v. Loomis Cycle Sales, Inc., 690
Grant v. Bethlehem Steel Corp., 568–570
Great Atlantic & Pacific Tea Co. and Amalgamated Food Employees Union, *in re*, 614
Great Dane Trailer v. Malvern Pulpwood, 341–342
Greater Boston Television Corp. v. FCC, 180
Greece v. Italy, 650
Greencastle Mfg. Co., 541
Grendell v. Kiehl, 201–202
Griggs v. Duke Power Co., 571, 572
Gun South Inc. v. Brady, 182–183
Gwaltney of Smithfield v. Chesapeake Bay Foundation, Inc., 636–637, 640

H. Rosenblum, Inc. v. Adler, 302
Hackbart v. Cincinnati Bengals, 308
Hagshenas v. Gaylord, 420–421
Hahn v. Hank's Ambulance Service, Inc., 689
Harper & Row v. Nation Enterprises, 384
Hauter v. Zogarts, 359
Heart of Atlanta Motel v. United States, 163–164
Helicopteros Nacionales de Colombia v. Hall, 37–38
Hendley v. Cameron-Brown Co., 664–665
Henningsen v. Bloomfield Motors, Inc., 358
Hessler, Inc. v. Farrell, 422
Hicklin v. Orbeck, 140–141
Hodel v. Virginia Surface Mining and Reclamation Assoc., 182, 183
Hoffman v. Red Owl Stores, Inc., 270–271
Hollon v. Pierce, 551
Holy Trinity Church v. United States, 115
Hoyem v. Manhattan Beach City School District, 301–302
HSL, Inc. v. Daniels, 503
Hunt v. Washington State Apple Advertising Commission, 132, 134
Hustler Magazine v. Falwell, 319

IBM v. United States, 461
Indvik, *in re*, 403
International Brotherhood of Teamsters v. United States, 574
International Shoe Co. v. Washington, 37

Japan Line, Ltd. v. County of Los Angeles, 135
Johnson Controls v. Phoenix Control Systems, Inc., 390
Johnson v. Lappo Lumber Co., 359
Johnson v. Nasi, 259
Jordache Enterprises, Inc. v. Hogg Wyld, Inc., 372

K.C. Roofing Center v. On Top Roofing, Inc., 422
K-Mart Corp. Store No. 7441 v. Trotti, 316
Kann v. United States, 243
Kardon v. National Gypsum Co., 487
Kassab v. Central Soya, 358
Kassell v. Consolidated Freightways Corp., 134
Kelly v. Hines-Rinalldi Funeral Home, Inc., 541
Kewanee Oil Co. v. Bicron Corp., 372
Kolender v. Lawson, 102, 229
Kori v. Wilco Marsh Buggies and Draglines, Inc., 390
Krell v. Henry, 282
Kulukundis Shipping Co. v. Amtorg Trading Corp., 711

Laaperi v. Sears, Roebuck & Co., 359
Laborers Local 859 v. NLRB, 625
Lamb v. Philip Morris, Inc., 725
Lampley v. Celebrity Homes, Inc., 268–269
Langston v. Brewer, 691
Lasher v. Kleinberg, 21
Lee v. Spicola, 502
Lehman v. Yellow Freight System, Inc., 587
Lehr v. Vance, 74–76
Linmark Associates v. Township of Willingboro, 146
Litton Industries, Inc. v. FTC, 689
Long v. Adams, 308
Los Angeles Department of Water & Power v. Manhart, 558–559
Louisiana Oil Corp. v. Renno, 318
Lowrey v. Horvath, 322
LTV Securities Litigation, *in re*, 492
Lumley v. Gye, 362

Mackey v. Montrym, 183
Maddux v. Donaldson, 114
Manufacturers Technologies v. Cams, Inc., 381
Mapp v. Ohio, 228
Marbury v. Madison, 119
Marshall v. Barlow's, Inc., 173, 531
Marshall v. Hendersonville Bowling Center, 541
Martin v. Johns-Manville Corp., 632
Mashburn v. Collins, 322
Mathews v. Eldridge, 160–161, 183
Matter of Parkview Assoc. v. City of New York, 184
Maxtone-Graham v. Burtchwell, 384
Mayo v. Satan and His Staff, 43
McBoyle v. United States, 106
McDonald v. Santa Fe Trail Transportation Co., 550

McGoldrick v. Gulf Oil Co., 130–131
McIntosh v. Milano, 322
McKeever v. New Jersey Bell Telephone Co., 540–541
McLain v. Real Estate Board of New Orleans, 124
McMahan & Co. v. Wherehouse Entertainment, Inc., 502
McNally v. United States, 489
Mead Data Central, Inc. v. Toyota Motor Sales, 390
Medo Photo Supply Corp. v. NLRB, 604–605
Meritor Savings Bank v. Vinson, 561, 563
Metromedia, Inc. v. San Diego, 148
Metropolitan Life Insurance Co. v. Estate of Cammon, 58
Michael v. Habnemann, 97
Midler v. Ford Motor Co., 317
Milkovich v. Loran Journal Co., 311
Miller Brewing Company v. G. Heileman Brewing Company, 390
Miller v. American Express Co., 690
Miller v. California, 145
Miller v. Central Chichilla Group, Inc., 474
Millstone v. O'Hanlon Reports, Inc., 690
Minnesota v. Clover Leaf Creamery Co., 152
Minnick v. Mississippi, 250
Miranda v. Arizona, 230
Mitchell v. W. T. Grant Co., 161
Mitsubishi Motors Corp. v. Soler Chrysler-Plymouth, Inc., 710–711
Mohasco Industries, Inc. v. Anderson Halverson Corp., 337–338
Montesano v. Donrey Media Group, 322–323
Motor Vehicle Manufacturers Ass'n v. State Farm Mutual Auto. Ins. Co., 178–180, 187
MRS Datascope v. Exchange Data Corp., 289

Nash v. CBS, Inc., 390
National Bond Co. v. Whithorn, 322
National Labor Relations Board v. Exchange Parts Co., 604–605
National Society of Professional Engineers v. United States, 447
National Treasury Employees Union v. Von Raab, 516, 517–519
Nebraska Seed Co. v. Harsh, 266
Nelson v. Saudi Arabia, 725
New Era Publications v. Carol Publishing Group, 384
New York City Transit Authority v. Beazer, 586
New York Times Co. v. Roxbury Data Interface, 384
New York v. Burger, 174–175
New York v. United States, 179
Newell Co. v. Vermont American Corp., 503
Nixon v. Mr. Property Management Co., 299
NLRB v. Bell Aerospace, 624
NLRB v. Bildisco, 688
NLRB v. Fruit Packers, 621, 622, 623
NLRB v. International Brotherhood of Electrical Workers, Local 1229, 625
NLRB v. Mackay Radio & Telegraph Co., 624
NLRB v. Retail Store Employees, 623
Nollan v. California Coastal Commission, 163
Noranda Aluminum, Inc. v. National Labor Relations Board, 597–598, 600
North Dixie Theatre, Inc. v. McCullion, 152

Northern Corporation v. Chugach Electric Association, 288–289
Northern Indiana Public Service Co. v. Carbon County Coal Co., 281–282
Northern Pac. R. Co. v. United States, 460–461
Northland Aluminum Products, Inc., *in re*, 389–390
Norton v. Worthen Van Service, Inc., 536–537

Oetjen v. Central Leather Co., 707
Orange County v. Piper, 68
Oregon v. Smith, 143
Orkin Exterminating Co., Inc. v. FTC, 659–661
Otis Engineering Corp. v. Clark, 296–297
Oulette v. Blanchard, 297
Owen v. Tunison, 266
Owens v. Palos Verdes Monaco, 405–407

Pacific Gas & Electric Co. v. Public Utilities Commission of California, 144
Palmateer v. International Harvester Co., 513
Palmore v. Sidoti, 152
Palsgraf v. Long Island R.R., 300
Paoli Railroad Yard PCB Litigation, *in re*, 631–632
Paradine v. Jane, 281
Paramount Communications, Inc. v. Time, Inc., 497
Parker v. Griswold, 95
Parker v. Port Huron Hospital, 94
Patterson v. Rohm Gesellschaft, 359
Peil v. Speiser, 492
Penny v. City of Chattanooga, 540
People v. Avila, 240–241, 246
People v. Mulder, 251
People's National Bank of Little Rock v. Linebarger Construction Co., 270
Pereira v. United States, 243
Perkins v. Benguet Consolidated Mining Co., 37
Perry v. Kalamazoo State Hospital, 94
Peters v. Jefferson Chemical Co., 555
Petrikis v. Hanges, 407
Pharmaceutical Society of New York v. Lefkowitz, 164
Philadelphia Newspaper, Inc. v. Hepps, 309
Philadelphia v. New Jersey, 132
Phillips v. Martin Marietta Corp., 558
Pierce v. Yakima Valley Hospital Ass'n., 97
Pilkenton v. Appalachian Regional Hospitals, 537
Pillars v. Reynolds Tobacco, 331
Pinkerton v. Georgia Pacific Corp., 649
Pipiles v. Credit Bureau of Lockport, 690
Posadas de Puerto Rico Associates v. Tourism Co. of Puerto Rico, 148, 164

Quivera Mining Co. v. EPA, 653

REA Express, Inc. v. Brennan, 530
Redd v. Woodford County Swine Breeders, Inc., 288
Reeves, Inc. v. Stake, 133
Regents of the University of Michigan v. Ewing, 165
Regina Corp. v. F.T.C., 661

CASE INDEX

Regina v. Dudley & Stephens, 21
Regina v. Ojibway, 100–101
Removatron International Corp. v. FTC, 689
Renfroe v. Higgins Rack Coating and Manufacturing Co., Inc., 113
Republic Steel v. Industrial Commission, 540
Revlon, Inc. v. MacAndrews & Forbes Holdings, Inc., 497
Ricaud v. American Metal Co., 707
Richards v. Flowers et al., 265–266
Richmond v. J. A. Croson Co., 153–154
Riley v. Willis, 67–68
Riverbank Canning Co., *in re*, 372
Robbins Tire and Rubber Co. v. NLRB, 593
Roberson v. McCarthy, 21
Robertson v. McKnight, 43
Rodriguez v. Bethlehem Steel Corp., 17
Roe v. Wade, 20–21
Rogers v. EEOC, 557
Rogers v. Grimaldi, 369
Rondeau v. Mosinee Paper Corp., 498
Rosenberg Bros. & Co. v. Curtis Brown Co., 38
Roto-Rooter Corp. v. O'Neal, 368
Rowland v. Christian, 295
RTE Corp. v. Coatings, Inc., 375

S&S Chopper Service, Inc. v. Scripter, 47
Sailors' Union of the Pacific [Moore Dry Dock Co.], 625
Samms v. Eccles, 294
Santa Fe Industries v. Green, 493
Sargia v. Skil Corp., 352
Scherk v. Alberto-Culver Co., 710, 711
Schlanger v. Four Phase Systems, Inc., 493
Schmuck v. United States, 243–244
Schock v. Ronderos, 286–287
Schoenbaum v. Firstbrook, 501
The Schooner Exchange v. McFadden, 693
Schreiber v. Burlington, 498–499
Schronk v. Gilliam, 322
Schultz v. Cheney School District, 298
Schupach v. McDonald's Systems, Inc., 278
Schweiker v. Hansen, 188–189
Seavy and Jensen v. Industrial Commission, 541
SEC v. Chenery Corp., 179
SEC v. Cherif, 488–489
SEC v. Clark, 489
SEC v. Glenn W. Turner Enterprises, Inc., 473
SEC v. Lund, 503
SEC v. Materia, 489
SEC v. McDonald Investment Co., 502–503
SEC v. Morgan F. Moore, 503
SEC v. W. J. Howey Co., 473
Sedima v. Imrex Co., Inc., 110–111
Segler v. The Industrial Commission, 523–524
Semmelroth v. American Airlines, 47
Serv-Air, Inc. v. NLRB, 624
Shaffer v. Heitner, 37
Sheets v. Yamaha, 390
Shlensky v. Wrigley, 416–417
Sinn v. Burd, 322
Skidmore v. Swift & Co., 537
Skinner v. Railway Labor Executives Ass'n, 516, 517

Smith v. Goodyear Tire & Rubber Co., 353–354
Smith v. Gross, 473–474
Smith v. Snap-On Tools Corp., 374–375
Smith v. Van Gorkom, 417
Smith v. Walter C. Best, Inc., 351
Smolowe v. Delendo Corporation, 485
Soar v. National Football League Players Ass'n, 422
Societe Nationale Industrielle Aerospacetiale v. U.S. District Court, 724
Soils v. City of Laredo, 363
Soldano v. O'Daniels, 7, 16–17, 95, 295
Sony Corp. v. Universal City Studios, 383
Sorrells v. United States, 236
Soucie v. David, 185–186
Southern Ohio Coal Co. v. Donovan, 160–161
Spier v. Barker, 353
Spur Industries, Inc. v. Del E. Webb Development Co., 629–630
Standard Oil Co. v. United States, 448
State v. Dame, 107
State v. Jay J. Garfield Bldg. Co., 102
State v. Joy, 238–239
State v. Marana Plantations, Inc., 170
State v. Speckman, 251
State v. Tolliver, 251
Steele v. Bulova Watch Co., 386
Steele v. Nimoy, 52
Stilphen v. Northrop Corp., 540

T&E Industries v. Safety Light Corp., 652
Tarasoff v. Regents of University of California, 16, 18
Taylor v. Allen, 114
Temple v. City of Petersburg, 114–115
Tennessee Valley Authority v. Hill, 109
Texas v. Johnson, 145, 231
Textile Workers v. Darlington Mills, 609
Theatre Enterprises, Inc. v. Paramount Film Distributing Corp., 466
Tierra Drilling Corp. v. Detmar, 421
Tiffany v. Boston Club, 371
Timberlane Lumber Co. v. Bank of America, 702, 703–704
Toibb v. Radloff, 688
Toomer v. Witsell, 140
Top Value Enterprises v. Carlson Marketing, 363
Towers World Airways v. PHH Aviation Systems, 669–670
Trail Smelter Arbitration, 650
The Trane Co. v. Randolph Plumbing & Heating, 258
Trans World Airlines v. Hardison, 552, 573
Truitt Manufacturing Co. v. NLRB, 624–625
TSC Industries, Inc. v. Northway, Inc., 478
Turman v. Central Billing, Inc., 319

U-Haul International, Inc. v. Jartran, Inc., 390–391
Union Carbide Class Action Securities Litigation *in re*, 502
Union Carbide Corp. Gas Plant Disaster at Bhopal, India in Dec. 1984, *in re*, 41
Union Electric Co. v. EPA, 653
Union of Transportation Employees v. Oil Transport Co., 624–625

United Automobile, Aerospace, & Agricultural Workers Union v. Johnson Controls, Inc., 575–577
United Housing Foundation, Inc. v. Forman, 502
United States v. Alcan, 647
United States v. Aluminum Co. of America, 465
United States v. American Future Systems, Inc., 674–675
United States v. Atlantic Richfield, 653
United States v. Biswell, 174–175, 188
United States v. Canada, 650
United States v. Cherif, 489
United States v. Colage & Co., 457
United States v. Continental Can Co., 465
United States v. Covino, 251–252
United States v. Doe, 229
United States v. Douglas Aircraft Co., 87
United States v. Dubilier Condenser Corp., 379
United States v. Fleet Factors Corp., 645–647
United States v. Frasch, 245
United States v. General Dynamics Corp., 446–447
United States v. Irving, 671
United States v. Kayser-Roth Corp., 644
United States v. Lee, 164
United States v. Leon, 228
United States v. LeRoy, 245–246
United States v. Locklear, 244
United States v. Mathews, 251
United States v. Matt, 251
United States v. Mirabile, 646
United States v. Moore, 87
United States v. National Dairy Products Corp., 104
United States v. Park, 249
United States v. Phoenix Petroleum Co., 188
United States v. Powell, 172, 173
United States v. Seeger, 551–552
United States v. Standard Oil Co., 653
United States v. Sun and Sand, 103–104
United Steelworkers of America v. Weber, 578
Universal City Studios, Inc. v. Nintendo Co., 370
Universal/Land Construction Co. v. City of Spokane, 289
Unocal Corp. v. Mesa Petroleum Co., 497

Vance v. Southern Bell Telephone & Telegraph Co., 557
Verlinden B. F. v. Central Bank of Nigeria, 706
Vietnamese Fishermen's Ass'n v. Knights of the Ku Klux Klan, 363
Village of Hoffman Estates v. The Flipside, Hoffman Estates, Inc., 103

Virginia Board of Pharmacy v. Virginia Citizens Consumers Council, 146
Volkswagenwerk Aktiengesellschaft v. Schlunk, 724

W.S. Kirkpatrick & Co. v. Environmental Tectonics Corporation, 707
Wagenseller v. Scottsdale Memorial Hospital, 513–514
Walcott & Steele, Inc. v. Carpenter, 358
Walker Bank & Trust Co. v. Jones, 690
Wallace v. Jaffree, 141
Walner v. Baskin Robbins Ice Cream Co., 389
Ward v. Rock Against Racism, 164
Ward v. Village of Monroeville, 164–165
Warner-Lambert v. FTC, 188
Waters, *in re*, 403
Weatherall Aluminum Products Company v. Scott, 678
Webster v. Blue Ship Tea Room, Inc., 333
Weeks v. Southern Bell Telephone & Telegraph Co., 587
Welch v. Fitzgerald-Hicks Dodge, Inc., 359
West Virginia State Board of Education v. Barnette, 142
Western Airlines, Inc. v. Criswell, 576–577, 579
Western Union Telegraph Co. v. Hill, 322
Westinghouse Electric Corp. Uranium Contracts Litigation, *in re*, 282
Whelan Assoc. v. Jaslow Dental Laboratory, 381
White Devon Farm v. Stahl, 335
Wickard v. Filburn, 124
Widlowski v. Durkee Foods, 322
Williams v. City of Detroit, 96
Williams v. Smith, 313
Wood Bros. Homes, Inc. v. Walker Adjustment Bureau, 42
World-Wide Volkswagen Corp. v. Woodson, 46
Wray v. Oklahoma Alcoholic Beverage Control Board, 188
Wrights Beauty College, Inc. v. Bostic, 422
Wydel Associates v. Thermasol Ltd, 86

Xerox Corp. v. Harris County, 129–131

Yellow Cab Corp. v. Clifton City Council, 188
Young v. Jackson, 317–318
Young v. Southwestern Savings & Loan Ass'n., 586

Zatrains, Inc. v. Oak Grove Smokehouse, 367

SUBJECT INDEX

AAA. *See* American Arbitration Association (AAA)
Absolute privilege, for defamation, 310–311
Acceptance, in contracts, 260, 262
Access Device and Computer Fraud and Abuse Act, 247
Accredited investors, 481
Acid rain, 640
Act of state doctrine, 706–707
Action at law, 44
Action in equity, 44
Actus reus, 232
ADA. *See* Americans With Disabilities Act (ADA)
ADEA. *See* Age Discrimination Employment Act (ADEA)
Adjudication, 24. *See also* Litigation
Adjudicative-legislative distinction, in due process, 158–159
Adjudicative power, of administrative agencies, 24n, 171, 180–182
Adjustment of Debts, 688–689
Administrative agencies
  adjudicative power of, 24n, 171 180–182
  cases, 172–175, 178–180, 182–183
  deregulation and, 187
  estoppel and, 184
  and Freedom of Information Act, 185–186
  functions and powers of, 171–183
  and Government in the Sunshine Act, 186
  growth of, 168–169
  investigative powers of, 171–176
  judicial review of rule making of, 177–180
  legislative delegation of lawmaking power to, 170
  ministerial and discretionary powers of, 171
  overview of, 169–170
  and Privacy Act, 186
  recent developments on, 185–187
  and Regulatory Flexibility Act, 186–187
  rule making powers of, 176–180
  search and seizure, 173–176
  subpoena power of, 171–172
Administrative law, 11
Administrative Law Judges (ALJs), 180, 595
Administrative Procedure Act (APA), 176, 180, 185, 716
ADR. *See* Alternative dispute resolution (ADR)
Adversarial system, 50–52, 50n
Adverse witness, 63
Affirmative action, 153, 548, 578
Affirmative defense, in pretrial proceedings, 54
Age Discrimination in Employment Act (ADEA), 172–173, 510, 576–577, 579–580
Agencies. *See* Administrative agencies
Agency, common law nature of, 90–91
Agency relationship
  case, 398–399
  creation of, 394–395
  definition of, 393–394
  duties of principal and agent, 395–396
  liability of the agent or employee to third parties, 399–401
  liability of the principal to third parties, 396–399
  termination of, 401–402
Agency shop, 618, 618n
Agent
  definition of, 394
  duties of, 395, 396
  in international trade, 721
  liability of the agent or employee to third parties, 399–401
Agents of capital, 218–219
Agents of society, 219–220
Agreement, in contracts, 260–266
Air pollution control, 638–641, 651
Airline Deregulation Act, 187
ALJs. *See* Administrative Law Judges (ALJs)
Ally doctrine, 621
Alternative dispute resolution (ADR)
  arbitration, 82–83

780

SUBJECT INDEX

Alternative dispute resolution (ADR) (cont.)
  future of, 86
  mediation, 84–85
  minitrial, 85
  negotiated settlement, 81–82
  regulatory negotiation, 85–86
  summary jury trial, 85
Amendments. *See* U.S. Constitution Amendments
American Arbitration Association (AAA), 83, 612–613, 709
American National Standards Institute, 529
American Psychological Association, 573
American Society for Testing and Materials, 529
Americans With Disabilities Act (ADA), 7, 580–585
  definition of disabilities, 581–582
  proving discrimination, 585
  qualification to do job in question, 582–585
  reasonable accommodation in, 583–584, 584n
  undue hardship in, 584–585
Annualized percentage rate (APR), 662–663
Answer, in pretrial proceedings, 53–55
Antidilution statutes, 371
Antitrust Division, Justice Department, 433, 445
Antitrust law
  cases, 438–439, 446–447, 450–452, 459–461
  coverage and exemptions of, 431–432
  enforcement of, 433
  federal antitrust statutes, 430–431
  horizontal restraints of trade, 447–455
  mergers and, 440–447
  monopolization and, 434–440
  objectives of, 426, 429–430
APA. *See* Administrative Procedure Act (APA)
Appearance, in personal jurisdiction cases, 33
Appearance requirements, for employment, 557
Appellate courts
  case, 74–76
  decision of, 73–74
  enforcement of judgments and, 76–77
  in federal court system, 26–27
  importance of, 27
  nature and role of, 71–72
  oral arguments in, 72
  process of appeal in, 72
  record in, 72
  review of trial court's factual determination, 73
  review of trial court's legal determination, 73
  in state system, 25
  written briefs in, 72
  written opinion of, 74
Appropriation of name or likeness, 317
APR. *See* Annualized percentage rate (APR)
"Arbitrary and capricious" test, 177–178
Arbitration
  in collective bargaining, 612–613
  in dispute resolution, 82–83
  for international trade disputes, 708–711
Arms Export Control Act, 713
Arson, 241
Articles of incorporation, 410
Assault and battery
  case, 306–307
  defenses in, 307–308

  definition of, 305
  elements of, 305–306
Assignees, in contracts, 276–277
Association, right of, 144
Assumption of risk, 352–353
Atomic Energy Act, 713
Attorneys. *See* Lawyers

Bank Export Services Act, 715
Bankruptcy
  Adjustment of Debts, 688–689
  business reorganization, 688
  claims against debtor in, 685
  creditors' meetings and, 683–684
  debtor's estate and, 684–685
  and discharge of debt, 687
  distribution of debtor's estate, 685–686
  duties of debtor in, 684
  historical development of legislation on, 681–682
  liquidation proceedings, 682–687
  nondischargeable claims in, 687
  reaffirming debt that has been discharged, 687
  trustee's role in, 683
Bankruptcy Reform Act of 1978, 681, 681n
Bankruptcy Reform Act of 1987, 681–682
Basel Convention, 650
Battery, definition of, 305. *See also* Assault and battery
Beneficiaries, in contracts, 276–277
Benefits
  discrimination in, 558
  of workers' compensation, 525–526
Berne Convention, 381–382, 386
BFOQ. *See Bona fide* occupational qualification (BFOQ)
Bilateral contracts, 257–258
Bill of Rights, 137–163, 138n, 228–231, 551.
  See also U.S. Constitution Amendments
Bills of lading, 696
Black Lung Act, 525n
Blue laws, 142
Bona fide occupational qualification (BFOQ), 554n, 574–575, 579
  case, 575–577
Boycotts, 453–454
  secondary, 620–624
Breach of contract. *See* Contracts
Bubble concept, 639
Burden of proof, 62
Bureau of Alcohol, Tobacco, and Firearms, 182–183
Burglary, 237
Business judgment rule, 417
Business torts
  cases, 364–365, 369–370, 374–375, 378–380, 383–385, 388–389
  copyright infringement, 380–385
  definition of, 320
  interference with business relationships, 362–366
  international protection of intellectual property, 385–386
  misuse of trade secrets, 371–375
  patent infringement, 375–380
  trademark infringement, 366–371
  unfair competition, 386–389

SUBJECT INDEX

Businesses. *See also* Corporations; International business
  government regulation of, 424–427
  search and seizure of, 173–176
  state statutes on, 113–114

CAB Sunshine Act, 187
Canada, Free Trade Act with United States, 720
Case law, 90, 91
Caveat emptor, 326
CCPA. *See* Consumer Credit Protection Act (CCPA)
Cellar-Kefauver Act, 440
CEQ. *See* Council on Environmental Quality (CEQ)
CERCLA. *See* Comprehensive Environmental Response, Compensation, and Liability Act of 1980 (CERCLA)
Certificates of origin, 697
Certioari, writ of, 595
Challenge for cause, 62
Checks and balances, in federal government, 119
Child labor, 535
Child Protection and Toy Safety Act, 681
Cigarette Labeling and Advertising Act, 680
Circumstantial context, 108
CISG. *See* Convention on Contracts for the International Sale of Goods (CISG)
Citizenship, discrimination based on, 550–551, 551n
Civil law
  criminal law compared with, 224–227
  definition of, 10
  jurisdiction of federal courts, 30–32
  in Louisiana, 90n
Civil Rights Act of 1866, 545
Civil Rights Act of 1964, 125, 153, 154n, 510, 547–578
Civil Rights Act of 1991, 549
Clayton Act, 431, 433, 461, 591, 713
Clean Air Act, 638–641
Clean Water Act, 635–637
Closely held corporations, 420–421
Coal Mine Health and Safety Act, 528
Coal Mine Safety Act, 528
COCOM. *See* Coordinating Committee for Multilateral Export Controls (COCOM)
Code of Federal Regulations, 176, 184
Coercion, as unfair labor practice, 615–618
Collective bargaining process
  arbitration in, 612–613
  cases, 609–610, 614
  duty to bargain in good faith, 610–611
  exclusive representative concept, 607
  grievance procedures and arbitration, 611–614
  illegal subjects of, 608
  mandatory subjects of, 607–608
  permissive subjects of, 608
  subjects of, 607–608
Collusion
  horizontal mergers and, 442
  in horizontal restraints of trade, 447–448
  vertical mergers and, 444
Color, discrimination based on, 549–551
Commerce clause, 123–135
Commerce Department, 712
Commercial arbitration, 83, 83n

Commercial defamation, 389
Commercial speech, 146
  case, 147–148
Commitments, 200
Commodity Futures Trading Commission, 432
Common law
  cases, 93–97
  change in, 95–97
  current status of, 90–91
  definition of, 10
  historical development of, 44
  judge's role in, 91–92
  legislative options and, 105
  legislative scope of, 105
  origin of, 90
  pollution and, 629–632
  precedent in, 92, 93–95
  processes and form of, 104
  social and political forces and, 104–105
    stare decisis doctrine and, 92–93, 92n
  statutory law compared with, 10, 104–105
Comparative negligence, 304
Compensation
  discrimination in, 545–546, 558
  minimum wage, 534, 534n
  overtime, 534, 538
Compensatory damages, 283
Complaint, in pretrial proceedings, 52, 53
Comprehensive Crime Control Act, 247
Comprehensive Environmental Response, Compensation, and Liability Act of 1980 (CERCLA), 643–647, 643n, 647n
Computer crime, 246–248
Computer Fraud and Abuse Act, 247
Conglomerate mergers, 441, 444–445
Consent, 307–308
Consideration, in contracts, 266–271
Constitutional law, 11. *See also* U.S. Constitution
Construct validity, of tests, 573
Consumer Credit Protection Act (CCPA)
  credit cards, 668–671
  Equal Credit Opportunity Act, 673–675
  Fair Credit and Charge Card Disclosure Act, 670–671
  Fair Credit Billing Act, 673
  Fair Credit Reporting Act, 666–668
  Fair Debt Collection Practices Act, 671–673
  garnishment, 666
  Home Equity Loan Consumer Protection Act, 665
  truth in lending, 661–665
Consumer Product Safety Act, 354–355
Consumer Product Safety Commission (CPSC), 187, 354–355, 681
Consumer protection
  bankruptcy, 681–689
  cases, 659–661, 664–665, 667–670, 674–678
  Consumer Credit Protection Act, 661–675
  Consumer Product Safety Act, 354–355
  credit cards, 668–670
  debtor default, 678–679
  deceptive trade practices, 656, 658–661
  Equal Credit Opportunity Act, 673–675
  Fair Credit and Charge Card Disclosure Act, 670–671
  Fair Credit Billing Act, 673

Consumer protection (cont.)
  Fair Credit Reporting Act, 666–668
  Fair Debt Collection Practices Act, 671–673
  garnishment, 666
  Home Equity Loan Consumer Protection Act, 665
  Magnuson-Moss Warranty Act, 355–356
  overview of federal laws on, 354–358, 657
  packaging and labeling, 680–681
  purpose of, 655–656
  Real Estate Settlement Procedures Act, 679
  truth in lending, 661–665
  Uniform Consumer Credit Code, 675–679
Consumer reports, 666
Contempt of court, 76
Content validity, of tests, 573
Contingency fee, of attorneys, 19
Contract clause, 137
Contract law, 42, 257, 291–292
Contracts
  acceptance in, 260, 262
  agreement in, 260–266
  bilateral contracts, 257–258
  cases, 259–260, 265–266, 268–271, 273–274, 278, 281–282, 286–287
  common law nature of, 90–91
  competent parties in, 271–272
  consideration in, 266–271
  counteroffer in, 263–264
  damages for breach of contract, 283–284
  decree of specific performance for breach of contract, 284
  definiteness in, 262–264
  definition of, 256–257
  discharge of, 279–282
  elements of, 260–274
  employment contracts, 507–508
  excused performance and, 280
  express contracts, 258
  with federal government, 546
  implied contracts, 258
  injunction for breach of contract, 284
  international sales contract, 696–700
  internationalization of, 287
  interpretation of, 282–283
  law governing, 257
  legality of, 272–274
  mail box rule, 264–265
  "mirror image" rule in, 263–264
  offer in, 260–261
  parol evidence rule, 276
  and plain meaning rule, 283
  preliminary negotiations in, 260–261
  remedies for breach of contract, 283–285
  rescission of, 274–275, 284
  sales contracts, 276, 284–285
  termination of, 261–262, 263
  third parties in, 276–278
  title and risk of loss, 285–287
  types of, 257–258
  unilateral contracts, 258
  warranties and, 280
  in writing, 275–276
Contractual liability

  of the agent or employee to third parties, 400
  of the principal to third parties, 396–397
Contributory negligence, 303
Convention on Conservation of Migratory Species of Wild Animals (1979), 651
Convention on Contracts for the International Sale of Goods (CISG), 287, 700
Convention on International Bills of Exchange and International Promissory Notes, 700
Convention on International Trade in Endangered Species and Wild Fauna and Flora (1973), 651
Conversion, 320
Coordinating Committee for Multilateral Export Controls (COCOM), 713
Copyright
  and copyrightability, 381
  definition of, 380
  international protection of, 381, 386
  procedure of, 381–382
  subject matter of, 380–381
Copyright Act of 1976, 382–383
Copyright infringement
  case, 383–385
  and copyright procedure, 381–382
  and copyrightability, 381
  definition of, 382
  and definition of copyright, 380
  and fair use doctrine, 382–383
  remedies for, 385
  and subject matter of copyright, 380–381
Copyright Office, 383
Corporate social responsiveness, 217–220
Corporations. See also Businesses
  as agents of capital, 218–219
  as agents of society, 219–220
  as defendants, and personal jurisdiction, 34–35
  cases, 414–417, 420–421
  closely held corporations, 420–421
  criminal liability of, 248–249
  criminal liablity of corporate officials, 249–250
  financing of, 411
  formation of, 410–411
  free speech clause and, 144
  involuntary dissolution of, 418–419
  lawyers for, 20
  as legal entity, 212, 410
  management of, 411–412
  as moral agents, 212–215
  nature of, 410
  officers of, 35
  registered agent of, 34
  rights and liabilities of corporate managers, 415
  rights and responsibilities of shareholders, 412–415
  social responsiveness of, 217–220
  state laws for, 409
  state statutes on, 114
  termination of, 417–420
  transnational corporations, 723–724
  voluntary dissolution of, 417–418
  winding up, 419–420
Council on Environmental Quality (CEQ), 634
Counterclaim, 54

Counteroffer, in contracts, 263–264
Court-annexed arbitration, 83
Courts. *See also* Litigation
  appellate courts 71–74, 76–77
  conflict of laws and, 41–43
  courts of equity, 44, 45
  courts of law, 44, 45
  federal court system, 26–32
  forum non conveniens and, 40–41
  judicial review of rule making of administrative agencies, 177–180
  jurisdiction in international trade disputes, 701–704
  jurisdiction of 29–43, 227
  of limited jurisdiction, 25
  and performance of judges, 77, 79–80
  personal jurisdiction of, 32–40
  removal from state to federal court, 32
  state court system, 25, 28–29
  subject matter jurisdiction of, 29–32
  venue and, 40
CPSC. *See* Consumer Product Safety Commission (CPSC)
Credit cards, 668–671
Crime
  arson, 241
  classification of, 226–227
  computer crime, 246–248
  definition of, 224
  degree of moral turpitude of, 227
  degree of seriousness of, 226–227
  federal crimes, 241–246
  forgery, 240–241
  Hobbs Act, 244–245
  jurisdiction for prosecution of, 227
  mail fraud, 242–244
  purpose of punishment, 227
  Racketeering Influenced and Corrupt Organizations Act (RICO), 109–111, 245–246, 472
  robbery, 239–240
  state crimes, 236–241
  theft, 237–239
  Travel Act, 244
  white collar crime, 248–250
  wire fraud, 242
Criminal conspiracy doctrine, 590
Criminal law
  cases, 233–234, 238–241, 243–246
  civil law compared with, 224–227
  classification of crime, 226–227
  computer crime, 246–248
  constitutional protections and, 228–231
  definition of, 11
  federal crimes affecting business, 241–246
  general criminal defenses, 234–236
  general elements of criminal responsibility, 231–234
  guilty act versus guilty mind, 232
  international criminal enforcement, 250
  jurisdiction of federal courts in, 30
  nature of, 224–227
  purposes of, 291
  state crimes affecting business, 236–241
  white collar crime, 248–250
Criterion-related validity, of tests, 573

Cross elasticity of demand, 436
Cross elasticity of supply, 436–437
Cross-examination, of witnesses in trial proceedings, 63
Currency controls, 721–722

Damages
  for breach of contract, 283–284
  compensatory damages, 283
  definition of, 10
  limitation on, in warranties, 340–341
  liquidated damages, 284, 340
  nominal damages, 283–284
  punitive damages, 284, 303
  treble damages, 433
  workers' compensation and, 521, 521n
Davis-Bacon Act, 538
De facto corporation, 411
De facto discrimination, 153
De jure corporation, 410
Death benefits, 526
Debt securities, 411, 472
Debtor default, 678–679
Deceptive trade practices, 113, 387, 656, 658–661
Decree of specific performance, 44, 284
Defamation
  commercial defamation, 389
  defenses for, 310–311
  definition of, 308
  elements of, 309–310
  injurious falsehood and, 311
  libel versus slander, 308–309
  as unprotected speech under First Amendment, 145
Default judgment, 56
Defective product, 348–349, 353
Defendants, 10
Defenses
  in assault and battery, 307–308
  criminal defenses, 234–236
  for defamation, 310–311
  failing company defense for mergers, 445
  for false imprisonment, 312–313
  for interference with business relationships, 363–365
  for negligence, 303–304
  for patent infringement, 377–378
  plaintiff misconduct defenses, 343, 352–353
  in pretrial proceedings, 54
  for price discrimination, 464
  privity defense, 342–343, 351
  sophisticated purchaser defense for, 351–352
  for strict liability, 351–354
  for trespass, 315–316
  for warranties, 342–343
Delegated powers, 121
Delegation of powers, in federal government, 120–121, 170
Denial, in pretrial proceedings, 53–54
Depositions, 56–57
Deprivation of life, liberty or property, 157
Deregulation, 187
Direct conflict, between state and federal laws, 128–129
Direct examination, of witnesses in trial proceedings, 63

SUBJECT INDEX 785

Disabilities
   Americans With Disabilities Act (ADA), 7, 580–585
   definition of, 581–582
Discipline, employee, 616
Disclaimers
   by custom or usage, 340
   definition of, 339
   by examination, 340
   excluding and limiting warranties, 339–342
   of express warranties, 339
   of implied warranties, 339–342
   by language, 339–340
   by limitation on damages, 340–341
Disclosure of embarrassing private facts, 317
Discovery stage, of pretrial proceedings, 56–57, 59–60
   case, 57–58
Discretionary powers, 171
Discrimination
   affirmative action, 578
   Age Discrimination in Employment Act, 172–173, 510, 576–577, 579–580
   Americans With Disabilities Act, 7, 580–585
   appearance requirements, 557
   and *bona fide* occupational qualification, 554n, 574–577, 579
   cases, 172–173, 558–559, 562–565, 568–570, 575–577
   Civil Rights Act of 1964, 125, 153, 154n, 510, 547–578
   compensation and benefits, 558
   Constitution and, 546
   coverage and enforcement of Civil Rights Act, 547–548
   de facto discrimination, 153
   disabilities, 580–585
   discriminatory impact, 565–574
   educational requirements and nonphysical skills, 571–572
   employer's rebuttal in, 555–556
   employer's rebuttal of discriminatory impact, 567
   employment rules concerning family, 557–558
   Equal Pay Act, 545–546, 546n
   federal government contracting and, 546
   harassment or intimidation, 557
   intentional discrimination, 553–559
   against interstate commerce, 131–133
   lack of U.S. citizenship, 550–551, 551n
   mixed motive cases of, 556
   overview of sources of law on, 544–547
   physical requirements, 570–571
   pregnancy, 557–558
   premise of employment discrimination law, 543–544
   pretext for, 556
   prima facie case of, 554–556
   prima facie case of discriminatory impact, 566–567
   proof of, 553–578, 585
   race, color and national origin, 549–551
   religion, 551–553, 584n
   remedies under Civil Rights Act, 548–549, 549n
   reverse discrimination, 578
   segregation, 557
   seniority systems, 573–574
   sex discrimination, 154, 154n, 545–546, 551, 574–575
   sexual harassment, 560–565
   state laws on, 547
   testing, 572–573
   as unfair labor practice, 615–616, 618–619

Dissolution
   of corporations, 417–419
   of partnerships, 408
District courts, 26
Diversity of citizenship cases, 31–32
Doctrine of incorporation, 138
Doctrine of substantial performance, 13, 279
Doing no harm, 200–201
Double jeopardy, 229
Drug testing, 515–517
   case, 517–519
Due process, 33, 36
Due process clause
   case, 160–161
   in criminal cases, 229
   definition of, 155
   procedural due process, 157–161
   substantive due process, 155–157
   takings clause, 162–163
   in U.S. Constitution, 37, 137–138
Duress, as criminal defense, 235
Durham rule, 235
Duty
   breach of, 297–299
   case, 296–297
   definition, 295
   of landowners, 297
Duty of candor, 378
Duty to warn, and products liability, 344

ECOA. *See* Equal Credit Opportunity Act (ECOA)
Educational requirements and nonphysical skills, 571–572
EEC. *See* European Economic Community (EEC)
EEOC. *See* Equal Employment Opportunity Commission (EEOC)
8-Ks, 477, 490
Eighth Amendment, 230–231
EIS. *See* Environmental impact statements (EIS)
Embarrassing private facts, disclosure of, 317
Embezzlement, 237
   case, 238–239
Emergency Planning and Community Right-to-Know Act, 652
Eminent domain, 162
Employee Polygraph Protection Act, 514–515
Employee security and welfare
   cases, 513–514, 517–519, 523–524, 536–537
   contractual protections of job security, 507–508
   distinction between employee and independent contractor, 506–507
   drug testing, 515–519
   employment-at-will, 509–514
   Fair Labor Standards Act, 533–538
   job security, 507–514
   lie detector testing, 514–515
   Occupational Safety and Health Act, 528–532
   privacy issues, 514–520
   protection for public employees, 508–509
   unemployment compensation, 538–539
   workers' compensation, 520–528
Employer-employee relationship, 394

Employer-independent contractor relationship, 394
Employer unfair labor practices, 615–617
Employers' liability, 320, 321
Employment-at-will
  case, 513–514
  definition of, 509
  exceptions to, 509–512
Employment law. See Discrimination; Employee security and welfare; Labor-management relations
Endangered species, 651
Entrapment, as criminal defense, 236
Entry barriers, 434, 442, 443–444
Environmental impact statements (EIS), 634
Environmental Protection Agency (EPA), 175–176, 187, 628, 634–635, 637–642, 644, 647, 648
Environmental protection law
  acid rain, 640
  air pollution control, 638–641, 651
  cases, 631–632, 636–637, 641, 645–646
  common law and pollution, 629–632
  environmental impact statements, 634
  Environmental Protection Agency, 634–635
  importance of, 627–628
  indoor pollution, 649
  industrial and societal considerations, 651–652
  international legal aspects of pollution, 649–651
  National Environmental Policy Act, 633–635
  noise pollution, 648–649
  oil spills, 638, 651
  pesticides, 648
  rationale for, 425
  solid waste disposal, 642–647, 650
  state laws, 632–633
  toxic substances, 647–648
  water pollution control, 635–638, 651
EPA. See Environmental Protection Agency (EPA)
Equal Credit Opportunity Act (ECOA), 673–675
Equal Employment Opportunity Commission (EEOC), 172–173, 547–548, 560, 567, 580
Equal opportunity. See Discrimination
Equal Pay Act, 545–546, 546n
Equal protection clause, 62, 151–155, 152n
Equity
  courts of, 44, 45
  law compared with, 43–46
Equity securities, 411, 472
Establishment clause, 141–142
Estoppel, 184
  promissory, 269
Ethics
  bad ethical behavior, 216
  business ethics, 194
  case, 201–202
  corporate social responsiveness, 217–220
  corporations as moral agents, 212–215
  definition of, 193–194
  doing no harm, 200–201
  and duty to "do good," 202–204
  economic benefits of, 215–217
  and excusing conditions, 204–205, 209
  honesty, 199
  keeping commitments, 200
  loyalty, 199–200
  moral dilemmas, 205–206
  moral minimum, 198–201
  moral reasoning and decision making, 206–212
  moral standards, 197–198
  morality compared with, 193–194
  relationship with law, 194–197
European Economic Community (EEC), 129, 713, 720–721, 720n
Evidence
  in federal courts, 64n
  hearsay evidence, 64–65
  irrelevant evidence, 64
  opinion evidence, 65–66
  presentation of, 62–63
  rules of, 63–66
Ex post facto laws, 231
Exclusive dealing, 463
Excused performance, and contracts, 280
Excusing conditions, 204–205, 209
Exemption laws, 77
Existing economic interests, 364
Export Administration Act, 712–713
Export license, 696
Export Trading Company Act, 714–715
Exports
  Export Administration Act, 712–713
  incentives for, 713–715
  regulations of the export/import process, 711–716
Express contracts, 258
Express preemption, 126
Express warranties, 326–328
  case, 329–330
  disclaimers of, 339
Externalities, 425
Extradition, Model Treaty on, 250

FAA. See Federal Arbitration Act (FAA); Federal Aviation Administration (FAA)
Failing company defense, for mergers, 445
Fair Credit and Charge Card Disclosure Act (FCCCDA), 670–671
Fair Credit Billing Act, 673
Fair Credit Reporting Act (FCRA), 666–668
Fair Debt Collection Practices Act, 671–673
Fair Labor Standards Act (FLSA)
  administration and enforcement of, 535–536
  case, 536–537
  child labor, 535
  coverage of, 509–510, 533–535
  minimum wage and overtime, 534–535, 534n
  statute of limitations in, 546
Fair Packaging and Labeling Act, 680–681
Fair use doctrine, 382–383
  case, 383–385
False arrest, 311
False imprisonment, 311–313
  case, 313–314
False light, 317–318
False pretenses, 237
Family, employment rules concerning, 557–558

Family Farmer Bankruptcy Act, 682n
FCC. *See* Federal Communications Commission (FCC)
FCCCDA. *See* Fair Credit and Charge Card Disclosure Act (FCCCDA)
FCPA. *See* Foreign Corrupt Practices Act (FCPA)
FCRA. *See* Fair Credit Reporting Act (FCRA)
Featherbedding, 619
FECA. *See* Federal Employees' Compensation Act (FECA)
Federal Arbitration Act (FAA), 83
Federal Aviation Administration (FAA), 170
Federal Bankruptcy Act, 666
Federal Communications Commission (FCC), 680
Federal courts
  civil cases in, 30–32
  criminal cases in, 30
  diversity of citizenship cases, 31–32
  federal question cases, 30–31
  judges in, 79–80
  personal jurisdiction in, 39
  removal from state courts to, 32
  rules of evidence in, 64n
  subject matter jurisdiction of, 29–32
  system of, 26–29
Federal Deposit Insurance Corporation, 471
Federal Employees' Compensation Act (FECA), 527
Federal Employers' Liability Act (FELA), 527
Federal Environmental Pesticide Control Act, 648
Federal Food, Drug, and Cosmetic Act, 680
Federal government
  authority of, compared with state governments, 121–137
  checks and balances in, 119
  contracting with, 546
  delegation of powers, 120–121
  interstate commerce and, 123–124
  judicial review, 119
  organization of, 118–121
  reasonable overlap of functions in, 120
  separation of powers, 119–121
Federal Insecticide, Fungicide, and Rodenticide Act (FIFRA), 648
Federal laws. *See also* names of specific laws
  Age Discrimination in Employment Act, 579–580
  air pollution control, 638–641
  Americans With Disabilities Act, 580–585
  antitrust statutes, 430–431
  on bankruptcy, 682–689
  Civil Rights Act of 1964, 547–578
  on computer crime, 247
  Consumer Credit Protection Act, 661–675
  consumer legislation, 354–356, 657
  crimes affecting business, 241–246
  deceptive trade practices, 656, 658–661
  on environmental protection, 633–649
  Equal Pay Act, 545–546, 546n
  export/import regulations, 711–716
  Fair Labor Standards Act, 533–538
  on labor-management relations, 591–594
  National Environmental Policy Act, 633–635
  National Labor Relations Act, 592–594
  noise pollution, 648–649
  Occupational Safety and Health Act, 528–532
  on packaging and labeling, 680–681

  products liability, 357–358
  Real Estate Settlement Procedures Act, 679
  on securities regulation, 471–472
  solid waste disposal, 642–647
  toxic substances, 647–648
  unemployment compensation, 538–539
  vs. state law, 10
  water pollution control, 635–638
  on workers' compensation, 527
Federal Mediation and Conciliation Service (FMCS), 613
Federal preemption, 125–126, 594
Federal Privacy Act, 186
Federal question cases, 30–31
Federal Register, 176, 177, 184, 186, 187
Federal Reserve Board (FRB), 170, 662
Federal Trade Commission (FTC), 169–171, 355, 356, 431, 433, 440, 441, 656, 658–661, 663, 667, 714
Federal Trade Commission Act, 387, 431, 433, 656, 658–659
  case, 659–661
Federal Warranty Act, 355
Federal Water Pollution Control Act, 635
Fees, of attorneys, 19
FELA. *See* Federal Employers' Liability Act (FELA)
Felonies, 11, 226–227
Fiduciary relationship, 404
Fifth Amendment, 155–163, 228–230
Fighting words, 145
Fines, for violation of criminal laws, 11
First Amendment, 141–150, 310, 311, 389, 546, 551
Fitness for a particular purpose
  implied warranty of, 334–335, 334n
  warranty of, 339–340
Flammable Fabrics Act, 354, 681
FMCS. *See* Federal Mediation and Conciliation Service (FMCS)
FOIA. *See* Freedom of Information Act (FOIA)
Food and Drug Administration (FDA), 680
Food, Drug and Cosmetic Act, 354
Foreign Corrupt Practices Act (FCPA), 216, 471–472, 713n
"Foreign-natural object" test, 332, 347
Foreign Sovereign Immunities Act (FSIA), 704–706
Foreign trade zone (FTZ), 715
Forgery, 240
  case, 240–241
Formal rule making, of administrative agencies, 176
Forum non conveniens, 40–41
Forum state, 33
Four-fifths rule, 567
Fourteenth Amendment, 37, 137–138, 151–155, 546
Fourth Amendment, 173, 228, 516, 517, 531
Franchising, in international business, 721, 722–723
Fraud
  and rescission of contracts, 274–275
  tort of, 14, 319
FRB. *See* Federal Reserve Board (FRB)
Free riding, 456
Free speech clause, 143–150
Free Trade Act (FTA), 720
Freedom of Information Act (FOIA), 185–186
Freedom of religion, 141–143, 551
Freedom of speech, 143–150
FSIA. *See* Foreign Sovereign Immunities Act (FSIA)

FTA. *See* Free Trade Act (FTA)
FTC. *See* Federal Trade Commission (FTC)
FTZ. *See* Foreign trade zone (FTZ)
Full disclosure, 493–494
Full faith and credit clause, 77, 136–137
Fungicides, 648

Garnishment, 76–77, 666
GATT. *See* General Agreement on Tariffs and Trade (GATT)
General Agreement on Tariffs and Trade (GATT), 715–716, 718–719
General creditors, 686
General denial, in pretrial proceedings, 53–54
General duty clause, of OSHA, 529–530
General trial courts, 25
Generic term, 367
Government agencies. *See* Administrative agencies; and names of specific agencies
Government in the Sunshine Act, 186
Government regulation of business. *See also* Antitrust law; Consumer protection; Discrimination; Employee protection and welfare; Environmental protection law; International business; Labor-management relations; Securities regulation
   externalities in market economy, 425
   inadequate information in market economy, 426
   and the market economy, 424
   market power and, 426
   natural monopolies and, 426–427
   rationale for, 424–427
   and societal goals not directly related to market economy, 427
Gramm-Rudman Act, 120
Grand jury, 228–229
Grievance procedures, in collective bargaining, 611–614
Group dynamics, 214–215
GTDA, 713
GTDR, 712–713

Hague Convention on Service Abroad of Judicial and Extrajudicial Documents in Civil or Commercial Matters, 708
Hague Convention on the Taking of Evidence Abroad in Civil or Commercial Matters, 708
Handicapped. *See* Disabilities
Harassment, 557
   case, 562–565
   hostile environment sexual harassment, 561–562
   quid pro quo sexual harassment, 560
   sexual harassment 560–568
Hazardous and Solid Waste Amendments, 642–643
Hazardous Materials Transportation Act, 652
Hazardous Substance Superfund, 644, 645
Hazardous Substances Act, 354
Hazardous waste, 642
Health and Human Services Department, 529
Hearsay evidence, 64–65
HELCPA. *See* Home Equity Loan Consumer Protection Act (HELCPA)

Herfindahl-Hirschman Index (HHI), 445
HHI. *See* Herfindahl-Hirschman Index (HHI)
Hobbs Act, 244–245
Home Equity Loan Consumer Protection Act (HELCPA), 665
Honesty, 199
Horizontal mergers, 441–443
   case, 446–447
Horizontal restraints of trade
   boycotts and, 453–454
   case, 450–452
   definition of, 447
   joint ventures, 454–455
   market division and, 453
   per se rule, 452–454
   price fixing and, 452
   requirement of collusion, 447–448
   rule of reason in, 448–450
   trade associations, 454
Hostile environment sexual harassment, 561–562
Hot cargo agreements, 620, 620n
Hourly fee, of attorneys, 19
Hybrid rule making, of administrative agencies, 176

IBRD. *See* International Bank for Reconstruction and Development (IBRD)
ICC. *See* International Chamber of Commerce (ICC); Interstate Commerce Commission (ICC)
ICSID. *See* International Centre for Settlement of Investment Disputes (ICSID)
IMF. *See* International Monetary Fund (IMF)
Immunity, as criminal defense, 236
Implied contracts, 258
Implied preemption, 126–128
   case, 129–131
Implied repeal, 108–109
Implied warranties
   disclaimers of, 339–342
   of fitness for a particular purpose, 334–335, 334n
   of merchantability, 331–333
Import licenses, 696–697
Imports
   protection from unfair competition, 716
   regulation of, 715–716
   Trade and Tariff Act, 716
Imprisonment, for violation of criminal laws, 11
In personam cases, 33, 37, 39
In rem cases, 33, 39–40
Income replacement, 525–526
Independent contractors, distinguished from employees, 506–507
Independent intervening cause, in negligence, 301
Indoor pollution, 649
Infancy, as criminal defense, 234
Informal rule making, of administrative agencies, 176
Injunction, 10, 284
Injurious falsehood, 311
Injury
   from assault and battery, 306
   defamation and, 310
   false imprisonment and, 312
   negligence and, 302–303, 302n

Innocent bystanders, 342–343
Inquisitorial system, 51–52, 51n
Insanity, as criminal defense, 235
Insecticides, 648
Insider trading, 484–489, 501
Insolvency, 413
Institutional investors, 482
Insurance, workers' compensation and, 525
Intellectual property
  copyright for, 380–385
  international protection of, 385–386
Intentional discrimination, 553–559
Intentional infliction of mental distress, 319
Inter-American Commercial Arbitration Commission, 709
Interbrand competition, 456
Interference with business relationships
  case, 364–365
  defenses for, 363–365
  definition of, 362, 362n
  elements of, 362–363
  manager's privilege, 366
Interlocking directorates, 431
Intermediate scrutiny, and equal protection clause, 154–155
International Bank for Reconstruction and Development (IBRD), 719
International business
  act of state doctrine, 706–707
  agent in, 721
  cases, 697–698, 703–707, 710–711, 722–723
  classification of international trade, 695–696
  Convention on Contracts for the International Sale of Goods, 700
  Convention on International Bills of Exchange and International Promissory Notes, 700
  currency controls, 721–722
  export/import regulations, 711–716
  Foreign Sovereign Immunities Act, 704–706
  franchising in, 721, 722–723
  General Agreement on Tariffs and Trade (GATT), 715–716, 718–719
  International Bank for Reconstruction and Development, 719
  international law and, 694
  International Monetary Fund, 719
  international sales contract, 696–700
  licensee in, 721
  organizing for international trade, 717–721
  regional trade agreements, 720–721
  resolving international trade disputes, 701–711
  transnational corporations, 723–724
International Centre for Settlement of Investment Disputes (ICSID), 709
International Chamber of Commerce (ICC), 83, 699n, 709
International Code of Marketing of Breast-Milk Substitutes, 724
International Convention on Civil Liability for Oil Pollution Damage, 651
International conventions, on pollution, 650–651
International Court of Justice, 650
International criminal enforcement, 250
International Emergency Economic Power Act, 713

International Fund for Compensation for Oil Pollution Damage, 651
International implications, of securities regulation, 500–502
International law
  definition of, 694
  on pollution, 649–651
  protection of intellectual property, 385–386
International Monetary Fund (IMF), 719
International organizations, on pollution, 650
International sales contract
  letter of credit, 696–698
  trade terms, 698–699, 699n
International trade. *See* International business
International trade disputes
  act of state doctrine, 706–707
  arbitration for, 708–711
  domestic court jurisdiction, 701–704
  Foreign Sovereign Immunities Act, 704–706
  international litigation for, 708
  resolution of, 701–711
Internationalization of contract law, 287
Interpretation
  aids to, 107–109
  of contracts, 282–283
  definition of, 106
  as necessary evil, 106
  and plain meaning rule, 283
  plain-meaning rule, 106–107
  rationale for, 107
Interrogatories, 57
Interstate commerce, 123–124, 131–135
Interstate Commerce Commission (ICC), 170
Intimidation, 557
Intoxication, as criminal defense, 235
Intrabrand competition, 456
Intrusion, 317
Invasion of privacy, 316–317
  case, 317–318
Investigative powers, of administrative agencies, 171–176
Investigative reports, 666
Investment Advisers Act of 1940, 471
Investment Company Act of 1940, 471
Investment contract, 473
Irrelevant evidence, 64

Joint and several liability, 321
Joint ventures, 454–455
Judges
  Administrative Law Judges, 180, 595
  performance of, 77, 79–80
  role in common law, 91–92
Judicial eccentricity, myth of, 12–13
Judicial review, 119, 177–180
Jurisdiction
  of civil cases by federal courts, 30–32
  conflict of laws and, 41–43
  in criminal law, 30, 227
  definition of, 29
  in diversity of citizenship cases, 31–32
  exclusive or concurrent, 31
  of federal courts, 29–32

Jurisdiction (*cont.*)
  in federal question cases, 30–31
  forum non conveniens and, 40–41
  in international trade disputes, 701–704
  personal jurisdiction, 32–40
  removal from state to federal court, 32
  subject matter jurisdiction, 29–32
  venue and, 40
Jury
  case, 67–68
  grand jury, 228–229
  impaneling of, 62
  instructions to, 66–67
  trial by jury, 61
Jury trial, 61–62
  summary jury trial, 85
Justice, and law, 13–14
Justice Department, 433, 440, 441, 445, 457, 486, 663
Justification, defense of, 363

Keeping commitments, 200

Labeling, and packaging, 680–681
Labor arbitration, 82
Labor Department, 529–532, 535, 538
Labor dispute, definition of, 595–596
Labor-management relations
  cases, 597–598, 604–605, 609–610, 614, 622–624
  collective bargaining process, 606–614
  decertification of unions, 606
  and employer free speech rights, 603–604
  federal laws on, 591–594
  history of, 590–591
  initial organizing to select bargaining representative, 598–599
  National Labor Relations Board, 594–595
  purpose of laws for, 426
  representation election to select bargaining representative, 599–601
  requirement of laboratory conditions, 602–603
  selecting bargaining representative, 598–606
  state laws on, 594
  unfair labor practices, 614–624
  union's campaign, 605–606
Labor-Management Relations Act, 592–593
Labor-Management Reporting and Disclosure Act, 593
Labor unions. *See* Unions
Landowners, duty of, 297
Landrum-Griffin Act, 246, 593
Lanham Act, 366–367, 369, 386, 387–389, 661
Larceny, 237
Law. *See also* Contracts; Criminal law; Federal laws; State laws; Tort law; and names of specific laws
  administrative, 11, 180–182
  civil vs. criminal, 10–11, 224–227
  classifications of, 9–12
  common law, 10, 90–97
  conflict of laws, 41–43
  constitutional law, 11
  courts of law, 44, 45
  definitions of, 4–6
  equity compared with, 43–46
  federal vs. state, 10
  justice and, 13–14
  misconceptions about the legal system, 12–13
  morals and, 14–17
  primary sources of, 5
  process-oriented approach to, 6
  processes by which law is made, 89–90
  public vs. private law, 11–12
  relationship with ethics, 194–197
  requisites of a legal system, 6–8
  rule-oriented approach to, 5–6
  secondary sources of, 5
  sources of, 5
  state laws, 112–114
  statutory law, 10, 97–114
  subject matter of, 9
Lawyers
  for corporations, 20
  fees of, 19
  for individuals, 18–20
  selection and use of, 18–20
Leading questions, 63
Leases, warranties in, 335
Legal detriment, 267
Legal entity, corporations as, 212, 410
Legal system. *See also* Courts; Litigation
  misconceptions concerning, 12–13
  and performance of judges, 77, 79–80
  requisites of, 6–8
  value in, 80
Legislative history, 108
Letter of credit, 696–698
Liability. *See also* Products liability
  of the agent or employee to third parties, 399–401
  civil liabilities under the 1933 Securities Act, 482–483
  contractual liability of the agent or employee to third parties, 400
  contractual liability of the principal to third parties, 396–397
  of corporate managers, 415
  criminal liability of corporations, 248–249
  criminal liablity of corporate officials, 249–250
  employers' liability, 320, 321
  joint and several liability, 321
  of partners to third-party creditors, 407–408
  of the principal to third parties in agency relationship, 396–399
  of shareholders, 413
  strict liability, 249, 345–354
  tort liability of the agent or employee to third parties, 401
  tort liability of the principal to third parties, 397–399
Libel, 308
Licensee, in international trade, 721
Lie detector testing, 514–515
Limited partnership, 409
Limited warranty, 356
Liquidated damages, 284, 340
Liquidation proceedings, 417, 682–687
Litigation
  appellate courts 71–74, 76–77
  discovery stage of, 56–57, 59–60

SUBJECT INDEX 791

Litigation (cont.)
  flow chart of, 78
  impaneling a jury, 62
  increase in, 81
  instructions to the jury, 66–67
  judgment after verdict, 69
  motion for directed verdict, 66
  and performance of judges, 77, 79–80
  pleading stage, 52–56
  presentation of evidence, 62–63
  pretrial proceedings, 52–60
  rules of evidence, 63–66
  summary judgment in, 60
  trial by jury, 61–62
  trial proceedings, 60–67, 69
  value in, 80
Local offerings, 481–482
Lockouts, 615
London Court of Arbitration, 83, 709
Long-arm statutes, 35–36
Longshoremen's and Harbor Workers' Compensation Act, 527
Loyalty, 199–200

MACT. *See* Maximum achievable control technology (MACT)
Madrid Agreement, 385–386
Magistrates, 59
Magnuson-Moss Warranty Act, 355–356
Mail box rule, 264–265
Mail fraud, 242
  case, 243–244
Malum in se, 227
Malum prohibitum, 227
Management, of corporations, 411–412, 415
Manager's privilege, 366
Mandatory authority, 93
  case, 93–94
Marine Protection, Research, and Sanctuaries Act, 638
Maritime Safety Act, 528
Market concentration, 442
Market demand, 436–437
Market division, 453
Market economy, 424
Market failure, 425
Market power, 434–435, 449
Market share, 434, 441–442
Master-servant relationship, 394
Materiality, 478
Maximum achievable control technology (MACT), 639
MBCA. *See* Model Business Corporation Act (MBCA)
MBEs. *See* Minority business enterprises (MBEs)
Mediation
  in collective bargaining, 613, 613n
  in dispute resolution, 84–85
Medical benefits, 526
Mental distress, intentional infliction of, 319
Mental impairment. *See* Disabilities
Merchantability
  implied warranty of, 331–333
  warranty of, 339

Mergers
  case, 446–447
  conglomerate mergers, 441, 444–445
  definition of, 440
  failing company defense for, 445
  guidelines for, 445
  horizontal mergers, 441–443
  types of, 441–445
  vertical mergers, 441, 443–444
Metal and Nonmetallic Mine Safety Act, 528
Mexico, free trade with United States, 720
Minimum wage, 534, 534n
Minitrial, 85
Minority business enterprises (MBEs), 153–154
"Mirror image" rule, in contracts, 263–264
Misdemeanors, 11, 226–227
Mistake, as criminal defense, 235–236
M'Naghten test, 235
Model Business Corporation Act (MBCA), 114, 409
Model Penal Code, 235
Model Treaty on Extradition, 250
Model Treaty on Mutual Assistance in Criminal Matters, 250
Model Treaty on the Transfer of Proceedings in Criminal Matters, 250
Monopolization
  case, 438–439
  defining the relevant market, 435–437
  definition of monopoly, 434
  geographic market and, 437
  intent to monopolize, 437–438
  measuring market power, 434–435
  product market and, 435–437
Monopoly, definition of, 434
Montreal Protocol, 651
Moral agents, corporations as, 212–215
Moral dilemmas, 205–206
Moral minimum, 198–201
Moral obligation to "do good," 202–204
Moral reasoning and decision making, 206–212
Moral standards, 197–198
Morals and morality. *See also* Ethics
  case, 16–17
  definition of, 193–194
  law and, 14–15
Motion for directed verdict, 66
Motion for judgment notwithstanding the verdict, 69
  case, 69–71
Motion for new trial, 69
Motion to dismiss, 55–56, 55n
Motor Carrier Act of 1980, 187

NASDAQ system. *See* National Association of Securities Dealers Automated Quotation (NASDAQ) system
National Association of Securities Dealers Automated Quotation (NASDAQ) system, 482
National Commission on State Workmen's Compensation Laws, 527
National Electrical Code, 529
National Environmental Policy Act (NEPA), 633–635

SUBJECT INDEX

National Fire Protection Association, 529
National Highway Traffic Safety Administration (NHTSA), 178–180
National Industrial Recovery Act (NIRA), 533
National Institute for Occupational Safety and Health (NIOSH), 529
National Labor Relations Act (NLRA)
  amendments to, 592–594
  case, 597–598
  collective bargaining in, 607
  coverage of, 592, 595–596
  exemptions under, 596
  secondary boycott, 621
National Labor Relations Board (NLRB), 170, 171, 180–181, 594–595, 599–606, 609–610, 613, 615
National origin, discrimination based on, 549–551
National Traffic and Motor Vehicle Safety Act of 1966, 178
Natural monopolies, 426–427
Negligence
  and all the circumstances, 298
  and breach of duty, 297–299
  case, 93–94
  comparative negligence, 304
  compared with strict liability, 347
  and conduct of others, 298–299
  contributory negligence, 303
  defenses for, 303–304
  definition of, 293–295
  duty and, 295–297
  independent intervening cause in, 301
  injury and, 302–303, 302n
  negligence *per se*, 299
  no fault systems, 304–305
  pollution and, 630
  in product design and manufacturing, 344–345
  products liability and, 344–345
  proximate cause in, 299–302
  statute of limitations for, 304
Negligence *per se*, 299
Negligent manufacture, 344
Negotiated settlement, 81–82
NEPA. *See* National Environmental Policy Act (NEPA)
New source performance standards (NSPSs), 639
New York Convention, 709
NHTSA. *See* National Highway Traffic Safety Administration (NHTSA)
NIOSH. *See* National Institute for Occupational Safety and Health (NIOSH)
NIRA. *See* National Industrial Recovery Act (NIRA)
NLRB. *See* National Labor Relations Board (NLRB)
No fault systems, 304–305
Noise Control Act of 1972, 648–649
Noise pollution, 648–649
Nominal damages, 283–284
Noncommercial speech, 148–150
Nonprice predation, 438
Norris-La Guardia Act, 591–592
NSPSs. *See* New source performance standards (NSPSs)
Nuclear Non-Proliferation Act, 713
Nuisance, 320, 629–630
Nutrition Labeling and Education Act, 680

Obscenity, 144–145
Occupational diseases, 525, 525n
Occupational Safety and Health Act (OSHA)
  appraisal of, 532
  citations for violations under, 531–532
  general duty clause, 529–530
  inspections under, 531–532, 531n
  protection against retaliation in, 510
  recordkeeping and notice requirements of, 530
  rights and responsibilities of employees, 530
  safety standards in, 528–529
  state enforcement plans, 532
Occupational Safety and Health Administration (OSHA), 170, 187, 528, 530–531
Occupational Safety and Health Review Commission, 531–532
OEA. *See* Office of Export Administration (OEA)
Offer, in contracts, 260–261
Office of Export Administration (OEA), 712
Officer, of corporation, 35
Oil spills, 638, 651
Oligopolies, 430
Omnibus Trade and Competitiveness Act, 695n
One right answer, myth of, 12
Opinion evidence, 65–66
OSHA. *See* Occupational Safety and Health Act (OSHA); Occupational Safety and Health Administration (OSHA)
Overtime, 534, 538

Packaging and labeling, 680–681
PACs. *See* Political action committees (PACs)
Palming off, 386
Parol evidence rule, 276
Partnerships
  business operations of, 404–408
  cases, 403, 405–407
  dissolution of, 408
  limited partnership, 409
  nature and formation of, 402
  partners' liability to third-party creditors, 407–408
  property of, 404
  relations between partners, 404
  relations with third parties generally, 405
  termination of, 408–409
  winding up, 409
Patent and Trademark Office, 27, 376–377
Patent infringement
  case, 378–380
  defenses for, 377–378
  definition of, 377
  definition of patent, 375–376
  and ownership of patents, 377
  and patent procedure, 376–377
  and patentability, 376
  remedies for, 378
  and subject matter of patents, 376
Patent misuse, 378
Patent Pending, 377
Patents
  definition of, 375–376

Patents (cont.)
　international protection of, 386
　ownership of, 377
　patentability and, 376
　procedure for, 376–377
　subject matter of, 376
Per se rule, 452–454
Peremptory challenges, 62
Perjury, 63
Permissive counterclaim, 54
Personal jurisdiction
　appearance, 33
　case, 37–38
　corporate defendants, 34–35
　definition of, 32–33
　due process and, 36
　in federal courts, 39
　foul-ups in service of summons, 38–39
　in rem cases, 33, 39–40
　long-arm statutes and, 35–36
　service of summons, 34
Personal service of summons, 34
Personal summons service, foul-ups in, 38–39
Persuasive authority, 94
Pesticides, 648
Petty offenses, 226
Physical impairment. *See* Disabilities
Physical requirements, 570–571
Picketing, 619, 620–621
Plain-meaning rule, 106–107, 283
Plaintiff carelessness, 352–353
Plaintiff misconduct defenses, 343, 352–353
Plaintiffs, 10
"Plant closing" law, 610
Pleading stage, of pretrial proceedings, 52–56
Poison Prevention Packaging Act, 354, 681
Political action committees (PACs), 105
Political speech, 148–150
Pollution. *See also* Environmental protection law
　air pollution control, 638–641
　common law and, 629–632
　indoor pollution, 649
　international legal aspects of, 649–651
　noise pollution, 648–649
　pesticides, 648
　solid waste disposal, 642–647
　toxic substances, 647–648
　water pollution control, 635–638
Polygraphs, 514–515
Potentially responsible parties (PRPs), 643, 643n
Precedent
　common law and, 92, 93–95
　definition of, 92
　in interpretation of statute, 108
　types of, 93–95
Predatory pricing, 437–438
Predispute arbitration agreements, 83
Preexisting duty rule, 267–268
Pregnancy, 557–558
Pregnancy Discrimination Act, 558
Preliminary negotiations, in contracts, 260–261

Pretrial proceedings, 52–60
　case, 57–58
Price discrimination, 463–464
Price fixing, 452
Prima facie case
　of discrimination, 554–556
　of discriminatory impact, 566–567
Principal
　definition of, 394
　duties of, 395, 396
　liability of, to third parties in agency relationship, 396–399
Principle 21 of the Stockholm Conference, 650
Privacy
　case, 517–519
　drug testing, 515–519
　employee privacy, 514–520
　lie detector testing, 514–515
　monitoring of employees, 519–520
　personality and psychological tests, 519
Privacy Act, 186
Private law, 11–12
Privilege of competition, 364
Privileges and immunities clause, 139
　case, 140–141
Privity defense, 342–343, 351
Privity of contract, 342–343
Probable cause, 228
Procedural due process, 33, 157–159
　case, 160–161
Process-oriented approach, to law, 6
Product misuse, 352
Products liability
　cases, 329–330, 333, 335, 337–338, 341–342, 349–350, 353–354
　Consumer Product Safety Act, 354–355
　federal consumer legislation, 354–356
　federal legislation on, 357–358
　legal theories of, 326
　legislative limitations on, 356–358
　Magnuson-Moss Warranty Act, 355–356
　negligence, 344–345
　strict liability, 345–354
　warranty, 326–343
Prohibition Amendment, 8
Promissory estoppel, 269
Property, of partnerships, 404
Protocol of 1984 to Amend the International Convention on Civil Liability for Oil Pollution Damage, 651
Protocol of 1984 to Amend the International Fund for Compensation for Oil Pollution Damage, 651
Proximate cause, in negligence, 299–302
Proxy, 493–494
Proxy contests, 494
Proxy regulation, 493–494
PRPs. *See* Potentially responsible parties (PRPs)
Public employees, job security for, 508–509
Public goods, 425
Public Health Cigarette Smoking Act, 680
Public law, 11
Public Utility Holding Company Act, 471
Puffing, 387
Punitive damages, 284, 303

QIB. *See* Qualified institutional buyer (QIB)
Qualified institutional buyer (QIB), 482
Qualified privilege, for defamation, 311
Question of law, 177
Quid pro quo sexual harassment, 560

Race, color and national origin, discrimination based on, 549–551
Racketeering Influenced and Corrupt Organizations Act (RICO), 109–111, 245–246, 472
Railway Labor Act, 591, 596
Real Estate Settlement Procedures Act (RESPA), 679
"Reasonable expectation" test, 332, 347
Recognitional picketing, 619
Redirect examination, of witnesses in trial proceedings, 63
Refrigerator Safety Act, 354
Regional trade agreements, 720–721
Register of Copyrights, 382
Registered agent, of corporation, 34
Regulatory environment. *See* Antitrust law; Consumer protection; Discrimination; Employee protection and welfare; Environmental protection law; International business; Labor-management relations; Securities regulation
Regulatory Flexibility Act (RFA), 186–187
Regulatory negotiation, 85–86
Rehabilitation Act of 1973, 580
Rehabilitation benefits, 526
Religion
  discrimination based on, 551–553, 584n
  freedom of, 141–143, 551
Remedies
  for breach of contract, 283–285
  under Civil Rights Act, 548–549, 549n
  for copyright infringement, 385
  damages, 283–284
  decree of specific performance, 284
  definition of, 44
  injunction, 284
  law and equity and, 43–45
  for patent infringement, 378
  rescission, 284
  in sales contracts, 284–285
  for trademark infringement, 371
Reorganization, 688
Reply, in pretrial proceedings, 53, 55
Requests for production of documents, 57
Requirement of certainty, 102
  case, 103–104
Res ipsa loquitur, 345, 345n
Res judicata doctrine, 77
Resale price maintenance (RPM), 456–458
Rescission, of contracts, 274–275, 284
Reserved powers, 121
Resource Conservation and Recovery Act (RCRA), 642–643
RESPA. *See* Real Estate Settlement Procedures Act (RESPA)
Respondeat superior doctrine, 249, 397
Restatement of the Foreign Relations Law of the United States (Revised), 701
Restatement of Torts, 372
Restatement (Second) of Torts, 326, 346–349

Restatement (Third) of the Foreign Relations Law of the United States, 708, 709
Reverse discrimination, 578
Revised Model Business Corporation Act (RMBCA), 114
Revised Uniform Limited Partnership Act (RULPA), 113–114
RFA. *See* Regulatory Flexibility Act (RFA)
RICO. *See* Racketeering Influenced and Corrupt Organizations Act (RICO)
Right of removal, 32
Right to Financial Privacy Act, 247
Right-to-know laws, 652
Rights. *See* Bill of Rights; Civil Rights Act
Risk of loss
  case, 286–287
  contracts and, 285–287
River and Harbors Act of 1890, 635
Rivers and Harbors Appropriations Act of 1899, 635
RMBCA. *See* Revised Model Business Corporation Act (RMBCA)
Robbery, 239–240
Robinson-Patman Act, 128, 431, 433, 463–464
Rodenticides, 648
RPM. *See* Resale price maintenance (RPM)
Rule making powers, of administrative agencies, 171, 176–180
Rule of reason, 448–450
  case, 450–452
Rule-oriented approach, to law, 5–6
Rules of evidence, 63–66
RULPA. *See* Revised Uniform Limited Partnership Act (RULPA)

Safe Drinking Water Act, 638
Safety legislation. *See* Occupational Safety and Health Act (OSHA)
Sales contracts, 276, 284–285
Sales law, 257
SARA. *See* Superfund Amendments and Reauthorization Act (SARA)
SBA. *See* Small Business Administration (SBA)
Scienter, 490
Search and seizure, 173–176, 228, 516, 531
  case, 174–175
SEC. *See* Securities and Exchange Commission (SEC)
Secondary boycotts, 620–624
Secondary meaning, 368
Securities, 411, 472–473, 475–477
Securities Act of 1933, 471, 474–483
Securities and Exchange Commission (SEC), 170, 250, 432, 471, 475–478, 480–482, 484, 486–489, 493–495, 501
Securities Exchange Act of 1934, 471, 484–499
Securities Investor Protection Act of 1970, 471
Securities Investor Protection Corporation (SIPC), 471
Securities regulation
  antifraud rules and, 494–495, 501
  cases, 473–474, 479–480, 485, 488–489, 491–493, 498–499
  civil liabilities under the 1933 Act, 482–483
  definition of securities, 472–473
  disclosure requirements, 477–480
  enforcement of 1933 Act, 482
  exemptions from requirements for, 480–482, 500, 501

Securities regulation (*cont.*)
   false or inadequate corporate disclosures, 490–493
   federal legislation on, 471–472
   full disclosure and, 493–494
   insider trading, 484–489, 501
   of institutional investors, 482
   international implications of, 500–502
   introduction to, 470
   of local offerings, 481–482
   proxy contests and, 494
   proxy regulation, 493–494
   purposes of, 426
   registration process for securities, 475–477, 499–500
   Securities Act of 1933, 474–483
   Securities Exchange Act of 1934, 484–499
   of small issues, 480–481
   state laws on, 499–500
   tender offers, 494–499, 502
Segregation, 557
Self-defense, 236, 307–308
Self-incrimination, protection against, 229–230
Seniority systems, 573–574
Separation of powers, 119–121
Service contract, 356, 356n
Service Contract Act, 538
Service marks, 366
Service of summons, 34
   foul-ups in, 38–39
Seventh Amendment, 61
Sex discrimination, 154, 154n, 545–546, 551, 574–575
Sexual harassment
   case, 562–565
   hostile environment harassment, 561–562
   as intentional discrimination, 560
   quid pro quo harassment, 560
Shareholders
   definition of, 411
   and involuntary dissolution of corporations, 418
   liabilities of, 413
   rights and responsibilities of, 412–415
   and voluntary dissolution of corporations, 418
Shelf registration, 477
Sherman Act, 430, 433, 440, 456, 461, 591, 713
Shop right doctrine, 377
Simple plaintiff carelessness, 352
SIPC. *See* Securities Investor Protection Corporation (SIPC)
Sixth Amendment, 230
SJT. *See* Summary jury trial (SJT)
Slander, 308–309
Slander *per se*, 308–309
Small Business Administration (SBA), 170, 186
Small issues, 480–481
Social Security Act, 538
Solid waste disposal, 642–647, 650
Solid Waste Disposal Act, 642
Sophisticated purchaser defense, 351–352
Sovereign compulsion, 706
Special appearance, 33
Specialized U.S. courts, 26
Speech
   analysis of free speech questions, 150
   commercial speech, 146–148
   corporate speech, 144
   free speech clause, 143–150
   noncommercial speech, 148–150
   political speech, 148–150
   scope of protection for, 146, 148–150
   unpopular views and, 145–146
   unprotected speech, 144–145
Stare decisis doctrine, 92–93, 92n
State courts
   powers of, 119n
   removal of cases to federal court, 32
   system of, 25, 28–29
State governments
   authority of, compared with federal government, 121–137
   limitations on, 135–137
   regulation of commerce by, 125–129
State laws, 112–114
   on computer crime, 248
   criminal law, 236–241
   deceptive trade practices acts, 387
   on discrimination, 547
   on environmental protection, 632–633
   on labor-management relations, 594
   for securities regulation, 499–500
   unemployment compensation, 539
   vs. federal law, 10
   on whistle blowing, 510
   workers' compensation, 520–528
State police power, 122
State supreme courts, 28
Statute of limitations
   for defamation, 310
   for negligence, 304
   for warranties, 343
Statutes of repose, 357
Statutory interpretation, 106–109
Statutory law
   cases, 103–104, 110–111
   common law compared with, 10, 104–105
   definition of, 10, 97, 97n
   interpretation of, 106–109
   legislative options and, 105
   legislative scope of, 105
   and limitations on legislative bodies, 99, 101–102
   processes and form of, 104
   profile of, 97–98
   rationale for, 98–99
   and requirement of certainty, 102
   social and political forces and, 104–105
   state statutes, 112–114
Statutory reforms, 321
Stockholm Conference, Principle 21 of, 650
Stress, work-related, 525
Strict liability
   advantages and disadvantages of, 353
   cases, 349–350, 353–354
   compared with negligence, 347
   and criminal liability of corporate officials, 249
   defenses for, 351–354
   definition of, 346
   elements of, 346–349
   limitations on, 350–351

Strict liability (cont.)
  plaintiff misconduct defenses for, 352–353
  pollution and, 630
  privity defense for, 351
  sophisticated purchaser defense for, 351–352
Strict scrutiny, and equal protection clause, 152–154, 152n
Strikes
  legality of, 619–620
  treatment of strikers, 616
  wildcat strike, 607
Subject matter jurisdiction, of federal courts, 29–32
Subpoena power, 171–172
"Substantial evidence" test, 177–178
Substantial performance, doctrine of, 13, 279
Substantive due process, 155–157
Summary judgment, 60
Summary jury trial (SJT), 85
Summons service, 34
  foul-ups in, 38–39
Superfund Amendments and Reauthorization Act (SARA), 644
Supremacy clause, 126
Supreme Court. See U.S. Supreme Court
Symbolic expression, protection for, 143

Taft-Hartley Act, 246, 592–593
Takings clause, 162–163
Tariff Act of 1930, 716
Tariff Schedules of the United States (TSUS), 715
10-Ks, 477, 490
10-Qs, 477, 490
Tender offers, 502
Tennessee Valley Authority, 109
Termination, of contracts, 261–262, 263
Territorial and customer restrictions, 458
Testimony, in trial proceedings, 62–63
Testing
  discrimination and, 572–573
  validation requirement for, 572–573
Textual context, 107–108
Theft, 237–239
Third parties, in contracts, 276–278
TILA. See Truth in Lending Act (TILA)
Title
  contracts and, 285
  warranties of, 336
Title of appealed case, 28–29
TNCs. See Transnational corporations (TNCs)
Tort law
  assault and battery, 305–308
  business torts, 320
  cases, 296–297, 301–302, 306–307, 313–314, 317–318
  conflict of laws in, 42–43
  conversion, 320
  defamation, 308–311
  employers' liability, 320, 321
  false imprisonment, 311–314
  fraud, 319
  intentional infliction of mental distress, 319
  invasion of privacy, 316–318
  joint and several liability, 321
  negligence, 293–305

  nuisance, 320
  scope and complexity of, 292–293
  statutory reforms, 321
  trespass, 314–316
  trespass to personal property, 320
Tort liability
  of the agent or employee to third parties, 401
  of the principal to third parties, 397–399
Torts. See also Business torts
  common law nature of, 90–91
  definition of, 292, 292n
Toxic substances, 647–648
Toxic Substances Control Act (TSCA), 647–648
Trade. See Deceptive trade practices; International business
Trade and Tariff Act, 716
Trade associations, 454
Trade deficits, 714, 714n
Trade restraints. See Horizontal restraints of trade; Vertical restraints of trade
Trade secrets
  case, 374–375
  definition of, 372
  elements of tort, of misuse of, 372–373
  misuse of, 371–375
  secrecy requirement and, 373
  wrongful acquisition requirement and, 374
Trade terms, 698–699, 699n
Trademark infringement
  antidilution statutes, 371
  case, 369–370
  and element of confusion, 368
  and registration, 366–368
  remedies for, 371
  and secondary meaning concept, 368
Trademark Revision Act of 1988, 389
Trademarks
  definition of, 366
  international protection of, 385–386
Trading with the Enemy Act, 713
Transnational corporations (TNCs), 723–724
Travel Act, 244
Treasury Department, 182
Treble damages, 433
Trespass, 314–316, 320, 630
Trial by jury, 61–62
Trial courts
  in federal court system, 26, 27, 28
  and questions of fact and law, 27
  in state system, 25
Trial proceedings, 60–67, 69
  cases, 67–71
Trial stage, 60–67, 69
Trust Indenture Act of 1939, 471
Trustees, of corporations, 419
Truth in lending, 661–664
  case, 664–665
Truth in Lending Act (TILA), 661–663
"Truth in Securities" law. See Securities Act of 1933
TSUS. See Tariff Schedules of the United States (TSUS)
Tying agreements, 461–463

SUBJECT INDEX 797

UCC. *See* Uniform Commercial Code (UCC)
UCCC. *See* Uniform Consumer Credit Code (UCCC)
ULPA. *See* Uniform Limited Partnership Act (ULPA)
UNCITRAL. *See* United Nations Commission on International Trade Law (UNCITRAL)
Underwriters, 475
Unemployment compensation, 538–539
UNEP (United National Environmental Programme), 650
UNESCO, 381
Unfair competition
  case, 388–389
  definition of, 386
  Lanham Act, 387–389
  state deceptive trade practices acts, 387
Unfair labor practices
  case, 622–624
  coercion, 615–618
  discrimination, 615–616, 618–619
  domination or assistance, 617
  employee discipline, 616
  employer unfair labor practices, 615–617
  featherbedding, 619
  lockouts, 615
  recognitional picketing, 619
  secondary boycotts, 620–624
  strikes, 619–620
  threatening behavior, 615–616
  treatment of strikers, 616
  union unfair labor practices, 617–624
Uniform Commercial Code (UCC)
  contracts, 257, 261–262, 276, 279–280, 283
  coverage of, 112
  definitions in, 699n
  historical background of, 112
  negligence, 345
  perfect tender rule in, 700
  products liability, 326, 328, 335–336
  revision of, 257n
  strict liability, 351
  warranties, 280, 339, 341, 343, 355
Uniform Consumer Credit Code (UCCC), 675–679
Uniform Customs and Practice for Documentary Credits, 696n
Uniform Guidelines on Employment Selection Procedures, 567
Uniform Limited Partnership Act (ULPA), 113
Uniform Partnership Act (UPA), 113, 402, 404, 405, 408, 409
Unilateral contracts, 258
Union shop, 618, 618n
Union steward, 607, 607n
Unions
  campaign of, 605–606
  cases, 245–246, 597–598, 604–605, 609–610, 614, 622–624
  coercion by, 617–618
  collective bargaining process, 606–614
  decertification of, 606
  discrimination by, 618–619, 618n
  and employer free speech rights, 603–604
  and employers' treatment of strikers, 616
  featherbedding, 619
  federal legislation on, 591–594
  historical development of, 590–591
  initial organizing of, 598–599
  National Labor Relations Act and its amendments, 592–594, 595–598
  National Labor Relations Board and, 594–595
  recognitional picketing by, 619
  representation election, 599–601
  requirement of laboratory conditions, 602–603
  secondary boycotts, 620–624
  selecting bargaining representative, 598–606
  strikes, 607, 616, 619–620
  unfair labor practices of, 617–624
United Nations
  Code of Conduct on Transnational Corporations, 724
  Commission on International Trade Law (CITRAL), 709
  Conference on the Environment and Development, 651
  Congresses on the Prevention of Crime and the Treatment of Offenders, 250
  Convention on Contracts for the International Sales of Goods, 287
  Convention on International Bills of Exchange and International Promissory Notes, 700
  Convention on the Enforcement of Arbitral Awards, 83
  Convention on the Recognition and Enforcement of Foreign Arbitral Awards, 709
  Criteria for Sustainable Development, 724
  Guidelines of Consumer Protection, 724
  World Intellectual Property Organization, 381
United States Code, 184
United States-Canada Free Trade Act, 720
U.S. Constitution
  authority of federal and state governments, 121–137
  Bill of Rights, 137–163, 138n, 228–231
  cases, 129–131, 140–141, 147–148
  categories of provision in, 118
  checks and balances, 119
  commerce clause, 123–135
  contract clause, 137
  delegation of powers, 120–121, 170
  discrimination and, 546
  Due Process Clause, 37, 137–138, 155–163, 229
  equal protection clause, 62, 151–155
  establishment clause, 141–142
  free exercise clause, 142–143
  freedom of religion, 141–143
  freedom of speech, 143–150
  full faith and credit clause, 77, 136–137
  judicial review, 119
  organization of federal government, 118–121
  privileges and immunities clause, 139–141
  protection of basic rights, 137–163
  protections for criminal defendants, 228–231
  reasonable overlap of functions, 120
  search and seizure, 228, 516, 531
  separation of powers, 119–121
  state limitations in, 135–137
  supremacy clause, 126
  takings clause, 162–163
  warrant clause, 173, 228
U.S. Constitution Amendments
  aFirst Amendment, 141–150, 310, 311, 389, 546, 551
  bFourth Amendment, 173, 228, 516, 517, 531
  cFifth Amendment, 155–163, 228–230

U.S. Constitution Amendments (*cont.*)
  dSixth Amendment, 230
  eSeventh Amendment, 61
  fEighth Amendment, 230–231
  Fourteenth Amendment, 37, 137–138, 151–155, 546
  Prohibition Amendment, 8
U.S. Court of Appeals for the District of Columbia, 27
U.S. Court of Appeals for the Federal Circuit, 27
U.S. International Trade Commission, 716
United States-Mexico free trade, 720
U.S. Supreme Court, 28
Universal Copyright Convention, 381, 386
UPA. *See* Uniform Partnership Act (UPA)
Usury, 655
Utilitarianism, 197

Vagueness test, 102
  case, 103–104
Validation requirement, for testing, 572–573
Venue, 40
Vertical integration, 443
Vertical mergers, 441, 443–444
Vertical nonprice restrictions (VNRs), 458–461
Vertical restraints of trade
  case, 459–461
  definition of, 455
  exclusive dealing, 463
  price discrimination, 463–464
  proving a vertical agreement, 457–458
  resale price maintenance, 456–458
  tying agreements, 461–463
  vertical nonprice restrictions, 458–461
Vicarious avengers, 388
Vienna Trademark Registration Treaty, 385
VNRs. *See* Vertical nonprice restrictions (VNRs)
Voir dire examination, of jury, 62

Wage and Hour Division, 535
Wagner Act, 592
Walsh-Healey Act, 538
Warrant clause, 173, 228
Warranty
  cases, 329–330, 333, 335, 337–338, 341–342
  conflicting and overlapping warranties, 336–338
  in contracts, 280
  defenses for, 342–343
  definition of, 326

  disclaimers excluding and limiting warranties, 339–342
  express warranties, 326–330
  of fitness for a particular purpose, 339–340
  implied warranties, 331–335
  in leases, 335
  limited warranty, 356
  of merchantability, 339
  notice requirements for, 343
  plaintiff misconduct defenses for, 343
  privity defense for, 342–343
  statute of limitations for, 343
  of title, 336
Warranty Act, 355
Water pollution control, 635–638, 651
Water Quality Act of 1987, 637–638
Webb-Pomerene, 713, 714
Whistle blowing, 205–206, 510, 511
White collar crime, 248–250
Wholesome Meat Act, 680
Wholesome Poultry Products Act, 680
Wildcat strike, 607
Williams Act, 495–496
Winding up
  of corporations, 419–420
  of partnerships, 409
Wire fraud, 242
Witnesses, testimony of, 62–63
Women's Business Ownership Act, 675
Worker Right-to-Know Rule, 652
Workers' compensation
  appraisal of, 527–528
  benefits of, 525–526
  case, 306–307, 523–524
  claims against outsiders, 522
  course of employment, 522–523
  coverage of, 521
  federal laws on, 527
  insurance requirements, 525
  as no-fault system, 304–305, 521–522
  occupational diseases, 525, 525n
  operation of laws, 521–523
  purpose of, 520
World Health Organization, 724
World Intellectual Property Organization, 381, 385
Writ of certiorari, 27, 27n, 595
Writ of execution, 76
Writ of garnishment, 76–77
Wrongful death, 15
  case, 16–17